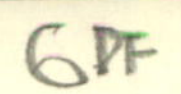

WORD INDEX TO POE'S FICTION

Edited
by
BURTON R. POLLIN

New York
GORDIAN PRESS
1982

GORDIAN PRESS, INC.
85 Tompkins Street
Staten Island, N.Y. 10304

First Edition

Processed July 1981-January 1982, in two computer facilities of The City University of New York: the main center on 57th Street and, chiefly, the Graduate Center on 42nd Street—Director, Dr. Leon F. Landowitz; Programmer-Analyst, Larry Powell.

Library of Congress Cataloging in Publication Data

Pollin, Burton Ralph.
Word index to Poe's fiction.

1. Poe, Edgar Allan, 1809-1849--Concordances.
I. Title.
PS2645.P63 818.309 82-2869
ISBN 0-87752-225-1 AACR2

CONTENTS

	Introduction	i
I.	Words in Poe's Fiction with Frequencies and Locations	1
II.	Compound Words	393
III.	Frequency List in Descending Order	399-485

INTRODUCTION

This volume was developed in response to an urgent need for an instrument to authenticate unsigned texts of Poe that he could have inserted into the journals that he edited during his energetic editorial career: *Southern Literary Messenger, Burton's Gentleman's Magazine, Graham's Magazine, The Mirror,* and the *Broadway Journal.* In addition it can and, I trust, will serve many other purposes for students of the words of Edgar Allan Poe: the analysis of his style and vocabulary, his characteristic and underlying concepts, his broad range of allusion, and his language transformations. There was an obvious need for such a key to the integrated body of his fiction, to accompany the 1941 Bradford Booth—Claude Jones concordance to the very small corpus of his poetry. The delay in preparing any concordance to Poe's prose could be explained largely in terms of the extended period of waiting for a definitive edition of his fiction, long promised and long prepared by the late Professor T.O. Mabbott. Surely only Poe's tales could comprise a truly significant and well defined corpus for such a source. The year 1978 saw the appearance of the Harvard edition, in two volumes, of the great bulk of his tales, posthumously completed through the admirable efforts of Maureen C. Mabbott and Eleanor D. Kewer. Proud to be involved in those volumes, as the Acknowledgments (I, v) indicate, I long cherished the idea of executing such a project upon the completion of the editing of the rest of Poe's fiction (*Arthur Gordon Pym,* "Hans Pfaall," and "Julius Rodman"). With the publication of this "third" volume of his works, under the imprint of G.K. Hall-Twayne, in August 1981, I looked forward to the editing of the rest of Poe's prose works, but without the necessary concordance tool for authenticating his vocabulary and his stylistic and rhetorical usages. My own *Dictionary of Names and Titles in Poe's Collected Works* (Da Capo, 1968) was useful for allusions, but it had to omit new works and variant forms not in the Harrison edition—the stipulated source. Likewise, my labors in the realm of "exceptional" or "creative" Poe vocabulary had served to produce *Poe, Creator of Words* (Baltimore: Enoch Pratt Library and Baltimore Poe Society, 1974; augmented, rev. ed. Bronxville: Nicholas Smith, 1981). But this was of limited scope compared to all of Poe's non-created but very creative words in his full texts. (The number of words in his fiction, my computer printout shows, is 468, 688, which merge into a total of 25,907 entries or indexed words in the main text which follows.)

Before I could be definitive about the unsigned "Marginalia" and "Pinakidia" type of paragraphs strewn, I suspected, by Poe in the *Messenger* or other magazines, I needed to consult a concordance; similarly, for authenticating as Poe's numerous unsigned and unattributed reviews, editorial miscellanies, obiter dicta, incidental remarks, footnotes, etc. in the *Broadway Journal.* Many difficulties of a practical nature immediately loomed: The text required three large volumes published by Harvard and Twayne, but a concordance furnishing the context of every word (or all save the high frequency auxiliary-type of words such as "the" or "is" or "and") would require even more space than the three volumes. Who would publish the fruits of such an enterprise? Moreover, how long would hand-culling such a collection of words and their context require?—many years, at the least. Two major solutions at once sprang out of the grim necessities of publishing in these adverse times and out of my own experience: since the texts might be assumed to have been defined in the three volumes, why not produce a "word index" referring to the context in those volumes thereby saving a great deal of space? The index to *Finnegans Wake* by Clive Hart even calls itself a "concordance" although not giving the context to the reader directly. There are also other examples of concordance-locations without contexts: R. Garcia and J. Karabatosos, *Concordance to the Short Fiction of D.H. Lawrence* (1972), Leslie Hancock, *Word Index to Joyce's Portrait of the Artist* (1967), and Gary Lane, *Word Index to...Dubliners* (1971). I was not unfamiliar with concordance making, since Alice M. Pollin, my wife, had compiled concordances to the poetry of Eugenio Florit (New York University, 1968) and the plays and poems of Federico García Lorca (Cornell Concordance Series, 1975). By my referring *to* but not giving the context (in the three volumes) a one-volume Index could be produced, if the proper format were devised.

The second aspect of the solution was to computerize the entire project, or at least the results of the editing and planning process for the sake of speed and potential accuracy conferred by the modern development of Babbage's Calculating Machine, as Poe called it in "Scheherazade" with prescience and admiration (B1166/35). But several conditions had to be met: availability of expensive computer machine time, of a programmer, of human "inputters" who could type the data "onto" the disk and, above all, of a publisher willing to issue a large and possibly expensive book. In June 1981 these conditions were miraculously fulfilled, when I found myself holding final page proofs of the third volume of Poe's fiction: called *Collected Writings of Edgar Allan Poe:* Volume I, *The Imaginary Voyages* (Boston: Twayne Publishers). Aware that the Gordian Press of New York, who had recently reissued Prescott's *Selections-...of Poe,* also put out the reprint of the Ostrom *Letters of...Poe,* I proposed a one-volume "Word Index to Poe's Fiction." The publisher, Mr. John Corta, liked the idea greatly. In rapid succession came the approval of Dr. Leon F. Landowitz, Director of the Computer Facilities of the Graduate Center of CUNY (42nd Street, New York City) and of Dr. Richard A. Styskal, Associate Dean of the Graduate School, CUNY. Dr. Landowitz assured me of the help of Mr. Larry Powell, of his organization, and of his staff. Eventually to be involved were also the work area and printer of the main computing facility of CUNY at 555 West 57th Street, New York City, where two and eventually three of the data inputters and I worked straight through the summer of 1981. The Hunter College Computer Facility also helped by providing me with a terminal where an efficient inputter spent many a night hour collecting data into the files of the project. (See the Acknowledgments at the end for more specific attributions.)

Various aspects of this Index might seem arbitrary and perhaps even incomprehensible if there were no description of the stages and circumstances of the development of the collection of the raw data for the text which had to be programed into the Index and its appendices. My three previous computer-aided texts (*Godwin Criticism,* the Poe *Dictiorary,* and *Music for Shelley's Poetry)* first involved the laborious key-punching of the data on IBM cards, with the consequent handling of these crude and precarious data-records. The development of word-processing instruments using a console screen set before the typewriter-like keyboard, with data files on central and safely stored disks, has greatly quickened and facilitated the collection and correction of considerable quantities of data—especially if one is willing to work almost around the clock. Having access to various terminals, for example, means that material can be inputted or stored and corrected during the night often far from the place where the central files or computer printers are kept. Thanks to the day and night functioning of the total computer system of the City University of New York, to the telephone-line linkages, and to accessibility to the central storage system, this Index was processed in all its stages in about six months. Almost incessant editing, proofreading, compilation of lists for correction, and consultation with the Graduate Center personnel were necessary. During the last three months, this Center chanced to install its own upper and lower case printer, so that time-consuming, inconvenient trips to the main facility (at 57th Street and 10th Avenue) were obviated, save for the final printout.

The first stage was the editing of the text of the three volumes (termed A, B, and C) after the Harvard University Press and the Twayne Publishers had both graciously granted their permission. My inserted markings next to and between the lines told the data inputters how to "type up" all the numbered lines. However. instead of numbers we used "T" and "M" and "V" for the words in Poe's titles and mottoes and variants, the last being at the foot of the page in "A" and "B". Ultimately, the locations would appear in this form: A0071/31 or B1137/28 or B806/M, meaning Vol. A, p. 71, l. 31; Vol. B, p. 1137, 1.28; Vol. B, p. 806, Motto. The fill-in zeroes reflect the fact that these locations were set by fixed columns at the head of the line, being extracted by the program through their position. While they could have been erased in the final printout text, before photographic copying of the text for publication, the uniformity of the columns improved both the general appearance and reading ease. With regard to copying out the text, we generally aimed at literal faithfulness, but only certain capitals and italics were to be preserved, even though both underlining and capitals were available to us in the CUNY printchain (first at

57th Street, later at 42nd Street). Proper nouns and the "I" (first person singular) of course retained the capital. There was a question about the numerous capitals used by Poe for rhetorical effect (Nature, Art, Death). Since almost every common noun that was occasionally capitalized would produce a separate entry in the list, there might be a considerable danger of swelling the number of entries beyond the scope of one volume or making it too bulky. Then too, the capitals might have been the reflection of an early editor's preference, not of Poe's deliberate wish as some of the variants might imply. Finally, the capitals in the titles, while deliberate on Poe's part, sometimes doubled several lower-case words to no great advantage, especially since a word in the title of a tale automatically exposed its location through the addition of "T" to the page number. This would not prevail, to be sure, for titles of other persons' works cited in the text by Poe, and some of these were arbitrarily lower-cased in my markings.

Finally, there was the large problem of capitals used to indicate the beginning of a sentence. Naturally, there was no purpose in signifying this purely grammatical function through a capitalized word (save for proper nouns which started sentences). All of these had to be lower-cased. On the other hand, it was my aim to cater to the habits of ordinary typists who knew the language of Wylbur sufficiently to input the text and make simple changes, such as corrections and insertions, and to recall lines from their disk numbers for subsequent alterations and corrections. Surely, I reasoned, it would be easier and quicker to type discursive prose with end punctuation uniformly reduced to periods. The programmer assured me that he would reduce initial capitals through his program and that we could add a special delimiter before every proper name (or I, first person) for retention of the capital. We therefore inserted a dollar sign ($) before all of these. The procedure was a mistake, I know now, for many of the dollar signs were inadvertently omitted by the typists; five months later I was still finding lower case words needing a restoration of their initial capital. On the other hand one of the typists (for a changing "crew" of four eventually produced the entire input text) casually lower-cased initial first person "I" and created a file of "i" which proved almost incorrigible in the long run. We also had enormous difficulties with capitals at the beginning of lines on the page through a gross misunderstanding of whether the program for "reading" final periods could operate from one line over to the next; this produced the need, eventually, for thousands of correctional changes through retrieval at the console, when it was found that the output Index contained numerous doublets of common words. We also found that the program for lower-casing unwanted capitals after periods was producing much trouble with initials in full proper names, including those enclosed in special symbols for reverse alphabetization (see below) and in abbreviations. One of the traces of this procedure is the presence in my Index of short abbreviations printed without their period, such as "Mr", "Mrs", "Capt" and "Lieut". In fact, we found it necessary eventually to devise a set of double delimeters ("plus" signs) around any words or abbreviations containing periods that we wished to keep in the index itself (see CHANGES...below).

Another editing necessity concerned italics, which Poe employs with a great deal of freedom. Sometimes these are used for the titles of books, articles and quotations; often for emphasized words or phrases, but sometimes the title is in quotation marks and the author's name is italicized; scientific names, in botany, for example, are inconsistently italicized. Since an italicized English word would often produce a doublet of an ordinary word, hence a new entry, I felt it better to keep doublets under one rubric or entry-name by canceling the italics, and the general rule that I followed was to use an underlining (italics in our Index) for all quoted foreign terms save when they were interjected into a passage of English prose. This led to few italics for the many French interjections of Madame Lalande, speaking passages of mongrel English in "The Spectacles." Poe's word coinages, as I indicate in *Poe, Creator of Words* (p. 16), were respectfully retained in almost every case, along with a few special words used for rhetorical emphasis. The method for designating italics in the inputting was somewhat awkward; since we early assumed that many whole phrases would need italics, we felt it best to enclose these phrases in two delimiters, to trigger the program into underlining all the individual words. The sign chosen was the percent sign, useless in our text for any other purpose. In practice this led to considerable trouble, largely through the machine's perplexity whenever a space erroneously intervened between the word and the sign or whenever one of the two signs had been omitted. Yet typing-in a tagging symbol attached to each word would have led to equivalent trouble. The treatment of Greek words and of dialectal non-standard English forms also required special symbols or handling. Brackets eventually designated (for the program) all Greek words, which were printed out in the index with a "(Gr.)" after each of the separate words, while the created dialect or distorted forms in "Why the Little Frenchman Wears his Hand in a Sling" were designated by an increase sign (>). The computer cannot print accent marks for foreign tongues, all of which have to be dropped. This means also that homonyms which would be differentiated to the eye, such as the English article "a" and French "à" are concorded together. In this case all of them are merged into one high-frequency rubric. The presence of homonyms in the Index must be realized. The user must be aware that "chest (17)" includes the word for "box" and also for "part of the body."

From the beginning of our inputting the data (in July 1981) it seemed to me necessary to keep names meaningfully together. What would be the use of having the name of Martin Luther concorded under Martin and Luther? Hence the programmer and I resolved this in terms of a pair of delimeters that would enable the machine to extract the names and turn them around to index them on the surname, thus: "Luther, Martin". This was done through the insertion of the signs for equals and plus before the name in the Index and a plus after the name: =+Martin Luther+ to be printed out in the index as "Luther, Martin". Even the names of characters, I judged, would often be most useful to the reader, under the surname (cf. Miller), rather than as separate entities for the first and sometimes the middle names or initials. In all these cases the names were preserved as phrases. This led to some difficulties, to be sure. For example: "Ferdinand Fitzfossilus Feltspar" could not be printed out in the space allotted to the entries. In a few cases I had to revise Poe's text slightly: e.g., this name became "Ferdinand F. Feltspar," to fit into the space. The second name of "Napoleon Bonaparte Froissart" became "B." This need for reduction applies to a few "words" humorously coined, such as "Alexander-the-Great-o-nopolis" (29 characters long), which became "Alexander-etc.-nopolis"—scarcely a desirable stratagem. In general, once our program functioned, the system proved feasible and, I trust, helpful to the reader. Originally I intended to keep all other meaningful phrases together, such as names of newspapers (*New York Sun*) or Poe's titles ("MS. Found in a Bottle") or special phrases often in foreign tongues ("comme il faut"). To do this required putting the words of an entire phrase on one line, that is ascribing the words entirely to the top line, on which the phrase began, rather than to two lines as in the book, since the index could properly print only one line number for each location. Moreover, the program for the Index could read each line as one unit but could not leap over from one line to the next. I spent the months of July and August 1981 editing the text into phrases and having the typists input it accordingly. This often entailed shifting a few words ending a phrase into the preceding or "upper" line to give the phrase only one line number, as was necessary according to space allowance. Then it appeared clear to me that I was really negating the basic nature of the entire "Word Index" by making it so often into a "phrase index." For one thing it would be almost impossible to find a specific word buried in a long or even short phrase. For another thing, the programmer found it impracticable to format the text to accept phrases of more than 25 characters in view of the need for leaving space for a frequency parenthesis plus 8 spaces for at least one location on the same line along with spaces between the separate sections of the entry and its accompaniments, all of which was limited to only 42 spaces for each half of the page. Although originally we intended to have entries of two-lines, if need be, we finally ruled this plan out. I therefore had to cut back all the preedited and "inputted" lines to single word lengths. A large number of errors, however, would have ensued if we had shifted back to their original pages the many words at the end of phrases that had been transferred or rather given the preceding line number. Hence a certain number of indexed words will be "off" by one line number in the text from their stipulated location in the Index. For example, the phrase "Glory of the East" was given in the text as "Glory of the" on AO128/7 and "East" on AO128/8. I had first edited it into +Glory of the East+ to be printed as a phrase and ascribed to AO128/7. With the abandonment of the plus signs or of the phrase units system, the individual words were concorded, when the plus signs were removed by a program directive. However, the word "East," having been assigned a new line number (7 in place of 8), retains this number still in my Index, although in the text it occurs at the start of the next line (line 8). This modification must be borne in mind when one consults the texts according to the number given in the Index. In short, if a word is supposed to be on a line and is not there, look at the beginning of the next line for its actual text location, always *below* the one given in the Index. Of course a very small number of words, almost all capitalized, are thus affected.

In order to preserve the meaningful unity of some short phrases, however, in an Index of individual words, I subsequently and at the end of the project resorted to the device of using a slash or virgule to keep together unitary phrases, such as "St. Louis" or "St. Pierre". To the computer the slash counts as a regular alphanumeric character, equivalent to a letter or a number. Hence the words on both sides of the slash would be linked together as one unit. For example, "United/States" as one parameter or word-unit is more significant and useful to the reader than would be the word "United" indexed with all other "United" words and, separately, 'States." It is true that the word "States" is eliminated from the Frequency List for capital "States" words, but the comprehensional value seemed to me to outweigh the merits of preserving the count, already somewhat tinctured by the variant forms of the same tale printed in the Harvard edition (see below). Other types of retained short phrases are magazine and newspaper titles (*Edinburgh/Review*), a few exclamations (he/he/he/, since scattering the phrase would make "he" identical with the personal pronoun, and it would disappear into the high frequency words with no locations designated), proper names having two parts in the surname (De/L'Omelette, de/-Stael, Le/Brun), real or putative institutions (Park/Theatre, States'/College, North/West Company, Folio/Club, Royal/Geographical/Society), song titles (Judy/O'Flannagan, Betty/Martin), ship's names (Jane/Guy, Mary/Pitts), and two-word unitary concepts (Post/Office). A slash also prevents the erasure by the program of the period (see above); St. Andrews would be printed out as "St Andrews" and, if taken by itself, "St" would also look like the word for "Street" with the period erased.

There were several dangers in this method of using slashes for short phrases: first, of extending a phrase beyond the limits for the Index entries (25 characters) and second, of inserting too many confusing slashes that might interfere with ready reading. For example, it seemed to me preferable to have "Cape of Good Hope" as one unit, but this would require three slashes. In this instance. I relied on the reader's intuition by yoking only "Good" and "Hope" together with one slash, producing "Good/Hope." In this matter of the slashes or the phrase units, I do not claim total consistency, as in "Rue/Morgue." It was indeed my expectation that the users of the Index might approach such phrases in various ways, e.g., through "Morgue" or through "Rue." Hence, the inconsistency might serve the reader's exact purposes, provided he eventually directs his attention to the different or possible elements. He must know that cross references are impossible in a computerized list.

THE TEXT AND THE VARIANTS

Since the "text" used as the source of index words includes significantly different "variants" I must explain how the variants were edited and how differently the Harvard and the Twayne editions print them. All of Poe's sketches, tales, and long narratives (i.e., *Pym* and "Julius Rodman") were "concorded" with the exception of "A Dream" (A/6-9, discussed below). The two volumes of the Harvard edition, which were paged continuously, were assigned the letters A and B, while the Twayne edition was designated as C. The line count differs slightly, with 37 lines to a full page in the Harvard and 41 in the Twayne edition, requiring the use of two different line-rulers (provided with this Index). In the Harvard edition the variants are printed at the foot of the page, whereas in the Twayne edition they are all listed after the text of *Pym* (pp. 211-214) and of "Hans Pfaall" (pp. 436-449). There are none for "Julius Rodman," and most of those for *Pym* concern accidentals. Typographical blunders are, of course, omitted, save that occasionally the Mabbott text fails to indicate when a variant is a blunder, as with "handsommest." In several instances I have allowed this oversight to prevail, especially since contemporary forms may make difficult the matter of determining the allowable usage of the day. In Vol. C, I have discussed more fully in my notes the variations then permitted, but verbal variants (for successive printings) are multifold only for "Hans Pfaall," not for *Pym.* Professor Mabbott has reprinted four of the tales which were only partially revised ("Loss of Breath," "Bon-Bon," "Lionizing," and "Morella"); and for these "essential" variants, it would have been impossible to match or trace duplicate words in parallel passages as I had been doing for the footnoted variants. That procedure had involved my elaborately red-lining the footnotes, word by word, so that the inputting typists could copy out those words which were different from the material in the text above. But in these so freely varied four tales, no such checking for parallelism and identity of words could be done. Each tale was therefore concorded as a separate entity. It should be mentioned here that it is easy to find the variant words at the foot of the page save when the variant is embedded in a deleted paragraph as in "Philosophy of Furniture" (A/495/V). In order to make it easier to trace the words in the very long detailed initial paragraph of "The Oval Portrait" (A/667), I have added putative line numbers for the 73 lines of the two-columned passage. The paucity of substantive variants for *Pym* and "Hans Pfaall" greatly eases finding the cited words on the pages totally devoted to variants in the Twayne edition (C).

For reasons given in his Introductions to the several articles, Professor Mabbott included as "Sketches" works of Poe which many would prefer to call "essays" (e.g., "The Folio Club" and "A Reviewer Reviewed" and "Autography"). For our concording purposes these increases in the "data bank" enhance the worth of this Index. But I cannot accept as authentic the dream-story, called "A Dream" in the Philadelphia *Saturday Evening Post* of August 13, 1831, which Killis Campbell in 1917 suspected might be Poe's work (p. A/5); and even Professor Mabbott cautiously states: "I feel a text of the story should be presented, with a caveat, as tentatively assigned to Poe." There are really no positive reasons for ascribing it to Poe, who never claimed or even mentioned it. Were I to include all of its words in my list I should negate a major purpose of the Index, that is, to test such passages against the totality of Poe's vocabulary. On these grounds, there are reasons to doubt Poe's authorship very strongly. He does not use any of the following words in his fiction (and only five in his poems): physiologist (7/1); Nazarene (7/10) gurgle (7/15); Judaea (7/25); beauteous (7/28); crape (7/35); requiem (8/12); expiatory (8/11); candlestick (8/15); babe (8/22); matted (9/15); enrobed (8/26); light-shot (8/30); amaranth (9/3); graveworm (9/14); parody (9/17). Since many of the situations in Poe concern death, torment, and guilt the absence of these connotative words among the others is a strong reason to reject the article. In addition, it is full of mawkish, sentimental, stereotyped, and fustian phrases that are inexpressive, tasteless, and unoriginal: p. 6—"the slumbers of night"; the "God of Nature"; "the wild vagaries of the imagination"; 7—"the bitterest woe that mortality ever felt"; "the mantle of clay"; life "shuddered to walk along"; "the chain of existence was broken, and a link dropped to eternity"; "a feeling of conscious pride...this pride of the eastern world"; "the skirts of mortal vision"; "a perfect loveliness had thrown itself over animated nature"; "a mantle of crape" over the sun; each star "had ceased to twinkle"; "enveloped in the badge of mourning"; 8—"they sang the hoarse requiem"; "the spirit of darkness spread his pinions"; "I could feel the flood of life slowly rolling back to its fountain"; "'twas lost in utter darkness"; "the living fire of the candlestick"; "'twas still as the sepulchre"; "Nature mourned"; "the habiliments of sorrow" over the earth; "the sables of mourning"; "a column of light shot athwart the gloom"; "still awfully plain and distinct"; 9—"amaranth which was wont to circle his brow"; "terror had tied up volition." Surely this does not "eminate" (a contained spelling Poe never used) from Poe, who was even then writing those matchless satires and burlesques of the early tales of the Folio Club. It is not difficult to oust this from the canon where it is only "tentatively" assigned by Professors Campbell and Mabbott.

The separate works which must be considered as sources of concordable words are eighty-three in the Harvard edition and three in the Twayne, two of which are novels (with 25 and 6 chapters). Several of the "sketches" in the Harvard Edition (volumes A and B) are brief newspaper pieces or short essays included for their fictive material (e.g., "Philosophy of Furniture"), but only the four-page "Dream" is excluded from this Index.

CHANGES MADE IN THE TEXT

I have tried to be as scrupulous as possible in adhering to the "copytext" provided by the Harvard and Twayne editions of Poe's fiction, even though this has produced some startling inconsistencies that look like errors in the lists of words that follow. Poe changed his spelling or punctuation habits from one period to another, thereby producing variations. It must be admitted, however, that he often wrote and published in a hurry; the evidence lies here. Even when one of his forms is incorrect, I have adhered to the text, although in every case I have checked into the source materials used by T. O. Mabbott or myself, to see what was actually printed. Very few changes have been needed: (A210/14) "wonderful" ("r" omitted); and "pre-eminently" (as in Griswold) for "preëminently" (A302/15). In one respect, however, I have had to supply an omission in the Harvard edition, the lack of a list of end-of-line hyphenations, for there was no way to verify whether the words with hyphens at the end of the lines coincided in spelling with the copytext being used save by going back to the source. It was necessary for me to indicate to my typists whether a word was to be inputted as a fused word or a hyphenated compound in every one of these. In a few cases, the text used by T. O. Mabbott itself showed a coinciding hyphen; for these, I consulted earlier texts and sought the most reasonable consensus according to the standard procedures in such cruxes. I can therefore claim that if one needs to know about hyphenations for the sake of exact quotations from the Harvard text, these indecisive appearances can be settled by consulting the form listed in my Index.

Some few changes in the cited texts were necessitated by the nature of the computer instrument and by the formatting of the text, in the two sets of four double columns, aiming to convey much, in little space. I have spoken about words that would not fit into the 25-character entry-span: others were "cock-a-doodle-de-dooooooh" (B1021/12), "good-for-nothing-to-nobody" (B1372/2, B1374/15), and the two instances of "Alexander-the-great-onopolis" (B1369/19 and 20). These are all obvious to the reader, in any event. The oddities of the machine's handling of alphabetization required some spelling changes. For one thing, the machine regards apostrophes as being of lower (or prior) order than any letter, so that in alphabetizing material, it inserts anything beginning with an apostrophe at the head of an alphabetized list: thus poeticisms or dialectical forms such as "'sembled" for resembled or "'tis" and "'twas" for "it is" and "it was" would begin the whole Index before letter "A" in a most confusing fashion. Similarly, Italian words, such as "'huomo" and "'io" go to the head of the list. My solution was to deprive eight such words of their apostrophe, have them appear in the order of their first letter (such as 't' for "'tis") and afterwards add the apostrophe by hand. another problem was with the machine's placing capitals after a lower-case letter. The programmer circumvented this process for a single capital letter beginning a doublet, such as "god" and "God," but not for a capitalized digraph in words taken from the Greek. Hence, the name "AEschylus" in the Harvard text twice had to be inputted as "Aeschylus" to avoid its appearing after the word "azure" in the Index. It would have been desirable to circumvent the machine for other marks of punctuation, such as the apostrophe and the hyphen, but too much programming would have been involved; hence the user of the Index must remember, for example, that apostrophes and hyphens appear before letters, in spelling. The letter D file, for example, reads thus (each entry being separated by a semicolon in my list here with "skips" not being marked): D; d; d; D.C.; D.U.K.; D—; d—d; d'autre; d'un; D'Alger; D'Avisson; dabble; dagger, etc. There is machine logic to this parade of forms and the pattern can be quickly grasped by the reader. Occasionally I substituted a full name for a letter designating a person previously mentioned (e.g., A735/36, "D." became "Deluc," a character in "Marie Roget"). This was to avoid multiplying the capital letters at the beginning and to render clear the meaning of the letter, which was, to Poe, a mere journalistic shorthand tolerated by editorial practice at the time. I did not do this consistently; hence, for example, the many instances of capital "P" ranging between B1032/20 to 1032/27. All represent "Mr. Poe," who is called "myself" in "Mesmeric Revelation" (B1032/17). I introduced a few other changes in the text designed to aid the inputting or the reading by users. There is no degree sign on the computer printer; yet in Poe's many nautical and geographical references this symbol was important. The inputters therefore used an "at" sign (@) for every degree sign, and these were programmed to appear as the word "degree." Of course they became merged as high frequency entries with the word degree or degrees as used by Poe, so that we find a total number of 132 instances of "degree" and 134 of "degrees." The dash presented its own problems since it was a mark of punctuation often at the end of a word, and by a sweeping program we had agreed to cancel end-punctuation early in the data-inputting. Hence, the inputters typed in two asterisks for Poe's numerous dashes, these to be eventually converted in the Index itself to two hyphens, serving as a dash. Often, however, the asterisk was confused by one of my input typists as a plus, with disastrous results, in view of the use made of plus signs to enclose names and set phrases; hence I cancelled the period and the asterisks in several instances of "—ult" (see A265: "your letter of the —ult.") and there are 7 of the "ult" in the list. The period at the end of the word always created trouble, in view of the program for erasing periods at the end of sentences, and I decided to allow several common abbreviations to stand without any period: "Mr" and "Mrs", "M" (for Monsieur), and "Capt". It was theoretically possibly to "save" the punctuation at the end of a word, by inputting a pair of plus symbols around the word outside the period. Points of the compass, such as N. and S./E., "No." for "number," "etc." and "A.M." were thus saved for selection. This proved extremely awkward for typing and led also to doublets of many abbreviations (such as Mr and Mr. or MSS and MSS.) which then had to be reconciled. Unfortunately, all corrections proved ultimately tedious and costly, to be made only on the input or original data, since we did not save a file of concorded output, to be corrected by itself. There were good reasons for this procedure, however, such as the fact that changes in any part of the index would also change frequencies and possibly the form and order of compound words, and both these categories formed separate appendices depending upon the original text for extraction and printing as a formatted string of entries.

There may be *apparent* errors, and despite a six month's nightmare of round-the-clock proofreading, I feel certain that some *real* ones are present, but it is to be noted that Poe and the editors of the copytext which was chiefly used (the Griswold or Redfield edition) allowed many errors and inconsistencies to persist, which I hesitate to change. For example, in "X-ing a Paragrab" the joke lies in substituting an "x" for every "o" in the printed copy. But B1374/8 shows "your" as "yzur" rather than "yxur" as in the Griswold copytext. Neither T.O. Mabbott nor I have changed the "z" to an "x". Nor have I changed Poe's error of "Coleridegy" in A495/V.

Poe's misconceptions, errors, and inconsistencies are not to be corrected, I feel. Here are a few of the "variants" or alternate forms: "mavourneen" and "mavoureen"; "Capricornuto" and "Capricornutti"; "mizen-mast" and "mizzen-mast"; "bouquets" and "boquets"; "Bordeau" and Bourdeau"; "Edinburg" and "Edinburgh"; "innuendo" and "inuendoes"; "villany" and "villainy"; "De Stael," "de Stael," and "Stael." While trying to preserve such distinctions, I have had to make changes in both the capitals and the italics, for many reasons. Accepting Poe's arbitrary use of capitals in titles and for rhetorical effects might have threatened to swell the number of entries beyond the permissible size of one volume. This is also true of many instances of italics, sometimes corresponding to no usage of our day and possibly not the norms of his own (e.g., A18/M: the author, not the Latin text, is in italics). It seemed most useful to take one of Poe's most common reasons for using italics as my own fundamental method, serving as a way to indicate a foreign quotation to the reader; the Latin, French, German, Spanish, Italian words are therefore in italics, save when they are briefly interjected into a passage of English, with no sense of being quoted (see "The Spectacles"). Also, Poe's regular habit, of italicizing what he thought to be his own word coinages, led me to italicize such words. Titles, unless in a foreign tongue, of magazines and books are not italicized, nor do I represent by italics words and phrases in quotation marks. In editorially inputting both capitals and italics, I must claim a large area of discretion, however; likewise, in dropping the period in such abbreviations as these: Capt (Captain), Lieut, M (Monsieur), Mr, Mrs, and viz (viz.).

FREQUENCIES

The frequency cut-off number proved one of the most crucial aspects of the entire Index, for the figure chosen and used in programming would determine the number of entries shown with all their locations, hence the length of the entire text. We considered as major determinants both the desirable size of the pages and the number of pages that could reasonably be contained within one volume in a book intended as a widely distributed tool for Poe studies. Our first cut-off was at the frequency of 41 occurrences, but Mr. Powell, the programmer, then had the happy thought of setting his program at 51, a felicitous conjectural thrust at half-a-hundred-plus-one. I kept in mind the virtual impossibility of a reader's looking up more than fifty locations in the three source-volumes in the course of fulfilling a research project. If this were a concordance with the texts of each entry exhibited, the cut-off point might be in the hundreds (omitting the auxiliary verbs, conjunctions, prepositions, etc.) Until the costliness of such a long text (undoubtedly in several volumes) can be overcome, perhaps by using microforms, this Word Index may make its own contribution to studies of Poe's style and vocabulary. Another partial solution to the lack of a text showing the multiple instances of interesting words beyond the level of 50 (such as "natural" and "opened" and "wilderness") may be the production of a printout text with the program set for 200 or even 300 instances. This printout, perhaps produced also in multiple carbon copies, can be bound in cardboard folders and placed in several centers for Poe materials around the country, for the sake of students who may wish to look up the more than 50 uses of some of Poe's words. Such centers might be in New York City, Baltimore or Washington, Bloomington, Iowa City, Austin, and Pasadena. This process will be subsequent to the publication of the bound volume. Similarly, the entire text of the Word Index has been placed on magnetic tape or disk pack, to be retained by the editor or the Graduate Center, City University of New York, for access in the future by data bank projects personnel, by Poe scholars, or by other institutions, who might even wish duplicates. There are many possibilities suggested by my own memory of the data-bank usage in Hitotsubashi University, Japan, of the tape of my computer-aided *Godwin Criticism* and in Oxford University of my *Music for Shelley's Poetry*.

It should be noted that the book was inputted through the Wylbur on-line text-editing system at terminals in various locations in New York City. The computer was an IBM 3033 mainframe with a Digital Data Printer, upper and lower case, at the

Graduate Center, CUNY, with the final printing executed at the CUNY Computer Center at 57th Street, New York City.

ACKNOWLEDGMENTS

Gratitude is owed and must be here expressed, inadequately, to many individuals and organizations for indispensable aid and encouragement in the processing and production of this volume:

To Dr. Alice M. Pollin, whose wise counsel and enduring interest was based only in part on her own experiences with the Florit and García Lorca concordances

To Dean Richard A. Styskal, who responded promptly to the proposal and most helpfully offered the support of the Computer Facility of the Graduate School, CUNY

To Dr. Leon F. Landowitz, Director of the Computer Facility, who afforded numerous types of aid and counsel throughout the project, despite his own great pressures of administrative work

To the officers and personnel of the CUNY Research Foundation, especially Brenda A. Newman and Elizabeth Walldov, who through ready and helpful responses and arrangements have furthered the development of the first volume of Poe's works and of the second, now in progress, to which this Word Index is directly ancillary and in whose support it has participated

To John Corta, head of the Gordian Press, who enthusiastically urged the production of the Index, offered useful advice about its format and dimensions, and evinced the keenest interest in its rapid completion and widespread distribution among students of Poe

To Larry Powell, programmer-analyst, in charge of operations at the Graduate Center Computer Facility, who developed the programs for sorting and for the formats of the Index and who most assiduously oversaw the successive printings of the varied outputs

To Dr. Leslie W. Dunlap, Dean of Library Administration, and Frank Paluka, in charge of Special Collections, Libraries of the University of Iowa, for the prolonged loan of various Mabbott Collection volumes, especially of old journals, for verifying end-of-line hyphenations and debatable spellings

To Harry S. Sigele, who generously supplied friendly and expert counsel that helped to solve problems and encourage the spirit

To David Hubbell, who worked unremittingly and assiduously at frequent intervals in typing, proofreading, and verification procedures, with commendable cheerfulness and alertness

To Phyllis F. Mirsky, Computer Liaison, CUNY, who graciously and patiently facilitated account transactions, often under emergency conditions

To a changing corps of data inputters, led in skill, speed, insight, constancy of work and purpose, selflessness, and aptness in problem-solving by Kevin Emerson Kalajan, Computer Science student at Columbia University, who was ultimately responsible for processing this introduction, subsequently typeset; also to Elizabeth Wood, a data inputter of noteworthy accuracy and reliability, and to Charles Ocheret, who helpfully learned key techniques rapidly.

INCLUSIVE PAGES OF POE'S WORKS IN VOLUMES A, B, AND C

[The Harvard University (The Belknap Press) edition of *Collected Works of... Poe* consists of Volume I, *Poems* (1969) and *Tales and Sketches,* Volumes II and III (1978). I designate the first of the latter as "A" and the second as "B" throughout the Index. Volume C in my Index designates Volume I, *Collected Writings of... Poe: The Imaginary Voyages* (1981).]

VOLUME A

18-29 METZENGERSTEIN
33-37 THE DUC DE L'OMELETTE
43-48 A TALE OF JERUSALEM
52-59 A DECIDED LOSS
61-81 and LOSS OF BREATH
85-94 THE BARGAIN LOST
96-114 and BON-BON
119-128 EPIMANES (FOUR BEASTS IN ONE)
135-146 MS. FOUND IN A BOTTLE
150-166 THE VISIONARY (THE ASSIGNATION)
172-183 LIONIZING
188-191 SHADOW—A PARABLE
195-199 SIOPE (SILENCE)
203-206 THE FOLIO CLUB (INTRODUCTION)
209-219 BERENICE
225-236 MORELLA
240-254 KING PEST
261-286 AUTOGRAPHY
292-304 VON JUNG (MYSTIFICATION)
310-330 LIGEIA
336-357 THE PSYCHE ZENOBIA (HOW TO WRITE A BLACKWOOD ARTICLE)
365-374 THE DEVIL IN THE BELFRY
378-389 THE MAN THAT WAS USED UP
397-417 THE FALL OF THE HOUSE OF USHER
426-448 WILLIAM WILSON
455-461 THE CONVERSATION OF EIROS AND CHARMION
464-470 WHY THE LITTLE FRENCHMAN WEARS HIS HAND IN A SLING
473-474 PREFACE FOR TALES OF THE GROTESQUE AND ARABESQUE
477-479 INSTINCT VS REASON—A BLACK CAT
481-491 PETER PENDULUM (THE BUSINESS MAN)
493-494 CABS

495-503 PHILOSOPHY OF FURNITURE
506-515 THE MAN OF THE CROWD
527-568 THE MURDERS IN THE RUE MORGUE
577-594 A DESCENT INTO THE MAELSTROM
599-605 THE ISLAND OF THE FAY
608-617 THE COLLOQUY OF MONOS AND UNA
621-631 NEVER BET YOUR HEAD (NEVER BET THE DEVIL YOUR HEAD)
638-645 ELEONORA
649-657 A SUCCESSION OF SUNDAYS (THREE SUNDAYS IN A WEEK)
662-667 LIFE IN DEATH (THE OVAL PORTRAIT)
670-677 THE MASQUE OF THE RED DEATH
681-697 THE PIT AND THE PENDULUM
702-712 THE LANDSCAPE GARDEN

VOLUME B (Harvard Edition)

723-774 THE MYSTERY OF MARIE ROGET
792-797 THE TELL-TALE HEART
806-844 THE GOLD-BUG
849-859 THE BLACK CAT
861-866 MORNING ON THE WISSAHICCON ("THE ELK")
869-880 RAISING THE WIND (DIDDLING)
886-916 THE SPECTACLES
922-934 THE OBLONG BOX
939-950 A TALE OF THE RAGGED MOUNTAINS
954-969 THE PREMATURE BURIAL
974-993 THE PURLOINED LETTER
1002-1022 THE SYSTEM OF DOCTOR TARR AND PROFESSOR FETHER
1029-1040 MESMERIC REVELATION
1044-1059 THOU ART THE MAN
1068-1082 THE BALLOON-HOAX
1089-1097 UNSIGNED CONTRIBUTIONS TO THE PUBLIC LEDGER
1100-1110 THE ANGEL OF THE ODD
1113-1116 PREFACE TO MARGINALIA
1119-1120 THE SWISS BELL-RINGERS
1121-1123 BYRON AND MISS CHAWORTH
1126-1145 THE LITERARY LIFE OF THINGUM BOB, ESQ.
1151-1170 THE THOUSAND-AND-SECOND TALE OF SCHEHERAZADE
1177-1195 SOME WORDS WITH A MUMMY
1206-1209 SOME SECRETS OF THE MAGAZINE PRISON-HOUSE

1211-1215 THE POWER OF WORDS
1219-1226 THE IMP OF THE PERVERSE
1233-1243 THE FACTS IN THE CASE OF M. VALDEMAR
1244-1245 THEATRICAL RATS
1246-1251 THE SPHINX
1256-1263 THE CASK OF AMONTILLADO
1267-1283 THE DOMAIN OF ARNHEIM
1291-1305 MELLONTA TAUTA
1310-1318 and A REMARKABLE LETTER
1320-1322 A PREDICTION
1324-1325 A WOULD-BE CRICHTON
1328-1340 LANDOR'S COTTAGE
1345-1354 HOP-FROG
1357-1364 VON KEMPELEN AND HIS DISCOVERY
1368-1375 X-ING A PARAGRAB
1378-1386 A REVIEWER REVIEWED
1390-1392 THE LIGHT-HOUSE

VOLUME C (Twayne Edition)

55-208 THE NARRATIVE OF ARTHUR GORDON PYM
211-214 VARIANT READINGS IN THE SOUTHERN LITERARY MESSENGER
387-433 THE UNPARALLELED ADVENTURE OF ONE HANS PFAALL
436-449 VARIANT READINGS
521-580 THE JOURNAL OF JULIUS RODMAN

<u>a</u> (56)
a (10861)
a (6) B0879/12 B1069/15
B1081/09 B1195/10 C0417/39 C0417/40
A.D. (1) B1304/18
A-- (3) A0112/20 A0113/01 A0113/V
a-kimbo (5) A0625/23
B0871/11 B0911/15 B1009/V C0425/12
a-piece (1) A0491/04
a-svigging (1) B1375/20
A/Goose (1) A0465/31
a's (1) A0267/06
Aaraaf (2) A0195/V B1384/33
ab (5) B1103/33
B1103/33 B1103/34 B1103/34 B1103/34
aback (3) A0585/16
B1374/05 C0105/37
abandon (19) A0351/02
A0403/17 A0408/10 A0515/15 A0532/28
A0556/11 B0807/29 B0898/16 B0978/20
B1270/28 B1277/23 C0071/38 C0083/08
C0094/41 C0096/23 C0124/26 C0132/17
C0132/32 C0187/19
abandoned (32) A0226/08
A0230/05 A0323/19 A0350/32 A0426/06
A0427/30 A0440/28 A0441/21 A0442/24
A0490/06 A0514/32 A0556/13 A0556/31
A0609/06 A0624/25 A0662/07 B0770/25
B0856/14 B0896/04 B0933/28 B1313/26
C0066/11 C0090/02 C0103/12 C0108/09
C0129/04 C0147/36 C0156/04 C0406/39
C0430/44 C0550/10 C0571/28
abandoning (3) A0567/23
A0643/20 B1369/10
abandonment (3) A0073/20
A0317/24 A0320/14
<u>abandonnement</u> (1) B1114/18
abased (1) A0444/12
abasement (1) A0432/14
abashed (1) B1014/07
abated (7) A0436/08
A0514/09 C0099/16 C0114/19 C0118/06
C0140/27 C0142/17
abatement (2) A0667/49 B0890/26
abating (4) B0930/27
C0066/06 C0114/20 C0115/18
Abbe (1) A0037/02
abbey (5) A0320/09
A0320/16 A0321/13 A0327/13 A0671/03
abbeys (1) A0670/14
abbreviation (2) B0746/31 B0746/34
abdication (1) B1126/05
abdomen (4) A0097/22
B0960/09 B1182/18 B1250/26
abductor (1) B1182/14
Abel-Phittim (7) A0043/01
A0043/10 A0044/05 A0044/21 A0046/29
A0047/07 A0047/18
Abel-Shittim (1) A0043/V
Abernethy (4) B0982/23
B0982/24 B0982/27 B0982/33
aberration (1) B0817/05
abet (1) B1354/16
abetting (1) B1183/17
abeyance (7) A0067/25

->A0402/22 A0613/09 B0963/20 B1037/25
B1187/17 B1242/28
abhor (3) A0228/18
A0232/23 A0240/M
abhorrence (2) A0403/15 B0955/10
abide (3) A0301/18
A0626/01 B0757/08
abiding (1) A0615/34
abilities (7) A0205/05
A0489/25 B0725/08 B0904/25 B1059/21
B1142/11 C0055/24
ability (28) A0071/26
A0295/17 A0298/V A0365/12 A0528/04
A0531/07 A0533/11 B0731/25 B0748/08
B0906/05 B0934/03 B0962/34 B1133/24
B1139/36 B1140/35 B1168/10 B1297/06
B1297/19 B1314/10 B1314/15 B1315/22
B1315/34 B1390/15 C0392/28 C0429/44
C0430/12 C0524/07 C0579/14
Abingdon (1) C0522/27
abject (4) A0509/33
A0644/17 B0769/01 C0134/24
able (97)
able-bodied (1) C0532/30
abnormal (8) A0213/19
A0613/03 B0742/01 B1030/01 B1031/34
B1162/30 B1246/20 B1273/36
abnormally (2) B0923/01 B0940/16
aboard (1) C0531/14
abode (2) A0081/38 C0522/27
abolish (1) A0203/03
abolished (1) A0072/15
abominable (8) A0053/01
A0062/06 A0122/11 A0174/20 A0179/35
A0374/05 A0374/V A0386/23
abomination (1) A0498/12
abominations (1) A0499/14
aboriginal (1) B1303/11
aborigines (1) A0055/34
abortion (2) A0092/10 A0111/23
abortions (2) A0070/28 B1128/15
abortive (2) A0704/28 B1269/27
abound (4) A0550/12
B0760/06 C0151/08 C0155/19
abounded (6) A0297/02 A0298/V
B0945/11 C0170/16 C0559/40 C0566/18
abounding (6) A0296/V B0749/21
B1162/24 C0536/40 C0547/40 C0570/14
abounds (5) A0266/01
B0960/05 B0989/12 C0155/31 C0576/12
about (939)
above (186)
above-ground (1) B1137/24
above-mentioned (2) B1184/14
C0400/09
above-named (1) A0542/04
aboveboard (1) C0070/14
abreast (2) C0181/08 C0573/41
abridgment (1) C0523/36
abroad (10) A0018/01 A0189/09
A0242/25 A0417/04 A0671/12 B0728/06
B0750/07 B0969/02 B1278/22 C0153/08
abrupt (10) A0211/14 A0266/18
A0276/33 A0281/17 A0298/V A0402/23
B0865/01 B1300/14 C0181/02 C0413/35

abruptly (16) A0025/06 ->B1013/25 B1018/28 B1130/27 B1167/18
A0160/09 A0165/09 A0166/06 A0273/14
A0347/11 A0409/15 A0412/13 A0414/26
A0443/16 B0896/08 B1017/10 B1330/20
C0396/34 C0573/14 C0575/15
abruptness (2) A0274/33 A0281/22
absconded (1) B1258/21
absence (49) A0028/22
A0054/30 A0063/31 A0430/06 A0547/19
A0557/01 A0625/30 A0626/11 A0654/22
A0709/29 A0710/18 B0726/07 B0727/12
B0734/01 B0753/11 B0753/15 B0756/02
B0756/14 B0756/20 B0763/30 B0769/08
B0771/10 B0833/18 B0857/31 B0877/10
B0900/08 B0926/33 B0942/21 B0967/24
B1038/16 B1070/13 B1123/18 B1123/19
B1274/31 B1275/21 C0070/12 C0071/30
C0083/38 C0085/06 C0092/35 C0095/03
C0110/33 C0128/10 C0171/12 C0177/38
C0180/16 C0422/25 C0429/01 C0575/34
absences (1) B0988/24
absent (16) A0313/V
A0508/11 A0655/03 A0655/08 A0655/V
A0689/V B0769/12 B0796/26 B0816/17
B0967/28 B0978/13 B1347/31 B1348/04
C0055/11 C0153/06 C0544/10
absented (1) B0733/04
absolute (61)
absolutely (85)
absolved (2) A0645/08 B1154/10
absorbed (33) A0063/18
A0088/15 A0102/27 A0146/13 A0211/31
A0215/32 A0352/34 A0353/12 A0440/04
A0458/17 A0507/29 A0511/13 A0515/27
A0534/04 A0581/28 A0582/06 A0592/10
A0592/17 A0592/23 A0592/30 A0602/21
A0603/30 A0605/02 B0728/05 B0811/05
B0814/20 B0863/26 B0894/22 B1057/22
B1077/17 B1371/26 C0392/15 C0422/19
absorbing (5) A0022/19
B0727/01 B0897/15 C0126/22 C0178/16
absorptive (1) B1322/25
abstains (1) B1207/15
absterrebitur (1) B0870/21
abstract (13) A0071/01
A0079/34 A0499/30 A0507/31 A0529/03
A0533/18 A0548/22 A0615/07 A0615/13
B0869/07 B0987/19 B1178/03 B1335/22
abstracted (3) A0297/08
B0811/04 B1053/24
abstractedly (2) A0496/V B1348/26
abstraction (8) A0079/15
A0162/01 A0214/08 A0405/29 A0610/15
A0695/16 B0724/28 B0843/05
abstractions (3) A0405/24
B1031/21 B1031/23
abstractly (2) A0496/14 B0987/14
abstruse (6) A0097/02 A0214/10
A0315/21 A0478/35 A0548/01 B0835/19
abstruseness (1) B0835/24
abstrusities (1) A0086/01
absurd (27) A0078/43
A0262/14 A0303/21 A0341/26 A0342/V
A0440/14 A0444/18 A0486/20 A0556/03
A0583/13 B0816/14 B0875/09 B0915/02
B1295/28 B1296/30 B1299/37 B1311/25
B1313/31 C0078/07 C0130/20 C0134/28
C0389/18 C0432/41
Absurdities (2) A0158/21 A0158/V
absurdities (4) A0078/41
A0295/30 A0320/27 B1017/25
absurdity (10) A0018/10 A0055/05
A0064/08 A0108/02 B1034/29 B1036/28
B1131/14 B1181/27 B1207/32 B1299/28
absurdly (2) A0529/11 B0759/24
absurdum (1) B1006/05
abundance (10) A0122/11 A0583/31
B1021/28 B1079/27 C0155/36 C0171/02
C0174/05 C0176/11 C0540/05 C0576/05
abundant (16) B0764/21
C0093/32 C0150/25 C0154/08 C0156/24
C0159/17 C0160/08 C0177/07 C0198/40
C0534/32 C0560/02 C0563/35 C0566/20
C0567/06 C0571/15 C0572/06
abundantly (3) B0768/06
B1077/34 C0178/10
abuse (5) A0341/24
A0342/V A0539/16 B1139/32 B1381/01
abused (2) A0490/28 A0710/02
abuses (1) B1275/06
abusing (1) B0854/30
abutting (1) B0865/26
abxut (1) B1374/20
abysmal (1) B1212/15
abyss (27) A0046/27
A0143/31 A0152/14 A0227/15 A0232/02
A0582/20 A0583/04 A0583/14 A0588/17
A0590/06 A0590/27 A0591/15 A0687/08
A0690/31 A0697/10 B0943/25 B1161/07
B1213/26 B1222/26 B1223/20 B1382/17
C0185/22 C0193/09 C0198/05 C0198/26
C0417/03 C0443/V
abysses (5) A0139/29
A0687/31 C0405/29 C0412/33 C0438/V
Academie/Pergola (1) A0079/08
academies (1) A0160/08
Academy (4) A0034/15
A0037/V A0086/18 A0096/18
academy (12) A0315/21
A0342/V A0429/02 A0430/20 A0432/22
A0434/08 A0436/06 A0437/28 A0437/34
A0440/02 B1364/02 C0057/13
acanthus (1) A0154/23
accede (1) B1236/22
accelerate (1) A0399/25
accelerated (4) B1281/13
C0402/37 C0406/11 C0423/01
accelerating (3) A0594/V
C0403/26 C0442/V
acceleration (3) C0144/02
C0403/05 C0412/13
accent (1) A0436/15
accents (4) A0191/16
A0562/22 B1157/29 C0072/23
accentuation (3) A0055/29
A0065/09 A0681/04
accept (5) A0263/20
A0271/12 B0908/01 B0965/24 B1130/09
acceptable (3) A0265/36

->B0906/V C0569/40
acceptance (1) A0642/21
acceptation (2) A0706/15 B1271/18
accepted (11) A0054/16
A0155/23 A0300/24 B0725/30 B0728/22
B0729/13 B1134/17 B1246/02 B1313/29
C0531/29 C0569/38
accepting (2) B0888/07 B1152/32
accepts (1) B1152/30
access (8) B1003/06
B1005/16 B1336/34 C0136/37 C0152/20
C0173/25 C0192/13 C0521/12
accessible (3) A0479/15
A0652/23 B0874/25
accession (2) A0120/03 B0940/18
accessory (2) A0405/33 A0600/15
accident (79)
accidental (8) A0441/13
A0514/25 A0530/18 A0652/18 B0741/25
B0752/10 B1054/11 C0573/23
accidentally (16) A0055/11
A0064/26 A0104/09 A0155/12 A0350/06
B0758/01 B0764/11 B0872/30 B0956/35
B1188/23 B1224/12 C0117/04 C0126/13
C0202/30 C0204/23 C0397/05
accidents (14) A0478/26 A0690/28
A0706/24 B0762/15 B0833/27 B0943/02
B1101/30 B1101/33 B1102/03 B1104/31
B1105/27 B1271/26 C0097/10 C0099/01
acclamation (1) B0758/14
accommodate (2) A0601/11 C0152/18
accommodated (4) A0057/14
A0067/32 A0090/21 A0601/12
accommodating (1) A0436/33
accommodation (4) A0100/35
A0249/14 B1038/34 C0069/20
accommodations (1) C0070/26
accompanied (32) A0079/35
A0406/13 A0537/14 A0541/20 B0735/23
B0807/27 B0816/26 B0856/17 B0897/22
B0905/01 B0959/33 B0968/10 B1072/32
B1080/21 B1157/24 B1241/32 B1242/10
B1282/15 B1379/22 C0093/08 C0102/25
C0125/31 C0128/20 C0139/31 C0158/28
C0161/28 C0164/32 C0176/13 C0403/33
C0411/27 C0561/04 C0568/15
accompanies (2) A0226/33 A0231/07
accompany (16) B0755/28
B0814/05 B0817/10 B0841/09 B0854/20
B0858/13 B1277/34 B1390/18 C0171/05
C0176/09 C0200/05 C0529/25 C0532/29
C0539/04 C0542/03 C0566/08
accompanying (7) A0265/31
A0530/19 A0546/33 B0916/02 B1130/03
B1322/12 C0180/28
accomplice (3) B0727/23
B0875/14 B1354/26
accomplices (1) B0768/19
accomplish (17) A0566/10
A0650/05 A0692/04 B0762/30 B1069/03
B1072/14 B1187/03 B1234/17 B1277/15
B1392/06 C0064/30 C0080/35 C0106/38
C0136/35 C0185/15 C0398/10 C0398/30
accomplished (50) A0056/04 A0263/32
A0295/V A0296/V A0479/25 A0553/21
->A0555/10 A0555/13 A0710/33 B0755/03
B0755/03 B0819/03 B0822/03 B0853/27
B0856/28 B0871/17 B0895/31 B0914/V
B0931/02 B0933/20 B0958/23 B1005/02
B1014/23 B1069/04 B1072/10 B1081/16
B1082/09 B1104/08 B1142/05 B1169/06
B1179/33 B1237/31 B1250/05 B1275/34
C0066/09 C0097/09 C0097/19 C0104/19
C0105/36 C0115/05 C0398/11 C0398/31
C0400/16 C0410/12 C0411/04 C0411/23
C0425/23 C0523/04 C0546/04 C0567/06
accomplishes (1) A0479/19
accomplishing (7) A0343/10
B0949/08 C0122/19 C0133/14 C0199/20
C0408/33 C0414/31
accomplishment (8) A0435/15
A0711/02 B0923/23 B1051/27 B1090/15
B1224/09 B1276/04 C0133/28
accomplishments (3) B1096/09
B1123/06 B1345/04
accord (7) A0554/01
B0741/12 B1020/15 B1380/01 C0138/24
C0152/15 C0429/04
accordance (15) A0025/22
A0252/04 A0275/16 A0559/26 A0671/28
B0752/21 B0984/36 B0991/25 B1032/01
B1054/18 C0202/08 C0403/37 C0426/11
C0429/08 C0442/V
accorded (1) A0027/02
according (28) A0079/43
A0173/19 A0178/28 A0251/09 A0270/36
A0353/16 A0483/02 B0733/33 B0747/32
B0747/33 B0810/08 B0831/24 B0869/16
B0879/26 B0929/31 B0981/03 B1091/28
B1095/02 B1164/30 B1237/04 B1299/14
B1321/02 C0106/13 C0167/36 C0178/38
C0548/20 C0551/39 C0574/40
accordingly (41) A0028/V
A0057/03 A0066/29 A0073/30 A0089/20
A0090/10 A0156/29 A0242/10 A0265/01
A0298/V A0338/16 A0340/14 A0347/11
A0353/05 A0384/15 A0398/27 B0744/16
B0841/02 B1052/04 B1054/02 B1092/22
B1108/05 B1152/27 B1182/27 B1187/06
B1351/04 C0107/31 C0110/33 C0121/21
C0127/10 C0158/16 C0170/37 C0172/27
C0177/30 C0181/40 C0390/34 C0396/32
C0398/22 C0424/38 C0432/34 C0565/22
accorto (1) A0344/31
accost (1) B0949/06
accosted (10) A0401/04 A0652/19
B0749/12 B0871/34 B0891/16 B0901/10
B1003/27 B1107/34 B1257/16 C0108/14
account (188)
accounted (7) A0218/11
A0240/20 A0406/11 B0756/16 B0853/29
B0979/23 B1346/12
accounting (8) A0293/19
B0731/17 B0844/13 B1018/02 B1382/33
C0123/27 C0401/36 C0419/27
accounts (10) A0484/13 A0581/07
B0955/05 B0955/08 B1293/13 B1370/15
C0387/01 C0525/11 C0550/07 C0565/05
accoutred (1) B1007/33
accoutrements (2) C0395/14 C0532/39

accredited (2) A0399/11 B0862/19
accruing (4) B1051/26
B1185/11 B1224/28 C0393/17
accumulate (2) A0704/23 B1269/22
accumulating (2) A0694/21 C0398/38
accumulation (1) B1322/27
accumulations (3) A0704/30
B0834/21 B1269/29
accumulative (2) B0746/15 B1035/30
accuracy (17) A0078/16
A0089/16 A0278/18 A0483/06 A0486/29
B0742/20 B0829/10 B0853/15 B0925/03
B0949/13 B0985/06 B1168/07 C0152/17
C0167/38 C0203/38 C0417/37 C0536/12
accurate (13) A0104/28
A0164/V A0250/23 B0948/31 B0979/24
B0981/05 B0981/26 B1069/22 B1090/06
C0193/06 C0195/22 C0416/28 C0418/14
accurately (14) A0027/07 A0406/23
A0457/29 A0590/28 A0601/09 A0615/15
B0827/26 B0984/36 B1180/08 B1214/09
B1248/29 B1250/31 C0172/13 C0388/14
accurse (1) A0074/01
accursed (9) A0045/25
A0163/10 A0195/V A0198/03 A0320/28
A0351/07 A0447/09 B0771/15 B1386/01
accusation (4) A0473/17
B1207/21 B1208/04 C0427/15
accusations (2) A0622/12 B1381/15
accuse (4) A0044/17
A0263/23 B0902/03 B1006/08
accused (8) A0090/10
A0295/11 B0906/26 B1053/15 B1053/20
B1054/03 B1054/12 B1369/04
accusing (3) A0055/04
A0064/07 C0071/18
accustomed (21) A0139/02
A0400/31 A0459/31 A0491/16 A0565/10
A0693/32 B0728/28 B0749/26 B0830/10
B0878/11 B0940/28 B0985/30 B1008/36
B1133/29 B1213/02 B1224/26 B1292/19
B1294/07 B1373/36 C0068/39 C0571/14
acetous (1) B0742/27
ached (2) B0797/01 C0071/11
achieved (6) C0521/T C0529/T
C0540/T C0550/T C0560/T C0571/T
achievement (2) B0819/04 C0399/39
achievements (1) A0120/11
achieves (1) B1126/12
Achilles (2) A0433/25 A0527/M
Achilles' (2) B1128/32 B1130/20
aching (1) A0510/29
achlus (Gr.) (1) A0507/11
acid (6) A0081/08 B1168/25
B1168/28 B1168/30 C0393/33 C0395/25
acknowledge (16) A0057/06
A0079/01 A0122/10 A0304/05 A0400/32
A0435/28 A0610/10 B0907/27 B1007/15
B1017/04 B1017/13 B1052/23 B1109/31
B1133/V C0428/13 C0578/40
acknowledged (7) A0389/13
A0432/04 A0676/33 B1054/11 B1129/27
B1133/12 B1188/12
acknowledgement (1) A0356/07
acknowledging (2) A0535/18 B0924/15
acknowledgment (2) A0159/20
C0087/27
acme (2) B1315/04 C0169/34
acquaint (3) B0909/10
C0089/08 C0133/10
acquaintance (52)
acquaintances (8) A0065/33
A0107/31 A0382/13 A0654/21 B0749/28
B0750/03 B0922/08 B1081/23
acquainted (27) A0027/V
A0089/35 A0099/16 A0146/11 A0163/17
A0310/02 A0433/V A0436/21 A0513/14
A0531/16 A0540/24 A0540/V A0549/28
B0843/10 B0900/V B0924/13 B0941/33
B0993/23 B1017/15 B1234/20 C0084/34
C0104/14 C0126/12 C0147/24 C0173/01
C0202/26 C0528/07
acquainting (3) B1155/22
C0077/04 C0090/03
acquiescence (5) A0112/07
A0650/13 B0966/V B1006/12 B1031/29
acquintance> (2) A0465/V A0467/05
acquired (18) A0298/01 A0441/02
A0580/08 A0610/11 A0667/15 B0725/08
B0956/21 B0969/02 B0969/02 B0986/18
B1037/20 B1070/10 B1322/01 C0170/34
C0391/25 C0398/21 C0418/43 C0529/07
acquirement (2) B1072/25 B1324/02
acquirements (3) A0090/22
A0099/32 A0163/19
acquires (1) C0402/33
acquisition (3) B1212/07
B1269/10 C0525/12
acquisitions (1) A0315/28
acquit (1) B0906/04
acquitted (1) C0104/20
acre (1) B1335/16
acres (4) C0152/12
C0156/01 C0540/20 C0543/17
acrid (2) A0691/06 C0150/30
acrimonious (1) A0069/11
across (67)
Act (1) B1131/33
act (48) A0022/06
A0162/06 A0325/20 A0372/11 A0438/28
A0589/32 A0608/15 A0623/34 A0704/30
B0771/12 B0829/05 B0832/07 B0875/07
B0888/06 B0891/14 B0898/31 B0901/02
B0957/30 B0977/19 B0993/02 B1038/32
B1072/06 B1134/24 B1135/01 B1140/13
B1213/31 B1220/25 B1220/27 B1225/09
B1269/28 B1269/29 B1296/26 B1313/27
C0093/24 C0096/18 C0107/31 C0109/14
C0109/34 C0110/13 C0113/14 C0113/17
C0125/33 C0146/27 C0199/19 C0527/17
C0531/06 C0535/14 C0561/21
acted (7) A0226/05
A0230/02 A0436/13 B1059/08 B1294/11
B1359/01 C0529/17
acting (7) A0398/08
A0478/12 A0478/18 A0478/28 A0478/28
B0840/19 B1010/13
action (63)
actions (15) A0161/15
A0196/21 A0197/02 A0197/10 A0197/19

->A0197/29 A0427/32 A0434/33 A0445/18
A0484/12 A0514/13 B1006/18 B1144/34
B1223/21 C0395/04
active (8) A0244/16
A0272/37 A0325/27 A0613/01 B1009/04
B1383/15 C0125/31 C0533/08
actively (1) A0508/19
activity (12) A0156/08
A0270/15 A0513/11 A0515/19 A0528/05
A0545/09 A0554/30 A0555/08 A0555/16
A0555/19 A0559/21 B1143/22
actors (1) A0557/09
acts (4) A0078/V
B1221/06 B1361/10 C0131/23
actual (33) A0034/09
A0080/27 A0157/04 A0244/25 A0340/32
A0457/34 A0527/V A0693/04 A0705/15
B0736/30 B0833/24 B0949/15 B0962/02
B0962/07 B0968/33 B1081/30 B1097/03
B1123/15 B1209/07 B1270/14 B1299/10
B1304/26 C0112/17 C0144/29 C0169/29
C0192/19 C0400/01 C0400/13 C0424/32
C0433/10 C0438/V C0525/11 C0543/12
actually (65)
actuated (9) A0073/13
A0105/13 A0432/11 B1093/04 B1213/36
C0082/30 C0104/21 C0152/16 C0545/32
acumen (10) A0278/16 A0296/V
A0296/V A0528/09 A0529/03 A0545/02
A0547/30 B0925/13 B0986/06 B1115/31
acumine (2) A0568/V B0974/M
acute (27) A0019/01
A0058/10 A0068/32 A0246/19 A0339/31
A0346/V A0366/05 A0398/21 A0416/08
A0528/31 A0621/20 A0696/26 B0749/02
B0789/04 B0941/13 B1030/22 B1030/28
B1303/17 B1350/04 C0072/24 C0141/09
C0389/21 C0419/39 C0428/40 C0428/43
C0532/02 C0567/27
acutely (2) B0758/23 B1047/18
acuteness (3) A0055/28
A0403/04 B0795/08
_ad_ (5) A0072/30
A0072/31 A0296/V B1006/05 B1193/34
ad (1) B0913/08
adage (1) A0336/13
Adam (3) B0736/37
B0871/25 B1095/06
Adam (1) B1190/24
Adam's (1) B1093/24
adamant (2) B0958/03 B1035/14
Adams, J. Q. (1) A0277/07
adaptation (8) A0400/11
A0478/23 A0497/15 A0707/17 A0707/20
B1039/32 B1272/15 B1272/21
adapted (34) A0098/27 A0240/12
A0263/31 A0310/13 A0347/17 A0486/V
A0501/11 A0545/05 A0601/07 B0831/13
B0838/03 B0857/04 B0871/35 B0901/19
B0908/04 B0916/13 B0961/19 B0986/01
B0988/17 B1037/14 B1037/32 B1054/06
B1081/26 B1240/17 B1274/04 B1337/04
C0065/13 C0181/09 C0182/28 C0202/22
C0394/35 C0410/30 C0549/17 C0560/21
adapting (4) A0709/23
->B1070/16 B1274/26 C0402/25
adapts (1) B0984/03
add (22) A0294/V A0337/24
A0341/27 A0382/01 A0382/02 A0500/11
A0568/03 B0746/16 B0768/14 B0887/06
B0907/12 B0916/12 B0930/33 B1022/03
B1305/10 C0074/08 C0081/13 C0095/20
C0112/14 C0114/32 C0143/02 C0430/01
added (26) A0021/17 A0024/09
A0045/18 A0105/10 A0141/29 A0402/33
A0408/21 A0438/20 A0440/16 A0446/06
A0580/09 A0666/V B0746/24 B0854/35
B1003/11 B1101/34 B1154/23 B1328/11
C0058/15 C0066/06 C0087/18 C0110/06
C0399/02 C0423/07 C0535/37 C0553/39
addenda (1) B1320/03
adders (1) A0161/16
addicted (3) A0086/01
A0210/25 A0427/24
adding (4) B0916/09
B1135/07 B1236/32 C0132/27
Addison (2) A0710/23 B1275/26
addition (13) A0128/27
A0433/14 A0558/05 B0727/26 B0746/07
B0748/03 B0813/26 B0888/26 B0965/33
C0141/22 C0407/10 C0423/08 C0535/02
additional (13) A0538/27
B0741/24 B0810/20 B0942/06 B1054/29
B1074/30 B1082/05 B1163/31 B1190/16
B1208/23 B1351/31 C0098/21 C0401/12
addle-headed (1) A0500/V
addling (1) B0988/04
address (19) A0074/02
A0159/22 A0264/30 A0264/31 A0264/31
B0872/03 B0876/25 B0877/01 B0899/02
B0925/31 B0977/07 B0977/11 B0991/16
B1055/18 B1188/30 B1361/08 C0056/20
C0105/28 C0108/18
addressed (26) A0240/16 A0267/17
A0273/34 A0279/13 A0286/03 A0345/22
A0548/23 A0625/09 A0628/15 A0628/27
B0894/18 B0977/12 B0991/07 B1010/15
B1012/06 B1014/04 B1059/15 B1157/28
B1183/02 B1241/04 B1241/13 C0142/26
C0174/33 C0175/22 C0390/32 C0523/19
addresses (2) B0873/35 B1221/29
addressing (6) A0265/06 A0299/32
B1010/20 B1015/30 B1040/16 B1310/13
adds (5) A0710/04
A0711/06 B1275/07 B1276/08 B1311/20
adduce (1) B0740/22
adduced (8) A0098/19
B0724/18 B0740/31 B0741/13 B0748/06
B0759/23 B0763/15 B0763/16
Adelaide (1) B1070/07
Adelaide/Gallery (2) B1070/33
B1072/09
Adelaide's/Island (1) C0162/01
ademptum (1) B1010/25
adept (4) A0440/22
A0510/12 B0989/33 B1009/15
adequate (6) A0211/24 A0347/16
B1169/10 C0397/08 C0421/18 C0424/29
adequately (3) A0447/25
B0905/09 C0182/25

adhered (3) B1145/20
B1301/11 B1354/19
adherence (2) A0484/11 B0747/17
adhesion (2) B1235/28 B1235/32
adieu (7) A0155/15
A0264/20 B0726/18 B0875/17 C0530/34
C0560/32 C0566/10
adjacent (3) A0631/07
B0853/20 B1048/11
adjective (3) B1294/02
B1295/24 B1311/21
adjoining (10) A0043/04 A0412/05
A0447/11 A0486/10 A0551/10 A0565/02
B0980/23 B0980/25 B1336/06 B1346/27
adjust (3) A0352/27
B0746/34 C0409/08
adjusted (11) A0058/22
A0069/12 A0388/33 A0508/05 A0615/09
B0893/17 B0911/02 B0911/V B1048/02
C0068/26 C0410/16
adjusting (6) A0056/23 A0066/13
B0842/12 B0910/23 B1186/04 C0079/40
adjustment (4) A0497/12
A0497/25 A0501/05 B0746/35
admeasured (1) B0985/06
admeasurement (3) B0981/05
B0984/13 C0165/13
administer (1) B1031/01
administered (1) A0429/01
administration (3) A0020/17
B0949/03 B1005/04
admirable (19) A0059/03
A0069/V A0070/03 A0102/14 A0174/28
A0180/14 A0302/23 A0348/18 A0664/11
B0890/09 B0890/22 B0908/02 B1121/02
B1133/04 B1138/05 B1270/37 B1279/11
B1300/28 B1304/32
admirably (5) A0379/26
A0434/33 B0857/V B1081/26 B1081/V
admirari (3) A0091/27
A0110/28 B1009/15
admiration (28) A0053/28
A0125/21 A0135/07 A0203/09 A0354/22
A0484/20 A0590/17 A0630/21 A0711/02
B0863/26 B0890/31 B0893/26 B0902/16
B0984/07 B1004/12 B1012/14 B1068/09
B1079/18 B1133/17 B1276/04 B1295/18
B1311/11 B1330/02 B1345/11 C0426/37
C0537/09 C0556/33 C0569/31
admire (4) A0064/17
A0107/14 A0214/08 A0611/31
admired (12) A0150/V
A0205/25 A0205/27 A0205/29 A0315/20
B0869/03 B0916/06 B1259/13 B1292/34
B1346/35 B1384/37 C0388/01
admirer (1) B0888/28
admirers (2) A0021/10 B0726/04
admires (1) A0204/34
admiring (2) A0125/32 A0533/09
admissible (4) A0498/07
B0902/30 B1315/36 B1315/37
admission (6) A0410/02 A0413/23
A0537/12 B0831/24 B0965/29 B1244/02
admit (48) A0141/22
A0302/07 A0347/11 A0352/26 A0401/28
->A0473/18 A0478/08 A0543/09 A0551/19
A0557/07 B0754/20 B0764/V B0797/28
B0961/12 B0965/26 B1034/27 B1108/16
B1126/09 B1136/33 B1140/15 B1153/10
B1178/04 B1192/34 B1220/20 B1221/04
B1234/33 B1250/34 B1274/02 B1292/18
B1298/23 B1314/13 B1315/22 B1316/34
B1369/33 B1380/09 C0076/12 C0091/28
C0105/39 C0136/36 C0169/01 C0171/12
C0183/32 C0189/09 C0202/20 C0409/26
C0418/14 C0432/24 C0439/V
admits (2) B0743/20 B1359/02
admittance (2) A0087/35 A0539/34
admitted (48) A0059/12
A0159/18 A0251/09 A0302/08 A0351/26
A0379/28 A0398/19 A0403/32 A0405/01
A0439/05 A0532/21 A0546/26 A0593/22
A0600/12 A0665/25 A0703/29 A0708/27
B0744/35 B0752/17 B0758/17 B0828/32
B0842/17 B0959/15 B0974/14 B1019/11
B1029/02 B1035/23 B1044/03 B1053/18
B1072/33 B1138/15 B1168/15 B1183/27
B1237/33 B1268/27 B1273/22 B1296/28
B1297/19 B1297/32 B1313/25 B1314/27
B1317/11 B1375/01 C0169/23 C0170/04
C0195/08 C0401/08 C0411/14
admitting (6) A0686/15 B0740/26
B0841/27 B1207/32 B1301/20 B1313/17
admixture (1) A0433/11
admonisher (1) A0445/30
admonition (3) A0439/20
C0080/16 C0080/17
ado (3) B0878/10 B1010/02 B1338/12
Adommin (1) A0045/17
Adonai (1) A0044/01
Adoni-Bezek (1) A0045/09
adopt (6) A0488/08 B0817/07
B0904/23 C0195/16 C0415/19 C0548/17
adopted (19) A0025/02
A0126/14 A0204/02 A0329/18 A0369/13
A0499/09 B0773/02 B0887/12 B0958/25
B0983/29 B0986/02 B1016/31 B1257/08
B1312/12 B1351/12 B1373/30 C0402/18
C0427/02 C0535/12
adopting (3) B0748/16
B0759/01 C0076/30
adoration (4) A0152/17
A0644/20 B0902/V B1107/14
adore (4) A0228/19
A0232/23 A0234/14 B1096/23
adored (5) A0122/22
A0122/27 A0458/25 B0909/24 B0933/25
adorn (1) B1122/16
adorned (6) A0045/01 A0093/08
A0112/20 B1192/12 B1340/21 C0552/15
Adramalech (1) A0046/12
Adriatic (1) A0087/27
adrift (8) B0771/24
C0061/24 C0088/07 C0088/13 C0088/25
C0089/14 C0092/28 C0100/24
adroitness (1) A0295/28
Aduanturier (1) C0430/29
adult (1) A0234/04
advance (20) A0128/30
A0250/27 A0322/21 A0478/26 A0609/20

->A0657/14 B0748/08 B0878/32 B0956/22 B1050/22 B1052/08 B1075/03 B1136/30 B1140/20 B1330/16 B1335/05 B1347/14 C0187/24 C0414/07 C0570/37

advanced (24) A0329/21 A0427/21 A0437/11 A0448/03 A0531/13 A0562/09 A0686/26 B0866/17 B0965/22 B1189/04 B1214/15 B1314/26 B1320/02 B1338/26 B1348/33 C0071/31 C0135/04 C0161/08 C0166/04 C0168/29 C0183/04 C0199/17 C0200/03 C0566/14

advancement (2) B1214/14 B1294/33

advances (6) B0754/24 B0962/23 B1281/12 B1295/30 B1311/27 B1348/02

advancing (2) C0183/09 C0200/30

advantage (25) A0074/12 A0094/16 A0098/05 A0114/11 A0379/21 A0433/32 A0502/15 A0529/23 A0583/37 A0654/15 A0707/19 B0931/08 B0978/12 B1051/22 B1077/26 B1114/26 B1168/31 B1272/17 B1294/13 B1315/03 B1338/02 C0128/10 C0177/28 C0540/15 C0570/31

advantageous (4) A0706/11 B0733/17 B1271/14 C0555/06

advantages (11) A0073/18 A0121/11 A0529/02 A0711/18 B0725/28 B0728/22 B1005/26 B1193/33 B1224/28 B1276/19 C0096/36

advent (6) A0293/15 A0294/02 A0429/18 A0533/04 B1295/12 B1311/04

adventitious (5) A0120/03 A0267/10 A0281/20 A0428/16 C0399/30

Adventure (2) C0158/29 C0387/T

adventure (31) A0156/27 A0242/32 A0304/01 A0352/19 A0486/26 B0829/36 B0843/09 B0866/08 B0947/26 B0968/10 B1072/35 B1076/09 B1078/30 B1165/13 C0055/02 C0062/39 C0067/02 C0078/39 C0084/13 C0102/02 C0104/18 C0165/02 C0176/28 C0193/25 C0197/23 C0422/02 C0424/04 C0563/33 C0565/29 C0569/16 C0574/34

adventurer (6) B0864/19 B0943/04 B0943/04 C0432/44 C0528/30 C0537/03

adventurers (6) A0638/14 B0725/27 B1075/16 C0536/21 C0544/22 C0550/18

adventures (22) A0293/06 A0347/16 A0347/16 B1154/34 B1158/23 B1159/13 B1170/06 C0053/T C0056/06 C0056/16 C0057/19 C0057/32 C0065/05 C0425/24 C0430/42 C0441/V C0521/22 C0524/39 C0528/26 C0532/19 C0541/12 C0560/17

adventuring (1) B1364/16

adventurous (2) B0864/12 C0532/17

advert (3) A0549/09 B0985/13 B1381/27

adverted (3) A0294/V A0567/V B0901/28

advertise (1) B0878/29

Advertisement (1) A0484/V

advertisement (10) A0560/21 A0561/14 A0561/19 A0562/03 B0770/27 B0770/31 B0876/23 B0876/24 B0877/07 B0879/16

advertisements (2) A0507/18 B0878/32

advertiser (2) A0488/13 A0561/30

advertisers (2) B0878/34 B0879/08

advertising (1) B0874/03

advice (22) A0121/24 A0179/11 A0347/14 A0435/25 A0435/25 A0625/26 A0626/19 A0650/22 B0816/23 B0892/19 B0928/12 B0981/25 B0982/33 B0982/35 B1142/09 B1143/07 B1153/03 B1182/27 B1352/01 C0115/04 C0131/02 C0166/30

advisable (9) B0727/14 B0753/36 B0772/05 B0879/06 B1142/34 B1177/08 B1193/23 B1239/02 C0179/36

advise (4) A0267/16 A0650/V B0864/19 B0981/21

advised (7) A0075/16 A0489/20 B0924/17 B1031/10 C0055/31 C0119/11 C0130/41

advisedly (1) B1137/28

advisers (1) C0055/26

advising (1) B1371/06

advocated (1) B0886/03

advocates (1) B1163/11

adzes (1) C0148/09

Aedepol (1) A0045/30

Aeolus (2) A0641/04 A0643/16

aerial (4) A0036/V A0210/01 B1070/01 B1072/14

aerienne (1) B0889/29

aeriforms (2) A0175/V A0182/05

Aeris (3) A0344/01 A0351/20 B1162/33

aerolites (1) B1322/20

aeronaut (6) B1072/04 B1080/32 B1108/27 B1294/25 C0390/06 C0408/13

aeronautic (1) C0401/05

aeronauts (2) B1069/18 C0403/36

aerostation (3) B1072/26 B1073/10 B1074/03

Aeschylus (3) A0078/27 A0175/31 A0181/31

aethera (1) A0603/35

Aetna (1) B1278/04

afar (8) A0079/12 A0088/12 A0154/21 A0190/21 A0197/14 A0198/17 B1274/16 C0405/29

aff> (5) A0464/09 A0465/19 A0466/25 A0469/V A0470/08

affability (2) A0245/28 A0383/12

affair (40) A0025/V A0074/25 A0382/29 A0383/31 A0384/20 A0385/33 A0386/09 A0439/31 A0493/06 A0538/30 A0544/25 A0558/02 A0563/V A0564/15 A0630/23 B0724/27 B0725/06 B0726/16 B0729/03 B0752/33 B0753/11 B0757/02 B0770/02 B0830/04 B0834/11 B0901/04 B0974/11 B0975/25 B0976/05 B1058/22 B1090/05 B1119/22 B1129/18 B1208/31 B1233/05 B1361/23 B1371/05 B1374/31 B1375/08 C0089/35

affaire (1) A0538/30

affairs (32) A0019/15 A0056/07 A0065/31 A0105/04 A0107/20 A0342/07 A0374/17 A0382/23 A0389/15 A0432/23 A0433/16 A0458/16 A0508/19 A0530/23 A0544/16 A0568/11 B0725/23

->B0733/28 B0810/22 B0977/16 B0978/29
B0979/16 B1005/05 B1135/21 B1178/03
B1299/35 B1302/14 C0065/01 C0077/04
C0122/12 C0412/18 C0422/01
affect (6) A0442/08 A0615/14
A0712/03 C0105/23 C0179/09 C0203/02
affectation (12) A0160/20
A0380/15 A0445/28 A0509/04 A0509/04
B0888/23 B0904/31 B0907/26 B0916/11
B1109/08 B1114/31 B1273/11
affectations (1) A0708/16
affected (32) A0022/04
A0053/16 A0062/24 A0093/02 A0112/14
A0210/16 A0298/V A0444/01 A0460/18
A0592/06 A0611/10 A0613/05 A0614/05
A0615/13 A0615/29 A0626/34 B0963/13
B1006/15 B1014/26 B1016/06 B1046/19
B1143/06 B1240/31 B1246/17 C0123/03
C0128/01 C0128/38 C0131/18 C0131/32
C0169/21 C0204/23 C0392/23
affectedly (3) A0536/04
B1295/16 B1311/09
affecting (2) A0211/V A0398/04
affection (21) A0028/07
A0108/12 A0225/01 A0228/20 A0229/01
A0233/01 A0233/21 A0235/05 A0311/07
A0317/17 A0350/04 A0402/33 A0642/12
B0850/16 B0851/15 B0906/10 B1052/31
B1122/30 B1123/21 C0073/08 C0073/26
affectionate (1) A0539/02
affectionately (1) A0262/26
affectionateness (3) A0297/13
A0432/16 C0523/40
affections (4) A0055/21
A0065/05 A0404/18 B0887/02
affects (1) A0496/21
affianced (1) B0755/31
afficiantur (1) A0622/19
affidavit (1) B0751/22
affidavits (6) B0731/16 B0751/21
B0751/26 B0752/26 B0752/33 B1119/M
affinity (7) A0175/12
A0181/02 A0399/35 A0493/06 B1038/12
B1073/16 C0429/24
affirm (2) A0027/19 A0319/16
affirmative (3) B0895/20
B1109/23 C0101/15
affixed (7) A0056/07
B1076/31 B1192/20 C0056/12 C0062/23
C0197/13 C0409/33
afflatus (3) A0173/27
A0179/09 B1127/18
afflict (1) B1032/25
afflicted (4) A0248/04
A0403/33 B1258/13 B1303/18
afflicting (1) C0191/20
affluence (1) B0899/15
afford (49) A0105/12
A0141/07 A0159/15 A0213/18 A0270/05
A0274/20 A0343/08 A0346/18 A0402/29
A0486/15 A0491/10 A0530/22 A0533/08
A0546/05 A0581/20 A0589/31 A0707/13
A0708/16 B0752/30 B0757/24 B0831/29
B0872/12 B0988/26 B1009/09 B1142/08
B1164/26 B1184/20 B1206/16 B1212/26
->B1270/15 B1272/12 B1273/11 B1315/02
B1318/05 C0129/03 C0185/10 C0190/26
C0192/19 C0205/08 C0207/15 C0207/23
C0208/04 C0407/11 C0422/34 C0428/13
C0438/V C0547/29 C0553/13 C0574/27
afforded (51)
affording (12) A0036/08
A0501/04 A0554/16 B0765/23 B0864/36
B1179/05 B1278/03 B1333/37 B1337/02
C0069/11 C0080/29 C0432/32
affords (5) A0478/20
B0916/25 B1113/03 B1113/10 B1208/14
affray (1) A0667/09
affright (5) A0568/01
B1057/17 B1157/35 B1352/11 C0562/30
affrighted (1) C0208/16
affront (4) A0300/06
A0302/10 B0869/13 B1313/11
affronted (4) A0356/28
A0711/01 B1107/30 B1276/03
afloat (7) A0021/07
A0432/21 B0731/34 B0732/15 B0834/02
B0931/21 B1361/23
afoot (1) A0486/08
afore (1) A0470/19
aforesaid (3) A0054/04
A0381/08 B1093/23
afraid (14) B0818/18 B1019/13
B1045/05 B1359/32 B1379/09 C0070/19
C0139/01 C0140/38 C0169/11 C0169/40
C0555/18 C0556/21 C0561/15 C0575/02
Afrasiab (1) B0969/16
Africa (3) B0870/28
B1294/04 C0407/38
African (3) A0409/07
A0550/11 A0623/04
Africans (1) A0550/12
aft (9) A0137/08
A0137/23 A0140/20 A0589/V B0930/32
C0061/39 C0106/24 C0110/37 C0124/15
after (521)
after-cabin (1) B0928/22
after-dream (1) A0397/16
after-sails (1) C0106/18
afterlife (1) B1129/08
afternoon (34) A0214/16 A0347/21
A0347/27 A0355/26 A0428/24 A0440/02
A0507/18 A0546/14 A0585/02 A0649/02
A0654/25 B0728/09 B0729/16 B0735/22
B0755/27 B0758/33 B0814/24 B0872/28
B0930/28 B1046/09 B1053/06 B1100/01
B1115/03 B1138/18 B1152/21 B1241/22
B1391/16 C0104/01 C0115/20 C0140/35
C0163/27 C0561/09 C0565/13 C0568/09
aftersail (1) B0930/17
afterward (58)
afterwards (83)
afterwords (1) B0866/12
afther> (9) A0466/07
A0466/17 A0468/01 A0468/05 A0469/03
A0469/29 A0470/07 A0470/17 A0470/20
ag (1) B0912/01
again (347)
against (151)
Agathos (22) B1211/01 B1211/03

->B1212/07 B1212/11 B1212/15 B1212/24
B1212/34 B1213/04 B1213/06 B1213/11
B1213/13 B1213/22 B1213/28 B1213/29
B1214/17 B1214/18 B1215/08 B1215/13
B1215/17 B1215/21 B1215/24 B1215/29
age (76)
aged (12) A0029/05
A0093/20 A0112/31 A0314/17 A0321/19
A0322/06 A0446/28 A0513/12 A0643/V
A0672/33 B0841/04 B0909/09
agencies (2) B0742/15 B0742/32
agency (14) A0243/10 A0295/16
A0457/19 A0457/30 A0459/03 B0762/17
B0762/29 B0762/35 B0763/04 B0770/31
B0831/34 B1214/10 B1224/12 B1352/33
agent (10) A0460/29 B0832/15
B0977/32 B0979/20 B1069/12 B1069/25
B1069/29 B1383/26 C0561/03 C0561/08
agents (6) A0546/27 A0547/30
A0690/24 B0737/04 C0529/06 C0530/13
ages (17) A0018/01
A0124/17 A0128/16 A0142/26 A0160/V
A0398/33 A0400/07 A0510/07 A0611/26
A0691/04 B0857/02 B1090/13 B1281/35
B1294/33 B1296/10 B1312/14 B1321/27
aggravated (4) A0211/V
A0500/07 C0083/29 C0183/40
aggregate (3) A0507/33
A0704/25 B1269/24
aggregated (1) B0987/25
aghast (14) A0078/27 A0125/21
A0145/09 A0153/21 A0162/25 A0191/12
A0234/11 A0294/V A0417/03 A0567/21
A0644/12 A0666/02 A0684/11 B0913/24
agile (2) A0210/23 C0563/09
agility (8) A0128/26
A0555/12 A0556/34 A0558/07 A0565/24
B1353/11 C0165/06 C0201/02
agin (1) B0912/25
agin> (1) A0467/V
agir (1) A0036/18
agitated (24) A0024/24
A0153/24 A0195/16 A0227/03 A0231/14
A0235/13 A0411/05 A0412/30 A0413/14
B0728/03 B0733/10 B0873/22 B1238/25
C0059/01 C0060/12 C0060/33 C0078/07
C0110/12 C0111/15 C0144/18 C0389/37
C0397/09 C0554/25 C0555/19
agitating (1) A0560/13
agitation (31) A0155/21
A0378/13 A0398/20 A0402/16 A0403/14
A0404/23 A0456/23 A0457/36 A0514/20
A0542/28 A0567/14 A0581/02 A0664/26
A0687/34 B0725/09 B0894/24 B0944/24
B0947/02 B1079/05 B1362/11 C0083/24
C0095/35 C0104/04 C0187/13 C0204/38
C0387/16 C0405/07 C0406/23 C0419/28
C0420/37 C0556/06
agitations (1) C0204/17
ago (78)
agog (1) C0391/14
agonies (14) A0209/08 A0344/30
A0448/06 A0498/08 A0687/21 A0691/19
A0696/04 B0959/09 B0964/21 B0966/05
B0966/05 C0063/17 C0083/12 C0145/31
agonizing (2) A0234/15 B0961/32
Agony (1) B0855/35
agony (40) A0029/03
A0029/10 A0079/33 A0326/24 A0328/26
A0353/26 A0354/28 A0444/33 A0514/08
A0540/05 A0567/14 A0580/35 A0589/30
A0681/01 A0685/04 A0690/33 A0695/11
A0697/04 B0764/32 B0797/24 B0859/05
B0899/16 B0913/23 B0955/20 B0967/36
B0983/14 B1057/19 B1079/09 B1106/23
B1237/07 C0060/39 C0072/24 C0082/40
C0119/39 C0124/24 C0143/35 C0149/05
C0182/25 C0397/19 C0567/41
agraffas (2) A0336/08 A0339/05
agraffas (1) A0349/14
agree (6) A0544/29 A0555/22
B0837/14 B1047/09 B1145/17 C0157/41
agreeable (12) A0055/14
A0064/28 A0090/20 A0651/01 B0850/25
B0904/20 B0905/V B0926/12 B1016/35
B1113/03 B1206/18 C0068/08
agreeably (2) B1055/12 C0411/25
agreed (31) A0300/22
A0350/14 A0457/16 A0549/12 A0549/19
A0583/12 A0630/02 B0908/12 B0910/09
B0962/05 B1105/16 B1181/13 B1193/11
B1235/04 B1236/06 B1239/17 B1390/02
C0066/30 C0067/10 C0096/34 C0104/14
C0104/37 C0111/10 C0121/21 C0134/09
C0134/40 C0152/03 C0179/34 C0526/20
C0529/26 C0539/15
agreeing (5) A0240/09
B1021/32 B1241/25 C0093/12 C0555/37
agreement (9) A0093/11
A0112/23 A0112/32 B0737/20 B0815/20
B0862/26 B0910/03 C0177/30 C0179/19
agreements (1) B1113/04
agrees (1) B1011/01
agressi (1) A0638/14
aground (1) C0201/07
ague (7) A0437/23
A0586/29 A0696/19 B1046/26 C0074/07
C0128/37 C0397/09
ah (2) A0033/17 B0905/23
ah (61)
aha (1) A0629/15
ahead (10) A0588/02 B0925/36
B1091/31 C0105/39 C0151/04 C0533/29
C0560/32 C0561/16 C0566/21 C0576/25
ahem (13) A0387/01
A0387/05 A0627/28 A0628/07 A0628/14
A0628/20 A0628/29 A0628/34 A0629/10
A0629/13 A0629/14 A0629/15 A0629/23
Ahmateaza (1) C0574/21
Ahnahaways (2) C0565/30 C0565/38
ai (2) C0430/35 C0430/37
aid (69)
aided (13) A0409/29
A0478/27 B1078/20 B1104/26 B1262/30
B1337/30 C0103/05 C0108/37 C0160/13
C0550/19 C0554/06 C0561/19 C0573/30
Aidenn (5) A0456/12
A0456/14 A0456/16 A0461/14 B1212/24
aides-de-camp (1) C0395/13
aiding (4) B1070/23

->B1183/16 C0117/38 C0179/40
aids (1) B0988/26
aiei (Gr.) (2) A0225/M A0229/M
aight (1) A0372/31
aigrette (1) B0890/11
ailment (1) B1031/02
ails (2) B0811/31 C0059/19
aim (8) A0387/V
  A0512/25 A0513/16 B0738/21 B0869/25
  B1104/08 C0433/04 C0546/14
aimable (1) A0100/15
aime (1) B1122/01
aimed (3) B0856/22
  B1379/01 B1380/30
aiming (2) A0705/10 B1270/09
aimless (1) A0320/08
aims (3) A0270/14
  A0706/04 B1271/08
Ainsworth (11) B1051/20
  B1072/32 B1075/27 B1075/29 B1076/23
  B1077/23 B1078/28 B1079/34 B1080/24
  B1081/09 B1081/20
Ainsworth, Harrison (3) B1068/04
  B1069/18 B1069/24
Ainsworth's (1) B1081/14
aint (9) B0809/01
  B0811/26 B0811/26 B0811/33 B0812/16
  B0821/11 B0821/22 B0824/09 B0826/27
air (2) A0037/V A0378/18
air (213)
air-boxes (1) C0063/10
air-bubble (1) A0588/20
air-tight (1) C0409/17
airing (1) C0540/03
airs (5) A0303/V
  A0355/08 A0432/18 A0603/12 B1012/07
airy (3) A0196/V
  A0311/25 A0501/17
aisles (1) A0235/22
aisy> (1) A0468/09
ajar (2) A0542/14 A0542/V
akimbo (1) B0912/V
akin (6) A0427/26 A0527/V
  A0600/31 A0614/30 A0711/28 B1276/31
Al (1) A0195/V
al (1) B0905/24
Al/ (1) B1384/33
alabaster (5) A0088/01
  A0088/21 A0090/05 B1145/24 B1280/14
alacrity (1) C0179/40
Aladdin's (1) B1361/24
alarm (18) A0161/25 A0411/26
  B0823/13 B0853/20 B1019/09 B1044/20
  B1226/03 B1353/01 C0061/02 C0129/02
  C0143/19 C0167/06 C0188/32 C0204/29
  C0406/09 C0423/02 C0553/20 C0562/34
alarmed (28) A0353/15
  A0625/20 B0726/21 B0814/26 B0857/28
  B0942/20 B1040/09 B1080/20 B1103/30
  B1182/01 B1182/02 B1249/20 C0059/05
  C0061/16 C0071/19 C0093/06 C0094/14
  C0121/30 C0122/30 C0140/20 C0146/25
  C0182/08 C0188/26 C0199/32 C0419/23
  C0420/03 C0561/30 C0577/27
alarmedly (1) A0694/11

alarming (9) A0324/05
  A0324/06 A0563/24 A0667/31 B0756/01
  B1134/31 B1259/20 C0092/11 C0553/33
alarmingly (2) C0141/02 C0424/26
alarummed (1) A0413/35
alas (49) A0077/03
  A0080/43 A0152/13 A0152/V A0154/19
  A0162/26 A0162/26 A0163/10 A0190/12
  A0211/05 A0214/29 A0215/18 A0317/24
  A0320/21 A0322/07 A0347/33 A0350/17
  A0350/29 A0351/17 A0353/18 A0356/28
  A0357/07 A0357/12 A0365/02 A0370/17
  A0428/12 A0507/01 A0608/19 A0610/05
  A0610/33 A0610/34 A0610/35 B0856/03
  B0856/15 B0900/07 B0903/02 B0907/02
  B0907/18 B0956/26 B0964/29 B0966/02
  B0969/14 B1154/19 B1222/25 B1225/23
  B1317/20 B1385/36 C0125/33 C0417/36
Albano (2) A0175/23 A0181/20
Albany (2) B0925/26 B0925/29
albatross (16) A0139/26
  C0151/30 C0151/31 C0151/37 C0152/01
  C0152/06 C0152/35 C0152/37 C0152/39
  C0153/13 C0153/20 C0159/17 C0163/23
  C0167/12 C0173/36 C0177/07
albatrosses (2) C0152/36 C0164/03
albeit (1) A0599/M
Albert (1) A0079/08
albuginea (1) B1181/33
Alceus (1) A0349/V
alchemy (1) A0036/13
Alcmaeon (2) A0341/23 A0342/V
Alcman (1) A0195/M
Alcohol (1) B0851/16
alcun (1) A0161/03
Alcyone (1) B1301/04
ale (5) A0242/10
  A0253/09 A0253/22 B0767/25 B0767/25
ale-house (2) A0240/06 A0240/07
Aleph (1) A0045/19
alert (3) C0105/26
  C0109/24 C0165/22
ales (2) A0250/26 A0251/18
Alex-- (1) B1369/25
Alexan (1) B1369/30
Alexander (6) A0037/23 A0037/23
  A0120/22 B0870/25 B1096/25 C0160/05
Alexander-etc.-nopolis (4) B1369/11
  B1369/19 B1369/20 B1369/22
Alexandria, (1) A0270/02
Alfred (1) A0349/34
Algae (1) B1163/12
algebra (3) B0987/06
  B0987/08 B0987/19
algebraic (4) A0365/22
  B1214/10 B1214/21 B1358/17
algebraists (2) B0987/12 B0988/01
alien (2) A0558/09 B1107/18
alienation (2) A0231/21 A0321/01
alight (2) B1003/28 B1075/13
alighted (2) B1370/07 C0191/15
alighting (3) A0057/07
  A0057/26 A0068/09
alike (11) A0267/07
  A0317/06 A0322/10 A0324/06 A0367/05

->A0367/21 A0432/09 A0434/19 B1156/33
B1313/04 C0200/37
aliment (1) B1068/12
alimentiveness (1) B1219/24
aliquantulum (2) A0209/M A0218/15
Aliquibus (1) A0515/34
alit (3) A0058/09
A0068/31 B1110/13
aliterque (3) A0301/10
A0302/20 A0303/17
Alive (1) A0339/25
alive (52)
All (1) B0806/M
all (1958)
all-absorbing (2) A0515/16 B0954/01
all-devouring (1) A0460/35
all-engrossing (1) A0297/07
all-fervid (1) A0461/22
all-important (1) B1194/26
all-pervading (1) A0294/V
all-sufficient (1) A0610/35
All/for/Love (1) A0033/V
Allah (2) A0198/27 B1155/03
Allamistakeo (5) B1185/14
B1185/20 B1185/30 B1190/14 B1190/34
Allamistakeo (1) B1179/31
Allamistakeo's (1) B1186/11
allay (3) A0019/20
A0458/33 B1212/26
allayed (3) B0816/09
B0858/24 C0561/24
allaying (2) A0458/21 B1273/34
Allbreath (1) A0071/31
alleged (2) B1047/32 C0546/13
allegorical (1) A0242/08
allegorically (1) B1010/01
allegory (1) A0240/T
Allen (9) C0102/40
C0105/16 C0108/14 C0108/32 C0110/33
C0112/11 C0181/37 C0181/40 C0183/23
Allen, Colonel Ethan (1) A0018/14
Allen, William (1) C0102/21
Allen, Wilson (1) C0181/26
alleviate (1) A0404/30
alleviating (2) A0320/18 B0941/13
alleviation (6) A0053/36 A0063/08
A0218/V A0398/24 B1208/08 C0128/32
alley (10) A0058/12 A0068/34
A0124/06 A0242/15 A0243/20 A0535/33
A0546/21 A0565/20 B1362/09 C0391/09
alleys (8) A0242/23
A0244/05 B0945/08 B0946/30 B0949/21
C0153/24 C0542/18 C0542/19
alliance (1) C0208/24
allied (1) A0296/V
allies (2) B1119/M C0557/13
allotted (5) A0065/10
A0098/32 A0455/12 B0871/17 C0182/33
allow (32) A0044/03
A0064/06 A0099/23 A0107/19 A0126/15
A0240/M A0299/08 A0300/02 A0427/11
A0485/20 A0629/28 B0732/32 B0739/05
B0815/33 B1010/20 B1010/21 B1013/24
B1128/01 B1153/05 B1193/02 B1381/27
C0056/05 C0068/09 C0068/27 C0071/31
->C0097/15 C0105/13 C0108/05 C0119/12
C0144/03 C0181/07 C0196/33
allowance (5) B0941/08
C0093/01 C0136/01 C0139/01 C0141/13
allowances (1) B0752/13
allowed (18) A0252/30 A0347/12
A0348/06 A0398/27 A0489/20 A0589/18
B0764/15 B0821/34 B0863/16 B0895/17
B1021/27 B1142/09 B1168/32 C0095/07
C0102/06 C0134/20 C0166/30 C0420/40
allowing (8) A0161/08
A0427/11 B0732/33 B0742/34 C0062/03
C0069/19 C0172/05 C0389/10
alloy (2) B1363/32 C0544/02
allude (14) A0120/18 A0266/26
A0275/26 A0277/06 A0280/33 A0294/V
A0343/05 B0764/16 B0842/03 B0984/11
B0987/03 B1191/11 C0207/25 C0522/01
alluded (20) A0099/06
A0263/04 A0270/28 A0324/15 A0380/06
A0406/15 A0693/23 B0725/V B0731/24
B0754/18 B0841/22 B0899/06 B0902/26
B0968/25 B1050/03 B1234/24 C0194/07
C0424/36 C0524/13 C0524/14
alludes (5) A0269/16
A0313/02 A0336/06 A0344/16 B1119/11
alluding (4) A0108/03
A0262/30 B0940/26 C0146/32
allured (1) A0690/07
allusion (14) A0283/14 A0434/23
A0602/05 A0654/06 B0763/21 B0850/30
B0915/25 B1050/32 B1122/09 B1145/12
B1186/24 B1358/12 C0448/V C0524/21
allusions (1) A0536/15
alluvia (1) C0536/32
alluvial (1) C0422/29
Alma/Mater (1) A0295/23
Almack's (2) A0182/18 A0182/27
Almacks (3) A0176/17
A0176/25 A0182/V
Almighty (2) A0601/06 B1276/25
almighty (3) A0139/31
A0711/24 B0797/21
almost (110)
aloft (5) A0126/17
A0319/20 A0676/20 B0930/11 C0431/07
alone (139)
along (97)
alongside (4) C0165/20
C0168/25 C0168/35 C0176/24
aloud (21) A0093/17
A0112/28 A0218/05 A0300/31 A0303/20
A0323/15 A0330/18 A0348/15 A0461/13
A0629/16 B0944/11 B0967/10 B0967/34
B0981/28 B1127/12 B1225/09 B1225/22
B1225/V B1263/16 C0116/07 C0145/01
alow (1) B0930/11
Alpha/Lyrae (3) B1300/30
B1300/33 B1302/15
alphabet (3) B0837/11
B0838/03 B0838/07
alphabetical (2) C0195/15 C0207/29
Alpheus (1) A0343/26
Alraschid, Haroun (1) B1166/19
already (135)

also (230)
altar (9) A0044/03
A0044/08 A0044/23 A0159/07 A0225/07
A0229/07 A0321/01 B0888/03 C0574/39
alter (8) A0369/14
A0488/08 A0510/32 A0704/17 B1051/36
B1269/16 C0523/34 C0538/20
alteration (28) A0025/19
A0026/18 A0159/08 A0213/17 A0216/05
A0299/24 A0320/17 A0415/05 A0457/24
A0458/16 A0580/19 A0629/12 A0695/24
A0696/29 A0709/03 B0851/07 B0866/04
B1069/27 B1235/11 B1333/17 B1370/34
C0081/23 C0203/29 C0394/34 C0418/41
C0419/35 C0423/34 C0424/13
alterations (2) A0412/22 A0459/16
altercation (4) A0353/11
A0389/01 A0436/12 A0437/02
altered (14) A0023/01 A0252/05
A0401/26 A0460/08 B0958/08 B0991/05
B1051/31 B1051/31 B1116/07 B1116/07
B1134/33 C0082/09 C0533/38 C0576/22
alterest (1) A0599/M
altering (4) A0053/21
A0062/26 B1077/02 C0056/18
alternate (4) A0640/10
A0641/V B0807/21 C0061/08
alternately (8) A0078/27
A0303/28 A0402/20 A0663/08 A0692/15
B1336/18 C0137/18 C0420/35
alternation (2) A0189/12 B1274/09
alternations (1) C0425/34
alternative (5) A0690/31
B0819/28 B0836/03 C0074/38 C0132/23
alternatively (1) C0078/13
althegither> (8) A0465/07
A0465/19 A0466/14 A0466/32 A0467/04
A0468/V A0469/13 A0470/03
although (389)
altitude (19) A0064/21
A0140/05 A0240/19 B1076/14 B1076/24
B1080/29 B1193/09 C0181/03 C0389/13
C0399/16 C0400/32 C0401/06 C0401/11
C0402/34 C0403/34 C0404/22 C0405/41
C0411/39 C0423/33
altitudes (3) C0157/33
C0157/33 C0417/38
alto (2) A0097/32 A0273/28
altogether (209)
aluit (1) A0681/M
alum (1) C0553/02
always (161)
am (331)
amassed (2) A0704/21 B1269/20
Amateaza (1) C0574/39
amativeness (1) B1220/03
Amatory (2) A0621/02 A0621/08
amazed (9) A0159/10
A0303/13 A0414/14 A0513/24 A0534/09
A0690/11 B0829/09 B0865/30 B0866/02
amazement (27) A0089/03
A0089/28 A0103/19 A0106/19 A0139/14
A0159/V A0163/22 A0163/25 A0248/15
A0328/02 A0414/27 A0439/18 A0515/14
A0535/17 B0826/18 B0895/15 B0943/31
->B1105/31 B1181/30 C0073/09 C0169/24
C0169/34 C0421/13 C0421/35 C0554/25
C0568/25 C0569/10
amazing (2) A0585/23 A0588/18
amazingly (1) B1359/05
Ambaaren (1) A0579/25
amber (1) B1162/06
ambiguity (2) A0217/11 C0430/34
ambiguous (4) A0056/16
A0264/22 A0428/17 C0097/02
ambition (18) A0162/V A0282/05
A0432/09 A0445/05 A0445/31 A0496/19
A0510/13 A0704/03 A0706/18 A0706/21
A0712/02 B0987/09 B1269/03 B1271/20
B1271/23 B1271/V B1277/05 C0569/34
Ambitious (2) A0176/09 A0180/30
ambitious (4) A0706/20
B0748/25 B1126/05 B1271/22
ambitus (1) B0987/09
ambuscade (1) C0181/09
Amen (1) A0075/13
amenable (1) A0497/09
amending (1) A0491/04
amendment (2) A0491/06 B1143/29
amends (1) C0062/38
amenity (2) A0175/23 A0181/20
amerement (1) A0036/17
America (16) A0389/09
A0496/24 A0628/26 B0861/01 B0862/02
B0862/25 B0863/04 B0864/30 B0874/17
B0914/19 B0941/22 B0942/18 B0958/06
B1126/15 B1234/27 C0525/28
American (29) A0263/19
A0490/07 A0498/25 A0512/31 A0580/05
B0818/29 B0827/31 B0864/04 B0894/03
B0904/12 B0958/16 B1031/12 B1081/13
B1151/05 B1151/05 B1184/19 B1207/02
C0053/T C0087/16 C0155/34 C0156/03
C0158/06 C0158/07 C0160/29 C0163/34
C0432/38 C0524/13 C0526/02 C0535/38
Americanism (1) B1093/32
Americans (7) A0292/V
A0493/01 A0495/V A0500/25 B0904/06
C0155/39 C0571/07
Amerique (1) B0913/06
ami (8) B0906/29
B0907/07 B0907/08 B0907/19 B0909/33
B0910/01 B1010/20 B1012/30
amiability (2) B0957/15 B1010/V
amiable (3) B0923/19
B0949/31 B1054/19
amicable (1) A0303/14
amicably (1) C0177/18
amicae (2) A0209/M A0218/15
amid (71)
amid-ships (1) C0102/32
amidships (1) C0118/29
amiss (1) C0152/06
amity (3) B1338/21
C0558/15 C0568/41
ammonia (1) B0853/27
Ammonites (1) A0044/01
ammunition (6) C0085/31 C0530/22
C0530/32 C0534/12 C0535/10 C0549/32
among (286)

amongst (1) B1160/36
Amontillado (18) A0181/16 B1256/T
B1257/24 B1257/25 B1257/28 B1257/30
B1257/32 B1257/34 B1258/03 B1258/15
B1258/17 B1260/31 B1260/34 B1261/20
B1262/01 B1262/03 B1263/08 B1263/09
amount (35) A0276/26
A0379/17 A0441/27 A0487/26 A0601/10
A0652/04 A0653/14 A0704/25 A0705/06
A0712/06 B0727/26 B0733/03 B0862/24
B0873/34 B0874/03 B0874/22 B0979/23
B0983/03 B0984/18 B0989/V B1045/30
B1054/17 B1073/18 B1209/01 B1269/24
B1270/05 B1277/11 B1296/09 B1312/13
B1329/34 B1373/26 C0135/41 C0403/23
C0429/48 C0521/15
amounted (8) A0296/V
A0317/19 A0705/19 B1031/08 B1154/24
B1270/17 C0065/22 C0123/17
amounting (6) A0282/04 B0834/24
B1073/21 C0141/26 C0400/06 C0412/01
amounts (4) B0739/03
B0745/33 B0879/04 B0986/08
amour (1) B0754/26
amphitheatre (8) A0128/09
A0146/03 B1283/01 B1331/29 B1332/22
B1333/07 B1334/31 B1335/34
ample (9) A0241/25
A0704/13 B0878/01 B1056/22 B1078/25
B1110/13 B1113/01 B1269/13 C0080/10
amplification (1) A0405/13
Amplitudine (1) A0213/04
amply (4) A0671/03
B0747/02 B0872/15 C0065/07
Amriccan (5) B1297/01
B1302/28 B1303/19 B1304/05 B1304/30
Amriccans (3) B1296/13
B1299/27 B1305/12
Amsterdam (1) A0541/01
amuse (4) A0205/34
A0430/23 B0927/05 B1031/23
amused (19) A0354/11
A0354/11 A0533/22 A0535/12 B0889/08
B0916/21 B0926/16 B0926/16 B0928/02
B0975/35 B1105/02 B1115/11 B1194/02
B1329/04 B1348/14 C0069/16 C0070/34
C0169/12 C0532/17
amusement (19) A0070/05
A0070/18 A0091/20 A0110/24 A0204/04
A0484/17 A0546/05 A0591/32 B0822/17
B0898/19 B1246/04 B1294/15 B1304/08
B1305/15 B1346/09 C0093/28 C0428/14
C0564/29 C0564/30
amusements (3) B0807/23
B1006/13 B1302/16
amusing (4) A0507/17
B0745/16 B1009/24 B1302/19
an (1) A0353/09
an (1811)
an> (2) A0469/22 A0470/16
Ana-Pest (3) A0250/16
A0253/02 A0254/06
Anacharsis (1) A0081/17
Anacreon (1) A0190/08
Anakim (1) B1008/33
analogical (2) C0401/04 C0429/47
analogically (1) A0601/22
analogies (3) A0314/07
B0989/13 B1300/25
analogist (1) B1114/20
analogous (16) A0387/16
A0457/14 A0489/07 A0497/02 A0531/09
B0757/06 B0877/04 B0987/33 B0990/03
B1168/23 B1168/23 B1296/14 B1312/17
B1359/19 B1359/24 C0426/05
analogy (14) A0298/V A0478/15
A0478/17 A0609/25 A0610/17 B1095/11
B1300/26 B1301/10 B1301/12 B1301/20
B1301/25 C0428/18 C0429/47 C0439/V
analyse (1) A0528/16
analysis (35) A0097/07
A0141/22 A0212/10 A0296/V A0303/V
A0398/04 A0511/19 A0527/02 A0527/V
A0528/15 A0529/18 A0530/30 A0708/22
B0751/28 B0751/V B0768/27 B0770/V
B0836/15 B0984/28 B0987/05 B0987/08
B1039/20 B1114/35 B1114/35 B1214/10
B1214/12 B1214/21 B1221/04 B1273/16
B1322/14 B1358/10 B1364/04 B1364/15
B1380/09 B1380/19
analyst (5) A0528/05
A0529/08 A0530/01 A0530/29 B1115/01
analytic (5) A0531/06
A0531/11 A0533/11 B1215/01 B1380/24
analytical (7) A0478/35
A0496/V A0527/01 A0530/28 B0725/08
B1092/34 B1143/32
analyze (3) A0214/09
A0250/24 A0314/12
analyzed (2) B1133/23 B1362/34
analyzing (4) A0078/18
B1295/15 B1311/08 B1362/32
Anamalech (1) A0046/12
Anamoo-moo (3) C0168/08
C0168/32 C0174/18
Anamoo-moos (1) C0175/24
anarchy (1) A0108/28
anatomical (2) A0559/19 B1114/20
anatomists (1) B0763/25
Anaxagoras (2) A0054/37 A0064/08
ancestor (4) A0022/09
A0704/32 B0912/15 B1269/31
ancestors (5) A0021/24
B0841/21 B1092/19 B1126/19 C0391/10
ancestral (2) A0234/V A0235/27
anchor (15) A0136/30
A0240/04 A0584/09 A0584/16 B0968/14
C0150/09 C0156/24 C0167/28 C0170/39
C0171/05 C0176/15 C0180/20 C0186/02
C0555/21 C0565/13
anchorage (5) A0584/02
A0585/21 C0150/39 C0150/41 C0151/03
anchored (1) C0538/04
anchors (2) C0147/20 C0557/35
ancient (35) A0019/08
A0019/21 A0075/10 A0286/06 A0310/12
A0374/19 A0398/31 A0404/04 A0428/02
A0430/12 A0497/27 A0509/03 A0609/35
B0806/02 B0841/01 B0850/30 B0865/18
B0871/04 B1049/35 B1294/02 B1294/09

->B1294/32 B1295/31 B1296/11 B1297/01
B1297/29 B1299/13 B1299/27 B1302/08
B1303/19 B1303/30 B1311/28 B1314/05
B1317/34 C0540/29
ancients (4) A0089/08
A0104/07 B1297/21 B1316/04
ancles (2) C0122/07 C0552/29
and (1) A0356/14
and (13921)
andava (1) A0344/32
Anderson (1) B0725/32
Andromache (2) A0033/V A0455/M
Andromache (1) A0033/01
Andronicus (1) A0110/21
anecdote (4) A0296/V
B1009/21 B1014/35 B1361/26
anecdotes (5) A0582/24
B1191/16 C0087/29 C0087/30 C0541/12
anemonae (1) A0345/26
anemone (2) A0345/26 A0345/27
anemonoe (1) A0345/V
aner (Gr.) (1) A0346/03
aneurism (1) B1235/34
anew (2) A0428/06 A0612/02
Anfangsgrunde (3) A0342/01
A0342/V A0342/V
Angel (20) B1100/T
B1103/25 B1103/35 B1104/10 B1104/15
B1104/20 B1104/25 B1105/03 B1106/04
B1106/15 B1107/02 B1107/34 B1108/34
B1109/17 B1109/25 B1109/29 B1109/34
B1110/04 B1110/08 B1110/22
angel (16) A0318/09
A0349/29 A0356/30 A0385/06 A0466/30
A0467/09 A0467/31 A0483/11 A0644/23
A0682/07 B0897/19 B0909/28 B1103/27
B1103/34 B1104/03 B1104/06
angelic (4) A0325/10
B0892/08 B1040/04 B1215/06
Angelo (1) A0161/01
angels (23) A0175/05
A0181/26 A0310/M A0314/28 A0319/15
A0319/24 A0320/01 A0349/29 A0406/26
A0461/22 A0642/30 A0643/25 A0682/04
A0711/32 B1039/02 B1040/01 B1122/02
B1128/27 B1130/05 B1212/02 B1213/13
B1276/35 B1316/01
anger (13) A0104/18
A0466/15 A0541/08 A0567/05 A0626/08
B0857/28 B0900/25 B1048/05 B1221/29
B1222/01 C0095/27 C0133/15 C0556/22
anges (2) B1121/01 B1121/03
angle (28) A0248/13
A0429/04 A0430/03 A0479/01 A0580/31
A0590/35 B0842/06 B1075/06 B1075/08
B1075/10 B1080/28 B1185/05 B1280/08
B1300/31 B1332/21 B1337/18 B1338/02
B1340/20 B1381/34 C0173/07 C0183/16
C0398/18 C0418/32 C0419/10 C0419/39
C0420/07 C0421/12 C0567/27
angler (1) B0870/26
angles (33) A0087/21
A0248/20 A0273/14 A0322/03 A0326/08
A0401/12 A0430/08 A0497/17 A0503/02
A0509/23 A0554/19 A0686/01 A0686/17

->A0688/27 A0688/29 A0691/30 A0696/26
B0762/19 B1009/V B1020/25 B1054/09
B1077/05 B1160/25 B1164/26 B1282/28
B1333/19 B1336/07 B1351/12 B1352/30
C0061/13 C0152/33 C0398/07 C0574/02
Anglo-Saxon (1) B1141/27
anglois (1) C0430/38
angrily (2) B0828/36 B1014/01
angry (14) A0177/11 A0183/04
A0197/32 A0262/14 A0353/06 A0434/08
A0441/32 A0537/16 A0540/07 A0579/19
B1104/34 C0061/29 C0079/02 C0579/23
anguish (5) A0209/08
A0317/03 C0124/28 C0129/37 C0143/22
angular (6) A0265/20 A0294/08
A0613/17 B1092/09 C0421/09 C0421/17
anima (1) A0638/M
animadversion (1) B0767/13
animadversions (1) A0072/04
Animae (2) A0515/31 A0515/34
animal (88)
animal's (6) A0026/30 A0125/30
B0853/16 B0866/06 B1046/23 C0546/11
animalculae (2) A0600/32 A0601/02
animalculae (1) B1213/21
Animals (2) B1093/19 B1131/33
animals (36) A0127/16
A0478/02 A0491/16 A0694/10 B0850/11
B1157/04 B1157/14 B1162/15 B1162/19
B1163/01 B1163/11 B1165/31 B1334/29
B1350/31 C0138/06 C0155/22 C0155/32
C0164/35 C0173/28 C0173/33 C0174/12
C0176/24 C0205/14 C0429/33 C0534/33
C0544/21 C0545/07 C0545/18 C0546/25
C0547/11 C0553/04 C0561/34 C0562/28
C0567/01 C0577/34 C0578/12
animate (1) A0600/26
animated (7) A0383/04
A0641/15 B0991/30 B1186/09 B1207/02
B1247/08 B1294/22
animation (6) A0059/19 A0067/10
A0322/28 B0956/02 B0959/28 C0198/27
animaux (1) A0019/04
animosity (5) A0020/01
A0385/26 A0433/12 B0946/25 C0082/02
ankle (5) A0035/22
A0535/26 C0090/28 C0127/01 C0397/32
ankles (7) A0103/26
A0243/33 A0348/34 A0368/09 C0092/38
C0168/18 C0411/28
annales (1) B1335/18
Annals (2) B1097/05 B1114/29
annals (2) A0293/29 C0404/21
annexed (3) A0282/02
B1071/V C0554/12
Annian (2) C0525/21 C0525/40
Annie (2) B1339/07 B1339/08
annihilate (1) A0398/08
annihilated (3) A0345/25
A0691/28 B1168/38
annihilation (3) B0963/05
B1223/08 C0421/28
anniversary (1) B1304/15
annotations (1) B1189/17
announce (1) B0769/22

announced (4) B0930/32
B1007/26 B1053/31 B1234/36
announcement (8) A0457/34
A0457/35 A0544/27 B1134/15 B1298/14
B1316/23 B1364/22 B1364/30
announcing (2) B0819/22 B0949/30
annoy (1) A0442/08
annoyance (6) A0434/04 A0434/30
B0854/28 B0940/26 B1164/19 C0393/08
annoyances (1) A0589/17
annoyed (10) B0844/04 B0854/27
B0888/16 B0908/V B0925/19 B0944/15
B1009/07 B1225/01 B1292/05 C0542/22
annoying (2) A0072/14 B0888/08
annoys (1) B0813/21
annual (8) A0243/03
A0440/06 A0705/18 B0941/08 B1134/19
B1270/17 B1321/19 C0561/35
annually (1) C0431/13
anointed (3) A0694/20
B1141/15 B1207/28
anomalies (4) A0294/16
A0313/25 A0413/16 C0170/19
anomalous (9) A0403/09
A0433/16 A0493/01 A0613/15 B0773/17
B0859/03 B0890/28 B0959/33 B1223/V
anomaly (7) A0053/32
A0063/03 A0080/22 A0087/06 A0164/18
A0214/01 B0724/04
anon (8) A0124/11
A0218/02 A0348/01 A0379/17 A0416/16
A0455/09 A0673/30 B1134/25
Anonymous (1) A0599/M
another (181)
another's (2) A0154/19 A0154/20
<u>Ansichten</u> (1) B0723/M
answer (57)
answered (19) A0178/19
A0191/08 A0218/05 A0240/22 A0372/31
B0766/14 B0796/34 B0858/06 B0858/35
B1035/16 B1142/29 B1188/28 B1260/28
C0070/11 C0100/21 C0101/15 C0180/31
C0197/26 C0557/31
answering (4) A0268/24
A0583/34 B0767/01 C0554/24
answers (3) A0026/07
A0251/24 A0341/18
ant (1) B1162/32
antagonist (8) A0037/24
A0433/28 A0441/20 A0443/27 A0447/25
A0448/05 A0703/10 B1268/09
antagonistical (2) B0740/31
B1221/17
antagonists (1) C0113/04
Antarctic (12) C0053/T
C0055/29 C0159/04 C0159/13 C0160/37
C0161/06 C0162/17 C0163/05 C0164/05
C0166/24 C0202/09 C0202/16
Antarctic/Ocean (1) C0201/36
Antares (1) B0898/03
ante-chamber (3) A0216/26
A0447/11 B1363/01
antediluvian (2) A0165/23 B1091/30
Antediluvians (1) A0621/21
antelope (9) B1055/18
->C0173/32 C0542/41 C0552/16 C0553/05
C0561/27 C0563/23 C0566/33 C0575/13
antelopes (8) C0542/20
C0543/32 C0559/41 C0561/33 C0561/36
C0562/13 C0562/28 C0563/09
<u>antennae</u> (5) B0808/35
B0810/14 B0810/15 B0810/17 B0810/23
antennae (1) B1250/25
Anthon (1) A0283/21
Anthon, Charles (1) A0283/17
anticipate (19) A0166/15
A0269/25 A0593/29 A0611/19 A0657/06
A0657/09 A0657/10 A0657/12 B0744/10
B0906/04 B0988/21 B0988/22 B1183/11
B1234/15 C0082/07 C0197/35 C0200/33
C0527/37 C0557/27
anticipated (30) A0106/22 A0417/02
A0552/22 B0854/25 B0979/08 B1059/12
B1107/20 B1181/24 B1352/08 B1372/22
C0068/08 C0104/39 C0108/13 C0112/23
C0120/41 C0127/03 C0133/21 C0133/39
C0139/29 C0189/34 C0191/28 C0397/19
C0398/16 C0400/17 C0406/23 C0414/11
C0416/13 C0419/36 C0422/04 C0555/03
anticipating (2) A0127/13 A0441/29
anticipation (3) A0127/06
B1222/10 C0391/38
anticipations (3) B0726/02
B0891/02 C0412/28
anticipative (1) C0111/39
<u>Antigone</u> (1) A0608/M
antimony (2) A0182/10 B1362/31
Antinous (2) A0160/23 A0621/18
Antioch (7) A0120/16
A0120/V A0121/10 A0121/18 A0121/18
A0123/25 A0128/V
Antiochia/Epidaphne (1) A0120/19
Antiochus (5) A0120/23
A0126/05 A0126/07 A0127/30 A0128/05
antipathies (1) C0427/17
antipathy (1) A0020/06
antipodes (3) A0241/V
B1296/26 B1313/27
antiquarian (4) A0089/13
B1089/09 B1293/09 B1304/04
antiquarians (2) A0124/21 B1303/08
antiquated (2) A0142/22 B1008/18
antique (16) A0100/34
A0209/17 A0235/V A0312/30 A0401/15
A0413/08 A0416/23 A0498/17 A0503/03
A0514/25 A0662/10 A0685/23 A0689/29
B0827/27 B1128/20 B1179/16
antiquities (3) A0145/04
B1299/26 B1302/28
antiquity (9) A0122/09
A0292/02 A0322/19 A0366/01 A0367/07
A0369/31 A0400/06 B0871/26 B1186/18
<u>antiquum</u> (1) A0536/18
Antoeus (1) A0079/44
Antony, Mark (1) A0069/18
<u>antro</u> (1) A0681/M
anxieties (2) A0612/20 C0425/19
anxiety (40) A0022/16
A0028/21 A0073/21 A0102/17 A0189/28
A0214/27 A0234/15 A0324/19 A0432/31

->A0442/25 A0456/25 A0530/19 A0566/05
A0614/11 B0726/07 B0756/16 B0756/21
B0795/23 B0813/17 B0826/13 B1031/03
B1132/33 B1133/09 B1137/08 B1195/03
B1370/10 C0062/22 C0077/12 C0080/12
C0083/17 C0089/05 C0094/28 C0114/18
C0134/12 C0134/36 C0141/23 C0395/20
C0417/31 C0419/28 C0446/V
anxious (33) A0073/26
A0263/08 A0263/09 A0263/10 A0264/25
A0371/02 A0378/08 A0435/16 A0593/06
A0703/10 B0768/21 B0810/33 B0816/10
B0819/30 B0923/24 B1076/35 B1195/15
B1236/10 B1268/09 B1383/32 B1383/34
B1384/01 C0092/01 C0100/01 C0139/04
C0170/22 C0192/35 C0545/02 C0555/17
C0558/27 C0560/08 C0565/02 C0574/32
anxiously (6) A0350/11 A0446/26
A0513/30 C0114/16 C0143/06 C0408/24
anxther (1) B1374/08
any (897)
anybody (4) A0340/04
A0342/07 A0385/17 B1299/28
anyone (1) B1046/19
anything (93)
anywhere (5) A0631/05
B1279/34 B1347/15 C0088/41 C0101/20
Aoede (1) A0343/21
aorta (1) B1235/34
apart (27) A0142/32
A0161/13 A0267/31 A0313/09 A0327/13
A0355/14 A0400/09 A0500/04 B0742/25
B0773/18 B0955/36 B0956/03 B0963/12
B0987/28 B0992/34 B1137/03 B1192/13
B1192/23 B1332/30 B1351/09 B1384/35
C0185/03 C0197/10 C0415/23 C0430/46
C0542/35 C0572/11
apartment (66)
apartments (15) A0067/08
A0159/11 A0294/02 A0296/11 A0410/27
A0436/34 A0500/25 A0551/11 A0662/08
A0671/21 A0672/07 A0674/11 A0674/12
B0929/04 B0976/12
apathetic (2) A0028/29 B0966/11
apathy (8) A0145/30
A0297/09 A0404/17 B0733/01 B0733/09
B0748/28 B0748/29 C0205/19
ape (7) A0124/19
A0565/15 A0565/V A0566/V A0566/V
A0567/20 B0945/21
apeak (1) C0180/20
Apennines (1) A0662/05
aper (1) B1142/15
aperture (23) A0246/25
A0351/25 A0352/01 A0352/07 A0352/23
A0538/11 A0557/11 A0695/23 B1184/13
B1263/20 B1362/21 C0068/35 C0075/21
C0076/05 C0091/28 C0094/08 C0100/06
C0101/32 C0189/06 C0194/14 C0194/23
C0410/21 C0545/21
apes (3) B1351/14
B1353/03 B1353/15
apex (7) A0354/23
A0579/07 B0762/20 B0841/14 B1248/21
B1336/02 C0388/28
aphelion (1) C0401/39
Aphrodite (1) A0166/19
Aphrodite, Marchesa (2) A0152/17
A0164/12
Apicius (1) A0033/03
apocryphal (1) B1358/23
Apollo (6) A0035/16 A0160/20
A0160/22 A0160/V A0312/27 A0379/24
Apollonius (2) A0176/02 A0182/01
apologetic (1) B0940/27
apologie (1) B0900/01
apologies (2) B1101/02 B1185/22
apologize (2) B1106/01 B1135/27
apologizing (1) B1185/12
apology (9) A0074/10
A0074/10 A0268/23 A0302/11 A0388/31
A0443/05 A0662/V B0923/28 B1140/01
apostrophising (1) A0345/10
apothecary (6) A0059/20 A0059/24
A0059/30 A0067/11 A0067/15 A0067/20
apothegm (1) A0143/03
apotheosis (2) A0710/23 B1275/26
apout (3) B1103/08
B1103/08 B1104/03
Appallachia (2) A0497/06 A0500/24
appalled (8) A0234/07
A0315/11 A0412/10 A0664/24 B0764/20
B1235/10 B1247/17 C0190/15
appalling (21) A0029/04
A0035/06 A0139/25 A0143/25 A0213/31
A0329/07 A0580/33 B0735/16 B0751/05
B0961/30 B1005/26 C0111/36 C0125/30
C0126/18 C0134/01 C0134/21 C0134/22
C0182/34 C0413/02 C0420/21 C0422/40
appals (1) A0674/08
Apparatus (1) B1167/37
apparatus (18) B1071/04 B1075/09
B1362/16 C0394/33 C0395/27 C0396/09
C0402/21 C0402/25 C0405/15 C0407/30
C0409/09 C0409/09 C0412/24 C0416/31
C0419/24 C0422/17 C0424/15 C0424/39
apparel (4) A0445/25
A0556/02 B1004/19 B1108/12
apparent (97)
apparently (101)
apparition (12) A0329/26
B0853/17 B0866/01 B0890/14 B1249/09
B1249/24 C0109/36 C0111/28 C0111/33
C0111/39 C0112/02 C0112/13
appeal (5) A0374/18
B0932/04 B1221/18 B1338/22 C0541/23
appealing (2) A0155/09 B0773/17
appeals (2) A0710/24 B1275/27
appear (65)
appearance (205)
appearances (10) A0124/15 A0413/02
A0543/23 A0556/01 A0672/15 B0956/17
B1235/29 C0166/19 C0191/28 C0547/28
appeared (200)
appearing (10) B1359/32 B1362/02
B1382/16 B1382/18 B1386/09 C0133/40
C0151/35 C0171/13 C0173/28 C0429/07
appears (56)
appease (2) C0128/30 C0569/08
appeased (2) B1142/06 C0135/32

appellation (15) A0120/17
A0145/16 A0150/V A0191/08 A0211/16
A0240/16 A0250/07 A0399/17 A0399/18
A0426/02 B1130/17 B1143/23 C0204/07
C0208/23 C0420/33
appellations (3) A0027/11
A0431/18 B0887/17
appendages (3) A0491/17
C0425/41 C0552/23
appended (9) A0265/02
A0622/12 A0690/20 B0723/07 B0727/24
B0730/33 B1073/32 B1075/28 B1136/02
appending (1) B1358/15
appendix (2) A0440/17 C0207/23
Appennine (1) A0667/03
appertain (1) B0833/08
appertaining (5) A0247/20
A0248/25 A0293/29 A0302/14 A0638/20
appertains (5) A0482/05
A0710/22 B0839/28 B1006/10 B1275/25
appetency (1) A0507/10
appetite (7) A0482/18
B1007/22 B1009/17 C0071/03 C0101/04
C0137/11 C0176/02
appetites (1) A0044/17
applause (6) A0177/V A0435/13
A0710/36 B1139/05 B1276/02 C0569/30
apple (8) A0253/10
B0980/12 B1010/28 B1092/28 B1383/20
B1383/20 B1383/28 B1383/29
apples (1) A0534/33
appliances (4) A0440/11
A0671/07 B0757/35 B1115/22
applicability (4) B0987/08
B0987/31 B1214/14 B1312/30
applicable (9) A0161/10
A0301/13 A0495/V B0723/17 B0764/03
B1051/24 B1162/29 B1240/11 C0394/35
application (21) A0105/19
A0345/03 A0346/13 A0381/V A0690/33
B0835/28 B0879/11 B0960/11 B0962/14
B0985/27 B0987/05 B1030/31 B1070/19
B1072/16 B1119/17 B1181/17 B1208/23
B1209/08 B1238/11 C0402/26 C0433/09
<u>applicationem</u> (3) A0301/12
A0302/19 A0303/04
applications (1) A0279/04
applied (33) A0056/34
A0066/24 A0071/18 A0142/30 A0161/09
A0246/20 A0312/08 A0482/06 A0536/04
A0546/06 A0609/13 A0609/34 A0611/19
A0705/34 B0724/05 B0910/22 B0950/04
B0959/23 B0981/06 B0987/17 B1008/26
B1070/04 B1070/21 B1130/18 B1137/15
B1139/28 B1182/15 B1185/27 B1214/15
B1270/33 C0187/41 C0393/35 C0544/33
applies (5) A0345/30
A0710/27 B1097/04 B1275/30 C0429/28
apply (11) A0044/07
A0059/33 A0065/23 A0280/24 A0341/04
A0356/04 A0459/31 B0879/07 B1096/36
B1130/08 C0536/08
applying (6) A0625/20 B0891/27
B0960/19 B1239/06 C0073/36 C0096/20
appoint (1) A0301/26
appointed (7) A0027/12
A0204/11 B0755/32 B1105/29 B1163/07
B1347/08 C0065/36
appointment (6) A0204/33 B0897/04
B1105/13 B1105/34 B1237/04 B1390/13
appointments (1) A0673/23
apposite (1) B1050/18
appreciable (7) A0560/17
A0691/03 A0705/05 B0836/07 B1037/19
B1270/05 B1363/32
appreciate (10) A0126/08 A0338/32
A0527/02 A0600/05 A0695/14 A0696/21
B0757/28 B1039/35 B1317/35 C0091/04
appreciated (5) A0613/15
A0613/31 A0616/03 B0738/14 B0895/27
appreciating (1) A0614/30
appreciation (10) A0159/23 A0383/26
A0495/06 A0545/25 A0682/12 A0709/15
B0926/32 B1135/28 B1209/11 B1274/19
apprehend (5) A0585/15
A0686/30 B1234/26 C0067/39 C0159/37
apprehended (14) A0092/23 A0111/33
A0138/04 A0458/27 A0710/27 B0763/10
B0958/23 B0960/33 B1015/07 B1082/01
B1275/29 C0097/38 C0160/36 C0548/21
apprehending (2) A0136/34 C0550/06
apprehension (17) A0138/08
A0141/04 A0387/V A0457/34 A0459/06
A0528/09 A0710/20 A0710/34 B0823/14
B1246/19 B1275/23 B1275/34 B1292/25
B1364/16 C0143/15 C0421/05 C0548/27
apprehensions (12) A0056/27
A0066/16 A0145/07 A0561/22 B0969/08
B1008/20 C0094/18 C0095/36 C0167/09
C0172/25 C0424/11 C0549/27
apprehensive (4) A0542/28
C0096/13 C0146/26 C0189/02
apprentices (3) A0338/21
B1101/11 B1127/12
apprize (1) C0186/08
approach (33) A0066/12
A0099/17 A0103/18 A0124/08 A0214/11
A0458/12 A0676/05 A0708/07 B0769/V
B0852/02 B1092/35 B1192/23 B1223/13
B1246/11 B1273/06 B1278/32 B1282/09
C0161/33 C0167/30 C0169/35 C0170/10
C0175/35 C0178/29 C0180/16 C0180/21
C0190/38 C0389/35 C0424/24 C0424/25
C0535/14 C0544/28 C0567/08 C0572/25
approached (41) A0179/31
A0232/16 A0415/20 A0437/13 A0459/20
A0511/31 A0567/20 A0589/28 A0627/12
A0676/20 B0744/34 B0818/06 B0853/13
B0854/08 B0862/31 B0866/15 B0889/25
B0897/20 B0966/10 B0968/12 B1141/23
B1156/28 B1188/16 B1238/07 B1238/14
B1279/03 B1281/19 B1338/29 C0127/39
C0133/17 C0140/21 C0162/37 C0169/03
C0169/32 C0173/24 C0174/16 C0186/38
C0200/40 C0201/03 C0545/33 C0568/36
approaches (7) A0128/06
A0427/04 B0767/31 B0767/32 B0875/32
B1282/34 C0401/38
approaching (35) A0080/11
A0127/06 A0214/15 A0314/03 A0314/04

->A0341/V A0342/17 A0403/35 A0489/14
  A0588/26 A0614/25 A0650/08 B0794/21
  B1019/34 B1076/20 B1155/35 B1179/19
  B1194/33 B1225/V B1234/22 B1236/08
  B1298/28 C0094/23 C0108/17 C0134/20
  C0144/24 C0150/21 C0165/26 C0205/34
  C0417/17 C0420/31 C0421/31 C0423/32
  C0446/V C0557/39
approbation (3) B1137/13
  B1138/10 C0569/33
approbatory (1) A0035/17
appropriate (5) A0098/33
  A0245/12 B0933/05 B1137/16 B1304/13
appropriated (1) A0435/01
appropriately (1) B0865/31
appropriating (1) A0044/17
approval (1) C0079/16
approved (3) A0675/13
  B0870/04 B1152/26
appurtenance (2) A0093/21 A0112/32
appurtenances (2) A0496/15 A0496/16
April (47) A0204/24
  B1075/33 B1291/13 B1293/32 B1294/15
  B1298/25 B1299/24 B1300/30 B1302/16
  B1302/25 C0155/26 C0212/V C0212/V
  C0213/V C0214/V C0395/18 C0416/16
  C0416/38 C0417/12 C0417/21 C0417/33
  C0417/39 C0418/01 C0418/40 C0419/14
  C0419/18 C0419/29 C0419/35 C0420/03
  C0420/11 C0420/19 C0420/34 C0421/07
  C0422/41 C0424/10 C0560/18 C0560/27
  C0560/29 C0561/18 C0563/32 C0563/32
  C0563/32 C0563/32 C0565/12 C0565/16
  C0565/16 C0565/25
apron (3) A0628/04
  A0630/01 A0630/28
aproposisms (1) B1050/19
apsides (1) C0420/13
apt (9) A0026/16
  A0092/01 A0111/13 B0840/16 B1018/06
  C0078/09 C0106/33 C0151/20 C0555/36
Apuleius (1) B0890/01
aqua (1) B0832/20
aqueduct (1) A0127/12
aquiline (2) A0298/V A0312/17
Arab (1) C0551/13
Arabella (2) A0383/13 A0383/18
Arabesque (9) A0087/23
  A0092/26 A0157/V A0320/V A0321/V
  A0402/12 A0498/16 A0502/02 B1386/08
arabesque (9) A0088/36
  A0166/03 A0322/15 A0322/17 A0473/01
  A0473/13 A0662/13 A0673/22 B1280/34
Arabian (3) A0336/07
  A0349/13 B1333/06
Arabian/Nights (3) B1152/05
  B1223/01 C0542/05
Arabian/Tales (1) B0945/03
Arabic (5) A0344/10
  B1091/30 B1155/13 C0171/39 C0208/05
Arago (2) B1357/01 B1363/37
arbitrary (5) A0431/26
  A0446/10 A0708/19 B1273/14 C0100/32
Arcadians (1) A0124/15
Arch (5) A0250/14
->A0250/16 A0253/02 A0254/06 B1092/32
arch (12) A0053/24
  A0062/28 A0127/11 A0150/V A0153/17
  A0190/33 A0209/03 A0630/29 A0631/10
  B1334/07 C0150/38 C0194/15
arch-angel (1) A0244/V
Arch-enemy (1) A0021/28
arch-enemy (2) A0445/33 A0626/09
arch-fiend (1) B1223/25
arch-way (1) A0626/27
Arch-Fiend (1) B0858/33
Archangel (1) B0943/33
Archangels (2) A0055/13 A0064/27
archbishop (1) B1105/08
arched (2) A0023/02 A0630/12
arches (2) B1261/01 C0207/41
Archilochus (1) A0111/06
Archimedean (2) B1070/28 B1071/V
Archimedes (4) A0593/35
  B1382/35 B1383/06 B1383/08
Archipelago (2) A0135/25 A0136/09
architect (5) A0044/27
  A0150/V A0478/21 A0486/11 A0611/14
architects (2) B1278/12 C0544/27
architectural (2) A0165/22 A0705/11
architecture (1) B1335/18
architecture (13) A0153/11
  A0157/16 A0158/13 A0321/04 A0352/22
  A0367/07 A0495/01 A0663/01 A0710/02
  B1192/04 B1275/05 B1283/11 B1337/29
archives (2) A0089/18 A0369/31
archway (9) A0151/13
  A0349/28 A0349/32 A0400/23 A0410/08
  A0416/14 B1258/28 B1382/19 C0184/24
Archytas (2) A0341/23 A0342/V
Arctic (5) C0164/35
  C0165/16 C0166/20 C0417/29 C0418/10
Arctic/ocean (1) C0525/31
Arctic/Ocean (3) C0202/16
  C0524/27 C0524/35
ardency (1) A0431/V
ardent (12) A0210/10
  A0212/15 A0644/17 B0888/27 B1158/31
  B1182/24 B1298/16 B1316/26 C0065/05
  C0073/26 C0093/35 C0569/06
ardently (1) A0653/23
ardor (8) A0028/07
  A0297/12 A0323/17 A0328/10 A0431/10
  A0440/12 A0638/01 A0665/26
ardour (1) A0328/V
arduous (1) A0347/22
are (1162)
area (12) A0686/22
  B1303/01 C0152/31 C0159/21 C0199/03
  C0387/25 C0404/38 C0405/04 C0411/40
  C0414/06 C0418/42 C0438/V
areas (2) A0315/26 B0862/30
Aregan (1) C0574/30
aren't (1) A0651/07
arena (1) B1189/14
Argand (2) A0499/06 A0503/08
Argelais (1) A0126/18
argent (1) B1135/18
Argostino (2) A0175/22 A0181/19
argue (2) A0209/25 B0732/19

argued (3) B0797/12
B1119/M C0401/17
argues (3) A0123/25
B0892/09 B0987/30
argument (18) A0099/03 A0109/18
A0601/13 B0723/16 B0734/29 B0738/19
B0739/18 B0740/27 B0740/32 B0743/34
B0745/11 B0745/18 B0745/19 B0902/21
B0989/15 B1006/04 C0132/16 C0132/34
argumentation (2) B0902/V B1315/24
argumentative (1) B0902/13
arguments (8) B0737/31
B0753/34 B0754/04 B0764/02 B0768/14
B1031/15 C0132/20 C0401/18
argumentum (1) B1006/V
aria (1) B1004/05
Arianus (2) A0175/15 A0181/05
Arickara (1) C0528/14
aridity (1) A0135/10
Ariel (4) C0057/26
C0063/22 C0064/11 C0064/34
Ariel's (2) C0063/16 C0065/29
Aries (6) A0189/14 B1296/05
B1310/19 B1311/10 B1311/12 B1312/06
Aries/Tottle (5) B1293/28
B1295/06 B1295/11 B1295/19 B1311/04
Aries/Tottle's (1) B1295/17
aright (10) A0191/02 A0226/03
A0436/11 A0457/09 A0535/20 A0600/17
A0663/30 B0985/05 B1017/10 B1056/07
Ariosto (2) A0344/33 A0356/12
Aripao (1) B1161/36
arise (19) A0080/08
A0162/20 A0322/25 A0402/14 A0432/17
A0459/14 B0752/14 B0774/01 B0887/03
B0964/05 B0964/13 B0964/13 B0976/18
B0984/37 B1168/19 B1281/02 B1281/20
C0080/01 C0205/05
arisen (18) A0020/V A0157/12
A0614/36 B0758/24 B0859/04 B0891/09
B0941/20 B1050/10 B1103/21 B1105/16
C0097/11 C0175/11 C0184/18 C0204/35
C0205/23 C0392/30 C0399/24 C0423/18
arises (7) A0550/26
A0703/12 B0752/05 B0794/08 B1268/11
C0154/35 C0573/04
arising (29) A0056/23
A0066/13 A0088/35 A0094/08 A0103/15
A0114/V A0136/23 A0160/01 A0249/12
A0329/18 A0408/01 A0433/27 A0530/V
A0531/23 A0561/01 B0757/05 B0767/03
B0767/04 B0824/15 B0854/24 B0916/01
B0944/29 B1247/10 B1292/32 B1330/13
C0084/35 C0097/29 C0392/32 C0392/38
Aristaeus (1) A0061/07
aristocracy (9) A0025/24
A0029/V A0247/23 A0496/06 A0496/08
A0496/25 A0500/23 B1092/28 B1094/06
aristocratic (1) A0496/26
Aristoeus (1) A0059/11
Aristolochia (1) B1163/25
Aristophanes (3) A0078/28
A0091/16 A0110/18
Aristotelian (4) A0086/08
A0097/05 B1295/22 B1311/18
Aristotelians (2) A0079/02 B1313/21
Aristotle (5) A0107/31
A0108/05 A0111/02 A0173/02 B1310/20
arithmetic (1) B0773/09
arithmetical (1) B0746/15
Arkansas (1) C0527/32
arm (94)
arm-chair (8) A0101/22
A0261/06 A0370/25 A0372/23 A0387/12
B0728/29 B1103/20 B1250/13
arm-chairs (2) A0373/21 C0397/41
arm-chests (1) C0147/19
arm-holes (1) A0248/09
arm-pits (2) C0559/27 C0572/31
armchair (1) B0808/11
armed (15) A0055/34
A0065/17 A0142/17 A0368/29 B0827/09
B1119/04 C0147/17 C0147/23 C0164/36
C0167/15 C0167/31 C0168/03 C0171/09
C0174/32 C0180/24
armful (1) B1325/06
arming (1) B0946/31
armorial (2) A0400/30 A0662/11
armory (2) A0209/17 B1119/07
arms (78)
army (3) A0045/11
A0697/11 B1021/10
Arnheim (6) A0210/33 B1267/T
B1278/28 B1278/32 B1283/04 B1328/T
Arnoldi (1) B1162/36
arointed (1) B1207/29
aromatic (2) B1180/06 B1334/21
arose (107)
Arouet (1) A0113/31
Arouet, Francois Marie (1) A0093/24
around (183)
arouse (11) A0166/20
A0412/02 B0811/06 B0826/29 B0944/10
B0968/07 B1050/V B1101/07 B1246/20
C0073/04 C0129/09
aroused (37) A0057/31
A0058/12 A0068/16 A0069/01 A0297/09
A0314/11 A0327/25 A0353/01 A0354/27
A0372/12 A0458/19 A0511/24 A0537/07
A0626/08 A0704/29 B0755/31 B0796/21
B0852/30 B0866/08 B0946/08 B0957/32
B0964/07 B1005/14 B1101/18 B1221/16
B1269/28 C0063/31 C0081/36 C0112/37
C0126/26 C0143/39 C0190/18 C0415/09
C0416/09 C0419/18 C0560/10 C0579/03
arousing (13) A0056/27
A0066/17 A0329/06 A0682/23 A0688/01
A0688/29 B0853/24 B1050/29 C0081/21
C0183/02 C0414/41 C0563/16 C0579/02
Arpino (2) A0175/22 A0181/19
arrange (9) A0301/25
B0839/10 B0922/05 B1120/02 B1135/21
C0094/05 C0110/29 C0134/37 C0549/20
arranged (34) A0074/13 A0264/34
A0500/10 A0532/10 A0601/12 B0737/20
B0834/35 B0837/20 B0904/17 B0910/21
B0933/29 B0979/29 B1048/21 B1059/15
B1073/23 B1155/15 B1156/23 B1180/21
B1181/20 B1186/05 B1234/34 B1273/29
B1339/16 C0060/32 C0066/01 C0069/11

->C0099/37 C0108/12 C0109/04 C0152/15
C0177/31 C0189/05 C0393/14 C0415/37
arrangement (35) A0074/29
A0107/29 A0398/06 A0408/14 A0408/17
A0478/23 A0497/16 A0530/21 A0622/16
A0707/30 A0708/25 B0734/22 B0761/31
B0761/35 B0762/02 B0827/21 B0838/13
B0838/25 B0838/35 B0908/V B0909/13
B0941/06 B0991/33 B1071/V B1272/30
B1274/04 B1335/27 B1351/08 C0134/14
C0169/02 C0190/40 C0531/29 C0535/20
C0548/32 C0562/20
arrangements (33) A0055/17
A0065/01 A0090/24 A0409/29 A0447/29
A0708/19 A0708/31 B0837/21 B0856/36
B0862/24 B0878/21 B0908/19 B0949/07
B0960/03 B0965/29 B1008/36 B1072/34
B1090/26 B1143/19 B1220/07 B1273/14
B1273/20 B1273/25 B1330/04 B1339/21
B1351/23 C0066/22 C0092/39 C0136/41
C0152/40 C0203/05 C0411/17 C0416/06
arranges (1) B0747/32
arranging (8) A0566/16
B0910/V B1311/09 B1347/06 C0066/08
C0076/13 C0085/07 C0139/33
arrant (5) A0482/22
A0483/10 B0765/11 B0765/11 B0984/14
array (4) A0101/02
A0101/15 A0152/26 B1274/20
arrest (9) A0676/16
A0692/06 A0692/22 A0692/23 B0725/17
B0957/04 B1049/36 B1187/12 C0429/34
arrested (46) A0138/23 A0244/06
A0405/21 A0410/15 A0412/05 A0414/09
A0444/15 A0511/13 A0537/05 A0544/22
A0565/21 A0610/26 A0674/24 A0683/06
A0686/32 A0691/17 B0731/13 B0753/40
B0842/08 B0856/24 B0889/11 B0914/24
B0943/29 B0957/30 B1052/04 B1106/06
B1109/16 B1115/10 B1136/26 B1212/18
B1225/08 B1233/23 B1241/27 B1261/24
B1277/21 B1335/05 B1335/06 B1340/05
B1362/02 C0062/31 C0076/19 C0085/14
C0159/37 C0191/29 C0403/22 C0526/26
arresting (2) A0027/17 B1187/17
arrests (2) B0727/33 B0876/04
arrival (18) A0138/29 A0404/22
A0409/26 A0434/07 A0437/28 A0584/12
B0808/12 B0904/15 B0924/33 B1068/03
B1155/25 B1236/15 B1239/03 B1247/14
B1369/30 C0153/30 C0155/30 C0156/19
arrivals (1) C0401/24
arrive (21) A0067/30
A0138/30 A0173/06 A0178/11 A0403/17
A0548/06 A0548/16 A0694/35 B0815/07
B0838/07 B0899/29 B0988/29 B1007/05
B1033/25 B1034/25 B1056/20 B1312/13
C0401/15 C0403/26 C0417/24 C0422/05
arrived (74)
arrives (9) A0127/05
A0621/28 B0871/33 B0872/06 B0877/34
B1222/14 C0152/08 C0402/34 C0432/02
arriving (9) A0537/20
B0875/04 C0160/21 C0166/17 C0193/17
C0199/35 C0417/29 C0419/09 C0567/10

arrogance (3) A0436/03
A0478/04 B1219/06
arrogated (1) A0609/33
arronde (1) A0443/V
arrondees (1) A0443/24
arrow (4) A0128/05
B0948/07 B0949/21 B1182/20
arrowhead (1) C0194/26
arrowheads (1) C0194/11
arrows (4) B0947/18
C0554/09 C0555/41 C0557/25
arrowy (2) A0144/01 B0862/13
Art (3) B1044/T B1141/07 C0542/07
art (1) A0295/17
art (70)
art-scarred (1) A0611/24
Artemis (2) A0175/29 A0181/24
arter (1) B0812/09
artery (2) A0615/03 B0950/08
artesian (1) B1193/15
arth> (1) A0468/28
Arthur (1) C0083/20
Article (1) A0336/T
article (69)
articles (48) A0205/24
A0338/19 A0338/29 A0339/23 A0388/15
A0389/09 A0473/33 A0538/02 A0556/02
A0556/04 A0591/26 A0592/11 B0728/07
B0736/05 B0751/14 B0758/27 B0758/29
B0759/09 B0759/23 B0759/26 B0760/22
B0760/27 B0760/29 B0761/05 B0761/07
B0761/08 B0761/24 B0761/32 B0762/01
B0764/09 B0827/01 B0828/11 B0980/01
B0988/32 B1073/29 C0056/13 C0077/11
C0098/02 C0099/28 C0102/36 C0129/31
C0140/12 C0144/21 C0148/11 C0170/13
C0393/20 C0394/31 C0395/15
articles' (1) B0763/08
articulate (5) A0324/V
A0623/11 C0088/12 C0123/02 C0184/13
articulation (1) B1102/12
articulo (1) B1233/18
artificers (1) C0525/37
artifices (2) A0441/23 B1224/16
artificial (27) A0158/04
A0283/25 A0322/27 A0406/02 A0406/16
A0709/22 A0709/31 A0710/03 A0711/04
B0761/31 B0841/13 B1274/25 B1274/34
B1275/06 B1276/06 B1281/24 B1335/02
B1338/31 C0422/31 C0430/02 C0430/13
C0430/14 C0540/24 C0543/36 C0573/06
C0574/02 C0577/06
artificialities (1) A0611/17
artificiality (1) A0276/35
artificially (1) C0184/34
artillery (2) B0958/19 C0156/12
artisan (1) A0189/21
artist (31) A0071/32
A0174/11 A0174/16 A0174/21 A0179/26
A0179/31 A0179/36 A0180/03 A0285/03
A0497/05 A0707/30 A0708/18 A0708/27
B0809/35 B0828/34 B0862/17 B0922/09
B0924/08 B0924/18 B0925/05 B0925/22
B0927/07 B0932/04 B0932/19 B0933/18
B1248/31 B1272/30 B1273/13 B1273/21

->B1330/03 B1337/35
artist's (1) B0925/30
artista (1) A0161/03
artistic (3) A0500/11
B0929/33 B1335/27
artistical (4) A0500/V
A0707/32 B0925/15 B1272/32
artists (2) A0499/02 B0929/13
artizan (1) C0391/02
artizans (2) A0510/27 C0544/41
artless (1) A0641/13
Arts (1) A0337/18
arts (9) A0263/22
A0381/31 A0440/21 A0610/08 A0611/15
A0652/08 B0915/05 B1303/16 C0547/08
as (2) A0034/01 A0034/02
as (3934)
asafoetida (2) A0092/07 A0111/19
asbestic (1) B1362/26
ascend (22) A0120/29 A0123/32
A0349/25 A0351/01 A0541/28 A0543/02
A0566/V B0818/27 B1074/12 B1074/31
B1076/10 B1294/15 B1391/23 C0085/09
C0183/36 C0198/23 C0199/35 C0401/15
C0567/17 C0567/21 C0575/08 C0577/13
ascendancy (7) A0431/12
A0511/01 A0611/06 B0976/30 B0976/32
B0977/23 B1017/28
ascended (19) A0057/30
A0071/02 A0350/24 A0428/31 A0551/10
A0566/07 A0580/01 B0858/23 B1079/25
C0400/28 C0401/13 C0404/24 C0408/04
C0414/15 C0416/32 C0417/36 C0538/08
C0565/37 C0568/21
ascendency (3) A0211/19
A0216/19 A0296/V
ascendere (1) A0043/M
ascending (20) A0547/25
B0817/14 B0819/09 B0905/20 B1070/24
B1074/06 B1074/15 B1076/06 B1079/22
B1135/05 B1294/27 C0086/16 C0127/17
C0189/25 C0399/15 C0403/11 C0541/35
C0545/28 C0569/35 C0571/24
ascension (9) A0085/06
B0818/33 C0394/14 C0401/10 C0401/12
C0402/38 C0407/03 C0407/13 C0407/31
ascensions (3) C0400/25
C0402/29 C0403/30
ascent (20) A0429/26
B1074/12 B1074/29 B1076/08 B1077/34
B1126/13 B1281/25 B1336/32 B1353/24
C0183/39 C0402/39 C0403/17 C0405/21
C0406/11 C0407/22 C0412/12 C0415/16
C0416/21 C0419/01 C0567/34
ascertain (30) A0053/15 A0062/23
A0094/20 A0106/21 A0114/V A0137/05
A0429/31 A0534/11 B0751/20 B0752/25
B0756/24 B0770/12 B0836/19 B1044/28
B1045/32 B1304/31 C0076/06 C0080/15
C0083/17 C0094/26 C0099/41 C0127/17
C0153/34 C0170/12 C0173/20 C0182/36
C0428/22 C0524/15 C0525/15 C0539/09
ascertained (27) A0114/15
A0460/31 A0560/28 A0582/15 B0729/23
B0729/27 B0751/13 B0754/32 B0759/08
->B0934/05 B0940/02 B0965/13 B1035/08
B1082/04 B1132/30 B1168/35 B1233/23
B1362/17 B1362/30 C0093/14 C0201/25
C0415/36 C0416/29 C0418/35 C0429/14
C0538/30 C0546/25
ascertaining (10) A0103/33 A0439/34
A0586/08 A0685/24 A0687/05 C0079/30
C0156/37 C0400/36 C0412/20 C0574/26
ascribed (1) C0546/16
ash (1) C0549/25
ashamed (16) A0145/07
A0298/V A0385/10 A0622/10 A0628/11
B0855/19 B0855/20 B1003/23 B1017/07
B1017/19 B1104/13 B1165/24 B1188/V
B1300/07 C0059/08 C0393/15
ashes (7) A0226/12
A0230/10 A0615/21 B1110/18 B1161/08
B1161/29 C0204/41
Ashimah (4) A0046/11
A0124/10 A0124/13 A0124/17
ashore (4) B0729/32
B0731/03 C0115/27 C0569/25
Ashtophet (1) A0311/13
ashy (2) C0205/21 C0205/31
Asia/Minor (1) A0205/30
Asiatic (1) A0550/11
Asiatic (1) B1160/43
Asiatics (1) A0550/11
aside (22) A0044/25 A0164/11
A0225/18 A0410/13 A0508/25 A0704/27
B0866/13 B0893/09 B0893/V B1002/08
B1106/16 B1181/09 B1184/01 B1235/21
B1262/05 B1269/26 C0069/15 C0132/12
C0199/16 C0564/25 C0564/29 C0564/41
ask (28) A0033/V
A0264/19 A0283/38 A0466/17 A0486/17
A0486/17 A0608/29 B0732/11 B0755/15
B0763/29 B0771/29 B0831/07 B0950/17
B0975/05 B1013/24 B1032/33 B1047/21
B1078/31 B1104/03 B1189/34 B1212/02
B1294/03 B1296/34 B1297/15 B1315/15
B1379/16 C0388/17 C0569/04
askance (1) C0078/02
askant (1) C0425/11
asked (60)
asking (9) A0465/17
B1091/25 C0066/31 C0070/08 C0117/29
C0127/38 C0133/18 C0539/04 C0540/06
asks (4) A0630/10
B0873/08 B0873/32 B0984/15
aslant (1) A0211/32
asleep (24) A0036/V
A0056/18 A0058/07 A0066/08 A0068/29
A0091/31 A0415/11 A0428/09 A0437/12
A0500/30 B0830/03 B1032/18 B1090/33
B1106/14 B1238/22 B1238/29 B1239/13
C0077/07 C0081/16 C0084/29 C0084/39
C0109/24 C0130/39 C0415/03
aspect (33) A0145/23
A0189/11 A0234/23 A0320/12 A0322/20
A0325/10 A0329/01 A0385/27 A0400/05
A0433/19 A0459/27 A0513/35 A0582/31
A0594/V A0603/24 A0627/31 A0682/03
A0688/09 A0695/30 B0757/36 B0840/05
B0942/32 B1003/21 B1049/29 B1223/29

->C0072/14 C0155/11 C0174/13 C0198/33
C0550/14 C0552/40 C0572/13 C0573/07
aspects (3) A0603/05
A0689/03 C0524/02
asphaltum (3) B1180/32
B1186/26 B1186/28
asphodel (4) A0213/15
A0640/03 A0640/33 A0641/V
Asphodel-interspersed (1) A0603/08
asphodels (1) A0643/08
asphyctic (1) B0959/07
aspirations (2) A0317/12 A0426/08
aspires (1) A0365/14
aspiring (1) B1329/12
asquint (2) A0056/03 A0065/25
ass (5) A0177/21
A0183/14 A0482/22 A0483/02 B1134/03
assailants (1) C0199/18
assailed (2) A0407/26 B1106/27
assassin (6) A0553/30 B0727/20
B0737/19 B0771/01 B0772/V B0773/03
assassinated (4) A0547/23
B0744/29 B0757/18 B0769/13
assassination (6) B0725/21 B0739/30
B0758/05 B0763/20 B0858/09 B0975/18
assassinations (1) B0738/34
assassins (12) A0078/30
A0551/08 A0552/32 A0557/04 B0727/21
B0728/12 B0737/19 B0739/26 B0744/20
B0769/15 B0769/25 B0769/31
assault (5) A0486/25
B0870/28 B1104/11 B1143/05 C0082/19
assaulting (1) B0947/03
assemblage (5) B0841/11
B0944/03 B1329/15 C0152/03 C0557/20
assemble (1) C0152/08
assembled (13) A0190/04
A0191/03 A0204/09 A0205/02 A0441/11
B0904/19 B1007/27 B1178/30 B1194/05
C0112/11 C0152/19 C0387/09 C0544/05
assembly (13) A0056/36
A0078/38 A0248/28 A0252/31 A0490/36
A0673/02 A0674/30 A0676/09 B1048/19
B1353/15 C0190/40 C0387/16 C0388/36
assent (6) A0339/17 B1031/26
B1077/29 B1109/28 B1116/05 B1178/19
assented (5) A0339/19
A0372/34 A0583/07 B1135/07 C0427/08
assert (16) A0018/06
A0028/12 A0096/17 A0113/20 A0341/V
A0342/15 A0528/21 B0750/V B0862/15
B0940/30 B0941/25 B1036/06 B1047/24
B1069/02 B1192/29 B1299/10
asserted (6) A0240/22 A0558/26
B0733/19 B0961/18 B1294/24 C0063/02
asserting (3) A0053/33
A0063/05 B0748/02
assertion (12) A0056/32
A0066/25 A0156/07 A0458/07 A0495/V
A0621/07 B0740/20 B0740/21 B0748/28
B0828/30 B0957/11 C0207/30
assertions (9) A0431/24
A0533/16 A0623/18 B0740/13 B0743/02
B0763/18 C0055/18 C0131/30 C0403/36
asserts (6) A0123/20 B0960/36

->B1299/19 B1315/14 B1383/04 C0156/36
asses (2) A0482/22 B1378/M
asseveration (1) B0958/35
asseverations (2) A0055/04 A0064/07
assiduity (1) A0059/33
assiduously (1) A0063/26
assign (6) A0366/30 A0426/14
A0500/15 B0742/20 B1069/04 B1223/29
assignable (1) A0366/01
Assignation (1) A0150/T
assigned (9) A0216/06
A0409/19 A0429/32 A0531/03 A0654/V
A0657/24 B0773/34 B1219/23 B1238/20
assimilate (1) A0611/32
Assiniboin (2) C0551/31 C0568/15
Assiniboins (7) C0551/30
C0551/32 C0568/30 C0568/41 C0569/21
C0569/35 C0572/01
assist (6) A0033/03 A0274/21
B0822/25 B1003/13 C0114/11 C0568/08
assistance (36) A0046/19
A0054/16 A0137/27 A0350/32 A0584/29
A0628/12 A0631/02 A0667/11 B0808/19
B0815/24 B0844/17 B0875/14 B0909/13
B0928/07 B1140/06 B1347/07 B1348/17
B1354/07 C0113/05 C0114/31 C0120/37
C0127/20 C0129/03 C0144/33 C0177/24
C0196/19 C0202/41 C0391/27 C0393/11
C0395/09 C0425/10 C0533/40 C0538/21
C0565/10 C0569/40 C0579/20
assistant (2) B0906/30 C0069/12
assistants (1) B1016/16
assisted (3) B0725/23
C0059/36 C0138/30
assisting (1) C0190/16
assists (1) A0340/33
associate (3) A0600/28
B0768/30 B0768/30
associated (1) A0296/05
associates (11) A0045/08
A0240/22 A0248/12 A0353/34 A0398/29
A0432/05 A0440/28 A0442/11 A0532/22
B0834/03 C0389/08
Association (1) B1305/06
association (12) A0203/08
A0204/06 A0204/20 A0337/14 A0337/27
A0337/32 A0510/12 A0681/07 B1123/14
B1249/10 B1304/20 B1349/30
assoilzie (1) A0252/24
assorted (1) B0827/22
assorting (1) A0530/10
assuaging (1) C0081/09
assume (20) A0071/19
A0080/11 A0099/08 A0299/22 A0339/12
A0428/16 A0675/14 A0711/29 B0739/05
B0826/21 B0837/16 B0837/22 B0969/12
B1276/33 B1347/14 C0094/25 C0205/23
C0443/V C0555/38 C0566/13
assumed (30) A0022/15 A0029/V
A0081/02 A0153/22 A0211/17 A0385/27
A0408/07 A0410/34 A0435/23 A0445/20
A0527/M A0555/V A0580/25 A0695/28
B0736/33 B0739/28 B0740/05 B0772/16
B0825/19 B0836/11 B0855/30 B0887/18
B0956/18 B1239/22 C0058/41 C0133/04

->C0419/15 C0432/33 C0535/36 C0550/14
assumes (3) A0580/17
B0908/V B1222/30
assuming (10) A0023/12 A0212/24
A0432/17 A0433/19 A0536/16 A0613/01
A0695/28 B0837/10 B1296/19 C0067/19
assumption (4) B0738/26
B0739/03 B0739/27 B1312/22
assumptions (6) A0251/12 A0317/11
A0446/07 A0527/V A0676/06 B1191/13
assunder (1) C0097/32
assurance (8) A0044/V
B0858/21 B0899/09 B1003/33 B1130/30
B1220/31 C0084/34 C0089/31
assure (19) A0053/18
A0263/22 A0277/24 A0284/16 A0303/10
A0347/04 A0352/09 A0381/33 A0389/11
A0487/33 A0601/03 B0813/29 B0907/22
B1181/30 B1292/13 B1295/26 B1311/23
B1379/10 C0400/37
assured (38) A0037/24 A0054/30
A0063/31 A0302/22 A0336/03 A0337/03
A0338/13 A0340/04 A0340/36 A0341/V
A0342/22 A0437/12 A0536/13 A0562/29
A0652/13 B0822/24 B0836/18 B0839/27
B0896/01 B0899/09 B0901/12 B0902/23
B1010/26 B1058/16 B1092/27 B1134/05
B1140/27 B1140/32 B1371/23 C0065/23
C0066/36 C0079/28 C0084/09 C0104/07
C0176/09 C0521/21 C0558/15 C0560/31
assuredly (13) A0415/05
A0432/15 A0432/26 A0437/26 A0443/18
A0559/V B0771/24 B0892/16 B0907/24
B0910/18 B1016/18 B1238/17 C0538/31
assurement (1) A0654/05
assures (4) A0683/13
B0839/08 B1293/22 B1314/05
assuring (1) C0175/26
assurity (1) A0044/07
Assyria (1) A0611/14
Ast (1) A0283/36
Astarte (1) A0035/25
astern (4) A0585/21
A0590/01 B0932/14 C0088/24
asteroids (1) B1302/17
asthma (1) B1030/30
astonish (5) A0264/31
A0432/12 A0534/28 B1005/23 B1012/26
astonished (41) A0028/28
A0062/31 A0106/18 A0158/11 A0158/16
A0163/20 A0240/05 A0251/26 A0356/10
A0513/03 A0532/05 A0535/15 A0630/30
A0706/02 B0810/35 B0824/03 B0924/16
B1012/30 B1014/04 B1080/08 B1152/03
B1162/14 B1169/30 B1186/14 B1188/10
B1270/32 B1350/17 B1353/24 B1359/08
B1363/10 B1379/11 C0058/11 C0104/10
C0123/15 C0159/32 C0170/15 C0390/02
C0397/33 C0408/01 C0416/38 C0420/22
astonishing (5) B0850/28
B0898/04 B1104/32 C0153/26 C0181/04
astonishingly (2) A0298/V B0897/26
astonishment (75)
Astor's (1) C0528/05
Astor's, John Jacob (1) C0527/37
Astoreth (1) A0035/25
Astoria (1) C0525/04
astound (1) A0157/17
astounded (6) B0893/20 B0893/20
B0983/05 B1103/21 B1261/29 B1280/28
astounding (8) A0027/08
A0316/01 A0558/07 B0877/14 B0943/34
B1068/01 B1358/04 B1364/22
astoundingly (1) B1137/34
astral (3) A0499/05
A0499/05 B1340/15
astride (1) C0431/06
astrologer (1) A0611/14
astrologers (1) A0313/24
astrology (1) C0432/29
astronomer (3) A0473/22
B1301/18 C0429/25
Astronomers (3) C0390/38
C0425/29 C0427/33
astronomers (10) A0457/15 A0457/35
A0458/04 A0459/26 B1035/24 B1302/09
B1317/13 C0427/17 C0427/35 C0429/11
astronomical (11) A0457/20
A0458/11 A0459/33 B1035/19 B1191/25
B1302/11 B1302/16 C0428/20 C0429/13
C0432/32 C0439/V
astronomically (1) C0448/V
Astronomy (3) C0390/34
C0392/11 C0393/02
astronomy (5) A0473/23
C0387/06 C0432/41 C0433/07 C0447/V
astute (2) A0346/09 B0978/21
astuteness (1) B0984/13
asunder (7) A0217/V
A0413/34 A0417/14 B1053/05 C0182/04
C0187/31 C0396/35
asylum (1) B1009/30
at (3614)
Atalanta (1) B1081/07
Atalantic (1) B1294/01
ate (7) A0686/10
B0735/30 B0767/19 B0942/11 B1166/11
C0137/12 C0145/38
Athenaeum (5) A0262/09
A0262/16 A0262/24 A0262/31 B1358/18
Athenian (3) A0160/V
A0160/V A0312/28
Athenians (1) A0611/33
Athens (3) A0075/14
A0108/14 A0108/19
athwart (5) A0145/02
A0693/09 C0064/06 C0131/09 C0172/10
Atlantic (13) B0834/03
B1068/01 B1069/08 B1077/19 B1079/03
B1080/07 B1081/16 B1081/30 B1294/02
B1294/V C0147/32 C0407/36 C0525/06
atmosphere (89)
atmospheric (15) B1161/39
C0394/33 C0400/27 C0402/32 C0402/34
C0403/08 C0404/04 C0404/07 C0404/13
C0404/28 C0407/14 C0411/31 C0413/16
C0419/33 C0424/33
atom (2) B1034/19 B1214/04
atomic (3) B1034/18
B1034/21 B1034/32

atomies (1) A0536/06
atoms (5) A0175/12
A0181/01 B1034/27 B1034/30 C0424/05
<u>Atree</u> (1) B0993/28
Atrevida (4) C0156/37
C0156/40 C0157/06 C0157/15
atrocious (7) A0026/20
A0298/V A0557/02 B0736/21 B0753/21
C0053/T C0062/39
atrocities (6) A0021/11 A0058/30
A0063/24 A0563/28 B0727/30 C0089/10
atrocity (18) A0547/09 A0547/20
A0560/21 B0723/19 B0725/15 B0726/27
B0736/27 B0753/33 B0757/22 B0757/29
B0844/14 B0851/29 B0853/02 B1052/01
B1207/07 C0061/36 C0133/13 C0556/38
attach (5) A0482/07
B0744/32 B0766/27 B1034/14 B1034/15
attached (27) A0246/16
A0594/01 A0623/27 B0730/13 B0730/32
B0744/31 B0766/28 B0771/09 B0817/02
B0888/08 B0949/02 B1050/28 B1162/34
B1336/03 C0057/07 C0063/18 C0144/36
C0160/01 C0185/05 C0185/06 C0185/19
C0202/39 C0396/04 C0409/21 C0409/28
C0411/13 C0554/11
attaching (2) A0225/09 A0229/09
attachment (6) A0026/28 A0026/29
A0296/02 B0957/25 B1122/19 C0090/31
attack (22) A0272/22 A0272/24
A0324/04 A0372/12 B0962/28 B0965/18
B1140/26 B1193/24 B1249/22 B1370/24
C0082/03 C0093/13 C0109/36 C0113/25
C0186/14 C0533/21 C0549/27 C0550/07
C0553/08 C0555/33 C0557/26 C0569/20
attacked (8) A0072/26
A0323/21 B1101/11 B1134/07 C0103/28
C0107/23 C0545/41 C0554/07
attacking (1) C0164/36
attacks (8) A0213/13
A0433/17 A0652/03 B0940/31 B0962/04
B0963/06 B1225/16 C0546/20
attaghan-maker (1) A0086/34
attain (6) A0026/29 A0271/25
B1360/30 C0159/33 C0186/25 C0574/33
attainable (9) A0667/03
A0703/32 B0747/19 B0766/35 B0767/04
B0843/01 B1268/31 B1269/04 B1299/07
attained (48) A0212/29
A0459/24 A0535/13 A0545/07 A0568/23
A0676/22 A0682/12 A0707/31 A0711/11
B0723/25 B0725/24 B0768/27 B0819/23
B0822/12 B0836/05 B0941/27 B0948/13
B0977/25 B0986/22 B1126/17 B1166/31
B1189/07 B1272/31 B1276/12 B1294/27
B1296/02 B1296/09 B1297/31 B1302/35
B1312/03 B1317/17 B1333/10 B1337/23
B1360/30 C0189/15 C0201/01 C0396/25
C0401/05 C0403/05 C0403/22 C0403/34
C0404/22 C0405/38 C0407/20 C0411/37
C0415/15 C0416/14 C0575/10
attaining (8) B0747/19
B0769/32 B0863/15 C0063/32 C0160/20
C0164/25 C0189/17 C0401/34
attainment (8) A0073/19
->A0145/25 A0704/10 A0704/14 A0704/19
B1269/13 B1295/04 B1297/25
attainments (1) B1361/15
attains (2) B0807/12 B1317/03
attempt (137)
attempted (27) A0075/15
A0261/13 A0496/22 A0534/18 A0549/22
A0552/21 A0684/18 A0692/22 A0692/23
B0861/08 B0911/20 B1030/32 B1080/24
B1082/10 B1240/31 C0074/41 C0075/12
C0075/39 C0080/16 C0109/23 C0133/09
C0142/29 C0143/06 C0183/03 C0200/02
C0203/04 C0432/23
attempting (30) A0071/10 A0102/10
A0373/V A0398/23 A0565/05 A0582/03
B0822/23 B0825/20 B0911/22 B0931/26
B0990/18 B1103/15 B1242/01 B1363/07
C0072/38 C0082/41 C0088/19 C0090/11
C0104/06 C0119/08 C0125/36 C0132/19
C0145/01 C0161/18 C0183/36 C0186/05
C0406/29 C0407/13 C0572/35 C0578/36
attempts (35) A0067/24
A0070/28 A0097/08 A0241/06 A0479/23
A0535/14 A0582/29 A0587/15 A0610/19
A0704/27 B0773/31 B0834/17 B0836/04
B0836/09 B0923/05 B1031/09 B1073/14
B1128/11 B1138/26 B1164/33 B1269/26
B1313/08 B1362/32 C0119/05 C0126/27
C0129/29 C0139/17 C0141/16 C0143/21
C0158/26 C0162/14 C0197/10 C0389/02
C0539/27 C0567/03
attend (18) A0026/07 A0026/V
A0123/18 A0279/32 A0286/09 A0369/02
A0369/27 A0372/19 B0732/34 B0733/11
B0736/34 B0819/16 B1134/09 B1372/10
C0133/30 C0171/08 C0399/10 C0412/25
attendance (13) A0056/12
A0066/01 A0386/29 A0484/04 B0725/29
B0770/21 B0807/30 B0901/11 B1009/04
B1091/12 B1235/20 B1236/11 B1334/28
attendant (8) A0142/33
A0352/27 A0500/12 A0667/05 B0924/06
B1281/06 C0097/12 C0097/30
attendants (10) A0080/34 A0081/04
A0325/02 A0615/10 B0947/06 B0959/34
B0992/31 B1258/21 C0171/27 C0175/32
attended (32) A0099/05
A0139/05 A0145/08 A0311/11 A0343/05
A0347/19 A0349/19 A0378/07 A0428/24
A0446/20 B0733/18 B0843/03 B0851/01
B0891/16 B0894/18 B0901/06 B0904/09
B0914/28 B0941/02 B0942/12 B0950/02
B0957/10 B1018/25 B1108/17 B1390/15
C0081/18 C0098/09 C0162/27 C0204/39
C0400/02 C0407/28 C0544/16
attending (25) A0020/17
A0053/30 A0063/01 A0103/07 A0368/03
A0368/16 A0380/13 A0381/17 A0482/02
A0552/25 A0686/30 B0723/12 B0733/14
B0875/16 B0887/22 B0974/12 C0066/21
C0390/27 C0399/30 C0403/31 C0407/16
C0411/30 C0413/24 C0424/21 C0531/02
attention (184)
attentions (3) B0813/21
B1241/34 B1261/34

attentive (5) A0211/22
A0212/32 A0286/18 A0535/28 B1352/19
attentively (8) A0136/14
A0529/26 A0552/28 A0689/31 B0894/14
B0925/01 C0059/16 C0545/33
Atticus, Herodes (1) A0441/01
attired (4) A0447/03
A0614/03 B1004/10 B1008/10
attitude (7) A0216/03
A0298/V A0411/09 A0603/19 A0604/20
A0604/30 B0865/34
attorney (3) A0487/11
B0959/29 C0057/03
attorneys (1) A0508/17
attract (5) A0298/V
A0511/32 A0562/02 A0564/26 B0941/21
attracted (17) A0028/20
A0098/13 A0136/17 A0325/06 A0370/23
A0531/05 A0593/15 A0690/03 B0725/25
B0729/22 B0731/20 B0894/03 B0929/10
B0984/07 B1353/27 B1380/01 C0181/29
attracting (5) A0142/09
A0513/20 A0556/21 B0758/32 B1139/04
attraction (9) A0581/27
A0582/27 B0889/02 B1321/24 C0401/34
C0403/27 C0422/05 C0422/06 C0432/45
attractions (1) C0401/26
attractive (2) B0989/26 C0547/21
attributable (2) A0119/02 B0863/23
attribute (7) A0043/14
A0144/03 B0813/08 B1038/17 B1191/05
C0396/36 C0546/15
attributed (24) A0026/18
A0059/29 A0067/19 A0099/21 A0140/28
A0226/02 A0229/19 A0243/09 A0266/19
A0434/30 A0560/03 A0566/22 B0853/09
B0985/02 B1036/04 B1123/14 B1234/18
B1334/17 C0062/07 C0098/15 C0111/37
C0411/33 C0419/23 C0430/01
attributes (1) A0459/32
attributing (4) A0104/22
A0624/20 B1070/29 C0413/11
Atys (1) A0135/M
au (15) A0019/03
A0034/29 A0096/M A0096/M A0268/30
A0340/22 A0378/M A0561/02 A0611/04
B0974/04 B0978/09 B0987/01 C0430/28
C0430/31 C0430/31
au-chat (3) B1011/07
B1011/09 B1011/14
auburn (2) A0641/V A0644/V
auction (1) B1141/05
audacious (4) A0371/17
B0870/27 C0140/20 C0404/20
audacities (1) A0027/02
audacity (9) A0022/06
B0796/31 B0870/01 B0870/27 B0900/27
B1052/23 B1129/22 B1348/37 C0522/06
audible (6) A0235/26 B0948/05
B1238/28 B1238/34 B1239/30 C0083/04
audibly (1) B1236/31
audience (12) A0514/06
A0514/11 B0889/08 B0890/32 B0894/05
B0894/26 B0895/01 B0896/07 B1050/27
B1156/09 B1244/05 B1245/02
Audiguier (1) A0301/03
auditory (1) A0406/05
Aug. (5) A0485/05
A0485/07 A0485/10 A0485/12 A0485/13
aught (1) A0397/20
augment (1) B0746/18
augmentation (1) A0500/08
augmented (3) B1282/22
C0421/16 C0555/05
augmenting (1) B1074/06
augos (Gr.) (3) A0108/21
A0108/V A0108/V
August (22) A0240/V A0279/18
A0301/32 A0302/29 C0142/13 C0142/36
C0143/26 C0143/38 C0145/35 C0146/05
C0146/13 C0148/16 C0155/26 C0539/20
C0539/38 C0540/14 C0541/01 C0541/24
C0542/01 C0542/23 C0542/30 C0543/03
august (14) A0090/12 A0296/06
A0323/09 A0456/20 A0601/20 A0610/01
A0670/16 A0706/04 B0955/12 B1127/07
B1133/07 B1188/15 B1271/08 B1272/18
Augustus (128)
Augustus's (6) C0100/38 C0101/11
C0114/11 C0127/08 C0136/31 C0141/07
aujourd'huy (1) C0430/36
aulos (Gr.) (2) A0108/20 A0108/V
aunt (6) B0729/09 B0731/27
B0749/33 B0755/22 B0756/13 B0756/27
aunt's (1) B0729/17
auram (1) A0072/31
Aurelian (1) A0125/35
auricle (1) A0246/25
auricula (1) A0349/15
auriculas (3) A0336/09
A0339/06 A0347/06
auriculas (1) A0349/33
Aurora (2) C0156/34 C0157/40
Aurora/Borealis (1) C0203/26
Auroras (4) C0156/31
C0157/13 C0157/40 C0158/10
auspices (2) B1304/19 B1305/05
Aussi (1) A0344/15
aussi (1) A0344/21
austere (2) A0627/05 A0665/01
austerity (1) A0433/23
Austrian (1) B1257/10
authentic (1) B1069/22
authenticated (2) B0956/07 B1361/27
authenticity (3) A0281/32
C0056/23 C0448/V
author (47) A0033/18
A0034/14 A0069/17 A0088/06 A0098/20
A0163/17 A0172/02 A0175/01 A0178/02
A0204/09 A0272/22 A0280/34 A0283/06
A0284/01 A0473/23 A0621/05 B0723/14
B0887/20 B1051/16 B1069/19 B1122/09
B1139/12 B1139/28 B1143/24 B1143/28
B1144/04 B1151/05 B1189/19 B1207/14
B1207/26 B1208/07 B1208/11 B1234/04
B1276/16 B1297/02 B1314/06 B1379/32
B1381/28 B1384/25 C0207/19 C0428/05
C0428/39 C0430/43 C0431/02 C0431/14
C0448/V C0522/34
author's (4) A0272/11

->A0276/34 A0711/04 B1276/06
authorities (4) A0018/11
A0365/13 B1094/04 B1325/11
authority (13) A0242/26
A0445/20 A0527/V B0873/30 B0950/19
B0950/22 B0958/14 B0958/16 B1003/31
B1137/35 B1158/26 B1295/27 C0388/21
authorized (1) B1047/24
authors (9) A0096/16
A0173/17 A0173/V A0178/25 A0621/24
B0761/10 B1140/31 B1207/04 B1379/25
authorship (2) B1359/14 C0055/35
auto (Gr.) (2) A0225/M A0229/M
auto-biography (1) A0483/12
Autobiographists (1) A0195/V
autocrat (1) A0021/25
autocrats (2) A0126/06 A0617/02
autograph (5) A0262/34
A0275/04 A0279/05 A0284/34 A0366/19
autographical (1) A0262/15
autographs (7) A0262/06
A0262/29 A0263/19 A0263/19 A0263/35
A0263/35 A0279/26
Autography (1) A0261/T
Automaton (3) B1119/15
B1120/03 B1166/34
automaton (1) B1119/M
automaton-chess-player (1) B1361/03
autor (1) A0621/01
autos (Gr.) (1) A0089/30
autos-da-fe (1) A0684/24
autremet (1) C0430/29
autres (2) A0600/01 C0430/38
autumn (7) A0397/02
A0437/V A0507/05 A0531/V B0974/01
B1002/01 C0561/36
autumnal (3) A0020/V
A0227/24 A0232/11
auyos (Gr.) (1) A0089/31
av (1) B0913/07
avail (7) A0127/18
A0276/11 B0901/01 C0142/18 C0145/27
C0430/14 C0555/30
availability (3) B0978/31
B0987/13 B1270/03
available (3) A0705/04
B0968/15 B1316/18
availed (6) A0059/02 A0069/V
A0070/02 B0723/20 B0733/07 C0185/14
availing (1) B0771/02
avails (1) B0966/03
avait (1) A0036/21
avalanche (1) A0692/23
avarice (4) A0044/21
A0073/23 A0445/33 A0511/22
avaricious (2) A0098/03 A0489/19
avast (2) A0249/25 A0249/25
avatar (1) A0670/02
ave (7) B0899/29
B0900/02 B0911/28 B0912/16 B0913/06
B1109/19 B1109/29
ave> (1) A0464/16
avec (1) A0037/V
aven> (1) A0467/15
avenged (1) B1256/04
avenger (1) B1256/09
avenging (2) A0034/28 B1058/02
avenue (10) A0025/04 A0029/05
A0514/02 B0877/09 B0877/12 B0946/19
B1107/25 B1192/24 B1330/01 C0192/26
avenues (6) A0428/05 A0709/34
B1101/20 B1275/02 B1295/23 B1311/19
average (9) B0749/25
B1190/01 C0098/07 C0193/12 C0203/26
C0400/02 C0400/04 C0400/14 C0400/20
averaged (1) C0181/02
Averni (1) B0993/08
averred (2) A0301/13 C0104/21
averse (3) B0733/34
B0747/16 C0568/14
aversion (5) A0434/04
B0748/19 B0825/08 B0855/07 B0871/08
avert (2) B0766/09 B0893/15
averted (5) A0447/28
A0697/06 B0893/V B0895/05 B1122/05
aves (1) A0500/V
avidity (6) A0686/10 B1127/06
C0076/28 C0083/35 C0137/04 C0165/18
avis (1) B1345/09
avoid (25) A0272/01
A0415/02 A0486/23 A0536/10 A0561/32
B0738/19 B0806/04 B0839/10 B0839/V
B0915/20 B1036/16 B1140/28 B1278/22
C0061/15 C0108/07 C0134/29 C0148/21
C0166/36 C0411/03 C0523/20 C0531/09
C0531/13 C0550/08 C0555/39 C0559/21
avoidance (2) A0710/28 B1275/27
avoided (15) A0436/10
A0499/24 A0502/V A0510/06 A0564/04
A0687/18 A0690/27 B0851/21 B0854/28
B0927/02 B0928/11 B1004/15 B1234/23
B1371/17 C0563/10
avoiding (4) A0436/10
A0694/19 A0710/24 C0199/33
avoids (1) A0496/21
avoirdupois (1) B0828/12
avowed (5) A0204/03
B1044/14 B1049/35 B1053/12 B1349/25
avowedly (1) B1137/14
await (6) A0684/26 B1054/35
B1155/25 C0070/24 C0085/09 C0426/25
awaited (16) A0140/20
A0387/12 A0458/12 A0508/11 A0685/16
A0687/25 A0690/32 B0757/23 B0808/12
B0899/16 B0956/27 B1132/32 B1143/30
B1165/08 B1370/10 C0139/28
awaiting (9) A0043/08
A0548/09 A0548/10 B0814/24 B0835/11
B1178/31 B1263/10 C0135/05 C0186/03
awake (21) A0022/19
A0189/30 A0433/08 A0687/34 B0794/14
B0928/34 B0946/05 B0959/19 B0968/08
B1032/28 B1033/09 B1040/09 B1153/V
B1178/27 B1385/31 C0057/22 C0072/31
C0415/08 C0422/14 C0541/11 C0574/23
awaken (8) A0625/08
B0959/18 B1153/12 B1153/14 B1241/28
B1242/01 B1242/29 B1242/32
awakened (12) A0217/05
A0324/18 A0326/28 A0340/13 A0348/01

->A0612/32 A0643/30 B1178/14 C0081/34
  C0100/39 C0148/36 C0414/37
awakening (5) A0431/02
  B0966/15 B1241/24 B1242/01 C0421/13
awakes (1) A0501/V
awaking (12) A0028/17
  A0210/06 A0616/25 A0638/09 A0686/08
  A0688/21 B0963/16 B0963/31 B0966/24
  B0968/27 C0070/37 C0071/08
aware (91)
away (169)
awe (31) A0078/27
  A0140/32 A0144/11 A0217/V A0217/V
  A0242/24 A0327/07 A0328/03 A0329/10
  A0401/25 A0405/26 A0429/06 A0430/09
  A0446/04 A0460/34 A0590/17 A0664/24
  A0676/06 B0764/22 B0794/09 B0850/06
  B0859/09 B0960/27 B0961/35 B1127/05
  B1248/33 C0109/11 C0125/23 C0169/33
  C0182/34 C0555/34
awe-inspiring (2) C0072/16 C0112/15
awe-stricken (2) A0437/32 B1372/27
awed (1) A0402/09
awful (16) A0028/V
  A0058/28 A0072/20 A0080/21 A0145/21
  A0248/14 A0490/29 A0541/03 A0591/35
  A0623/09 A0630/19 B0959/19 B0967/33
  B1157/21 B1371/20 C0134/29
awfulest (1) B1374/02
awfully (4) A0102/02
  A0240/V B1193/28 C0126/10
awhile (6) A0023/12 A0137/12
  A0190/28 B0932/28 B1046/31 B1155/32
awkward (7) B0993/07
  B1157/08 C0123/18 C0173/32 C0413/27
  C0552/28 C0579/12
awkwardly (2) A0436/29 A0562/21
awoke (8) A0081/25
  B0963/06 B1105/30 B1106/24 B1135/31
  C0084/39 C0128/34 C0392/16
awry (1) B1141/28
axe (14) A0692/31 B0856/21
  B0856/26 C0086/01 C0086/21 C0105/08
  C0136/13 C0136/15 C0136/27 C0136/31
  C0143/20 C0143/30 C0169/14 C0545/16
axes (8) B1160/03
  C0085/36 C0107/07 C0114/23 C0136/10
  C0148/09 C0189/30 C0534/13
axiom (14) B0987/26 B1296/22
  B1296/22 B1314/19 B1314/22 B1314/24
  B1314/24 B1314/27 B1314/32 B1314/33
  B1314/36 B1315/11 B1315/11 B1315/22
axiomatic (7) B1297/07
  B1297/20 B1314/11 B1314/27 B1315/05
  B1315/23 B1315/35
axioms (16) B0987/22
  B0987/22 B1295/09 B1296/24 B1296/28
  B1296/31 B1296/33 B1310/28 B1310/32
  B1313/19 B1313/23 B1313/25 B1313/30
  B1314/02 B1314/20 B1314/30
axis (13) A0656/29
  B1071/10 B1071/18 B1071/20 B1071/21
  B1075/07 B1077/16 B1321/04 B1321/04
  B1322/11 C0398/06 C0401/28 C0426/12
ay (4) B1370/31
  ->C0110/34 C0110/34 C0559/18
aye (1) B0857/34
Ayesher (1) B1294/05
azimuth (4) C0161/05
  C0163/11 C0164/05 C0164/21
Aznac (1) B1192/16
azote (2) B1359/17 C0393/36
Azoth (2) A0059/12 A0061/07
Azrael (2) A0029/V A0316/25
Azrael's (1) B1040/14
azure (5) A0702/M
  A0702/M B1259/34 B1267/M B1267/M
B (1) B0733/27
b (1) C0194/22
B.A.T.C.H. (1) A0338/12
B.L.U.E. (1) A0338/12
B-- (3) A0036/21 B0733/25 B0748/21
B--'s (3) B0892/17
  B0896/20 C0528/26
B/flat (1) B1012/09
Baal (2) A0043/14 A0498/21
Baal-Peor (1) A0046/13
Baal-Perith (1) A0046/13
Baal-Zebub (2) A0034/20 A0046/13
Baalzebub (1) A0080/20
Babbage's (1) B1166/35
Babel (1) A0128/18
babies (3) A0622/27
  A0623/13 B1131/13
baboon (4) A0124/20
  A0177/12 A0183/06 A0340/02
baboons (3) A0303/22
  B0912/04 B1021/11
baby (3) A0622/31
  A0625/27 B1359/01
Babylon (2) A0068/14 C0198/35
bac (2) A0096/M A0096/M
Bacchanalian (1) B0828/09
Back (1) C0535/33
back (236)
back-ground (1) C0159/25
back-water (1) C0117/12
backed (5) A0297/04
  B0862/35 B1261/15 C0164/09 C0399/32
backing (1) A0623/18
backs (5) B0931/26
  C0086/17 C0134/12 C0568/01 C0579/26
backward (4) A0515/06
  B1145/22 B1223/19 B1321/18
backwards (7) B0927/16
  B1058/07 B1093/22 B1163/38 B1167/15
  B1335/14 C0563/04
backwoods (1) C0575/42
Bacon (1) A0311/29
Bacon-engendered (1) B1313/13
Baconian (4) B1295/22
  B1295/23 B1311/18 B1311/20
Baconianism (1) B1312/23
Bad (1) A0487/11
bad (32) A0091/08
  A0110/14 A0177/10 A0268/14 A0268/14
  A0270/22 A0274/06 A0277/27 A0299/05
  A0466/09 A0473/16 A0485/13 A0584/21
  A0656/03 B0840/01 B1039/19 B1047/14
  B1114/31 B1114/31 B1115/01 B1292/19

->B1360/07 C0130/14 C0149/30 C0154/13
C0387/12 C0436/V C0447/V C0535/09
C0549/21 C0555/12 C0567/02
bade (18) A0105/13 A0108/15
A0318/04 A0562/21 A0663/03 B0726/18
B0796/24 B0796/27 B0858/13 B0902/04
B0992/07 B0992/25 B1003/05 B1109/17
C0395/07 C0395/12 C0560/32 C0566/10
badger (1) A0653/12
Badger, Samuel (1) C0146/42
badges (1) B1157/15
badly (2) C0121/22 C0557/33
baffled (6) A0404/16 B0956/14
C0071/36 C0090/15 C0525/26 C0526/10
baffles (1) B0975/26
baffling (1) C0103/27
Bag (2) A0487/14 A0487/25
bag (15) A0089/09
A0093/12 B1292/26 C0138/07 C0138/23
C0138/31 C0389/36 C0409/17 C0409/17
C0409/19 C0409/21 C0409/31 C0409/34
C0409/39 C0410/10
bag-pipes (1) A0071/29
bagatelle (1) B1015/01
Bagdad (2) B1160/11 B1167/25
baggage (3) B0923/13
B0924/30 B0925/05
bags (8) A0537/33
A0541/22 A0541/23 A0556/14 B1073/23
C0138/11 C0390/10 C0534/41
bah (1) A0035/V
Baiae (1) B0871/05
bail (2) B1054/15 B1054/23
bailed (1) C0058/30
bailing (1) C0534/15
baissee (1) B1145/23
bait (1) C0547/21
bait> (1) A0467/12
baize (1) C0062/33
baked (1) A0340/06
balance (4) A0213/11
A0272/31 A0383/08 C0393/10
balanced (1) B0741/22
balancez (1) A0371/30
balancing (1) B1279/10
Balbec (1) A0145/05
balconies (1) B0945/10
bald (3) A0103/29
A0508/35 C0087/13
balderdash (3) B1129/24
B1137/06 B1137/15
bales (2) C0069/08 C0165/28
ball (9) A0671/14
B0992/22 B1054/01 B1058/24 B1093/31
B1238/27 C0146/24 C0415/04 C0579/21
ball-room (2) A0152/26 A0447/11
ballad (3) A0408/01
A0417/V A0510/26
ballast (28) A0138/03
A0251/18 B1073/23 B1073/30 B1074/08
B1074/09 B1074/25 B1074/32 B1074/35
B1077/35 B1079/26 C0077/13 C0098/15
C0114/36 C0114/39 C0127/13 C0390/10
C0394/41 C0396/22 C0399/13 C0403/23
C0404/25 C0405/19 C0405/35 C0406/10
->C0406/22 C0407/24 C0424/39
ballast's (1) C0097/15
ballet-dancers (1) A0671/08
Balloon (3) B1068/05
B1069/09 B1069/31
balloon (102)
balloon-bag (1) B1294/16
Balloon-Hoax (1) B1068/T
balloon's (1) C0403/05
balloons (8) B1292/35
B1294/21 B1298/28 C0118/18 C0394/08
C0402/29 C0403/02 C0405/37
balls (5) A0613/09
B1347/06 C0189/30 C0534/04 C0577/41
balm (2) A0696/10 B1107/13
Baltimore (3) A0273/02
A0275/02 B0956/10
Baltimore/Museum (1) A0417/V
balustrade (6) A0710/06 B0890/01
B1275/09 B1336/32 C0121/34 C0121/35
Balzac (1) A0602/33
Balzac (1) A0096/M
bamboozled (1) B1129/09
ban (2) A0242/26 A0670/06
band (12) A0217/V
A0693/10 B0766/19 B1055/18 C0107/41
C0388/33 C0551/07 C0556/40 C0561/02
C0564/03 C0569/19 C0569/39
bandage (19) A0057/33
A0068/17 A0072/05 A0247/28 A0330/05
A0693/07 A0693/15 A0694/07 A0694/20
A0694/26 A0695/02 B0766/11 B0766/13
B0766/23 B0766/30 B0766/35 B0767/01
B0768/31 B0968/29
bandaged (2) A0247/13 B1185/26
bandages (3) A0329/14
B1180/11 C0119/28
banditti (1) A0667/09
bands (7) A0514/32
B0754/01 B0826/05 B1071/14 C0550/02
C0551/26 C0551/35
bandy (1) C0569/30
banish (3) A0081/35
C0197/25 C0197/31
Bank (2) B0874/17 B1053/11
bank (22) A0602/30 B0735/19
B0807/V B0947/07 B1281/22 B1281/24
B1281/29 B1281/34 B1333/29 C0173/07
C0183/08 C0530/01 C0535/17 C0537/06
C0538/11 C0554/04 C0558/31 C0566/22
C0567/15 C0567/30 C0570/32 C0577/08
bank-notes (1) A0624/23
banked (1) B0862/35
banker (5) A0541/11
A0556/14 B0870/09 B0887/26 B0957/19
banking (1) A0541/13
bankrupt (1) A0486/04
banks (40) A0489/02
A0642/04 B0729/11 B0753/24 B0863/36
B0864/05 B0864/24 B0864/27 B0865/02
B0870/19 B0945/24 B0945/32 B0968/12
B1162/06 B1246/03 B1247/23 B1279/03
B1333/26 B1334/15 C0522/20 C0526/04
C0535/13 C0538/19 C0540/08 C0542/37
C0543/13 C0546/21 C0548/15 C0552/35

->C0553/16 C0553/35 C0553/37 C0555/03
C0555/06 C0561/29 C0570/17 C0571/22
C0572/27 C0575/06 C0576/36
banned (1) A0244/V
banners (3) A0406/34
B0945/14 B0945/16
Banquo (1) A0080/33
banter (4) A0433/18
C0428/03 C0443/V C0448/V
Bantry/Bay (1) C0433/03
baptism (2) A0235/12 B1346/05
baptismal (3) A0209/11
A0235/14 B0887/V
Baptista (1) A0087/03
Baptiste (1) A0033/17
bar (9) A0087/25
A0353/28 A0354/26 A0355/21 A0544/02
A0631/11 A0631/20 B0875/32 B0924/34
Barac (2) A0101/V A0181/14
Barac (1) A0439/V
barb (2) B0947/21 B1381/05
Barbadoes (1) B1161/30
barbarian (2) A0045/V C0065/20
barbarians (1) C0202/31
barbaric (2) A0673/13 B1008/33
barbarity (1) C0146/28
barbarous (5) A0034/09
A0100/09 A0301/09 B1346/22 C0180/10
barber (1) A0566/27
barbers (1) B1142/32
Barclay (1) A0071/30
bard (3) A0641/22
B0863/35 B1123/18
bards (1) A0654/16
bare (12) A0103/29
A0152/24 A0369/30 A0551/12 B1008/02
B1045/14 B1181/22 C0066/03 C0072/28
C0125/01 C0413/03 C0531/38
barefooted (1) C0572/28
barely (20) A0099/28
A0164/22 A0327/04 A0351/33 A0400/18
A0557/12 A0653/13 B0978/28 B1235/15
B1238/28 C0077/39 C0079/35 C0081/05
C0091/32 C0144/37 C0183/01 C0183/32
C0394/28 C0425/04 C0559/29
barely-discernible (1) A0417/09
Bargain (1) A0085/T
bargain (9) A0094/06
A0098/02 A0098/04 A0114/01 B0878/08
B1145/04 B1257/29 C0177/30 C0394/41
bargaining (2) A0491/18 B0923/16
bargains (2) A0098/18 A0102/14
barge (2) B0754/07 B0754/09
barge-office (2) B0770/20 B0770/29
bargeman (2) B0770/19 B0770/24
bargemen (2) B0754/05 B0754/07
bark (17) A0603/10
A0604/13 A0640/09 B0761/18 B0818/31
B1160/39 B1279/11 B1281/11 C0061/21
C0202/21 C0202/21 C0532/41 C0545/18
C0545/41 C0546/34 C0546/41 C0547/03
Barlow's (1) B1101/04
Barnabas (1) B1044/09
barnacles (2) C0145/18 C0145/39
Barnard (14) C0057/14 C0057/15
->C0065/36 C0067/37 C0084/16 C0085/06
C0085/31 C0088/08 C0091/21 C0092/27
C0093/16 C0097/06 C0128/05 C0137/23
Barnard, Augustus (1) C0058/25
Barnard's (2) C0058/02 C0064/25
Barnes (1) B1182/33
barometer (10) B1076/13 C0396/05
C0396/23 C0399/16 C0400/25 C0404/35
C0405/40 C0411/37 C0417/40 C0439/V
barometers (1) B1073/24
Baron (46) A0020/10 A0020/18
A0020/V A0022/04 A0023/04 A0023/15
A0024/05 A0024/16 A0025/01 A0025/06
A0025/14 A0025/20 A0026/04 A0026/05
A0026/11 A0026/V A0026/V A0027/09
A0028/06 A0029/V A0177/05 A0292/01
A0292/V A0293/13 A0294/01 A0294/16
A0294/V A0294/V A0294/V A0295/06
A0296/06 A0296/13 A0296/18 A0296/V
A0296/V A0297/07 A0299/03 A0299/09
A0299/17 A0300/20 A0301/19 A0301/31
A0303/09 A0303/13 A0303/31 C0150/13
baron (2) A0177/12 C0150/17
Baron's (5) A0021/18
A0026/28 A0177/26 A0296/V A0297/19
baron's (1) A0294/V
barque-rigged (1) C0147/15
barques (1) B1293/14
barred (2) A0062/01 B1282/24
barrel (10) A0142/13 A0590/09
A0593/08 A0594/V B1071/28 B1102/10
C0077/26 C0077/32 C0078/17 C0199/15
barrels (6) A0591/27 A0593/17
B1073/25 C0069/08 C0097/21 C0394/29
barren (5) A0579/12
B1160/27 C0153/33 C0154/14 C0154/37
Barrett (1) B1380/16
barricade (2) C0409/12 C0409/14
barricaded (1) B0946/34
barrier (3) A0020/V
A0642/33 C0198/36
Barriere (3) B0726/25
B0734/22 B0737/15
Barriere/du/Roule (15) B0729/30
B0731/34 B0734/11 B0734/16 B0734/21
B0734/31 B0735/19 B0755/14 B0755/26
B0758/05 B0758/26 B0761/03 B0767/11
B0768/07 B0768/29
barriers (7) A0242/29
A0243/04 A0243/18 A0695/13 C0521/05
C0527/09 C0528/39
barring (1) C0055/14
Barronissy> (1) A0464/10
Barronit> (2) A0464/V A0468/V
Barronitt> (8) A0464/03
A0464/13 A0465/14 A0465/23 A0466/14
A0467/04 A0468/14 A0470/17
barroques (1) B0850/02
barrow (1) B1059/19
Barry, Littleton (3) A0037/V
A0470/V A0304/07
Barry, Lyttleton (1) A0075/18
bars (5) B1008/26
C0438/V C0538/18 C0559/35 C0576/23
Bartas (1) A0303/24

barterings (1) C0177/15
Bartholinus (4) A0173/03
A0173/19 A0176/12 A0178/28
bas (3) B0853/14
B0898/08 B0898/09
bas-reliefs (1) B1179/08
Bas-Bleu (8) A0174/07
A0174/08 A0174/09 A0179/22 A0179/23
A0179/24 A0385/16 A0385/19
Bas-Bleus (1) A0385/26
base (25) A0417/11
A0426/14 A0445/15 A0580/36 A0695/20
B0752/16 B0755/02 B0817/24 B1003/18
B1080/27 B1080/30 B1080/37 B1163/26
B1280/09 B1334/35 B1337/31 C0061/35
C0163/29 C0199/35 C0204/41 C0388/28
C0408/07 C0408/10 C0408/18 C0567/11
based (6) A0529/28 A0560/16
B0723/09 B0747/31 B0985/28 B1295/17
baseless (4) B0763/24
B0902/09 B1297/22 B1316/06
basement (2) A0045/05 B0725/26
baseness (1) B1131/29
bases (2) B1283/02 B1296/31
basest (2) A0484/24 A0486/30
Bashan (1) A0047/22
bashfulness (1) B1141/24
basin (4) B1280/03
B1280/12 C0151/02 C0415/04
basin-full (1) C0406/39
basinful (1) C0172/05
basis (12) A0399/27
A0486/07 B1039/25 B1123/19 B1220/13
B1220/15 B1297/34 B1313/22 B1313/32
B1317/13 B1392/08 C0112/01
basket (12) A0045/22
A0045/24 A0046/20 A0047/09 A0047/27
A0534/33 A0535/22 B1071/08 C0393/19
C0411/09 C0413/32 C0414/02
baskets (2) B1154/14 B1154/23
basso (1) A0244/18
Batavia (3) A0135/24
A0136/14 C0179/18
batch (1) A0279/26
bate> (1) A0465/18
bath (1) B0826/24
bathe (1) C0145/40
bathed (7) A0328/11
A0351/17 A0406/03 A0643/28 A0687/02
B0944/13 C0064/19
bathing (7) B0945/25
B1246/06 C0140/37 C0142/17 C0143/07
C0143/13 C0143/35
bathing-places (1) B0945/V
Batrachomyomachia (1) A0621/13
battalions (1) A0509/27
batten (1) A0586/03
batter (1) A0488/14
Battery (1) A0059/29
battery (15) A0067/20
A0144/V A0439/24 A0486/25 A0664/V
A0682/07 B0927/27 B0948/15 B0959/23
B0959/26 B0960/11 B0960/19 B1119/20
B1181/20 B1182/15
battle (2) A0356/16 A0488/24
battle-lantern (1) C0109/10
battle-lanterns (2) A0140/10
A0145/02
battledoor (1) B1072/01
battlement (1) A0120/29
battlements (4) A0028/23
A0029/24 A0045/20 A0675/26
bauble (1) A0691/12
bawled (4) A0385/16
C0062/14 C0110/33 C0553/14
bawling (1) A0124/23
bay (18) B1280/27 B1281/04
B1282/12 C0155/03 C0165/29 C0170/40
C0171/01 C0176/15 C0179/22 C0186/02
C0186/19 C0186/29 C0186/41 C0189/09
C0190/13 C0201/28 C0201/33 C0525/19
bayonet (1) A0539/35
bazaar (2) A0513/13 A0513/28
bazaars (1) B0945/11
be (2578)
beach (11) A0136/17
B0807/10 B0807/24 B0933/11 B1081/25
C0155/03 C0189/31 C0190/19 C0200/13
C0200/30 C0205/15
beads (8) A0685/03
B1180/21 C0148/08 C0175/28 C0177/12
C0177/39 C0534/25 C0558/18
beak (2) B1281/02 C0125/08
beaker (1) B1348/08
beam (1) B1382/01
beam-ends (8) A0137/07
A0590/36 C0098/06 C0099/18 C0104/27
C0114/36 C0143/33 C0149/37
beaming (3) A0164/17
A0166/22 A0298/V
beams (2) A0158/03 A0244/23
bean (1) C0543/24
beant (1) B1372/33
bear (58)
bear-skins (1) C0535/11
bear's (2) A0128/09 C0579/20
beard (6) A0044/10 A0044/15
B0945/20 B1152/14 C0531/38 C0560/02
beards (1) A0046/30
bearer (3) A0093/21
A0112/32 C0426/23
bearing (33) A0029/06
A0161/06 A0265/09 A0271/27 A0283/30
A0412/07 A0434/08 A0461/08 A0503/03
A0515/06 A0564/13 A0593/33 A0604/12
A0672/12 A0675/07 A0704/25 B0728/20
B0739/29 B0757/16 B0761/34 B0770/14
B0991/06 B1140/14 B1165/04 B1269/24
B1302/20 C0101/26 C0122/35 C0123/14
C0165/27 C0181/34 C0399/19 C0541/34
bearings (3) A0434/28
B0842/28 C0167/36
bears (21) A0023/30
A0265/26 A0274/08 A0344/01 A0351/20
A0582/25 A0609/26 A0710/01 B0764/25
B1079/15 B1096/02 B1096/10 B1137/05
B1275/04 B1311/03 C0150/11 C0150/28
C0572/07 C0577/32 C0578/08 C0578/22
bearskins (1) C0087/17
beast (37) A0027/21

->A0047/10 A0099/23 A0125/30 A0126/02
A0126/10 A0559/30 A0561/25 A0561/31
A0562/03 A0565/01 A0566/20 A0566/V
A0567/10 B0851/28 B0854/35 B0855/17
B0855/26 B0855/37 B0856/01 B0857/24
B0859/13 B0944/06 B1053/34 B1057/34
B1156/28 B1157/27 B1158/07 B1158/20
B1159/08 B1159/19 B1159/28 B1161/14
B1166/26 C0072/38 C0165/07 C0579/29
beast-like (1) B1350/34
beastly (1) C0059/25
Beasts (1) A0119/T
beasts (14) A0123/10 A0127/V
A0128/18 A0478/05 B1162/16 B1350/16
B1352/10 C0200/16 C0562/37 C0567/12
C0567/29 C0567/38 C0578/24 C0579/04
beat (18) A0069/29 A0197/24
A0327/08 A0372/06 A0459/28 A0483/06
A0581/29 A0592/05 A0612/35 A0643/27
A0674/13 B0795/29 B0858/16 B0922/14
B1078/08 B1292/12 C0061/01 C0113/17
beaten (6) A0109/18 B0828/03
B0862/27 B1020/06 B1102/10 B1166/18
Beati (1) A0213/04
beating (18) A0078/05 A0078/10
A0372/09 A0416/18 A0622/28 A0683/27
B0789/M B0795/10 B0795/11 B0795/22
B0797/29 B0812/08 B0943/30 B1021/13
B1077/27 C0061/11 C0062/25 C0075/25
beau (2) A0273/12 B0889/23
beaucoup (2) A0036/06 B1105/09
beauties (11) A0035/29
A0079/05 A0079/05 A0297/11 A0383/28
A0399/04 A0603/06 B0864/04 B0914/13
B1381/01 C0564/32
beautiful (97)
beautiful-minded (1) A0611/30
beautifullest> (1) A0466/29
beautifully (5) A0165/V
A0278/15 B1076/12 B1294/05 C0570/30
beauty (104)
Beauvais (22) B0729/29 B0730/01
B0731/04 B0732/21 B0732/24 B0732/29
B0732/40 B0733/13 B0733/22 B0733/25
B0733/28 B0733/30 B0733/36 B0745/20
B0745/22 B0745/31 B0746/03 B0747/22
B0747/28 B0748/22 B0748/24 B0755/08
Beauvais' (1) B0748/13
beaver (17) A0478/15
C0388/32 C0536/22 C0543/08 C0544/13
C0544/41 C0546/08 C0546/20 C0546/24
C0546/28 C0547/22 C0547/28 C0558/02
C0564/22 C0566/26 C0570/04 C0572/07
beaver-traps (1) C0535/10
Beaver/Island (1) C0547/35
beavers (8) C0544/19
C0544/26 C0545/06 C0545/34 C0546/34
C0566/22 C0566/23 C0570/32
becalmed (1) A0585/25
became (222)
because (92)
Beckford (1) B1051/18
beckoned (2) A0385/19 B1225/19
beckoning (1) A0318/03
become (76)
becomes (28) A0123/32
A0249/24 A0474/02 A0583/12 A0710/34
B0738/24 B0741/32 B0742/05 B0742/12
B0743/22 B0746/20 B0747/34 B0756/06
B0772/26 B0818/31 B0870/06 B1074/34
B1079/03 B1163/35 B1220/30 B1275/35
B1281/10 C0098/04 C0105/37 C0106/08
C0430/17 C0575/38 C0577/01
becoming (23) A0022/22
A0093/30 A0113/09 A0205/07 A0381/15
A0427/22 A0534/18 A0616/19 B0762/18
B0851/17 B0910/20 B0949/07 B0976/36
B0982/13 B1020/02 B1127/19 B1234/20
C0121/30 C0130/39 C0131/40 C0134/29
C0418/29 C0558/12
becomingly (2) B1008/10 B1349/01
bed (120)
bed-chamber (3) A0024/17
A0217/V B1339/23
bed-clothes (1) B0980/16
bed-post (1) A0482/15
bed-posts (1) A0663/20
bed-room (3) A0386/28
A0565/02 B1224/16
bed-side (2) A0232/12 B1236/03
bedclothes (4) C0094/05
C0109/02 C0120/39 C0145/14
bedding (2) B0968/18 C0138/38
bedecked (4) A0321/08
A0643/15 A0662/10 B1008/01
bedevilled (1) B1115/13
bedewed (1) A0631/19
bedight (1) A0318/09
bedizzened (3) A0159/19
A0498/09 A0500/14
Bedlam (1) A0320/24
bedlam (1) A0320/V
Bedlamite (1) B1316/03
bedlamite (1) B1129/16
Bedlo (4) B0949/33
B0950/18 B0950/27 B0950/V
Bedlo, Augustus (1) B0949/31
Bedloe (10) B0941/06 B0941/23
B0942/04 B0942/18 B0946/16 B0947/29
B0947/33 B0948/29 B0949/04 B0950/23
Bedloe, Augustus (1) B0939/03
bedposts (1) B0979/32
bedroom (1) A0437/04
beds (7) A0197/26
A0243/32 A0506/04 A0514/29 A0542/14
B0980/16 B1212/32
bedside (1) B1030/27
bedstead (7) A0537/27
A0538/04 A0543/20 A0551/30 A0553/02
A0557/V A0567/16
bee (6) A0298/V A0478/32
A0478/33 B0839/35 B0943/16 C0546/26
bee-line (3) A0254/03
B0840/24 B0842/20
bee'nt (1) C0067/22
beef (1) C0100/35
beefsteak (1) A0352/12
been (1588)
beer (3) A0246/13
A0252/09 A0622/21

bees (7) A0479/03
B1102/06 B1163/10 B1164/04 B1164/09
B1164/23 B1164/23
beetle (24) B0810/01
B0810/23 B0812/33 B0815/11 B0815/23
B0816/11 B0818/14 B0818/19 B0820/22
B0820/26 B0821/25 B0821/30 B0822/06
B0824/26 B0824/32 B0829/09 B0830/20
B0830/32 B0831/22 B0844/01 B0844/07
B1383/17 B1383/19 B1383/19
beetle's (1) B0822/33
beetling (2) A0579/04 A0639/10
befall (1) A0641/20
befallen (3) A0662/V
B0811/14 C0063/30
befell (2) C0072/12 C0122/23
befitting (1) A0407/13
before (598)
befriended (1) B0933/09
befriends (1) B1078/36
befxre (1) B1374/08
beg (18) A0072/16 A0108/13
A0121/29 A0124/16 A0263/21 A0284/16
A0302/16 A0656/06 B0761/31 B0873/34
B1005/03 B1119/M B1139/11 B1158/35
B1189/29 B1189/30 B1310/01 C0124/24
began (82)
Begebenheit (1) B0723/M
Begebenheiten (1) B0723/M
begetting (1) C0521/21
beggar (1) B0963/09
beggarly (1) A0384/11
beggars (1) A0509/34
beggary (2) A0055/21 A0065/05
begged (12) A0303/05
A0623/32 B0822/15 B0830/23 B0900/11
B0902/06 B1003/01 B1003/28 B1140/23
B1191/33 B1236/27 C0132/32
begging (2) B1133/18 C0132/15
begin (16) A0072/17
A0099/07 A0204/01 A0262/21 A0345/28
A0608/31 B0771/32 B0976/04 B1033/01
B1178/23 B1317/35 B1353/34 B1379/32
B1381/04 C0152/24 C0197/35
begin'd> (1) A0468/27
beginned> (1) A0467/18
beginning (35) A0204/01
A0276/19 A0614/18 B0737/12 B0739/06
B0823/31 B0837/06 B0838/24 B0839/03
B0843/20 B0912/29 B1031/18 B1033/01
B1033/02 B1033/02 B1033/03 B1101/12
B1101/14 B1128/01 B1128/31 B1169/25
B1190/21 B1213/06 B1321/V B1353/01
B1370/16 B1385/18 B1390/06 C0095/14
C0122/31 C0161/37 C0430/02 C0522/04
C0526/05 C0576/08
begins (5) A0345/V
A0612/30 B0955/27 B1074/24 B1163/40
begirdled (1) B1156/14
begirt (2) A0447/04 B1283/01
begrimed (1) A0160/V
begs (1) B0878/15
beguile (1) A0136/08
begun (6) A0445/01 B0836/08
B1329/05 C0132/20 C0398/39 C0548/17
behalf (10) A0067/05 A0070/09
A0079/25 A0357/10 A0365/08 A0704/16
B1050/24 B1055/33 B1269/15 C0065/16
behave (5) A0352/09
B1010/07 B1013/34 B1016/22 C0101/13
behaved (14) A0653/22 B0735/29
B0767/19 B0915/02 B0926/03 B1013/30
B1018/20 B1018/23 B1048/01 C0110/40
C0179/39 C0560/24 C0566/06 C0569/04
behaves (1) B1207/14
behaving (1) A0443/06
behavior (16) A0249/09
A0261/04 A0374/01 A0432/17 A0443/05
A0468/25 A0468/V A0625/13 B0875/09
B0894/29 B0992/20 B1011/33 B1055/01
B1105/04 B1134/31 C0558/13
behaviour (11) A0021/08
A0025/21 A0026/21 A0303/10 A0355/10
A0513/24 B1183/04 C0062/39 C0076/19
C0081/35 C0092/02
beheld (42) A0035/26 A0085/11
A0121/V A0139/34 A0190/05 A0195/V
A0195/V A0198/18 A0215/13 A0215/23
A0236/08 A0298/V A0312/14 A0316/13
A0326/V A0371/19 A0379/25 A0381/05
A0411/08 A0578/33 A0590/29 A0605/12
A0665/21 A0695/07 B0853/17 B0889/15
B0891/01 B1158/17 C0087/06 C0089/10
C0112/19 C0124/35 C0130/06 C0149/28
C0404/38 C0405/04 C0417/12 C0417/33
C0418/05 C0420/35 C0422/28 C0425/13
behemoth (1) A0197/16
behild> (1) A0470/16
behind (64)
behold (42) A0053/29 A0062/33
A0078/25 A0099/30 A0107/11 A0122/14
A0123/01 A0125/24 A0150/03 A0154/28
A0160/22 A0165/21 A0191/05 A0245/22
A0250/12 A0253/14 A0263/33 A0318/V
A0357/01 A0383/22 A0412/34 A0545/24
A0600/17 A0600/18 A0601/28 A0706/25
A0707/17 A0707/20 B0858/03 B0863/05
B0864/19 B0892/05 B0910/20 B0964/23
B1141/21 B1195/12 B1272/16 B1272/21
C0124/37 C0128/15 C0135/25 C0414/12
beholder (3) A0029/V
A0581/11 B0991/22
beholding (6) A0511/16 B1157/01
B1250/32 B1384/32 C0169/39 C0556/32
beholds (1) A0683/03
behooved (1) B0826/31
behould> (5) A0464/02
A0465/19 A0468/10 A0468/25 A0470/13
bei (1) B0723/M
being (582)
beings (26) A0123/01 A0161/13
A0191/14 A0226/35 A0231/09 A0313/08
A0709/13 B0768/25 B1036/21 B1038/18
B1038/20 B1038/21 B1038/25 B1039/32
B1040/01 B1051/05 B1119/13 B1165/06
B1274/15 B1276/31 C0130/04 C0145/07
C0146/30 C0153/27 C0180/05 C0564/09
bejewelled (1) A0510/10
Bekker (1) A0283/36
bel-esprit-ism (1) A0343/14

belabor (1) A0123/06
belave> (1) A0469/20
belaved> (1) A0469/12
belay (2) A0251/26 A0251/28
beldame (1) A0510/11
Belfry (1) A0365/T
belfry (7) A0350/34
A0351/09 A0351/13 A0369/19 A0372/01
A0372/09 A0374/10
belfry-man (5) A0369/27
A0370/09 A0372/02 A0372/07 A0374/10
Belgium (1) A0296/V
Belial (2) A0034/22 A0046/13
belied (3) A0156/07
A0388/20 B0899/21
belief (23) A0018/04
A0209/20 A0316/28 A0408/10 A0431/24
A0436/20 A0527/V A0582/24 B0733/08
B0745/17 B0748/08 B0748/13 B0833/25
B0849/02 B0902/31 B1219/07 B1247/06
B1247/07 C0055/20 C0107/25 C0111/40
C0125/20 C0125/41
believe (140)
believed (33) A0066/23
A0075/11 A0078/08 A0086/12 A0086/12
A0097/11 A0097/12 A0163/17 A0216/10
A0233/20 A0304/03 A0340/04 A0483/13
A0539/03 A0540/13 A0587/34 A0612/11
A0653/V B0733/02 B0808/20 B0987/34
B0988/02 B1031/28 B1091/34 C0103/30
C0169/10 C0402/09 C0405/16 C0412/18
C0414/29 C0438/V C0529/06 C0557/08
believes (3) A0550/02
A0708/18 B1273/13
believing (10) A0138/06 A0548/20
A0601/24 A0612/12 B0748/30 B0761/29
B0887/19 B0942/33 B1302/09 C0179/11
Bell (1) A0340/10
bell (23) A0059/19
A0067/10 A0086/20 A0340/13 A0340/28
A0351/18 A0370/01 A0372/14 A0372/20
A0372/27 A0372/30 A0372/35 A0373/04
A0674/18 B0796/16 B0872/14 B0965/36
B1103/11 B1178/13 B1186/07 B1244/06
B1338/25 C0396/07
bell-metal (1) A0056/20
Bell-ringers (5) B1119/01
B1119/03 B1119/13 B1119/T B1119/M
bell-rope (4) A0374/12
B0967/22 B1134/32 B1140/10
bell-tones (1) A0614/13
belle (3) A0602/07
A0602/08 B0913/05
Belles (1) C0430/36
belles (3) A0337/13
A0337/26 A0652/08
bellies (1) C0568/22
belligerents (2) A0057/35 A0068/18
Bellini (2) B0905/26 B1004/05
bellowed (3) A0087/35
A0347/31 B1017/26
bellowing (1) A0146/07
bellowings (1) A0582/02
bellows (5) A0054/24
A0252/14 C0391/02 C0391/12 C0391/26
bellows-maker (1) A0071/10
bellows-mender (1) C0438/V
bells (8) A0078/09
B1120/02 B1257/19 B1258/33 B1259/26
B1260/03 B1263/22 B1345/20
belly (5) A0367/V
A0370/V A0374/V B1156/14 B1165/02
belong (3) A0123/04
A0322/24 C0430/03
belonged (10) A0023/27 A0044/11
A0508/15 A0561/11 B0866/22 B0904/V
C0102/11 C0173/02 C0398/04 C0523/24
belonging (27) A0022/08
A0079/19 A0240/02 A0323/07 A0509/07
A0554/27 A0560/29 A0561/04 A0561/13
A0638/18 B0809/21 B1017/05 B1052/15
B1304/05 C0065/35 C0090/38 C0102/16
C0103/33 C0104/11 C0128/04 C0146/30
C0146/37 C0156/35 C0202/04 C0409/09
C0532/07 C0532/11
belongs (2) C0394/05 C0524/37
beloved (25) A0218/V
A0234/16 A0253/09 A0310/05 A0313/01
A0313/21 A0317/21 A0321/08 A0323/09
A0326/20 A0357/02 A0404/01 A0608/02
A0642/34 A0666/04 B0890/25 B0907/17
B0909/08 B0910/15 B0926/35 B0957/17
B0957/31 B1215/31 B1259/13 C0531/24
below (104)
Belphegor (1) A0408/30
belt (9) A0447/05
A0578/31 A0580/28 A0588/15 A0589/11
A0589/20 A0590/14 A0591/15 B1180/23
belted (1) C0425/18
Belus (1) A0045/13
Ben-Levi (5) A0044/05
A0045/18 A0047/03 A0047/15 A0047/V
Ben/Nevis (1) A0241/21
Benares (1) B0949/14
benches (2) A0429/14 A0430/12
bend (5) C0173/13
C0183/14 C0183/31 C0194/17 C0550/01
bended (1) A0251/07
bending (4) A0143/20
A0416/02 B1015/29 C0528/16
Bendis (2) A0175/28 A0181/23
bends (2) B1282/15 C0145/17
beneath (121)
beneficial (1) C0129/10
benefit (18) A0365/05 B0941/05
B1051/23 B1051/26 B1089/25 B1195/11
B1346/36 B1347/32 C0095/09 C0129/21
C0141/11 C0142/04 C0145/21 C0177/02
C0186/07 C0200/04 C0411/24 C0564/11
benefits (4) A0297/10
B1185/11 B1358/31 C0145/26
Benevenuta (2) A0087/09 A0100/19
benevolence (1) A0650/10
benevolent (1) A0059/23
Bengal (1) A0490/19
Bengalee (1) B0949/22
benighted (1) A0316/15
benign (2) A0428/33 B1135/03
benignity (4) A0053/24
A0062/29 A0078/38 A0629/05

benignly (1) A0348/09
Benjamin (2) A0043/05 A0045/03
Bennet's/Islet (2) C0166/02
C0204/06
Bennett's (1) B1141/V
Bennett's/Islet (1) C0203/12
bent (22) A0142/14 A0143/13
A0153/V A0166/06 A0298/V A0316/07
A0319/29 A0369/05 A0415/31 B0730/07
B0896/11 B0942/27 B0948/16 B1080/19
C0088/37 C0090/13 C0093/22 C0118/39
C0170/24 C0187/03 C0197/31 C0567/25
Bentham (3) B1113/11
B1297/04 B1314/09
Bentham, Jeremy (1) B0869/02
Benthams (1) A0498/22
Bentinck's (1) B1069/17
Bentley (1) A0179/19
Benton (1) B1304/30
benumbed (2) C0060/17 C0118/30
bepuffed (2) A0053/22 A0062/27
bequeath (1) B1142/12
bequeathed (4) A0056/08
A0653/01 A0704/24 B1269/23
bequest (4) A0704/27
B0887/14 B1126/06 B1269/26
Beranger (1) A0397/M
bereavement (3) A0026/22
A0055/20 A0055/20
bereft (1) A0347/26
Berenice (16) A0209/T
A0210/21 A0210/28 A0210/29 A0211/07
A0213/18 A0213/30 A0214/06 A0214/07
A0214/20 A0215/12 A0216/09 A0216/27
A0217/07 A0217/V A0217/V
Beresina (1) B0955/05
Bergerac (1) C0432/37
Berlifitzing (13) A0019/05
A0019/11 A0019/17 A0019/V A0020/03
A0021/15 A0022/05 A0023/14 A0023/27
A0024/11 A0024/30 A0026/10 A0027/17
Berlifitzing, Wilhelm Von (1) A0024/03
Berlifitzings (1) A0019/21
Berlin (2) A0445/06 C0392/12
Bermuda (1) C0088/31
berries (3) C0167/13
C0535/03 C0547/40
berry (10) B0811/18 B0811/22
B0811/27 B0812/10 B0812/17 B0812/21
B0819/32 B0820/14 B0820/17 B0821/05
berth (22) B0928/28 B0929/20
B0929/22 C0068/15 C0089/30 C0089/33
C0090/02 C0090/23 C0090/30 C0091/14
C0092/37 C0093/03 C0094/06 C0095/05
C0099/35 C0100/02 C0100/13 C0100/38
C0101/11 C0101/32 C0109/31 C0136/26
berths (9) B0922/19
B0922/20 B0968/16 B0968/17 C0068/04
C0069/17 C0093/40 C0109/27 C0136/14
Berwick (1) C0156/10
beseamed (1) A0430/14
beseech (3) A0072/18
A0128/22 A0264/12
beseechingly (1) A0510/01
beset (8) A0427/25
->A0627/05 A0644/13 A0654/07 B0760/10
B1163/27 C0122/18 C0564/18
besets (1) B1169/08
beside (9) A0218/07
A0404/V A0510/24 A0566/18 A0665/29
A0686/08 A0692/20 C0058/13 C0415/05
besides (67)
besieged (3) A0653/18
C0143/08 C0391/33
besieging (2) A0044/06 A0045/10
besmeared (2) A0537/28 B1053/30
besotted (1) A0441/16
besought (2) B0901/21 B0907/09
bespeak (1) A0144/09
bespotted (1) C0552/17
besprinkled (4) A0036/01
A0640/02 A0675/16 C0387/13
bess (1) B1103/24
Bessarion (1) A0097/12
Bessop (1) B0840/35
Bessop's/Castle (1) B0841/05
best (131)
best-hearted (1) C0529/14
bestir (1) A0531/20
bestow (6) A0554/25 A0711/13
B0815/06 B0910/05 B1276/14 C0390/30
bestowed (7) A0317/24
A0530/11 B0958/04 B1133/28 B1158/27
B1182/19 B1346/16
bestowing (2) A0705/13 B1270/12
bestows (1) B0978/01
bestrode (1) A0026/01
bestudded (2) A0087/07 A0100/16
bet (12) A0621/T
A0623/29 A0624/05 A0624/12 A0624/12
A0624/13 A0624/13 A0624/14 A0624/26
A0626/03 A0626/31 A0627/23
betaken (1) A0404/21
Bete (1) A0183/11
bete (1) A0177/16
bethinking (1) A0415/18
bethought (7) A0667/12
B0766/29 B0891/27 B0914/18 B1003/05
B1102/21 C0071/03
betook (14) A0057/27 A0068/10
A0079/44 A0101/20 A0328/10 A0625/10
B0830/03 B1101/08 B1105/29 B1108/14
B1128/08 C0087/19 C0416/07 C0416/34
betray (6) A0105/32 A0298/V
A0509/12 C0059/09 C0208/24 C0413/14
betrayal (1) B0768/21
betrayed (8) A0047/28
A0099/17 A0626/03 B0754/22 B0768/19
B0768/22 B1183/31 C0429/32
betrayer's (1) B0754/24
betrays (1) B0768/21
betrothed (6) A0311/04 A0654/21
B0729/15 B0736/12 B0908/20 B1107/24
bets (1) A0623/18
Betsey (1) C0155/34
better (140)
betting (3) A0624/10
A0624/22 B0773/22
Betty/Martin (1) C0388/30
betwane> (1) A0468/11

between (212)
between-decks (1) C0092/16
betwixt (1) B1164/37
beverage (1) B1045/33
bevy (1) B1015/04
beware (1) A0046/15
bewilder (2) A0413/02 B0764/31
bewildered (23) A0150/01
A0153/V A0166/20 A0243/27 A0329/20
A0403/01 A0456/05 A0466/33 A0644/07
A0683/05 A0705/04 B0764/24 B0947/14
B1107/31 B1247/18 B1261/24 B1270/04
B1279/36 B1281/16 B1330/02 B1348/26
C0073/09 C0563/04
bewildering (6) A0234/27 A0411/20
A0581/11 A0590/22 B0765/13 C0060/06
bewilderment (4) A0470/01
B0895/16 B0963/18 B1134/26
bewinged (1) A0318/09
bewitched (2) A0373/26 B0913/15
bewitching (1) A0385/05
bewitchingly (1) B0901/14
beyond (167)
Bi-chloride (2) B0742/25 B0826/03
bi-part (2) A0175/12 A0181/02
Bi-Part (1) A0533/22
Bianca (2) A0152/V A0166/V
bias (6) A0550/V A0652/18
A0706/10 B0835/25 B0968/24 B1271/14
Bias, Fanny (1) A0079/09
Bible (3) B0878/27
B0880/09 C0541/20
bible (1) C0427/25
biblical (1) A0458/34
bibliographical (2) A0337/13
A0337/26
Bibliotheca/Forensica (1) B1234/03
bibliotheque (1) A0101/05
biche/de/mer (10) C0170/17 C0170/36
C0176/10 C0176/20 C0177/22 C0177/37
C0177/40 C0178/36 C0179/10 C0179/24
Bichloride (1) B1186/31
bickering (1) B1047/26
bid (10) A0264/19 A0352/09
A0655/06 A0671/04 B0756/17 B0756/18
B0756/23 B0964/13 C0088/22 C0530/34
bidden (3) B1236/04
B1281/06 B1317/24
bidding (9) A0034/15
A0155/15 A0212/09 A0318/18 A0675/V
B0875/V B1181/28 C0068/32 C0074/18
bids (1) B0875/17
bien (5) A0035/05
A0037/V B0907/07 B0907/08 B1154/22
bienseance (2) A0158/10 A0158/V
big (49) A0173/05
A0174/08 A0179/23 A0205/30 A0337/15
A0339/08 A0340/28 A0341/22 A0342/10
A0342/V A0367/11 A0367/V A0368/20
A0368/31 A0369/09 A0369/32 A0371/11
A0372/04 A0372/06 A0372/27 A0372/33
A0373/04 A0374/14 A0388/15 A0464/15
A0468/08 A0468/22 A0468/23 A0469/25
A0483/V A0490/21 A0627/09 A0685/03
B0812/08 B0818/18 B0819/19 B0821/06
->B0875/18 B0911/11 B0913/04 B0913/04
B1012/02 B1021/11 B1046/05 B1056/23
B1102/11 B1164/07 B1372/33 C0535/08
big-horn (1) C0572/07
Big/Devils (1) C0551/33
bigger (8) A0045/20
A0348/24 A0368/34 A0369/10 A0370/14
B1096/24 B1164/21 B1166/09
biggest (1) B1164/21
bight (1) C0186/36
bigness (1) C0432/17
bignonia (1) B1337/11
bigoted (3) B1294/35
B1298/09 B1316/14
bigots (2) B1313/03 B1317/08
bijou (2) B1137/05 B1137/17
bilge-water (2) A0251/24 C0059/27
bill (19) A0056/36
A0059/16 A0066/26 A0067/06 A0484/28
A0485/15 A0491/08 A0631/22 B0872/03
B0872/22 B0873/12 B0873/15 B0878/14
B0878/18 B0879/26 B1349/19 C0125/02
C0151/16 C0178/19
billet (1) A0559/13
billet-doux (1) A0055/08
billets (1) B0916/30
billets (1) C0109/19
billets-doux (1) A0064/14
billiard-ball (1) B1090/18
Billingsgate (1) B1141/08
billow (2) A0139/17 A0163/11
billows (2) A0143/31 B1156/16
bills (1) B0889/02
Billy (1) B1245/04
bin (5) A0414/19
B0812/16 B0812/21 B0821/01 B1373/02
binary (2) B1300/36 B1302/14
bind (4) A0625/31
A0642/10 C0537/24 C0564/02
binder (1) B0981/10
binding (3) A0088/16
A0090/09 A0100/14
bindings (1) B0981/07
biography (1) A0483/12
Biot (1) C0401/06
biped (1) B0869/15
bipeds (1) A0056/16
Bipont (1) A0283/35
birch (3) B1333/34
C0532/41 C0540/04
birch-bark (1) C0534/17
bird (19) A0033/07
A0100/21 A0152/V B1108/11 B1164/35
B1164/36 B1165/09 B1292/21 B1337/14
C0125/04 C0125/19 C0126/16 C0151/39
C0153/08 C0164/04 C0174/03 C0188/27
C0191/10 C0409/04
Bird, Robert (1) A0273/37
Bird, Robert M. (2) A0273/35
A0274/02
Bird, William (1) A0541/26
bird's (3) A0035/03
A0274/06 C0178/13
birds (38) A0033/15 A0509/25
A0640/34 A0643/13 B0809/07 B0850/25

->B0862/36 B1127/35 B1163/10 B1164/05
B1164/09 B1164/18 B1166/06 B1283/07
B1292/12 C0118/18 C0151/17 C0151/26
C0151/38 C0152/08 C0152/15 C0152/19
C0153/03 C0153/15 C0155/21 C0158/35
C0159/17 C0160/23 C0164/03 C0164/27
C0173/36 C0205/41 C0208/20 C0428/30
C0430/47 C0431/02 C0432/22 C0543/01
Birds, Robert (1) A0273/38
birds' (1) C0177/08
birth (11) A0164/07
A0233/16 A0378/19 A0406/09 A0603/29
A0613/34 B0834/17 B0957/17 B1166/13
B1168/12 B1215/32
birth-day (2) A0704/31 B1269/31
birthday (1) B1348/03
biscuit (3) C0081/12
C0534/29 C0542/28
bisected (1) B1182/15
Bishop (5) A0150/M
A0166/09 A0172/M A0178/M A0388/04
bishop (1) A0346/10
bishop's (2) B0839/31 B0840/03
Bishop's/hostel (1) B0840/21
Bishop's/Hostel (1) B0840/34
Bishop's/Hotel (3) B0840/30
B0842/26 B0843/03
bismuth (1) B1364/02
bison (1) C0428/39
bit (33) A0176/24
A0182/26 A0249/26 A0299/06 A0339/32
A0355/22 A0464/20 A0465/27 A0466/06
A0468/15 A0469/17 A0469/28 A0469/V
A0470/05 A0470/06 A0483/16 A0483/17
A0483/25 A0486/13 B0809/02 B0810/11
B0812/21 B0813/02 B0817/02 B0821/02
B0821/22 B0844/06 B0927/26 B1046/13
B1185/02 B1373/12 B1373/13 C0541/20
bite (5) B0812/25
B0812/27 B0812/33 B0830/09 C0539/30
bits (1) B1363/13
bitten (6) A0029/13 A0341/06
A0347/03 A0543/27 B0806/M B0812/32
bitter (27) A0020/01
A0151/06 A0225/04 A0227/21 A0229/04
A0232/09 A0236/11 A0326/19 A0348/05
A0385/25 A0397/17 A0410/29 A0416/28
A0444/09 A0445/19 A0536/13 A0593/22
B0825/19 B1130/11 B1131/30 B1348/05
B1369/34 B1379/27 B1380/31 C0143/11
C0150/29 C0565/09
bitterest (5) B0823/29
B0852/22 B1106/18 C0134/12 C0391/36
bitterly (11) A0139/11
A0213/24 A0214/12 A0405/02 A0435/35
A0446/10 A0642/20 A0696/17 B1158/22
C0146/06 C0411/20
bittern (3) C0188/27
C0191/12 C0204/11
bitterness (10) A0152/21 A0158/V
A0190/18 A0404/03 A0461/06 A0645/02
A0685/17 B0854/28 B1129/30 C0197/38
bitther> (1) A0468/04
bituminous (1) C0571/18
bivalve (1) B0808/18
bivouac (1) B1329/03
bizarre (2) B1009/12 B1141/26
bizarre (7) A0273/24
A0296/V A0528/24 A0654/07 A0663/01
A0671/21 A0673/25
bizarrerie (1) A0532/27
bizarreries (1) A0338/30
Blab (2) A0072/24 A0072/26
Black (3) A0366/17
A0477/T B0849/T
black (147)
black-looking (4) A0367/23
C0573/33 C0574/13 C0577/21
black-robed (1) A0681/10
black-striped (1) C0543/01
black-tailed (1) C0559/41
black-walnut (1) C0549/24
Black/Bear (1) C0527/01
Black/Hills (3) B1160/21
C0087/03 C0572/21
Black/Hole (1) B0955/08
Black/Strap (3) A0251/06
A0251/25 A0252/22
blackamoor (1) C0569/11
blackberries (1) A0380/05
blacken (1) B1142/34
blackened (3) A0166/24
B1239/32 B1354/21
blacker (3) A0330/16
A0604/08 C0444/V
blackest (1) A0603/16
blackfish (1) C0174/06
blackguard (4) B0750/27
B0760/13 B0766/07 C0067/23
blackguards (7) B0735/21
B0754/02 B0757/03 B0760/04 B0765/11
B0765/11 B0767/28
blacking (2) A0489/10 A0489/17
blackish (1) C0576/19
blackness (17) A0145/11
A0273/17 A0400/29 A0604/29 A0605/02
A0616/11 A0674/07 A0682/15 A0684/14
A0685/07 B0950/12 B0961/23 B1156/11
B1234/10 C0182/29 C0397/23 C0418/35
blacksmith (1) A0482/34
Blackwood (21) A0061/T
A0174/06 A0179/21 A0336/T A0338/13
A0338/13 A0338/18 A0338/21 A0338/24
A0338/33 A0340/04 A0340/20 A0340/23
A0343/15 A0346/07 A0346/18 A0346/20
A0346/21 A0347/13 A0347/23 A0354/06
Blackwood, Blackwood (1) A0205/23
Blackwood's (1) A0339/01
bladders (1) A0247/12
blade (12) A0685/30
B0825/25 B0943/15 B1052/16 C0076/10
C0165/08 C0168/05 C0172/10 C0172/13
C0192/23 C0406/36 C0543/23
blades (1) A0603/22
blame (5) A0074/16
A0151/10 A0622/24 B0815/18 B1152/07
blandest (3) A0303/05
A0650/09 A0703/01
blandly (2) A0299/13 B1135/14
blank (8) A0265/01

->A0683/27 B0838/17 B0993/19 B0993/24
B1336/31 C0078/23 C0192/32
blanket (2) C0129/30 C0552/08
blankets (6) B1078/26 C0069/22
C0082/19 C0082/25 C0101/29 C0534/25
blanks (2) B0875/01 B0875/02
blarney (1) B0870/31
Blas, Gil (1) C0430/42
blasphemer (1) A0046/08
blasphemies (1) A0150/V
blaspheming (1) A0044/16
blasphemous (1) A0675/24
blasphemy (1) A0053/27
blast (6) A0137/09 A0138/03
A0145/08 A0697/08 C0106/09 C0115/21
blaze (7) A0106/06
A0514/36 B0808/23 B0832/12 B1106/28
C0562/18 C0562/28
blazed (4) A0157/10
A0316/20 A0587/11 B1004/04
blazing (7) A0101/22
B0808/10 B0832/04 B0852/31 B1354/05
C0396/28 C0563/03
blazoned (1) A0150/V
bleak (2) A0397/13 C0552/41
bleak-looking (1) A0579/08
bleating (1) A0047/19
bled (2) B0928/09 B0958/24
bleed (1) C0407/25
bleeding (6) A0028/V A0670/04
B0950/03 C0115/02 C0403/33 C0406/17
Bleitziz (2) A0366/10 A0366/10
blemish (3) A0502/10
A0709/05 B1274/10
blemishes (1) B1381/11
blend (2) B0769/05 B1212/20
blende (1) A0182/08
blended (5) A0209/04
A0602/30 B1122/15 B1133/16 C0542/08
bless (14) A0124/19 A0173/26
A0179/08 A0371/14 A0380/32 A0382/28
A0383/20 A0384/03 A0384/26 A0386/10
A0387/08 B0874/09 B1305/08 C0067/17
Bless-my-soul (3) A0174/12
A0174/17 A0176/16
Bless-my-Soul (2) A0179/27 A0182/17
blessed (12) A0078/38
A0317/20 A0464/12 A0642/13 A0667/52
B0812/07 B0898/14 B1039/23 B1212/09
B1375/20 C0117/26 C0146/05
blessing (1) B0856/03
blessings (1) A0071/23
blew (15) A0138/21
A0487/20 A0584/12 A0584/37 A0585/31
A0603/12 A0624/05 C0058/33 C0118/27
C0120/02 C0162/25 C0162/32 C0203/18
C0536/29 C0548/41
blieve (1) B0814/17
blind (22) A0078/27 A0107/17
A0125/26 A0157/05 A0160/21 A0487/06
A0501/15 A0589/15 A0610/28 B0747/35
B0896/03 B1107/28 B1109/31 B1128/29
B1128/33 B1129/01 B1132/04 B1226/08
B1294/12 B1296/23 B1313/19 B1313/24
blinded (5) A0667/58
->B1296/16 B1312/19 C0126/04 C0145/25
blindfold (1) B1372/20
blindly (6) A0499/13 A0644/V
A0707/05 B0856/14 B1038/34 C0181/16
blindness (2) A0432/05 A0703/15
blink (1) A0355/15
blinking (2) A0355/09 A0469/V
bliss (12) A0209/08
A0608/15 A0640/28 A0703/10 A0703/30
B0898/20 B0901/23 B0901/24 B1039/25
B1268/09 B1268/29 B1385/32
bliss> (1) A0464/24
blissful (4) A0610/01
A0612/07 B0857/30 B1274/04
Blitzen (2) A0177/13 A0373/19
Blitzen (2) A0183/07 A0366/11
bloated (1) A0070/23
Block (3) C0061/29
C0061/39 C0063/06
block (4) A0160/24
B1303/33 C0074/10 C0074/32
Block, E. T. V. (1) C0061/24
blockading (1) C0186/24
blocked (5) C0075/09
C0094/29 C0164/01 C0170/32 C0549/18
blockhead (1) B0810/05
blocks (5) A0536/01
B0734/12 B0749/07 B0749/11 C0198/40
blood (74)
blood-bedewed (1) A0676/35
blood-chilling (3) A0243/12
B0765/04 B1058/05
blood-colored (1) A0674/07
blood-red (6) A0035/09 A0319/05
A0417/08 B1156/13 B1156/24 C0389/28
blood-spot (1) B0796/13
blood-stained (1) B1052/26
blood-thirstiness (1) A0511/22
blood-thirsty (2) A0034/V C0086/41
blood-tinted (1) A0672/17
blood-vessels (1) C0404/05
bloodless (2) A0613/08 B0940/11
bloodshed (1) C0095/21
bloodthirsty (3) A0021/V
C0180/11 C0201/17
bloody (14) A0021/V A0382/30
A0387/23 A0469/26 A0560/11 A0567/13
B1046/21 B1052/17 B1057/07 B1058/27
C0086/26 C0111/11 C0133/10 C0166/29
bloody-minded (1) A0058/26
bloom (5) A0163/02
A0503/01 A0503/V B1333/37 C0543/28
bloomed (1) A0407/30
blooming (2) A0613/07 B1280/16
Bloomsbury (1) A0464/04
blossoming (1) B1334/22
blossoms (4) B1332/36
B1333/04 B1337/11 C0542/10
blossomy (1) B1329/35
blot (1) A0644/04
blotted (3) A0162/09
B1161/08 B1168/13
blotting (1) B1039/01
blow (25) A0553/22
A0622/32 B0855/14 B0856/22 B0856/24

->B0930/08 B0930/28 B1048/02 B1226/V
C0085/18 C0086/01 C0086/04 C0089/15
C0112/33 C0113/25 C0113/29 C0115/19
C0116/12 C0119/39 C0149/25 C0149/38
C0165/09 C0199/12 C0199/26 C0547/14
blowing (14) A0180/08 A0487/02
A0579/16 B1080/18 C0058/21 C0062/41
C0071/29 C0102/24 C0113/36 C0117/18
C0118/07 C0149/19 C0162/35 C0392/01
blown (7) A0138/04
A0562/04 B1101/23 B1154/29 B1156/31
C0201/26 C0566/15
blowpipe (1) B1161/38
blows (5) A0413/31
A0544/05 B0730/16 B0844/19 B0858/34
Bluddennuff (3) A0183/03
A0183/05 A0183/22
Bludenuff (2) A0177/05 A0177/27
Bludenuff, Baron (1) A0177/10
bludgeon (1) C0073/35
Blue (1) A0409/03
blue (49) A0088/16
A0106/23 A0121/V A0227/10 A0231/24
A0249/28 A0267/11 A0269/08 A0316/22
A0348/22 A0368/04 A0447/04 A0587/11
A0610/01 A0644/V A0671/30 A0671/30
A0675/27 A0676/01 A0676/13 A0702/M
B0789/13 B0795/02 B0862/13 B0864/33
B0990/36 B1153/30 B1165/32 B1192/05
B1267/M B1361/06 C0108/39 C0151/27
C0164/04 C0174/06 C0175/28 C0177/12
C0177/39 C0184/05 C0189/07 C0387/15
C0387/26 C0388/31 C0407/34 C0416/40
C0542/10 C0543/28 C0577/01 C0578/27
blue-eyed (2) A0321/02 A0330/04
blueish (1) A0280/09
bluff (4) C0537/35
C0541/03 C0541/03 C0574/13
bluffs (8) C0538/25
C0559/15 C0567/11 C0571/16 C0572/10
C0572/11 C0573/26 C0576/19
bluish (4) A0268/19
A0269/37 A0275/17 A0276/01
blunder (4) A0107/33
B1383/16 C0075/07 C0079/03
blunderbuss (1) C0392/02
blunderbusses (1) C0147/19
Blunderbuzzard (1) A0366/16
blundering (1) A0556/15
blunders (3) B1050/19
B1381/20 C0432/31
blunt (1) A0339/09
Blunt's/Lunar/Chart (1) C0429/04
blurred (3) A0089/05
A0689/07 A0695/27
blush (12) A0035/24
A0056/20 A0066/09 A0155/03 A0379/22
A0410/23 A0487/18 B0851/06 B0851/29
B0893/14 B0901/28 B0906/27
blushed (7) A0407/30
A0588/33 A0603/06 B0895/05 B1014/06
B1107/15 B1195/04
blushes (1) B1384/23
blushing (2) A0155/09 B1300/12
bluster (1) A0345/28
blustering (1) C0550/12
Boanerges (2) A0048/V A0048/V
boar (3) A0026/06
B1142/15 B1248/16
board (95)
board-bill (1) B1119/M
boarded (1) B0732/38
boarding (3) B0878/10
C0125/29 C0187/41
boarding-nettings (2) C0171/10
C0180/17
boards (6) B0796/11 B0797/18
B0980/15 B0981/13 C0075/22 C0098/19
boast (1) B0862/14
boasted (8) A0160/22
A0315/21 A0350/17 A0477/02 A0533/13
A0547/30 B1312/21 B1317/03
boasting (1) A0588/29
boat (116)
boating (2) B1246/05 C0539/24
boatman (1) C0532/02
boatmen (3) C0530/38
C0536/07 C0537/39
boats (34) A0581/35 B0735/21
B0767/30 B0931/07 B1158/19 C0153/31
C0155/04 C0164/32 C0165/29 C0167/30
C0168/25 C0168/30 C0168/40 C0201/29
C0202/24 C0204/03 C0532/40 C0535/20
C0539/36 C0540/05 C0548/16 C0548/39
C0549/16 C0555/21 C0557/39 C0558/24
C0563/24 C0563/30 C0565/22 C0568/16
C0568/30 C0569/19 C0572/24 C0576/15
Bob (16) B1126/T
B1132/15 B1133/05 B1135/05 B1135/06
B1135/17 B1135/22 B1142/30 B1373/05
B1373/08 B1373/14 B1373/15 B1373/20
B1373/24 B1373/34 B1375/14
Bob, Thingum (9) B1137/10
B1138/03 B1139/12 B1143/27 B1144/03
B1145/13 B1145/13 B1145/13 B1145/14
Bob, Thomas (5) B1127/01
B1127/16 B1137/12 B1138/04 B1142/33
Bob's (1) B1138/05
bobbing (3) A0246/25
A0253/09 C0553/24
Bobby (3) A0651/03
A0651/07 A0657/27
bobby (2) A0651/V A0656/20
Bobby's (1) A0656/V
bobolink (1) B1337/15
bobtail (1) A0485/05
boded (1) B0814/03
bodies (48) A0457/22
A0489/05 A0540/15 A0543/19 A0544/10
A0545/21 A0546/32 A0592/25 A0601/08
A0601/09 B0732/07 B0732/07 B0740/08
B0740/08 B0740/16 B0740/17 B0740/23
B0741/06 B0741/11 B0743/03 B0743/03
B0743/11 B0743/18 B0743/18 B0964/28
B1035/07 B1035/10 B1037/05 B1038/23
B1038/27 B1089/23 B1162/27 B1168/25
B1212/20 C0114/09 C0114/21 C0124/20
C0126/09 C0137/37 C0192/09 C0199/29
C0418/50 C0424/32 C0429/13 C0429/14
C0429/41 C0438/V C0539/35

bodiless (1) B1037/03
bodily (35) A0020/07
A0085/05 A0101/V A0136/29 A0145/32
A0212/06 A0233/24 A0298/V A0329/21
A0380/09 A0398/21 A0426/15 A0438/20
A0582/28 A0616/05 B0859/10 B0928/10
B0932/23 B0948/05 B0961/19 B1030/34
B1031/02 B1089/04 C0082/24 C0099/19
C0129/37 C0142/37 C0182/28 C0399/06
C0404/29 C0529/15 C0532/04 C0532/32
C0546/17 C0573/22
boding (1) A0189/25
body (260)
body-snatchers (1) B0960/04
body's (1) A0028/10
bog (3) A0465/22 B1160/37 B1372/03
bog-throthing> (1) A0464/09
bog-throtting> (1) A0469/26
Boggs (3) B0879/13
B0879/17 B0879/24
boggy (1) C0578/13
Bogs (1) B1055/22
bogs (1) A0467/26
bogthrotter> (1) A0468/21
boiled (3) C0083/34
C0178/41 C0179/02
boiling (5) A0580/14
B1166/02 B1166/11 C0534/40 C0535/34
boilings (1) A0085/09
Bois (2) A0560/26 A0561/24
Bois-Brules (1) C0551/19
boisterous (10) A0087/35 A0102/18
A0296/14 A0581/24 A0581/33 A0584/13
B0928/03 C0161/34 C0532/34 C0541/09
boisterously (2) B0735/29 B0767/19
bold (33) A0143/08
A0162/V A0265/19 A0272/37 A0273/17
A0276/33 A0278/14 A0279/12 A0281/17
A0348/11 A0385/05 A0628/33 A0672/19
A0673/13 A0675/29 A0690/25 A0693/30
B0870/27 B0874/24 B0893/21 B0977/01
B0988/19 B0991/18 B1077/29 B1182/08
B1260/07 C0155/02 C0399/40 C0536/35
C0549/05 C0550/11 C0555/38 C0568/17
bolder (5) A0226/09
A0284/26 A0510/34 C0531/17 C0559/05
boldest (2) A0694/14 B0865/36
boldly (13) A0555/03
A0609/16 B0793/13 B0899/05 B0944/10
B1114/17 C0058/32 C0110/37 C0136/25
C0162/20 C0163/20 C0202/13 C0557/36
boldness (3) A0278/18
A0281/22 A0564/12
Bolingbroke (1) A0096/V
Bologna (2) C0069/23 C0071/21
bolsters (1) B1169/20
bolt (6) A0242/12 A0586/15
A0590/01 B0910/24 B0911/V C0062/33
bolted (5) A0057/16
A0067/34 A0068/33 A0540/02 C0068/13
bolts (5) A0243/04
A0429/05 A0671/01 B0826/12 C0189/30
bomb (1) A0628/25
bombarded (1) A0294/V
bombast (1) B1131/05
Bombay (1) A0136/01
bombshell (1) B1370/08
bon (6) A0033/17 A0096/M
A0431/08 A0508/28 A0652/11 B1105/09
Bon-Bon (37) A0096/12
A0096/T A0097/02 A0097/03 A0097/09
A0097/09 A0097/12 A0098/15 A0098/27
A0099/07 A0099/12 A0099/14 A0099/28
A0102/30 A0102/V A0105/22 A0106/07
A0106/18 A0107/03 A0107/11 A0107/20
A0107/23 A0108/13 A0108/26 A0109/01
A0109/18 A0109/22 A0110/12 A0110/28
A0111/08 A0111/09 A0111/22 A0112/25
A0112/V A0113/05 A0113/14 A0113/V
Bon-Bon (3) A0096/10
A0100/30 A0101/12
Bon-Bon, Pierre (12) A0096/01
A0096/04 A0097/26 A0097/27 A0100/20
A0101/17 A0101/19 A0104/25 A0106/26
A0107/06 A0108/02 A0112/04
Bon-Bon's (1) A0103/V
Bon-Bonist (1) A0097/13
bona (1) A0062/16
bona (2) A0034/V A0053/10
bond (3) A0093/21
A0654/12 B1057/34
Bond, Peter (1) C0526/08
bonds (3) A0691/21
B0878/06 C0537/28
bone (5) B1166/09
C0074/04 C0137/09 C0570/26 C0577/40
Bones (1) A0071/27
bones (23) A0252/25
A0298/V A0356/30 A0443/04 A0543/32
A0616/29 B0741/06 B0742/01 B0743/32
B0795/03 B0825/23 B1166/02 B1223/05
B1260/05 B1260/10 B1261/08 B1261/11
B1262/04 B1262/17 B1263/25 C0090/20
C0389/03 C0551/40
Bonfanti's (1) A0389/08
bonfire (1) A0123/31
bonheur (1) B1105/09
Bonhomme (1) C0538/08
Bonhomme/Island (1) C0548/06
bonhommie (1) B1361/09
bonne (2) B0875/03 C0566/24
Bonner, Jim (2) C0102/10 C0102/11
bonnet (6) A0245/26 B0730/32
B0730/33 B0730/34 B0747/05 B0747/05
bonnet-ribbon (1) B0768/32
Bonnet/Lake (1) C0526/38
Bonneville (2) C0528/24 C0546/12
bono (6) B1051/09 B1051/14
B1051/20 B1051/21 B1051/23 B1051/28
bonum (1) A0622/20
bonus (1) A0486/15
Book (1) A0461/03
book (65)
book-case (1) B1250/09
book-closet (1) B0974/04
book-cover (1) B0981/05
book-stall (1) B1128/19
booked (2) A0487/24 B0747/16
books (44) A0078/25
A0087/29 A0102/26 A0210/11 A0212/34

->A0278/23 A0280/08 A0314/22 A0401/15
A0408/26 A0408/26 A0430/13 A0486/33
A0503/07 A0531/26 A0621/06 B0807/22
B0900/13 B0962/32 B0969/04 B0980/33
B0990/32 B1004/03 B1006/15 B1113/01
B1115/13 B1123/01 B1132/01 B1141/17
B1164/07 B1246/06 B1247/03 B1321/01
B1325/06 B1329/33 B1340/14 C0068/18
C0068/18 C0069/21 C0070/32 C0071/23
C0415/03 C0417/11 C0543/38
bookseller (3) B0958/16
B1128/21 C0399/32
bookseller's (4) A0269/17
C0392/08 C0392/39 C0395/05
booksellers (1) B1206/02
bookshelves (1) A0300/29
bookworm (1) A0343/07
boomed (1) C0060/23
booming (1) C0420/28
booms (1) A0143/23
boon (4) A0398/16
B0760/19 B0907/13 B0916/16
boosed (1) B0826/27
Booshoh (1) A0047/14
Booshoh/he (2) A0047/13 A0047/16
boot (3) B0825/32
B1115/22 C0552/21
boot-black (1) A0489/17
boot-blacks (1) A0263/06
boots (7) A0489/14
A0508/24 A0691/01 B1090/29 B1093/29
B1185/35 C0425/02
booty (3) B0827/11
C0093/15 C0189/33
boquets (1) B1340/V
Bordeaux (1) A0101/V
border (4) A0191/10
A0501/V C0425/16 C0563/25
bordered (2) A0354/12 A0531/04
bordering (6) A0099/31 A0444/22
C0064/17 C0074/24 C0078/25 C0564/41
borders (5) A0055/32
A0065/14 A0146/03 A0195/03 C0536/33
bore (59)
bored (4) B0985/32
B0985/35 C0415/30 C0533/20
boredom (1) B1131/20
boring (3) B0985/24
B1093/07 B1298/07
born (25) A0078/22
A0172/03 A0178/03 A0209/07 A0209/23
A0210/06 A0339/28 A0383/02 A0432/28
A0539/11 A0608/01 A0608/02 A0611/21
A0703/04 B0750/30 B1046/04 B1108/07
B1122/27 B1131/07 B1183/08 B1268/04
B1299/31 B1360/35 C0057/02 C0413/23
borne (28) A0154/21
A0177/10 A0183/04 A0189/34 A0294/V
A0404/20 A0406/V A0582/04 A0588/19
A0591/23 A0594/14 B0734/06 B0766/21
B0865/24 B0947/13 B1079/02 B1195/06
B1256/01 B1280/33 B1332/14 C0064/29
C0161/24 C0188/02 C0400/05 C0431/06
C0436/V C0567/28 C0579/05
Borneo (2) A0564/20 B1351/14
Bornese (1) A0560/28
borough (18) A0365/02 A0365/17
A0366/24 A0369/12 A0369/21 A0370/02
A0370/11 A0371/27 A0374/19 B1044/11
B1044/22 B1045/14 B1048/34 B1052/02
B1054/07 B1054/20 B1055/02 B1056/19
borrow (1) C0393/14
borrowed (1) B0875/27
borrows (1) B0871/13
bosky (1) B1283/07
bosom (60)
bosoms (5) A0295/27
A0459/29 A0533/15 A0608/17 B1008/02
Bossarion (2) A0086/12 A0342/V
Bossuet (1) B0958/05
Bossuet, Julien (1) B0957/14
Boston (7) A0035/10
A0267/15 A0271/09 A0272/20 A0278/02
C0146/31 C0146/33
Bostonians (1) B1193/26
botanical (2) A0343/34 C0523/02
botanically (1) B1293/02
botanist (1) C0522/34
Botany (1) B1163/42
Botany/Bay (1) A0490/19
bote (1) B0912/19
both (183)
botheration (3) A0467/15
A0468/17 A0470/01
bothered (1) B0869/17
Bothnia (1) A0583/05
Bottle (2) A0135/T A0146/10
bottle (42) A0055/11 A0064/27
A0092/11 A0092/37 A0094/21 A0098/25
A0100/29 A0108/24 A0109/19 A0110/10
A0112/V A0114/16 A0142/06 A0206/03
A0487/24 A0547/V B1011/26 B1015/V
B1020/29 B1077/08 B1109/12 B1109/23
B1222/31 B1259/22 B1260/16 B1305/15
B1310/05 B1340/14 C0082/11 C0082/32
C0083/28 C0093/40 C0094/33 C0095/28
C0127/18 C0127/24 C0128/11 C0130/01
C0137/06 C0138/33 C0153/36 C0427/18
bottle-nosed (1) B1208/18
bottles (23) A0101/15
A0105/16 A0110/29 A0245/11 A0245/14
A0248/V A0253/30 B1017/30 B1020/18
B1055/29 B1056/28 B1081/03 B1101/02
B1102/28 B1103/20 B1104/22 B1104/22
B1106/22 B1110/21 B1178/05 C0069/24
C0142/41 C0571/06
bottom (99)
bottoms (2) B0979/32 C0168/20
<u>bouche</u> (3) B0875/03
C0178/08 C0566/24
<u>boudoir</u> (5) A0062/33
A0064/30 A0155/05 A0500/24 B0977/03
boudoir (2) A0053/29 A0055/15
bought (8) A0172/06
B0865/21 B1141/05 B1143/17 B1143/21
B1257/13 C0439/V C0529/12
Bougive (1) B0985/V
bould> (1) A0467/28
<u>bouleversement</u> (2) B1144/19
C0422/02

Boullard (2) B1013/15 B1013/23
Boulogne (2) A0560/26 A0561/24
bounced (1) A0371/29
Bound (1) A0710/31
bound (31) A0123/07
A0136/10 A0204/15 A0217/V A0225/07
A0301/07 A0330/12 A0503/07 A0564/08
A0586/31 A0624/11 A0689/14 B0734/19
B0866/02 B0967/11 B0968/30 B1091/03
B1158/20 B1291/19 C0061/05 C0065/26
C0072/27 C0086/20 C0103/26 C0114/11
C0147/06 C0147/26 C0148/19 C0186/11
C0562/17 C0562/22
boundaries (5) A0079/39
B0955/25 B1329/25 B1333/18 B1334/31
boundary (10) A0021/02 A0195/14
A0195/14 A0477/03 A0479/33 B1302/32
B1334/37 C0418/08 C0429/15 C0429/16
boundary-line (1) C0412/39
bounded (11) A0028/19
A0029/17 A0219/02 A0461/10 B0865/25
B1226/02 B1338/19 C0113/06 C0160/13
C0173/17 C0566/36
bounden (3) A0320/25
A0403/09 B1189/22
bounding (1) C0562/35
boundless (2) B1128/05 C0407/33
bounds (10) A0437/30 A0675/02
B0752/03 B0901/03 B1010/03 B1214/13
B1295/30 C0062/02 C0169/24 C0565/03
bouquets (1) B1340/21
Bourdeaux (1) A0554/13
Bourdon (3) A0034/16
A0034/24 A0079/03
bout (10) B0811/27 B0811/32
B0811/V B0812/22 B0813/02 B0813/03
B0813/V B0821/14 B0912/13 B1373/02
Bovis (1) A0353/08
bow (27) A0142/22
A0160/V A0461/17 A0465/18 A0466/04
A0507/06 A0586/03 A0586/10 B0895/04
B0915/03 B0924/15 B1105/07 B1119/23
B1339/17 C0106/26 C0123/33 C0131/08
C0164/30 C0165/21 C0200/37 C0201/09
C0202/36 C0203/08 C0533/28 C0533/30
C0536/05 C0569/15
bow-knot (1) C0389/30
bow-legs (2) A0241/10 A0348/31
bow-wow-wow (2) A0353/32 B1372/05
bowed (23) A0037/21
A0087/26 A0089/21 A0094/19 A0114/14
A0144/23 A0159/20 A0263/33 A0297/V
A0302/01 A0389/11 A0458/24 A0508/13
A0541/24 A0562/21 A0644/16 B0866/19
B1010/18 B1107/15 B1195/08 B1258/28
C0087/10 C0533/10
bowels (8) A0146/13
B1158/02 B1160/09 B1187/29 B1187/31
B1322/22 C0190/01 C0191/21
Bowen, Walter G. (1) B1378/T
bower (3) A0165/20
B0762/04 C0151/04
Bowie (3) C0180/26
C0184/02 C0188/34
bowing (3) A0034/30
->A0381/03 B1145/24
bowl (4) A0253/10
A0667/22 B0955/34 B1372/08
Bowling-Green (2) B1192/07 B1193/01
bows (16) A0140/14
A0371/09 B0872/05 B0875/16 B1107/26
C0060/10 C0060/20 C0098/05 C0103/05
C0103/14 C0106/25 C0147/09 C0163/36
C0200/18 C0534/08 C0554/08
bowsprit (4) C0115/07
C0123/34 C0124/31 C0124/40
bowstring (2) B1154/29 B1170/02
bowstringing (1) B1154/03
bowstrung (1) B1153/21
Box (1) B0922/T
box (90)
boxed (1) C0534/07
boxes (8) A0430/08
A0542/14 A0591/27 B0889/12 B1157/10
B1363/03 C0074/35 C0095/39
Boy (1) A0018/15
boy (16) A0078/23
A0482/11 A0483/24 A0650/14 A0651/07
A0657/29 B0872/29 B0873/03 B0984/11
B0984/31 B1097/06 B1127/28 B1331/04
B1373/01 B1373/06 C0543/12
boyhood (5) A0210/11
A0398/16 A0401/29 A0431/28 B1122/35
boyish (3) A0402/18
B0761/23 B1122/06
boys (20) A0368/15
A0368/16 A0368/32 A0372/25 A0373/14
A0398/29 A0483/29 A0490/09 A0584/29
B0734/30 B0758/34 B0759/09 B0759/09
B0761/06 B0761/07 B0761/17 B0761/20
B0761/23 B0770/13 B1096/24
Boz (1) B1138/02
brace (2) A0631/10 A0631/13
bracelet (1) B0890/10
bracelets (1) B1008/01
brackets (1) B1133/03
braggadocio (3) A0627/21
B1136/12 B1136/33
bragging (1) B1194/08
brain (49) A0035/08
A0058/34 A0063/22 A0078/02 A0195/V
A0215/18 A0217/V A0236/02 A0317/10
A0327/V A0328/V A0329/25 A0417/14
A0430/22 A0437/25 A0466/33 A0600/32
A0613/27 A0615/04 A0643/02 A0644/08
A0663/V A0683/05 A0693/24 B0739/08
B0789/08 B0814/01 B0856/26 B0895/12
B0927/33 B0963/25 B1009/29 B1037/36
B1038/05 B1038/05 B1038/13 B1128/17
B1181/07 B1221/V B1322/09 B1340/12
B1348/11 C0073/01 C0078/07 C0083/12
C0198/12 C0413/01 C0440/V C0579/32
brain-scattering (1) B1115/08
brains (25) A0253/21
A0459/35 A0488/12 A0488/16 A0494/09
A0499/01 A0556/16 A0624/23 B0870/32
B0988/04 B1006/02 B1090/24 B1109/14
B1127/30 B1165/27 B1166/26 B1187/29
B1187/32 B1207/34 B1300/21 B1363/24
C0113/17 C0199/25 C0392/01 C0577/39

brambles (9) B0734/37
B0817/31 B0822/11 B0827/02 B1049/04
B1057/34 B1059/04 C0194/10 C0194/25
bran (1) A0485/03
branch (23) A0074/20
A0097/18 A0399/07 A0528/13 B0724/09
B0724/10 B0773/05 B0773/12 B0819/07
B0839/33 B0840/23 B0842/15 B1250/08
B1279/33 C0191/29 C0528/02 C0528/18
C0544/28 C0544/34 C0545/01 C0547/20
C0551/15 C0575/29
branches (17) A0429/27
A0602/15 B0758/11 B0818/02 B0818/30
B0821/34 B1160/38 B1332/05 C0173/10
C0174/38 C0207/41 C0426/19 C0525/38
C0545/05 C0546/04 C0546/40 C0551/12
brand (1) A0215/22
branded (1) A0024/01
branding (1) B1312/08
brandish (1) B1167/20
brandished (1) B0913/17
brandishing (1) C0557/24
Brandreth's (2) A0341/02 B1195/02
brands (2) C0563/03 C0563/15
brandy (6) B0767/16 B0876/01
B0876/02 B0876/05 B0876/07 B0876/08
brandy-saturated (1) B1108/09
Bransby (2) A0430/05 A0436/31
Bransby's (4) A0432/27
A0438/03 A0440/02 A0446/01
brant (1) C0560/01
Brantome's (2) A0301/04 A0301/V
bras (1) A0096/M
brass (19) A0140/08
A0189/21 A0190/29 A0414/18 A0415/26
A0494/08 A0690/21 B0990/36 B1071/10
B1071/18 B1166/17 B1363/13 B1363/17
B1363/24 B1363/27 C0147/19 C0177/12
C0410/30 C0533/33
brat (1) C0110/08
brats (1) B1128/24
bravado (3) A0431/31
B0858/30 C0550/18
brave (6) A0244/10 B0756/05
B0789/M C0058/24 C0096/04 C0532/03
bravo (3) A0126/28
A0126/28 A0128/04
brawling (1) C0173/26
brawny (1) C0168/14
braying (1) B1020/32
brazen (5) A0087/25
A0190/33 A0415/18 A0672/25 B1017/26
brazier (1) A0672/12
Brazil (1) C0148/17
breach (3) C0115/12
C0149/38 C0544/35
breaches (1) A0137/32
bread (10) A0341/V A0341/V
A0341/V A0341/V A0342/15 A0342/17
A0342/19 A0342/20 B0992/18 B1021/28
breadth (28) A0035/05
A0081/38 A0156/14 A0312/25 A0312/V
A0352/30 A0401/33 A0443/28 A0501/04
A0554/22 A0554/23 A0558/02 A0631/11
B0806/08 B0925/01 B1164/13 B1164/38
->B1167/02 B1302/35 B1303/01 B1331/14
B1345/12 C0183/32 C0193/12 C0202/23
C0421/09 C0525/15 C0531/21
break (12) A0654/V
A0682/24 B0820/18 B0820/22 B0840/15
B0870/19 B0908/22 B0929/02 B1169/25
B1281/14 B1383/17 C0202/36
breakbones (1) C0151/32
breakers (2) A0137/18 B1076/29
breakfast (10) B0896/27 B0909/21
B0909/24 B0942/10 B1045/30 C0064/26
C0140/06 C0561/02 C0563/31 C0577/13
breakfasted (1) C0538/14
breaking (22) A0057/05 A0066/31
A0070/20 A0081/41 A0162/V A0415/19
A0416/11 A0428/07 A0542/21 A0567/15
A0568/04 B0818/21 B0899/01 B1010/V
B1015/06 C0107/13 C0121/39 C0191/36
C0397/15 C0526/01 C0534/38 C0546/40
breaks (2) B1091/16 B1154/11
breast (24) A0262/19
A0351/07 A0415/11 A0437/18 A0460/16
A0512/34 A0514/09 A0564/17 A0642/20
A0693/18 B0765/11 B0854/13 B0855/14
B1156/04 B1238/33 B1248/29 B1248/32
B1262/20 C0112/36 C0151/16 C0168/36
C0389/16 C0408/31 C0579/07
breast-pocket (1) A0104/07
breasts (1) C0567/27
Breath (1) A0061/T
breath (83)
breathe (12) A0052/M
A0061/M A0217/V A0235/19 A0507/14
B0741/30 B0981/24 B1220/31 C0064/02
C0081/17 C0142/06 C0414/25
breathed (24) A0228/34
A0228/34 A0233/16 A0233/16 A0236/08
A0319/28 A0401/17 A0460/03 A0612/34
A0640/27 A0642/29 A0685/08 A0696/01
B0795/13 B0858/02 B0969/03 B1030/29
B1127/17 B1163/04 C0060/25 C0073/03
C0205/20 C0407/27 C0411/24
breathes (3) A0315/25
A0318/12 A0710/26
breathing (27) A0154/10
A0214/06 A0218/27 A0326/14 A0330/06
A0437/12 A0614/26 A0708/07 B0943/17
B1032/14 B1080/03 B1237/10 B1237/15
B1238/10 B1273/07 C0094/16 C0094/20
C0096/20 C0096/36 C0128/21 C0404/06
C0404/11 C0404/29 C0405/10 C0407/04
C0413/12 C0413/18
breathings (2) A0081/04 A0324/27
breathless (8) A0053/33
A0053/33 A0063/04 A0063/05 A0214/28
A0609/07 A0612/25 B0906/08
breathlessly (1) A0694/09
bred (2) A0280/05 B1104/02
breeched (2) A0172/07 A0178/08
breeches (7) A0087/04
A0100/14 A0104/34 A0253/06 B1110/02
C0389/25 C0397/28
breeches' (1) B1184/02
breed (3) A0345/13
C0079/12 C0137/22

breeding (6) A0354/20 A0378/19
B0893/25 B0895/31 B1007/29 C0151/39
breeze (31) A0585/03
A0585/16 A0585/24 B0814/21 B0923/36
B0928/24 B0944/29 B1076/04 B1079/14
B1079/23 B1330/23 C0058/10 C0071/41
C0102/13 C0103/07 C0118/27 C0120/02
C0120/22 C0123/14 C0131/41 C0133/39
C0139/02 C0139/31 C0140/01 C0145/35
C0160/33 C0165/22 C0166/10 C0204/20
C0536/29 C0540/14
breezes (5) C0099/11
C0136/05 C0148/32 C0159/03 C0559/04
Bremen (3) B1361/17
B1361/30 B1363/27
brethren (3) A0088/12
A0478/28 B1273/19
breve (1) A0033/03
Brevet (9) A0378/02
A0380/02 A0381/10 A0382/13 A0382/23
A0382/31 A0385/01 A0388/23 A0389/16
brevity (1) B0738/21
brewing (1) B1018/22
Brewster (1) C0430/01
briar-bushes (1) C0578/09
bribing (1) C0562/25
brick (6) A0078/21 A0428/21
B0871/08 B0980/29 B1166/10 C0391/08
brick-work (2) B0857/18 B0858/31
bricks (8) A0367/09
B0857/10 B0857/14 B0980/30 B1336/18
B1336/19 C0573/39 C0574/04
bridal (3) A0321/05
A0322/02 A0323/01
bride (9) A0321/06
A0326/06 A0665/02 A0665/09 A0665/16
A0704/12 B0924/08 B0926/26 B1269/12
bridge (16) A0321/01
A0591/09 A0626/25 A0627/12 A0627/30
A0629/02 A0629/26 A0630/12 A0630/19
A0631/08 B0874/26 B0874/26 B0923/28
B1334/04 B1338/06 B1338/16
Bridge/of/Sighs (3) A0151/17
A0152/05 A0156/09
brief (79)
briefer (1) B1035/23
briefly (4) A0473/05
B0736/16 C0092/26 C0415/36
brig (82)
brig's (4) C0085/33
C0088/16 C0103/03 C0117/06
Brigadier (10) A0378/02 A0380/02
A0381/11 A0382/13 A0382/23 A0382/32
A0385/02 A0386/06 A0388/24 A0389/17
bright (33) A0046/03
A0087/01 A0100/11 A0162/19 A0262/04
A0328/02 A0437/15 A0489/14 A0494/02
A0508/24 A0587/11 A0602/03 A0603/09
A0642/18 A0644/21 B0865/11 B0895/18
B0895/19 B0940/20 B1016/20 B1040/10
B1123/27 B1144/33 C0065/18 C0080/09
C0136/08 C0149/22 C0149/33 C0151/16
C0389/27 C0543/28 C0562/11 C0573/26
brighten (1) B1347/34
brightened (2) A0053/19 A0536/02
brighter (3) A0379/04
A0639/19 A0642/18
brightest (6) A0153/05 A0213/32
B0865/07 B0887/04 B1078/23 B1097/05
brightly (2) A0585/03 C0062/12
brilliancy (15) A0139/34
A0150/01 A0205/03 A0312/22 A0313/14
A0345/27 A0461/22 A0695/29 B0827/35
B1004/22 B1138/17 B1281/26 C0080/07
C0208/06 C0418/43
brilliant (37) A0087/17
A0100/13 A0103/27 A0156/13 A0164/23
A0298/V A0313/10 A0325/23 A0459/21
A0502/08 A0513/35 A0640/12 A0640/29
B0808/32 B0809/09 B0897/26 B1050/01
B1127/10 B1132/08 B1144/29 B1168/04
B1215/27 B1215/32 B1340/19 B1369/33
C0150/24 C0151/13 C0164/04 C0167/16
C0167/20 C0389/21 C0416/22 C0425/16
C0432/14 C0543/14 C0543/27 C0559/36
brilliantly (8) A0157/13
A0379/10 A0512/32 B1180/30 B1331/02
B1333/25 C0123/37 C0416/20
brilliantly-plumed (1) B1334/27
brim (6) B0827/19 B1185/35
B1362/22 B1363/12 C0388/32 C0415/35
brimful (1) A0244/10
brimfull (1) B1182/24
brimming (1) B1349/03
bring (88)
Bringhurst, Everard (3) B1069/16
B1072/23 B1072/30
bringing (35) A0102/15
A0295/20 A0436/17 A0457/24 A0484/21
A0528/07 A0629/13 A0709/25 A0710/14
A0711/18 B0730/12 B0832/15 B0930/18
B1274/28 B1275/17 B1276/19 B1383/26
C0075/08 C0079/14 C0084/23 C0088/14
C0090/35 C0092/40 C0101/07 C0105/33
C0106/10 C0118/21 C0129/29 C0135/27
C0137/01 C0171/25 C0186/06 C0399/20
C0407/12 C0529/26
brings (6) A0612/15 B0751/V
B0765/28 B1364/14 C0402/27 C0430/46
brink (17) A0143/30
A0398/09 A0555/27 A0578/14 A0589/28
A0687/04 A0696/10 A0697/06 B0739/31
B0764/32 B0766/34 B1222/26 B1223/12
B1281/V C0121/02 C0191/33 C0196/18
brinks (1) A0639/V
Briscoe (2) C0161/26 C0162/08
brisk (5) A0382/26
B1186/17 C0141/34 C0146/05 C0548/36
briskly (3) B0944/11
C0181/35 C0200/01
Brisky> (1) A0464/15
bristles (1) A0582/07
bristly (2) A0043/M B0807/08
Bristol/Channel (2) B1076/05
B1076/28
Britain (1) C0407/36
Britannia-ware (1) B1009/31
Britannica (1) A0583/02
British (21) A0261/25
A0261/28 A0261/28 A0499/32 A0500/24

->B0861/08 B0946/29 B0949/19 B1206/11
B1257/10 B1317/12 C0053/T C0147/04
C0156/05 C0156/08 C0156/12 C0157/12
C0160/16 C0399/21 C0525/24 C0571/07
British/Channel (2) B1072/22
B1075/12
broach (5) A0381/19
A0653/28 C0060/11 C0066/05 C0133/23
broached (1) C0523/17
broaching (1) B1056/03
Broad (1) B1093/18
broad (38) A0035/V A0044/29
A0121/03 A0121/07 A0152/14 A0157/02
A0278/35 A0298/V A0501/17 A0502/11
A0508/34 A0544/02 A0554/17 A0580/28
A0675/15 A0690/20 B0826/04 B0878/27
B0880/09 B0940/10 B1079/03 B1208/17
B1226/10 B1226/V B1281/25 B1334/04
B1336/01 B1337/26 C0087/09 C0099/36
C0151/15 C0168/12 C0388/33 C0389/17
C0389/22 C0405/25 C0416/35 C0533/18
broad-leaved (1) C0577/19
broadcloth (1) A0485/02
broader (2) A0501/V B0864/02
broadest (4) A0352/30
B1316/17 C0525/16 C0526/11
broadside (4) C0106/40
C0187/10 C0187/21 C0187/24
Broadway (3) A0512/29
B0933/15 B1384/08
Brobdingnag (1) B0870/10
brocade (2) B1010/09 B1185/34
brochures (1) C0433/04
Broglio, Duke Di (1) A0446/21
broils (2) A0431/04 A0431/24
broke (37) A0056/23
A0066/12 A0080/24 A0139/30 A0151/26
A0216/21 A0382/34 A0440/12 A0447/10
A0533/34 A0613/36 A0695/25 B0728/23
B0793/13 B0931/07 B1020/15 B1106/28
B1153/18 B1154/01 B1242/22 B1260/14
C0058/05 C0100/41 C0102/37 C0108/23
C0114/19 C0114/35 C0115/39 C0117/15
C0118/05 C0120/32 C0124/30 C0138/33
C0184/27 C0194/16 C0540/12 C0557/22
broken (57)
brooded (1) A0405/15
brook (9) B0863/31
B0864/26 B0865/23 B0866/05 B1335/11
B1337/07 B1338/07 B1339/25 C0171/26
Brooks (2) A0276/33 A0285/19
Brooks, James (1) A0276/29
broom (1) A0488/20
broomstick (1) C0431/06
broth (2) A0466/04 A0470/21
brother (17) A0404/12
A0404/22 A0409/20 A0410/15 A0416/32
A0584/28 A0585/35 A0586/07 A0586/22
A0587/15 A0589/25 A0593/34 B0875/18
B1045/23 B1046/25 C0426/40 C0531/27
brother-in-law (1) B1379/19
Brother/Jonathan (1) B0731/38
brother's (1) A0593/16
brotherhood (1) B1260/21
brothers (12) A0432/22
->A0432/26 A0583/20 A0585/06 B0986/21
C0180/33 C0444/V C0531/16 C0531/24
C0531/33 C0537/26 C0564/01
Brougham (2) A0337/28 B1013/04
Brougham's (2) A0337/22 B1141/06
brought (154)
brow (11) A0196/26
A0511/10 A0536/V A0614/27 A0643/28
A0675/16 A0675/22 B0823/25 B1040/13
B1330/24 B1338/08
brow-beating (1) B1140/30
brown (8) A0087/20
A0265/25 A0508/33 B1160/33 B1279/34
C0176/37 C0577/32 C0578/02
Brown/Stout (2) B1178/05 B1182/03
Browne, Thomas (4) A0173/03
A0176/12 A0527/M B1114/19
Brownson (2) B1031/12 B1369/06
brows (6) A0128/27 A0313/11
A0508/03 A0512/35 A0628/17 A0672/33
Bruges (1) C0427/21
bruin (1) C0579/33
bruise (2) A0543/28 C0121/22
bruised (5) A0510/16
A0543/21 A0543/34 B1057/07 C0580/04
bruises (6) A0057/20 A0538/15
A0557/25 A0558/29 B0730/06 B0730/15
bruited (1) A0426/05
Brunswick (1) B1358/22
brush (4) A0142/14
A0665/31 A0665/33 B1335/29
brushed (2) A0510/20 B1292/24
brushes (5) A0489/10
A0489/18 A0543/12 A0665/05 B1163/38
brushing (2) A0535/23 B0762/06
brushwood (1) C0189/05
brusquerie (1) B0813/15
Brussels (2) A0498/07 B1008/08
brutal (3) A0557/25
A0558/08 B0730/21
brutality (1) C0089/02
brutally (1) B0753/28
brute (15) A0028/V
A0447/21 A0477/01 A0561/25 A0566/02
A0566/V A0568/02 B0850/19 B0852/19
B0855/37 B0856/01 B1170/04 B1351/03
C0165/09 C0188/01
brute's (2) A0026/V B0823/18
Brutii (1) A0286/06
Brutus (2) A0074/08 A0379/03
Bryant (1) B0987/32
Bubastis (2) A0175/28 A0181/23
bubbled (1) C0543/33
bubbles (1) C0577/23
Buchan (1) B0969/05
buck (3) C0538/14
C0539/12 C0566/32
buck-wheat (2) A0341/V A0342/17
bucket (2) A0430/17 C0169/19
Buckholm (1) A0579/26
Buckhurst's (1) A0240/M
Buckingham (12) B1183/01
B1184/04 B1184/09 B1184/11 B1184/15
B1184/26 B1185/06 B1186/12 B1186/22
B1186/28 B1188/01 B1371/19

Buckingham, Silk (2) B1182/07
B1190/33
buckle (6) C0388/34 C0398/04
C0398/05 C0398/07 C0398/12 C0398/15
buckles (3) A0103/27
A0368/20 C0389/26
buckskin (3) A0368/19
A0489/31 B1009/32
buds (1) C0576/08
Buffalo (1) C0527/01
buffalo (13) C0536/23
C0540/11 C0548/03 C0552/09 C0552/19
C0552/31 C0552/33 C0553/04 C0558/33
C0562/17 C0568/02 C0572/07 C0575/43
buffaloes (7) A0580/05
B1248/14 C0550/22 C0559/41 C0567/07
C0567/09 C0575/12
Buffon (2) A0494/06 B1145/17
buffoon (1) B1133/34
buffooneries (1) A0295/14
buffoonery (1) A0337/35
buffoons (1) A0671/07
Bug (1) B1380/06
bug (31) B0808/28
B0808/32 B0809/02 B0809/02 B0809/04
B0810/11 B0812/19 B0812/21 B0812/25
B0812/28 B0814/18 B0814/20 B0815/01
B0815/03 B0815/09 B0815/10 B0815/25
B0816/21 B0816/32 B0818/15 B0818/15
B0818/16 B0818/24 B0818/24 B0820/17
B0820/17 B0821/27 B0822/30 B0833/26
B0843/12 B0844/02
bug-bear (2) A0080/28 B0901/23
Bugaboo (6) A0378/T A0380/31
A0381/09 A0381/17 A0382/15 A0388/15
bugaboo (1) B0969/06
Bugaboos (3) A0383/31
A0385/09 A0387/24
bugbears (2) A0165/26 C0550/23
build (8) A0142/18
A0548/14 A0710/30 B1275/32 B1303/10
C0123/09 C0125/40 C0570/16
building (51)
building-sites (1) B0863/37
buildings (13) A0121/05
A0243/13 A0244/V A0367/05 B0807/06
B1192/16 B1278/13 B1336/07 B1337/31
B1338/01 B1338/07 C0177/33 C0179/20
builds (1) C0153/02
built (18) A0120/21 A0136/01
A0142/27 A0560/08 A0587/27 B0807/16
B1072/29 B1159/31 B1192/30 B1219/20
B1335/28 B1337/27 C0063/09 C0173/12
C0525/41 C0533/10 C0560/21 C0573/29
bulk (24) A0099/27
A0143/07 A0143/29 A0601/05 A0601/13
B0741/05 B0741/21 B0742/06 B0742/11
B0743/22 B0979/23 B0980/04 C0097/17
C0097/18 C0097/32 C0165/03 C0191/13
C0387/24 C0396/11 C0423/01 C0423/05
C0535/36 C0535/37 C0535/40
bulkhead (5) C0090/23
C0094/05 C0096/15 C0099/32 C0100/11
bulkheads (3) C0068/12
C0068/16 C0089/31
bulky (3) A0593/04
B1155/24 B1383/03
bull (4) A0056/20
A0066/10 A0123/21 A0347/04
bull-dog (1) A0295/10
bull-roarings (1) A0244/18
bulldog (1) C0165/17
bullet (13) B0842/19
B0842/22 B0843/24 B0844/02 B1054/05
B1054/08 B1054/13 B1058/01 B1058/22
B1058/28 C0122/37 C0412/09 C0577/38
Bullet-head (11) B1369/01
B1369/02 B1369/24 B1370/21 B1370/30
B1370/34 B1371/21 B1371/25 B1374/33
B1375/05 B1375/18
Bullet-head, Touch-and-go (4) B1368/02
B1369/08 B1370/26 B1370/29
Bullet-head's (2) B1369/36 B1374/25
bullet-headed (1) B1296/01
bullet-proof (1) C0533/19
bullets (2) C0533/32 C0550/17
bullock (1) B1300/20
bullocks (1) C0156/23
bulls (5) A0175/05
A0181/26 A0347/30 B0945/21 B1017/26
bully (1) A0509/15
bulwark (2) C0089/26 C0124/36
bulwarks (9) B0930/21
C0102/32 C0103/16 C0108/19 C0109/16
C0113/41 C0115/14 C0123/12 C0205/30
Bulwer (1) B1051/19
bump (3) A0173/20
A0178/29 A0482/16
bumper (9) A0092/31
A0107/23 A0108/08 A0112/06 A0165/15
A0650/04 A0651/20 B1347/30 B1349/27
bumpers (1) A0092/12
bumpkin (2) A0500/13 B1358/32
bunch (2) A0368/11 B0943/35
bunches (1) A0371/09
bundle (16) A0055/08
A0064/13 A0093/13 A0262/19 A0263/14
A0386/32 A0387/01 A0387/08 A0387/20
A0387/V A0387/V A0556/12 B0734/20
B0872/21 B0872/23 B0872/31
bundles (2) B1155/23 B1158/15
bung-hole (1) C0416/10
Bunker-Hill (1) B1138/35
Buonaparte (3) B0887/V
B0914/V B0914/V
Buonaparte, Napoleon (1) B0887/16
buoy (1) B1076/33
buoyancy (1) A0080/05
buoyant (1) A0592/09
buoyantly (1) B0948/11
buoyed (4) A0078/31
C0063/26 C0134/23 C0398/39
buoys (2) B1076/31 B1077/33
buppy (1) B1104/02
burden (12) A0073/27
A0410/12 A0562/29 A0567/20 A0642/V
B0765/30 B0771/01 B0857/34 B1225/V
B1249/29 C0146/33 C0147/09
burdens (1) C0391/29
<u>bureau</u> (2) A0538/01 A0568/09

bureau (5) A0033/09
A0155/V A0556/01 B0749/12 C0523/24
Buren, Vanny (1) A0354/30
burgher (1) A0371/19
burghers (7) A0370/06
A0371/15 B1048/22 B1049/14 C0388/02
C0388/23 C0427/05
burglars (1) B1093/08
burgomaster (5) C0388/05
C0390/05 C0390/13 C0427/08 C0437/V
burgomaster's (1) C0427/03
burgomasters (1) C0427/17
Burial (1) B0954/T
burial (4) A0057/12
A0217/01 B0961/20 B0963/24
burial-ground (1) A0409/24
buried (52)
buries (1) A0033/12
burn (6) A0323/12 A0465/12
A0468/28 A0608/27 B0809/07 B0851/29
burned (12) A0136/25
A0157/10 A0218/07 A0225/03 A0226/13
A0229/03 A0230/11 A0608/17 A0615/26
A0696/14 B0858/20 B0969/05
burning (31) A0023/26
A0057/32 A0068/16 A0122/17 A0190/02
A0215/02 A0442/23 A0446/17 A0456/25
A0510/13 A0644/12 A0665/18 A0688/02
A0693/25 A0696/33 B0893/13 B0895/09
B1106/14 B1360/03 B1371/03 C0066/17
C0070/27 C0071/25 C0072/25 C0073/40
C0188/20 C0387/M C0396/28 C0425/35
C0524/01 C0564/35
burning-glasses (1) B1191/30
burnings (1) B1322/17
burnished (4) A0502/13
B0815/17 B0821/31 B1282/24
burns (1) C0394/02
burnt (4) A0230/V
B1360/06 C0073/42 C0572/12
burr (1) A0681/08
burst (38) A0047/15 A0057/32
A0068/16 A0151/V A0157/04 A0166/17
A0219/05 A0245/06 A0249/06 A0253/23
A0417/13 A0443/31 A0460/10 A0461/21
A0514/36 A0580/02 A0580/14 A0587/10
A0587/24 A0590/29 A0640/30 A0685/03
B0795/23 B1053/05 B1057/17 B1135/22
B1213/27 B1226/10 B1354/03 C0072/29
C0123/06 C0128/13 C0130/37 C0189/26
C0396/34 C0421/22 C0421/23 C0562/29
bursting (13) A0078/05
A0245/11 A0248/V B1243/01 B1262/23
C0099/19 C0110/27 C0115/40 C0122/13
C0135/04 C0166/25 C0198/15 C0419/24
bursts (2) A0614/21 B1283/04
burthen (9) A0047/11
A0141/15 A0507/02 A0583/21 A0642/19
B0735/01 B0764/27 B0766/25 B1225/03
burthened (1) B0863/01
burthening (1) B0807/13
burthens (1) B0827/13
Burton (1) B1114/20
Bury (1) B0871/03
bury (3) A0603/26
->B0965/21 C0182/08
burying (1) B0826/23
bush (3) B0735/14
C0167/12 C0197/01
bushel (4) A0465/24
A0466/09 C0098/25 C0098/25
bushes (13) B0734/37
B0735/12 B0758/12 B0762/08 B0762/10
B0866/13 C0186/23 C0186/40 C0188/26
C0197/24 C0542/17 C0543/30 C0570/21
bushy (1) C0173/31
busied (27) A0070/20
A0081/37 A0081/41 A0211/26 A0404/29
A0439/28 A0440/35 A0533/02 A0611/V
A0688/15 A0694/19 A0695/16 B0731/19
B0841/16 B0923/02 B0943/20 B0964/09
B1185/24 B1241/02 B1262/04 B1300/12
C0066/10 C0077/10 C0081/03 C0119/34
C0143/28 C0549/30
busies (1) A0683/24
busily (9) A0316/04
A0614/04 C0061/06 C0125/01 C0188/25
C0202/18 C0404/33 C0540/02 C0545/08
Business (2) A0481/T A0481/V
business (93)
business-like (1) A0508/02
buskin (1) A0536/16
Bussy (1) A0164/26
bust (2) A0379/19 A0379/19
bustle (11) A0058/13
A0069/01 A0086/22 A0347/28 A0515/19
B0913/16 B0924/06 C0070/06 C0084/04
C0085/14 C0097/12
bustled (1) B0808/15
busy (11) A0019/16
A0125/28 A0280/08 A0368/03 A0513/13
B0844/20 B1364/10 C0067/36 C0116/21
C0390/08 C0547/09
busy-body (1) B0747/24
busy-bodyism (1) B0748/15
busying (6) A0705/09 B0834/16
B1270/09 C0073/22 C0181/21 C0412/23
but (2616)
butcheries (1) A0548/11
butchery (9) A0544/V
A0557/02 A0557/V A0558/08 A0561/24
A0567/23 C0053/T C0086/20 C0200/36
butefulle (1) B0899/28
Butler (2) A0203/M B1114/20
buts (2) B0876/16 B0876/18
butt (7) A0058/18
A0388/16 A0388/17 B0927/25 B1057/32
C0196/33 C0201/08
butt-end (2) A0069/07 B1057/V
butter (8) A0341/V
A0341/V A0341/V A0341/V A0342/15
A0342/17 A0342/19 A0342/21
buttercup (1) A0640/02
butterflies (1) A0603/14
butterfly (3) A0314/14
A0336/05 B1037/06
button (2) C0411/09 C0413/33
button-headed (1) A0483/19
buttons (8) A0368/20
A0509/16 B0825/24 C0409/33 C0409/34

->C0409/38 C0410/01 C0410/03
buttresses (2) A0019/18 A0209/16
buy (1) B0911/28
buyers (1) A0513/16
buying (1) B0814/12
Buzi-Ben-Levi (5) A0043/01
A0043/10 A0043/16 A0046/08 A0047/08
buzz (4) A0293/15
A0674/27 B0894/05 B0894/26
buzzard (1) C0174/03
buzzing (1) B1155/31
bxg (1) B1374/16
bxw-wxw-wxw (1) B1374/18
bxwl (1) B1374/21
by (2853)
by-and-by (6) A0072/17 B1105/03
C0059/13 C0059/14 C0116/09 C0190/38
by-gone (2) A0141/23 A0439/23
by-path (3) B1003/17
B1048/35 B1049/08
by-paths (1) A0244/04
by-the-by (5) A0388/18
B1016/30 B1138/06 B1359/02 B1370/18
by-the-bye (1) A0340/11
by/gosh (1) B1046/08
bye (8) A0512/20
A0512/20 B0858/25 B0910/V B1105/V
B1305/13 B1316/13 C0395/12
bye-street (2) A0513/10 A0541/25
bypaths (1) B0863/04
Byron (2) A0708/08 B1121/T
Byron's (1) A0385/22
bystanders (2) A0613/35 A0613/37
C (1) B1311/02

c (1) C0194/23
c.o.r.d.a. (1) A0271/29
C-- (3) B0888/V B0909/20 B0922/11
C'est (1) A0037/20
c'est (2) A0034/08 A0036/05
c'etait (1) A0109/31
c's (1) A0267/07
Cab (1) B1091/24
cab (14) A0493/05 B1091/28
B1091/31 B1092/07 B1092/09 B1092/15
B1092/16 B1092/36 B1093/15 B1093/21
B1093/22 B1093/28 B1093/32 B1093/36
cab-hire (1) B1092/25
cab-introduction (1) A0494/04
caba (1) B1091/30
cabalistic-looking (1) A0351/30
cabalistical (2) A0242/02 B1374/22
cabbage (6) A0367/18 A0367/27
A0367/28 A0368/11 A0496/03 C0150/29
cabbaged (1) B1373/03
cabbages (6) A0367/04 A0367/25
A0368/25 A0369/17 A0373/23 C0155/36
cabin (67)
cabinet (7) A0159/11
B0813/26 B0871/32 B0872/11 B0978/16
B0979/24 B1347/23
cabinets (2) A0500/27 B0979/25
cabins (2) A0137/26 B0928/27
cable (3) A0137/29
C0187/10 C0188/11

cables (1) C0147/20
cabman (5) A0494/05
B1092/35 B1093/01 B1093/08 B1094/02
cabmen (2) B1092/18 B1092/26
caboose (2) B0930/21 C0114/01
cache (4) C0564/22
C0571/03 C0575/41 C0576/02
caches (1) C0575/33
cachinnated (1) A0387/V
cachinnatio (1) A0091/13
cachinnatory (1) A0241/01
cadaverous (2) A0106/V B1239/23
cadaverous-looking (1) B1011/16
cadaverously (3) A0104/12
A0299/27 A0412/08
cadaverousness (1) A0401/30
cadence (1) A0683/06
cadences (3) A0191/14
A0613/31 B0905/20
Cadet (1) A0033/11
Caesar (2) A0283/30 B1096/25
Cafe (1) A0096/03
Cafe (4) A0099/11
A0100/25 A0101/01 A0101/12
Cafes (1) A0101/V
cage (1) A0033/04
cage-wires (1) B1349/19
caged (1) C0438/V
cages (2) B1038/19 B1337/13
Cain (2) A0093/04 A0112/16
Cairo (1) B1160/24
cajole (1) B1059/06
cajoled (1) B1302/09
cake (2) A0341/V A0342/18
cakes (6) B0767/16 B0767/25
B0767/25 C0158/33 C0162/33 C0163/37
calamities (5) A0073/27
B0955/13 B1294/08 C0098/32 C0133/06
calamitous (1) A0365/09
calamity (16) A0028/V
A0053/18 A0062/26 A0065/04 A0065/04
A0072/20 A0074/06 A0075/08 A0213/22
A0457/09 A0457/13 A0459/07 B0955/14
C0053/T C0072/11 C0182/37
calamo (1) A0269/36
Calbrinachus (1) A0056/09
calc (1) A0182/07
calcedony (1) A0182/10
calculate (4) A0381/30
A0528/15 B0752/08 B1191/22
calculated (22) A0019/V A0055/20
A0065/04 A0093/37 A0099/24 A0102/18
A0458/01 A0478/33 B1240/33 C0095/24
C0115/28 C0133/24 C0144/02 C0153/28
C0176/29 C0201/27 C0394/39 C0400/32
C0404/37 C0418/04 C0430/17 C0439/V
Calculating (1) B1166/35
calculating (3) A0139/12
A0527/V A0529/14
calculation (5) B0752/18
B0857/13 B1214/02 B1234/33 C0546/15
calculations (5) A0694/29
B1166/22 C0084/29 C0400/38 C0423/05
Calculus (4) B0724/02
B0724/03 B0773/13 B0986/23

Calcutta (1) B0949/02
calcutta (1) B0955/08
calf (4) A0047/22
A0368/V A0379/32 B1010/27
calico (1) C0148/11
calicoes (1) C0534/23
California (4) B1361/25
B1364/13 B1364/16 B1364/31
Caligula (4) A0021/14
A0093/05 A0112/17 A0112/27
caliph (3) B1159/V
B1159/V B1166/19
caliphs (3) B1156/10
B1160/24 B1164/22
call (102)
called (221)
calling (28) A0088/30
A0103/09 A0122/02 A0161/13 A0247/17
A0339/01 A0353/31 A0485/34 A0485/34
A0545/06 A0599/02 B0740/03 B0755/32
B0756/23 B0793/14 B0908/15 B0910/12
B0975/12 B1056/32 B1126/14 B1133/14
B1312/07 C0152/03 C0162/01 C0182/12
C0529/18 C0558/09 C0564/30
calls (15) A0226/34
A0320/06 A0336/03 A0337/05 A0337/09
A0338/30 A0338/31 A0710/06 B0875/05
B0966/33 B1222/08 B1241/31 B1275/09
C0178/09 C0526/31
calm (31) A0026/33
A0029/21 A0053/33 A0063/04 A0087/37
A0136/24 A0214/17 A0315/08 A0507/16
A0581/31 A0584/09 A0663/27 A0691/11
B0850/04 B0871/03 B0871/03 B0891/07
B1081/09 B1081/21 B1391/19 C0097/41
C0118/28 C0126/29 C0142/13 C0142/36
C0164/31 C0192/38 C0200/27 C0397/20
C0421/33 C0432/20
calmer (1) B1351/25
calmest (3) A0581/22
A0586/34 B0723/01
calmly (13) A0025/17
A0088/23 A0094/07 A0103/03 A0114/03
A0235/29 A0639/04 B0789/06 B0858/16
B1234/22 B1247/35 C0124/04 C0186/01
calmness (4) A0693/05
B1249/25 B1249/30 C0139/28
calms (1) C0148/21
caloric (4) B0832/29
B1034/11 B1168/30 B1322/27
calumet (1) C0553/22
calumny (1) A0086/16
Calvin, John (1) A0621/17
cambric (7) A0246/29
A0371/19 A0371/20 B1381/14 C0393/18
C0394/11 C0395/01
Cambyses (1) A0120/01
came (324)
camel (2) B1166/09 C0138/07
Cameleopard (1) A0128/04
cameleopard (5) A0125/29
A0126/04 A0126/10 A0127/14 A0127/20
Cameleopards (2) A0127/03 A0128/02
camelopard (1) A0125/V
cameos (1) B1191/36
camp (13) A0043/06
A0045/11 B0945/31 B1258/14 C0532/18
C0534/13 C0538/14 C0542/39 C0543/07
C0543/39 C0544/05 C0574/21 C0580/03
camp-meeting (1) B0874/24
Campaign (1) A0378/T
campaign (2) A0381/09 A0382/15
Campanella (2) A0409/04 B0985/03
Campanile (1) A0151/22
camphor (1) B1181/01
Campi/Phlegraei (1) C0422/34
Can (1) A0342/12
can (357)
can't (25) A0284/32
A0337/30 A0341/13 A0341/13 A0345/17
A0378/11 A0385/13 A0388/20 A0486/15
A0487/13 A0489/V A0490/27 A0562/30
A0656/06 B0812/13 B0873/30 B1019/18
B1103/13 B1103/14 B1103/14 B1169/23
B1208/27 B1372/29 C0070/17 C0541/17
Canada (1) B1164/40
Canadas (1) C0525/12
Canadian (15) C0526/03
C0529/16 C0530/08 C0539/29 C0548/33
C0553/14 C0555/16 C0556/05 C0561/22
C0561/40 C0562/03 C0562/18 C0562/24
C0563/11 C0578/28
Canadians (17) C0530/36
C0531/05 C0531/15 C0534/30 C0536/03
C0544/06 C0548/26 C0548/35 C0549/03
C0549/21 C0550/20 C0555/13 C0555/37
C0557/38 C0560/10 C0564/04 C0570/36
canaille (1) B1291/19
canal (5) A0151/19
A0151/25 A0152/10 A0154/09 A0191/11
canaries (1) B1337/16
cancel (1) B0875/10
candelabra (2) A0321/29 B1009/02
candelabrum (5) A0503/03
A0663/05 A0663/14 A0664/25 A0672/08
candid (3) A0271/36
A0507/13 B1140/15
candidly (2) A0355/33 B1194/34
candle (14) A0136/25 A0442/30
A0672/10 B0810/31 B0829/12 B0871/20
B0940/22 B1106/11 B1106/25 B1224/12
B1239/28 C0094/02 C0094/12 C0095/05
candles (7) A0663/18
A0664/01 A0682/03 A0682/14 A0684/V
B1009/02 C0077/30
candlestand (1) B1224/16
candor (5) A0204/28
A0532/04 B0903/07 B0906/11 B0907/23
candy (1) B1096/04
cane (6) A0511/28 B0858/30
B1071/30 B1142/24 B1185/35 B1340/10
canine (1) C0101/06
caning (1) B1142/26
canis (1) B0870/21
canister (2) C0180/18 C0394/22
canisters (3) C0180/19
C0394/24 C0394/26
cannibal (1) C0133/10
cannibals (1) B1305/02
Canning, Launcelot (1) A0413/09

cannister (1) C0550/17
cannister-shot (1) C0557/05
cannon (15) A0140/08
B0732/10 B0740/11 B0742/30 B0743/06
B0743/15 C0189/30 C0394/24 C0533/33
C0533/35 C0534/05 C0550/16 C0553/38
C0555/17 C0556/04
cannot (155)
canoe (31) A0604/19
B1280/34 B1281/08 B1281/18 B1282/33
B1333/34 C0165/35 C0168/24 C0170/17
C0180/20 C0187/15 C0187/25 C0187/38
C0200/28 C0200/34 C0200/37 C0201/05
C0201/14 C0201/20 C0201/37 C0202/17
C0203/06 C0204/15 C0204/39 C0205/01
C0205/31 C0530/31 C0533/13 C0533/39
C0540/04 C0541/07
canoe-load (1) C0176/37
canoe's (1) B1282/09
canoes (25) C0168/02
C0168/11 C0168/21 C0168/28 C0168/33
C0169/03 C0171/03 C0172/21 C0174/21
C0175/23 C0176/16 C0176/28 C0186/19
C0186/29 C0186/39 C0187/11 C0187/22
C0188/09 C0189/31 C0200/19 C0201/23
C0201/33 C0204/03 C0526/08 C0530/23
canonicals (1) A0294/V
canopy (3) A0101/02
A0322/03 A0322/12
canos (1) A0043/M
Canova (1) A0160/20
canst (2) A0045/18 B0964/19
Cant (1) B1295/11
cant (7) A0338/07
A0338/07 A0568/23 A0601/04 A0610/07
B0976/24 B1132/24
canteen (1) B1102/31
canteens (1) B1102/30
Canton (1) C0179/13
canvas (2) A0405/V A0663/V
canvas-backs (1) B1209/02
canvass (11) A0142/22
A0143/22 A0145/32 A0405/25 A0664/01
A0665/11 A0665/27 A0665/29 A0707/26
B1272/26 C0389/36
canvass-back (2) C0174/02 C0176/27
caoutchouc (6) A0513/21 B1073/04
B1293/05 B1293/07 C0393/19 C0394/12
cap (14) A0059/27 A0078/34
A0086/28 A0100/05 A0368/04 B0889/29
B0910/23 B0913/19 B1008/08 B1102/31
B1257/19 B1258/33 C0123/38 C0389/27
capabilities (5) A0027/06
A0097/20 A0710/13 B1275/16 B1329/32
capability (1) A0216/07
capable (19) A0027/22
A0295/09 A0318/02 A0436/32 A0478/21
A0706/27 A0707/01 B0835/18 B1071/27
B1160/43 B1271/29 B1272/02 C0128/29
C0141/40 C0163/07 C0182/20 C0185/21
C0423/24 C0532/31
capacious (3) A0321/13
A0429/12 A0443/12
capacities (5) A0098/19
A0458/19 B1015/V B1036/03 C0390/33
capacity (21) A0097/14
A0123/18 A0126/08 A0128/03 A0398/08
A0527/V A0529/20 A0545/28 A0600/03
A0710/34 B0879/03 B0988/17 B0989/21
B1072/20 B1139/10 B1214/12 B1275/34
B1317/25 C0425/28 C0530/24 C0535/14
caparisoned (1) B0945/16
Cape (10) A0655/23 B1021/11
C0148/20 C0148/24 C0149/11 C0150/12
C0151/28 C0156/06 C0156/17 C0525/25
Cape/Clear (1) B1077/21
Cape/Francois (1) C0150/35
Cape/Hatteras (1) B0930/07
Cape/Horn (1) A0655/22
Cape/Madeira (1) C0137/21
Cape/St./Roque (1) C0148/27
Cape/Verd (3) C0088/39
C0093/13 C0148/14
Cape/Verds (4) C0099/39
C0101/23 C0103/12 C0148/16
capered (2) A0348/14 A0371/12
capers (1) A0345/13
capital (35) A0267/34
A0338/08 A0339/25 A0344/04 A0383/09
A0387/20 A0388/10 A0388/15 A0483/16
A0483/17 A0483/25 A0489/09 A0490/03
A0583/34 A0650/28 B0874/23 B0910/V
B0957/26 B1012/25 B1019/29 B1020/22
B1021/33 B1058/29 B1114/23 B1153/15
B1155/V B1178/09 B1183/02 B1184/V
B1311/30 B1346/12 B1349/35 B1350/13
C0531/28 C0535/03
capital-O (1) B1372/26
capital/S (2) B1372/18 B1372/19
capitally (1) A0487/23
capitals (8) A0267/28
A0272/32 A0277/13 A0285/03 A0622/15
B0925/24 B1068/09 B1131/30
Capitol (1) B1192/09
Capitols (1) B1192/30
capon (1) A0345/13
caprice (4) A0248/21
A0311/08 B0825/19 C0100/32
caprices (5) A0427/24
A0484/04 A0499/13 B1018/02 B1370/35
capricious (2) A0514/27 C0093/05
Capricornutc (2) A0177/04 A0177/09
Capricornutti (1) A0182/36
caprioles (1) A0652/24
caps (3) B1078/14
B1129/29 B1345/19
capsising (1) C0559/29
capsize (1) B0931/33
capsized (3) C0101/35
C0146/38 C0533/39
capsizing (2) C0105/40 C0114/39
Capt (7) A0655/03
A0655/10 A0655/V A0656/V A0656/V
A0656/V A0656/V
Captain (95)
captain (34) A0071/29 A0136/28
A0136/34 A0137/25 A0144/07 A0384/27
A0384/29 A0384/31 B0873/10 B0873/27
B0874/11 B0874/14 B0923/26 B0924/03
B0928/12 B0931/21 B0931/36 B0932/09

->B1292/25 C0057/14 C0061/24 C0061/37
C0062/37 C0067/37 C0088/10 C0099/05
C0146/36 C0147/22 C0153/32 C0156/34
C0159/26 C0170/31 C0190/30 C0527/25
captain's (3) A0142/01
B1300/31 C0110/08
Captains (4) C0160/04
C0548/07 C0551/22 C0566/39
captains (1) C0527/16
captious (1) B1380/32
captivated (1) B0924/25
captivating (1) B1141/22
captive (6) A0564/24 C0200/24
C0201/25 C0202/29 C0203/31 C0208/18
captives (2) B1346/30 C0086/34
captivity (2) C0065/19 C0185/29
capture (5) A0561/01
B1351/13 C0053/T C0141/16 C0186/01
captured (4) A0564/21
C0140/26 C0191/15 C0562/34
capturing (1) C0187/03
Capuletti (1) B0905/15
caput (1) B0810/12
car (1) B0987/01
car (64)
carabine (1) C0555/40
Caraccas (1) B1161/34
caracols (1) B0824/14
Carathis (1) B0969/13
Caravaggio (2) A0175/22 A0181/20
carboy (3) C0137/20
C0142/02 C0146/07
carboys (2) A0253/28 C0535/04
carbuncle-nosed (1) B1185/02
carcase (1) A0056/18
carcases (2) A0057/01 C0567/08
carcass (15) A0021/V
A0070/22 A0111/15 A0128/10 A0244/05
A0415/20 B0853/27 B1058/23 B1102/27
C0165/11 C0167/13 C0190/28 C0190/37
C0208/17 C0396/02
carcasses (4) A0021/30
A0066/28 B1162/20 C0568/03
card (7) A0037/19
A0176/20 A0182/23 A0388/V A0465/29
A0530/19 B1135/05
card-rack (3) B0990/35
B0992/15 B0993/16
card-table (1) A0384/15
carded (1) B0922/16
cards (15) A0037/15
A0177/V A0183/08 A0438/28 A0441/12
A0441/22 A0443/21 A0443/25 A0464/01
A0530/10 A0530/25 A0623/11 A0671/V
B0991/02 B1006/14
care (69)
cared (4) B1328/11
C0396/01 C0553/35 C0564/08
career (13) A0020/V
A0027/V A0029/09 A0296/V A0354/02
A0515/12 A0566/09 A0703/11 B0866/10
B1126/07 B1144/30 B1268/10 C0067/29
careered (2) A0589/21 A0604/11
careering (2) A0412/25 C0559/26
careful (17) A0124/03
->A0284/12 A0296/V A0343/24 A0441/12
A0474/04 A0552/25 A0685/22 B0821/26
B0956/31 B1009/31 B1090/37 B1383/30
C0097/07 C0140/04 C0192/10 C0547/03
carefully (76)
careless (7) A0213/16
A0272/30 A0440/34 B0934/06 B1045/07
C0097/09 C0108/17
carelessly (5) A0210/26
A0578/07 B0959/13 B0991/08 B1363/06
carelessness (3) A0080/39
A0530/19 C0089/05
Careme (1) A0653/20
cares (6) A0712/06 B0870/19
B1277/11 B1293/19 C0126/22 C0399/10
caressed (1) B0832/09
caresses (9) A0152/22
A0154/19 B0809/22 B0854/19 B0855/11
B0957/33 C0073/11 C0073/25 C0076/16
caressing (1) B0850/13
Carey (1) A0277/33
Carey, Matthew (1) A0277/29
cargo (22) A0139/20 A0251/20
A0252/01 B0930/36 C0097/13 C0097/15
C0097/19 C0097/30 C0097/37 C0098/03
C0098/10 C0098/15 C0098/16 C0098/33
C0098/38 C0098/38 C0099/04 C0099/08
C0116/11 C0116/14 C0146/34 C0148/07
cargoes (3) C0098/21
C0098/40 C0179/17
caricature (1) A0435/06
Carlyle (3) A0035/V
A0625/04 A0627/19
Carlyle-ism (1) B1114/29
Carnac (3) B1192/21
B1192/33 B1193/13
carnal-minded (1) B1044/06
Carne (1) A0213/06
Carnival (1) A0446/20
carnival (3) B1257/16
B1257/26 B1340/03
carnivorous (3) C0125/18
C0151/31 C0174/04
carols (1) C0544/08
carousal (1) A0438/22
carousals (2) A0296/14 B0906/17
carouse (1) C0086/30
carousing (2) B0760/04 C0109/28
Carpaccio (2) A0175/22 A0181/19
carped (1) A0158/05
carpenter (1) B0930/32
carpenters (1) A0554/11
carpet (23) A0322/10
A0325/08 A0325/19 A0466/26 A0497/29
A0497/31 A0498/09 A0501/24 A0501/V
A0640/31 A0643/07 A0672/04 A0674/09
A0676/25 B0981/12 B1008/24 B1339/28
C0068/05 C0068/23 C0068/28 C0068/34
C0175/04 C0535/10
carpet-bags (1) B1073/26
carpeted (2) A0639/33 C0543/13
carpets (1) B0980/17
carpets (6) A0165/24 A0320/24
A0497/27 A0498/01 A0498/15 B0981/11
carriage (15) A0380/11

->A0508/26 B0863/07 B0897/20 B0898/12
B0908/22 B0909/15 B0909/23 B1090/17
B1090/23 B1092/09 C0151/17 C0174/26
C0526/28 C0533/33
carriage-road (1) B0864/18
carriage-track (1) B1329/08
carriages (1) C0118/18
carried (54)
carrier-pigeons (1) C0430/47
carriers (1) B1090/16
carries (5) A0369/01
A0493/08 B0870/28 B1072/13 C0448/V
carronades (1) C0147/18
carrot (1) C0534/24
carrots (1) C0558/17
carry (29) A0145/31
A0342/09 A0488/V A0494/08 B0724/21
B0764/27 B0765/17 B0765/24 B0818/19
B0911/21 B0961/29 B0965/10 B1072/22
B1155/24 B1292/22 B1321/23 C0056/23
C0102/15 C0110/25 C0138/08 C0151/17
C0182/33 C0404/27 C0430/48 C0532/39
C0533/02 C0533/40 C0546/41 C0557/15
carrying (15) A0055/26
A0295/04 A0534/32 B0816/29 B1053/23
B1089/13 B1089/14 B1293/14 B1325/06
C0104/38 C0105/39 C0152/26 C0162/36
C0190/24 C0396/21
cars (1) B1299/02
Carson, John (1) C0179/30
cart (7) A0058/05
A0058/09 A0058/18 A0068/27 A0069/03
B0924/31 B1094/03
carted (1) B1363/28
cartel (2) A0302/02 B1140/14
cartes (1) A0037/10
Carthaginian (1) A0430/34
cartilaginous (1) B1235/24
carts (1) A0347/30
carve (1) A0367/18
carved (9) A0036/16
A0087/20 A0373/25 A0502/12 B0945/11
B1193/21 B1282/25 C0534/02 C0573/19
Carver (1) C0525/13
Carver, Jonathan (1) C0525/04
Carver's (1) C0525/32
carvers (1) A0367/17
carving (2) A0367/15 C0165/35
carving-knife (2) C0082/12 C0083/14
carvings (4) A0140/07
A0157/22 A0320/23 A0400/28
Caryatides (2) B1351/34 B1353/09
cascade (2) B1335/06 C0171/34
Case (2) B1233/T B1380/09
case (172)
case-knives (1) C0129/29
casement (6) A0413/05 A0552/20
A0553/03 A0554/07 A0567/20 B0992/14
casements (3) A0412/16
A0414/10 A0671/33
Caserta (1) B1161/28
cases (37) A0136/04
A0300/06 A0339/24 A0478/09 A0487/32
A0528/30 B0725/12 B0737/01 B0742/01
B0757/08 B0773/07 B0817/26 B0828/17
->B0835/32 B0840/19 B0956/02 B0986/02
B1039/20 B1051/24 B1057/01 B1160/39
B1213/22 B1237/21 B1315/26 B1345/34
B1373/32 B1382/09 B1385/24 C0058/03
C0111/30 C0111/37 C0122/24 C0158/07
C0171/38 C0197/35 C0398/29 C0438/V
cash (2) A0094/12 B0870/04
Cask (1) B1256/T
cask (9) A0590/01
A0593/14 A0593/23 A0594/01 C0099/33
C0394/21 C0394/27 C0394/29 C0395/24
casks (5) B1260/05
C0091/34 C0393/29 C0394/17 C0396/17
Casneau (2) C0146/35 C0146/41
cassimere (1) A0439/V
Cassini (1) C0423/32
cassock (1) B0916/17
cast (24) A0068/18
A0122/16 A0142/06 A0142/21 A0191/05
A0247/32 A0310/06 A0442/24 A0487/28
A0502/04 A0610/08 A0690/10 A0706/09
B0771/21 B0771/24 B0873/30 B0874/11
B0874/14 B0983/15 B1030/01 B1160/31
C0199/16 C0432/46 C0533/10
cast-off (1) A0508/29
castas (1) A0621/03
caste (1) C0569/17
castellated (3) A0321/12
A0670/14 B0862/12
casting (11) A0102/21
A0139/34 A0343/12 A0511/06 A0536/10
B0744/31 B0856/35 B0873/19 C0058/36
C0131/38 C0430/07
Castle (3) A0019/17
A0021/15 A0023/27
castle (6) A0022/V A0024/04
A0415/21 A0568/16 B0841/06 B0841/11
castles (3) A0020/20
B1313/22 C0395/11
castor (1) B1141/19
casual (17) A0144/09
A0267/04 A0270/20 A0283/23 A0530/18
A0651/31 A0689/28 B0810/27 B0840/05
B0974/06 B1002/07 B1225/16 B1360/28
C0087/26 C0151/21 C0439/V C0524/19
casually (2) A0432/27 B0939/02
Cat (3) A0477/T B0849/T B1097/06
cat (53)
cat-aplasm (1) B1095/13
cat-au-rabbit (1) B1011/14
cat-egory (1) B1095/13
cat-erect (1) B1095/10
cat-heads (1) A0491/04
cat-like (1) B1225/V
cat-nip (1) B1096/02
cat-peltries (1) B1293/25
cat-worshippers (1) B1095/03
Cat-Act (1) A0491/03
Cat-Growing (1) A0490/31
cat's (2) B0850/35 C0167/19
catacombs (9) A0191/09
B1186/20 B1188/20 B1258/32 B1260/06
B1261/06 B1261/15 B1262/28 B1263/23
Catalani (3) A0057/26
A0068/09 B0993/09

catalepsy (5) B0962/05
B0962/22 B0965/12 B0966/25 B1187/05
cataleptic (2) B0964/02 B0969/09
cataleptical (2) A0404/19 A0410/23
catalogue (2) A0440/17 B0955/15
catalpa (1) B1332/10
catalpas (1) B1337/08
catamites (1) A0124/V
catapult (2) A0128/06 B1182/21
cataract (11) A0145/19
A0195/22 A0580/34 A0582/36 B1095/10
B1280/25 C0205/24 C0205/32 C0206/04
C0417/04 C0444/V
cataracts (3) A0087/33
A0158/03 A0581/25
catastrophe (5) A0457/07
B1021/03 C0059/36 C0065/03 C0189/35
catch (8) A0374/09
B1225/06 B1225/V C0135/39 C0145/15
C0406/16 C0547/16 C0578/12
catch-word (1) A0366/18
catching (10) A0072/22 A0623/12
A0685/06 B0911/29 B1095/06 C0139/19
C0141/36 C0146/08 C0191/16 C0199/08
catechism (2) B0879/21 B1032/12
category (5) B0743/21
B1296/05 B1296/05 B1312/06 B1312/06
caterpillar (2) B1163/15 B1207/35
caterpillars (2) B1159/32 C0178/17
caterwauled (1) A0347/31
caterwauling (1) A0374/03
cathead (1) C0124/40
cathedral (4) A0087/10
A0349/22 A0349/27 A0353/29
catholic (2) A0227/30 A0232/V
Catholique (2) A0104/11 A0106/02
Cato (1) B1275/32
Catone (1) A0043/M
Cats (1) B1095/T
cats (23) A0057/24
A0068/07 A0294/V A0347/31 A0373/30
A0479/11 A0479/12 A0490/34 B0850/31
B1095/01 B1095/06 B1096/06 B1096/09
B1096/23 B1096/25 B1096/28 B1096/37
B1096/37 B1097/02 B1097/03 B1158/05
B1168/11 C0413/28
Catskills (1) B0862/09
cattymount (1) B0968/05
Catullus (4) A0086/14
A0091/19 A0099/01 A0110/22
caught (48) A0023/25
A0027/16 A0035/24 A0072/23 A0073/05
A0078/33 A0092/08 A0093/14 A0111/19
A0112/25 A0177/01 A0249/32 A0299/19
A0353/24 A0415/12 A0446/31 A0512/04
A0552/30 A0560/26 A0568/06 A0580/02
A0582/04 A0623/11 A0630/28 A0697/10
B0796/14 B0825/12 B0825/32 B0832/12
B0895/02 B0898/07 B1081/31 B1145/29
B1181/19 B1299/01 B1362/15 C0120/39
C0141/39 C0145/16 C0183/02 C0189/27
C0198/17 C0547/12 C0547/14 C0547/24
C0553/08 C0566/33 C0570/32
cauliflowers (3) A0175/19
A0181/08 B1007/24
Caus, Solomon de (1) B1194/22
causality (3) A0298/V
A0527/V B1220/04
cause (72)
caused (33) A0028/01
A0214/23 A0410/10 A0440/01 A0547/11
A0627/06 A0663/03 A0689/30 B0753/06
B0794/24 B0830/09 B0854/07 B0857/08
B0890/32 B0950/10 B0956/33 B0964/25
B1008/12 B1109/13 B1155/34 B1158/07
B1261/02 B1292/25 B1329/35 B1352/05
C0095/41 C0139/15 C0150/24 C0167/05
C0405/23 C0416/12 C0562/23 C0578/37
causeless (3) A0411/26
B0794/16 C0569/12
causes (14) A0019/13 A0104/24
A0225/16 A0324/11 A0338/02 A0611/28
B0742/28 B0747/32 B0850/07 B0956/01
B0962/07 B1215/03 C0055/25 C0106/12
causeway (4) A0400/21
A0417/05 A0535/24 B1331/32
causeways (1) B1193/08
causing (8) A0071/18
A0248/20 A0673/29 B0756/15 B1134/23
B1278/27 B1321/28 C0128/39
caustic (1) B1370/07
caution (27) A0511/21
A0513/19 A0686/23 B0740/02 B0748/20
B0770/23 B0789/19 B0830/10 B0832/12
B0976/04 B1004/30 B1259/20 C0067/34
C0077/20 C0079/24 C0100/30 C0105/14
C0119/16 C0140/38 C0184/25 C0192/05
C0393/13 C0398/02 C0531/12 C0549/29
C0549/42 C0577/15
cautioned (1) B0928/13
cautious (13) A0341/V
A0342/19 A0350/31 A0365/13 A0695/01
B0793/19 B0877/35 B0929/10 B1004/20
B1258/30 C0098/03 C0137/12 C0548/22
cautiously (17) A0366/08
A0511/32 A0685/05 A0685/10 B0793/07
B0793/08 B0793/08 B0818/25 B0842/08
B0866/12 B0895/06 B0929/01 B0990/27
B1304/29 C0079/40 C0199/10 C0575/39
cavalier (2) B1019/05 B1102/31
cavalierly (1) A0100/17
cavalry (1) C0118/14
cave (5) B1160/08
C0537/33 C0537/34 C0537/39 C0538/05
caved (2) C0182/22 C0567/33
cavern (9) B0969/14
B1162/31 B1240/19 B1259/03 C0199/12
C0537/37 C0537/41 C0538/35 C0564/24
cavernous (1) B0967/07
caverns (6) B0943/27 B1162/16
B1162/22 C0173/15 C0173/18 C0195/25
caves (2) A0195/M B1163/22
cavilled (1) B1314/21
caving (1) C0183/25
cavities (5) B0741/33
B0742/09 B0742/28 B0742/35 C0194/02
cavity (6) A0198/30 B0979/32
B0979/34 B1054/04 B1304/01 C0194/03
Cayley, George (2) B1069/33
B1070/15

Cayley's, George (2) B1070/30
B1070/34
ce (9) A0033/19
A0033/20 A0431/08 A0506/M A0568/24
A0568/25 A0654/05 B1114/02 C0430/38
cease (6) A0121/12 A0327/08
A0351/03 B0747/33 C0076/21 C0395/25
ceased (46) A0026/10 A0059/33
A0089/01 A0190/21 A0198/03 A0198/06
A0212/04 A0328/14 A0329/07 A0440/03
A0508/10 A0531/20 A0532/23 A0537/15
A0537/19 A0540/04 A0590/13 A0594/V
A0612/35 A0615/02 A0615/29 A0644/11
A0672/30 A0673/02 A0674/15 A0695/07
B0725/10 B0795/31 B0896/19 B0948/06
B0956/20 B0965/02 B1013/12 B1090/35
B1105/32 B1110/06 B1155/11 B1237/15
B1262/17 B1352/04 C0060/41 C0132/21
C0204/26 C0406/15 C0414/10 C0428/36
ceaseless (1) A0061/03
ceases (3) B0747/34
B1081/19 C0432/25
ceasing (4) A0140/22
A0443/15 A0515/26 C0546/06
Cecil (1) B1051/16
cedar (2) B1180/05 C0559/17
Cedar/Lake (1) C0526/39
ceder (1) A0611/04
ceiling (23) A0501/19 A0035/06 A0087/18
A0087/19 A0094/22 A0101/V A0114/17
A0157/V A0248/14 A0248/19 A0321/20
A0344/03 A0351/22 A0401/13 A0430/02
A0503/10 A0672/03 A0689/23 A0695/08
B1354/23 C0068/06 C0069/06 C0429/37
ceilings (2) A0400/28 A0551/12
celebrated (23) A0059/02
A0160/07 A0337/11 A0338/15 B0864/03
B0890/19 B0892/10 B0909/30 B0914/15
B0915/09 B1016/32 B1017/05 B1017/12
B1136/13 B1136/34 B1137/31 B1138/28
B1144/04 B1245/04 C0176/21 C0178/09
C0428/02 C0448/V
celebration (2) A0128/12 A0128/29
celebrity (4) A0101/V
A0342/04 B1278/29 B1310/25
celery (3) C0138/12
C0176/37 C0177/01
celeste (1) A0087/05
cell (10) A0478/31 A0478/33
A0478/37 A0690/02 A0695/19 A0696/08
A0696/20 B0855/20 B1006/27 B1224/01
cellar (7) B0856/18
B0856/34 B0857/02 B0857/04 B0857/09
B0858/15 B0858/17
cellars (4) A0243/04
A0248/V B0981/16 B1019/21
cells (5) A0684/29
B1018/25 B1019/04 B1021/25 B1164/23
cellular (3) B0730/05
B0742/08 B0742/34
Cemeteries (1) A0034/23
cemeteries (1) B0958/28
cemetery (3) A0081/01
B0958/29 B0959/17
censer (6) A0165/18 A0321/25
->A0325/05 A0325/09 A0326/10 A0326/12
censers (7) A0036/05
A0157/26 A0165/14 A0166/03 A0642/30
A0643/25 B0828/08
cent (10) A0485/26 A0486/16
A0705/18 B0872/02 B0874/28 B1094/03
B1138/31 B1270/17 B1364/33 B1364/34
centigrade (1) C0396/24
centime (1) B0982/V
central (8) A0138/26
A0321/23 A0489/09 B1301/12 B1301/13
B1301/18 B1301/21 C0395/24
centre (50) A0101/25 A0137/06
A0212/27 A0245/13 A0253/17 A0367/02
A0369/06 A0582/18 A0583/03 A0601/21
A0640/09 A0689/09 A0696/08 A0696/36
B0822/13 B0842/10 B0962/14 B1071/05
B1120/04 B1160/41 B1239/25 B1301/02
B1301/03 B1301/24 B1301/26 B1301/36
B1302/15 B1303/31 B1321/05 B1321/24
B1321/28 B1322/28 B1351/19 B1351/30
B1352/26 B1353/10 C0139/23 C0152/01
C0152/35 C0154/34 C0157/04 C0174/35
C0394/20 C0400/07 C0403/06 C0418/30
C0418/36 C0430/24 C0438/V C0543/33
centres (4) A0676/10
B1030/31 B1164/31 C0400/02
centrifugal (4) B1322/01
B1322/24 B1382/05 C0401/33
centripetal (1) C0401/33
cents (1) A0018/12
cents (13) A0484/32
A0485/08 A0487/27 A0487/29 A0487/30
A0487/32 A0494/03 B1092/15 B1092/24
B1136/18 B1136/39 B1137/36 B1138/33
centuries (16) A0019/06
A0144/31 A0150/V A0189/02 A0399/13
A0408/22 A0609/14 A0640/26 B0986/31
B1092/06 B1188/34 B1190/13 B1215/30
B1299/20 B1311/32 B1317/06
centurion (1) A0046/06
century (18) A0059/13 A0062/02
A0101/24 A0103/24 A0121/17 A0612/14
A0612/17 A0704/23 B0899/17 B1079/10
B1079/12 B1164/28 B1195/14 B1263/26
B1269/22 B1300/35 B1318/05 B1321/01
Cerberus (2) A0091/18 A0110/20
cerebral (1) B1165/35
cerement (1) A0217/V
cerements (2) A0330/13 A0676/30
ceremonial (1) B0733/19
ceremonies (1) B1304/13
ceremony (8) A0235/12
A0253/09 B0909/15 B0968/06 B1010/19
B1056/33 B1154/04 B1185/24
certain (181)
certainly (69)
certainty (20) A0022/18
A0027/19 A0105/V A0242/31 A0302/16
A0429/24 A0459/27 A0530/14 B0752/V
B0753/38 B0834/24 B1296/11 B1312/15
B1312/16 B1313/18 C0065/02 C0080/35
C0092/07 C0094/25 C0537/21
certum (1) A0213/08
Cervantes, Miguel de (1) A0344/26

Cervantes, Miguel De (1) A0354/29
ces (2) A0019/04 A0036/06
cessation (5) A0138/05
A0589/09 A0609/05 A0674/17 A0694/11
cessations (2) B0955/28 B0955/29
cet (1) A0034/01
cette (1) C0430/37
Chabert (1) B1167/27
Chacun (1) A0119/M
chafed (7) A0058/33
A0078/35 A0328/11 A0543/23 A0592/12
B0730/10 B0992/01
chaff (1) B1316/32
chafing (4) A0078/01
A0102/16 C0061/07 C0119/34
chagrin (7) A0381/12
A0435/21 A0530/14 A0568/11 B0756/04
B0915/15 C0545/02
chagrined (2) A0037/22 C0397/30
chain (42) A0035/09 A0087/22
A0094/21 A0101/V A0114/16 A0321/24
A0503/10 A0535/08 A0553/11 B0831/05
B0833/06 B0853/03 B0942/13 B1054/28
B1160/21 B1248/27 B1261/27 B1262/15
B1281/20 B1351/05 B1351/11 B1351/19
B1352/20 B1352/26 B1352/29 B1353/12
B1353/17 B1353/20 B1354/09 B1384/09
B1385/21 C0075/40 C0127/15 C0127/27
C0172/16 C0180/36 C0183/34 C0208/16
C0521/05 C0528/01 C0547/19 C0547/26
chain-bridle (1) A0027/18
chain-cable (3) C0076/10
C0089/20 C0107/15
Chained (2) B1345/V B1350/07
chained (4) A0124/26
B0759/33 B1262/24 B1350/23
chaining (1) B1351/08
chains (14) A0509/03 A0509/16
A0610/08 B0828/06 B0903/09 B1226/18
B1350/20 B1352/05 B1354/21 C0127/01
C0127/12 C0136/10 C0143/34 C0187/40
chair (46) A0063/18 A0089/20
A0091/31 A0102/08 A0102/21 A0105/17
A0108/19 A0174/15 A0179/30 A0214/28
A0294/V A0354/23 A0368/29 A0415/07
A0415/30 A0493/08 A0537/28 A0544/02
A0656/15 B0797/17 B0832/06 B0855/10
B0910/24 B0913/01 B0913/15 B0913/24
B0947/31 B0975/16 B0976/03 B0979/25
B0980/05 B0980/08 B0981/34 B1013/13
B1017/09 B1057/25 B1105/02 B1128/10
B1135/04 B1186/07 B1188/11 B1249/22
B1250/30 C0068/18 C0392/08 C0415/05
chair-leg (2) B0985/32 B0985/35
chairs (9) A0367/22
A0369/23 A0502/22 A0502/V B0796/29
B0841/21 B0980/06 B1340/08 B1340/10
chaise (1) B0904/31
chaise-longue (1) A0166/V
Chaldaea (1) A0190/32
Chaldaean (1) B1051/17
chalice (1) B1379/27
chalk (4) A0241/32
A0498/10 B1392/09 C0109/05
Chalk-Farm (1) A0183/09
chalky (1) C0107/38
challenge (1) A0122/V
challenged (1) B1139/03
chamber (105)
Chamberlaine's (1) A0426/V
Chamberlayne's (1) A0426/M
chambermaid (1) A0263/29
chambermaids (2) A0263/03 A0263/06
chambers (13) A0301/24
A0436/27 A0438/22 A0441/08 A0444/11
A0672/11 A0673/18 A0673/27 A0676/18
B0724/30 B0829/34 B0967/34 C0207/42
Chambers/Street (1) B0925/34
Chambertin (6) A0099/04 A0101/V
A0108/25 A0109/19 A0110/10 A0181/12
Chamfort (1) B0986/33
champagne (6) A0487/24 B1011/26
B1011/32 B1015/V B1020/28 B1209/03
champion (2) A0414/13 A0415/17
Champollion (2) B1298/04 B1317/05
chance (49) A0046/16
A0072/25 A0142/08 A0152/01 A0195/V
A0341/22 A0342/V A0347/26 A0353/23
A0371/27 A0384/33 A0386/24 A0427/02
A0510/02 A0630/24 B0724/02 B0752/14
B0752/17 B0756/10 B0773/27 B0817/07
B0823/08 B0870/15 B1017/32 B1114/09
B1155/25 B1208/14 B1224/09 B1244/06
B1292/17 B1299/01 B1373/06 C0056/01
C0060/26 C0070/12 C0084/07 C0089/14
C0090/05 C0116/12 C0134/08 C0135/07
C0143/35 C0175/18 C0186/05 C0199/32
C0200/34 C0403/16 C0407/12 C0563/28
chanced (4) A0602/12
B0734/31 C0392/07 C0398/27
chances (10) A0037/04 A0037/04
A0528/29 B0754/27 B0876/35 C0122/23
C0134/21 C0135/10 C0430/45 C0548/29
chandelier (5) B1351/19
B1351/26 B1351/31 B1352/21 B1352/31
chandelier-chain (1) B1352/33
chandeliers (1) A0499/25
change (63)
changeable (4) A0270/19
A0314/18 A0322/20 C0172/02
changed (21) A0198/10
A0215/12 A0594/23 A0689/12 B0964/34
B1006/31 B1015/17 B1015/19 B1015/21
B1015/V B1015/V B1015/V B1015/V
B1090/12 B1237/19 B1382/05 C0072/24
C0130/07 C0200/38 C0423/33 C0526/27
changes (5) A0213/29
A0556/08 A0641/17 A0641/V B1119/08
changing (7) A0106/03
A0216/20 A0567/02 A0580/07 B0830/26
B1074/22 B1119/07
channel (27) A0020/V
A0152/03 A0268/29 A0433/18 A0582/17
A0583/03 A0584/01 A0584/12 A0586/33
A0594/14 A0639/29 B0758/23 B1279/03
B1279/14 B1279/37 B1282/17 B1282/34
C0184/32 C0192/29 C0521/19 C0531/40
C0533/38 C0542/24 C0559/16 C0559/21
C0576/26 C0576/30
channels (6) A0461/11 A0580/13

->B1030/07 C0399/01 C0552/38 C0577/06
Channing (1) A0278/06
Channing, W. E. (1) A0278/09
Channing's (3) A0278/14
A0278/17 A0342/11
chanticleer-note (1) B1222/23
Chantilly (8) A0534/13
A0534/17 A0535/02 A0535/08 A0536/14
A0536/23 A0536/28 A0537/01
chanting (1) A0297/21
chaos (10) A0145/12 A0158/V
A0159/03 A0280/04 A0594/01 A0614/35
B1121/02 C0069/06 C0190/04 C0205/36
chaotic (6) A0029/19 A0316/03
B1382/17 C0184/33 C0198/36 C0577/11
chap (5) A0372/03
A0374/V A0466/16 A0470/13 B1373/24
chapeau-de-bras (2) A0371/10
A0372/04
chapel (2) A0294/V C0530/06
Chapman (1) A0502/06
Chapman's (1) A0164/26
Chapter (1) B1089/T
chapter (4) A0301/15
A0302/19 A0303/20 B1193/25
chapters (4) A0078/25
A0301/11 C0207/03 C0207/16
character (207)
characteristic (6) A0027/11
A0142/34 A0213/02 A0240/16 B1220/23
B1240/16
characteristically (1) A0435/12
characteristics (4) A0065/27
A0216/03 A0269/07 A0284/05
characterization (1) A0246/18
characterize (2) A0098/31 B0960/13
characterized (6) A0275/35 A0293/29
A0337/35 A0411/03 A0484/12 A0560/06
characterizes (2) A0269/24 C0126/11
characters (51)
charadrai (Gr.) (1) A0195/M
charcoal (6) A0248/24 B0834/32
B1092/29 B1185/02 C0071/26 C0405/24
charge (33) A0097/24
A0097/25 A0242/03 A0262/17 A0262/17
A0311/06 A0473/16 A0485/16 A0485/21
A0494/03 A0546/27 A0622/05 B0733/05
B0733/14 B0764/33 B0771/15 B0816/33
B0874/02 B0925/27 B1015/08 B1143/04
B1240/06 B1293/32 B1314/13 B1329/05
B1332/19 C0534/17 C0535/16 C0535/17
C0539/32 C0544/09 C0557/38 C0562/19
chargeable (1) B1207/20
charged (4) A0564/09
B0769/18 B1092/24 C0066/33
chargee (1) B1090/05
charger (1) A0026/29
charges (2) A0561/01 B0873/12
chariot-wheels (1) A0080/02
charicted (1) A0045/29
charitable (4) A0026/18
A0056/08 B0748/17 B1305/06
Charite (1) C0538/23
charities (1) B1271/01
charity (9) A0399/02
->A0509/35 A0652/06 A0682/03 A0705/14
B0878/07 B1048/02 B1096/30 B1270/13
charlatanerie (1) A0535/04
Charles (5) A0037/12
B1031/12 B1045/01 B1045/08 B1045/17
Charles/the/Twelfth (1) B0870/32
Charleston (9) B0806/06
B0807/07 B0808/05 B0811/12 B0922/01
B1068/03 B1068/13 B1069/13 B1082/03
Charley (18) B1045/22 B1045/25
B1045/27 B1046/02 B1047/08 B1047/27
B1048/01 B1048/18 B1048/23 B1048/25
B1049/13 B1050/24 B1051/06 B1054/18
B1056/12 B1056/22 B1056/29 B1058/18
Charley's (2) B1045/32 B1047/19
Charlottesville (7) B0939/01
B0942/14 B0942/27 B0949/29 B0949/32
B0950/11 C0524/18
charm (4) A0711/12
B0760/03 B1276/13 B1277/26
charming (1) B0902/02
Charmion (15) A0455/03
A0455/05 A0455/08 A0455/T A0456/05
A0456/07 A0456/15 A0456/18 A0456/21
A0456/31 A0457/02 A0457/05 A0461/04
A0461/18 B1322/31
charms (4) B0726/03
B0915/05 B1277/26 B1385/37
charnal (2) B0963/22 B0969/08
charnel (3) A0236/12
A0329/15 A0689/02
charnel-house (2) A0228/16 A0232/V
Charon (1) A0096/M
Charonian (1) A0191/10
chart (5) B0989/31
B0989/35 C0418/07 C0422/22 C0429/05
Chartreuse (1) A0408/29
charts (2) A0141/18 A0144/22
chas'd (1) A0318/V
chase (6) A0020/09 A0027/V
A0565/18 B0896/10 C0546/06 C0566/31
chased (6) A0087/25 A0318/24
A0628/31 B0828/09 B0907/05 B1096/23
chasing (1) B1096/22
chasm (28) A0139/33
A0246/24 A0687/09 B1279/26 B1280/07
B1330/35 B1331/07 C0184/16 C0185/31
C0188/18 C0189/08 C0192/11 C0192/27
C0192/32 C0193/07 C0193/22 C0194/01
C0194/16 C0194/21 C0194/24 C0194/27
C0195/04 C0195/07 C0196/03 C0196/08
C0196/23 C0197/24 C0206/05
chasm-like (2) B1280/31 B1282/11
chasms (7) C0207/25
C0207/27 C0207/29 C0207/40 C0208/23
C0208/24 C0405/31
chassez (2) A0371/30 B1330/34
chastened (1) B1122/08
chastise (1) B0813/23
chastisements (1) A0622/35
chastity (2) A0165/23 B0733/05
Chateau (3) A0019/V
A0293/06 B1055/32
Chateau (1) B1045/33
chateau (4) B1003/20

->B1008/28 B1019/21 B1021/32
chateau (10) A0023/V A0024/V
A0025/V A0025/V A0028/V A0029/V
A0662/01 A0663/01 A0667/06 B1014/25
Chateau-Margaux (7) B1055/18
B1055/29 B1055/V B1056/V B1056/V
B1059/07 B1059/V
Chateau/Margaux (3) B1046/06
B1056/07 B1056/20
Chateaubriand (1) B1144/31
chatted (4) B0796/35
B0797/02 B0797/20 B1017/24
chatter (1) B0964/17
chattered (2) B0947/32 C0421/21
chattering (1) B0945/22
chatty (2) B0926/13 B0926/13
Chaucer (1) B1095/10
Chaussee (1) A0033/05
Chaworth (2) B1121/T B1123/05
Chaworth, Mary (2) B1122/10
B1122/31
Chayenne (3) B1160/20
C0551/23 C0551/25
che (3) A0161/04
A0344/31 A0356/13
cheap (3) A0491/10
B1141/06 B1169/21
cheat (1) A0675/12
cheats (1) B0869/22
check (10) A0180/22 A0427/27
A0608/15 B0982/11 B0983/02 B0983/10
B0983/19 B0988/16 B1074/12 B1223/18
check-book (1) B0983/02
checked (1) A0541/15
checking (1) B1003/22
cheek (16) A0053/25
A0062/29 A0196/28 A0227/10 A0231/24
A0241/30 A0298/V A0327/19 A0328/08
A0641/V B0893/14 B0906/29 B0962/14
B1011/29 B1239/25 C0551/40
cheek-bones (2) A0241/02 B1235/14
cheeks (11) A0247/11
A0327/05 A0330/07 A0330/08 A0442/23
A0640/11 A0665/29 B1242/19 C0142/11
C0389/22 C0406/03
cheer (3) B0931/09
B1009/17 B1281/07
cheered (2) C0117/26 C0125/25
cheerful (4) A0562/15
B1004/04 B1030/33 C0123/36
cheerfully (2) B0908/12 B0910/08
cheerfulness (1) A0398/24
cheerily (2) B0796/34 B0963/10
cheering (2) A0405/03 C0127/20
cheerless (4) A0510/04
C0072/04 C0162/31 C0571/13
cheers (3) B1049/13
B1077/08 B1078/13
cheese (1) B1011/20
chef (3) A0160/V
A0160/V A0568/V
chef-d'oeuvres (1) A0160/V
chefs (1) A0160/06
chemical (4) B0742/23
B0832/17 B1362/16 C0429/24
chemically (2) C0404/07 C0413/22
chemin (2) A0053/13 A0062/21
chemise (1) B1185/34
chemist (2) B1358/08 B1359/09
chemist's (1) B1363/02
chemistry (1) B0987/25
Chenes (1) C0522/35
Cheops (1) A0045/12
chequered (2) C0436/V C0573/17
cher (2) B0906/29 B0910/01
cherished (1) B0850/16
cherishing (1) A0665/04
cherry (1) C0543/30
cherub (2) A0165/11 B0967/20
chesnut (1) C0549/25
chess (5) A0528/17
A0528/24 A0529/16 A0529/19 B1166/18
chess-board (1) A0367/10
Chess-player (2) B1120/03 B1166/34
chess-player (4) A0528/16
A0529/18 A0529/27 B1361/04
chest (17) A0566/16
B0730/07 B0826/01 B0826/07 B0827/05
B0827/19 B0828/02 B0828/18 B1046/23
B1054/04 B1057/12 B1080/05 C0081/18
C0089/22 C0093/03 C0404/11 C0407/29
Chestnut (2) B1092/32 B1093/17
chestnut (1) B1339/09
chestnuts (1) B1332/04
cheval (1) A0019/03
Chevalier (3) B0724/14
B0724/26 B0772/07
Chevalier's (1) B0725/07
chew (2) C0130/41 C0131/02
chewing (1) C0128/33
chez (2) C0430/30 C0430/31
Chian (1) A0189/18
chibouc (1) B1167/09
chicanery (1) C0111/33
Chichester (2) A0150/M A0166/09
Chickasaw (2) A0344/10 B1051/17
chicken (6) A0344/19 A0345/11
B0869/13 B0869/15 B1006/10 B1103/30
chicken-bone (6) A0344/21 A0344/30
A0345/05 A0345/22 A0346/16 A0347/02
chicken-cock (1) B1013/29
chickens (4) B0869/19
B1006/06 B1166/13 C0151/29
chided (1) B0879/28
Chief (2) A0274/28 A0274/31
chief (61)
chiefly (33) A0123/15
A0225/16 A0296/V A0380/23 A0485/15
A0502/04 A0549/03 A0555/11 B0725/27
B0750/11 B0754/15 B0763/18 B0855/16
B0904/19 B0904/29 B0905/11 B0962/09
B0978/15 B0983/23 B1035/11 B1128/09
B1185/11 C0068/18 C0071/19 C0097/37
C0123/15 C0135/26 C0138/11 C0149/09
C0156/16 C0413/12 C0544/09 C0552/36
chiefs (3) C0550/04
C0554/10 C0555/41
chieftain's (1) C0552/24
chien (2) A0019/03 A0033/17
Chienne (1) B1160/20

child (38) A0020/V A0078/23
A0152/08 A0152/20 A0153/09 A0153/21
A0154/03 A0154/10 A0154/18 A0228/21
A0228/21 A0228/33 A0228/35 A0233/02
A0233/03 A0233/15 A0233/17 A0233/23
A0234/03 A0234/20 A0235/04 A0235/25
A0270/21 A0316/14 A0510/11 A0622/30
A0642/21 A0653/02 A0691/11 B0859/01
B0888/01 B1091/09 B1215/17 C0082/32
C0086/03 C0094/32 C0123/07 C0130/38
child-like (2) A0316/02 A0320/17
child's (1) B0725/19
Childe (1) B1122/09
childhood (7) A0020/V
A0141/19 A0320/19 A0430/22 A0430/32
B1225/V C0130/18
childish (4) A0399/21
A0539/18 A0610/11 B0856/21
childishly (2) B0740/30 C0079/06
childlike (1) C0145/10
children (19) A0058/29
A0128/V A0347/29 A0427/30 A0498/21
A0499/22 B0878/11 B0914/18 B0931/22
B0992/21 B1091/10 B1096/23 B1096/23
B1122/35 B1129/17 C0145/01 C0174/24
C0391/29 C0522/28
Chili (1) A0158/06
chill (2) A0214/26 B1225/12
chilled (4) A0329/26
A0694/24 B0795/03 C0060/33
chillily (1) C0080/23
chilliness (4) A0328/16
A0428/04 B0808/02 B0964/18
chilling (2) A0413/05 C0441/V
chills (1) B1223/04
chilly (6) B0809/18 B0832/03
B0963/03 B1100/01 C0571/23 C0579/08
chimaeras (1) B0855/22
chime (5) A0483/07
A0652/24 A0673/33 A0674/22 B0865/31
chimed (2) A0534/05 B1015/21
chimera (5) A0703/07
A0708/16 B1268/06 B1273/11 B1363/36
chimerical (3) A0459/27
B1077/25 B1318/11
Chimerique (1) C0430/27
chimes (1) A0672/31
chiming (3) A0673/05
A0673/08 B0822/32
chimney (16) A0102/01
A0340/30 A0538/09 A0543/15 A0543/22
A0547/26 A0549/05 A0557/04 A0557/06
A0567/17 B0794/18 B0832/06 B0857/08
B1110/13 B1330/29 B1336/18
chimneys (4) A0542/17
A0543/08 A0543/11 A0551/17
chimpanzees (2) B1021/10 B1351/13
chin (23) A0156/11
A0176/V A0182/19 A0241/03 A0246/28
A0298/V A0298/V A0312/24 A0330/09
A0368/31 A0370/15 A0401/34 A0512/33
A0543/24 A0641/V A0686/33 A0687/01
B0734/25 B0750/19 B0766/04 B1013/04
C0121/16 C0389/21
China (3) A0367/29
->A0611/13 C0525/24
Chinese (8) A0097/21
A0344/06 A0344/09 A0348/19 A0495/07
B1101/13 C0178/11 C0179/10
chins (2) A0369/09 C0568/22
chip (1) B1329/22
Chiponchipino (1) A0380/01
chirography (9) A0274/06
A0276/17 A0277/12 A0278/18 A0278/36
A0281/19 A0283/26 A0284/12 A0285/35
Chiromancy (1) A0409/02
chirp (1) B0794/19
Chirurgical/Journal (1) B0958/15
chisel (3) A0367/20
B0929/14 B1057/04
chiseled (1) B1303/33
chiselled (2) B0893/10 B1281/35
chiselling (1) A0209/16
chisels (1) C0148/09
chit-chat (1) B1114/10
chivalrous (4) A0240/02
A0279/12 A0303/10 B1054/19
chivalry (1) B1371/03
cho-o-ose (1) A0386/05
chocolate (1) A0494/02
Choctaw (1) B1128/30
Choctaws (1) B1144/21
choice (8) A0036/23
A0583/29 A0687/21 B0904/21 B0989/06
B1014/03 B1277/19 C0546/27
chokeberries (1) C0576/05
choked (6) A0244/01 A0344/20
A0345/05 A0347/02 B0930/34 C0194/25
choking (3) A0166/17
A0345/22 A0347/30
Cholera (1) B1246/01
cholera (2) A0092/09 A0111/20
cholic (1) B1097/02
choose (8) A0026/V
A0091/35 A0111/11 A0292/V A0338/06
A0366/13 B0732/04 B1079/31
chooses (2) B1207/34 B1364/04
chopped (1) B0925/36
chopping (3) A0580/06
A0586/05 C0149/17
chops (1) B0821/15
chords (1) A0675/03
Chorum (1) A0409/11
chorus (2) A0105/28 B1350/13
chorused (1) B1348/20
chose (3) A0033/20
A0602/07 A0602/08
chose (6) A0337/15 B1107/30
B1139/33 C0088/14 C0091/14 C0189/12
chosen (7) A0160/04
A0204/31 A0497/21 B0831/18 C0065/34
C0142/01 C0152/13
choses (1) A0036/06
Christ (1) A0120/05
Christchurch-steeple (1) B1092/11
Christendom (4) A0498/14
A0529/18 B1370/35 C0058/10
christened (2) B1045/17 B1127/25
Christi (1) A0213/06
Christian (6) A0266/01 A0431/15

->B0725/16 B0887/15 B0887/16 B1048/02
Christmas (2) A0429/20 B1093/08
Christmas/Harbour (4) C0150/09
C0150/33 C0153/30 C0154/18
chronic (2) A0324/08 B0906/19
chronicle (1) A0625/07
chronicled (1) B0862/19
Chronicles (1) B0887/21
chronicles (1) A0142/26
Chronology, Chronologos (1) A0205/29
chronometer (2) C0085/28 C0416/10
chronometers (1) C0157/02
chrysalis (3) A0314/15
A0711/01 B1276/02
chucking (1) A0176/V
chuckle (2) A0435/11 B0823/20
chuckled (4) A0252/18
B0793/25 B0794/13 B0925/13
chuckling (2) A0533/14 C0397/34
chum (1) A0298/V
chums (1) A0296/V
church (9) A0340/13
A0349/22 A0352/21 A0382/18 A0409/11
A0428/28 A0428/29 B0750/12 B1303/22
church-bell (1) A0428/07
church-yards (1) B0969/06
churches (1) B1303/19
Cicero (1) B1013/02
Cicero (1) A0109/31
cigar (3) A0071/11
A0507/16 C0396/14
cigar-girl (1) B0725/18
cigars (1) B1186/08
Cimabue (4) A0160/03
A0160/03 A0175/22 A0181/19
cipher (9) B0835/17
B0835/33 B0836/06 B0837/08 B0837/29
B0838/23 B0991/06 B0991/15 B0992/18
ciphers (2) B0836/01 B0839/26
circle (32) A0314/07
A0318/26 A0580/26 B0822/13 B0823/26
B0825/04 B0904/27 B1279/09 B1293/31
B1301/29 B1301/30 B1302/04 B1351/10
B1351/12 B1352/30 B1370/15 C0159/05
C0160/37 C0161/06 C0162/17 C0163/05
C0164/06 C0190/39 C0388/29 C0394/19
C0394/20 C0417/30 C0418/07 C0418/10
C0543/21 C0562/20 C0575/35
circled (1) C0543/32
circles (7) A0146/03
A0146/06 B1092/17 B1242/03 B1242/19
B1301/34 C0557/23
circonscriva (1) A0161/04
circuit (19) A0021/03
A0243/16 A0513/02 A0589/20 A0591/20
A0605/03 A0672/24 A0685/25 A0686/02
A0686/17 A0688/10 A0688/20 A0688/22
B0990/34 B1192/27 B1283/03 B1301/06
B1302/01 C0559/10
circuitous (2) B0946/26 B0948/12
circular (30) A0366/27 A0367/04
A0368/31 A0498/11 A0502/18 A0587/10
A0590/24 A0602/28 A0687/05 A0689/09
B0730/08 B0822/02 B0842/09 B0842/30
B0842/33 B1092/01 B1239/24 B1280/03

->B1335/14 B1339/29 B1351/16 C0154/24
C0190/02 C0389/15 C0398/16 C0410/17
C0410/29 C0418/30 C0418/36 C0423/33
circulate (7) B1383/32
B1383/33 B1383/35 B1383/35 B1384/01
B1384/02 C0119/13
circulated (2) B0731/19 B1378/01
circulation (6) A0107/04 A0265/10
B1136/14 B1136/36 B1137/32 B1138/29
circumambient (2) A0461/V B1214/05
circumference (20) A0085/05
A0366/28 A0559/13 A0590/20 A0656/28
A0656/V A0656/V B1159/30 B1192/22
B1302/03 B1302/05 B1322/28 B1381/32
C0154/30 C0155/10 C0161/14 C0165/25
C0196/07 C0418/36 C0420/37
circumgyratory (2) A0070/29
C0390/29
circumjacent (1) C0410/36
circumlocution (1) B1221/24
circumnavigating (2) B1159/06
C0160/05
circumscribed (3) B1275/28
C0157/37 C0550/32
circumscribing (1) B1261/16
circumscription (1) B1114/25
circumstance (56)
circumstanced (1) B0741/19
circumstances (130)
circumstantial (7) A0024/21
A0564/V A0581/09 B0752/02 B0758/31
B1054/29 C0546/09
circumvallatory (1) A0044/30
circumvents (1) B0870/24
circumvolutions (1) C0390/18
citadel (1) A0159/02
citation (1) B0740/21
cited (2) A0499/27 B1325/11
cities (8) A0059/07
A0078/24 A0120/17 A0509/08 A0610/22
B0727/30 B1076/20 C0407/39
citing (1) B0740/16
citizen (4) A0705/08
B1270/07 C0391/15 C0394/05
citizens (14) A0087/34 A0126/01
A0128/23 B0727/25 B0949/32 B0956/12
B1044/10 B1052/02 B1055/02 B1058/19
B1370/08 C0388/35 C0390/25 C0414/13
citizenship (1) C0153/15
cito (1) A0072/30
City (3) A0213/05
A0409/04 B1385/01
city (109)
City/Fathers (1) B1092/21
City/Museum (1) B1178/19
civil (4) A0387/01
A0387/05 B1294/04 B1339/19
civilities (2) B1338/24 C0569/38
civility (7) A0056/25
A0066/14 A0155/23 A0339/02 A0346/27
B1107/35 C0566/07
civilization (3) A0609/13
A0611/12 C0565/03
civilize (2) A0337/14 A0337/27
civilized (14) A0495/V B1350/33

->C0171/17 C0174/26 C0202/26 C0521/T
C0524/30 C0528/32 C0529/T C0540/T
C0550/T C0560/T C0564/37 C0571/T
clad (2) A0349/02 B0946/28
claim (12) A0070/10
A0474/01 B0854/18 B0873/14 B0958/11
B0958/11 B0977/18 B1358/21 C0056/27
C0393/09 C0432/32 C0528/40
claimant (1) B0873/29
claimed (3) A0023/25
B0897/11 C0156/13
claiming (1) A0561/32
claims (2) A0478/09 B0760/12
clairvoyance (1) B1234/17
clamber (6) A0243/23 A0351/29
B0855/13 C0075/03 C0096/27 C0143/41
clambered (15) A0138/19
A0321/19 A0565/24 A0603/25 B0817/30
B0823/29 B0841/14 B0862/11 B0945/21
B1337/20 B1353/12 B1354/22 C0095/30
C0196/22 C0542/13
clambering (4) A0567/21
B0864/23 C0096/01 C0545/03
clamminess (2) A0327/22 A0694/24
clammy (2) A0079/42 A0687/02
clamor (2) A0124/01 B0945/18
clamored (1) B1262/29
clamorer (1) B1262/31
clamorous (1) B1049/35
clamorously (1) B0877/20
clandestinely (2) B0988/06 B1114/27
clang (1) A0672/23
clanging (1) A0088/03
clangor (2) A0416/12 A0644/06
clangorous (1) A0415/28
clanking (1) B1262/18
clans (1) C0551/02
clap (1) B1090/35
clapped (3) A0372/04
A0465/11 A0486/22
clapper (2) A0340/13 A0370/03
clapping (2) C0131/22 C0168/36
claret (1) B1058/29
Clarke (11) C0070/33
C0523/04 C0523/21 C0524/12 C0527/16
C0527/27 C0528/37 C0548/08 C0551/23
C0566/39 C0574/40
Clarke, Lewis G. (1) B1141/08
Clarke's, Lewis (1) B1141/31
clashing (2) A0591/11 C0142/33
clasp (3) A0019/V
B0745/32 B0746/28
clasp-garter (1) B0746/33
clasped (5) A0628/01
A0644/V A0696/30 B0890/11 B1215/30
clasping (1) A0104/15
clasps (2) A0093/13 A0104/09
class (24) A0100/06
A0150/V A0431/23 A0484/34 A0485/01
A0508/06 A0508/30 A0556/22 A0559/V
A0703/34 A0709/13 B0750/24 B0869/21
B0946/13 B1034/16 B1163/11 B1163/12
B1250/19 B1268/33 B1274/15 B1314/34
B1332/07 C0178/34 C0420/32
classes (10) A0293/29 A0432/22
->A0508/15 B0758/24 B0759/19 B1006/15
B1037/30 B1037/31 B1278/28 C0546/25
classic (3) A0101/03
A0312/02 A0352/18
classical (11) A0087/30
A0098/29 A0152/27 A0311/28 A0315/17
A0348/16 A0354/01 A0430/10 B0880/04
B1370/07 B1385/17
classically (1) A0156/16
classics (1) B1385/25
classification (1) B0747/35
classify (2) B1220/12 B1220/13
classifying (2) B1295/15 B1311/08
clatter (1) A0374/13
clattering (2) A0029/14 C0387/16
Claude (3) A0707/26
A0707/V B1272/27
clause (2) A0204/01 A0491/05
claws (10) B0812/24 B0825/22
B0855/13 B1292/22 C0167/16 C0167/21
C0190/29 C0578/04 C0579/17 C0579/34
clay (12) A0227/18
A0232/05 C0151/03 C0173/08 C0567/19
C0572/27 C0576/19 C0577/01 C0577/03
C0578/20 C0578/27 C0579/34
clayey (1) C0576/31
clean (9) A0267/35
A0286/17 A0488/25 A0543/11 A0564/17
A0627/33 B1046/22 B1279/35 B1333/02
cleanest (2) A0485/18 B0829/30
cleanly (2) B1331/29 C0545/15
cleanness (1) B1281/21
clear (89)
clear-sighted (1) B1138/10
cleared (11) A0388/28
B0822/02 B1157/26 B1298/21 B1316/32
C0146/37 C0156/01 C0550/14 C0563/02
C0567/10 C0570/30
clearer (4) A0381/05
B1299/19 B1333/24 C0571/20
clearest (1) A0440/29
clearing (3) A0029/16
B0822/11 C0179/21
clearly (36) A0021/03
A0298/09 A0315/28 A0370/V A0388/22
A0461/07 A0535/05 A0557/29 A0600/08
A0601/15 A0622/03 A0675/29 A0687/15
B0842/04 B0869/15 B0886/V B0928/34
B0976/16 B0978/36 B1034/04 B1057/10
B1058/21 B1058/26 B1078/22 B1106/27
B1139/20 B1178/03 B1212/22 B1298/09
B1315/21 B1329/20 C0142/20 C0146/22
C0161/30 C0184/08 C0536/30
clearness (3) A0273/17
A0379/12 A0545/14
cleft (2) B1331/29 C0183/36
clefts (1) C0571/25
clematis (1) B1282/02
Clematitis (1) B1163/25
clenched (4) A0299/31
A0588/06 B0730/08 B0824/06
Cleomenes (3) A0160/V
A0160/V A0312/27
clergyman (3) A0509/17
B0908/26 B0916/15

clerically (1) A0428/33
clerk (5) A0104/06
A0541/17 A0541/19 B0879/07 C0088/07
clerk's (1) A0272/13
clerks (4) A0508/22
A0508/23 A0508/31 B0879/01
clever (11) A0089/23
A0093/25 A0107/25 A0107/28 A0113/04
A0176/14 A0179/16 A0182/15 A0621/07
B0876/20 B0923/20
cleverest (2) B1297/01 B1314/05
cleverly (6) A0585/33 A0587/31
B0796/11 B1116/09 B1209/02 C0062/01
cleverness (1) C0397/35
clew (9) A0242/08
A0538/26 A0544/17 A0553/16 A0561/27
B0772/04 C0079/27 C0125/38 C0388/06
click-clack (3) A0354/13
A0354/14 A0354/14
cliff (26) A0045/06 A0578/06
A0578/07 A0578/10 A0579/04 B0841/19
B0865/26 B0865/29 B1331/22 B1332/06
B1334/36 C0185/20 C0189/16 C0197/19
C0197/32 C0198/03 C0198/18 C0198/36
C0199/33 C0538/01 C0554/16 C0567/34
C0578/12 C0578/29 C0579/09 C0579/26
cliffs (20) B0841/12
B0864/35 B1076/07 B1332/15 B1334/30
B1338/15 C0193/12 C0536/36 C0537/40
C0541/38 C0549/23 C0567/17 C0572/32
C0572/41 C0573/06 C0573/16 C0577/02
C0577/30 C0578/09 C0578/17
Climah (1) A0047/V
climate (11) A0055/18
A0065/02 A0092/19 A0111/29 A0459/16
B1161/20 B1183/15 C0093/31 C0156/15
C0202/15 C0425/33
climates (1) C0171/23
Climax (2) A0383/14 A0384/08
climax (2) B1021/03 C0569/32
climb (5) B0818/04
B0818/09 B1346/19 B1354/09 C0074/37
climber (1) B0819/05
climbing (2) B0993/09 C0544/23
clime (2) A0033/M A0163/14
clinched (1) C0115/36
cling (1) A0154/18
clinging (3) B0961/21
B1353/20 C0425/04
clip (1) B1311/31
cliverly> (1) A0468/10
cloak (17) A0048/V
A0087/05 A0100/15 A0154/07 A0154/12
A0246/03 A0442/32 A0444/04 A0444/06
A0444/15 A0444/27 A0447/04 A0448/07
B1260/32 C0067/12 C0067/18 C0082/13
cloaks (2) B1073/25 B1078/26
clock (36) A0033/12
A0151/20 A0352/24 A0352/27 A0353/20
A0354/14 A0369/20 A0369/24 A0369/28
A0370/27 A0372/18 A0372/21 A0430/18
A0483/06 A0513/27 A0533/03 A0615/10
A0672/22 A0672/25 A0672/32 A0673/05
A0673/08 A0673/30 A0673/32 A0674/09
A0674/15 A0674/18 A0676/29 A0677/02
->B0896/19 B1104/10 B1105/18 B1105/32
B1106/02 B1222/22 B1352/04
clocks (5) A0369/17
A0370/02 A0370/07 A0373/25 A0689/29
clockwork (1) B1153/33
clod (1) A0601/26
cloister (1) A0210/24
<u>Clos</u> (2) B1007/24 B1016/28
Clos/de/Vougeot (2) A0099/03
A0181/15
close (118)
close-fitting (1) B0890/05
close-hauled (1) C0399/21
close-reefed (2) C0104/34 C0106/21
close-veiled (1) B0945/V
closed (51)
closely (45) A0278/07
A0278/15 A0416/02 A0442/32 A0511/31
A0512/26 A0514/16 A0628/03 A0672/02
A0691/06 A0709/07 B0761/17 B0818/34
B0829/14 B0829/20 B0854/10 B0915/26
B0924/14 B0957/22 B0967/13 B1030/02
B1160/35 B1258/19 B1274/13 B1296/16
B1300/34 B1312/19 B1332/36 B1352/27
B1354/02 C0069/06 C0074/34 C0076/05
C0082/13 C0084/36 C0091/13 C0096/20
C0124/31 C0158/33 C0175/11 C0175/18
C0181/23 C0190/38 C0416/33 C0431/06
closely-buttoned (1) A0512/03
closely-interlocking (1) C0543/19
closeness (2) B0944/18 C0094/14
closer (14) A0102/V A0404/32
A0405/01 A0532/01 A0676/05 B0833/02
B0896/09 B1010/26 B1322/14 C0076/38
C0090/16 C0167/24 C0418/49 C0432/19
closes (1) A0479/15
closest (3) A0675/11
B0962/17 C0117/30
closet (15) A0054/33
A0055/06 A0055/06 A0064/01 A0064/23
A0064/24 A0108/24 A0437/10 A0565/02
A0565/07 B0871/18 B1362/15 B1362/17
B1362/35 C0068/16
closets (2) A0436/32 B0989/02
closing (14) A0216/28 A0324/16
A0404/21 A0507/05 A0515/09 A0650/08
A0687/12 A0697/01 C0085/01 C0086/09
C0110/38 C0410/24 C0411/12 C0411/36
cloth (20) A0087/05
A0100/09 A0103/22 A0158/05 A0165/V
A0205/31 A0322/14 A0322/16 A0484/34
A0692/09 B1157/07 C0177/13 C0177/39
C0409/30 C0409/32 C0409/33 C0409/37
C0410/19 C0410/25 C0552/07
clothe (1) A0612/02
clothed (11) A0246/01
A0510/18 B0864/28 B1279/04 B1280/09
B1334/34 B1337/10 C0150/23 C0154/36
C0168/15 C0174/31
clothes (20) A0411/33
A0484/16 A0508/05 A0511/35 A0539/06
A0566/15 A0685/29 B0731/09 B0736/11
B0871/19 B0931/25 B1014/15 B1019/20
B1048/02 B1108/06 B1183/15 C0058/27
C0120/09 C0121/06 C0140/36

clothing (3) B1003/18
C0108/39 C0138/39
cloths (1) A0498/18
clotted (4) A0218/28
A0557/20 B0859/11 C0125/08
cloud (26) A0029/23 A0136/12
A0426/08 A0439/29 A0457/03 A0585/22
A0641/05 A0643/20 B1157/25 B1161/29
B1222/29 B1222/30 B1223/01 B1280/24
B1391/22 C0119/38 C0143/21 C0145/31
C0387/14 C0387/24 C0390/23 C0405/14
C0405/17 C0405/22 C0405/33 C0412/06
clouded (2) C0063/39 C0425/17
clouds (16) A0035/07
A0138/20 A0195/22 A0198/05 A0228/07
A0233/22 A0397/02 A0412/23 A0590/24
B0931/07 B1161/25 C0154/37 C0159/19
C0412/39 C0418/46 C0432/11
cloudy (3) A0578/29
B0865/06 C0542/31
Club (2) A0203/13 A0681/M
club (7) A0204/12
A0204/21 A0205/33 A0544/02 B1250/26
C0199/12 C0199/24
Club/Vingt-un (1) A0037/07
club's (1) A0204/30
clubs (5) A0123/06
B1089/09 C0168/18 C0174/32 C0186/37
clue (6) A0544/V A0553/V
A0561/V B0727/13 B0993/23 B1224/23
clump (3) B1334/21
C0562/16 C0577/34
clumps (2) B1329/26 C0570/21
clumsily (4) A0136/04
A0497/17 B1193/06 C0099/25
clumsy (2) C0120/40 C0174/28
clung (8) A0227/18
A0232/05 A0578/15 A0581/01 A0586/15
A0694/17 B0945/23 C0062/19
cluster (4) A0579/12
B1301/17 C0416/18 C0543/34
clustered (2) A0152/26 B1340/22
clutch (1) B1372/22
clutched (4) A0510/22
A0558/22 C0198/06 C0406/28
clutches (3) C0073/30
C0391/37 C0561/41
clutching (1) C0399/06
Co. (4) B0879/13
B1055/22 B1361/32 C0058/29
co-exist (1) B1297/13
co-mates (1) A0617/07
coach (12) A0056/13
A0056/36 A0057/03 A0066/02 A0066/30
A0069/26 A0077/03 B1090/25 B1090/27
B1090/27 B1090/32 B1091/23
coachman (2) A0278/04 A0493/09
coadjutor (1) A0557/27
coadjutors (1) B0844/20
coal (5) B1073/05
B1073/08 C0552/05 C0570/27 C0571/17
coal-gas (1) B1073/17
coal-heavers (1) A0510/25
coalesce (1) B1034/31
coalescence (2) B1035/06 B1035/11
coals (1) A0683/02
coarse (3) A0685/30
C0150/27 C0165/15
coarser (1) C0543/21
coast (38) A0136/07 A0138/16
A0578/27 A0580/12 A0582/13 A0583/36
A0592/09 A0594/15 B0830/07 B0834/03
B0834/19 B0926/01 B1076/29 B1077/28
B1078/06 B1079/02 B1079/02 B1081/13
B1081/15 B1081/21 B1161/14 C0063/11
C0088/35 C0148/17 C0148/22 C0154/01
C0154/08 C0155/03 C0157/35 C0158/11
C0161/33 C0165/24 C0165/39 C0167/29
C0170/41 C0176/09 C0525/17 C0526/39
coasting (2) C0097/12 C0098/39
coastmen (1) A0583/25
coasts (3) C0160/25
C0178/10 C0407/36
coat (23) A0104/08
A0104/34 A0106/16 A0205/17 A0262/19
A0349/06 A0371/06 A0371/22 A0563/V
A0629/10 B0810/37 B0823/31 B0872/19
B0916/18 B1052/12 B1108/14 B1185/32
B1354/02 B1362/30 C0068/40 C0404/31
C0407/07 C0425/02
coat-pocket (5) B0910/V
B1052/V C0092/21 C0101/17 C0204/21
coat-tail (1) A0370/12
coat-tails (1) B1194/29
coated (1) B1180/12
coating (4) B0834/28
B1351/04 B1351/05 C0394/11
coatings (1) C0533/19
coats (8) A0368/20
A0369/10 A0508/24 A0508/33 A0509/29
B0869/22 B1248/14 C0394/41
cobalt (1) B0832/22
Cobbett (1) B1115/02
Cobbett's (1) B1141/06
cobbler (1) A0534/17
cobbler's (2) A0536/15 A0536/25
cobler (1) A0087/03
Cocaigne (1) B1101/30
cock (2) B1021/V B1372/04
cock-a-doodle (2) B1015/V B1021/V
cock-a-doodle-de-doo (2) B1015/V
B1016/01
cock-a-doodle-de-doo-doo (1) B1013/32
cock-a-doodle-de-doooooh (1) B1021/02
cock-a-doodle-doo (2) B1013/32
B1013/32
cock-a-doodleing (1) B1021/04
cock-crowing (1) B1153/11
Cock-neighs (1) B1158/36
Cock/Robin (1) A0621/22
cock's (1) A0498/10
cocked (3) A0247/V
A0368/18 A0482/15
cocking (1) C0436/V
cocks (2) A0175/05 A0181/26
cocoa (1) B0945/29
cocoa-nuts (1) A0136/03
cod (2) C0155/06 C0174/06
code (1) A0297/11
codfish (1) A0568/22

codicil (1) A0056/07
coeur (3) A0096/M
A0397/M B1122/01
coexist (2) A0527/V B1315/06
coffee (3) B0942/11
B1073/27 B1195/16
coffee-plant (1) C0156/02
coffee-warmer (1) B1073/27
Coffee-House (1) A0507/06
coffer (1) B0826/10
coffin (35) A0020/V
A0034/21 A0070/16 A0080/34 A0080/37
A0081/08 A0081/23 A0217/V A0217/V
A0217/V A0248/07 A0248/V A0249/16
A0249/20 A0252/17 A0253/04 A0254/01
A0339/29 A0410/14 A0416/09 A0416/13
A0614/03 A0615/26 A0616/08 A0616/30
B0956/33 B0957/03 B0957/29 B0959/04
B0965/31 B0965/31 B0966/01 B0967/18
B0967/31 B1179/13
coffin-shaped (3) B1179/21
B1179/34 B1180/04
coffin-tressels (1) A0245/17
coffins (4) A0070/19
A0081/40 A0248/25 B1183/15
cognizance (8) A0561/29
A0600/31 A0600/31 A0690/23 B0770/21
B0770/34 B0961/13 B1030/04
cognizant (14) A0550/05 A0560/09
A0561/17 A0561/28 A0638/07 B0837/31
B0966/23 B1034/09 B1037/11 B1038/31
B1047/22 B1138/32 B1212/05 B1212/05
cognomen (2) A0122/25 A0150/V
Cognoscenti (1) A0384/10
Cognoscenti, Miranda (1) A0383/13
coherence (1) A0558/20
cohesion (2) C0172/08 C0172/14
cohort (1) B0985/09
coin (4) A0045/25
B0825/27 B0827/24 B1363/04
coinage (1) B1363/31
coincide (3) B0723/M
B0928/12 B1187/30
coincided (1) C0549/12
coincidence (19) A0414/08
A0414/35 A0432/29 A0432/V A0434/12
A0556/28 A0655/07 A0655/13 B0758/01
B0829/16 B0829/21 B0829/27 B0887/22
B0888/V B0974/13 B1044/26 B1135/27
B1144/17 B1350/05
coincidences (10) A0556/18 A0556/21
B0723/03 B0723/04 B0724/09 B0772/10
B0772/21 B0829/22 B0833/27 B1144/17
coincident (5) A0366/08
B0738/08 B0739/35 B0757/30 C0527/27
coins (5) A0496/25
B0827/30 B1303/09 B1304/02 B1304/07
coir (1) A0136/03
Col. (1) B0740/33
Col--e (1) A0035/V
cold (47) A0079/42
A0092/08 A0111/20 A0138/17 A0151/01
A0226/11 A0230/09 A0243/31 A0312/08
A0353/13 A0444/05 A0685/03 A0685/22
A0694/22 B0742/16 B0789/14 B0950/01
->B0964/10 B1078/24 B1080/02 B1183/15
B1185/31 B1238/12 B1258/12 B1258/15
C0058/22 C0058/34 C0064/04 C0069/23
C0071/03 C0083/34 C0094/01 C0120/03
C0159/01 C0159/16 C0163/21 C0163/38
C0185/33 C0187/04 C0416/32 C0417/09
C0425/34 C0559/09 C0563/35 C0565/12
C0565/17 C0570/22
colder (1) C0560/07
coldly (1) A0235/29
coldness (3) A0327/22
B1040/13 B1237/17
Coleridgey (1) A0495/V
Coleridge (4) A0079/07
A0297/22 A0340/01 A0625/03
collapsed (2) B1305/08 C0396/40
collar (8) A0447/03
A0485/03 A0627/33 B0824/03 B1180/20
B1180/23 B1184/04 C0062/33
collars (1) B1157/15
collate (1) B0760/29
collated (3) B0863/18
C0428/10 C0448/V
collateral (7) A0399/14
A0709/12 B0752/02 B0752/10 B0752/21
B0757/13 B1369/01
collaterally (1) C0524/19
collation (4) A0365/13
B0836/15 B1191/19 B1315/11
collect (5) A0586/21
B0964/10 C0182/05 C0406/32 C0530/24
collected (18) A0172/07 A0535/24
A0540/21 A0625/10 A0693/05 B0736/07
B0853/10 B1322/08 C0188/23 C0188/40
C0389/20 C0398/02 C0532/15 C0536/21
C0552/26 C0570/06 C0575/32 C0577/24
collectedly (1) B0763/06
collectedness (1) A0406/14
collecting (13) A0705/12
B0751/02 B0968/25 B1239/10 B1270/10
C0078/16 C0139/21 C0155/27 C0156/16
C0172/05 C0177/24 C0539/27 C0564/20
collection (4) A0027/10
B0807/25 B0873/17 C0172/31
collectively (1) B0747/07
collector (1) B0873/16
College (1) C0427/33
college (5) A0071/27
A0293/16 A0294/V A0294/V B0906/16
colleges (2) C0427/34 C0427/35
collision (4) A0582/33
A0601/08 C0549/13 C0550/09
collocation (2) A0408/13 B0837/18
collocations (1) A0708/31
colloquialism (1) B1140/28
Colloquy (1) A0608/T
colloquy (4) B0821/29
B1030/19 B1059/05 B1188/17
Cologne (1) A0301/05
Colonial (1) B1162/28
colonnades (1) A0122/17
colony (2) B1159/31 C0152/24
color (52)
color-grouping (1) B1273/33
colored (5) A0022/08

->A0280/29 A0325/23 A0349/14 B1250/21
coloring (5) A0320/26
A0441/11 B0814/31 B1163/21 C0538/35
colorless (3) A0500/05
A0563/V B1104/21
colors (18) A0181/20 A0495/03
A0497/14 A0497/28 A0501/22 A0628/31
A0673/11 A0689/07 A0695/27 A0695/28
A0708/03 B0832/23 B1165/04 B1180/02
B1273/02 B1340/17 C0532/24 C0542/08
colossal (9) A0027/02
A0029/24 A0035/21 A0066/05 A0144/01
A0297/V A0380/18 A0600/26 B1261/14
colour (11) A0312/V
A0313/V A0328/V C0065/09 C0151/15
C0167/23 C0171/21 C0171/41 C0193/19
C0203/30 C0204/13
colouring (1) A0320/V
colourless (1) C0171/41
Colquhoun (1) C0155/34
Columbia (6) C0070/34 C0525/20
C0527/26 C0527/39 C0528/02 C0528/19
Columbia/River (1) C0527/24
Columbiad (2) B1101/05 B1275/V
column (2) B1101/09 B1101/10
columnar (2) B1180/17 B1333/02
columns (10) A0075/01 A0145/04
A0195/V B0734/09 B1101/10 B1143/31
B1192/12 B1192/21 B1385/16 C0577/09
com'd (2) B1103/07 B1103/09
com'd> (2) A0465/05 A0469/12
Combat (1) A0301/01
combat (1) A0356/14
combat (4) A0303/30
A0345/01 A0356/15 B0740/15
combating (1) B0734/08
combativeness (4) B1220/04
B1221/08 B1221/09 B1221/14
combats (1) B0949/14
combattendo (1) A0344/32
Combe (1) A0507/V
combed (2) A0086/27 A0100/04
combination (9) A0294/12
A0580/23 A0707/11 B0837/28 B0838/12
B0838/29 B0839/04 B1272/10 B1272/24
combinations (6) A0398/03 A0707/24
A0708/06 B0838/23 B1272/V B1273/05
combine (3) A0536/22
A0536/23 A0558/07
combined (4) A0711/25
B1134/20 B1276/28 B1335/20
combing (2) A0566/26 C0060/16
combings (1) C0067/37
combining (4) A0531/01
A0707/10 B1145/03 B1272/09
combustibility (1) B1354/18
combustible (1) A0410/06
combustion (2) A0460/27 A0460/35
come (168)
come-at-able (1) A0653/14
comedies (1) B0878/06
comers (1) C0174/20
comes (17) A0085/11
A0124/27 A0125/23 A0143/04 A0252/23
A0319/14 A0581/27 A0674/09 A0683/19
->B0733/24 B0769/07 B1091/18 B1091/29
B1091/33 B1163/18 C0430/04 C0543/06
comet (11) A0457/35
A0458/12 A0459/10 A0459/24 A0460/04
A0461/05 B0870/11 C0401/24 C0401/30
C0401/35 C0423/09
comet's (5) A0458/30
C0401/28 C0401/32 C0401/37 C0402/10
cometary (1) A0458/18
cometh (2) A0195/12 A0383/03
comets (5) A0457/21
A0457/29 A0459/05 B1035/21 B1214/35
comfort (14) A0642/24 B0794/20
B0878/01 C0069/18 C0073/25 C0083/36
C0120/09 C0120/13 C0127/22 C0138/40
C0140/37 C0141/12 C0145/23 C0561/21
comfortable (17) A0101/03
A0205/03 B0875/15 B0879/27 B0975/16
B1008/21 B1158/22 B1186/07 B1337/03
B1347/26 C0066/37 C0068/02 C0070/09
C0070/26 C0101/30 C0545/25 C0561/13
comfortably (4) A0508/34
C0099/33 C0146/03 C0541/10
comforted (1) B1317/27
comforter (1) B0967/23
comfortless (1) A0401/14
comforts (3) A0101/21
C0066/41 C0068/19
comic (2) A0091/17 A0110/19
comicality (1) A0123/08
coming (77)
command (13) A0654/17
B0901/20 B0944/26 B1077/34 B1348/03
C0065/36 C0074/28 C0095/33 C0103/35
C0146/35 C0182/18 C0200/25 C0528/09
commandant (1) C0539/32
commanded (4) A0447/14
B1167/26 C0537/40 C0568/21
commander (4) C0156/34
C0157/14 C0166/26 C0387/M
commander-in-chief (1) C0554/12
commanding (4) A0312/09
A0349/11 A0378/17 B1247/22
commands (2) C0178/12 C0179/13
comme (2) A0035/05 B1207/06
commemorated (1) A0109/10
commemorates (1) B1304/36
commence (13) A0128/12
A0173/19 A0178/28 A0206/02 A0609/05
A0609/06 B0837/10 B0878/34 B0927/23
B1127/19 B1236/10 C0186/28 C0199/37
commenced (46) A0054/32 A0059/17
A0063/33 A0067/08 A0092/26 A0112/01
A0128/13 A0253/07 A0293/05 A0303/01
A0382/25 A0444/32 A0479/33 A0674/14
B0836/15 B0898/V B1004/31 B1020/21
B1075/19 B1075/34 B1076/32 B1144/29
B1178/33 B1236/34 B1277/20 B1333/29
C0070/22 C0073/07 C0077/05 C0091/12
C0108/35 C0126/31 C0136/30 C0168/06
C0169/16 C0176/04 C0187/34 C0191/26
C0193/18 C0406/37 C0536/15 C0536/28
C0554/17 C0554/25 C0567/35 C0568/27
commencement (13) A0161/26
A0278/37 A0323/20 A0348/18 B0737/14

->B0754/27 B0837/30 B1270/35 B1372/16
C0113/25 C0130/13 C0204/07 C0428/08
commencements (1) B0837/26
commences (5) A0241/27
B0738/01 B1131/05 B1282/35 C0056/31
commencing (5) A0126/23
A0246/23 B0838/02 B1130/19 C0194/21
commendable (3) A0294/V
A0380/17 B1005/08
commendation (2) B1139/04 B1380/23
commensurate (3) A0577/M
B0989/20 C0421/32
comment (10) A0380/20 A0408/25
A0434/27 B0810/36 B0849/07 B0862/24
B1030/18 B1318/10 C0207/27 C0523/17
commentaries (1) B1115/23
commentary (5) A0499/10
A0531/13 A0621/12 B1091/24 B1115/11
commentators (1) B1189/16
commented (3) B0748/04
B0766/02 B1115/37
commenting (2) A0300/32 A0381/22
comments (10) A0101/18 A0544/26
A0568/09 B0728/25 B0735/03 B0735/04
B0908/28 B0924/19 B1113/05 B1114/09
commerce (4) A0381/31
C0176/22 C0178/01 C0178/07
Commercial/Advertiser (1) B0740/33
commincement> (1) A0468/16
commingle (1) C0172/07
commingled (4) A0414/10
A0568/01 A0662/04 C0444/V
commingling (1) A0614/13
Commire, P. (1) A0603/35
commiseration (4) A0071/16
A0071/21 A0078/37 C0567/32
commission (5) A0144/24
A0483/16 A0483/25 B0747/09 C0539/31
commit (7) A0366/14
B0901/02 B0932/34 B0993/06 B1113/06
B1158/09 B1359/30
commits (1) B1383/16
committal (1) B1054/26
committed (48) A0055/27
A0065/08 A0345/19 A0353/07 A0440/28
A0528/28 A0544/14 A0544/15 A0548/13
A0549/02 A0549/07 A0551/V A0556/19
A0688/16 B0726/28 B0732/02 B0732/16
B0734/21 B0736/27 B0737/13 B0738/27
B0738/31 B0738/33 B0739/04 B0739/09
B0739/10 B0739/25 B0739/28 B0744/22
B0744/26 B0757/26 B0757/29 B0757/30
B0757/31 B0764/04 B0764/19 B0769/29
B0895/09 B0900/04 B0977/30 B0991/33
B1050/31 B1054/14 B1192/02 C0079/02
C0197/09 C0389/07 C0419/12
committee (1) B0727/25
committing (3) B0852/11
B0852/25 C0399/28
commodious (1) B1298/26
commodities (3) A0073/16
C0097/25 C0179/40
Commodus (1) A0156/17
Common (1) B1092/23
common (98)
common-place (7) A0091/11
A0173/01 A0272/09 A0341/10 A0548/V
B0850/03 B1314/32
common-places (1) A0508/18
common-sense (1) B0843/28
commonalty (1) A0242/01
commoner (1) A0440/31
commonest (5) A0210/16
A0314/06 A0314/V B0989/02 B1168/10
commonly (5) A0529/31
A0548/24 A0689/26 C0404/11 C0432/26
commotion (10) A0123/25 A0127/13
A0512/11 A0610/07 B0958/33 B1352/28
C0147/03 C0205/03 C0205/15 C0545/36
communicate (6) A0072/12 A0266/30
B1038/04 B1247/19 C0090/09 C0425/33
communicated (12) A0024/22
A0056/28 A0058/16 A0066/17 A0069/05
A0446/29 B1081/20 C0096/11 C0136/17
C0392/19 C0394/06 C0565/06
communicates (2) B1038/09 B1119/20
communicating (2) A0436/27 B1071/24
communication (13) A0054/06
A0063/14 A0267/16 A0268/06 B0926/10
B1130/01 C0112/08 C0207/42 C0390/36
C0391/06 C0525/18 C0525/23 C0527/23
communications (12) B0753/32
B0753/37 B0760/32 B0760/33 B0761/04
B0761/10 B0761/11 B0769/02 B0770/05
B0770/07 B0770/11 C0426/17
communicative (2) A0382/20 C0549/38
communion (7) A0101/04
A0217/V A0445/10 A0532/01 B1122/33
C0065/27 C0094/38
community (4) A0293/25
C0156/19 C0544/36 C0546/05
compact (5) A0144/13
B0772/07 C0094/13 C0159/09 C0395/32
compactly (1) C0098/17
compacts (1) A0054/15
companies (1) A0498/24
companion (46) A0139/19 A0139/30
A0240/15 A0241/09 A0244/17 A0251/05
A0253/15 A0381/02 A0401/28 A0404/01
A0415/03 A0445/35 A0547/02 A0564/21
A0564/22 A0578/15 B0755/25 B0825/14
B0889/06 B0891/27 B0897/24 B0905/V
B0913/08 B0916/16 B0949/08 B1002/06
B1003/27 B1021/22 C0058/37 C0061/03
C0064/34 C0066/35 C0069/14 C0073/28
C0083/07 C0091/05 C0096/35 C0101/31
C0143/09 C0182/14 C0183/23 C0197/18
C0198/30 C0199/21 C0408/33 C0532/14
companion-hatch (4) C0110/31
C0120/32 C0136/21 C0140/24
companion-ladder (4) A0137/03
C0089/21 C0109/25 C0121/16
companion-way (12) B0932/22
C0085/23 C0088/41 C0090/26 C0105/21
C0108/33 C0109/17 C0111/05 C0111/26
C0115/40 C0122/26 C0129/12
companion's (4) A0105/17
A0251/27 C0100/21 C0183/27
companionless (1) A0025/26
companions (50) A0056/14 A0066/03

->A0190/06 A0218/V A0245/19 A0295/27
A0348/21 A0398/16 A0431/29 A0432/V
A0433/15 A0530/02 A0589/03 A0594/19
B0760/19 B0850/10 B0891/17 B0947/09
B1353/33 B1363/15 C0110/37 C0111/21
C0116/07 C0116/20 C0118/07 C0118/35
C0124/11 C0126/26 C0127/33 C0128/10
C0128/34 C0129/25 C0130/25 C0131/10
C0131/28 C0134/11 C0134/30 C0135/05
C0136/17 C0181/27 C0184/14 C0185/22
C0186/12 C0187/35 C0191/30 C0205/07
C0388/40 C0530/38 C0545/24 C0569/16
companionship (2) A0712/04 B0768/33
Company (4) B0879/17
B0879/24 C0525/09 C0529/17
company (78)
company's (1) B1091/15
comparable (1) B0864/07
comparative (6) B0948/06 B1162/30
C0136/02 C0138/40 C0139/16 C0575/07
comparatively (22) A0426/15 A0513/10
A0529/01 B0761/28 B0831/28 B0836/14
B0862/02 B0897/12 B0980/29 B1074/15
B1074/33 B1235/30 C0095/16 C0096/37
C0118/28 C0120/25 C0159/24 C0396/11
C0400/40 C0402/30 C0403/09 C0418/12
compare (7) A0397/15
B0770/05 B0770/07 B0770/10 B1133/08
B1157/25 B1340/03
compared (15) A0356/V
A0553/15 B0898/01 B1011/24 B1071/26
B1080/31 B1191/06 B1193/07 B1280/03
C0387/20 C0401/07 C0402/32 C0408/11
C0433/05 C0531/25
compares (2) B0749/14 B1136/10
comparing (3) A0356/15
A0530/08 C0401/23
comparison (21) A0122/09
A0298/V A0401/31 A0488/02 A0527/V
A0611/13 A0644/19 A0667/61 B0741/14
B0862/01 B1039/19 B1072/12 B1075/04
B1080/29 B1128/14 B1162/31 B1248/03
B1281/27 B1300/16 C0408/09 C0571/13
comparisons (2) A0081/33 B0863/16
compartment (2) B0853/06 B1336/08
compartments (3) A0081/36
B0980/20 B0991/02
compass (10) A0405/20 B1075/05
C0060/03 C0088/23 C0166/10 C0167/37
C0396/06 C0429/06 C0439/V C0533/34
compassion (4) A0023/02
A0108/02 B1130/35 C0147/36
compassionating (1) A0071/22
compassless (1) A0638/12
compatible (1) B1164/27
compeers (1) A0708/24
compel (1) B0948/18
compelled (4) A0234/14
B0856/18 B0890/20 B1123/15
compels (3) B0771/28
B1114/26 B1220/01
compendious (1) B0871/30
compendium (1) A0058/29
compensated (1) B1296/11
compensation (3) B0767/26
->B1135/10 B1346/16
compete (1) A0431/23
competent (2) A0650/V B0879/01
competing (1) A0183/25
competition (6) A0432/06 A0488/11
A0708/02 B1136/08 B1138/26 B1273/01
competitors (1) B1311/16
compilation (1) C0056/15
compilations (1) A0283/29
compiled (1) B1082/03
compiler (1) B1234/03
complacent (1) A0241/17
complacently (1) B0944/16
complain (8) A0246/10
A0277/23 B0739/28 B0811/20 B1091/09
B1208/01 B1297/21 C0411/29
complained (3) B0990/25
B1080/04 C0141/08
complaining (1) C0561/10
complains (1) B1091/09
complaint (3) A0085/05
B0900/26 C0130/12
complaisance (1) B0816/31
complate> (1) A0470/V
complately> (1) A0467/24
Complete (1) B1141/07
complete (40) A0088/09
A0351/10 A0427/28 A0470/01 A0553/25
A0586/02 A0591/20 A0600/04 A0613/08
B0809/18 B0825/23 B0852/33 B0905/17
B0941/31 B0977/23 B1035/29 B1037/05
B1070/24 B1129/13 B1179/15 B1242/31
B1351/09 B1354/20 B1380/12 C0069/06
C0075/06 C0115/07 C0115/12 C0117/18
C0124/06 C0189/23 C0208/16 C0389/28
C0402/27 C0409/22 C0529/02 C0533/06
C0543/18 C0569/27 C0573/20
completed (30) A0102/24 A0104/19
A0105/16 A0141/09 A0217/02 A0299/16
A0691/26 B0773/25 B0815/23 B0818/08
B0831/31 B0913/26 B0980/18 B1071/16
B1081/32 B1105/25 B1143/23 B1178/12
B1262/33 C0091/26 C0092/39 C0188/14
C0190/40 C0203/05 C0207/03 C0394/37
C0411/17 C0416/06 C0523/06 C0575/40
completely (57)
completeness (1) C0190/15
completes (1) B1208/15
completing (1) A0686/02
completion (1) C0393/10
complex (6) A0294/12 A0528/25
B0907/04 B1039/08 B1072/12 B1164/31
complexion (16) A0246/33
A0401/30 A0509/19 B0735/23 B0736/04
B0768/31 B0768/31 B0769/08 B0769/09
B0770/14 B0940/10 B1114/07 B1360/24
C0168/14 C0169/09 C0533/11
complexity (1) B1039/13
compliance (4) A0107/27
A0264/36 A0441/32 B0818/23
complicate (1) B1317/04
complicated (1) B1072/16
complied (1) B1057/02
compliment (6) A0108/11 A0159/24
B0728/16 B0728/21 B1136/25 B1381/08

complimented (2) B1380/05 B1380/33
compliments (5) A0270/26
B1049/13 B1133/20 B1381/04 B1381/09
comply (6) A0074/11 A0074/22
A0285/24 A0441/33 B1110/05 C0555/27
complying (3) A0278/25
A0653/27 C0055/25
component (2) A0707/29 B1272/29
compose (4) A0338/17
A0473/12 B0899/28 B1208/12
composed (24) A0069/19
A0318/05 A0340/02 A0588/25 A0681/M
B0723/18 B0811/02 B0823/07 B0944/03
B1037/13 B1037/16 B1073/03 B1105/23
B1133/35 B1144/02 B1179/24 B1192/24
B1292/29 B1301/29 C0183/35 C0388/20
C0572/11 C0573/08 C0578/26
composedly (1) B1372/11
composing (4) A0340/22
B1130/23 B1134/07 B1371/13
composite (1) B1013/02
composition (24) A0204/08
A0278/17 A0280/34 A0281/05 A0281/23
A0282/08 A0338/34 A0707/33 A0708/24
A0708/28 B0840/15 B0905/20 B1128/11
B1128/29 B1131/21 B1132/21 B1133/23
B1137/18 B1141/26 B1272/34 B1273/19
B1273/23 B1330/11 B1371/26
compositions (8) A0266/15
A0272/11 A0275/16 A0474/03 B1133/08
B1137/40 B1138/08 B1139/11
composure (8) A0024/25
A0092/28 A0112/03 A0249/34 A0444/01
B0894/27 B0932/04 B1277/27
compound (5) A0460/24
B0869/27 B0922/12 B1154/24 C0403/15
comprehend (49) A0069/01
A0262/22 A0378/12 A0388/34 A0514/12
A0535/05 A0555/26 A0559/30 A0583/11
A0609/03 A0624/24 A0683/31 A0696/13
B0736/26 B0752/09 B0761/24 B0855/09
B0922/22 B0927/32 B0939/05 B1010/11
B1035/25 B1037/01 B1039/28 B1105/07
B1108/24 B1115/26 B1131/26 B1134/13
B1135/13 B1137/32 B1158/31 B1185/01
B1190/16 B1191/10 B1213/15 B1220/16
B1233/12 B1260/19 B1291/03 B1293/36
B1294/11 B1301/08 B1339/04 C0063/30
C0176/36 C0190/36 C0392/28 C0537/29
comprehended (13) A0096/19
A0302/16 A0383/18 A0593/19 A0706/04
B0986/13 B1035/33 B1194/35 B1208/11
B1240/21 B1271/07 C0170/14 C0388/01
comprehending (2) A0058/13 B0748/17
comprehensible (3) A0529/29
B1220/25 B1313/15
comprehension (19) A0080/31
A0086/07 A0096/20 A0112/07 A0217/09
A0252/29 A0389/15 A0529/22 A0534/08
A0545/28 A0555/26 B0975/13 B1037/33
B1038/02 B1130/26 B1138/29 B1222/13
B1302/01 C0427/14
comprehensive (6) A0086/15 A0611/33
B0752/28 B0990/17 B1294/18 C0178/04
comprehind> (1) A0466/06
compressed (3) B0853/25
B0967/13 B0980/03
compressing (1) C0397/39
compression (4) A0509/20
C0400/40 C0401/41 C0404/10
comprising (3) A0430/04
C0053/T C0152/11
compromised (1) A0487/26
comptant (1) B1135/18
compting-house (1) A0276/03
comptoir (1) B0753/08
compulsory (1) A0022/22
computation (1) A0138/12
computations (1) B1186/17
computed (1) C0423/19
comrades (1) C0563/18
Comus (1) A0347/26
con (1) A0621/01
con (2) B1144/22 C0065/01
concated> (1) A0468/V
concave (3) B1080/13
B1336/11 C0418/30
concavity (4) B1080/35
C0408/02 C0408/16 C0412/05
conceal (23) A0053/17
A0055/20 A0062/24 A0065/03 A0127/11
A0150/V A0163/24 A0326/01 A0564/07
A0567/V A0568/11 B0906/10 B0977/05
B0979/30 B0985/31 B0990/16 B0990/18
C0087/13 C0091/15 C0092/35 C0094/07
C0100/06 C0185/30
concealed (31) A0054/33
A0063/34 A0296/V A0434/22 A0552/22
A0675/10 B0759/14 B0769/V B0834/07
B0834/15 B0842/24 B0889/29 B0899/05
B0906/09 B0906/21 B0978/24 B0978/27
B0986/03 B0988/32 B1337/08 B1374/24
C0068/35 C0072/19 C0080/28 C0105/05
C0523/30 C0536/32 C0542/33 C0548/39
C0571/07 C0575/41
concealing (8) A0163/19
A0567/13 B0856/29 B0901/27 B0958/05
B1052/12 B1182/05 C0068/10
concealment (18) A0018/V A0141/02
A0141/10 A0141/33 A0530/20 A0564/07
B0796/05 B0858/12 B0986/01 B0986/03
B0986/13 B0988/35 B1053/26 B1057/36
C0069/12 C0186/32 C0189/04 C0199/09
concealments (1) B0756/29
conceals (1) B1018/07
conceded (1) A0458/02
conceit (2) A0079/39 B1114/18
conceited (1) A0483/V
conceits (1) B0865/23
conceivable (7) A0295/13
A0379/11 B1074/20 B1214/13 B1299/31
B1315/08 C0201/15
conceive (44) A0073/03
A0136/25 A0145/20 A0275/25 A0294/12
A0374/06 A0381/18 A0432/16 A0482/04
A0579/01 A0710/31 B0762/21 B0764/05
B0764/05 B0855/23 B0864/37 B0962/19
B1034/01 B1034/24 B1034/33 B1035/01
B1078/29 B1194/07 B1275/33 B1297/06
B1297/17 B1297/19 B1302/22 B1314/10

->B1314/15 B1315/18 B1315/22 B1315/26
B1315/27 B1315/35 B1332/36 B1333/10
B1340/13 B1350/22 C0059/39 C0063/07
C0143/23 C0182/10 C0427/14
conceived (42) A0053/21 A0096/15
A0226/24 A0230/23 A0353/25 A0402/30
A0473/33 A0592/21 A0615/19 A0667/63
A0704/22 A0705/26 B0789/09 B0904/20
B0960/34 B0966/V B0982/26 B1070/27
B1101/13 B1129/07 B1130/25 B1269/21
B1270/24 B1274/06 B1297/10 B1337/34
B1358/08 B1363/26 B1374/23 C0087/23
C0127/19 C0145/02 C0182/35 C0185/27
C0196/25 C0197/16 C0398/29 C0402/20
C0404/12 C0421/33 C0425/24 C0432/43
conceiving (2) B0807/32 B1037/36
concentrate (1) B0751/30
concentrated (1) A0546/02
concentration (3) A0406/15
A0707/16 B1272/14
concentrations (1) A0499/V
concentrative (2) A0528/31 A0529/27
concentric (1) A0146/02
conception (33) A0071/01
A0079/34 A0104/05 A0158/12 A0276/36
A0293/03 A0555/24 A0581/09 A0615/05
A0707/02 B0829/35 B0869/10 B0895/14
B1034/18 B1035/02 B1038/01 B1039/30
B1115/35 B1115/36 B1160/29 B1213/30
B1239/34 B1248/09 B1277/14 B1301/33
B1315/30 B1315/31 B1322/20 C0124/10
C0182/02 C0185/10 C0404/20 C0573/30
conceptions (9) A0078/18
A0141/26 A0141/27 A0234/03 A0405/28
A0673/13 C0073/17 C0078/12 C0197/33
concern (6) A0085/09 B0756/30
B0948/10 C0055/08 C0190/36 C0538/32
concerned (9) A0234/15
B0728/13 B0836/02 B0993/02 B1184/24
B1233/04 C0086/18 C0092/29 C0528/06
concerning (16) A0263/07
A0275/23 A0301/11 B0734/18 B0890/17
B0988/31 B1031/02 B1129/16 B1189/24
B1190/23 B1303/10 C0205/06 C0207/36
C0389/02 C0395/20 C0413/16
concerns (9) A0250/19
A0250/19 A0286/10 A0428/12 A0434/11
A0445/03 B0877/15 B1357/09 C0093/04
concert (3) A0355/15
B1015/03 B1046/V
concerted (3) A0094/20
A0355/18 C0151/41
<u>concerto</u> (1) B1015/05
concessions (1) C0555/29
<u>concetto</u> (1) A0161/03
<u>concierge</u> (1) A0546/20
conciliate (1) C0393/07
conciliation (1) B0866/18
concise (2) A0386/25 A0654/V
concision (1) A0402/22
conclave (1) B1127/12
conclude (6) A0075/05 A0109/19
A0150/V B0819/29 B0879/19 C0082/40
concluded (50) A0054/02 A0063/11
A0107/15 A0323/25 A0414/02 A0631/01
->B0728/16 B0822/35 B0828/22 B0844/18
B0892/28 B0899/13 B0913/18 B0915/07
B0991/11 B1005/21 B1052/02 B1056/06
B1076/09 B1102/11 B1106/19 B1115/31
B1135/07 B1135/24 B1140/06 B1157/12
B1178/07 B1193/14 B1239/18 B1248/05
C0056/21 C0076/10 C0076/25 C0077/29
C0084/21 C0092/14 C0092/30 C0117/31
C0118/02 C0126/06 C0141/32 C0159/26
C0168/22 C0172/26 C0174/15 C0184/09
C0425/31 C0539/11 C0539/26 C0558/21
concludes (1) B0772/08
concluding (15) A0299/05
A0319/30 A0356/11 B0724/10 B1114/29
B1139/15 B1185/14 B1226/14 B1240/05
B1318/03 B1331/05 C0080/13 C0129/35
C0175/27 C0429/28
conclusion (53)
conclusions (7) A0212/21
A0402/18 A0535/13 A0709/11 B0991/26
C0208/13 C0439/V
conclusive (12) A0150/V
A0553/14 A0583/12 B0732/29 B0738/03
B0738/04 B1054/32 B1136/01 C0207/31
C0429/48 C0546/10 C0546/23
conclusively (1) B0751/V
concocted (4) A0433/22
B0915/19 B1194/06 B1219/17
concocting (1) B0916/29
concoctor (1) B1101/30
Concord (2) B1371/31 B1372/03
concordance (1) B0815/V
concrete (1) A0405/27
concretely (1) B1178/04
concubines (2) A0126/17 A0127/22
concur (1) C0162/08
concurred (1) A0491/06
concurrence (2) A0655/15 A0708/24
concussion (8) A0079/17
C0115/27 C0181/41 C0184/09 C0184/27
C0190/05 C0396/34 C0446/V
concussions (1) B1080/20
<u>Condamnes</u> (1) A0106/05
condemn (1) C0134/41
condemnation (1) A0252/11
condemned (4) A0204/34
A0684/24 A0684/29 B1224/02
condemning (1) C0095/01
condensation (7) A0408/20
C0394/33 C0401/41 C0410/38 C0420/18
C0424/33 C0535/41
condense (2) C0402/22 C0419/32
condensed (6) B1236/24 B1321/02
B1321/04 B1321/14 C0402/13 C0409/15
condenser (9) C0407/06
C0409/09 C0409/14 C0410/34 C0411/07
C0416/11 C0420/39 C0424/07 C0424/12
condensing (4) C0396/09
C0405/15 C0407/30 C0424/39
condescended (5) A0251/02
A0625/23 B1109/06 B1208/18 C0188/15
condescends (1) B1381/03
condescension (1) A0045/27
condiment (1) B1178/06
condition (122)

conditionally (1) C0394/06
conditioned (1) B0887/14
conditions (20) A0252/05
A0408/08 A0408/12 A0638/17 A0687/29
A0703/17 B0742/21 B0757/04 B0890/30
B1037/06 B1090/13 B1207/11 B1213/17
B1214/06 B1220/30 B1268/16 B1268/28
C0097/31 C0099/28 C0134/14
condor (2) A0152/04 A0318/20
Condorcet (5) A0109/32
A0176/09 A0180/30 A0703/05 B1268/05
conduct (44) A0021/07
A0026/18 A0151/10 A0248/29 A0300/02
A0386/18 A0432/19 A0442/19 B0747/26
B0810/35 B0812/14 B0843/34 B0894/15
B0895/29 B0899/11 B0926/05 B1014/01
B1032/12 B1054/19 B1116/03 B1183/12
B1183/23 B1207/12 B1221/07 C0059/30
C0066/12 C0076/23 C0080/32 C0081/23
C0093/06 C0100/31 C0101/04 C0123/25
C0128/13 C0129/01 C0131/19 C0131/32
C0134/34 C0169/12 C0177/16 C0555/29
C0566/36 C0569/09 C0569/18
conducted (9) A0104/21
A0296/V A0400/23 B0731/25 B1007/26
B1059/02 B1329/07 C0139/23 C0175/05
conducting (1) A0508/20
conductor (1) B1127/10
conduit (2) A0053/14 A0062/21
cone (4) A0122/30
C0154/35 C0154/36 C0388/29
cones (1) B1092/17
confectioner (2) A0543/01 A0560/06
confederacy (1) B1299/29
confederation (1) A0204/03
confer (1) B0874/01
conference (7) A0024/24
A0045/10 A0339/17 A0339/19 B0925/07
B1128/07 C0066/23
conferred (2) B1152/19 B1346/05
confess (33) A0163/21
A0205/02 A0251/29 A0324/26 A0355/33
A0366/04 A0388/25 A0533/13 A0564/08
B0809/27 B0840/04 B0851/06 B0855/16
B0908/08 B0923/02 B0924/15 B0926/28
B0932/32 B0993/12 B1017/07 B1017/18
B1101/06 B1104/13 B1133/11 B1190/18
B1191/09 B1225/17 B1271/04 B1310/08
B1358/23 B1382/32 C0166/25 C0415/01
confessed (9) A0106/01
A0145/26 A0166/V A0583/11 B0907/21
B1359/04 B1375/10 C0064/36 C0569/12
confessing (1) A0166/12
confession (12) A0058/28
B0724/21 B0772/V B0887/05 B0906/13
B0906/24 B0906/25 B1057/28 B1058/11
B1225/11 B1225/V B1363/33
Confessions (1) A0339/29
confessions (2) A0317/20 B0723/22
confessor (1) B1154/12
confessors (1) A0506/04
confide (2) B0816/07 C0563/38
confided (2) A0532/10 B0976/07
confidence (23) A0037/11
A0075/12 A0205/04 A0301/17 A0316/02
->A0350/04 A0389/10 A0446/29 B0748/26
B0755/12 B0764/22 B0765/10 B0765/10
B0796/29 B0941/15 B0983/25 B1006/18
B1142/07 B1313/19 C0091/25 C0172/27
C0404/15 C0416/07
confident (6) A0297/V A0350/10
A0384/14 B1369/17 C0095/36 C0166/17
confidential (2) A0303/08 C0527/20
confidentially (1) B1092/27
confidently (6) A0667/67 B0730/20
B1059/20 B1360/32 C0088/02 C0402/25
confiding (3) B0906/10
C0094/37 C0199/22
configuration (1) A0215/V
confine (9) A0069/18
A0247/33 A0352/18 B0752/03 B1038/19
B1297/26 B1316/10 C0198/03 C0536/24
confined (29) A0070/31
A0079/39 A0081/05 A0144/02 A0173/07
A0178/12 A0248/19 A0330/14 A0406/08
A0565/03 A0601/18 A0616/08 B0749/20
B0811/25 B1004/23 B1006/24 B1089/14
B1090/16 B1295/31 B1311/28 C0071/26
C0081/39 C0084/36 C0112/04 C0402/10
C0410/41 C0418/09 C0552/30 C0562/29
confinement (7) B1004/15
B1016/34 B1163/38 C0094/16 C0095/14
C0095/22 C0096/14
confines (4) A0530/06
A0582/35 C0182/32 C0399/41
confining (5) A0056/05
A0065/28 A0496/20 B1163/06 C0090/19
confirm (4) B0946/07
B1052/07 C0208/10 C0413/15
confirmation (8) A0064/15
A0536/09 B0822/28 B1049/30 C0208/05
C0407/19 C0423/25 C0439/V
confirmed (15) A0059/24
A0684/13 A0689/33 A0708/23 B0723/23
B0837/24 B0842/01 B0916/06 B1030/24
B1058/28 B1234/21 B1273/18 B1349/23
C0094/18 C0192/12
conflagration (3) A0027/16
A0123/29 B0852/33
conflict (3) B1314/25
C0186/32 C0579/03
conflicting (7) A0157/25
A0298/V A0414/35 A0580/13 B0747/18
B1189/14 C0157/17
conformation (10) A0103/33 A0104/31
A0216/04 A0293/09 A0298/V A0379/32
A0402/19 A0460/18 B1247/29 B1249/27
conformity (1) B1055/15
confound (6) A0437/24 A0496/28
A0705/17 B0982/04 B1139/11 B1270/16
confounded (21) A0212/13
A0245/21 A0262/27 A0410/V A0434/13
A0499/30 A0530/28 A0547/19 A0613/03
A0650/15 A0664/23 A0690/11 B0737/05
B0894/28 B0914/05 B0987/20 B1114/30
B1144/01 B1178/03 B1207/35 B1247/18
confounding (2) A0547/31 B1138/08
confounds (2) A0581/11 A0600/02
confront (1) B0894/25
confronted (4) A0330/02

->A0676/23 B0894/33 B1225/18
confronting (3) A0299/23
B0911/14 B1102/22
confronts (1) B1280/30
Confucius (1) A0089/27
confused (19) A0078/12
A0151/15 A0217/05 A0354/04 A0436/17
A0590/28 A0608/09 A0673/01 B0826/15
B0826/34 B0873/13 B0908/08 B1096/19
C0059/35 C0063/39 C0068/37 C0070/37
C0077/06 C0116/15
confusedly (6) A0046/22 A0511/20
B0961/01 B0990/30 B1283/10 B1328/05
confusion (43) A0078/13
A0079/12 A0079/13 A0140/28 A0280/03
A0280/09 A0281/24 A0347/28 A0374/05
A0447/30 A0508/14 A0515/21 A0589/14
A0599/V A0626/02 A0686/30 A0688/23
B0726/05 B0744/25 B0839/10 B0839/V
B0894/06 B0907/01 B0908/23 B0930/35
B0945/18 B0977/11 B1020/09 B1033/33
B1036/16 B1076/19 B1325/04 B1350/20
C0073/18 C0089/16 C0110/27 C0116/22
C0165/01 C0166/36 C0198/20 C0422/09
C0429/07 C0557/34
confutation (2) A0067/29 A0074/33
confute (1) A0067/16
confuted (1) B0740/26
congeal (1) A0218/V
congealed (1) A0218/17
congealing (1) C0060/41
congenial (1) A0025/24
congeniality (1) A0433/07
conger (1) C0174/06
conglomeration (2) B1038/22
B1191/04
congratulate (3) B1179/18
C0115/10 C0129/14
congratulated (6) A0382/21 A0413/19
A0687/16 B0909/12 C0070/22 C0189/10
congratulating (1) C0188/35
congregated (2) B1332/36 C0549/04
congregation (1) C0562/26
Congress (3) A0623/34
B0956/13 C0527/20
conic (2) A0176/02 A0182/01
conical (6) A0086/28 A0100/04
B1257/19 C0415/31 C0422/31 C0576/29
conjecture (5) A0445/15
A0527/M A0667/44 A0695/17 C0208/13
conjectures (3) B0923/03
C0073/23 C0126/16
conjoined (3) A0189/14
A0432/19 C0207/39
conjoining (1) B1123/02
conjointly (2) B0859/05 B1283/13
conjunction (2) B1298/25 C0392/18
conjured (2) A0414/31 A0683/12
conjurer (1) C0427/18
conjuror (2) B0817/03 B1166/25
conjurors (2) B1166/16 B1169/06
Connaught (3) A0465/05
A0467/26 A0468/22
connect (2) A0402/11 C0073/19
connected (37) A0209/21
->A0320/13 A0329/24 A0408/11 A0427/33
A0428/16 A0432/25 A0478/31 A0536/20
B0754/05 B0828/26 B0830/28 B0835/29
B1047/23 B1069/29 B1071/13 B1137/11
B1138/06 B1139/09 B1180/13 B1248/26
B1334/03 B1361/02 B1362/19 C0055/13
C0065/30 C0075/40 C0079/29 C0085/08
C0087/04 C0118/22 C0193/10 C0207/01
C0207/11 C0392/27 C0394/25 C0409/38
connecting (4) B1071/21
B1077/12 B1159/02 C0071/07
connection (18) A0079/11 A0097/20
A0262/01 A0282/16 A0296/19 A0315/02
A0486/24 B0754/20 B0771/22 B0816/11
B0831/07 B1301/27 B1352/35 B1364/08
C0207/35 C0425/28 C0426/03 C0426/05
connections (3) A0704/22
B0902/06 B1269/21
connexion (15) A0315/V
A0436/04 B0731/28 B0751/08 B0757/26
B0770/32 B0770/33 B0829/23 B0831/04
B0831/23 B0833/07 C0064/12 C0101/06
C0208/14 C0208/16
connexions (1) A0539/27
connings (1) A0431/03
connivance (2) A0295/16 B0733/03
connoisseur (1) A0379/27
connoisseurship (1) B1257/07
conoissance (1) C0430/36
conquer (2) B0907/19 B0907/26
conquered (4) A0155/15
A0155/17 A0319/22 A0448/13
Conqueror (2) A0319/18 B0961/24
conqueror (2) A0319/22 A0414/19
conquerors (1) A0046/01
conquers (2) A0528/31 B0870/28
consated> (1) A0468/25
Conscience (1) A0426/M
conscience (18) A0021/13 A0108/17
A0490/27 A0507/02 A0568/15 A0626/18
A0629/27 B0853/30 B1045/05 B1059/21
B1153/15 B1169/26 B1178/09 B1185/20
B1207/13 B1271/01 C0107/21 C0558/41
conscientiously (8) A0065/16
A0386/09 A0474/01 A0627/17 B0871/06
B0873/33 B1050/13 B1192/34
conscientiousness (1) B1054/30
conscious (14) A0081/10 A0091/28
A0105/05 A0110/30 A0227/08 A0231/19
A0231/20 A0379/23 A0567/12 B0830/29
B0894/11 B0959/12 B1372/11 C0198/22
consciousness (26) A0022/14 A0079/29
A0080/10 A0166/24 A0226/32 A0226/33
A0231/06 A0399/24 A0406/20 A0612/31
A0615/33 A0616/01 A0616/17 A0663/V
A0682/19 A0683/29 B0944/10 B0948/01
B0961/27 B0962/36 B1279/02 B1317/24
C0063/33 C0130/21 C0397/12 C0397/32
consecrated (3) A0044/18
A0123/21 B1089/19
consecutive (2) B0928/33 B1104/11
consekvence (1) B1375/20
consent (9) A0651/12
A0653/12 A0653/13 B0901/21 B1096/01
B1107/13 B1346/06 C0135/33 C0141/37

consented (13) A0243/07
B0841/09 B0907/31 B0908/07 B0941/08
B0963/31 B1032/13 B1185/08 B1295/03
B1310/16 C0056/08 C0128/03 C0171/06
consenting (2) B0755/27 B0830/23
consequence (1) B1114/03
consequence (46) A0142/32 A0209/07
A0240/19 A0274/12 A0295/21 A0296/01
A0351/06 A0483/17 A0488/11 A0538/06
A0592/35 A0601/01 A0629/18 A0651/26
A0690/13 B0736/09 B0761/04 B0930/16
B0969/10 B1005/10 B1045/18 B1046/01
B1074/24 B1105/13 B1143/21 B1163/40
B1234/11 B1296/18 B1301/27 B1321/17
B1321/18 B1352/34 C0064/21 C0092/13
C0094/19 C0392/30 C0405/36 C0410/26
C0416/04 C0417/20 C0420/01 C0424/03
C0446/V C0542/27 C0547/35 C0549/14
consequences (29) A0019/14
A0053/30 A0063/01 A0227/02 A0231/13
A0249/21 A0542/28 A0567/22 A0625/20
A0706/33 B0723/M B0765/05 B0849/08
B1214/23 B1222/05 B1233/25 B1271/34
B1300/09 B1364/28 C0097/29 C0098/07
C0131/05 C0137/07 C0162/34 C0390/26
C0396/31 C0406/30 C0414/27 C0424/20
consequent (17) A0286/08
A0399/14 A0499/03 B0735/17 B0752/34
B0806/04 B0962/22 B0989/V B1074/29
B1081/01 C0097/35 C0098/01 C0145/12
C0404/04 C0410/24 C0426/01 C0556/06
consequently (39) A0035/27
A0072/26 A0109/03 A0136/04 A0140/23
A0152/02 A0266/27 A0276/25 A0280/26
A0337/07 A0343/01 A0459/16 A0696/26
B0851/17 B0863/27 B0887/02 B0926/02
B1052/13 B1075/03 B1314/24 B1369/15
C0056/10 C0056/24 C0061/12 C0070/41
C0084/32 C0088/31 C0090/12 C0128/41
C0133/06 C0136/34 C0148/04 C0182/23
C0402/34 C0411/40 C0415/16 C0420/16
C0430/10 C0535/41
conservatione (1) A0638/M
conservatories (1) B1007/18
considdeble (1) B1373/21
consider (27) A0034/08
A0097/02 A0300/08 A0340/25 A0341/08
A0491/18 B0727/29 B0756/V B0758/04
B0765/19 B0819/03 B0842/14 B0890/20
B0965/18 B0979/02 B0985/12 B1007/34
B1040/04 B1040/05 B1107/30 B1183/32
B1233/01 B1301/31 B1329/05 C0179/10
C0407/18 C0521/01
considerable (21) A0103/30
A0138/01 A0263/16 A0441/05 A0538/11
B0874/03 B1054/03 B1179/02 B1280/03
B1282/31 B1334/25 B1361/34 B1379/34
C0079/14 C0095/40 C0148/02 C0169/14
C0188/38 C0394/34 C0403/31 C0419/30
considerably (18) A0278/34 A0589/11
B0903/05 B0928/25 B1073/35 B1079/16
B1179/34 B1331/27 B1336/06 C0123/20
C0140/01 C0398/22 C0418/44 C0424/14
C0535/20 C0540/19 C0572/09 C0576/15
considerate (4) A0352/10
->A0650/10 B0897/03 B1104/25
consideration (67)
considerations (21) A0398/05
A0458/08 A0547/27 B0961/29 B0990/04
B0993/01 B1032/06 B1096/35 B1214/18
B1302/13 C0074/12 C0095/20 C0112/15
C0126/22 C0161/20 C0166/15 C0182/31
C0399/38 C0400/21 C0402/14 C0404/18
Considered (1) B0869/T
considered (93)
considering (2) A0544/29 B1273/36
considers (2) A0530/09 B1281/09
consigned (9) A0092/23
A0111/33 B0831/12 B0859/14 B0962/29
B1132/31 B1186/20 B1226/14 C0098/26
consignee (1) C0098/25
consigning (3) B0771/12
B0897/01 B1240/05
consist (4) A0226/30
A0231/04 B0864/28 B1280/13
consisted (25) A0087/28
A0211/20 A0245/25 A0293/21 A0296/18
B0732/27 B0826/12 B0841/11 B0889/08
B0984/33 B1187/16 B1192/21 B1333/25
B1340/07 C0093/01 C0168/18 C0173/03
C0173/15 C0174/40 C0175/33 C0180/23
C0530/36 C0534/22 C0542/11 C0548/14
consistency (15) A0080/11
B0843/26 B0843/29 B1276/26 B1298/10
B1298/12 B1298/22 B1298/23 B1316/21
B1316/34 B1316/34 B1316/35 C0171/39
C0204/14 C0535/36
consistent (2) B1301/13 B1316/19
consisting (10) A0100/28 A0136/31
A0246/27 A0262/36 A0262/37 A0263/01
A0611/27 C0098/21 C0546/36 C0551/03
Consistory (1) B1390/14
consists (15) A0161/08
A0341/12 A0342/06 A0582/08 A0710/24
B0806/07 B1071/10 B1160/15 B1163/28
B1169/17 B1275/27 C0151/14 C0152/38
C0154/24 C0577/21
consolation (7) A0435/07
A0510/02 B0900/26 B0965/24 B1170/02
B1346/10 C0145/01
consolations (1) B0900/14
consolatory (3) A0054/12
A0063/19 C0100/25
console (3) B0898/11
C0088/32 C0120/18
consoled (1) A0385/03
consoles (1) B0873/05
consolidation (1) B1194/09
consoling (4) A0057/22
A0068/05 B0896/11 C0076/17
consort (1) A0250/12
conspicuous (8) A0178/10
A0240/14 A0247/22 A0382/V B0850/09
B0861/08 B0864/31 C0423/32
conspicuously (3) A0104/08
B0764/15 B0991/07
conspiracy (2) B1018/35 B1092/19
conspire (1) B0865/09
conspired (1) B0726/29
constables (3) B0879/31

->B1053/20 B1053/27
constant (19) A0225/21
A0229/18 A0415/14 A0612/13 A0613/34
A0623/12 B0949/08 B0989/21 B1078/19
B1278/16 B1278/17 B1279/12 C0084/04
C0089/13 C0121/25 C0138/08 C0167/04
C0425/36 C0576/11
Constantinople (1) A0667/14
constantly (24) A0368/01
A0434/10 A0500/09 A0579/18 A0582/10
B0928/24 B1126/08 B1136/16 C0055/06
C0089/12 C0095/20 C0114/14 C0117/09
C0123/37 C0141/18 C0157/38 C0180/17
C0203/18 C0203/23 C0401/14 C0401/34
C0403/24 C0416/20 C0548/25
consternation (2) A0053/11 A0062/17
constituent (4) A0271/04
A0273/16 A0527/V C0393/36
constitute (7) A0631/10
A0708/19 A0708/20 B1273/14 B1273/15
C0173/35 C0207/43
constituted (10) A0141/24 A0429/12
A0431/22 B0724/16 B0747/25 B0765/12
B0769/10 B0854/05 B0855/25 B1021/28
constitutes (3) A0638/21
A0654/18 B0869/20
constituting (1) A0496/19
constitution (13) A0059/05
A0204/02 A0324/09 A0486/27 A0704/17
B1034/18 B1034/21 B1034/32 B1194/06
B1234/15 B1269/16 C0130/15 C0404/16
constitutional (7) A0402/31
A0427/25 A0433/27 A0435/01 A0440/11
B0900/27 B1346/11
constitutionally (1) A0378/10
constrained (7) A0099/22
A0106/29 A0401/22 A0672/28 B1139/05
B1381/10 C0406/34
constraint (1) A0380/15
constriction (2) A0460/16 B1080/04
construct (3) B0835/27
B1072/19 B1132/09
constructed (20) A0046/19
A0689/24 B0836/20 B0857/05 B0858/26
B0858/28 B1074/16 B1132/17 B1166/20
B1168/03 B1261/13 B1292/35 B1300/02
B1337/25 C0151/41 C0152/35 C0174/36
C0430/21 C0547/16 C0576/01
constructing (3) B0835/19
B1164/23 C0394/08
construction (19) A0081/37
A0100/35 A0143/18 A0298/V A0479/16
B0889/24 B0889/V B0895/29 B1034/V
B1069/26 B1072/29 B1383/31 C0106/14
C0147/16 C0393/21 C0411/38 C0425/40
C0540/24 C0552/32
<u>constructionem</u> (3) A0301/12
A0302/19 A0303/04
constructive (1) A0530/30
constructiveness (2) B0870/23
B1220/04
constructs (1) C0432/45
construed (2) A0159/23 B1105/04
consubstantialism (2) A0175/15
A0181/05
consul (1) A0294/V
consult (7) A0059/20
A0067/11 A0366/18 B0817/18 B0975/05
B1151/02 B1191/27
consultation (1) C0088/25
<u>Consultations</u> (1) C0430/32
consulting (2) B1257/28 C0537/26
consults (1) B1221/19
consumed (15) A0323/22
A0353/10 A0688/02 A0689/20 B0890/25
B0898/11 B1133/09 B1145/20 C0081/11
C0135/32 C0141/32 C0188/20 C0191/18
C0198/02 C0569/07
consuming (8) A0214/27
A0226/10 A0227/16 A0232/03 A0235/01
A0323/17 A0329/10 B1371/26
consummate (4) A0295/17
A0432/17 B0852/18 B1195/05
consummated (4) B0732/02
B0738/28 B1100/01 B1144/27
consummation (5) A0263/22
A0461/08 B1226/04 C0135/25 C0181/09
consumption (2) A0020/V A0247/01
consumptive (1) A0249/17
contact (21) A0457/28
A0457/28 A0458/05 A0458/27 A0459/14
A0510/05 A0615/32 A0631/15 A0693/04
B0960/21 B1057/26 B1107/15 B1168/29
B1181/26 B1182/18 B1182/30 B1352/26
C0061/15 C0113/19 C0144/29 C0410/42
contagion (1) A0671/05
contain (13) A0079/32
A0373/27 B0793/22 B0925/08 B1302/27
B1381/13 C0128/06 C0131/14 C0207/17
C0390/35 C0393/29 C0394/38 C0533/17
contained (16) A0057/10
A0067/04 A0267/32 A0556/05 B0931/20
B1071/01 B1128/25 B1160/09 B1322/14
C0069/17 C0095/12 C0396/10 C0414/02
C0424/30 C0524/17 C0535/37
containing (18) A0240/T A0264/27
A0367/27 A0537/33 B0950/05 B1004/02
B1010/24 B1011/03 B1073/04 B1073/25
B1135/35 B1304/01 B1362/30 C0068/17
C0082/11 C0137/20 C0394/22 C0415/20
contains (2) B1096/07 B1163/28
contaminated (1) C0180/11
contemns (1) A0601/27
contemplate (1) A0611/38
contemplated (7) A0105/08
A0440/04 A0441/13 A0602/16 C0522/37
C0523/03 C0536/22
contemplating (1) B0809/26
contemplation (38) A0029/03 A0104/13
A0140/16 A0166/01 A0211/27 A0215/10
A0215/32 A0314/14 A0348/02 A0352/34
A0397/22 A0405/26 A0435/21 A0486/09
A0507/29 A0515/27 A0545/20 A0600/16
A0663/09 A0696/36 A0705/33 B0756/21
B0763/19 B0772/25 B0862/11 B0929/05
B1057/23 B1128/13 B1157/20 B1192/08
B1269/36 C0130/33 C0199/30 C0391/32
C0422/10 C0422/21 C0438/V C0537/15
contemplations (1) A0353/10
contemplative (4) A0135/04

->A0610/33 B0976/03 B1102/01
contemporaries (2) B1136/30
B1293/22
contemporary (2) A0101/10 B1310/14
contempt (20) A0068/18
A0297/17 A0355/06 A0444/01 A0652/09
A0681/14 A0704/03 A0706/18 A0712/02
B1105/04 B1106/18 B1269/03 B1271/20
B1277/05 B1298/01 B1298/32 B1317/35
B1371/11 C0175/30 C0425/12
contemptible (12) A0055/09
A0064/12 A0487/03 B0975/01 B1101/28
B1137/06 B1138/06 B1138/12 B1138/13
B1191/19 B1370/32 C0432/48
contemptuous (2) B1165/24 C0557/24
contemptuously (5) B0855/37
B0991/09 B1162/21 B1191/23 B1363/28
contend (3) B1207/24
C0149/14 C0401/21
contended (2) A0101/V A0297/16
contending (2) A0609/16 B1247/10
content (12) A0639/26
A0703/14 B0747/11 B0862/07 B0871/29
B0888/25 B0948/23 B1032/29 B1268/13
B1278/10 C0073/23 C0537/05
contented (4) A0340/31
B0817/01 C0071/15 C0140/06
contentedly (2) A0706/22 B1271/24
contenting (3) B0981/03
B1304/27 B1311/15
contention (11) A0068/10
A0537/16 A0540/07 A0541/28 A0542/21
A0542/29 A0547/22 A0548/27 A0549/09
A0560/01 B0946/27
contento (1) B0905/24
contents (36) A0209/19
A0245/12 A0273/03 A0273/35 A0277/26
A0300/31 A0302/V A0356/05 A0530/24
A0538/05 A0566/18 A0694/02 B0826/35
B0827/20 B0828/18 B0925/32 B0977/08
B0983/16 B1053/24 B1056/26 B1073/17
B1136/32 B1310/09 B1340/21 B1349/03
B1362/26 B1363/17 C0056/13 C0080/15
C0140/32 C0390/12 C0392/15 C0403/19
C0409/41 C0410/05 C0579/32
Contes (1) A0599/01
contest (7) A0356/16
A0447/17 A0589/34 B0822/26 B1222/20
C0187/07 C0579/27
contested (1) C0201/01
context (5) B0833/19
B1115/20 B1115/21 B1115/27 B1359/21
contiguous (1) A0019/15
continent (20) A0444/32
B1075/15 B1165/13 B1165/19 B1298/35
B1299/23 B1303/13 C0150/15 C0159/28
C0166/24 C0407/38 C0419/03 C0521/14
C0524/24 C0524/27 C0525/05 C0525/16
C0526/11 C0526/32 C0527/35
continental (1) B1345/18
continents (3) A0478/21
B1299/21 C0420/19
contingencies (1) B0772/19
continual (16) A0161/14
A0321/27 A0322/27 A0348/04 A0373/28
->A0432/31 B0727/12 B0963/24 B1241/34
C0071/40 C0142/19 C0146/05 C0167/36
C0203/10 C0388/30 C0540/30
continually (28) A0026/01
A0026/V A0080/32 A0143/30 A0191/05
A0195/16 A0246/25 A0270/16 A0296/03
A0479/03 A0545/11 B0797/19 B0940/26
B0987/35 B1104/31 B1119/06 B1375/19
C0089/03 C0102/26 C0148/22 C0153/21
C0163/39 C0203/19 C0205/21 C0391/35
C0444/V C0538/19 C0562/14
continuance (3) C0141/07
C0142/13 C0565/16
continuation (2) B1334/08 C0194/05
continue (11) A0064/11
A0142/03 A0630/23 A0686/21 B0732/23
B0825/30 B0852/18 B1220/02 C0399/35
C0403/14 C0408/35
continued (141)
continues (5) B0744/21
B1312/11 B1316/04 B1317/37 C0418/18
continuing (6) A0533/05 B0724/29
B0825/01 B1162/24 C0123/40 C0439/V
continuity (1) C0546/34
continuous (21) A0348/05
A0350/05 A0366/33 A0500/04 A0507/24
A0614/17 A0702/02 A0704/07 A0711/36
B0834/V B0859/02 B0944/29 B0967/35
B1020/32 B1106/22 B1115/04 B1212/18
B1269/07 B1281/32 C0162/04 C0185/16
continuously (6) A0602/24 A0614/12
B0834/05 B1127/07 C0205/41 C0414/18
contortions (2) A0059/27 A0067/17
contour (11) A0023/13
A0215/02 A0234/27 A0294/07 A0312/07
A0312/26 A0434/19 A0437/27 B0746/08
B0893/10 B0914/09
contra-distinction (1) A0611/37
contract (2) B0879/20 C0401/38
contracted (4) A0623/17
B0806/01 B0950/02 C0193/15
contraction (1) B0940/18
contradicted (3) B0986/30
B1006/01 C0207/20
contradiction (4) A0433/01
A0651/27 A0651/V B1220/26
contradictions (3) A0432/15
B0738/11 B1315/05
contradictories (2) B1297/12
B1297/17
contradictory (1) B0731/18
contradistinction (3) B1301/32
B1338/31 C0149/08
contralto/D (1) B0905/17
contraries (1) B1183/27
contrary (32) A0022/15
A0045/04 A0078/20 A0080/05 A0087/04
A0204/14 A0263/30 A0460/29 A0528/32
A0657/17 A0667/66 B0888/10 B0903/04
B1006/02 B1092/16 B1096/02 B1300/25
B1382/26 B1383/05 C0056/21 C0065/04
C0072/09 C0115/04 C0131/33 C0148/21
C0390/17 C0402/12 C0423/06 C0538/33
C0557/19 C0564/01 C0568/17
contrast (7) A0315/14

->A0626/28 B1039/20 B1050/02 B1122/11
B1234/10 B1350/26
contrasted (1) B0861/01
contrasting (1) A0692/13
contre (1) B1104/V
contre-temps (2) B1005/10 B1050/19
contree (1) B0899/29
contretemps (1) B1104/30
contribute (1) A0206/01
contributed (6) A0205/05 A0400/26
A0446/25 B0928/16 C0145/23 C0406/25
contribution (1) B1135/11
contributions (10) B1132/30 B1134/17
B1136/10 B1136/16 B1136/38 B1137/34
B1138/32 B1138/37 B1206/16 B1208/28
contributors (3) B1136/19
B1137/01 B1137/38
contrivance (5) A0322/18
B0817/19 C0120/40 C0410/23 C0428/40
contrivances (4) A0382/03
B1037/29 B1157/13 C0098/34
contrive (8) A0141/05
B1292/09 C0066/35 C0069/39 C0107/14
C0119/02 C0400/08 C0414/40
contrived (39) A0295/29
A0297/26 A0321/26 A0405/25 A0433/03
A0441/04 A0441/11 A0445/26 A0651/26
A0655/01 B0807/33 B0843/06 B0914/12
B0965/34 B0966/04 B1039/09 B1058/03
B1059/06 B1073/27 B1119/14 B1120/06
B1153/08 B1206/09 C0060/29 C0101/30
C0111/10 C0129/10 C0135/39 C0142/15
C0143/40 C0146/09 C0196/18 C0198/26
C0202/33 C0393/14 C0395/35 C0415/38
C0431/03 C0561/35
control (11) A0427/08
A0446/13 A0609/19 B0772/14 B0890/30
B0907/24 B1018/14 B1069/10 B1234/16
B1277/28 C0156/14
controversy (3) A0057/28
A0075/02 B1311/17
controvert (3) B0773/31
B1122/24 C0132/19
contusion (1) B0958/21
conundrums (1) A0528/07
convalescent (2) A0324/01 A0507/07
convenience (5) A0057/13
A0248/11 A0301/23 B1321/07 C0547/24
conveniences (2) A0485/22 A0563/01
conveniency (1) B1207/31
convenient (20) A0141/07
A0347/01 A0581/21 A0650/23 B0813/27
B0923/33 B0965/30 B0988/11 B1048/04
B1069/08 B1107/05 B1298/27 C0068/04
C0068/16 C0150/33 C0165/30 C0179/23
C0391/31 C0553/13 C0565/21
conveniently (2) A0340/29 C0156/26
convention (1) B0986/34
conventional (3) B0899/23
B0903/13 B1009/14
conventionalities (1) B0760/15
convenu (1) B0987/01
converge (1) B1163/37
conversant (7) A0484/26
A0549/26 B1005/31 B1074/03 B1158/36
->B1359/14 C0171/18
Conversation (1) B1322/31
conversation (67)
conversational (1) A0382/09
conversations (4) A0592/31
A0612/09 C0064/36 C0065/10
converse (11) A0241/08
A0456/27 A0507/09 A0549/26 A0641/22
B0959/31 B1075/11 B1158/30 C0537/12
C0555/14 C0574/04
conversed (10) A0527/V A0536/17
A0540/27 A0543/07 A0550/03 B0950/27
B1007/17 B1360/29 B1361/13 C0574/31
converses (1) B0977/16
conversible (1) B1299/25
conversing (5) A0533/03
B0897/14 B1008/19 C0129/18 C0182/20
convert (2) B0941/11 B0941/17
converted (9) A0296/11
A0303/02 A0567/11 A0604/14 B0890/15
B1013/17 B1044/05 B1160/30 B1189/13
convertible (1) B1339/06
converting (1) B1167/11
convex (4) A0443/24
A0443/25 B1080/12 C0404/39
convexity (6) B1080/38 C0408/03
C0416/17 C0417/01 C0443/V C0444/V
convey (29) A0145/09
A0211/23 A0212/04 A0296/V A0317/01
A0402/06 A0405/08 A0405/33 A0533/29
A0555/V A0615/04 A0711/17 B0733/20
B0739/23 B0753/24 B0835/17 B0940/23
B1115/34 B1155/26 B1185/06 B1240/17
B1240/33 B1248/08 B1276/18 B1276/30
B1293/35 B1333/01 C0080/17 C0094/06
conveyance (2) B1089/12 C0447/V
conveyed (17) A0033/07
A0403/25 A0511/20 A0603/20 A0613/33
A0622/17 A0681/06 B0865/03 B0869/07
B0916/18 B0933/31 B0959/06 B1006/26
B1158/20 B1181/21 B1193/08 C0394/31
conveying (6) A0294/13 A0581/16
B1184/31 B1277/14 C0393/28 C0567/36
conveys (4) A0538/31
B0870/07 B0987/08 B1038/05
convict (2) B1224/23 B1313/35
convicted (1) B0772/V
conviction (23) A0225/05
A0229/05 A0459/04 B0727/20 B0727/21
B0737/19 B0752/33 B0829/26 B0843/22
B0905/11 B0961/36 B0967/33 B0978/03
B0988/28 B0988/29 B1031/08 B1220/V
B1226/17 B1236/20 B1317/22 C0056/21
C0171/15 C0555/27
convictions (2) A0226/04 A0230/01
convince (18) A0053/04 A0062/10
A0107/08 A0209/26 A0302/22 A0500/02
A0583/18 B0728/31 B0773/20 B0823/01
B0839/25 B1048/20 B1129/09 B1299/27
B1359/28 B1369/06 C0130/37 C0183/05
convinced (39) A0073/04
A0209/25 A0356/02 A0378/06 A0401/23
A0540/26 A0550/06 A0552/23 B0737/32
B0745/01 B0796/33 B0842/32 B0894/13
B0902/03 B0927/31 B0946/05 B0977/28

->B1013/05 B1031/20 B1031/21 B1048/19
B1079/24 B1119/13 B1132/01 B1183/34
B1195/14 B1248/02 B1351/02 B1359/33
C0071/29 C0073/38 C0080/19 C0096/20
C0107/07 C0107/17 C0118/23 C0160/34
C0195/16 C0432/22
convinces (1) B1031/34
convincing (6) B0902/17 B1031/17
B1031/V B1053/03 B1247/33 B1371/08
convolute (1) A0157/25
convolutions (2) A0294/V A0689/15
convulsed (5) A0235/24
A0675/21 B1353/16 C0081/38 C0087/26
convulsion (6) A0506/05 A0580/14
B1303/35 C0182/22 C0185/11 C0195/20
convulsions (7) A0058/36
A0069/28 A0069/V B0989/11 C0107/32
C0142/22 C0204/24
convulsive (14) A0023/18 A0029/10
A0080/40 A0089/01 A0155/10 A0195/07
A0317/07 A0328/V A0459/11 A0616/V
B0960/14 C0072/27 C0135/14 C0441/V
convulsively (9) A0103/17
A0217/V A0415/V A0684/34 A0692/25
B0967/06 C0083/01 C0198/06 C0397/09
cooing (1) C0408/24
Cook (7) C0150/19
C0158/27 C0158/35 C0159/11 C0159/26
C0159/32 C0526/16
cook (27) B1012/22
B1012/23 C0085/29 C0086/02 C0086/21
C0086/35 C0089/02 C0089/33 C0090/01
C0093/09 C0093/19 C0099/38 C0100/02
C0100/16 C0102/20 C0103/10 C0103/33
C0103/37 C0104/01 C0110/24 C0110/35
C0112/30 C0146/36 C0159/36 C0169/13
C0169/16 C0544/08
cook's (4) C0102/11
C0102/17 C0102/21 C0103/29
cooked (1) C0151/33
cooking (2) C0535/01 C0562/14
cooks (2) A0263/03 A0263/05
cool (14) A0499/02 A0500/30
A0513/08 B0833/30 B0852/20 B0871/02
B0871/03 B1363/22 B1372/03 B1372/03
B1372/03 C0541/11 C0542/31 C0562/11
cooled (1) C0065/04
cooler (1) A0033/M
coolly (8) A0441/29
B0732/41 B0733/12 B0931/29 B1009/16
B1139/37 C0058/13 C0103/35
coolness (3) A0511/22
A0696/09 C0059/33
cools (1) B0832/24
coop (1) A0589/26
cooped (1) B1291/18
Cooper, J. Fenimore (1) A0268/10
Cooper's (1) A0268/14
Copernicus (1) C0432/25
copied (8) B0754/15
B0993/24 B1069/23 B1128/23 B1236/25
B1360/18 C0428/10 C0448/V
copies (6) A0264/02 B0876/24
B1129/03 B1141/06 B1166/29 B1167/01
copious (3) C0069/37
->C0092/24 C0203/15
copiously (2) C0119/21 C0406/17
copper (9) A0410/09
A0488/25 B1074/34 B1193/22 C0062/30
C0189/30 C0415/04 C0425/14 C0525/29
copper-colored (1) A0585/22
copper-fastened (2) A0136/01
C0062/24
copper-plate (1) A0465/30
copperas (1) C0553/02
coppered (2) A0416/14 C0062/24
coppice (2) B0807/13 B0807/15
copy (24) A0056/09
A0160/21 A0160/V A0180/11 A0284/17
A0434/34 A0435/17 A0487/01 A0652/14
B0729/02 B0876/28 B0925/09 B0925/09
B1119/M B1128/02 B1137/22 B1138/20
B1193/24 B1304/07 B1371/22 B1372/14
B1384/11 C0195/23 C0429/20
Copy-Right (1) B1206/01
copying (1) C0085/07
copyist (1) A0435/18
coquet (1) B0926/16
coquetries (1) A0510/13
coquetry (1) A0160/19
coquetted (1) B0748/25
coquettish (2) A0053/24 A0062/28
coral (4) A0157/V
B1282/01 C0167/16 C0178/35
coral-worm (1) A0478/20
coralliferi (1) C0546/26
cord (12) A0344/03
A0351/22 A0501/26 A0693/08 B0955/33
B1339/34 C0069/34 C0070/28 C0090/21
C0396/19 C0397/04 C0398/27
cordage (5) A0351/18
B1073/24 C0119/22 C0139/03 C0188/07
corded (1) C0165/28
cordial (3) A0026/09
B0808/14 B1339/19
cordiality (6) A0155/27 A0158/15
A0205/07 A0401/21 B0811/10 C0110/39
cordially (5) A0104/20
A0435/35 A0629/04 B0909/12 B1003/28
cordials (3) A0245/15
C0069/24 C0081/07
Cordova (1) B1011/20
cords (9) A0502/14
A0503/06 C0185/04 C0185/06 C0185/18
C0185/19 C0389/16 C0393/26 C0562/22
Corinnos (1) A0189/22
corio (1) B0870/21
cork (7) A0248/02
A0387/21 A0388/02 B1011/30 B1305/15
C0127/21 C0138/34
corked (2) B1291/06 B1310/04
corn (8) B1006/11
B1108/10 B1166/03 B1304/35 C0099/05
C0099/09 C0099/18 C0566/03
corned (1) C0576/04
Corneille (1) A0378/M
cornelian (1) A0093/13
corner (57)
corner-stones (1) B1305/07
corners (12) A0035/18

->A0044/10 A0044/15 A0104/14 A0469/18
A0629/13 B0831/16 B1048/27 B1336/15
B1337/26 B1370/09 C0387/19
cornice (3) B1336/19
C0573/10 C0573/24
cornices (7) A0153/12
A0158/02 A0161/17 A0320/23 A0367/11
A0501/15 B0945/22
corns (1) B0871/12
Cornwallis (4) B1304/16
B1304/35 B1304/37 B1305/05
corolla (2) B1163/25 B1163/34
coroner's (1) B1224/18
corporal (2) A0478/18 C0156/12
corporate (2) B1036/23 B1036/29
corporation (2) A0486/04 A0486/18
corporations (3) A0489/04
A0489/04 B1089/20
corpore (2) A0092/34 A0112/11
corporeal (2) A0093/10 A0112/21
corps (1) A0019/03
corps (2) B0960/04 B1127/04
corpse (116)
corpse-like (1) A0676/30
corpses (6) A0244/V A0539/13
B1014/29 B1167/20 B1354/21 C0126/05
corpulent (4) A0064/18
A0348/31 A0368/23 B1345/06
correct (9) A0067/13
A0078/15 A0267/08 A0299/09 A0374/18
A0552/24 A0557/29 B1119/12 C0208/01
corrected (2) B1298/20 B1316/31
correcting (3) A0078/17
B1154/21 B1189/23
correction (3) A0653/06
B1189/35 B1273/34
corrective (2) A0069/25 A0077/02
correctly (2) A0043/V A0536/13
correctness (1) C0162/07
correspond (4) A0672/05
B0984/38 B1292/03 C0409/35
corresponded (1) B1054/10
correspondence (3) A0264/27
B0901/01 B0991/19
correspondent (3) B1055/16
B1318/01 C0429/30
correspondents (3) B0753/35
B1129/14 B1143/26
corresponding (7) A0337/11
B0742/11 B0746/04 B0746/21 B1037/06
C0194/03 C0410/20
corridor (1) A0671/26
corridors (2) A0672/11 C0573/23
corroborate (1) A0709/13
corroborated (3) A0541/04
A0544/10 B1160/19
corroborates (2) A0540/19 A0543/06
corroboration (5) A0552/23
B0769/03 B0771/34 B0771/35 C0438/V
corroborative (5) A0556/28
B0746/20 B0751/25 B0771/08 B0991/27
corrosion (1) B0828/17
corrosive (1) A0617/07
corrumpitur (2) A0072/01 A0072/31
corrupted (2) B1310/21 C0550/28

corruption (6) A0336/04 A0337/03
A0500/21 A0612/11 A0616/11 B0742/24
Corsican (1) B1385/11
corslet (1) B1250/29
corty (1) A0356/13
corvette (2) C0156/37 C0156/40
cosmogony (1) A0536/10
cost (12) A0159/15
A0247/18 A0432/03 A0486/16 A0487/29
A0496/29 A0499/10 B1132/07 B1134/19
B1391/23 C0530/28 C0556/29
costliness (1) A0496/21
costly (4) A0444/17
A0496/15 B1073/09 C0536/25
costs (1) B1094/05
costumbres (1) A0621/01
costume (8) A0058/04
A0068/25 A0086/31 A0100/08 A0446/30
A0447/03 A0675/07 B1347/06
costumed (1) B1119/04
costumes (3) A0128/17
A0673/V B1347/11
cosy-looking (1) B0878/02
cot> (1) A0470/23
cotch (2) B0812/26 B0812/29
cotch'd> (1) A0468/29
Cote (13) C0529/05
C0529/31 C0530/01 C0530/25 C0530/35
C0530/37 C0532/39 C0533/13 C0533/38
C0533/41 C0534/30 C0535/24 C0536/26
cotelette (1) A0094/06
cotemporaries (2) B1122/23 B1294/28
cotemporary (1) B0752/24
Cotes/du/Rhone (1) A0098/33
Cotopaxi (3) B1079/V
B1080/02 C0400/29
Cottage (1) B1328/T
cottage (1) B1246/03
cottage (5) B0864/37
B1247/14 B1335/26 B1337/09 B1337/34
cottage-built (2) A0427/V A0428/V
Cottle (1) B1358/06
cotton (10) A0247/25 A0252/15
A0482/31 B0795/10 B0797/10 B0929/16
B0979/36 C0097/30 C0165/28 C0534/22
cotton-wood (11) C0536/34
C0539/02 C0541/28 C0541/30 C0543/18
C0560/16 C0566/14 C0566/17 C0570/21
C0572/16 C0577/19
cotton-wool (1) A0136/02
cottons (1) C0534/24
cottonwood (1) C0574/22
couch (7) A0322/01
A0322/02 A0325/19 A0327/24 A0411/17
B1106/16 B1153/09
cough (6) A0627/27 B0906/18
B1259/07 B1259/17 B1259/18 B1260/11
could (1145)
could/n't (1) A0094/07
couldn't (10) A0072/25 A0114/03
A0346/15 A0384/09 A0470/03 A0488/06
A0489/02 A0489/21 A0563/08 B1363/12
couldst (2) A0228/17 A0232/22
Council (2) A0369/18 B1385/17
council (4) A0250/18

->B1347/23 B1350/27 C0549/04
Council/of/Nice (2) A0175/15
A0181/05
Council/Bluffs (1) C0541/40
councillors (2) B1353/27 B1354/16
Councils (1) B1092/23
councils (3) A0250/09
A0251/04 C0104/16
counsel (5) A0439/32
A0626/17 B0815/24 B0982/21 B1142/14
counsels (1) A0435/34
Count (28) A0020/03
A0024/13 A0026/10 A0177/04 A0177/09
A0182/36 A0465/31 B1185/29 B1186/02
B1186/14 B1186/27 B1187/01 B1188/11
B1188/22 B1189/33 B1190/14 B1191/09
B1191/15 B1191/22 B1191/34 B1192/14
B1192/34 B1193/04 B1193/28 B1193/32
B1194/14 B1194/17 B1194/28
count (4) A0372/19
A0443/29 B0819/17 B1130/24
count's (1) A0023/28
counted (10) A0081/38 A0686/03
A0686/13 A0686/14 A0688/18 A0691/02
A0694/13 B1059/21 B1167/14 C0532/04
countenance (91)
countenanced (1) A0366/11
countenances (11) A0145/29
A0509/32 A0510/21 A0672/18 B1353/32
C0111/15 C0127/33 C0130/06 C0190/21
C0556/32 C0568/24
counter (11) A0587/32
A0589/26 A0593/15 A0593/24 B0726/12
C0060/16 C0060/24 C0114/02 C0124/14
C0124/21 C0162/33
counter-balance (1) B1351/20
counter/revolution (1) B1019/06
counteract (1) A0478/30
counteracted (3) B1051/34
B1074/26 B1074/30
counterbalance (2) B1345/24
C0403/04
counterbalanced (1) B1312/15
counterbalances (1) B1301/28
counterfeit (5) A0058/14
A0058/36 A0532/29 B0760/19 B0874/22
counterfeiting (1) B1362/11
counterfeits (1) B1018/09
counterpart (4) A0023/22
A0069/02 A0414/31 A0444/25
counters (1) B0827/29
counties (1) B1328/02
counting (5) A0530/10
A0530/20 B0836/20 B1081/32 C0551/27
counting-house (1) A0483/15
countless (4) A0436/26
B0945/20 B0964/32 C0575/12
countries (5) A0120/17
A0496/10 B0863/26 B1155/21 C0154/14
country (93)
countrymen (3) A0549/24
B1257/11 C0205/07
counts (2) A0037/18 A0037/19
county (2) B0874/27 B1054/35
coup (1) B1331/03
coup-de-grace (1) B1129/10
coupa (1) A0037/V
couple (21) A0173/08
A0178/13 A0241/23 A0245/05 A0347/03
A0379/14 A0532/31 B0735/28 B0817/01
B0844/19 B0875/23 B0875/32 B0916/18
B1053/19 B1056/10 B1068/13 B1138/31
B1195/17 B1302/18 C0122/36 C0143/31
coupled (4) A0027/04
B0865/36 B0908/09 C0107/06
couples (1) B0837/12
couplet (1) A0161/02
couplets (1) B1244/07
cour (1) B1007/31
courage (34) A0061/02 A0127/28
A0244/10 A0263/13 A0298/03 A0380/24
A0385/11 A0411/06 A0554/30 A0578/20
A0583/24 A0583/34 A0590/16 A0650/01
A0676/26 A0686/25 A0687/30 B0795/12
B0906/15 B0966/29 B1104/06 B1379/12
B1380/26 C0080/36 C0116/10 C0119/03
C0142/27 C0183/41 C0198/20 C0399/03
C0529/08 C0532/33 C0559/04 C0560/13
courageous (2) A0059/05 C0529/15
courageously (1) B0793/14
Courier (2) B0753/39 B0753/42
Courier (1) C0430/29
Courier/and/Enquirer (2) B1358/20
B1359/03
course (278)
courses (4) A0440/30
A0639/20 B0773/08 C0157/36
court (16) A0443/21
A0644/06 A0644/14 A0670/13 B0747/14
B0747/15 B0978/29 B1054/31 B1345/18
B1345/29 B1345/31 B1346/12 B1346/23
B1347/03 B1347/11 C0204/02
Court-Yard (1) B1075/20
courteous (1) B1339/11
courtesy (8) A0300/02
A0347/12 A0531/21 B0858/25 B0924/11
B1003/02 B1004/07 B1338/22
courtezan (1) A0123/V
courtier (1) B0988/19
courtiers (8) A0123/07
A0127/22 A0670/17 A0671/04 A0675/23
A0676/02 B1348/33 B1349/18
courts (2) B0747/12 B0752/03
Cousin (1) B1031/10
cousin (9) A0211/10
A0215/17 A0639/07 A0639/16 A0654/24
A0656/20 B1179/01 C0392/19 C0399/33
cousins (1) A0210/21
cove (2) A0583/35 B0814/22
covenant (1) A0209/06
cover (9) A0368/09
A0502/23 A0502/25 B0990/26 B1134/15
B1336/33 C0068/33 C0075/26 C0534/14
covered (52)
covering (18) A0152/29 A0298/V
A0322/11 A0498/04 A0498/05 B0854/12
B0855/11 B1071/16 B1157/07 C0068/06
C0092/01 C0107/40 C0174/39 C0174/40
C0410/07 C0410/16 C0573/38 C0577/39
coverings (1) A0498/15

covers (4) A0247/20
B1132/06 B1163/39 B1303/32
covert (8) A0197/10
A0197/18 A0197/29 A0433/18 B0773/01
B0927/23 B1139/31 C0188/27
coveted (1) A0216/12
cow (5) A0175/07
A0181/28 B1165/16 B1165/20 B1165/32
cowardice (1) A0676/18
cowardly (1) C0548/27
cowards (1) A0687/31
Cowper (1) A0033/M
cows (2) A0294/V A0347/31
coxcombry (1) A0444/19
Crab (25) B1133/21
B1133/28 B1133/30 B1133/31 B1134/03
B1134/05 B1134/08 B1134/11 B1134/21
B1135/14 B1135/23 B1136/18 B1137/02
B1137/38 B1138/37 B1140/09 B1140/18
B1140/23 B1140/25 B1140/33 B1142/06
B1142/20 B1142/22 B1142/28 B1143/07
Crabbe (2) A0070/32 A0079/04
crabs (1) C0145/37
crack (7) A0356/21
A0625/V A0630/V B0878/06 B1051/15
B1051/19 C0183/15
cracked (2) A0166/24 A0413/33
cracking (1) A0414/06
crackling (4) A0028/24
B0808/12 C0419/19 C0420/04
cracks (2) C0076/04 C0109/22
cradle (2) A0703/01 B1268/01
craft (2) A0583/32 B0859/13
crafty (2) A0611/15 B0857/27
crag (4) A0046/17
A0577/01 A0582/21 A0583/16
craggy (6) A0579/12 A0582/08
B1332/02 C0412/32 C0521/07 C0564/23
crags (6) A0046/06 A0195/M
A0241/20 A0578/12 B0817/25 B1076/18
crammed (2) A0056/13 A0066/02
cramp (1) A0081/26
cramped (2) A0081/26 C0071/01
cranium (1) A0248/23
crank (1) A0136/05
crannies (1) A0102/01
crash (5) C0082/35
C0094/32 C0095/28 C0128/09 C0546/03
crashing (1) A0195/18
crate (5) C0074/29
C0074/32 C0075/03 C0075/11 C0075/17
crates (4) C0069/08
C0070/03 C0071/02 C0083/01
Cratinus (2) A0091/15 A0110/18
crature> (1) A0465/21
cravat (7) A0089/12
A0103/34 A0627/34 B0877/36 B1186/02
C0398/10 C0398/12
cravats (1) A0508/34
craved (1) A0691/20
craving (3) A0511/26
B1222/16 B1222/17
cravings (2) C0146/09 C0191/20
crawl (2) C0074/21 C0178/26
crawled (5) B1363/10
->C0091/01 C0119/15 C0192/07 C0580/01
crawling (8) A0319/04
B1295/31 B1296/08 B1297/26 B1311/29
B1311/29 B1312/12 B1316/09
<u>crayons</u> (1) B1339/35
crazy (1) B1021/21
creak (1) A0429/08
creaked (2) A0102/04 B0793/08
creaking (1) C0114/02
cream (1) A0280/28
creamy (1) B1340/09
creases (1) B0992/04
create (10) A0496/16 A0710/35
B0732/42 B0738/06 B0890/30 B1036/21
B1074/05 B1213/04 B1276/01 C0176/29
created (14) A0243/15 A0295/30
B0943/09 B0958/31 B0959/30 B1011/31
B1036/09 B1038/34 B1158/03 B1166/16
B1191/20 B1213/06 C0189/16 C0410/37
creates (3) B1036/09
B1215/12 B1281/13
creating (9) A0099/28
A0253/13 A0374/05 A0600/03 B0772/14
B1068/12 C0110/27 C0144/25 C0197/39
Creation (1) B1190/12
creation (30) A0294/V A0477/01
A0527/V A0611/35 A0670/15 A0706/07
A0706/13 A0707/07 A0709/31 A0710/19
A0710/27 A0710/36 B0808/30 B0902/09
B1168/13 B1213/02 B1213/18 B1213/20
B1213/23 B1213/23 B1214/31 B1215/11
B1220/19 B1271/11 B1271/16 B1272/07
B1274/33 B1275/22 B1275/29 B1276/01
creations (2) A0156/V A0457/26
creative (3) A0533/23
B0942/06 B1213/09
Creator (1) B1188/15
creator (6) A0295/29 A0478/29
A0711/22 B1213/03 B1220/11 B1276/23
creature (30) A0023/29 A0176/17
A0182/18 A0246/31 A0357/10 A0478/21
A0565/10 A0568/22 B0852/04 B0854/16
B0854/28 B0856/04 B0857/31 B0950/08
B1036/34 B1102/34 B1156/20 B1158/27
B1166/20 B1247/31 B1248/03 B1249/18
B1249/27 B1250/34 C0073/27 C0164/34
C0165/39 C0169/10 C0563/24 C0566/34
creature's (1) B1157/03
creatures (26) A0348/21 A0385/09
A0478/13 A0478/17 A0482/25 A0494/05
B0869/21 B1036/35 B1038/29 B1038/30
B1157/15 B1157/36 B1163/06 B1164/27
B1188/13 B1190/27 B1213/07 B1220/18
B1302/20 B1352/10 C0173/29 C0429/41
C0545/10 C0548/27 C0562/33 C0577/36
Crebillon's (4) A0119/M
A0534/19 A0534/V B0993/28
credence (1) C0088/01
credential (1) B1003/09
credentials (1) A0546/26
<u>credibile</u> (1) A0213/07
credible (1) B1138/32
credit (17) A0164/05
A0534/09 A0622/15 A0639/01 B0738/10
B0925/03 B1050/17 B1081/30 B1152/19

->B1206/05 B1361/24 C0207/24 C0391/15
C0401/25 C0528/36 C0538/32 C0569/17
credited (1) A0440/19
creditors (8) A0531/22
C0393/07 C0395/13 C0406/30 C0426/22
C0427/28 C0438/V C0439/V
credulity (2) A0438/08 C0087/41
creed (2) B1313/04 C0401/23
creek (22) B0807/02 B0817/13
C0538/23 C0541/24 C0542/32 C0543/05
C0543/06 C0543/16 C0544/01 C0544/17
C0544/19 C0548/10 C0548/39 C0549/17
C0553/18 C0553/29 C0558/32 C0559/12
C0560/19 C0560/20 C0565/23 C0565/25
creek's (1) C0547/35
creeks (3) C0538/09
C0542/06 C0553/37
creep (4) A0583/16
B1225/13 C0070/15 C0178/17
creeping (7) A0411/11
A0437/32 A0558/13 B0947/20 B1297/25
B1316/09 C0068/41
creese (1) B0947/19
Creoles (1) C0530/08
crept (7) A0139/07
A0234/11 A0639/18 A0674/19 A0692/12
C0109/17 C0544/22
Crepuscularia (1) B1250/18
crescent (8) A0690/16
A0691/31 A0692/07 A0693/09 A0693/19
B1281/03 C0425/15 C0429/15
cresset (1) A0035/11
crest (1) A0579/06
crevice (5) A0685/31
B0794/27 B0794/30 C0397/05 C0398/28
crevices (2) C0163/31 C0181/34
crew (41) A0136/31
A0140/29 A0143/09 A0143/27 A0144/31
A0145/28 A0240/03 B0931/13 B0968/28
C0053/T C0061/35 C0062/14 C0062/38
C0085/28 C0086/18 C0091/19 C0092/11
C0092/34 C0093/08 C0093/18 C0095/34
C0099/21 C0104/19 C0104/26 C0106/29
C0107/08 C0107/22 C0110/01 C0112/09
C0114/09 C0125/27 C0125/41 C0146/25
C0147/22 C0166/15 C0169/12 C0170/30
C0177/34 C0430/44 C0539/06 C0564/10
Cribalittle (2) B1138/33 B1139/01
Crichton (3) B1324/03
B1324/T B1325/05
Crichton's (1) B1325/09
cricket (1) B0794/19
cried (25) A0047/06
A0139/31 A0182/36 A0233/11 B0815/26
B0818/15 B0819/24 B0819/34 B0820/08
B0820/20 B0820/34 B0897/17 B0903/11
B0908/11 B1010/V B1011/06 B1013/22
B1014/18 B1103/28 B1192/07 B1296/03
B1348/27 B1350/04 C0110/34 C0183/26
cries (11) A0162/22
A0537/15 A0614/02 B0873/23 B0874/15
B0965/04 B1350/25 C0128/37 C0130/38
C0399/05 C0408/29
Crime (1) B0855/35
crime (24) A0021/17
->A0135/11 A0163/12 A0426/11 A0430/26
A0507/04 A0514/24 A0515/28 A0551/V
A0564/09 B0736/21 B0753/33 B0758/21
B0760/13 B0769/06 B0771/22 B0851/32
B0855/16 B0906/26 B1051/11 B1057/28
B1224/24 C0108/04 C0426/21
crimes (2) A0548/13 B0732/04
criminal (1) B1054/28
criminate (1) A0544/23
criminating (1) B1058/20
crimped (1) A0246/V
crimpled (1) A0246/28
crimson (27) A0087/07
A0087/19 A0089/09 A0100/17 A0154/29
A0157/V A0196/09 A0197/01 A0227/10
A0231/23 A0336/07 A0339/05 A0349/12
A0447/05 A0501/13 A0501/23 A0501/25
A0502/03 A0502/20 A0503/06 A0563/V
A0602/25 A0641/07 A0696/04 B1283/07
C0542/10 C0543/29
crimson-tinted (3) A0158/01
A0501/09 A0503/08
crimsoned (1) C0125/05
cripple (5) B1345/29
B1347/25 B1348/30 B1350/07 B1354/22
crisis (9) A0054/04
A0063/13 A0610/29 B0963/01 B0966/35
B1006/26 B1222/08 C0197/34 C0197/35
crisp (1) A0351/11
criterion (6) B1297/07 B1297/20
B1314/11 B1314/15 B1315/23 B1315/35
critic (4) A0279/25
A0708/12 B1273/07 C0432/40
critic's (1) B1386/07
critical (11) A0710/29
B1113/05 B1119/M B1135/34 B1258/02
B1275/31 B1330/11 B1381/11 C0113/07
C0150/18 C0175/09
criticise (2) A0663/11 B1101/17
criticism (15) A0033/01
A0708/04 A0710/22 B1133/27 B1142/01
B1273/03 B1275/25 B1371/12 B1379/27
B1379/30 B1380/18 B1380/19 B1381/07
C0432/39 C0432/40
criticisms (1) B1380/22
critics (6) A0473/14 A0621/11
A0621/27 A0622/08 B1101/17 B1379/04
critique (1) A0282/25
critiques (1) B1136/03
croak (1) B1012/08
croaked (1) B1020/30
crockery-ware (1) C0148/11
Croissart (10) B0887/25 B0887/25
B0888/04 B0912/23 B0912/25 B0912/26
B0912/30 B0913/03 B0913/26 B0913/27
croit (1) A0019/V
Crommelin (1) B0729/35
crone (1) A0019/V
cronies (2) B1045/31 B1059/06
crony (1) B1046/01
crooked (11) A0268/19
A0274/34 A0275/17 A0367/23 A0368/29
A0513/32 B1316/08 B1362/07 C0389/21
C0541/28 C0570/28
crooked-looking (1) A0367/32

crops (1) A0491/15
cross (25) A0512/20
A0584/17 A0586/04 A0626/26 A0686/22
A0686/26 A0691/31 B0735/21 B0736/02
B1072/21 B1075/12 B1215/21 B1282/28
C0148/17 C0149/41 C0521/05 C0525/05
C0525/13 C0525/26 C0526/11 C0526/17
C0527/23 C0527/35 C0567/03 C0574/01
cross-questioning (1) C0176/05
crossed (32) A0080/30
A0265/21 A0266/09 A0445/17 A0445/17
A0512/24 A0535/22 A0585/06 A0588/34
A0614/04 A0693/15 B0767/29 B0769/24
B0817/13 B0945/07 B0967/15 B1068/02
B1069/09 B1081/16 B1081/17 B1352/30
C0082/30 C0148/12 C0159/04 C0160/37
C0162/18 C0163/05 C0171/26 C0174/14
C0524/11 C0527/09 C0542/18
crosses (2) B1160/28 C0429/16
crossing (12) A0417/04
A0430/11 A0488/25 A0586/33 A0631/10
B0794/18 B1080/09 B1081/30 C0152/33
C0528/01 C0528/39 C0567/28
crotchet (6) B0813/33 B1009/29
B1013/16 B1013/26 B1169/12 B1169/14
crotchets (2) B1291/09 B1310/08
crouch (1) B0855/10
crouched (1) C0072/26
crouching (1) A0105/28
Crow (2) A0066/29 A0067/03
crow (5) B0869/22
B1013/31 B1108/09 B1110/02 B1371/28
crow-bar (3) A0537/V
A0539/V B0857/13
crowbar (2) A0537/13 A0539/35
Crowd (1) A0506/T
crowd (53)
crowded (31) A0079/12
A0176/25 A0182/28 A0234/01 A0278/16
A0383/15 A0398/01 A0446/23 A0507/22
A0542/14 A0674/12 B0889/03 B0891/22
B0924/05 B0931/13 B0949/21 B1226/03
B1293/13 B1298/30 B1333/32 B1351/29
C0069/18 C0076/02 C0122/24 C0144/28
C0175/06 C0190/03 C0190/37 C0193/26
C0535/11 C0576/17
crowding (6) A0046/V B0840/19
B0946/18 C0057/29 C0197/40 C0533/18
crowds (1) C0185/36
crowing (1) B1372/04
crown (9) A0128/27
A0245/26 B1109/13 B1385/16 C0087/12
C0114/07 C0388/33 C0552/01 C0566/15
crowned (6) A0127/05 A0491/02
B0864/29 B1162/08 B1334/38 C0154/05
Crows (3) A0057/04
A0057/09 A0058/06
crows (3) B0821/02
B0824/23 C0579/37
Crozet (1) C0150/07
Crozet's/group (1) C0154/19
crucible (5) B1168/24
B1168/26 B1168/29 B1362/19 B1362/22
crucibles (3) B1362/19
B1362/20 B1362/25
crucifixes (1) B0828/07
crude (4) A0135/20
B0835/21 B1360/03 C0392/32
cruel (7) A0072/06
A0120/10 A0354/10 A0354/35 B0852/29
B1158/02 B1249/30
cruelly (5) A0356/30
A0498/23 A0654/26 C0147/36 C0580/04
Cruelty (2) B1093/19 B1131/33
cruelty (3) B0853/25
B0854/30 B1109/08
cruise (4) C0053/T
C0093/21 C0148/06 C0154/01
cruised (1) C0158/18
cruises (1) B0754/34
cruising (1) C0101/22
crumbled (2) A0197/27 B1243/03
crumbling (2) A0400/11 C0150/26
crumbs (1) B1345/21
crumple (2) B0810/26 B0828/35
crumpled (1) B0991/03
crumpling (1) B0829/05
crushed (2) A0320/03 B1292/31
crushes (1) B1259/34
crushing (2) A0639/14 C0577/33
crustily (1) C0058/39
crusty (1) A0649/01
crxw (1) B1374/07
crxwing (1) B1374/17
Cry (1) A0336/M
cry (20) A0216/21
A0218/23 A0242/20 A0416/31 A0676/24
B0852/30 B0859/01 B0964/20 B0967/10
B0967/34 B1109/16 B1250/28 B1262/12
B1262/12 C0062/15 C0063/03 C0063/14
C0104/24 C0108/19 C0208/16
crying (3) A0666/02
B0793/33 C0072/22
crypt (4) B1261/02
B1261/04 B1261/07 B1261/V
cryptogamous (1) B1163/22
cryptograph (5) B0836/11
B0837/15 B0839/03 B0839/28 B1298/03
cryptographist (3) B0840/07
B1298/03 B1317/03
cryptographs (1) B0835/19
crystal (9) A0600/V
A0603/01 B1104/09 B1106/05 B1248/19
B1279/34 B1333/23 B1337/06 B1340/14
crystallic (1) B0862/35
cub (1) A0128/09
cubic (3) B1071/01
B1073/05 C0394/38
cubical (1) B1303/33
cubits (2) A0045/03 A0045/07
cucumber (1) B0871/03
cud> (3) A0464/12
A0465/13 A0465/30
cuddy (6) C0057/27 C0058/35
C0060/32 C0063/16 C0063/23 C0550/17
cuddy-cabin (1) C0533/16
cudgel (4) A0562/20
A0563/20 B1135/01 B1140/11
cue (5) A0105/05
A0295/03 A0434/32 B0901/13 B1244/02

cuff (2) A0443/11 B0890/06
cuffed (1) A0623/03
cuffs (1) A0100/08
cui (6) B1010/25 B1051/09
  B1051/14 B1051/20 B1051/23 B1051/28
cul-de-sac (1) C0195/11
cul-de-sac (1) A0096/03
Cul-de-Sac (3) A0099/11
  A0100/25 A0101/V
culpable (2) A0564/05 B0756/V
culprit (2) A0070/07 A0079/23
cultivated (6) A0296/V B0862/17
  B0987/14 B1167/22 B1303/16 C0156/01
cultivating (4) A0709/24
  B1274/27 B1313/11 C0530/09
cultivation (2) A0611/36 B1278/36
culture (6) A0610/28 A0711/16
  A0711/27 B1276/16 B1276/30 B1280/20
cum (3) A0271/29
  A0515/34 B1364/03
cum (3) B0812/25 B0814/18 B0826/26
cum'd (4) A0373/14
  A0373/16 A0373/18 A0467/11
cum'd> (4) A0465/28
  A0466/03 A0468/21 A0469/07
cunning (10) A0189/10 A0401/03
  A0545/02 A0568/19 B0983/22 B0984/18
  B0985/16 B1018/06 B1019/10 C0105/23
Cunningham (1) A0135/M
cunningly (2) B0793/02 B0796/11
cup (5) A0248/17
  B0942/11 B1195/16 B1381/11 C0413/31
cupboard (1) A0101/15
cupola (1) B1351/22
cur-tailed (1) A0356/V
Cur-Spattering (1) A0489/07
curas (2) A0209/M A0218/15
curbstone (1) B1090/22
curdled (1) A0245/04
cure (4) B1006/07
  C0177/26 C0179/05 C0555/31
cured (5) A0629/21
  B1010/04 C0179/04 C0179/05 C0179/06
Curio, Caelius Secundus (1) A0213/04
Curiosities (2) B1101/05 B1151/05
curiosities (1) B1160/14
curiosity (47) A0024/23
  A0106/21 A0145/21 A0214/27 A0250/01
  A0293/15 A0352/20 A0382/11 A0383/11
  A0433/13 A0512/06 A0546/17 A0564/26
  A0588/35 A0591/28 A0686/21 B0726/18
  B0853/13 B0893/11 B0894/08 B0923/17
  B0928/16 B0939/04 B0949/11 B0959/34
  B0993/21 B1003/03 B1126/11 B1137/08
  B1137/09 B1153/23 B1186/09 B1189/03
  B1233/24 B1238/01 B1381/22 C0123/33
  C0169/22 C0181/35 C0190/21 C0388/13
  C0416/24 C0417/31 C0545/26 C0566/36
  C0569/07 C0571/08
curious (5) A0067/21
  A0143/03 A0409/10 B1302/27 B1381/27
curiously (5) A0034/22
  A0087/01 A0100/12 A0164/21 A0247/19
curiously-pannelled (1) A0087/24
curl (1) A0020/V
curlin> (1) A0464/08
curling (7) A0156/13
  A0274/09 A0351/11 A0464/V B0888/12
  B0974/08 C0165/15
curls (2) A0152/28 B0909/06
curly (1) A0367/14
curmudgeon (1) A0651/29
curous (1) B0821/05
currant-bushes (1) C0541/34
Currant/River (1) C0547/40
currants (1) C0576/07
currency (2) B0742/18 B0834/18
current (49) A0026/26
  A0054/07 A0063/16 A0140/01 A0144/06
  A0145/16 A0145/25 A0152/02 A0322/27
  A0406/19 A0434/21 A0496/25 A0580/07
  A0580/08 A0582/06 A0584/27 B0834/01
  B0865/17 B1077/18 B1079/26 B1079/31
  B1108/08 B1292/20 B1294/27 C0111/13
  C0159/14 C0163/09 C0164/15 C0164/20
  C0167/03 C0167/05 C0170/27 C0203/19
  C0204/28 C0432/32 C0536/31 C0537/38
  C0538/16 C0540/16 C0549/23 C0553/40
  C0555/08 C0558/28 C0561/09 C0567/14
  C0567/24 C0571/19 C0572/10 C0572/37
currente (1) A0269/36
currents (11) A0088/04
  A0584/17 A0604/11 B1079/31 B1382/19
  C0148/21 C0160/07 C0160/13 C0536/14
  C0575/23 C0576/16
curry-comb (1) B1141/10
curse (9) A0197/21
  A0197/32 A0445/07 A0642/14 A0644/V
  A0645/01 A0650/19 B0821/12 B1212/09
cursed (8) A0037/16
  A0197/21 A0197/32 A0198/31 A0227/21
  A0232/08 A0317/21 A0587/01
curses (2) A0245/07 C0441/V
cursing (3) A0490/28
  A0623/17 C0131/18
cursory (5) A0074/17
  A0141/03 A0554/26 B1358/01 C0526/14
curt (3) A0298/V
  A0341/11 B1221/25
curtail (1) A0074/07
curtain (8) A0319/13
  A0496/02 B1244/04 B1245/01 B1331/09
  C0205/26 C0205/40 C0208/20
curtained (1) A0501/10
curtains (22) A0036/V A0101/02
  A0102/02 A0158/02 A0217/V A0217/V
  A0322/12 A0437/14 A0496/03 A0497/21
  A0497/22 A0498/15 A0501/13 A0501/22
  A0501/27 A0502/26 A0663/06 B0852/30
  B0980/17 B1008/25 B1106/17 B1339/30
curtchy> (1) A0467/08
Curtis, Adelaide (2) B0925/26
  B0925/29
curvature (2) B1302/10 B1330/08
curve (6) A0379/30 A0401/32
  B1282/30 B1301/29 B1336/11 C0194/22
curved (3) A0312/17
  A0497/18 A0613/17
curves (2) A0501/29 B1281/30
curveted (1) A0025/03

curvets (1) B0824/14
curvetted (1) A0371/17
cushion (1) C0536/09
cushioned (1) B1119/05
cushions (1) B0979/26
cusps (2) C0423/13 C0423/17
custody (1) B1052/06
custom (19) A0057/23
A0068/07 A0536/V A0586/03 B0725/27
B0808/08 B0901/06 B0901/V B0904/20
B0904/V B0929/31 B1105/13 B1114/01
B1135/12 B1187/28 B1187/30 B1234/21
C0414/33 C0431/13
customarily (1) A0247/21
customary (22) A0102/08 A0140/07
A0324/28 A0441/15 A0443/26 A0685/17
B0753/08 B0760/12 B0907/29 B0924/08
B0943/13 B0960/12 B0965/15 B0968/31
B1071/07 B1181/07 B1225/09 B1242/07
C0105/08 C0107/04 C0171/35 C0404/03
customer (4) A0484/21
A0484/32 A0485/10 B0872/25
customers (2) C0391/19 C0392/09
customs (6) B0903/13 B1009/14
B1303/11 C0203/33 C0425/39 C0433/05
cut (98)
cut-glass (2) A0499/07 A0499/12
cut-throat (3) A0058/27
B1139/09 B1139/26
Cut/and/Comeagain (3) A0484/22
A0484/30 A0485/27
cuteness (1) A0467/31
cutlasses (2) C0180/25 C0184/15
cutlery (2) B0945/13 C0534/23
cuts (4) A0338/24
A0443/26 A0443/27 B0730/15
cutter (6) B1293/32 B1294/03
B1390/05 B1391/08 C0161/28 C0171/14
cutting (24) A0037/20
A0068/14 A0371/12 A0443/28 A0486/23
A0630/19 B0856/32 B0931/01 B1049/01
B1053/14 B1155/02 B1179/23 B1281/32
C0090/25 C0091/13 C0114/17 C0136/30
C0141/24 C0173/25 C0184/01 C0194/09
C0196/24 C0197/09 C0545/09
Cuvier (4) A0494/06
A0559/18 A0559/30 C0178/09
cxck (1) B1374/17
cxme (1) B1374/16
Cxncxrd (2) B1374/10 B1374/16
cxw (1) B1374/14
cxxl (3) B1374/16
B1374/16 B1374/16
cyanite (1) A0182/09
Cybele (1) A0161/V
cycle (3) A0601/20
A0601/20 A0604/25
cycles (2) A0601/06 A0615/08
cycloid (1) A0498/11
Cygni (1) B1168/34
cylinder (6) A0592/30 A0592/33
A0593/02 B0818/34 B1337/14 B1383/01
cylindrical (5) A0543/10
A0559/13 A0592/29 B1180/20 B1391/02
cynic (1) A0069/11

cynosure (1) B0725/11
cypher (1) A0366/18
cyphers (1) B1317/04
cypress (4) A0228/23
A0233/04 A0236/04 A0603/21
cypresses (1) B1332/25
Cyrus (3) A0057/30
A0068/13 A0120/01
cythern (1) A0047/26
D (1) B0905/17
d (1) B0838/28
d̄ (1) C0194/22
D.C. (1) B1192/09
D.U.K. (1) A0337/20
D-- (24) A0294/V
A0507/06 B0976/35 B0977/09 B0978/19
B0978/30 B0979/07 B0983/25 B0985/23
B0990/21 B0991/06 B0991/08 B0991/15
B0991/22 B0992/13 B0992/18 B0992/23
B0992/30 B0993/19 B1235/04 B1235/20
B1236/04 B1237/04 B1238/02
D--/Hotel (2) A0513/34 A0515/18
D--'s (1) B0980/32
d--d (10) A0177/27 A0386/03
A0482/14 B0812/08 B0812/25 B0816/32
B0816/V C0061/33 C0067/32 C0110/20
d--dest (1) A0106/11
d--l (4) B1371/23
B1372/35 B1373/10 C0447/V
d--n (8) A0389/05
A0389/06 B0812/V B0812/V B0812/V
B0818/17 B1373/07 B1373/23
d'autre (1) A0033/20
d'ecarte (1) A0037/03
d'esprit (5) B1068/08
C0428/07 C0432/47 C0448/V C0448/V
d'etre (2) A0019/V A0037/26
d'expliquer (1) A0568/25
d'objection (1) A0037/25
d'oeil (1) B1331/03
d'oeuvre (1) A0160/06
d'oeuvres (2) A0160/V A0160/V
d'or (2) A0112/31 B1259/34
d'oreon (Gr.) (1) A0195/M
d'oro (1) B1386/04
d'un (2) A0498/02 B1122/01
d'une (1) B1335/18
d'ye (3) A0469/27
B0873/30 B0914/02
d'Alger (1) A0537/33
D'Ambois (1) A0164/26
d'Amerique (1) C0522/35
D'Anan, Thomas (1) C0430/39
D'Antin (1) A0033/05
d'Atree (1) B0993/27
D'Avisson (1) C0430/34
D'Avisson (1) C0430/35
D'Indagine, Jean (1) A0409/02
D'Israeli, I. (1) A0018/13
dabble (1) A0046/10
dabbled (4) A0448/03
A0485/33 A0537/30 A0675/15
dabbler (1) A0488/15
Daddy (4) B1139/23
B1139/23 B1139/31 B1139/33

Daddy-Long-Legs (7) B1138/20
B1138/21 B1139/17 B1139/20 B1139/37
B1140/02 B1140/15
Daddyship (1) B1140/04
dagger (4) A0022/12
A0512/05 A0676/20 A0676/24
daggers (2) A0110/09 B0870/29
Dagon (1) A0046/13
Daguerreotype (1) B1168/33
daily (41) A0027/V
A0227/09 A0231/23 A0234/03 A0234/V
A0298/V A0382/03 A0436/02 A0479/18
A0490/20 A0547/03 A0594/19 A0601/19
A0611/23 A0624/21 A0665/20 A0708/08
B0728/08 B0731/V B0771/27 B0871/16
B0876/22 B0876/31 B0942/01 B1021/29
B1068/11 B1130/23 B1137/22 B1143/31
B1164/01 B1168/40 B1241/31 B1246/10
B1321/19 B1322/02 B1322/04 C0065/11
C0096/36 C0098/40 C0207/02 C0565/10
Daily/Polyglot (1) A0272/23
daintiest (1) A0034/16
daintiness (1) B1280/19
dainty (3) A0036/01
A0599/M C0389/29
dais-chamber (1) A0250/08
daisies (1) A0640/32
daisy (1) A0640/03
dalliance (1) A0161/15
dallied (1) A0407/02
dallying (2) A0640/13 A0696/24
dam (5) C0544/26
C0544/29 C0544/38 C0545/07 C0545/30
damage (8) C0101/36
C0102/33 C0104/30 C0106/02 C0115/09
C0395/23 C0544/38 C0559/25
damaged (2) A0484/34 B1292/28
damages (2) A0487/12 B1185/25
damaging (1) C0405/14
Damascus (3) A0086/34
A0121/23 B1160/11
damascus (1) B1167/25
dames (3) A0022/02
A0670/13 B0945/15
damme (6) A0093/31 A0093/31
A0093/35 A0093/38 A0113/11 A0113/17
dammed-up (1) A0514/30
damming (1) C0544/19
Dammit (19) A0624/17
A0624/30 A0625/12 A0625/27 A0626/05
A0626/30 A0627/16 A0628/12 A0628/13
A0628/18 A0628/20 A0628/24 A0628/28
A0629/03 A0629/07 A0630/01 A0630/25
A0631/01 A0631/23
Dammit, Toby (4) A0622/22
A0623/20 A0627/20 A0629/17
Dammit's (3) A0624/08
A0625/05 A0626/10
damn (1) A0072/27
damnable (3) A0263/12
A0446/33 B0851/29
damnation (1) B0859/06
damned (10) A0035/28 A0036/14
A0037/08 A0183/23 A0443/17 A0489/05
A0692/14 B0795/05 B0859/05 B1128/28
damning (3) B1053/03
B1054/30 B1139/29
damp (11) A0070/17
A0243/V A0410/01 A0616/29 A0684/07
A0689/08 B0759/11 B0961/21 B1258/31
B1261/32 C0182/31
dampened (1) B1055/08
dampness (6) A0081/28 A0683/23
B0857/06 B1078/24 B1263/22 C0179/08
damps (1) B1259/21
damsel (1) B1153/06
damsels (1) B0871/04
dan (3) B0814/17 B0814/18 B0912/02
dance (6) A0022/03 B0911/27
B1167/21 B1298/37 C0544/08 C0569/31
danced (6) A0347/32 A0347/32
A0347/33 A0348/14 B0913/22 C0123/03
dancer (1) B1346/26
dances (1) A0163/08
dancing (8) A0347/33
A0354/18 A0373/26 A0484/04 B0806/M
B0913/V B1006/14 C0118/14
dandies (1) A0509/27
dandled (1) A0371/V
dandy (4) A0351/20
A0489/14 A0489/16 B0863/12
danger (61)
dangerous (19) A0027/19
A0123/10 A0123/12 A0156/11 A0413/05
A0438/25 A0483/20 A0565/07 A0581/34
B0977/27 B1005/14 B1299/15 C0098/41
C0149/16 C0197/10 C0440/V C0549/06
C0560/09 C0564/24
dangerously (3) A0512/15
B1016/06 C0557/40
dangers (16) A0020/08
B1006/34 C0074/39 C0117/26 C0122/17
C0134/19 C0139/14 C0147/24 C0155/02
C0413/06 C0414/29 C0425/20 C0523/41
C0527/06 C0532/22 C0564/18
dangle (2) A0248/21 A0499/26
dangled (3) A0351/18
A0371/07 B1102/27
dangling (5) A0241/12
B0990/35 B1077/15 C0397/03 C0552/21
dank (2) A0417/16 B1003/18
dans (6) A0019/02 A0096/M
A0096/M B1335/18 C0430/27 C0430/36
danseuse (1) A0294/V
Dante (1) B1132/03
Dante's (1) B1128/23
Daphne (1) A0120/20
Daphnis (1) B1302/19
dapperness (1) A0508/25
dar (1) A0344/25
dar (3) B0811/22 B0821/11 B0821/28
dar's (1) A0387/V
Darcotas (1) C0551/02
Darcotas (1) C0550/29
dare (22) A0069/22 A0078/03
A0078/26 A0078/42 A0104/03 A0122/25
A0284/20 A0345/25 A0591/13 A0624/13
A0639/V B0812/17 B0812/19 B0821/V
B0821/V B0942/02 B0976/34 B1046/34
B1102/37 B1109/07 B1109/10 C0396/01

dare-devil (1) A0562/17
dare's (1) B0821/06
dared (20) A0191/04
A0416/06 A0416/07 A0416/07 A0416/10
A0416/10 A0578/16 A0590/10 A0624/V
A0684/09 A0692/04 B0855/33 B0965/10
B0966/30 B0977/19 B1295/34 B1297/26
B1311/34 B1316/10 C0135/20
dares (4) A0345/V
A0675/23 A0675/24 B0976/35
Darien (1) C0521/07
daring (5) A0408/07
B0771/29 B0961/31 B0990/11 B1349/04
dark (117)
darkened (3) A0233/21
C0153/20 C0548/03
darker (7) A0234/21
A0509/31 A0605/07 B0769/V B1161/09
C0417/16 C0418/33
darkest (4) A0440/34
B0856/11 B1161/09 C0541/09
darkling (1) A0616/28
darkly (3) B0902/11
B0902/11 B1371/20
darkness (54)
darling (2) A0356/27 B1339/08
darlint> (3) A0465/22
A0469/07 A0470/08
darned (1) B1046/05
<u>darry</u> (1) A0354/33
dart (2) B1101/22 B1101/25
darted (1) B0944/06
darting (1) C0203/24
darty (1) C0067/23
<u>das</u> (1) B0723/M
dash (4) A0279/15
A0286/21 B1090/24 C0562/27
dashed (11) A0140/09
A0687/09 B0911/12 B0913/21 B1090/22
B1108/21 B1333/13 C0082/33 C0199/25
C0424/04 C0563/02
Dashers (1) A0044/11
dashes (1) A0286/19
dashing (7) A0044/12
A0279/12 A0440/34 A0509/06 A0579/20
B0990/11 C0201/09
<u>dass</u> (1) B0723/M
dastardly (1) A0120/10
dat (34) B0811/23 B0811/26
B0812/09 B0812/21 B0812/22 B0812/30
B0812/31 B0815/09 B0816/32 B0820/24
B0821/14 B0821/14 B0821/27 B0824/23
B0826/27 B0826/28 B0899/29 B0900/01
B0911/28 B0912/06 B0912/08 B0912/16
B0912/16 B0912/17 B0912/23 B0912/27
B0912/27 B0913/10 B0913/10 B1102/06
B1103/02 B1103/07 B1103/09 B1103/13
dat's (6) B0811/22 B0811/26
B0813/05 B0814/17 B0820/15 B0821/11
data (5) A0294/04
B1303/09 C0065/02 C0401/03 C0427/14
date (27) A0018/02
A0025/19 A0085/02 A0093/20 A0163/21
A0310/12 A0365/19 A0365/22 A0366/21
B0760/29 B0760/30 B0761/09 B0761/10
->B0761/28 B0827/27 B0901/27 B0901/29
B0948/34 B1235/30 B1310/08 B1345/17
B1358/28 B1381/23 C0160/32 C0160/39
C0389/01 C0550/31
dated (1) B1127/09
dates (6) A0204/01 A0264/37
B1089/10 C0167/36 C0167/39 C0203/38
dating (1) B0737/22
daubed (2) A0142/12 A0689/01
daughter (37) A0228/35
A0233/17 A0234/V A0235/04 A0235/08
A0321/08 A0537/10 A0538/10 A0539/01
A0539/12 A0539/18 A0539/23 A0539/28
A0540/27 A0549/02 A0556/06 A0566/15
A0566/27 A0567/17 A0599/M A0639/05
A0642/11 B0724/26 B0725/18 B0725/22
B0732/32 B0737/11 B0753/22 B0753/26
B0887/25 B0887/27 B0912/09 B0912/18
B0912/24 B0912/26 B1152/04 B1152/22
daughter's (3) A0549/05
B0912/24 B0912/25
daughters (7) A0196/V
A0228/13 A0232/18 A0311/27 B1169/02
B1169/05 C0522/22
daunt (1) C0532/34
daunted (1) A0245/03
dauntless (1) A0670/10
David (3) A0043/05
A0044/27 A0188/M
Davidson (1) C0430/34
Davy, Humphrey (2) B1359/12
B1359/29
Davy, Sir Humphrey (1) B1358/06
dawdling (1) B0990/22
dawn (17) A0080/24
A0328/24 A0407/28 A0438/26 A0439/05
A0444/31 A0532/30 A0592/06 B0771/32
B0827/14 B0908/15 B0910/11 B0930/01
B0960/16 B0966/10 C0091/35 C0142/36
dawned (6) A0216/15 B0829/25
B0896/15 C0120/21 C0129/38 C0559/03
dawns (1) B0963/08
day (365)
day-book (1) A0483/04
day-break (6) A0515/03 A0543/19
B1238/04 B1371/25 B1391/15 C0548/38
day-dream (1) A0212/21
day-dreamer (1) A0212/33
day-dreams (1) A0712/07
day-time (1) B0934/03
Day-Book (3) A0487/01
A0487/04 A0487/34
day's (3) A0538/27
C0099/11 C0561/17
daybreak (15) A0296/17
B0929/25 B1075/19 B1076/01 C0060/05
C0091/26 C0095/05 C0100/39 C0102/13
C0114/16 C0126/27 C0136/39 C0143/38
C0146/13 C0396/13
daydreams (1) B1277/12
daylight (11) B0768/06
B0826/32 B0909/27 B0909/32 B0915/26
C0070/17 C0099/36 C0167/35 C0203/11
C0416/35 C0539/05
days (196)

days' (3) B0732/10
 B0740/11 B0743/07
dazzle (1) A0157/17
dazzled (3) A0705/04
 B0826/16 B1128/13
dazzling (4) A0604/12
 A0639/28 B0945/13 C0416/41
De (8) A0037/25
 A0043/M A0096/M A0213/04 A0213/06
 A0366/17 A0601/33 B1382/35
de (62)
de (113)
De/la/Chambre (1) A0409/03
De/Grat (2) B1390/02 B1390/13
De/Grat's (1) B1391/05
De/Grave (1) B1260/14
De/Kock (5) B1010/07
 B1010/14 B1010/16 B1010/18 B1010/V
De/L'Omelette (9) A0033/02
 A0033/06 A0034/07 A0034/13 A0035/04
 A0036/06 A0036/19 A0037/17 A0037/V
De/L'Omelette, Duc (1) A0033/T
De/L'Orme's (1) A0388/11
De/Stael (5) A0176/09
 A0176/V A0180/30 A0712/07 B1277/13
Dead (1) A0339/25
dead (106)
deaden (2) A0310/13 A0583/17
deadened (1) B0929/15
deadly (27) A0019/07
 A0144/V A0324/29 A0514/V A0577/07
 A0582/27 A0615/36 A0642/19 A0676/19
 A0681/16 A0682/05 A0693/13 A0694/V
 A0696/10 B0760/V B0826/20 B0852/25
 B0947/23 B0966/18 C0063/07 C0073/01
 C0082/02 C0083/13 C0122/29 C0126/11
 C0440/V C0579/27
deaf (4) B0892/20
 B1226/08 B1371/21 B1371/24
deafen (1) A0589/15
deafening (1) C0168/39
deal (42) A0128/V A0205/14
 A0264/34 A0274/32 A0281/27 A0286/16
 A0342/07 A0343/22 A0367/13 A0490/05
 A0588/27 B0732/33 B0737/27 B0911/V
 B0975/06 B0975/25 B0980/26 B0982/09
 B1009/19 B1057/03 B1138/07 B1157/07
 B1233/09 B1301/35 B1346/32 C0088/28
 C0098/25 C0102/25 C0102/38 C0104/28
 C0110/27 C0118/06 C0123/10 C0140/29
 C0183/18 C0395/02 C0414/11 C0521/25
 C0529/20 C0542/36 C0548/21 C0564/06
dealer (3) A0145/03
 A0482/33 B1304/35
dealers (1) A0243/07
dealings (1) A0486/32
deals (1) A0611/37
dealt (6) A0037/15 A0037/21
 A0047/23 A0441/24 B1059/17 C0536/20
dear (97)
dearest (8) A0153/V
 A0611/22 A0650/15 B0903/17 B0903/V
 B0949/22 B0965/14 B1215/32
dearly (2) C0110/14 C0201/02
Death (13) A0250/30
 ->A0319/27 A0329/17 A0608/05 A0608/10
 A0608/13 A0609/03 A0615/25 A0616/23
 A0662/V B0794/21 B0855/35 B1233/22
death (195)
death-agonies (1) A0416/32
death-bed (2) B1239/33 B1317/27
death-condemned (2) A0589/17
 A0693/01
death-cry (1) A0416/12
death-furniture (2) A0253/28
 A0253/V
death-hour (1) A0514/34
death-producing (1) A0609/29
death-purged (1) A0612/05
death-refined (1) B1274/19
death-struggles (1) A0590/11
death-watches (1) B0794/04
Death's (2) A0070/14 A0081/15
death's-head (16) B0809/28
 B0809/31 B0810/25 B0828/30 B0829/08
 B0831/08 B0831/09 B0831/15 B0832/26
 B0833/01 B0833/16 B0833/33 B0835/05
 B0839/33 B0840/24 B0842/17
Death's-headed (1) B1250/26
death's-heads (1) B0840/03
Death's/Head (1) B1248/28
deathful (1) B1274/06
deathlike (1) A0081/24
deaths (6) A0158/19 A0304/04
 A0690/30 B0724/25 C0076/01 C0134/21
debasement (1) A0099/18
debated (1) C0157/26
debating (1) C0122/26
debauch (1) B0851/31
debaucheries (3) A0021/10
 A0438/23 B0753/17
debbil (1) B0814/17
debbil's (1) B0814/13
debbils (1) B0814/V
debilitated (1) C0131/01
debility (1) C0133/14
debouche (1) C0577/07
debouches (1) C0570/12
debris (1) B1281/23
debt (1) A0442/02
debtor (1) A0441/27
debts (1) B0906/17
debut (1) A0204/31
decade (1) B1188/34
decadence (1) B0759/21
decamped (1) B0977/20
decamps (1) B0877/03
decanter (5) A0299/30
 A0300/11 A0300/15 A0325/03 B1056/32
decay (10) A0081/28 A0121/19
 A0320/16 A0400/16 A0612/21 A0615/36
 A0677/03 B0764/15 B0962/23 B0964/26
decayed (13) A0141/17
 A0397/14 A0400/01 A0400/V A0408/15
 A0427/V A0687/03 B0825/25 B0859/11
 B1160/32 C0058/28 C0126/05 C0142/29
decaying (5) A0244/23
 A0310/10 A0320/05 B1037/18 B1057/09
decays (1) C0534/39
decease (17) A0020/18

->A0034/04 A0059/31 A0227/17 A0232/04
A0404/02 A0704/23 B0933/32 B0949/35
B0959/35 B1101/21 B1208/37 B1234/36
B1246/09 B1269/22 B1359/13 C0390/21
deceased (27) A0217/V
A0409/22 A0410/17 A0538/16 A0538/35
A0539/12 A0540/29 A0544/05 A0546/29
A0561/11 A0613/28 A0622/22 B0730/20
B0731/10 B0735/27 B0746/26 B0751/14
B0757/19 F0764/16 B0768/30 B0768/33
B0933/05 B0949/10 B0950/17 B1126/02
B1179/10 C0108/38
deceased's (1) B0933/35
deceit (2) B0751/25 B0751/26
deceitful (1) C0150/24
deceive (4) B0901/11
B0957/22 B1008/14 C0151/20
deceived (21) A0155/16
A0326/27 A0355/25 A0414/03 A0512/02
A0592/02 A0663/27 A0688/26 B0857/13
B0915/04 B0915/15 B1035/03 C0124/33
C0131/31 C0144/12 C0147/02 C0187/09
C0424/27 C0428/14 C0429/10 C0532/06
December (5) C0146/34
C0146/41 C0158/16 C0158/29 C0159/15
decency (1) A0440/13
decent (7) A0484/03
A0508/16 A0653/V B0877/30 B1141/11
B1207/12 C0564/25
decently (2) A0057/13 A0486/34
deception (8) B0916/01
B0916/10 B0987/06 C0064/30 C0066/19
C0112/05 C0112/22 C0112/38
decide (5) A0075/02
A0497/11 A0558/26 B1046/28 B1384/11
Decided (1) A0052/T
decided (23) A0022/06
A0023/V A0056/28 A0062/09 A0063/24
A0066/18 A0267/03 A0337/28 A0478/03
A0482/16 A0529/06 A0676/15 B0773/15
B0916/03 B0957/17 B0984/25 B0991/18
B1056/25 B1069/32 B1163/15 B1333/16
C0108/17 C0578/36
decidedly (18) A0035/16 A0075/04
A0275/37 A0339/32 A0388/01 A0528/22
A0583/05 B0754/03 B0924/22 B0926/21
B1006/33 B1142/22 B1297/01 B1314/05
B1358/02 B1371/21 C0207/27 C0422/29
decides (1) B0875/24
deciding (2) A0385/20 B0958/12
deciphering (1) B1298/06
decision (18) A0273/24 A0379/V
A0497/12 A0551/07 A0562/13 A0627/02
A0654/26 A0706/03 B0757/08 B0817/17
B0899/01 B1259/12 B1270/32 B1338/29
B1347/13 C0109/15 C0134/32 C0135/18
decisions (1) B1136/05
decisive (8) A0138/20
A0441/07 A0443/09 B0729/03 B0990/14
B1181/27 B1302/10 B1362/02
decisively (1) B1339/31
deck (94)
decked (1) A0165/V
decks (8) A0137/08
C0114/05 C0123/29 C0124/19 C0146/23
->C0188/06 C0189/28 C0189/41
declaration (2) B0899/14 B0958/31
declare (5) A0128/24
A0151/V B0880/01 C0157/20 C0432/10
declared (13) A0027/V
A0056/36 A0353/02 A0707/01 B0877/13
B1155/32 B1234/21 B1272/02 B1294/30
B1301/05 C0130/29 C0165/19 C0388/38
declares (4) A0059/11
A0061/07 B0960/36 B1364/23
declaring (2) B0877/08 B1134/16
decline (6) A0204/19 A0271/11
A0479/02 A0547/06 B0923/29 C0563/05
declined (10) A0227/23 A0232/10
B0733/17 B0822/19 B0960/01 B1140/13
B1328/02 C0175/40 C0199/22 C0207/10
declines (1) B0875/19
declining (8) A0108/10
A0278/23 A0301/25 B1054/15 B1091/07
B1248/20 B1280/28 C0055/07
declivities (2) B1331/23 C0171/33
declivity (8) B1330/21
B1332/11 B1334/11 C0171/38 C0188/39
C0191/26 C0196/13 C0527/08
<u>decollavimus</u> (2) A0125/01 A0125/02
decomposed (1) B0732/21
decomposition (14) B0732/09 B0740/10
B0742/07 B0742/08 B0742/14 B0742/21
B0742/25 B0743/05 B0743/11 B0743/16
B0743/30 B0744/12 B0956/23 B0965/22
<u>decora</u> (2) A0157/18 A0673/12
decoration (4) A0321/04
A0495/01 A0498/26 B1340/18
decorations (6) A0411/23 A0497/22
A0500/29 A0662/09 A0671/28 A0672/06
decorative (1) A0497/01
decorist (1) A0166/01
decorists (1) A0496/01
decorously (1) B1317/29
decorum (5) A0249/01
A0675/02 B0901/23 C0179/39 C0181/25
<u>decouuert</u> (1) C0430/28
decrease (4) C0401/29
C0420/06 C0420/11 C0421/10
decreased (2) C0166/06 C0418/36
decreases (2) A0581/20 C0161/09
decreasing (3) C0401/14
C0403/37 C0424/09
decree (3) A0252/08
A0252/11 A0704/29
decrees (2) A0681/14 B0891/23
decrepid (1) A0511/12
decrepitude (2) A0020/V A0143/14
decrying (2) A0478/07 C0427/11
decypher (2) A0196/15 A0218/01
decyphered (1) A0284/28
decyphering (1) A0241/34
deduce (4) A0684/18
B1298/11 B1316/20 C0065/01
deduced (10) A0274/13 A0279/22
A0402/18 A0473/31 A0497/29 A0498/26
A0688/27 B0902/19 B1032/12 B1317/10
deducible (1) B1214/19
deducing (1) B1220/10
deduct (1) C0400/12

deductions (8) A0212/20
A0212/26 A0530/07 A0550/20 A0550/24
A0550/25 B0749/01 B1317/22
deductive (3) B1295/08
B1310/27 B1317/17
Dee, Dubble L. (5) A0652/20
A0655/14 A0655/21 A0655/26 A0657/16
Dee's, Dubble L. (1) A0657/31
deed (22) A0210/19 A0218/04
A0251/22 A0551/04 A0558/14 A0561/26
B0764/22 B0768/24 B0769/21 B0795/28
B0797/28 B0820/28 B0851/35 B0852/29
B0854/29 B0858/04 B0869/08 B1051/25
B1224/06 B1257/01 B1379/07 C0559/07
deed's (1) B1051/27
deeds (9) A0226/07
A0230/04 A0399/01 A0515/30 A0557/25
A0567/13 B0793/24 C0111/11 C0551/17
deem (3) A0599/M
B1038/34 B1223/24
deemed (8) A0293/21
A0685/13 A0703/06 B0727/08 B0811/08
B0879/06 B1268/06 C0414/34
deep (137)
deep-seated (1) B0843/22
deep-set (2) B0814/28 B1338/35
deep-toned (1) A0609/37
deepen (3) A0399/23
B0943/08 B1050/V
deepened (7) A0510/30
A0510/30 A0602/04 A0605/01 A0640/31
B0943/21 C0418/34
deepening (4) B0794/11
B1031/28 B1050/28 B1280/01
deeper (12) A0020/15
A0509/31 A0582/36 A0589/32 A0696/03
B0861/03 C0192/11 C0407/34 C0407/34
C0419/15 C0575/24 C0576/26
deepest (8) A0055/31
A0073/32 A0078/37 A0161/27 A0304/02
A0682/21 B0905/31 C0568/23
deeply (27) A0067/23
A0086/30 A0099/09 A0104/13 A0190/08
A0213/22 A0226/07 A0264/04 A0315/18
A0353/12 A0436/16 A0441/24 A0457/02
A0532/02 A0578/14 A0675/07 B0755/12
B0886/03 B0890/23 B0895/05 B1144/05
B1249/28 C0183/27 C0207/17 C0425/26
C0552/37 C0565/01
deeply-burthened (1) B0945/26
deeply-laid (1) C0180/08
deeply-shadowed (1) A0428/04
deer (9) B1334/27
B1335/01 C0536/24 C0540/06 C0542/41
C0553/04 C0559/41 C0559/41 C0576/03
deer-stalking (1) B1052/25
defaced (1) B1180/02
default (5) B0962/05
B0968/30 B0985/09 B1116/02 C0404/08
defeat (3) A0528/28
B0986/17 B1195/06
defeated (2) A0568/16 A0654/26
defect (10) A0433/31 A0435/02
A0497/07 A0622/25 A0707/28 B0888/14
B0983/36 B1272/28 B1334/15 B1361/08
defective (4) A0708/25
A0708/28 B1273/19 B1273/23
defects (8) A0707/28
A0709/29 A0710/18 B0906/V B1133/24
B1272/28 B1274/32 B1275/21
defence (10) A0058/20 A0069/09
A0447/16 A0652/04 B1050/02 C0112/32
C0186/05 C0187/06 C0533/34 C0550/16
defenceless (2) B0763/33 B1354/15
defend (3) A0628/21
B1247/08 B1259/21
defended (3) A0044/30
C0395/22 C0577/39
defer (2) A0139/23 C0132/33
deference (3) A0160/04
B1091/32 B1382/03
deferred (2) A0268/26 B1236/32
deferring (1) B0933/24
defiance (10) A0064/V A0212/10
A0438/17 A0444/31 A0671/04 B1093/33
B1136/08 B1222/05 B1317/24 C0075/34
deficiencies (2) A0240/21 B0915/12
deficiency (11) A0135/10
A0356/06 A0399/09 A0399/14 A0624/07
B0750/16 B1156/21 B1184/19 B1346/16
C0087/14 C0207/08
deficient (11) A0055/30
A0065/11 A0065/25 A0272/14 A0499/12
B0888/09 B0907/06 B1137/19 B1373/30
C0148/03 C0411/34
defied (1) B0993/14
defies (1) B1383/08
define (12) A0161/11
A0225/06 A0229/06 A0314/12 A0433/09
A0436/24 A0479/01 A0609/04 A0682/20
B0855/19 B0869/09 B1329/25
defined (12) A0021/03
A0173/16 A0178/25 A0473/05 A0509/26
A0527/V B1089/01 B1239/25 C0152/24
C0387/24 C0418/31 C0422/24
defines (1) A0231/04
defining (2) A0667/59 B0869/10
definite (24) A0079/40
A0217/09 A0234/22 A0303/V A0378/09
A0385/29 A0430/29 A0482/06 A0550/29
A0551/07 A0580/26 A0625/02 A0693/26
B0841/27 B0842/23 B0864/35 B1044/05
B1293/15 B1374/23 C0112/06 C0134/18
C0172/16 C0401/19 C0430/05
definitely (3) A0621/09
A0705/01 B0944/20
definiteness (1) A0365/20
definition (9) A0508/30
A0615/V A0707/05 B0869/16 B1034/13
B1272/05 B1314/34 B1329/26 B1335/22
definitive (2) A0273/05 B0962/06
definitively (3) A0621/V
B0944/V B1256/05
definitiveness (5) A0365/V
A0711/26 B0797/05 B1256/05 B1276/29
deflect (1) B0751/27
deformed (4) A0604/21
A0610/24 B1303/23 C0087/12
deformities (1) A0028/10
deformity (4) A0035/20

->A0298/V B1303/24 C0108/41
defraud (1) A0047/03
Defuncti (1) A0622/19
defy (2) B1272/29 B1315/16
defying (2) A0138/12 A0324/06
degage (2) A0247/03 A0247/V
degenerating (1) B1189/27
degradation (1) A0127/28
degraded (1) C0198/35
degree (132)
degrees (134)
Dei (2) A0213/04 A0213/07
deigning (1) A0136/35
deities (2) B0900/25 B1180/22
Deity (10) A0036/16 A0068/06
A0601/17 B1106/13 B1213/04 B1215/04
B1219/23 B1220/01 B1220/15 B1272/19
deity (6) A0122/28 A0124/20
A0156/11 A0196/24 A0478/18 B0772/17
dejected (2) C0195/26 C0392/06
dejection (2) C0142/37 C0549/22
dejeuner (1) C0176/03
del (2) A0344/24 A0662/V
Del/Rio (2) A0173/03 A0176/11
Delaware (1) B0864/06
delay (18) A0227/20 A0232/07
A0537/11 A0593/22 B0767/01 B0872/07
B0896/19 B0924/31 B1091/11 B1222/07
B1222/17 C0107/10 C0119/17 C0133/35
C0135/03 C0170/24 C0549/14 C0557/28
delayed (1) A0266/24
delectable (2) A0387/V B1300/17
delegates (1) B1207/28
deleterious (2) A0217/V C0101/05
deliberate (12) A0271/19
A0499/12 A0541/V A0676/04 B0862/22
B0877/35 B0990/32 B1017/17 B1136/05
B1384/13 C0202/03 C0427/01
deliberated (1) B0856/34
deliberately (15) A0025/14
A0053/26 A0136/32 A0262/16 A0296/V
A0474/03 B0851/28 B0893/18 B0989/05
B1103/19 B1114/12 C0085/26 C0086/03
C0125/28 C0579/31
deliberateness (1) A0533/20
deliberating (1) C0152/09
deliberation (12) A0488/20
B0823/18 B0825/11 B0826/33 B0856/29
B1013/28 B1132/31 B1224/07 B1315/32
C0186/16 C0398/03 C0546/36
deliberations (2) C0104/23 C0104/36
delicacies (3) B1008/32
C0068/21 C0176/01
delicacy (12) A0063/07
A0269/21 A0301/17 A0302/13 A0381/18
A0641/V B1122/15 B1135/29 B1167/13
B1280/19 B1339/33 B1371/16
delicate (35) A0020/V
A0033/15 A0074/25 A0074/25 A0128/11
A0152/30 A0154/29 A0156/V A0246/31
A0247/07 A0298/V A0311/V A0312/13
A0343/32 A0352/22 A0366/05 A0383/28
A0401/33 A0486/27 A0488/03 A0495/06
B0890/07 B0902/24 B0902/V B0906/11
B0926/36 B1020/29 B1090/03 B1119/09
->B1160/40 B1337/16 B1340/17 C0079/36
C0130/14 C0400/35
delicately (4) A0100/31
A0164/24 B0907/03 B1350/25
delicately-granulated (1) B1333/02
delicious (22) A0150/V A0316/08
A0507/28 B0863/03 B0889/27 B0890/V
B0896/05 B0904/24 B0942/32 B1011/04
B1013/31 B1019/30 B1136/07 B1337/02
C0145/37 C0536/27 C0542/14 C0543/02
C0543/23 C0560/29 C0568/11 C0570/01
deliciously (3) A0348/10
A0348/33 B1333/08
deliciousness (1) C0093/31
Delight (3) A0127/02
A0127/23 A0128/01
delight (36) A0057/20
A0068/03 A0078/18 A0078/29 A0078/37
A0102/15 A0135/07 A0247/16 A0265/35
A0316/05 A0409/09 A0428/06 A0529/16
A0533/12 A0613/25 A0613/26 A0614/37
A0614/37 A0663/V A0702/M B0858/24
B0905/31 B1079/11 B1138/11 B1223/05
B1224/27 B1267/M B1278/07 B1391/14
C0121/04 C0122/22 C0137/22 C0168/36
C0419/37 C0420/35 C0523/38
delighted (14) A0315/11 A0381/21
A0439/02 B0820/34 B0854/15 B0872/01
B0894/28 B0903/08 B1056/01 B1279/36
B1280/28 C0104/10 C0177/13 C0542/21
delightful (6) A0090/03 A0486/30
C0058/20 C0540/14 C0543/11 C0568/06
delightfully (4) A0339/33
A0381/10 B1080/08 B1186/35
delighting (1) A0528/04
delights (1) A0491/15
delikittest> (1) A0468/V
delineate (1) A0245/18
delineated (3) B0833/01
B0945/06 B1122/14
delineation (3) A0164/13
C0193/23 C0208/03
delirious (7) A0438/27
A0591/32 A0640/28 A0673/23 A0673/24
A0681/18 B0895/16
delirium (13) A0166/04
A0461/11 A0612/22 A0644/19 A0644/V
A0663/02 A0667/55 A0682/22 B0894/30
C0081/15 C0127/35 C0398/39 C0561/15
deliver (4) A0490/21
B0858/33 B1152/16 C0104/17
deliverance (16) A0235/13
A0693/22 B0932/33 C0053/T C0062/05
C0065/07 C0073/13 C0096/33 C0117/19
C0122/19 C0124/06 C0125/28 C0127/11
C0131/20 C0562/09 C0563/27
delivered (10) A0059/15 A0067/06
A0074/13 A0556/17 A0695/11 C0066/34
C0067/05 C0139/14 C0175/23 C0188/11
deliverer (3) A0154/17
B0875/18 C0579/30
deliverers (1) A0694/35
delivers (1) B0875/26
delivery (6) A0065/24 A0465/29
A0556/19 A0556/26 C0523/09 C0523/22

dell (1) C0181/02
delly (1) A0354/32
Delos (2) A0196/V A0311/27
Deluc (18) B0723/22 B0734/30
B0735/18 B0735/33 B0735/36 B0761/16
B0767/07 B0767/10 B0767/14 B0767/18
B0767/24 B0767/34 B0768/01 B0768/03
B0768/08 B0768/28 B0769/11 B0770/12
Deluc's (2) B0735/26 B0763/13
delude (1) B0991/22
deluge (4) A0079/08
A0087/34 A0204/25 A0253/24
deluged (4) A0137/26
A0586/14 B1134/01 C0060/16
deluging (1) B1106/21
delusion (1) A0436/23
delusive (1) A0342/12
dem (1) B0813/03
demagogue-ridden (1) B1207/28
demand (18) A0155/03 A0250/17
A0272/21 A0386/22 A0445/11 A0626/01
A0684/28 B0738/30 B0879/06 B0907/13
B0977/23 B0983/23 B1110/06 B1128/03
B1129/22 B1130/30 C0097/09 C0554/19
demande (1) A0033/19
demanded (26) A0023/20 A0178/22
A0180/11 A0191/07 A0217/V A0228/29
A0263/13 A0301/16 A0438/33 A0675/23
B0748/33 B0809/06 B0869/14 B0907/10
B0915/06 B0931/29 B0964/14 B1157/35
B1184/16 B1193/14 B1194/20 B1208/27
B1212/01 B1349/11 C0148/31 C0430/09
demanding (5) A0561/19
B0878/31 B0906/14 B0976/05 C0089/25
demands (4) A0548/19
B0875/32 B0984/09 C0555/28
demarcates (1) A0477/01
demeanor (27) A0025/20
A0027/21 A0104/04 A0105/24 A0161/09
A0311/19 A0317/08 A0329/24 A0412/10
A0414/16 A0415/06 A0436/14 A0479/14
A0508/02 A0512/22 A0513/15 B0811/02
B0816/31 B0825/10 B0843/05 B0877/35
B1140/09 B1249/13 B1249/26 C0531/27
C0562/08 C0568/17
demeanour (9) A0311/V
A0329/V C0059/32 C0081/22 C0093/04
C0133/04 C0170/09 C0176/29 C0190/17
demented (1) B0825/14
demerit (1) A0710/24
demeure (1) A0019/02
demi-god (1) A0078/28
demijohns (1) C0393/32
demnition (1) A0490/09
Democracy (2) B1193/31 B1250/04
democracy (2) A0610/20 B1300/28
Democratic (2) A0075/01 A0490/08
Democritus (2) A0313/21 A0577/M
demolished (4) A0055/11
A0064/27 B1056/29 C0188/08
demolition (1) B1104/09
Demon (7) A0029/08
A0151/V A0195/01 A0198/29 A0198/31
A0199/01 B0865/19
demon (16) A0140/V
->A0190/12 A0198/27 A0235/19 A0242/23
A0296/09 A0323/07 A0403/V A0641/V
A0690/30 A0695/31 B0851/23 B1158/02
B1223/03 C0086/36 C0087/29
demon-like (1) A0026/30
demoniac (2) A0696/07 B1223/V
demoniacal (1) B0856/25
demoniacally (1) B1223/14
demons (7) A0144/02
A0144/02 A0691/16 B0859/06 B0969/16
C0060/37 C0072/13
demonstrable (3) B1214/24
B1314/18 C0429/41
demonstrably (2) B1295/35 B1312/01
demonstrate (9) A0621/20
B0763/29 B0763/30 B1030/15 B1054/02
B1250/16 B1296/32 B1300/28 B1384/09
demonstrated (6) A0458/29 A0624/02
B1164/25 B1167/32 B1189/06 C0535/40
demonstrates (2) B0767/02 B1070/12
demonstrating (1) A0066/21
demonstration (9) B0823/02
B0829/36 B1030/16 B1310/22 B1351/02
B1359/35 C0207/31 C0429/48 C0550/13
demonstrations (5) A0708/17
B1273/12 C0073/08 C0131/16 C0180/02
Demosthenes (4) A0065/16
A0346/01 A0356/24 B1013/02
demur (2) B0841/08 B0904/31
demure (3) A0479/13
A0711/01 B1276/03
demurely (2) A0428/32 C0404/31
demureness (1) B0888/21
den (16) A0372/31
A0510/35 B0811/34 B0812/01 B0812/16
B0812/17 B0812/27 B0820/18 B0854/02
B0911/27 B0912/06 B0912/12 B0912/25
B1102/06 B1102/19 B1103/32
denial (2) B0907/27 B1275/30
denied (8) A0079/02
A0445/22 A0460/17 B0827/16 B0872/08
B0955/25 B1053/27 B1219/15
denies (1) A0601/27
denizen (2) A0233/20 C0425/24
denizens (3) A0298/V
A0550/09 C0431/12
denn (2) A0150/V A0345/07
denominate (5) A0655/14
B0907/10 B1158/30 B1213/20 C0403/08
denominated (2) A0340/23 B1303/19
denominating (1) B1379/24
denomination (1) C0430/04
denoted (1) A0122/30
denoting (1) A0112/06
denouement (4) B0772/29
B0916/22 B1021/16 B1152/06
denounce (1) A0151/11
denouncement (1) B0769/30
denouncing (1) B0769/25
dens (1) B1162/19
dense (29) A0028/25
A0035/07 A0087/21 A0297/V A0426/08
A0507/24 B0758/06 B0761/13 B0807/10
B0819/10 B0853/10 B0943/09 B1003/18
B1035/13 B1076/17 B1157/24 B1161/21

->B1247/31 C0189/26 C0190/07 C0396/27
C0402/02 C0405/14 C0411/02 C0411/14
C0418/45 C0423/04 C0423/35 C0424/27
densely (5) A0512/20
A0674/12 B0817/24 B1279/25 B1303/02
denseness (1) A0508/08
denser (4) A0601/11
C0413/25 C0424/24 C0442/V
densest (1) B0760/05
densities (1) C0402/35
density (13) A0412/23
A0412/27 A0457/22 A0458/30 B0865/09
B1035/11 B1035/12 C0394/01 C0404/07
C0404/28 C0424/01 C0424/14 C0424/29
dental (1) A0219/06
dents (1) A0216/10
denuded (2) B1247/24 C0545/05
denunciations (1) A0461/02
deny (20) A0209/25
A0241/34 A0279/21 A0409/24 A0495/V
A0563/29 A0710/28 B0740/26 B0763/11
B0772/13 B0907/28 B1031/05 B1090/31
B1182/08 B1221/20 B1240/31 B1314/13
B1379/33 C0202/10 C0403/36
denying (5) A0024/04
A0478/05 A0550/12 B1031/06 B1358/02
depart (7) A0020/V
A0264/20 A0314/05 A0674/01 B0858/19
B0872/13 C0399/34
departed (48) A0070/12
A0081/13 A0155/V A0156/26 A0190/17
A0190/24 A0191/16 A0215/17 A0215/18
A0217/V A0218/02 A0233/19 A0247/22
A0311/21 A0318/03 A0322/22 A0323/18
A0323/V A0357/01 A0430/17 A0443/15
A0443/V A0455/V A0541/24 A0594/V
A0605/09 A0612/35 A0615/25 A0616/01
A0617/01 A0639/06 A0642/25 A0643/10
B0764/20 B0811/09 B0820/02 B0901/V
B0942/18 B0948/06 B0957/32 B0992/29
B1004/34 B1096/17 B1105/08 B1179/28
B1385/32 C0134/23 C0206/04
departing (2) A0048/V A0166/06
department (1) C0068/22
departs (4) A0228/21
A0233/02 A0507/11 B0978/02
departure (41) A0025/01
A0057/17 A0078/19 A0128/11 A0136/13
A0286/09 A0300/20 A0347/10 A0429/18
A0440/05 A0547/02 A0685/31 B0728/33
B0732/12 B0735/24 B0735/28 B0755/01
B0755/17 B0874/22 B0908/24 B0981/31
B0992/07 B1044/16 B1049/23 B1053/07
B1075/23 B1105/10 B1239/26 B1331/10
C0069/36 C0170/07 C0179/33 C0390/09
C0396/14 C0401/39 C0412/22 C0419/12
C0425/21 C0522/13 C0554/28 C0570/36
depend (8) A0344/13
A0346/17 B0836/02 B0976/32 B1209/07
B1352/32 C0103/21 C0177/37
dependance (1) C0533/25
depended (22) A0089/08 A0103/17
A0103/30 A0114/17 A0321/24 A0662/13
A0672/09 B0822/22 B1020/31 B1059/20
B1108/22 B1261/27 B1279/25 B1310/22
->B1311/11 B1321/20 C0083/02 C0094/35
C0104/20 C0113/05 C0424/02 C0531/05
dependence (2) B1359/05 C0410/02
dependencies (1) A0293/30
dependent (1) B0890/29
depending (8) A0063/15
A0497/25 B1312/29 B1351/19 C0059/06
C0388/28 C0426/06 C0552/28
depends (14) A0054/07 A0350/27
A0497/V A0503/09 A0710/12 B0906/30
B0961/36 B0985/05 B0985/08 B0986/05
B1275/15 C0080/14 C0092/31 C0431/09
depict (5) A0069/14
A0665/19 B0724/13 C0524/07 C0532/23
depicted (7) A0665/23
B0809/25 B0831/06 B1057/19 B1152/05
C0065/17 C0190/21
depicting (1) B0724/16
deplorable (4) A0403/10
A0514/24 B1187/10 C0145/14
deplorably (2) A0579/01 C0432/42
deplored (1) B1194/15
depopulated (2) A0242/21 A0670/11
depopulating (1) B1152/25
deportment (2) A0099/18 A0104/27
deposed (2) A0542/04 A0542/V
deposes (10) A0538/34 A0539/09
A0539/32 A0540/17 A0541/19 A0541/26
A0542/25 A0543/01 A0543/18 B0732/38
deposit (10) A0410/06 B0834/25
B0842/24 B0879/06 B0980/02 B1053/10
B1074/27 B1113/07 B1119/05 C0575/34
deposite (1) C0089/19
deposited (44) A0070/12
A0081/13 A0106/17 A0247/14 A0325/03
A0410/12 A0615/25 A0616/09 B0761/08
B0761/28 B0761/30 B0762/09 B0796/10
B0811/01 B0827/01 B0827/13 B0830/30
B0857/14 B0925/20 B0929/19 B0956/24
B0960/07 B0979/31 B0979/35 B0983/12
B0983/31 B0990/08 B1009/02 B1058/27
B1059/09 B1155/28 B1179/11 B1325/06
B1352/16 C0077/09 C0188/24 C0394/22
C0395/16 C0415/29 C0426/34 C0533/30
C0534/07 C0534/27 C0576/01
depositing (2) B1010/23 B1305/07
deposition (1) B1074/23
deposits (1) A0541/15
depot (1) C0394/31
depot (1) C0576/40
depraved (1) A0557/09
deprecates (1) B1221/28
depredations (1) A0243/15
depressed (10) A0189/33 A0248/V
B0981/31 B1246/16 B1276/25 B1336/06
C0418/29 C0537/14 C0549/02 C0549/21
depresses (1) B1278/15
depressing (1) C0143/12
depression (6) A0023/15 A0282/06
A0397/15 B1277/27 B1331/36 B1334/09
depressions (2) A0688/30 A0688/33
deprivation (1) C0138/09
deprive (4) A0612/27
B1187/28 C0394/15 C0399/02
deprived (17) A0059/18

->A0121/16 A0529/08 A0631/04 A0665/06
A0667/33 A0694/04 B0741/23 B0760/12
B0834/13 B0855/02 B0905/05 B1154/07
C0207/40 C0413/29 C0421/36 C0562/04
depriving (1) B1170/05
depth (43) A0086/18
A0087/22 A0096/18 A0337/35 A0398/05
A0405/34 A0410/02 A0545/18 A0560/17
A0577/M A0581/18 A0581/20 A0581/27
A0582/14 A0582/18 A0590/20 B0742/17
B0823/21 B0823/27 B0981/V B1162/05
B1261/11 B1261/18 B1262/12 B1280/12
B1381/32 C0152/39 C0169/15 C0173/24
C0185/17 C0191/32 C0194/04 C0196/04
C0196/15 C0197/28 C0202/24 C0394/21
C0438/V C0439/V C0536/02 C0537/37
C0567/17 C0575/37
depths (14) A0190/19 A0191/06
A0234/26 A0245/11 A0589/01 A0603/27
A0639/30 A0644/24 B0964/31 B1144/14
B1168/08 B1281/19 C0205/29 C0413/03
deputed (2) A0338/33 B0796/22
deputes (1) B1152/28
der (6) A0342/01 A0342/02
A0342/V A0342/V B0723/M B0723/M
der (5) A0373/06
A0373/09 B0913/07 B1109/07 B1110/08
deranged (1) B1012/34
derangement (1) A0667/30
derided (1) A0435/V
deriding (1) A0054/28
derision (4) A0063/28
B0797/25 C0085/26 C0087/34
derisive (1) B0773/32
derivable (2) A0600/02 B0850/18
derivation (6) A0124/21 A0366/03
A0366/11 A0366/22 A0536/V B1091/28
Derivationibus (1) A0366/17
derive (6) A0122/24 B0862/32
B0987/07 C0137/29 C0142/04 C0200/04
derived (20) A0073/19
A0209/05 A0314/09 A0430/25 A0459/12
A0507/14 A0529/23 A0533/13 A0599/04
B0725/29 B0850/14 B0942/06 B1089/03
B1115/14 B1162/27 B1170/01 B1194/21
B1382/04 C0120/09 C0538/36
derives (2) A0528/06 B1162/34
deriving (2) B1092/33 C0077/33
derogate (1) A0478/06
Derome (1) A0301/07
des (15) A0053/14
A0062/21 A0102/10 A0106/05 A0216/09
A0216/10 A0216/10 A0216/11 A0568/07
A0600/01 A0600/01 B0723/M C0430/36
C0430/36 C0522/35
des (5) A0534/02
A0537/02 A0537/04 A0546/31 B0729/09
Des/Moines (1) C0551/15
descant (2) B1131/14 C0530/08
descanted (1) A0161/20
descend (13) A0124/02
B0755/13 B0821/30 B0905/26 B1070/15
B1074/09 B1074/24 B1074/31 B1081/24
B1352/22 C0121/28 C0405/30 C0408/27
descendant (1) A0427/18
descendants (1) C0522/28
descended (41) A0020/03
A0028/18 A0085/08 A0217/V A0353/21
A0370/30 A0507/33 A0543/14 A0592/18
A0593/32 A0603/28 A0616/29 A0690/14
B0856/23 B0858/15 B0945/24 B0946/15
B0946/17 B0947/04 B1154/13 B1261/01
B1303/29 C0068/31 C0084/28 C0094/12
C0095/37 C0113/41 C0121/15 C0121/37
C0127/26 C0137/01 C0192/01 C0192/27
C0197/14 C0197/29 C0387/19 C0389/09
C0389/32 C0446/V C0528/03 C0575/22
descending (21) A0054/29
A0063/30 A0140/23 A0509/30 A0562/11
B0905/20 B1071/19 B1106/32 B1261/01
B1294/27 B1330/24 C0075/10 C0111/09
C0111/26 C0136/19 C0191/25 C0193/07
C0196/05 C0196/13 C0196/21 C0197/22
descends (3) B0993/11
B1163/34 B1280/34
descensus (1) B0993/08
Descent (2) A0577/T B1380/07
descent (54)
descents (2) A0580/17 A0591/33
describe (27) A0352/17
A0373/11 A0433/10 A0435/07 A0436/19
A0443/16 A0549/22 A0582/01 A0591/14
A0663/11 A0682/21 A0693/21 B0796/05
B0826/17 B0857/30 B0905/09 B0944/33
B0946/10 B1224/15 B1247/34 B1277/16
B1330/27 B1335/32 B1370/22 B1372/21
B1391/12 C0079/01
described (53)
describing (5) A0585/31
B1240/10 B1250/15 B1381/29 C0116/23
descried (4) A0509/13
C0146/13 C0161/29 C0571/17
description (34) A0054/13 A0124/28
A0241/07 A0244/V A0245/24 A0293/02
A0389/09 A0444/16 A0510/27 A0559/25
A0581/15 B0732/27 B0750/24 B0877/07
B0980/08 B0981/26 B0981/30 B0989/16
B0991/14 B1014/05 B1057/14 B1163/14
B1277/16 C0072/11 C0166/18 C0172/36
C0178/01 C0185/08 C0422/36 C0429/19
C0431/03 C0433/05 C0533/05 C0548/06
descriptions (4) B0924/18
C0152/05 C0198/34 C0544/15
descriptive (2) A0559/19 B0876/23
dese (1) B0912/07
desecrate (1) B0760/07
desecrating (1) B1130/02
desecration (1) B0760/V
desert (9) A0139/07
A0195/09 A0198/09 A0198/15 A0354/09
B1160/26 C0138/07 C0522/10 C0528/17
deserted (9) A0062/19
A0151/22 A0349/21 A0513/10 A0532/15
B0750/13 B1049/34 C0527/39 C0576/18
deserting (2) A0513/28 C0548/28
desertion (1) C0104/17
deserts (2) A0053/12 C0072/15
deserve (2) C0073/27 C0391/15
deserved (9) A0317/20
A0317/21 A0433/04 A0567/12 B1131/37

->B1136/25 B1375/16 B1379/02 C0546/05
deserves (3) A0297/18
B1139/05 C0150/21
deshabille (1) A0034/01
desideratum (1) B1072/14
design (100)
designate (1) B0768/03
designated (9) A0024/20
A0431/20 A0664/28 B0750/15 B1133/32
B1249/17 B1293/03 B1358/30 C0560/20
designates (2) A0561/30 B0769/01
designation (1) B1317/34
designations (1) A0235/05
designed (19) A0550/25
A0691/31 B0733/20 B0831/24 B0832/16
B0923/27 B0966/01 B1157/13 B1237/05
B1248/31 B1274/05 B1340/12 B1351/18
B1359/13 B1383/27 C0158/15 C0394/20
C0530/18 C0554/03
designedly (1) A0350/06
designs (14) A0160/07 A0250/28
A0405/21 A0502/14 A0711/16 B0755/02
B0984/03 B1158/10 B1219/18 B1276/17
C0103/10 C0133/10 C0522/04 C0557/17
desirable (3) B1178/21
C0092/05 C0147/14
desire (55)
desired (24) A0183/08
A0266/28 A0303/08 A0386/20 A0473/09
A0583/19 A0696/30 B0762/25 B0772/05
B0796/30 B0874/20 B0892/V B0901/26
B0977/32 B1077/07 B1140/33 B1194/34
B1300/05 B1349/26 C0121/21 C0132/21
C0147/25 C0181/38 C0569/03
desires (4) A0054/35
B0760/16 C0065/22 C0065/22
desirous (6) A0073/28 A0366/15
A0567/12 B0960/18 B1159/07 C0076/16
desist (2) A0667/31 C0139/25
desk (1) B1145/20
deskism (1) A0508/26
desks (1) A0430/12
desolate (16) A0021/21
A0121/22 A0145/14 A0214/12 A0244/14
A0397/10 A0407/28 A0532/17 A0579/01
B0817/16 B0963/09 B1160/30 C0065/21
C0199/03 C0201/36 C0528/31
Desolation (1) A0196/18
desolation (8) A0122/18
A0196/07 A0196/31 A0320/04 A0514/31
B0942/32 B1247/26 C0524/06
Desolation/Island (2) C0150/08
C0150/20
Desoulieres (1) B1012/V
Desoulieres (1) B1012/24
Desoulieres, Jules (1) B1012/20
despair (62)
despaired (2) A0402/32 C0077/32
despairing (4) A0677/01
B0965/04 B1107/22 C0201/34
despairingly (1) A0593/20
despatch (2) C0082/05 C0201/12
despatched (6) B1057/32 B1082/03
B1129/05 C0113/03 C0113/13 C0160/04
despatches (1) B1208/16
despera-a-ado (1) A0385/34
desperado (4) A0380/25
A0384/01 A0384/24 A0385/12
desperadoes (2) B0734/06 C0187/02
desperate (24) A0022/V
A0037/04 A0037/05 A0053/20 A0072/05
A0086/01 A0272/17 A0281/27 A0297/04
A0347/16 A0351/34 A0372/11 A0446/18
A0509/15 A0514/24 A0583/33 B0725/27
B0824/11 B0992/30 B1134/26 C0075/16
C0092/11 C0186/21 C0196/12
desperately (10) A0253/30 A0316/24
A0430/13 A0611/01 A0662/02 A0695/09
B0989/06 B1177/02 C0182/16 C0190/12
desperation (3) A0684/12
B1370/25 C0200/41
despicable (1) A0440/22
despise (3) A0481/02
B0988/35 B1072/13
despised (4) A0435/35
A0611/02 A0625/26 A0644/V
despises (2) B0760/14 B0878/23
despising (1) B0899/23
despite (6) A0610/17 B1113/11
B1153/02 B1153/V B1166/V C0062/18
despoiled (1) B0751/13
despondency (1) C0078/38
despondingly (1) C0120/30
desposition (1) C0522/09
despotic (1) A0293/26
despotism (4) A0431/27
A0431/27 B1194/11 B1300/16
dessein (1) B0993/26
dessert (2) B1101/02 B1110/20
destination (4) A0069/08
B1208/22 C0067/35 C0098/24
destined (6) A0690/24 B1263/01
C0147/01 C0147/13 C0172/17 C0394/30
destinies (5) A0408/23
A0600/30 A0601/25 C0426/07 C0426/08
destiny (17) A0141/31
A0146/05 A0234/13 A0235/14 A0349/27
A0350/28 A0428/18 A0444/34 A0707/19
B0869/23 B0966/03 B1108/16 B1123/04
B1220/10 B1272/18 C0065/25 C0094/35
destitute (5) A0432/09
B0750/25 C0161/16 C0165/25 C0576/32
destroy (4) A0144/03
B0855/14 B1034/20 C0389/14
destroyed (14) A0054/02 A0063/11
A0078/36 A0121/19 A0216/11 A0549/01
A0551/04 B0789/03 B0831/17 B0849/08
B0855/26 B0856/01 B0978/35 B1223/20
destroyer (5) A0211/05
A0404/24 A0445/30 A0461/14 C0061/22
destroying (3) A0693/19
B0856/33 C0205/07
destruction (26) A0137/14 A0145/25
A0455/V A0457/17 A0457/31 A0459/02
A0586/07 A0590/10 A0610/27 A0690/32
A0696/08 B0852/33 B0993/06 B1294/12
C0060/02 C0060/22 C0063/08 C0116/03
C0165/07 C0180/08 C0185/24 C0186/06
C0405/35 C0420/25 C0446/V C0568/14
Desultory (1) B1095/T

desultory (3) A0165/17
A0214/10 B1114/09
detach (1) A0693/10
detached (1) A0281/05
detaching (3) B0957/30
B1304/01 C0535/12
detachment (3) C0156/05
C0186/38 C0539/33
detachments (1) C0172/22
detail (31) A0204/29
A0283/07 A0299/03 A0320/27 A0328/22
A0440/14 A0709/08 B0723/15 B0774/02
B0828/25 B0829/11 B0830/35 B0850/05
B0861/02 B0906/12 B0949/12 B0979/14
B1030/18 B1126/16 B1144/35 B1192/10
B1274/13 B1277/17 B1312/20 B1320/01
B1340/23 C0198/39 C0399/38 C0426/15
C0428/05 C0522/32
detailed (17) A0087/12
A0403/01 A0532/03 A0544/24 A0564/V
B0757/13 B0853/30 B0915/02 B0983/24
B1057/27 B1069/14 B1191/12 B1357/02
C0404/17 C0431/09 C0522/03 C0550/25
detailing (5) A0533/26
B0853/02 B0949/26 B0988/31 C0055/15
details (41) A0074/18
A0075/05 A0100/23 A0321/09 A0340/22
A0352/18 A0398/07 A0427/09 A0428/14
A0456/25 A0461/02 A0507/33 A0581/16
A0708/01 B0723/25 B0724/07 B0724/21
B0763/22 B0772/03 B0839/25 B0888/25
B0908/19 B0975/22 B1005/32 B1074/03
B1187/11 B1224/15 B1273/01 B1296/17
B1303/29 B1358/25 B1361/21 B1363/33
C0053/T C0096/12 C0134/02 C0147/29
C0207/11 C0425/30 C0429/12 C0433/06
detain (4) A0548/18
C0203/34 C0390/08 C0549/11
detained (7) B0771/27
B0873/26 B0900/10 B0942/25 C0558/25
C0569/37 C0570/29
detaining (1) A0317/17
detect (13) A0135/09
A0278/17 A0312/05 A0326/26 A0509/21
B0840/19 B0857/12 B0961/12 B0962/15
B0980/11 B1054/04 C0079/37 C0415/17
detected (5) A0555/23
B0796/12 B0979/34 C0198/40 C0438/V
detecting (10) A0136/28 A0513/04
A0675/12 A0709/25 A0710/14 B1274/28
B1275/16 C0428/11 C0428/29 C0448/V
detection (4) B0980/14
B1224/09 B1300/06 C0553/23
detects (1) C0547/27
detention (1) C0091/39
deter (4) A0242/31
C0144/23 C0187/23 C0406/31
<u>deteriora</u> (1) A0495/04
deteriorate (1) B1071/03
determinate (1) C0109/35
determination (20) A0056/37
A0058/34 A0066/26 A0078/02 B0737/29
B0748/22 B0902/22 B0950/02 B0986/07
B1047/12 B1048/11 B1048/13 B1053/13
B1371/03 C0075/28 C0104/01 C0104/05
->C0156/37 C0192/31 C0576/13
determine (21) A0078/14
A0161/07 A0250/24 A0501/23 A0688/08
B0929/19 B1081/10 B1142/02 B1158/16
B1164/29 B1214/02 B1317/02 B1317/08
B1333/30 B1337/12 B1345/09 C0105/11
C0110/13 C0120/24 C0406/33 C0525/16
determined (72)
determines (1) A0226/30
determining (5) B1072/07
B1082/11 B1214/06 B1214/36 C0070/41
deterred (3) B0769/17
C0055/10 C0103/36
deters (2) B0901/23 B1223/12
detestable (9) A0079/03
A0262/29 A0351/09 A0434/12 A0445/02
A0499/21 B1106/17 B1163/05 B1243/05
detestably (1) A0624/08
detestation (1) A0426/04
detested (2) B0857/31 C0096/14
detract (1) B1380/15
detracts (1) B0865/11
detriment (2) B0863/13 B1115/20
detrimental (1) B1351/28
deuced (3) B0812/V
B0812/V B0816/V
<u>deux</u> (2) A0018/12 A0037/08
dev-- (4) A0091/34
A0092/14 A0111/11 A0111/24
devastated (1) A0670/01
develop (1) A0622/08
develope (1) B0891/11
developed (3) A0298/V
A0427/22 C0127/10
developing (2) A0128/03 B0835/30
development (11) A0215/27
A0234/02 A0404/V A0430/26 B0724/20
B0728/15 B0839/27 B1191/04 B1221/12
B1301/12 B1312/31
developments (1) B1364/13
deviate (2) A0300/05 B1302/07
deviations (4) A0078/17
A0548/01 A0615/11 A0615/12
device (7) A0211/30
A0267/37 A0271/27 A0321/23 A0405/32
B0765/27 B1347/09
devices (9) A0036/01
A0100/17 A0165/23 A0498/18 A0501/21
A0502/02 A0689/02 B1281/01 C0573/20
Devil (10) A0034/05 A0252/24
A0365/T A0387/V A0624/05 A0624/14
A0624/26 A0626/03 A0626/31 A0627/23
devil (34) A0024/10 A0054/05
A0054/15 A0072/18 A0088/20 A0090/17
A0103/01 A0105/24 A0108/27 A0109/06
A0109/17 A0110/V A0112/02 A0128/V
A0249/26 A0280/05 A0621/T A0629/V
A0630/12 B0808/23 B1092/30 B1130/23
B1207/03 B1207/13 B1208/19 B1208/24
B1208/32 B1208/34 B1372/12 B1372/14
B1375/14 B1379/25 C0393/05 C0395/32
devil-me-care (1) A0285/07
Devil's (1) B0843/30
devil's (5) A0372/09
B0839/31 B0840/03 B0842/29 B0968/02

devil's-seat (1) B0841/22
Devil's/seat (1) B0840/21
devilish (1) B1018/22
devils (5) B1019/22
B1316/02 B1373/02 C0064/33 C0388/03
devious (3) A0514/04
A0639/29 B1334/12
devise (5) C0130/13
C0132/34 C0134/07 C0176/05 C0198/20
devised (2) B1007/13 C0077/03
devising (2) A0705/11 C0120/08
devoid (5) A0274/31
A0278/32 A0558/10 B1129/20 C0087/21
devolving (1) B0924/11
devote (1) B0941/08
devoted (11) A0250/09
A0560/23 A0704/12 A0712/04 B0888/27
B0900/24 B0992/31 B1269/12 C0148/03
C0187/38 C0393/03
devotedly (1) A0663/12
devotees (1) A0044/13
devoting (3) A0711/34
B0979/17 B1277/01
devotion (8) A0311/09
A0317/19 A0399/02 A0624/27 B0747/35
B0894/32 B0899/10 B0902/15
devotional (1) C0537/30
devour (3) B0969/17
C0074/03 C0175/36
devoured (11) A0127/19
A0356/30 A0694/01 B1299/24 C0076/28
C0077/29 C0083/34 C0135/35 C0137/03
C0143/09 C0165/18
devouring (3) A0123/20
C0170/18 C0567/08
devours (1) B0875/08
devout (4) A0457/03
A0642/12 B0888/V B1152/20
devoutest (1) A0313/24
devoutly (2) A0150/V A0663/12
Dew (2) A0281/17 A0284/06
dew (6) A0196/26 A0643/10
A0702/M B1074/07 B1074/10 B1267/M
dew-drop (1) B0943/16
Dew, T. R. (1) A0281/13
dews (2) A0195/19 C0559/04
dexterity (6) A0344/07 A0445/24
A0479/17 B1018/08 B1166/28 B1346/18
dexterous (3) A0125/V
A0388/34 B1011/30
dexterously (1) A0068/20
dey (2) B0809/01 B0812/16
DeGrat's (1) B1391/V
di (2) A0151/14 B1386/04
Di/Broglio (1) A0446/28
di/Mentoni (1) A0164/V
Diable (4) A0037/01
A0037/02 A0037/26 C0538/12
diable (2) A0540/11 A0541/10
Diable/rapid (1) C0538/15
diablerie (1) A0054/17
diablerie (1) A0099/09
diabolical (4) A0203/07
B1374/24 C0086/15 C0135/13
diagnosis (4) A0404/19
->A0627/01 B0962/07 B1235/35
diagonal (1) C0157/36
diagonally (10) A0101/04 A0274/34
A0276/01 A0279/14 B0832/33 B0833/16
B1008/26 B1336/32 C0106/24 C0107/40
Dial (4) A0342/09
A0622/02 A0627/03 B1193/25
dial (1) B1104/09
dial-plate (3) A0352/24
A0354/17 A0367/30
dialect (2) B1092/05 B1158/36
dialects (1) A0315/19
dialogue (1) B1032/17
diameter (36) A0322/15
A0351/27 A0458/15 A0459/20 A0580/27
B0822/02 B0822/13 B0823/26 B1071/28
B1161/35 B1192/13 B1248/04 B1248/25
B1280/04 B1333/03 B1333/23 C0153/01
C0393/30 C0394/20 C0400/33 C0401/37
C0404/40 C0410/30 C0418/06 C0418/31
C0418/41 C0419/14 C0419/29 C0420/06
C0420/11 C0421/17 C0425/14 C0428/32
C0429/42 C0430/23 C0575/35
diameters (1) B1351/11
diametrically (1) B1352/30
diamond (5) A0512/05
B0877/05 B0877/16 B0877/24 B0890/08
diamond-like (2) B1137/40 B1138/15
diamonds (4) A0152/27
A0384/20 B0827/33 B1160/12
Dian (2) A0175/29 A0181/24
Diana (14) A0120/06 A0347/20
A0348/21 A0348/23 A0349/20 A0350/12
A0350/13 A0350/16 A0350/18 A0352/09
A0353/16 A0353/32 A0356/28 A0599/M
Dianam (1) A0056/09
diaphragm (1) A0097/23
diaries (1) B1069/24
Diary (9) A0340/08
B1358/06 B1358/13 B1358/16 B1358/17
B1359/12 B1360/03 C0523/15 C0523/22
diary (3) B1390/02
C0522/30 C0522/32
diatribe (1) B1139/15
Diavolo (1) A0177/08
Diavolo (1) A0182/36
diavolo (1) A0177/04
dice (2) B0773/22 B0773/30
dicebant (2) A0209/M A0218/14
Dick (3) A0347/08
B0876/V B1183/14
Dick/street (1) B0876/29
Dickens (1) B1051/19
dickey (3) A0485/03
A0485/16 A0485/17
dickeys (1) A0485/18
dicta (1) A0096/17
dictate (1) B1219/19
dictated (1) A0343/19
dictates (2) B0899/22 C0147/35
dictation (1) A0431/26
dictatorial (1) A0265/24
diction (1) A0611/34
dictionary (1) B1128/02
Dictu, Horribile (1) A0205/21

dictum (1) A0527/V
did (457)
did'st (1) A0162/V
didactic (1) A0341/10
Didcot (1) B1166/32
diddle (1) B1158/33
diddle (23) B0869/07
B0869/23 B0869/24 B0869/M B0869/M
B0870/09 B0870/14 B0870/14 B0871/09
B0871/22 B0871/23 B0871/31 B0872/16
B0873/10 B0873/17 B0874/23 B0874/24
B0874/33 B0875/26 B0875/31 B0876/20
B0877/04 B0877/30
diddled (1) B0869/26
diddler (30) B0870/03 B0870/08
B0870/13 B0870/18 B0870/23 B0870/25
B0870/27 B0870/30 B0870/33 B0871/06
B0871/10 B0871/15 B0871/21 B0871/24
B0871/25 B0872/09 B0873/16 B0874/26
B0874/30 B0875/01 B0875/04 B0875/07
B0875/08 B0875/13 B0875/14 B0875/31
B0876/03 B0876/16 B0876/24 B0877/01
Diddler, Jeremy (1) B0869/V
diddler's (4) B0874/33
B0875/05 B0875/08 B0875/14
diddles (4) B0869/12
B0869/17 B0869/18 B0869/23
diddling (8) B0869/07
B0869/09 B0869/11 B0869/21 B0869/27
B0869/T B0870/07 B0877/26
didn't (9) A0345/23
A0465/12 A0488/05 A0655/17 B0811/24
B0812/27 B0876/07 B0876/11 B0900/V
didst (6) A0162/20 A0228/18
A0228/20 A0232/23 A0233/01 A0448/15
die (2) B0723/M B0723/M
die (47) A0020/V
A0058/31 A0069/20 A0077/01 A0150/V
A0150/V A0158/18 A0158/18 A0158/V
A0190/16 A0228/12 A0232/17 A0235/02
A0316/24 A0345/09 A0345/09 A0345/12
A0345/32 A0506/03 A0506/05 A0564/17
A0588/30 A0642/02 A0651/18 A0673/33
B0797/26 B0849/05 B0956/15 B1032/24
B1032/28 B1057/29 B1108/04 B1108/07
B1126/03 B1142/12 B1235/36 B1238/29
B1259/18 C0073/04 C0119/13 C0132/05
C0134/41 C0135/10 C0144/11 C0398/36
C0432/04 C0562/01
died (63)
dies (3) B0916/28
B1163/19 B1208/36
diet (2) B1006/09 B1166/04
dieth (3) A0310/M
A0314/26 A0318/V
Dieu (6) A0034/01 A0101/V
A0541/10 A0541/31 A0560/05 B1016/08
dieu (1) B1014/18
differ (8) A0098/15
A0101/12 A0269/03 B0766/17 B1092/20
B1168/16 B1257/12 C0552/26
differed (4) A0018/11
B0813/32 B0962/31 C0575/25
difference (38) A0027/08 A0079/36
A0161/06 A0161/08 A0181/16 A0366/25
->A0368/33 A0388/25 A0512/30 A0530/03
A0531/07 A0552/34 A0589/35 A0592/15
A0603/05 A0655/18 A0696/27 B0741/32
B0741/34 B0749/15 B0855/25 B1035/18
B1074/05 B1105/35 B1168/17 B1168/20
B1168/21 B1178/01 B1207/23 B1207/24
B1382/11 C0056/31 C0148/40 C0157/02
C0171/37 C0403/09 C0421/36 C0562/07
differences (3) A0530/13
B0991/20 B1113/04
different (67)
Differential (1) B0986/23
differently (1) A0210/22
differing (5) B0980/03
C0171/16 C0174/02 C0202/24 C0565/39
differs (5) A0550/04
B0736/20 B0903/15 C0544/14 C0577/17
difficult (55)
difficulties (20) A0073/14
A0486/33 A0584/20 B0736/34 B1096/06
C0066/05 C0072/03 C0074/38 C0076/14
C0079/23 C0114/07 C0122/14 C0147/24
C0160/18 C0166/13 C0191/27 C0424/21
C0522/30 C0532/22 C0574/34
difficulty (173)
diffident (1) C0392/28
diffuse (2) A0281/23 B0955/19
diffused (3) A0696/04
C0078/19 C0430/18
diffuseness (1) B1114/27
Diffusion (1) A0337/18
diffusion (5) A0496/24
B1250/04 B1250/05 B1322/17 C0430/11
diffusive (1) A0341/15
dig (4) B0823/01
B0856/34 B1162/16 C0196/31
digest (1) B0924/02
digested (1) B0832/20
digestion (1) B1153/15
digestive (1) C0535/39
diggers (2) B0834/V B1312/26
digging (5) B0822/15
B0825/03 B0843/12 B1303/31 C0432/44
digits (1) A0559/25
digne (2) B0993/27 B0993/27
dignified (9) A0107/01
A0246/27 A0249/11 A0383/08 B0942/14
B1132/32 B1295/25 B1311/22 B1370/10
dignitaries (2) A0021/25 C0390/35
dignitary (1) A0370/11
dignitary's (1) B0990/15
dignities (1) A0204/12
dignity (26) A0026/23 A0086/23
A0097/17 A0100/24 A0126/11 A0126/16
A0141/19 A0203/12 A0249/34 A0251/12
A0263/17 A0266/17 A0295/23 A0372/02
A0380/18 A0433/05 A0706/05 B0903/07
B1003/31 B1056/31 B1103/04 B1194/34
B1271/09 B1372/13 C0390/28 C0426/35
digress (1) B1051/12
digression (1) C0107/04
dilapidated (1) B1003/20
dilapidation (1) A0400/09
dilatation (1) B0940/V
dilate (7) A0086/25

->A0100/01 A0295/V A0317/23 A0352/16
B1089/17 C0401/39
dilation (2) B0940/19 C0400/40
dilemma (9) B0930/33
B0933/29 B1132/15 C0079/08 C0175/19
C0397/36 C0414/28 C0554/15 C0559/28
dilemma'd (1) B1116/01
diligence (3) A0545/09
B1145/17 C0395/24
diligent (3) A0365/13
B0840/28 C0157/13
diligently (2) A0135/05 A0478/29
dilikittest> (1) A0468/17
dillikittest> (1) A0467/29
diluted (2) B0832/21 B1104/26
dim (30) A0079/29 A0138/27
A0140/15 A0151/03 A0152/09 A0162/24
A0189/19 A0191/10 A0198/26 A0217/12
A0227/26 A0227/35 A0232/12 A0235/22
A0320/05 A0328/04 A0403/29 A0427/06
A0436/17 A0514/25 A0545/25 A0602/02
A0639/17 B0794/29 B0942/16 C0073/02
C0109/10 C0397/32 C0412/38 C0443/V
dim-remembered (1) A0407/31
dimension (2) B0738/24 B1248/16
dimensions (17) A0034/25
A0066/05 A0297/V A0380/16 A0430/18
A0685/25 A0688/14 B0933/31 B1008/22
B1071/27 B1073/04 B1192/15 C0389/31
C0393/21 C0393/25 C0409/18 C0533/17
diminish (2) B1364/17 C0404/14
diminished (21) A0438/10
A0512/28 A0528/33 A0615/28 B0745/15
B0750/06 B0756/19 B0931/05 B1014/33
B1359/18 B1359/20 B1359/23 C0139/38
C0164/21 C0181/07 C0400/10 C0407/04
C0419/14 C0421/10 C0424/08 C0558/28
diminishing (5) B1074/06
C0401/27 C0402/35 C0403/05 C0403/25
diminution (8) A0446/16
B0940/18 C0117/27 C0146/02 C0402/38
C0418/40 C0419/29 C0430/10
diminutive (19) A0064/19
A0160/16 A0246/30 A0267/30 A0283/02
A0370/29 A0380/13 A0502/09 A0534/14
A0536/27 B0901/V B0991/07 B0991/17
B1008/09 B1293/13 B1302/20 C0191/12
C0418/13 C0425/06
diminutively (1) A0099/29
dimmer (1) A0639/21
dimness (4) A0509/19
A0641/09 A0643/21 C0205/33
dimpled (1) A0245/27
dimples (2) A0312/20 A0330/09
din (6) A0374/05 A0587/16
B1353/05 C0116/22 C0168/38 C0415/04
dine (1) B1007/23
dined (1) A0205/07
dingy (2) A0140/07 A0367/V
dining (2) B1008/16 B1178/32
dining-room (7) A0205/02
A0650/V A0654/15 B0928/20 B1008/21
B1100/03 B1110/13
dining-table (1) B1020/18
dinner (24) A0068/01
->A0175/02 A0180/25 A0204/10 A0204/15
B0871/13 B0875/V B1007/09 B1007/23
B1007/26 B1008/14 B1017/35 B1020/30
B1045/30 B1091/19 B1100/02 B1105/13
B1142/10 B1158/34 B1167/10 C0093/07
C0101/22 C0175/31 C0566/26
dinner-table (1) B1013/08
dinners (1) B1136/29
dint (14) A0212/04 A0403/27
A0490/11 A0689/17 B0773/10 B0932/22
B0990/01 B1206/08 B1300/21 B1317/20
B1362/08 C0113/19 C0184/01 C0188/08
Diodorus (2) A0059/09 A0061/05
Diogenes (3) A0037/23
B0870/25 B1091/35
Dionysius (2) A0093/05 A0112/17
Dios (1) A0183/01
dios (2) A0177/03 A0177/08
dip (1) B1282/06
diplomacy (4) A0092/16
A0111/26 B0976/25 B1178/19
diplomatist (2) A0105/03 B0957/19
dipped (2) A0037/01 B1076/33
dipping (1) B1115/05
dips (2) B0875/02 B1281/22
dire (2) A0602/07 A0681/M
direct (44) A0073/18
A0080/30 A0101/04 A0264/30 A0399/07
A0500/08 A0510/05 A0533/16 A0546/02
A0548/07 A0614/04 A0652/05 A0686/26
A0707/14 B0728/18 B0729/12 B0746/V
B0760/28 B0888/05 B0903/22 B0956/04
B1050/26 B1079/26 B1116/11 B1139/24
B1169/19 B1188/30 B1193/07 B1213/09
B1214/06 B1223/25 B1272/13 B1282/25
B1321/23 C0066/02 C0101/25 C0418/47
C0420/14 C0430/13 C0438/V C0525/23
C0536/11 C0536/18 C0559/11
directed (29) A0218/30
A0249/15 A0268/28 A0673/17 B0734/11
B0758/23 B0761/05 B0770/15 B0795/05
B0836/04 B0982/31 B1057/17 B1072/03
B1075/14 B1119/21 B1168/05 B1182/12
B1249/16 B1298/04 B1360/06 B1361/33
C0080/31 C0144/37 C0390/26 C0392/17
C0393/22 C0422/20 C0437/V C0553/15
directing (6) A0286/04 A0704/24
B0761/01 B1237/08 B1269/23 C0195/17
direction (119)
directions (33) A0153/20
A0353/16 A0514/26 A0537/26 A0552/06
A0614/08 A0685/01 A0693/19 A0695/32
B0762/23 B0762/31 B0763/32 B0810/34
B0817/29 B0841/30 B0945/07 B1294/20
B1294/26 B1301/23 B1335/12 B1352/25
C0108/06 C0144/18 C0169/03 C0171/11
C0173/26 C0190/32 C0524/38 C0542/18
C0543/31 C0543/41 C0556/15 C0577/04
directly (41) A0124/06
A0140/02 A0141/35 A0295/15 A0298/V
A0300/01 A0300/16 A0478/18 A0497/04
A0565/26 A0689/31 A0710/25 B0850/19
B0940/30 B1037/25 B1057/06 B1058/20
B1091/03 B1188/15 B1207/21 B1275/27
B1292/21 B1300/25 B1331/33 C0064/06

->C0077/24 C0078/01 C0080/34 C0082/07
C0125/07 C0143/18 C0147/04 C0156/36
C0162/12 C0182/14 C0192/12 C0396/38
C0410/25 C0416/26 C0418/11 C0420/16
directness (2) A0276/36 A0459/01
Directorium (1) A0409/05
directors (2) B1105/17 B1178/19
direful (2) A0616/03 B1130/20
direst (1) A0687/21
dirges (1) A0405/12
dirt (5) A0349/06
B0834/29 B0991/20 B1094/02 C0182/17
dirteen (3) A0373/09
A0373/09 A0373/10
dirty (13) A0242/07
A0512/02 A0533/31 B0809/16 B0829/04
B0990/36 B1008/08 B1091/13 B1291/18
C0067/18 C0388/18 C0427/24 C0427/24
dis (19) A0373/15
A0373/17 A0373/19 B0811/34 B0813/03
B0813/11 B0819/20 B0819/32 B0820/02
B0820/33 B0821/05 B0824/09 B0824/27
B0826/26 B0900/01 B0900/V B0912/V
B0913/05 B1104/18
disabled (1) C0558/22
disabuse (1) B0725/08
disabused (1) B1133/30
disadvantage (2) A0490/07 C0555/33
disadvantages (2) B1006/33 B1114/01
disagreeable (10) A0078/11 A0355/24
B0906/20 B0907/25 B0925/24 B1156/36
B1157/29 C0177/11 C0203/09 C0541/01
disagreeably (1) C0571/23
disagreed (2) A0097/21 A0549/21
disagreement (2) A0302/10 A0549/13
disappear (5) A0582/28
B0832/23 B0908/V B1245/01 C0427/04
disappearance (20) A0024/19
B0726/05 B0726/21 B0729/27 B0734/01
B0738/22 B0745/06 B0746/17 B0753/06
B0753/14 B0754/19 B0929/09 B1047/23
B1049/28 B1052/23 B1258/25 C0145/14
C0391/10 C0397/29 C0414/02
disappeared (23) A0029/18
A0253/11 A0327/19 A0356/23 A0404/07
A0459/32 A0511/30 A0580/20 A0594/07
B0811/03 B0944/04 B1107/29 B1142/03
B1249/01 B1330/32 B1354/23 C0388/40
C0391/03 C0423/27 C0536/31 C0539/10
C0568/02 C0570/37
disappearing (3) B0932/27
B1239/22 B1247/30
disappears (5) A0591/35
B1080/37 B1222/24 B1281/07 C0408/19
disappointed (12) A0025/21
A0591/36 B0891/03 B0891/04 B1234/14
C0115/18 C0131/12 C0133/28 C0189/35
C0192/29 C0416/08 C0530/14
disappointment (11) A0057/34
A0068/19 A0384/14 B0823/29 B0825/29
B0896/11 C0079/05 C0124/28 C0125/30
C0147/35 C0201/14
disapprobation (1) A0674/27
disarmed (2) C0562/02 C0562/16
disarrangement (1) C0422/16
disaster (11) A0054/31
A0063/32 A0345/11 B0811/14 B0853/02
B0933/16 B0955/18 C0064/12 C0065/29
C0080/18 C0126/14
disasters (2) B0806/04 C0076/02
disastrous (3) B1303/05
C0097/10 C0123/11
disastrously (1) A0444/26
disbelief (4) B1233/10
B1240/02 C0207/12 C0423/07
disbelieve (1) A0189/03
disbelieving (2) B0763/06 B1031/15
disburse (2) B1135/17 B1206/16
disburses (4) B1136/16
B1136/37 B1137/34 B1138/31
disc (1) C0416/24
discard (3) A0556/15
B0751/29 B0838/01
discarded (4) A0458/17
B0969/04 B1074/09 C0564/16
discern (1) A0299/07
discerned (6) A0244/04 A0508/22
C0077/39 C0388/15 C0399/20 C0417/37
discernible (11) A0164/22
A0400/02 A0406/02 A0514/27 A0567/10
A0579/09 B1299/10 B1338/25 C0079/41
C0082/10 C0407/35
discernment (1) A0302/21
discharge (15) A0094/21
A0114/15 A0300/10 A0484/10 B1163/30
C0119/25 C0186/13 C0187/14 C0187/21
C0187/29 C0390/09 C0405/34 C0557/28
C0557/31 C0579/23
discharged (5) B0727/35
B0731/13 B0753/40 C0407/24 C0410/37
discharges (1) B0873/14
discharging (9) B1074/25
B1079/25 B1182/20 C0097/13 C0097/22
C0113/17 C0143/22 C0404/25 C0406/22
disciple (1) A0242/04
disciples (3) B1295/11
B1310/33 B1313/08
discipline (1) C0105/27
disclaim (1) A0023/29
disclose (4) A0296/V
A0616/13 B0728/19 C0525/23
disclosed (3) A0215/12
B1317/12 C0174/28
disclosing (4) A0328/01
B0895/19 B1239/31 C0394/04
disclosure (2) B0906/14 B0976/27
disclosures (1) C0398/31
discoloration (2) A0400/06 B0730/05
discolored (3) A0543/26
A0543/34 C0571/18
discomfited (3) A0022/11
A0628/27 B1194/23
discomfiture (2) A0253/14 C0190/15
discomfort (4) A0614/15
B0925/22 B1143/11 C0416/13
discomposed (2) B0982/34 C0390/07
disconcert (3) A0672/31
A0673/09 B0894/31
disconcerted (5) B0823/24
B0943/28 B1019/32 B1141/33 B1193/23

disconsolate (1) B1107/11
disconsolately (1) A0605/10
discontinuance (1) A0442/12
discord (2) A0175/12 A0181/02
discordant (6) A0046/05 A0407/37
A0500/12 A0613/16 A0697/07 B1096/19
discordantly (2) A0215/07 A0510/28
discountenanced (1) A0623/33
discourage (2) B1128/14 C0136/38
discouraged (4) B0737/04
B0870/18 B1077/11 C0164/38
discourages (1) C0160/26
discourse (19) A0072/14
A0073/04 A0113/10 A0297/10 A0297/19
A0298/12 A0383/09 A0498/V A0548/23
A0555/29 A0568/15 A0625/24 B0863/28
B1040/16 B1104/28 B1106/04 B1185/10
B1250/13 C0558/14
discoursed (7) A0181/18
A0527/01 A0611/23 A0641/17 B0728/26
B0901/16 B1130/16
discoursing (2) A0498/01 B0903/12
discover (31) A0062/26
A0104/10 A0104/29 A0106/27 A0196/21
A0234/19 A0276/26 A0283/37 A0313/22
A0434/29 A0611/25 B0737/23 B0746/25
B0763/14 B0768/V B0771/31 B0837/19
B0903/30 B1152/03 B1181/05 B1189/19
B1300/08 B1353/23 B1374/29 C0157/16
C0189/02 C0403/10 C0419/25 C0424/08
C0432/44 C0555/40
discoverable (1) A0408/21
discovered (165)
discoveries (12) B0727/16
B0752/11 B0841/31 B0886/03 B0898/05
B0948/23 B1058/20 B1361/25 C0053/T
C0162/08 C0429/29 C0524/40
discovering (18) A0488/04 B0871/09
B1054/01 C0071/05 C0074/16 C0089/18
C0096/03 C0158/14 C0167/27 C0176/06
C0192/28 C0192/35 C0202/14 C0208/17
C0525/29 C0527/25 C0547/28 C0561/30
Discovery (1) A0142/15
discovery (71)
discreditable (1) A0299/10
discredited (1) B1160/19
discredits (1) C0546/13
discrepancy (6) A0649/05 B0768/11
B0902/27 B0903/01 C0408/04 C0574/38
discretion (4) B1005/17
B1006/19 B1047/08 B1142/09
discretionary (1) C0148/06
discriminating (2) A0527/V
B0990/11
discrimination (3) A0098/30
A0280/16 A0302/13
discursive (2) B0749/23 B1291/17
discuss (2) A0300/26 B1044/08
discussed (4) A0535/21
A0536/07 A0664/27 C0558/36
discussing (4) B0726/V
B0974/09 B1359/09 C0109/37
discussion (21) A0097/09
A0226/27 A0231/02 A0337/34 A0457/14
A0458/17 A0460/20 A0706/02 A0709/18
->B0752/03 B0861/05 B0875/06 B0991/30
B1233/03 B1241/23 B1242/03 B1249/31
B1250/08 B1270/31 B1274/21 C0061/28
discussions (2) A0459/19 B1247/09
discussioN (1) B0726/32
disdain (3) A0351/12
B0911/V B1107/18
disdained (1) A0026/12
disdaining (1) A0435/19
disease (27) A0020/V
A0211/01 A0211/01 A0211/15 A0211/16
A0212/31 A0213/26 A0242/23 A0282/05
A0324/08 A0404/16 A0410/21 A0433/27
A0610/24 A0627/02 A0638/05 A0670/09
B0742/19 B0789/02 B0851/16 B0851/16
B0962/07 B0963/01 B1234/32 C0126/07
C0177/03 C0522/02
diseased (3) A0533/28
A0610/07 A0695/V
diseases (2) A0611/17 B0955/28
disembogued (1) C0525/20
disemboweled (1) B1056/26
disembowelling (1) B1185/12
disenchained (1) A0461/04
disenchanted (1) A0499/17
disenfranchised (1) A0609/17
disengage (1) A0582/02
disengaged (4) A0538/14
B0929/18 C0062/28 C0409/37
disengagement (1) C0414/01
disentangle (1) A0495/V
disentangled (2) A0558/21 B0725/04
disentangles (1) A0528/05
disfigure (1) C0536/33
disfigured (4) A0218/26
A0592/14 A0689/05 B0948/08
disfigures (1) B0888/19
disfiguring (1) B1122/12
disgrace (2) B1130/26 B1133/13
disgraceful (1) A0536/15
disgracefully (1) B1140/16
disguise (5) A0111/04
A0439/29 B0850/31 B1381/06 C0113/10
disguised (2) A0641/14 C0110/34
disguising (1) C0108/35
disgust (14) A0034/03 A0196/29
A0374/17 A0430/21 A0490/30 A0673/26
A0674/29 A0694/23 B0854/27 B0893/22
B0927/11 B0955/02 B1101/15 C0399/29
disgusted (7) A0298/V
A0434/09 B0854/26 B0893/21 B1058/13
B1138/07 C0086/26
disgusting (12) A0023/07
A0114/13 A0355/09 A0435/22 B0925/25
B1130/04 B1139/08 C0074/41 C0107/41
C0112/02 C0124/25 C0137/36
dish (5) A0101/05
A0689/18 A0689/22 A0694/02 B1010/24
Dish-Clout (1) B1137/37
dishearten (1) C0575/04
disheartened (1) B1277/16
dished (1) A0343/28
dishevelled (1) A0330/15
dishonored (1) B1089/07
dishonour (1) A0150/V

disinclined (1) C0389/34
disingenuous (1) B0745/21
disinheritance (3) B1051/02
B1051/04 B1051/30
disinter (2) B0960/02 B1049/16
disinterested (1) A0264/10
disinterment (1) B0733/15
disinterred (1) B0731/07
disinterring (2) B0957/27 B1056/33
disjointed (2) C0080/24 C0208/08
disk (2) B1300/31 C0420/36
diskiver> (1) A0464/05
diskivered> (1) A0469/17
dislike (4) B0852/04
B0854/24 B0888/18 B1359/31
dislikes (1) B0878/11
dislocated (3) A0056/26
A0066/15 A0487/23
dislodged (1) B0857/14
dislodging (1) A0687/07
dismal (8) A0242/28
A0426/08 A0430/23 A0614/07 C0074/41
C0537/34 C0538/35 C0567/36
Dismal/Swamp (1) A0502/05
dismally (2) A0139/24 A0430/01
dismasted (1) C0061/23
dismay (11) A0033/16
A0138/06 A0216/22 A0370/26 A0372/03
B0818/16 C0064/38 C0075/38 C0200/13
C0398/36 C0562/34
dismayed (1) B1353/18
dismembered (1) B0796/07
dismiss (4) A0547/15
B0747/23 B0751/24 B1006/28
dismissed (5) B0724/26
B0830/01 B0923/17 B0969/08 C0526/30
dismissing (3) A0459/25
B0830/V B0841/10
dismounted (1) C0533/33
disobey (2) C0061/38 C0555/18
disorder (25) A0087/30
A0213/01 A0213/03 A0213/29 A0243/32
A0324/03 A0326/03 A0330/01 A0398/21
A0410/30 A0413/15 A0537/25 A0547/25
A0558/06 A0610/14 A0685/33 B0962/05
B0967/01 B0969/09 B0980/12 B1006/16
B1006/27 B1274/16 C0071/07 C0557/23
disordered (8) A0029/07
A0215/18 A0408/07 A0439/26 B0730/24
B1108/01 B1234/19 C0145/05
disorders (1) A0546/29
disorganization (1) C0404/05
disorganized (1) A0102/02
disparity (1) B1186/02
dispassionate (1) B0760/21
dispelief (1) B1103/02
dispelled (4) A0664/17
B0760/03 B0866/07 B1008/20
dispensation (1) B1055/33
dispensations (1) A0090/14
dispense (4) B1006/20
B1073/28 C0403/22 C0575/31
dispensed (1) B1008/24
dispeptic (1) B1100/V
disperate> (1) A0467/19

disperse (1) B1048/15
dispersed (1) C0556/34
dispersing (1) B1048/11
dispirate> (1) A0467/12
dispirited (3) A0665/20
B0811/14 C0196/01
displace (1) B0857/10
displaced (5) A0514/28
A0616/08 B0741/21 B0742/13 C0403/20
displaces (2) B0741/06 B0742/06
displacing (1) B1261/10
display (16) A0105/25
A0320/18 A0321/11 A0496/09 A0496/10
A0496/25 A0533/12 A0707/09 B1013/07
B1015/V B1238/26 B1272/09 B1325/09
B1380/09 C0123/37 C0397/35
displayed (12) A0089/12
A0101/15 A0301/03 A0402/34 B0889/29
B0945/12 B1005/08 B1078/V B1349/24
B1380/19 C0069/15 C0428/16
displaying (6) A0073/21 A0128/03
A0371/02 A0398/33 C0082/09 C0205/11
displays (2) A0265/35 B1032/10
displeased (3) A0624/27
A0624/28 A0663/14
displeases (1) B1221/25
displeasing (2) A0500/13 B1004/25
displeasure (2) A0652/13 C0066/13
disported (1) C0570/05
disposal (11) A0654/18
A0705/03 B0739/34 B0761/V B0828/19
B0986/03 B0986/03 B1132/27 B1134/06
B1179/15 B1270/03
dispose (4) A0072/09
A0557/05 B0762/01 C0393/13
disposed (18) A0242/10 A0286/02
A0497/21 A0568/10 A0601/11 A0671/22
B0769/15 B0822/30 B0926/02 B1047/09
B1162/17 B1221/20 B1224/22 B1247/08
C0056/19 C0539/03 C0556/22 C0557/41
disposes (1) B0764/33
disposing (1) B0764/25
disposition (21) A0057/25
A0059/23 A0098/01 A0104/26 A0431/11
A0443/26 A0624/24 A0654/13 B0822/24
B0850/09 B0850/22 B0851/11 B0854/20
B0910/18 B0926/15 B1046/34 B1074/07
C0170/06 C0177/23 C0180/08 C0523/11
dispossessed (1) A0204/13
disproportion (2) B0750/02 C0105/02
disproved (3) B0729/04
B0732/23 B0733/21
dispute (11) A0096/04
A0120/21 A0385/21 A0409/20 A0707/23
B0987/13 B0987/15 B1105/16 B1272/24
C0157/23 C0564/01
disputed (3) A0440/29
A0485/15 A0638/18
disputes (1) B0744/26
disputing (2) B1297/08 C0086/30
disquieting (1) C0078/06
disquietude (6) A0323/03 A0427/23
C0071/06 C0081/19 C0403/30 C0414/28
disquisitions (2) A0226/20 A0230/19
disregard (2) B0747/18 B0752/01

disregarded (3) A0610/31
A0673/12 B0757/04
disregardful (1) A0435/12
disregarding (1) B0894/26
disreputable (1) B1029/04
disrepute (2) B1295/20 B1311/13
disrespect (1) C0523/27
disruption (1) B1081/01
disruptured (1) C0198/36
dissatisfaction (3) A0500/16
B0877/22 C0395/27
dissatisfied (2) A0539/16 C0419/28
dissect (1) B0960/03
dissecting-room (1) B0961/06
dissection (3) A0067/14
B0960/17 B1181/12
dissemble (2) B0797/28 C0392/02
dissension (1) B0861/04
dissent (1) B1116/05
dissertation (1) A0054/09
dissertations (1) A0295/V
disservice (1) B1360/12
disshevelled (1) A0330/V
dissimilar (4) A0064/17
A0431/21 A0612/28 C0193/16
dissimulation (1) B0789/20
dissimuler (1) A0135/M
dissipate (3) A0664/02
B0944/14 B1322/29
dissipated (4) A0210/11
A0381/11 B1047/13 B1330/25
dissipating (1) B1362/23
dissipation (2) A0020/V A0438/21
dissolute (3) A0025/20
A0438/22 A0440/17
dissolution (11) A0211/13
A0329/06 A0403/35 A0448/06 A0604/07
A0609/15 A0670/05 B1234/22 B1236/08
B1241/29 C0182/04
dissolved (1) B0832/22
dissolves (1) C0577/22
dissonant (1) A0123/32
dissuade (2) B1046/29 C0132/13
dissuaded (1) B1140/14
Distance (1) A0409/03
distance (145)
distances (10) A0275/38 A0277/36
A0278/35 A0279/14 A0283/25 B1164/30
B1164/32 B1212/15 C0204/17 C0403/25
distant (33) A0102/22
A0398/18 A0414/29 A0435/27 A0579/15
A0614/12 A0614/17 A0644/14 B0726/25
B0887/13 B0914/20 B1044/15 B1161/28
B1247/23 B1250/35 B1251/04 B1261/26
B1274/11 B1278/22 C0131/10 C0146/19
C0150/12 C0154/27 C0199/07 C0200/12
C0201/05 C0201/28 C0202/02 C0202/04
C0403/27 C0417/02 C0428/23 C0570/17
distantly (1) B1274/14
distantly-observed (1) A0709/09
distaste (2) A0621/14 A0675/22
distasteful (3) A0436/01
A0706/25 B1271/27
distemper (1) A0323/26
distempered (3) A0212/25
->A0405/10 B0929/36
distend (1) B0742/35
distended (5) A0023/06
A0143/01 B1012/11 B1240/08 C0410/10
distending (3) B0741/33
B0742/08 C0411/16
distension (2) B0742/10 B0742/28
distention (2) C0404/05 C0411/28
distillation (1) C0425/37
distilled (1) B1259/05
distinct (69)
distinction (8) A0479/04
A0496/26 A0531/V B0743/18 B0743/20
B0757/10 B0962/18 B1314/21
distinctions (1) C0538/37
distinctive (8) A0268/14
A0473/26 A0508/14 A0549/17 B0870/06
B0962/25 B1221/22 B1279/17
distinctly (64)
distinctness (18) A0080/11 A0216/19
A0315/12 A0533/20 A0587/13 A0613/11
A0615/28 B0770/01 B0795/02 B0832/02
B0855/30 B1078/14 B1235/17 B1383/10
C0205/24 C0399/01 C0420/20 C0422/25
distingue (1) A0378/18
distinguish (29) A0081/08
A0267/30 A0283/28 A0365/14 A0416/17
A0439/11 A0540/09 A0540/10 A0540/25
A0541/06 A0542/30 A0682/32 B0842/11
B0929/17 B1031/30 B1155/33 B1169/22
B1250/12 B1258/17 C0063/03 C0086/32
C0096/19 C0118/09 C0150/36 C0168/08
C0174/18 C0417/18 C0420/26 C0438/V
distinguishable (1) A0550/17
distinguished (30) A0027/11 A0056/14
A0066/03 A0071/26 A0099/22 A0107/15
A0246/18 A0302/15 A0319/29 A0367/06
A0427/27 A0482/19 A0509/18 A0537/16
A0540/V A0543/03 A0549/27 A0578/26
A0640/26 A0676/12 A0703/21 B0857/17
B0950/12 B1136/27 B1138/04 B1187/24
B1268/20 B1278/30 C0110/06 C0523/32
distinguishes (2) B0943/06 C0575/27
distinguishing (3) A0226/34
A0231/08 B0855/05
distorted (7) A0028/16
A0053/22 A0062/28 A0078/12 A0190/13
B1189/18 C0406/07
distorting (1) C0056/18
distortion (4) A0078/13
A0213/31 B1346/13 C0128/15
distracted (4) A0685/19
B0726/07 B0733/12 B0794/12
distress (11) B0820/04
B0933/10 B0961/20 B0963/22 B1104/16
C0114/33 C0117/37 C0131/03 C0182/28
C0411/20 C0567/31
distressed (7) A0108/15
B1012/17 C0076/25 C0081/15 C0148/31
C0399/26 C0406/18
distresses (1) C0139/13
distressing (16) A0073/18
A0211/11 A0324/17 A0349/29 A0374/07
A0541/03 B0943/28 B0958/18 B1030/24
C0053/T C0081/18 C0089/06 C0098/31

->C0128/41 C0140/09 C0207/01
distressingly (1) A0294/V
distribute (1) B1048/16
distributed (1) C0387/14
distributio (1) B0986/19
district (5) A0044/28
A0243/16 A0578/28 A0592/32 B1162/24
districts (5) A0242/26
A0244/V B0862/05 B0863/24 C0422/34
distrust (5) A0685/23
C0055/24 C0171/09 C0172/24 C0568/16
disturb (9) A0102/09
A0235/18 A0434/22 A0445/18 A0663/15
B0793/03 B0826/09 B1239/02 B1313/06
disturbance (17) A0166/16
A0400/14 A0434/23 A0709/04 B0753/05
B0890/32 B0980/10 B0992/19 B1014/36
B1185/13 C0071/14 C0091/17 C0092/29
C0105/17 C0133/18 C0175/11 C0549/35
disturbances (8) A0459/15
A0612/33 B1273/33 B1273/33 B1273/36
B1274/05 C0401/26 C0424/36
disturbed (22) A0139/28 A0215/16
A0233/V A0414/12 A0434/01 A0690/14
A0694/19 B0857/20 B0858/04 B0891/12
B0892/27 B1106/15 B1169/04 B1179/13
B1263/26 B1300/01 C0145/32 C0421/14
C0539/08 C0545/31 C0562/27 C0576/20
disturber (1) C0539/10
disturbing (5) A0211/04
A0218/23 A0348/05 A0348/06 B0822/21
disuse (1) B1304/26
dit (2) A0096/V C0430/29
ditch (1) A0045/05
Dithyrambics (1) A0176/03
dithyrambics (1) A0182/02
ditty (1) A0650/05
divarsion> (1) A0468/10
divarted> (1) A0467/24
dive (1) C0128/01
dived (2) B1134/34 C0544/31
diver (2) C0121/11 C0122/01
diverged (1) B0770/V
divergent (1) B1059/01
diverging (2) B1282/31 B1332/29
divers (2) B1291/09 B1310/08
diverse (2) B0985/16 B1180/21
diversified (1) C0552/36
diversion (2) B1349/35 B1350/06
diversity (2) B0749/26 C0156/32
divert (1) B0752/23
diverted (4) A0022/23
A0249/22 A0438/30 C0531/39
diverting (2) B0760/27 B0773/08
divest (5) A0034/15
A0578/17 A0705/26 B1270/25 C0546/41
divested (8) A0162/V
A0457/21 B1036/22 B1036/26 B1036/29
B1036/31 B1036/32 B1183/30
divesting (1) B1108/06
divests (1) B0871/19
divide (8) B0840/06
B0955/26 B1295/21 B1311/14 C0172/29
C0428/23 C0428/25 C0546/40
divided (8) A0694/32
->B0827/10 B0980/20 C0091/18 C0093/11
C0137/10 C0531/31 C0557/01
divides (1) B0762/19
dividing (1) B0985/25
divil> (7) A0465/12
A0466/06 A0466/28 A0468/28 A0469/17
A0470/05 A0470/15
divilish> (1) A0466/01
Divine (3) A0319/21
A0601/23 B1213/09
divine (21) A0108/03
A0141/33 A0173/27 A0179/09 A0179/20
A0311/25 A0312/08 A0313/23 A0383/05
A0478/12 A0641/04 A0643/17 A0644/23
B0889/17 B0889/18 B1036/22 B1039/07
B1096/07 B1096/16 B1127/18 B1317/35
divinely (2) A0316/10 B1340/04
divinest (1) B1281/14
diving (2) C0121/04 C0546/07
divining (1) A0410/16
divinities (2) A0159/06 B1180/15
divinity (4) A0120/20
A0122/26 A0128/25 A0532/28
division (18) A0429/17 A0508/31
A0705/29 B0745/03 B0751/08 B0836/18
B0840/06 B0840/12 B0840/20 B0840/26
B1270/27 B1332/32 B1336/22 C0091/27
C0093/21 C0204/41 C0429/16 C0533/30
divisions (8) A0343/16
A0508/23 A0550/09 B0836/13 B0836/14
B0991/09 B1190/30 C0551/29
divorce (1) B0929/05
Divorum (1) A0091/13
divulge (1) A0411/06
divulged (1) B0768/23
dizzily (5) A0045/14
A0137/17 A0146/02 A0578/33 A0580/32
dizziness (4) A0670/04
A0683/16 B1222/29 C0197/37
dizzy (6) A0036/04 A0139/26
A0157/05 A0587/36 B0963/03 B1222/27
dizzying (1) A0591/18
do (438)
Dobson, Tom (2) A0490/16 A0490/28
doch (2) A0150/V A0345/07
docility (1) B0850/08
Doctor (35) A0382/34
A0652/20 A0655/14 A0655/15 A0655/26
A0657/03 B0941/10 B0941/16 B0941/23
B0946/16 B1002/T B1017/12 B1018/03
B1022/04 B1181/11 B1182/06 B1182/19
B1182/29 B1182/35 B1183/04 B1183/17
B1184/01 B1185/07 B1185/17 B1186/33
B1187/22 B1188/18 B1189/29 B1189/34
B1190/08 B1190/15 B1192/02 B1193/01
B1194/24 B1194/33
doctor (8) A0337/31
A0382/18 A0655/20 B0941/07 B0982/31
B1185/31 B1186/03 B1186/07
Doctor's (3) B1178/29
B1192/30 C0428/43
doctor's (2) B1091/32 B1181/21
Doctors (3) B1235/20
B1236/04 B1237/04
doctrine (2) A0108/22 B0724/01

doctrines (13) A0018/04
A0018/05 A0018/13 A0086/06 A0086/17
A0089/33 A0089/35 A0096/19 A0226/27
A0231/01 A0703/05 B0941/11 B1268/04
document (12) B0976/11
B0976/17 B0976/27 B0976/30 B0977/01
B0978/31 B0981/29 B0990/12 B0991/23
B0991/24 C0426/31 C0448/V
documents (2) B1119/M B1304/02
dod (1) B1373/04
dodged (1) B1104/08
Dodona (1) A0198/26
Dodona's (1) B1115/23
doer (1) B1051/25
doers (1) A0551/04
does (70)
doesn't (2) B0873/03 B1373/22
doffed (2) B0916/17 B1019/19
Dog (1) B1245/04
dog (65)
dog-days (1) A0071/04
dog-leaf (1) A0078/22
dog-meat (1) A0483/V
Dog-Head/Lake (1) C0526/38
Dog/Street (1) B0879/14
dog's (4) A0622/23
A0631/23 A0653/03 C0079/10
dogged (8) A0241/05
A0261/05 A0432/07 A0437/28 B0816/31
B0823/18 B0958/35 B1206/08
doggedly (1) C0392/09
doggrel (1) B0979/12
dogless (1) A0357/10
dogma (3) A0703/08
B0989/14 B1268/08
dogmas (2) A0079/02 B1034/26
dogmatic (1) B0761/27
dogmatically (1) A0109/15
dogmaticians (2) B1297/29 B1317/02
dogmatizing (1) B1312/01
dogs (15) A0046/02
A0099/32 A0347/04 A0347/32 A0348/14
B1015/04 B1096/10 B1101/10 B1157/16
B1158/05 B1168/11 B1299/30 B1300/27
B1300/29 C0073/25
doing (62)
doings (3) A0072/28
A0243/10 C0110/21
dolce (1) A0296/09
doll (1) B1372/01
dollar (10) A0487/32 A0624/12
B0820/27 B0872/17 B0872/22 B0872/28
B0926/24 B1091/12 B1207/14 B1363/19
dollar-manufacture (1) A0500/22
Dollar/Newspaper (1) B0806/T
dollar's (1) B1054/24
Dollars (1) B0806/T
dollars (35) A0059/16
A0067/07 A0485/14 A0487/29 A0487/29
A0496/09 A0496/V A0704/33 A0705/20
A0705/23 B0827/25 B0828/15 B0828/19
B0872/23 B0872/33 B0874/31 B0877/06
B0877/23 B0879/06 B0879/23 B1206/11
B1209/02 B1269/32 B1270/18 B1270/22
C0057/27 C0179/14 C0179/14 C0179/15
->C0179/15 C0179/15 C0179/16 C0179/16
C0179/17 C0529/30
Dolores (1) C0157/41
dolphins (1) C0174/06
dolt (3) A0177/19
A0183/13 B0979/21
Domain (2) B1267/T B1328/T
domain (12) A0025/25
A0320/12 A0397/12 A0399/33 A0428/23
A0639/18 A0643/15 B1278/27 B1282/04
B1282/07 B1334/38 B1335/07
domains (3) A0708/15
B1271/28 B1273/10
dome (1) B1385/15
domes (1) B1164/22
Domestic (1) B1137/36
domestic (6) A0710/01 B0850/23
B0866/22 B1275/04 B1278/34 C0155/31
domesticated (4) A0127/16
B0854/22 B1165/31 C0173/29
domestication (1) C0173/37
domestics (1) A0028/21
domiciliary (1) A0625/30
dominant (1) A0617/02
domination (5) A0292/V
A0294/01 A0295/06 A0296/V A0446/03
dominator (2) A0294/V A0294/V
Dominican (1) A0409/06
Dominie (1) A0430/06
dominion (8) A0123/20
A0406/29 A0411/18 A0444/35 A0603/02
A0610/11 A0677/04 B0966/22
dominions (8) A0021/02
A0210/09 A0250/03 A0250/29 A0670/11
B1039/V B1152/16 C0550/30
domino (2) C0399/19 C0441/V
Don (4) A0177/03
A0177/09 A0183/01 A0621/01
don't (57)
donations (1) C0555/29
donc (1) A0033/19
donce (1) B0913/04
Donder (1) A0373/19
Donder (1) A0366/10
Dondergat (1) B1362/07
done (170)
donjon (1) A0411/16
donjon-keep (1) A0410/05
donkey (5) B1010/01
B1010/12 B1020/33 B1092/02 B1160/35
donkeys (1) B0874/29
donna (1) B0889/10
donned (2) B0916/V B1178/07
Donner (1) A0177/13
Donner (1) A0183/07
dont (1) A0033/19
doo (2) A0372/28 B1103/01
doom (6) A0589/19 A0591/30
A0687/15 A0690/22 B0932/18 B0961/17
doomed (8) A0143/30
A0348/03 A0587/02 B1057/29 B1157/19
B1292/08 B1384/28 C0135/23
doomsday (1) A0489/32
door (156)
door-nail (1) B0820/01

doors (19) A0216/25
A0367/12 A0416/26 A0442/27 A0469/14
A0498/28 A0514/06 A0515/08 A0551/15
A0671/18 B0750/11 B0864/11 B0871/02
B0877/21 B1057/15 B1336/25 B1337/01
B1352/14 C0110/27
doorway (2) A0190/33 A0241/33
dormant (2) A0096/M A0096/M
dormant (2) A0189/31 B1163/19
dormitories (2) A0209/16 A0436/32
dose (7) A0325/12
A0341/02 A0667/46 A0667/64 B0942/09
B1133/07 C0557/05
dost (5) A0073/33
A0074/02 A0074/06 B0964/17 B1385/29
dot-and-carry-one (1) A0630/10
dotage (3) A0320/21
A0612/19 B1186/16
doth (4) A0310/M
A0314/28 A0319/23 A0320/01
doting (2) A0020/04 A0446/28
dots (3) A0272/34
B0838/18 B0838/33
dotted (4) A0266/10
A0277/36 C0443/V C0443/V
Double (4) A0655/V
A0655/V A0655/V A0656/V
double (24) A0055/13
A0143/13 A0314/18 A0368/31 A0369/09
A0370/15 A0441/29 A0467/16 A0490/23
A0533/23 A0540/02 A0688/22 B0727/15
B0893/16 B0906/31 B1046/09 B1055/18
B1059/10 B1059/10 B1299/12 C0118/39
C0157/32 C0389/23 C0569/15
double-bass (1) A0372/09
double-dealers (1) C0569/18
double-headed (1) C0187/30
double-padded (1) A0485/05
double-reefed (4) A0579/17
B0930/13 C0099/14 C0106/18
double-shotted (1) C0180/18
double-winded (1) A0073/33
doubled (8) A0487/10
A0655/23 B0735/10 B0759/05 B0837/12
B0837/14 B0982/14 B1168/16
doublet (1) A0244/16
doublets (1) A0242/11
doubly (8) A0037/08
A0315/14 A0327/20 A0434/08 B0858/21
B1055/02 C0059/40 C0425/27
doubt (235)
doubted (16) A0310/12
A0317/14 A0402/07 A0527/V B0727/31
B0832/14 B0835/26 B0965/14 B1122/17
B1247/32 B1362/34 B1383/25 C0187/04
C0207/17 C0208/08 C0569/27
doubters (1) B1029/03
doubtful (8) A0247/V
B0732/14 B1097/05 B1364/19 C0084/15
C0164/07 C0167/30 C0200/32
doubting (1) B0946/04
doubtless (4) A0600/09
B1384/26 C0185/37 C0540/11
doubts (5) B0751/07
B1159/26 B1257/24 B1257/27 B1257/31

dough (2) B0913/07 B0913/V
doughty (1) A0413/26
doux (1) B0916/30
Dover (1) B1070/26
down (441)
down-east (1) B1370/19
down-right (1) A0098/15
Down-East (1) A0486/12
Down-East/Review (1) A0205/11
Down-Easter (1) A0622/02
downcast (1) A0190/06
downfall (4) A0094/23
A0114/18 B0993/07 C0424/34
Downing, Jack (1) A0285/14
downright (8) A0343/24
A0380/26 A0380/29 B0888/22 B1182/05
B1381/01 C0428/04 C0448/V
downward (15) A0164/21
A0232/02 A0538/10 A0547/26 A0557/04
A0590/31 A0591/21 A0692/13 B1163/36
B1194/28 B1237/08 B1321/22 C0118/32
C0193/08 C0397/03
downwardly (1) B1248/15
downwards (12) A0153/04
A0227/14 A0501/V B0834/31 B1072/03
B1163/27 B1194/V B1381/33 C0408/34
C0418/44 C0440/V C0579/33
downy (1) B1250/24
doze (2) A0602/15 C0058/08
dozen (31) A0091/22
A0110/26 A0160/V A0178/13 A0578/13
B0734/17 B0749/11 B0764/30 B0767/10
B0824/01 B0844/21 B0859/10 B0875/02
B0896/22 B0943/10 B1014/18 B1052/14
B1055/29 B1296/27 C0069/24 C0093/02
C0147/33 C0160/41 C0176/23 C0390/10
C0390/14 C0390/18 C0390/19 C0393/32
C0570/13 C0577/41
dozing (1) B1105/28
Dr (35) A0273/35
A0273/36 A0274/06 A0278/06 A0278/14
A0278/17 A0337/04 A0337/14 A0337/19
A0337/22 A0337/29 A0338/07 A0338/20
A0338/29 A0349/04 A0354/05 A0354/16
A0388/20 A0430/05 A0432/27 A0436/31
A0438/03 A0440/02 A0446/01 A0535/09
A0628/V B0946/14 B0950/03 B1091/29
B1238/02 B1238/03 B1238/08 B1239/03
B1242/14 C0428/40
drab (2) A0349/03 C0388/32
Draco (1) B1096/25
Draconian (1) A0429/02
drag (8) A0557/12
B0766/25 B1166/04 B1352/34 C0117/14
C0120/31 C0135/40 C0170/02
drag-rope (1) B1292/24
drag-ropes (1) B1293/10
dragged (26) A0071/13 A0217/V
A0538/10 A0584/16 A0587/22 A0599/M
A0643/03 A0653/15 B0735/01 B0765/30
B0765/34 B0766/26 B0766/34 B0795/27
B0932/23 B1049/09 B1049/V B1057/33
C0065/20 C0086/21 C0089/21 C0096/25
C0114/20 C0120/35 C0188/35 C0200/05
dragging (11) A0447/12

->A0567/15 B0765/32 B0765/35 B0771/01
B1089/22 B1353/17 C0082/24 C0185/29
C0192/09 C0536/14
draggled (1) A0127/26
dragon (5) A0414/15
A0414/20 A0414/22 A0415/18 A0416/12
dragon-fly (1) B1156/23
dragon's (1) A0414/32
drags (1) B1075/02
drain (3) B1049/16
B1160/37 C0544/33
drained (5) B1348/08
B1349/27 C0082/33 C0139/23 C0540/21
draining (1) B1049/12
dram (4) A0058/17
A0069/06 A0173/08 B1078/11
drama (10) A0065/09 A0318/22
A0328/24 A0385/21 A0438/06 A0446/02
B0725/01 B0916/22 B1021/03 C0134/13
dramas (1) A0055/29
drams (1) A0178/14
drank (16) A0189/33
A0190/08 A0242/V A0249/V A0251/V
A0416/03 A0487/24 A0686/10 A0688/V
B0735/30 B0767/20 B0928/18 B1017/23
B1127/06 C0138/35 C0141/38
Draper (1) B1359/09
draperied (1) B0890/03
draperies (14) A0157/22 A0189/23
A0190/22 A0190/24 A0190/28 A0191/04
A0214/23 A0320/23 A0322/28 A0329/15
A0401/13 A0411/21 A0682/01 A0684/02
drapery (10) A0036/V A0152/29
A0155/07 A0164/11 A0326/09 A0497/23
A0501/19 A0502/26 A0674/08 B1280/10
draping (1) A0322/06
draught (12) A0251/07
A0441/28 A0688/03 B1259/21 B1260/12
C0083/31 C0092/19 C0131/04 C0142/04
C0147/12 C0147/14 C0563/22
draughts (3) A0528/23
A0528/32 A0529/04
draw (18) A0055/22 A0065/05
A0447/15 A0536/26 B0810/03 B0829/03
B1241/08 B1363/07 C0056/05 C0075/13
C0077/23 C0090/28 C0100/15 C0115/38
C0133/41 C0134/39 C0135/16 C0409/07
draw-back (1) B1128/12
drawer (14) A0054/33 A0055/06
A0055/06 A0064/01 A0064/24 A0064/24
B0809/13 B0830/33 B0977/06 B0979/19
B0979/20 B0979/21 B0983/01 C0523/24
drawers (10) A0034/25 A0067/32
A0247/25 A0252/15 A0538/01 A0556/01
A0556/05 A0556/05 B1350/37 B1363/03
drawing (41) A0034/05
A0034/19 A0080/37 A0248/02 A0387/17
A0558/28 A0559/04 A0559/14 A0559/26
B0809/16 B0810/23 B0810/30 B0818/15
B0828/29 B0829/09 B0829/20 B0829/28
B0831/13 B0831/22 B0831/31 B0832/27
B0905/03 B0948/25 B1016/15 B1017/09
B1101/24 B1189/33 B1258/19 B1262/32
B1282/10 B1350/09 C0064/03 C0109/03
C0121/14 C0133/12 C0134/08 C0390/03
->C0398/13 C0406/01 C0533/04 C0557/25
drawing-room (3) A0650/03
B0904/16 B0916/03
drawing-rooms (1) A0499/26
drawings (2) B1004/03 B1340/02
drawling (1) A0385/31
drawlingly (1) B0982/16
drawn (35) A0104/14
A0540/05 A0556/34 A0592/23 A0593/03
A0640/23 A0665/29 A0676/20 A0695/08
B0767/12 B0832/06 B0842/20 B0854/03
B0907/14 B1049/08 B1092/02 B1092/13
B1093/23 B1185/03 B1233/14 B1352/21
B1352/33 B1383/02 C0103/14 C0115/36
C0118/34 C0119/30 C0121/21 C0135/18
C0162/04 C0401/35 C0409/19 C0410/36
C0439/V C0523/07
draws (1) C0178/19
dread (20) A0403/11
A0404/08 A0460/06 A0567/V A0608/20
A0681/03 B0769/17 B0824/12 B0855/16
B0855/18 B0855/18 B0856/21 B0957/02
B1003/22 B1226/13 B1246/01 C0059/16
C0139/35 C0143/25 C0555/24
dreaded (16) A0323/04
A0417/V A0446/01 A0457/28 A0567/11
A0645/01 A0684/09 A0685/01 B0814/03
B0830/26 B0855/32 B0965/14 B1132/29
C0145/20 C0553/09 C0577/35
dreadful (18) A0385/08 A0414/24
A0510/12 A0581/25 A0591/30 B0765/07
B0794/11 B0795/20 B0844/14 B1156/26
B1169/24 C0076/01 C0120/17 C0133/27
C0144/38 C0148/34 C0184/27 C0185/26
dreadfully (5) A0070/17
A0543/34 B0789/01 B0825/06 C0187/33
dreading (6) A0567/22 A0665/05
A0693/16 C0074/25 C0075/28 C0137/13
dreads (1) B1221/28
Dream (1) B1122/12
dream (42) A0162/19 A0165/17
A0165/19 A0212/02 A0214/07 A0217/06
A0229/10 A0311/25 A0312/27 A0329/20
A0400/04 A0404/31 A0427/15 A0455/07
A0456/30 A0587/01 A0587/36 A0638/06
A0638/08 A0641/V A0682/25 B0793/24
B0796/25 B0813/01 B0849/04 B0946/03
B0946/06 B0946/09 B0946/10 B0946/11
B0946/11 B0947/26 B0948/19 B0961/32
B0968/23 B1212/23 B1215/27 B1246/14
B1247/34 C0072/31 C0072/32 C0148/35
dream-like (2) A0428/03 B1283/06
dreamed (20) A0035/14
A0071/05 A0225/08 A0325/21 A0329/16
A0513/11 A0564/03 A0644/05 A0682/26
A0683/11 B0765/24 B0865/32 B0871/28
B0944/09 B0944/25 B0946/01 B1212/04
B1369/18 C0543/12 C0573/28
dreamer (3) A0212/18
A0616/04 C0078/11
dreamers (1) A0638/V
dreaminess (2) B0866/07 C0204/33
dreaming (4) A0409/08
A0585/14 B0813/33 C0579/27
Dreamland (1) B1380/21

dreams (41) A0087/34
A0163/05 A0165/20 A0166/05 A0195/V
A0196/V A0210/18 A0216/21 A0320/26
A0323/13 A0455/09 A0456/32 A0533/02
A0611/23 A0614/14 A0616/25 A0640/07
A0644/04 A0654/08 A0673/27 A0673/28
A0673/32 A0674/02 A0710/21 B0724/32
B0724/33 B0813/04 B0856/05 B0862/06
B0946/06 B0946/07 B0964/01 B1106/15
B1122/07 B1123/25 B1212/24 B1215/33
B1275/24 B1280/21 C0072/10 C0444/V
dreamy (9) A0022/18
A0078/29 A0158/V A0602/27 A0612/22
A0664/02 A0681/06 A0695/16 C0412/29
dreariness (2) A0397/19 B0865/10
dreary (24) A0070/17
A0195/02 A0197/06 A0217/08 A0227/14
A0232/02 A0320/11 A0397/04 A0578/28
A0614/21 B0817/22 B0896/17 B0942/13
B0942/32 B1391/01 C0072/20 C0073/24
C0078/22 C0083/30 C0139/33 C0154/14
C0198/35 C0524/02 C0577/11
dree (1) A0372/31
drenched (4) A0154/12
C0060/21 C0139/34 C0549/19
drenching (1) C0542/31
dress (37) A0089/04
A0103/20 A0103/28 A0126/12 A0153/18
A0246/27 A0248/11 A0336/07 A0349/12
A0349/13 A0368/05 A0368/32 A0371/05
A0434/34 A0507/35 A0509/14 B0730/24
B0730/28 B0734/36 B0735/26 B0736/01
B0758/11 B0762/27 B0763/05 B0855/13
B0877/35 B0908/V B1008/11 B1014/14
B1185/32 B1194/27 B1257/18 B1292/35
C0058/17 C0123/31 C0203/37 C0552/24
dressed (10) A0124/24 A0343/28
A0387/21 B0924/24 B0930/05 B1178/28
B1186/06 C0389/25 C0552/04 C0552/16
dresser (1) A0101/06
dresses (5) B1008/03
B1093/02 B1351/29 C0125/41 C0174/31
dressing (3) A0386/27
B1010/29 B1129/15
dressing-case (2) A0055/11 A0064/26
dressing-wrapper (1) A0100/16
drew (54)
dried (6) C0174/05 C0177/01
C0179/03 C0534/36 C0535/03 C0575/41
drift (2) C0162/33 C0542/25
drifted (7) A0101/V
A0153/V A0584/16 C0147/27 C0148/28
C0390/23 C0405/08
drifting (5) A0136/29
A0152/04 A0585/25 C0064/03 C0412/04
driftwood (1) C0164/02
drill (1) C0185/01
drily (1) A0024/16
drink (27) A0107/23
A0165/09 A0165/10 A0165/13 A0441/24
B0900/13 B1019/22 B1020/30 B1056/08
B1091/18 B1259/24 B1259/27 B1347/27
B1347/34 B1348/04 B1348/29 B1348/31
B1375/19 C0074/03 C0083/37 C0101/16
C0111/02 C0120/27 C0128/06 C0128/10
->C0129/41 C0171/27
drinking (14) A0248/17 A0252/23
A0296/10 A0621/16 B1257/17 C0068/22
C0091/20 C0101/02 C0103/28 C0107/24
C0127/36 C0140/10 C0530/39 C0544/05
drinks (1) B0871/13
dripped (1) A0665/10
drippings (1) B1351/27
drissed> (1) A0464/14
drive (3) A0464/15
B1093/16 C0117/23
drivel (2) B1130/30 B1138/07
driven (25) A0135/02
A0215/19 A0246/13 A0320/14 A0509/35
A0553/07 A0584/14 A0599/M B0822/12
B0946/33 B0977/29 B0989/04 B1299/22
B1375/05 B1379/01 C0068/33 C0069/32
C0070/16 C0081/40 C0140/18 C0144/01
C0175/02 C0184/39 C0399/27 C0526/28
driver (6) A0057/06 A0058/07
A0066/33 A0068/29 A0081/07 B1093/15
drives (3) A0340/14
A0622/32 B1093/08
driving (11) A0485/31
A0585/29 A0586/36 B0822/05 B0909/16
B1077/20 C0098/35 C0118/18 C0120/31
C0196/33 C0196/36
drizzling (1) C0395/19
drole (1) B1012/30
droll (9) A0293/06
A0296/V A0370/29 A0494/07 A0652/11
B0728/16 B0864/09 B1013/16 C0437/V
drolleries (1) A0295/20
drollery (2) A0053/28 A0062/31
drollest (1) A0301/11
dromedary (4) B1169/22
B1169/27 B1303/28 C0138/07
Dromeo (1) C0147/28
Dromes (1) B0729/10
dronk (4) B1102/19
B1102/37 B1104/16 B1109/31
droop (2) B1163/40 B1215/25
drooping (2) B0931/10 C0151/18
droopingly (1) A0603/22
drop (28) A0058/31
A0069/13 A0069/24 A0077/02 A0195/19
A0251/23 A0251/24 A0264/28 A0443/15
A0584/01 B0820/17 B0820/V B0821/25
B0830/10 B0842/19 B0908/26 B1034/10
B1108/02 B1108/02 B1168/26 B1383/15
B1383/17 C0082/28 C0082/33 C0099/15
C0106/28 C0399/35 C0409/40
drop-curtain (1) B0896/06
dropped (34) A0054/04 A0063/13
A0089/32 A0111/23 A0158/15 A0160/17
A0218/12 A0249/03 A0253/V A0351/04
A0415/10 A0426/15 A0514/17 A0676/24
A0676/34 A0693/20 B0824/V B0834/11
B0840/30 B0844/V B0877/04 B0894/08
B1077/08 B1080/25 B1280/02 B1383/18
C0083/15 C0108/30 C0125/09 C0408/05
C0408/31 C0412/09 C0426/32 C0438/V
dropping (20) A0092/11
A0099/19 A0105/24 A0299/18 A0355/17
A0373/01 A0373/07 A0380/27 A0397/17

->A0443/V A0530/18 A0553/31 B0844/V
B0913/15 B1108/31 B1109/13 C0171/05
C0396/14 C0553/41 C0573/21
drops (5) A0325/23
B1168/28 B1260/09 B1348/05 B1383/20
dropsical (1) A0247/10
dropsy (2) A0033/V A0246/11
dross (2) A0229/16 B1298/21
drove (10) A0584/18 A0586/31
A0684/31 B0916/18 B1370/25 C0092/36
C0143/30 C0162/32 C0190/39 C0197/04
drown (2) B1372/07 C0061/33
drown'd (1) A0318/V
drowned (28) A0056/19
A0066/08 A0252/09 A0253/31 A0318/10
A0340/17 A0341/06 A0347/02 A0588/12
B0730/05 B0732/07 B0740/08 B0740/16
B0740/17 B0743/03 B0743/11 B0743/18
B0744/01 B0744/04 B0851/34 C0064/06
C0064/33 C0102/18 C0102/31 C0107/36
C0117/24 C0117/32 C0568/02
drowning (6) A0651/11 A0657/04
B0742/03 B0743/22 C0060/28 C0190/13
drownthed> (1) A0465/22
drowsily (1) B0728/28
drowsiness (3) C0141/09
C0204/24 C0415/06
drowsy (6) A0087/34 A0384/05
A0688/05 B1105/11 B1105/19 B1177/03
Drs. (1) A0484/31
drug (3) A0323/14
A0667/16 A0667/39
drugged (2) A0035/14 A0688/04
drum (5) B0795/12
B0943/30 B0943/31 B1009/06 B1017/25
drummers (1) A0372/09
Drummummupp (2) A0382/18 A0382/34
drums (4) A0078/10
B0789/M B0945/16 C0406/04
drunk (19) A0036/04
A0058/08 A0068/30 A0069/19 A0158/13
A0240/22 A0296/17 A0487/06 A0625/V
A0688/04 B0978/15 B1102/09 C0058/12
C0059/25 C0059/25 C0059/29 C0092/40
C0101/10 C0104/26
drunkard (3) A0037/V
A0402/25 B0992/23
drunkards (1) A0510/14
drunken (8) A0243/27
A0245/05 A0413/28 B1103/11 B1262/12
C0086/29 C0397/02 C0427/27
drunkenness (1) A0069/V
drxwn (1) B1374/20
dry (18) A0413/34 B1059/03
C0078/35 C0119/33 C0120/25 C0138/37
C0138/39 C0140/02 C0175/03 C0178/31
C0179/06 C0188/41 C0191/06 C0191/09
C0552/38 C0559/36 C0572/22 C0575/34
dry-goods (1) A0482/33
drying (4) C0140/36
C0177/37 C0178/20 C0540/02
dryness (1) A0460/17
Du (1) A0303/24
du (3) A0096/M B1154/22 C0430/39
du (2) B0726/26 B0737/15

Du/Bois (1) C0538/23
Du/Bois (1) C0538/43
Du/Pont (1) A0071/09
dub (1) A0292/V
Dub-- (2) A0655/15 A0657/03
dubiously (1) C0112/21
Dublin (1) A0179/18
Dubourg, Pauline (1) A0538/34
Duc (16) A0033/06
A0033/08 A0033/17 A0034/03 A0034/13
A0034/27 A0034/30 A0035/11 A0035/16
A0036/06 A0036/21 A0037/05 A0037/14
A0037/18 A0037/19 A0037/24
Duc (1) A0036/10
Duc's (1) A0036/03
Ducal (3) A0151/23
A0152/06 A0164/15
ducal (1) B0991/15
Duchess (10) A0174/12 A0174/17
A0176/22 A0176/29 A0179/27 A0182/24
A0182/32 A0250/16 A0253/02 A0254/06
Duchess' (1) A0179/28
Duchess's (1) A0174/13
Duck (1) A0337/21
duck (5) A0337/20
B1134/24 B1134/30 B1140/11 B1156/31
ducks (5) B1334/27
C0151/27 C0174/02 C0176/27 C0176/34
Ducrow (1) A0388/07
Dudevant (1) B1121/01
dudgeon (4) A0110/V
A0386/16 A0652/16 B0876/17
due (31) A0064/22
A0070/12 A0143/22 A0155/07 A0205/04
A0267/16 A0268/03 A0272/14 A0300/03
A0302/07 A0379/31 A0380/18 A0411/20
A0554/23 A0639/02 B0863/16 B0874/34
B0896/13 B1077/32 B1079/17 B1091/32
B1132/31 B1193/33 B1215/01 B1321/13
B1330/05 C0401/26 C0404/08 C0419/04
C0422/18 C0570/09
duel (2) A0303/22 A0384/29
Duelli (3) A0301/10
A0302/20 A0303/16
duelling (1) A0297/17
duellist (2) A0297/28 A0300/24
duello (4) A0297/03
A0298/04 A0300/30 A0304/07
duello (1) A0303/V
Duels (2) A0301/03 A0301/04
dug (11) A0631/23
B0823/10 B0825/11 B0825/26 B0981/V
C0173/09 C0197/04 C0394/18 C0394/21
C0575/33 C0575/39
duk (3) A0357/05
A0357/06 A0357/06
Duke (4) A0033/V
A0250/14 A0250/15 A0250/15
duke (2) A0037/V A0673/11
duke's (1) A0671/21
dull (25) A0081/02
A0138/24 A0139/32 A0397/01 A0400/02
A0414/06 A0458/14 A0599/M A0614/16
A0615/31 A0667/55 A0672/23 A0690/01
B0724/32 B0795/02 B0795/09 B0797/09

->B0940/23 B0962/35 B0966/11 B1261/17
B1337/32 C0071/28 C0425/14 C0551/41
dulled (2) A0502/12 B0789/03
duller (1) A0316/18
dully (2) A0616/06 B0961/01
duly (4) A0100/27
A0251/20 A0252/08 A0279/03
Dumas (5) A0543/29
A0544/09 A0544/11 A0557/26 A0559/01
Dumas, Paul (1) A0543/18
dumb (1) B1079/09
Dumbarton (1) C0428/35
dumpy (2) A0244/16 A0368/22
dun (1) A0357/05
dunder-headed (2) A0346/15 A0649/01
Dundergutz (1) A0366/16
Dunderheadism (1) A0203/01
dungeon (10) A0684/26 A0684/29
A0685/25 A0686/04 A0686/16 A0687/29
A0688/14 A0689/10 A0690/29 C0077/03
dungeons (4) A0074/30
A0685/12 A0693/02 C0083/10
duns (3) C0391/31
C0395/23 C0396/19
duodecimal (1) A0101/07
duodecimo (1) A0058/29
dupe (3) A0441/14
A0442/20 A0443/26
Dupin (68)
Dupin, C. Auguste (3) A0531/16
B0724/14 B0974/03
Dupin's (2) B0724/18 B0752/32
duplicate (5) A0097/V
B1207/10 B1280/16 B1362/19 C0092/18
duguel (1) C0430/41
durability (2) B1293/04 C0391/25
durable (2) A0430/33 B0831/11
duration (18) A0612/16 A0615/18
A0615/34 A0667/02 B0744/19 B0827/17
B0962/16 B0964/02 B0965/15 B1188/31
B1191/01 B1277/29 B1353/25 C0122/16
C0166/13 C0387/13 C0399/04 C0419/20
durch (4) A0150/V
A0150/V A0345/08 A0345/08
dure (1) A0430/07
during (283)
dusk (12) B0729/15
B0735/31 B0753/23 B0767/21 B0767/27
B0767/33 B0768/05 B1257/15 C0141/35
C0143/21 C0548/35 C0566/33
duskily (1) A0191/15
dusky (4) A0428/08
C0198/14 C0392/21 C0418/32
dusky-red (1) A0136/17
dusky-visaged (1) B0943/36
dust (11) A0320/03
A0444/12 A0616/33 A0616/33 B0759/33
B0807/07 B0825/24 B1017/15 C0192/02
C0207/32 C0208/27
dusted (1) B1141/20
Dutch (15) A0143/04
A0365/02 A0368/12 A0486/13 A0496/02
A0592/01 A0621/19 B1115/30 B1328/13
B1336/18 B1337/26 C0123/08 C0125/41
C0154/26 C0155/23
Dutchman (2) A0549/28 B1311/01
duties (11) A0097/16
A0268/26 A0484/10 A0490/12 A0622/26
B0873/13 B0879/03 B0983/23 B1180/14
C0416/11 C0568/08
duty (36) A0024/14
A0066/23 A0109/19 A0123/07 A0128/27
A0249/24 A0251/05 A0327/09 A0328/06
A0365/11 A0369/27 A0369/27 A0407/20
A0443/06 A0486/20 A0623/31 A0626/14
B0733/11 B0759/33 B0771/28 B0949/30
B0985/30 B1020/13 B1052/29 B1053/19
B1093/17 B1126/12 B1189/22 B1316/25
B1390/17 C0055/06 C0088/13 C0097/05
C0153/07 C0416/36 C0531/02
Duval, Henri (1) A0540/17
dvelf (2) A0373/01 A0373/03
dwarf (19) B1345/29
B1345/32 B1346/04 B1346/34 B1348/07
B1348/26 B1348/32 B1349/12 B1349/23
B1350/14 B1350/33 B1351/01 B1351/25
B1352/27 B1353/30 B1354/11 B1354/19
C0427/18 C0578/09
dwarf's (2) B1348/03 B1352/16
dwarfish (2) B0807/04 B1346/24
dwarfs (1) B1345/29
dwell (15) A0230/13
A0296/V A0317/09 A0428/11 A0532/29
B0754/14 B0895/22 B1384/30 B1384/34
B1390/05 C0071/35 C0134/01 C0135/28
C0413/05 C0528/25
dwelled (2) A0639/07 A0643/04
dweller (1) C0206/07
dwellers (1) B1213/32
dwelleth (1) A0198/32
dwelling (16) A0191/07
A0191/09 A0314/09 A0320/04 A0367/03
A0398/10 A0403/23 A0413/23 A0478/27
A0546/25 A0692/06 B0761/16 B1105/15
B1339/21 C0174/01 C0427/03
dwelling-house (1) B1335/17
dwelling-place (1) A0612/04
dwellings (9) A0242/33
A0247/22 A0367/21 A0498/17 A0499/32
C0172/36 C0173/28 C0530/07 C0547/04
dwells (2) B0772/12 C0550/24
dwelt (13) A0197/15
A0216/04 A0297/10 A0458/34 A0533/21
A0641/20 A0692/05 B0725/22 B0767/24
B0902/17 C0093/28 C0132/06 C0551/11
dwindled (1) C0443/V
dx (3) B1374/11 B1374/16 B1374/19
dxes (1) B1374/08
dxg (1) B1374/15
dxll (1) B1374/14
dxn't (7) B1374/07
B1374/11 B1374/12 B1374/13 B1374/17
B1374/17 B1374/18
dye (1) B0769/V
dyed (2) A0165/V C0567/40
dying (34) A0151/23 A0227/23
A0228/15 A0228/19 A0228/33 A0232/10
A0232/20 A0232/25 A0233/15 A0252/16
A0427/15 A0442/30 A0447/25 A0498/08
A0510/36 A0564/22 A0604/04 A0642/23

->A0653/01 A0653/V B0744/04 B0828/24
B1014/33 B1090/21 B1235/09 B1237/14
B1239/01 B1239/10 B1239/13 C0072/40
C0085/25 C0142/21 C0204/21 C0565/20
dynamically (1) B1301/14
Dynamics (1) C0436/V
dynamics (1) B1072/17
dyspeptic (1) B1100/02
DOMITIAN (1) A0093/15
e (6) A0344/32 A0662/V
A0662/V B0837/10 B0837/12 B0837/16
e (3) B0950/20 B0950/23 B0950/27
E. (10) C0150/05 C0150/07
C0150/39 C0158/31 C0159/02 C0160/31
C0160/37 C0161/29 C0162/05 C0163/13
E./E. (1) A0271/28
E./S./E. (1) C0161/31
e.g. (3) B1383/16
B1383/21 B1383/25
e-clench-eye (1) A0353/07
Eac (1) A0096/M
each (229)
eager (13) A0155/04
A0165/14 A0225/05 A0317/27 A0409/22
A0438/31 A0442/05 A0533/11 B0814/25
B0853/12 B1178/30 C0082/36 C0125/14
eagerly (16) A0228/29
A0404/12 A0656/16 A0664/26 B0725/30
B0768/21 B0825/11 B0948/17 B0992/10
B1152/30 B1249/16 C0075/18 C0091/40
C0129/39 C0183/02 C0392/39
eagerness (10) A0145/29 A0323/17
A0499/08 A0530/21 A0692/27 C0073/08
C0077/05 C0101/03 C0176/12 C0545/23
eagle (2) A0163/03 B1311/32
eagle's (1) C0433/02
ear (57)
ear-ring (1) A0537/32
ear-rings (1) B1008/02
Earl (5) A0174/14
A0174/19 A0179/28 C0430/21 C0430/23
earl (1) A0179/34
Earl's/Hotel (1) B1361/12
earldoms (1) A0440/09
earlier (17) A0078/26
A0241/24 A0297/08 A0316/04 A0326/21
A0354/08 A0638/22 B0756/20 B0906/07
B0974/11 B1005/30 B1126/07 B1384/08
C0056/06 C0132/31 C0160/10 C0521/30
earliest (13) A0034/28
A0085/12 A0209/21 A0301/23 A0427/20
A0427/33 A0436/17 B0908/14 B0910/11
B1262/11 C0107/12 C0423/02 C0524/41
early (59)
earn (2) A0651/27 B0835/13
earned (1) B0874/31
earnest (36) A0028/04
A0212/11 A0227/16 A0232/03 A0268/31
A0299/26 A0317/26 A0324/22 A0382/27
A0398/22 A0402/28 A0404/29 A0408/10
A0409/V A0413/10 A0439/28 A0608/16
A0614/31 A0683/09 A0683/31 B0734/08
B0746/02 B0825/34 B0906/06 B0932/03
B1122/20 B1122/24 B1181/20 B1221/23
C0109/27 C0179/25 C0207/33 C0428/04
->C0438/V C0448/V C0550/08
earnestly (11) A0064/11
A0300/32 A0411/28 A0664/18 B0809/06
B0907/09 B1050/24 B1242/29 C0072/15
C0170/23 C0197/32
earnestness (3) A0458/33
A0684/04 C0532/20
earns (1) B0738/10
ears (70)
earth (182)
earth-angels (1) B1274/17
earth-worm (1) B1292/29
earth's (24) A0611/11
A0612/19 B1080/37 B1212/35 B1213/35
B1273/30 B1274/04 B1274/11 B1322/22
C0400/03 C0400/07 C0400/33 C0403/27
C0404/38 C0405/04 C0411/40 C0414/05
C0416/17 C0417/28 C0418/05 C0418/40
C0419/14 C0420/06 C0432/34
earthen (2) A0689/18 C0415/29
earthenware (1) C0069/02
earthliness (1) B1122/11
earthly (13) A0071/16
A0071/21 A0109/02 A0214/V A0397/15
A0455/05 A0456/09 B1274/02 B1301/31
B1316/02 B1385/03 C0117/19 C0446/V
earthquake (4) A0340/30
B0955/06 B1161/34 B1303/05
earthquakes (1) A0121/20
earthy (2) A0214/08 B0968/29
ease (26) A0101/10 A0135/08
A0248/05 A0275/34 A0311/19 A0568/15
B0736/31 B0770/26 B0796/34 B1030/35
B1035/16 B1145/19 B1329/04 C0061/17
C0119/24 C0136/28 C0145/24 C0155/22
C0177/22 C0396/21 C0397/41 C0409/01
C0411/25 C0413/18 C0533/02 C0578/15
easier (2) B0766/33 C0575/28
easiest (1) C0535/29
easily (92)
easing (1) C0113/38
East (13) A0124/09
A0126/06 A0127/02 A0127/24 A0128/01
A0128/07 A0128/15 B0827/14 B0908/27
B1077/18 B1078/23 B1368/01 B1369/10
east (36) A0438/27
A0602/22 A0655/24 A0657/01 A0657/06
A0657/12 B0839/33 B0840/23 B0841/29
B0842/15 B1048/33 B1331/35 B1332/23
B1333/15 B1335/13 B1336/21 B1336/22
B1336/30 B1337/23 B1368/02 C0103/27
C0149/13 C0160/14 C0162/10 C0193/05
C0203/24 C0203/25 C0389/05 C0393/28
C0429/08 C0432/26 C0524/36 C0530/06
C0559/09 C0565/34 C0575/15
East/Indiaman (1) A0140/06
East/Indian/Islands (1) A0559/20
East/Indies (2) C0148/20 C0525/24
easterly (4) C0150/41
C0161/05 C0163/11 C0207/28
Eastern (5) A0018/11
A0321/29 B1095/04 B1283/06 C0444/V
eastern (25) A0120/26
A0136/07 A0495/07 A0603/04 A0603/10
A0603/16 A0644/V A0671/29 A0675/27

->B0807/15 B0841/17 B0862/01 B1076/20
B1333/18 B1334/30 B1336/31 B1338/04
B1338/16 C0179/21 C0184/37 C0193/03
C0525/17 C0527/08 C0527/39 C0567/19
Eastern-looking (1) B0945/02
eastward (29) A0122/21
A0136/15 A0370/23 A0580/08 A0580/16
B0830/07 B1077/03 C0089/15 C0103/07
C0131/08 C0146/14 C0157/32 C0163/17
C0163/40 C0163/41 C0165/23 C0191/22
C0191/35 C0196/03 C0405/09 C0407/35
C0412/03 C0414/06 C0414/14 C0417/18
C0419/39 C0420/10 C0443/V C0538/21
eastwardly (3) C0150/41
C0157/34 C0160/07
easy (37) A0254/04
A0434/34 A0547/18 A0642/22 A0667/32
A0705/08 B0736/23 B0737/09 B0750/V
B0750/V B0764/27 B0821/27 B0836/14
B0871/04 B0871/04 B0961/08 B0993/10
B1032/15 B1079/19 B1092/09 B1141/04
B1153/10 B1153/15 B1163/41 B1214/02
B1224/15 B1237/27 B1270/07 B1296/32
B1313/35 B1314/01 B1381/05 C0070/24
C0402/11 C0422/12 C0547/08 C0559/19
eat (10) A0085/M A0085/M
B1010/03 B1177/05 B1219/23 C0091/07
C0128/06 C0128/31 C0534/41 C0544/08
eaten (10) A0347/06 B0767/16
B1160/39 C0071/04 C0071/21 C0081/13
C0137/09 C0204/11 C0545/18 C0547/04
eater (2) A0145/01 A0402/26
eating (15) A0078/30
A0127/20 A0296/10 A0344/20 A0621/16
B1010/05 B1012/25 B1108/09 B1220/01
C0068/22 C0126/14 C0164/28 C0165/19
C0191/11 C0543/02
eats (3) B0871/12
B1011/12 B1163/17
eau (1) A0378/M
eave (1) B1336/33
eaves (3) A0355/04
A0367/12 A0400/08
ebb (5) A0235/20
A0581/24 A0581/31 A0592/20 C0060/01
ebber (4) B0812/05
B0818/09 B0819/14 B0820/10
ebbing (1) A0329/V
eberry (1) B1103/03
ebery (3) B0809/02
B0812/25 B0821/02
ebon (1) A0400/29
ebony (23) A0139/07
A0190/04 A0190/19 A0191/06 A0218/V
A0322/03 A0322/11 A0324/21 A0326/24
A0328/21 A0416/25 A0511/02 A0590/21
A0591/22 A0605/02 A0605/10 A0640/10
A0672/22 A0673/30 A0674/09 A0676/29
A0677/02 B1161/01
ebullition (1) B1048/05
ecarte (6) A0441/20 A0441/V
A0443/08 A0443/21 A0443/V A0443/V
Eccaleobion (1) B1166/33
eccentric (9) A0482/01
A0482/32 A0484/05 A0670/16 B1008/18
->B1016/11 B1123/24 C0057/10 C0529/13
eccentrically (1) A0613/01
eccentricities (3) A0262/05
B1016/10 C0433/01
eccentricity (3) A0159/22
B0926/07 C0400/06
Ecclesiae (1) A0409/11
ecclesiastic (1) A0104/03
ecclesiastical (1) A0088/08
ecclesiastics (1) A0107/15
Eccossois (1) C0430/39
echo (14) A0217/V A0244/14
A0370/05 A0414/06 A0435/04 A0608/07
A0630/13 A0630/14 A0673/30 B0747/11
B0794/11 B0896/19 B1391/02 C0082/35
echoed (7) A0093/29
A0113/V A0372/22 B0735/04 B0809/31
B1109/10 C0190/06
echoes (10) A0190/21 A0218/05
A0407/20 A0673/01 A0673/33 A0674/21
A0687/11 B1031/12 C0417/04 C0444/V
echoing (2) B0747/12 B1092/10
eclat (2) B1347/10 B1347/V
eclipse (2) B1092/37 C0419/13
eclipsed (1) B1332/35
eclipses (1) B1191/23
ecliptic (1) C0419/10
economic (1) A0436/31
economize (1) A0498/22
economy (6) A0079/01 A0102/03
A0485/30 A0531/24 B1096/03 B1096/04
ecrivaient (1) A0109/31
ecstacies (1) B1268/V
ecstasies (4) A0209/09
A0704/02 B1268/32 B1303/37
ecstasy (9) A0612/22
A0613/36 A0644/20 B0895/23 B0913/23
B1178/28 B1391/11 C0058/23 C0131/21
ecstatic (4) A0036/05
B0959/24 C0122/34 C0136/27
eddies (4) A0583/23
A0584/03 A0585/20 B0974/08
eddy (3) C0540/15
C0541/32 C0554/07
eddying (1) A0604/11
Eden (2) B1095/02 B1154/15
Edens (1) B0862/21
eder (1) B1104/16
Edgarton (2) C0057/05 C0057/16
edge (44) A0044/31
A0354/03 A0578/07 A0578/10 A0580/27
A0589/24 A0631/13 A0690/18 A0690/19
A0692/11 B0762/27 B0762/28 B0762/30
B0762/32 B0832/27 B1102/32 B1155/35
B1223/02 B1223/15 B1280/08 B1332/06
C0075/18 C0152/22 C0159/21 C0163/17
C0176/18 C0185/04 C0185/20 C0191/31
C0192/04 C0196/30 C0389/14 C0398/28
C0410/31 C0416/22 C0419/17 C0544/28
C0544/41 C0545/14 C0545/21 C0553/24
C0554/16 C0559/22 C0578/29
edge-tools (1) B1193/22
edges (19) A0142/12
A0215/21 A0267/11 A0271/27 A0273/25
A0352/31 A0503/05 A0553/20 A0641/08

->B0762/24 B0832/26 B0832/27 B0929/22
B0991/36 B0992/04 C0425/15 C0430/24
C0542/06 C0552/39
edgeways (1) A0072/25
edible (1) C0178/13
edifices (1) C0407/38
edified (1) B0916/11
Edina (4) A0347/28
A0349/21 A0351/25 A0352/18
Edinburg (1) A0174/05
Edinburgh (6) A0174/V A0179/17
A0347/16 A0352/17 A0352/17 C0429/31
Edinburgh/Review (1) B1132/22
edit. (1) B1161/33
edited (4) A0071/26
B0731/38 B0735/37 B0740/33
editing (2) A0269/17 B1369/22
edition (16) A0071/27
A0174/32 A0180/24 A0265/10 A0276/09
A0276/10 A0283/35 A0366/17 A0409/05
A0537/03 A0544/18 B1022/06 B1141/08
B1383/16 B1384/15 C0428/38
editions (1) A0283/35
Editor (3) A0074/32
B1126/T B1378/01
editor (49) B0732/19
B0733/23 B0747/08 B0747/29 B0748/01
B0748/12 B0750/23 B0759/15 B0759/V
B0950/15 B1127/14 B1127/22 B1127/33
B1130/33 B1132/09 B1132/30 B1133/07
B1133/14 B1133/29 B1133/32 B1133/V
B1136/19 B1137/02 B1137/39 B1137/40
B1138/37 B1139/18 B1140/04 B1140/34
B1141/35 B1143/28 B1143/34 B1207/10
B1208/17 B1208/23 B1208/33 B1208/37
B1358/19 B1361/05 B1369/02 B1369/15
B1369/35 B1370/04 B1371/06 B1371/07
B1375/06 B1379/08 B1381/25 C0055/29
editor's (1) B1133/22
editorial (5) B1101/11
B1127/04 B1128/10 B1135/33 B1137/03
editorials (1) B1137/24
Editors (2) A0058/30 B1291/01
editors (4) B0772/09
B1127/34 B1129/09 B1207/25
Edmund's (1) C0067/15
Edouard (1) A0062/21
Eds. (8) C0530/40
C0533/11 C0535/42 C0538/42 C0538/43
C0540/32 C0541/40 C0576/40
educated (4) A0545/11
A0556/23 B0807/20 B1009/20
education (14) A0121/11 A0135/03
A0164/07 A0173/23 A0179/04 A0225/15
A0229/14 A0610/35 A0611/25 A0611/28
A0706/08 B1271/12 C0392/26 C0522/16
educe (1) A0405/19
educed (2) B0941/16 B0987/15
Edward (1) A0240/02
eel-skinning (1) B1370/22
eels (2) B1156/32 C0174/07
eend (2) B0820/29 B0820/32
efface (2) A0612/01 C0134/03
effaced (1) C0574/08
effect (134)
effected (34) A0098/05 A0204/29
A0211/09 A0242/14 A0441/19 A0442/15
A0485/19 A0554/31 A0555/32 A0593/29
B0730/14 B0756/29 B0762/28 B0960/04
B0984/32 B1006/04 B1019/06 B1044/03
B1049/16 B1077/04 B1145/04 B1180/32
B1271/03 B1354/27 C0094/08 C0105/32
C0106/12 C0109/01 C0155/04 C0165/29
C0172/14 C0185/09 C0538/03 C0550/12
effecting (7) A0074/29
B1163/41 C0122/10 C0136/39 C0185/13
C0186/04 C0572/39
effective (5) A0315/14
B1119/17 B1350/31 C0523/37 C0555/41
effects (33) A0058/23
A0067/19 A0324/28 A0406/07 A0500/13
A0502/09 A0511/04 A0528/01 A0528/18
A0594/13 A0600/06 A0667/27 A0673/12
A0689/07 B0850/07 B0851/18 B0956/01
B0960/12 B1053/32 B1168/19 B1214/01
B1215/03 C0064/22 C0084/35 C0088/11
C0101/33 C0111/14 C0141/18 C0148/33
C0391/18 C0411/33 C0538/33 C0572/23
effectual (9) A0056/15
A0066/04 A0226/02 A0229/19 B1007/13
B1035/14 B1236/35 C0565/10 C0568/32
effectually (13) A0163/23
A0441/05 B0823/17 B0915/28 B1014/23
C0065/04 C0074/32 C0075/09 C0075/36
C0082/27 C0086/09 C0415/05 C0575/40
effeminacy (1) A0266/11
effeminate-looking (1) B0947/04
Effendi (1) A0086/34
effervescent (1) A0253/12
efficacious (1) C0547/15
efficacy (1) C0181/17
efficiency (2) B1077/01 C0416/08
efficient (4) A0342/08
B1058/12 C0165/05 C0530/16
efficiently (2) A0074/V B1351/03
effort (55)
efforts (25) A0028/27
A0127/18 A0154/01 A0295/22 A0411/24
A0427/28 A0430/15 A0552/21 A0650/05
A0707/15 B0741/30 B1165/29 B1272/13
C0062/26 C0075/34 C0127/06 C0129/31
C0130/40 C0133/13 C0140/11 C0183/33
C0185/34 C0190/16 C0567/32 C0579/34
effrontery (3) A0028/12
B0893/25 B1131/15
effudit (1) A0125/06
effulgence (2) A0316/21 B1282/26
effusion (5) A0127/04
B1127/14 B1131/18 B1133/28 B1137/40
Egaeus (1) A0209/11
Egeria (1) B1123/25
egg (4) B1141/16
C0152/39 C0168/21 C0170/11
egg-shells (1) C0061/30
egg'd (1) B1141/20
eggs (5) A0495/V
A0623/25 C0153/08 C0153/11 C0177/08
eglantine (1) B1282/01
egli (1) A0662/V
egotism (1) B1131/18

egotist (1) B1325/11
egregious (5) A0295/13
  B0987/20 C0079/02 C0181/11 C0388/23
egress (14) A0547/24 A0551/01
  A0551/08 A0551/20 A0552/06 A0554/24
  A0555/31 A0671/02 B1106/30 B1277/26
  B1335/08 C0074/11 C0152/23 C0192/02
egressions (1) A0429/07
Egypt (17) A0122/18
  A0157/22 A0165/24 A0175/28 A0181/24
  A0311/13 A0320/23 A0445/33 A0611/14
  B1183/07 B1186/34 B1187/12 B1187/28
  B1191/17 B1193/02 B1194/25 B1317/07
Egyptian (19) A0035/20
  A0190/32 B1160/35 B1181/21 B1183/02
  B1183/09 B1184/07 B1184/24 B1185/01
  B1186/05 B1188/06 B1188/07 B1189/30
  B1191/08 B1194/04 B1194/16 B1195/04
  B1337/29 C0208/09
Egyptian's (1) B1184/01
Egyptians (6) B1179/06 B1191/06
  B1192/01 B1193/08 B1194/35 B1318/07
eh (3) A0037/V B0907/07 B0907/08
eh (29) A0072/22
  A0090/29 A0092/22 A0094/03 A0094/11
  A0107/04 A0111/32 A0112/V A0113/27
  A0114/06 A0158/13 A0262/24 A0284/32
  A0386/06 A0386/10 A0657/15 B0809/33
  B0812/11 B0982/19 B0982/22 B1016/02
  B1016/07 B1016/23 B1016/23 B1016/29
  B1017/11 B1135/13 B1142/15 B1373/23
eider-down (1) A0036/V
eides (Gr.) (2) A0225/M A0229/M
Eight (2) B1345/V B1350/07
eight (77)
eighteen (26) A0020/13 A0121/16
  A0429/33 A0484/07 A0508/29 A0584/28
  B0725/20 B0730/29 B0766/18 B0827/35
  B0841/18 B0968/19 B0993/02 B1015/17
  B1071/10 B1235/23 B1336/02 C0065/29
  C0137/38 C0156/25 C0159/09 C0178/23
  C0181/31 C0428/32 C0522/17 C0533/04
eighteen-thousandth (1) B1167/30
eighteenth (5) A0020/13
  C0135/36 C0150/07 C0158/17 C0190/30
eighth (9) A0176/02
  A0182/01 A0411/15 A0490/31 A0553/V
  B0793/19 B1262/33 C0103/28 C0179/16
eighty (12) A0176/01
  A0181/33 A0348/30 B1161/35 B1331/17
  B1332/31 C0147/08 C0154/32 C0181/03
  C0400/33 C0401/07 C0565/33
eighty-doo (1) B0912/02
eighty-fifth (1) C0161/22
eighty-four (1) C0201/37
eighty-fourth (2) C0053/T C0170/26
eighty-second (1) C0423/25
eighty-seven (1) B1138/33
eighty-six (2) A0705/21 B1270/20
eighty-three (3) A0175/31
  A0181/31 B0828/07
eighty-two (2) B0912/03 B0914/08
eighty-two-hundred (1) B0912/03
eine (1) B0723/M
Eiros (12) A0455/01
  ->A0455/02 A0455/06 A0455/T A0456/01
  A0456/13 A0456/17 A0456/29 A0456/32
  A0457/01 A0457/12 B1322/31
either (178)
ejaculated (25) A0025/14
  A0046/05 A0047/30 A0062/10 A0080/13
  A0088/20 A0092/10 A0103/01 A0111/22
  A0166/09 A0180/14 A0183/02 A0250/31
  A0263/11 A0264/31 B0866/11 B0897/19
  B0912/03 B0933/03 B1016/03 B1017/09
  B1019/35 B1104/02 B1262/01 B1349/15
ejaculating (1) B1109/09
ejaculation (6) A0029/V A0442/14
  A0627/28 B1159/35 C0073/03 C0429/38
ejaculations (4) A0056/19
  A0066/08 B1242/35 C0169/26
ejected (3) C0411/01
  C0411/08 C0420/30
ejecting (1) A0374/20
ekidnato (Gr.) (1) B1385/18
el (1) A0344/24
El/Elohim (2) A0046/05 A0046/07
El/Emanu (2) A0047/30 A0048/01
elaborate (10) A0405/15 A0459/15
  A0528/23 B0877/30 B0899/03 B0965/25
  B0967/09 B1357/01 B1384/07 C0432/39
elaborately (2) A0321/21 B1282/24
elaboration (1) A0474/05
Elah-Gabalus (1) A0427/02
Elah/Gabalah (1) A0122/23
elapse (1) A0081/20
elapsed (23) A0046/25
  A0310/03 A0324/02 A0327/02 A0327/27
  A0398/17 A0410/29 A0590/12 A0612/15
  A0684/20 B0726/22 B0727/16 B0729/24
  B0731/05 B0744/01 B1190/09 B1239/09
  B1246/08 B1247/19 C0070/38 C0078/38
  C0089/13 C0094/35
elapses (1) B0955/32
elapsing (4) A0542/20
  A0566/20 B0754/32 B0758/32
elastic (5) A0514/35
  A0604/32 B0746/33 B1167/15 C0178/16
elasticity (4) A0080/08
  A0311/20 A0460/05 B0948/03
elated (1) B1372/19
elbow (17) A0090/06
  A0144/28 A0442/13 A0512/18 A0578/10
  A0627/27 A0692/19 A0692/22 B0890/04
  B0977/20 B1100/04 B1191/33 B1260/07
  B1382/33 B1383/04 C0118/30 C0204/22
elbowed (2) B0733/32 B0889/05
elbowing (1) B0748/19
elbows (5) A0241/29
  B0826/23 B1012/10 B1185/03 B1194/19
Eld (1) A0144/30
elder (8) A0240/15
  A0485/20 A0541/12 A0586/07 A0586/22
  B0891/20 B1169/32 C0531/27
elderly (1) B1134/24
elders (1) A0510/14
eldest (7) A0584/28
  B0735/34 B0768/01 B0887/25 B0887/27
  C0529/12 C0531/18
Eleatic (2) A0341/23 A0342/V

eleben (1) A0372/34
Elector (1) A0183/03
elector (1) A0183/21
electric (10) A0366/12 A0459/17
A0460/21 B0887/03 B0966/18 B1033/23
B1033/23 B1119/19 B1119/24 B1182/32
electrical (2) A0413/03 B0905/07
electricity (4) A0615/31
B0948/02 B1034/11 B1181/17
electrified (1) A0507/12
electrify (1) B1120/08
Electro-tintinnabulic (1) B1119/19
Electro-Magnetic (1) B1119/18
Electro-Telegraph (2) B1167/35
B1167/37
electro/magnetics (1) A0381/33
electrometer (1) C0396/06
Electrotype (1) B1167/28
elegance (4) A0248/10
A0278/19 A0283/27 B1008/22
B0889/29
elegant (1) A0269/01
elegantly (1) A0087/29
elegantly-bound (1) B1179/02
Eleithias (2) B1186/21
element (2) A0603/27 B1123/22
elementary (3) A0703/30
B1221/05 B1268/28
elements (17) A0044/18
A0197/21 A0457/29 A0458/01 A0495/06
A0527/V A0531/V A0610/12 A0703/14
A0707/11 B0863/22 B1221/04 B1247/12
B1268/13 B1272/10 B1278/05 B1322/29
elenchi (3) A0345/19
A0345/19 A0345/24
Eleonora (16) A0638/T
A0639/06 A0639/19 A0640/11 A0640/17
A0641/05 A0641/12 A0642/09 A0642/18
A0643/17 A0643/24 A0643/34 A0643/V
A0644/09 A0644/V A0645/09
elephant (4) A0070/26
B1248/12 C0137/32 C0156/17
elephantfish (1) C0174/07
elephants (4) B0945/15
C0151/08 C0154/08 C0155/20
elevate (4) A0710/23
B0741/26 B1139/21 B1275/26
elevated (19) A0245/19
A0252/12 A0341/15 A0348/07 A0446/05
A0610/09 A0625/15 A0693/17 B0893/17
B0911/05 B1133/25 B1165/23 B1193/19
B1237/30 B1278/02 B1312/34 B1351/20
B1379/13 C0154/31
elevates (1) B0743/24
elevating (1) A0068/12
elevation (40) A0139/25
A0356/18 A0426/12 A0460/32 A0687/01
B0842/03 B0842/07 B0864/29 B0893/28
B0967/17 B1054/11 B1076/21 B1076/25
B1076/35 B1079/25 B1080/01 B1080/10
B1080/25 B1080/36 B1128/10 B1279/21
B1298/31 B1332/31 B1334/37 C0400/29
C0402/31 C0404/36 C0405/01 C0405/02
C0405/17 C0405/38 C0407/20 C0408/17
C0412/17 C0415/14 C0416/27 C0417/06
C0418/03 C0418/49 C0422/33
eleven (20) A0120/08
A0204/21 A0204/26 A0372/33 A0513/27
B0750/14 B0879/11 B0888/12 B0928/34
B1076/03 B1076/27 B1178/23 B1237/18
C0095/12 C0102/31 C0107/32 C0145/37
C0416/06 C0424/14 C0535/21
eleven-knot (1) C0160/33
eleventh (3) B1262/34
C0154/12 C0160/28
elfin (1) A0599/M
elicit (4) A0098/11
A0105/07 B0770/15 C0153/28
elicited (12) A0297/13
A0435/14 A0538/33 A0544/12 A0550/08
B0727/34 B0729/01 B0731/08 B1030/12
B1123/13 C0149/03 C0569/30
eliciting (2) A0262/34 A0264/01
elite (2) B0889/09 B1107/25
Elizabeth (1) A0112/27
Elizabethan (3) A0427/34
A0710/01 B1275/05
elk (14) B0865/22 B0866/03
B0866/15 B0866/18 B0866/21 C0536/24
C0543/32 C0552/19 C0553/04 C0559/41
C0566/22 C0566/30 C0572/07 C0575/13
elk-skin (1) C0552/28
Elk/river (2) C0526/08 C0527/02
elks (2) B0865/36 C0542/20
elle (1) B0987/01
Elline (1) A0126/18
ellipse (6) C0400/06 C0400/07
C0401/28 C0402/11 C0419/41 C0420/09
ellipsoid (2) B1070/34 B1073/V
elliptical (3) B1321/06
B1321/17 B1321/32
Ellison (31) A0702/02
A0703/08 A0703/24 A0704/07 A0704/26
A0704/31 A0705/26 A0706/28 A0707/03
A0707/21 A0709/01 A0709/07 A0710/09
A0711/05 A0712/05 B1268/02 B1268/07
B1268/23 B1269/07 B1269/25 B1269/30
B1270/24 B1271/30 B1272/03 B1272/22
B1274/01 B1275/12 B1276/07 B1277/10
B1277/33 B1278/25
Ellison, Seabright (2) A0704/20
B1269/19
Ellison's (4) A0704/19
B1269/18 B1277/19 B1278/04
elm (4) B1332/08
B1332/16 B1332/18 C0541/30
elongated (1) B1250/26
elongation (2) B1250/23 C0423/33
eloped (2) A0440/03 B0754/28
elopement (11) B0754/21
B0754/23 B0754/23 B0754/29 B0754/29
B0754/33 B0755/06 B0755/20 B0756/09
B0769/04 B0770/02
eloquence (9) A0297/12
A0310/07 A0625/06 B0901/20 B1013/06
B1050/12 B1050/23 B1092/33 B1139/07
eloquent (4) A0135/07
A0234/18 A0682/31 B1050/02
elp (2) B1109/10 B1109/10
else (57)
else's (1) A0072/23

elsewhere (13) A0247/21
A0580/17 A0584/03 B0766/22 B0978/27
B1051/15 B1193/03 B1335/02 B1345/32
C0055/02 C0199/04 C0523/01 C0576/39
elucidation (2) B0727/33 B0736/35
elude (2) B0727/06 B0756/11
eluded (2) A0438/18 B1317/24
eludes (1) B1040/06
eluding (2) A0055/16 A0064/31
Elwood (1) B1031/12
Elysium (2) A0151/04 A0642/V
Elzevir (1) A0301/05
em (4) B0814/14
B1373/03 B1373/09 B1373/09
emaciated (8) A0245/22
A0311/18 A0324/20 A0404/14 A0416/29
B0940/10 C0130/04 C0142/07
emaciation (3) A0215/01
A0246/11 B1235/12
emanate (1) A0244/03
emanated (1) B1137/14
emanating (1) A0672/10
emanation (2) A0711/31 B1276/34
emancipated (1) A0047/31
embalm (1) B1187/12
embalmed (9) B0933/30
B1180/16 B1187/06 B1187/21 B1188/23
B1188/24 B1188/27 B1189/09 B1195/17
embalming (3) B1181/10
B1187/07 B1189/01
embalmment (4) B1180/32
B1187/16 B1187/19 B1187/29
embankment (1) B1331/30
embark (1) B0814/08
embarrass (2) B0989/32 B1075/33
embarrassed (9) A0264/29
A0442/20 A0532/12 B0766/31 B0772/26
B0989/23 B1328/03 C0095/02 C0548/37
embarrassing (1) B0903/23
embarrassment (11) A0106/08
A0355/29 A0378/08 A0431/30 A0530/21
B0737/17 B0823/11 B0858/12 B0978/05
B1236/17 C0545/28
embellish (1) B0989/15
embellishment (3) A0120/03
A0283/28 A0499/23
embellishments (4) A0157/16
A0165/22 A0673/17 B1136/31
ember (1) B1206/19
embers (1) A0212/02
embittered (2) A0019/07 C0521/29
emblem (2) B0831/08 B1371/15
emblematic (1) A0271/20
emblematical (1) C0552/14
embodied (2) A0435/34 B1135/34
embodies (2) C0521/04 C0550/25
embodiment (4) A0615/06
A0711/34 B0728/29 B1277/01
embody (4) A0426/10
B0731/23 B1033/30 C0578/15
embolden (2) B0894/31 B1102/14
emboldened (1) B0915/01
embossed (1) B0828/10
embouchure (2) C0527/08 C0527/25
embrace (11) A0081/05
->A0591/24 A0616/26 A0640/19 A0673/06
A0695/02 B0772/19 B0961/22 B1034/12
B1385/22 C0072/14
embraced (5) A0021/03
A0671/22 B0736/08 B0905/16 C0160/33
embraces (1) C0206/04
embracing (1) B0818/34
embroidered (2) A0247/20 A0443/13
embroidery (1) A0100/14
embryo (1) C0429/24
emendation (7) A0708/25
A0708/26 A0708/30 B1273/20 B1273/21
B1273/24 B1330/12
emendations (1) B1189/17
emerald (4) A0157/27
A0603/01 B1281/28 B1333/26
emeralds (1) B0827/36
emerge (3) B0932/21
C0201/33 C0387/25
emerged (7) A0343/27
A0349/33 A0513/32 B0866/13 C0194/27
C0200/13 C0390/24
emergency (8) A0059/21
A0067/11 A0156/11 A0593/21 A0667/43
B0985/20 C0080/36 C0141/03
emerging (2) B0966/08 C0422/19
Emeritus (1) A0295/12
Emerson (1) A0625/04
emeutes (1) B0727/18
emigrate (1) B1364/20
emigrated (1) C0522/16
eminence (5) A0045/12
B0821/33 B0956/12 B0957/19 B1070/03
eminences (1) B1331/25
eminent (9) B0863/19
B1131/V B1135/26 B1137/02 B1137/38
B1138/37 B1169/06 B1335/28 B1359/09
emissaries (1) B0725/02
emit (2) B0809/09 B0940/21
emits (1) B1163/23
emitted (8) A0138/V
B0925/24 B1157/24 B1180/06 C0076/06
C0079/23 C0205/27 C0390/18
emitting (3) A0138/20
B1102/34 B1351/33
Emmet (1) C0066/32
Emmons (1) B1126/02
Emmons, William (1) A0279/08
emotion (20) A0162/08
A0164/V A0166/18 A0296/V A0299/29
A0316/24 A0319/26 A0431/07 A0459/33
A0507/28 A0673/05 A0675/04 B0731/06
B0889/13 C0082/38 C0087/22 C0122/21
C0198/04 C0397/34 C0537/20
emotions (4) A0024/25
A0329/09 B1021/07 C0543/11
Emperor (2) A0156/17 B1130/03
emperor (2) A0122/24 C0432/06
emperor's (2) B1302/30 B1303/31
emperors (1) A0120/26
emphasis (8) A0264/06
A0324/17 A0672/27 B1226/13 B1315/34
B1373/13 C0550/25 C0556/40
emphasized (1) B1135/14
emphasizing (1) A0547/10

emphatic (1) A0674/10
emphatically (4) A0086/09
A0097/13 A0262/20 B0880/02
empire (9) A0033/07
A0057/30 A0250/04 A0704/12 B0989/30
B1164/02 B1164/11 B1269/11 B1311/14
empires (1) B1167/04
empirical (1) B1359/32
employ (21) A0278/04
A0299/31 A0539/07 A0557/04 A0684/09
B0726/04 B0838/12 B0871/07 B0888/19
B0907/29 B0976/20 B0979/27 B0982/21
B1037/26 B1050/12 B1074/34 B1144/21
B1279/15 B1373/35 C0057/14 C0161/26
employed (55)
employer (2) A0499/12 B0770/29
employers (1) A0484/22
employing (8) A0707/18
B0976/19 B1070/27 B1222/V B1272/16
C0554/01 C0556/24 C0560/05
employment (11) A0482/26
A0485/27 A0490/10 A0499/31 A0557/14
B0767/02 B0978/01 B0978/01 B1184/30
B1208/13 C0391/16
employments (1) C0542/02
employs (2) B0759/16 B1030/05
Empress (2) C0526/23 C0526/27
empressement (2) B0814/26 B0907/07
emptied (4) A0688/03
B0736/14 B1260/14 C0416/10
empties (1) B0863/32
empty (20) A0241/25
A0337/16 A0589/25 B0754/06 B0957/01
B1102/10 B1110/21 B1372/24 C0069/03
C0074/02 C0077/26 C0109/29 C0116/14
C0128/17 C0129/30 C0142/01 C0390/11
C0533/12 C0571/03 C0571/06
emptying (1) B1094/02
en (21) A0033/03
A0037/21 A0037/V A0096/M A0096/M
A0175/20 A0181/10 A0253/V A0345/14
A0378/M B1044/22 B1048/22 B1122/01
B1182/22 B1350/21 C0412/09 C0430/29
C0430/38 C0430/38 C0448/V C0572/33
enable (10) A0440/07 B0741/26
B1076/22 B1191/36 B1261/19 B1277/32
C0079/37 C0127/30 C0390/10 C0578/14
enabled (58)
enables (3) B1031/33
B1144/31 C0059/31
enact (1) B1350/09
enacted (3) B1350/01
B1350/08 C0133/33
enactments (1) A0491/02
enamel (1) A0215/20
enamelled (2) A0165/05 A0165/V
enamored (6) A0033/04 A0033/15
A0498/27 A0532/26 A0706/29 B1271/31
encamp (3) C0539/03
C0558/32 C0565/20
encamped (7) C0538/11
C0540/01 C0560/14 C0569/41 C0570/20
C0576/27 C0576/33
encamping (2) C0541/02 C0570/31
encampment (15) C0152/21
->C0152/29 C0540/12 C0541/33 C0542/01
C0542/21 C0543/06 C0544/10 C0560/09
C0565/23 C0572/03 C0575/32 C0576/09
C0576/19 C0577/17
encampments (3) C0152/03
C0153/18 C0571/26
encased (2) B1350/36 B1362/25
enchained (2) A0403/22 A0511/04
enchanted (6) A0036/13 A0603/34
B0903/08 B1279/09 C0542/04 C0573/27
enchanter (1) B0944/34
enchanting (5) A0707/27
B0890/V B0897/21 B1272/27 C0575/17
enchantingly (1) B1331/10
enchantment (4) A0415/19
A0429/22 B1122/20 C0543/37
encircle (3) A0164/23
B0746/01 C0167/33
encircled (7) A0379/08
A0460/23 A0639/18 B0890/10 C0076/37
C0116/24 C0172/17
encircles (2) A0501/18 C0153/25
encircling (1) B1333/14
Encke, Professor (1) C0392/12
Encke's (2) C0401/24 C0423/09
enclose (3) A0142/05
B1315/01 C0574/02
enclosed (6) A0217/V A0273/34
B0815/12 B0900/16 B1130/18 C0411/15
enclosing (1) B1077/08
enclosure (14) A0027/14 A0243/26
A0429/11 A0430/03 A0686/22 A0688/26
A0689/01 B0761/13 B1335/02 C0409/22
C0410/12 C0438/V C0561/32 C0561/39
encoffined (1) A0409/30
encompass (2) B0764/29 B0902/18
encompassed (9) A0428/22
A0430/20 A0579/12 A0684/14 B1331/18
B1337/31 C0081/04 C0083/30 C0122/14
encompassing (1) C0423/36
encore (1) C0430/39
encored (2) A0070/01 A0127/04
encounter (4) A0686/02
C0399/03 C0574/35 C0578/24
encountered (27) A0023/16
A0138/14 A0217/V A0253/29 A0400/25
A0584/21 A0685/20 B0893/12 B0915/10
B0915/23 B0941/03 B0945/V B0948/14
B0988/04 B1165/13 B1215/26 B1257/16
C0076/03 C0095/10 C0097/39 C0112/29
C0149/11 C0159/19 C0160/10 C0405/37
C0527/06 C0577/33
encountering (5) C0064/24
C0160/18 C0208/18 C0539/30 C0565/28
encounters (1) B0749/30
encourage (2) B1127/35 B1207/13
encouraged (9) A0351/01
B0906/10 B1006/03 B1379/14 C0120/19
C0183/07 C0194/12 C0537/16 C0576/26
encouragement (1) B0866/18
encouraging (1) C0123/35
encrimsoned (1) A0401/09
encroached (1) B0961/13
encroachments (2) B1021/05 B1233/22
encrusted (3) B1081/02

->B1258/14 C0570/18
encumber (2) A0556/12 C0442/V
encumbered (7) A0079/31
A0643/10 B0945/27 B1076/01 B1300/19
C0113/10 C0152/14
Encyclopaedia (1) A0583/02
end (185)
endanger (1) C0204/15
endangered (1) C0532/36
endeared (3) B0855/03
B0949/32 B1055/02
endeavor (27) A0065/03
A0069/V A0107/20 A0142/05 A0245/18
A0269/25 A0300/08 A0338/09 A0354/23
A0405/19 A0683/31 A0684/04 B0750/22
B0751/18 B0754/03 B0770/11 B0840/05
B0896/V B0966/21 B0967/35 B0977/06
B0988/12 B1158/27 B1213/29 B1242/27
C0393/07 C0555/22
endeavored (37) A0067/16
A0081/34 A0081/39 A0110/29 A0166/20
A0411/19 A0412/01 A0511/18 A0552/01
A0589/30 A0695/22 A0696/21 B0724/13
B0732/42 B0817/08 B0832/01 B0896/29
B0929/22 B0944/09 B0957/04 B0959/16
B0961/06 B0965/19 B0967/05 B1035/24
B1046/29 B1053/25 B1081/05 B1160/03
B1241/10 B1241/16 B1261/17 B1348/01
C0176/01 C0397/29 C0406/32 C0562/24
endeavoring (17) A0125/29
A0356/04 A0356/21 A0539/34 A0686/25
B0738/19 B1020/05 B1052/34 B1077/16
B1078/08 B1348/25 B1348/27 B1353/23
C0160/06 C0539/13 C0559/21 C0567/18
endeavors (19) A0154/V
A0295/25 A0313/27 A0327/17 A0404/30
A0433/20 A0435/13 A0683/08 A0688/15
B0728/11 B0740/14 B0826/09 B0964/10
B1022/05 B1091/06 B1154/02 B1233/07
B1241/03 B1246/20
endeavour (10) A0055/19 C0072/06
C0075/02 C0105/19 C0119/03 C0126/33
C0128/11 C0182/36 C0184/13 C0186/20
endeavoured (22) A0059/25 A0353/27
C0064/07 C0077/09 C0077/15 C0079/10
C0082/39 C0088/32 C0111/08 C0114/15
C0120/17 C0125/38 C0126/24 C0128/14
C0128/31 C0129/09 C0131/36 C0143/03
C0170/12 C0197/30 C0198/19 C0201/05
endeavouring (4) C0116/29
C0121/18 C0130/12 C0182/10
endeavours (2) A0313/V C0204/10
ended (7) A0461/23
A0688/24 B0866/21 B1107/19 B1128/07
B1194/09 B1333/29
Enderby (2) C0065/31 C0161/26
ending (1) A0512/09
endings (1) B0879/27
enditing (1) C0066/33
endless (10) A0122/16 A0322/24
A0430/11 A0707/10 B0865/04 B1214/08
B1272/09 C0072/18 C0118/19 C0575/03
endlessly (1) B1035/29
endorsed (1) A0264/34
endorsement (1) B0900/18
endcw (2) B0893/02 B0905/12
endowed (6) A0078/20 A0204/12
A0348/34 A0379/14 B1166/17 C0072/21
endowing (2) A0705/13 B1270/12
endowment (1) A0601/15
endowments (6) A0093/18 A0112/29
A0380/09 A0703/27 B0888/09 B1268/25
ends (16) A0104/02
A0263/31 A0367/09 A0436/30 A0443/25
A0445/09 A0664/07 B0955/27 B1071/19
B1145/11 B1382/02 C0056/30 C0069/14
C0147/29 C0185/15 C0202/33
endued (2) A0157/V A0321/27
enduing (1) B0943/13
endurable (1) A0403/04
endurance (8) A0408/16
A0446/24 B0813/21 B0966/11 C0391/34
C0399/29 C0407/14 C0413/16
endure (18) A0057/01 A0066/27
A0128/12 A0234/25 A0320/04 A0435/09
B0962/26 B0963/30 B1195/06 C0080/37
C0081/41 C0082/04 C0096/17 C0117/36
C0404/15 C0413/26 C0421/02 C0424/23
endured (19) A0026/08
A0412/11 A0498/14 A0578/01 A0673/34
A0675/13 A0694/29 B0757/19 B0955/20
B0963/21 B0968/32 C0134/12 C0139/15
C0143/01 C0149/01 C0205/18 C0391/28
C0411/19 C0411/32
endures (1) A0204/13
endureth (1) B0967/03
enduring (14) A0228/24 A0233/05
A0399/06 A0609/24 A0611/13 A0616/27
B0763/32 B0887/04 B0924/26 B1122/24
B1298/05 C0134/36 C0532/31 C0564/19
enemies (7) A0336/02
A0697/12 B1049/35 C0201/28 C0555/25
C0556/18 C0565/36
enemy (9) A0045/11
A0059/07 A0061/03 A0071/04 A0125/36
A0499/08 C0533/21 C0550/19 C0568/39
enemy-werrybor'em (1) A0353/09
energetic (15) A0023/05
A0026/17 A0154/01 A0272/37 A0316/26
A0327/08 A0402/22 A0431/28 A0460/29
A0707/15 B0817/07 B0947/09 B0990/23
B1044/23 B1272/13
energies (4) A0151/12
A0625/11 B1239/10 B1300/22
energy (34) A0056/03 A0210/23
A0253/19 A0273/23 A0284/08 A0315/13
A0329/12 A0339/10 A0351/29 A0402/01
A0416/22 A0430/32 A0432/10 A0447/18
A0515/12 A0531/19 A0693/27 B0902/17
B0907/14 B1020/17 B1020/24 B1069/12
B1222/08 B1222/24 C0059/34 C0074/28
C0078/27 C0095/24 C0134/23 C0136/30
C0148/04 C0182/17 C0200/41 C0537/04
enfeeble (2) A0438/03 A0545/29
enfeebled (2) C0074/35 C0078/06
enflamed (1) A0567/V
enforce (1) B1005/15
enforced (2) A0459/04 C0105/27
enforcing (1) A0593/06
engage (3) B0725/12

->B1236/12 C0187/06
engaged (35) A0180/22
A0441/03 A0508/19 B0728/04 B0753/22
B0757/35 B0763/14 B0832/13 B0879/05
B0879/22 B0895/02 B0922/01 B0922/18
B0933/18 B0933/33 B0933/36 B0946/29
B0949/26 B0968/28 B0978/18 B0985/12
B0992/11 B1072/28 B1258/01 C0065/31
C0067/38 C0109/27 C0134/19 C0413/08
C0522/38 C0530/31 C0531/06 C0531/14
C0540/11 C0566/08
engagement (5) B1245/03
B1258/10 B1258/11 B1258/12 C0188/12
engagements (2) A0268/05 B0831/09
engaging (3) A0705/08
B1155/24 B1270/07
Engedi (1) A0047/17
engender (1) A0550/22
engendered (7) A0107/12
A0326/V A0434/14 A0460/33 A0556/16
B1123/05 B1222/02
engendering (1) A0107/V
engenders (1) B0747/21
Engine (1) B0865/19
engine (2) B0855/35 B1194/21
engineer (1) A0478/24
engineers (1) B1193/17
enginery (1) B1044/02
engirdle (1) B1214/04
engirdled (2) B1213/33 B1331/25
England (18) A0163/V A0242/19
A0247/21 A0320/10 A0428/01 A0496/14
A0496/18 A0654/22 A0704/35 B0807/12
B0863/12 B0863/34 B1031/22 B1269/34
B1329/21 C0190/32 C0430/21 C0522/14
English (39) A0162/10
A0163/16 A0275/17 A0279/17 A0315/03
A0346/16 A0430/10 A0495/02 A0542/31
A0547/05 A0550/02 A0621/04 A0651/22
A0709/35 A0710/01 B0827/28 B0836/08
B0836/12 B0837/01 B0837/13 B0866/22
B0901/17 B0911/18 B1010/28 B1092/08
B1092/11 B1095/09 B1096/38 B1097/05
B1131/12 B1275/04 B1275/05 C0156/08
C0162/02 C0188/23 C0430/33 C0542/19
C0543/25 C0550/28
Englishman (9) A0164/08
A0541/27 A0542/01 A0542/30 A0549/21
A0549/31 A0550/01 C0085/40 C0156/11
engraved (1) B1052/16
engraven (1) A0196/12
engraving (5) A0602/V
B1071/V B1073/V B1122/33 C0431/04
engravings (1) B1122/V
engrossed (2) A0286/07 C0166/33
engrosses (1) B1324/03
engulfed (1) A0438/V
enigma (9) A0707/22
B0835/12 B0835/27 B0840/01 B0842/14
B0923/06 B1044/01 B1272/23 B1364/05
enigmas (2) A0528/07 C0399/35
enigmatically (1) A0273/05
enim (1) A0599/M
enjoy (8) A0344/03
A0351/22 A0382/10 B0748/26 B1016/26
->C0414/15 C0432/03 C0522/09
enjoyed (9) A0105/06
A0265/08 A0600/07 B0909/31 B1193/33
C0093/30 C0412/21 C0537/17 C0544/12
enjoying (10) A0433/24 B0826/24
B0974/02 B1038/30 B1137/22 B1155/20
B1178/08 C0138/40 C0153/15 C0413/18
enjoyment (9) A0352/13
A0507/14 A0528/03 A0600/04 A0703/21
B1268/20 C0398/35 C0544/02 C0564/35
enjoyments (1) A0609/36
enkindle (1) B0975/09
enkindled (4) A0532/06
A0640/24 A0696/11 C0205/37
enkindling (1) A0230/08
enlarged (1) B0823/26
enlighten (3) A0098/07
A0105/08 A0385/14
enlightened (4) A0105/13
B1128/13 B1293/18 B1317/26
enlisted (2) C0065/16 C0531/34
enlisting (1) A0365/08
enmity (1) A0019/08
ennui (7) A0070/18
A0081/34 A0507/09 B0990/23 B1115/05
B1292/04 B1299/24
ennuied (1) A0153/V
ennuye (3) A0153/20
A0153/V A0401/22
enormities (3) A0021/18
A0054/21 A0427/02
enormity (3) A0079/44
A0248/15 A0440/25
enormous (22) A0022/07 A0101/V
A0143/28 A0240/19 A0248/V A0440/23
A0690/04 A0705/01 B0978/20 B1010/24
B1137/35 B1160/37 B1270/01 B1277/01
C0069/23 C0137/32 C0141/14 C0388/32
C0418/49 C0422/41 C0572/31 C0577/32
enormously (7) A0428/V
A0436/V B0773/11 B0817/34 C0087/09
C0140/21 C0389/19
enough (98)
enraged (4) A0023/06
A0414/14 C0082/17 C0578/24
enrapt (1) A0641/V
enraptured (6) A0294/V B0902/02
B0909/28 B1208/13 B1277/35 C0564/38
enriching (2) A0705/28 B1270/26
Ens (1) A0079/20
ensanguined (1) C0125/12
ensconce (1) A0124/10
ensconced (5) A0056/16
A0062/33 A0126/09 B0761/21 C0541/06
ensemble (3) A0087/08
A0100/18 A0281/05
ensheathed (1) B1180/20
enshrine (1) A0164/23
enshrined (1) A0641/V
enshrouded (10) A0138/31 A0190/11
A0191/03 A0217/V A0218/26 A0326/18
A0329/21 A0412/33 A0416/26 B0773/01
enslaved (1) A0446/19
enslaving (1) B1163/05
ensue (8) A0138/08

->A0204/10 B1032/07 B1082/10 C0097/33
C0137/14 C0399/36 C0414/27
ensued (26) A0182/35 A0249/21
A0373/11 A0442/27 A0443/20 A0558/11
A0560/14 B0731/18 B0823/23 B0927/11
B1020/09 B1032/16 B1057/02 B1057/14
B1186/17 B1353/25 C0061/29 C0080/07
C0086/07 C0086/20 C0089/17 C0134/02
C0135/29 C0140/09 C0165/01 C0186/33
ensues (2) B0873/24 C0528/41
ensuing (6) A0140/28 A0404/28
B0837/30 C0092/24 C0101/25 C0522/22
ensured (2) B1277/02 C0531/30
entablature (2) A0190/33 A0501/17
entailed (2) A0624/08 B1316/14
entangle (2) A0441/05 C0120/36
entangled (7) A0686/28
B0762/18 B0947/14 B0957/06 C0121/34
C0397/07 C0413/32
entanglement (1) B1107/17
entangling (1) C0398/15
entende (1) A0033/20
entendre (1) A0545/06
enter (34) A0027/14 A0099/11
A0099/12 A0100/25 A0100/26 A0143/25
A0296/V A0365/07 A0437/34 A0539/22
A0546/03 A0707/11 B0871/34 B0872/12
B0908/25 B0929/01 B1091/14 B1093/29
B1119/03 B1162/11 B1187/11 B1272/10
B1297/35 B1317/14 C0079/13 C0104/08
C0105/15 C0112/14 C0132/23 C0173/11
C0177/25 C0177/30 C0181/30 C0558/38
entered (97)
entereth (1) A0414/19
entering (25) A0024/20
A0057/25 A0068/08 A0322/20 A0412/18
A0414/13 A0439/11 A0447/13 A0500/13
A0554/10 A0580/23 A0592/19 A0704/32
B1003/15 B1163/17 B1163/34 B1269/30
C0068/12 C0069/27 C0158/22 C0165/12
C0168/01 C0180/35 C0203/22 C0524/22
enterprise (9) A0274/19
C0148/04 C0526/15 C0526/33 C0528/05
C0529/07 C0531/31 C0564/06 C0565/08
enterprises (1) C0525/08
enterprize (2) C0525/35 C0528/36
enters (4) B0762/20
B0872/17 B0977/09 C0429/30
entertain (10) A0600/08 A0682/13
B0773/19 B1114/27 B1119/M B1155/07
B1190/19 B1301/34 B1316/02 C0100/26
entertained (44) A0096/13
A0105/02 A0127/15 A0143/05 A0203/08
A0265/11 A0298/V A0300/30 A0441/09
A0488/15 A0583/09 A0626/33 A0652/08
A0671/13 B0736/32 B0747/08 B0755/20
B0758/28 B0767/26 B0814/27 B0819/27
B0823/03 B0902/31 B0922/09 B0931/06
B0932/32 B0977/35 B0991/35 B1052/07
B1058/32 B1302/08 B1374/23 C0078/15
C0088/29 C0107/11 C0125/36 C0130/25
C0132/13 C0133/22 C0159/11 C0180/05
C0180/09 C0180/13 C0431/01
entertaining (5) B0975/01
B1090/20 B1159/14 C0110/35 C0521/22
entertainment (5) A0664/18
B0871/18 B1009/09 B1015/28 B1089/02
entertainments (1) A0204/19
entertains (1) B0872/24
enthral (1) A0155/06
enthralling (1) A0310/06
enthroned (2) A0610/08 B0761/21
enthusiasm (24) A0160/11
A0297/14 A0352/13 A0379/07 A0431/10
B0796/29 B0807/21 B0808/17 B0811/03
B0861/04 B0891/07 B0896/02 B0896/03
B0901/19 B0905/31 B0908/11 B0922/13
B0923/22 B0929/33 B1128/05 B1192/07
B1257/08 B1338/33 C0538/27
enthusiast (1) A0212/18
enthusiastic (15) A0021/09
A0341/10 B0830/28 B0888/27 B0889/23
B0891/07 B0893/03 B0899/13 B0902/16
B0924/18 B0927/08 B0942/05 C0065/14
C0532/05 C0576/13
enthusiastically (1) B0915/06
enthusiasts (1) B0941/16
enticed (1) C0561/39
enticing (1) C0175/37
entire (105)
entirely (140)
entitle (1) C0538/31
entitled (17) A0071/16
A0071/21 A0126/06 A0247/14 A0250/22
A0311/12 A0406/22 B0724/12 B0869/V
B0907/13 B0942/31 B1138/34 B1139/08
B1144/03 B1247/13 B1361/23 B1363/37
entitling (1) B1075/16
entity (4) A0141/29
A0615/34 A0616/19 B1034/22
entombed (16) A0234/12
A0323/09 A0339/26 A0407/32 A0410/21
A0603/32 A0642/05 B0834/07 B0964/35
B1303/35 B1317/06 B1385/33 C0075/39
C0182/24 C0185/27 C0444/V
entombment (5) A0409/30
A0411/V B0956/32 B1190/09 B1192/18
entomological (1) B0807/25
Entozoa (1) B1165/34
entrails (5) B1181/04
B1292/29 C0135/34 C0175/33 C0178/39
entrance (29) A0029/06
A0059/31 A0081/13 A0100/28 A0152/14
A0189/13 A0189/20 A0244/29 A0245/10
A0245/19 A0311/21 A0401/19 A0413/24
A0515/04 A0540/20 A0554/30 A0662/02
B0943/03 B0977/04 B1004/06 B1020/05
B1262/08 B1332/20 B1352/15 B1382/21
C0122/10 C0150/38 C0164/11 C0173/19
entranced (5) A0180/05
A0317/11 A0665/34 B1037/24 B1278/08
entrances (1) A0242/29
entrancing (1) B1283/04
entrapment (1) A0690/28
entrapped (2) B0926/22 C0105/24
entre (1) C0430/38
entreated (3) A0624/02
C0088/12 C0113/27
entreaties (4) B0907/11
B0910/03 B1236/19 B1371/22

entreating (3) B0900/16 C0085/41 C0134/30

entreats (1) B0875/17

entrust (1) B1140/04

entrusted (5) A0498/03 B1072/28 B1372/14 C0523/08 C0544/09

entry (2) B1390/02 C0160/39

enuff (1) B0812/24

enumerated (1) C0394/31

enunciated (1) B1371/21

enunciation (4) A0402/23 A0533/21 A0624/32 B1226/12

envelop (2) A0139/01 B1029/01

envelope (2) B1129/05 C0552/11

enveloped (28) A0029/21 A0241/15 A0243/13 A0296/03 A0512/04 A0579/10 A0588/09 A0591/07 A0616/25 A0663/07 A0693/08 A0693/18 B0794/22 B0795/10 B0797/10 B0819/10 B0929/16 B1143/24 B1180/10 B1189/18 B1277/09 B1328/10 B1354/03 C0067/12 C0082/21 C0125/39 C0389/29 C0414/08

envelopes (1) B1133/V

enveloping (2) A0217/V A0501/20

envelops (3) A0366/21 B1133/09 C0182/30

enviable (2) A0348/08 A0348/09

envied (1) B0807/26

environed (2) A0688/14 B0946/24

environs (2) B0729/26 C0387/22

envy (3) A0336/11 A0562/25 C0524/05

enwrapped (3) A0610/15 A0682/01 B0865/32

enwrapt (1) B1279/29

enwreathed (1) B1337/17

enwritten (1) A0414/18

eo (1) A0638/15

eos (Gr.) (1) B1385/18

ep'aian (Gr.) (1) B1385/18

epeen (Gr.) (1) A0507/11

ephemera (1) A0642/V

ephemeron (1) A0642/01

Ephesus (1) A0120/06

Epic (1) B0869/M

epics (1) A0628/V

Epictetus (1) A0073/26

epicures (1) A0626/22

Epicurus (7) A0109/05 A0109/07 A0109/08 A0109/08 A0109/V A0535/09 A0536/06

Epidaphne (5) A0122/02 A0123/23 A0126/02 A0128/09 A0128/23

Epidaphnians (1) A0127/V

Epidendron (1) B1162/33

Epidendrum (1) A0344/01

epidermis (1) B1180/31

Epigoniad (1) B1101/04

epigram (8) A0093/10 A0112/22 A0602/08 B0738/13 B0738/15 B0916/09 B1378/02 B1379/13

epigrammatic (1) A0281/04

epilepsis (1) A0072/26

epilepsy (2) A0211/12 A0216/27

epileptic (1) A0216/V

Epimanes (1) A0119/V

Epimanes, Antiochus (1) A0126/07

Epimenides (1) A0075/15

Epiphanes (4) A0126/25 A0126/27 A0126/29 A0128/04

Epiphanes, Antiochus (3) A0119/01 A0126/04 A0127/29

epistle (14) A0266/08 A0268/24 A0270/20 A0272/16 A0272/31 A0273/05 A0279/16 A0285/04 A0302/01 A0303/01 B0899/13 B1311/23 B1318/10 C0390/31

epistles (4) A0262/32 A0262/34 A0490/16 A0490/24

epistolary (1) A0264/19

epitaphs (1) B0963/23

epithet (4) A0053/04 A0062/09 A0312/12 B1298/01

epithets (5) A0473/01 B1139/26 B1140/17 B1162/30 B1240/10

Epizoae (1) B1163/11

epoch (46) A0020/04 A0098/10 A0098/12 A0212/34 A0236/03 A0242/18 A0294/01 A0295/06 A0296/08 A0324/05 A0366/24 A0426/12 A0436/22 A0457/20 A0459/23 A0491/01 A0609/10 A0612/10 A0638/19 A0641/V A0642/32 A0652/22 A0683/13 B0767/09 B0772/24 B0772/28 B0922/23 B0966/07 B1127/10 B1144/33 B1189/24 B1190/01 B1192/18 B1214/24 B1214/34 B1224/29 B1234/33 B1241/19 B1247/07 B1250/04 B1312/02 B1350/32 C0403/17 C0421/07 C0439/V C0558/39

epochs (1) B1215/03

Epsilon (1) A0346/09

equal (51)

equality (2) A0432/01 A0610/16

equalization (1) A0615/07

equalled (3) A0311/24 A0581/25 C0524/09

equalling (1) A0138/13

equally (31) A0019/14 A0065/23 A0080/16 A0089/10 A0097/10 A0341/04 A0366/04 A0441/09 A0593/04 A0621/20 A0640/27 A0675/05 A0711/07 B0723/M B0749/16 B0816/09 B0827/11 B1141/33 B1158/13 B1162/29 B1167/05 B1219/04 B1256/08 B1383/03 C0060/06 C0087/11 C0121/01 C0121/40 C0123/03 C0394/12 C0423/35

equals (1) A0026/13

equanimity (1) B0822/21

equations (1) B1358/16

equator (5) C0140/19 C0148/17 C0402/07 C0418/07 C0418/39

equatorial (3) B1321/V C0400/03 C0425/18

equerries (3) A0023/17 A0023/24 A0024/23

equerry (1) A0024/02

equilibrium (1) C0389/14

equilibrium (1) C0098/11

Equinoctial (1) C0432/26

equip (2) B1350/14 C0108/40

equipment (3) A0142/18 C0389/28 C0393/21

equipments (3) A0205/04
C0529/31 C0530/14
equipped (2) C0085/30 C0147/23
equipping (2) B1350/30 C0093/20
equitably (1) B0958/14
equity (1) B0747/37
equivalent (4) A0547/05
B1034/02 B1295/24 B1311/21
equivocal (16) A0026/26
A0054/20 A0063/23 A0099/26 A0247/09
A0299/16 A0399/17 A0403/21 A0599/V
A0625/13 B0851/33 B0898/15 B0926/15
B0944/14 B1139/27 C0095/23
equivocation (1) A0386/24
er (2) A0506/01 A0515/32
era (2) A0344/31 A0344/32
era (4) A0019/V
A0293/29 A0638/21 A0643/01
eradicated (1) A0324/09
eram (1) A0018/M
erase (1) C0065/08
erat (1) A0043/M
ere (24) A0069/08
A0189/02 A0233/21 A0324/02 A0439/24
A0444/31 A0445/01 A0501/V A0676/15
A0691/06 B0796/35 B0907/18 B0968/04
B1103/01 B1103/07 B1239/09 B1260/10
B1373/01 B1373/09 B1373/21 B1374/01
B1375/20 C0387/05 C0425/06
ere-while (1) A0427/12
Erebus (1) B0897/02
erect (25) A0218/17
A0248/12 A0298/V A0299/23 A0603/09
A0604/18 A0676/29 B0859/11 B0865/34
B0911/13 B0947/31 B0957/08 B0959/04
B0964/06 B1160/15 B1208/06 B1304/28
C0060/40 C0070/02 C0075/04 C0075/26
C0111/27 C0151/17 C0195/14 C0577/09
erected (10) A0044/31 A0068/23
A0165/21 A0242/29 A0681/M B1167/03
B1263/02 B1313/22 C0098/19 C0202/35
erecting (3) A0166/08
C0152/40 C0177/33
erection (3) A0075/17
C0076/35 C0177/25
erections (1) C0573/40
Ermengarde (5) A0644/21
A0644/22 A0644/23 A0644/V A0645/07
ermined (1) B1281/04
ero (1) A0018/M
Eros (3) A0225/04
A0229/04 A0640/23
err (4) A0226/06
A0230/01 A0271/24 A0497/28
errand (2) B0856/17 B0873/04
Errant (1) B1270/37
erred (4) A0545/11
A0694/29 A0708/08 A0708/08
erring (1) A0601/24
erroneous (2) A0488/16 B1119/12
erroneously (2) A0531/02 C0526/31
error (48) A0104/22
A0135/14 A0261/27 A0267/17 A0279/24
A0282/16 A0427/10 A0498/25 A0498/26
A0528/26 A0529/12 A0545/20 A0547/31
->A0561/15 A0688/16 A0708/05 B0746/32
B0747/21 B0751/31 B0773/09 B0773/33
B0773/33 B0843/17 B0843/19 B0950/23
B0950/28 B0987/02 B0987/03 B0987/18
B0987/20 B0987/33 B1035/19 B1152/04
B1154/21 B1221/01 B1249/33 B1273/05
B1278/13 B1296/12 B1296/14 B1312/16
B1312/24 B1383/21 B1383/24 C0195/17
C0197/09 C0419/12 C0438/V
errors (8) A0435/29
A0440/33 A0459/08 A0459/09 A0497/02
A0615/17 B0747/35 B1050/31
errs (2) B0946/08 B0984/03
erry (1) A0356/14
erscheint (1) B0723/M
erudite (3) A0204/03
A0342/02 A0342/V
erudition (10) A0210/09 A0225/11
A0229/11 A0284/10 A0315/21 A0339/28
A0343/08 B1091/32 B1163/10 B1325/09
eruption (2) B1161/25 C0422/37
eruptions (2) B1321/28 B1322/V
erysipelas (1) C0107/39
Es (1) B0723/M
escape (82)
escaped (44) A0024/23
A0029/12 A0137/14 A0415/17 A0551/05
A0551/13 A0551/22 A0552/32 A0553/31
A0558/01 A0558/02 A0558/15 A0560/12
A0568/04 A0586/07 A0687/17 A0689/10
A0695/10 B0723/20 B0753/30 B0816/32
B0889/12 B0900/06 B0947/06 B0977/09
B0981/08 B1237/14 B1248/05 B1294/32
B1317/24 B1350/21 B1360/07 C0063/08
C0063/27 C0084/16 C0096/33 C0120/17
C0144/37 C0185/23 C0207/38 C0414/22
C0554/08 C0568/02 C0568/33
escapes (5) A0144/04
B0819/02 B1037/16 C0095/22 C0425/20
escaping (9) A0078/32
A0081/22 A0248/27 B0949/17 B1021/29
B1040/04 B1280/10 C0134/21 C0176/11
eschew (2) A0342/09 B0955/01
eschewed (2) B0878/31 B1178/06
eschewing (1) A0529/16
escondida (2) A0344/22 A0354/30
escort (1) B0904/03
escorted (2) B0729/15 B0905/03
escorting (1) B0916/03
escritoire (2) B0875/07 B0983/13
escrutoire (1) A0090/03
escutcheon (2) A0150/V A0631/20
escutcheons (2) A0247/21 A0253/V
Espagnol (1) C0430/29
especial (29) A0102/15
A0126/14 A0247/16 A0298/11 A0378/11
A0380/22 A0499/17 A0667/44 B0822/17
B0833/07 B0843/05 B0924/V B0949/36
B0963/19 B0987/14 B0990/29 B1055/33
B1207/32 B1233/24 B1261/13 B1317/07
B1325/02 B1345/11 B1347/05 B1371/14
C0153/03 C0427/16 C0523/28 C0525/08
especially (116)
espouse (1) B1152/15
esprit (1) B1206/14

Esq. (53)
->A0108/15 A0108/21 A0108/V A0108/V
Esqr (1) A0205/15
Esquimau (1) A0486/14
Esquimaux (1) A0091/24
Esquire (1) B1055/14
essais (1) A0098/31
essay (4) A0281/10
A0703/28 B0877/27 B1268/26
essays (3) A0096/07
B0738/01 B1115/24
essence (11) A0209/V
A0216/02 A0226/32 A0231/06 A0507/03
A0528/11 B0724/03 B0869/20 B1096/15
B1221/10 C0438/V
essential (10) A0384/17 A0443/21
A0527/V A0611/28 A0706/18 B0723/15
B0955/17 B1116/11 B1271/20 C0535/41
essentiality (1) B1123/13
essentially (11) A0018/11
A0161/12 A0212/17 B1034/14 B1297/37
B1317/33 C0171/16 C0401/02 C0402/20
C0403/08 C0414/34
esset (1) A0638/15
est (17) A0033/03
A0091/14 A0213/07 A0213/07 A0213/07
A0213/08 A0213/08 A0397/M A0568/24
A0599/03 A0599/M A0602/06 A0602/08
B0880/04 B0986/34 B0993/27 B1154/21
est-il (1) A0652/10
establish (13) A0086/04
A0484/03 A0486/34 B0740/31 B0752/30
B0829/23 B0833/06 B0837/25 B0853/01
B0961/09 B0962/18 C0428/15 C0525/17
established (15) A0382/19
A0457/22 A0497/01 A0498/23 A0662/07
B0747/03 B0822/10 B0831/03 B0835/29
B0837/25 B0842/05 B1296/24 B1384/10
C0177/13 C0522/19
establishes (1) B0874/27
establishing (4) B0751/V
B1220/10 B1369/16 C0527/17
establishment (8) A0440/07
B0843/19 B1002/09 B1003/33 B1019/08
B1021/21 C0428/35 C0527/38
estate (7) A0057/14
A0370/16 A0399/17 A0407/26 A0440/20
A0491/09 B1274/05
estates (4) A0019/14
A0020/19 A0085/11 B1123/02
esteem (7) A0266/03
A0433/12 A0609/12 B0807/19 B1133/25
B1165/23 C0180/10
esteemed (4) A0044/28
A0128/V B1055/16 B1314/06
estimate (14) A0073/16 A0100/27
A0266/15 A0266/16 A0315/10 B0828/13
B1078/17 B1090/09 B1168/37 B1250/02
B1250/06 B1292/15 C0418/03 C0575/07
estimated (6) A0600/10 B0828/18
B1073/20 B1135/32 C0115/35 C0125/34
estimating (4) A0613/19
B0827/25 B0827/32 B1248/03
estimation (4) A0064/22
A0097/17 A0270/04 A0555/16
estin (Gr.) (5) A0089/30
estomac (1) A0096/M
estrange (2) A0055/21 A0065/05
estranged (1) A0135/02
estray (1) A0023/28
Et (1) B0767/17
et (20) A0034/01
A0036/16 A0062/21 A0072/30 A0213/07
A0301/10 A0301/12 A0302/19 A0302/20
A0303/04 A0303/17 A0378/M A0430/07
A0534/27 A0568/24 A0654/08 B1105/09
B1114/03 C0430/31 C0430/37
et (3) A0408/29 A0541/11 B1131/18
et/cetera (4) A0073/01
A0073/01 A0073/01 A0073/01
etaient (2) A0216/09 A0216/10
etait (1) B1335/18
etait (1) B1335/V
etc. (48) A0052/M
A0053/08 A0054/09 A0061/M A0062/13
A0072/31 A0262/25 A0278/27 A0279/07
A0280/36 A0337/01 A0337/19 A0337/19
A0490/01 A0601/34 B0739/07 B0837/14
B1069/19 B1095/13 B1130/21 B1130/21
B1130/21 B1130/21 B1168/18 B1168/19
B1180/22 B1188/13 B1189/16 B1303/11
B1303/11 B1303/11 B1304/07 B1304/07
B1369/28 B1369/28 B1381/32 B1382/02
C0396/07 C0396/07 C0396/07 C0426/28
C0528/23 C0528/24 C0534/25 C0534/25
C0572/07 C0572/07 C0578/10
ete (1) A0037/25
eternal (15) A0138/32
A0145/12 A0217/V A0235/V A0348/03
A0354/13 A0608/10 A0684/14 A0696/31
B0966/14 B1219/15 B1298/08 B1316/15
C0175/27 C0206/01
eternally (8) A0071/28
A0195/18 A0225/M A0229/V A0426/09
B0856/08 B0903/08 C0061/30
Eternity (1) A0615/23
eternity (9) A0079/36
A0080/20 A0080/21 A0143/30 A0591/10
A0600/30 A0638/09 B1371/16 B1384/35
Ethelred (6) A0413/22 A0413/26
A0414/13 A0414/21 A0414/23 A0416/11
ether (20) A0461/20
B0960/30 B1034/12 B1034/15 B1034/22
B1034/24 B1034/24 B1034/25 B1035/13
B1035/14 B1035/19 B1035/19 B1035/21
B1035/22 B1035/27 B1038/03 B1038/14
B1038/14 B1214/22 B1215/10
ethereal (11) A0163/08
A0164/14 A0316/06 A0323/11 A0348/10
A0502/07 A0641/V A0644/21 A0663/V
C0401/31 C0402/01
ethereality (1) B1122/16
etherial (1) A0163/V
ethical (6) A0097/09 A0105/07
A0473/23 A0706/09 B0886/04 B1271/13
ethics (4) A0101/07
A0102/12 A0175/11 A0209/06
Ethiopian (2) C0207/43 C0208/25
Ethix, Aestheticus (1) A0181/01
Etienne (2) A0557/27 A0559/01

Etienne, Alexandre (1) A0544/09
etiquette (4) A0297/11
A0297/17 A0298/04 A0302/14
Etoile (1) B0738/03
Eton (3) A0438/02
A0438/11 A0445/30
etre (2) A0018/08 A0506/M
Etruscan (2) A0165/06 B1293/37
Ettrick (2) B1295/12 B1311/05
eu (1) C0430/35
Euclid (2) B1310/33 B1314/37
eudosin (Gr.) (1) A0195/M
Euenis (1) A0621/17
Eugenie (10) B0903/05 B0903/11
B0903/17 B0903/24 B0907/17 B0907/20
B0910/07 B0910/18 B0911/10 B0911/17
Eulalie (1) B1384/15
eulogies (1) B1133/21
Eupatrids (1) A0508/18
euphonious (2) B1295/24 B1311/22
euphonous (1) A0150/V
euphorbium (1) B1293/01
eureka (1) B1302/25
Euripides (1) A0455/M
Europe (17) A0056/11
A0154/15 A0157/09 A0159/10 A0315/19
A0440/18 A0550/09 B0861/03 B0863/11
B1022/04 B1151/04 B1207/06 B1207/31
B1364/32 C0098/40 C0148/19 C0387/05
European (2) B0946/28 B1031/11
Europeans (1) C0168/13
Eusebius (3) A0101/09
A0175/14 A0181/04
ev'ning (1) A0702/M
evacuation (1) C0156/07
evade (1) B0910/19
evanescent (2) A0439/27 B0966/21
evaporated (3) B1321/29
C0059/40 C0128/36
evaporates (1) B1168/26
evaporating (1) B1074/10
evaporation (1) B0957/01
Eve (2) B1095/02 B1154/13
eve (1) A0286/04
even (551)
Evening (3) B0753/13
B0754/04 B0754/35
evening (72)
evening's (1) A0301/24
evenly (1) B0730/30
evenness (1) C0152/13
event (33) A0301/25
A0347/22 A0427/02 A0439/26 A0456/26
A0457/28 A0578/23 B0725/15 B0749/27
B0752/24 B0757/13 B0807/36 B0958/18
B0961/18 B1044/08 B1132/33 B1322/26
C0074/26 C0090/22 C0095/08 C0104/16
C0119/39 C0124/04 C0139/02 C0139/28
C0143/29 C0158/14 C0170/32 C0170/35
C0171/13 C0431/09 C0547/03 C0579/14
eventful (11) A0019/14
A0075/06 A0161/10 A0241/22 A0242/18
A0446/02 B0989/22 B1144/30 C0438/V
C0528/20 C0536/15
events (86)
eventuality (1) A0298/V
eventually (5) A0311/V
B1321/28 C0141/02 C0146/21 C0163/16
ever (255)
ever-blossoming (1) B1162/08
ever-memorable (2) B1127/09
B1317/37
ever-placid (1) A0315/08
ever-prevalent (1) B0966/27
ever-remembered (1) A0446/33
ever-victorious (1) B1346/28
Everard (1) B1080/04
everchanging (1) C0412/30
Everett, Edward (1) A0271/14
evergreens (1) B0808/03
everlasting (13) A0140/V
A0151/12 A0195/11 A0195/19 A0241/25
A0303/16 A0348/03 B0898/24 B1133/13
B1347/34 B1385/21 B1390/21 C0174/18
everlastingly (3) A0229/M
B0914/05 B1305/17
evermore (4) A0236/10
A0318/V A0407/19 B0967/04
every (465)
every-day (11) A0210/18
A0296/V A0397/17 A0431/17 A0507/12
A0588/02 A0601/31 A0642/08 A0706/15
B1208/09 B1271/18
every-man-for-himself (1) B1299/29
everybody (10) A0336/01 A0337/10
A0338/19 A0338/31 A0365/01 A0370/31
B1048/25 B1091/01 B1347/12 B1375/11
everybody's (1) B1299/36
everything (53)
everywhere (9) A0215/24
A0244/01 A0709/27 B1038/32 B1126/10
B1145/06 B1274/30 B1329/27 B1330/10
evidence (89)
evidences (5) B0764/11
B0764/26 B1122/22 C0561/01 C0564/12
evidencing (2) A0056/31 A0066/V
evident (96)
evidently (78)
Evil (1) B0793/12
evil (48) A0053/30
A0064/18 A0098/21 A0136/33 A0141/25
A0189/25 A0209/06 A0214/13 A0402/32
A0407/25 A0427/03 A0427/27 A0444/34
A0445/33 A0459/27 A0460/12 A0489/06
A0499/18 A0500/07 A0500/11 A0500/19
A0608/20 A0610/06 A0610/06 A0610/20
A0610/21 A0622/33 A0626/23 A0638/12
A0664/31 B0855/18 B0856/10 B0856/11
B0968/34 B0993/20 B1093/05 B1108/16
B1158/03 B1158/06 B1167/05 B1169/14
B1248/33 B1296/10 B1312/14 C0139/16
C0430/11 C0555/31 C0565/09
evils (6) A0459/14 B1294/09
B1300/13 C0080/37 C0120/19 C0145/08
evince (6) A0045/26 A0086/18
A0090/16 A0344/08 A0483/04 C0141/08
evinced (24) A0028/V
A0096/17 A0156/08 A0508/05 A0530/01
A0650/10 B0854/20 B0926/15 B1032/09
B1093/02 B1104/10 B1143/07 B1302/21

->C0119/26 C0145/09 C0153/27 C0168/35
C0170/08 C0175/37 C0409/06 C0539/36
C0548/24 C0568/16 C0569/22
evinces (1) A0269/33
evincing (8) A0278/38
A0442/14 C0061/35 C0171/09 C0172/26
C0413/19 C0537/09 C0569/02
evolution (2) A0387/16 A0601/07
evolutions (2) A0672/30 A0674/16
evolving (1) A0609/27
ex (6) A0704/28 B0740/03
B0745/11 B1269/27 B1296/25 B1313/26
Ex-President (1) A0277/12
exacerbate (1) B0810/36
Exact (1) B0869/T
exact (43) A0023/12
A0058/14 A0089/15 A0102/24 A0226/20
A0230/19 A0300/12 A0338/34 A0355/15
A0405/08 A0410/V A0414/05 A0414/31
A0429/28 A0444/25 A0479/01 A0479/06
A0508/27 A0548/V A0559/26 A0587/38
A0651/08 A0652/V B0724/04 B0773/16
B0869/05 B0878/03 B0878/08 B0910/15
B1120/03 B1214/02 B1234/33 B1235/35
B1244/04 C0077/09 C0105/30 C0166/01
C0401/25 C0415/33 C0419/40 C0422/05
C0440/V C0447/V
exacted (3) A0478/11
B0965/20 C0395/03
exactions (3) A0073/23
A0488/02 B0993/05
exactitude (1) B0772/26
exactly (38) A0069/01 A0094/20
A0378/12 A0533/12 A0585/18 A0655/08
B0821/08 B0855/18 B0873/24 B0888/V
B0891/04 B0946/23 B0975/24 B0985/32
B0991/25 B1013/21 B1019/03 B1020/16
B1054/06 B1074/26 B1079/20 B1101/27
B1120/04 B1128/31 B1182/02 B1207/06
B1241/33 B1336/08 B1336/22 B1369/28
C0077/19 C0103/01 C0152/32 C0193/21
C0195/21 C0415/28 C0564/05 C0573/37
exaggerate (3) B0985/21
B1292/13 C0562/41
exaggerated (13) A0212/30
A0244/V A0297/01 A0299/04 A0499/31
A0705/35 B0864/05 B0962/11 B1079/30
B1233/07 B1270/35 C0532/23 C0550/07
exaggeration (9) A0157/08
A0212/16 A0402/05 A0681/10 B0985/27
C0055/14 C0538/28 C0538/39 C0538/40
exaggerations (1) C0549/07
exalt (1) B1050/27
exaltation (6) A0708/32 A0709/02
B1030/22 B1031/33 B1273/26 B1274/07
exalted (14) A0250/12 A0303/09
A0382/09 A0399/01 A0609/23 A0612/05
A0638/06 A0708/05 B0891/06 B0891/V
B0976/29 B0977/05 B1030/09 B1273/04
exalting (1) A0348/07
examination (40) A0059/24
A0067/31 A0098/23 A0267/33 A0365/13
A0511/04 A0545/01 A0547/01 A0552/09
A0554/26 A0703/10 B0733/14 B0751/10
B0752/32 B0754/18 B0810/33 B0815/23
->B0827/18 B0828/22 B0832/13 B0960/01
B0986/12 B0991/32 B1048/16 B1052/20
B1053/34 B1054/10 B1058/29 B1178/20
B1178/32 B1181/14 B1237/20 B1268/09
C0113/31 C0150/18 C0157/38 C0193/06
C0413/17 C0418/14 C0575/23
examinations (2) A0544/20 A0546/03
examine (20) A0250/24
A0443/10 A0551/07 B0738/18 B0741/02
B0751/07 B0752/26 B0841/10 B0904/02
B0975/09 B1105/32 B1223/21 B1237/32
B1353/13 C0090/23 C0169/27 C0169/33
C0181/35 C0194/08 C0540/17
examined (37) A0074/14
A0312/06 A0538/29 A0540/31 A0544/13
A0549/30 A0551/14 A0554/20 A0641/15
B0727/12 B0763/22 B0795/31 B0818/07
B0875/33 B0979/18 B0980/07 B0980/19
B0980/30 B0981/12 B0983/12 B1052/11
B1052/29 B1108/01 B1160/41 B1363/17
C0066/12 C0076/05 C0076/26 C0076/32
C0078/40 C0079/26 C0179/07 C0397/24
C0399/11 C0419/24 C0564/32 C0571/05
Examiner (4) A0338/23
A0338/25 A0338/26 A0338/26
examines (1) A0530/08
examining (17) A0081/37
A0511/33 A0538/12 A0546/22 A0552/03
B0761/17 B0853/11 B0874/16 B1054/13
B1106/02 C0154/02 C0169/07 C0181/27
C0192/31 C0196/02 C0412/23 C0429/14
example (77)
examples (3) B0724/18
B0740/22 B0740/24
exasperated (3) B0856/20
B1189/16 C0558/08
excadingly> (1) A0464/19
excavated (2) B0823/25 B0979/31
excavation (2) A0405/34 C0575/37
exceed (10) A0027/08 A0688/11
A0707/29 B0903/01 B0903/03 B1105/22
B1272/V C0400/21 C0422/32 C0536/27
exceeded (12) A0140/05
A0241/09 A0704/09 B0828/12 B0891/02
B1269/09 B1334/14 B1336/02 C0169/24
C0190/09 C0199/23 C0542/05
exceeding (20) A0405/34
A0412/23 A0412/27 A0458/24 A0460/06
A0640/04 A0641/V A0642/16 B0823/11
B0902/16 B0925/22 B0968/21 B1182/16
B1250/15 B1364/14 C0075/21 C0164/35
C0201/37 C0400/32 C0400/33
exceedingly (95)
exceeds (1) B0807/01
excel (4) A0432/10
B1136/12 B1136/33 B1138/27
excelled (3) B0904/27
B1122/14 B1122/15
excellence (6) A0384/23 A0528/15
B0878/04 B0892/10 B0986/32 C0550/24
excellence (4) A0380/08
B1128/14 B1136/09 C0112/18
excellences (2) A0710/28 B1275/V
Excellencies (12) C0390/37
C0391/01 C0391/05 C0399/25 C0399/26

->C0404/17 C0409/10 C0418/08 C0422/35
C0425/19 C0425/25 C0426/09
excellencies (1) B1275/30
Excellencies' (2) C0426/25 C0426/28
Excellency (2) C0390/06 C0390/28
excellency (1) C0065/38
excellent (69)
excellently (2) A0367/V B0858/27
excelling (1) A0045/12
except (92)
excepted (1) B1332/13
excepting (4) A0245/23
A0546/32 B1322/08 B1362/29
exception (60)
exceptions (4) A0610/04
B0740/24 B1315/36 C0174/20
excess (17) A0460/31
A0566/12 A0581/02 A0705/09 A0707/28
B0760/19 B0816/31 B0851/34 B0895/24
B0969/01 B1047/32 B1058/12 B1270/08
B1272/28 B1278/11 B1329/31 C0538/34
excesses (3) A0446/22
A0707/28 B1272/28
excessive (39) A0215/01
A0282/04 A0398/30 A0400/06 A0402/16
A0459/12 A0461/18 A0488/11 A0497/V
A0509/11 A0511/23 A0667/01 A0686/06
B0827/06 B0903/09 B0909/11 B0963/26
B0991/20 B1012/12 B1020/10 B1054/22
B1235/14 B1257/17 B1334/18 B1362/12
C0115/02 C0133/13 C0141/09 C0141/23
C0159/16 C0163/39 C0168/38 C0183/10
C0187/18 C0400/34 C0406/23 C0419/32
C0420/25 C0549/01
excessively (62)
Exchange (2) A0487/09 C0387/09
exchange (7) A0337/12
A0337/25 B1019/03 B1250/11 C0070/25
C0148/40 C0177/13
exchanged (5) A0177/V
A0183/08 A0685/29 B0916/13 B1237/V
exchanging (2) B0898/21 B1237/07
excipting> (1) A0466/07
excitability (2) A0161/23 A0324/11
excitable (7) A0427/19
B0814/01 B0850/04 B0894/16 B0942/05
B1246/15 B1348/11
excitation (1) A0252/19
excite (7) A0508/21
A0621/14 B0756/20 B0807/19 B0990/33
B0991/31 C0081/08
excited (65)
excitement (53)
excites (3) A0144/17
B0955/10 B1278/15
exciting (21) A0025/15
A0027/23 A0098/17 A0098/25 A0145/24
A0217/06 A0227/01 A0231/12 A0234/10
A0313/26 A0415/02 A0592/07 B1004/25
B1078/29 C0055/16 C0065/09 C0078/32
C0166/32 C0208/13 C0418/15 C0574/33
exclaimed (18) A0113/08 A0182/32
A0534/21 B0826/25 B0897/18 B0907/02
B0907/14 B0910/26 B0912/20 B0980/25
B1014/10 B1101/28 B1187/22 B1188/07
->B1192/04 B1250/33 B1260/30 B1350/18
exclaims (1) B0872/30
exclamation (4) A0047/15
A0500/18 C0208/18 C0388/38
exclamations (2) A0567/25 C0061/07
exclude (1) B1352/12
excluded (6) A0189/26 A0210/02
A0684/30 B0737/13 B1315/33 C0189/11
excluding (1) C0535/35
exclusion (3) B1005/16
B1037/31 B1313/12
exclusive (3) A0261/06
A0564/23 C0578/03
exclusively (7) A0478/09
A0600/11 B0892/21 B0941/09 B0974/07
B1089/19 B1312/12
exclusiveness (1) A0624/26
excoriated (1) A0543/21
excoriations (3) A0538/12
B0730/09 B0730/13
excrescence (2) A0173/20 A0178/29
excretory (1) C0178/16
excruciating (2) C0064/37 C0196/12
excursion (6) A0347/18 A0564/20
B0949/36 B1291/19 C0542/21 C0552/19
excursions (6) A0026/V B0807/26
C0177/20 C0529/17 C0530/37 C0571/32
excuse (9) A0278/25
A0653/27 B0926/08 B0965/18 B1005/04
B1293/37 B1304/30 B1338/11 C0133/32
excused (1) B1247/17
excuses (2) B0899/10 C0522/05
execrable (3) A0250/35
B1093/07 B1096/08
execrations (1) B1054/27
execute (2) B1277/32 C0133/26
executed (6) A0365/11 A0473/33
B0905/19 B0916/07 B0983/36 B1193/20
executing (2) A0123/07 B0824/14
execution (23) A0034/10
A0053/21 A0055/26 A0058/02 A0058/19
A0068/23 A0079/22 A0445/26 A0622/11
A0664/12 A0693/27 A0706/26 B0905/29
B1103/18 B1128/18 B1271/28 B1350/28
C0108/12 C0110/24 C0187/23 C0392/01
C0393/05 C0525/36
executioner (1) B1152/17
executive (1) A0109/01
executors (2) B1188/25 B1189/09
exemplary (1) B1048/01
exemplification (1) B0863/30
exemplifications (1) A0293/04
exemplifying (2) A0703/06 B1268/05
exemption (3) A0712/05
B1075/16 B1277/10
exequy (1) A0150/M
exercise (25) A0213/19
A0243/25 A0293/24 A0444/35 A0456/24
A0498/V A0513/06 A0533/12 A0600/05
A0614/37 A0684/17 A0703/32 A0706/12
A0711/35 B0822/20 B0832/05 B0965/09
B0969/03 B1029/06 B1031/23 B1090/12
B1158/26 B1268/30 B1271/15 B1277/02
exercised (9) A0019/15
A0070/09 A0079/25 A0212/32 A0399/13

->B1167/05 B1215/06 B1250/03 C0429/23
exercises (3) A0528/04
B1006/14 B1346/19
exergues (1) A0430/34
exert (2) C0086/37 C0127/10
exerted (7) A0557/21
B0982/17 B1108/25 B1108/27 B1158/24
B1237/02 B1246/16
exerting (1) A0374/08
exertion (46) A0022/23 A0029/11
A0072/05 A0073/15 A0081/27 A0244/25
A0246/26 A0327/12 A0328/12 A0459/11
A0529/07 A0554/29 A0578/04 A0689/17
A0706/25 B0741/20 B0758/25 B0826/31
B0932/11 B0944/17 B1050/11 B1237/26
B1271/27 C0060/08 C0072/09 C0074/08
C0081/21 C0122/11 C0127/01 C0144/31
C0151/36 C0157/22 C0183/03 C0184/12
C0185/13 C0195/11 C0200/33 C0201/29
C0398/14 C0398/35 C0406/26 C0420/41
C0538/02 C0559/24 C0560/10 C0579/02
exertions (30) A0025/12 A0055/05
A0064/23 A0137/28 A0154/02 A0244/17
A0324/07 A0325/01 A0337/32 A0354/24
B0727/02 B0731/04 B0825/30 B0967/21
C0062/18 C0074/33 C0109/35 C0114/30
C0121/25 C0125/18 C0127/29 C0140/28
C0143/18 C0154/06 C0159/28 C0175/16
C0177/38 C0192/14 C0559/29 C0567/27
Exeter (1) B1166/30
exhalation (1) A0412/32
exhalations (1) A0136/23
exhaling (1) A0217/V
exhaust (1) B1074/17
exhausted (32) A0319/26
A0510/27 A0577/02 A0594/16 A0654/16
A0667/04 A0686/09 B0826/18 B0957/01
B1058/07 B1073/22 B1082/01 B1109/02
B1208/26 B1300/22 B1372/09 C0076/15
C0116/06 C0119/40 C0121/27 C0127/03
C0128/26 C0129/32 C0130/39 C0144/10
C0145/22 C0179/12 C0184/11 C0192/14
C0192/22 C0396/08 C0567/29
exhausting (3) A0152/22
A0604/06 C0129/35
exhaustion (6) A0028/V A0157/14
C0064/09 C0096/09 C0142/37 C0421/01
exhibited (6) B1070/09 B1070/19
B1072/25 B1119/16 B1330/30 C0405/26
exhibiting (3) A0528/08
B0946/19 C0423/14
exhibition (4) A0123/28
A0710/08 B0960/30 B1275/11
exhibitions (1) B1007/22
exhort (1) B1123/17
exhorted (2) C0116/09 C0117/39
exhumed (1) B1160/38
exigencies (2) A0302/12 B0900/V
exigency (3) B1373/27
B1373/29 C0067/19
exile (1) A0243/08
exist (33) A0210/05
A0267/02 A0448/15 A0478/30 A0546/30
A0552/22 A0602/09 A0615/20 A0649/06
A0707/24 B0832/17 B0942/09 B1003/10
->B1035/08 B1122/20 B1168/12 B1188/20
B1272/V B1293/19 B1296/26 B1310/17
B1313/23 B1314/20 C0071/25 C0081/05
C0132/37 C0138/01 C0399/35 C0401/16
C0401/17 C0428/09 C0429/14 C0448/V
existed (37) A0018/03
A0028/07 A0106/28 A0303/27 A0365/18
A0366/24 A0369/19 A0410/19 A0427/12
A0461/21 A0532/24 A0675/08 B0733/10
B0739/08 B0749/26 B0772/25 B0832/17
B0834/04 B0949/05 B1007/03 B1019/07
B1031/06 B1046/15 B1233/19 B1233/20
B1235/28 B1295/04 B1299/18 B1299/28
B1313/03 B1313/23 B1369/15 C0095/23
C0122/15 C0156/32 C0158/03 C0563/15
existence (69)
existences (1) A0314/09
existent (1) B1274/05
existing (18) A0433/16 A0434/24
A0615/19 B0988/01 B1034/06 B1036/20
B1039/35 B1048/27 B1160/17 B1206/19
B1219/03 B1300/36 B1317/13 C0092/07
C0160/26 C0409/13 C0423/38 C0424/01
exists (12) A0355/13
A0369/19 A0531/07 B0727/17 B0773/27
B0863/11 B0863/12 B1033/20 B1214/26
B1221/17 B1272/25 C0151/40
exit (5) A0404/V
A0554/01 A0602/21 B1058/26 B1325/05
exonerate (1) C0523/25
exonerated (1) B0753/34
exorbitant (2) B0863/36 B1134/17
expand (1) B1248/36
expanded (4) A0156/06
B1282/35 C0151/35 C0396/40
expanding (2) A0316/08 B1074/11
expanse (8) A0502/03
A0578/33 B1074/33 B1334/19 B1339/34
C0159/20 C0159/21 C0163/15
expansion (7) A0315/10
A0402/03 B1080/23 C0097/32 C0190/02
C0404/10 C0411/15
expatiate (3) A0072/11
A0100/22 B1144/15
expatiating (2) A0707/01 B1272/02
expect (24) A0137/27
A0336/13 A0353/34 A0473/34 A0533/10
A0563/08 A0564/15 A0588/04 A0594/24
B0816/01 B0849/02 B0849/03 B0876/13
B1107/35 B1134/15 B1246/10 C0074/27
C0083/07 C0092/28 C0095/15 C0121/10
C0177/17 C0410/25 C0424/04
expectation (28) A0025/21
A0137/29 A0161/27 A0355/25 A0548/15
B0752/15 B0814/25 B0825/13 B0899/16
B0903/20 B0926/25 B1055/31 B1347/11
C0066/17 C0093/14 C0100/05 C0116/35
C0120/30 C0126/25 C0133/29 C0143/10
C0190/09 C0192/28 C0192/35 C0420/24
C0424/27 C0553/08 C0562/22
expectations (5) A0021/09
A0027/08 A0316/13 B0872/02 C0137/05
expected (66)
expecting (3) B0925/17
C0086/24 C0117/20

expectoration (1) B1235/14
expediency (4) B0826/30
  B1049/11 C0166/21 C0167/30
expedient (15) A0055/25
  A0488/07 B0723/09 B0765/25 B0844/18
  B0857/01 B0960/17 B0990/17 B1141/23
  C0092/05 C0142/18 C0144/26 C0406/40
  C0415/10 C0535/11
expedients (3) C0078/08
  C0078/08 C0142/02
expedite (1) A0347/10
expedition (36) A0584/05
  B0816/05 B0816/06 B0816/12 B0817/09
  B0843/03 B0942/24 B0968/11 B1075/15
  C0088/38 C0156/40 C0159/30 C0207/20
  C0401/05 C0406/13 C0521/24 C0522/25
  C0522/37 C0524/12 C0525/27 C0527/16
  C0528/19 C0529/04 C0529/25 C0530/35
  C0532/09 C0532/29 C0532/36 C0533/35
  C0536/17 C0537/09 C0537/25 C0539/33
  C0546/38 C0564/11 C0564/28
expeditions (3) C0070/33
  C0525/11 C0544/11
expeditious (2) A0443/09 B1292/09
expel (1) B1310/24
expelled (1) A0108/06
expence (1) A0204/13
expending (1) B1134/18
expenditure (4) A0057/11
  A0440/08 B1008/34 B1058/31
expense (10) A0159/09 A0159/V
  A0437/06 A0440/23 A0532/13 A0638/06
  B0733/16 B1139/21 B1325/02 B1329/34
expenses (5) A0631/21
  B1136/14 B1136/35 B1137/32 B1138/29
expensive (5) B1006/20
  B1073/06 B1073/12 C0394/10 C0395/02
experience (52)
experienced (58)
experiences (1) B1102/08
experiment (33) A0399/21
  A0536/01 A0559/15 A0624/06 B0832/32
  B0836/03 B0838/02 B0842/32 B0959/23
  B0960/11 B0988/08 B1032/13 B1070/31
  B1093/21 B1093/25 B1132/01 B1181/16
  B1182/11 B1234/13 B1236/09 B1236/29
  B1241/35 B1242/02 B1382/28 C0079/37
  C0129/14 C0393/27 C0406/33 C0411/08
  C0412/07 C0413/12 C0413/30 C0424/20
experimental (4) A0337/13
  A0337/26 A0340/33 C0400/38
Experimentalist (1) A0340/05
experimentally (1) B1358/09
experimenting (1) C0535/39
experiments (13) A0067/21
  A0583/01 B0941/19 B1070/06 B1168/14
  B1168/23 B1182/26 B1213/19 B1233/15
  B1234/31 B1237/33 B1238/16 C0415/32
expert (1) C0536/03
expiated (1) B1352/13
expiration (13) A0046/26
  A0073/07 B0727/08 B0753/12 B0894/23
  B0956/25 B1154/10 B1189/12 B1208/22
  B1237/13 B1240/08 C0138/05 C0415/40
expire (4) B1145/15
  ->C0083/09 C0169/40 C0527/18
expired (13) A0034/03
  A0061/06 A0455/12 A0567/07 A0677/03
  B0823/21 B0959/24 B0965/03 B1040/11
  B1053/32 B1105/15 C0133/40 C0142/22
expiring (1) C0095/06
explain (23) A0250/22
  A0369/03 A0535/05 A0656/18 B0829/33
  B0926/17 B1031/32 B1032/30 B1037/04
  B1046/33 B1183/V B1187/11 B1188/26
  B1213/05 B1223/28 B1225/14 B1242/17
  B1249/04 B1301/22 B1361/35 C0107/27
  C0399/25 C0408/04
explained (21) A0303/22
  A0338/20 A0592/34 B0725/05 B0915/13
  B0915/24 B1059/23 B1185/16 B1188/19
  B1191/02 B1192/11 B1237/04 B1274/02
  B1292/28 B1298/02 C0061/10 C0092/27
  C0129/17 C0411/18 C0424/35 C0443/V
explaining (3) A0213/20
  B0850/17 C0067/02
explains (2) B1119/23 B1370/15
explanation (24) A0059/28
  A0212/10 A0277/04 A0301/24 A0302/08
  A0302/24 A0303/11 A0339/03 A0536/20
  A0592/34 A0707/21 B0723/10 B0754/13
  B0948/24 B1074/02 B1080/25 B1096/21
  B1135/23 B1190/16 B1272/22 B1281/15
  C0097/01 C0409/10 C0422/02
explanations (4) A0073/12
  A0608/04 B0728/24 B0983/20
explanatory (1) B0940/27
expletive (1) A0624/09
expletives (1) A0623/28
explicit (8) A0085/04
  A0353/16 A0386/22 B0842/26 B0976/21
  B1190/11 B1258/23 B1305/04
explicitly (2) A0277/05 A0626/01
exploded (1) B1006/34
exploit (2) A0124/26 C0558/36
exploits (2) B1021/19 C0550/24
exploration (1) A0688/18
exploraturi (1) A0638/15
explore (10) A0589/01 B0969/13
  C0165/31 C0189/20 C0192/35 C0525/39
  C0526/31 C0529/10 C0564/34 C0575/05
explored (4) B0862/16
  B0981/11 B1155/27 C0543/41
explorer (1) B1332/07
exploring (7) B1391/22
  C0101/40 C0159/30 C0192/17 C0523/16
  C0527/25 C0527/27
explosion (7) A0026/15
  C0189/38 C0190/11 C0190/35 C0201/26
  C0396/37 C0403/14
expose (2) A0204/28 C0056/26
expose (5) B0773/34
  B1093/05 C0192/06 C0531/12 C0556/03
exposed (11) A0088/10
  A0102/04 A0409/23 A0444/26 B1194/20
  B1261/10 C0117/05 C0178/31 C0180/22
  C0534/34 C0534/39
exposes (1) C0432/40
exposing (1) B1384/04
Exposition (3) A0103/11

->A0103/12 A0103/13
exposition (4) A0088/09
A0088/32 A0088/33 A0088/33
expostulated (1) C0132/13
expostulating (1) A0543/04
expostulation (3) A0387/V
A0560/07 A0625/11
exposure (3) B0773/35
B0843/32 B0895/10
expound (2) B0849/09 B1044/02
expounded (1) A0459/01
Express (1) B0753/39
express (27) A0026/11
A0033/V A0159/V A0271/35 A0303/09
A0353/V A0378/15 A0380/12 A0382/04
A0408/09 A0458/06 A0499/21 A0534/24
A0708/23 B0729/21 B0889/18 B1047/05
B1068/01 B1104/33 B1129/V B1134/04
B1138/16 B1273/17 B1349/01 C0106/16
C0162/20 C0405/03
expressed (25) A0066/26
A0069/05 A0550/25 A0710/10 A0711/08
B0734/19 B0755/29 B0905/30 B1116/04
B1139/24 B1139/35 B1155/10 B1159/15
B1185/21 B1186/10 B1239/04 B1275/13
B1276/09 B1375/17 C0055/27 C0104/01
C0104/05 C0107/24 C0129/17 C0395/27
expresses (6) B0875/10 B0877/14
B0877/21 B1092/08 B1276/16 C0161/19
expressing (6) A0159/22 A0318/02
A0629/16 B1135/27 B1379/09 C0056/21
expression (90)
expressions (16) A0234/31
A0343/17 A0344/05 A0442/13 A0482/07
A0614/07 A0623/26 B0768/09 B0853/13
B0926/27 B0926/36 B1039/27 B1373/21
C0084/15 C0130/19 C0190/20
expressive (2) A0674/27 B1248/37
expressly (1) B0806/T
exquisite (28) A0053/28
A0087/02 A0091/16 A0100/13 A0110/19
A0311/29 A0312/04 A0348/16 A0354/27
A0354/28 A0383/12 A0435/05 B0889/15
B0890/02 B0899/27 B0924/24 B0926/31
B1167/01 B1279/29 B1281/21 B1332/16
B1339/35 B1346/25 B1346/34 B1350/18
C0135/31 C0540/09 C0544/41
exquisitely (7) A0273/23
A0298/V B0828/10 B0892/25 B1128/16
B1333/36 B1334/25
extacy (1) C0543/38
extant (1) C0525/11
extend (18) A0267/29 A0272/32
A0285/03 A0293/01 A0561/31 A0601/17
A0601/V B0966/01 B0985/21 B1032/01
B1080/27 B1160/31 B1302/33 B1336/23
C0174/39 C0418/18 C0552/27 C0571/32
extended (48) A0023/03
A0025/04 A0079/40 A0079/41 A0248/08
A0298/V A0315/18 A0321/19 A0387/V
A0631/11 A0639/30 A0685/05 B0842/22
B0859/12 B0890/04 B0903/05 B0941/26
B0956/11 B0965/06 B0965/27 B0967/16
B0983/27 B0983/28 B1009/V B1030/12
B1156/05 B1156/18 B1178/31 B1194/31
->B1213/34 B1239/31 B1336/08 C0069/30
C0087/19 C0107/40 C0115/32 C0124/38
C0181/30 C0407/35 C0408/07 C0411/38
C0414/26 C0432/34 C0443/V C0549/36
C0550/30 C0558/15 C0566/19
extending (27) A0319/19
A0400/18 A0417/10 A0460/01 A0601/19
A0695/20 B0840/32 B0905/17 B1180/17
B1248/17 B1331/35 B1336/11 B1338/24
C0076/35 C0098/18 C0152/28 C0159/07
C0159/23 C0162/04 C0183/15 C0185/19
C0195/06 C0402/08 C0413/20 C0541/36
C0553/16 C0575/16
extends (8) A0366/33
B0864/35 B1145/10 B1281/30 C0154/34
C0402/05 C0524/27 C0552/34
extension (7) A0460/33
A0509/22 B0773/01 B0773/14 B0825/01
B1336/16 C0527/19
extensive (26) A0027/V A0293/26
A0343/09 A0400/16 A0428/21 A0429/11
A0484/08 A0497/23 A0670/15 A0705/14
B0734/08 B0862/30 B0878/34 B1032/09
B1115/31 B1235/28 B1259/30 B1270/12
B1272/04 B1282/30 C0150/15 C0204/17
C0525/35 C0571/17 C0572/18 C0575/09
extensively (1) B1360/18
extent (111)
exterior (9) A0099/22
A0104/27 A0400/07 A0501/15 A0545/22
B1179/34 B1182/13 C0078/01 C0438/V
exterminated (1) B1096/33
external (26) A0100/02 A0215/29
A0317/08 A0320/15 A0400/15 A0430/22
A0495/01 A0530/07 A0612/32 A0613/12
A0626/29 A0671/05 A0703/03 B0890/30
B0943/14 B0980/V B0981/29 B0991/33
B1030/05 B1037/25 B1038/09 B1038/09
B1038/11 B1057/24 B1299/02 B1336/29
externally (2) B0962/12 B1179/14
externals (1) B0992/16
extinct (5) A0611/21
A0613/33 B1168/40 C0062/36 C0183/30
extinction (1) A0687/32
extinguish (3) A0044/24
B1138/02 B1212/28
extinguished (9) A0088/03
A0138/27 A0190/14 A0437/33 A0442/29
A0616/32 B0958/13 B1110/18 C0070/35
extinguishment (1) B1239/27
extolled (1) A0545/01
extort (4) A0711/02
B0840/02 B1053/25 B1276/04
extorted (4) A0029/V
A0652/04 B0724/21 B1058/11
extortion (1) B1094/06
extortions (1) B1092/33
extra (9) A0485/01
B0923/13 B0924/30 B0925/05 B0925/20
B0929/02 B0929/06 B0929/09 B0933/36
Extract (1) A0064/V
extract (4) A0055/13
B0760/30 B1310/03 C0389/38
extracted (4) A0088/07
B1128/26 B1181/04 C0160/32

extraction (1) A0460/34
extracts (5) A0487/33
B0753/04 B0754/10 B0754/15 B0757/14
extraneous (1) A0120/V
extraordinary (80)
extravagance (5) A0438/27
A0440/14 A0440/34 A0613/19 B0891/14
extravagances (5) A0705/09
B0900/05 B0906/16 B1270/08 C0130/27
extravagant (13) A0071/08
A0073/V A0157/V A0441/30 B0825/10
B1101/31 B1381/08 C0073/08 C0123/04
C0131/16 C0180/02 C0532/34 C0537/20
extravagantly (3) A0444/16
A0626/V B1007/30
Extravaganza (2) A0365/V B1100/T
extravaganza (1) A0473/34
extreme (94)
extremely (10) A0024/05 A0110/31
A0264/22 B1055/05 C0401/30 C0408/23
C0420/11 C0438/V C0530/08 C0548/22
extremeness (2) A0413/16 B1280/20
extremes (6) B0955/19 B0955/23
B1277/18 C0122/22 C0428/41 C0429/01
extremities (8) A0241/12
A0603/04 B0766/27 B0966/14 B1071/14
B1108/14 B1237/17 B1282/07
extremity (53)
extricate (3) C0082/26
C0091/02 C0542/26
extricated (2) C0096/05 C0571/03
extricating (3) C0175/18
C0183/28 C0397/35
extrinsic (1) B1070/04
exuberance (1) B1056/01
exuberant (1) B0862/32
exult (1) B0859/06
exultation (3) A0444/34
A0610/11 A0708/V
exultingly (2) A0312/23 B0909/07
exults (1) A0528/03
Eye (1) B0793/12
eye (160)
eye-balls (1) A0543/26
eye-brows (2) B1014/06 B1193/15
eye-glass (14) B0888/22 B0893/16
B0894/25 B0906/31 B0908/05 B0908/14
B0908/14 B0908/V B0910/10 B0910/10
B0914/24 B0916/08 B1186/01 B1188/29
eye-lids (1) B1238/26
eye-like (3) A0397/13
A0398/13 A0643/09
eye-sore (4) A0485/28
A0486/07 A0486/23 A0488/13
eye-witnesses (1) A0128/26
eyeballs (2) C0073/02 C0081/31
eyebrow (2) A0298/V B1156/25
eyebrows (1) A0625/15
eyed (2) A0078/37 C0390/01
eyeing (5) A0241/30
A0263/14 A0444/08 C0404/31 C0425/11
eyelashes (1) A0205/21
eyelid (2) A0327/19 B0966/17
eyelids (7) A0080/02
A0327/06 A0329/13 A0609/08 A0613/08
->A0613/23 B1350/10
eyes (335)
eying (2) C0085/26 C0125/05
eyrie (1) B1165/04
Ezekiel (1) A0119/02
ELIZABETH (1) A0093/16
F-- (8) B1235/04
B1235/20 B1236/04 B1237/04 B1238/03
B1238/08 B1239/03 B1242/15
Fable (1) A0195/T
fable (8) A0188/V
A0198/27 A0638/V B1076/20 B1189/28
B1299/30 C0056/16 C0056/20
fables (1) A0096/V
fables (5) A0196/28
A0622/18 A0685/13 B0987/34 B0988/02
fabric (11) A0400/16
A0406/32 A0501/16 B0762/22 B0762/24
B0902/13 B1070/14 B1115/21 B1192/11
B1262/28 B1292/29
fabricated (1) C0204/02
fabrication (1) B1359/03
fabrications (1) C0065/13
fabrics (1) B0762/17
fabulous (4) A0313/09
A0664/V A0687/19 B1300/16
fac-simile (5) A0558/28
B0877/23 B0877/24 B0992/16 B0992/28
fac-similes (3) A0443/22
B1304/07 B1305/10
face (185)
faced (2) A0086/31 A0100/10
faces (14) A0123/02 A0369/24
A0369/26 A0374/04 A0494/08 A0508/07
A0510/18 A0511/05 A0530/26 A0683/02
C0117/11 C0387/18 C0557/09 C0579/30
facetious (1) B1379/24
facie (2) A0303/23 B1191/29
facili (1) A0097/07
facilis (1) B0993/08
facilitate (1) C0525/18
facilities (3) A0295/04
B0736/34 B0808/06
facility (12) A0053/20
A0144/01 A0406/10 A0548/05 A0548/V
B0872/12 B0924/20 B1089/24 B1113/03
B1214/11 B1386/07 C0091/29
facing (2) B1057/06 C0193/21
facsimile (1) A0508/27
facsimiles (2) A0264/01 A0264/36
fact (254)
factions (2) C0093/18 C0557/01
facto (2) A0704/28 B1269/27
factory (1) A0086/33
Facts (1) B1380/09
facts (41) A0209/V
A0343/17 A0343/20 A0365/13 A0544/24
A0547/22 B0723/15 B0732/24 B0740/01
B0751/05 B0773/06 B0853/03 B0876/24
B1029/02 B1054/30 B1183/31 B1190/04
B1206/17 B1233/11 B1233/T B1295/16
B1296/18 B1296/18 B1296/19 B1296/20
B1311/08 B1312/21 B1312/21 B1312/27
B1312/28 B1312/31 B1313/07 B1358/27
C0056/07 C0056/22 C0207/34 C0207/37

->C0428/18 C0538/28 C0538/38 C0538/39
faculties (24) A0056/21
A0066/10 A0067/19 A0078/19 A0093/10
A0093/30 A0112/21 A0113/09 A0212/09
A0234/04 A0245/V A0293/V A0479/36
B0852/09 B0963/18 B0967/02 B1030/08
B1219/01 C0055/16 C0064/13 C0073/20
C0078/12 C0100/14 C0406/33
faculty (14) A0053/19 A0294/V
A0478/08 A0527/V A0528/12 A0529/17
A0530/V A0531/03 A0610/29 B1167/11
B1215/03 B1220/06 C0125/31 C0422/20
faded (16) A0021/22
A0080/27 A0103/22 A0104/18 A0190/23
A0226/17 A0230/16 A0236/06 A0436/23
A0614/10 A0614/33 A0643/07 A0687/14
A0689/07 B1191/17 C0407/39
fag (1) A0622/18
faggots (2) A0101/22 A0105/14
fail (51)
failed (53)
faileth (1) A0311/V
failing (3) A0378/11
B1101/08 B1242/28
failings (3) A0097/26
A0097/27 A0097/28
fails (9) A0244/03
A0311/16 A0488/V A0711/02 B0946/07
B0987/26 B0987/26 B1256/09 B1276/03
failure (13) A0070/29
A0252/07 A0295/25 A0427/28 B0728/11
B0757/28 B0834/29 B1070/24 B1070/29
B1234/18 B1301/22 C0187/15 C0407/18
failures (1) B1069/32
fain (3) A0414/24
A0427/07 A0568/12
faint (37) A0106/12
A0106/12 A0263/04 A0297/20 A0320/18
A0324/V A0325/10 A0326/13 A0326/28
A0327/V A0403/06 A0410/23 A0439/10
A0685/06 A0687/13 A0693/16 B0767/26
B0827/V B0832/31 B0895/19 B0912/29
B0931/06 B0943/17 B0964/26 B0966/10
B1139/07 B1139/30 B1186/29 B1223/29
B1339/34 C0073/03 C0077/14 C0120/35
C0128/05 C0192/28 C0423/14 C0575/19
fainted (7) A0046/06
A0059/01 A0190/V B0948/30 B1057/16
C0440/V C0440/V
fainter (2) A0502/02 A0605/06
faintest (7) A0581/09
A0667/62 B1169/32 B1240/04 C0064/11
C0130/34 C0198/07
fainting (6) A0036/03 A0325/02
A0325/15 A0697/10 B0875/25 B1249/02
faintly (11) A0034/05
A0400/02 A0412/32 A0438/26 B0821/33
B0829/34 B0944/20 B0962/12 B1239/12
B1329/17 C0423/15
faintly-detailed (1) C0208/15
faints (1) A0036/18
fair (50) A0152/20 A0213/23
A0228/12 A0228/13 A0232/17 A0232/18
A0235/17 A0294/08 A0320/10 A0330/08
A0370/17 A0406/27 A0406/32 A0407/17
->A0426/01 A0559/11 A0563/11 A0610/23
A0641/V A0702/M A0710/07 B0725/29
B0814/21 B0865/06 B0894/18 B0959/22
B1005/27 B1079/33 B1129/03 B1153/01
B1159/15 B1215/18 B1215/25 B1267/M
B1275/10 B1379/17 B1385/28 C0086/12
C0105/41 C0133/32 C0158/02 C0170/28
C0392/03 C0533/29 C0544/38 C0552/10
C0568/06 C0570/10 C0570/23 C0570/30
fair-haired (3) A0321/02
A0330/03 A0644/V
faire (1) A0037/20
fairest (8) A0153/V
A0608/02 A0611/22 A0707/09 B1272/08
B1314/31 B1379/32 B1385/28
Fairies (1) B1283/14
fairies (1) B1280/21
fairly (43) A0021/09
A0345/02 A0353/24 A0387/06 A0387/V
A0473/06 A0479/30 A0484/07 A0486/08
A0603/07 B0739/21 B0741/13 B0793/25
B0814/04 B0820/30 B0825/35 B0929/18
B1020/20 B1046/18 B1076/30 B1081/16
B1134/V B1144/29 B1240/16 B1269/01
B1295/27 B1311/24 B1331/19 B1333/36
B1337/23 B1364/07 B1379/01 B1379/28
C0070/22 C0116/26 C0169/37 C0200/12
C0417/41 C0421/35 C0530/33 C0538/08
C0554/27 C0579/02
Fairmount (1) B1091/18
fairy (6) A0162/17 A0164/21
A0210/08 A0502/05 B1215/27 B1281/11
fairy-like (3) A0604/V
B0902/12 B1330/01
fairy-looking (1) C0543/10
faisant (1) A0096/M
fait (6) A0036/V A0268/30
A0340/22 B0978/09 B1144/32 C0430/28
fait> (2) A0464/07 A0468/19
faith (28) A0034/12
A0128/24 A0339/16 A0460/09 A0464/V
A0468/V A0594/24 A0653/09 B0772/12
B0878/33 B0988/07 B1004/29 B1006/13
B1115/31 B1115/33 B1219/08 B1219/08
B1219/08 B1247/09 B1271/04 B1296/30
B1390/10 C0055/21 C0095/26 C0172/27
C0177/15 C0179/38 C0564/01
faithful (7) A0265/13
A0348/21 A0352/12 B0850/16 B0985/15
C0073/15 C0532/28
faithfully (4) A0271/13
A0286/11 A0438/24 A0642/33
fal/lal (1) B1166/15
Fall (1) A0397/T
fall (89)
fallacy (2) B0823/02 B1221/09
fallen (1) B0723/M
fallen (55)
falling (53)
falls (10) A0121/04 A0320/07
A0674/08 B0738/09 B1037/17 B1130/12
B1168/31 B1282/33 C0106/39 C0538/26
Falls/of/St./Anthony (1) C0551/05
false (18) A0055/07 A0064/13
A0107/05 A0350/30 A0499/19 A0499/27

->A0499/V B0734/10 B0756/24 B0857/08
B0914/11 B0914/11 B0914/11 B0987/23
B1096/32 C0106/11 C0108/41 C0143/16
falsehood (1) B1101/28
falsely (3) A0262/16
A0311/28 A0445/32
falsities (2) A0079/04 A0135/09
falsity (8) A0018/05
A0160/V A0530/V B1314/18 B1314/26
C0162/12 C0438/V C0538/40
Falstaffian (1) B1102/25
faltered (2) A0166/17 B1058/06
fama (2) A0072/01 A0072/30
Fame (2) C0146/42 C0147/28
fame (4) A0121/27
B0863/23 B1145/10 B1310/22
familiar (18) A0074/02 A0142/24
A0190/27 A0191/16 A0400/32 A0439/22
A0456/27 A0550/10 A0645/05 A0683/02
B0796/35 B0901/12 B1144/35 B1212/35
B1363/34 C0112/13 C0174/13 C0431/11
familiarised (1) C0535/32
familiarity (3) A0071/15
B1165/25 C0388/37
familiarly (2) A0021/25 B1259/26
families (5) A0019/05
A0019/23 A0261/20 B1137/12 C0156/08
family (80)
famine (7) B1093/10
C0053/T C0065/19 C0076/01 C0128/24
C0134/20 C0185/33
famous (3) A0296/13
B1135/32 C0079/12
fan (1) A0691/06
fanatico (2) B0889/06 B0897/03
fancied (38) A0217/V A0270/34
A0299/25 A0325/11 A0351/19 A0351/19
A0354/05 A0406/19 A0436/14 A0448/12
A0603/28 A0640/14 A0641/V A0689/32
B0797/01 B0824/30 B0825/13 B0851/21
B0866/03 B0906/27 B0929/17 B0941/05
B0949/25 B1006/06 B1009/27 B1012/34
B1155/31 B1224/03 B1225/V B1242/31
B1335/27 C0071/12 C0072/39 C0118/16
C0128/32 C0165/36 C0417/17 C0531/37
fancies (32) A0054/13
A0063/20 A0262/04 A0329/24 A0397/23
A0401/01 A0457/32 A0578/21 A0589/04
A0601/29 A0613/05 A0640/26 A0673/23
A0673/24 B0725/02 B0736/32 B0764/30
B0771/25 B0865/32 B0896/05 B0943/27
B0943/28 B1006/01 B1123/18 B1296/15
B1312/18 B1318/11 B1318/12 C0197/39
C0387/M C0412/39 C0429/45
fanciful (11) A0062/17
A0067/27 A0100/10 A0531/10 B0831/03
B0855/29 B0927/09 B0969/15 B1206/18
C0207/29 C0554/10
fancifully (1) B1119/04
fancy (90)
fancying (6) A0437/23 B1115/13
B1330/29 C0395/38 C0428/09 C0448/V
fandango (2) A0371/23 B0913/22
fanfaronnade (1) A0297/17
fang-like (2) A0105/26 B1353/30
fangs (6) A0021/14 A0694/06
B0858/33 B1259/35 C0072/35 C0082/10
fanned (2) B1123/23 C0391/23
fanning (1) C0391/23
fans (3) A0071/09
B1070/07 C0432/07
fantasias (1) A0406/12
fantastic (28) A0087/23
A0101/V A0157/01 A0210/32 A0215/07
A0320/22 A0321/11 A0326/06 A0406/09
A0411/12 A0444/18 A0482/26 A0532/14
A0601/32 A0613/06 A0640/07 A0641/V
A0644/V A0662/V A0672/15 B0862/34
B1003/20 B1297/23 B1316/06 B1337/10
C0388/31 C0389/30 C0563/41
fantastical (3) A0225/20
A0326/V A0371/13
fantastical-looking (1) C0425/07
fantastically (6) A0165/05 A0407/36
A0602/V A0664/V B0945/11 C0542/07
fantasy (2) A0670/V B0902/08
far (1) A0296/09
far (360)
far-distant (5) A0054/20
A0063/23 A0601/21 A0602/10 C0205/25
far-famed (1) B1278/05
far-searching (1) A0602/01
far-seeing (1) A0479/06
far-stretched (1) A0610/26
farce (2) B0823/23 B1134/01
fare (2) A0381/29 B1091/13
fared (1) B1153/26
farewell (4) B0992/25
B1236/04 C0088/22 C0395/07
Farmers' (1) B1053/10
farmhouse (1) B1328/13
farming (1) B0833/09
Farnesian (1) A0297/V
farrago (1) A0299/07
farrago (2) A0500/12 B1116/05
farther (126)
farthest (15) A0105/30
A0353/17 A0355/24 A0384/28 A0387/07
B0810/32 B1082/07 B1321/11 C0142/09
C0414/25 C0421/26 C0423/15 C0425/38
C0447/V C0575/30
farthing (1) B0878/09
farthingale (1) B1008/07
fascinated (2) A0511/24 B0893/08
fascinating (1) B0894/16
fascination (2) A0022/21 B1016/21
Fashion (1) B1303/21
fashion (48) A0086/29
A0087/25 A0089/07 A0100/06 A0104/06
A0159/13 A0190/26 A0209/18 A0246/03
A0248/08 A0294/11 A0298/V A0337/18
A0439/09 A0444/17 A0469/04 A0498/08
A0499/13 A0623/21 A0654/10 A0654/16
A0673/12 A0681/16 B0878/29 B0886/01
B0890/04 B0891/24 B0975/12 B0981/04
B0984/35 B1008/26 B1010/28 B1011/27
B1031/22 B1046/04 B1091/27 B1097/04
B1114/18 B1129/15 B1130/19 B1134/30
B1152/26 B1261/06 B1299/29 B1303/16
B1345/18 B1351/12 C0522/20

fashionable (11) A0159/12
A0484/17 A0499/26 A0599/04 A0705/09
B0878/22 B0908/17 B0908/28 B0910/13
B1143/01 B1270/08
fashionably (1) A0348/23
fashioned (14) A0164/21 A0165/06
A0189/21 A0243/24 A0247/19 A0367/08
A0494/08 A0496/08 B0772/19 B0856/02
B0965/33 B1165/01 B1166/25 B1248/21
fashioning (1) A0166/04
fashions (1) A0673/24
fast (29) A0018/10
A0151/23 A0285/05 A0324/V A0340/30
A0373/21 A0467/23 A0490/26 A0513/08
A0513/27 A0540/21 B0766/34 B0830/03
B0931/04 B1158/13 B1236/21 C0059/08
C0063/20 C0072/41 C0095/03 C0106/33
C0108/23 C0108/27 C0196/28 C0390/20
C0390/21 C0398/12 C0406/04 C0539/01
fast-sinking (1) B1282/26
fasten (7) A0080/38
B0753/33 B1051/10 C0121/02 C0129/11
C0409/23 C0410/12
fastened (48) A0057/15
A0067/33 A0072/07 A0104/08 A0156/21
A0189/22 A0247/28 A0248/18 A0325/17
A0368/10 A0368/15 A0542/09 A0551/32
A0552/16 A0552/18 A0554/02 A0593/23
A0694/05 B0730/18 B0730/34 B0793/28
B0821/03 B0950/08 B0966/02 B1008/25
B1157/15 B1340/01 C0062/31 C0068/29
C0076/39 C0082/01 C0085/35 C0100/11
C0121/07 C0122/06 C0126/32 C0127/28
C0136/24 C0139/06 C0140/05 C0175/01
C0197/24 C0389/26 C0409/27 C0415/26
C0547/25 C0552/14 C0562/24
fastening (11) A0552/18
B0771/19 B0793/32 B0822/07 B0855/12
C0069/28 C0120/34 C0197/08 C0197/12
C0547/18 C0547/26
fastenings (8) A0057/33
A0068/17 A0692/21 B0826/11 C0117/14
C0119/07 C0119/31 C0432/46
fastens (1) B0821/07
faster (2) B1225/21 B1225/21
fastest (1) C0147/10
fastidious (6) A0265/37 A0444/18
B0890/12 B0926/30 B1278/09 B1280/22
fastidiously (1) B1330/11
fastness (1) C0087/02
fastnesses (3) C0185/31
C0200/18 C0531/41
fat (39) A0046/30
A0054/25 A0069/25 A0091/22 A0092/16
A0110/26 A0111/26 A0254/02 A0342/12
A0368/03 A0368/14 A0369/09 A0372/07
A0485/11 A0487/16 A0487/18 A0489/10
B0741/06 B1009/26 B1089/21 B1183/05
B1207/04 B1208/37 B1292/31 B1345/07
B1345/07 B1345/34 B1347/19 B1348/15
B1361/06 B1369/22 C0138/04 C0138/22
C0534/39 C0535/35 C0538/14 C0540/07
C0561/27 C0570/31
fatal (18) A0211/01 A0211/09
A0253/22 A0297/04 A0383/05 A0403/V
->A0670/02 B0758/33 B0768/27 B0769/28
B0771/34 B0856/23 B0916/15 B0949/20
B1224/11 B1224/22 C0394/03 C0406/13
fatalities (1) B1169/10
fatality (4) A0018/01
A0427/10 B1169/08 B1246/10
fatally (2) B0949/34 C0390/27
Fate (2) A0225/07 A0227/09
fate (54)
fated (1) C0124/23
fates (5) A0654/20
A0685/09 B1107/23 B1281/07 C0147/36
Father (1) A0319/21
father (51)
father's (4) A0235/05
B1153/02 C0100/22 C0529/24
fathered (1) A0262/17
fatherly (1) B1133/17
fathers (2) A0210/13 B1169/09
fathom (4) A0313/19
A0534/22 A0580/30 C0204/31
fathomed (2) B0747/23 B1219/19
fathomless (2) A0227/15 A0232/V
fathoms (16) A0136/21
A0581/19 A0582/16 B0931/28 B0977/12
C0089/20 C0144/06 C0150/10 C0151/02
C0156/25 C0163/08 C0163/28 C0164/14
C0167/03 C0167/28 C0170/41
fatigue (7) A0594/16
A0686/06 B1007/10 C0096/27 C0114/18
C0141/23 C0532/31
fatigued (3) A0354/24
B0822/20 C0064/28
fatigues (2) B0796/30 B1278/15
fatness (1) B1165/02
Fatquack (4) B1137/35
B1137/39 B1139/02 B1145/29
fatted (1) A0047/22
fattened (1) A0345/13
fatter (1) B1209/01
fatty (1) B0742/02
fatui (1) A0135/17
Faubourg (1) A0561/02
Faubourg/Saint/Germain (1) B0724/30
Faubourg/St./Germain (2) A0532/17
B0974/05
faucial (1) A0433/29
faugh (2) A0091/18 A0110/20
fault (18) A0109/07 A0284/09
A0286/02 A0315/20 A0315/22 A0366/04
A0379/20 A0457/20 A0500/29 A0544/16
A0547/29 A0553/10 A0561/26 B0975/28
B1134/10 B1383/09 C0061/32 C0407/18
fault-finding (1) B1380/32
faultless (2) A0266/10 A0312/07
faults (1) A0097/28
faulty (1) B0926/31
faut (4) A0035/05
A0036/18 A0602/07 B1207/06
favor (19) A0073/11
A0145/27 A0269/15 A0271/10 A0282/32
A0286/03 A0624/22 A0652/18 B0740/30
B0754/03 B0874/01 B0907/09 B0910/04
B1051/29 B1142/06 B1158/28 B1345/03
B1379/15 C0552/22

favorable (6) B0738/18 B1079/27
B1114/16 B1294/27 C0555/21 C0567/24
favored (1) C0415/18
favoring (1) B1080/19
favorite (23) A0025/12
A0071/31 A0071/31 A0099/09 A0229/18
A0348/26 A0380/22 A0409/04 A0413/06
A0413/09 A0441/20 A0664/06 B0807/03
B0822/32 B0850/35 B0854/23 B1009/23
B1045/32 B1055/03 B1247/06 C0529/20
C0537/11 C0571/29
favors (2) A0277/23 B1207/26
favour (2) C0067/10 C0086/34
favourable (6) C0104/09 C0104/37
C0129/02 C0145/30 C0156/14 C0158/15
favourite (3) A0225/21
B0863/22 C0058/06
Favyn (1) A0301/02
fawn (1) A0665/04
Fay (6) A0286/16 A0286/21
A0599/T A0604/09 A0604/24 A0605/09
fay (2) A0599/M A0604/30
Fay, Theo. (1) A0286/12
Fays (2) A0604/02 A0604/16
fear (50) A0090/16 A0135/13
A0141/23 A0142/20 A0211/23 A0273/04
A0299/13 A0324/12 A0403/19 A0433/13
A0455/11 A0458/21 A0512/18 A0541/08
A0547/14 A0567/12 A0667/71 A0689/35
B0729/21 B0755/17 B0793/28 B0796/18
B0796/24 B0809/35 B0816/29 B0856/06
B0870/29 B0899/11 B0965/17 B0981/20
B1020/01 B1078/12 B1079/29 B1080/16
B1152/32 B1212/29 B1236/32 B1240/20
B1248/01 C0056/24 C0070/11 C0081/36
C0105/09 C0133/28 C0395/07 C0395/34
C0537/20 C0548/17 C0550/20 C0556/22
fear-enkindled (1) A0458/34
feared (11) A0432/01
A0684/10 B0811/14 B0812/17 B0943/24
B1257/06 C0055/11 C0090/15 C0141/02
C0207/03 C0534/32
fearful (41) A0019/09
A0028/29 A0053/29 A0062/33 A0080/26
A0213/V A0217/11 A0234/10 A0242/20
A0329/04 A0442/04 A0559/07 A0567/07
A0684/31 A0685/16 A0689/04 A0691/10
A0693/11 A0696/26 B0768/21 B0822/21
B0823/13 B0944/24 B0956/27 B0961/15
B0961/17 B0961/17 B0992/13 B1222/16
B1223/04 B1235/10 B1246/07 B1257/29
C0060/06 C0126/07 C0128/23 C0133/22
C0134/13 C0135/29 C0189/19 C0197/34
fearfully (19) A0139/30
A0197/17 A0456/28 A0456/30 A0456/30
A0510/21 A0538/23 A0543/26 B0947/30
B0950/04 B0968/33 B1136/38 B1372/26
C0060/15 C0072/15 C0081/37 C0142/36
C0422/37 C0567/30
fearing (3) A0413/30
C0201/29 C0417/31
fearlessly (2) A0140/20 B1375/16
fears (12) A0054/29
A0063/29 A0136/34 B0764/28 B0794/15
B1003/07 B1077/31 C0075/05 C0188/04
->C0192/12 C0420/28 C0541/08
feasibility (1) B1241/24
feasible (3) B1070/02
B1078/34 B1294/32
feast (4) A0046/29
B0929/34 B1298/37 C0143/10
feasted (3) B0893/05
B1008/33 C0570/03
feasting (4) A0078/30
C0091/21 C0125/06 C0544/05
feasts (1) A0608/13
feat (8) A0479/31
A0555/09 A0565/27 B1078/34 B1080/09
C0096/29 C0106/37 C0562/32
feather (10) A0053/35 A0063/06
A0079/12 A0509/25 A0582/28 A0586/01
B0932/17 B1349/07 C0061/18 C0552/15
feathered (3) B1021/24
C0151/08 C0153/27
feathers (12) A0498/10
B0869/15 B1021/27 B1161/22 B1166/08
B1351/01 C0134/23 C0404/24 C0412/08
C0412/14 C0553/23 C0553/27
Featherstone (1) C0147/26
Featherstonhaugh (1) B1115/15
feathery (1) B1281/05
feats (1) B1346/17
feature (15) A0212/31
A0245/23 A0246/17 A0400/06 A0403/21
A0434/19 A0484/12 A0499/20 A0509/32
B0759/21 B0823/30 B0888/20 B1279/17
B1380/24 C0422/27
features (47) A0056/14
A0066/03 A0088/26 A0156/15 A0196/24
A0196/24 A0196/26 A0196/V A0235/24
A0271/01 A0276/34 A0294/13 A0311/27
A0312/02 A0313/14 A0397/12 A0402/02
A0402/05 A0404/V A0410/30 A0415/09
A0439/10 A0445/27 A0447/V A0448/03
A0473/26 A0509/28 A0510/32 A0527/01
A0547/18 A0675/16 B0724/14 B0764/14
B0861/02 B0863/01 B0870/06 B0890/27
B0948/32 B1030/15 B1038/29 B1040/11
B1050/14 B1135/03 C0149/17 C0539/23
C0564/41 C0569/14
Feb. (2) A0487/26 A0487/28
February (8) A0280/24
A0282/24 C0056/11 C0160/30 C0161/28
C0161/38 C0180/12 C0192/22
fed (3) B0851/01 B0898/11 B1292/30
feeble (57)
feebleness (3) B0906/02
C0074/20 C0096/29
feebler (1) A0605/06
feeblest (4) A0459/12
A0533/01 B0965/34 C0532/32
feebly (7) A0405/30
B1030/05 B1236/31 B1238/19 B1348/21
C0117/33 C0118/09
feed (4) A0491/10
A0611/31 C0178/34 C0411/10
feeding (1) B0850/13
feel (94)
feeling (84)
feelings (56)

feels (5) A0548/02
A0614/11 B0736/36 B0873/07 B0986/19
feerd (1) B0819/32
feered (1) B0818/24
feet (315)
feigned (1) C0110/39
feint (2) A0530/17 C0100/21
felicitous (1) A0269/23
felicity (2) B0858/07 B1137/28
feline (1) B0940/19
Felix, Minutius (2) A0173/02
A0176/12
fell (200)
felled (4) A0058/17
C0112/33 C0179/26 C0545/04
felling (4) C0199/12
C0545/26 C0546/29 C0546/30
fellow (64)
fellow-citizens (1) C0391/07
fellow-collegians (1) A0440/24
fellow-commoner (1) A0441/08
fellow-creature (1) C0135/12
fellow-men (3) A0483/08
A0670/07 B1052/30
fellow-sojourners (1) B1361/11
fellow-sufferers (2) C0131/15
C0134/39
fellow-traveller (1) A0066/20
fellow-wayfarers (1) A0508/04
fellow's (2) B0822/33 B1373/18
fellows (29) A0347/04
A0372/34 A0482/03 A0498/02 A0498/V
A0508/32 A0621/20 B0734/26 B0750/20
B0750/22 B0766/06 B0842/10 B0872/26
B0878/06 B0983/31 B0984/28 B1009/07
B1015/11 B1018/23 B1021/18 B1101/31
B1108/10 B1158/26 B1259/23 B1301/36
C0391/33 C0529/14 C0544/07 C0564/05
<u>felo</u> (1) B1379/07
felon (5) A0058/14
A0069/03 B0985/16 B0985/17 B1108/15
felon's (1) B0855/20
felons (1) A0589/17
felt (219)
Feltspar, F. F. (1) A0182/04
Feltzpar (1) A0175/25
female (21) A0151/25
A0218/03 A0483/27 A0499/16 A0502/06
A0623/13 B0731/34 B0735/34 B0745/02
B0757/21 B0768/02 B0889/14 B0889/21
B0890/19 B0905/02 B0991/07 B1236/11
B1292/34 B1340/04 C0138/21 C0153/06
females (4) B1007/34
B1015/10 C0124/20 C0547/10
feminine (4) A0269/02
A0384/27 B0991/17 B1096/36
<u>feminis</u> (1) A0072/30
<u>femoris</u> (1) A0379/30
fence (4) A0036/24
B0765/32 B0765/34 B1335/01
fences (2) B0734/39 B0765/29
fender (1) B1100/04
fens (1) A0197/15
<u>fer</u> (1) A0431/09
fer (1) B0815/09
ferment (1) C0387/06
fermentation (2) B0742/27 C0097/34
ferments (1) C0534/38
ferocious (8) A0026/30
A0565/08 C0072/13 C0087/35 C0530/20
C0547/11 C0548/23 C0575/01
ferocious-looking (2) B1352/09
C0087/06
ferocity (10) A0447/21 A0557/25
A0558/08 A0559/22 A0564/24 B0946/32
C0087/18 C0550/07 C0577/37 C0578/40
<u>ferrades</u> (2) A0554/11 A0554/21
ferret (1) B0728/12
Ferrex (1) A0240/M
Ferroe (1) A0582/33
ferry (3) B0736/03
B1104/16 B1104/17
ferry-boat (1) B0769/25
fertile (3) B1329/01
C0572/17 C0573/18
fertility (1) B1278/02
ferule (1) A0429/02
fervent (4) A0227/33
A0228/36 A0233/19 C0138/24
fervid (5) A0297/21
A0406/10 A0665/18 A0710/21 B1275/24
fervor (10) A0026/32 A0227/30
A0232/V A0532/07 A0641/14 A0644/19
B1122/03 B1122/15 C0521/25 C0537/30
fervour (1) A0644/V
feshionable> (1) A0466/18
festered (1) A0514/29
festivals (1) A0026/05
festooning (1) A0501/26
<u>fete</u> (2) A0673/18 B1347/08
Fether (5) B1002/T
B1017/05 B1017/12 B1018/04 B1022/04
fetid (3) A0244/01
B1354/21 C0579/30
fetter (1) A0248/19
fettered (2) A0323/14 B1261/25
fetterless (1) B1226/19
fetters (3) A0329/17
B0887/05 B1224/01
feudal (2) A0019/19 A0410/04
fever (21) A0033/V
A0323/22 A0483/19 A0512/14 A0609/06
A0612/21 A0667/01 A0667/50 B0807/08
B0815/32 B0815/33 B0894/30 B0950/01
B0959/33 B1347/11 C0073/40 C0078/37
C0081/08 C0126/07 C0561/15 C0561/24
fever-demons (1) A0243/11
feverish (1) B0815/29
feverishly (1) A0674/13
few (295)
fewer (3) B0964/29
B1165/16 C0571/20
fewest (1) C0191/27
fiat (1) A0021/27
Fibalittle (1) B1139/02
fibe (3) A0372/31
B0819/19 B0819/19
fibre (4) A0613/36
A0682/06 A0684/34 B0851/26
fibres (2) B1333/35 C0533/01

fibula (1) A0379/31
Fichte (1) A0230/25
fickle-minded (1) A0043/15
fickle-mindedness (1) A0043/13
fiction (19) A0281/34
A0340/35 A0621/10 A0621/12 A0684/22
B0723/16 B0862/31 B0950/27 B0955/01
B0957/11 B1121/03 B1151/M B1361/26
C0055/23 C0056/08 C0056/10 C0056/12
C0428/17 C0429/32
fictitious (3) A0150/V
A0431/21 C0429/40
fiddle (5) A0371/10
A0372/06 A0372/07 A0374/14 B0869/M
Fiddle/de/dee (1) B1162/01
fiddles (2) B1009/06 B1017/25
fiddlestick (1) A0483/17
fiddling (1) A0349/18
fide (1) A0062/16
fide (2) A0034/V A0053/10
fidelity (3) B0850/21
B0965/14 B1333/35
fidgetty (1) A0270/13
fie (1) A0656/03
field (29) A0296/V
A0434/30 A0552/31 A0706/12 A0706/32
A0707/09 B0752/28 B0945/30 B1126/04
B1167/29 B1206/07 B1259/34 B1270/15
B1271/15 B1272/09 B1369/17 C0159/27
C0160/38 C0160/40 C0162/18 C0162/24
C0162/35 C0163/20 C0164/01 C0164/13
C0199/27 C0208/13 C0417/22 C0534/03
fields (6) A0428/26 A0702/M
B1267/M C0158/31 C0160/22 C0163/06
Fiend (1) B0851/06
fiend (12) A0081/34
A0135/27 A0227/21 A0232/08 A0235/21
A0235/24 A0442/18 A0511/18 A0515/02
B0964/16 B1212/09 B1226/09
fiendish (11) A0022/13
A0245/02 A0249/32 A0568/01 A0695/30
B0851/25 B1058/15 C0085/26 C0146/27
C0198/14 C0201/17
fiends (4) A0249/27
A0689/03 B1079/09 B1348/31
fier (1) A0096/M
fierce (15) A0087/37
A0253/24 A0315/13 A0317/07 A0323/04
A0367/32 A0417/12 A0612/21 B0943/26
B1215/28 B1260/15 C0060/01 C0072/26
C0138/26 C0531/26
fiercely (7) A0101/24
A0373/21 A0513/35 B0964/10 B1348/27
B1354/05 C0081/31
fierceness (3) A0317/02
B1223/05 C0135/11
fiercer (1) A0213/14
fiercest (5) A0565/10
B1140/34 B1392/01 C0151/37 C0550/14
fierte (1) A0037/V
fiery (15) A0023/05
A0028/08 A0144/23 A0196/01 A0414/16
A0457/30 A0459/05 A0461/02 A0612/10
A0640/25 A0673/13 A0696/08 A0697/09
B1354/26 B1369/36
fiery-colored (3) A0023/19
A0025/27 A0035/07
fiery-faced (2) A0052/03 A0062/05
fievre (1) A0033/20
fifes (1) B1009/06
fifteen (53)
fifteenth (6) B0922/03 B1030/26
C0146/37 C0146/41 C0192/22 C0421/10
fifth (22) A0059/13 A0062/02
A0138/17 A0151/21 A0177/20 A0183/15
A0437/01 A0653/04 A0653/17 A0671/11
A0672/01 B0760/30 B0941/29 B1183/01
B1262/19 B1375/04 C0156/29 C0179/15
C0550/06 C0550/13 C0567/22 C0567/28
fiftieth (1) B0979/24
fifty (90)
fifty-eight (1) C0158/30
fifty-five (1) B0912/07
fifty-four (2) A0175/31 A0181/31
fifty-one (2) C0164/23 C0174/10
fifty-six (1) C0156/20
fifty-three (3) C0157/29
C0157/42 C0167/02
fifty-two (3) A0686/13
A0688/18 C0157/31
fig-pedler (1) A0336/M
figgur> (1) A0464/16
figgurs (2) B0812/04 B0812/04
fight (8) A0345/02
A0346/05 A0356/V A0387/24 B1167/21
B1373/26 C0555/22 C0578/05
fighting (3) B0946/32
B1021/09 C0531/04
figs (1) A0336/M
figurative (1) C0430/03
figuratively (4) A0382/04
B1089/26 B1182/31 B1187/26
figure (97)
figure/V (1) A0354/19
figurehead (1) C0123/09
figures (30) A0022/02 A0080/32
A0145/01 A0236/07 A0322/15 A0322/16
A0324/27 A0326/09 A0354/17 A0430/15
A0498/05 A0498/11 A0614/03 A0673/22
A0682/13 A0683/15 A0689/03 A0695/26
A0705/17 A0705/17 B0828/09 B0834/35
B1180/15 B1270/15 B1339/29 C0207/26
C0207/27 C0207/34 C0208/11 C0552/13
filagreed (6) A0087/01 A0100/12
A0502/12 A0509/16 A0664/10 B0907/05
filamentous (1) C0178/19
filbert (2) C0181/35 C0188/23
filbert-bushes (2) C0188/21
C0196/27
filberts (4) C0191/05
C0191/19 C0192/20 C0196/11
file (1) C0553/21
filed (1) A0101/11
files (2) B0753/03 C0148/09
filius (1) A0213/07
fill (11) A0601/15
B0983/02 B0983/19 B1073/14 C0098/12
C0099/10 C0106/23 C0202/37 C0207/10
C0415/35 C0423/02
fillagree (1) B0990/35

filled (61)
filleted (1) B0945/20
filling (7) A0023/13
A0343/05 A0611/30 A0642/29 B1337/04
C0109/03 C0115/41
fillip (1) A0108/20
filliping (2) B1105/03 B1106/03
fills (1) B0741/34
film (3) A0455/10
A0507/10 B0789/13
filmy (4) A0509/19
B0940/23 B1259/04 C0198/14
Fils (1) A0541/11
filtered (1) A0036/12
filth (4) A0086/22
A0122/12 A0510/09 A0514/29
filthy (9) A0104/01
A0242/23 A0251/01 A0351/08 A0510/17
A0511/35 B0945/21 B1093/29 B1300/20
final (24) A0019/25
A0143/31 A0274/09 A0355/29 A0409/17
A0416/32 A0429/18 A0441/07 A0457/17
A0459/02 A0625/11 A0697/05 B0726/18
B0852/06 B0852/16 B0932/33 B1072/34
B1213/18 B1236/04 C0080/39 C0179/37
C0185/31 C0197/37 C0207/16
finale (1) C0424/04
finale (1) B0905/21
finally (102)
finances (1) C0526/24
financial (1) B0870/09
financier (1) B0870/07
find (152)
finder (5) B0873/28
B0873/32 B0874/19 B0876/35 B0877/20
finding (56)
finds (13) A0212/22
A0286/04 A0478/07 A0488/12 A0683/01
B0749/15 B0852/V B0871/35 B0872/18
B0984/21 B1282/23 B1302/22 C0432/03
fine (118)
fine-looking (4) A0378/02
A0380/04 B1003/29 C0147/08
finely (2) A0298/V A0401/34
fineness (1) B1033/25
finer (8) A0381/05
B1033/22 B1033/22 B1160/40 B1332/18
B1363/30 C0174/29 C0531/17
finery (1) B1007/31
finesse (3) A0296/V
A0441/15 C0134/38
finest (11) A0247/04
A0338/14 A0365/01 A0379/19 A0583/30
B0863/05 B0864/03 B0864/19 B0902/V
B1012/09 B1167/02
finest-tempered (1) B1160/03
finger (20) A0108/20
A0136/27 A0217/V A0386/07 A0439/17
A0467/29 A0538/16 A0558/30 A0559/06
A0641/25 B0812/29 B0828/06 B1012/18
B1180/29 C0068/27 C0076/36 C0079/38
C0092/24 C0109/06 C0397/23
finger-nails (1) A0558/V
fingers (34) A0046/16 A0079/42
A0085/12 A0108/09 A0227/06 A0231/17
->A0234/29 A0246/32 A0316/21 A0404/15
A0509/23 A0510/23 A0543/26 A0553/19
A0558/22 A0559/02 A0559/08 A0587/19
A0609/08 A0613/23 A0625/22 A0694/06
B0730/06 B0890/07 B0899/27 B0906/31
B1120/05 B1166/27 B1372/21 C0076/04
C0134/26 C0197/41 C0198/06 C0569/28
finicky (1) A0268/18
finish (8) A0252/30
A0270/37 A0272/11 A0274/12 A0278/17
A0281/03 A0283/27 B1153/20
finished (20) A0088/31
A0103/11 A0108/23 A0110/V A0112/V
A0124/25 A0173/24 A0179/04 A0271/05
A0301/15 A0303/04 B0736/18 B0857/19
B1020/02 B1137/21 B1153/19 B1262/18
B1262/33 C0176/02 C0556/05
finishing (3) B0981/30
B1153/29 C0426/31
finite (1) B0987/30
finnicky (1) A0370/32
fins (3) A0241/13
B1156/30 C0566/25
Fior (1) B1386/04
fioriture (1) B0905/21
fir (1) A0591/34
fire (86)
fire-dogs (1) A0368/01
fire-eater (2) A0380/26 A0380/29
fire-guns (3) C0556/09
C0556/16 C0557/12
fire-light (2) A0102/23 A0672/16
fire-place (7) A0101/13
A0101/14 A0253/27 A0538/08 B1021/01
B1339/25 B1340/18
fire-places (1) A0367/32
firearms (1) C0181/18
fired (10) B0732/10 B0740/11
B0743/06 B0992/20 B1078/12 C0164/37
C0184/17 C0186/08 C0533/21 C0579/20
Firefly (1) C0099/03
fireplace (3) A0242/12
B0857/08 C0191/08
fires (23) A0036/09
A0138/26 A0140/09 A0151/V A0157/V
A0175/V A0182/05 A0225/03 A0225/04
A0229/03 A0229/04 A0321/28 A0323/13
A0326/10 B1207/01 C0189/28 C0532/18
C0562/12 C0562/14 C0562/19 C0563/05
C0563/11 C0563/14
firing (6) B0742/30 B0743/15
C0184/14 C0186/16 C0199/18 C0199/32
firm (28) A0091/24
A0351/02 A0386/16 A0484/23 A0485/20
A0510/21 A0541/11 A0553/27 A0555/01
A0559/05 A0653/09 A0697/03 B0752/33
B0826/08 B0879/24 B1055/15 B1081/27
B1127/15 B1127/22 B1183/11 B1329/18
C0061/41 C0065/30 C0075/32 C0163/15
C0398/08 C0536/07 C0537/25
firma (2) B1292/01 C0389/35
firmament (7) A0227/28
A0232/14 A0236/08 A0546/01 C0072/29
C0387/15 C0396/35
firmamental (1) A0615/08

firmer (1) A0695/31
firmest (1) A0021/V
firmly (22) A0182/33 A0295/05
A0299/30 A0304/03 A0513/25 A0542/09
A0543/15 A0555/V A0686/25 B0826/05
B0857/25 B1119/13 B1372/11 C0080/19
C0116/01 C0118/23 C0127/13 C0159/22
C0182/26 C0201/07 C0557/05 C0576/38
firmness (4) A0446/15
A0681/13 B1369/27 C0116/34
firms (1) A0508/31
firs (1) A0582/05
First (6) A0240/V A0250/04
A0251/12 A0252/33 B0806/T C0569/35
first (543)
first-mentioned (1) B1152/02
firstling (1) A0047/18
fish (23) A0205/20
A0252/16 A0583/28 A0585/08 A0585/13
A0641/01 A0643/14 B1017/33 B1156/30
B1161/01 B1333/31 C0126/15 C0127/40
C0143/17 C0155/06 C0156/23 C0174/04
C0174/09 C0177/01 C0540/08 C0560/02
C0570/01 C0572/08
fish-oil (1) C0084/35
fished (1) C0135/40
fisher (1) C0536/23
fishermen (4) A0594/16
A0594/25 B0729/33 B0730/12
fishes (1) B1156/11
fishing (6) A0583/22 A0583/23
A0584/31 B0807/23 B1246/06 C0120/38
fishy (2) C0165/18 C0177/10
fiss (1) B1158/34
fissure (16) A0400/18
A0417/09 A0417/12 A0553/25 A0695/19
B1331/30 C0181/28 C0181/41 C0182/21
C0183/13 C0183/22 C0185/09 C0189/15
C0194/07 C0195/08 C0195/18
fissures (1) C0192/33
fist (7) A0384/08
A0487/10 A0649/03 B0913/18 B1182/35
B1184/01 B1185/04
fists (2) A0241/12 B1142/34
fit (4) A0096/M
A0652/15 B1296/25 B1313/26
fit (32) A0045/27
A0091/10 A0110/16 A0216/V A0247/19
A0247/26 A0344/14 A0437/23 A0586/28
A0612/04 A0623/06 A0652/16 A0696/19
B0745/34 B0815/05 B0927/08 B0928/15
B0966/35 B1046/26 B1140/12 B1141/27
B1185/30 B1225/10 B1379/18 C0061/37
C0108/28 C0134/26 C0168/16 C0389/34
C0397/09 C0529/24 C0533/23
Fitche (3) A0079/07
A0226/25 A0342/V
fitful (6) A0138/21 A0139/34
A0164/18 A0248/24 A0511/01 C0436/V
fitfully (4) A0158/04
A0318/12 A0411/22 C0112/21
fitly (1) B0769/07
fitness (3) A0338/03
A0348/17 A0482/27
fits (7) B0808/16
->B0924/08 B0929/33 B0962/25 B0965/12
B1225/13 C0082/31
fitted (14) A0103/23 A0436/31
A0552/02 A0552/04 A0553/06 B1008/04
B1262/35 B1347/09 B1362/16 C0063/10
C0068/02 C0099/40 C0410/30 C0415/30
fitter (1) A0166/03
fitting (14) A0099/33 A0160/05
A0441/03 A0687/25 B0730/31 B0766/16
B1144/16 B1157/07 B1180/08 C0065/32
C0079/27 C0195/21 C0207/31 C0405/28
five (159)
five-and-twenty (4) A0067/V
A0473/04 C0148/28 C0411/39
five-pound (2) C0405/18 C0406/10
five-sevenths (1) C0428/26
fix (2) A0557/V B0874/17
fixed (7) A0559/05
B0893/31 B1071/22 B1168/26 B1168/V
C0423/32 C0425/14
fixedly (6) A0153/08 A0415/31
A0434/28 A0663/29 B1057/08 B1349/14
fixtures (1) A0553/01
fizz (2) B1011/27 B1145/30
fizzes (1) B0874/21
fizzing (2) B1011/31 B1020/28
flaccid (1) B0742/02
Flaccus (2) B0869/M B0870/10
Flaccus, Quintus (1) A0110/23
flacon (1) B1260/14
flag (4) A0528/27
B0831/09 B0843/26 C0147/04
flagon (2) A0241/31 C0544/07
flagons (2) A0245/15 A0253/29
flagrant (2) A0021/10 A0054/21
flags (3) A0155/21
B1078/V C0554/11
flagstones (2) A0152/14 A0154/11
flakes (4) A0604/12
A0604/13 C0162/37 C0195/19
flambeau (3) B1351/32
B1353/09 B1354/02
flambeaux (1) A0152/05
flambeaux (3) B1258/27
B1261/03 B1262/21
flame (19) A0029/21
A0136/25 A0212/01 A0457/21 A0460/01
A0460/30 A0461/21 A0614/23 A0665/32
A0682/08 B1123/19 B1123/19 B1261/03
B1354/04 C0066/06 C0143/02 C0189/26
C0190/03 C0394/03
flames (18) A0023/31 A0025/13
A0028/26 A0029/15 A0071/05 A0150/02
A0189/34 A0677/03 A0682/15 A0710/26
B0852/31 B0853/27 B1106/30 B1275/29
B1282/27 B1354/08 B1360/07 C0562/39
flaming (4) A0022/24
B1079/07 B1322/27 C0420/26
flamingo (2) A0640/34 A0643/11
flannel (3) A0100/05
C0123/38 C0558/18
flannels (1) C0064/19
flapped (3) B1013/30
B1185/34 C0167/20
flapping (4) A0081/10

->A0318/20 C0149/35 C0174/40
flapping-to (1) A0566/22
flaring (5) A0157/26
C0146/16 C0203/23 C0204/23 C0204/40
flash (9) A0023/09
A0142/23 A0198/05 A0508/23 B1057/24
B1157/24 B1302/02 C0130/23 C0405/22
flash-name (1) B1362/07
flashed (17) A0166/25
A0197/V A0314/V A0587/22 A0631/08
A0687/13 A0688/17 A0693/21 B0826/15
B1260/15 C0059/24 C0060/06 C0079/03
C0085/17 C0125/11 C0136/07 C0578/16
flashes (2) A0161/16 A0311/02
flashiness (1) A0499/09
flashing (6) A0152/05 A0412/29
A0509/32 A0567/05 A0664/01 C0081/31
flashy (1) A0485/33
flask (2) A0090/03 C0101/16
flasks (1) A0189/18
flat (28) A0366/33
A0374/11 A0500/04 A0502/14 A0586/09
A0587/07 A0630/11 A0630/25 A0631/11
B0928/05 B1072/03 B1129/19 B1156/17
B1159/21 B1337/01 B1363/20 C0106/23
C0116/02 C0117/11 C0155/12 C0179/21
C0185/37 C0191/07 C0197/32 C0563/10
C0568/03 C0569/15 C0578/14
flat-bottomed (2) C0201/33 C0204/03
flatboats (1) C0186/34
flatness (1) A0683/23
Flatplatz (1) B1362/09
flattened (4) B1071/14
C0097/22 C0417/29 C0418/29
flatter (7) A0608/18
A0696/35 A0696/35 B0810/04 B0977/34
B1035/02 B1115/07
flattered (3) A0090/19
A0109/14 A0301/19
flattering (3) A0268/24
A0271/12 A0382/22
flatteringly (1) B0903/29
flattish (1) C0178/24
flatu (2) A0072/01 A0072/31
flaunted (2) A0641/01 A0643/11
flaunting (1) A0515/04
flavor (4) A0110/25
B1056/09 B1181/01 C0542/38
flavour (2) A0091/21 C0188/23
flaw (3) A0553/11
B1054/09 C0101/34
flaws (2) A0138/12 B1383/12
flax (2) B1351/04 B1354/18
flaxen (1) B1354/02
flayed (3) A0059/04
A0069/V A0070/04
fled (15) A0027/16
A0198/17 A0328/14 A0417/03 A0444/34
A0445/09 A0515/14 B0771/23 B0852/02
B0858/03 B0958/06 B0967/23 C0522/10
C0558/11 C0567/08
fledged (1) B1038/19
flee (4) A0316/V
A0445/08 B0760/08 B0854/33
Fleece (1) B1303/15
fleeces (1) B1278/35
fleeing (1) A0317/26
flees (1) B0765/07
fleet (2) B0837/13 C0201/32
fleeting (1) B0789/M
fleets (1) B0945/26
flesh (20) A0044/18
A0047/21 A0048/02 A0106/30 A0241/14
A0245/26 A0354/04 A0379/29 A0557/20
A0558/13 A0616/04 B0730/14 B0730/17
B0743/31 B1166/09 B1180/24 C0125/02
C0125/23 C0177/09 C0534/33
fleshly (3) A0244/28
B1166/24 B1223/V
fleshy (1) B0741/06
Fletcher, Giles (2) A0702/M
B1267/M
flew (33) A0138/11
A0166/20 A0228/03 A0323/08 A0373/12
A0412/25 A0445/03 A0567/06 A0590/02
A0616/15 A0643/12 A0663/13 A0705/24
B1057/05 B1078/04 B1164/12 B1164/14
B1270/22 B1347/19 B1353/17 C0058/35
C0059/24 C0060/20 C0061/41 C0163/23
C0164/03 C0164/27 C0187/27 C0205/41
C0432/23 C0545/37 C0562/39 C0566/34
flexibility (1) C0087/11
flexible (3) A0247/06
B0940/11 C0409/17
flicker (1) C0078/12
flickered (2) A0514/34 A0665/32
flickering (3) A0157/26
A0499/21 C0205/02
flickeringly (1) A0615/26
flickerings (1) C0204/18
flies (8) A0128/05
A0346/05 A0673/07 B0875/14 B1168/29
B1222/24 C0429/37 C0432/46
Flight (1) C0432/47
flight (14) A0210/28 A0537/15
A0616/16 B0851/25 B1070/09 B1166/06
B1215/27 B1298/34 B1299/02 C0199/37
C0403/21 C0433/02 C0568/27 C0578/07
flights (4) B0945/24
B0947/18 C0164/26 C0167/12
Flimen (2) A0579/27 A0584/18
flimsy (2) A0507/13 B1207/34
fling (1) A0487/22
flinging (1) C0089/26
flint (1) C0168/20
Flint, Timothy (1) A0270/09
Flint's (2) A0270/20 A0275/37
flints (3) C0194/11
C0194/26 C0572/32
flinty (1) A0020/V
flippant (4) A0337/34
A0602/05 B1114/13 B1324/02
flipper (9) A0468/01
A0468/05 A0468/13 A0468/22 A0469/05
A0469/23 A0470/08 A0470/19 A0470/V
flirt (1) B1298/36
flirtations (1) B0906/17
flirting (2) A0174/14 A0179/29
flit (1) B1221/V
flitted (11) A0054/18

->A0063/21 A0078/21 A0079/11 A0214/05
A0326/07 A0511/06 A0555/25 A0614/04
B0895/V B0948/11
flitting (5) A0080/32
A0236/07 A0616/24 B1322/08 C0205/36
float (9) A0406/35
B0741/13 B0741/19 B0742/02 B0866/10
B1074/36 B1161/39 C0147/31 C0412/08
floated (31) A0022/02
A0087/06 A0100/17 A0153/25 A0164/24
A0216/20 A0253/V A0254/01 A0402/10
A0591/31 A0604/25 A0604/26 A0604/32
A0613/30 A0641/06 A0643/26 A0693/24
B0895/11 B1092/05 B1156/12 B1156/14
B1279/12 B1330/26 C0063/15 C0063/25
C0064/04 C0118/12 C0140/12 C0164/02
C0205/14 C0412/06
floating (28) A0036/V
A0589/22 A0593/01 A0593/16 A0683/03
B0726/23 B0729/33 B0734/22 B0738/23
B0740/18 B0740/23 B0744/01 B0744/05
B0754/06 B0757/16 B0865/14 B1282/22
B1291/07 B1293/33 B1310/05 C0063/18
C0121/26 C0131/35 C0139/12 C0144/20
C0418/38 C0418/49 C0547/01
floats (1) A0674/01
flock (5) A0047/18
B1164/13 B1164/15 B1164/37 B1334/26
flocked (1) A0026/V
flocks (3) B1283/07
C0160/23 C0163/23
floe (5) C0162/24
C0163/17 C0164/09 C0164/29 C0164/33
floes (3) C0159/09
C0160/13 C0165/40
flog (1) B0812/12
flogged (1) A0622/30
flogging (3) A0622/26
B0813/25 B0843/09
floggings (1) A0653/05
flood (14) A0079/07 A0089/16
A0326/17 A0406/03 A0581/22 A0581/31
A0582/36 A0590/25 A0592/20 A0599/M
A0605/11 B1106/22 C0073/16 C0130/38
flooded (1) A0253/25
floods (2) A0101/25 A0197/25
floor (92)
floor-cloths (1) A0498/17
flooring (2) B0796/09 C0068/25
floors (6) A0367/22 A0400/29
A0551/12 A0684/30 B0981/11 B1337/01
<u>Flora/Boreali-Americana</u> (1) C0522/34
<u>florem</u> (1) A0603/35
Florence (4) A0100/19
A0175/21 A0181/18 B0925/10
Florentine (1) A0085/08
florid (1) A0442/02
<u>Flos</u> (3) A0344/01
A0351/20 B1162/33
<u>flos</u> (1) A0072/30
flounces (2) A0336/08 A0349/14
floundered (2) A0253/28 A0253/V
floundering (3) C0108/11
C0111/20 C0140/23
flounders (1) C0174/08
flour (3) C0097/20
C0097/25 C0170/12
flourish (6) A0057/26 A0068/09
A0121/29 A0125/20 A0274/32 A0465/20
flourished (5) A0096/16
B1161/17 B1191/17 B1295/11 B1311/04
flourishes (3) A0271/23
A0629/30 A0630/19
flourishing (3) A0120/24
A0485/31 A0566/26
flow (8) A0195/06
A0235/V A0406/35 A0639/23 A0644/V
B0864/33 B1221/28 C0092/24
flow'rs (1) A0702/M
flowed (8) A0438/24
A0614/24 B1127/07 B1161/01 B1279/20
C0119/21 C0171/33 C0172/01
flower (15) A0212/03
A0213/15 A0344/02 A0351/21 A0383/03
A0683/05 A0707/14 B0746/22 B1163/25
B1163/30 B1163/32 B1163/40 B1272/12
B1384/21 C0543/36
flower-blossoms (1) B1280/10
flower-enamelled (1) B1386/02
flower-garden (1) C0542/19
flower-pot (1) A0367/27
flowering (1) C0543/35
flowers (43) A0035/15
A0162/17 A0162/18 A0195/20 A0228/27
A0236/03 A0403/06 A0426/07 A0498/12
A0503/02 A0603/07 A0613/06 A0613/06
A0639/15 A0640/29 A0640/30 A0641/14
A0643/05 A0702/M B0745/31 B0746/21
B0747/05 B1004/03 B1122/29 B1162/09
B1163/04 B1215/27 B1215/32 B1267/M
B1267/M B1329/27 B1333/37 B1337/31
B1340/17 B1340/17 B1385/28 C0412/36
C0428/29 C0542/06 C0543/27 C0559/04
C0566/15 C0568/10
flowery (1) B0862/35
flowing (10) A0135/M A0379/04
A0407/18 A0407/18 A0407/18 A0428/33
B0863/34 B0945/20 C0085/24 C0406/37
flown (4) B0830/11
B0900/09 B1080/05 B1106/04
flows (3) A0674/06
B0864/03 B0865/08
Floyd's (1) C0548/09
fluctuating (3) A0594/V
B1033/04 B1280/12
Flud, Robert (1) A0409/02
flue (1) A0543/12
fluency (1) B1184/27
fluent (1) A0381/14
fluently (3) A0629/20
B0797/07 B0901/17
fluid (8) A0325/23
A0366/12 B0741/34 B1104/21 B1167/19
B1182/15 B1214/01 C0146/11
fluidiforms (2) A0175/V A0182/06
<u>fluido</u> (2) A0593/35 B1382/35
flummery (1) A0339/33
flung (2) A0023/10 A0587/24
flurried (1) A0586/13
flurry (2) A0563/18 B0871/02

flush (1) A0586/02
flushed (6) A0154/28 A0327/05
A0329/12 A0438/28 A0508/07 A0563/19
fluttered (2) A0088/17 B0866/16
fluttering (1) C0408/24
fluvial (1) B0863/24
flux (2) A0582/09 A0582/34
Fly (9) A0034/20
B1127/15 B1133/31 B1133/32 B1134/07
B1134/V B1137/16 B1139/20 B1139/33
fly (15) A0217/V
A0270/18 A0316/14 A0318/16 A0356/25
A0416/15 B0961/26 B0965/28 B1059/13
B1059/V B1108/11 B1222/17 C0429/44
C0432/07 C0549/34
flying (11) A0023/25
A0105/29 A0374/04 A0589/21 B1068/03
B1069/20 B1078/04 C0123/16 C0125/07
C0151/34 C0429/20
flying-fish (1) B1333/32
foam (20) A0137/07
A0139/05 A0197/26 A0253/11 A0579/21
A0580/21 A0588/09 A0590/15 A0591/15
A0591/34 A0594/01 B0730/04 B1123/27
B1156/03 B1382/18 C0060/10 C0116/24
C0144/25 C0149/37 C0438/V
foamed (3) A0087/35
B0797/17 B1353/31
foaming (4) A0023/26
A0137/20 B0911/15 B1333/13
foamless (1) A0145/12
fob (1) A0587/22
focal (3) C0430/03
C0430/15 C0430/25
focus (3) A0141/31
B0842/12 C0400/08
foe (3) A0021/V A0329/01 C0186/14
foes (2) A0021/30 C0555/03
fog (12) A0046/23
A0512/08 B0943/09 B0944/34 B1076/01
B1330/25 B1330/32 C0067/10 C0133/35
C0133/39 C0159/16 C0163/32
fog-canopy (1) B1331/13
fogs (1) C0136/04
foible (2) A0654/06 B1369/04
foible (1) B1369/03
foibles (1) A0097/30
foiled (1) B0988/V
foils (2) A0036/20 B0985/17
fois (3) A0019/02
A0037/08 A0096/06
Fol-Lol (1) B1143/23
fold (1) B0992/04
folded (11) A0089/12
A0164/20 A0247/13 A0276/01 A0490/17
B0735/10 B0759/05 B0766/20 B0858/17
B0992/03 B1108/34
folder (1) B0992/03
folding (8) A0047/19
A0056/02 A0442/27 A0540/02 A0554/14
A0671/18 B0910/23 C0082/13
folding-doors (1) A0444/21
folds (14) A0089/06 A0153/02
A0154/13 A0322/09 A0444/08 A0501/16
A0672/04 B1076/02 B1260/29 B1280/24
->C0063/35 C0082/22 C0173/04 C0410/13
Folgen (1) B0723/M
foliage (16) A0460/10
A0602/22 A0603/10 A0639/13 B0760/05
B0760/18 B0818/02 B0819/10 B0842/09
B0865/09 B1279/05 B1279/10 B1282/08
B1332/30 C0173/06 C0184/24
Folio (2) A0203/13 A0366/17
folio (4) A0100/28
A0102/03 B1101/16 B1141/08
Folio/Club (2) A0203/01 A0203/T
folios (1) A0144/21
folks (1) B1375/19
follies (6) A0320/19 A0435/30
A0440/16 A0440/32 A0440/32 B0903/14
follow (34) A0020/V A0096/20
A0126/22 A0173/28 A0179/06 A0179/11
A0279/29 A0296/V A0300/21 A0447/10
A0512/06 A0512/26 A0515/26 A0515/29
A0533/15 A0564/V A0566/06 A0585/05
A0664/29 B0816/22 B0864/22 B1142/13
B1241/10 B1379/31 B1384/25 C0068/32
C0088/19 C0131/01 C0175/07 C0197/21
C0524/25 C0527/23 C0539/18 C0550/26
followed (55)
follower (1) C0073/15
followers (5) A0370/04
A0673/15 B0834/14 C0168/37 C0528/02
following (64)
follows (20) A0206/04
A0302/V A0528/17 A0531/12 A0622/33
B0984/33 B1101/19 B1136/06 B1137/25
B1190/34 B1221/13 B1242/16 B1369/01
B1370/11 B1371/27 C0056/27 C0402/06
C0521/04 C0548/32 C0556/15
folly (39) A0080/17
A0141/33 A0166/02 A0227/08 A0231/19
A0317/06 A0403/11 A0413/16 A0438/12
A0438/18 A0445/29 A0473/29 A0483/18
A0497/03 A0499/28 A0585/31 A0667/58
A0671/06 A0673/04 B0732/01 B0738/27
B0738/31 B0738/33 B0739/06 B0739/09
B0739/12 B0746/27 B0754/19 B0763/17
B0859/07 B0899/V B1158/22 B1318/10
B1345/24 B1360/14 C0079/04 C0181/12
C0202/11 C0578/06
fond (14) A0111/03 A0370/06
A0528/07 A0561/08 B0850/11 B0926/33
B0976/24 B1177/06 B1347/24 B1384/03
C0529/09 C0529/18 C0529/19 C0547/13
fondez-vous (1) A0378/M
fondness (2) B0854/26 B1093/04
font (1) A0235/14
Fontaine (1) C0430/30
Fonthill (1) B1278/31
food (46) A0235/01 A0296/V
A0298/08 A0319/08 A0403/04 A0616/34
A0689/18 A0689/22 A0691/20 A0693/24
A0693/32 B0965/30 B1166/03 B1220/V
C0078/33 C0083/37 C0120/27 C0120/36
C0129/31 C0129/41 C0138/01 C0138/11
C0138/15 C0139/10 C0142/12 C0145/19
C0151/33 C0153/06 C0169/26 C0173/35
C0173/37 C0175/37 C0177/10 C0188/36
C0188/40 C0192/20 C0199/06 C0203/15

->C0430/45 C0535/03 C0535/42 C0545/18
C0546/34 C0547/14 C0561/36 C0566/24
fool (44) A0090/10
A0090/10 A0160/21 A0177/17 A0183/12
A0262/26 A0262/27 A0297/26 A0298/V
A0345/21 A0353/07 A0564/16 A0587/01
A0625/29 A0628/17 A0696/32 B0812/09
B0873/06 B0880/08 B0900/14 B0913/04
B0915/17 B0923/08 B0979/07 B0979/09
B0979/10 B0986/17 B1011/23 B1014/10
B1019/26 B1096/34 B1108/28 B1131/36
B1169/27 B1183/05 B1194/21 B1225/11
B1225/17 B1296/07 B1312/08 B1345/23
B1345/27 B1345/27 B1372/04
fool-hardiness (1) C0411/21
fool's (1) B1346/02
fool's-cap (1) C0388/25
foolish (2) A0588/31 B0813/15
foolishly (2) B0808/27 C0181/16
fools (17) A0072/27
A0080/19 A0088/13 A0089/29 A0124/21
A0175/09 A0175/10 A0180/32 A0180/33
A0482/01 A0490/23 A0656/26 B0986/18
B0986/20 B1258/04 B1345/19 B1345/30
foolscap (5) A0274/38
A0485/23 B0809/16 B1141/16 B1141/20
foot (99)
foot-fall (1) A0325/18
foot-hold (1) C0567/18
foot-note (2) A0341/27 A0342/V
foot-notes (1) B0723/07
foot-path (1) A0631/10
foot-race (1) A0128/28
footfall (1) A0311/20
foothold (3) A0697/03
C0075/11 C0183/38
footing (5) A0143/27
A0591/02 B0914/13 B1337/03 C0143/27
footman (6) B0896/21 B0898/25
B0900/18 B1004/32 B1103/12 B1325/06
footpads (1) B0979/04
footstep (5) A0141/09
A0163/07 A0416/17 A0639/09 B0817/17
footsteps (8) A0063/30
A0243/30 B0807/30 B0855/08 B0959/15
B1220/09 B1225/V C0564/37
footstool (4) A0644/16
B0734/33 B0758/08 B0761/14
foppery (1) B0888/23
for (3160)
foraging (1) C0546/38
forbade (6) A0204/02 A0381/18
B0725/09 B0933/23 B1054/31 C0526/27
forbear (14) A0069/14 A0100/22
A0106/31 A0300/26 A0352/16 B0753/19
B0961/09 B1014/19 B1223/17 C0125/25
C0146/32 C0432/08 C0539/18 C0541/22
forbearance (1) B1139/16
forbid (2) A0085/03 B1133/20
forbidden (14) A0035/29 A0044/15
A0144/03 A0195/V A0226/10 A0230/08
A0230/08 A0242/27 A0243/13 A0316/11
A0589/18 A0609/29 A0623/34 A0683/24
forbidding (3) A0704/30
B1269/29 C0155/11
forbids (2) B0773/14 B0773/14
forbore (3) A0325/24
A0552/26 C0066/09
force (108)
forced (68)
forces (4) A0121/03
B0762/22 B1193/10 C0105/02
forcible (8) A0278/32
A0550/29 A0662/01 B0989/21 B1144/21
B1247/04 B1315/07 B1383/11
forcibly (15) A0216/V
A0281/04 A0340/19 A0406/18 A0557/11
A0579/04 B0753/37 B0984/03 B1059/11
B1346/26 C0076/19 C0118/36 C0131/37
C0165/37 C0438/V
forcing (15) A0121/V
A0353/23 A0446/24 A0479/29 A0542/08
A0685/30 B1206/03 B1347/27 C0062/34
C0092/06 C0158/34 C0200/04 C0200/24
C0201/31 C0537/32
fore (2) A0209/M A0218/15
fore (6) A0137/08 B0812/07
B0812/17 B0813/03 C0082/08 C0545/20
fore-chains (1) B0932/12
fore-finger (4) A0071/18
A0630/V B0927/29 C0397/40
fore-ground (1) A0022/10
foreboded (1) A0242/06
foreboding (1) B0814/34
forebodings (2) C0142/24 C0143/12
forebore (10) A0099/15 A0381/15
A0626/18 B0857/29 B0975/09 C0131/11
C0169/33 C0184/19 C0186/17 C0205/17
forecastle (29) A0138/11
C0067/37 C0085/35 C0086/09 C0086/15
C0089/31 C0090/01 C0090/26 C0091/05
C0091/19 C0092/34 C0093/38 C0095/01
C0095/03 C0095/38 C0100/37 C0101/21
C0104/35 C0108/15 C0110/08 C0110/29
C0121/01 C0123/32 C0124/34 C0135/04
C0136/13 C0136/18 C0149/30 C0189/26
forecastle-way (1) C0136/22
forechain-plates (1) C0139/22
forechains (2) C0126/32 C0143/30
foredoomed (1) B0966/05
forefathers (6) A0408/12 A0609/11
A0640/25 B0806/05 B1294/11 B1313/18
forefinger (5) A0380/V
A0387/V B1101/34 C0079/40 C0205/11
forego (2) B1079/11 C0564/22
foregoing (1) C0080/24
foreground (1) A0165/07
forehead (34) A0020/V A0024/02
A0086/27 A0100/04 A0104/13 A0144/18
A0156/14 A0215/04 A0227/11 A0231/24
A0232/19 A0234/28 A0245/25 A0252/13
A0294/08 A0298/V A0312/07 A0316/23
A0328/07 A0641/V A0685/04 A0687/02
B0940/10 B0964/03 B1013/03 B1103/19
B1104/12 B1134/26 B1237/01 C0074/28
C0085/23 C0086/01 C0552/25 C0577/40
foreheads (1) B1190/32
Foreign (1) A0179/16
foreign (14) A0023/28 A0055/18
A0065/02 A0135/23 A0142/25 A0144/27

->A0205/24 A0235/16 A0436/14 A0558/09
A0654/23 B0746/35 B1107/27 B1155/21
foreign-looking (1) A0370/30
foreigner (6) A0540/12 A0549/23
B0862/23 B1190/16 B1193/19 B1300/18
foreman (7) B1371/22
B1371/23 B1372/28 B1372/31 B1373/04
B1373/12 B1373/17
foremast (4) A0586/11
C0115/04 C0115/11 C0136/09
foremost (4) B1044/23
C0136/25 C0201/03 C0579/01
forenoon (6) A0251/18 B0942/11
B1278/33 C0107/32 C0141/15 C0162/32
forerunner (2) B1249/21 C0149/23
foreruns (1) A0427/04
foresail (11) A0586/09
C0099/14 C0102/15 C0104/34 C0106/14
C0106/17 C0106/18 C0106/21 C0115/11
C0123/16 C0163/02
foresaw (1) C0574/34
foresee (2) A0478/26 B0808/25
foreseen (7) A0496/12
A0585/04 A0693/14 B0756/04 B0988/23
B1054/26 B1300/12
foreshadowed (1) A0710/25
foreshadowing (2) A0703/04 B1268/04
foreshortened (1) C0418/12
foresight (2) A0460/09 B0789/19
forest (30) A0028/19 A0029/05
A0045/V A0078/23 A0195/15 A0196/V
A0197/27 A0198/01 A0214/04 A0227/28
A0232/14 A0413/35 A0602/19 A0610/02
A0639/13 B0862/35 B0864/30 B0943/18
B1003/18 B1160/14 B1160/20 B1160/24
B1160/32 B1161/18 B1161/36 B1247/31
B1248/05 B1282/27 C0444/V C0542/12
foresters (1) B0818/29
forests (5) A0600/23
A0601/30 B1160/01 B1331/33 C0412/32
forethought (2) B0825/11 B1005/09
foretold (2) A0233/15 A0459/07
foretopmast (1) C0123/12
foretopsail (5) B0930/12
B0930/22 C0101/36 C0102/16 C0146/24
foretopsails (1) C0106/19
forever (44) A0020/V
A0080/23 A0080/23 A0080/23 A0195/06
A0195/06 A0195/22 A0198/32 A0226/37
A0231/11 A0318/V A0323/19 A0385/04
A0405/12 A0407/40 A0426/07 A0593/34
A0608/21 A0608/24 A0639/27 A0641/10
A0642/06 A0644/01 B0742/24 B0765/07
B0789/16 B0858/03 B0898/30 B0901/24
B0916/30 B0926/36 B0927/01 B0932/27
B0934/10 B0969/08 B1005/22 B1138/24
B1142/22 B1292/08 B1302/03 B1302/04
B1371/01 C0390/24 C0425/13
forevermore (1) A0318/24
forfeit (1) B1169/31
forfeiting (1) A0204/18
forgave (1) B1050/07
forged (1) C0092/18
forgery (1) B1361/32
forget (40) A0057/07
->A0066/33 A0151/17 A0226/04 A0230/02
A0264/13 A0298/01 A0348/29 A0350/16
A0404/03 A0455/04 A0482/12 A0584/36
A0590/17 A0651/12 A0656/01 A0687/31
B0878/17 B0889/13 B0987/35 B1021/07
B1036/01 B1048/17 B1057/18 B1114/04
B1128/26 B1153/08 B1259/33 B1347/01
C0057/28 C0060/39 C0068/20 C0073/10
C0083/06 C0122/34 C0124/19 C0396/34
C0432/18 C0432/41 C0573/27
forgetful (1) A0321/10
forgetfulness (2) A0684/03 C0148/39
forgets (1) B1154/09
forgettest (1) A0044/05
forgetting (6) A0026/20 B0856/21
B1096/34 B1300/24 C0396/08 C0440/V
forgive (5) A0300/06
B0927/12 B1155/03 B1183/06 C0125/10
forgiveness (1) B1050/04
forgot (4) A0318/23
A0644/V B0894/32 C0426/35
forgotten (42) A0121/29 A0152/16
A0155/06 A0156/21 A0156/22 A0161/26
A0212/23 A0264/25 A0278/05 A0311/10
A0313/28 A0378/07 A0402/04 A0409/10
A0410/32 A0431/05 A0494/06 A0536/21
A0592/34 A0611/02 A0629/19 A0643/24
B0726/17 B0727/02 B0761/23 B0876/05
B0891/V B0897/03 B0897/04 B0910/04
B1031/18 B1048/07 B1054/22 B1058/23
B1093/32 B1128/21 B1158/35 B1191/18
B1391/04 C0109/07 C0432/30 C0438/V
fork (8) A0091/21
A0101/09 A0110/25 B0819/03 C0566/09
C0572/01 C0574/09 C0575/09
forked (1) C0173/12
forks (1) C0572/25
forlorn (2) C0072/16 C0200/31
form (144)
formae (1) A0638/M
formal (4) A0428/27
A0497/22 B0899/12 C0179/34
formalities (1) B1075/17
formality (3) A0266/11
B0731/02 B0897/13
formally (4) A0104/02
B1339/31 C0066/40 C0104/02
formation (10) A0242/05 A0267/30
A0282/07 A0283/22 A0312/24 A0313/14
A0691/27 C0184/09 C0193/13 C0193/22
formations (3) A0175/V
A0182/05 A0401/34
formed (79)
former (67)
formerly (19) A0025/23
A0099/05 A0205/11 A0324/14 A0349/04
A0536/19 A0539/14 B0914/06 B1296/28
B1298/01 B1313/29 C0057/05 C0075/31
C0155/22 C0156/12 C0171/18 C0391/19
C0424/36 C0541/30
formidable (4) A0101/15
C0174/13 C0551/20 C0577/35
forming (30) A0045/07 A0154/05
A0294/01 A0631/12 A0638/19 B0734/32
B0746/06 B0758/07 B0761/14 B0808/18

->B0825/23 B0826/06 B0838/01 B1071/15
B1115/11 B1250/22 B1261/09 B1281/25
B1384/37 C0150/37 C0152/32 C0173/14
C0195/10 C0203/37 C0394/19 C0409/30
C0410/19 C0521/07 C0533/16 C0562/20
formless (3) A0190/30
A0318/18 B1225/V
forms (38) A0021/24 A0210/01
A0292/V A0293/28 A0311/30 A0322/24
A0407/36 A0434/21 A0445/13 A0497/30
A0501/V A0593/01 A0601/08 A0614/05
A0615/29 A0624/25 A0682/07 A0689/04
A0706/07 A0707/10 A0710/07 B0725/21
B0773/36 B0807/13 B1037/18 B1037/19
B1037/30 B1037/31 B1184/31 B1214/31
B1271/11 B1272/10 B1275/10 B1280/30
B1321/32 B1340/11 C0150/35 C0522/25
formula (1) A0623/26
formulae (1) B0752/19
formulae (2) A0079/03 A0365/22
forsaken (1) A0645/04
forsooth (1) A0074/03
Forsyth (3) B1069/29
B1075/26 B1081/20
Fort (1) C0525/30
fort (5) B0808/27
B0830/23 B1081/28 C0525/41 C0560/21
Fort/Moultrie (4) B0807/06
B0814/22 B1081/23 B1082/04
Fort/Osage (1) C0528/27
forte (2) A0430/07 B1369/05
forten> (1) A0465/16
forth (63)
forthcoming (4) B0875/12
B0923/37 B1195/04 B1248/33
forthwith (49) A0024/V
A0057/11 A0059/17 A0067/05 A0179/12
A0251/08 A0340/37 A0346/21 A0384/11
A0386/21 A0398/28 A0484/03 A0490/20
A0603/34 A0614/20 A0623/07 A0625/09
A0705/27 B0727/35 B0742/13 B0830/24
B0856/28 B0873/14 B0875/08 B0877/19
B0878/26 B0900/17 B0909/24 B0959/06
B1014/02 B1017/17 B1019/04 B1056/26
B1077/02 B1093/30 B1105/24 B1123/22
B1140/34 B1143/08 B1155/06 B1178/10
B1182/11 B1189/V B1220/03 B1372/15
C0136/18 C0186/10 C0409/08 C0432/47
fortification (1) C0548/04
fortified (2) A0044/28 A0122/03
fortin> (1) A0465/V
fortitude (6) C0060/35 C0075/02
C0076/18 C0117/39 C0120/19 C0145/08
fortnight (10) A0409/16 B0898/22
B1073/25 B1136/37 B1246/02 C0066/32
C0139/11 C0148/31 C0425/35 C0540/10
fortuitous (2) A0703/17 B1268/16
fortunate (16) A0173/28
A0179/10 A0482/10 A0704/35 B0813/07
B0891/25 B1269/34 C0057/03 C0091/23
C0092/09 C0094/33 C0109/23 C0126/26
C0127/26 C0128/39 C0145/36
fortunately (7) A0073/05
A0551/05 B0891/16 C0086/39 C0116/36
C0139/35 C0399/12
Fortunato (14) B1256/01 B1257/02
B1257/05 B1257/10 B1257/22 B1258/18
B1258/27 B1260/07 B1261/17 B1262/10
B1263/04 B1263/11 B1263/17 B1263/19
Fortune (2) B0815/03 B0815/05
fortune (43) A0021/06
A0065/09 A0482/16 A0561/22 A0702/03
A0704/08 A0704/21 A0704/33 A0705/27
B0822/34 B0833/23 B0877/16 B0892/24
B0909/11 B0931/09 B0933/08 B1059/24
B1080/19 B1108/04 B1108/21 B1133/15
B1142/19 B1179/18 B1187/20 B1269/08
B1269/20 B1269/32 B1270/25 B1360/07
C0062/07 C0092/20 C0100/08 C0107/20
C0119/41 C0137/19 C0138/19 C0144/30
C0149/40 C0191/36 C0521/01 C0529/29
C0569/34 C0579/07
fortunes (4) A0531/21
A0539/04 A0539/21 B0931/18
fortunittest> (1) A0468/21
fortunnittest> (1) A0466/21
forty (28) A0043/04
A0176/03 A0182/02 A0581/19 A0582/16
A0689/24 B0865/26 B0877/06 B0877/23
B1077/22 B1092/36 B1160/08 B1164/13
B1248/18 B1334/05 C0064/33 C0142/09
C0175/10 C0181/06 C0187/31 C0193/07
C0194/27 C0391/07 C0394/38 C0412/26
C0442/V C0538/24 C0578/19
forty-eight (4) A0686/14
B0930/14 B1310/10 C0418/48
forty-five (11) A0121/16
A0248/13 A0580/31 A0590/35 B1071/27
B1280/08 B1332/22 B1381/34 C0173/07
C0183/16 C0398/19
forty-four (2) B1192/21 C0161/04
forty-nine (1) C0429/27
forty-one (7) A0705/22
B0839/V B0840/V B0841/V B0842/V
B0842/V B1270/21
forty-pinny> (1) A0466/27
forty-seven (2) C0161/04 C0164/16
forty-sixth (1) C0525/14
forty-third (1) C0525/14
forward (54)
forwarding (1) B1055/17
forwards (5) A0351/06
B0927/16 B1163/38 B1167/16 C0563/04
fosse (1) A0045/04
Fosters (1) B1206/10
fought (4) A0382/30
B0947/12 C0112/39 C0579/30
foul (8) A0191/10
A0249/27 B0796/21 B1044/12 B1046/18
C0184/18 C0389/06 C0410/42
fouled (1) A0584/15
foulness (1) B1261/02
Found (2) A0135/T A0146/10
found (614)
foundation (6) A0028/24 A0197/28
A0269/16 A0366/22 B0828/33 B0834/04
foundations (4) A0578/18
B1192/16 B1322/30 C0182/03
founded (12) A0527/V
B0723/16 B0738/09 B0749/03 B0750/22

->B0773/03 B1070/02 B1128/09 B1358/26
C0095/37 C0400/38 C0427/15
founder (1) B1310/25
foundered (2) A0586/06 C0098/14
foundering (1) C0116/17
fount (1) B1312/24
Fountain (2) B1192/07 B1192/35
fountain (2) A0162/16 B1302/30
fountain-head (1) A0386/21
fountains (2) A0210/33 A0602/25
Four (1) A0119/T
four (188)
four-footed (1) A0127/20
fourpence (1) A0491/04
fours (2) A0126/16 B1182/09
fourteen (6) B0888/02 B0931/17
C0078/31 C0211/V C0528/15 C0539/39
fourteenth (7) B0922/04
B0923/25 B0933/21 C0120/21 C0160/39
C0164/11 C0421/09
fourth (43) A0021/15
A0035/21 A0043/06 A0151/14 A0177/19
A0183/14 A0326/05 A0537/09 A0537/21
A0539/08 A0539/30 A0542/13 A0543/09
A0554/10 A0565/22 A0640/19 A0671/33
A0704/03 B0726/22 B0729/26 B0765/16
B0858/09 B0858/15 B0968/05 B1005/33
B1014/32 B1128/33 B1182/35 B1239/11
B1261/08 B1262/14 B1269/03 B1278/24
B1375/02 C0084/12 C0084/23 C0122/07
C0161/38 C0179/15 C0410/20 C0423/28
C0538/13 C0567/22
fourthly (1) C0427/27
fourths (1) C0098/23
fowl (8) B1164/20
B1165/01 B1372/01 C0176/34 C0191/11
C0191/17 C0570/02 C0572/08
fowl-house (1) B1334/01
fowls (4) B1164/13
B1164/16 C0173/34 C0174/02
fox (2) B0869/22 C0536/23
fox-hunter (2) A0704/02 B1268/32
Fox/river (1) C0528/12
foxes (1) C0572/07
fraction (5) A0655/09
B0878/09 B1168/17 B1350/05 C0404/36
fracto (1) A0681/M
fracture (2) A0553/20 B1107/07
fractured (5) A0057/08
A0067/01 B0958/22 B1106/04 C0201/20
fractures (1) C0573/24
fragile (3) A0227/17
A0232/04 A0604/19
fragility (2) A0379/29 A0641/V
fragment (7) A0685/34
A0686/12 A0687/07 A0688/19 B0957/03
C0109/09 C0420/30
fragmentary (1) C0080/20
fragments (26) A0300/18 A0417/17
A0535/25 A0557/20 A0581/30 A0591/25
A0592/16 A0593/01 B0734/36 B0758/11
B0856/33 B1110/19 B1160/30 C0063/01
C0063/25 C0077/25 C0078/16 C0079/21
C0081/12 C0115/15 C0116/02 C0117/10
C0139/03 C0190/07 C0207/32 C0573/22
fragrance (5) A0344/03
A0351/22 A0428/05 B0807/14 C0543/26
fragrant (1) A0639/14
frail (10) A0404/04 A0682/25
B0890/05 B1073/33 B1115/21 C0061/21
C0063/06 C0095/23 C0201/37 C0202/18
frailness (1) C0134/16
frame (54)
frame-work (3) A0137/33
A0627/29 A0694/15
framed (3) A0165/20
A0303/25 B1093/34
frames (6) A0036/01 A0502/11
A0662/12 A0663/V B0922/23 B1340/01
framework (8) A0689/13
A0693/28 B1071/08 B1071/15 C0127/02
C0136/21 C0179/27 C0202/35
framings (1) A0501/10
France (18) A0386/06 A0495/03
A0538/30 B0888/03 B0957/10 B0958/07
B1002/02 B1006/34 B1008/23 B1009/30
B1031/22 B1129/10 B1135/17 B1137/20
B1141/26 B1378/M C0394/05 C0407/37
France (1) B0913/05
Francis (1) A0037/12
Francois (1) C0430/30
francs (11) A0538/01
A0541/17 A0541/21 A0556/12 B0727/10
B0727/19 B0727/26 B0727/28 B0982/12
B0982/36 B0983/11
Frank (4) C0531/17
C0535/17 C0538/13 C0548/34
frank (10) A0342/03 A0342/V
A0440/30 B0844/04 B0899/14 B0899/22
B0977/02 B1361/08 B1379/31 C0568/17
frank-hearted (1) B1045/02
frankest (1) A0629/08
Frankfort (1) B1164/37
frankincense (1) A0047/01
frankly (6) A0302/07 A0532/09
B1053/18 B1234/28 C0064/36 C0549/36
frankness (3) A0509/11
B0906/12 B1058/13
frantic (6) A0447/17 B0933/23
B0947/11 B0992/19 C0399/05 C0562/38
frantically (5) A0691/09
B0733/13 B0825/22 B0932/13 B0957/34
Fraser (1) A0179/20
fraternity (2) A0708/29 B1273/23
fraud (2) A0485/26 B1300/08
frauds (1) A0489/02
fraudulent (1) B1300/04
fraught (1) C0063/06
fray (1) A0691/32
fraying (1) A0692/03
Frazer's (1) C0527/14
freak (6) A0532/25 B0753/12
B0816/21 B0914/V B0927/08 B0929/36
freaks (4) A0704/15
B1269/14 C0057/30 C0545/34
Frederick (7) A0020/10
A0020/12 A0020/V A0024/10 A0024/24
A0026/V A0029/V
Frederick's (1) A0022/13
free (41) A0126/01

->A0128/23 A0138/V A0251/08 A0266/12
A0269/33 A0312/17 A0692/18 A0692/19
A0694/30 A0695/04 A0695/05 A0695/10
A0703/31 A0711/35 B0874/26 B0965/29
B0969/03 B1019/04 B1019/20 B1075/03
B1075/23 B1159/07 B1194/04 B1222/24
B1268/30 B1277/02 B1299/31 C0081/07
C0119/04 C0119/06 C0135/06 C0135/09
C0136/37 C0143/15 C0160/40 C0182/16
C0202/17 C0535/08 C0560/31 C0564/27
Free/and/Easy (2) A0240/03 A0254/03
freebooters (2) C0553/35 C0555/23
freed (4) B0729/03
B0737/14 C0091/09 C0093/39
freedom (18) A0266/17 A0269/02
A0276/19 A0326/14 A0460/03 B0742/19
B1021/30 B1133/23 B1136/28 C0060/26
C0064/02 C0093/30 C0100/22 C0120/26
C0174/26 C0404/29 C0405/11 C0411/24
freely (22) A0247/30 A0299/23
A0323/12 A0412/17 A0438/24 A0446/22
A0458/28 A0685/08 B0797/04 B0899/05
B1212/02 B1212/29 B1234/31 B1236/07
C0071/21 C0093/03 C0115/33 C0137/08
C0191/21 C0537/13 C0558/36 C0563/40
freeman (1) B0858/02
freer (1) C0407/02
freestone (3) C0572/12
C0573/11 C0573/24
freezing (1) C0147/35
freight (3) C0097/19
C0098/24 C0200/21
freighted (1) A0136/02
French (42) A0035/21 A0096/M
A0267/08 A0344/15 A0344/17 A0344/V
A0352/25 A0384/23 A0470/V A0540/23
A0540/31 A0546/V A0549/30 A0562/22
A0697/11 B0827/28 B0836/09 B0901/18
B0903/22 B0904/05 B0914/14 B0987/06
B1011/04 B1095/08 B1115/29 B1144/20
B1154/21 B1224/10 B1339/33 C0154/26
C0155/24 C0178/08 C0522/40 C0530/38
C0534/03 C0544/08 C0550/04 C0550/27
C0551/03 C0551/09 C0555/12 C0571/07
French-horn (1) A0071/29
Frenchman (26) A0036/18 A0301/09
A0464/T A0532/04 A0533/27 A0535/17
A0540/09 A0541/06 A0541/29 A0542/29
A0543/03 A0549/13 A0549/22 A0549/26
A0549/29 A0550/04 A0560/02 A0560/09
A0560/20 A0561/13 A0561/18 A0563/26
A0565/15 A0602/05 C0150/14 C0392/13
Frenchman's (1) A0567/25
Frenchwoman (1) B0899/21
frenzied (2) A0215/31 A0692/12
frenzy (4) A0447/01
A0461/04 A0671/03 B1005/14
frequency (5) B0727/30
B0837/12 B1030/11 C0421/04 C0422/40
frequent (42) A0026/09 A0144/04
A0212/04 A0244/26 A0282/06 A0295/V
A0344/16 A0404/18 A0412/22 A0435/23
A0541/14 A0614/21 A0642/28 A0683/08
B0764/32 B0771/29 B0836/19 B0850/20
B0850/30 B0856/13 B0926/34 B0940/V
->B0941/19 B0945/28 B0988/24 B1101/07
B1169/04 B1180/10 B1277/29 B1279/27
B1282/05 B1337/05 C0065/11 C0087/37
C0097/12 C0102/09 C0137/26 C0410/42
C0412/27 C0532/35 C0560/04 C0571/30
frequented (11) A0065/14
A0096/02 A0296/13 A0320/10 A0512/31
A0514/18 B0853/36 B0898/18 B1310/07
C0147/32 C0155/24
frequenting (2) A0539/26 B0771/27
frequently (83)
frequents (1) A0479/15
fresco (1) B1179/08
frescos (1) A0209/15
fresh (23) A0026/30
A0162/09 A0343/29 A0445/02 A0544/20
A0585/13 A0694/16 B0741/05 B0741/11
B0760/16 B0956/08 B0960/10 B1160/27
C0072/07 C0138/10 C0170/30 C0176/33
C0177/01 C0177/05 C0538/20 C0539/12
C0545/11 C0559/03
fresh-water (1) C0137/30
freshened (7) B0930/12
B0930/17 B1078/03 B1078/21 C0102/14
C0139/30 C0160/33
fresher (1) C0559/04
freshets (1) C0530/04
freshly (3) B0949/25
B1114/17 C0058/33
freshly-spread (1) B0853/26
freshness (2) A0532/07 B0893/01
fret (1) C0438/V
fretted (5) A0087/20
A0321/21 A0401/13 A0428/09 B1282/25
Frey/Herren (1) B0870/29
fricandeau (1) A0113/30
fricandeaux (1) A0096/09
fricasee (1) A0094/04
fricaseed (2) A0093/27 A0093/29
Fricassee (2) A0175/17 A0181/07
fricassee (1) A0097/07
fricassee (1) A0113/28
fricasseed (3) A0113/07
A0113/08 A0113/11
friction (3) A0692/09
B1035/27 C0064/19
Friday (1) B1241/35
friend (195)
friend's (9) A0264/37
A0624/23 B0817/04 B0819/28 B0822/21
B0924/26 B1119/M C0068/40 C0093/01
friendless (1) B0963/08
friendliness (3) A0473/15
C0560/24 C0566/01
friendly (9) A0056/24
A0066/14 A0101/V B0769/V B1223/18
C0170/08 C0177/23 C0387/13 C0550/09
friends (70)
friendship (15) A0433/09
A0436/05 B0807/18 B0850/21 B0851/04
B0922/10 B0949/06 C0089/07 C0095/26
C0151/40 C0175/27 C0181/19 C0537/25
C0561/01 C0569/02
frieze (1) C0573/10
fright (7) A0589/34

->B0851/22 B0912/14 B1182/05 B1350/12
  C0073/01 C0182/19
frighten (1) C0562/13
frightened (7) A0090/13
  A0578/05 B1014/28 C0059/19 C0187/34
  C0427/04 C0578/28
frightening (1) B1165/09
frightful (16) A0021/V
  A0137/31 A0197/22 A0217/V A0538/29
  A0547/26 A0559/31 B0851/37 B1165/07
  C0117/15 C0120/08 C0125/16 C0128/16
  C0133/31 C0143/14 C0148/35
frightful-looking (1) C0142/39
frightfully (2) C0142/07 C0424/11
frigid (2) A0533/17 C0171/19
frigidity (1) C0425/36
Frinch> (1) A0470/09
Frinchman> (6) A0464/21 A0466/02
  A0467/02 A0467/18 A0468/06 A0469/21
frind> (2) A0464/24 A0467/05
fringe (2) A0501/22 C0543/18
fringed (3) A0501/13
  A0663/06 C0552/39
frisked (1) A0348/14
frisking (1) A0373/28
frivolity (3) A0528/23
  A0692/10 B1316/05
frivolous (10) A0097/08 A0211/30
  A0212/12 A0212/19 A0212/24 A0444/19
  A0529/16 A0687/19 B1299/15 C0564/17
fro (44) A0081/11
  A0140/10 A0144/31 A0158/01 A0195/11
  A0219/08 A0246/04 A0252/15 A0318/19
  A0411/23 A0412/03 A0416/30 A0513/16
  A0514/33 A0515/22 A0582/09 A0590/04
  A0603/14 A0614/04 A0672/09 A0672/23
  A0673/26 A0674/02 A0675/20 B0749/09
  B0749/20 B0753/24 B0762/06 B0797/15
  B0817/03 B0858/18 B1005/13 B1238/16
  B1322/09 C0072/22 C0077/21 C0084/06
  C0112/20 C0120/35 C0124/37 C0125/18
  C0153/23 C0412/06 C0542/11
Frobisher, Joseph (1) C0526/06
frock (8) A0439/08
  A0485/05 B0730/28 B0735/11 B0735/13
  B0762/10 B0762/11 B0763/02
frocks (1) A0623/V
Frog (2) A0467/22 A0469/14
frog (7) A0078/28
  A0469/26 B1012/04 B1012/07 B1015/V
  B1346/20 B1372/03
frog-like (1) A0065/20
frog-man (1) B1020/30
frogged (1) A0509/29
Frogpondium (1) B1370/29
Frogs (4) B0879/13
  B0879/17 B0879/24 B1055/22
frogs (1) A0054/09
Froissart (11) B0887/19
  B0887/24 B0888/04 B0897/29 B0912/23
  B0912/27 B0912/29 B0912/30 B0913/03
  B0913/03 B0913/26
Froissart, Napoleon B. (3) B0913/09
  B0913/27 B0914/03
frolic (4) A0564/30
->B1352/13 C0058/17 C0058/25
frolicksome (1) A0665/03
frolics (1) B1349/35
from (2410)
front (31) A0196/12
  A0367/03 A0367/11 A0367/25 A0368/28
  A0400/19 A0429/15 A0486/10 A0515/24
  A0539/28 A0542/09 A0542/11 A0542/12
  A0546/25 A0551/21 A0562/08 A0613/14
  A0627/34 B0864/35 B0889/04 B0892/24
  B1143/12 B1336/04 B1336/12 B1337/19
  B1338/16 B1339/14 C0067/15 C0075/10
  C0162/35 C0566/05
frontal (1) C0577/40
frontem (1) A0043/M
fronting (6) A0154/06 A0245/19
  A0248/03 A0415/06 B1280/05 C0122/28
frontis (1) A0298/V
fronts (1) B1338/04
frost (2) C0534/35 C0534/38
frosts (1) C0563/35
frosty (1) A0056/09
froth (2) A0438/13 A0594/07
frothing (2) A0587/07 B1011/32
frown (2) B1372/04 B1373/08
frowned (2) A0429/04 A0662/04
frowningly (1) C0164/10
frowns (1) A0509/29
frows (2) A0175/24 A0181/21
froze (1) A0140/01
frozen (5) A0217/V
  B1131/10 B1131/10 C0159/20 C0159/24
Frozen/Ocean (1) C0417/24
fru (2) B0819/14 B0821/28
frugal (1) B1178/07
fruit (5) A0609/29
  B1004/33 B1292/30 C0542/15 C0543/19
fruiterer (7) A0534/25
  A0534/28 A0534/28 A0534/32 A0535/07
  A0535/10 A0535/22
fruitful (1) A0434/29
fruitless (11) A0055/05
  A0064/23 A0213/09 A0266/27 A0325/01
  A0411/24 A0495/V A0537/12 A0582/02
  C0077/11 C0192/17
fruits (3) A0162/17
  B0768/26 C0190/10
frustrate (1) A0445/18
frustrated (6) A0102/12 A0693/16
  B0755/07 B1246/21 B1273/32 C0104/18
frxg (1) B1374/15
frxwn (1) B1374/17
Fry (1) B1134/04
frying (1) A0101/10
Fuci (1) B1163/12
fudder (1) B0819/12
fuddled (1) A0055/25
fudge (1) A0628/11
fuel (6) A0447/08 C0066/06
  C0143/02 C0161/16 C0166/14 C0170/30
fugitive (2) A0566/07 C0558/20
fugitive's (1) A0565/21
fugitives (1) B0807/07
fuit (2) A0382/15 A0681/M
fulfil (4) A0300/11

->B0862/25 B1158/09 C0065/26
fulfilled (9) A0252/06
A0408/13 A0491/11 B0724/17 B0772/06
B1058/17 B1152/18 B1178/11 B1273/30
fulfilling (2) A0097/15 A0443/06
fulfillment (2) A0461/01 B1163/07
fulfilment (9) A0043/07
A0067/22 A0252/07 A0707/19 B1153/25
B1272/17 B1371/20 C0066/18 C0177/36
full (252)
full-grown (1) C0178/33
full-length (4) A0103/06
A0158/09 A0164/11 A0166/13
fuller (4) A0100/07
A0196/16 A0313/04 C0063/38
fuller's (1) C0173/17
fullest (12) A0074/12
A0105/25 A0249/04 A0313/04 B0748/26
B0824/04 B1226/16 B1237/25 B1271/09
B1314/23 C0190/05 C0414/40
fullness (2) A0312/26 B1096/35
fully (99)
fulness (4) A0312/V
B0889/27 B1215/02 C0411/28
fulsomely (1) B1133/22
fulvous (1) A0559/20
Fum-Fudge (7) A0172/03
A0174/02 A0177/28 A0178/03 A0179/13
A0181/22 A0183/24
Fum-Fudge/University (1) A0175/27
fumbled (1) A0090/01
fumes (8) A0122/13
A0245/29 B0851/31 B0874/21 B0961/21
C0059/40 C0128/36 C0182/31
fun (4) A0124/02
A0433/19 B1019/14 C0058/25
functionaries (1) B0737/10
functionary (4) A0568/10
B0983/14 B0986/15 C0390/29
functions (5) A0613/02
A0616/02 B0955/29 B1187/13 B1187/17
fund (2) A0053/27 A0530/13
fundamental (1) A0108/22
funds (3) A0114/07
A0241/24 A0653/14
funeral (10) A0057/14 A0153/V
A0319/13 A0340/14 A0631/21 B0789/M
B0956/22 B0958/28 B0960/06 B1179/25
funereal (2) A0153/26 B1279/26
funeris (1) A0681/M
funeste (1) B0993/26
fungi (1) B1293/08
fungi (2) A0400/07 A0408/15
fungus (1) B1163/22
fungus (2) A0687/03 B0759/19
funnel (9) A0580/29
A0590/20 A0591/11 A0594/05 B1102/31
B1105/05 B1162/17 B1381/31 B1382/14
funnel-cap (1) B1106/20
funniest (1) A0387/02
funnin (1) B0818/24
funny (1) B1291/20
Fur (2) C0525/09 C0529/17
fur (10) A0444/16 B0819/14
B1375/19 C0151/07 C0154/06 C0155/20
->C0526/03 C0552/08 C0552/22 C0575/33
fur-trader (1) C0087/03
Furies (3) A0053/25
A0349/17 B1142/05
furies (2) A0053/13 A0062/30
furious (19) A0023/23
A0059/26 A0067/17 A0227/20 A0232/07
A0461/11 B0795/01 B0825/21 B0947/02
B0959/05 B1143/22 B1178/12 B1262/14
C0082/19 C0106/09 C0108/11 C0387/M
C0390/19 C0563/07
furiously (17) A0300/V
A0351/10 A0416/19 A0447/13 A0671/12
A0692/18 B1056/32 B1349/12 B1362/23
C0082/33 C0118/18 C0144/05 C0144/17
C0387/21 C0396/40 C0549/19 C0557/23
furled (1) A0136/30
furlong (1) B1279/08
furnace (3) B0834/32
B1168/04 B1362/18
furnaces (2) A0610/23 A0671/01
Furneaux (1) C0158/29
furnish (7) A0125/19
A0204/15 A0496/04 B0879/09 B1069/13
B1206/11 C0530/16
furnished (15) A0440/V
A0500/17 A0613/27 A0662/08 A0671/33
B0862/25 B0876/02 B0904/10 B1069/21
B1073/36 B1138/36 B1163/33 C0101/29
C0156/03 C0522/31
furnishing (4) A0440/06
A0532/13 B0839/01 C0191/06
Furniture (2) A0495/T A0495/V
furniture (30) A0079/32 A0087/28
A0189/32 A0320/24 A0367/21 A0373/25
A0401/14 A0411/20 A0495/V A0496/29
A0497/14 A0497/22 A0499/16 A0501/05
A0503/08 A0537/25 A0551/29 A0567/15
A0591/27 B0854/05 B0872/13 B0979/18
B0979/30 B0980/01 B0980/09 B0980/19
B1339/27 B1340/07 C0099/27 C0393/09
furores (1) A0681/M
furrener> (2) A0464/21 A0466/02
furrenner> (3) A0467/02
A0468/06 A0470/10
Furrier (1) B1293/24
furrowed (1) A0104/13
furrows (1) A0196/28
furs (7) A0444/04
A0444/06 B1293/25 C0536/21 C0547/32
C0558/04 C0575/34
further (28) A0062/25
A0067/V A0366/V A0539/07 A0550/V
B0738/07 B0763/19 B0892/20 B0916/01
B0965/V B1093/02 B1106/10 B1219/14
C0061/26 C0072/07 C0078/05 C0094/39
C0103/36 C0106/29 C0108/07 C0125/03
C0133/30 C0140/30 C0185/10 C0198/30
C0199/21 C0390/07 C0524/21
furtherance (3) B0733/20
B1223/26 C0066/14
furthering (2) B0745/17 B0815/24
furthermore (3) A0250/22
B0732/16 B0744/21
furtively (1) B0895/17

fury (43) A0025/03
A0029/20 A0102/04 A0102/18 A0137/09
A0138/03 A0138/22 A0213/14 A0215/27
A0339/31 A0373/27 A0412/18 A0415/17
A0447/08 A0567/10 A0578/18 A0580/11
A0581/33 A0587/04 A0587/26 B0764/21
B0795/11 B0797/15 B0851/23 B0856/14
B1006/26 B1050/30 B1248/05 B1318/08
B1374/29 C0073/05 C0075/33 C0104/32
C0108/08 C0112/39 C0115/19 C0149/15
C0162/35 C0190/05 C0200/16 C0422/38
C0556/38 C0578/22
Fuseli (1) A0405/27
fusion (2) B1362/20 C0167/34
fuss (3) B0812/26
B0818/23 B0820/18
fustian (2) A0086/29 B0969/05
fusty (1) A0649/02
fut (2) A0033/20 A0033/20
fut> (2) A0464/17 A0464/20
futile (7) A0028/28
A0402/15 A0704/27 B0897/07 B1036/34
B1073/14 B1164/33
futility (3) A0405/02
B1296/32 B1314/01
futmen> (1) A0470/20
Future (2) B0724/30 B0773/27
future (27) A0057/01
A0066/27 A0124/17 A0144/20 A0162/22
A0228/09 A0403/12 A0456/20 A0478/30
A0601/25 A0608/M A0611/16 B0772/20
B0858/07 B0898/31 B1037/09 B1131/21
B1304/28 C0110/41 C0134/04 C0152/20
C0393/16 C0539/16 C0549/05 C0555/24
C0558/13 C0576/04
futurity (1) A0141/23
fxr (1) B1374/12
fxwl (1) B1374/14
fxxl (1) B1374/17
fy (1) B1164/17
G (2) A0282/07 B0905/27
g (1) B0838/21
G-- (18) A0546/08 B0728/09
B0731/16 B0736/26 B0737/04 B0737/26
B0808/27 B0974/15 B0976/35 B0978/03
B0979/09 B0981/23 B0982/01 B0982/17
B0983/24 B0988/28 B0990/12 C0533/11
G--/M** (7) C0530/40
C0535/42 C0538/42 C0538/43 C0540/32
C0541/40 C0576/40
G--, Lieutenant (1) B0814/30
G--'s (1) B0975/04
G--n (8) A0292/V
A0293/12 A0294/02 A0295/05 A0296/08
A0296/V A0297/05 A0298/01
G'zette (1) B1373/01
gable (6) B1336/28 B1336/31
B1337/23 B1338/04 B1338/16 B1338/19
gables (2) A0367/10 B1336/19
gad-abouts (1) A0495/05
Gad-Fly (10) B1127/10 B1128/02
B1132/09 B1132/28 B1133/08 B1133/25
B1133/29 B1139/18 B1140/34 B1141/35
gagged (1) B0753/28
gagne (1) A0037/09

gaieties (1) A0674/11
Gaillard, Petit (1) B1012/16
gaily (2) B0795/28 C0565/27
gain (10) A0487/31 A0539/34
A0663/26 B0756/16 B0838/08 B0963/16
B1006/19 B1020/05 C0103/05 C0114/30
gained (16) A0137/17
A0350/33 A0435/26 A0460/08 A0511/01
A0561/17 A0610/16 B0797/04 B0931/04
B0941/18 B1017/28 B1178/19 C0103/02
C0201/32 C0407/34 C0557/28
gaining (8) A0211/18
A0493/05 B0756/29 B0840/31 B0947/10
C0102/11 C0114/14 C0393/13
gains (1) B1321/23
gainsay (1) B0744/35
gainsayed (1) A0602/08
gait (8) A0141/11
A0434/34 A0437/29 A0448/04 A0507/35
A0536/26 B1258/33 B1346/08
gaiters (1) A0508/35
gala (1) A0318/07
galaxy (3) B1139/03
B1301/02 B1301/36
gale (52)
gale's (1) C0115/17
gales (4) B1079/01
C0064/24 C0098/14 C0159/16
Gall (1) B1191/16
gall (4) A0092/01
A0111/13 B1131/31 B1300/20
gallant (4) A0245/V
A0249/15 A0349/19 A0381/20
gallant-looking (1) C0554/11
galled (1) A0434/20
Gallery (1) B1070/07
gallery (2) A0209/17 A0428/31
galley (2) C0124/21 C0169/13
galling (1) A0444/13
Gallipago (5) C0137/22
C0137/30 C0174/11 C0176/27 C0200/22
Gallipagos (2) C0137/28 C0170/16
gallon (3) A0251/05
C0136/01 C0533/41
gallons (9) A0125/18
A0252/22 C0137/21 C0138/10 C0163/08
C0393/29 C0415/20 C0535/04 C0535/05
gallop (2) A0630/05 C0555/05
galloped (3) C0553/31
C0554/16 C0554/27
galloping (2) A0247/01 C0557/23
Gallows (1) B0855/34
gallows (6) A0058/04 A0068/25
A0069/14 A0070/06 A0079/23 C0061/37
Galvanic (2) A0059/29 A0144/V
galvanic (8) A0067/19
A0439/24 A0664/V A0682/06 B0948/15
B0959/23 B0959/26 B1181/25
Galvanism (1) B1187/03
galvanized (1) C0189/37
gamble (1) A0623/23
gambler (2) A0440/21 A0443/28
gambler's (1) A0441/04
gamblers (1) A0509/13
gambols (1) B0809/23

game (35) A0037/13
A0441/20 A0443/30 A0528/17 A0528/23
A0529/03 A0529/22 A0529/29 A0530/06
A0530/07 A0655/29 B0870/22 B0984/06
B0984/07 B0989/28 B0989/32 B1350/11
B1380/31 C0534/32 C0535/13 C0535/19
C0540/05 C0542/40 C0559/40 C0560/15
C0562/14 C0563/35 C0566/20 C0566/37
C0567/06 C0568/12 C0570/14 C0572/01
C0572/06 C0576/03
game-keeper (1) C0433/01
game's (1) B0824/18
gammoned (1) B1019/14
gander's (1) B1141/16
gang (33) B0734/06
B0735/29 B0749/05 B0753/27 B0757/03
B0757/13 B0757/20 B0757/32 B0757/33
B0761/02 B0763/20 B0763/29 B0763/30
B0763/33 B0764/17 B0765/09 B0767/08
B0767/12 B0767/14 B0767/18 B0767/28
B0768/06 B0768/14 B0768/18 B0768/20
B0769/12 B0770/07 C0090/38 C0102/11
C0102/17 C0102/40 C0103/33 C0108/34
gangs (3) B0765/12
B0767/10 C0558/21
gangway (2) C0086/21 C0086/39
gannets (1) C0174/03
ganzas (3) C0431/07
C0431/11 C0432/43
gaping (3) A0028/01
A0651/16 B0980/13
garb (1) C0056/08
garbled (1) B1233/07
Garcia (2) A0089/18 A0089/32
Garcia, Pedro (4) A0085/02
A0085/12 A0090/09 A0092/29
Garcio, Alfonzo (1) A0542/25
Garden (1) A0702/T
garden (19) A0367/03
A0368/16 A0603/06 A0702/M A0710/03
A0711/06 B0853/20 B0853/20 B0864/37
B0968/14 B1095/02 B1154/15 B1162/10
B1267/M B1275/07 B1276/07 B1302/31
B1303/31 C0543/36
garden-gate (1) A0295/10
Gardening (1) B1329/33
gardening (6) A0709/29 A0710/17
A0711/04 B1274/31 B1275/21 C0530/11
gardens (2) B1007/18 C0574/02
Gargantua (2) B1234/05 B1345/14
garish (1) A0511/02
garment (9) A0100/10
A0444/08 A0692/08 A0696/31 B0730/25
B0762/16 B0765/19 B0766/32 B1049/25
garments (9) A0103/24
A0218/28 A0349/02 A0403/05 A0510/17
B0946/28 B0961/22 B0964/32 B1157/05
garnered (1) A0135/05
Garnier (1) A0079/03
garret (6) A0057/13 A0067/31
B1128/01 B1336/34 B1362/08 B1362/15
garrets (1) A0542/18
garter (2) B0745/29 B0745/32
garter's (1) B0746/31
garters (7) A0340/36
->B0745/30 B0745/34 B0746/26 B0746/27
B0747/01 B0747/04
gas (33) A0071/32
A0400/V A0458/31 A0498/28 A0513/35
B0742/08 B0742/26 B0742/35 B0743/17
B1034/11 B1071/01 B1071/03 B1073/05
B1073/05 B1073/08 B1074/11 B1074/14
B1074/14 B1074/32 B1076/09 B1076/31
B1079/28 B1080/23 B1298/25 C0393/33
C0393/34 C0394/09 C0394/14 C0394/38
C0402/32 C0403/01 C0403/11 C0403/19
gas-lamps (1) A0510/35
gas-lighted (1) A0499/25
gas-litten (1) A0499/V
gaseous (3) A0412/32
A0461/07 B1321/30
gases (1) A0460/24
gash (4) B0960/20
C0119/19 C0169/14 C0169/18
gashes (1) A0430/V
gasp (3) A0411/27
A0514/07 C0121/32
gasped (16) A0139/25
A0252/16 A0373/06 A0461/09 A0628/30
A0676/29 A0684/V A0692/24 A0696/05
B0797/10 B0947/23 B0967/08 B1226/07
C0111/21 C0124/11 C0397/08
Gasperitch/Iane (1) B1361/34
gasping (7) A0072/04
A0437/20 B1348/30 B1372/29 C0083/02
C0135/23 C0406/16
gaspingly (1) A0614/01
gasps (3) B0743/24
B0743/25 B0743/26
gasteropeda (2) C0178/09 C0178/21
gate (15) A0023/16
A0043/04 A0045/03 A0429/05 A0540/02
A0540/03 B1281/18 B1282/10 B1282/24
B1282/27 B1282/34 B1332/17 B1335/08
B1338/11 B1338/13
gate-way (4) A0029/16
B1003/25 B1282/V B1282/V
gates (7) A0062/01
A0075/11 A0128/08 A0670/17 A0681/M
B1160/25 C0561/34
gateway (3) A0537/13
A0539/34 A0546/18
gather (5) A0297/20
A0303/19 B0823/33 C0147/29 C0560/13
gathered (12) A0197/22
A0228/25 A0233/06 A0356/09 B0902/11
B1370/09 C0077/34 C0133/36 C0155/27
C0178/10 C0178/11 C0420/23
gathering (14) A0046/22 A0141/31
A0154/23 A0154/24 A0216/16 A0218/24
A0530/13 A0530/15 B0770/01 C0060/02
C0177/27 C0181/36 C0188/25 C0410/13
gathers (2) A0643/01 B1222/17
gaudiness (1) C0538/41
gaudy (5) A0165/14
A0499/14 A0672/15 B0908/V C0543/29
gaudy-colored (1) A0247/17
gaunt (4) A0071/14
A0245/21 A0675/08 C0531/26
gauntlet (1) A0584/22

gauntleted (1) A0413/32
gauze-like (1) A0152/29
gave (195)
gay (15) A0152/18
A0440/30 A0446/27 A0640/34 A0643/12
A0644/14 A0672/31 A0673/10 A0677/02
B0768/33 B0862/36 B0898/06 B0943/18
B0947/03 C0125/28
Gay-Lussac (1) C0401/06
gayest (1) A0152/17
gaze (1) B0889/29
gaze (15) A0022/26
A0087/34 A0153/08 A0590/30 A0639/25
A0663/28 B0893/08 B0893/13 B0894/33
B1057/22 B1212/16 B1237/08 B1330/01
B1381/32 C0565/03
gazed (42) A0022/19 A0157/08
A0191/05 A0210/10 A0211/02 A0234/17
A0318/V A0326/08 A0329/26 A0398/10
A0401/25 A0417/11 A0437/24 A0515/25
A0580/08 A0583/07 A0590/18 A0602/02
A0602/04 A0641/V A0663/12 A0666/02
A0689/31 A0690/06 A0696/V B0795/01
B0826/17 B0889/V B0890/14 B0909/27
B0932/23 B0944/21 B0948/30 B0960/23
B0964/36 B1021/08 B1057/08 B1330/03
B1348/30 B1354/05 C0405/29 C0438/V
gazelle (1) A0313/04
gazes (2) A0227/14 A0232/01
Gazette (13) A0058/29
A0075/02 A0546/31 A0547/14 B1369/29
B1369/35 B1371/07 B1371/09 B1371/11
B1371/12 B1371/14 B1371/17 B1381/22
gazette (1) B1369/23
Gazette's (1) B1371/18
Gazetteer (1) A0537/04
gazing (9) A0035/29
A0190/19 A0217/V A0326/20 A0411/08
A0546/16 B1278/08 C0126/20 C0425/12
Ge-Henna (2) A0226/19 A0230/17
gear (1) C0163/07
geese (2) C0151/29 C0570/16
gelasma (Gr.) (1) A0159/05
gelatinous (3) B1240/22
C0142/38 C0178/13
gelebt (1) A0150/V
geliebet (1) A0150/V
gem (5) B0877/07
B0908/03 B1137/04 B1137/17 B1144/02
gemmary (1) B1257/10
gems (2) B0945/14 B1160/12
gendarme (5) A0539/32
A0546/33 B0733/26 B0733/27 B0748/21
gendarmes (1) A0537/14
gender (1) B1096/36
gendering (1) C0178/27
genera (2) A0311/30 B1190/27
General (28) A0269/19
A0378/03 A0379/19 A0380/02 A0380/19
A0381/02 A0381/11 A0382/08 A0382/13
A0382/24 A0382/28 A0382/32 A0383/19
A0383/30 A0384/19 A0385/02 A0385/08
A0385/32 A0386/06 A0386/22 A0386/27
A0388/24 A0388/29 A0389/10 A0389/17
A0697/11 B1304/17 B1304/35

general (183)
General's (1) A0389/01
generalities (2) A0610/15 B0955/18
generality (2) B0745/24 B1277/17
generalization (3) A0708/13
B1273/09 B1313/08
generalizing (1) A0507/31
generally (64)
generally-educated (1) B1316/26
generally-received (1) C0202/09
generals (1) B1346/28
generate (2) B1038/03 B1072/05
generated (2) B0743/17 C0393/34
generation (2) B0742/08 B0742/26
generic (2) B1039/29 C0172/34
generical (1) B1190/25
generis (1) A0493/06
generosity (7) A0043/12
A0044/03 A0044/22 A0264/10 B1054/18
B1128/05 B1209/10
generous (5) A0440/30
B0899/23 B1055/11 B1137/13 B1138/10
generously (2) B1021/27 B1209/02
Geneva (1) B1078/11
Genii (1) B1283/14
genii (4) A0198/23
B1158/03 B1158/10 B1169/14
genio (1) A0599/M
Genius (1) A0053/12
genius (61)
geniuses (1) A0482/21
Genoa (1) A0100/11
Genoese (1) B1329/19
Gens/de/Feuilles (1) C0551/32
Gens/des/Feuilles (1) C0551/09
Gens/du/Lac (1) C0551/03
gentaal> (2) A0466/14 A0468/05
gentaalest> (1) A0468/17
genteel (1) B1153/22
Gentiles (1) A0046/09
gentilhomme (1) C0430/39
gentility (1) A0509/30
gentle (52)
gentle-footfall (1) A0325/V
gentleman (133)
gentleman-like (1) B1143/10
gentleman's (4) A0072/14
A0339/26 B0879/22 B1011/06
gentlemanly (2) A0440/20 B1183/12
gentlemen (51)
gentleness (4) A0312/25
B1108/01 B1139/16 B1139/18
gentler (3) A0510/32
B1015/14 B1332/08
gentlest (1) B1385/29
gentlewoman (1) B1015/29
gently (28) A0033/14
A0217/V A0218/29 A0228/03 A0294/10
A0353/18 A0553/26 A0610/32 A0614/26
A0639/24 A0650/08 A0682/11 B0789/23
B0865/17 B0866/15 B0927/29 B0929/23
B1075/23 B1076/04 B1189/30 B1238/16
B1282/22 B1330/18 B1333/12 B1385/16
C0129/27 C0197/02 C0198/27
gently-flowing (1) B0944/30

gentry (2) A0508/29 A0509/08
Genuine (1) B1127/13
genuine (7) A0338/18
A0340/23 A0346/12 A0346/20 B0766/07
B1144/06 B1304/05
genus (2) A0534/27 A0654/08
genus (3) B0808/18
B1250/18 C0543/26
geographer (3) A0638/14
B1291/08 B1310/06
geographer's (1) A0578/35
geography (1) C0524/14
geological (6) A0459/15 B1160/23
B1273/33 C0402/15 C0422/27 C0424/35
geologist (1) A0175/25
geometrical (1) B0746/15
geometrician (1) B1310/33
geometry (3) B1164/01
B1301/31 C0404/38
George (5) A0086/12
A0097/12 A0112/27 B0887/V B1070/18
Georges (1) C0146/37
Georgia (3) C0157/35
C0160/14 C0162/10
geranium (1) B1340/19
geraniums (1) B1334/22
germ (2) A0580/25 B1270/35
German (21) A0018/V
A0091/24 A0099/10 A0101/08 A0135/06
A0225/18 A0229/16 A0297/02 A0344/11
A0345/09 A0357/04 A0473/20 A0473/28
A0506/01 A0542/02 A0542/03 A0549/31
A0549/32 B0827/28 B1360/19 C0432/48
Germanic (2) A0473/19 A0473/27
Germanism (2) A0473/16 A0473/19
Germans (1) B1115/08
Germany (3) A0473/30
B1031/22 B1140/25
germen (2) B1163/28 B1163/30
germinated (1) B1190/28
germination (3) B1190/26
B1190/28 B1247/01
gesticulate (1) A0565/16
gesticulated (1) A0508/07
gesticulating (1) A0123/02
gesticulation (1) B1260/16
gesticulations (9) A0508/10
B0797/13 C0123/40 C0200/15 C0205/10
C0397/40 C0554/17 C0555/19 C0557/24
gesture (3) A0439/12
A0513/09 C0131/30
get (151)
gets (6) A0486/04 A0488/V
B0871/20 B0872/03 B1154/10 C0570/27
getting (115)
gewohnlich (1) B0723/M
ghastliest (1) A0533/01
ghastlily (1) A0665/15
ghastliness (1) B0814/27
ghastly (41) A0036/09
A0152/V A0195/10 A0196/08 A0196/11
A0197/07 A0215/19 A0217/V A0244/02
A0245/28 A0321/17 A0322/24 A0327/21
A0330/13 A0398/13 A0402/07 A0406/04
A0407/38 A0410/34 A0413/04 A0509/36
->A0579/06 A0590/23 A0672/17 A0683/20
A0685/14 A0695/32 B0764/33 B0771/15
B0855/34 B0859/V B0955/19 B0963/25
B1057/19 B1208/08 B1223/09 B1223/09
C0072/13 C0072/34 C0182/31 C0405/31
ghastly-looking (1) A0244/30
Gheber (1) A0035/13
ghee (1) A0136/03
ghost (11) A0295/11
A0357/02 A0605/09 B0764/19 B1109/16
B1115/35 B1142/04 B1222/23 B1225/18
B1303/10 B1374/28
ghostly (1) A0506/04
ghosts (3) A0080/32
A0144/31 B1345/10
giant (6) A0318/V A0427/01
A0639/10 A0640/14 B1076/20 B1300/19
giants (1) B1248/04
gib (3) B0812/06 B0812/08 B0814/14
gibbering (4) A0416/01
B0964/04 B0964/11 B1014/30
gibbous (1) C0429/15
Gibraltar (1) C0443/V
giddiest (1) A0672/32
giddiness (3) A0227/14
A0232/01 B1292/20
giddy (10) A0046/21 A0140/16
A0154/08 A0227/13 A0232/01 A0349/26
A0578/06 A0578/31 B1226/09 C0073/12
giebt (1) B0723/M
gift (2) A0241/34 A0242/01
gifted (2) A0044/14 A0478/24
gifts (3) A0702/03
A0704/08 B1269/07
gigantic (56)
Gil-Blas (1) B1105/08
gilded (4) A0160/17
A0664/09 B0945/17 B1180/30
gilden (1) B0945/V
gilding (1) A0502/V
gill (4) C0081/09
C0082/29 C0138/34 C0145/30
gilt (9) A0267/11
A0271/26 A0273/25 A0368/14 A0368/25
A0372/25 A0509/16 B1180/13 C0123/09
giltwork (1) A0501/18
gimlet-dust (1) B0980/11
gimlet-hole (4) A0552/01
A0553/19 B0985/32 B0985/34
gimlets (2) B0989/03 C0148/09
Gin (1) A0515/02
gin (2) B0812/26 B0854/04
gin-nurtured (1) B0851/26
gingerly (1) B0910/22
gingham (1) B1185/33
gintaal> (1) A0469/02
gintleman> (5) A0464/02
A0464/09 A0465/15 A0467/03 A0469/10
girded (1) A0047/01
girdle (3) B0893/16
C0552/06 C0552/30
girdled (2) A0639/33 A0670/16
girdles (1) C0184/15
girl (42) A0567/06 A0644/18
A0653/10 A0653/13 A0663/21 A0664/04

->B0723/10 B0725/14 B0726/01 B0726/17
B0727/29 B0729/23 B0731/11 B0733/07
B0735/23 B0735/26 B0735/31 B0745/08
B0746/05 B0746/22 B0747/04 B0750/07
B0755/21 B0757/02 B0757/15 B0757/18
B0763/33 B0767/21 B0769/01 B0769/13
B0769/24 B0924/12 B0934/01 B0957/13
B1008/05 B1014/09 B1091/02 B1346/24
B1349/04 B1349/32 B1354/15 C0146/37
girl's (6) A0627/34 B0734/01
B0734/24 B0738/32 B0750/18 B0766/04
girlhood (2) B0914/10 B1122/35
girls (3) A0510/03
B0923/20 C0118/14
Gironne, Eymeric de (1) A0409/06
girt (1) B1280/05
girth (1) C0163/29
girting (1) A0136/15
git (2) B0811/32 B0815/10
git> (3) A0466/15
A0469/19 A0470/03
gits> (2) A0467/07 A0467/V
gitting (1) B0812/05
gitting> (1) A0464/11
giunge (1) B0905/23
giv'd> (6) A0467/V A0468/08
A0468/15 A0468/22 A0468/23 A0469/05
give (127)
gived> (3) A0467/16
A0467/26 A0470/21
given (141)
givers (1) B1136/29
gives (28) A0280/13
A0283/23 A0285/06 A0340/15 A0379/18
A0428/10 A0502/V A0559/04 A0626/12
B0832/23 B0838/21 B0838/27 B0875/03
B0908/15 B0910/11 B0976/22 B0976/29
B1016/01 B1152/32 B1164/39 B1164/40
B1168/18 B1168/19 C0194/01 C0521/09
C0522/13 C0565/37 C0571/28
giving (67)
Gizbarim (4) A0043/10
A0044/26 A0047/10 A0047/28
gizzard (1) B1129/V
gizzards (1) B1373/23
glad (12) A0279/27
A0355/19 A0381/01 B0820/05 B0873/12
B0965/18 B1379/08 C0102/02 C0176/11
C0395/11 C0398/08 C0404/26
gladdens (1) A0708/08
glades (1) B1329/06
gladiatorial (1) A0123/28
gladly (3) A0054/16
A0567/23 C0531/28
glance (48) A0022/14
A0022/21 A0068/18 A0141/03 A0155/09
A0164/25 A0227/12 A0231/26 A0267/04
A0270/20 A0283/24 A0313/V A0401/23
A0404/11 A0415/12 A0511/07 A0511/09
A0529/10 A0531/V A0557/02 A0558/27
A0578/16 A0582/20 A0587/37 A0587/38
A0627/29 A0651/31 A0684/10 A0689/28
B0728/30 B0755/23 B0759/22 B0810/27
B0829/06 B0840/05 B0887/05 B0932/18
B0983/15 B1181/30 B1221/08 B1297/05
->B1314/09 C0087/26 C0112/07 C0151/21
C0422/27 C0438/V C0524/23
glanced (10) A0035/08 A0155/22
A0164/V A0587/23 A0602/23 A0663/22
B0728/07 B0895/17 B0991/11 B1194/28
glances (14) A0163/06 A0215/02
A0314/16 A0326/14 A0410/19 A0442/23
A0510/05 A0530/11 A0545/21 A0567/08
B0894/19 B0898/21 B0899/07 C0198/03
glancing (6) A0158/01 A0312/21
A0535/30 B1105/18 B1190/33 B1372/25
Glanvill (2) A0314/23 A0319/30
Glanvill, Joseph (2) A0310/M
A0318/V
glare (21) A0022/23
A0026/32 A0029/23 A0139/32 A0145/02
A0157/04 A0190/05 A0326/12 A0498/25
A0512/01 A0626/29 A0673/20 A0696/11
B0823/05 B0826/16 B0865/07 B1009/01
C0112/20 C0142/31 C0205/29 C0205/40
glared (6) A0087/26 A0217/V
A0695/32 A0696/04 B0814/28 B1353/31
glaring (8) A0693/30
B0944/05 B1248/29 B1301/23 B1330/35
C0073/02 C0107/39 C0122/32
glaringly (2) A0672/13 B1385/26
Glass (4) C0156/12
C0156/18 C0156/26 C0158/18
glass (54)
glass-house (1) C0428/34
glass-like (1) C0559/36
Glass's/Islands (1) C0162/22
glasses (18) A0103/31 A0106/16
B0728/31 B0888/17 B0907/03 B0909/04
B0910/21 B0910/V B0911/01 B0911/V
B0915/27 B0916/12 B1020/19 B1056/29
B1102/13 B1105/10 B1110/21 C0067/32
glassy (5) A0215/10
A0235/26 A0294/09 A0602/32 B1237/19
glauber (1) C0553/02
Glaumba (1) B1161/26
glazed (4) A0245/29
A0546/19 A0567/V C0059/26
gleam (4) A0417/06
A0687/13 B0944/19 C0136/09
gleamed (8) A0023/05
A0152/24 A0156/14 A0663/V A0695/33
B0827/14 B1338/35 B1348/10
gleaming (16) A0151/V
A0234/06 A0565/21 A0580/28 A0590/23
A0676/24 B0826/14 B0907/05 B0943/16
B1248/15 B1278/V B1279/07 B1283/02
B1317/30 B1333/22 C0072/35
gleams (5) A0036/08
A0163/07 A0401/09 B1259/03 B1280/V
glean (3) B0734/04
B1304/24 C0575/21
gleaned (2) B1104/29 B1358/03
glee (9) A0249/18
A0487/24 A0664/31 A0665/03 B0858/19
B1352/08 C0538/15 C0543/39 C0560/15
gleichfalls (1) B0723/M
Glendinning (5) A0440/36
A0441/19 A0442/05 A0442/15 A0443/08
glens (1) A0323/16

Gliddon (14) B1179/28 B1180/31
B1182/06 B1183/01 B1183/06 B1184/03
B1184/16 B1184/18 B1184/26 B1184/32
B1186/06 B1188/05 B1188/10 B1193/16
Gliddon's (1) B1185/10
glide (2) A0143/32 A0144/31
glided (2) A0604/22 A0639/29
glides (4) A0604/V
B1034/33 B1282/17 B1282/35
gliding (1) A0567/21
glimmer (5) B0829/34
C0077/18 C0080/09 C0183/04 C0397/32
glimmering (2) C0077/14 C0111/31
glimpse (26) A0093/14 A0112/26
A0124/09 A0299/19 A0374/09 A0397/06
A0404/24 A0412/28 A0446/31 A0512/05
A0566/10 A0566/11 A0580/02 B0771/31
B0819/09 B0842/30 B1156/15 B1299/02
B1330/28 B1334/33 B1338/05 C0108/02
C0183/12 C0418/47 C0543/20 C0553/08
glimpses (5) A0078/30
A0253/19 A0638/08 B1280/15 C0065/25
glistened (2) A0143/15 B0821/31
glistening (2) A0217/V A0692/31
glitter (5) A0499/20
A0499/29 A0500/12 A0500/12 A0673/20
glittering (4) A0353/19
A0690/16 A0691/11 B1283/12
gloaming (1) B0901/V
globe (24) A0426/05
A0457/27 A0458/26 A0583/04 A0656/28
A0657/11 B0821/31 B1159/06 B1160/22
B1180/22 B1190/30 B1213/37 C0160/05
C0180/11 C0182/03 C0201/18 C0396/07
C0400/31 C0405/05 C0408/02 C0429/23
C0432/19 C0432/24 C0432/35
globes (2) B1301/03 B1301/05
globular (2) B1163/26 B1163/28
gloom (42) A0122/15 A0139/06
A0151/20 A0152/07 A0175/22 A0181/19
A0210/23 A0217/V A0233/22 A0243/16
A0397/07 A0398/14 A0401/18 A0403/33
A0405/05 A0442/21 A0457/03 A0473/16
A0532/14 A0579/04 A0603/17 A0605/01
A0605/07 A0626/29 A0662/04 A0687/13
B0901/08 B0906/28 B0927/17 B0940/16
B0963/36 B1246/21 B1247/26 B1279/26
B1280/01 B1280/27 C0068/39 C0072/35
C0078/03 C0080/25 C0081/31 C0151/21
gloomily (3) A0021/23
A0139/22 C0136/07
gloominess (1) B0865/10
gloomy (25) A0080/24
A0087/22 A0153/09 A0154/02 A0156/30
A0189/23 A0209/13 A0217/V A0320/11
A0348/01 A0351/26 A0410/27 A0411/20
A0437/V A0514/18 B0926/06 B1003/19
C0065/15 C0071/13 C0075/41 C0122/12
C0128/23 C0140/16 C0142/24 C0201/23
gloomy-looking (1) A0321/20
glories (6) A0071/03 A0175/23
A0528/05 A0639/14 A0643/23 B0863/10
glorifying (1) B1139/31
glorious (30) A0020/V A0036/10
A0128/04 A0158/18 A0158/18 A0198/22
->A0247/20 A0252/11 A0263/23 A0263/32
A0316/21 A0339/30 A0352/33 A0406/34
A0498/19 A0556/24 A0556/25 A0638/04
A0644/V A0707/12 B1162/04 B1222/10
B1272/11 B1278/10 B1294/03 B1301/23
C0058/10 C0124/06 C0146/15 C0575/11
gloriously (5) A0071/32
A0093/30 A0113/V A0639/27 A0663/13
Glory (4) A0127/02
A0127/24 A0128/01 A0128/07
glory (13) A0158/03
A0407/13 A0407/29 A0590/25 A0600/17
A0600/18 A0640/05 A0641/11 A0665/12
B1278/11 B1302/25 B1332/35 C0421/40
gloss (1) A0379/04
glossy (12) A0087/17
A0156/V A0267/11 A0312/11 A0428/33
A0502/01 A0603/11 B0815/16 B0862/36
B1180/26 B1332/33 C0151/13
glove (3) A0101/08
B0871/04 B0992/06
Glover's (1) B1101/03
gloves (6) A0034/19 B0734/34
B0758/09 B0761/33 B1186/01 B1362/25
glow (13) A0138/24
A0227/27 A0232/13 A0328/07 A0644/V
A0683/02 A0696/03 A0696/34 B0826/16
B1261/03 B1318/01 C0079/22 C0080/01
glow-worm-like (1) B0829/35
glowed (7) A0603/06
A0673/13 A0707/26 A0712/07 B1163/01
B1272/26 B1277/12
glowing (11) A0248/V
A0405/27 A0407/16 A0412/31 A0640/34
A0643/12 A0696/07 B0832/30 B1362/18
C0065/15 C0443/V
glowworm (1) B0898/02
Gluck (1) C0427/25
glueing (1) B0980/13
glut (1) C0555/31
glutinous (2) B1240/22 C0566/25
gluttony (1) A0097/24
gnarled (2) A0428/01 B0818/31
gnashed (2) B0913/17 B1353/31
gnashing (1) A0567/05
gnawed (2) C0545/20 C0545/39
gnawing (2) A0623/11 C0128/28
gnawings (1) A0081/31
Gnomes (1) B1283/14
go (167)
go-ahead (1) B1091/31
goaded (2) B0856/24 B1158/08
goading (3) A0397/19
A0706/24 B1271/26
goal (2) A0316/10 A0535/16
goat (6) A0124/14 B0833/02
B0833/08 B0833/10 B0835/05 C0566/22
goats (5) B0833/08
C0155/31 C0156/23 C0559/41 C0560/01
gobble (1) B0821/02
goblet (7) A0166/24
A0325/21 B1104/20 B1348/05 B1348/12
B1348/29 B1349/03
goblet-ful (1) A0325/14
gobletful (1) A0325/V

goblets (3) A0165/05
A0165/16 A0189/33
goblin (1) A0599/M
goblins (1) B1128/28
God (117)
god (10) A0045/28 A0045/29
A0124/12 A0146/09 A0190/31 A0190/32
A0312/V A0371/14 A0387/08 B1188/12
God's (15) A0465/09
A0469/11 A0470/19 A0534/V A0588/33
B0873/28 B1139/11 B1191/33 B1220/02
B1242/24 B1385/17 C0059/18 C0083/23
C0426/13 C0529/21
Goddess (1) A0568/21
goddesses (1) B0911/11
Goddin (1) C0067/22
Godhead (2) A0601/21 B1214/33
godlike (1) A0348/07
Gods (2) A0357/01 B1145/19
gods (7) A0240/M
A0351/03 A0351/15 B0911/11 B1127/06
B1188/06 B1188/09
Godwin, William (2) A0055/01
A0064/04
goes (17) A0338/18
A0340/13 A0343/34 A0379/32 A0628/34
A0650/26 B0740/07 B0766/25 B0850/19
B0871/18 B0874/30 B1152/07 B1208/24
B1299/09 B1312/33 B1373/20 C0574/19
Goethe (1) A0150/V
Gog (1) A0119/01
goggle (1) A0248/14
goggling> (2) A0464/22 A0469/04
going (99)
Golconda (1) B0835/11
Gold (1) B1380/06
gold (61)
gold-fish (1) B0850/25
gold-flowered (1) A0502/21
gold-seeker (1) B0823/28
gold-threaded (1) A0502/24
Gold-Bug (1) B0806/T
Golden (1) B1303/15
golden (27) A0033/04
A0036/01 A0087/22 A0165/11 A0175/23
A0215/V A0316/18 A0321/29 A0325/08
A0406/34 A0426/08 A0503/05 A0590/25
A0602/25 A0641/01 A0643/13 A0643/22
A0662/13 A0672/08 B0827/13 B0828/08
B0955/34 B1212/19 B1280/26 B1283/07
B1318/07 B1385/21
golly (1) B0824/09
gondola (4) A0151/24
A0152/11 A0153/26 A0155/22
Gondola, Convulvulus (1) A0205/13
gondolier (1) A0151/28
gone (77)
gongs (1) B0945/17
Gonzales (3) C0431/05
C0432/10 C0432/43
Gonzales, Dominique (1) C0430/28
Good (2) A0558/V B1017/09
good (375)
good-by (1) B1003/05
good-bye (1) A0655/06
good-for-nothing (2) A0346/14
C0067/33
good-for-nothing-to-nobody (1) B1372/02
good-hearted (2) A0482/11 B0926/20
good-humored (1) B1009/21
good-humoredly (1) B0993/20
good-humour (2) C0089/04 C0101/11
good-humouredly (1) A0091/21
good-looking (1) B0888/18
good-natured (1) B1045/02
good-tempered (1) C0531/23
good-will (1) B1158/25
Good/Hope (8) A0655/23
B1021/11 C0148/20 C0149/11 C0150/12
C0156/06 C0156/17 C0525/25
Goodfellow (24) B1045/22
B1047/18 B1049/11 B1050/01 B1050/07
B1050/08 B1050/11 B1050/16 B1050/V
B1050/V B1052/07 B1052/27 B1052/33
B1053/33 B1054/03 B1054/16 B1054/24
B1055/30 B1057/10 B1057/18 B1058/23
B1058/31 B1059/01 B1059/06
Goodfellow, Charles (3) B1044/24
B1055/14 B1055/27
Goodfellow, Charley (1) B1044/25
Goodfellow, Old Charley (4) B1044/25
B1045/09 B1046/19 B1055/01
Goodfellow's (6) B1053/05 B1053/08
B1054/30 B1056/18 B1058/12 B1059/18
goodly (5) A0250/27
A0347/28 C0124/27 C0388/12 C0436/V
goodness (5) B0910/26
B0910/28 B1116/10 B1370/05 B1370/14
goods (14) B0872/27 B0873/06
C0180/01 C0534/08 C0534/14 C0534/18
C0534/20 C0534/24 C0535/09 C0540/03
C0559/25 C0571/08 C0575/34 C0575/43
goodwill (1) C0175/27
goole (3) B0809/02
B0813/02 B0818/15
goole-bug (6) B0812/22 B0813/02
B0813/03 B0826/26 B0826/26 B0826/27
goose (3) B1103/02
B1372/07 C0151/23
goose-quill (1) B1133/07
Goose's (1) B1130/29
gooseberries (1) C0576/07
Goosetherumfoodle (24) B1126/T
B1129/26 B1130/09 B1130/13 B1130/28
B1130/36 B1131/01 B1131/32 B1134/20
B1136/12 B1136/33 B1137/29 B1138/26
B1143/25 B1143/30 B1143/33 B1143/34
B1143/35 B1144/04 B1144/10 B1144/12
B1144/13 B1144/23 B1145/09
goot (3) B0912/17
B0912/17 B1104/18
Gordon (2) C0067/17 C0067/32
Gore (1) B1051/15
gore (4) A0125/18
A0218/29 A0319/10 B0859/11
gores (1) B1071/16
gorge (24) A0639/21
A0643/14 B0865/08 B0942/28 B1279/14
B1279/17 B1280/04 C0180/35 C0180/37
C0181/33 C0183/23 C0183/35 C0184/30

->C0184/33 C0184/38 C0191/30 C0192/12
C0549/25 C0553/12 C0553/21 C0553/31
C0559/09 C0567/14 C0572/34
gorgeous (23) A0020/V
A0036/V A0210/32 A0316/09 A0320/22
A0322/12 A0503/01 A0641/07 A0643/23
A0663/V A0705/11 B0862/04 B0862/31
B0907/V B1138/23 B1162/09 B1248/20
B1280/10 B1332/35 B1337/11 B1337/30
B1340/17 B1347/08
gorgeously (3) B0945/15
B1334/22 B1350/25
gorges (2) B1076/17 C0552/37
Gorgias (3) A0341/23
A0342/V A0507/14
gorging (1) C0125/01
gose (1) B0812/01
gospel (1) C0531/36
gossamer (5) A0402/10
A0682/24 B0850/21 B0890/V B1207/36
gossip (3) B1007/06
B1390/20 C0427/10
gossiping (1) B1291/15
got (74)
Gotham (3) A0292/V
A0294/V A0298/V
Gothic (9) A0349/22
A0366/17 A0400/23 A0409/10 A0428/09
A0430/02 A0671/25 A0710/01 B1275/04
Gott (5) A0373/09
B1102/06 B1103/29 B1104/15 B1104/16
gotten (3) A0092/36
A0109/11 C0062/17
Gottingen (2) A0086/02 A0205/22
gouge (3) A0388/19
B0824/12 B1373/22
gouges (1) C0148/09
Gould (1) A0281/01
gould> (1) A0465/11
Gould H. F. (1) A0280/37
gout (4) A0033/V
A0253/01 A0253/21 B0906/20
gouty (2) A0247/11 A0252/13
governed (2) B1299/27 C0203/35
government (21) A0019/16
A0203/04 A0547/30 A0704/29 B1018/32
B1018/33 B1031/18 B1250/07 B1269/28
B1299/37 B1300/10 B1300/29 C0150/16
C0156/05 C0156/09 C0207/20 C0391/24
C0523/02 C0525/17 C0526/21 C0527/30
governor (4) A0491/08
B1142/20 C0156/13 C0156/19
gown (2) B0732/25 B0734/19
grabs (1) A0136/09
Grace (7) A0035/01
A0036/19 A0036/25 A0037/11 A0037/13
A0037/20 A0182/16
grace (36) A0033/13
A0034/04 A0035/V A0036/23 A0037/09
A0037/V A0176/15 A0179/32 A0180/01
A0250/14 A0250/15 A0250/15 A0266/18
A0271/20 A0280/25 A0357/03 A0383/07
A0383/24 A0641/V A0644/V A0652/07
A0704/09 B0889/22 B1109/16 B1128/28
B1130/05 B1170/01 B1184/27 B1195/06
->B1208/05 B1269/08 B1281/04 B1333/02
B1338/31 B1346/34 C0174/26
grace's (1) A0035/08
graceful (17) A0154/14
A0210/23 A0247/03 A0269/34 A0312/14
A0349/14 A0379/30 A0385/06 A0503/05
A0603/10 B0945/31 B1004/07 B1096/21
B1330/06 B1332/10 B1332/21 B1340/13
gracefully (3) A0640/08
B0890/06 B1138/14
gracefulness (1) B0889/21
graces (6) A0065/27 A0298/V
A0464/11 A0508/29 B0924/26 B1051/35
gracious (5) A0629/03
B0910/26 B0910/28 B1019/35 B1370/05
graciously (1) A0249/10
gradation (8) A0435/17
A0610/18 A0667/32 B0963/07 B0966/10
B1034/10 B1299/32 C0406/12
gradations (5) A0431/12
B1033/20 B1033/24 B1222/30 B1224/30
grade (3) A0509/28
B0769/01 B0989/23
gradu (1) A0097/07
gradual (12) A0225/05
A0229/05 A0231/21 A0404/17 A0408/19
A0510/32 B0962/24 B1076/33 B1282/09
C0143/40 C0411/05 C0422/13
gradually (52)
graduated (1) A0205/22
Graham (1) B1380/18
grain (10) B0980/11 B1162/32
C0098/21 C0098/22 C0098/26 C0098/29
C0098/35 C0098/38 C0099/08 C0118/13
grains (1) C0404/33
grammar (4) B1114/31
B1114/31 B1114/33 B1383/12
grammarians (2) B1114/32 B1114/34
Grampus (11) C0053/T
C0065/32 C0066/21 C0066/36 C0087/33
C0097/05 C0099/25 C0099/40 C0101/09
C0106/20 C0137/23
Grand (3) A0175/04
A0181/25 A0279/16
grand (3) A0506/M
B0987/01 C0430/31
grand (10) A0649/03 A0653/12
B0862/17 B0942/31 B1152/22 B1152/29
B1152/33 B1152/33 B1347/01 B1351/15
grand-uncle (2) A0651/22 A0652/23
Grand/Canal (2) A0151/24 A0157/01
Grand/Portage (1) C0526/37
Grand, Bouffon Le (1) B1012/33
grandames (1) B1044/06
grande (1) B0912/26
grande-daughter (1) B0913/V
grandest (1) B1166/05
grandeur (8) A0157/V
A0158/V A0320/11 A0590/29 A0641/11
A0662/04 B1278/14 B1278/17
grandfather (5) C0057/03
C0066/03 C0067/17 C0521/30 C0522/29
grandiloquence (1) B0843/34
grandiloquent (1) B0815/22
Grandjean (1) B1107/16

Grandjean's (1) A0064/27
grandly (1) A0630/19
grandmother (5) B0914/04
B0914/07 B0915/10 B0916/01 B0916/24
grandmother's (1) B0914/23
granite (16) A0322/04
B0864/32 B1161/35 B1261/16 B1261/25
B1279/35 B1303/33 B1331/20 B1331/29
B1337/02 C0192/02 C0192/32 C0193/20
C0194/06 C0196/04 C0199/01
grano (1) B1364/03
Grant (1) C0428/35
grant (9) A0183/23
A0279/05 A0638/16 B0767/09 B0987/02
B1078/31 B1186/23 B1314/19 B1314/22
Grant's (1) C0428/35
granted (12) A0339/15
B0736/31 B0834/22 B0903/15 B0906/25
B0985/31 B1016/06 B1183/19 B1190/10
B1220/15 C0401/01 C0413/22
granting (4) A0478/05
B0749/28 C0072/01 C0402/19
granulated (2) C0193/11 C0199/02
grape (8) A0085/M
C0180/18 C0185/05 C0540/09 C0542/14
C0542/38 C0542/39 C0543/19
grape-vine (1) B1337/19
grape-vines (1) B1334/34
grapes (1) A0085/M
graphic (1) B0828/33
grapnel (3) B1073/36
B1081/27 B1081/31
grapple (2) A0397/23 A0456/22
grasp (24) A0073/30
A0146/07 A0154/11 A0351/18 A0458/09
A0555/01 A0559/07 A0561/23 A0567/07
A0586/22 A0589/31 A0695/05 B0763/34
B0841/22 B0856/26 B0965/02 B1226/06
C0085/20 C0138/27 C0142/30 C0181/36
C0197/41 C0198/10 C0579/15
grasped (10) A0219/03 A0563/20
A0565/24 B0814/25 B0851/27 B0964/10
B0964/24 B0983/14 B1317/19 C0127/16
grasping (2) A0586/10 B1108/22
grass (42) A0155/02 A0243/33
A0514/29 A0578/30 A0599/M A0603/08
A0603/21 A0639/08 A0640/01 A0640/06
A0640/28 A0641/16 A0642/05 A0643/04
A0643/23 A0644/05 B0735/08 B0759/02
B0759/06 B0759/11 B0759/15 B0903/26
B0943/15 B0944/21 B0961/25 B1052/10
B1281/25 B1329/20 B1329/20 B1331/08
B1333/07 B1333/26 C0150/28 C0176/37
C0177/02 C0192/21 C0541/34 C0542/12
C0543/14 C0543/21 C0543/25 C0575/40
grass-grown (1) B1003/17
grass-hopper (1) C0556/13
grasshopper (6) A0466/13 C0556/27
C0556/29 C0557/18 C0557/19 C0558/09
grasshoppers (2) A0382/05 A0382/05
grate (1) C0534/34
grated (1) B0797/18
grateful (7) A0354/16
A0356/04 A0483/26 C0083/36 C0139/36
C0146/11 C0398/32
gratification (7) A0706/06
B0850/18 B1003/02 B1155/10 B1371/14
C0166/30 C0532/16
gratified (6) A0090/18 A0268/04
B1136/22 B1189/03 B1277/06 B1391/13
gratify (6) A0024/23 A0034/V
A0250/01 A0279/24 A0709/33 B1275/01
gratifying (2) A0265/33 A0270/05
grating (7) A0410/10
A0414/30 A0416/13 A0697/08 B1349/08
B1353/26 C0061/20
gratis (1) B1092/14
gratitude (7) A0045/26
A0346/29 B0875/21 B1107/14 C0061/08
C0131/21 C0563/29
Grave (2) A0101/V A0181/14
grave (41) A0054/21
A0080/25 A0153/05 A0216/28 A0217/V
A0218/26 A0218/V A0268/26 A0302/01
A0316/22 A0329/15 A0369/04 A0457/08
A0507/03 A0527/V A0612/13 A0616/09
A0616/28 A0617/06 A0631/19 A0642/02
A0675/09 A0676/30 A0682/10 A0682/23
A0703/01 B0789/M B0815/11 B0823/19
B0856/34 B0957/24 B0957/29 B0958/32
B0959/01 B0959/10 B0959/13 B0960/06
B0963/32 B0967/32 B1249/13 B1268/01
gravel (4) A0429/13
B1006/11 B1160/27 C0396/27
gravelly (1) C0575/27
gravely (2) A0534/08 C0541/16
graven (3) A0189/05
B0853/14 C0208/27
graves (4) A0603/24
B0964/23 B0964/25 B0965/03
gravest (1) A0627/10
graveyard (1) B0961/13
gravitating (2) C0403/06 C0432/07
gravitation (7) B1297/32
B1317/10 C0403/24 C0404/28 C0422/07
C0422/08 C0432/33
gravities (1) B0741/20
gravity (21) A0080/04
A0294/14 A0300/27 B0741/04 B0741/08
B0741/13 B0742/05 B0742/12 B0892/29
B1003/30 B1136/05 B1301/03 B1301/24
B1301/27 B1302/15 B1321/24 B1382/04
B1382/05 C0402/31 C0424/32 C0556/14
gray (33) A0106/22
A0143/16 A0144/19 A0195/22 A0196/10
A0196/11 A0196/12 A0209/13 A0210/29
A0214/03 A0214/23 A0328/24 A0398/12
A0400/01 A0403/29 A0408/11 A0430/29
A0438/26 A0485/04 A0502/01 B0888/13
B0901/08 B0942/34 B0966/10 B1337/32
B1339/09 C0072/18 C0151/12 C0203/23
C0204/35 C0389/19 C0555/11 C0557/07
gray-mottled (1) C0408/22
grayer (1) A0144/20
grayish (1) C0192/40
grayish-white (1) C0416/41
grayness (1) C0204/36
grazed (1) B1278/34
grease (2) B1128/32 C0552/05
greasy (1) A0561/07

Great (3) A0120/22
B1193/18 C0407/36
great (666)
Great/Bend (1) C0559/10
Great/Britain (4) A0164/04
A0261/21 A0440/10 C0525/12
Great/Sioux (1) C0548/09
Great/Spirit (1) C0558/03
greater (90)
greatest (72)
greatly (74)
greatness (3) A0183/24
B1126/12 B1130/03
Grecian (3) A0035/20
B0909/06 B0914/10
Grecque (2) A0101/02 A0109/32
Greece (5) A0175/29
A0181/24 A0190/31 B1091/35 B1130/20
greedily (1) C0170/18
greedy (3) A0057/24
A0068/07 B0768/20
Greek (25) A0091/22
A0110/26 A0124/21 A0157/20 A0160/V
A0189/11 A0312/26 A0336/04 A0337/06
A0337/06 A0340/09 A0344/12 A0346/01
A0346/07 A0346/12 A0536/09 A0536/V
A0612/37 A0622/28 A0641/V B0889/28
B1091/33 B1092/04 B1128/30 B1340/04
Greeks (3) A0097/22
A0160/03 B1095/07
Greely (14) C0102/20 C0102/40
C0112/41 C0113/17 C0531/16 C0562/02
C0562/16 C0562/40 C0563/11 C0579/01
C0579/05 C0579/19 C0579/24 C0579/27
Greely, John (7) C0531/18
C0535/23 C0557/38 C0560/03 C0561/40
C0575/08 C0577/12
Greely, Meredith (2) C0535/16
C0548/34
Greely, Poindexter (4) C0535/17
C0538/13 C0548/30 C0548/32
Greely, Robert (1) C0570/15
Greelys (5) C0537/06
C0541/05 C0548/31 C0549/05 C0558/33
Green (2) A0018/14 C0403/35
green (59)
Green/Bay (1) C0528/12
Green, Charles (1) B1073/11
Green's (1) B1074/13
greenest (2) A0406/25 B1215/26
greenish (1) C0394/03
Greenwich (1) C0524/29
greet (2) B0901/13 B1107/26
greeted (2) A0401/20 B1030/33
greeting (1) B1325/05
Grenouille (1) A0183/02
Gresset (1) A0408/30
grew (121)
Grey (3) A0079/06
A0079/06 A0079/06
grey (6) A0328/V A0537/30
A0557/16 A0600/23 A0638/08 C0065/21
gridiron (1) A0101/08
grief (18) A0217/V A0233/22
A0316/12 A0320/21 A0410/29 A0589/02
->A0589/32 B0732/32 B0733/12 B0794/07
B0933/23 B1046/27 B1047/05 C0074/31
C0089/18 C0122/09 C0140/02 C0552/03
griefs (1) A0608/23
grieve (3) A0365/20
A0626/23 A0671/06
grieved (6) A0642/04 B0852/03
B0902/03 B1135/25 B1169/29 C0563/36
grievous (2) B1155/02 C0124/28
grim (7) A0244/13
A0316/25 A0403/18 A0426/M B0963/27
B0966/26 B0969/14
grimace (1) A0058/37
grimaces (1) C0397/41
Grimm (1) C0402/21
Grimm's (1) C0394/32
grin (6) A0098/16 B0870/02
B0871/15 B0871/15 B0871/23 B1103/15
grind (2) A0489/31 A0489/32
grinders (1) A0490/01
grinding (1) C0081/38
grinning (7) A0161/17
A0371/03 A0371/16 B0808/15 B0911/15
B0916/21 C0425/10
grins (2) B0871/16 B0871/21
grip (1) C0399/07
gripings (1) C0191/20
grisette (3) B0723/14
B0726/04 B0745/16
grisette (1) B0773/03
Griswold's (1) B1101/05
gritting (1) B1349/22
grizzly (2) C0087/16 C0191/12
groan (6) B0794/06 B0794/06
B0794/07 B0856/27 C0086/02 C0182/11
groaned (5) A0174/19
A0179/34 A0317/03 A0373/09 A0458/23
groans (2) A0542/07 A0614/06
grocery (2) A0484/01 A0484/02
grog (1) C0103/29
groggy (1) A0487/05
Grogswigg (1) A0366/07
groin (1) C0119/21
grooming (1) A0027/12
grooms (2) A0023/29 A0027/16
grope (3) B1262/26
C0068/37 C0182/37
groped (4) A0081/30
A0141/16 A0687/26 C0070/27
groping (7) A0316/15
A0686/01 A0687/06 B0943/22 C0077/13
C0094/12 C0127/15
gross (10) A0298/V A0547/31
A0624/22 B0768/11 B0773/33 B1055/29
B1122/11 B1207/32 B1383/21 C0428/19
grosser (3) A0515/31
B1033/21 B1033/22
grossest (2) B1314/01 C0071/19
grossly (8) A0271/24
A0458/19 A0667/06 A0705/35 B0987/23
B1186/19 B1270/35 C0429/06
Grotesque (1) B1386/08
grotesque (17) A0099/V
A0120/15 A0122/02 A0240/11 A0245/V
A0295/29 A0298/07 A0303/V A0321/22

->A0430/14 A0473/01 A0532/15 A0673/20
B1260/18 C0093/05 C0437/V C0537/40
grotesquely (1) B0945/16
grotesqueness (1) A0681/12
grotesquerie (2) A0293/02 A0558/08
grotesquerie (1) A0690/29
grotesques (1) A0157/20
grottoes (2) A0502/05 B1179/03
ground (82)
ground-glass (3) A0499/06
A0503/09 B1340/15
ground-moles (2) B1298/15 B1316/24
groundlessness (1) B1247/09
grounds (28) A0428/20
A0473/17 A0498/11 A0583/27 A0584/11
A0584/21 A0594/15 B0760/26 B0817/14
B0958/29 B0959/17 B0980/28 B0980/29
B1004/18 B1123/02 B1208/04 B1340/12
C0107/29 C0177/33 C0566/15 C0566/18
C0568/04 C0572/16 C0575/08 C0576/06
C0577/16 C0577/21 C0577/26
groundwork (1) B0837/06
group (30) A0143/09 A0153/24
A0675/V A0676/01 A0676/03 B0823/07
B0898/12 B1332/20 B1333/13 B1353/13
C0053/T C0137/28 C0150/11 C0150/20
C0154/24 C0154/30 C0155/09 C0155/23
C0156/31 C0157/28 C0167/25 C0170/32
C0171/31 C0174/09 C0202/04 C0202/29
C0203/07 C0203/35 C0204/02 C0539/02
groups (6) A0240/11 A0240/13
B0945/28 B1282/04 B1370/08 C0176/21
grouse (2) C0540/07 C0542/41
grove (1) C0544/20
grovelled (1) B1110/17
grovelling (3) A0710/20
B1275/23 C0182/06
groves (6) A0640/06 B0755/14
B0759/32 B0901/08 B0943/27 C0546/38
grow (27) A0143/07
A0146/06 A0327/09 A0402/10 A0426/14
A0500/22 A0500/22 A0503/V A0591/29
A0600/20 B0759/11 B0962/25 B1096/24
B1156/08 B1163/11 B1207/04 B1212/13
B1222/27 B1318/02 B1345/07 B1363/22
C0392/17 C0395/22 C0444/V C0546/17
C0552/25 C0561/20
growing (35) A0079/38
A0226/21 A0230/20 A0458/17 A0459/20
A0500/19 A0604/08 A0616/21 A0643/18
A0652/V B0760/03 B0794/15 B0810/36
B0826/30 B0904/02 B1006/26 B1017/27
B1089/15 B1126/01 B1130/32 B1160/16
B1163/15 B1163/16 B1282/03 B1350/28
C0070/35 C0150/25 C0155/12 C0181/34
C0192/24 C0197/28 C0401/28 C0417/08
C0560/07 C0575/19
growl (7) B0909/19
B1372/05 C0081/32 C0082/15 C0113/06
C0549/34 C0577/27
growled (5) A0174/20
A0179/35 A0183/03 A0253/04 B1372/31
growling (1) C0113/31
grown (17) A0064/21
A0214/V A0330/10 A0434/21 A0442/04

->A0614/18 A0616/17 A0623/21 A0665/26
B0725/03 B0735/08 B0759/02 B0759/06
B0941/24 B1127/32 B1369/22 C0073/32
grows (4) A0545/25
A0683/05 B1162/33 B1223/02
growth (3) A0623/21
B0850/14 C0171/18
Gruff (5) A0487/06
A0487/15 A0487/18 A0487/28 A0487/33
gruff (10) A0540/08 A0541/09
A0541/29 A0541/33 A0542/29 A0543/03
A0549/13 A0549/19 A0550/21 B0968/01
gruffest (1) C0067/20
grumble (1) B1158/34
grumble (1) B0874/29
grumbling (3) A0388/31
B1102/35 C0085/39
Grunninger (1) A0515/34
grunt (1) B1158/33
grunt (1) A0047/28
grunted (2) C0388/09 C0388/10
Gruntundguzzell (1) A0366/20
grxwl (1) B1374/18
gry (1) B1104/18
Gualtier (1) A0037/02
guarantee (1) B1304/31
guard (12) A0058/07
A0068/29 A0180/14 A0414/16 A0436/13
A0479/20 A0479/20 B0827/02 B1006/18
B1332/16 C0097/39 C0171/11
guarda (1) A0183/01
guarda (2) A0177/03 A0177/08
guarded (2) A0159/15 A0509/21
guardian (2) A0349/28 A0483/11
guardianship (1) B0807/34
guarding (1) A0581/36
guards (1) C0562/25
guerre (2) B1136/24 B1138/01
guess (18) A0138/22 A0139/12
A0252/28 A0272/31 A0280/06 A0294/04
A0556/03 A0686/18 B0835/16 B0837/07
B0842/07 B0900/02 B0984/10 B0984/19
B0984/26 B1360/25 C0069/41 C0118/21
guessed (5) B0984/22
B1297/33 B1297/36 B1317/11 B1317/15
guesser (2) A0545/10 B0984/10
guesses (9) A0536/09
A0560/15 A0560/19 A0560/V A0592/02
B0984/19 B0984/26 B1189/15 B1189/16
guessing (3) B0925/04
B0984/06 B0984/12
guest (4) A0105/06
A0107/22 A0300/04 B1281/06
guest's (2) A0106/03 A0106/21
guests (8) A0176/15
A0182/16 A0250/02 A0250/21 B1007/32
B1056/22 B1351/29 B1352/09
guffaw (1) B1134/01
guidance (9) A0152/02
A0226/08 A0230/06 A0316/02 A0427/31
A0609/18 C0069/35 C0074/36 C0170/38
guide (7) A0228/06
A0578/21 A0583/08 B0771/32 B0841/06
B1126/13 C0570/14
guide-rope (9) B1073/36

->B1074/13 B1074/19 B1075/01 B1076/10
B1076/31 B1078/04 B1108/22 B1110/10
guided (8) A0179/10
A0577/03 B0870/13 B1116/02 B1317/05
B1351/25 C0079/22 C0126/03
guides (2) A0710/16 B1275/20
guiding (2) A0673/19 B0747/15
Guido's (2) A0160/11 A0160/13
guile (1) A0641/14
guilt (10) A0426/V A0561/29
B0748/16 B0764/11 B0764/26 B0770/09
B0858/04 B1052/18 B1054/03 B1362/13
guiltlessness (1) B0858/22
guilty (21) A0322/25
A0487/04 A0561/V A0564/05 B0732/04
B0761/10 B0851/32 B0979/12 B0986/19
B1054/33 B1058/06 B1154/30 B1225/18
B1383/31 C0104/22 C0107/21 C0130/27
C0200/28 C0406/22 C0411/22 C0426/21
Guinea (1) C0148/22
guineas (4) A0340/18
A0346/23 B0827/28 B0878/07
guitar (3) A0153/19
A0404/32 A0406/09
gulf (14) A0140/15 A0162/24
A0583/05 A0588/25 A0591/06 A0594/03
A0594/08 A0594/V A0682/31 A0682/32
A0697/01 C0185/04 C0194/04 C0196/18
gulfs (1) C0405/31
gull (3) B1391/18
C0125/20 C0151/38
gulled (2) C0428/12 C0448/V
gullet (1) B1106/20
gulley (1) C0553/24
Gulley's (1) A0338/23
gullibility (1) B1101/31
Gulliver (1) A0096/V
gully (2) C0553/17 C0572/34
gum (7) A0513/V
B1073/03 B1113/08 B1293/05 C0171/39
C0394/12 C0534/16
gum-elastic (6) C0409/17 C0410/08
C0410/35 C0411/16 C0424/18 C0424/40
gummy (1) C0178/19
gums (2) B0913/17 B1181/02
gun (3) B1329/05 C0399/21 C0557/35
gun-trigger (1) A0479/21
gunning (2) B0807/23 B0968/11
guns (11) B1078/13
C0169/31 C0171/10 C0177/14 C0180/18
C0187/07 C0187/30 C0188/01 C0533/40
C0534/02 C0534/04
gunwale (7) A0586/10
B0931/33 C0165/04 C0202/38 C0533/04
C0533/15 C0536/09
gurnards (1) C0174/07
gush (1) B1283/04
gushed (1) C0567/40
gust (3) A0412/18
A0416/25 B0944/33
gusty (1) B0974/01
Gutsmuth (1) B1361/32
Gutt-stuffin/University (1) B1091/29
gutta (1) B1293/06
gutta (1) B1298/26
gutter (8) A0341/07
A0355/04 A0355/07 A0355/10 A0355/19
A0355/31 B1090/21 B1143/03
gutters (1) A0514/30
guttural (10) A0054/05 A0054/07
A0055/31 A0056/19 A0063/13 A0063/15
A0065/12 A0066/08 A0402/24 A0433/29
Guy (21) C0147/06
C0148/01 C0150/02 C0153/35 C0154/12
C0156/26 C0162/20 C0164/31 C0165/36
C0166/01 C0166/16 C0167/08 C0168/05
C0168/31 C0168/39 C0170/20 C0171/06
C0172/25 C0175/26 C0177/25 C0190/31
Guy's (3) C0148/24
C0157/21 C0158/09
guzzle (1) B1046/04
gwine (1) B0820/28
gx (8) B1374/09
B1374/10 B1374/11 B1374/12 B1374/12
B1374/12 B1374/13 B1374/20
gxt (1) B1374/12
gxxd (1) B1374/18
gxxd-fxr-nxthing-tx-nxbxdy (1) B1374/15
gxxse (1) B1374/20
gymnastic (1) B1006/14
gymnastics (1) A0611/27
gypsum (2) A0175/V A0182/07
gypsy (1) B0945/31
gyrating (1) A0580/15
gyrations (2) A0593/33 A0594/06
gyratory (1) A0580/24
h (1) B1095/08
H.F.B./&/Co. (2) B1055/26 B1055/28
ha (1) A0161/03
ha (71)
ha> (6) A0465/18 A0466/32
A0467/11 A0467/15 A0468/24 A0469/12
hab (1) B0812/05
habe (1) A0150/V
habet (1) A0125/05
habiliment (6) A0086/25 A0089/10
A0100/02 A0556/08 B0746/06 B1014/13
habiliments (7) A0037/17
A0248/06 A0429/01 A0508/15 A0675/09
B1007/30 B1186/04
habit (39) A0135/14
A0161/13 A0226/02 A0229/20 A0241/17
A0274/29 A0274/30 A0281/27 A0283/05
A0283/07 A0479/18 A0479/36 A0509/01
A0536/V A0539/10 A0583/22 A0623/12
A0623/31 A0652/11 A0667/15 B0761/17
B0771/27 B0901/05 B0926/06 B0987/31
B1030/21 B1046/07 B1053/23 B1130/23
B1194/08 B1207/15 B1224/13 B1370/18
B1379/24 B1383/12 C0057/29 C0066/28
C0099/06 C0562/31
habitation (3) A0081/30
A0099/33 A0120/15
habitations (3) A0244/05
C0172/31 C0425/06
habited (9) A0058/04
A0068/25 A0248/06 A0349/12 A0439/08
A0446/30 A0566/15 A0614/08 B1350/25
habits (24) A0025/23
A0135/08 A0211/03 A0293/24 A0437/29

->A0438/19 A0478/14 A0483/05 A0485/30
A0486/29 A0488/18 A0488/26 A0509/25
B0724/28 B0866/22 B0878/12 B0978/11
B0991/22 B1047/14 B1055/05 B1089/05
C0544/12 C0546/32 C0547/08
habitual (14) A0028/15 A0073/13
A0099/20 A0240/18 A0296/01 A0398/31
A0402/15 A0437/31 A0694/03 B0942/07
B1373/33 C0407/14 C0413/16 C0414/36
habitually (8) A0315/15
A0323/14 A0411/03 A0434/04 A0440/22
A0446/04 B0853/35 B0908/06
habituated (1) C0404/13
habitudes (1) A0483/08
hack (1) B0916/18
hackmen (1) B1092/19
hackneyed (1) B1113/09
hacknied (1) A0341/02
had (3306)
Hades (2) A0033/18 A0682/17
hadn't (1) B0812/09
hadst (1) A0128/07
haematite (1) A0182/09
hag (2) A0062/04 B0911/30
haggard (2) A0019/V A0078/38
hail (9) A0251/25
B1128/34 B1131/07 B1131/09 C0099/20
C0102/29 C0163/22 C0163/39 C0168/04
hailed (7) B0988/25
C0102/30 C0121/04 C0136/27 C0146/14
C0415/11 C0419/06
hailing (1) A0127/01
hair (79)
hair-like (1) C0087/15
hair-splitting (1) A0299/07
hairs (10) A0143/16 A0144/19
A0218/16 A0557/18 A0557/22 A0578/03
B1163/27 B1163/36 B1163/41 B1263/02
hairy (3) B0746/08
B0746/12 C0428/38
hake (1) C0174/08
Halcyon (2) A0214/18 A0227/26
Hale (1) A0284/26
Hale, Sarah J. (1) A0284/23
half (216)
half-a-dozen (1) C0408/26
half-breed (1) C0055/19
half-credence (2) B0723/02 B0723/05
half-deck (1) C0057/27
half-empty (1) B1090/27
half-engendered (1) C0093/27
half-formed (3) A0555/24
A0691/23 A0691/25
half-holidays (1) A0431/03
half-insane (1) B1348/13
half-naked (1) B0943/36
half-negligent (1) B1329/25
half-north (1) B0909/17
half-parted (1) A0664/V
half-past (1) B1076/27
half-pleasurable (1) A0397/09
half-precise (1) B1329/25
half-quizzical (1) A0241/19
half-sentiment (3) B0853/33
B1031/07 B1031/07
half-shut (1) A0604/10
half-slumber (1) A0323/23
half-slumberous (1) B0865/32
half-subdued (1) A0673/34
half-way (1) A0486/11
half-wondrous (1) A0241/19
half-Indian (1) B0946/V
halibut (1) C0566/26
hall (10) A0036/12 A0189/19
A0400/23 A0438/33 A0673/31 B0761/21
B1156/09 B1347/08 B1351/32 B1352/25
Hall, Lieut. F. (1) B1164/41
Hall's (2) A0172/M A0178/M
Halleck (1) A0280/24
Halleck, Fitz Greene (1) A0269/28
Halleck's (2) A0269/33 A0269/35
halloo (1) B0819/11
hallooed (2) A0137/22 A0264/23
hallooing (1) C0146/18
halls (8) A0209/13
A0210/22 A0323/01 A0437/34 A0676/35
B1207/30 B1317/30 C0405/30
hallucination (1) C0531/39
halt (2) B0873/21 C0542/27
halted (1) C0171/27
halter (1) B0866/20
halts (1) C0539/25
ham (9) B1011/11
C0069/23 C0076/28 C0081/11 C0137/06
C0137/08 C0137/20 C0138/41 C0140/04
ham-skin (2) C0082/10 C0082/28
Hamadryad (1) A0599/M
hammer (5) A0165/11
A0489/27 A0553/22 B1057/04 C0391/27
hammering (1) C0189/29
hammers (3) A0671/01
B0828/04 C0148/10
hammock (1) C0108/05
hampers (1) C0069/08
hams (1) C0175/10
hand (281)
hand-bells (1) B1119/05
hand-cuffed (1) B1362/27
hand-cuffing (1) B1362/13
hand-writing (5) A0265/19
A0266/37 A0282/01 A0282/27 B1075/28
handcuff (1) C0090/27
handcuffs (4) C0089/28
C0090/14 C0092/37 C0099/36
handed (19) A0264/03
A0264/33 A0303/17 A0387/20 A0465/31
A0560/25 A0667/16 B0809/18 B0810/20
B0813/11 B0828/27 B0828/35 B0873/15
B0875/33 B0909/24 B0983/11 B1372/11
C0088/23 C0175/32
handful (4) C0088/22
C0412/07 C0565/36 C0577/22
handing (1) A0302/V
handiwork (4) A0711/32
B1213/28 B1276/35 B1283/13
handkerchief (20) A0067/34
A0068/04 A0371/07 A0371/21 A0512/15
B0734/35 B0758/10 B0764/16 B0766/09
B0766/11 B0767/04 B0911/02 B0968/30
B1058/04 B1058/28 B1161/32 C0127/24

->C0168/05 C0204/22 C0389/29
handkerchiefs (9) B0750/25
B1078/14 C0196/28 C0196/30 C0196/37
C0197/03 C0197/07 C0197/13 C0534/22
handle (5) B0765/23
B1009/V B1052/16 B1302/23 C0169/27
handled (4) A0676/31
B0925/28 B0955/02 C0534/27
handling (2) A0341/V C0169/31
handmaiden (1) A0600/29
hands (120)
handsome (8) A0123/30
A0248/07 A0294/06 A0368/27 A0484/18
B0888/11 B1093/35 C0067/26
handsomely (4) A0266/12
A0629/29 B1110/12 B1208/12
handsomest (2) A0379/08 A0468/20
handsommest (1) A0468/V
handspike (2) C0085/19 C0105/08
handspikes (1) C0107/07
handwriting (3) B0900/21
B0977/10 C0092/19
hang (9) A0046/17
A0340/37 A0426/09 A0502/14 A0675/26
B0982/24 B0982/25 C0398/27 C0447/V
hanged (3) A0058/20
A0069/17 C0061/38
hangeth (1) A0292/V
hanging (18) A0069/09 A0080/26
A0104/02 A0244/16 A0298/V A0320/16
A0341/01 A0400/08 A0444/23 A0501/12
A0503/05 A0590/19 B1153/21 B1381/30
C0068/18 C0144/01 C0173/04 C0406/20
hangings (3) A0021/22
A0081/11 A0672/16
hangman (4) A0058/22
A0069/12 B0859/15 B1226/15
hangman's (3) A0058/05
A0059/27 A0068/27
hangmen (1) A0496/03
hangs (5) A0153/03
A0456/10 B1075/09 B1260/08 C0552/25
Hans (4) B1386/08
C0428/06 C0428/10 C0447/V
Hans/Pfaal (1) C0448/V
Hans/Pfaall (3) C0433/08
C0448/V C0448/V
hap-hazard (1) B1189/13
haply (2) A0066/10 A0190/16
haporth> (1) A0469/18
happen (19) A0062/16
A0189/01 A0436/29 A0473/11 A0478/27
A0556/20 A0706/21 B0877/23 B1090/23
B1106/09 B1144/23 B1271/23 B1390/04
C0060/34 C0099/02 C0120/20 C0144/05
C0415/32 C0573/24
happened (52)
happening (3) B1181/28
C0431/14 C0560/18
happens (14) A0496/06 A0581/22
A0581/37 A0616/22 B0850/33 B0960/01
B0985/18 B1015/05 B1057/01 B1186/33
B1358/30 B1373/30 B1380/27 C0432/44
happier (3) A0020/V
A0435/33 B1269/01
happily (11) A0056/21
A0088/10 A0242/13 B1006/34 B1059/26
B1137/09 B1154/30 B1271/05 C0147/02
C0148/36 C0425/31
happily-timed (1) B1058/11
happiness (30) A0225/10 A0225/10
A0228/24 A0229/10 A0229/10 A0233/05
A0350/26 A0354/12 A0355/23 A0600/16
A0608/19 A0610/01 A0703/03 A0703/28
A0704/05 A0706/18 A0712/06 B0858/04
B0895/24 B0898/31 B1039/12 B1182/23
B1212/07 B1268/03 B1268/26 B1269/05
B1271/21 B1277/12 B1337/32 C0432/03
happy (43) A0033/07
A0036/25 A0055/23 A0065/07 A0107/33
A0225/09 A0229/10 A0235/17 A0249/24
A0272/24 A0275/24 A0280/17 A0282/33
A0301/25 A0351/20 A0354/09 A0357/11
A0370/16 A0407/07 A0507/09 A0608/18
A0639/12 A0642/06 A0670/10 A0703/18
A0704/01 B0832/04 B0850/13 B0850/22
B0916/18 B1007/10 B1017/04 B1039/21
B1101/16 B1136/25 B1141/33 B1159/04
B1212/05 B1212/11 B1259/14 B1268/17
C0391/36 C0419/06
harangue (4) A0300/29
B1106/19 C0168/22 C0175/26
harangues (1) A0354/16
haranguing (1) C0531/38
harassed (4) A0435/05
A0439/31 B1224/31 C0399/29
harassing (6) A0348/05 B0947/17
B1224/30 C0081/20 C0095/01 C0572/26
harbour (5) C0150/28
C0150/36 C0151/01 C0186/10 C0186/36
harbours (1) C0150/33
hard (44) A0053/36
A0063/07 A0191/09 A0351/08 A0429/13
A0465/20 A0467/19 A0467/23 A0611/25
A0684/07 B0730/31 B0735/07 B0758/34
B0761/24 B0766/16 B0807/10 B0815/16
B0878/05 B0941/17 B0967/12 B1081/26
B1104/11 B1141/12 B1142/32 B1160/02
B1166/04 B1180/26 B1184/02 B1193/16
B1333/09 B1336/18 C0063/37 C0076/08
C0078/35 C0119/39 C0127/16 C0140/29
C0151/03 C0191/10 C0556/28 C0559/35
C0566/03 C0572/26 C0573/12
hard-a-lee (1) C0061/41
hard-burned (1) A0367/09
hard-hearted (1) A0649/01
hardening (1) B0857/07
harder (2) B1163/20 C0184/03
hardest (1) B1161/38
hardihood (1) C0404/16
hardly (40) A0140/31
A0300/26 A0440/19 A0527/V A0628/26
B0815/18 B0825/31 B0850/17 B0876/34
B0947/25 B1077/10 B1137/21 B1322/22
B1391/09 B1391/10 C0058/17 C0059/39
C0060/36 C0062/02 C0065/34 C0067/24
C0070/26 C0087/09 C0088/12 C0089/33
C0115/15 C0120/41 C0121/10 C0146/25
C0148/25 C0170/34 C0183/04 C0187/08
C0192/25 C0387/11 C0392/09 C0406/37

->C0408/30 C0414/29 C0536/28
hardness (1) B0826/02
hardships (3) C0523/41
C0527/06 C0532/19
hardware (3) A0483/16
A0483/24 C0558/18
Hardy (6) B0922/03 B0923/32
B0931/30 B0931/36 B0933/15 B0933/29
hardy (2) B0862/15 C0063/04
Hardy's (1) B0930/01
hare (2) A0203/V B1010/29
harem (1) A0603/06
hark (3) A0123/01
A0124/27 B0797/26
harken (2) A0357/03 A0672/29
harkened (3) A0411/29
A0413/18 A0413/18
Harlaem (1) B1234/06
Harlem (1) B1234/V
harm (4) A0561/14
A0563/25 C0186/16 C0579/36
harmless (9) A0409/28
A0458/31 A0532/20 B0818/19 B0927/30
B1016/02 B1016/02 B1016/03 C0170/11
harmonies (1) A0611/34
harmoniously (1) A0312/17
harmonized (1) A0711/24
harmony (8) A0611/29
A0709/24 A0709/30 B1119/09 B1212/30
B1274/27 B1274/33 B1276/26
Harold (1) B1122/09
harp (2) A0047/25 A0641/04
Harper's/Ferry (1) B0862/09
Harpies (1) A0621/19
harpooner (1) C0102/10
harpooners (1) C0093/08
Harris, Alfred (1) C0179/30
harrowing (1) C0080/19
Harry (1) B1183/14
Harry/street (1) B0876/29
harsh (15) A0294/08
A0414/23 A0414/30 A0499/01 A0541/08
A0541/09 A0549/15 A0550/14 A0555/20
A0611/07 A0697/08 B1157/29 B1240/12
B1349/08 B1353/26
harsher (1) A0510/33
harshness (2) A0711/20 B1276/20
Hartford (1) A0265/30
Hartley (2) C0428/35 C0428/35
harvest (1) B1360/14
has (632)
hashish (1) A0078/30
hasn't (3) A0488/12
B0811/30 B1370/17
hasp (1) B1363/06
hast (10) A0046/09 A0155/15
A0155/16 A0195/V A0195/V A0227/36
A0448/16 A0599/M A0599/M C0559/02
haste (25) A0028/19
A0090/01 A0155/04 A0198/17 A0356/25
A0411/33 A0416/16 A0438/32 B0735/32
B0744/16 B0767/22 B0767/23 B0767/23
B0767/28 B0767/29 B0767/33 B0771/18
B0958/28 B1002/10 B1109/21 B1162/13
C0095/38 C0134/06 C0553/28 C0558/26
hasten (3) A0043/04
A0043/12 A0446/01
hastened (9) A0044/27
A0325/04 A0447/23 B0742/15 B0771/16
B0956/22 B1135/26 B1263/23 C0198/23
hastening (4) A0108/18
A0166/15 B1107/26 C0059/36
hastens (1) B0872/03
hastily (4) B0731/02
B0796/06 B0960/20 C0181/37
Hastings (2) B0949/16 B0949/19
Hastings, Warren (1) B0949/03
hasty (4) A0474/01
B0835/15 B0862/07 B1305/10
hat (14) A0104/33 A0465/20
A0482/15 A0511/28 B0745/31 B0746/21
B1090/29 B1185/35 B1195/07 C0388/32
C0388/35 C0388/39 C0425/02 C0437/V
hatch (7) A0586/02
A0586/03 C0085/37 C0091/30 C0091/33
C0091/38 C0136/23
hatchet (1) C0534/12
hatchets (1) C0148/09
hatchway (7) A0140/30
C0092/33 C0094/11 C0095/07 C0099/19
C0099/31 C0113/40
hatchways (2) C0095/19 C0115/41
hate (3) A0433/01
A0482/21 A0608/22
hated (3) A0036/19
A0435/35 A0445/35
hath (12) A0045/16
A0045/V A0047/09 A0150/03 A0165/03
A0195/V A0228/16 A0232/V A0347/26
A0383/02 A0414/19 B0806/M
hating (1) A0665/04
hatred (7) A0323/07
A0433/12 A0436/09 B0854/28 B0854/35
B0856/12 C0135/13
hats (5) A0300/V
A0368/18 A0509/02 C0188/24 C0534/23
Haubrion (2) A0101/V A0181/13
haughtiest (1) A0440/09
haughty (3) A0026/07
A0026/23 A0321/06
haul (1) C0535/29
hauled (3) A0138/18
C0061/11 C0106/23
hauling (3) C0147/04
C0188/09 C0538/07
haunches (2) A0105/28 C0576/04
haunt (1) A0604/01
Haunted (2) A0406/22 A0417/V
haunted (6) A0135/27 A0641/02
B0789/09 B0963/25 B1123/08 B1224/31
haunting (1) B1224/30
haunts (3) B0851/21
B0853/35 B0934/09
<u>haut</u> (1) A0247/02
<u>hauteur</u> (3) A0034/06
A0380/17 B1016/15
<u>have</u> (1) A0356/14
have (2342)
haven't (2) B0914/04 B1373/04
having (470)

havoc (3) C0188/06
C0190/09 C0547/32
hawk (2) A0205/11 A0509/32
hawk-nose (1) A0241/02
Hawk, Thomas (7) B1140/21
B1140/23 B1140/28 B1140/33 B1141/03
B1141/15 B1142/07
Hawk, Tommy (1) B1140/29
hawk's (1) C0552/15
hawthorn (1) C0167/13
hay (1) C0575/41
Haydn (1) B1119/10
hazard (5) A0293/V
B1238/20 C0090/10 C0196/25 C0578/18
hazarded (2) B0728/27 B0932/30
hazardous (3) A0555/08
B1018/15 C0097/07
hazards (6) B0891/16 C0066/07
C0074/12 C0082/05 C0104/06 C0187/03
haze (1) C0158/02
hazel (3) A0106/23
A0156/13 A0379/15
hazy (4) A0101/V
C0103/26 C0131/40 C0156/29
he (3084)
he-aw (6) A0387/V A0387/V
A0387/V A0387/V A0387/V A0387/V
he/he (1) B1263/05
he/he/he (12) A0034/05
A0105/22 A0113/06 A0387/V A0387/V
A0650/27 B1012/28 B1103/13 B1263/07
B1263/07 B1263/09 B1263/09
he'll (4) A0346/16
A0487/06 A0487/07 A0488/14
he's (12) A0337/16
A0380/34 A0382/32 A0384/03 A0384/26
A0385/14 A0386/10 A0388/19 A0483/02
B0869/26 B0979/09 B1373/02
head (317)
head-board (2) A0553/02 A0565/V
head-piece (1) A0248/07
head-teuffel (1) B1103/34
headache (7) B1080/02
B1169/24 B1177/02 C0081/14 C0191/21
C0411/27 C0424/19
headboard (1) A0565/26
headed (8) A0585/24
B0876/26 B0876/28 B0949/19 B1144/01
C0093/18 C0103/08 C0168/20
heading (5) A0292/V
B0876/25 B0930/24 B1068/08 C0131/13
headland (1) C0161/40
headless (1) A0357/11
headlong (25) A0048/01
A0145/19 A0154/09 A0245/05 A0351/08
A0567/19 A0580/09 A0590/06 A0593/34
A0708/13 B0763/17 B0856/20 B1108/07
B1110/12 B1273/08 C0061/02 C0110/26
C0190/08 C0197/38 C0399/08 C0417/02
C0425/07 C0443/V C0578/22 C0579/16
heads (37) A0078/36
A0144/02 A0175/06 A0181/27 A0195/11
A0491/05 A0502/06 A0507/27 A0508/36
A0603/21 A0625/24 A0664/06 A0682/08
B0738/19 B0761/20 B1013/01 B1141/34
->B1157/09 B1157/13 B1157/18 B1162/15
B1164/13 B1165/10 B1169/15 B1353/08
C0116/25 C0151/17 C0175/32 C0186/07
C0187/16 C0391/13 C0429/42 C0536/08
C0545/21 C0551/34 C0551/41 C0554/27
headsail (1) C0149/35
headway (9) A0585/20
B1079/32 C0062/17 C0542/30 C0553/41
C0554/06 C0567/05 C0570/23 C0579/09
heady (1) B1016/28
health (33) A0026/33
A0068/24 A0176/10 A0180/31 A0210/22
A0252/24 A0275/24 A0330/09 A0330/V
A0488/02 A0507/07 A0624/29 A0665/15
A0703/32 B0726/10 B0814/29 B0858/24
B0928/10 B0942/22 B0958/03 B0958/20
B0960/31 B0963/12 B1234/19 B1259/12
B1268/31 B1347/30 C0130/14 C0133/06
C0170/29 C0412/27 C0413/18 C0416/38
healthily (1) B0789/06
healthy (1) B1274/32
heap (2) B0826/15 C0194/11
heaped (3) A0616/10
B0827/22 C0173/08
heaps (2) A0244/26 A0694/21
hear (62)
heard (181)
hearer (1) C0532/24
hearers (2) A0297/14 B1120/09
hearin> (1) A0466/12
hearing (21) A0153/23
A0385/01 A0542/20 A0613/17 B0724/22
B0789/04 B0794/26 B0905/06 B1020/27
B1053/08 B1108/32 B1153/26 B1183/19
B1190/22 C0086/04 C0086/13 C0100/40
C0103/11 C0110/18 C0186/13 C0198/21
hearken (3) B0789/06
B1262/16 C0558/41
hearkened (4) A0317/11
A0687/08 B1263/15 B1294/28
hearkening (1) B0794/04
Hearne, Samuel (1) C0525/28
hears (1) B0764/30
hearse (3) A0080/45
A0616/09 B0963/29
hearse-plumes (2) A0246/04 A0253/V
Heart (1) B0789/T
heart (181)
heart-rending (1) C0564/19
heart-sick (1) B1278/22
heart-stirring (1) A0162/06
heart's (1) A0683/19
heart's-ease (1) B1212/32
heartfelt (3) B1370/10
B1381/06 C0419/05
hearth (8) A0102/08
A0537/29 A0557/15 A0557/V B0808/10
B0832/04 B1004/04 B1110/14
hearths (1) A0551/18
heartiest (1) B1046/03
heartily (8) A0481/02
B0975/30 B1195/13 B1249/12 C0059/19
C0067/01 C0100/36 C0571/02
heartless (2) A0020/V C0061/35
heartlessness (2) C0128/13 C0135/01

heartrending (2) C0131/37 C0135/16
Hearts (1) A0337/05
hearts (18) A0047/10 A0245/04
A0384/24 A0459/28 A0459/34 A0608/12
A0608/20 A0640/04 A0640/17 A0675/03
B0789/M B0901/15 B0932/V B1215/34
B1339/01 C0120/16 C0124/04 C0183/30
hearty (10) A0080/07 A0562/15
B0793/15 B0974/16 B1045/06 B1077/08
B1100/02 B1181/27 C0176/02 C0409/04
hearty-looking (1) A0510/18
heat (27) A0071/03
A0345/01 A0356/15 A0460/27 A0461/22
A0696/18 B0742/16 B0759/34 B0832/15
B0832/25 B0832/31 B0834/27 B0865/15
B0904/13 B0928/31 B0944/28 B1050/06
B1080/23 B1168/24 B1321/27 B1383/26
C0178/31 C0204/12 C0204/37 C0205/17
C0425/34 C0536/31
heated (6) A0136/23 A0313/08
A0696/02 B0832/05 B0834/33 B1168/29
heathen (4) A0043/13
A0047/23 A0085/M A0311/29
heaved (2) A0437/18 A0594/13
Heaven (19) A0054/23
A0055/13 A0064/V A0075/11 A0408/30
A0580/35 A0610/19 A0626/12 A0642/10
B0932/01 B1039/26 B1131/07 B1185/05
B1267/M B1305/07 B1314/17 B1385/15
B1385/22 B1390/09
heaven (45) A0044/24
A0074/01 A0175/06 A0181/27 A0190/26
A0195/10 A0195/17 A0196/02 A0197/01
A0197/05 A0197/22 A0197/23 A0198/01
A0198/04 A0198/22 A0198/24 A0217/V
A0227/24 A0228/13 A0232/11 A0232/18
A0233/21 A0235/27 A0236/06 A0314/17
A0399/35 A0426/09 A0448/14 A0461/23
A0602/03 A0645/09 A0691/08 A0702/M
B0789/04 B0820/03 B0969/03 B1122/08
B1280/02 B1280/16 B1333/27 B1333/27
B1384/32 C0205/26 C0412/34 C0443/V
Heaven's (2) A0534/21 B1384/35
heavenly (7) A0312/19
A0348/07 A0353/12 A0460/07 A0545/21
B1035/07 C0438/V
heavens (31) A0106/25
A0122/26 A0123/09 A0125/22 A0128/02
A0183/25 A0189/11 A0217/V A0350/16
A0357/04 A0397/03 A0459/34 A0461/12
A0585/01 A0587/08 A0591/13 A0603/12
A0709/06 B0975/32 B1017/09 B1019/35
B1079/07 B1161/08 B1165/05 B1168/01
B1213/27 B1301/01 B1382/16 B1382/26
C0387/18 C0425/15
heavier (6) B0741/03 B0741/32
B0743/22 B1049/07 B1321/22 C0410/06
heaviest (1) C0106/06
heavily (31) A0029/24
A0037/19 A0046/20 A0047/11 A0137/11
A0219/04 A0329/14 A0330/05 A0415/26
A0416/31 A0592/05 A0603/26 A0616/10
A0626/30 A0630/28 A0643/03 A0643/27
A0684/06 B0729/16 B0858/30 B0928/05
B0943/07 B0960/25 B1057/26 B1260/33
->C0072/33 C0080/23 C0101/32 C0182/07
C0399/22 C0579/35
heaviness (1) A0189/27
heaving (3) A0136/21
A0580/14 C0132/30
heavy (92)
hebby (3) B0809/03
B0811/27 B0820/17
Hebrew (3) A0156/V
A0298/V A0401/33
Hebrews (2) A0075/10 A0312/14
Hebrides (1) A0195/15
Hebron (1) A0047/21
Hecla (1) B1161/25
hectic (4) A0246/33
B0906/18 B1239/24 B1242/19
Hedelin (2) A0301/09 A0302/18
heed (2) B1095/09 C0091/22
heeded (2) A0088/03 A0325/12
heeding (2) A0252/18 B0820/08
heedlessness (1) C0099/02
heel (12) A0433/25
A0626/06 B0896/30 B0950/25 B1013/19
B1259/35 C0114/04 C0117/07 C0124/40
C0144/03 C0426/36 C0552/21
heeled (2) B0928/25 C0559/23
heeling (1) C0143/39
heels (11) A0127/V
A0243/23 A0252/08 A0482/12 B1010/06
B1141/34 B1158/11 B1245/02 B1261/22
B1352/28 C0429/37
heels-over-head (1) A0483/V
heerd (1) B0813/03
Hegel (1) A0495/V
heigho (1) B1292/07
height (82)
heighten (2) A0400/26 B0928/16
heightened (11) A0024/17
A0241/17 A0322/26 A0382/08 A0512/06
A0581/34 B0797/08 B0855/22 B0891/12
B0944/08 C0538/38
heir (18) A0021/08 A0025/V
A0486/04 A0704/32 A0704/35 A0705/16
B0914/20 B0914/26 B0916/28 B1050/04
B1050/32 B1138/03 B1142/11 B1145/01
B1154/13 B1269/31 B1269/34 B1270/14
heiress (1) B0957/16
heirs (1) A0440/09
helas (2) B0900/01 B0900/02
held (89)
Heliogabalus (1) A0122/25
Hell (3) A0408/30
B0961/33 B0969/12
hell (10) A0139/27 A0143/25
A0690/25 B0789/05 B0859/05 B1226/15
B1384/32 B1384/35 B1385/05 C0405/27
hellish (3) A0695/07
B0795/15 C0124/10
Hellofagabaluses (1) B1300/17
helm (8) C0058/34
C0060/25 C0061/28 C0061/40 C0062/11
C0106/30 C0106/32 C0106/34
helmsman (1) C0123/27
help (69)
helped (4) A0107/22

->B1051/17 C0120/12 C0431/04
helping (3) A0247/29
A0250/31 B1056/27
helpless (6) A0329/09 B0911/16
B1313/14 C0072/39 C0134/24 C0579/13
helplessly (1) A0079/42
helplessness (2) A0446/09 C0398/37
Helseggen (5) A0578/29
A0579/32 A0581/14 A0582/21 A0585/16
helter-skelteriness (1) B1115/10
Helusion (2) A0191/10 A0642/15
hem (13) A0386/05
A0387/01 A0650/14 A0685/34 A0686/27
B0730/26 B0735/12 B0735/14 B0762/11
B0763/02 B0763/03 B0765/21 B0896/12
hemi-syncope (1) B0962/V
hemisphere (7) A0613/11
B1321/11 C0418/06 C0418/34 C0422/29
C0423/16 C0423/21
hemispheres (1) B1274/20
hemispherical (1) C0388/33
hemlock (1) A0236/04
hemmed (6) A0512/35 A0695/13
B0762/33 C0096/06 C0160/19 C0162/30
hen (3) B0880/02 B1166/08 B1166/12
hence (12) A0482/18
B1005/15 B1080/35 B1091/31 B1163/31
B1207/07 B1207/08 B1207/09 B1385/04
C0178/21 C0408/16 C0423/34
henceforth (1) B1386/02
henceforward (5) A0026/01
A0448/13 A0455/04 B1102/04 B1209/01
hencoop (1) B0869/18
Henderson (4) C0061/33
C0062/13 C0062/40 C0064/08
Hennepin (1) C0525/01
Henry (1) C0158/06
hens (1) C0151/27
Henson (5) B1068/04
B1069/19 B1069/32 B1072/12 B1072/32
Henson's (2) B1070/01 B1070/29
Hephestion, Ptolemy (2) A0213/13
B1310/06
her (1079)
Heraclides (1) A0124/06
Heraclitus (1) A0295/11
Herald (1) B0753/39
herald (1) A0124/08
heralded (1) A0150/V
heraldic (1) A0496/10
herbage (2) A0581/01 C0552/41
herbaged (1) B0864/36
herbs (1) C0561/23
Herculean (2) A0156/09 C0087/08
Hercules (1) A0297/V
herd (12) A0580/04
A0710/20 B1140/31 B1275/24 B1378/M
C0561/33 C0562/35 C0563/27 C0567/12
C0567/35 C0568/02 C0570/33
herds (3) B1189/15
C0548/03 C0575/12
here (582)
here's (2) A0347/07 B1373/23
hereafter (23) A0079/37
A0080/19 A0122/23 A0150/V A0262/02
->A0266/29 A0296/V B0750/22 B0751/08
B0754/04 B0850/02 B0891/20 B1081/18
B1097/07 B1138/24 C0087/38 C0152/05
C0207/14 C0394/13 C0400/23 C0432/28
C0534/06 C0555/32
hereby (3) A0093/20
A0112/31 B1109/22
hereditarily (1) A0438/09
hereditary (11) A0019/24
A0026/15 A0026/25 A0097/16 A0135/03
A0209/13 A0296/V A0446/12 B0906/20
B1247/01 C0522/01
herein (7) A0065/15
A0209/23 A0339/12 A0414/19 B0723/14
B0739/27 B1261/20
hereinafter (1) C0522/26
heresy (2) A0175/15 A0181/05
heretical (3) A0369/30
B1213/12 B1373/34
heretofore (4) A0486/28
B1242/14 B1249/31 C0103/18
hereupon (21) A0035/01
A0066/22 A0106/15 A0107/22 A0388/31
B0815/10 B0831/27 B0968/05 B1047/25
B1049/33 B1051/09 B1102/21 B1104/20
B1109/21 B1140/33 B1155/09 B1181/13
B1184/11 B1194/33 B1349/23 C0206/02
herewith (1) A0281/09
Hermann (14) A0297/24 A0298/11
A0298/V A0299/06 A0299/16 A0299/24
A0299/32 A0299/V A0300/09 A0300/16
A0300/20 A0302/03 A0303/01 A0304/04
Hermann, Johan (2) A0301/30
A0302/28
Hermann's (2) A0303/14 A0303/32
hermaphrodite (1) C0123/08
hermetically (1) A0558/03
hermit (4) A0413/23
A0413/29 A0414/15 C0522/20
hermit's (1) A0416/11
Hernani (1) A0673/22
Hero (1) B1194/22
hero (36) A0065/10
A0085/04 A0086/21 A0087/15 A0088/02
A0088/20 A0088/36 A0089/09 A0089/21
A0090/07 A0091/11 A0091/27 A0092/29
A0093/30 A0097/16 A0100/03 A0103/01
A0103/16 A0103/32 A0104/16 A0104/35
A0105/13 A0112/03 A0113/09 A0183/23
A0319/18 A0345/01 A0356/15 A0356/V
A0381/08 A0382/31 A0384/24 A0413/22
B1031/16 C0433/01 C0523/18
hero's (2) A0089/28 B1382/34
Herod (3) A0021/09
A0440/15 A0675/01
heroes (1) A0242/14
heroine (1) B0957/11
heroines (1) B1152/26
Herr (1) A0302/28
hers (7) A0210/23
A0317/15 A0330/10 B0733/02 B0905/13
B0930/06 B0993/04
Herschel (4) B1169/32
C0428/40 C0430/01 C0430/22
Herschel's, John (1) C0428/28

herself (36) A0225/09
A0229/09 A0318/05 A0325/16 A0352/09
A0357/10 A0404/21 A0436/18 A0532/29
A0539/17 A0546/01 A0586/18 A0586/19
A0642/09 B0726/17 B0733/04 B0877/15
B0891/18 B0899/25 B0906/04 B0914/18
B0914/25 B0926/12 B0926/34 B0927/05
B0930/15 B1014/14 B1014/22 B1096/34
B1153/30 C0110/02 C0187/02 C0412/30
C0413/10 C0438/V C0559/01
hervor (1) B0723/M
hesitate (19) A0026/25
A0446/14 A0515/12 A0533/13 A0534/09
A0550/19 A0561/18 A0562/10 A0667/38
A0686/25 B0761/22 B0841/28 B1053/03
B1277/17 B1364/12 C0084/19 C0095/41
C0133/11 C0136/24
hesitated (12) A0235/14
A0400/32 A0447/15 A0593/13 A0631/18
B0866/09 B0888/07 B0947/29 B0965/09
B1262/25 B1347/17 B1348/32
hesitates (2) A0490/22 B0755/12
hesitating (3) B1033/07
B1133/24 C0199/37
hesitatingly (2) A0512/24 B1190/17
hesitation (32) A0065/07
A0252/07 A0264/16 A0398/27 A0403/32
A0530/21 A0593/25 A0667/19 B0726/01
B0730/01 B0814/05 B0822/23 B0908/10
B0943/23 B0961/18 B0989/24 B1032/23
B1036/27 B1237/07 B1277/35 B1296/28
B1313/29 C0075/01 C0083/21 C0103/22
C0402/18 C0413/11 C0414/32 C0416/23
C0417/34 C0424/16 C0578/23
Hesper (2) A0641/06 A0643/22
Hessian (1) B1102/29
heterodox (1) A0621/V
heterogeneous (6) A0342/06 A0342/24
A0347/23 A0433/11 C0069/07 C0387/26
Hetty (1) A0349/18
Hevelius (1) C0423/31
Hewitt's (2) A0055/12 A0064/V
hewn (2) A0044/30 B0945/16
hey (1) B0869/M
hey-day (1) A0020/V
hey-diddle (1) B1158/33
Hey-Diddle-Diddle (3) B1143/27
B1144/01 B1144/06
Heywood (1) C0155/38
hi (9) A0105/23
A0105/23 A0105/23 A0650/27 A0650/27
A0650/27 B1012/28 B1012/28 B1012/28
hic (1) A0681/M
hiccup (26) A0093/31 A0094/06
A0108/07 A0109/04 A0109/16 A0109/24
A0110/05 A0110/11 A0111/08 A0111/16
A0111/22 A0111/22 A0111/35 A0111/35
A0112/12 A0113/08 A0113/11 A0113/12
A0113/12 A0113/15 A0113/19 A0113/21
A0113/21 A0114/01 A0114/06 A0114/12
hickories (1) B1332/03
hickory (3) B1332/17
B1333/14 C0541/30
hickory-nut (1) B0808/33
Hicks (1) C0113/19
Hicks, Absalom (2) C0102/22
C0113/01
hid (6) A0196/20 A0527/M
A0709/27 B1274/29 C0200/11 C0549/16
hid> (2) A0469/12 A0469/17
hidden (19) A0018/04
A0551/30 A0552/26 A0562/19 A0621/21
A0703/09 B0730/17 B0985/13 B0985/14
B0986/11 B0990/15 B1049/04 B1059/03
B1119/20 B1268/08 B1282/33 C0154/37
C0420/17 C0421/39
hide (5) A0126/09
A0234/08 C0552/33 C0562/17 C0576/38
hideous (49) A0021/17
A0026/32 A0054/27 A0072/29 A0080/21
A0145/23 A0216/19 A0217/12 A0226/18
A0230/17 A0248/23 A0298/V A0322/28
A0328/24 A0397/17 A0407/40 A0416/03
A0459/32 A0557/19 A0566/12 A0587/22
A0670/02 A0683/16 A0685/09 A0687/22
A0689/02 B0795/03 B0797/29 B0855/34
B0856/28 B0859/13 B0911/07 B0961/33
B0968/34 B1057/28 B1157/01 B1162/16
B1239/34 B1240/13 B1242/22 B1247/29
B1350/34 B1354/21 C0125/39 C0201/21
C0205/34 C0405/31 C0420/25 C0426/10
hideously (7) A0234/22
A0243/V A0245/25 A0510/22 A0579/11
B0928/01 B1053/30
hideousness (2) A0506/06 B0964/19
hiding (2) A0163/V C0126/20
hiding-place (11) A0141/05
C0066/36 C0066/36 C0069/31 C0070/01
C0100/04 C0100/40 C0101/30 C0102/37
C0188/17 C0191/04
Hierocles (2) A0176/06 A0180/28
hieroglyphical (6) B0833/14
B1136/01 B1179/27 B1184/19 C0208/01
C0573/20
hieroglyphics (6) A0528/08 B1180/18
B1192/29 B1298/06 B1317/07 B1374/25
Hieronymus (1) A0072/01
Hieronymus (1) A0072/31
High (1) B0856/02
high (142)
high-backed (1) A0368/28
high-heeled (1) B1008/07
high-minded (1) A0487/03
high-mindedness (1) B0872/25
high-spirited (1) A0027/22
high-toned (1) B1136/22
high-water (1) B1392/07
higher (26) A0197/01 A0497/11
A0528/21 A0578/30 A0582/36 A0583/35
A0600/10 B0819/09 B0819/09 B0819/21
B0906/14 B1076/07 B1179/04 B1337/21
B1354/09 B1392/04 C0069/26 C0161/01
C0166/20 C0432/36 C0543/21 C0545/03
C0551/09 C0553/25 C0572/02 C0575/16
highest (28) A0045/02
A0045/V A0275/27 A0406/16 A0478/35
A0528/13 A0529/14 A0582/21 A0611/12
A0613/22 A0706/20 A0707/29 B0813/29
B0814/01 B0893/25 B0942/04 B1160/43
B1271/22 B1272/29 C0111/24 C0153/37

->C0184/30 C0190/18 C0422/32 C0538/32
C0540/22 C0543/39 C0564/15
highlands (2) C0542/34 C0544/17
highly (34) A0074/20 A0090/19
A0264/09 A0264/29 A0269/21 A0276/34
A0405/10 A0410/06 A0503/04 A0703/17
B0746/15 B0761/31 B0820/34 B0928/02
B0984/01 B1056/01 B1056/18 B1103/28
B1133/25 B1136/27 B1180/06 B1242/12
B1268/16 B1348/14 B1380/05 B1380/16
C0138/15 C0145/19 C0389/18 C0406/12
C0409/12 C0413/21 C0544/13 C0560/09
highly-agitated (1) B1134/23
highly-concentrated (1) C0059/30
highly-polished (1) A0087/20
highly-scented (1) A0055/12
Highly-Scented (1) A0064/V
Highness (3) A0174/15
A0174/20 A0179/29
highness (4) A0175/02
A0176/14 A0179/35 A0250/16
highway (6) B1069/08 B1207/32
B1298/10 B1312/28 B1316/19 C0569/01
highways (1) B0863/25
hilarity (3) A0412/09
B0760/20 C0536/27
hill (34) A0044/29 A0071/02
A0371/12 B0817/24 B1159/23 B1159/23
B1159/29 B1159/29 B1247/23 B1247/28
B1249/02 B1249/19 B1250/34 B1338/08
C0057/13 C0181/30 C0185/05 C0185/21
C0188/18 C0188/39 C0189/03 C0189/13
C0189/20 C0191/04 C0191/23 C0192/04
C0192/18 C0193/08 C0196/01 C0196/13
C0196/23 C0198/33 C0199/09 C0204/11
hill-side (1) A0210/24
hill-sides (1) B1332/15
hill-top (1) C0191/29
hill-tops (1) B1278/13
hillo (2) B0968/01 B0968/01
hillock (1) C0152/40
hillocks (2) A0603/23 C0540/24
Hills (2) C0526/09 C0527/03
hills (53)
hillsides (1) C0138/14
hilly (1) C0150/31
Him (2) A0461/20 B1212/12
him (1143)
himself (356)
himsilf> (2) A0466/V A0470/V
hinc (1) B0767/17
hind (7) A0057/05
A0066/32 A0353/17 A0479/27 A0479/29
B1313/16 C0545/19
hinder (3) A0104/33
A0127/21 A0253/06
hinder-part (1) A0103/29
Hindoo (2) B1293/28 B1295/06
hindrances (1) C0570/20
hinges (7) A0410/11
A0416/14 A0429/09 B0793/08 B1051/25
B1363/06 C0109/22
Hinnom (1) A0230/17
Hinnon (1) A0226/18
hint (23) A0074/22
->A0086/17 A0100/03 A0108/01 A0231/22
A0304/04 A0341/V A0341/V A0342/14
A0342/17 A0346/16 B0773/01 B0810/11
B0840/19 B0877/27 B1059/07 B1185/15
B1208/17 B1297/10 B1358/14 B1360/09
C0110/10 C0168/25
hinted (10) A0123/22 A0248/V
A0378/19 A0408/11 A0435/26 B1190/22
B1213/01 C0103/19 C0104/03 C0394/05
hinting (1) B1208/21
hints (5) A0026/26
A0098/17 A0276/08 A0403/21 B1032/12
hip (1) B1009/V
hipped (1) A0626/31
Hippocrates (3) A0054/09
A0092/06 A0111/18
Hippocratian (1) A0067/28
Hippodrome (1) A0123/28
hippodrome (5) A0126/22
A0127/05 A0127/29 A0128/06 A0128/21
hippopotami (2) A0197/14 A0197/16
hips (2) A0055/08 A0064/13
hire (1) B1206/07
His (3) A0110/V A0577/M C0390/06
his (3039)
hiss (1) B1158/34
hissed (1) A0690/21
hisses (1) A0294/V
hissing (8) A0029/V
A0439/20 A0580/14 A0692/01 B0824/05
B1011/31 C0081/29 C0204/09
hissingly (1) A0236/01
hist (2) B0866/11 B0866/11
Histoire (1) C0522/35
historian (4) A0365/15
B1189/07 B1189/22 C0521/24
historian's (1) B1189/35
historians (1) A0120/10
historical (3) A0100/23
A0459/31 A0630/V
Histories (1) B0810/13
histories (5) A0198/22
A0664/27 B0961/08 B1190/05 B1190/10
History (4) B0830/29
B1097/06 B1126/15 B1250/10
history (32) A0019/V
A0097/31 A0241/27 A0340/12 A0365/09
A0413/15 A0511/09 A0511/25 A0532/03
A0611/15 A0611/38 A0622/12 A0622/13
B0752/09 B0770/03 B0772/25 B0955/09
B1090/19 B1144/31 B1144/33 B1145/10
B1153/18 B1153/34 B1154/32 B1155/16
B1159/16 B1170/03 B1189/05 B1189/27
B1302/11 B1311/27 C0178/05
hit (11) A0055/25
A0340/28 B0856/37 B0869/12 B1235/06
B1328/12 C0092/04 C0107/20 C0187/15
C0415/10 C0574/30
hitch (4) B0730/27
B0765/22 B0766/31 B0768/31
hitched (1) B0766/23
hither (7) A0195/18
A0318/16 A0603/22 B0880/01 B1329/06
B1337/05 C0563/15
hitherto (49) A0139/05

->A0145/08 A0265/33 A0328/03 A0329/06
A0404/19 A0437/07 A0446/08 A0514/22
A0640/34 A0663/19 A0708/34 B0734/10
B0752/24 B0856/22 B0865/28 B0888/23
B0890/18 B0900/28 B0906/21 B0944/14
B0948/27 B1031/04 B1052/31 B1055/06
B1107/03 B1152/03 B1159/13 B1169/09
B1233/16 B1239/24 B1303/12 B1317/31
B1330/20 B1332/14 B1370/08 C0116/15
C0145/15 C0158/26 C0171/16 C0184/23
C0398/39 C0411/27 C0416/41 C0418/09
C0419/07 C0524/10 C0547/37 C0571/19
hitting (4) A0177/26
A0183/21 B1103/19 C0066/25
ho (16) A0105/23
A0105/23 A0105/23 A0650/27 A0650/27
A0650/27 B0806/M B0806/M B0975/34
B0975/34 B0975/34 B0985/34 B1012/29
B1012/29 B1012/29 B1371/28
hoarded (1) C0095/14
hoarhound (1) B1096/03
hoarse (1) A0045/23
hoarsely (2) A0675/23 B0947/33
hoary (2) A0143/12 C0412/32
Hoax (1) C0448/V
hoax (5) B0916/09
B1101/29 C0427/12 C0427/12 C0428/37
hoaxes (4) C0428/03
C0428/04 C0448/V C0448/V
hobbies (2) A0654/11 B0929/32
hobbled (1) C0067/30
hobbling (2) A0710/22 B1275/25
hobby (3) A0298/06
A0299/06 A0652/24
Hock (1) B0900/13
Hoeyholm (1) A0579/25
Hog (8) B1295/12
B1295/32 B1296/05 B1311/05 B1311/10
B1311/33 B1312/06 B1313/08
hog (6) A0047/28 B1106/33
B1107/03 B1372/02 C0173/30 C0177/09
Hog-ian (3) B1295/24
B1311/21 B1312/34
Hog-ishly (1) B1317/29
Hog-ites (1) B1312/21
hog's (1) B1295/18
Hogarth (1) B1145/17
Hoggishly (1) B1296/17
Hoggs (1) B1055/22
Hogs (4) B0879/13
B0879/17 B0879/24 B1316/14
hogs (2) C0156/23 C0175/34
hogshead (3) A0252/09
A0253/22 B0854/06
hogsheads (3) B0854/04
C0097/21 C0097/36
hoisted (4) B0831/09
C0058/31 C0147/36 C0168/40
Holberg (1) A0409/02
hold (151)
holder (3) B0976/23
B0976/29 C0134/10
holders (1) A0530/11
holding (38) A0174/13 A0179/28
A0243/26 A0387/V A0545/13 A0589/25
->A0610/30 A0615/16 B0824/11 B0832/10
B0866/15 B0892/V B0904/04 B0930/10
B0984/14 B1079/17 B1187/17 B1262/21
B1353/12 C0068/40 C0069/29 C0108/23
C0112/08 C0119/11 C0129/07 C0138/34
C0139/21 C0141/39 C0142/01 C0163/07
C0163/26 C0166/22 C0390/20 C0394/23
C0398/08 C0419/03 C0420/14 C0579/06
holds (10) A0162/28 B0821/04
B0874/33 B0878/32 B0984/08 B1296/16
B1312/19 B1321/27 B1385/22 C0106/35
hole (50) A0057/25 A0068/08
A0351/30 A0351/31 A0351/32 A0351/33
A0352/02 A0356/29 A0367/30 B0821/28
B0823/18 B0825/21 B0827/01 B0844/11
B0966/01 B0985/33 B1058/24 B1102/30
B1102/33 B1102/33 B1106/26 B1162/31
B1372/18 B1372/25 C0068/33 C0075/35
C0091/01 C0092/35 C0094/04 C0096/15
C0096/30 C0099/32 C0100/12 C0100/37
C0138/30 C0150/37 C0152/38 C0196/31
C0196/35 C0197/02 C0197/04 C0197/05
C0198/06 C0394/19 C0394/21 C0394/27
C0415/30 C0415/34 C0571/05 C0575/36
holes (19) A0535/31
B0827/12 B1048/27 B1071/20 B1141/13
B1156/34 C0173/09 C0196/04 C0196/05
C0197/09 C0197/30 C0394/19 C0394/22
C0394/29 C0533/20 C0533/22 C0566/05
C0573/29 C0575/33
holiday (1) C0546/05
Holland (6) A0138/16 B1072/30
B1077/26 B1080/04 C0388/18 C0427/23
Holland, Robert (2) B1068/04
B1069/18
Hollander (1) A0549/22
Hollanders (1) C0123/31
Hollands (1) A0340/03
hollo (2) B0820/24 B1372/05
hollow (16) A0150/M
A0166/11 A0215/06 A0372/08 A0415/27
A0416/09 A0428/07 B1058/06 B1071/10
B1071/18 B1106/17 B1108/32 B1240/12
B1391/28 C0189/14 C0192/37
hollow-backed (1) B0841/20
hollow-sounding (2) A0402/23
A0413/34
Holy (2) A0461/03 B1131/07
holy (22) A0020/V A0043/11
A0044/18 A0046/18 A0059/08 A0061/04
A0080/15 A0198/25 A0198/25 A0227/34
A0228/37 A0234/18 A0235/23 A0252/11
A0312/22 A0457/17 A0610/01 A0643/26
B0945/20 B1128/34 B1131/09 B1131/11
Holy/of/Holies (1) A0120/07
Holy/Moses (1) A0047/04
Holy/River (1) B0949/14
holydays (1) A0429/20
homage (2) A0640/14 B1385/11
home (132)
Home/Journal (2) B1360/18 B1360/33
homely (1) B0849/01
Homer (5) A0086/14
A0099/01 A0621/17 B0870/10 B1385/17
Homer/Junior (2) A0176/04 A0182/02

Homeric (1) A0312/12
homes (2) A0513/09 B1346/26
homewards (4) B0842/29
  B0896/11 B0948/17 B1052/05
homily (1) A0479/08
homines (1) B0987/10
hominis (1) B0810/12
homme (2) A0019/03 B1122/01
hommes (1) A0036/22
hommy (1) A0356/13
homo (2) A0125/01 B1372/01
Homo-Cameleopard (1) A0119/T
Homocameleopard (1) A0119/V
homoeopathists (2) A0631/06
  A0631/16
Homoomeria (1) A0175/13
homoomeria (1) A0181/03
Homouioisios (2) A0175/16 A0181/06
Homousios (2) A0175/16 A0181/06
hon> (4) A0467/11
  A0468/30 A0469/15 A0470/10
honest (16) A0249/28
  A0371/15 A0582/23 B0767/15 B0874/01
  B1019/27 B1045/02 B1047/10 B1055/02
  B1091/03 B1137/24 B1140/20 B1206/08
  B1379/10 B1381/06 C0391/15
honesti (1) B0987/10
honesty (2) B1132/02 B1381/13
honey (3) A0047/21
  B1163/34 B1381/11
honeysuckle (2) B1282/01 B1337/18
Honor (1) A0301/02
honor (48) A0026/04
  A0059/11 A0061/07 A0101/V A0105/05
  A0106/13 A0107/28 A0119/02 A0176/V
  A0182/20 A0275/04 A0281/09 A0297/02
  A0298/05 A0302/24 A0379/03 A0385/34
  A0443/27 A0445/30 A0466/05 A0485/16
  A0530/11 A0530/11 A0563/26 A0564/08
  A0654/09 B0728/13 B0813/08 B0816/20
  B0892/14 B0976/28 B0976/31 B0978/19
  B1010/17 B1013/27 B1017/06 B1055/17
  B1127/13 B1194/35 B1208/18 B1258/22
  B1291/02 B1349/21 B1357/08 B1371/06
  C0394/16 C0426/28 C0524/37
honorable (1) B0987/10
honorable (5) A0303/11
  A0440/26 A0509/05 B0755/08 C0426/20
honorably (1) B1379/29
honors (2) A0426/07 A0443/24
honour (5) A0204/20
  A0298/V C0162/02 C0166/02 C0186/11
Honourable (1) A0204/32
honourable (1) A0128/V
honourably (1) A0020/V
hoo (3) B0821/11 B1155/12 B1161/19
hood (1) A0248/09
hoof (1) B1160/31
hoofs (3) A0029/14
  A0125/30 C0563/09
hook (8) A0484/01
  B0858/14 B1185/35 B1352/31 B1352/34
  B1373/06 C0155/06 C0411/13
hookah (1) A0667/23
hookahcase (1) A0667/14

hooked (2) A0371/01 B1352/23
hooks (3) C0115/31
  C0115/32 C0115/35
hoop (15) B1008/07
  B1071/19 B1073/30 C0393/25 C0409/21
  C0409/24 C0409/25 C0409/26 C0409/28
  C0409/31 C0409/40 C0409/40 C0410/07
  C0411/14 C0447/V
Hop (1) A0621/22
Hop-Frog (28) B1345/T
  B1345/V B1346/02 B1346/04 B1346/07
  B1346/13 B1346/21 B1346/24 B1346/31
  B1346/37 B1347/04 B1347/04 B1347/20
  B1347/24 B1347/27 B1347/29 B1347/31
  B1348/01 B1348/17 B1348/21 B1349/28
  B1350/11 B1350/18 B1350/29 B1351/11
  B1353/04 B1353/20 B1354/17
Hop-Frog's (1) B1352/01
hope (111)
hoped (5) A0593/26
  A0696/29 C0114/16 C0126/35 C0531/07
hopeless (6) A0036/14 A0404/04
  B0958/25 B0961/28 C0077/30 C0187/14
hopelessness (3) A0139/21
  A0329/07 C0088/01
hopes (20) A0054/29
  A0063/29 A0228/10 A0426/09 A0448/V
  A0560/08 A0566/02 A0654/27 B0931/06
  B1107/19 B1128/09 B1129/11 B1178/11
  B1385/33 C0066/24 C0100/26 C0120/01
  C0416/25 C0563/40 C0565/06
hoping (3) B0830/34
  C0090/02 C0145/29
Hopkinson, Joseph (1) A0278/28
hopperer> (1) A0464/14
Horace (2) A0111/02 A0652/14
hordes (2) B1190/29 C0065/20
horizon (42) A0136/15 A0138/20
  A0196/01 A0209/02 A0209/04 A0460/01
  A0460/02 A0580/31 A0585/22 A0588/23
  B0842/03 B1080/28 B1080/28 B1080/32
  B1080/35 B1155/35 B1280/30 C0129/39
  C0159/07 C0159/21 C0163/41 C0166/12
  C0203/23 C0204/36 C0205/23 C0205/27
  C0397/18 C0398/20 C0402/06 C0408/07
  C0408/08 C0408/13 C0408/16 C0416/15
  C0416/23 C0417/03 C0417/05 C0417/23
  C0417/27 C0418/08 C0443/V C0575/16
horizontal (5) B0842/04
  B1382/15 C0410/18 C0415/25 C0573/11
horizontally (3) A0631/11
  B1261/27 B1382/17
horn (4) A0690/17
  A0690/17 B1296/22 C0437/V
horn-blende (1) A0182/08
hornblende (2) A0175/25 A0175/V
Hornet (1) C0110/02
horns (6) A0175/08 A0181/29
  A0690/17 B1162/15 B1165/16 B1165/32
horrendum (2) B0993/12 B1010/25
horresco (1) A0382/16
Horreur (2) A0033/17 A0036/24
horrible (63)
horribly (6) A0303/21 A0543/31
  C0182/08 C0197/34 C0446/V C0579/29

horrid (8) A0382/29
A0383/30 A0384/20 A0414/23 B0732/04
B1163/06 C0107/34 C0125/08
horridly (1) A0579/03
horrific (1) B0911/06
Horror (2) B0850/01 B0855/35
horror (108)
horror-inspiring (1) A0461/02
horror-stricken (2) B1354/06
C0397/34
horrorless (1) B0949/11
horrors (22) A0080/10 A0235/V
A0243/15 A0243/30 A0247/27 A0253/31
A0328/22 A0443/17 A0559/23 A0644/V
A0685/12 A0687/22 A0690/24 A0696/05
B0768/24 B0959/19 B1239/33 C0081/04
C0117/16 C0134/20 C0197/39 C0413/01
Horse (1) B1293/34
horse (46) A0019/10 A0022/08
A0022/09 A0023/07 A0023/19 A0023/20
A0024/04 A0024/07 A0024/07 A0024/12
A0026/01 A0026/14 A0027/02 A0027/22
A0027/V A0027/V A0028/09 A0029/25
A0398/09 A0400/22 B0958/20 B1003/22
B1044/16 B1046/20 B1046/33 B1053/31
B1057/31 B1057/33 B1058/23 B1058/25
B1090/20 B1093/09 B1093/10 B1093/10
B1093/11 B1093/13 B1093/17 B1093/20
B1153/32 B1159/02 B1166/01 B1166/10
C0387/M C0541/07 C0555/11 C0557/07
horse-jockey (1) A0388/32
Horse-Shade (1) A0018/V
horse's (3) A0027/14
B1048/32 B1160/31
horseback (5) A0397/03
B0863/07 B1044/14 C0118/18 C0553/26
horseman (1) A0029/09
horses (17) A0020/07
A0023/28 A0081/05 A0175/05 A0181/26
A0347/31 A0535/20 B0874/28 B1089/22
B1090/19 B1093/12 B1093/12 C0535/15
C0535/18 C0541/05 C0548/31 C0557/23
horses' (1) C0554/27
Horsley (1) A0652/27
horticulturists (1) B0807/11
Hortulus (2) A0515/31 A0515/34
hose (3) A0247/25
A0508/35 C0534/23
hospitable (2) A0057/09 A0067/03
hospital (3) B0959/06
B0961/04 B1003/11
hospitality (2) A0104/30 B1055/04
hospitals (2) B0960/08 B1006/30
host (33) A0112/06
A0205/25 A0343/13 A0348/01 A0348/13
A0402/34 A0444/03 A0513/16 A0515/09
A0530/01 B0811/07 B0990/28 B1004/35
B1007/04 B1007/26 B1009/16 B1009/20
B1010/V B1011/06 B1014/01 B1015/23
B1017/09 B1055/11 B1056/20 B1057/06
B1059/07 B1215/06 B1246/15 B1249/25
B1301/22 C0068/21 C0122/14 C0388/02
host's (1) B1019/31
hostages (1) C0171/07
hostel (2) B0839/31 B0840/30
hostelrie (1) A0241/26
hostess (1) A0384/16
hostile (1) C0175/20
hostilities (2) C0540/31 C0555/39
hostility (7) A0019/07
A0120/06 A0433/20 C0539/36 C0548/24
C0549/08 C0569/22
hosts (1) B0808/13
hot (17) A0028/19
A0136/22 A0152/30 A0340/03 A0388/05
A0610/23 B0856/06 B0944/02 B1089/26
B1168/26 B1373/12 C0064/19 C0072/34
C0141/14 C0142/14 C0142/36 C0579/29
hot-corn (1) B1092/29
hot-headedness (1) B1050/20
hot> (1) A0464/06
Hotel (3) B0978/19
B0981/24 B0983/25
hotel (12) A0507/29
B0898/23 B0909/03 B0915/24 B0923/31
B0978/04 B0980/08 B0989/02 B0990/21
B0992/12 B0992/31 B1361/16
hotels (1) B0840/03
hotly (3) A0242/16
B1158/18 C0140/35
Hotte (1) B1163/14
Hottentot (1) A0486/14
Hottentots (1) A0496/04
houl> (6) A0464/06 A0464/22
A0465/04 A0465/24 A0465/32 A0467/05
hould> (5) A0467/28
A0470/04 A0470/11 A0470/14 A0470/19
houly> (1) A0464/11
hound (1) B1329/02
hour (162)
hour's (3) A0059/13
C0145/32 C0191/36
Houri (2) A0313/09 A0664/V
hourly (15) A0211/18
A0234/06 A0234/21 A0243/12 A0353/21
A0458/27 A0616/17 A0653/06 B0731/12
B0856/05 B1122/32 B1212/13 B1213/27
C0093/14 C0419/15
hours (119)
hours' (2) A0028/22 B0827/17
House (8) A0366/13
A0397/22 A0397/T A0399/18 A0405/07
A0417/17 A0495/V A0681/M
house (135)
housed (1) B0826/32
household (12) A0166/16
A0189/32 A0218/24 A0296/05 A0427/30
A0457/04 A0495/05 A0498/25 B0725/03
B0849/07 B0856/17 C0393/09
housekeeper (1) B0871/31
houseless (1) B0963/08
houses (25) A0019/06
A0121/13 A0122/15 A0243/33 A0244/25
A0367/01 A0428/02 A0490/21 A0508/24
A0554/V A0582/13 B0945/09 B0947/15
B0980/23 B0980/25 B0980/28 B1101/09
B1303/03 B1337/27 B1360/16 C0177/26
C0179/27 C0527/18 C0530/05 C0548/14
hove (1) A0140/27
hovel (1) A0486/12

hovels (1) A0122/11
hover (4) A0143/30
A0711/32 B1215/25 B1276/35
hovered (9) A0078/32
A0140/03 A0196/V A0311/26 B0963/35
C0125/07 C0205/28 C0419/02 C0539/36
hovering (3) A0162/24
A0327/17 C0153/21
how (344)
however (618)
howiver> (1) A0467/12
howl (4) B0859/03
B1015/03 B1372/05 C0169/16
howled (1) A0692/16
howling (7) A0145/17
A0579/06 A0582/22 B1021/10 C0131/36
C0200/16 C0564/18
howlings (3) A0036/14
A0582/02 B0825/17
howls (1) C0123/05
Hoyle (1) A0529/28
hu (15) A0105/23
A0105/23 A0105/23 A0113/06 A0113/06
A0113/06 A0650/27 A0650/27 A0650/27
B1012/29 B1012/29 B1012/29 B1103/13
B1103/13 B1103/13
hubbub (2) A0128/21 C0387/23
huddled (2) A0280/08 C0136/06
huddling (1) C0099/27
Hudibras (1) A0346/04
Hudson (5) A0491/19
B0726/33 B0862/08 B1246/03 B1334/12
Hudson/Bay (1) C0525/09
Hudson/Bay/fur/company (1) C0561/03
Hudson's (1) C0525/19
Hudson's/bay (1) C0525/30
hue (30) A0195/05 A0246/32
A0313/10 A0316/22 A0321/16 A0328/16
A0367/15 A0410/34 A0502/02 A0502/V
A0578/34 A0663/V A0671/28 A0672/04
A0673/28 A0674/03 B0943/15 B1160/33
B1235/12 B1239/23 B1281/35 C0126/05
C0172/07 C0204/14 C0204/38 C0206/07
C0417/16 C0418/32 C0538/36 C0543/14
hues (8) A0209/02
A0209/03 A0235/25 A0329/12 A0497/30
A0498/19 A0641/V C0172/02
huge (96)
hugely (1) C0560/25
huggab (1) A0047/25
Hugh (2) A0249/15 A0250/35
Hugo, Jacobus (1) A0621/16
Huguenot (1) B0806/02
hulk (19) A0138/11
A0143/V C0065/33 C0115/07 C0117/23
C0118/05 C0126/36 C0129/28 C0134/10
C0139/25 C0140/14 C0141/15 C0141/24
C0143/07 C0143/38 C0144/16 C0144/25
C0146/20 C0149/02
Hull (1) C0146/42
hull (13) A0140/06
A0251/29 A0579/18 B0830/16 B1248/08
C0062/26 C0125/36 C0126/28 C0141/05
C0143/31 C0144/06 C0144/13 C0144/35
hum (11) A0512/12
->A0681/06 A0697/07 B0821/11 B0944/31
B1155/12 B1159/33 B1160/05 B1161/03
B1161/13 B1294/23
Hum-drum (1) A0270/06
Hum-Drum (14) B1129/14 B1130/08
B1130/12 B1130/27 B1131/22 B1131/25
B1134/19 B1136/11 B1136/32 B1137/28
B1138/25 B1144/26 B1145/02 B1145/07
human (145)
human-looking (1) A0028/05
human-perfectibility (2) A0176/08
A0180/29
humane (1) B1093/24
humanely (1) B1089/21
humanities (2) A0652/17 B1096/24
Humanity (4) B0855/37
B1293/19 B1293/20 B1294/07
humanity (23) A0337/14
A0337/27 A0402/12 A0478/25 A0538/24
A0558/09 A0641/20 A0703/12 A0709/14
A0711/28 A0712/06 B0850/08 B0855/04
B0969/12 B1005/28 B1178/11 B1219/15
B1240/14 B1268/11 B1274/16 B1276/31
B1277/11 B1302/21
humble (20) A0227/33
A0263/18 A0268/09 A0268/23 A0274/01
A0296/V A0301/29 A0348/20 A0665/09
B0727/29 B0864/08 B1129/20 B1145/15
B1359/06 B1371/18 B1382/28 C0085/41
C0391/01 C0426/28 C0438/V
humbled (3) A0059/07
A0444/12 B1017/15
humbly (1) B1348/05
Humboldt (1) C0403/36
humbug (3) A0090/31
A0109/23 B1091/27
Humdrum (2) A0268/07 A0622/09
Hume, David (1) B1314/16
humid (1) A0512/08
humility (2) A0104/15 A0509/33
humming (7) A0137/04
A0251/20 B0898/06 B0943/16 B1108/33
B1155/31 C0071/28
humming-stuff (2) A0241/31 A0244/11
humming-top (1) A0341/17
humor (17) A0098/10
A0110/25 A0386/33 A0547/06 A0626/20
A0626/32 B0724/29 B0725/09 B0810/22
B0817/06 B1056/24 B1115/09 B1208/05
B1278/20 B1347/24 C0387/12 C0531/03
humored (1) B1006/01
humorous (1) B1119/M
humour (2) A0053/27 C0092/40
hump (2) B1169/20 C0558/35
humph (9) A0093/31
A0093/32 A0094/15 A0113/12 A0113/13
A0113/19 A0180/10 B1102/18 B1162/12
Humphrey's (1) B1358/16
Hundred (1) B0806/T
hundred (198)
hundreds (6) A0694/18 B0746/25
B0874/09 B1159/30 B1295/31 C0098/39
hundredth (1) C0400/32
hundredths (1) B1314/17
hung (77)

Hungarian (3) A0018/09
A0029/V A0292/01
Hungarians (1) A0018/10
Hungary (2) A0018/03 A0020/20
hunger (7) A0081/31
B1145/26 C0120/14 C0126/22 C0128/28
C0132/10 C0191/20
hungry (1) C0076/27
Hungry/Hill (1) C0433/03
hunks (1) A0486/03
Hunt (1) C0146/36
hunt (2) A0026/06 C0571/31
Hunt, John (2) C0102/22 C0112/30
Hunt, Wilson Price (1) C0528/10
hunted (2) A0078/23 B0808/18
hunter (4) A0024/30
C0532/03 C0532/22 C0566/21
hunter's (1) C0562/05
hunters (13) C0531/03
C0531/28 C0535/12 C0540/05 C0542/39
C0561/25 C0561/40 C0562/15 C0562/21
C0562/36 C0563/28 C0566/30 C0568/13
hunting (12) A0020/07
A0025/12 A0026/06 C0522/03 C0529/09
C0529/27 C0530/11 C0536/17 C0539/24
C0540/10 C0544/11 C0571/29
'huomo (1) A0344/31
hurdy-gurdy (1) A0294/V
hurl (2) A0140/25 A0690/31
hurled (19) A0137/07
A0300/15 A0356/23 A0459/11 A0567/18
B1104/07 B1162/21 B1354/22 C0088/16
C0112/25 C0114/35 C0116/28 C0140/25
C0144/05 C0149/36 C0190/05 C0397/02
C0421/27 C0578/30
hurling (1) C0185/21
Hurlygurly, Tim (2) A0252/27
A0252/31
hurrah (2) A0128/V B0824/13
hurricane (15) A0137/30
A0140/13 A0582/28 A0584/37 A0585/31
A0586/36 A0594/13 B0930/17 B1078/21
B1392/02 C0062/41 C0106/38 C0117/18
C0149/19 C0396/27
hurried (34) A0023/15 A0068/01
A0080/33 A0139/17 A0155/V A0166/V
A0267/33 A0410/33 A0412/16 A0416/01
A0444/32 A0508/06 A0513/30 A0537/20
A0567/22 A0590/07 A0594/15 A0631/02
A0694/16 A0694/35 A0696/23 B0841/31
B0924/12 B0947/09 B0960/21 B0977/06
B0977/13 B1069/28 B1114/11 B1357/04
B1373/20 C0110/30 C0389/37 C0421/22
hurriedly (19) A0138/26
A0155/15 A0198/13 A0216/V A0324/24
A0329/25 A0439/11 A0511/27 A0642/08
A0655/27 A0663/22 A0676/18 A0690/06
B0827/04 B0944/24 B0959/01 B1350/27
C0073/13 C0568/27
hurry (23) A0043/01
A0044/22 A0088/18 A0088/29 A0098/18
A0102/30 A0265/21 A0269/36 A0272/17
A0281/28 A0329/03 A0341/19 A0347/09
A0490/20 A0529/12 B0879/19 B0900/22
B1182/24 B1226/13 B1258/20 B1370/19
->B1372/15 C0097/12
hurrying (7) A0145/24
A0416/16 A0446/31 A0608/20 C0058/27
C0060/02 C0204/27
hurt (5) A0353/30
A0631/02 B0873/08 C0076/27 C0579/23
hurting (1) C0169/11
hurts (1) B1091/15
husband (20) A0057/15
B0732/38 B0902/28 B0903/01 B0910/15
B0914/V B0916/24 B0916/26 B0926/35
B0926/35 B0929/03 B0929/11 B0933/22
B0956/27 B0958/05 B0958/14 B1107/12
B1153/12 B1169/05 B1170/04
husband's (3) B0914/21
B1159/35 C0552/27
husbands (1) B1169/09
hush (7) A0088/35
A0103/15 A0490/01 A0651/11 B0907/31
B0933/04 C0083/23
hushed (4) A0675/30
B0726/13 B0731/05 B0753/11
hushing (1) A0639/23
huskiness (1) A0411/02
husky (3) A0023/21
A0218/21 A0447/07
hut (10) B0807/17 B0808/03
B0808/07 B0811/07 B0814/23 B0827/05
B0827/12 B0945/30 C0175/05 C0561/12
huts (1) A0122/11
huzzy (1) A0655/19
hx (1) B1374/07
hxg (1) B1374/15
hxllx (1) B1374/18
hxme (2) B1374/09 B1374/10
hxmx (1) B1374/14
hxw (2) B1374/07 B1374/19
hxwl (1) B1374/18
hyacinth (2) A0036/02 A0152/28
hyacinthine (2) A0312/13 B1386/03
hyacinths (1) B1283/08
hybrid (4) C0093/34
C0100/31 C0104/10 C0117/32
Hyde (1) A0464/15
hydrangea (1) B1334/20
hydrogen (5) B1071/02
B1073/06 B1073/14 B1073/19 C0394/02
hydrophobia (2) B1093/14 C0101/02
hyena (3) B0944/07
B0948/14 B1300/21
hymn (5) A0124/28
A0125/34 A0227/30 A0227/36 A0232/V
Hymns (1) A0176/03
hymns (1) A0182/01
hyper-exquisite (1) B1371/16
hyper-fizzitistical (1) A0625/V
hyperbole (1) B1122/04
Hyperion (1) B1136/11
hyperobtrusive (1) B0991/24
hyperquizzitistical (1) A0625/04
hypochondria (1) C0522/01
hypochondriac (3) A0405/24
A0409/14 A0413/14
hypocrisy (3) B0746/30
C0066/14 C0066/14

hypocritical (2) B0797/25 C0201/16
hypothenuse (6) B1080/28 B1080/30
B1080/37 C0408/08 C0408/10 C0408/18
hypothesis (7) B0748/15
B0871/21 B1031/32 B1052/33 B1119/M
B1301/10 B1322/06
hypothetical (1) B0723/24
hysteria (1) A0412/10
hysterical (3) A0151/26
A0190/07 B0934/09
hysterics (6) A0059/01 A0069/V
A0070/02 A0253/27 B1183/21 C0066/02
I (7883)
i.e. (1) B1093/12
i' (1) A0034/12
I'd (2) B0815/09 C0067/22
I'en (1) C0430/35
I'll (27) A0094/06
A0113/30 A0292/M A0343/09 A0387/25
A0388/V A0470/08 A0623/29 A0624/12
A0624/12 A0624/13 A0624/13 A0624/14
A0624/26 A0651/08 A0651/08 A0651/11
A0656/18 A0657/30 B0820/22 B0820/26
B1046/04 B1046/10 B1103/32 B1373/08
B1373/09 B1383/17
I'm (8) A0285/12
A0336/05 A0385/12 A0465/03 A0651/19
B0812/17 B0812/21 B0820/28
I's (2) A0267/34 B1373/22
i's (2) A0277/35 B1373/07
I've (3) A0373/14
A0464/09 A0708/10
Iago (1) A0383/14
Iamblichus (1) A0176/05
Iamblicus (1) A0180/27
ibid. (1) A0611/32
Ibis (1) B1188/13
ice (57)
ice-cream (1) B1092/30
icebergs (2) C0163/27 C0163/41
Iceland (1) B1161/24
ices (1) C0416/24
ich (1) A0150/V
ichor (1) B1242/11
iciness (2) A0397/18 A0437/17
icy (7) A0214/26
A0328/16 B0964/03 B1225/12 B1237/17
C0160/01 C0160/13
id (2) A0534/27 A0654/08
iddication> (1) A0464/11
idea (219)
ideal (2) A0273/12 B0889/23
ideal (9) A0230/03
A0322/V A0708/11 B0723/M B0723/M
B0924/21 B1089/15 B1123/08 B1123/20
idealische (1) B0723/M
idealischer (1) B0723/M
ideality (7) A0298/V
A0405/11 A0413/12 A0527/V A0527/V
A0533/10 B1220/04
idealized (2) A0318/V B1273/04
ideas (48) A0028/11
A0079/11 A0086/11 A0097/11 A0105/07
A0105/09 A0107/12 A0108/06 A0210/17
A0282/06 A0296/05 A0345/21 A0353/05
->A0356/03 A0429/28 A0496/28 A0500/22
A0511/21 A0536/22 A0558/07 A0603/20
A0610/16 A0703/28 B0822/32 B0826/34
B0985/12 B0990/19 B1034/14 B1089/13
B1089/14 B1089/14 B1128/17 B1190/18
B1234/24 B1268/27 B1293/23 B1310/24
B1311/28 C0073/19 C0161/22 C0392/32
C0398/02 C0421/22 C0423/24 C0438/V
C0442/V C0551/39 C0564/04
idee (2) A0096/10 B0986/34
idees (5) A0096/11
A0216/10 A0216/10 A0216/11 A0216/V
identical (20) A0073/07
A0241/V A0270/35 A0435/03 A0553/05
A0559/29 A0708/29 B0769/14 B0865/36
B0906/31 B0989/17 B1164/08 B1180/15
B1273/24 B1358/10 C0143/08 C0388/20
C0388/38 C0391/06 C0547/30
identically (3) A0404/V
A0404/V A0448/V
identification (8) B0745/20
B0745/22 B0828/04 B0984/29 B0984/32
B0985/04 B0985/10 B1035/31
identified (6) A0399/16 A0473/28
B0730/01 B0731/10 B0736/06 B0877/20
identifies (1) A0529/09
identify (4) A0079/26
A0563/03 A0685/31 B0770/24
identifying (2) A0560/30 B0769/23
identity (30) A0035/02 A0211/05
A0213/31 A0226/27 A0226/29 A0226/36
A0226/37 A0231/01 A0231/03 A0231/09
A0231/10 A0234/24 A0356/02 A0401/28
A0432/20 A0439/30 A0445/25 A0448/10
B0732/26 B0736/05 B0737/29 B0744/33
B0746/19 B0747/03 B0748/10 B0748/31
B0751/11 B0915/04 B0915/16 B0993/22
idiocy (2) A0531/05 C0078/26
idiom (1) B0836/03
idiosyncracy (1) A0511/14
idiosyncrasy (10) A0079/19 A0213/26
B0724/18 B0757/07 B0946/03 B0963/14
B1038/10 B1038/25 B1247/V C0524/01
idiosyncratic (1) B1038/16
idiot (6) A0073/33 A0556/31
A0625/V A0691/29 B0745/22 B0769/26
idiotic (5) A0216/11
C0130/19 C0131/17 C0205/10 C0398/35
idiots (4) A0125/28
A0499/22 C0395/31 C0425/10
idle (8) A0547/15
A0561/22 A0583/06 B1113/10 C0195/16
C0395/10 C0427/28 C0564/29
idleness (2) A0209/23 A0438/01
idly (2) A0028/28 B0753/23
idolaters (1) A0043/07
idolator (1) A0046/11
idolatrous (5) A0044/16
A0045/28 A0122/13 A0311/13 A0323/11
idolatry (1) A0317/19
idolised (1) B0899/20
idols (3) B0945/16
B1303/20 C0169/29
if (803)
Iflesen (1) A0579/25

ignes (1) A0135/17
ignited (3) A0248/24
B1321/09 C0405/24
igniting (1) C0396/15
ignoble (2) A0033/02 B1123/24
ignoramus (1) A0353/07
ignoramus (5) A0488/12
B1007/08 B1012/03 B1144/02 B1261/21
ignoramuses (1) A0622/06
ignorance (16) A0313/16
B0726/14 B0756/25 B0761/27 B1017/13
B1095/09 B1187/10 B1194/16 B1325/11
C0097/11 C0169/20 C0392/27 C0426/01
C0428/19 C0431/10 C0432/41
ignorant (23) A0228/27
A0233/08 A0236/03 A0267/19 A0353/31
A0457/34 A0458/19 A0601/04 A0707/23
B0743/30 B0915/14 B1131/15 B1272/24
B1313/15 B1316/10 B1317/20 C0114/06
C0139/09 C0202/27 C0393/12 C0429/07
C0447/V C0568/04
ignoratio (3) A0345/19
A0345/19 A0345/24
ignotum (1) B1080/10
igualmente (1) A0621/03
ihre (1) B0723/M
Il (1) A0344/31
il (14) A0035/05 A0036/06
A0036/18 A0036/21 A0036/22 A0036/25
A0037/25 A0273/29 A0356/13 A0397/M
A0602/07 B0897/03 B0986/33 B1207/06
iligant> (2) A0464/15 A0466/32
ill (40) A0059/06
A0063/01 A0068/24 A0107/32 A0135/01
A0176/10 A0180/31 A0189/11 A0210/22
A0228/01 A0248/05 A0316/20 A0385/03
A0442/17 A0500/02 A0507/07 A0545/04
B0810/22 B0813/25 B0815/33 B0851/19
B0854/31 B0928/18 B1052/32 B1145/27
B1158/09 B1169/15 B1195/06 B1208/05
B1259/15 B1347/23 B1349/28 C0078/37
C0122/32 C0139/16 C0421/01 C0430/43
C0432/42 C0561/11 C0563/36
ill-adapted (1) A0486/26
ill-admeasurement (1) B0985/10
ill-advised (1) A0135/07
ill-bred (1) B0923/02
ill-breeding (2) A0249/30 A0386/18
ill-conceived (1) B1193/06
ill-constructed (1) C0403/02
ill-contrived (1) A0240/08
ill-directed (1) A0427/28
ill-disposed (1) B0747/28
ill-fated (1) A0150/01
ill-favored (2) A0240/V A0252/25
ill-fitted (1) B0930/27
ill-fortune (1) A0061/01
ill-founded (1) A0527/V
ill-furnished (1) A0499/03
ill-health (2) A0026/25 A0058/03
ill-humor (1) B1372/32
ill-looking (1) A0203/02
ill-luck (2) A0058/08 A0068/31
ill-made (1) C0551/38
ill-mannered (1) B1159/35
ill-natured (1) A0437/05
ill-omened (1) A0311/14
ill-regulated (1) C0392/33
ill-timed (2) A0249/07 C0166/26
ill-treated (2) B0933/12 B0957/21
ill-used (1) B0851/12
ill-ventilated (1) B1224/14
illae (1) B0767/17
illegibility (1) A0281/24
illegible (6) A0265/20 A0267/06
A0267/37 A0272/30 A0280/04 A0281/18
illiberality (4) B1207/18
B1207/19 B1207/27 B1208/02
illigant> (4) A0465/29
A0466/26 A0467/16 A0467/25
illimitable (7) A0198/09
A0198/15 A0535/15 A0677/04 B0895/23
B1316/12 B1346/09
Illinois (1) C0207/14
illness (11) A0323/21
A0398/21 A0403/35 B0812/14 B0956/13
B1032/22 B1224/11 C0409/03 C0561/19
C0565/09 C0565/21
illnesses (1) A0324/05
illuminated (9) A0087/29
A0093/30 A0113/09 A0190/01 A0245/V
A0695/V B1351/18 C0423/15 C0423/17
illuminating (1) B1156/04
illumination (1) C0078/23
illumine (1) C0414/10
illumined (4) A0672/14
A0695/19 A0696/11 B0821/33
illusion (3) A0663/V
A0663/V C0574/03
illusions (1) B1330/30
illustrate (1) B1010/10
illustrated (1) A0579/05
illustration (2) A0556/25 B1321/07
illustrations (2) B1179/05 B1179/07
Illustrious (1) A0126/05
illustrious (21) A0019/06
A0021/24 A0127/30 A0250/02 A0349/04
A0531/18 A0704/11 B0750/31 B0957/13
B0976/30 B1092/18 B1130/03 B1130/18
B1137/12 B1144/30 B1164/34 B1269/11
B1310/32 B1358/08 C0426/39 C0437/V
illy (2) A0486/V A0545/V
Ils (1) A0109/31
ilse> (1) A0466/28
image (15) A0124/12
A0156/24 A0210/31 A0300/11 A0311/01
A0399/29 A0448/02 A0448/15 A0675/18
A0689/28 B0855/33 B0856/02 B0909/07
C0112/03 C0405/28
imaged (1) A0616/23
images (18) A0153/15 A0244/08
A0397/10 A0398/12 A0401/01 A0405/18
A0614/06 A0640/21 A0641/22 A0689/05
B0963/36 B1180/21 B1184/28 B1223/09
C0118/12 C0124/25 C0205/36 C0537/40
imaginable (7) B0889/V
B0898/14 C0067/20 C0151/13 C0172/36
C0193/01 C0568/37
imaginary (3) A0022/03
A0411/10 B0982/29

imagination (67)
imaginations (5) A0189/17
B0736/28 B1301/37 C0093/35 C0112/18
imaginative (13) A0027/09
A0213/01 A0226/28 A0231/03 A0348/02
A0427/18 A0502/04 A0527/V A0531/10
A0623/28 B1122/27 C0055/16 C0078/12
imagine (69)
imagined (50) A0035/13 A0036/V
A0058/32 A0078/29 A0106/23 A0139/18
A0145/16 A0164/24 A0284/12 A0353/26
A0355/36 A0408/13 A0704/34 A0705/06
A0707/04 B0732/29 B0733/09 B0739/08
B0755/06 B0759/32 B0763/33 B0765/14
B0766/10 B0767/05 B0768/17 B0833/18
B0977/33 B1010/12 B1013/02 B1214/27
B1250/35 B1269/33 B1270/05 B1297/36
B1317/16 B1350/23 B1362/10 B1370/24
C0076/29 C0078/04 C0123/21 C0129/37
C0135/30 C0139/29 C0182/25 C0197/39
C0403/07 C0407/14 C0424/01 C0531/16
imagines (2) B0744/10 B0987/32
imagining (4) A0036/10
A0340/31 B0772/17 B0940/07
imaginings (1) C0075/41
imbecile (3) A0691/29
B1297/23 C0134/34
imbecilities (1) C0130/27
imbecility (2) A0610/13 C0145/10
imbedded (9) A0036/V
A0428/09 A0553/22 A0559/07 A0567/06
B0742/32 B1115/22 B1259/35 B1337/02
imbibe (1) A0478/24
imbibed (5) A0145/04
A0251/06 A0320/20 A0611/12 B0876/02
imbibes (1) A0604/08
imbitter (1) C0134/04
imbodied (1) A0079/37
imbue (2) A0711/16 B1276/17
imbued (9) A0144/30
A0319/10 A0437/09 A0703/19 B0905/10
B0946/21 B1268/19 C0080/19 C0521/24
imitate (6) A0496/23 A0708/02
B0947/20 B1273/02 C0059/32 C0204/09
imitated (4) A0708/05
B1015/V B1273/05 C0092/19
imitating (1) B0992/17
Imitation (1) A0018/V
imitation (15) A0241/06
A0270/21 A0434/32 A0435/07 A0437/29
A0437/32 A0566/26 B0905/25 B1011/32
B1092/18 B1120/06 B1385/26 B1386/07
C0108/41 C0112/18
imitations (1) B1350/33
imitative (1) A0559/22
immaculate (2) A0096/07 B1383/13
immaterial (2) B0989/13 B1033/12
immateriality (2) B1033/13 B1040/06
immature (2) A0435/30 A0510/12
immeasurable (3) A0590/V
A0613/25 A0653/14
immeasurably (4) A0442/06
A0582/18 A0711/12 B1249/20
immediate (72)
immediately (235)
immemorial (1) A0322/06
immense (59)
immensely (8) A0405/31
A0478/31 B0892/11 B0914/17 B0976/24
B1233/25 C0072/17 C0107/35
immensity (4) A0099/33
A0600/30 B1186/25 C0536/38
immerse (1) B0741/24
immersed (5) A0316/17
B0741/15 B0741/18 B0744/13 B0964/02
immersion (7) B0732/11
B0740/12 B0741/29 B0743/07 C0127/36
C0129/18 C0129/21
immethodical (1) B0943/19
imminency (1) C0144/38
imminent (16) A0023/17
A0053/19 A0144/V B0949/17 B1194/23
C0060/28 C0062/27 C0063/06 C0096/33
C0106/39 C0114/06 C0116/17 C0117/25
C0198/19 C0398/23 C0556/31
immoderate (4) A0211/V
A0249/07 A0325/12 C0179/12
immoderately (1) C0202/17
immolation (2) A0536/25 B1257/04
immoral (1) A0623/32
immortal (12) A0099/33
A0382/31 A0384/01 A0384/25 A0612/07
A0664/12 B0852/26 B0887/20 B1037/09
B1145/12 B1293/20 B1361/20
immortality (9) A0019/10
A0150/V A0617/06 A0682/23 B1031/05
B1031/20 B1038/31 B1211/02 B1274/02
immortalize (1) A0105/09
immortalized (1) A0071/26
immovably (1) C0425/14
immoveable (1) A0681/13
immoveably (1) A0461/V
immutable (2) B1296/31 B1313/32
Imp (2) B1219/T B1224/05
imp (1) B1103/34
impaired (4) A0282/09
A0545/12 A0663/V B1233/21
impalpability (2) B1296/33 B1314/01
impalpable (7) A0074/17
A0461/07 B1161/39 B1312/20 C0194/05
C0194/15 C0559/37
impart (2) A0581/09 C0553/03
imparted (2) A0106/07 A0329/15
impartiality (1) A0365/12
imparts (2) B1038/02 B1114/08
impassable (1) C0159/23
impassioned (2) B0905/13 C0537/22
impatience (14) A0439/13 A0508/05
A0513/09 A0612/16 B0828/24 B0833/34
B0896/16 B0901/22 B0924/02 B1178/31
B1223/V C0096/13 C0123/17 C0569/20
impatient (10) A0387/V A0446/13
B0900/12 B0964/04 B1163/37 B1178/13
B1222/14 B1223/14 B1263/15 C0083/37
impatiently (3) B0892/01
B1348/23 C0062/15
impede (1) B1039/06
impeded (16) A0054/03
A0063/12 A0243/21 A0508/09 A0627/13
A0671/19 A0685/02 B1070/08 B1077/33

->B1282/08 C0094/40 C0159/06 C0164/13
C0183/08 C0194/10 C0418/44
impediment (6) A0613/08 B1039/07
B1039/10 B1329/22 B1352/05 C0061/18
impediments (5) A0139/15
A0244/08 B1039/13 C0096/28 C0163/13
impeding (1) A0508/12
impelled (4) B0948/11
B1030/17 B1055/06 B1249/11
impelling (1) B1033/21
impels (4) B1033/23
B1033/28 B1221/02 B1221/02
impended (2) A0696/09 B1055/09
impending (2) A0028/V B0833/23
impends (1) B0767/30
impenetrable (5) A0373/22
B0807/13 B1279/09 B1282/08 C0445/V
imperatively (3) B0891/24
B0933/23 B0988/34
imperceptible (9) A0028/14
A0682/01 B0855/28 B0893/06 B1044/27
B1113/08 B1222/30 B1237/10 B1238/09
imperceptibly (3) A0212/19
A0664/08 A0706/10
imperfect (8) A0690/10
B0723/M B0723/M B0749/03 B0832/29
B0853/04 B1072/09 C0172/09
imperfection (1) B1039/12
imperfectly (3) A0080/29
A0495/V B0767/01
imperial (3) A0157/V
A0159/18 A0671/16
imperious (2) A0026/08 A0446/03
imperiously (1) A0445/20
imperiousness (1) A0431/10
imperishable (2) B0831/11 B1317/32
imperor> (1) A0464/11
impertinence (4) B0726/18
B0870/02 B0871/10 C0390/16
impertinences (2) B0903/V B1291/16
impertinent (6) A0293/21 A0432/07
A0445/14 B0871/10 B1224/15 B1318/10
impetuosity (10) A0028/V A0029/08
A0442/29 A0580/10 A0582/12 A0676/21
B1372/20 C0079/04 C0424/38 C0562/38
impetuous (11) A0020/V
A0025/27 A0027/V A0144/06 A0253/24
A0412/18 A0581/24 B0901/19 C0421/24
C0424/25 C0552/38
impetuously (10) A0102/01 A0316/23
B0907/16 B0947/17 B0963/03 B1223/13
B1223/V C0072/30 C0190/06 C0446/V
impetus (9) A0479/29
A0479/30 B0989/V B1070/10 B1070/11
B1321/23 C0098/02 C0144/03 C0578/30
impia (1) A0681/M
impiety (1) A0627/26
impinging (1) B1070/05
impious (1) A0120/10
impiously (1) A0044/06
implacable (2) A0120/06 B1107/23
implanted (2) A0098/20 B1272/19
implements (5) B0816/30
B0823/06 C0394/39 C0396/04 C0399/12
implicate (2) A0561/29 B0727/34
implicated (4) A0548/12
A0563/29 B0727/21 B1051/28
implicit (5) A0075/12
A0431/24 A0446/10 B0924/17 C0564/01
implicitly (4) A0226/08
A0230/05 B0816/23 B1361/28
implied (5) A0019/25
A0103/28 A0108/11 B0907/27 B1322/26
impliedly (1) B1314/33
implies (2) A0529/19 B0987/09
implore (2) B0932/02 B1261/32
implored (3) A0624/03
B1348/34 C0122/17
imploring (2) B1109/03 C0111/22
imploringly (1) A0386/12
imply (7) A0019/25
A0550/25 B0844/15 B0880/03 B0910/19
B1109/24 B1339/05
implying (1) C0131/30
impolicy (1) B1221/V
impolitic (1) C0550/10
import (9) A0106/04
A0226/13 A0354/01 A0416/03 A0538/30
B0835/31 B0929/13 B1092/10 C0080/23
importa (1) A0621/03
importance (55)
important (62)
importunate (2) A0398/19 A0408/22
importuning (1) C0395/25
importunities (2) A0045/28 A0653/19
impose (1) B1258/09
imposed (4) A0104/27
A0252/06 B0825/08 B1258/16
imposing (2) A0488/28 C0562/41
imposition (1) A0488/27
impositions (2) A0057/02 A0066/27
impossibile (1) A0213/08
impossibilities (3) A0551/26
A0551/27 A0552/11
impossibility (15) A0210/04
A0251/V A0251/V A0547/21 A0551/19
B0826/10 B0942/02 B1116/07 B1183/28
B1315/26 B1315/29 C0061/14 C0186/20
C0394/10 C0414/26
impossible (136)
impost (1) B1302/18
impostor (1) A0447/08
imposts (1) B1193/12
imposture (1) B1257/09
impotent (4) A0317/01
A0612/23 A0667/48 B1079/09
impracticable (1) B0896/24
imprecations (2) B1020/03 C0123/05
impregnated (1) C0553/01
impregnating (1) A0603/27
impregnation (3) B0742/16
B1163/31 B1163/40
impress (15) A0099/24
A0218/30 A0316/27 A0446/08 A0514/23
A0555/11 A0641/V B0733/07 B0988/27
B1029/06 B1214/04 B1214/25 B1240/22
C0135/30 C0166/16
impressed (24) A0025/15
A0317/16 A0406/18 A0479/32 A0559/28
A0614/06 B0825/11 B0831/01 B0833/22

->B0892/28 B0940/28 B1030/04 B1109/14
B1182/25 B1240/20 B1299/33 B1325/01
B1329/18 B1331/04 B1331/04 C0109/11
C0125/19 C0182/02 C0420/12
impresses (3) B0878/25
B0888/20 B0955/14
impressing (2) B1030/10 B1193/32
impression (43) A0266/20
A0273/27 A0276/11 A0283/30 A0346/27
A0398/08 A0399/23 A0430/29 A0438/14
A0496/16 A0543/25 A0550/18 A0558/12
A0559/02 A0581/17 A0622/17 B0725/01
B0732/42 B0733/20 B0734/04 B0853/15
B0853/31 B0865/02 B0905/07 B0915/03
B0916/07 B1030/11 B1080/35 B1080/35
B1091/15 B1103/27 B1338/32 B1358/03
B1364/19 B1369/14 C0112/16 C0167/07
C0392/20 C0400/22 C0408/16 C0408/16
C0573/09 C0574/07
impressions (24) A0228/23
A0233/04 A0235/10 A0310/14 A0378/09
A0403/22 A0429/06 A0545/23 A0559/08
A0613/21 A0682/30 A0682/31 A0682/33
B0730/06 B0748/09 B0943/08 B1004/20
B1031/03 B1107/10 B1240/35 B1247/04
B1280/18 C0438/V C0538/38
impressive (6) A0028/02 A0298/V
A0339/10 A0411/12 A0641/23 B1003/31
impressively (2) B1047/21 B1057/10
impressiveness (1) A0297/12
imprimis (1) C0427/16
imprinted (1) B0823/29
imprisoned (9) A0544/22
A0544/27 A0564/09 B1021/25 B1057/29
B1093/26 B1279/08 C0084/37 C0090/06
imprisonment (1) C0081/06
improbabilities (1) A0164/06
improbability (1) A0163/V
improbable (11) A0527/V
B0732/16 B0739/25 B0744/21 B0807/31
B0813/16 B1101/32 B1168/40 B1188/19
B1358/24 C0088/03
impromptus (1) A0406/10
improper (3) B0723/21
B0902/01 C0524/23
improperly (2) A0226/29 B1383/23
impropriety (3) A0624/22
B0895/09 B1383/21
improve (4) A0708/03
A0709/07 B1273/02 B1274/13
improved (3) A0107/30
B1080/17 C0523/37
improvement (10) A0337/28 A0609/13
A0707/31 A0708/33 A0709/01 B0752/13
B1271/02 B1272/31 B1273/27 B1298/26
improvements (2) B1301/07 C0394/32
improves (1) A0489/28
improvisations (2) A0404/31
A0406/14
improvisatori (1) A0671/08
improvisatrice (2) A0087/09
A0100/19
improvised (1) A0405/11
improviso (1) A0343/24
imprudence (2) B0902/04 B0915/18
imprudent (1) A0653/28
imprudently (2) B0901/24 C0406/09
imps (1) A0243/11
impudence (2) B1109/08 B1134/02
impudent (2) B1337/15 C0055/23
impulse (21) A0297/05
A0676/10 B0769/21 B0946/21 B0947/V
B0984/23 B1213/35 B1214/03 B1214/07
B1214/08 B1214/22 B1214/25 B1214/28
B1215/01 B1215/23 B1219/10 B1221/05
B1222/02 B1222/27 B1249/03 B1372/28
impulses (10) A0296/V A0671/02
B0852/08 B0899/23 B1214/01 B1215/07
B1215/09 B1215/18 B1219/01 C0131/21
impulsion (1) B1033/26
impulsive (2) A0663/25 B0934/07
impune (1) B1260/01
impunity (8) A0034/27
A0440/27 A0564/06 B0969/14 B1131/24
B1225/V B1256/07 C0390/17
impurity (1) A0162/07
imputed (1) A0135/11
in (18) A0043/M A0056/09
A0072/30 A0161/04 A0244/18 A0296/V
A0365/V A0593/35 A0638/15 B0870/09
B1017/29 B1233/18 B1263/26 B1345/09
B1364/06 B1382/35 C0425/37 C0569/25
in (9631)
in-X-plicable (1) B1375/09
inability (12) A0054/01
A0063/10 A0304/05 A0583/11 A0710/35
B1276/01 B1297/06 B1297/19 B1314/10
B1315/22 B1315/35 B1346/06
inaccessibility (1) C0112/04
Inaccessible (1) C0155/09
inaccessible (5) A0401/08
A0529/25 B0817/24 B0943/02 C0567/20
inaccuracy (2) B1275/19 C0207/11
inaccurate (3) B1104/08
B1152/06 B1383/31
inadapted (1) B1273/V
inadequate (7) A0141/23
A0294/V A0705/16 C0075/15 C0096/29
C0400/36 C0410/02
inadmissible (3) A0457/31
A0498/28 A0499/24
inadvertence (1) A0528/33
inadvertent (1) A0530/18
inadvertently (1) B0762/12
inanimate (2) A0029/04 A0601/01
inanition (1) A0691/19
inapplicability (1) B1312/30
inapplicable (2) B0983/36 B1279/15
inappreciable (2) A0293/V B0773/09
inapprehension (1) B0990/03
inappropriate (3) A0406/04
A0432/15 A0496/01
inarticulate (2) A0324/26 A0510/15
inartistical (1) A0497/16
inasmuch (3) A0614/37
B1092/08 C0433/08
inattention (1) C0071/19
inaudible (2) A0536/V B0929/27
inaudibly (2) A0415/10 B1239/12
incalculable (5) A0027/V

->A0181/28 B0826/13 B1301/22 C0177/02
incantations (1) C0395/30
incapable (10) A0457/27 A0460/29
A0530/30 B1049/33 B1107/34 C0059/41
C0095/36 C0401/02 C0406/25 C0531/02
incapacitated (1) C0074/13
incapacity (3) A0020/08
A0054/28 A0063/28
incarceration (2) C0083/39 C0085/12
incarnate (3) B0856/07
B0889/22 B1036/21
incarnated (1) B1036/24
incarnation (2) B1037/08 B1123/08
incarnations (1) A0511/18
incautiously (1) C0121/22
incendiary (1) A0021/17
incense (1) A0122/13
incensed (3) B0875/09
B1103/28 B1370/23
inception (1) B0741/30
incessant (1) C0175/15
incessantly (4) A0371/13
B1021/01 B1048/28 C0571/21
inch (31) A0247/16
A0298/V A0354/03 A0464/08 A0501/25
A0542/16 A0553/18 A0654/V A0691/03
A0691/03 A0695/20 A0697/03 B0865/24
B0865/24 B0980/22 B0980/V B1167/30
B1168/16 B1168/20 B1185/27 B1251/03
B1251/04 B1363/10 B1392/08 C0074/33
C0090/24 C0115/41 C0157/19 C0178/38
C0394/28 C0552/07
inches (53)
incident (30) A0078/20 A0079/18
A0106/18 A0136/07 A0142/07 A0281/33
A0281/34 A0296/V A0350/07 A0403/13
A0430/23 A0431/07 A0704/34 B0832/02
B0960/35 B1078/16 B1107/24 B1247/15
B1269/33 C0065/06 C0094/34 C0094/34
C0122/20 C0125/34 C0164/26 C0182/27
C0203/16 C0547/39 C0569/37 C0576/36
incidental (2) A0073/V B0752/10
Incidentibus (1) B1382/35
incidentibus (1) A0593/35
incidents (16) A0343/03
A0608/27 A0670/09 B1079/33 B1122/13
C0055/17 C0073/21 C0087/39 C0101/26
C0149/02 C0149/03 C0149/06 C0208/15
C0537/31 C0539/17 C0548/26
incipient (5) A0320/21
A0663/02 B1237/23 C0065/04 C0440/V
incision (11) A0059/22
A0067/13 B0960/09 B1181/08 B1182/13
B1182/28 C0092/23 C0178/38 C0545/15
C0545/22 C0545/39
incitamentum (1) A0212/22
incited (1) B1021/V
inciting (1) B1352/28
inclination (8) A0098/24
A0098/25 A0251/02 B0852/13 B0879/22
B1034/16 C0071/40 C0546/02
inclinations (4) A0098/20
B0895/20 B1164/24 B1331/35
inclined (21) A0342/15
A0580/31 A0590/32 B0878/13 B0879/10
->B0879/18 B0880/06 B1070/03 B1070/10
B1071/11 B1072/05 B1091/32 B1105/12
B1105/26 B1279/23 B1293/22 B1381/33
C0084/38 C0398/18 C0417/07 C0419/09
inclines (1) B1092/03
include (6) A0399/18 A0601/09
A0603/03 B0980/28 B1360/05 C0087/39
included (10) A0263/35 A0611/34
B0828/13 B1072/35 B1072/36 B1113/06
B1335/16 B1353/15 C0093/22 C0536/22
includes (2) A0529/22 B0743/20
including (6) B0922/06 B0980/22
B1073/26 B1187/14 B1340/08 C0535/06
inclusive (1) A0600/28
incognizant (2) B0769/28 B1316/12
incoherence (5) A0402/13
A0535/15 A0667/57 B0738/19 B0743/10
incoherent (7) A0022/18
A0158/V A0166/18 A0437/25 A0558/19
B1131/04 B1291/17
incoherently (2) B0928/08 C0127/37
income (5) A0440/23
A0491/14 A0531/23 A0705/18 B1270/17
incommoding (2) C0555/16 C0556/05
incommunicativeness (1) B0927/13
incomparable (1) B1137/05
incomparably (2) B1007/13 B1169/02
incomprehensible (14) A0073/01
A0141/31 A0164/18 A0164/V A0211/19
A0250/25 A0311/20 A0313/25 A0355/35
A0429/23 B0955/31 B1221/21 B1302/12
C0426/03
inconceivable (24) A0155/21
A0429/27 A0457/26 A0459/35 A0565/24
A0705/15 B0940/20 B0946/21 B1078/04
B1136/17 B1156/02 B1170/05 B1182/19
B1220/17 B1224/24 B1270/13 B1301/18
B1302/03 C0062/06 C0063/34 C0124/11
C0149/22 C0200/40 C0396/21
inconceivably (5) B0968/34
B1069/11 B1168/35 B1334/03 C0403/18
incongruities (4) A0709/29
A0710/18 B1274/32 B1275/22
incongruity (1) A0080/07
incongruous (2) A0165/25 B0760/09
inconnue (1) B1335/18
inconsequence (1) B0743/10
inconsequential (2) A0213/02
B0739/15
inconsiderable (7) B1115/14
B1358/09 C0393/16 C0397/14 C0406/06
C0422/23 C0425/03
inconsiderately (1) B1359/26
inconsistency (5) A0400/10
A0402/14 B1141/25 B1298/21 B1316/33
inconsistent (5) A0684/22
B0733/01 B0748/29 B0907/23 B0991/21
incontestably (1) C0441/V
incontrollable (1) C0556/38
incontrovertible (4) A0711/08
B0751/V B1276/09 C0107/26
incontrovertibly (1) A0110/03
inconvenience (22) A0058/32 A0069/23
A0078/03 A0080/05 A0093/04 A0112/16
A0143/27 A0489/03 B1114/26 C0085/12

->C0090/18 C0097/27 C0403/37 C0404/29
C0405/11 C0405/34 C0411/03 C0413/24
C0414/37 C0418/50 C0422/16 C0424/17
inconveniences (1) B1292/08
inconvenient (8) A0355/12
B0888/14 B0906/21 B1073/06 B1110/04
B1187/32 C0403/33 C0555/15
inconveniently (1) B1333/31
increase (33) A0138/21
A0233/24 A0324/07 A0324/10 A0399/24
A0399/25 A0446/15 A0458/15 A0705/11
B0742/12 B0746/10 B0746/13 B0746/14
B0840/12 B0855/08 B1033/24 B1058/31
B1074/25 B1080/23 B1102/02 B1168/21
B1270/10 C0117/18 C0163/21 C0401/33
C0404/02 C0405/21 C0407/22 C0412/21
C0419/30 C0422/41 C0430/09 C0430/45
increased (45) A0106/19
A0248/V A0507/23 A0512/12 A0587/16
A0652/17 A0690/12 A0696/18 A0696/27
B0727/14 B0731/12 B0742/11 B0795/11
B0795/15 B0797/08 B0797/12 B0797/14
B0797/16 B0797/19 B0843/20 B0856/12
B0932/20 B1078/03 B1136/15 B1136/36
B1137/33 B1138/30 B1155/36 B1233/21
B1246/10 B1279/05 B1364/12 C0059/07
C0104/34 C0149/26 C0205/18 C0205/39
C0417/27 C0420/40 C0424/14 C0431/01
C0445/V C0549/27 C0553/30 C0562/34
increases (4) A0123/31
B1030/11 B1222/02 B1260/08
increasing (23) A0022/05
A0047/12 A0299/01 A0414/10 A0440/23
A0500/09 A0515/20 A0580/04 A0623/15
B0834/27 B0843/32 B0928/04 B1071/29
B1077/19 B1350/20 B1354/08 C0060/15
C0081/14 C0134/16 C0203/28 C0412/19
C0417/06 C0575/29
incredible (14) A0135/19 A0513/31
B0931/11 B1020/27 B1166/28 B1358/34
C0053/T C0138/02 C0145/10 C0146/28
C0163/27 C0171/22 C0541/15 C0567/02
incredibly (1) B1106/29
incredulity (3) A0018/07
B1104/33 C0056/25
incredulous (1) C0569/21
incredulously (1) B0983/07
incrustations (1) C0577/24
incrusted (1) A0553/21
incubation (3) C0152/08
C0153/04 C0173/39
incubus (3) A0296/09
A0411/26 A0459/34
inculpate (1) B0770/06
incumbent (8) A0301/23
A0461/20 A0497/30 B0856/08 B0944/34
B0967/08 B1380/34 C0400/31
incumbrance (1) A0107/18
incurred (1) B1017/35
incurring (2) A0074/27 C0537/20
ind> (2) A0467/27 A0467/28
indebted (18) A0086/03 A0097/03
A0122/03 A0341/28 A0342/V A0483/09
A0556/25 B0752/11 B1069/25 B1073/11
B1154/20 B1295/34 B1311/35 B1358/13
->C0129/17 C0144/26 C0193/25 C0197/17
indecent (7) A0110/31
B0767/33 B0958/27 B1014/13 B1139/10
B1207/15 C0557/24
indecision (5) A0402/21
B0906/03 B1347/15 C0088/04 C0094/37
indecisive (1) C0173/32
indecorous (5) A0057/27
A0068/10 A0105/32 B0901/03 B0902/01
indeed (375)
indefatigability (1) A0278/38
indefatigable (1) B1303/07
indefinable (4) A0250/24
A0609/04 C0080/20 C0198/04
indefinite (17) A0089/05
A0140/32 A0141/27 A0190/30 A0210/03
A0325/10 A0365/20 A0411/30 A0675/02
A0695/27 B0732/28 B0854/12 B0855/28
B0894/04 B0966/09 B0966/19 B1214/13
indefinitely (4) B1187/12
B1213/34 C0402/09 C0443/V
indefinitive (2) A0190/V A0293/27
indelible (1) C0392/20
indelicate (1) A0354/21
indemnification (1) B1184/12
indemnify (2) A0057/10 A0067/04
indemnity (1) A0445/21
indentation (3) A0553/24
A0558/30 C0087/12
indentations (2) A0538/16 A0559/28
indented (1) A0218/30
indenture (1) A0215/21
indentures (9) C0195/10
C0195/12 C0195/20 C0195/21 C0207/28
C0207/32 C0207/45 C0208/04 C0422/23
Independence (3) B0922/02
B0923/34 B0933/14
independence (2) A0355/06 B1136/28
independent (5) A0485/29
B1070/16 B1070/31 B1143/09 B1371/13
independently (4) A0142/31
A0615/20 B1235/33 C0156/09
indescribable (15) A0242/05
A0248/09 A0510/15 A0625/21 B0895/26
B0942/31 B0943/22 B1102/23 B1145/15
B1240/13 B1338/30 C0059/15 C0127/22
C0128/35 C0143/13
indescribably (2) B0926/28 C0577/10
indeterminate (4) A0496/02
A0681/06 B0743/14 B1340/05
indeterminately (1) A0693/24
index (3) A0315/05
B0815/07 B0822/34
India (4) A0247/04
A0324/21 B1293/07 C0093/20
Indian (25) A0244/15
A0322/02 A0498/09 B0880/07 B0946/28
B0949/14 B1328/10 C0055/20 C0087/01
C0087/05 C0178/07 C0527/18 C0530/19
C0531/08 C0533/39 C0534/18 C0539/12
C0549/10 C0549/35 C0553/09 C0553/21
C0558/01 C0559/25 C0565/28 C0571/26
Indian/Archipelago (1) A0564/19
Indian/Summer (2) B0942/18 B0943/07
Indiana (1) B1164/37

Indians (39) A0380/31
A0385/10 B1096/31 B1096/32 C0527/19
C0528/14 C0530/12 C0531/09 C0534/20
C0535/14 C0536/19 C0537/41 C0539/35
C0540/09 C0540/25 C0541/13 C0548/22
C0550/28 C0553/29 C0554/15 C0554/22
C0557/32 C0560/23 C0560/31 C0561/04
C0561/36 C0561/41 C0562/20 C0563/07
C0563/16 C0565/05 C0568/15 C0568/34
C0569/08 C0574/20 C0574/31 C0575/01
C0576/19 C0577/35
indicate (11) A0270/14
A0284/08 A0473/02 A0612/11 A0650/29
B0758/16 B0842/23 B1075/06 B1093/03
B1302/13 C0540/29
indicated (14) A0243/19 B0824/28
B0825/02 B0842/04 B1076/13 B1179/09
C0157/14 C0157/27 C0158/18 C0203/21
C0204/30 C0405/41 C0411/38 C0572/22
indicates (3) A0286/22
B0876/29 B1075/07
indicating (8) A0113/03
A0263/28 A0282/25 A0546/20 B0754/24
B0834/13 C0417/38 C0576/40
indication (16) A0136/29
A0298/V A0400/15 B0815/31 B1181/25
B1241/11 B1242/08 B1262/11 B1304/28
C0114/03 C0118/38 C0157/16 C0424/08
C0547/29 C0571/17 C0571/28
indications (14) A0106/27 A0247/01
A0298/V A0530/22 A0557/14 A0642/28
A0644/09 B0824/31 B1004/02 C0101/01
C0105/07 C0158/36 C0160/24 C0400/25
indicative (11) A0272/10
A0274/37 A0276/34 A0283/05 A0284/28
A0562/23 A0604/21 B0736/33 B0865/34
C0087/28 C0169/17
indifference (1) A0241/05
indifferent (3) A0272/17
A0340/09 C0569/02
indifferent-looking (1) B0926/20
indigenous (2) A0261/29 B1334/24
indigestible (1) B1068/12
indignant (3) A0426/05
B0873/08 C0061/34
indignantly (2) A0510/04 B1012/23
indignation (18) A0055/22 A0057/32
A0065/06 A0068/16 A0073/32 A0204/27
A0241/32 A0351/19 A0371/22 A0443/31
A0579/01 A0653/21 B1092/34 B1139/14
B1192/04 B1349/01 B1370/21 C0166/25
indignity (2) B1094/01 C0557/06
indigo (1) B1153/34
indirect (1) B1213/09
indirectly (1) B1058/21
indiscernible (1) C0423/29
indiscretion (3) B1154/30
B1225/V C0192/06
indiscretions (1) B0906/16
indiscriminate (2) A0075/07
B1133/22
indispensable (12) A0056/12
A0107/08 A0107/20 B0737/28 B0750/27
B1073/26 B1074/01 B1105/14 B1108/12
B1115/37 B1189/06 C0108/24
indisposed (1) B0923/29
indisposition (1) C0407/09
indisputable (2) B1044/04 B1373/29
indisputably (3) A0029/09
A0109/29 B1122/06
indissolubly (1) B0910/02
indistinct (13) A0142/24
A0195/12 A0196/23 A0214/24 A0354/04
A0430/30 A0605/06 A0615/05 A0616/18
A0643/28 C0079/22 C0205/36 C0423/28
indistinctly (8) A0047/14
A0145/13 A0311/09 A0356/09 A0414/04
A0588/17 A0683/15 A0689/11
indistinctness (1) C0073/18
indistinguishable (2) A0190/V
B1354/22
indite (2) B1167/25 B1370/30
indited (2) A0262/31 A0262/34
inditer (3) B0738/04
B0739/09 B0750/30
inditing (2) A0108/19 A0242/02
individual (84)
individualities (2) B1036/12
B1036/18
individuality (3) A0216/01
A0378/16 B0773/09
individualized (1) B1036/22
individually (5) A0262/35
A0612/12 A0707/29 B1272/29 B1358/33
individuals (21) A0296/18
A0486/35 A0489/03 A0490/27 A0509/06
A0538/28 A0674/23 B0727/11 B0731/12
B0740/17 B0742/01 B0742/02 B0749/21
B0749/27 B0959/08 B0968/07 B1276/12
B1294/13 B1313/02 B1370/09 C0130/08
individuationis (2) A0226/36
A0231/10
indivisible (2) B0852/09 B1033/26
indolent (3) A0033/05
B0725/09 C0530/09
indubitable (1) B1049/30
indubitably (3) A0072/02
A0090/36 A0109/27
induce (8) B0742/28
B0941/18 B0941/28 B1382/27 C0087/27
C0103/19 C0131/28 C0205/04
induced (35) A0212/08
A0441/23 A0446/14 A0473/14 A0489/07
A0611/08 A0686/06 A0708/14 B0807/29
B0914/29 B0927/09 B0949/06 B0989/05
B1040/09 B1052/33 B1153/24 B1236/18
B1237/03 B1238/23 B1240/35 B1277/23
C0056/14 C0063/04 C0085/10 C0086/05
C0094/39 C0120/16 C0122/20 C0126/16
C0150/22 C0157/17 C0158/12 C0170/20
C0429/21 C0522/33
inducement (3) A0135/26
B1052/01 C0095/30
induces (2) A0629/19 B1380/26
inducing (6) B0817/10 C0086/13
C0166/28 C0392/29 C0400/19 C0561/23
induct (1) A0455/13
induction (2) A0561/12 B1220/20
inductions (3) A0553/09
B0725/04 B1317/23

inductive (3) B1295/14
B1311/06 B1317/17
indulge (7) A0440/07
A0568/12 A0674/11 B0965/09 B1223/16
B1318/07 C0130/36
indulged (10) A0212/14 A0337/34
A0413/13 A0446/22 A0491/12 A0625/12
B0850/11 B1006/03 B1222/05 C0191/21
indulgence (3) A0098/28
A0474/01 A0667/33
indulgences (1) A0589/18
indulges (2) A0532/04 B0760/18
indulging (7) B0924/19
B0929/32 C0065/39 C0071/24 C0128/40
C0131/16 C0137/08
industriously (1) B0731/04
Industry (1) C0155/25
industry (5) A0055/09
A0064/12 B0751/02 B0816/31 B1089/07
indwelling (1) B1038/32
inebriates (1) A0515/03
ineffable (5) A0144/17
A0638/13 B0914/01 B1130/26 B1372/13
ineffective (1) A0145/11
ineffectual (11) A0127/V
B1070/23 C0062/26 C0090/19 C0119/05
C0127/06 C0130/40 C0133/12 C0183/33
C0567/21 C0579/33
inefficient (1) A0099/28
inelastic (1) A0400/V
ineptum (1) A0213/07
inequalities (1) B1076/26
inertia (1) B1090/13
inertiae (1) B0989/16
inessential (1) B0723/15
inestimable (2) A0096/09 A0250/26
inevitable (17) A0069/10
A0140/24 A0294/V A0351/06 A0458/05
A0496/08 B0955/36 B0969/01 B1123/03
B1162/11 B1300/13 B1352/34 C0200/36
C0422/03 C0443/V C0443/V C0446/V
inevitably (17) A0075/11
A0138/07 A0403/V A0434/12 A0550/26
A0581/28 A0692/24 B0764/23 B0962/29
B0993/06 B1034/33 B1108/21 B1223/16
B1292/27 B1364/14 C0117/05 C0198/25
inexhaustible (1) C0556/16
inexorable (2) A0102/22 B1054/36
inexperience (3) A0435/30
B1133/18 B1141/24
inexplicable (4) A0350/28
A0387/16 A0411/07 B1247/15
inexpressible (8) A0033/16
A0330/11 A0404/23 B0834/34 C0074/30
C0122/09 C0147/34 C0183/15
inexpressibles (1) C0440/V
inexpressibly (4) A0353/14
A0691/18 B0815/02 C0397/30
inexpressive (1) B1139/27
inextinguishable (1) A0356/17
inextricable (2) B1076/19 C0429/07
inextricably (1) A0613/03
infallible (2) B1364/01 B1369/09
infallibly (2) B0770/23 C0074/40
infamous (3) A0489/V
->B1133/33 C0181/20
infamy (3) A0426/06
A0510/35 B0854/02
infancy (8) A0234/05
A0400/32 A0427/20 A0436/17 B0725/19
B0850/08 B0871/24 B1187/03
infant (4) A0609/31
A0622/26 B1090/09 B1097/01
infantine (1) A0610/13
infantry (2) A0058/08 A0068/30
infants (4) B1090/02
B1090/07 B1090/11 B1168/10
infarm> (1) A0469/01
infatuate (1) B1316/07
infatuation (4) A0440/13
B0902/07 B1295/32 B1311/32
infect (1) B1006/27
infected (5) A0411/11
A0610/14 A0611/19 B0807/20 B0822/27
infection (1) B0742/19
infer (1) B1320/01
inference (6) A0530/04 A0550/12
B0763/27 B0766/21 B1385/25 C0162/09
inferences (5) A0530/02
B0763/23 B0987/35 B0988/02 C0065/01
inferior (13) A0298/V
A0478/08 A0478/10 A0515/19 B0989/22
B1192/20 B1250/24 B1364/27 C0175/39
C0418/04 C0543/26 C0546/25 C0573/31
inferiority (3) A0099/18
A0379/23 B1191/05
infernal (6) A0342/14 B0816/11
B0820/20 B0824/06 B0900/24 B1335/18
infernally (1) A0072/06
Inferno (3) A0710/31
B1128/23 B1275/33
inferorum (1) A0091/13
inferred (5) A0473/06
A0473/06 B0763/26 B0976/16 C0417/41
inferring (1) B0986/20
infest (3) A0600/32
B0754/02 B1158/05
infested (4) A0490/34
A0509/08 C0530/18 C0552/34
infesting (2) B0725/27 B1303/13
infidelity (1) B1044/05
infinite (24) A0057/20
A0316/01 A0478/08 A0601/14 B0773/36
B0852/27 B0916/25 B0945/12 B0967/19
B1009/08 B1034/20 B1034/27 B1039/V
B1057/03 B1212/26 B1213/31 B1214/20
B1214/27 B1293/30 C0186/16 C0401/17
C0407/08 C0414/11 C0562/23
infinitely (20) A0126/18
A0436/22 A0479/05 B0817/22 B0865/04
B1035/04 B1035/13 B1038/14 B1050/21
B1136/31 B1157/17 B1164/20 B1214/23
B1248/16 B1278/29 B1333/05 C0139/13
C0145/24 C0543/36 C0546/26
infinitesimally (1) B1207/24
infinitude (2) B0963/22 B1034/28
infinitum (1) A0296/V
infinity (17) A0079/35
A0122/10 A0429/30 A0495/V A0533/07
A0601/14 A0612/18 B1038/25 B1038/35

->B1039/28 B1164/07 B1164/32 B1164/33
B1212/22 B1212/25 B1281/30 B1301/30
infirm (3) A0020/04
B0729/20 B1091/05
infirmities (2) A0427/26 B0906/14
infirmity (8) A0020/07
A0058/02 A0068/23 A0141/13 A0143/13
A0213/21 B0907/28 B0907/28
inflamed (2) A0567/05 B0957/25
inflammatory (1) C0389/21
inflated (4) A0345/30
B1073/07 B1163/26 C0396/04
inflation (6) B1071/03 B1073/07
B1073/12 B1075/19 B1075/34 C0394/18
inflections (2) B0877/27 C0208/06
inflict (4) B1030/16
B1131/19 B1131/20 B1169/15
inflicted (7) A0435/12
A0544/01 A0544/05 A0557/28 B0851/22
B0852/19 C0113/33
inflicting (1) B1158/03
infliction (1) B1291/15
inflictions (1) C0207/44
influence (66)
influenced (4) A0225/14
B0741/09 B1237/01 C0407/13
influences (5) A0323/26
A0411/12 A0459/17 A0478/30 B1214/29
influencing (1) B1321/21
influential (1) A0020/02
inform (13) A0127/12
A0266/26 A0275/24 A0277/05 A0280/32
A0281/33 A0383/25 B1131/10 B1140/23
B1249/03 C0186/09 C0192/18 C0432/20
informality (1) B0901/02
information (43) A0067/21
A0173/22 A0179/01 A0205/32 A0266/28
A0268/27 A0274/19 A0281/10 A0366/15
A0381/14 A0385/05 A0385/30 A0386/20
A0443/10 A0530/03 A0563/13 A0564/02
B0729/03 B0729/04 B0734/28 B0736/07
B0770/16 B0770/17 B0796/21 B0840/31
B0877/14 B0904/01 B0914/29 B0976/10
B1069/26 B1082/06 B1090/06 B1152/09
B1191/27 B1302/27 C0102/07 C0150/15
C0158/11 C0158/23 C0207/13 C0392/14
C0393/23 C0574/35
informe (1) B1010/25
informed (19) A0182/04
A0303/31 A0409/15 B0729/32 B0770/31
B0915/08 B0923/26 B0961/26 B0961/28
B1008/17 B1072/35 B1105/33 B1108/02
B1130/22 B1165/21 C0072/02 C0522/29
C0556/36 C0572/02
informing (1) B0859/14
informs (1) B0874/27
infuriated (1) B1353/34
infusion (1) C0171/39
infusions (1) B0742/23
ingenious (23) A0067/26
A0382/01 A0486/13 A0530/29 A0530/29
A0531/09 A0621/V B0842/25 B0870/23
B0977/01 B0983/22 B0984/01 B1048/17
B1119/14 B1153/07 B1194/06 B1294/29
B1330/30 C0055/23 C0176/05 C0402/21
->C0428/17 C0430/26
ingeniously (3) A0303/25
C0056/17 C0546/02
ingens (1) B1010/25
ingenuity (25) A0263/18
A0344/13 A0367/20 A0436/31 A0530/29
A0531/01 A0531/06 A0568/24 A0654/14
A0690/23 B0835/27 B0835/28 B0842/31
B0870/01 B0870/23 B0985/12 B0985/15
B0985/29 B0990/12 B1166/17 B1192/35
B1302/21 B1380/14 C0197/17 C0430/07
ingenuous (1) B1045/18
Inglitch (3) B1296/12
B1296/37 B1297/34
inglorious (2) A0706/23 B1271/25
ingrain (1) B1339/28
ingrates (1) A0484/24
ingratitude (1) A0355/12
ingredients (1) B0869/27
ingress (7) A0555/31
A0566/20 A0671/02 B1277/25 B1335/07
C0074/11 C0152/23
ingressions (1) A0429/08
ingulfed (2) A0137/20 A0438/13
ingulfs (1) A0604/09
inhabit (2) B0856/19 B0964/15
inhabitant (2) C0205/13 C0426/23
inhabitants (21) A0019/17
A0365/09 A0369/11 A0370/18 A0372/12
A0458/26 A0537/07 B0945/08 B1039/33
B1081/27 B1303/11 C0153/11 C0202/25
C0203/33 C0204/02 C0426/07 C0426/08
C0428/42 C0428/44 C0432/16 C0530/08
inhabited (5) B1165/22
B1329/01 C0425/28 C0548/14 C0548/23
inhalation (2) C0407/28 C0413/24
inhale (1) A0428/05
inhaling (2) A0071/32 C0078/28
inherent (2) A0405/03 C0392/34
inherit (1) C0057/08
inheritance (5) A0043/V
A0705/19 B0887/13 B1270/17 B1270/29
inherited (6) A0427/20 A0705/02
B1059/24 B1154/23 B1269/35 B1270/02
inhuman (1) B0859/03
inhumation (6) A0080/43 B0957/09
B0962/27 B0966/05 C0182/29 C0185/09
inhumed (1) B0959/12
inimitable (9) A0036/23
A0383/24 A0440/33 B1127/12 B1136/18
B1137/39 B1184/27 B1345/06 B1350/26
iniquities (1) A0074/01
iniquity (3) A0052/03
A0062/05 A0623/15
initial (4) A0280/10
A0430/14 B1031/15 B1128/V
initials (8) A0024/03
A0271/27 A0280/29 A0337/17 A0337/24
A0337/29 B1052/16 B1053/29
injudicious (3) B0906/24
B1005/14 B1048/19
injunction (3) A0107/27
A0491/11 A0622/20
injure (3) A0624/29
A0709/08 B1274/14

injured (9) A0348/25
A0502/16 B1141/29 C0113/09 C0187/15
C0542/28 C0559/26 C0563/29 C0579/28
injuria (1) A0622/19
Injuriae (3) A0301/11
A0302/19 A0303/03
injuries (4) A0432/14
A0544/01 B1256/01 C0578/01
injury (23) A0138/01
A0343/27 A0349/32 A0427/23 A0457/27
A0458/26 A0528/28 A0563/27 A0631/04
B0852/19 B1141/14 B1179/32 B1221/11
B1303/35 C0076/25 C0113/29 C0114/28
C0145/21 C0187/26 C0199/15 C0540/04
C0563/10 C0579/24
ink (8) A0339/08
B0809/12 B0875/01 B1128/01 B1143/22
C0069/21 C0080/08 C0092/22
inkling (2) A0652/12 B1322/06
inky (1) A0578/34
inlaid (1) A0034/21
inland (3) C0152/27
C0171/15 C0189/34
inlet (1) C0168/01
inmate (1) B1047/33
inmates (2) A0019/V A0566/14
inmost (5) A0590/26
A0641/15 A0696/12 B0807/15 B1260/06
inn (9) B0735/18
B0735/23 B0735/31 B0735/35 B0760/17
B0767/21 B0768/02 B0909/24 B0916/21
innate (3) A0086/11
A0097/11 B1220/21
inner (11) A0044/31
A0214/19 A0303/16 A0443/11 A0589/24
B0857/15 B1037/18 B1037/18 B1037/19
B1219/V C0410/31
innermost (5) B0897/02
B0964/27 B0967/33 C0080/26 C0413/03
innocence (3) A0348/25
B0752/34 B0858/17
innocent (15) A0047/19
A0490/27 A0548/13 A0560/10 A0560/21
A0561/17 A0561/20 A0563/28 A0564/09
A0564/16 A0623/28 A0641/13 A0642/31
B0769/22 B0769/28
innocently (1) B1135/25
innocui (1) A0681/M
innuendo (2) A0341/V A0342/14
innumerable (48) A0036/05
A0087/21 A0093/02 A0112/15 A0121/04
A0122/V A0140/09 A0153/16 A0215/06
A0252/13 A0314/22 A0429/27 A0430/12
A0507/34 A0510/14 A0580/15 A0584/17
A0603/14 A0610/22 B0742/14 B0742/15
B0822/27 B0862/15 B0887/06 B0896/17
B0945/06 B0945/24 B0963/36 B1078/07
B1079/08 B1219/21 B1278/35 B1298/05
B1313/20 B1317/05 B1333/03 C0068/41
C0070/28 C0076/14 C0077/24 C0093/29
C0161/13 C0164/26 C0167/11 C0174/08
C0422/30 C0527/06 C0572/08
inny> (4) A0464/02
A0464/20 A0465/16 A0469/03
inopportuneness (1) B1364/14

inordinate (5) A0020/05
A0402/02 A0473/07 A0510/28 C0180/09
inordinately (4) A0104/32
A0428/V A0528/02 C0071/08
inorganic (5) B1039/05
B1039/05 B1039/16 B1039/23 B1040/01
inorganization (1) A0408/09
inornate (1) A0509/17
inquest (1) B0763/22
inquietude (2) A0161/V A0608/08
inquire (8) A0293/21
A0432/23 A0532/16 A0561/16 B0872/14
B1014/35 B1338/11 C0147/31
inquired (16) A0090/27
A0163/26 A0174/23 A0178/20 A0180/03
A0180/09 A0264/16 A0383/20 B0814/09
B0818/12 B0896/20 B0898/23 B1007/14
B1109/26 B1193/11 B1194/25
inquirendo (1) B0747/10
Inquirer (2) B0753/39 B0753/42
inquirer (1) B0725/08
inquiries (20) A0251/03
A0263/02 A0263/27 A0266/25 A0266/27
A0275/23 A0311/07 A0409/22 A0442/05
A0550/30 B0729/30 B0737/22 B0814/28
B0841/03 B0858/05 B0897/07 B0914/27
B0915/20 B1191/24 C0523/02
inquiring (4) B0793/15
B0872/01 B0984/31 B1004/35
inquiringly (1) B1142/15
inquiry (19) A0064/02
A0106/32 A0382/12 A0382/27 A0439/28
A0546/05 A0554/04 B0726/12 B0751/18
B0752/01 B0752/23 B0752/31 B0753/34
B0770/26 B0840/28 B0872/07 B1031/09
B1089/05 B1359/08
Inquisition (2) A0687/20 A0693/02
inquisition (3) A0695/05
A0697/12 B0727/07
inquisitive (5) A0507/16
B0923/01 B0934/07 B1152/10 C0569/25
inquisitively (2) A0625/14 B1012/26
inquisitiveness (4) A0509/09
B0865/35 B0924/29 C0169/07
Inquisitorial (1) A0696/23
inquisitorial (4) A0681/05
A0684/17 A0685/28 A0690/24
Inquisitorum (1) A0409/05
insane (1) B1009/30
insanity (5) B0772/16
B0819/28 B0928/13 B1249/13 C0104/21
inscribed (2) B0734/03 B1104/23
inscription (7) A0662/V
B1180/17 B1303/37 B1303/37 B1304/08
B1304/32 B1304/36
inscriptions (3) A0365/16
B0827/31 B1303/09
inscrutability (1) B0858/12
inscrutable (1) A0445/07
insect (12) B0810/17
B0815/17 B0818/26 B0822/03 B0828/32
B0830/11 B0830/22 B1163/14 B1163/16
B1163/21 B1163/34 B1163/42
Insecta (1) B1250/19
insects (2) B1250/19 C0562/31

insensibility (7) A0683/32
A0684/32 A0691/13 B0959/13 C0063/37
C0074/24 C0118/11
insensible (5) B0958/21
B0961/01 B1241/16 C0059/37 C0061/02
insensibly (3) A0496/28
C0432/24 C0432/35
inseparable (3) A0164/19
A0433/15 C0073/28
insert (9) A0263/37
B0857/10 B1129/23 B1130/31 B1131/15
B1131/23 B1131/23 B1379/12 C0409/39
inserted (15) A0091/12
B0876/30 B0980/05 B1057/03 B1101/23
B1102/26 B1184/13 B1282/27 B1336/14
B1352/31 C0178/19 C0185/02 C0409/30
C0410/17 C0536/06
inserting (1) B1106/20
insertion (4) B1129/06
B1129/22 B1135/15 B1144/06
inserts (1) B0876/22
inside (19) A0054/32
A0063/33 A0367/21 A0490/14 A0493/08
A0537/22 A0542/06 A0542/12 A0551/17
A0552/15 B0809/03 B0992/06 B1014/14
B1391/25 C0115/36 C0168/17 C0175/13
C0410/14 C0534/39
insight (4) A0293/09
A0293/10 B0839/26 C0413/29
insignia (3) A0250/13
A0496/V B1250/29
insignificance (2) A0053/05
A0062/10
insignificant (3) A0028/09
B1078/32 B1192/33
insignium (2) B1187/23 B1187/26
insignium (1) B0843/27
insinuate (10) A0097/24 A0341/V
A0342/18 A0386/08 A0621/17 B0770/27
B0940/30 B1090/02 B1207/18 B1314/13
insinuated (5) A0435/26
A0439/32 B0928/02 B0982/28 B0987/05
insinuating (1) B1131/28
insinuations (6) A0381/07 A0625/26
B0733/03 B0747/22 B0927/23 B1370/21
insipid (1) A0403/04
insipidity (1) A0159/13
insist (9) A0442/12
A0489/21 A0555/15 B0756/V B0844/02
B0874/04 B0878/14 B1006/07 B1114/33
insisted (17) A0299/02
A0458/32 A0599/02 A0623/16 A0627/16
B0740/18 B0816/28 B0960/19 B1047/16
B1120/03 B1134/16 B1153/01 B1315/12
C0088/06 C0133/23 C0175/24 C0179/35
insisting (8) A0438/28
B0740/27 B0770/09 B0828/29 B1010/04
B1249/32 C0055/34 C0068/09
insists (4) B0745/16
B0745/32 B0759/16 B0875/15
insolence (1) A0355/11
insolent (3) A0355/06
B1130/01 B1300/20
insolubility (1) A0548/07
insoluble (5) A0397/23
->A0544/29 A0547/16 A0548/V B0835/21
insommary (1) A0353/08
insomnia (1) A0345/28
inspect (2) B1003/32 B1005/15
inspected (1) A0264/33
inspecting (3) A0121/24
B0832/07 B0909/03
inspection (20) A0267/09
A0280/04 A0493/02 B0830/26 B0835/04
B0835/15 B0837/20 B0862/08 B0893/29
B0907/04 B0909/31 B0979/05 B1179/14
B1214/36 B1305/10 B1359/15 B1359/27
C0388/27 C0390/31 C0523/07
Inspector (1) A0034/23
inspiration (4) A0160/22
A0446/17 B0967/09 B1127/09
inspire (11) A0205/05
A0314/25 A0403/08 A0429/06 A0711/26
B0961/19 C0121/05 C0130/12 C0182/28
C0198/19 C0555/23
inspired (23) A0140/11
A0251/13 A0446/08 A0461/05 A0652/09
A0676/07 A0685/23 B0765/09 B0855/21
B0941/14 B1003/22 B1126/11 C0080/20
C0081/35 C0116/13 C0127/23 C0130/21
C0136/08 C0175/38 C0393/06 C0521/18
C0537/07 C0550/08
inspires (3) B0764/23
B1127/04 B1371/12
inspiring (2) C0536/27 C0555/34
inst. (2) A0282/32 A0560/27
instability (1) A0400/16
installed (1) C0066/41
instalments (2) B1189/05 B1191/02
instance (70)
instanced (2) A0704/01 B1268/32
instances (29) A0027/21
A0098/19 A0211/14 A0314/23 A0445/16
B0725/13 B0727/32 B0740/16 B0740/21
B0740/30 B0747/17 B0748/11 B0749/03
B0871/30 B0887/07 B0955/17 B0956/07
B1115/33 B1116/06 B1213/22 B1359/25
B1383/25 C0073/29 C0097/27 C0098/14
C0138/02 C0138/09 C0167/40 C0538/28
instant (114)
instantaneous (8) A0104/22
A0389/02 B0947/22 B1035/27 B1049/36
B1348/12 C0149/17 C0413/35
instantaneously (9) A0021/V
A0137/31 B0941/34 B1142/03 B1167/35
C0113/20 C0199/26 C0394/03 C0416/04
instanter (1) B0877/09
instanter (2) A0298/V B0980/V
instantiae (2) B1295/16 B1311/08
instantly (38) A0023/21 A0139/18
A0156/21 A0336/10 A0437/18 A0444/11
A0500/14 A0567/11 A0568/07 A0664/17
A0676/25 B0851/23 B0856/23 B0893/13
B0895/16 B0900/V B0980/11 B1077/04
B1077/25 B1090/22 B1162/18 B1338/26
B1354/03 C0077/01 C0088/28 C0100/08
C0112/32 C0121/22 C0127/18 C0127/27
C0135/28 C0137/05 C0143/04 C0146/16
C0172/12 C0200/23 C0557/30 C0563/16
instead (16) A0341/18

->A0583/34 A0617/01 B0723/M B0740/22
B0843/13 B0844/02 B1014/14 B1105/27
B1106/23 B1166/09 B1177/03 B1317/27
C0398/25 C0398/28 C0567/23
instigated (1) C0100/31
instigation (5) A0019/24
B1223/25 C0093/17 C0522/02 C0522/33
instil (1) B0807/33
Instinct (1) A0477/T
instinct (15) A0477/01
A0478/07 A0478/10 A0478/16 A0478/20
A0479/04 A0479/34 A0586/11 A0711/03
B0795/05 B1013/26 B1206/08 B1276/04
C0106/36 C0392/35
instinctive (5) A0411/29
A0703/23 A0708/23 B1268/21 B1273/18
instinctively (8) A0164/27
A0295/03 A0404/11 A0590/08 A0590/30
A0706/06 B1271/10 B1381/32
Institute (1) B1163/13
institute (2) A0122/24 A0311/07
instituted (8) A0458/18
A0544/21 B0729/25 B0731/08 B0858/06
B1048/22 B1058/34 B1303/20
instituting (1) B1044/23
institution (3) A0438/18
B1004/13 B1305/07
institutions (4) A0500/19
A0705/14 B1270/13 C0425/39
instruct (3) A0205/33
B1212/34 C0177/36
instructed (6) A0381/13 A0708/01
A0710/29 B1272/35 B1275/32 C0426/24
instruction (1) A0204/04
instructions (11) A0339/21
A0341/03 A0346/18 A0354/07 B0872/33
B0878/17 B1059/18 B1164/01 B1189/09
B1390/17 C0180/15
instrument (14) A0089/07 A0104/07
A0544/08 A0557/24 A0557/28 A0557/29
B0833/18 B0893/30 B0916/12 B0944/02
B1169/34 B1180/33 C0087/36 C0398/09
instrumental (4) B0904/27
C0096/24 C0135/26 C0166/31
instrumentality (2) B0851/05
C0100/27
instruments (23) A0071/08
A0124/01 A0128/19 A0141/17 A0143/18
A0144/21 A0219/06 A0314/21 A0401/15
A0403/08 A0406/07 A0665/06 B0931/25
B0990/31 B1004/04 B1020/14 B1181/12
B1185/18 C0161/16 C0388/29 C0393/26
C0439/V C0572/24
insufferable (11) A0214/26
A0397/07 A0397/08 A0460/17 B0856/02
B0964/19 B1106/23 C0083/28 C0094/14
C0118/34 C0124/10
insufferably (2) A0122/14 B1258/13
insufficient (8) A0086/15
A0243/08 B0741/35 B0922/21 C0079/32
C0404/07 C0413/22 C0447/V
insulated (6) A0303/V A0708/29
B0841/13 B1273/23 B1332/15 B1333/14
insulation (2) B1277/25 B1391/04
insult (22) A0034/29 A0300/12
->A0300/28 A0366/27 A0386/15 A0625/28
A0626/14 A0652/V A0675/24 B0772/17
B0789/11 B0875/29 B1050/05 B1207/29
B1256/02 C0388/23 C0436/V C0550/03
C0556/37 C0557/03 C0558/09 C0561/07
insulted (4) A0034/27
A0626/14 B0875/13 B1131/24
insulting (2) A0626/09 B0993/19
insultingly (1) A0445/22
insults (2) A0026/08 A0432/14
insuperable (3) A0685/33
B1279/09 B1322/19
insupportable (2) B1194/10 C0128/28
insurance (3) B1105/15
B1105/21 B1107/08
insure (3) B0980/14
B1241/29 B1258/25
insurmountable (2) B1035/05
C0183/41
insurrection (1) B0949/15
intangible (2) A0294/V B0724/05
integrity (4) A0485/30
B0879/03 B1169/31 B1370/24
intellect (54)
intellects (4) B0986/02
B0989/21 C0125/33 C0145/04
intellectual (5) A0293/V
A0354/17 B0926/30 B1030/08 B1219/17
intellectually (2) B1031/20
B1031/27
intelligence (21) A0025/09
A0027/21 A0166/21 A0175/13 A0181/02
A0228/36 A0233/23 A0298/V A0458/06
A0533/28 A0600/V A0615/05 A0638/03
B0728/08 B0756/01 B0850/29 B1167/35
B1209/11 B1246/07 C0389/02 C0425/29
intelligences (2) A0711/28 B1215/06
intelligent (8) A0019/02
A0226/31 A0231/05 A0354/17 A0369/08
A0486/06 B0879/01 B0924/12
intelligibility (2) A0303/26
B1115/21
intelligible (13) A0410/18
A0498/20 A0558/11 A0560/18 B0724/09
B0731/14 B1069/29 B1102/36 B1131/06
B1131/08 B1223/24 B1241/01 C0580/05
Intemperance (1) B0851/06
intemperance (2) A0515/01 A0611/08
intemperate (1) B0851/09
intemporal (1) A0615/22
intend (12) A0113/20
A0205/33 A0563/27 A0622/01 A0622/03
A0625/28 B1017/11 B1036/17 B1102/04
B1213/30 B1220/23 B1379/21
intended (49) A0088/05
A0102/28 A0103/25 A0273/36 A0347/18
A0435/11 A0479/08 A0621/28 A0622/03
B0732/37 B0732/39 B0739/23 B0833/03
B0840/06 B0841/30 B0915/30 B0925/15
B0925/31 B0965/31 B0990/13 B1009/08
B1059/20 B1093/18 B1102/36 B1140/12
B1152/30 B1153/13 B1157/11 B1179/27
B1180/16 B1185/17 B1220/15 B1305/03
B1322/06 B1329/07 B1336/36 B1359/22
C0058/12 C0058/37 C0089/34 C0092/08

->C0168/23 C0179/29 C0208/02 C0394/17
C0394/35 C0395/26 C0402/25 C0429/27
intending (8) B0756/07
B1109/23 B1110/04 B1361/16 B1371/10
C0084/25 C0141/31 C0523/26
intends (3) B0750/23
B1097/07 C0390/20
intense (78)
intensely (8) B0946/21
B1050/02 C0065/11 C0072/20 C0077/37
C0122/21 C0166/32 C0197/33
intensest (2) A0460/21 C0083/17
intensities (2) A0338/31 A0339/08
intensity (31) A0029/13
A0078/36 A0099/08 A0211/25 A0225/06
A0229/07 A0315/04 A0317/04 A0317/V
A0317/V A0323/08 A0339/12 A0347/17
A0405/25 A0545/12 A0681/13 A0684/15
B0850/17 B0893/07 B0894/31 B0899/10
B0941/28 B0943/14 B1138/16 B1155/10
B1168/16 B1168/18 B1245/03 C0132/10
C0418/33 C0420/23
intent (4) B0990/28
B1108/18 B1300/13 B1339/20
intention (50) A0034/09 A0203/03
A0204/29 A0262/33 A0269/17 A0409/16
A0437/07 A0441/07 A0621/15 A0624/01
B0729/08 B0744/10 B0755/30 B0756/26
B0811/06 B0910/05 B0991/28 B1010/15
B1044/14 B1127/22 B1134/33 B1139/20
B1221/25 B1236/05 B1259/19 B1273/29
B1273/32 B1274/03 B1304/31 B1381/07
C0066/07 C0077/17 C0086/16 C0103/08
C0103/20 C0123/25 C0124/14 C0132/31
C0133/16 C0148/24 C0156/30 C0157/21
C0158/09 C0202/06 C0409/13 C0525/13
C0546/11 C0550/03 C0553/22 C0569/06
intentional (1) C0195/13
intentionally (1) B1139/26
intentions (9) B0734/19
B1050/21 B1082/04 B1144/11 B1219/20
B1219/20 C0093/36 C0102/08 C0394/07
intently (3) A0160/12
B0893/17 B0974/07
intentness (3) A0310/M
A0314/28 A0318/V
inter (1) A0081/17
inter-communication (1) C0426/03
inter-planetary (1) B1322/18
inter-Tritonic (1) B1312/26
intercept (4) A0566/V
C0539/31 C0551/20 C0556/19
intercepted (2) A0566/04 C0088/39
interchange (1) C0065/28
interchanging (1) C0569/37
intercourse (4) A0235/07
A0315/06 B1123/10 C0556/20
interest (105)
interested (20) A0067/23
A0212/19 A0403/01 A0414/12 A0436/16
A0441/21 A0442/11 A0532/02 A0544/25
A0624/32 B0734/14 B0825/09 B0914/26
B0929/07 B0978/19 B1154/01 B1339/21
C0057/24 C0539/33 C0564/28
interesting (20) A0054/04
->A0057/08 A0063/12 A0067/01 A0074/20
A0240/13 A0263/36 A0348/26 A0379/17
B0863/28 B1008/05 B1075/31 B1082/08
B1152/09 B1154/34 B1169/07 B1304/25
C0425/26 C0524/38 C0544/13
interestingly (1) A0104/12
interests (9) A0044/02
A0074/26 A0215/31 A0458/17 B0770/34
B0992/32 B1134/09 B1189/04 C0564/14
interfere (4) A0431/25
B1003/02 B1234/28 C0109/20
interfered (3) A0282/05
A0439/31 B1107/24
interference (11) A0432/07
A0435/24 A0435/24 A0445/26 A0711/17
B0856/25 B1047/12 B1276/18 C0062/08
C0089/27 C0133/17
interfering (1) C0153/17
interim (2) B0898/22 C0414/24
interior (40) A0018/03
A0100/33 A0122/28 A0154/04 A0405/31
A0410/07 A0497/05 A0510/09 A0545/24
A0555/33 A0564/20 A0566/11 A0580/01
A0580/29 A0590/19 A0613/14 A0626/29
B0751/29 B0762/28 B0763/04 B0862/04
B0993/18 B1165/06 B1180/02 B1261/07
B1261/11 B1339/08 B1381/31 B1391/28
C0069/16 C0109/21 C0153/35 C0154/13
C0167/26 C0171/06 C0172/19 C0177/21
C0189/07 C0191/01 C0415/21
interiorly (1) B0957/07
interjectional (2) A0341/15
B1346/08
interlarding (1) A0623/23
interleaf (1) A0162/10
interlinked (1) B1096/18
interloper (2) A0384/28 B0823/08
intermediate (3) A0295/15
A0711/30 B1276/33
intermedium (1) B1276/27
interment (7) A0080/11
A0080/33 A0327/V A0409/17 B0962/20
B1186/23 C0076/02
interments (3) B0956/03
B0956/05 B0961/10
interminable (2) A0080/02 B1391/24
interminableness (1) A0683/17
intermingled (11) A0216/23
A0219/06 A0502/V B0825/23 B0944/30
B1110/20 C0123/05 C0168/07 C0199/01
C0572/12 C0575/12
intermingling (2) B1260/05 B1283/06
intermixed (1) B1166/26
internal (8) A0080/07
A0175/V A0182/05 A0495/01 B0981/28
B1090/26 B1181/14 C0422/15
internally (3) B0878/05
B1163/27 C0438/V
International (1) B1206/01
interpose (1) B0820/05
interposed (6) A0252/03 A0261/21
B0816/01 B0831/21 B0976/32 B1011/23
interpret (1) C0531/08
interpretation (3) B0748/17
B0842/17 C0395/37

interpretations (1) C0208/10
interpreted (1) A0043/V
interpreter (9) A0540/31
A0549/30 C0555/10 C0556/07 C0557/07
C0557/20 C0566/08 C0568/40 C0577/12
interpreters (2) B1184/27 C0531/06
interred (5) A0070/11
A0079/26 A0217/07 B0731/02 B0959/29
interregnum (1) B0942/17
interrogatories (2) A0088/29
A0103/07
interrupt (3) A0072/13
B0903/21 B1189/31
interrupted (40) A0024/02
A0034/31 A0044/20 A0072/03 A0106/14
A0178/30 A0249/25 A0251/26 A0261/27
A0261/27 A0264/06 A0264/11 A0381/02
A0447/02 A0497/17 A0536/28 A0614/20
A0628/06 B0754/34 B0809/02 B0825/17
B0896/06 B0977/04 B1010/08 B1013/20
B1014/01 B1015/19 B1016/14 B1070/21
B1152/21 B1159/24 B1261/21 B1349/08
B1373/12 C0091/15 C0104/24 C0412/05
C0554/12 C0559/16 C0575/14
interrupting (3) A0655/16
B0815/26 B0909/33
interruption (16) A0381/06
A0405/32 A0439/01 A0442/26 A0513/07
B0756/11 B0823/15 B1070/30 B1226/13
B1262/19 C0164/18 C0416/37 C0548/38
C0558/24 C0562/33 C0576/31
interruptions (4) A0072/14
B1169/04 C0416/12 C0576/11
interrupts (1) B0876/16
intersected (2) C0553/15 C0577/04
intersection (2) B1352/29 C0152/34
interspaces (4) A0045/01
B1034/30 B1035/12 B1329/27
intersperse (1) A0367/19
interspersed (8) A0430/11
B0817/25 B1068/09 B1179/26 B1332/04
C0425/06 C0543/26 C0572/15
intersperses (2) A0338/24 B1121/01
interspersing (1) B0728/24
interstices (1) C0097/35
interstriped (1) B1340/10
intertangled (1) B1283/09
intertwining (1) B1279/25
interval (34) A0070/12 A0438/02
A0511/09 A0682/34 A0684/20 A0691/13
B0738/22 B0738/24 B0745/06 B0745/13
B0811/11 B0825/35 B0866/02 B0905/28
B0966/12 B1179/35 B1180/07 B1235/11
B1239/10 B1241/30 B1261/14 B1334/06
C0084/12 C0137/19 C0168/27 C0193/12
C0193/15 C0400/02 C0400/04 C0400/13
C0421/03 C0545/27 C0548/02 C0560/19
intervals (49) A0145/13
A0153/20 A0156/15 A0213/21 A0241/18
A0271/22 A0271/22 A0276/37 A0313/05
A0322/14 A0403/20 A0411/31 A0579/12
A0581/30 A0609/19 A0614/13 A0688/30
A0691/04 B0749/20 B0832/23 B1009/07
B1127/11 B1237/11 B1237/16 B1337/05
C0063/03 C0064/07 C0078/26 C0081/01
->C0116/29 C0130/20 C0131/02 C0142/19
C0200/11 C0205/34 C0393/06 C0393/18
C0395/19 C0401/24 C0405/09 C0406/16
C0407/25 C0409/34 C0409/35 C0412/25
C0414/19 C0414/38 C0415/09 C0573/31
intervene (1) A0546/13
intervened (3) A0217/08
C0409/32 C0413/35
intervening (2) A0350/23 B1068/13
intervention (4) B0833/31
B1038/13 C0389/15 C0573/11
interview (6) A0654/14 B0728/30
B0989/07 B1004/30 B1133/10 B1140/18
interviews (1) B0747/29
intervolved (1) B1276/32
interweaving (2) A0161/15 A0641/21
interwoven (1) C0426/08
interwreathed (1) B0862/34
intestinal (1) B1165/34
intestines (1) B1181/07
intheristhin> (1) A0464/03
intheristhing> (1) A0464/V
inthroduction> (1) A0466/18
intimacy (5) A0293/10
A0405/01 B0748/26 B0806/01 B1346/30
intimate (19) A0097/19
A0107/31 A0344/08 A0398/29 A0441/09
A0533/16 A0703/10 B0749/04 B0768/29
B0926/14 B1017/06 B1045/22 B1045/27
B1046/15 C0057/13 C0065/27 C0094/38
C0425/27 C0537/25
intimated (2) B1242/15 B1371/20
intimately (4) A0209/03
A0611/29 A0667/24 B1047/22
intimates (1) B0856/11
intimation (3) A0105/04
A0609/30 A0613/33
intirely> (3) A0467/24
A0469/13 A0470/V
into (1018)
intolerability (1) B1116/11
intolerable (26) A0078/08 A0081/31
A0106/V A0122/14 A0403/14 A0405/25
A0406/06 A0432/32 A0436/03 A0437/19
A0438/V A0442/25 A0562/29 A0685/04
A0689/20 B0944/28 B0961/30 B1249/29
B1313/02 B1390/20 C0073/41 C0095/18
C0145/32 C0391/30 C0409/08 C0558/08
intolerably (3) A0136/22
A0684/16 C0137/15
intolerant (1) B1313/02
intonation (6) A0540/26 A0542/32
A0548/24 A0550/01 A0550/06 B1240/16
intonsos (1) A0043/M
intoxicated (10) A0243/29 A0644/07
B0851/20 B1020/13 B1056/30 C0058/03
C0058/14 C0089/03 C0109/30 C0128/18
intoxication (13) A0245/29
A0438/28 A0441/25 B1259/05 B1262/10
B1349/14 C0059/31 C0064/39 C0086/40
C0093/09 C0100/20 C0140/09 C0143/03
intractable (2) A0027/02 A0564/24
intreated (1) C0569/07
intrench (1) A0313/16
intricacies (3) A0230/07

->A0399/03 B1153/31
intricacy (3) A0226/09
B0945/18 C0398/01
intricate (7) A0243/28
A0244/22 A0400/24 B0736/19 B0989/01
B1279/27 C0074/26
intriguant (1) B0988/19
intrigue (2) A0088/08 B1270/09
intrigues (3) A0431/05
A0705/10 B0978/29
intriguing (1) A0152/19
intrinsic (3) B0940/22
B1360/16 B1364/23
intrinsically (4) A0079/02
A0150/V B0908/V C0448/V
introduce (6) A0338/09 A0378/03
B0892/15 B0924/10 B1003/13 B1007/11
introduced (17) A0125/34
A0343/18 A0344/17 A0417/V A0493/03
A0710/12 B0796/19 B0875/18 B0896/13
B0950/06 B1021/22 B1168/28 B1275/15
B1295/07 C0126/13 C0155/32 C0409/37
introducing (4) A0344/07
B0897/13 C0178/03 C0409/14
introduction (19) A0322/27
A0378/07 A0389/04 A0441/12 A0466/V
B0857/33 B0891/20 B0898/16 B0899/12
B0900/V B0905/04 B0915/20 B1073/10
B1095/12 B1184/28 B1295/19 B1311/12
C0057/32 C0429/29
Introductory (1) C0521/01
intrude (4) A0242/27
A0319/04 A0626/19 C0445/V
intruded (3) A0027/24
A0104/30 C0412/35
intruder (6) A0089/14 A0103/07
A0443/02 A0676/03 B1102/16 B1104/07
intruders (1) A0249/10
intruding (1) A0161/15
intrusion (6) A0251/04 A0436/07
A0447/24 A0662/V A0662/V B0760/04
intuition (12) A0528/11
A0610/34 A0616/03 A0704/11 B0757/06
B1212/02 B1247/V B1269/10 B1316/12
B1317/20 B1317/22 C0392/35
intuitive (6) A0098/30 A0295/18
A0296/V A0530/22 B1295/30 B1311/28
intuitively (1) B1317/28
inuendoes (1) B0927/24
inutility (1) B1070/13
invalid (4) A0408/27
B0941/09 B0941/35 B1030/28
invalid's (1) B1236/03
invalids (1) A0509/36
invaluable (2) A0354/07 C0532/37
invariable (2) A0592/03 B0988/31
invariably (17) A0212/24
A0263/24 A0381/24 A0443/27 A0545/17
A0622/28 A0706/20 B0741/27 B0768/09
B1051/14 B1189/12 B1295/30 B1362/05
C0076/22 C0162/27 C0166/12 C0443/V
invent (1) B1315/17
invented (6) A0498/23 A0653/26
B1018/32 B1095/01 B1295/24 B1311/21
invention (30) A0055/23 A0097/07
->A0381/22 A0381/34 A0382/11 A0384/22
A0385/12 A0444/18 A0498/20 A0499/08
A0527/V A0707/10 A0710/26 B1007/14
B1017/01 B1018/34 B1070/20 B1072/19
B1074/13 B1077/09 B1101/29 B1194/22
B1292/07 B1300/13 B1347/32 B1358/22
C0394/16 C0411/24 C0415/11 C0416/08
inventions (3) B0752/14
B0955/10 B1361/23
inventive (4) A0382/29
A0383/32 A0386/01 B1347/05
inventor (4) A0071/08
A0073/11 B1127/14 B1361/04
invents (1) B0870/24
inventus (1) B0880/04
inversion (2) A0210/15 C0422/15
inverted (2) A0398/12 B1280/16
invest (2) A0128/27 B0748/14
invested (5) A0491/08
A0706/30 B0866/07 B1271/32 C0148/06
investigate (2) A0708/22 B1273/17
investigated (1) B0978/22
investigation (38) A0064/11 A0098/28
A0213/09 A0250/23 A0316/03 A0338/01
A0338/02 A0410/01 A0460/20 A0496/V
A0538/18 A0550/23 B0723/17 B0723/19
B0727/10 B0732/31 B0732/34 B0737/12
B0752/28 B0830/04 B0858/11 B0956/31
B0983/26 B1143/32 B1185/17 B1233/06
B1241/04 B1295/08 B1295/31 B1296/04
B1296/12 B1298/14 B1311/28 B1314/32
B1316/23 B1317/12 C0170/21 C0401/23
investigations (14) A0545/12
A0548/03 A0552/32 A0601/03 B0726/09
B0737/03 B0751/09 B0751/24 B0751/31
B0978/09 B0985/19 B0988/24 B1151/02
B1249/33
investiture (2) B1036/23 B1036/30
investment (2) A0704/24 B1269/23
inveterate (1) A0020/05
invidious (1) A0339/22
invigorate (1) C0120/11
invigorated (3) A0528/12
B1030/09 C0129/15
inviolable (1) A0654/12
inviolate (2) B1017/14 B1039/11
invisible (15) A0023/04
A0055/02 A0064/05 A0318/21 A0325/07
A0325/22 A0329/01 A0484/35 A0553/26
A0695/08 A0709/14 B1167/13 B1182/07
B1226/09 B1274/15
invitation (1) B1246/02
invitations (4) A0026/03
A0026/09 B1056/05 B1339/11
invited (6) A0175/02 A0180/25
A0438/21 B0871/34 B1056/02 C0171/05
invitingly (1) A0349/27
invoice (1) A0034/22
invoke (1) A0046/08
invoked (3) A0642/15
A0644/V A0645/01
involuntarily (2) A0215/09 A0588/05
Involuntary (1) A0340/05
involute (1) A0528/29
involutions (1) B1222/01

involve (5) A0431/06
B0740/28 B0879/04 B0907/25 C0575/03
involved (22) A0349/31 A0405/09
A0478/07 A0478/34 A0624/17 A0642/16
A0707/03 B0724/25 B0752/22 B0773/33
B0829/17 B0834/25 B0960/36 B0978/30
B1077/17 B1129/30 B1224/09 B1273/36
C0126/17 C0126/18 C0414/06 C0417/13
involves (4) A0267/17
A0508/30 B1223/08 C0535/42
involving (4) A0074/26
A0164/06 B0733/04 B1164/25
inward (3) A0271/05
A0416/31 B1237/20
inwardly (4) A0087/24
A0226/16 A0230/15 B0897/01
inwards (2) B1057/22 C0552/19
'io (1) B0905/24
Ionia (1) A0165/23
Ionic (4) A0086/10
A0097/09 A0341/22 A0342/V
iota (2) B1152/34 B1190/06
irae (1) B0767/17
irascibility (3) A0053/30
A0063/01 B1369/03
Irdonozur (1) C0432/06
Ireland (1) B1160/37
iris (2) A0343/30 B1242/09
Irish (7) A0482/11
A0483/V A0485/V A0625/07 B1293/24
C0093/02 C0433/01
irksome (2) A0227/19 A0232/06
iron (49) A0101/V
A0103/17 A0107/19 A0112/01 A0136/23
A0189/05 A0190/01 A0243/01 A0323/V
A0351/32 A0353/28 A0410/09 A0410/26
A0416/13 A0429/05 A0429/06 A0538/03
A0544/02 A0566/16 A0631/11 A0670/17
A0688/32 A0692/02 A0695/13 A0696/02
A0696/25 A0696/33 B0825/32 B0826/06
B0826/07 B0957/04 B0965/28 B1008/26
B1035/15 B1160/31 B1161/21 B1166/02
B1166/09 B1261/26 C0076/09 C0099/40
C0115/31 C0163/07 C0189/30 C0391/25
C0398/04 C0404/16 C0534/04 C0536/04
iron-bound (4) A0198/21
C0069/01 C0074/29 C0393/29
iron-chest (1) A0566/V
iron-clasped (1) A0144/21
iron-grooved (1) B1193/07
iron-riveted (1) B1392/06
iron-work (1) B0957/07
ironed (1) A0246/27
ironmongery (1) C0534/23
irons (2) C0090/16 C0093/39
irradiating (1) B1040/10
irrational (2) A0486/17 B1013/16
irreclaimable (1) A0402/26
irreconcilable (2) A0497/24
A0557/08
irreconcileable (1) A0086/09
irrecoverable (1) B0965/16
irrecoverably (3) A0245/V
B0890/V C0207/05
irredeemable (3) A0328/26
->A0401/18 A0579/V
irreducible (2) B1219/04 C0393/36
irregular (17) A0265/19
A0272/37 A0280/02 A0313/12 A0322/14
A0428/20 A0429/11 A0430/30 A0501/29
A0613/18 B0841/11 B1281/03 B1333/21
B1337/02 B1363/19 C0155/17 C0570/24
irregularities (2) A0615/09
C0200/10
irregularity (3) A0312/05
A0430/11 A0688/28
irregularly (3) A0671/22
B0945/07 B1335/11
irrelevant (4) A0558/16
B0752/06 B0754/11 C0430/42
irreparably (2) B0955/34 B1107/30
irrepressible (3) A0144/10
A0411/24 C0198/02
irresistible (8) A0140/25
A0215/29 A0460/35 B0768/16 B0967/27
B1034/16 B1220/30 C0564/33
irresistibly (2) A0688/04 B0833/22
irresolute (2) C0059/41 C0112/31
irresolution (1) B0966/33
irreverence (1) B1035/32
irrevocable (3) B0852/06
B1036/36 B1053/12
irrevocably (3) A0245/04
B0890/24 B1089/21
irritability (2) A0211/20 A0324/V
irritable (2) A0019/20 B0851/08
irritate (1) A0212/34
irritated (4) A0446/24
B0828/34 C0145/39 C0547/11
irritating (1) A0355/11
irritation (2) A0324/10 B0852/05
Irving (4) C0525/04
C0527/24 C0528/07 C0528/26
Irving, Washington (1) A0272/04
Irving's (1) A0272/09
is (3414)
is/n't (2) A0093/08 A0112/20
Isaeus (2) A0175/32 A0181/32
Ise (3) B0812/05 B0812/09 B0813/02
Isis (1) A0350/19
Isitsoornot (7) B1151/02
B1152/10 B1154/20 B1154/27 B1155/09
B1159/10 B1169/29
Island (4) A0599/T
B0806/07 B0841/02 C0057/23
island (86)
islanders (4) C0177/23
C0180/09 C0202/27 C0429/20
Islands (6) C0088/31 C0088/39
C0093/13 C0093/20 C0148/14 C0178/11
islands (60)
Isle (1) B1091/33
isle (4) A0162/15
A0603/16 B1385/28 B1386/03
islet (4) A0603/04
A0604/23 C0165/24 C0166/01
islets (1) C0155/16
isn't (11) A0285/13
A0387/14 A0387/19 A0389/08 A0464/17
A0467/03 A0467/04 A0469/06 A0470/06

->A0651/13 B0876/12
Isola (1) B1386/04
isolated (3) A0136/12
C0112/03 C0576/29
Ispan, Pan (1) A0086/33
Israelitish (1) A0124/26
iss (1) A0373/03
issue (13) A0045/24
A0053/35 A0063/07 A0399/14 A0501/17
B0898/31 B1048/09 B1208/30 B1270/36
B1300/14 B1314/31 B1358/11 C0568/28
issued (22) A0379/12 A0417/06
A0603/31 A0605/11 A0639/22 A0641/02
A0690/04 B0730/03 B0930/04 B0964/26
B0967/06 B1056/05 B1161/07 B1238/28
B1240/08 B1333/12 B1334/08 B1353/29
B1369/30 C0185/32 C0194/24 C0208/20
issues (5) A0551/11
A0551/13 A0551/15 C0106/26 C0575/27
issuing (9) A0212/21
A0327/28 A0537/08 A0583/04 A0605/04
A0614/23 A0681/15 C0082/36 C0113/32
Isthmus (1) C0521/07
istorein (Gr.) (1) A0611/38
it (5166)
it'll (1) A0487/25
it's (34) A0107/28 A0109/V
A0109/V A0252/27 A0285/11 A0338/17
A0345/18 A0385/17 A0464/01 A0464/01
A0464/06 A0464/10 A0464/15 A0465/02
A0465/15 A0465/15 A0465/17 A0465/23
A0466/20 A0466/22 A0466/22 A0468/04
A0468/19 A0469/02 A0469/10 A0470/19
A0488/01 A0656/18 B0808/25 B0814/18
B0820/06 B1363/12 B1374/02 C0541/20
Italia (1) A0286/05
Italian (21) A0151/21
A0157/21 A0162/03 A0163/09 A0213/04
A0344/11 A0344/33 A0501/09 A0540/22
A0540/25 A0540/26 A0543/07 A0549/21
A0550/02 A0550/05 A0662/V B0923/17
B1257/13 B1275/03 B1330/07 B1340/16
italian (1) A0709/35
Italians (2) A0495/02 B1257/07
Italic (3) A0086/10
A0097/10 A0342/V
italicised (1) C0432/31
italics (2) B1130/14 B1133/03
Italicus, Silius (1) A0345/29
Itasca/Lake (1) C0527/29
Itchiatuckanee (1) B1332/25
item (5) A0484/25
A0485/15 B0732/40 B1100/03 B1250/06
items (4) B0736/07
B0751/01 B0863/19 B1304/24
ither> (1) A0467/27
itmost> (1) A0465/10
its (1205)
itself (255)
iver> (4) A0467/08
A0469/02 A0469/09 A0470/05
ivory (7) A0034/21
A0090/03 A0156/15 A0312/09 B1280/34
B1281/14 C0156/27
ivory-looking (1) A0219/07
ivy (2) B1282/01 B1334/32
ivy-wreathed (1) A0153/11
ixpicted> (1) A0467/11
iz (6) B1103/02 B1103/03
B1103/07 B1103/24 B1103/33 B1109/10
izzards (1) B1373/07
II (3) A0265/29 A0279/18 A0406/33
III (2) A0266/22 A0407/06
IV (2) A0267/14 A0407/15
IX (1) A0270/24
J./B./D./A. (1) C0430/30
J./Goignard (1) C0430/31
J./S. (1) A0280/10
J-- (2) C0526/14 C0526/16
j'advoue (1) C0430/41
j'ai (1) B1144/32
j'ay (1) C0430/41
j'irois (2) A0096/M A0096/M
jabbering (3) A0468/26
C0168/06 C0168/23
jabberings (1) A0568/01
Jack/o'/Dandy (1) A0482/07
Jack/Sheppard (1) B1069/19
jackanapes (1) B1370/27
jackass (1) C0151/23
jacket (5) A0056/05
B1018/12 C0062/33 C0100/11 C0202/34
Jacobin (1) A0681/M
jaconet (1) B1339/30
Jacques (2) C0551/14 C0551/16
Jacques/river (1) C0548/09
jade (1) A0655/25
jaded (1) C0064/28
jagged (4) A0105/26
A0429/06 C0429/17 C0570/24
jaggeree (2) A0136/03 A0138/10
jail (3) A0068/22
A0486/22 B1054/35
jam (1) A0470/22
James/River (1) B0968/12
jammed (1) A0137/16
Jan. (7) A0487/05
A0487/09 A0487/15 B1390/01 B1391/11
B1391/19 B1392/10
Jane (8) C0162/16
C0169/10 C0170/39 C0186/01 C0186/28
C0187/01 C0188/05 C0529/21
Jane/Guy (6) C0053/T C0147/06
C0147/08 C0148/30 C0201/26 C0202/07
jangling (1) B1350/21
January (20) A0432/28
B1381/27 C0056/11 C0157/01 C0157/11
C0159/04 C0159/39 C0160/28 C0162/30
C0163/03 C0163/12 C0163/25 C0163/33
C0164/07 C0164/12 C0164/26 C0166/34
C0167/22 C0190/30 C0527/21
Japan (2) A0087/02 A0100/13
jar (2) B0950/05 C0137/02
Jardin (1) A0568/07
jargon (1) B0840/02
jarred (3) A0079/17
A0510/28 B1240/14
jarring (1) A0215/07
jars (3) C0137/20
C0140/03 C0141/04

jasmine (1) B1337/17
jauntily (1) C0389/27
jaunty (1) A0246/05
Java (4) A0135/25
A0136/07 A0344/01 A0351/20
jaw (4) A0045/25
A0099/19 A0249/03 B1239/30
jaws (20) A0057/16
A0057/21 A0067/34 A0072/05 A0217/V
A0244/12 A0246/V A0247/27 A0253/03
A0416/25 A0588/25 A0689/09 B0967/10
B0968/29 B1240/09 B1242/21 B1248/35
B1250/23 B1332/21 C0164/40
Je (3) A0037/V A0547/05 C0430/37
je (11) A0033/19
A0037/07 A0037/07 A0037/09 A0037/09
A0096/M A0096/M A0380/07 B1114/02
B1114/03 B1114/03
jealous (4) A0704/29
B0981/06 B1152/13 B1269/28
jealousy (2) A0019/24 B1132/29
Jefferson (5) C0522/37
C0526/13 C0526/21 C0526/30 C0527/21
Jefferson's (1) C0523/16
Jeffrey (1) C0156/10
Jehoshaphat (1) A0047/17
Jehovah (1) B1219/20
jellies (2) A0175/20 A0181/09
Jennings' (1) B1185/32
jeopardize (1) B0852/25
jeopardized (1) B0976/31
Jeremiad (1) B0869/02
Jeremy (1) B1314/09
Jeremys (1) B0869/01
jerk (4) A0069/24
A0077/01 A0270/18 B1239/30
jerked (4) B1077/13
C0121/20 C0121/32 C0399/06
jerkin (2) A0086/29 A0100/05
jerking (1) A0374/12
jerks (1) A0591/19
Jermyn (1) A0174/32
Jermyn/street (1) A0180/23
Jerusalem (4) A0043/11
A0043/T A0044/28 A0045/10
Jeruschalaim (1) A0043/V
jest (11) A0413/10
A0675/06 B0850/10 B0927/19 B1181/20
B1260/30 B1263/06 B1345/12 B1348/01
B1354/17 B1374/02
Jest-Book (1) A0261/25
jested (1) B1017/24
jester (7) B1345/27
B1345/32 B1347/29 B1353/16 B1353/34
B1354/09 B1354/17
jesters (2) B1345/17 B1345/33
jesting (2) A0650/20 B0828/31
jests (2) A0240/24 A0675/05
jet (4) A0156/13
B0808/33 C0168/14 C0191/12
jet-black (1) A0580/30
jetty (7) A0215/05
A0313/11 A0322/16 A0379/04 A0578/03
B1156/11 C0416/19
jeu (6) A0037/03 B1068/08
->C0428/07 C0432/47 C0448/V C0448/V
jeu-d'esprit (1) C0448/V
jeune (1) B1122/01
Jew (4) A0093/06
A0482/25 A0509/31 B0923/17
jewel (2) A0469/06 A0469/20
jewelled (2) A0599/M B0828/17
jeweller (1) A0539/14
jewelry (2) B0751/14 B1008/01
jewels (10) A0047/20 B0826/16
B0827/32 B0828/20 B0835/11 B0890/11
B0907/05 B0908/V B0945/13 B1019/21
Jewish (1) C0533/10
Jews (3) A0120/06
A0123/31 A0126/15
jews-harp (1) A0466/28
jib (6) C0058/31 C0060/09
C0060/23 C0106/17 C0106/17 C0123/16
jib-boom (1) A0240/23
jiffy (2) A0465/10 A0468/02
jig (1) C0569/31
jingled (3) B1258/34
B1259/26 B1260/03
jingling (2) B0943/35 B1263/21
jis (1) B0824/27
jist (3) B1373/08
B1373/24 B1375/V
jist> (22) A0464/07 A0464/13
A0464/21 A0465/04 A0465/16 A0465/26
A0466/03 A0467/03 A0467/16 A0467/24
A0467/28 A0468/02 A0468/08 A0468/14
A0468/19 A0468/25 A0469/04 A0469/27
A0469/V A0470/12 A0470/18 A0470/24
Jo-Go-Slow (1) A0348/19
Job (1) A0653/21
job (1) B1132/19
Jochaides, Simeon (1) B1151/03
jocular (1) C0088/06
Jod (1) A0045/21
Joe (1) B1314/16
jog-trot (1) B1292/10
jogged (1) A0485/33
Johannisberger (2) A0165/08
A0165/V
John (12) A0173/V
A0173/V B1305/12 B1371/28 B1371/30
B1371/32 B1371/34 B1371/34 B1372/06
C0531/16 C0531/25 C0548/34
John/A./B./C. (8) A0382/32
A0383/19 A0383/30 A0384/19 A0385/08
A0385/32 A0386/06 A0386/10
John/Donaldson (1) C0057/18
Johnson (1) C0158/06
join (4) A0026/05
B1017/22 B1018/35 C0186/41
joined (15) A0105/28
A0337/33 A0338/09 B0900/19 B0946/30
C0090/23 C0133/23 C0159/27 C0168/37
C0172/22 C0173/39 C0212/V C0525/33
C0532/09 C0550/20
joining (3) B1191/12
C0086/35 C0131/20
joint (4) B0760/20
B1069/24 B1075/26 C0397/31
joint-stock (1) A0498/24

jointings (1) B0980/08
joints (2) A0688/33 B0980/13
joke (15) A0295/10
A0433/18 A0650/17 B1263/05 B1345/01
B1345/02 B1345/08 B1347/18 B1348/14
B1348/20 B1374/32 C0067/01 C0128/14
C0558/37 C0569/24
joker (2) B1345/09 B1349/24
jokers (2) B1345/05 B1345/06
jokes (5) A0098/16
A0433/24 A0626/22 B1345/15 B1347/26
joking (4) A0261/24
B0810/06 B1345/02 B1345/07
joli (2) A0177/02 A0177/08
jollity (1) B1055/07
jolly (2) B1019/19 C0063/08
jolly-boat (2) B0931/18 C0062/09
jolly/golly (1) B1046/08
Jolly/Tar (3) A0240/07
A0242/17 A0251/21
jollyboat (3) C0099/23
C0114/02 C0154/16
Jones (12) C0102/20
C0103/33 C0103/34 C0104/03 C0104/11
C0104/15 C0110/11 C0112/41 C0113/01
C0113/08 C0113/11 C0113/31
Jones, Davy (1) A0250/31
Jones, Robert (1) A0178/03
Joseph (1) A0314/23
jostle (1) A0512/12
jostled (2) A0508/12 A0513/29
jostlers (1) A0508/13
jostling (2) A0253/15 C0061/39
jottings (1) B1114/06
joue (1) A0036/25
jouissent (1) A0600/01
Jourdain's (1) A0545/06
Journal (21) B0864/13
B1075/32 B1384/08 C0429/26 C0429/31
C0521/04 C0521/16 C0521/T C0522/05
C0529/T C0539/22 C0540/13 C0540/T
C0546/31 C0548/02 C0548/13 C0550/31
C0550/T C0553/05 C0560/T C0571/T
journal (29) A0142/03
A0487/27 A0487/30 B0732/42 B0737/32
B0740/06 B0743/V B0744/22 B0745/28
B0746/V B0748/V B0753/14 B0766/03
B1075/26 B1075/27 B1081/19 B1130/V
B1136/04 B1136/13 B1138/10 B1143/25
B1145/02 B1390/03 C0055/10 C0101/27
C0160/32 C0167/39 C0414/17 C0538/38
Journal/des/Scavans (1) A0283/15
Journal/of/Commerce (1) B0734/40
journal's (1) B0738/19
journalist (2) B0739/24 B0957/15
journalists (1) B0731/19
journals (6) B0768/12 B0769/03
B1138/27 B1206/09 C0525/07 C0535/33
Journey (2) A0409/03 C0432/39
journey (23) A0444/32
B0764/28 B0816/33 C0070/31 C0074/19
C0077/08 C0080/30 C0402/23 C0522/03
C0522/39 C0523/20 C0524/06 C0524/16
C0524/21 C0525/13 C0527/05 C0527/11
C0528/06 C0528/08 C0530/14 C0549/28
->C0564/27 C0564/38
journeyed (3) B0817/21
B0943/12 C0412/37
journeyings (1) A0602/10
journeys (2) B0957/26 C0528/24
Jove (1) A0657/30
Jovis (1) A0345/28
joy (51)
Joyeuse (7) B1013/25
B1013/34 B1014/05 B1014/05 B1014/10
B1016/09 B1020/33
joyful (2) C0165/21 C0388/38
joyfully (1) A0429/19
joyous (1) A0608/08
joys (1) A0455/13
Ju-Kiao-Li (1) A0344/06
Judge (1) A0275/33
judge (19) A0104/35
A0157/13 A0275/37 A0484/28 A0497/30
A0497/31 A0544/32 B0809/10 B0904/12
B1007/05 B1081/10 B1127/33 B1380/17
C0126/09 C0144/17 C0417/37 C0421/25
C0432/16 C0557/01
judged (7) A0157/V
A0413/17 A0544/26 A0667/66 B1005/30
B1073/28 C0422/22
judges (7) A0530/15
A0542/32 A0550/01 A0681/10 A0682/13
A0684/01 A0685/18
judging (1) C0413/06
judgment (9) A0271/24
A0272/01 A0656/17 A0657/28 B0727/11
B0757/22 B0757/23 B0852/14 B1351/25
judgments (2) A0601/16 B1381/11
judicial (2) B0958/11 B1226/16
judicious (2) A0064/07 A0342/24
Judy/O'Flannagan (1) A0374/16
jug (18) B1110/21 B1291/07
C0069/22 C0071/20 C0074/02 C0088/22
C0090/06 C0095/13 C0129/30 C0138/31
C0139/23 C0141/21 C0142/02 C0142/14
C0142/38 C0142/40 C0145/16 C0146/07
jugglers (1) B1119/08
jugs (3) A0245/15
A0253/28 C0109/29
juicy (2) A0091/24 C0176/35
Juif (1) B1270/37
Jules (8) C0556/05
C0556/14 C0557/41 C0561/22 C0568/32
C0577/12 C0578/35 C0580/03
Julie (1) A0062/22
Julien's (1) B1339/35
Julius (1) C0523/24
July (27) A0484/32
A0484/33 A0484/34 A0485/01 A0485/03
A0584/35 B0728/10 C0056/32 C0101/10
C0101/29 C0102/05 C0102/13 C0102/24
C0102/35 C0103/07 C0103/16 C0103/26
C0139/07 C0139/38 C0140/27 C0140/34
C0141/01 C0141/07 C0141/14 C0141/23
C0147/28 C0148/12
jumble (1) A0128/16
jump (4) A0630/10
A0630/11 B0875/03 C0432/06
jumped (7) A0469/28

->B0913/15 B0913/16 B1105/32 C0062/10
C0138/29 C0559/27
jumping (4) A0055/25
A0656/16 C0131/17 C0396/19
jumps (1) B0875/08
junction (7) A0501/18
B1280/23 C0526/09 C0530/02 C0571/09
C0573/39 C0576/02
juncture (5) B0977/09
B1053/31 B1070/25 C0406/09 C0554/07
June (27) A0293/16
A0602/14 B0729/06 B0729/29 B0731/26
B0745/10 B0753/13 B0753/20 B0753/31
B0753/36 B0754/04 B0754/09 B0770/19
B0922/04 B0933/21 B1055/23 C0053/T
C0066/29 C0066/29 C0067/04 C0069/40
C0084/02 C0101/08 C0146/41 C0530/04
C0530/34 C0538/13
Jung (3) A0292/V
A0293/06 A0299/09
Jung, Ritzner Von (10) A0292/01
A0292/V A0293/13 A0294/01 A0294/V
A0294/V A0295/06 A0296/07 A0296/V
A0301/31
junior (1) A0508/23
juniors (1) A0432/24
Juniper (1) A0340/02
Junius (2) A0172/02 A0178/02
junk (3) A0253/30
C0091/06 C0100/35
Junot (1) C0529/03
Junot, Pierre (4) C0529/11
C0532/07 C0535/22 C0548/33
Junot's (1) C0532/27
Junto (1) A0252/V
junto (2) A0203/01 B0968/06
Jup (10) B0808/29 B0809/05
B0811/16 B0813/07 B0813/21 B0814/09
B0818/09 B0818/18 B0818/22 B0819/24
Jupiter (51)
Jupiter's (13) B0808/19
B0809/08 B0814/02 B0819/31 B0821/29
B0822/22 B0822/29 B0824/26 B0825/20
B0826/19 B0833/25 B0843/12 C0423/27
jurisprudence (1) B0747/33
Jurmains (1) B1296/12
jury (1) B1054/32
just (326)
Justice (2) A0274/28 A0274/31
justice (18) A0057/06 A0066/33
A0096/07 A0242/03 A0280/28 A0352/12
A0435/28 A0441/09 A0621/08 A0623/25
B0737/28 B0747/35 B1009/17 B1056/22
B1133/11 B1369/13 B1379/20 C0088/15
justifiable (3) A0113/V
B1048/05 C0401/40
justification (2) A0075/01 A0445/20
justified (3) A0113/02
A0263/28 B1383/12
justify (1) A0122/02
justly (21) A0024/08
A0065/27 A0074/06 A0089/30 A0125/30
A0337/11 A0338/15 A0435/06 A0560/05
A0610/35 A0708/01 B0746/10 B1022/01
B1269/36 B1272/35 B1369/04 B1380/07

->B1383/09 C0061/34 C0078/14 C0145/06
jut (1) C0538/16
jutted (1) A0097/32
jutting (2) C0537/36 C0576/12
juxta-position (1) A0555/19
juxtaposition (2) B0838/09 B0977/15
Jxhn (6) B1374/07 B1374/09
B1374/11 B1374/13 B1374/13 B1374/19
K (2) A0338/08 B1311/02
k (1) B1095/08
Kabbala (3) B1190/02
B1190/03 B1219/08
<u>kabos</u> (2) B1091/34 B1092/04
kai (Gr.) (3) A0195/M
A0195/M A0346/03
kaleidoscope (1) A0498/23
<u>kam</u> (1) B0723/M
Kamschatka (2) C0526/17 C0526/26
Kanadaw (3) B1298/34
B1299/08 B1299/21
kanadaw (1) B1302/26
Kanawdian (1) B1302/27
Kanawdians (1) B1299/21
Kant (6) A0079/07 A0086/03
A0097/03 A0342/V A0625/03 B1311/01
Kanzas (2) C0527/33 C0539/35
Kate (11) A0650/16
A0650/21 A0651/16 A0653/03 A0653/09
A0655/16 A0655/22 A0656/03 A0656/16
A0656/25 A0657/27
Kate's (2) A0653/26 A0654/13
kath'auto (Gr.) (2) A0225/M
A0229/M
Katholim (1) A0046/28
Katy-Did (1) B1138/34
Katy-Didn't (1) B1138/35
Keats (2) A0033/01 A0710/32
keel (10) A0590/03 A0590/33
B1279/10 C0061/22 C0062/21 C0143/32
C0144/17 C0144/34 C0145/18 C0145/18
keel-boat (1) C0533/12
keen (7) A0609/36
A0615/18 A0690/18 A0692/31 A0693/05
B0926/31 B1212/V
keener (3) A0093/10
A0112/22 A0435/32
keenest (3) A0507/10
A0588/35 B1335/20
keenly (4) A0189/30
B1030/06 B1345/01 C0537/12
keenness (2) A0456/05 B1137/23
keep (73)
keepers (9) B0828/16
B1006/21 B1016/14 B1018/24 B1018/27
B1019/02 B1019/04 B1021/23 B1350/22
keeping (43) A0019/23
A0080/06 A0138/V A0157/18 A0273/26
A0296/V A0321/11 A0370/02 A0370/26
A0371/25 A0387/V A0399/10 A0408/28
A0486/32 A0497/07 A0497/07 A0497/08
A0497/13 A0556/33 A0561/01 A0563/01
A0586/16 A0711/10 B0725/23 B1004/20
B1134/29 B1164/05 B1276/11 B1293/25
C0063/20 C0077/23 C0088/06 C0104/28
C0107/28 C0109/16 C0144/04 C0157/37

->C0171/03 C0172/28 C0179/36 C0391/34
C0419/40 C0523/31
keeps (7) A0070/14
A0081/15 A0369/05 A0500/21 B0735/18
B0812/03 B0812/04
keer (1) B0818/24
keg (7) C0069/22
C0394/23 C0394/24 C0415/24 C0415/29
C0415/30 C0416/11
kegs (4) B1074/34
B1102/26 C0415/20 C0533/30
Keith, Rev. P. (1) B1163/42
Kemble, Fanny (1) B0864/09
Kempelen (1) B1361/04
ken (1) B1037/13
Kennebeck (1) C0147/29
Kennedy (3) A0273/21
A0282/23 B1160/18
Kennedy, John P. (2) A0273/08
A0275/13
Kennedy's (1) A0282/24
kennel (2) A0046/02 A0122/12
Kentucky (4) B1161/23
C0522/19 C0522/39 C0531/20
Kepler (7) B1297/32
B1297/32 B1297/36 B1317/11 B1317/11
B1317/15 B1317/33
Kepler's (1) B1321/21
Keplers (2) B1316/27 B1316/30
kept (78)
Kerguelen (1) C0150/14
Kerguelen's (1) C0150/08
Kerguelen's/Island (1) C0151/07
Kerguelen's/Land (4) C0148/25
C0151/22 C0154/03 C0160/29
Kergulen (1) C0150/13
kerseymere (2) A0371/07 A0439/08
kettle (2) A0101/07 C0534/13
key (17) A0024/28
A0141/24 A0303/27 A0435/03 A0439/21
A0537/22 A0538/04 A0542/12 A0563/17
B0797/13 B0808/09 B0835/22 B0839/10
B1017/32 B1153/34 B1261/30 B1364/05
key-hole (4) A0565/06
B0734/02 B0748/18 B1106/05
key-stone (1) A0150/V
keyhole (1) A0352/25
keys (4) A0551/17
B0943/36 B0978/15 B1352/16
<u>Khoda</u> (1) A0626/12
kick (11) A0345/04
A0368/25 A0386/34 A0627/11 B0812/25
B1103/12 B1131/37 B1142/23 B1167/21
B1182/19 C0563/12
Kickapo-o-o-os (1) A0385/33
Kickapoo (6) A0378/T A0380/31
A0381/09 A0382/15 A0486/14 B1145/23
Kickapoos (5) A0382/30
A0384/21 A0387/24 A0388/19 A0496/04
kicked (8) A0125/30
A0173/25 A0179/07 A0470/21 A0489/05
A0565/27 A0622/35 A0624/04
kicking (6) A0059/26 A0067/16
A0091/30 A0110/32 B1010/05 B1142/25
kicks (1) B0871/14
kid (3) B0833/03 B0833/11 B1186/01
Kidd (8) B0833/13
B0834/03 B0834/07 B0835/18 B0836/07
B0843/25 B0844/15 B0844/15
Kidd's (1) B0834/21
Kieldholm (1) A0579/26
Kilkenny (1) A0468/31
kill (10) B1089/22 B1093/20
B1096/14 B1096/26 B1127/35 B1259/18
C0140/05 C0141/22 C0550/03 C0556/19
killed (12) A0345/02
B0789/21 B1090/22 B1101/26 C0137/39
C0154/09 C0187/31 C0203/14 C0547/14
C0557/32 C0560/03 C0578/31
killing (6) B1046/23 C0081/41
C0138/09 C0141/24 C0199/25 C0577/38
kind (160)
kind-hearted (1) A0483/27
kinder (1) B0789/20
kindest (1) B1050/21
kindle (2) A0230/V C0405/23
kindled (3) B0832/29
C0191/08 C0562/12
kindly (3) B1017/21
B1071/V B1119/M
kindness (10) A0264/05 A0264/13
A0389/13 B1104/25 B1143/06 B1159/18
C0089/01 C0101/37 C0148/30 C0180/07
kindred (4) A0509/25
A0641/V B0749/22 B1384/21
kinds (16) A0478/14
A0510/06 A0627/19 B0993/09 B1009/13
B1078/07 B1080/08 B1166/01 B1337/13
C0097/19 C0151/10 C0151/23 C0174/01
C0177/05 C0536/25 C0560/01
King (11) A0044/27
A0126/05 A0240/T A0240/V A0250/04
A0251/12 A0252/21 A0252/33 A0253/15
B1213/28 C0569/35
king (97)
King, Henry (1) A0150/M
King's (1) B0768/17
king's (5) A0123/08
A0128/13 B1153/23 B1348/14 B1353/11
Kingdom (1) B1297/35
kingdom (7) A0250/09
A0251/07 A0408/08 B1155/26 B1162/10
B1162/13 B1317/14
kingly (1) A0020/V
kings (3) A0240/M
A0322/05 A0529/04
kiosk (5) B0946/34
B0947/02 B0947/11 B0947/14 B0949/18
kip> (1) A0469/V
kipt> (4) A0466/16
A0467/25 A0469/22 A0469/V
Kircher (1) A0583/03
Kirschenwasser (4) B1104/24
B1106/21 B1109/12 B1110/22
kiss (3) A0053/24
A0062/29 A0125/29
Kissam (6) B1358/22 B1358/27
B1358/29 B1358/35 B1359/02 B1359/02
Kissam's (1) B1359/10
kissed (5) A0182/33

->A0232/19 A0342/23 B0900/04 B1010/18
kisses (1) B0871/14
kissing (1) A0623/13
kitchen (3) A0101/05
A0479/14 B1339/26
kitt-fox (1) C0536/23
kitten (1) B1096/21
kittens (7) C0407/09
C0407/17 C0409/05 C0411/08 C0413/10
C0413/13 C0414/04
Klimm, Nicholas (1) A0409/01
Klock-klock (1) C0180/38
Klock-klock (1) C0177/16
Klock-Klock (1) C0172/33
knack (1) A0107/33
knapsack (1) B1329/02
knee (7) A0249/06
A0369/04 A0543/29 B0866/09 B0880/02
B1182/17 C0552/28
knee-breeches (2) A0368/19 A0371/08
knees (32) A0056/02
A0065/26 A0141/13 A0143/13 A0217/V
A0251/07 A0373/08 A0437/18 A0586/16
A0623/07 B0818/35 B0824/04 B0824/15
B0826/22 B0832/11 B0855/10 B1010/28
B1090/12 B1127/20 B1127/27 B1348/34
C0059/17 C0082/18 C0122/17 C0124/39
C0134/27 C0134/30 C0138/23 C0192/08
C0197/40 C0389/26 C0421/20
knell (4) A0235/V
B1222/22 B1249/01 C0198/01
knelt (1) B1107/14
knew (150)
Knickerbocker (3) B1303/13
B1304/06 B1304/08
Knickerbockers (1) B1303/30
knife (28) A0430/15
A0685/27 B0820/11 B0825/26 B1011/20
B1052/14 B1052/16 B1058/01 B1110/09
B1142/21 C0076/07 C0092/36 C0094/07
C0095/41 C0105/06 C0128/30 C0133/12
C0165/08 C0172/10 C0172/12 C0175/29
C0175/30 C0178/38 C0180/26 C0180/26
C0188/34 C0534/12 C0562/05
knight (2) B1303/14 B1349/21
knights (1) A0670/13
knit (4) A0508/03
A0512/35 A0536/V A0628/16
knitting-needle (1) B0980/04
knives (8) C0109/30
C0148/10 C0177/12 C0177/39 C0184/02
C0196/24 C0201/12 C0577/31
knob (1) B0990/36
knock (2) A0166/15 B0988/12
knock-down (1) A0487/12
knocked (20) A0069/07
A0070/16 A0125/15 A0341/05 A0372/05
A0389/07 A0482/15 A0487/10 A0488/04
A0628/25 B1020/26 B1047/31 B1103/20
B1109/14 B1165/05 B1259/22 B1293/11
C0085/18 C0113/24 C0563/07
knocker (2) A0489/31 B1178/14
knocking (6) A0246/07 A0253/20
A0383/01 B0796/17 C0114/37 C0134/27
knocks (1) A0622/34
knoll (1) C0568/21
knot (16) A0044/11
A0069/21 A0078/01 A0139/23 A0501/21
A0561/09 B0730/18 B0730/31 B0730/33
B0730/35 B0766/17 B0768/32 B0916/15
B1079/14 C0197/11 C0398/10
knots (1) C0543/30
know (236)
knowest (3) A0228/29
A0228/29 A0233/11
knoweth (3) A0310/M
A0314/26 A0318/V
knowing (29) A0090/11
A0098/08 A0246/05 A0272/24 A0300/22
A0301/34 A0372/11 A0388/32 A0405/17
A0435/09 A0470/03 A0484/20 A0547/11
A0548/20 A0585/19 A0639/15 B0749/12
B0814/29 B0900/21 B0914/26 B1011/12
B1101/27 B1101/31 B1194/15 B1212/08
C0058/11 C0392/10 C0397/27 C0565/34
knowingly (3) A0089/24
A0107/26 B0927/28
Knowledge (1) A0337/18
knowledge (74)
Knowles, Ned (1) A0292/M
known (154)
knows (21) A0091/35
A0111/11 A0262/28 A0338/10 A0338/20
A0365/01 A0365/10 A0466/28 A0486/06
A0498/04 A0629/02 A0708/18 B0831/25
B0852/12 B1033/21 B1183/05 B1273/13
B1293/26 B1313/16 B1313/17 C0098/36
knuckles (2) B1372/23 C0068/23
knxw (5) B1374/07
B1374/09 B1374/12 B1374/13 B1374/19
Koran (2) B1165/33 B1166/29
koruphai (Gr.) (1) A0195/M
kraken (1) A0139/28
kraut (2) A0373/16 A0374/18
Kreutzenstern (2) C0160/04 C0160/09
Kritik (2) A0341/28 A0342/V
krokopepeplos (Gr.) (1) B1385/18
Kroutaplenttey (1) A0366/08
Kupris (1) A0035/25
L (1) B0908/24
L--l (6) B1236/22 B1236/28
B1238/04 B1240/33 B1241/03 B1241/21
L--l, Theodore (1) B1236/16
L'an (1) A0018/12
l'autre (1) A0378/M
l'ennemi (1) B1154/22
l'etudier (1) B0899/30
l'histoire (2) A0033/03 B1144/32
L'homme (2) A0033/19 C0430/27
l'oiseau (1) A0033/17
l'original (1) C0430/35
l'ottimo (1) A0161/03
l'oublie (1) B1114/03
l'Ame (1) A0096/08
l'Andromache (1) A0033/21
L'Enclos, Ninon De (3) B0898/09
B0914/15 B0915/25
L'Espanaye (29) A0537/10
A0538/07 A0539/04 A0539/11 A0539/16
A0539/21 A0539/27 A0540/27 A0541/12

->A0541/21 A0541/22 A0542/06 A0543/15
A0543/20 A0543/30 A0546/28 A0547/23
A0549/04 A0551/03 A0551/09 A0556/06
A0557/26 A0558/23 A0559/01 A0566/14
A0566/25 B0724/26 B0737/04 B0737/11
L'Espanaye, Camille (1) A0537/11
L'Espanaye's (1) A0565/22
l'Esprit (1) A0096/08
L'Etoile (23) B0731/25
B0733/08 B0733/16 B0733/19 B0738/17
B0739/05 B0739/07 B0739/19 B0740/18
B0740/20 B0743/02 B0743/29 B0744/07
B0744/26 B0744/34 B0745/16 B0745/21
B0745/24 B0746/30 B0747/08 B0747/29
B0748/12 B0748/28
l'Etoile (1) B0737/31
L'Etoile's (4) B0739/18
B0740/02 B0740/25 B0740/30
L'Omelette (1) A0035/23
L'Omelette (1) A0037/25
La (1) A0599/01
la (38) A0019/04 A0053/14
A0062/22 A0096/06 A0096/07 A0096/M
A0101/02 A0102/10 A0102/11 A0109/31
A0109/31 A0175/19 A0175/20 A0181/08
A0181/09 A0344/16 A0344/25 A0378/M
A0386/05 A0545/07 A0599/03 A0602/06
A0602/07 A0662/V B0913/05 B1007/23
B1010/21 B1010/31 B1012/24 B1335/18
C0430/27 C0430/28 C0430/30 C0430/31
C0430/36 C0430/37 C0430/41 C0430/41
la (2) A0057/26 A0068/09
La/Bellissima (1) A0033/06
La/Bruyere (3) A0018/07
A0506/M B0985/03
La/Chaise (1) A0037/V
La/Charette (1) C0538/43
La/Fontaine (1) A0622/16
La/Scala (1) A0079/08
La/Seine, Pierre (1) A0621/14
labelled (3) A0034/22
A0101/15 B0736/13
labels (2) B1104/23 B1104/23
labor (37) A0510/04
A0583/34 A0665/24 A0704/10 B0737/26
B0760/12 B0823/32 B0825/08 B0843/23
B0844/17 B0844/17 B0857/23 B0913/14
B0931/11 B0982/05 B1057/34 B1164/06
B1166/23 B1189/08 B1206/03 B1222/25
B1263/23 B1269/10 B1281/34 B1329/34
C0394/36 C0395/27 C0402/24 C0419/32
C0420/17 C0420/39 C0424/07 C0424/15
C0541/02 C0545/35 C0572/34 C0577/15
labor-saving (1) B1093/09
labored (4) A0490/06
B1050/24 B1128/15 B1145/18
laborer (1) B1206/07
laborers (3) A0510/27
B0968/28 B1302/29
laboring (5) A0411/05
A0707/18 B1030/24 B1047/01 B1272/17
laborious (2) A0213/09 B1280/21
labors (11) A0027/V
A0270/05 A0311/29 A0320/26 B0796/15
B0823/07 B0871/17 B0983/26 B0983/28

->B1128/09 B1262/17
labour (12) B0981/V
C0069/12 C0075/20 C0086/26 C0114/11
C0114/15 C0114/28 C0115/02 C0120/38
C0140/29 C0152/21 C0203/01
laboured (4) C0113/36
C0132/10 C0149/29 C0197/12
labours (3) C0137/14
C0154/04 C0189/39
labyrinth (3) B1362/06
C0096/06 C0575/03
labyrinths (2) A0296/V C0075/01
lac (2) A0096/M A0096/M
lace (4) B0730/16
B0730/32 B0890/06 B1008/08
lacerated (2) A0029/12 C0116/32
lacerating (1) A0044/12
lacessit (1) B1260/01
Lachadive/islands (1) A0136/02
lachrymatory (2) A0054/13 A0063/20
lachrymose (1) A0298/V
lack (6) A0320/05 A0408/09
A0621/10 B0753/41 B1123/22 C0391/16
lack-lustre (2) A0510/16 B1057/09
Lacko'breath (1) A0078/42
Lackobreath (3) A0064/16
A0064/22 A0072/06
laconic (4) A0026/07
A0341/11 A0628/09 B1221/26
Lacroix (1) A0079/03
ladder (8) A0350/06
B1106/32 B1107/06 B1109/37 B1294/16
C0121/23 C0121/34 C0121/38
laden (7) A0046/20
A0587/28 A0643/28 B0968/14 C0189/01
C0189/33 C0542/14
ladies (16) A0059/01
A0069/V A0070/01 A0253/27 A0380/23
A0464/16 A0556/10 B0904/29 B0922/07
B0926/14 B0926/19 B1007/32 B1009/19
B1016/13 B1047/05 B1090/10
ladle (1) A0368/13
Lady (12) A0020/12
A0020/V A0020/V A0204/34 A0205/26
A0321/02 A0323/02 A0323/21 A0330/04
A0330/06 B0871/03 B1159/09
lady (108)
lady's (8) A0064/15
A0270/35 B0730/34 B0877/10 B0877/18
B0877/19 B0933/32 B0958/08
lady's-maid (1) B0933/35
Lady's/Book (1) B1291/01
ladye-love (1) B1123/21
Laertes, Diogenes (1) A0109/10
Laertius (1) A0075/16
laffin> (2) A0468/24 A0470/13
Lafitte (5) A0101/V
A0181/14 B1101/07 B1102/13 B1105/10
Lafourcade, Victorine (1) B0957/12
laid (42) A0020/V A0035/V
A0037/V A0057/12 A0079/31 A0225/15
A0229/V A0236/12 A0242/03 A0253/18
A0262/17 A0262/20 A0415/V A0446/V
A0551/12 A0621/09 A0623/24 A0623/25
B1181/09 B1192/16 B1262/09 B1262/13

->B1304/13 B1304/29 B1382/14 C0072/28
C0078/17 C0093/23 C0104/27 C0104/33
C0104/39 C0106/13 C0106/21 C0106/22
C0125/31 C0136/13 C0184/11 C0201/29
C0392/39 C0544/35 C0573/40 C0575/36
laider> (1) A0464/06
lain (7) A0195/V
A0399/09 B1317/06 C0107/36 C0138/03
C0184/24 C0524/10
lair (1) A0199/V
Lake (4) C0526/09
C0526/37 C0527/03 C0528/23
lake (14) A0502/05 A0602/03
B1079/03 B1161/16 B1161/35 B1281/09
B1333/21 B1334/02 B1334/08 B1334/13
C0412/38 C0422/26 C0444/V C0444/V
Lake/Huron (1) C0526/35
Lake/Nipissing (2) C0526/35
C0528/10
Lake/Superior (1) C0526/36
Lake/Winnipeg (3) C0526/39
C0528/23 C0551/01
lakelet (1) B1333/22
Lakes (1) C0527/01
lakes (6) B0862/09 B0865/04
B1076/17 B1283/08 C0419/03 C0528/11
Lalande (29) B0892/10
B0892/23 B0894/07 B0894/21 B0895/03
B0896/02 B0896/09 B0897/08 B0898/12
B0898/27 B0899/19 B0899/20 B0901/04
B0901/17 B0903/21 B0904/25 B0904/30
B0905/V B0906/23 B0909/16 B0909/31
B0911/10 B0911/17 B0912/08 B0915/09
B0915/21 B0915/26 B0915/29 B0916/26
Lalande, Eugenie (2) B0909/09
B0914/06
Lalande, Stephanie (5) B0913/09
B0914/22 B0915/V B0916/08 B0916/26
Lama-Lama (3) C0168/08
C0168/32 C0174/19
Lama-Lamas (1) C0175/25
Lamartine (1) A0535/33
Lamartine's (1) B1101/04
lamb (1) A0124/14
lambent (1) A0316/18
Lambert, Jonathan (1) C0155/40
lambs (3) A0043/08
A0044/03 A0044/07
lame (3) A0627/30
B1123/25 B1313/14
lament (1) C0166/28
lamentable (12) A0121/18
A0352/19 A0354/25 A0354/25 A0373/12
B1312/23 C0097/28 C0099/02 C0128/37
C0136/07 C0192/25 C0567/35
lamentation (1) A0460/15
lamented (3) B0990/26
B1055/10 C0416/27
lamenting (1) A0214/12
lamentingly (1) B0767/24
lamma (1) A0108/20
lamp (36) A0087/23
A0088/03 A0089/01 A0092/26 A0094/23
A0101/V A0103/17 A0112/01 A0114/18
A0212/02 A0218/07 A0412/07 A0412/16
->A0437/03 A0437/10 A0437/20 A0437/33
A0439/04 A0499/05 A0499/05 A0499/06
A0503/03 A0503/08 A0512/01 A0514/25
A0514/34 A0614/23 A0665/33 A0672/07
A0672/10 B0904/16 B0956/34 B0975/03
B1168/24 B1340/15 B1361/24
lamp-black (1) A0486/21
lampoon (1) B1134/02
lamps (5) A0122/16
A0165/14 A0190/01 A0507/24 A0615/26
lances (1) C0174/32
lancet (1) C0406/34
Land (1) C0162/10
land (83)
land-animal (1) C0167/14
land-slide (2) B1247/24 B1248/05
landed (6) A0564/20 B0933/09
C0147/28 C0557/39 C0568/05 C0570/34
landing (7) A0537/18
A0540/06 C0155/04 C0161/41 C0165/30
C0180/28 C0567/24
landlady (5) A0057/14
A0242/16 B0878/16 B0879/26 B0880/06
landlady's (1) B0878/25
landlocked (2) C0151/02 C0170/40
landlord (4) A0057/09
A0067/03 A0242/V B0854/17
landmarks (2) B0817/19 B1126/13
Landon (1) B1340/V
Landor (2) B0747/37 B1339/18
Landor's (2) B1328/T B1340/24
lands (4) A0088/12
A0235/16 C0158/15 C0202/14
Landscape (2) A0702/T B1329/33
landscape (12) A0397/12
A0600/21 A0707/33 A0708/12 A0708/31
A0711/25 B0861/02 B1272/34 B1273/07
B1273/25 B1274/08 B1276/28
landscape-garden (4) A0709/16
A0711/12 B1272/07 B1276/13
landscape-gardener (1) B1272/05
landscape-gardening (5) A0709/21
A0710/03 B1274/22 B1274/24 B1275/06
landscape-gardens (1) B1274/20
landscape-painter (1) B1335/28
Landscape-Garden (2) A0702/V
A0707/07
Landscape-Gardener (1) A0707/06
landscapes (4) A0502/04
A0707/27 B0863/05 B1272/27
landsman (1) A0587/30
landward (1) A0579/16
lane (6) A0514/18 B0864/21
B0864/22 B1049/03 B1049/04 B1329/24
lanes (2) A0242/23 A0513/32
language (45) A0074/03
A0141/16 A0162/28 A0163/16 A0227/06
A0231/17 A0299/31 A0303/25 A0310/07
A0327/07 A0344/08 A0344/18 A0444/13
A0447/25 A0456/27 A0540/14 A0540/25
A0542/31 A0549/25 A0555/14 A0555/V
A0558/19 A0599/V B0766/15 B0835/33
B0836/07 B0837/16 B0851/09 B0911/18
B1091/30 B1097/01 B1104/05 B1105/08
B1114/35 B1154/27 B1157/30 B1158/30

->B1159/01 B1160/06 B1221/26 B1279/15
B1305/04 C0061/33 C0100/25 C0156/40
languages (1) A0128/18
languidly (1) A0033/09
<u>langve</u> (1) C0430/29
lank (1) A0205/10
lantern (15) B0789/24
B0793/07 B0793/31 B0794/28 B0795/14
B0795/25 B1189/19 B1391/05 B1391/25
C0068/31 C0069/37 C0074/01 C0083/36
C0094/02 C0094/21
lanterns (4) B0817/01
B0823/04 B0826/14 C0112/20
lanyards (1) C0114/24
lap (2) A0374/14 A0507/17
lap-dog (1) A0347/19
Laplace (6) A0479/03 B1010/16
B1010/19 B1010/V B1015/20 B1321/03
Laplaces (1) B1316/27
lapse (16) A0397/17
A0399/13 A0438/01 A0672/27 A0673/06
A0683/32 B0723/08 B0726/10 B0740/18
B0898/22 B0899/17 B0958/13 B0966/13
B0988/03 B1189/11 C0562/35
lapsed (2) A0683/10 B1249/13
lapsing (1) A0691/14
larboard (22) A0588/10 A0588/21
B0930/21 C0071/40 C0085/29 C0089/26
C0102/32 C0108/10 C0110/26 C0114/01
C0114/40 C0117/08 C0117/11 C0130/29
C0131/08 C0136/14 C0154/20 C0164/30
C0187/27 C0187/29 C0188/01 C0559/22
large (325)
large-boned (1) B0741/08
largely (6) A0213/01 A0282/02
A0473/24 B1093/33 B1257/14 C0423/05
largeness (1) B1321/12
larger (44) A0066/06
A0108/24 A0284/26 A0313/03 A0459/20
A0535/08 A0592/25 B0752/05 B0752/20
B0825/04 B1049/07 B1073/34 B1075/10
B1156/26 B1158/05 B1160/12 B1164/20
B1248/06 B1281/07 B1300/33 B1321/11
B1332/18 B1336/05 B1336/10 C0147/13
C0151/22 C0153/17 C0164/33 C0165/16
C0174/35 C0181/22 C0186/38 C0206/06
C0393/30 C0394/23 C0397/26 C0429/23
C0429/27 C0432/15 C0432/20 C0534/33
C0545/08 C0562/20 C0576/24
largest (22) A0057/07 A0066/34
A0429/12 A0429/34 A0582/26 B0752/13
B0773/22 B0819/07 B1332/30 B1332/37
B1333/03 C0143/19 C0151/11 C0151/37
C0154/30 C0155/34 C0164/35 C0167/30
C0168/30 C0173/29 C0203/14 C0551/26
lark (1) C0390/22
<u>las</u> (1) A0621/01
Lasalle (1) A0697/11
lash (2) A0593/13 B0932/33
lashed (10) A0580/11 A0585/36
A0589/26 C0089/29 C0106/30 C0106/33
C0116/01 C0117/04 C0120/03 C0143/33
lashes (1) A0313/11
lashing (5) A0145/19
C0060/31 C0139/27 C0140/15 C0141/03
lashings (9) A0593/23
C0116/19 C0116/34 C0117/20 C0117/34
C0118/29 C0119/17 C0119/37 C0139/33
lasm (Gr.) (1) A0159/04
lasping (1) B0959/13
<u>lasst</u> (2) A0506/01 A0515/32
Last (1) B1384/20
last (198)
Last/Supper (3) B0925/09
B0925/10 B0927/13
laste> (2) A0468/15 A0470/06
lasted (15) A0541/02
A0683/30 A0688/06 B0851/04 B1011/32
B1262/15 C0084/32 C0086/30 C0102/24
C0135/38 C0141/35 C0142/03 C0191/17
C0406/14 C0419/21
lasting (3) A0228/23
A0233/04 C0146/06
lastly (12) A0078/10
A0209/18 A0248/03 A0643/20 A0712/03
B0748/22 B1145/04 C0151/30 C0190/05
C0427/32 C0527/05 C0557/15
latch (6) A0447/23 A0479/20
A0479/26 A0479/28 A0479/30 B0789/22
latches (1) A0479/16
Late (3) A0340/08
A0378/T B1126/T
late (107)
lately (32) A0142/16
A0166/22 A0341/12 A0365/10 A0369/30
A0398/17 A0564/18 A0641/17 A0662/07
B0724/22 B0857/05 B0887/11 B0898/28
B0982/14 B1015/17 B1057/20 B1091/30
B1151/01 B1215/18 B1296/36 B1380/18
C0055/29 C0059/40 C0095/21 C0139/14
C0389/04 C0392/19 C0413/26 C0425/13
C0430/21 C0430/26 C0571/27
lately-acquired (1) A0026/28
lateness (1) A0540/21
latent (2) B1247/02 C0073/04
later (13) A0121/15
A0293/10 A0326/21 A0403/17 A0410/05
A0426/11 A0426/12 A0639/01 A0683/13
A0684/03 B0907/25 B1379/26 C0555/32
lateral (9) A0429/27
A0692/13 B0818/30 B1237/01 B1237/08
B1237/22 B1332/05 C0193/19 C0207/41
laterally (1) B1248/15
latest (1) A0101/07
lath-like (1) A0064/20
lather (2) B1127/08 B1127/21
lathered (1) A0565/04
Latin (15) A0124/28
A0265/26 A0301/09 A0343/35 A0344/11
A0345/17 A0345/18 A0536/16 B0987/09
B1051/13 B1051/20 B1089/04 B1142/16
B1143/14 B1143/15
latitude (57)
latitudes (5) C0166/20
C0167/39 C0171/20 C0176/21 C0199/05
Latour (2) A0175/18 A0181/11
latter (173)
latter's (2) A0244/17 B1052/32
latterly (4) A0460/32
B1031/28 C0084/33 C0166/08

lattice (3) A0057/34
A0154/06 A0645/03
latticed (1) A0554/15
laudable (5) A0123/07
A0295/21 A0346/32 B0751/02 B1189/03
laudanum (2) A0667/36 B0736/13
laudatory (1) B1380/18
lauded (1) A0122/09
lauding (2) A0124/27 A0626/22
lauft (1) B0723/M
laugh (23) A0080/07
A0098/16 A0105/32 A0158/17 A0158/V
A0158/V A0198/31 A0198/32 A0236/11
A0407/41 A0533/14 B0833/04 B0928/03
B0934/09 B1181/27 B1263/02 B1263/06
B1325/05 B1345/32 B1345/33 B1348/20
C0067/01 C0128/14
laughable (1) B0744/25
laughably (1) B1157/08
laughed (24) A0080/07
A0105/26 A0158/07 A0190/06 A0198/30
A0236/11 A0433/25 A0603/07 A0624/03
A0652/25 A0692/15 B0793/02 B0898/V
B0926/18 B0983/33 B0988/13 B0989/07
B1017/24 B1225/V B1249/12 B1260/15
B1348/21 B1349/23 C0571/02
laughing (11) A0158/18
A0158/20 A0300/26 B0975/29 B1333/36
B1349/24 B1350/04 C0131/17 C0167/09
C0168/37 C0174/28
laughingly (2) B0902/04 B0906/23
Laughter (1) A0159/07
laughter (13) A0123/32
A0158/16 A0249/08 A0673/02 A0674/01
B1013/18 B1353/02 B1353/16 C0061/08
C0067/24 C0087/26 C0128/15 C0541/22
laughter-like (1) A0245/02
Launcelot (2) A0414/07 A0415/16
launch (2) A0053/03 A0062/08
laundress (1) A0538/34
laurels (2) B1126/04 B1137/29
Lauzanne, Jacques (1) C0539/29
lave> (1) A0465/03
laved (1) B1283/02
Laverna (1) A0568/21
lavish (1) B1008/34
lavished (4) A0702/03
A0704/08 B1133/21 B1269/08
Law (5) A0294/V
B0852/14 B1206/01 B1312/32 B1321/21
law (27) A0078/41
A0078/41 A0399/26 A0407/10 A0427/30
A0491/03 A0497/31 A0555/14 A0555/17
A0622/19 B0747/34 B0747/36 B0874/27
B1033/26 B1034/05 B1039/07 B1039/11
B1039/12 B1039/15 B1054/36 B1092/32
B1093/11 B1093/33 B1213/25 B1311/17
C0391/35 C0432/04
law-encumbered (1) B1039/08
lawn (1) A0247/04
lawn's (1) B1334/25
Laws (1) A0429/02
laws (28) A0046/09
A0438/17 A0497/10 A0498/12 A0609/19
A0610/18 A0652/27 A0703/12 A0703/29
->B0772/17 B0772/18 B1003/11 B1030/14
B1039/14 B1213/16 B1268/11 B1295/17
B1297/33 B1297/33 B1297/33 B1299/32
B1311/09 B1317/11 B1317/11 B1317/12
B1317/15 B1383/05 C0400/39
lawyer (3) A0482/34
B0956/12 B1127/31
lawyers (1) B0747/11
laxity (1) B0751/10
lay (225)
layer (2) B1180/12 C0098/18
layers (1) C0185/12
laying (5) B1181/22
B1182/29 B1189/30 C0105/31 C0177/32
lazily (2) B1108/33 C0125/06
lazy (2) A0368/23 B0865/23
lbs (1) C0179/05
Le (1) B0753/19
Le (2) A0036/10 A0537/V
le (16) A0037/21
A0037/26 A0053/13 A0062/21 A0096/M
A0096/M A0096/V A0397/M A0431/08
A0599/03 B1122/01 B1154/21 C0430/27
C0430/29 C0430/39 C0430/41
Le/Blanc (5) B0725/28
B0726/06 B0726/13 B0753/07 B0753/09
Le/Blanc's (1) B0753/16
Le/Bon (3) A0544/27
A0546/06 A0568/07
Le/Bon, Adolphe (2) A0541/19
A0544/22
Le/Brun (1) A0037/06
Le/Commerciel (10) B0734/07 B0748/34
B0749/26 B0750/06 B0750/07 B0750/17
B0758/19 B0766/01 B0766/10 B0766/18
le/Commerciel (1) B0749/04
Le/Commerciel's (1) B0734/29
Le/Diligence (1) B0754/09
Le/Febvre (4) A0096/03
A0099/11 A0100/25 A0101/V
Le/Mercurie (1) B0769/04
Le/Monde (1) A0560/22
Le/Moniteur (3) B0740/14
B0740/20 B0740/26
Le/Soleil (9) B0735/03
B0750/29 B0751/06 B0758/29 B0758/34
B0759/16 B0761/27 B0762/13 B0763/18
Le/Tribunal (1) A0547/V
lead (21) A0136/21
A0236/01 A0296/V A0316/18 A0381/23
A0527/V A0551/06 A0555/18 A0709/12
B0835/V B0988/34 B1166/26 B1213/29
B1331/31 B1362/20 B1363/21 B1364/08
B1364/27 B1364/33 C0181/21 C0533/31
lead-work (1) A0243/01
leaden (7) A0241/V
A0246/33 A0321/16 A0402/24 B1235/12
B1304/01 C0396/22
leaden-footed (1) B0728/33
leaden-hued (1) A0400/02
leader (4) B1019/25
B1374/06 C0521/24 C0533/06
leading (37) A0105/06
A0297/10 A0339/16 A0343/07 A0445/14
A0479/04 A0484/11 A0498/25 A0499/20

->A0509/28 A0542/11 A0551/15 A0601/17
A0610/21 B0727/16 B0728/07 B0770/33
B0945/25 B1048/23 B1048/34 B1133/02
B1187/15 B1294/16 B1336/34 B1339/14
B1339/26 B1369/33 B1371/14 C0069/33
C0073/31 C0096/10 C0129/11 C0180/35
C0192/11 C0523/11 C0536/16 C0547/01
leading-strings (1) A0427/31
leads (7) A0124/06
A0145/26 A0599/V A0641/V B0907/26
B1278/12 C0538/34
leaf (8) B0830/11
B0943/15 B0981/02 B1059/25 B1161/18
B1279/33 B1280/11 B1349/07
leafless (1) C0072/18
leafy (1) A0602/14
league (4) A0145/13
C0163/30 C0165/24 C0167/28
leagues (7) A0581/26
B1161/26 B1161/28 C0150/13 C0157/05
C0161/33 C0202/05
leak (7) B0931/03
C0103/02 C0103/06 C0103/12 C0114/13
C0114/31 C0146/38
leaky (1) C0106/05
lean (10) A0103/21 A0487/17
A0487/21 B0741/07 B1012/02 B1345/09
C0534/33 C0535/34 C0546/17 C0567/01
leaned (8) A0196/30
A0350/04 B0895/07 B1105/01 B1145/21
B1145/22 B1250/30 B1260/33
leaning (9) A0136/11
A0160/01 A0179/30 A0249/02 A0349/19
B0913/01 B1108/34 C0123/33 C0124/36
leans (1) A0616/05
leant (1) A0249/V
leap (8) A0027/07
A0630/18 A0630/23 B0863/08 B1013/08
B1057/25 B1346/08 C0196/19
leap-year (1) B1152/27
leaped (22) A0058/10 A0068/08
A0243/25 A0252/31 A0415/29 A0586/23
A0594/03 A0694/14 A0694/17 B0771/17
B0795/26 B0809/21 B0832/08 B1020/19
B1134/32 B1178/27 B1353/10 C0090/29
C0124/04 C0168/30 C0562/39 C0578/28
leaping (13) A0029/07
A0068/33 A0319/19 A0627/16 B0825/21
B0911/13 B1014/21 B1020/20 B1021/08
B1353/V C0146/17 C0165/07 C0537/07
leaps (3) A0128/05
A0128/06 B1311/28
leapt (2) A0057/25 A0694/V
learn (17) A0098/27
A0515/30 A0638/10 B0899/V B1007/05
B1096/24 B1130/24 B1132/22 B1136/38
B1138/02 B1169/29 B1185/21 B1293/33
B1380/05 C0061/01 C0083/37 C0523/25
learned (28) A0124/16
A0226/23 A0230/22 A0338/06 A0366/05
A0399/04 A0403/20 A0404/24 A0410/17
A0432/27 A0458/20 A0459/15 A0592/33
A0609/04 B0908/20 B0933/17 B0987/33
B1017/12 B1096/10 B1096/10 B1096/13
B1246/10 B1294/03 C0102/22 C0137/07
->C0203/34 C0432/29 C0536/19
learnedly (2) B0728/27 B0986/23
learning (6) A0059/30 A0310/05
A0315/16 A0343/14 B0958/01 B1051/17
least (231)
leather (9) A0086/32
A0112/24 A0368/10 B1053/22 B1166/17
C0128/04 C0128/30 C0130/41 C0391/24
leather-bottomed (5) A0101/21
A0368/28 A0369/22 A0370/25 A0372/22
leather-jackets (1) C0174/07
leave (68)
leaves (27) A0020/V
A0088/17 A0198/26 A0227/27 A0232/14
A0368/24 A0610/22 A0640/12 A0702/M
B0764/25 B0840/26 B0872/03 B0944/20
B1113/07 B1267/M B1282/16 B1325/04
B1332/34 B1337/34 C0153/09 C0175/03
C0175/07 C0191/07 C0192/15 C0543/20
C0543/29 C0566/14
leavestaking (1) C0179/34
leaving (90)
lecture (4) A0271/13
A0625/12 A0629/21 B0916/10
lecturer (1) A0652/20
lecturing (1) A0294/V
led (78)
Leda (1) A0313/24
leddy-ship> (1) A0465/24
leddyship> (11) A0466/19
A0467/14 A0467/19 A0467/24 A0468/12
A0468/16 A0468/23 A0468/27 A0469/04
A0469/27 A0470/07
leddyship's> (1) A0470/20
ledge (19) B0841/17
B0841/18 B0841/33 B0843/02 B0956/33
B1331/20 B1335/06 B1338/14 C0155/16
C0165/27 C0165/28 C0173/16 C0173/25
C0196/17 C0196/27 C0530/03 C0572/37
C0579/04 C0580/01
ledger (2) A0483/04 A0487/07
ledges (1) B1334/36
Ledyard (2) C0526/14 C0526/20
Ledyard's (1) C0526/30
lee (6) A0583/16 A0584/18
B0932/10 B0932/15 C0059/08 C0062/11
lee-lurch (2) A0242/05 C0114/25
Lee, Nat (1) B1130/06
leech (2) B0950/09 B0950/12
leeches (2) B0950/04 B0950/06
leer (1) B1259/25
lees (1) B1101/29
leetle (2) B0820/15 B0900/V
leeward (7) B0928/25
B0928/26 C0112/25 C0113/39 C0114/36
C0125/27 C0143/18
lef (10) B0821/01 B0821/11
B0821/14 B0821/21 B0821/21 B0821/23
B0821/23 B0824/09 B0824/27 B0913/05
left (282)
left-handed (2) A0622/29 B0821/16
left-handedly (1) A0622/30
leg (19) A0247/14
A0368/08 A0369/04 A0383/29 A0387/17
A0387/20 A0387/21 A0388/02 A0485/07

->A0485/08 A0487/23 A0543/32 B0979/31
B1011/22 B1185/03 B1313/14 C0069/23
C0142/29 C0404/32
leg-bail (1) A0128/03
legacies (1) A0056/08
legacy (2) A0653/01 B0888/08
legal (2) B0753/34 B1051/23
legally (2) A0108/29 B0958/14
lege (1) A0366/10
legend (1) A0414/18
legging (1) C0562/07
leggings (2) C0552/16 C0552/27
legible (14) A0150/V A0159/04
A0265/27 A0267/05 A0271/21 A0271/28
A0274/07 A0274/29 A0277/12 A0277/33
A0278/32 A0283/02 B0835/29 B1303/37
legion (2) B0969/14 B0975/13
legions (2) A0197/07 B0945/21
legislative (2) A0491/13 B1269/28
legislatively (1) B0887/12
legislature (3) A0490/36
B0747/36 B0888/06
legitimate (16) A0473/31
A0473/32 A0496/21 A0507/15 A0529/23
A0550/20 A0550/24 A0706/11 B0954/02
B1132/14 B1271/15 B1312/31 B1369/10
B1374/29 B1385/25 C0438/V
legitimately (1) B1317/29
Legrand (44) B0807/16
B0807/32 B0808/16 B0808/24 B0809/05
B0809/21 B0809/31 B0809/35 B0810/15
B0811/12 B0813/10 B0813/33 B0814/24
B0815/10 B0815/26 B0816/14 B0816/27
B0817/01 B0817/17 B0818/03 B0819/07
B0819/13 B0819/24 B0819/34 B0820/03
B0820/20 B0820/30 B0820/34 B0822/01
B0822/15 B0823/15 B0823/24 B0824/02
B0824/05 B0824/13 B0824/26 B0825/10
B0826/18 B0828/23 B0833/12 B0835/03
B0835/14 B0840/04 B0840/27
Legrand, William (2) B0806/01
B0813/30
Legrand's (1) B0815/19
Legs (17) A0240/16
A0241/28 A0242/08 A0243/20 A0244/13
A0245/01 A0245/21 A0245/V A0247/31
A0249/02 A0249/14 A0249/25 A0249/34
A0251/11 A0251/28 A0253/16 A0254/01
legs (36) A0127/21
A0127/28 A0248/18 A0297/V A0353/17
A0367/23 A0368/29 A0373/07 A0379/27
A0379/28 A0380/02 A0630/20 A0652/25
A0686/28 B0796/08 B1090/15 B1102/27
B1165/20 B1167/21 B1237/28 B1346/13
C0082/08 C0087/10 C0119/09 C0119/14
C0119/16 C0151/19 C0167/15 C0173/31
C0178/15 C0533/10 C0545/19 C0563/25
C0569/15 C0569/30 C0579/12
Leibnitz (3) A0086/09
A0097/06 A0507/13
Leipsic (1) B0958/15
leisure (14) A0098/19 A0274/22
A0352/21 A0443/11 A0508/19 A0630/30
A0674/23 B0904/03 B0924/02 B0960/03
C0169/28 C0184/07 C0391/32 C0432/28
leisurely (6) B1003/03 B1102/15
B1109/01 B1188/29 B1354/23 B1372/12
lemon (1) B1092/30
Lempriere (1) A0286/07
lend (6) A0711/12 B0875/22
B1276/13 B1348/17 C0104/07 C0127/40
lending (2) C0104/21 C0185/37
length (413)
lengthen (4) A0227/22
A0227/22 A0232/09 A0232/09
lengths (3) A0235/12
C0128/29 C0575/18
lens (4) C0428/22
C0428/25 C0428/31 C0430/09
lenses (2) B1191/31 C0430/07
lent (3) A0442/03
B0808/28 B1056/27
lenticular-shaped (1) C0402/02
Leonardo's (1) B0925/09
Leonidas (1) B1101/03
Leonville (2) A0101/V A0181/13
leopard (1) A0123/16
leper (1) A0510/10
lepidolite (1) A0182/09
Lepidoptera (1) B1250/19
les (9) A0035/10
A0037/10 A0547/05 A0600/01 B1121/01
B1121/03 B1335/18 C0430/32 C0430/38
lesen (2) A0506/02 A0515/33
Leslie (4) A0270/34
A0271/03 A0274/09 A0281/01
Leslie's (2) A0270/26 A0270/37
less (277)
lessen (1) C0548/29
lessened (1) C0388/27
lessening (1) C0535/20
lesser (4) A0101/V
A0123/15 A0583/01 B1282/33
lesson (7) A0631/19
A0695/09 B0958/04 B1092/31 B1093/37
B1300/23 C0555/35
lessons (4) A0141/23
A0234/04 B1059/25 B1095/06
lest (23) A0044/22
A0090/12 A0135/18 A0228/05 A0344/27
A0684/11 A0685/02 B0814/03 B0943/24
B0965/12 B1006/27 B1051/11 B1320/01
C0071/24 C0075/28 C0082/40 C0111/39
C0119/39 C0131/11 C0188/32 C0189/19
C0399/37 C0548/27
let (303)
lethargic (3) A0081/02
A0616/03 B0962/35
lethargy (6) A0688/29 B0957/33
B0962/11 C0081/28 C0112/37 C0126/19
lets (3) A0479/26
B0870/22 C0523/41
Letter (3) B0974/T
B1310/T B1378/M
letter (168)
letter-writer (4) B1310/20
B1311/20 B1312/11 B1316/04
letter's (1) A0285/12
lettered (3) B0925/24
B0989/33 B0989/35

letters (59)
lettest (1) A0046/15
letting (23) A0047/31
A0151/28 A0293/22 A0555/02 A0588/14
A0667/07 B0809/07 B0824/14 B0843/12
B0843/24 B0844/02 B0927/V B1134/29
B1165/09 B1194/30 C0059/21 C0068/24
C0091/16 C0107/01 C0121/11 C0188/32
C0197/02 C0405/29
Lettres (1) C0430/37
lettres (3) A0337/13
A0337/26 A0652/08
Levante (1) B1386/04
levatas (2) A0209/M A0218/16
levee (1) B0904/05
level (29) A0045/05
A0106/30 A0198/06 A0249/05 A0366/32
A0429/13 A0591/03 A0592/22 A0593/09
B0817/35 B0945/05 B1074/22 B1076/27
B1080/33 B1193/07 B1262/20 B1331/36
C0116/23 C0152/10 C0152/27 C0203/25
C0398/20 C0408/13 C0422/28 C0444/V
C0571/14 C0572/22 C0577/16 C0577/26
levelled (3) A0387/V
B0747/22 C0196/34
levelling (1) B0841/30
levem (1) A0072/31
lever (1) B0965/27
leverage (1) C0185/20
levigue (2) A0071/32 A0072/31
levities (1) A0438/15
levity (6) A0161/20 A0538/30
B0940/V B1044/09 B1074/29 B1074/29
Lewis (14) C0070/33 C0087/05
C0523/04 C0523/21 C0524/12 C0527/16
C0527/25 C0527/27 C0528/36 C0537/41
C0548/08 C0551/23 C0566/39 C0574/40
Lewis's (1) C0538/27
Lex (3) A0301/10
A0302/20 A0303/16
liability (1) B1249/34
liable (10) A0107/18 A0135/16
A0509/17 A0562/01 B0747/27 B0749/17
C0097/13 C0098/30 C0117/06 C0395/23
liars (1) C0569/18
lib. (2) A0611/27 A0611/32
lib/2 (1) B1382/35
libel (1) C0447/V
liber (1) A0593/35
liberal (9) A0440/31
A0491/12 A0706/35 A0707/02 B0725/30
B0728/18 B0879/01 B0941/08 B0982/09
liberality (4) A0204/28
B1046/14 B1058/31 B1127/15
liberally (1) A0652/07
liberate (1) C0104/41
liberties (2) B0739/06 C0523/35
liberty (30) A0055/14 A0055/37
A0056/17 A0064/28 A0065/20 A0066/06
A0088/30 A0096/04 A0103/09 A0203/06
A0409/20 A0466/05 A0689/16 B0728/19
B0760/20 B0772/02 B0897/13 B0927/05
B0965/35 B1004/17 B1018/15 B1047/32
B1236/12 B1362/03 B1363/37 C0101/15
C0114/10 C0188/17 C0391/18 C0408/21

libitum (1) B1193/34
libraries (1) A0096/12
Library (1) B1358/18
library (12) A0209/18
A0214/05 A0214/19 A0216/25 A0217/04
A0218/19 A0531/28 B0974/04 B0980/33
B1022/03 B1115/06 B1246/22
library's (1) A0209/19
libre (1) A0037/V
Libya (1) A0195/02
lice (1) B1191/20
license (2) A0674/32 B0760/17
lichen (1) C0150/28
licked (2) A0091/09 A0110/V
licking (3) A0241/18
C0073/07 C0076/20
lid (18) A0070/16 A0080/38
A0081/27 A0217/V A0410/14 A0410/26
B0826/11 B0925/25 B0929/18 B0929/21
B0930/03 B0959/04 B0965/32 B0967/21
B1057/02 B1059/11 B1102/31 B1141/19
lids (11) A0070/20
A0081/41 A0322/06 A0356/22 A0588/06
A0625/V A0663/24 B0966/34 B1181/33
B1237/23 B1242/12
lie (61)
Lieber (3) A0284/05
A0284/10 A0284/27
Lieber, Francis (1) A0284/02
lied (1) A0458/11
lieden (1) B1360/23
lies (43) A0097/22
A0122/20 A0160/19 A0162/24 A0338/28
A0339/12 A0341/V A0365/03 A0398/04
A0466/09 A0500/30 A0530/03 A0545/18
A0674/05 A0703/09 B0739/27 B0764/20
B0864/15 B0957/27 B0962/10 B0962/27
B0985/01 B0986/17 B0987/18 B1169/18
B1169/24 B1207/27 B1268/08 B1271/16
B1273/34 B1281/03 B1281/08 B1350/11
B1383/29 C0098/10 C0105/35 C0106/23
C0159/34 C0178/25 C0402/31 C0438/V
C0524/34 C0530/02
lieth (3) A0310/M
A0314/26 A0318/V
lieu (3) A0044/04
A0302/16 A0689/27
Lieut (1) A0283/08
Lieutenant (3) A0283/01
B0808/27 C0158/29
Lieutenant/G-- (1) B0830/22
Life (3) A0178/V
A0662/V B1126/T
life (202)
life-boats (1) C0063/11
life-like (3) A0412/25
A0455/10 B1180/28
life-likeliness (1) A0664/22
life-likeliness (2) B0960/V
B1182/V
life-likeness (2) B0960/14 B1182/16
life-preserver (1) B1293/17
life-time (1) C0579/31
life's (1) A0609/05
lifeless (4) A0215/08

->B0736/11 B0736/11 C0165/09
lifelessly (1) B1134/29
lifetime (1) C0065/20
lift (4) A0125/22
A0353/28 A0487/22 C0142/29
lift> (5) A0465/02
A0465/31 A0467/14 A0470/19 A0470/V
lifted (16) A0070/19
A0080/36 A0080/44 A0081/41 A0145/32
A0253/08 A0412/18 A0442/25 A0683/15
B0765/33 B1056/25 C0059/28 C0063/24
C0086/03 C0133/39 C0389/36
lifting (4) A0372/05
C0115/25 C0133/36 C0138/30
lifts (1) A0580/35
Ligeia (31) A0310/02
A0310/12 A0310/12 A0310/T A0311/01
A0311/06 A0311/17 A0312/02 A0312/29
A0313/07 A0313/18 A0313/V A0315/03
A0315/08 A0315/16 A0315/22 A0315/28
A0316/14 A0316/20 A0316/V A0317/V
A0317/V A0319/19 A0320/06 A0321/02
A0323/09 A0323/V A0323/V A0326/16
A0327/26 A0328/19
Ligeia, Lady (1) A0330/20
Ligeia's (3) A0314/03
A0314/08 A0317/23
Light (1) B1131/07
light (217)
light-coloured (1) C0199/38
light-headed (1) A0589/07
light-hearted (1) A0670/12
light-heartedness (1) A0210/31
light-house (2) B1390/01 B1391/22
light-looking (1) B1334/03
Light-House (1) B1390/T
lighted (10) A0157/13 A0196/10
A0507/24 A0512/32 A0532/V A0671/33
B0834/32 B1106/25 B1336/35 C0396/14
lighten (4) A0023/15
A0081/39 B0930/36 C0114/17
lightened (2) B0826/34 C0576/15
lightening (1) A0023/V
lighter (5) B0741/03
B0741/07 B1073/31 B1074/35 C0403/15
lightest (2) A0586/01 C0444/V
lighting (2) A0532/31 B0975/03
lightly (3) A0104/32
A0325/08 A0352/10
lightness (2) A0139/19 A0311/20
lightning (13) A0027/V
A0053/21 A0088/16 A0197/28 A0197/V
A0198/05 A0412/29 B1167/26 B1302/02
C0139/19 C0141/35 C0405/22 C0563/06
lightning-rod (5) A0554/08
A0554/29 A0561/11 A0565/23 A0566/07
lightning-rods (1) A0071/24
lights (15) A0151/22
A0155/19 A0216/20 A0319/11 A0443/19
A0499/22 A0499/24 A0533/06 A0614/19
B0764/31 B0904/13 B0965/03 B1009/01
B1168/04 B1301/07
ligulate (1) B1163/26
like (365)
liked (1) A0107/32
likely (20) A0104/26
A0138/08 A0278/05 A0354/02 A0438/10
A0496/15 A0556/09 A0693/13 B0836/17
B0861/05 B0893/22 B1075/33 B1234/28
C0066/25 C0078/05 C0098/39 C0132/35
C0179/09 C0187/20 C0395/29
liken (1) C0205/24
likened (1) A0511/03
likeness (2) B0949/01 C0428/09
likens (1) A0549/24
likes (4) A0468/09
A0468/26 A0469/03 A0470/17
likewise (6) A0107/07 A0189/23
A0581/36 B1015/V B1164/30 C0410/19
liking (2) B1144/13 C0532/24
lilach (1) C0151/12
Lilienthal (1) C0423/11
lilies (7) A0155/01
A0196/06 A0196/06 A0197/02 A0197/14
A0198/01 A0641/V
lily (2) A0708/03 B1273/03
lily-fringed (1) B1283/08
lily-looking (1) C0412/35
limb (28) A0248/19
A0687/26 B0819/19 B0819/21 B0819/23
B0819/25 B0819/32 B0819/32 B0819/34
B0820/15 B0820/18 B0820/25 B0820/31
B0821/03 B0824/21 B0824/22 B0839/33
B0840/23 B0842/15 B0852/21 B1163/26
B1182/18 B1241/09 C0060/17 C0072/36
C0418/38 C0423/17 C0423/29
limbs (52)
lime (1) B0853/26
limestone (1) C0171/36
limit (13) A0428/23
A0561/31 B0740/04 B0823/27 C0138/35
C0193/14 C0401/16 C0401/19 C0401/22
C0411/37 C0418/17 C0430/05 C0430/06
limited (12) A0204/21
A0706/33 B0727/09 B0749/10 B0749/19
B1038/10 B1270/15 B1271/34 C0065/18
C0202/19 C0392/26 C0574/35
limiting (1) B0752/01
limitless (6) A0426/08 A0683/21
B1280/31 C0072/16 C0164/09 C0205/24
limits (32) A0025/25
A0235/11 A0293/23 A0296/V A0365/10
A0406/08 A0496/20 A0498/14 A0529/32
A0683/21 B0762/04 B0773/34 B0862/16
B0941/26 B0945/27 B0986/12 B0987/29
B0990/15 B1074/32 B1113/06 B1274/12
C0087/41 C0097/10 C0112/06 C0152/24
C0162/09 C0397/17 C0417/26 C0418/10
C0521/13 C0528/28 C0537/05
limped (1) A0629/02
limpid (2) C0138/22 C0171/36
limpidity (1) C0171/35
limping (1) A0630/27
linden (1) B1332/09
line (85)
line-manager (2) C0086/41 C0093/34
lineally (1) B1154/13
lineament (1) A0295/25
lineaments (2) A0437/21 A0448/09
lined (3) A0501/14

->B1261/05 C0575/41
linen (10) A0034/24 A0047/01
A0512/02 A0556/12 A0694/33 B1180/11
C0128/07 C0198/25 C0203/02 C0204/23
linen-draping (1) A0483/V
lines (51)
linger (2) A0226/14 A0230/12
lingered (2) A0217/V B0932/28
lingering (5) A0410/24
A0459/26 A0604/20 B1206/14 C0128/24
lingeringly (1) B0767/24
lingers (1) B0962/13
lingo (1) A0466/01
lining (1) A0443/20
linings (1) A0443/11
link (5) A0553/11
B0833/06 B0853/03 B1159/02 C0172/16
linked (2) B1092/12 B1385/15
links (6) A0087/23 A0101/V
A0321/25 A0535/08 B0831/04 B1261/28
linsey-woolsey (1) A0368/06
lintels (2) B1193/13 B1302/18
Lion (1) A0178/V
lion (7) A0123/16
A0177/28 A0177/29 A0177/29 A0183/24
A0183/26 C0072/26
lion-ant (3) A0478/14
B1162/29 C0546/26
lion-izing (1) A0172/T
lion's (1) A0273/28
lionizing (2) A0172/V A0178/T
lions (4) A0175/03
A0180/26 B0862/08 C0155/20
Lionship (2) A0173/06 A0178/11
lip (17) A0020/V
A0022/13 A0154/22 A0154/22 A0154/V
A0154/V A0247/07 A0298/V A0298/V
A0298/V A0312/20 A0410/24 A0509/20
B0962/15 B1239/28 B1379/28 C0205/11
lips (71)
<u>liqueur</u> (1) B1101/03
liqueur (5) A0250/32
A0253/08 C0081/10 C0082/11 C0082/30
liqueurs (3) A0250/27
A0251/19 C0069/24
liquid (14) A0154/24 A0156/12
A0156/V A0401/31 A0591/22 B1073/03
B1074/35 B1243/05 B1362/22 C0142/12
C0171/32 C0172/06 C0429/17 C0547/21
liquid-looking (1) A0158/05
<u>liquidum</u> (1) A0603/35
liquor (9) A0240/V
A0243/25 A0251/16 A0253/12 A0253/24
C0086/33 C0102/17 C0123/28 C0531/02
liquors (3) A0243/05
A0247/30 C0058/12
<u>Liriodendron</u> (2) B0818/28 B0864/31
<u>liriodendron</u> (1) B1332/26
Lisbon (1) B0955/06
Lisiausky (1) C0160/04
lisped (2) A0174/18 A0179/33
lisping (1) A0627/09
list (7) A0021/17
A0158/21 B0922/07 B0922/17 B0923/09
B1136/19 B1136/36
listen (23) A0022/04
A0045/28 A0126/23 A0128/13 A0166/07
A0195/01 A0226/14 A0262/02 A0413/07
A0587/20 B0820/25 B0892/04 B0910/08
B0932/06 B0965/24 B1047/15 B1054/13
B1104/27 C0086/38 C0094/20 C0170/28
C0541/14 C0545/33
listened (18) A0022/04 A0101/17
A0197/08 A0198/14 A0326/24 A0327/29
A0383/08 A0404/31 A0437/11 B0906/08
B0944/32 B1021/15 B1140/09 B1194/01
C0083/17 C0109/33 C0175/25 C0556/33
listener (4) A0025/10
B1221/24 C0066/01 C0537/22
listening (8) A0161/27
A0411/09 B0794/03 B0929/11 B1014/30
B1155/32 C0417/03 C0443/V
listens (2) A0048/V A0048/V
listless (1) B1115/04
listlessly (3) B0832/10
B1225/V C0149/35
listlessness (1) C0205/17
lit (5) A0587/13
B0823/04 B0904/16 C0068/30 C0094/12
lit> (3) A0466/14
A0468/08 A0470/05
<u>litera</u> (1) A0536/18
literal (3) A0354/01
B0731/24 C0429/19
literally (9) A0693/29
B1048/31 B1089/18 B1182/31 B1302/31
C0186/22 C0190/13 C0391/33 C0401/15
Literary (6) B1126/15 B1126/T
B1386/10 C0055/30 C0428/07 C0448/V
literary (29) A0090/22
A0262/32 A0267/08 A0269/07 A0270/37
A0281/03 A0281/21 A0283/03 A0285/36
A0294/V B1114/10 B1126/05 B1130/09
B1132/23 B1133/31 B1136/05 B1136/10
B1136/32 B1143/32 B1144/14 B1152/03
B1189/14 B1206/03 B1207/01 B1207/04
B1207/31 B1379/10 B1381/15 B1384/13
Literary/Gazette (3) B1381/18
B1381/25 B1381/26
Literary/World (1) B1360/32
Literati (1) B1381/20
<u>literati</u> (1) A0263/36
literatim (1) B1131/18
Literature (1) B1151/05
literature (7) A0203/03
A0229/17 A0344/09 A0381/32 A0473/28
B0738/12 B1145/05
lithe (1) A0603/09
lithographs (1) B1339/35
litten (4) A0196/V
A0507/V A0512/V A0671/V
litter (1) C0407/09
<u>litterateur</u> (2) A0096/09 B0957/14
litters (1) B0945/15
Little (1) A0464/T
little (632)
little-o (3) B1372/20
B1372/25 B1372/25
Little/Sioux (1) C0548/08
Little/Snake (1) C0560/32

littleness (2) B1034/27 B1034/28
live (44) A0092/15
A0111/25 A0176/V A0182/22 A0228/12
A0228/15 A0228/21 A0229/11 A0232/17
A0232/20 A0233/02 A0296/04 A0344/02
A0351/21 A0381/26 A0383/03 A0383/32
A0509/26 A0532/10 A0655/04 A0655/V
A0674/02 B0889/13 B0897/17 B0927/04
B1010/13 B1057/18 B1187/32 B1206/15
B1206/15 B1293/17 B1345/02 C0060/39
C0087/02 C0135/10 C0399/31 C0399/34
C0414/04 C0430/46 C0432/05 C0522/28
C0530/11 C0565/31 C0577/41
lived (39) A0044/16
A0044/18 A0085/01 A0150/V A0209/24
A0228/35 A0233/17 A0327/11 A0328/10
A0341/V A0342/22 A0460/05 A0466/02
A0539/19 A0541/27 A0556/06 A0590/13
A0612/12 A0639/15 A0652/29 A0702/01
A0706/29 B0731/21 B0969/07 B0975/13
B1019/23 B1163/04 B1165/27 B1186/15
B1188/34 B1189/25 B1271/31 B1295/06
B1310/19 B1369/20 C0118/35 C0124/23
C0549/38 C0551/07
liveliest (1) A0528/03
livelihood (2) A0486/26 B1208/14
liveliness (1) B0864/11
Lively (1) C0161/27
lively (4) A0626/33
B0947/28 C0128/38 C0409/05
liver-like (1) C0125/08
Liverpool (5) C0065/31
C0102/05 C0147/06 C0148/12 C0149/12
livers (1) A0631/19
livery (3) A0563/02
B0901/07 B1004/32
lives (26) A0023/18 A0093/08
A0112/19 A0156/19 A0295/02 A0388/V
A0464/21 A0535/12 A0556/21 A0604/03
A0704/35 B0738/16 B0769/16 B0852/08
B1079/10 B1079/10 B1221/22 C0072/36
C0092/12 C0100/07 C0119/02 C0138/16
C0184/02 C0426/07 C0426/08 C0541/21
liveth (1) A0198/27
livid (11) A0028/25
A0152/07 A0166/22 A0197/23 A0217/V
A0246/32 A0328/16 A0543/25 A0559/02
B0897/01 C0059/17
living (63)
Livius, Titus (1) A0111/06
Livre (1) C0430/38
Lloyd (3) C0057/14
C0065/30 C0067/38
lo (4) A0033/14
A0036/08 A0190/23 A0318/07
load (10) A0141/14 B0968/29
B1094/02 B1166/04 C0097/20 C0097/25
C0097/30 C0176/23 C0534/26 C0550/17
loaded (15) A0136/22
A0253/25 A0585/08 B0809/22 B0944/28
B1008/31 B1008/32 C0177/22 C0180/19
C0418/46 C0533/04 C0533/15 C0540/06
C0543/18 C0543/25
loading (1) C0155/29
loaf (2) A0686/09 A0688/02
loam (3) C0573/34
C0577/21 C0578/20
loan (1) A0278/23
loathed (2) A0323/07 B0855/32
loathing (1) B0854/32
loathsome (12) A0242/30
A0328/17 A0510/09 A0610/24 B0855/11
B1223/09 B1223/09 B1243/05 C0083/10
C0107/34 C0124/22 C0142/28
loathsomeness (1) C0112/17
lobe (1) B1235/30
local (4) A0611/17
A0611/18 B0770/34 B1382/19
locale (1) B1277/24
localities (3) A0513/14
B0723/21 B0877/33
locality (17) A0428/17
A0429/32 A0532/21 A0616/18 B0757/32
B0757/34 B0770/31 B0771/27 B0771/28
B0834/13 B0876/30 B0961/06 B0964/08
B1277/19 B1278/25 B1278/26 B1301/17
location (5) A0489/08
A0527/V B1358/28 C0560/22 C0576/40
lock (2) A0226/30 B1363/06
Locke (10) A0231/04 A0341/25
A0342/V C0428/02 C0428/25 C0428/28
C0429/12 C0430/14 C0448/V C0448/V
Locke, Richard Adams (1) B1381/21
Locke's (2) C0428/08 C0448/V
locked (15) A0024/28
A0101/20 A0537/22 A0542/06 A0542/11
A0542/12 A0551/16 A0563/16 A0602/11
A0640/19 B0733/29 B0811/02 B0928/23
B1352/15 C0122/09
lockers (1) C0190/34
locking (2) A0054/32 A0063/33
locks (5) A0243/04
A0297/V A0509/29 A0557/19 B0871/19
locomotion (1) B1311/30
locomotive (1) B1089/05
locus (1) A0599/M
locust (1) B1332/09
locusts (2) A0045/16 B1337/08
locution (1) A0681/16
lodge (1) C0547/33
lodged (7) A0355/04
A0355/31 B0729/14 B0796/21 C0124/39
C0579/07 C0580/06
lodges (2) C0566/05 C0572/04
lodging (3) A0564/25
B1106/05 B1107/27
lodgings (2) B0957/34 B0992/17
Lofoden (10) A0578/28 A0580/01
A0581/18 A0581/23 A0582/03 A0582/17
A0583/25 A0592/09 A0594/11 A0594/25
loft (1) B1336/34
loftier (3) A0638/V
A0710/26 B1275/29
loftiest (6) A0045/09 A0271/25
A0496/18 A0577/01 A0638/03 B1156/08
loftily (1) A0020/03
lofty (43) A0019/09
A0019/18 A0036/V A0044/29 A0104/13
A0152/09 A0189/21 A0195/15 A0196/27
A0198/24 A0245/25 A0250/10 A0294/08

->A0312/07 A0316/22 A0318/V A0321/21
A0322/07 A0323/10 A0401/06 A0406/21
A0413/12 A0416/26 A0478/19 A0503/09
A0587/36 A0670/16 B0872/25 B0895/31
B1092/12 B1161/04 B1281/20 B1282/19
B1282/27 B1332/07 B1351/16 B1391/23
C0150/32 C0154/35 C0194/17 C0203/24
C0433/03 C0537/35
log (5) B1372/02
C0059/27 C0112/26 C0117/17 C0560/21
loge (1) A0546/20
Logic (1) B1297/02
logic (10) A0064/V B0772/16
B0987/17 B1297/22 B1313/12 B1314/06
B1314/29 B1315/13 B1316/06 B1369/06
logical (10) A0297/28 A0601/18
A0652/12 B0850/04 B0987/15 B1031/09
B1031/14 B1031/15 B1114/20 B1219/17
logically (2) B1295/10 B1310/32
logician (1) B1315/03
logicians (1) B1296/34
Logs (3) B0879/13
B0879/17 B0879/24
logs (3) B0808/12
C0058/30 C0542/25
loins (4) A0047/01
B0766/30 B1237/29 C0118/36
loiter (2) B0873/02 B0873/03
loitered (2) A0210/11 C0564/40
loll (1) C0541/18
Lollipop (32) B1129/25
B1130/08 B1130/13 B1130/16 B1131/01
B1131/22 B1131/26 B1132/32 B1133/14
B1134/05 B1134/16 B1134/16 B1135/35
B1136/07 B1136/10 B1136/13 B1136/20
B1136/30 B1136/34 B1137/25 B1137/26
B1137/31 B1138/23 B1138/27 B1138/28
B1140/05 B1140/22 B1141/02 B1142/08
B1142/12 B1145/01 B1145/07
lolls (1) B0864/33
lombardy (1) A0071/25
lombardy-poplars (1) A0073/11
London (34) A0163/22 A0164/01
A0240/06 A0262/09 A0262/16 A0262/24
A0262/31 A0262/33 A0283/37 A0381/30
A0464/V A0493/06 A0507/06 A0512/30
A0514/23 A0514/33 A0515/13 A0655/V
A0657/07 A0657/13 A0657/20 B0955/06
B0959/29 B0960/05 B1101/20 B1166/30
B1358/07 B1380/12 B1380/14 B1381/18
C0156/10 C0161/27 C0162/03 C0179/31
Londonderry (1) A0465/25
lone (2) A0665/15 B1364/26
lonely (7) A0320/04
A0541/25 A0602/10 A0667/05 B0765/03
B0771/01 B1093/26
lonesome (2) A0318/08 B1322/28
long (488)
long-abiding (1) B1122/21
long-boat (1) B0931/12
long-cherished (1) C0066/18
long-continued (3) A0027/V
A0028/15 A0403/35
long-desired (1) C0399/07
long-drawn (1) B0773/16
long-enduring (1) B0723/12
long-forgotten (1) A0144/22
long-imprisoned (1) B1226/10
long-interred (1) B0940/24
long-lost (1) A0644/V
long-sustained (1) C0181/19
Long/Tom (1) C0067/33
Long, Stephen H. (1) C0528/21
longas (1) A0681/M
longboat (2) C0115/08 C0115/14
longed (9) A0215/30
A0227/16 A0232/03 A0612/23 A0643/33
A0684/09 B0855/14 C0186/03 C0537/06
longer (130)
longest (2) A0352/29 B0756/15
Longfellow (1) B0789/M
longing (10) A0080/22 A0196/29
A0317/25 A0317/27 A0323/17 B0852/16
B1222/03 B1222/04 C0065/05 C0198/09
longings (1) A0098/20
Longinus (1) A0345/V
longitude (35) C0088/30
C0147/27 C0148/13 C0148/18 C0148/27
C0150/05 C0150/07 C0150/38 C0154/23
C0155/10 C0155/15 C0157/02 C0157/08
C0157/09 C0157/10 C0157/26 C0158/14
C0158/31 C0159/02 C0159/15 C0159/33
C0160/07 C0160/31 C0161/29 C0161/39
C0162/05 C0162/17 C0162/23 C0163/04
C0163/14 C0163/38 C0164/19 C0166/03
C0167/22 C0526/05
longitudes (1) C0167/39
longitudinal (5) B0762/19
B1141/13 C0194/18 C0195/01 C0545/17
longitudinally (3) B0766/20
B0981/10 C0544/30
longue (1) B0904/31
lonon> (1) A0464/06
look (121)
look-aisy (1) A0465/32
look-out (5) C0061/13
C0061/27 C0102/30 C0103/32 C0559/39
looked (137)
looking (96)
looking-glass (3) A0565/04
B1093/36 C0109/09
looking-glasses (3) A0500/03
C0148/08 C0175/40
lookout (3) A0298/07
C0149/33 C0157/37
looks (10) A0218/20 A0268/18
A0343/23 A0383/05 B0813/25 B0870/16
B0897/27 B1281/16 B1361/09 B1363/21
loom (1) A0214/V
loop (2) B1335/15 C0413/32
loop-hole (1) B0947/01
looped (1) A0242/11
loophole (1) C0189/22
loops (6) C0409/28 C0409/29
C0409/31 C0409/35 C0409/36 C0409/37
loose (37) A0248/20
A0535/25 A0566/25 A0593/14 A0654/V
B0825/26 B0825/33 B0828/02 B0873/19
B0890/03 B0901/19 B1015/06 B1019/36
B1076/03 C0058/36 C0075/19 C0098/02

->C0101/13 C0102/37 C0106/31 C0106/33
C0118/29 C0119/17 C0119/19 C0122/05
C0165/34 C0173/04 C0182/07 C0182/15
C0183/03 C0184/16 C0389/25 C0425/02
C0432/46 C0548/31 C0559/25 C0567/33
loosed (1) B0955/34
loosely (11) A0501/12
A0501/20 B0730/31 B0766/16 B0817/26
B0857/05 B0959/13 C0098/29 C0099/09
C0142/11 C0552/25
loosen (2) B0742/31 C0091/38
loosened (6) A0079/28 A0152/26
A0243/32 C0083/21 C0091/40 C0413/33
loosening (3) A0694/26
C0117/35 C0126/37
Lor-gol-a-marcy (1) B0820/32
Lord (16) A0044/03
A0047/09 A0062/21 A0093/23 A0121/16
A0311/30 A0313/02 A0337/21 A0337/28
B1013/03 B1069/17 B1141/06 B1169/34
B1304/37 B1305/04 B1372/05
Lord (1) A0096/V
lord (6) A0023/03 A0024/12
A0025/08 A0385/22 A0443/08 B1304/16
Lord/Auckland/Islands (1) C0174/10
Lord's (2) A0630/05 A0630/06
lore (1) A0198/24
lorgnette (2) B0891/V B0891/V
lose (19) A0098/30
A0212/01 A0212/05 A0561/22 A0608/14
B0737/26 B0743/32 B0816/25 B0976/06
B1076/08 B1078/06 B1236/20 C0067/10
C0074/40 C0090/13 C0143/29 C0163/33
C0547/08 C0561/16
loser (2) B0876/22 B0876/33
loser's (2) B0976/33 B0977/24
loses (4) A0212/19
B0870/06 B0984/10 B0984/16
losing (8) A0442/02
A0512/18 B0926/01 B1257/29 C0139/01
C0204/36 C0406/34 C0569/17
Loss (2) A0052/T A0061/T
loss (52)
Lost (1) A0085/T
lost (101)
lot (10) A0070/25 A0071/12
A0320/07 A0486/09 A0486/16 B0814/13
B0955/23 B1363/27 C0134/32 C0393/19
loth (1) B1331/10
Lothario (1) B0753/18
Lotophagi (1) A0621/18
lots (5) B0863/36
C0133/41 C0134/14 C0135/08 C0135/17
lottery (1) C0134/07
loud (60)
loud-toned (1) A0513/27
louder (19) A0435/02
A0541/33 B0795/16 B0795/16 B0795/17
B0795/18 B0795/22 B0795/23 B0797/19
B0797/20 B0797/20 B0797/26 B0797/27
B0797/27 B0797/27 B1014/31 B1155/33
B1155/34 C0085/03
loudest (4) A0581/25
A0710/36 B1276/02 C0447/V
loudly (11) A0054/24
->A0105/27 A0197/17 A0675/29 B0854/14
B1337/16 C0084/29 C0096/02 C0110/07
C0124/24 C0387/21
loudness (1) B1137/30
louis (1) A0112/31
Louis/d'or (1) A0093/19
Louisiana (4) A0270/02
B0862/05 B0862/29 B0863/02
lounging (2) B0990/21 B1249/10
love (102)
love-litter> (1) A0465/28
love-passages (1) B1123/09
love-poems (1) B1122/12
loved (24) A0150/V
A0214/01 A0214/13 A0228/36 A0233/19
A0234/31 A0317/14 A0323/05 A0458/22
A0593/34 A0639/04 A0639/25 A0653/02
A0653/03 A0664/31 A0665/20 B0789/10
B0852/04 B0852/23 B0895/25 B0896/02
B1122/32 B1347/26 C0524/06
loveliest (3) A0704/12
B0808/30 B1269/12
loveliness (28) A0160/12
A0164/24 A0312/03 A0499/16 A0641/12
A0642/01 A0644/07 A0664/V A0706/13
A0707/15 A0708/06 B0760/02 B0862/30
B0863/17 B0863/19 B0863/34 B0864/10
B0890/19 B0894/33 B0909/30 B0909/31
B0924/19 B1123/26 B1169/19 B1271/16
B1272/14 B1273/06 B1277/09
lovely (19) A0152/18
A0384/13 A0499/04 A0613/06 A0664/30
A0665/03 B0862/30 B0889/20 B0890/31
B0892/05 B0892/25 B0897/V B0914/21
B0914/V B0915/21 B0933/20 B1340/20
C0565/27 C0566/13
lover (12) A0665/07
B0732/37 B0754/34 B0755/10 B0755/15
B0759/33 B0768/29 B0862/17 B0902/14
B0957/26 B0957/33 B0958/06
lovers (3) A0266/02
A0374/18 B0754/21
loves (4) B1122/02
B1297/27 B1316/11 B1339/06
loving (1) A0665/04
low (121)
low-pitched (2) A0100/34 A0240/08
low-tide (1) B1391/27
low-water (1) B1391/24
lowed (1) A0347/31
lower (60)
lowered (8) A0046/20
A0437/20 A0616/10 B0931/19 B1351/20
C0062/09 C0088/17 C0196/29
lowering (2) B1242/10 B1350/10
lowest (4) A0045/02
B0738/14 B0750/23 C0172/37
lowing (1) C0567/36
lowness (2) A0509/21 B1131/28
loyalty (1) A0033/10
lozenge (4) A0696/29
A0696/35 B1336/25 B1336/27
lozenges (1) B1195/01
lubber (1) A0251/28
lubbers (1) C0110/20

Lucan (2) A0043/M A0345/25
luce (2) A0702/M B1267/M
Luchesi (6) B1258/01 B1258/03 B1258/10 B1258/16 B1259/16 B1261/20
Luchresi (6) B1258/V B1258/V B1258/V B1258/V B1259/V B1261/V
Lucian (1) A0510/08
lucid (5) A0213/21 A0281/25 A0638/18 A0683/13 C0423/35
Lucilius (1) A0110/22
luck (11) A0059/06 A0385/04 A0464/22 A0466/09 A0584/19 B0827/09 B1179/28 B1194/24 B1208/36 C0060/13 C0554/14
luckily (15) A0513/20 B0826/11 B0962/24 B1257/22 C0061/26 C0064/26 C0075/19 C0079/20 C0082/21 C0110/28 C0116/01 C0149/39 C0184/17 C0193/23 C0399/04
lucky (1) B0984/28
lucrative (3) A0485/28 A0490/32 C0391/12
Lucretius (1) A0109/31
ludicrous (8) A0158/17 A0247/V A0284/17 A0296/02 A0303/02 A0303/29 C0425/10 C0554/24
luggage (1) B1093/16
lui (1) C0430/37
lui-meme (1) A0600/01
luke-warm (1) C0521/26
lull (2) C0095/31 C0096/03
lulled (2) B1391/15 C0115/18
lulling (2) A0641/03 A0643/15
lulls (1) C0110/18
Lully, Raymond (1) A0638/M
lumber (11) C0068/37 C0069/32 C0074/26 C0075/07 C0083/04 C0083/26 C0085/05 C0094/31 C0096/06 C0146/34 C0564/25
lumber-yard (1) C0058/28
Lumberskull (1) B1091/29
lumen (1) B1010/25
luminary (2) B1168/06 C0414/13
luminiferous (5) B1034/11 B1034/15 B1034/23 B1038/03 B1038/14
luminous (16) A0089/10 A0093/12 A0314/11 A0316/16 A0381/10 A0401/31 A0407/08 A0412/32 A0641/V B0909/05 B0940/21 B1038/02 B1168/14 B1221/26 C0205/29 C0423/21
luminousness (1) A0411/01
lump (3) A0667/69 B1168/31 B1168/32
lunacy (5) B0819/29 B0822/31 B1003/14 B1006/17 B1009/23
lunae (1) B1191/29
lunar (6) C0404/19 C0419/13 C0419/40 C0423/08 C0429/05 C0429/07
lunar-lunatic (1) A0079/04
Lunarian (1) C0433/05
lunarians (1) B1302/20
lunatic (13) B0822/23 B0992/22 B0992/26 B1003/01 B1004/25 B1006/17 B1009/29 B1016/19 B1018/05 B1018/16 B1018/31 B1018/33 B1021/18
lunatico (1) B0747/10
lunatics (7) B1008/16 B1015/02 B1015/13 B1018/26 B1018/26 B1019/18 B1019/35
lung (1) B1235/23
lungs (18) A0054/27 A0063/27 A0075/12 A0244/19 A0460/16 A0672/25 B0741/31 B0743/26 B0961/21 B0962/16 B0967/07 B1101/26 B1108/26 C0146/18 C0182/30 C0183/10 C0411/01 C0578/01
lurch (7) A0127/22 A0590/06 B0930/29 C0062/20 C0099/17 C0110/25 C0140/22
lurches (4) C0062/26 C0098/09 C0108/11 C0113/15
lurid (5) A0036/07 A0189/24 A0398/10 A0461/16 A0695/33
lurked (2) A0164/17 A0215/02
lurking (5) A0054/34 A0064/01 A0512/14 B1120/07 C0188/33
lurking-place (1) C0553/13
lustily (3) A0054/25 A0105/28 A0611/10
lustra (2) A0235/03 A0616/33
lustre (28) A0138/19 A0190/03 A0227/07 A0231/18 A0316/17 A0321/17 A0325/09 A0398/10 A0402/08 A0405/11 A0459/21 A0502/13 A0511/02 A0545/25 A0545/25 A0587/12 A0664/V A0673/14 A0688/08 A0695/33 B0809/09 B0814/28 B0940/22 B1050/01 B1144/03 B1330/35 C0402/05 C0416/41
lustreless (3) A0215/09 B0956/19 B1235/12
lustrous (2) A0153/04 A0379/16
lustrum (6) A0020/V A0059/11 A0061/06 A0430/21 A0653/V B1135/08
lustrums (1) A0235/V
lute's (1) A0407/10
luth (1) A0397/M
Luther, Martin (2) A0018/M A0621/18
Lutheranism (1) B0723/M
Lutherthum (1) B0723/M
Luxor (1) A0322/05
luxuriance (4) A0460/10 B1282/20 B1334/35 B1337/20
luxuriant (8) A0312/11 B0901/08 B0909/06 B0957/28 B1107/15 B1161/18 B1162/10 B1277/21
luxuriantly (2) B1281/20 B1329/27
luxuries (2) A0531/26 C0083/32
luxurious (4) A0033/V A0087/31 A0312/15 A0444/04
luxuriously-cushioned (1) B1294/19
luxuriousness (1) A0157/05
luxury (8) A0035/28 A0212/22 A0430/25 A0440/08 B0826/24 B0974/02 B1340/02 C0179/11
Lvne (1) C0430/28
lvne (1) C0430/27
lxg (1) B1374/15
Lxrd (1) B1374/18
lxxk (1) B1374/19
Lybian (1) B1179/02

Lyceum (2) A0086/19 A0096/18
lyceum (1) A0342/V
Lycophron/Tenebrosus (1) B1115/24
Lyell (1) B1115/15
lying (82)
lynching (1) B1375/07
lynn (1) C0549/24
lynx (4) A0198/32
B0977/10 B1048/26 C0536/22
Lyons (1) A0554/13
Lyra (1) A0314/19
lyre (1) A0600/12
lyrics (1) B1130/29
Lysias (2) A0176/01 A0181/33
M (29) A0543/29
A0544/09 A0544/11 B0732/24 B0732/29
B0732/37 B0732/40 B0733/13 B0733/25
B0733/28 B0733/30 B0745/22 B0745/31
B0746/03 B0747/28 B0748/13 B1233/02
C0394/32 C0401/40 C0402/21 C0522/34
C0522/35 C0523/06 C0523/09 C0523/15
C0523/23 C0524/18 C0529/03 C0532/27
M. (1) B1233/T
M.S. (1) A0206/03
M-- (1) C0533/11
M--'s (1) C0523/09
m'auoir (1) C0430/38
ma (2) A0378/M B1114/03
Ma-a-a-a-n (1) A0386/02
ma-a-an (1) A0386/11
Ma'mselle (7) B0912/V
B0912/V B0912/V B1010/16 B1010/19
B1010/V B1015/20
macaroni (1) C0151/23
Macassar (1) A0491/15
mace (2) A0413/31 A0414/21
maces (1) B0945/17
mache (1) B1179/24
Machi-- (1) A0112/26
Machiavelian (1) A0203/M
Machiavelli (4) A0085/10
A0408/30 B0985/03 B1153/07
Machine (1) B1166/35
machine (29) A0269/08
A0355/01 A0388/33 A0689/30 A0695/07
B1068/03 B1069/11 B1069/20 B1070/08
B1070/11 B1070/16 B1071/04 B1071/25
B1072/12 B1072/29 B1073/07 B1073/33
B1074/09 B1074/24 B1075/07 B1080/22
B1108/29 C0388/31 C0394/34 C0410/34
C0410/37 C0431/03 C0431/08 C0547/19
machinery (9) A0046/19
A0296/V A0351/31 A0351/32 A0354/11
A0692/30 B1071/22 B1093/09 B1317/19
Mackenzie (3) C0527/26
C0527/36 C0528/37
Mackenzie, Alexander (2) C0525/07
C0526/34
Mackenzie's/river (3) C0527/04
C0527/07 C0528/32
mackerel (1) C0174/06
Mackinaw (1) C0528/12
maculae (1) C0423/34
Mad (1) A0413/08
mad (54)
mad-houses (1) B1003/10
Mad'selle (1) A0216/V
madam (8) A0339/04
A0339/06 A0339/12 A0339/V A0346/09
A0383/23 A0383/27 B0875/22
Madame (99)
madame (1) B0735/17
maddened (1) A0243/24
maddening (3) A0446/12
A0676/17 B1225/22
maddest (1) C0057/30
made (666)
Madeira (4) C0099/04
C0099/12 C0099/21 C0137/06
Madeline (5) A0404/05
A0404/16 A0409/15 A0411/15 A0416/27
Mademoiselle (24) A0177/02
A0177/09 A0216/08 A0537/11 A0541/22
A0542/06 A0543/15 A0543/20 A0543/30
A0546/28 A0547/23 A0551/03 A0551/09
A0558/30 B0731/26 B0753/15 B0887/25
B0888/01 B0912/18 B0912/24 B0912/26
B0957/12 B1138/32 B1139/01
madly (7) A0146/06
A0216/12 A0438/27 A0601/24 A0643/V
B0890/23 B0947/13
madman (20) A0126/07
A0416/18 A0416/20 A0558/14 A0558/21
A0589/33 A0673/23 B0793/06 B0932/20
B1006/05 B1006/19 B1013/23 B1013/23
B1018/10 B1019/26 B1130/05 B1226/02
B1294/29 C0123/04 C0399/37
madmen (10) A0125/28 A0532/19
A0532/20 A0558/17 A0558/18 B0789/17
B1018/02 B1019/03 B1019/16 B1019/22
madness (27) A0135/08
A0190/08 A0319/01 A0320/21 A0330/11
A0349/24 A0411/08 A0638/03 A0644/V
A0683/23 A0683/23 B0746/30 B0795/07
B0824/30 B0856/20 B0898/27 B1240/09
B1257/15 B1268/14 B1347/25 B1347/25
C0059/31 C0101/06 C0131/21 C0397/20
C0441/V C0578/06
Madonna-like (1) B0891/08
Madonna/della/Pieta (1) A0160/10
Madrid (1) C0156/38
Maelstrom (4) A0577/T
A0581/04 A0583/04 B1382/34
Maelstroom (2) B1380/07 B1381/29
Maelzel (1) B1361/02
Maelzel's (3) B1119/15
B1120/03 B1166/34
Magazine (6) A0264/27 B0772/30
B1162/28 B1206/T B1378/01 B1379/08
Magazine (1) B1160/43
magazine (25) A0268/06
A0269/17 A0284/17 A0338/15 A0338/28
B1135/12 B1135/17 B1136/07 B1136/34
B1137/31 B1138/23 B1138/28 B1143/23
B1144/07 B1145/05 B1207/09 B1207/19
B1207/25 B1208/02 B1209/09 B1291/02
B1324/01 C0055/30 C0056/13 C0521/28
magazines (8) A0205/24
B1129/06 B1129/12 B1132/07 B1206/04
B1206/15 B1207/07 B1207/08

Magellan (2) B1392/05 C0158/10
magi (4) A0198/20
A0198/21 B1166/20 B1169/03
Magian (1) A0068/13
magic (10) A0442/29 A0590/19
A0641/10 B0889/20 B0955/33 B1331/01
B1381/31 C0149/37 C0187/01 C0188/08
magical (7) A0294/V
A0296/V A0315/12 A0503/11 A0605/12
A0663/V B1385/36
magical-looking (1) C0173/27
magically (3) A0682/14
B1282/17 C0190/03
magicians (3) B1165/26
B1165/31 B1167/19
magistrate (4) B1052/19
B1053/19 B1053/24 B1054/13
magna (1) A0382/15
magnanimity (1) B1049/36
magnanimous (3) B1055/12
B1056/15 B1304/31
magnetic (10) A0459/17 B0890/20
B0941/12 B0941/25 B0941/28 B1089/11
B1233/20 B1293/11 B1293/32 C0396/06
magnetism (3) B0886/04
B1123/15 B1191/14
magnetoesthetics (1) B0887/01
magnificence (14) A0019/19 A0036/04
A0099/31 A0157/10 A0158/14 A0320/19
A0496/29 A0499/30 A0581/10 A0641/09
A0671/14 A0711/26 B1192/35 B1276/29
magnificent (45) A0020/14
A0028/22 A0036/V A0122/08 A0151/03
A0158/22 A0165/19 A0166/01 A0293/05
A0298/V A0312/19 A0352/08 A0503/V
A0588/30 A0591/08 A0670/15 A0673/10
A0707/08 B0818/29 B0829/36 B0864/30
B0870/05 B0889/18 B0890/11 B0899/20
B0907/04 B0907/V B0945/13 B0945/33
B1068/08 B1082/10 B1138/37 B1145/05
B1160/10 B1162/03 B1179/04 B1194/05
B1272/08 B1280/21 B1294/06 B1298/37
B1332/03 B1332/24 C0536/40 C0575/10
magnificently (1) A0503/07
magnifico (1) B1080/10
magnifiers (1) B1160/42
magnifying (2) C0428/24 C0448/V
magnitude (8) A0079/34
A0314/18 A0705/03 B0807/05 B0870/08
B0986/09 B1270/03 C0423/32
magnolias (1) B1332/27
Magpies (1) A0284/18
Maguntinae (1) A0409/12
mahogany (2) A0248/07 A0502/V
Mahomet (1) A0087/32
maid (1) B1102/34
maiden (16) A0162/V
A0216/26 A0311/24 A0321/08 A0641/13
A0642/07 A0644/15 A0664/30 A0665/02
B0945/32 B1122/31 B1132/26 B1135/16
B1152/15 B1385/34 C0522/18
mail (3) A0056/10
A0065/32 A0268/04
mail-robber (2) A0057/37 A0068/21
Maillard (21) B1003/08
->B1003/12 B1003/29 B1004/13 B1007/17
B1008/05 B1008/13 B1010/20 B1012/01
B1012/27 B1015/01 B1015/26 B1015/29
B1016/14 B1017/18 B1017/29 B1020/01
B1020/10 B1021/17 B1021/26 B1021/33
Maillard's (1) B1003/33
mails (1) B1068/13
maimed (1) C0187/35
main (1) C0430/38
main (91)
main-chains (1) C0062/19
main-hatchway (1) C0189/25
main-road (1) B1003/16
mainchains (1) C0141/05
Maine (1) B1358/22
mainland (1) B1092/06
mainly (10) A0086/03 A0097/03
A0140/11 A0371/22 A0399/25 A0560/08
A0690/14 B1310/22 B1339/12 C0408/01
mainmast (5) A0585/35
C0101/20 C0114/03 C0114/17 C0114/22
mainsail (4) C0058/31
C0060/09 C0060/19 C0123/16
maintain (11) A0143/27
A0473/30 A0495/05 B0757/11 B0795/14
B0947/26 B1033/31 C0064/07 C0106/35
C0143/27 C0168/26
maintained (33) A0054/37
A0059/09 A0061/05 A0064/09 A0104/32
A0216/18 A0277/17 A0408/05 A0432/02
A0442/22 A0458/05 B0974/06 B0991/29
B1011/19 B1013/01 B1015/24 B1073/19
B1249/17 B1272/03 B1279/18 B1294/25
B1295/09 B1295/22 B1296/08 B1301/24
B1310/27 B1312/12 B1353/20 B1364/29
C0059/09 C0131/35 C0188/13 C0545/27
maintaining (10) A0299/04 A0445/25
A0591/01 B0818/25 B0822/30 B1247/09
B1353/V C0388/08 C0549/06 C0567/26
maintains (6) A0018/12 A0279/21
A0549/28 A0656/21 B1169/32 C0432/25
mais (8) A0033/20
A0036/06 A0036/18 A0036/25 A0037/V
A0109/31 A0602/07 C0430/39
Maison (4) A0558/15
B1002/03 B1003/19 B1009/22
Maisons (2) B1006/34 B1007/08
Maiter-di-dauns> (7) A0465/32
A0466/23 A0467/10 A0467/13 A0468/06
A0468/26 A0469/01
majestic (17) A0021/23
A0339/04 A0446/05 A0608/09 A0610/34
A0641/V B0889/26 B0894/33 B0914/09
B0945/01 B0945/28 B1333/05 C0523/39
C0536/34 C0542/12 C0542/15 C0564/32
majestically (1) A0057/33
Majesty (24) A0035/24
A0036/23 A0036/24 A0037/11 A0037/13
A0037/16 A0037/18 A0037/20 A0037/22
A0090/12 A0106/14 A0107/01 A0107/25
A0108/10 A0109/18 A0110/13 A0111/08
A0111/17 A0112/27 A0113/02 A0114/02
A0114/05 A0174/32 A0180/23
majesty (33) A0034/11
A0037/V A0099/25 A0106/27 A0109/14

->A0110/32 A0110/V A0114/V A0114/V
A0251/15 A0251/16 A0251/22 A0252/25
A0252/33 A0253/05 A0311/19 A0312/08
A0312/26 A0318/V A0456/19 A0458/24
A0461/18 A0610/10 A0706/05 B0818/03
B0893/02 B0955/03 B1158/35 B1271/08
B1349/32 B1349/33 B1350/22 C0175/39
Majesty's (1) A0113/10
Major (3) A0285/12
A0285/18 C0527/28
major (4) C0400/06
C0401/27 C0418/05 C0528/21
majority (5) A0293/02
A0704/19 B1015/13 B1269/13 B1269/V
make (294)
make-weight (1) C0395/10
maker (2) B0870/26 B1052/30
makes (43) A0033/18
A0091/25 A0226/33 A0231/07 A0346/07
A0367/26 A0388/06 A0458/10 A0467/07
A0530/01 A0655/18 A0655/20 A0705/32
B0742/13 B0795/09 B0797/10 B0838/20
B0872/17 B0873/16 B0873/21 B0875/03
B0876/03 B0876/17 B0876/32 B0878/10
B0878/26 B1091/15 B1092/30 B1096/27
B1096/34 B1097/01 B1152/14 B1152/28
B1208/33 B1269/35 B1282/32 B1295/30
B1311/27 B1358/11 C0106/03 C0106/31
C0428/25 C0522/21
makesetai (Gr.) (1) A0346/03
making (135)
mal (1) B1050/19
mal-apropos (1) A0297/V
mal-practice (1) B0752/02
Malabar (1) A0136/01
maladies (2) A0211/08 A0410/22
malady (10) A0213/17 A0214/V
A0330/11 A0398/25 A0402/31 A0404/20
A0409/22 B0962/23 B0963/14 B1006/25
Malay (1) B0947/20
Malays (1) A0136/31
Malcontent (2) A0070/13 A0081/14
male (6) B0733/32 B0748/19
B0887/13 B0897/08 B1236/11 C0153/06
males (3) C0174/29
C0547/06 C0547/12
malevolence (2) A0651/31 B0851/26
malevolent (1) A0150/V
malheur (1) A0506/M
Malibran (1) B0905/25
malice (3) A0086/16
A0437/09 A0511/22
maliceful (2) A0413/29 A0414/15
malicious (2) B1158/10 B1381/10
maliciously (1) A0262/16
malignancy (1) A0024/26
malignant (2) C0073/31 C0090/38
malignity (1) A0028/16
mallet (2) B0929/14 B0930/04
Malninas (1) C0157/03
Maltese (4) A0560/29
A0561/04 A0561/10 A0561/13
maltreated (1) B0734/07
maltreating (2) B0851/13 B0851/14
Mam'selle (2) B1014/18 B1014/21

Mam'selle (1) B1010/14
mamma (2) A0025/23 A0626/10
mammalia (1) A0559/22
Mammon (1) A0498/22
Mammoth/Cave (1) B1161/23
Man (10) A0319/30 A0340/10
A0378/T A0481/T A0481/V A0506/T
A0703/16 B0850/21 B0852/10 B1044/T
man (495)
man-animal (4) B1158/25
B1159/18 B1165/21 B1165/23
man-animals (3) B1157/26
B1158/36 B1165/25
man-at-arms (1) A0123/21
man-bat (1) C0429/19
man-bats (1) C0429/44
man-of-war (1) A0628/32
man-traps (1) A0381/27
Man-Fred (3) A0385/16
A0385/18 A0385/23
Man-Friday (2) A0385/18 A0385/23
man's (20) A0540/23
A0589/05 A0609/09 A0615/06 A0703/08
B0793/04 B0795/04 B0795/11 B0795/17
B0795/25 B0869/25 B0958/34 B0969/07
B1188/31 B1235/09 B1268/08 B1273/30
C0430/07 C0523/41 C0534/26
manacle (1) C0090/19
manacles (1) C0091/09
manage (9) A0092/25
A0111/35 A0355/02 B0975/20 B1301/21
B1390/15 C0114/13 C0395/08 C0402/26
manageable (1) B1298/27
managed (13) A0338/20
A0342/08 A0531/24 B0888/23 B1004/14
B1073/09 B1153/14 B1194/07 B1353/08
C0057/06 C0064/25 C0119/06 C0394/40
management (5) A0498/03
C0059/05 C0066/20 C0099/23 C0187/06
manages (1) B1119/22
managing (3) A0092/32
A0112/09 C0060/01
Manchester (1) C0534/24
Mandans (5) C0565/30
C0565/32 C0565/40 C0566/05 C0566/10
mandate (1) A0242/28
Mandeville (2) A0055/02 A0064/05
mandibles (1) B1250/24
mandragora (1) A0384/04
manganese (1) A0182/10
manger (1) B1007/27
mangled (5) B0732/13
B0744/07 B1182/22 C0190/12 C0396/28
manhood (3) A0210/13
A0430/25 B0850/14
mania (2) B1004/28 C0129/24
mania (3) A0027/05
B1007/03 B1249/22
maniac (5) A0028/18
A0217/V A0558/14 A0589/33 B1006/29
maniacal (1) B1353/32
maniere (2) B0900/01 B0900/V
manifest (9) A0189/16
A0355/11 A0408/02 B0823/22 B0866/04
B0902/19 B1313/33 C0175/38 C0416/17

manifestation (3) A0080/42
A0351/12 A0588/33
manifestations (4) A0612/22
A0644/10 B0962/24 C0524/03
manifested (5) A0399/01
A0531/02 B0992/02 B1329/31 C0180/03
manifesting (1) B0757/05
manifold (6) A0209/01 A0528/29
A0529/24 A0547/04 A0643/22 A0662/11
Manilla (1) C0179/17
manipulations (3) A0388/24
B1030/25 B1237/25
mankind (37) A0058/28
A0165/26 A0189/17 A0196/29 A0212/14
A0213/28 A0430/28 A0457/08 A0457/33
A0459/21 A0461/05 A0604/03 A0611/09
A0703/13 A0711/11 B0856/13 B0964/25
B1069/08 B1104/30 B1133/13 B1144/34
B1158/04 B1163/05 B1166/18 B1194/05
B1195/12 B1250/03 B1268/12 B1294/10
B1298/05 B1300/23 B1317/05 B1360/12
C0126/12 C0173/01 C0404/21 C0407/39
manly (3) A0440/26
B0899/01 B1045/02
Mann (6) A0384/27 A0384/27
A0384/29 A0384/31 A0386/03 A0386/V
manned (1) C0186/29
manner (291)
mannerisms (1) A0294/V
manners (13) A0025/23
A0293/24 A0599/05 B0949/31 B1091/01
B1093/28 B1114/23 B1303/11 C0057/10
C0105/32 C0106/13 C0529/13 C0532/34
manoeuvre (8) A0180/15
A0441/19 B1078/02 C0094/08 C0105/35
C0106/03 C0396/18 C0398/11
manoeuvres (6) A0296/02 A0372/19
B1191/18 C0076/29 C0172/28 C0192/05
manoeuvring (3) A0025/22
B1058/18 C0104/40
manor (1) B1183/08
manor-house (1) B0841/01
mansarde (1) B1362/14
mansardes (1) A0542/18
mansion (12) A0209/15
A0210/13 A0398/14 A0399/20 A0399/33
A0403/27 A0412/33 A0414/04 A0417/03
A0429/29 A0532/15 B0904/10
mansions (2) A0554/13 B0904/12
mantel (2) A0615/10 B1340/21
mantel-piece (4) A0650/04
B0991/01 B1104/10 B1105/18
mantel-pieces (2) A0367/24 A0373/26
mantelet (1) A0336/07
mantelet (1) A0349/13
mantle (5) A0196/25
A0426/15 A0460/01 C0552/09 C0552/31
mantled (1) B0893/14
manual (2) A0409/10 A0557/03
manufacture (3) A0343/17
B1191/31 B1195/01
manufactured (4) A0100/12
B1161/38 C0388/17 C0534/32
manufacturer (1) A0482/31
manufacturing (1) B1364/24
manumitted (1) B0807/28
manuscript (4) A0102/27
A0135/V A0339/15 B1358/19
manuscripts (3) A0101/10
A0365/16 B0949/23
Manuscrit (1) C0430/39
many (406)
many-colored (7) A0639/08
A0640/28 A0641/16 A0642/05 A0643/04
A0643/23 A0644/05
map (6) B0945/06 B0989/29
C0422/33 C0429/08 C0521/11 C0524/25
maple (2) B1332/10 B1340/09
maps (2) A0146/11 C0524/33
mar (1) A0499/15
marble (26) A0036/16 A0045/02
A0087/36 A0152/14 A0152/25 A0153/03
A0154/11 A0154/26 A0154/27 A0154/28
A0156/17 A0161/01 A0165/03 A0311/23
A0327/20 A0379/23 A0502/25 A0510/09
B0864/34 B0956/19 B1057/21 B1238/12
B1303/36 B1304/08 C0059/02 C0124/12
marbles (3) A0495/03
B0984/08 B0984/11
marcescit (1) A0072/31
March (18) A0568/V B1381/23
C0150/23 C0156/10 C0160/11 C0160/39
C0203/21 C0203/31 C0204/12 C0204/20
C0204/26 C0204/35 C0205/06 C0205/14
C0205/21 C0205/28 C0205/39 C0530/25
march (5) A0381/22
A0381/34 B0925/15 C0181/14 C0391/22
marches (1) B0789/M
Marchesa (5) A0153/17
A0154/07 A0154/11 A0154/17 A0154/22
marching (1) C0153/24
Marchioness (2) A0174/13 A0174/18
Mare (3) A0578/35
B1291/07 B1310/05
mare (1) A0638/14
Mare/Foecunditatis (1) C0429/11
Mare/Nubium (1) C0429/10
Mare/Tranquillitatis (1) C0429/10
mares (1) B1096/38
Mareschino (1) A0175/18
Margaux (2) A0101/V B1055/32
Margaux (1) B1045/33
margin (21) A0045/04
A0211/30 A0218/V A0274/35 A0277/15
A0278/35 A0284/07 A0286/18 A0301/06
A0639/28 A0687/07 A0696/16 B0878/27
B0880/09 B0945/02 B1055/19 B1113/02
B1113/06 C0546/17 C0548/01 C0571/16
marginal (4) A0276/02
A0366/19 B1114/06 B1116/12
Marginalia (1) B1113/T
marginalia (2) B1114/11 B1114/16
marginalic (1) B1114/24
margins (1) A0639/30
Maria (2) A0227/31 A0227/36
Marian (1) B0924/12
Marie (48) B0723/18
B0723/T B0725/16 B0725/23 B0725/29
B0726/10 B0726/14 B0729/14 B0729/21
B0729/30 B0731/15 B0732/35 B0732/38

->B0733/01 B0733/03 B0734/03 B0734/05
B0736/04 B0736/06 B0736/16 B0737/24
B0737/25 B0738/23 B0740/05 B0744/29
B0745/13 B0746/03 B0746/09 B0746/12
B0746/14 B0746/29 B0747/01 B0748/01
B0748/02 B0748/18 B0749/04 B0749/23
B0749/31 B0754/20 B0754/28 B0755/09
B0755/11 B0755/17 B0756/V B0757/15
B0757/24 B0769/20 B0772/28
Marie/Roget (1) B0723/07
Marie's (6) B0736/12 B0738/22
B0744/28 B0745/06 B0748/25 B0755/17
Marinade (2) A0175/20 A0181/09
marine (1) C0126/15
mariners (1) C0525/37
Marion's/Island (1) C0154/19
mark (23) A0096/18
A0177/26 A0183/21 A0228/16 A0232/V
A0339/09 A0339/11 A0514/20 A0559/17
A0657/29 B0746/12 B0747/06 B0795/18
B0830/08 B0855/24 B0855/27 B0898/15
B1379/02 B1391/25 B1392/07 C0085/38
C0169/32 C0576/39
Markbrunnen (2) A0175/18 A0181/12
marked (28) A0025/19
A0182/35 A0227/02 A0231/13 A0245/24
A0431/11 A0441/03 A0448/09 A0485/32
B0824/32 B0874/19 B0941/24 B0962/24
B1004/27 B1053/29 B1055/19 B1059/15
B1073/24 B1140/05 B1191/05 B1194/01
B1226/13 B1239/20 B1299/09 C0152/22
C0521/12 C0524/33 C0562/07
markedly (2) B0991/18 B1234/12
market (3) A0681/M
C0177/14 C0178/11
marking (1) C0198/35
marks (9) A0023/30
A0143/12 B0732/26 B0732/27 B0744/27
B0757/16 B0771/06 B1136/02 C0184/41
marl (8) A0175/V
A0182/06 C0193/11 C0195/07 C0195/10
C0195/19 C0199/01 C0199/38
marlin-spike (1) A0252/21
marling-spike (1) A0252/V
<u>marmo</u> (1) A0161/04
Marmontel (1) A0599/01
Marquis (1) A0179/28
marquis (1) A0179/33
marriage (8) A0164/02
A0214/14 A0316/05 A0323/03 A0323/20
A0642/10 B0901/21 B0957/19
marriages (2) A0311/14 B0888/03
married (14) A0651/14 B0850/22
B0887/24 B0887/27 B0887/28 B0888/01
B0908/26 B0913/V B0914/04 B0923/20
B0926/25 B1169/26 C0522/27 C0529/21
marrow (6) A0252/25 A0443/04
B0795/03 B1223/04 C0165/09 C0535/02
marry (6) B0912/07 B0912/18
B0912/25 B0912/26 B1153/02 B1153/04
marrying (1) B1153/02
marsh (2) A0055/33 A0065/15
marsh-hen (1) B0807/03
marsh-hens (1) B0808/16
Marshall (1) A0274/24
marshy (2) B0864/06 C0536/32
Marston's (2) A0070/13 A0081/14
Marsyas (3) A0059/04
A0069/V A0070/04
mart (1) A0515/17
marten (1) C0536/22
Martial (1) A0111/05
martins (1) C0573/28
martyrdom (1) A0383/08
marvel (3) A0328/20
A0665/22 A0682/35
marvellous (17) A0176/14
A0182/15 A0491/11 A0557/15 B0723/04
B0758/01 B0853/15 B1016/20 B1018/08
B1044/26 B1102/02 B1178/29 B1335/26
B1346/25 B1361/22 C0055/17 C0532/21
marvellously (1) A0379/V
marvels (2) B1191/13 B1277/15
Marx, Issachar (1) B1234/04
Mary (4) A0020/12
A0020/V A0020/V B1122/19
Mary/Pitts (1) C0137/24
masculine (2) A0037/16 A0284/28
mashed (1) C0077/32
mask (9) A0172/02
A0178/02 A0386/13 A0447/05 A0448/07
A0670/V A0675/10 A0676/31 B1258/19
masked (4) A0671/13
A0674/24 B0927/27 B1347/06
maskers (3) A0674/06
B1353/21 B1354/14
masks (1) A0161/17
Mason (5) B1068/04
B1072/18 B1072/30 B1075/28 B1080/03
mason (3) B1260/25
B1260/26 C0573/38
mason-work (1) B1262/21
Mason, Monck (4) B1069/17
B1069/24 B1070/25 B1075/27
Mason's (2) B1079/13 B1080/14
Mason's, Monck (1) B1068/02
masonry (10) A0081/39 A0400/10
A0551/12 A0685/21 A0685/31 A0687/06
A0688/32 B1262/09 B1263/25 B1391/29
masons (1) B1260/23
Masque (1) A0670/T
masquerade (11) A0446/21
A0671/15 A0674/32 B1161/27 B1161/27
B1347/02 B1347/02 B1347/10 B1349/29
B1350/23 B1351/15
masquerader (1) B1352/18
masqueraders (5) A0673/19
B1350/16 B1352/03 B1352/07 B1352/36
masquerades (1) B1350/01
Mass (1) A0387/V
mass (61)
Massa (13) B0807/31
B0809/01 B0811/27 B0811/33 B0812/21
B0812/26 B0814/12 B0818/15 B0819/06
B0820/10 B0820/28 B0821/27 B0824/09
massa (22) B0811/18 B0811/32
B0812/16 B0812/19 B0812/24 B0813/09
B0813/11 B0814/10 B0814/15 B0815/09
B0818/09 B0818/12 B0818/22 B0819/19
B0820/01 B0820/13 B0820/24 B0820/32

->B0821/05 B0821/09 B0824/23 B0824/27
massacre (6) A0123/29 A0126/15
B0949/15 B0955/06 C0053/T C0203/33
masse (7) A0253/V
B1044/22 B1048/22 B1182/22 B1350/21
C0412/09 C0572/33
masses (16) A0101/V
A0158/05 A0330/15 A0412/30 A0457/24
A0507/32 A0591/25 A0592/26 A0592/29
B1302/23 C0387/14 C0387/24 C0412/06
C0418/46 C0565/18 C0570/24
massive (8) A0165/05
A0298/V A0322/V A0410/09 A0501/10
A0501/16 B0828/06 B1226/V
massive-looking (1) A0322/09
massy (8) A0165/V
A0321/20 A0322/V A0430/05 A0430/20
A0532/30 A0671/01 A0690/19
mast (11) A0593/08
C0058/35 C0060/21 C0088/23 C0114/04
C0114/23 C0146/39 C0149/35 C0533/27
C0533/29 C0534/15
mast-head (1) A0240/23
master (33) A0028/12
A0045/27 A0099/17 A0123/14 A0299/29
A0387/V A0388/32 A0400/25 A0401/05
A0405/07 A0427/32 A0565/06 A0566/V
A0567/09 A0568/23 B0811/17 B0811/30
B0812/32 B0816/30 B0817/33 B0822/26
B0823/33 B0824/16 B0824/17 B0825/29
B0826/29 B0873/08 B0900/19 B0900/25
B1046/21 B1277/07 B1371/10 C0129/06
master-mind (1) A0431/27
master-minds (1) A0609/20
master-stroke (2) A0568/V B1144/27
master's (4) A0024/18
B0824/12 B0978/14 B1046/21
mastered (2) A0172/07 A0178/08
masterly (1) A0435/18
masterpiece (1) B1139/06
masters (3) B0810/04
C0113/21 C0199/27
mastery (2) A0227/20 A0232/07
masthead (5) C0157/38
C0160/25 C0164/29 C0165/20 C0167/24
masticating (1) C0142/11
mastication (1) A0127/25
mastiff (2) B1334/28 B1338/19
Mastodon (1) B0870/11
masts (7) A0137/11
A0585/34 B0931/01 C0110/26 C0189/27
C0202/38 C0202/39
mat (1) A0087/16
match (12) A0464/19
B0892/12 B0916/29 B0926/22 B0984/38
B1258/04 B1340/11 C0068/30 C0113/12
C0389/26 C0394/28 C0396/16
matches (5) C0077/06
C0077/26 C0078/16 C0094/04 C0187/41
mate (49) A0141/35
C0061/34 C0062/09 C0062/19 C0085/26
C0085/37 C0085/41 C0086/12 C0086/28
C0086/37 C0088/08 C0088/17 C0089/24
C0093/04 C0093/18 C0099/38 C0100/16
C0100/18 C0101/10 C0102/11 C0102/21
->C0102/30 C0102/40 C0103/08 C0103/31
C0103/35 C0104/02 C0104/04 C0104/12
C0105/09 C0105/22 C0107/05 C0107/21
C0107/25 C0107/29 C0108/02 C0108/25
C0110/05 C0110/19 C0110/34 C0110/39
C0111/15 C0112/23 C0146/36 C0147/23
C0153/31 C0154/16 C0164/33 C0171/12
mate's (7) C0090/38
C0093/16 C0102/01 C0102/23 C0103/19
C0108/34 C0154/01
material (70)
materialism (2) A0706/09 B1271/13
materiality (1) B1040/04
materially (20) A0510/31
A0551/05 B0742/11 B0766/17 B0813/32
B0965/22 B1077/33 B1078/20 B1140/V
B1257/13 B1303/01 B1364/17 B1391/16
C0205/39 C0400/09 C0417/27 C0418/36
C0431/04 C0544/14 C0576/22
materials (8) A0142/02
A0510/19 A0613/27 B1262/06 C0092/15
C0208/19 C0393/26 C0393/34
maternal (3) A0625/29
A0626/V C0057/02
mates (3) A0137/25
A0594/18 B0933/09
mathematical (19) A0143/18
A0315/27 A0430/10 A0528/13 A0601/03
A0611/07 B0724/03 B0752/19 B0773/18
B0986/31 B0987/15 B0987/17 B0987/21
B0987/29 B1164/25 B1301/29 B1301/32
C0152/16 C0572/24
mathematician (12) A0478/32
B0773/19 B0986/24 B0986/26 B0986/26
B0987/30 B0988/05 B0988/15 B0988/16
B1207/23 B1297/34 B1375/10
mathematicians (8) A0365/21
B0987/01 B1163/10 B1164/28 B1164/34
B1213/37 B1214/07 B1214/15
mathematics (4) A0708/16
B0987/16 B1273/11 B1313/12
matronly (1) B0891/08
Mattee (1) C0180/32
matter (265)
matter-of-course (1) B1183/30
matter-of-fact (1) A0100/24
mattered (2) B1295/35 B1311/35
matters (60)
matting (1) C0069/04
mattock (1) B0844/19
mattress (12) C0069/16
C0073/13 C0073/18 C0076/15 C0080/41
C0081/21 C0081/27 C0082/25 C0091/10
C0091/16 C0110/24 C0112/23
mattresses (1) C0109/26
mature (4) A0430/29
B1013/28 B1132/16 C0186/16
matured (5) A0105/19
A0474/04 A0708/21 B1273/16 C0067/05
maturing (1) A0234/18
maturity (5) A0234/06
A0410/22 A0711/02 B0875/04 B1276/03
Maury, Lieutenant (1) B1357/03
Mavis, Martin Van Buren (1) B1291/04
mavoureen (1) A0468/19

mavourneen (5) A0465/14
A0467/22 A0468/04 A0469/10 A0469/24
maxime (1) A0072/31
maximum (2) B0747/19 B1312/13
Maximus (1) A0176/06
May (19) B1161/29
C0530/26 C0566/10 C0566/12 C0566/28
C0567/05 C0568/06 C0568/29 C0570/10
C0570/17 C0570/22 C0570/29 C0570/34
C0571/09 C0574/18 C0574/23 C0576/10
C0576/21 C0576/30
may (400)
maybe (1) A0470/12
Mayor (1) B1097/07
Maza-- (1) A0112/26
mazes (4) A0022/02
A0028/19 A0446/25 B1279/37
mazurka (1) A0354/19
Mazurkiad (1) A0034/14
mazy (2) A0639/20 C0542/18
McHenry's (1) A0628/V
me (4) A0053/14
A0062/21 A0344/25 B1260/01
me (1851)
meadow (1) A0495/V
meadows (5) B1212/31
B1278/36 B1283/08 C0118/13 C0412/35
meagre (1) B0768/26
meal (4) B1045/26
B1178/07 C0176/04 C0409/04
meals (2) B0729/14 C0145/37
mean (106)
meandered (1) B1162/04
meandering (3) B1333/20
B1334/08 B1335/11
meaning (76)
meaningless (5) A0294/09
A0430/V A0437/28 A0682/07 C0432/37
meanness (1) A0263/24
means (294)
meant (17) A0489/32
A0543/10 A0586/29 A0587/21 A0621/17
A0622/03 B0915/07 B0986/11 B1033/09
B1048/06 B1134/02 B1139/29 B1184/17
B1348/19 B1359/27 B1360/05 C0146/27
meantime (76)
meanwhile (3) A0189/30
A0546/22 C0412/28
meas (2) A0209/M A0218/15
measurable (1) A0711/25
measure (62)
measured (13) A0027/07
A0240/17 A0242/21 A0380/12 A0415/29
A0615/09 A0676/12 A0694/18 B0981/04
C0098/24 C0137/37 C0157/01 C0566/32
measurement (1) A0688/16
measures (10) A0036/22 A0460/25
B0773/02 B0773/03 B0817/07 B0983/29
B0983/35 B0988/17 C0138/35 C0427/02
meat (10) A0631/23 A0689/22
A0690/07 B0821/02 C0074/05 C0141/26
C0141/33 C0165/17 C0534/41 C0535/34
meats (1) B1008/33
Mecca (3) A0228/28
A0233/10 A0405/V
mechanical (6) A0381/22 A0382/03
A0382/11 B1193/10 B1302/21 C0400/39
mechanically (1) A0022/27
mechanically-moved (1) B1120/05
mechanician (1) B1119/22
Mechanics (1) C0393/01
Mechanics' (1) B1053/11
mechanism (3) A0529/29
B0955/31 B1119/14
medallion (1) A0298/V
medallions (2) A0156/V A0312/14
medals (3) A0365/16
A0430/34 B1303/09
meddled (2) B0981/07 B1299/34
medecin (1) C0430/35
media (1) B1188/14
Median (3) A0252/05
A0498/12 B1311/17
mediate (3) A0600/29
B0949/35 B1213/08
medical (19) A0324/V
A0328/13 A0409/23 B0730/19 B0941/09
B0956/04 B0958/01 B0959/23 B0959/34
B0962/18 B0962/32 B0969/04 B0982/27
B1002/04 B1016/35 B1192/10 B1236/16
B1241/32 C0129/22
Medicean (1) B1014/22
Medici (1) A0160/16
medicinal (2) B0950/09 B0950/12
medicine (12) A0384/06
C0555/16 C0556/06 C0556/12 C0556/17
C0556/22 C0556/26 C0556/28 C0557/02
C0557/16 C0557/21 C0558/07
medicines (1) B1235/17
medii (1) B0986/19
meditate (2) B1090/25 C0398/01
meditated (1) C0392/24
meditates (1) B1223/15
meditating (1) C0419/26
meditation (20) A0021/20
A0057/18 A0063/19 A0068/02 A0142/08
A0151/03 A0210/26 A0211/26 A0213/19
A0216/18 A0298/V A0343/21 A0349/18
A0429/10 A0673/01 A0673/09 B0963/26
B0974/02 C0392/38 C0397/38
meditations (12) A0079/11
A0102/10 A0141/32 A0189/17 A0205/06
A0212/28 A0226/07 A0534/06 A0535/06
A0536/28 A0601/29 A0674/20
meditatively (1) A0533/21
Mediterranean (4) A0121/07
A0121/09 B0864/34 C0443/V
medium (18) A0156/05 A0212/25
A0485/12 B0764/33 B0889/25 B1037/26
B1184/24 B1184/26 B1215/11 B1330/05
B1338/28 C0207/02 C0401/31 C0401/32
C0402/01 C0402/10 C0403/07 C0413/23
medley (4) A0165/22
B1131/04 B1374/31 C0069/08
Medoc (7) A0086/14
A0099/01 A0101/V A0181/13 B1259/21
B1260/04 B1260/13
meee (1) B0914/03
meek (2) A0600/28 B1145/14
meekly (2) A0665/09 B1188/05

meerschaum (5) B0974/03
B0979/12 B0982/17 B1109/05 B1390/21
meet (32) A0150/M
A0155/17 A0166/11 A0302/11 A0384/14
A0448/03 A0488/V A0489/15 A0609/30
B0755/25 B0756/08 B0837/13 B0857/26
B0864/25 B0913/08 B0933/15 B1090/20
B1105/16 B1129/24 B1138/19 B1182/23
B1292/17 B1375/15 C0084/21 C0157/39
C0174/17 C0186/14 C0400/08 C0402/19
C0421/27 C0530/13 C0572/03
meeting (26) A0057/04 A0066/30
A0136/09 A0139/15 A0151/16 A0204/05
A0204/16 A0205/01 A0225/03 A0229/03
A0301/27 A0378/04 A0398/17 A0441/07
A0531/28 B0749/34 B0762/20 B0898/20
B0899/07 B0958/10 B1107/24 C0093/14
C0149/07 C0162/22 C0164/17 C0565/28
meetings (2) A0369/12 C0531/09
meets (1) B0755/11
mein (8) A0373/09
A0373/14 A0373/16 A0373/18 B1102/06
B1103/29 B1104/15 B1104/16
Mela, Pomponius (2) A0409/07
A0601/33
melancholy (32) A0026/25
A0150/V A0157/23 A0164/18 A0189/V
A0195/V A0198/21 A0215/08 A0227/13
A0231/18 A0234/20 A0320/12 A0321/23
A0357/03 A0379/02 A0397/05 A0404/30
A0602/12 A0614/14 A0641/V B0807/22
B0865/35 B0940/15 B0964/32 B1055/09
B1250/28 B1281/15 C0065/24 C0128/41
C0143/12 C0444/V C0444/V
Melancthon, Philip (1) A0621/12
melanges (1) A0101/07
Melanie (1) A0280/15
melee (2) A0253/29 A0253/V
melee (1) C0563/07
Melete (1) A0343/21
meliora (1) A0495/03
Mellen (1) A0282/01
Mellen, G. (1) A0281/36
Mellonta (1) B1291/T
mellonta (Gr.) (1) A0608/M
Melnotte (1) A0623/V
Melodies (3) A0052/M
A0061/M B1130/29
melodies (1) A0036/11
melodious (3) A0036/V
A0354/14 A0614/24
melodrama (1) B1331/06
melodrame (1) B0738/15
melody (16) A0022/03
A0150/V A0226/15 A0230/13 A0315/12
A0317/11 A0379/12 A0389/03 A0407/37
A0641/03 A0643/16 B1096/07 B1096/18
B1281/14 B1283/05 C0083/16
Melrose (1) B0865/06
melt (1) B1322/29
melted (7) A0227/12
A0231/25 A0664/07 B1161/05 B1337/33
C0205/32 C0534/40
melting (1) A0033/05
melts (1) B0933/02
Melty (1) A0349/17
Mem (6) A0337/01 A0337/02
A0487/06 A0487/06 A0487/13 B1080/10
Mem. (2) A0280/27 A0280/28
member (22) A0034/14 A0037/07
A0204/18 A0204/31 A0246/07 A0292/02
A0299/11 A0708/29 B0733/18 B0768/18
B0956/12 B1005/01 B1181/05 B1183/31
B1191/25 B1191/32 B1226/V B1239/32
B1241/16 B1273/23 C0525/34 C0563/38
members (14) A0203/02 A0204/02
A0205/09 A0337/33 A0444/28 A0600/26
B0904/V B1008/19 B1020/12 B1047/26
B1184/25 B1347/22 C0523/19 C0544/10
membrane (1) C0394/08
membranous (1) B1250/21
meme (2) A0019/03 A0386/05
memoire (1) B1114/03
Memoirs (1) A0301/04
memoirs (2) B1122/23 B1224/10
memorable (7) A0349/11
A0490/36 A0654/26 B0969/07 B1049/26
C0135/36 C0527/16
memoranda (7) B1114/01
B1126/15 B1195/11 B1235/19 B1236/23
C0193/26 C0203/40
memorandum (1) A0036/V
memorandum (8) A0091/12
B0831/19 B0834/12 B0878/26 B0880/08
B1114/06 C0533/07 C0570/15
memorandum-book (2) B0862/26
B0981/27
memorial (1) A0644/24
memorials (2) A0121/27 A0189/02
memories (9) A0320/13
A0326/16 A0436/18 A0439/23 A0456/24
A0643/34 A0682/31 B1225/02 B1385/30
memory (71)
men (228)
men (Gr.) (1) B1385/18
men-mathematicians (1) B1164/07
men-of-war (1) B0754/34
men-vermin (1) B1158/18
menace (1) A0689/04
menaced (1) B1106/18
menagais (1) A0547/V
menageais (1) A0547/05
menages (2) B1006/01 B1006/V
Menander (1) A0111/04
Menatopae/Assiniboins (1) C0551/30
mended (3) A0339/11
B0735/13 B0762/12
mender (2) A0534/26 C0391/02
mendicant (2) B1139/09 B1139/26
mendicants (1) A0509/34
mending (2) A0281/18 C0391/12
menial (2) A0217/V A0218/20
menials (1) A0326/04
Mennais (3) B0753/33
B0753/40 B0770/10
Menschen (1) B0723/M
mental (46) A0020/08 A0085/04
A0093/10 A0093/18 A0112/21 A0112/29
A0212/08 A0216/01 A0216/02 A0234/02
A0270/33 A0279/22 A0280/06 A0283/05

->A0293/09 A0294/V A0296/V A0298/V
A0320/28 A0398/21 A0403/21 A0406/14
A0408/27 A0410/30 A0413/15 A0430/26
A0431/05 A0507/10 A0511/08 A0511/21
A0527/01 A0528/18 A0533/07 A0615/05
A0638/17 A0667/30 A0682/28 B0724/14
B0939/V B0961/19 B0963/18 B1235/16
B1316/13 C0059/34 C0129/37 C0182/28
mentally (6) A0057/22 A0068/05
A0080/13 B0974/09 B1030/34 C0132/12
mention (44) A0034/V
A0069/20 A0092/05 A0111/17 A0164/04
A0204/22 A0209/11 A0251/18 A0268/30
A0278/24 A0282/33 A0283/35 A0285/25
A0342/05 A0399/30 A0408/03 A0436/24
A0547/28 A0654/06 B0850/32 B0887/22
B0929/26 B0959/26 B0978/19 B0980/02
B1046/13 B1056/06 B1241/09 B1345/26
B1380/03 B1386/07 B1390/21 C0066/03
C0087/37 C0125/12 C0132/17 C0137/27
C0394/12 C0400/22 C0427/35 C0526/10
C0528/08 C0534/04 C0534/16
mentioned (86)
mentioning (9) A0028/12
A0583/07 B0902/24 B1154/22 C0090/34
C0119/10 C0132/31 C0177/29 C0196/01
mentions (4) A0034/18
B0987/33 B1101/21 C0525/04
Mentoni (3) A0152/19
A0153/18 A0155/12
Mentoni, Marchesa di (3) A0153/12
A0164/01 A0166/V
Mentoni's (1) A0166/16
mer (1) C0178/08
mercantile (2) A0269/33 A0276/18
Mercator (1) A0146/12
merchandise (2) B0933/32 B1155/23
merchandize (1) B0856/36
merchant (7) A0482/31
A0483/16 A0483/25 A0484/30 A0592/01
B1137/13 B1138/03
merchant-barber (1) B1127/02
merchant-barbers (1) B1127/16
merchants (3) A0486/08
A0508/17 B1059/17
Mercier (1) A0018/12
mercies (1) A0515/32
Merciful (1) B0852/27
merciful (2) B0955/21 C0558/41
merciless (1) B0964/16
Mercurie (1) B0753/19
Mercury (4) B0731/37
B0742/25 B0826/03 B1186/31
mercury (1) C0411/36
mercy (19) A0152/V
A0447/20 A0608/22 B0852/27 B0932/15
B0986/28 B1131/01 B1313/08 C0072/23
C0106/41 C0113/27 C0116/08 C0117/17
C0117/25 C0139/12 C0147/01 C0201/18
C0426/13 C0554/05
mere (152)
Meredith (2) C0531/17 C0541/07
merely (157)
merest (8) A0079/37
A0195/V A0436/32 A0690/27 B0855/22

->B0863/12 B1358/32 C0139/12
merge (4) A0399/16
A0459/29 A0489/07 A0496/12
merged (7) A0456/20
A0615/33 A0616/19 A0681/06 B1145/01
B1222/29 B1279/01
meridian (8) C0157/04
C0157/30 C0157/33 C0157/34 C0157/35
C0159/33 C0162/10 C0524/29
meridians (2) C0148/18 C0161/06
merit (22) A0054/26 A0063/27
A0245/24 A0271/36 A0304/03 A0338/28
A0340/08 A0342/06 A0497/01 A0500/26
A0710/21 A0710/24 A0710/26 B0738/14
B0958/16 B1132/23 B1136/10 B1275/25
B1379/34 B1380/14 B1383/10 C0432/36
meritorious (2) A0204/15 B1152/28
merits (12) A0069/01
A0075/07 A0100/27 A0126/08 A0265/09
A0265/11 A0495/V A0497/11 B1143/32
B1144/14 B1275/30 B1379/32
merrily (3) A0674/02
B1224/V C0576/10
merriment (9) A0161/16
A0190/15 A0190/16 A0511/23 B0989/10
C0087/28 C0087/28 C0168/38 C0558/38
merry (8) A0159/09
A0190/07 A0296/11 A0594/25 B1258/22
B1347/28 C0544/05 C0570/03
Merry-Andrewism (1) A0627/05
mes (2) A0037/10 A0378/M
meself> (11) A0464/V
A0465/V A0465/V A0465/V A0466/V
A0467/V A0468/V A0468/V A0468/V
A0469/V A0470/V
mesilf> (11) A0464/07
A0465/16 A0465/17 A0465/23 A0466/20
A0467/24 A0468/14 A0468/30 A0468/V
A0469/14 A0470/12
Mesmer (2) B0941/12 B1191/18
Mesmeric (1) B1029/T
mesmeric (15) B1030/23
B1031/31 B1032/01 B1032/10 B1032/14
B1032/29 B1037/21 B1234/13 B1237/19
B1238/01 B1241/11 B1241/17 B1241/27
B1242/06 B1242/35
mesmerical (1) B1031/33
mesmerism (3) B1029/01
B1030/14 B1233/14
mesmerist (1) B0941/29
mesmerized (3) B1032/08
B1233/17 B1236/31
mesmerizing (2) B1030/21 B1236/29
message (4) B0813/10
B0924/03 B1140/04 C0527/21
Messenger (12) A0263/37
A0280/27 A0280/28 A0285/36 A0286/20
B1386/10 C0055/30 C0056/07 C0056/10
C0056/18 C0428/07 C0448/V
messenger (7) B1246/12
C0056/30 C0110/30 C0426/25 C0427/04
C0523/22 C0523/30
Messieurs (10) A0541/V A0559/V
A0653/19 B1183/01 B1184/26 C0065/31
C0161/26 C0401/06 C0523/04 C0544/39

Messrs (8) A0484/22 A0484/30 A0485/27 A0559/01 B0879/12 B0879/17 C0428/35 C0428/35

met (81)

metal (2) A0537/33 A0537/V

metal (18) A0035/09 A0321/25 A0688/32 A0696/08 B0825/24 B1034/10 B1034/14 B1034/25 B1161/06 B1248/24 B1363/23 C0190/04 C0199/02 C0396/28 C0415/05 C0430/23 C0432/44 C0534/02

metallic (7) A0415/27 A0689/01 B0809/09 B1156/16 B1250/22 C0193/11 C0393/31

metals (1) B1167/11

Metamora (2) A0055/28 A0065/08

metamorphosis (3) B1037/07 B1037/11 B1038/30

metaphor (1) B0989/14

metaphysical (7) A0211/21 A0297/27 A0316/03 A0341/21 A0342/V A0350/08 C0426/19

metaphysician (21) A0085/02 A0087/11 A0088/25 A0089/19 A0090/28 A0094/22 A0097/26 A0099/21 A0100/02 A0101/01 A0102/07 A0103/05 A0104/19 A0106/31 A0108/07 A0109/11 A0109/24 A0114/04 A0114/17 B1018/09 B1317/21

metaphysicianism (2) A0078/43 B1219/16

metaphysicians (5) A0107/16 B1033/31 B1036/14 B1295/02 B1310/15

Metaphysics (1) B1193/24

metaphysics (10) A0086/03 A0097/04 A0108/22 A0338/05 A0339/27 B0989/17 B1004/28 B1297/36 B1313/12 B1317/15

Metaphysische (2) A0342/01 A0342/V

Metempsychosis (2) A0018/04 A0018/13

metempsychosist (1) A0018/15

meteor (1) A0314/16

meteoric (6) B1321/09 B1322/V C0402/05 C0420/33 C0421/04 C0422/39

meth'auton (Gr.) (2) A0225/M A0229/M

methinks (3) A0044/02 A0318/V A0610/25

method (42) A0055/16 A0064/31 A0204/17 A0296/V A0338/34 A0338/35 A0408/13 A0481/01 A0481/M A0482/01 A0482/05 A0484/12 A0484/13 A0485/26 A0488/17 A0528/11 A0534/21 A0534/22 A0545/02 A0545/03 A0549/03 A0611/25 B0824/31 B0977/01 B1007/02 B1152/19 C0069/28 C0077/04 C0090/14 C0097/28 C0098/32 C0134/07 C0139/33 C0178/02 C0391/31 C0393/23 C0394/08 C0414/41 C0426/03 C0534/09 C0536/01 C0546/08

methodical (7) A0481/01 A0482/07 A0486/29 B0749/18 B0830/04 B0878/12 B0991/21

methodically (1) B0751/20

methodise (1) A0135/05

methods (5) A0081/39 A0445/14 A0529/10 B1213/01 C0120/08

methought (2) B0964/01 B1106/16

metropolis (6) A0071/03 A0164/04 A0242/19 A0250/27 B0759/34 B0914/14

mets (1) B1114/02

Metzengerstein (21) A0018/T A0019/05 A0019/10 A0019/18 A0019/V A0019/V A0020/10 A0021/01 A0021/21 A0021/29 A0022/12 A0024/10 A0025/04 A0026/06 A0026/06 A0027/01 A0028/03 A0028/17 A0028/23 A0029/06 A0029/V

Metzengerstein, Frederick Von (1) /20

meuble (1) A0096/M

mewed (1) C0406/19

Mexican (1) B0931/22

Mexican/Gulf (1) C0419/17

Miantinimoh (1) A0055/28

miasma (1) A0413/04

mica-slate (2) A0175/26 A0182/08

mice (2) A0491/10 A0653/23

Michael (1) A0161/01

Michau (4) C0522/36 C0523/06 C0523/15 C0523/23

Michau, Andre (1) C0522/34

Michau's (1) C0524/18

Michilimackinac (1) C0528/11

microscope (7) A0180/12 B0980/09 B0980/23 B0981/06 B0981/13 B0985/25 B1167/31

microscopes (2) B0989/03 B1191/36

microscopical (1) B1312/26

mid (4) B1103/33 B1283/11 B1301/17 C0072/25

mid-air (3) A0683/03 B1279/V B1353/19

mid-channel (1) C0555/09

mid-day (1) B1161/31

mid-summer (2) A0152/30 A0313/V

midday (2) C0117/26 C0164/29

middle (55)

middle-aged (1) B0877/33

midehed (1) A0626/12

midnight (39) A0086/20 A0137/02 A0151/17 A0151/V A0152/30 A0173/19 A0178/27 A0217/06 A0244/03 A0326/21 A0330/16 A0501/01 A0547/V A0615/24 A0663/13 A0674/14 B0732/03 B0738/30 B0739/01 B0739/03 B0739/12 B0739/14 B0739/27 B0771/34 B0789/22 B0793/10 B0794/10 B0796/16 B0957/29 B1145/21 B1161/09 B1235/05 B1236/01 B1237/31 B1262/32 B1352/02 B1371/26 C0115/23 C0562/26

midst (10) A0143/10 A0245/06 A0371/30 A0442/33 B1020/32 B1056/28 B1362/11 C0111/27 C0562/28 C0562/39

midsummer (4) A0313/19 A0429/20 A0612/30 B0901/09

midway (5) A0579/24 A0581/06 A0590/19 A0602/27 B1333/17

mienne (1) C0430/41

mieux (3) A0545/06 B1154/21 C0430/36

Mige-Gush (2) A0057/30 A0068/13

might (502)

mightiest (1) B1167/04

mighty (19) A0195/18
A0198/23 A0413/27 A0415/23 A0417/14
A0429/09 A0515/13 A0580/34 A0641/17
A0642/13 A0665/22 B0812/06 B0812/26
B0821/27 B1166/16 B1166/25 C0205/37
C0420/30 C0444/V
Mignaud (3) A0541/11
A0541/12 A0556/14
Mignaud/et/Fils (1) A0541/19
Mignaud, Jules (1) A0541/11
migrate (1) C0431/13
migrated (2) B1369/11 C0540/31
mihi (2) A0209/M A0218/14
Milan (1) A0086/02
mild (8) A0234/18
A0499/02 C0133/04 C0159/03 C0161/01
C0161/08 C0164/22 C0566/12
milder (4) A0690/32
A0690/32 C0166/08 C0202/15
mildew (5) A0608/12
B0735/08 B0759/02 B0759/15 B0759/18
mildewed (4) B0735/07
B0735/10 B0758/34 B0759/05
mile (44) A0144/29
A0366/28 A0513/11 A0579/25 A0580/27
A0581/35 A0588/02 B0807/01 B0830/07
B0864/17 B1049/02 B1075/21 B1164/13
B1164/14 B1164/38 B1164/39 B1298/31
B1302/35 C0123/30 C0142/34 C0159/23
C0163/09 C0163/18 C0164/16 C0164/21
C0167/04 C0170/39 C0180/20 C0180/39
C0187/12 C0190/02 C0191/31 C0199/07
C0425/01 C0541/36 C0560/20 C0561/32
C0567/15 C0567/25 C0572/41 C0573/13
C0574/10 C0576/02 C0580/02
mile-stone (1) B0864/21
miles (142)
military (4) A0069/22
A0509/28 C0153/24 C0552/14
militates (1) B0755/24
militating (1) B0740/21
Milk (1) C0551/34
milk-weed (1) B1293/02
milky (3) C0204/14
C0204/38 C0205/29
Milky/Way (1) B1301/04
Mill (13) B1113/11
B1297/03 B1297/06 B1297/10 B1297/13
B1314/07 B1314/10 B1314/18 B1314/21
B1314/30 B1315/07 B1315/14 B1315/32
mill (2) A0489/30 B1292/31
mill-horse (2) B1297/04 B1314/08
mill-race (1) A0588/03
mill-wheel (2) A0137/05 A0681/08
Mill's (1) B1315/19
Mille (2) A0183/02 B1010/14
mille (16) A0018/12
A0124/30 A0124/30 A0124/30 A0124/31
A0124/31 A0124/31 A0125/02 A0125/02
A0125/02 A0125/02 A0125/03 A0125/03
A0125/03 A0125/04 A0125/04
milled (2) A0485/02 C0534/25
Miller (22) A0261/22 A0261/25
A0261/29 A0262/18 A0262/26 A0263/12
A0263/16 A0263/29 A0264/02 A0264/23
->A0264/23 A0264/24 A0264/26 A0264/33
A0268/17 A0270/26 A0272/16 A0277/35
A0279/13 A0282/15 B1297/03 B1314/07
Miller, Joseph (3) A0261/01
A0261/10 A0262/22
Miller, Joseph A. (3) A0261/02
A0265/16 A0279/35
Miller, Joseph A. etc. (1) A0279/19
Miller, Joseph B. (3) A0261/03
A0266/06 A0280/21
Miller, Joseph C. (3) A0261/03
A0266/35 A0280/38
Miller, Joseph D. (3) A0261/10
A0267/24 A0281/15
Miller, Joseph E. (2) A0261/11
A0268/12
Miller, Joseph E. F. (1) A0281/37
Miller, Joseph F. (2) A0261/11
A0268/35
Miller, Joseph G. (2) A0261/17
A0269/30
Miller, Joseph G. H. (1) A0282/20
Miller, Joseph H. (2) A0261/22
A0270/11
Miller, Joseph I. (2) A0261/27
A0270/31
Miller, Joseph J. K. (1) A0282/37
Miller, Joseph K. (2) A0262/13
A0271/17
Miller, Joseph L. (2) A0262/18
A0272/07
Miller, Joseph L. M. (1) A0283/19
Miller, Joseph M. (2) A0272/22
A0272/29
Miller, Joseph N. (2) A0262/23
A0273/10
Miller, Joseph N. O. (1) A0284/03
Miller, Joseph O. (2) A0262/28
A0274/04
Miller, Joseph P. (2) A0263/01
A0274/26
Miller, Joseph P. Q. (1) A0284/24
Miller, Joseph Q. (2) A0263/10
A0275/10
Miller, Joseph R. (2) A0263/23
A0275/31
Miller, Joseph R. S. (1) A0284/37
Miller, Joseph S. (2) A0264/04
A0276/15
Miller, Joseph T. (2) A0264/06
A0276/31
Miller, Joseph T. V. (1) A0285/16
Miller, Joseph V. (2) A0264/08
A0277/09
Miller, Joseph W. (3) A0264/14
A0264/15 A0277/31
Miller, Joseph W. X. (1) A0285/30
Miller, Joseph X. (2) A0264/18
A0278/12
Miller, Joseph Y. (2) A0264/21
A0278/30
Miller, Joseph Y. Z. (1) A0286/14
Miller, Joseph Z. (2) A0264/32
A0279/10
Miller's (1) A0270/27

million (13) A0124/01
A0140/V A0557/22 A0705/20 B0828/18
B0833/05 B0900/04 B0945/19 B1138/30
B1270/19 B1302/07 B1332/37 C0184/34
millionaires (2) B1092/27 B1257/10
millions (13) A0639/14
A0704/33 A0705/19 A0705/32 B0964/29
B1164/16 B1164/16 B1167/16 B1168/12
B1269/32 B1269/36 B1270/18 B1294/23
Mills'/Point (2) C0522/21 C0532/09
millstone (1) B1142/20
Milton (2) A0706/22 B1271/24
mimes (2) A0318/14 A0319/08
mimic (2) A0319/03 B1333/29
mimicking (1) B0912/11
minarets (3) B0945/10
B0945/23 B1283/12
mind (270)
mind's (2) A0500/28 C0118/15
minding (2) A0470/18 A0568/13
minds (17) A0399/19
A0535/13 B0726/30 B0758/24 B1220/30
B1347/13 B1347/19 B1364/20 B1364/21
C0109/34 C0111/41 C0112/14 C0127/34
C0172/03 C0392/33 C0562/01 C0578/16
mine (42) A0024/09 A0092/19
A0097/15 A0111/29 A0160/V A0162/18
A0196/09 A0198/12 A0210/24 A0226/12
A0228/22 A0233/03 A0311/01 A0311/15
A0314/05 A0326/V A0382/21 A0427/29
A0431/17 A0443/23 A0448/02 A0448/10
A0608/23 A0608/24 A0643/V A0644/11
A0685/08 B0793/21 B0811/06 B0813/16
B0830/13 B0923/04 B1101/34 B1105/04
B1139/34 B1238/20 B1240/19 B1379/19
C0130/26 C0137/13 C0531/32 C0564/38
mineral (5) A0241/33
B0742/16 B1364/21 C0553/01 C0572/13
mineralizing (1) B0826/03
minerals (1) C0564/24
mines (4) B1163/22
B1364/18 C0525/29 C0531/40
mingle (2) A0019/V C0410/38
mingled (19) A0058/21
A0102/17 A0144/11 A0157/25 A0158/04
A0161/20 A0253/29 A0265/25 A0265/36
A0271/20 A0319/28 A0401/03 A0432/14
A0667/24 B0738/15 B1004/11 C0142/39
C0153/20 C0190/20
mingling (3) A0614/28
B1333/04 C0061/20
miniature (4) B0903/26
B0909/03 B0912/04 B0948/31
minion (1) B1131/28
minions (1) A0693/13
Minister (13) B0976/35
B0977/09 B0982/03 B0986/17 B0986/22
B0988/14 B0988/34 B0990/07 B0990/17
B0991/16 B0991/30 B0992/07 B0993/03
minister (9) B0977/20
B0977/37 B0978/12 B0978/26 B0979/01
B0991/08 B1348/15 C0156/03 C0522/40
Minister/G-- (1) A0020/11
minister's (1) B0978/04
Ministerial (1) B0992/33
ministerial (3) A0705/10
B0990/21 B1270/09
ministers (9) B1128/27
B1130/05 B1345/04 B1345/26 B1346/06
B1347/16 B1350/06 B1350/36 C0526/26
ministry (1) B1350/13
mink (1) C0536/22
Minnackenozzies (1) C0551/24
Minnakenozzies (1) C0551/18
Minnetaree (1) C0566/06
Minnetarees (5) C0565/30
C0565/38 C0571/31 C0572/04 C0574/40
minnows (1) B1312/26
minor (7) A0087/28
A0088/30 A0459/14 B0763/13 B0817/11
B0906/12 C0194/02
minute (89)
minute-hand (3) A0353/20
A0355/26 A0672/24
minute's (2) A0489/18 B1353/25
minutely (18) A0074/18 A0103/22
A0296/V A0321/09 A0328/21 A0428/34
A0553/03 A0704/23 B0810/30 B0989/33
B1192/10 B1249/17 B1269/22 C0124/01
C0169/33 C0194/08 C0539/18 C0568/24
minuteness (7) A0546/24
B0753/02 B0763/16 B0870/01 B0870/03
B1034/20 B1250/15
minutes (149)
minutes' (1) A0583/37
minutest (9) A0404/V
A0444/25 B0857/21 B0905/19 B0949/13
B1073/02 B1333/35 C0134/02 C0190/07
mio (1) B0905/14
miracle (12) A0055/37
A0065/19 A0137/14 A0139/19 A0143/28
B0757/31 B0762/29 B0931/19 B1044/03
B1044/04 B1233/03 B1283/11
miracles (9) A0143/28
A0709/31 A0710/19 B0905/29 B0942/01
B1191/20 B1274/34 B1275/22 C0172/16
miraculous (17) A0024/V
A0315/10 A0402/08 A0445/24 B0725/07
B0760/25 B0894/27 B0905/16 B0949/05
B1165/29 B1169/09 B1280/20 B1382/19
C0065/06 C0069/09 C0150/03 C0426/11
miraculously (4) A0122/15
B0948/31 B1303/26 B1333/09
Miranda (1) A0383/20
Mirror (3) A0284/22
B1119/01 B1119/M
mirror (23) A0053/36
A0063/07 A0121/08 A0152/25 A0153/15
A0156/24 A0156/25 A0190/03 A0190/19
A0191/06 A0300/09 A0300/11 A0300/16
A0447/30 A0500/04 A0502/17 B0962/14
B1238/11 B1239/06 B1241/07 B1333/36
C0172/04 C0405/06
mirror-like (2) A0156/25 A0602/32
mirrors (4) A0499/31
A0500/10 B0980/15 C0169/34
mirth (5) A0190/12
A0609/37 A0641/V B0833/05 B0927/22
mirthful (1) A0603/09
mis (3) A0378/M

->C0430/29 C0430/38
mis-calculation (1) A0584/08
mis-called (1) C0422/39
misadmeasurement (1) B1250/01
misadventure (3) A0340/31
A0341/04 A0662/V
misanthrope (2) B1360/26 B1361/10
misanthropic (2) B0925/33 B1277/24
misanthropy (3) B0807/21
B0922/13 B0924/09
misapprehended (2) A0212/11
B1079/30
misapprehensions (1) B1360/19
miscalculation (3) A0529/12
A0592/03 B0981/18
miscalculations (1) B0773/07
miscellaneous (6) A0338/28 B0990/30
B1101/02 B1110/20 B1115/06 B1360/05
mischief (4) A0242/15
A0243/11 A0445/19 B0773/33
mischievous (1) A0490/09
misconceived (3) A0299/26
B1051/14 B1360/22
misconception (1) B1381/27
misconduct (1) B1155/03
miscreants (3) B0735/29
B0767/19 B0767/33
misdemeanor (1) C0427/19
misdemeanors (1) A0021/18
miser (2) B0982/26 B0982/30
miserable (14) A0120/07 A0416/06
A0438/16 A0546/12 A0626/16 B0807/06
B1057/23 B1139/09 B1183/17 C0074/41
C0078/38 C0172/36 C0185/29 C0549/22
miserably (6) A0025/13 A0071/10
A0374/17 B1313/14 C0083/09 C0563/29
miseries (4) B0955/16
B0967/19 C0072/12 C0399/30
misery (13) A0209/01
A0218/V A0350/27 A0426/11 A0428/12
A0428/12 A0687/30 B1158/04 C0080/40
C0117/36 C0131/24 C0149/01 C0563/30
misfortune (10) A0064/V A0070/30
A0622/29 B0814/03 B0876/34 B1107/07
C0097/39 C0163/33 C0414/04 C0559/22
misfortunes (2) A0457/14 B0806/03
misguided (1) A0078/16
mishap (1) C0097/14
misinformed (1) B1369/24
misjudged (1) B1186/19
mislaid (1) A0073/07
misled (4) A0561/15
B1007/09 B1360/33 C0428/19
Misquash (5) C0568/39
C0569/03 C0571/10 C0572/02 C0574/19
misrepresentations (2) B1233/09
C0131/31
misrepresented (1) C0056/28
misrule (1) A0610/04
Miss (27) A0174/08
A0174/09 A0179/23 A0179/24 A0268/37
A0269/06 A0270/37 A0271/02 A0274/09
A0281/01 A0281/01 A0339/09 A0339/22
A0340/11 A0340/19 A0341/V A0342/20
A0345/03 A0346/30 A0382/21 A0382/25
->A0383/18 A0385/16 A0385/19 B1121/T
B1123/05 B1380/16
miss (5) A0270/26
A0270/34 A0336/10 B1120/05 C0170/07
Miss/Lucy/Long (1) B1119/10
missed (7) B0843/11
B0980/21 B1259/14 B1298/09 C0070/19
C0096/13 C0563/37
Misses (2) A0383/13 A0384/10
misshapen (1) A0028/09
missing (16) A0080/38
B0737/30 B0746/04 B0746/22 B0747/04
B0981/29 B1044/11 B1044/20 B1046/24
B1048/12 C0077/11 C0079/20 C0107/07
C0183/23 C0397/28 C0427/20
Missinipi (1) C0527/01
missionaries (1) C0526/04
Mississippi (15) B0862/10
C0522/20 C0527/28 C0527/30 C0528/13
C0530/02 C0530/30 C0531/14 C0533/14
C0534/19 C0541/13 C0548/29 C0550/30
C0550/32 C0551/04
Missouri (34) C0087/03 C0522/14
C0525/38 C0526/18 C0527/20 C0527/22
C0527/27 C0528/14 C0529/03 C0529/27
C0530/01 C0533/36 C0536/16 C0536/33
C0539/19 C0540/13 C0542/15 C0548/16
C0550/32 C0551/11 C0551/22 C0551/31
C0552/35 C0553/16 C0553/34 C0556/10
C0570/08 C0571/09 C0571/32 C0572/19
C0574/06 C0574/41 C0575/26 C0576/37
missure> (1) A0464/17
mist (15) A0047/12
A0087/07 A0100/18 A0196/09 A0196/25
A0227/26 A0232/12 A0591/07 A0591/10
A0591/13 B0943/06 B0943/21 B0944/04
B1328/09 B1330/22
mistake (25) A0164/03
A0189/15 A0270/21 A0270/28 A0276/27
A0380/26 A0380/29 A0465/08 A0470/06
A0470/18 A0508/32 B0795/07 B0843/14
B0950/10 B1017/05 B1096/28 B1143/35
B1144/10 B1237/22 B1293/26 B1304/23
B1381/05 C0130/37 C0150/19 C0446/V
mistaken (43) A0024/12
A0113/05 A0230/04 A0267/18 A0267/34
A0272/35 A0283/38 A0298/V A0330/18
A0350/11 A0350/13 A0509/10 A0528/26
A0554/03 A0590/21 A0603/14 A0623/04
A0651/31 A0656/07 A0664/15 A0688/10
B0736/05 B0816/01 B0890/12 B0944/06
B0957/33 B0958/09 B0986/25 B1097/02
B1153/32 B1157/30 B1234/11 B1361/03
B1370/27 B1370/28 B1379/01 C0067/21
C0178/09 C0402/05 C0424/03 C0447/V
C0447/V C0525/06
mistakes (3) B0774/01
B0934/06 B1144/12
mistaking (3) A0242/13
A0652/19 B1329/09
Mister (1) C0449/V
mister (1) A0285/11
Misthress> (5) A0464/23
A0465/08 A0466/10 A0466/23 A0466/30
mistook (2) A0612/23 B1012/03

mistranslated (1) B1051/14
mistress (4) A0166/18
A0166/18 B0916/07 B0934/04
mistress' (1) B0934/01
mistrust (4) A0457/36
A0643/02 C0392/29 C0550/20
mists (2) A0216/16 C0575/20
misty (9) A0080/24
A0163/14 A0214/17 A0214/21 A0243/31
B0942/16 B1156/17 B1300/33 B1382/24
misty-looking (1) A0427/34
misty-winged (1) A0311/13
misunderstanding (3) A0269/18
A0353/05 C0154/15
misunderstood (7) A0499/V
A0528/18 A0553/09 B0890/V B1051/11
B1224/03 C0537/13
mit (1) B1103/28
mitigating (1) A0622/12
mittens (1) C0109/03
mixed (7) A0142/24
A0709/35 B1275/03 C0140/08 C0389/03
C0534/40 C0566/03
mixing (2) C0142/16 C0143/04
mixture (12) A0141/18
A0342/24 A0433/V A0667/26 A0710/03
A0711/05 B1141/14 B1141/20 B1275/06
B1276/07 B1362/31 C0140/09
mizen-mast (1) A0139/11
mizzen-mast (1) B0930/29
Mneme (1) A0343/21
mo-o-o-on (1) A0386/V
mo-o-on (1) A0386/14
moaning (9) A0102/05
A0416/31 A0580/04 A0614/16 A0696/27
B1262/11 C0118/01 C0567/36 C0567/41
moanings (1) A0216/23
moans (1) B1385/03
moat (1) A0029/17
Mob (3) B1194/14 B1300/15 B1300/17
mob (8) A0125/27
A0127/18 A0431/19 A0510/01 A0511/11
B0738/10 B0992/13 B1050/30
mobile (2) B1219/13 B1220/24
mobilia (1) B1219/02
moccasin (1) C0579/15
moccasins (4) C0552/19
C0552/26 C0559/20 C0572/29
mock (1) B1056/31
mockery (4) A0410/23
A0599/03 A0675/25 B0797/22
mocking (1) B1337/14
mode (40) A0530/09
A0539/03 A0551/06 A0551/06 A0554/05
A0555/31 A0593/28 A0685/18 A0705/03
B0736/28 B0739/34 B0747/18 B0754/11
B0766/24 B0822/20 B0830/35 B0908/06
B0983/24 B0984/27 B1014/13 B1038/08
B1049/34 B1070/19 B1071/V B1115/19
B1270/02 B1292/09 B1292/19 B1295/08
B1295/17 B1311/10 B1350/30 B1379/31
C0152/07 C0535/26 C0546/15 C0546/33
C0547/15 C0548/17 C0554/03
model (16) A0073/31
A0142/21 A0165/07 A0297/V A0322/02
->A0338/15 A0339/23 A0401/33 B1070/19
B1070/32 B1072/08 B1073/32 B1073/35
B1073/V B1114/23 B1132/08
modelled (5) A0298/V
A0379/26 A0645/04 C0098/05 C0200/37
modelling (1) C0106/11
models (4) A0312/30
A0496/27 A0577/M B1070/06
moderate (24) A0300/07
A0457/22 A0485/15 A0500/25 A0631/21
B0873/12 B0900/12 B1168/37 B1237/29
C0105/33 C0118/27 C0119/41 C0127/22
C0137/07 C0140/26 C0147/10 C0185/13
C0401/06 C0402/30 C0406/39 C0417/19
C0417/21 C0521/20 C0554/04
moderated (1) C0102/34
moderately (2) A0489/19 C0145/22
moderation (1) B1048/01
modern (31) A0088/11
A0089/07 A0097/05 A0104/06 A0121/11
A0128/11 A0176/05 A0180/27 A0235/15
A0303/30 A0315/19 A0621/19 A0621/V
A0622/28 A0654/16 A0662/12 B0752/07
B0871/30 B0886/03 B1089/10 B1092/05
B1184/29 B1185/07 B1194/21 B1295/21
B1297/08 B1298/28 B1299/15 B1310/07
B1311/14 C0178/05
moderns (4) B0871/27
B1191/07 B1191/35 B1194/26
modes (16) A0497/15
A0545/20 A0553/01 A0557/05 A0704/24
A0706/V B0736/28 B0736/30 B0985/13
B0985/22 B0988/21 B1009/13 B1213/01
B1269/23 B1296/11 C0536/13
modest (7) A0510/03
B1014/12 B1091/02 B1096/09 B1325/03
B1332/11 B1338/29
modeste (1) A0034/01
modestly (5) A0108/10
A0381/15 B1130/07 B1142/25 B1208/21
modesty (2) B1133/20 B1380/20
modification (8) A0461/10
A0613/20 B0772/18 B0908/04 B1221/07
B1221/14 B1279/31 C0401/02
modifications (7) A0460/19
B1017/04 B1021/31 B1214/30 C0396/05
C0439/V C0527/19
modificiren (1) B0723/M
modified (10) A0226/26 A0230/25
A0267/10 A0281/19 B0742/14 B0905/25
B1033/27 C0402/14 C0402/15 C0426/01
modifies (1) B1033/V
modify (7) A0398/07
B0723/M B0772/14 B0772/17 B1160/17
B1220/26 B1322/15
modistes (1) B0914/12
modo (1) B1143/16
modulated (1) A0402/24
modulation (1) A0315/12
moeurs (1) A0599/04
Mogul (1) A0279/16
moiety (3) A0693/23
B0875/27 C0393/09
Moissart (16) B0888/01
B0888/02 B0888/04 B0912/09 B0912/10

->B0912/11 B0912/13 B0912/18 B0912/20
B0912/22 B0912/30 B0912/V B0913/02
B0913/25 B0913/27 B0914/06
moist (3) A0686/04
B0967/27 B1329/18
moistened (1) A0613/05
moisture (7) A0512/15
B1074/23 B1260/09 C0395/22 C0406/02
C0425/36 C0544/33
moitie (1) A0378/M
Mole (5) B1137/22
B1138/11 B1138/16 B1138/19 B1139/35
mole (1) B1137/25
moles (1) B1298/02
molest (3) C0154/11
C0549/40 C0560/12
molestation (2) C0177/21 C0189/18
molesting (1) C0569/06
mollified (1) B1104/25
mollusca (3) C0178/07
C0178/22 C0178/39
molluscae (1) C0178/14
molten (3) A0158/03
A0236/01 B1363/22
Molucca (1) A0345/13
moment (1) A0135/M
moment (224)
moment's (5) A0252/07
A0593/25 B0814/05 B0978/32 B1345/21
momentarily (12) A0078/V
A0106/03 A0106/V A0211/V A0244/V
A0672/28 A0695/28 C0081/14 C0134/16
C0172/21 C0203/29 C0446/V
momentary (25) A0022/26
A0137/28 A0161/27 A0556/21 A0615/17
A0664/18 A0676/18 B0893/29 B1035/29
B1058/16 C0074/10 C0078/26 C0080/09
C0081/01 C0100/05 C0110/18 C0116/34
C0130/22 C0139/35 C0143/10 C0204/40
C0205/35 C0387/13 C0414/33 C0562/21
momently (13) A0078/04
A0211/18 A0244/23 A0299/01 A0507/23
A0515/20 A0594/05 A0603/31 A0605/01
A0672/V A0673/V C0412/19 C0424/24
momentous (9) A0350/08
A0352/18 B0727/01 B1316/21 B1317/09
B1360/11 B1360/11 C0058/01 C0425/23
moments (50) A0098/33 A0156/06
A0161/15 A0227/22 A0232/09 A0313/05
A0313/07 A0350/11 A0401/24 A0406/16
A0412/14 A0442/21 A0533/17 A0565/09
A0586/06 A0586/14 A0625/13 A0663/28
A0681/18 A0683/10 B0818/06 B0820/14
B0866/01 B0903/24 B0911/26 B0940/06
B0940/19 B0960/27 B0969/11 B1057/08
B1142/28 B1222/17 B1249/23 B1282/28
B1330/19 B1348/36 B1360/01 C0060/07
C0065/17 C0074/30 C0079/14 C0082/22
C0083/19 C0094/14 C0114/38 C0140/23
C0182/10 C0187/18 C0420/22 C0578/41
moments' (1) A0267/33
momentum (2) B0989/19 B0989/V
mon (16) A0096/M
A0096/M A0096/M A0541/10 A0541/31
A0560/05 B0906/29 B0907/07 B0907/08
->B0907/19 B0909/33 B0910/01 B1010/20
B1012/30 B1014/18 B1016/08
monarch (17) A0120/02
A0126/12 A0126/16 A0144/25 A0242/28
A0250/03 A0406/29 B1152/13 B1153/12
B1154/07 B1347/23 B1349/20 B1349/27
B1350/13 C0069/27 C0175/29 C0176/04
monarch's (2) A0407/26 B1348/34
monarchical (1) A0496/10
monarchs (1) B1345/30
monarchy (1) A0120/24
monastic (1) A0210/09
Monday (9) B0729/23
B0745/13 B0753/13 B0754/05 B0770/19
B0770/32 B1080/14 B1082/06 C0067/05
Monday's (1) B0738/03
Monde (1) C0430/28
money (48) A0047/04
A0080/01 A0174/31 A0247/18 A0347/05
A0441/V A0443/08 A0482/24 A0484/13
A0488/01 A0489/06 A0539/05 A0539/20
A0541/18 A0556/17 A0556/19 A0705/06
B0814/13 B0822/28 B0827/28 B0827/32
B0833/05 B0834/02 B0834/11 B0834/V
B0843/27 B0871/13 B0872/08 B0873/07
B0879/05 B1053/10 B1092/19 B1134/18
B1143/10 B1143/19 B1144/28 B1206/16
B1208/31 B1270/05 B1362/01 C0057/06
C0391/17 C0393/01 C0393/17 C0395/06
C0395/39 C0402/24 C0427/30
money-finders (1) B0834/10
money-lovers (1) A0498/21
money-seekers (1) B0834/10
Moneypenny (10) A0337/04 A0337/14
A0337/19 A0337/22 A0337/29 A0338/07
A0338/20 A0338/30 A0349/05 A0354/05
mongers (1) A0510/26
monitions (1) A0428/18
monk (1) A0322/26
monkey (5) A0490/07
B0850/26 B0851/14 B1346/20 B1353/11
monkey-exhibiters (1) A0510/25
monkish (1) A0690/22
monks (2) A0689/03 B0857/02
mono (Gr.) (2) A0225/M A0229/M
Monody (1) B1136/39
monologue (1) A0298/12
monomania (3) A0211/20
A0215/28 B1303/18
monomaniac (1) A0211/17
monopoly (1) A0246/21
Monos (14) A0608/02 A0608/07
A0608/14 A0608/17 A0608/23 A0608/29
A0608/30 A0608/T A0609/02 A0609/03
A0609/09 A0612/09 A0612/17 A0612/18
monosyllable (2) A0349/30 B1109/09
monotone (1) A0614/25
monotonous (3) A0297/21
A0615/27 A0672/23
monotonously (3) A0055/31
A0065/12 A0212/03
monotony (3) A0136/08
A0430/24 B1090/31
Monsieur (54)
Monsieur (1) C0430/35

monsieur (11) A0557/26
B0725/28 B0726/06 B0726/13 B0887/27
B1010/V B1016/30 B1017/17 B1020/09
B1021/17 B1021/33
monster (28) A0058/28
A0073/32 A0073/33 A0357/01 B0855/33
B0858/02 B0859/15 B0944/08 B1102/29
B1156/01 B1156/15 B1156/35 B1157/22
B1157/36 B1162/29 B1165/04 B1247/29
B1247/35 B1248/07 B1249/01 B1249/15
B1250/16 B1250/32 B1348/31 C0072/33
C0140/22 C0164/39 C0579/31
monsters (3) C0143/08
C0144/28 C0578/37
monsters' (1) B1162/19
monstrosities (2) A0322/21 A0689/06
monstrosity (1) B1331/06
monstrous (6) A0157/V A0429/03
A0500/07 A0580/08 B1162/15 C0541/19
monstrously (1) B1056/23
monstrum (2) B0993/12 B1010/25
Montani (1) A0560/06
Montani, Alberto (1) A0543/01
montantes (1) A0292/M
Montesquieu (2) A0386/26 A0654/V
Montesquieu-ism (1) B1114/28
Montfleury (1) A0033/18
month (45) A0043/02
A0093/20 A0112/31 A0240/01 A0323/03
A0323/20 A0623/15 A0623/15 A0671/11
A0705/21 B0728/06 B0753/13 B0811/11
B0878/15 B0878/19 B0879/16 B0879/25
B0922/03 B0933/14 B0981/33 B1019/17
B1021/26 B1046/31 B1131/23 B1136/16
B1208/13 B1208/15 B1208/16 B1208/19
B1208/20 B1235/32 B1270/20 B1292/01
B1347/14 C0053/T C0066/24 C0135/37
C0145/23 C0157/25 C0161/32 C0161/41
C0179/33 C0196/10 C0530/34 C0547/37
monthly (10) A0204/05 A0205/01
B1129/14 B1136/37 B1137/34 B1138/31
B1143/26 B1322/01 B1322/03 C0055/30
months (60)
Monticello (1) C0523/09
Montreal (4) C0526/35
C0527/10 C0527/35 C0528/10
Montresor (1) B1263/13
Montresors (2) B1258/32 B1259/31
Monument (2) B1304/20 B1305/06
monument (2) B1304/10 B1304/28
monuments (3) A0071/24
B1304/26 C0573/19
mood (4) A0101/21
B0811/08 B0857/29 B1115/04
moodily (3) A0514/02
B0897/07 B0927/19
moodiness (3) A0323/04
B0810/36 B0856/11
moods (13) A0062/20
A0282/06 A0507/09 A0507/10 A0533/21
A0565/11 A0638/05 A0641/V A0706/13
B0807/21 B1220/19 B1271/16 B1278/14
moody (6) A0665/13 B0724/28
B0851/08 B0922/23 B0924/09 C0130/33
Moon (1) B1322/10
moon (83)
moon-day (1) B1322/V
moon-hoax (1) C0448/V
moon-hoax-y (1) B1359/05
Moon-Hoax (2) C0428/10 C0428/12
Moon-Story (2) C0428/02 C0448/V
moon's (8) C0400/01
C0400/05 C0420/36 C0422/41 C0423/19
C0428/21 C0428/26 C0429/34
moonless (1) C0430/19
moonlight (7) A0027/V
A0499/07 A0587/23 B0865/06 C0561/25
C0573/26 C0577/08
moons (4) B1321/30
B1321/31 B1322/V C0429/03
moonshine (1) B1145/28
Moore's (2) A0052/M A0061/M
Moore's, Tom (1) B1384/20
Moral (1) A0599/02
moral (42) A0100/24 A0108/03
A0161/11 A0211/10 A0213/18 A0216/07
A0243/29 A0293/V A0315/27 A0350/08
A0402/01 A0405/04 A0434/15 A0435/31
A0528/05 A0610/07 A0610/31 A0613/30
A0615/06 A0615/14 A0621/10 A0621/26
A0621/27 A0621/T A0622/07 A0622/07
A0622/13 A0687/22 A0704/17 A0710/05
B0906/13 B0907/21 B0939/05 B0963/22
B0990/03 B1090/09 B1187/15 B1220/06
B1269/16 B1275/08 B1299/33 B1317/25
morale (1) A0403/31
Moralische (1) B0723/M
moralist (2) A0315/03 A0433/13
moralists (3) A0135/06
B1031/22 B1219/05
morality (5) A0101/08
A0225/19 A0226/23 A0230/23 B0879/10
morally (1) B1182/31
morals (7) A0105/11
A0473/24 A0531/06 A0621/04 A0621/06
A0622/09 B0987/23
morass (5) A0196/05
A0196/13 A0196/16 A0197/13 A0197/15
morasses (1) C0072/19
Moraux (1) A0599/01
moraux (1) A0599/04
morbid (8) A0026/25
A0211/20 A0212/12 A0213/V A0403/03
A0406/05 A0439/29 C0523/32
morbidity (1) A0296/V
morbidly (2) A0325/27 B1359/32
morbus (2) A0092/09 A0111/21
morceau (2) A0204/14 B1011/05
more (1222)
More, Thomas (3) A0158/19
A0158/19 A0158/20
Moreau, Pierre (1) A0539/09
Morella (30) A0225/02 A0225/T
A0226/11 A0226/22 A0226/28 A0227/03
A0227/25 A0228/11 A0228/15 A0228/20
A0228/30 A0229/02 A0229/T A0229/V
A0230/09 A0230/21 A0231/03 A0231/14
A0232/12 A0232/21 A0232/24 A0232/V
A0233/02 A0233/11 A0233/11 A0234/12
A0235/24 A0236/08 A0236/10 A0236/13

Morella's (10) A0225/11 A0225/21
A0227/17 A0228/22 A0229/11 A0232/04
A0233/03 A0234/25 A0234/27 A0235/07
moreover (41) A0019/16
A0024/V A0027/04 A0085/05 A0128/25
A0150/V A0263/26 A0279/21 A0284/18
A0285/26 A0296/V A0403/20 A0412/08
A0428/15 A0483/06 A0509/20 A0550/04
A0561/08 A0684/29 A0693/13 A0706/04
B0733/15 B0743/14 B0756/01 B0771/19
B0857/07 B0876/30 B1030/08 B1036/03
B1052/15 B1144/05 B1163/05 B1271/08
B1279/29 B1349/25 C0400/35 C0428/05
C0521/13 C0540/07 C0555/08 C0569/13
Moresque (1) A0664/10
Morgan (2) A0204/34 A0205/26
Morgue (3) B0723/T
B0724/12 B0731/02
moriens (1) A0018/M
morir (1) A0344/24
morn (1) A0227/35
mornin> (3) A0465/14
A0465/26 A0468/13
Morning (3) B0753/20
B0753/31 B0753/36
morning (159)
morning-gown (1) A0087/06
Morning/Post (1) B1380/13
morning's (2) A0431/02 B1371/08
mornings (1) C0563/34
Morocco (1) A0086/32
morocco (1) C0389/38
morose (1) B0926/06
morphine (4) A0354/V
A0667/36 B0942/07 B0943/13
Morrell (2) C0158/06 C0161/17
Morrell, Benjamin (1) C0160/28
morrow (21) A0088/06
A0102/28 A0407/27 A0473/20 A0640/23
B0808/21 B0895/11 B0896/14 B0896/15
B0907/11 B0908/20 B0923/31 B1053/09
B1056/02 B1056/11 B1056/17 B1153/13
B1236/01 C0092/08 C0093/07 C0570/04
morry (1) A0354/32
mors (2) A0018/M A0681/M
morsel (5) B1010/21
C0082/28 C0125/09 C0128/32 C0178/08
mort (1) A0033/19
mortal (23) A0071/04
A0317/11 A0319/07 A0405/22 A0405/22
A0466/21 A0577/06 A0603/20 A0615/35
A0691/02 A0709/03 B0794/07 B0964/16
B0965/23 B1057/19 B1226/V B1263/26
B1274/08 B1317/31 B1317/31 C0122/19
C0537/28 C0573/38
mortality (10) A0019/10 A0070/21
A0071/23 A0081/42 A0217/V A0317/12
A0327/07 A0600/14 B0955/23 B1213/02
mortalium (1) A0091/14
mortally (2) C0563/08 C0579/28
mortals (1) A0320/07
mortar (2) A0428/22 B1262/06
mortem (2) B0959/35 B1053/34
mortification (6) A0067/23 A0295/24
B0806/04 B1195/07 B1222/04 C0141/08
mortified (3) A0177/23
A0183/18 B1183/04
mortify (1) A0432/12
mortis (1) B1233/18
morto (1) A0344/32
mortuis (1) A0622/20
Mortuorum (1) A0409/11
Mortuus (1) A0213/07
mortuus (1) A0265/27
morty (1) A0356/14
morus (1) B1207/37
mos (7) B0819/32
B0820/29 B1102/37 B1103/01 B1104/03
B1104/17 B1104/17
Mosaic (1) B1179/09
mosaics (1) A0157/03
mosaiques (3) A0175/20
A0181/10 A0345/14
Moscow (2) A0445/06 C0526/24
Moses (1) B1370/14
Moses (1) B1370/06
moshe (1) B0900/03
Moskoe (9) A0579/24
A0579/27 A0580/11 A0581/06 A0581/18
A0581/23 A0582/04 A0582/17 A0583/22
Moskoe-strom (10) A0581/06 A0582/18
A0583/18 A0584/01 A0584/23 A0586/25
A0588/01 A0588/02 A0592/10 A0594/12
Moslemin (3) A0228/28
A0233/09 A0405/V
mosques (1) B0945/22
moss (6) B0980/30 B1260/08
B1279/24 B1279/35 C0150/26 C0543/35
moss-covered (3) A0710/06
B0864/32 B1275/09
Most (2) B0852/27 B0852/28
most (783)
Most/High (2) A0044/07 B1212/10
mostly (4) B0749/10
C0525/02 C0530/08 C0541/30
moth (1) A0314/14
Mother (1) B1130/29
mother (40) A0020/11
A0020/V A0152/08 A0152/19 A0154/04
A0172/05 A0178/06 A0209/23 A0228/02
A0228/34 A0233/16 A0234/20 A0235/08
A0484/01 A0543/31 A0611/15 A0622/25
A0624/08 A0626/02 A0639/06 A0639/16
A0643/V B0725/21 B0729/05 B0731/10
B0748/29 B0753/10 B0755/29 B0887/24
B0888/02 B0925/30 B0932/01 B0933/25
B1090/07 B1166/14 B1371/29 C0066/02
C0407/18 C0413/15 C0421/38
mother-of-pearl (1) A0368/21
mother-tongue (1) B1184/27
Mother/Carey's (2) C0151/29
C0151/29
mother's (13) A0155/05
A0234/24 A0468/19 B0726/19 B0731/26
B0731/31 B0731/36 B0732/38 B0734/18
B0738/32 B0745/08 B0749/05 B1183/10
mothers (1) B1090/01
motion (60)
motioned (1) A0302/02
motioning (1) A0158/07

motionless (31) A0022/10
A0029/V A0059/14 A0066/15 A0080/22
A0089/02 A0162/25 A0190/03 A0198/05
A0214/29 A0216/17 A0566/28 A0609/07
A0612/25 A0612/30 A0639/26 A0676/29
B0764/20 B0795/14 B0859/09 B0962/12
B0964/09 B0983/06 B1240/09 B1281/09
B1382/20 C0113/26 C0123/02 C0142/25
C0182/10 C0412/37
motionlessness (2) A0683/19
A0693/31
motions (11) A0323/24
A0324/14 A0324/23 A0350/12 A0354/21
A0528/25 A0566/27 B0950/13 B1167/15
C0189/22 C0567/13
motive (15) A0442/12
A0446/27 A0547/19 A0556/16 A0556/29
A0556/30 A0556/32 A0557/01 A0558/08
B0736/28 B0987/26 B1051/32 B1220/24
B1220/24 C0205/10
motives (5) A0044/20
B0736/28 B0736/30 B0987/26 C0205/06
motivirt (1) B1220/24
motley (6) A0318/22 A0433/11
B0943/19 B0989/31 B1257/18 B1345/19
motto (4) A0088/10
A0265/26 A0273/29 B1259/36
mouff (3) B0812/24
B0812/28 B0812/31
mought (3) B0811/19
B0820/14 B0820/14
mould (6) A0311/28 A0616/10
B0825/21 B0968/14 B1259/23 C0087/08
moulded (4) A0401/34
A0408/23 C0428/34 C0533/32
mouldering (2) A0144/21 A0616/29
moulds (1) B1054/11
mound (1) B1261/10
mounds (3) C0540/18
C0540/21 C0540/29
Mounseer> (9) A0465/31
A0466/22 A0467/09 A0467/13 A0467/22
A0468/06 A0468/25 A0469/01 A0469/14
Mount/Moriah (1) A0045/07
Mountain (1) A0018/15
mountain (19) A0080/09
A0195/M A0578/18 A0578/29 A0580/36
A0602/11 A0602/11 B0944/35 B0967/08
B1003/18 B1161/05 B1161/11 B1161/26
B1278/05 B1278/21 B1329/12 C0118/17
C0433/03 C0576/28
mountain-slopes (1) A0612/03
mountain-top (1) A0587/36
mountain-tops (1) A0545/19
mountainous (10) A0121/04 A0137/19
A0139/16 A0589/12 A0594/13 B0863/24
B1079/08 C0561/37 C0572/21 C0575/27
Mountains (1) B1179/02
mountains (34) A0071/05 A0071/06
A0137/V A0587/07 A0600/24 A0601/30
A0639/17 A0639/33 A0641/09 A0643/21
B0942/28 B0948/13 B1076/21 B1115/33
B1282/20 B1283/02 B1331/32 B1378/M
C0159/26 C0160/01 C0161/31 C0164/09
C0422/30 C0521/06 C0521/09 C0525/26
->C0525/39 C0527/02 C0527/13 C0528/01
C0528/17 C0565/04 C0572/19 C0575/14
mountebanks (1) A0123/04
mounted (1) C0553/21
mounting (1) A0028/18
mourn (2) A0407/27 B0869/24
mourned (2) A0456/32 A0457/02
mournful (6) A0410/12 A0603/18
A0613/31 B0794/23 B0855/34 B1179/25
mournfully (2) A0604/05 B0964/16
mourning (2) B1004/10 B1008/10
mouse (2) B0794/18 B0870/11
mouse-trap (1) B1163/37
Mouse/River (1) C0551/31
mouser (1) A0653/22
mousike (Gr.) (2) A0610/34 A0611/32
Mousseux (4) A0101/V
A0108/09 A0108/24 A0181/12
Mousseux (1) A0105/16
moustaches (3) A0498/03
A0623/16 B1097/03
mouth (126)
mouthful (1) B1177/05
mouths (8) A0146/12
A0261/13 B1093/36 B1127/08 B1296/31
C0146/11 C0387/20 C0577/06
mouton (1) A0498/02
move (28) A0080/30
A0153/22 A0217/V A0217/V A0329/08
A0407/36 A0513/21 A0536/02 A0593/20
A0601/07 A0684/01 A0685/01 B0794/02
B0966/29 B0967/22 B1081/11 B1091/06
B1157/18 B1346/14 B1363/12 C0074/33
C0119/08 C0119/10 C0119/14 C0119/24
C0120/26 C0151/35 C0563/25
moveable (4) A0673/17
B1089/02 B1336/27 C0188/08
moved (26) A0190/34 A0247/08
A0322/23 A0410/11 A0439/19 A0539/17
A0567/15 A0593/11 A0664/13 A0685/05
B0793/02 B0793/26 B0842/08 B0911/V
B0967/06 B0989/23 B1119/24 B1156/29
B1163/02 B1163/04 B1213/31 B1238/27
C0077/17 C0125/03 C0133/03 C0168/04
movement (47) A0081/06
A0319/20 A0380/13 A0415/29 A0512/26
A0513/05 A0529/07 A0591/18 A0610/06
A0615/07 A0625/22 A0663/26 A0675/19
A0676/03 A0676/15 A0690/01 A0694/04
A0694/11 A0694/18 A0695/01 B0866/06
B0894/04 B0960/22 B0965/34 B0967/10
B1011/30 B1077/14 B1091/22 B1102/15
B1182/16 B1193/27 B1213/36 B1241/12
B1260/17 B1281/10 B1292/10 B1346/09
B1354/10 C0062/25 C0072/36 C0074/07
C0082/14 C0083/04 C0099/19 C0143/16
C0198/07 C0437/V
movements (13) A0416/09
A0508/07 A0616/07 B0989/22 B1193/28
B1362/04 C0169/30 C0197/25 C0390/30
C0533/22 C0548/22 C0549/05 C0549/39
moves (5) A0128/V
A0528/29 A0528/32 B0793/20 C0552/13
Moving (1) B1089/T
moving (11) A0407/09

->A0562/11 B0865/17 B1070/23 B1157/18
B1245/02 B1382/10 C0077/20 C0083/25
C0118/19 C0118/40
Mr (551)

Mrs (45) A0064/16
A0064/22 A0174/07 A0179/22 A0266/15
A0266/37 A0267/05 A0284/26 A0384/13
A0384/30 A0384/30 A0384/32 A0385/06
A0385/07 A0385/17 A0385/20 A0385/24
A0465/21 A0466/10 A0466/31 A0467/02
A0484/V A0662/05 B0872/32 B0873/01
B0873/05 B0909/16 B0911/14 B0911/22
B0911/V B0913/13 B0923/28 B0924/14
B0924/22 B0925/26 B0925/29 B0926/12
B0926/18 B0928/34 B0929/09 B0930/05
B1051/15 B1139/01 B1139/02 B1385/07
much (669)
much-bethumbed (1) A0430/13
much-talked (1) C0178/12
mud (16) A0122/10
A0127/26 A0467/21 A0486/12 A0488/15
A0489/13 B0742/31 B1044/19 B1049/18
B1107/03 C0540/22 C0544/32 C0547/19
C0561/33 C0562/29 C0578/02
mud-dabble (1) A0488/16
Mud-Dabbling (1) A0488/09
Mud-Puddle (1) B1136/39
mud> (1) A0467/01
muddy (5) A0218/28
A0490/08 C0536/02 C0552/38 C0565/19
Mudler (2) B1301/09 B1301/13
muerte (1) A0344/22
muffled (10) A0154/07 A0415/28
A0442/32 A0444/27 A0674/09 B0789/M
B0795/29 B0859/01 B0929/15 B0930/04
mulberries (1) B1292/30
Mulciberian (1) A0054/23
mulct (2) A0251/05 A0252/04
mule-deer (1) C0572/07
mullets (1) C0174/07
multicaulis (1) B1207/37
multicolor (2) A0707/14 B1272/12
multicoloured (1) B0862/36
multifarious (1) A0296/V
multiform (6) A0209/01 A0529/24
A0604/13 A0662/11 A0707/13 B1272/12
multiple (4) B0746/24
B1168/17 B1168/17 B1168/18
multiplication (2) B0773/10
B1089/24
multiplicity (1) A0128/16
multiplied (6) A0215/29 A0430/15
A0445/16 A0528/30 B0746/25 C0156/20
multiplies (1) A0153/15
multiply (2) B0744/20 B0961/08
multiplying (1) B0770/01
multitude (23) A0026/27
A0029/01 A0046/21 A0055/21 A0065/05
A0070/01 A0151/08 A0191/14 A0366/04
A0437/25 A0440/16 A0447/19 A0672/14
A0673/27 B0945/20 B1009/01 B1354/05
C0071/13 C0073/28 C0078/07 C0187/02
C0387/12 C0431/07
multitudinous (5) A0157/26

->B0944/31 B1038/22 B1116/04 B1212/16
mum (1) A0087/14
mumble (1) A0318/15
mumbled (1) C0077/29
Mumblethumb (4) B1136/38
B1137/02 B1137/39 B1139/02
mummer (3) A0675/14
A0676/07 A0676/28
mummies (5) B1181/06
B1183/11 B1185/12 B1188/02 B1188/21
Mummy (13) B1177/T
B1178/20 B1178/22 B1178/31 B1179/15
B1181/17 B1181/29 B1184/23 B1185/14
B1186/18 B1188/07 B1188/28 B1191/30
mummy (4) B1182/17
B1184/03 B1184/27 B1194/34
Mummy's (2) B1183/29 B1195/07
munching (1) B1105/02
Munday, George (1) B1091/35
munificent (5) A0399/02
A0705/13 B1156/10 B1164/22 B1270/11
Munroe (1) B1358/06
Murchison (1) B1115/15
Murder (1) B1380/04
murder (60)
murdered (11) A0448/16
A0557/06 B0723/11 B0734/07 B0745/02
B0769/12 B1047/17 B1047/25 B1053/31
B1057/07 B1225/19
murderer (10) A0023/14 A0544/31
B0727/06 B0737/23 B0765/03 B0766/21
B0766/29 B0771/10 B0771/15 B0771/35
murderers (12) A0551/02
A0551/23 A0552/13 B0732/03 B0732/14
B0738/29 B0739/11 B0744/09 B0744/17
B0744/31 B0744/32 B0763/08
murdering (1) C0555/26
murderous (4) B1057/23
B1059/22 C0086/29 C0184/36
Murders (5) A0527/T
A0527/V B0723/T B0724/12 B0737/33
murders (4) A0537/06
A0544/28 A0546/03 A0563/14
Muriton (2) A0175/18 A0181/08
murky (1) A0152/21
murmur (12) A0195/12
A0197/08 A0198/07 A0319/29 A0416/01
A0446/13 A0536/V A0639/23 A0641/03
A0674/27 B0944/29 B1330/18
murmured (4) A0035/V
A0236/09 A0410/16 A0536/03
murmuring (6) A0227/29 A0232/V
A0415/10 B0929/26 B1225/09 B1333/12
murmurings (1) C0204/25
murmurs (5) A0078/10
A0155/16 A0643/18 A0643/29 B0875/20
Murray (2) B1161/33 B1161/37
mus (7) B0815/10
B0818/12 B0818/16 B0819/06 B0821/05
B0821/23 B1102/19
muscle (9) A0028/16
A0615/02 B0794/02 B0858/16 B0911/V
B1181/23 B1182/14 C0177/06 C0397/10
muscles (9) A0054/08
A0063/17 A0241/02 A0528/04 B0960/20

->B1165/35 B1359/19 B1359/25 C0577/39
muscular (8) A0021/29
A0567/03 B1093/26 B1346/15 C0112/40
C0168/13 C0398/14 C0404/11
muscular-looking (1) A0562/17
Muse (1) B1272/07
muse (3) A0211/29
A0706/30 A0707/08
mused (3) A0216/05
A0604/10 A0604/15
Musee (1) A0536/14
muses (2) A0343/21 A0652/13
Muset (2) A0540/19 A0540/V
Muset, Isidore (1) A0539/32
Museum (1) B1179/11
museums (1) B1270/11
mushrooms (2) A0345/14 A0382/04
Music (1) A0611/32
music (28) A0033/14
A0150/V A0157/23 A0159/21 A0226/15
A0230/13 A0244/18 A0311/22 A0318/13
A0354/15 A0406/06 A0600/04 A0600/10
A0600/15 A0611/27 A0611/35 A0673/29
A0674/01 A0674/15 A0675/30 A0706/29
B1006/14 B1009/09 B1096/08 B1120/07
B1246/06 B1271/31 B1281/15
music-mill (1) A0489/25
musical (20) A0210/01
A0227/06 A0231/17 A0234/30 A0297/21
A0310/07 A0320/V A0399/04 A0401/15
A0611/28 A0613/32 A0672/26 A0682/09
A0683/06 B0889/06 B0904/04 B0904/25
B0915/27 B0990/31 B1004/04
musically (3) A0407/09
A0614/08 B1282/35
musician (5) A0706/14
A0706/28 B1119/22 B1271/17 B1271/30
musicians (3) A0671/08
A0672/28 A0673/02
Musing (1) B1385/07
musing (3) A0024/05
A0091/07 A0142/11
musingly (8) A0110/13
A0159/01 A0165/10 A0180/03 A0383/20
A0604/24 B0913/V B1142/28
musings (1) A0212/23
Musique (1) A0599/01
musique (2) A0545/07 A0599/03
Muskau, Puckler (2) A0705/31
B1269/35
Muskau's (1) B1270/38
musket (8) B0992/20
C0109/25 C0113/18 C0122/37 C0192/30
C0197/23 C0199/14 C0201/08
musket-balls (1) C0180/19
muskets (7) A0058/18
A0069/07 C0085/30 C0109/31 C0112/35
C0180/25 C0184/15
muslin (9) A0246/29
A0247/28 B0730/28 B0730/32 B0766/19
B1339/30 C0393/18 C0394/11 C0395/01
muslins (1) B0945/12
musn't (1) A0387/24
musquash (1) C0536/22
musquitoes (1) C0542/22
Musselmen (1) A0626/13
Mussulman (1) A0035/13
Mussulmen (1) A0591/09
must (377)
mustache (1) A0562/V
mustachio (1) A0562/19
mustachio (1) A0298/V
mustachios (2) A0371/03 A0498/V
mustard (2) A0626/22 B1030/31
muster (2) A0344/11 B0908/12
mustn't (1) A0651/12
musty (2) A0300/30 A0649/02
mutability (1) B1313/33
mutantur (1) B1293/37
mute (4) A0162/25
A0548/08 A0706/22 B1271/25
mutely (1) B0824/16
mutilated (3) A0538/23
A0543/32 A0567/20
mutilation (1) A0547/26
mutineer (1) C0112/35
mutineers (15) C0085/36
C0086/08 C0086/23 C0086/32 C0088/09
C0088/24 C0088/37 C0089/08 C0090/05
C0093/27 C0101/40 C0102/08 C0102/29
C0111/09 C0111/41
mutiny (11) A0127/16
C0053/T C0086/18 C0086/35 C0087/34
C0090/35 C0091/20 C0092/27 C0093/15
C0104/22 C0111/11
mutter (1) A0318/15
muttered (7) A0035/16
A0141/15 A0144/25 A0183/01 A0253/03
A0535/26 A0590/07
muttering (5) A0508/10
B1048/03 B1373/21 C0067/31 C0093/07
mutteringly (2) B0950/25 B1033/18
mutton (5) C0069/24
C0071/03 C0071/22 C0074/04 C0078/33
mutual (1) A0608/16
mutually (1) A0019/07
muy (1) A0621/03
muzzle (1) B0825/20
mxther (1) B1374/08
My (1) A0621/22
my (3702)
Mynheer (4) A0299/32
A0300/09 C0388/05 C0426/33
myriad (2) A0144/19 B1294/13
myriad-tinted (1) B1280/22
myriads (6) A0478/27 B1160/12
B1162/14 B1212/19 C0543/27 C0573/28
Myrmeleon (1) B1162/29
myrmeleon (1) B1162/31
myrmidons (2) B0736/25 B0768/13
myrtle (2) A0233/08 B0807/11
myrtles (1) B0807/24
myself (488)
mysteries (12) A0145/21
A0159/18 A0310/M A0314/26 A0316/16
A0318/V A0455/09 A0506/06 A0589/03
A0624/29 B0962/V C0426/10
mysterious (19) A0023/22
A0025/V A0026/01 A0027/V A0150/01
A0277/04 A0277/06 A0301/08 A0350/28

->A0355/34 A0381/17 A0444/35 A0490/16
A0544/13 A0552/24 B0753/14 B0814/15
B0955/32 B0962/08
mysteriously (2) A0608/15 C0208/25
Mystery (2) B0723/18 B0723/T
mystery (50) A0081/25 A0089/11
A0210/34 A0217/V A0231/15 A0295/07
A0303/22 A0314/06 A0327/03 A0349/30
A0378/12 A0380/28 A0386/23 A0388/27
A0389/15 A0397/22 A0427/16 A0429/09
A0533/26 A0538/25 A0544/30 A0547/16
A0548/06 A0550/24 A0559/31 A0568/17
A0695/24 A0708/34 B0723/12 B0725/04
B0727/13 B0727/31 B0728/16 B0736/23
B0772/29 B0829/32 B0831/27 B0891/10
B0929/06 B0974/12 B0975/31 B0989/08
B1133/09 B1273/27 C0061/09 C0080/22
C0080/30 C0126/18 C0388/06 C0567/10
mystic (3) A0400/02
A0406/19 A0609/28
mystical (6) A0227/02 A0229/15
A0231/V A0608/03 A0625/03 B1374/22
mysticism (3) A0099/08
A0226/05 A0230/03
mystific (1) A0296/01
Mystification (1) A0292/T
mystification (7) A0295/01
A0296/V A0298/08 B0751/23 B0844/06
B0925/31 B0927/26
mystified (2) B0986/16 B1359/07
mystifique (1) A0295/17
mystify (1) C0554/22
Mythology (1) B0987/33
MACHIA (1) A0093/15
MAZA (1) A0093/15
MDCXLVIII (1) C0430/32
MS. (64)
MSS. (16) A0086/04
A0088/05 A0090/02 A0090/33 A0262/20
A0263/14 A0264/03 A0264/12 A0267/01
A0278/37 A0282/28 B0770/11 B0772/03
B1075/26 B1304/07 C0522/31
N. (7) C0136/05
C0147/27 C0412/04 C0412/04 C0526/07
C0527/32 C0528/15
N./B. (1) A0091/13
N./E. (1) C0527/02
N./L. (1) C0527/15
N./N./E. (1) C0099/12
N./P./W. (1) A0280/29
N./W. (3) A0136/12
C0120/02 C0120/23
N./Y. (2) B0731/37 B0731/38
n.e.i. (1) B0880/03
N.B. (1) B0950/11
n'a (2) A0135/M A0135/M
n'aurait (1) A0037/25
n'est (3) A0019/04
A0568/25 B0993/27
n'etait (2) A0037/V A0654/05
n'eut (1) A0037/25
n'ose (1) A0037/02
Naevius (1) A0110/21
Naiad (2) A0210/33 A0599/M
nail (20) A0552/02
->A0552/04 A0552/20 A0552/28 A0552/30
A0553/06 A0553/13 A0553/17 A0553/23
A0553/25 A0553/28 A0554/03 B0762/18
B0821/06 C0068/33 C0069/32 C0070/15
C0070/31 C0075/25 C0092/24
nailed (4) A0542/19
B0824/21 B0967/30 C0075/36
nails (15) A0218/30
A0538/16 A0552/07 A0552/25 A0553/01
A0558/03 A0558/30 B0930/03 B1059/12
B1180/30 C0120/32 C0120/40 C0148/10
C0177/12 C0397/24
naiteral (1) B1375/20
naive (1) C0432/32
naivete (1) B0902/02
naked (15) A0103/26
A0123/02 A0457/07 B0819/01 B0826/23
B1247/28 B1249/18 B1300/32 B1334/33
C0072/25 C0125/24 C0148/37 C0174/20
C0174/30 C0198/12
nakedness (2) A0405/21 A0426/V
name (194)
named (18) A0173/V A0341/V
A0583/06 B0725/14 B0872/02 B0907/18
B0941/02 B1045/01 B1128/24 B1130/03
B1137/11 B1369/20 C0057/17 C0155/40
C0163/34 C0181/26 C0203/36 C0532/08
nameless (6) A0140/V A0235/04
A0676/06 B0967/32 B0976/28 B1222/16
names (22) A0078/V A0101/V
A0160/08 A0337/17 A0337/24 A0430/14
A0473/28 A0579/28 B0887/21 B0887/22
B0887/V B0922/08 B0989/33 B1130/18
B1136/19 B1139/01 B1180/19 B1303/21
B1304/02 B1310/20 B1385/29 C0551/35
namesake (6) A0431/21 A0432/27
A0433/22 A0435/10 A0436/25 A0445/35
Nantucket (14) C0053/T C0057/02
C0058/26 C0061/05 C0061/11 C0064/24
C0064/31 C0071/37 C0073/31 C0084/15
C0087/30 C0101/09 C0127/38 C0142/08
Nantz (3) C0392/20
C0394/05 C0399/33
nap (3) B1081/13 B1105/12 B1105/30
nape (1) A0487/22
Naples (1) A0445/32
Napoleon (1) B0887/V
Napoleons (1) A0537/31
Napoli (1) A0155/01
narcotic (2) A0663/V A0667/18
nare (1) A0603/35
nare (4) A0203/M
A0250/V B0869/20 B1123/13
narrated (3) A0685/13
B0962/01 C0055/17
narrating (2) B1153/17 B1358/27
narration (9) A0341/09
A0403/03 A0568/08 B1153/31 B1155/01
C0096/10 C0203/39 C0207/12 C0523/35
narrations (1) A0150/V
Narrative (2) C0207/22 C0574/40
narrative (50) A0020/04 A0086/23
A0098/12 A0413/25 A0415/15 A0431/19
A0528/20 A0531/12 A0564/V A0608/31
B0723/23 B0725/21 B0728/20 B0772/28

->B0849/01 B0906/09 B1082/03 B1159/17
B1240/01 B1345/17 C0053/T C0055/06
C0056/06 C0056/22 C0057/T C0058/01
C0087/38 C0087/38 C0097/01 C0101/26
C0134/05 C0137/26 C0147/29 C0158/23
C0167/34 C0207/04 C0207/36 C0208/15
C0389/01 C0431/09 C0521/02 C0521/18
C0522/01 C0523/18 C0524/10 C0524/39
C0528/40 C0538/36 C0548/18 C0550/25
narratives (4) A0599/V
A0685/23 B0961/34 C0549/02
narrator's (1) C0523/29
narrow (79)
narrowed (2) A0552/31 B0838/05
narrower (3) A0353/25
A0353/25 B1336/24
narrowly (6) A0400/05 A0616/15
B0831/32 B0838/23 C0547/31 C0553/11
narrowness (1) B0865/08
nascent (1) B1129/10
nascitur (1) A0652/15
Naso (3) A0091/19
A0110/23 A0111/04
Nassau (3) A0381/28
B1070/26 B1075/16
Nassau-balloon (1) C0403/35
Nassau/balloon (1) B1072/22
Nassau/Street (1) B0725/31
nasty (1) A0652/15
nate> (3) A0465/15
A0469/10 A0470/21
nation (12) A0495/V
A0496/03 A0549/25 A0558/19 B0747/34
B1165/26 B1166/16 B1167/07 B1168/09
B1168/13 B1188/11 C0568/15
National (2) A0294/V B1163/13
national (3) A0600/09
B1207/30 C0159/29
nationality (2) A0157/19 A0555/21
nations (6) A0128/17 A0558/10
B1095/04 C0202/26 C0558/01 C0565/40
native (9) A0162/03
A0541/01 A0542/26 A0543/07 A0550/03
B1165/22 B1360/32 C0163/35 C0522/14
natives (23) A0344/02
A0351/22 B1163/21 C0057/23 C0173/35
C0174/14 C0175/06 C0176/29 C0177/12
C0177/19 C0177/36 C0179/31 C0181/18
C0186/22 C0186/40 C0189/01 C0189/32
C0191/24 C0200/14 C0201/01 C0201/10
C0202/29 C0208/16
nativity (3) A0242/24
A0432/30 B0957/24
natur> (2) A0466/29 A0467/29
Natura, De Rerum (1) A0205/15
Naturae (1) B1311/08
naturae (1) B1295/16
Natural (3) B0810/13
B1168/14 B1250/10
natural (115)
naturalibus (1) C0569/25
naturalists (1) B0815/13
naturally (43) A0055/27
A0059/22 A0065/07 A0104/24 A0106/29
A0204/19 A0244/09 A0496/V A0510/21
->A0554/25 A0561/18 A0566/22 A0655/01
B0738/30 B0758/22 B0758/28 B0761/13
B0761/35 B0762/01 B0769/14 B0771/04
B0836/10 B0840/16 B0888/18 B0915/12
B0933/16 B0934/06 B0941/14 B0956/02
B0968/23 B1044/19 B1102/13 B1128/14
B1219/22 B1233/09 B1234/15 B1238/12
B1372/09 B1383/32 B1383/34 B1384/01
C0063/23 C0546/22
naturally-curling (1) A0312/11
naturally-waving (1) A0641/V
naturalness (1) B1126/09
Nature (9) A0123/20
A0610/10 B0772/12 B1213/16 B1272/13
C0524/01 C0537/16 C0542/07 C0564/36
Nature (1) A0096/07
nature (229)
Naturelle (1) C0430/37
Naturwissenschaft (2) A0342/02
A0342/V
naught (2) A0654/12 B0986/31
nausea (2) A0682/05 C0397/11
nauseated (1) B1133/06
nauseous (1) C0553/03
nautical (2) C0059/06 C0167/36
naval (4) A0654/21
B0753/16 B0754/18 B0769/05
navigable (1) B0864/02
navigation (9) A0141/18
A0142/32 B1070/01 B1072/15 B1079/19
C0091/22 C0538/17 C0560/04 C0575/28
navigator (7) A0143/04
C0065/06 C0137/34 C0147/24 C0150/22
C0159/36 C0160/17
navigators (7) A0139/14
A0140/32 C0149/14 C0152/02 C0155/32
C0157/17 C0166/05
navy (3) B0770/33
C0157/12 C0160/16
Naxos (1) B1091/33
nay (3) A0348/09 A0355/34 B0825/09
ne (9) A0018/08
A0019/02 A0033/19 A0379/27 A0380/07
A0506/M A0622/19 A0652/12 B1121/03
ne (1) A0085/06
Neal (3) A0274/29
A0274/30 A0277/34
Neal, John (3) A0272/26
B0869/03 B1141/V
Neal's (2) A0272/30 A0272/36
Neal's, John (1) B1141/V
Neapolitans (1) B0978/15
near (166)
nearer (24) A0089/34
A0437/21 A0579/11 A0589/23 A0589/23
A0591/29 A0591/30 A0665/24 B0866/10
B0891/22 B1014/31 B1157/03 B1282/10
B1382/21 C0123/38 C0131/13 C0161/33
C0167/30 C0389/34 C0401/35 C0528/03
C0530/06 C0566/37 C0566/37
nearest (21) A0704/25
B0822/08 B0824/34 B0824/V B0832/27
B0842/21 B0843/16 B0843/18 B0959/06
B1108/06 B1168/V B1247/23 B1269/24
B1270/27 C0068/16 C0420/15 C0540/23

->C0545/14 C0546/21 C0547/01 C0575/40
nearing (1) C0131/34
nearly (265)
nearly-new (1) A0349/03
neat (14) A0273/26 A0275/15
A0278/32 A0283/01 A0283/21 B0874/33
B0877/36 B1004/02 B1019/29 B1022/01
B1135/29 B1330/06 B1334/38 C0552/32
neatly (5) A0089/12
A0264/34 A0371/05 A0627/33 C0068/26
neatly-folded (1) A0142/12
neatness (4) A0270/37
A0281/02 B1128/23 B1334/18
nebber (2) B0812/24 B0821/23
neber (2) B0809/03 B0811/22
nebula (1) A0536/11
nebulae (4) B1038/23
B1038/23 B1169/32 B1214/V
nebular (1) A0536/10
Nebular/Hypothesis (1) B1320/02
nebulosity (1) C0401/38
nebulous (2) A0616/31 B1317/14
necessaries (3) A0531/24
A0531/V C0148/15
necessarily (33) A0436/29
A0530/29 A0545/14 A0610/20 A0706/20
B0743/13 B0879/05 B0901/18 B0959/15
B0987/27 B0988/33 B1016/34 B1017/03
B1019/26 B1070/14 B1072/08 B1074/16
B1096/19 B1115/25 B1163/32 B1271/22
B1296/15 B1312/18 B1321/13 B1357/09
C0055/18 C0066/19 C0095/04 C0097/08
C0098/12 C0410/42 C0549/11 C0574/34
necessary (126)
necessities (1) B1208/10
necessity (56)
neck (53)
neck-handkerchief (1) B1053/29
necked (1) B1106/22
neckerchief (1) A0509/15
necks (5) A0195/11
B1102/28 B1104/23 B1157/15 C0191/36
necromancers (1) B1167/07
necromancy (3) B0889/20
B1123/17 B1156/30
necromantic (1) B1168/10
need (47) A0120/02
A0122/26 A0205/32 A0246/18 A0341/26
A0342/V A0368/32 A0408/24 A0426/02
A0457/15 A0461/04 A0547/28 A0621/25
A0631/02 A0639/12 B0736/18 B0747/09
B0751/27 B0756/30 B0765/18 B0816/07
B0850/16 B0879/07 B0900/02 B0944/33
B0955/15 B0961/09 B0968/17 B1031/04
B1039/10 B1119/01 B1133/05 B1178/27
B1207/36 B1219/10 B1224/14 B1224/15
B1277/30 B1311/29 B1348/18 B1358/25
B1363/33 C0116/31 C0180/32 C0391/27
C0430/06 C0528/08
needed (7) A0611/01
B0747/02 B1051/18 B1107/04 B1335/03
B1336/13 B1369/02
needing (1) B1336/14
needle (5) B1101/22
B1101/24 B1101/25 B1381/14 C0396/06
needles (3) B0979/26
B0981/10 C0148/10
needless (14) A0240/V A0353/14
A0382/07 A0485/23 A0690/15 B0894/15
B0900/24 B0981/23 B1030/16 B1078/05
B1144/35 B1278/26 C0419/22 C0422/18
needn't (2) B0820/24 B1046/11
needs (1) B0773/35
nefarious (1) A0262/14
negative (9) A0142/18
A0500/26 A0710/22 A0710/35 B1039/11
B1109/22 B1110/03 B1275/24 B1275/35
neglect (10) A0277/23 A0345/04
A0610/28 B0756/18 B0879/27 B1003/21
B1155/04 B1381/02 C0097/06 C0097/11
neglected (13) A0139/09
A0155/05 A0225/17 A0400/14 A0410/32
A0707/05 B0771/10 B0851/11 B0957/20
B1271/19 B1272/05 C0180/14 C0564/16
neglects (1) B1208/13
negligence (1) C0411/21
negligently (1) A0246/02
negotiation (1) C0177/25
negro (29) A0348/28
A0386/29 A0387/V A0388/31 B0807/27
B0811/13 B0814/05 B0818/15 B0818/18
B0819/08 B0819/14 B0820/13 B0820/28
B0821/20 B0824/03 B0824/14 B0824/28
B0866/13 B0866/17 B0901/06 B0931/22
C0085/29 C0100/05 C0146/36 C0430/44
C0532/07 C0532/29 C0569/10 C0569/29
negro-servant (1) A0347/19
negro's (2) B0822/24 B0826/21
negroes (2) B0841/03 C0087/13
neider (1) B0913/V
neighbor (10) A0073/06 A0073/25
A0464/24 A0540/17 A0553/05 B0748/10
B0795/24 B0796/20 B1045/29 C0529/12
neighborhood (28) A0021/16
A0026/03 A0028/28 A0241/24 A0243/07
A0539/11 A0546/23 B0725/28 B0726/25
B0735/19 B0758/20 B0760/24 B0761/02
B0840/28 B1019/08 B1045/12 B1048/28
B1052/25 B1328/15 B1362/06 C0402/11
C0525/22 C0543/09 C0547/33 C0559/33
C0566/01 C0575/05 C0576/37
neighboring (14) A0025/24 A0067/11
A0121/01 A0428/26 A0558/15 A0709/25
B0950/07 B0956/10 B1247/27 B1274/27
C0427/20 C0543/40 C0548/25 C0576/39
neighbors (9) A0019/16
A0101/18 A0537/14 A0539/21 A0539/25
A0564/27 B0856/31 B1045/24 C0551/05
neighbour (1) A0055/08
neighbourhood (6) B0864/05 C0072/01
C0149/13 C0158/19 C0161/31 C0188/33
neighbouring (3) A0059/20
C0172/09 C0189/34
neighed (1) A0347/31
neither (103)
Nellies (1) C0164/03
nelly (1) C0151/28
nem./con. (2) A0491/07 B1056/25
nemo (2) A0125/05 B1260/01
Neopolitan (1) A0446/21

Nep (3) C0541/16 C0541/17 C0541/18
nephew (10) B1047/13 B1047/14
B1047/33 B1051/03 B1052/18 B1053/08
B1053/12 B1055/10 B1069/17 C0154/12
nephew's (1) B1051/36
Neptune (7) B1321/14
B1321/14 B1321/V B1390/08 C0544/23
C0566/31 C0568/37
Neptune's (1) C0545/29
Neptunian (1) B1302/17
Nereus (1) C0155/38
Nergal (1) A0046/10
Nero (3) A0022/V
A0093/05 A0112/17
nerve (11) A0406/06
A0615/02 A0692/29 A0692/32 A0694/34
B0890/02 B0992/31 B1038/05 B1038/05
C0111/08 C0397/10
nerves (18) A0021/30 A0211/V
A0227/19 A0232/06 A0354/35 A0578/04
A0588/28 A0687/23 A0692/10 A0695/31
B0871/01 B0965/07 B1007/25 B1014/26
B1177/02 B1182/16 B1248/37 C0578/40
nerving (1) A0328/06
nervous (31) A0102/17
A0135/26 A0161/22 A0189/29 A0211/25
A0262/21 A0276/35 A0324/10 A0378/10
A0398/20 A0402/16 A0402/33 A0542/27
A0567/14 A0581/02 A0667/06 A0693/27
B0789/01 B0789/01 B0795/19 B0814/25
B0871/01 B0928/18 B0943/23 B0946/32
B1030/31 B1102/13 B1182/04 B1234/12
B1391/03 C0111/24
nervously (2) A0695/12 B1348/12
nervousness (5) A0274/08
A0411/18 A0415/03 A0441/25 A0673/03
nest (6) C0152/35 C0152/35
C0152/37 C0153/02 C0153/09 C0178/21
nestled (1) C0173/05
nestling (1) C0153/09
nests (7) C0151/40
C0152/02 C0153/03 C0153/16 C0178/13
C0570/16 C0573/29
net (2) A0487/29 C0552/26
net-work (10) B1292/24 C0393/24
C0409/21 C0409/24 C0409/25 C0409/25
C0409/27 C0409/39 C0410/11 C0425/04
nether (4) A0035/10
A0690/16 B1102/25 B1108/14
nethermost (1) B0961/33
nettings (1) C0187/41
nettled (2) A0249/21 B0810/03
network (3) A0501/14
B1071/07 B1081/02
Neuclid (1) B1295/11
Neufchatel-ish (1) A0562/22
neuralgia (1) B0949/33
neuralgic (1) B0940/31
neutral (1) B1337/33
neutralize (1) B1314/27
never (423)
never-ceasing (1) A0156/22
never-dying (1) A0036/11
never-to-be-forgotten (1) A0443/03
never-to-be-imparted (1) A0145/24
nevertheless (69)
New (8) A0138/16
B0863/17 B1081/04 B1141/07 B1192/08
B1328/02 C0428/09 C0522/18
new (92)
new-fledged (1) B1211/01
new-style (1) A0485/07
new-touch (1) A0485/V
New-Bank (1) C0057/05
New-York (4) A0493/04
B1246/01 C0056/32 C0163/35
New-York/Sun (1) B1068/10
New/Bedford (5) C0057/11
C0057/15 C0066/27 C0066/34 C0067/06
New/Compendium (1) A0338/23
New/London (1) C0061/25
New/Monthly (1) A0174/04
New/Orleans (2) A0490/18 B0806/05
New/Year's (1) A0487/05
New/York (29) A0266/23
A0268/02 A0268/23 A0269/14 A0271/32
A0276/07 A0494/02 B0723/11 B0724/11
B0734/40 B0740/33 B0753/39 B0753/39
B0753/39 B0753/42 B0754/35 B0754/35
B0862/09 B0922/02 B0925/16 B0925/26
B0925/34 B0933/13 B0933/24 B1234/06
B1304/21 B1361/01 B1361/16 C0448/V
New/York/Sun (2) C0428/08 C0448/V
New/Zealand (1) B1163/14
Newfoundland (5) B0809/20
B0832/08 B1092/02 C0073/10 C0532/15
newly (6) A0157/27 A0217/05
A0246/27 A0247/27 B0759/13 B0923/20
news (8) B0732/40
B0733/12 B0770/34 B1068/01 B1069/01
B1246/09 B1294/04 C0101/18
newspaper (11) A0507/17
B0729/01 B0753/03 B1068/11 B1090/16
B1090/21 B1101/08 B1110/20 B1145/12
B1369/15 C0391/23
newspapers (13) A0058/25
B0723/19 B0734/05 B0736/08 B0738/06
B0752/26 B0760/30 B1304/03 B1305/11
B1358/04 C0388/18 C0427/22 C0427/23
Newton (5) A0479/03
B1035/10 B1167/32 B1297/32 B1317/10
next (108)
next-door (1) B1045/24
_ni_ (1) A0096/M
Niagara (3) A0580/34
B0862/08 C0387/21
Niagara/Falls (1) B1017/33
nib (1) A0339/09
nibble (1) A0128/10
nibbled (1) C0545/17
nibblers (2) C0545/31 C0545/41
nibbling (1) C0545/06
nibblings (1) B1158/07
Nibhaz (1) A0046/11
Nicander (1) A0111/04
Nicanor, Seleucus (1) A0120/22
nice (11) A0098/26
A0299/10 A0339/32 A0345/17 A0486/09
A0488/21 A0709/26 A0710/14 B1274/28
B1275/17 C0178/08

nicely (3) B0741/21
B1129/05 B1337/04
nicer (1) C0068/13
nicest (1) C0124/32
niceties (1) B1345/13
nicety (4) A0298/05
A0302/20 B0822/05 B1279/11
niche (8) A0035/21
A0153/09 A0154/05 A0663/19 B0841/19
B1261/23 B1262/08 B1263/02
niches (3) A0035/18
A0688/30 C0573/20
Nichol (1) A0535/09
nicht (2) A0506/02 A0515/33
Nick (1) A0373/24
Nicolino (3) B0923/16
B0925/07 B0925/11
Niebuhr (1) B1089/08
niece (1) B1005/01
niente (1) A0296/09
nier (1) A0568/24
Niger (1) B1162/28
niggardly (1) A0346/25
nigger (6) A0348/V A0388/13
B0818/23 B0820/19 B0820/24 B0826/28
niggerless (1) A0357/11
nigh (4) B1091/06
B1384/22 C0147/33 C0562/01
Night (1) B0969/05
night (289)
night-cap (1) B1178/07
night-clothes (1) A0566/V
night-fall (1) A0512/08
Night-Mare (1) B0856/07
night's (3) B0829/36
B0851/31 B1277/23
nightcap (1) B0968/31
nightfall (1) C0537/33
Nightingale (1) A0710/32
Nightingale/Island (2) C0155/14
C0156/21
nightly (4) A0163/05
A0242/33 A0431/02 A0506/03
nightmare (3) A0079/29
B0968/23 B1225/20
nights (16) A0101/23
A0138/09 A0323/23 B0793/10 B0928/19
B0928/33 B0929/08 B0930/02 B0979/17
B1154/09 C0069/41 C0084/33 C0095/12
C0120/27 C0154/15 C0563/34
nihil (2) B1296/25 B1313/26
nihility (2) B1034/17 B1039/33
nihilo (2) B1296/25 B1313/26
Nil (1) B0974/M
nil (5) A0091/27
A0110/28 A0568/V A0622/20 B1009/15
Nile (3) B1179/03
B1188/20 B1192/23
nill (2) A0385/20 B1153/04
nill-I (1) B1220/01
nimbleness (1) B1108/15
nimbly (1) A0630/18
nimio (2) A0568/V B0974/M
Nimmy (1) A0349/18
Nimrod (2) A0093/04 A0112/17

nincompoop (3) A0093/32
A0113/13 A0374/15
nine (48) A0043/03
A0066/22 A0125/36 A0240/V A0284/18
A0349/03 A0352/30 A0372/29 A0484/15
A0528/30 A0705/21 B0729/06 B0738/35
B0745/10 B0750/08 B0750/09 B0750/11
B0808/05 B0942/26 B1071/06 B1077/08
B1078/28 B1079/14 B1135/20 B1167/16
B1181/20 B1233/14 B1270/20 B1299/09
B1303/01 B1310/15 C0064/23 C0085/32
C0105/03 C0122/23 C0157/05 C0172/19
C0405/41 C0411/18 C0411/35 C0412/02
C0412/07 C0417/40 C0419/17 C0424/10
C0558/30 C0562/10 C0565/32
nine-tenths (4) B0888/11
B0933/27 B1278/09 B1303/22
nineteenth (6) A0121/17 A0432/28
B1195/13 C0135/36 C0135/38 C0425/21
ninety (6) A0705/32 B1185/05
B1269/36 B1331/20 C0154/32 C0179/14
ninety-four (1) C0399/21
ninety-fourth (1) A0189/13
ninety-gun (1) A0587/03
ninety-nine (3) B0757/07
B1314/17 B1345/33
ninety-ninth (2) A0174/32 A0180/23
ninety-one (3) A0175/32
A0181/32 C0146/40
ninety-seven (1) B0828/13
Nineveh (2) A0059/10 A0061/05
ninny (2) A0177/18 A0183/15
Ninon (3) B0898/08
B0898/08 B0898/08
ninth (3) A0302/18
B1262/33 C0147/28
Niobe (1) A0153/03
nisi (1) A0622/20
nitre (6) B0832/23 B1258/14
B1259/06 B1259/07 B1260/08 B1261/32
nitrogen (5) A0460/24
A0460/25 A0460/29 A0460/34 C0403/15
niver> (4) A0465/30
A0467/18 A0468/27 A0470/15
nixt> (2) A0464/23 A0465/26
No (1) A0020/V
No (1) A0344/25
no (4) A0161/03
A0344/23 A0354/31 A0621/03
no (1876)
No. (7) A0561/01
B0876/28 B0876/29 B0876/29 B0877/08
B0877/12 B0879/14
No./1 (1) B1055/29
No./33 (1) B0974/04
No./79 (1) A0388/V
no-o-o (1) A0386/14
Noah (1) A0285/01
Noah, M. (1) A0284/36
nobility (8) A0026/09
A0086/29 A0496/19 A0496/20 A0705/11
B0903/07 B0907/22 B1270/10
noble (27) A0024/15
A0025/08 A0027/22 A0045/25 A0085/08
A0126/01 A0128/23 A0189/19 A0213/04

->A0250/11 A0264/09 A0271/19 A0292/01
A0356/12 A0431/17 A0536/09 A0610/04
B0864/28 B0866/16 B0899/21 B1055/01
B1139/34 B1390/13 C0073/29 C0537/02
C0554/09 C0567/32
noble-spirited (1) B0900/04
nobleman (7) A0020/20
A0021/20 A0023/08 A0025/02 A0026/19
A0028/08 A0440/36
noblemen (1) A0508/17
nobles (1) A0496/23
noblest (5) A0440/31
A0706/03 A0706/24 B1271/07 B1271/26
Noblet (1) A0079/08
nobody (21) A0252/26
A0336/02 A0337/08 A0372/18 A0468/20
A0488/24 A0490/22 A0623/30 B0731/28
B0732/35 B0733/31 B0748/23 B0871/16
B0928/27 B0990/24 B1045/11 B1048/27
B1167/19 B1292/01 B1292/09 B1371/33
nobody's (3) B1299/36
B1373/18 C0061/32
nocturnal (1) A0244/06
nod (2) A0195/11 B1109/21
Nodaway (1) C0541/04
nodded (7) A0246/04
A0249/11 A0253/V B1109/28 B1109/30
B1109/32 B1259/25
nodding (2) C0123/36 C0124/36
nods (1) B0895/V
noffin (4) B0811/33
B0812/16 B0813/01 B0821/01
noin (1) A0372/31
noise (46) A0123/25 A0128/V
A0137/04 A0195/21 A0326/28 A0341/17
A0413/34 A0414/24 A0482/13 A0581/26
A0582/12 A0588/12 A0690/03 B0794/14
B0795/20 B0797/05 B0797/12 B0797/14
B0797/16 B0797/19 B0823/16 B0929/28
B0979/37 B1014/33 B1092/30 B1097/01
B1155/06 B1156/36 B1157/25 B1262/15
B1349/11 B1349/34 C0083/17 C0094/19
C0095/39 C0106/31 C0110/16 C0188/32
C0408/25 C0412/33 C0419/23 C0420/04
C0539/08 C0539/11 C0545/31 C0552/12
noiselessly (2) A0437/10 A0602/24
noises (9) A0074/33
A0078/09 A0078/11 A0414/10 A0542/07
B0929/10 B1009/08 B1080/20 B1102/35
noisome (4) A0243/28
A0244/21 A0514/22 C0552/22
noisy (1) A0510/28
nom (4) B0723/26
B1136/24 B1138/01 B1234/04
nom-de-guerre (1) B1139/13
nom-de-plume (1) B1137/10
nombre (1) B0987/01
nommy (1) A0354/33
non (14) A0161/04 A0301/10
A0302/20 A0303/17 A0344/31 A0356/13
A0652/15 A0662/V A0681/M B0880/04
B0905/23 B0986/19 C0180/32 C0430/38
non-admeasurement (1) B0985/11
non-appearance (2) B0962/23
B0976/17
non-entity (1) B1213/26
non-epistolary (1) A0264/19
non-luminosity (1) B1301/19
non-luminous (1) B1301/21
non-plused (1) A0628/10
nonce (2) B0872/10 B0923/18
nonchalance (5) B0870/02
B0893/24 B0907/V C0058/41 C0404/32
nonchalance (1) B0870/33
nonchalant (1) B0870/33
nondescript (3) A0126/21
A0387/15 B1102/23
none (93)
nonentities (1) B1039/01
nonentity (3) A0210/07
B0947/35 B0966/16
nonplussed (1) A0105/20
nonsense (13) A0093/26
A0113/V A0153/13 A0303/24 A0708/11
B0808/32 B0820/21 B0975/29 B1116/11
B1130/26 B1165/30 B1391/03 C0061/31
noodle (2) A0177/20 A0183/16
nook (6) A0627/29 A0629/02
B0863/13 B0945/05 B0978/22 C0154/03
nooks (6) A0436/30 A0663/01
B0760/06 B0862/16 B0986/01 B0988/35
noon (45) A0026/32
A0138/22 A0173/17 A0178/26 A0210/12
A0227/35 A0318/03 A0330/07 A0370/21
A0370/28 A0371/29 A0372/13 A0484/21
A0512/29 A0541/20 A0547/07 A0612/30
A0616/06 B0731/32 B0731/33 B0958/30
B1079/24 B1178/08 B1391/09 C0100/34
C0102/14 C0108/01 C0115/17 C0130/29
C0137/16 C0139/30 C0140/16 C0146/06
C0162/23 C0163/03 C0163/37 C0164/18
C0387/15 C0540/17 C0542/31 C0553/14
C0559/09 C0565/22 C0566/29 C0570/34
noon-day (1) A0640/09
noonday (3) A0214/04
B0865/07 C0412/34
noose (5) A0027/18
A0058/23 A0069/12 B0852/20 C0141/16
nooses (1) C0409/28
Nootka (1) C0526/18
noovers (1) B0812/06
Nopolis (4) B1369/25
B1369/31 B1370/08 B1374/05
nor (200)
Nordland (2) A0578/28 B1391/V
Norfolk (2) B1068/01 C0103/26
Norland (1) B1391/09
normal (2) B1030/03 B1032/02
Norman (1) A0322/25
North (4) B0874/17
B0909/17 B1075/22 B1077/22
north (56)
North-east (1) B0909/17
north-eastern (1) B1338/14
north-west (2) B1333/12 C0525/18
north-western (1) B1332/20
north-westwardly (1) C0525/29
North-Eastern (1) A0478/01
North-West/Company's (1) C0530/12
North-Western (1) C0524/24

North/America (11) B1077/28
C0419/03 C0521/14 C0521/T C0524/25
C0524/41 C0529/T C0540/T C0550/T
C0560/T C0571/T
North/American (2) A0622/09
C0575/01
North/West/Fur/Company (1) C0527/34
northeast (10) B0839/32 B0840/22
B0842/04 B1080/18 C0149/20 C0150/34
C0155/17 C0162/26 C0162/32 C0167/01
northerly (1) C0195/12
Northern (1) B1299/20
northern (32) A0146/13
B0862/01 B1302/32 B1331/15 B1331/19
B1334/02 B1334/33 B1336/15 B1338/05
B1338/15 C0150/35 C0157/07 C0159/21
C0166/10 C0171/19 C0192/04 C0407/37
C0417/34 C0418/06 C0419/17 C0525/27
C0526/32 C0526/36 C0527/04 C0528/02
C0532/12 C0535/33 C0551/12 C0554/02
C0558/31 C0572/18 C0574/10
Northern/Liberties (1) A0273/37
Northman (1) A0322/V
northward (29) A0138/18
A0579/25 B0814/22 B0841/02 B0925/36
C0104/32 C0129/27 C0129/40 C0139/25
C0140/18 C0140/35 C0149/15 C0149/20
C0149/26 C0154/21 C0156/28 C0159/12
C0161/35 C0163/39 C0165/23 C0165/26
C0198/37 C0202/06 C0203/10 C0204/21
C0407/32 C0416/21 C0417/08 C0417/15
northwardly (3) C0207/45
C0208/11 C0418/15
northwest (2) C0158/32 C0163/24
Northwest/Fur/Company (2) C0529/06
C0534/31
northwesterly (2) B0817/15 C0140/18
northwestern (1) C0155/03
northwesternly (1) B0817/V
Norway (2) A0581/34 A0585/32
Norwegian (1) A0578/26
Norwegians (3) A0579/24
A0581/05 A0583/10
nose (108)
noses (6) A0173/13 A0176/13
A0178/21 B1157/20 C0388/19 C0388/20
Nosology (12) A0173/11
A0173/12 A0174/01 A0175/01 A0177/25
A0178/07 A0178/19 A0178/20 A0179/12
A0180/24 A0182/13 A0183/20
nosology (1) A0172/06
nostril (1) A0401/33
nostrils (11) A0312/17
A0615/29 A0687/03 A0691/07 A0696/01
B0741/18 B0741/30 B0967/26 B1106/27
B1156/34 C0567/40
not (2838)
not-over-acute (1) B0761/35
notable (1) C0395/08
note (57)
note-book (3) B0949/24
B1359/27 B1360/05
notebook (1) B1189/13
noted (13) A0398/32
A0508/15 A0529/13 A0638/01 A0640/27
->B0731/09 B0750/03 B0753/17 B0850/08
B0863/18 B0878/07 B0899/02 B1345/04
Notes (1) B1095/T
notes (15) A0283/13
A0366/19 A0406/12 A0530/12 B0736/19
B0747/28 B0757/01 B0874/03 B0874/08
B1036/29 B1068/09 B1113/13 B1115/19
B1236/23 B1325/08
nothing (363)
nothingness (4) A0617/06
A0682/14 A0683/10 B1302/12
notice (49) A0091/30
A0110/32 A0136/17 A0140/28 A0142/10
A0164/10 A0298/V A0337/32 A0338/16
A0350/09 A0415/15 A0445/23 A0536/08
A0547/24 A0551/22 A0556/21 A0690/03
B0725/25 B0729/07 B0731/20 B0750/12
B0760/29 B0761/31 B0768/11 B0829/32
B0854/15 B0877/30 B0914/24 B0957/16
B0977/09 B0978/32 B1136/22 B1137/01
B1159/35 B1338/17 B1339/13 B1345/21
C0059/12 C0064/28 C0068/05 C0110/32
C0122/32 C0123/40 C0130/32 C0178/04
C0525/35 C0531/12 C0548/02 C0548/13
noticeable (9) A0313/07
A0327/04 A0445/16 A0459/07 B1181/32
B1234/07 B1238/10 B1361/09 B1364/32
noticed (33) A0120/09
A0274/30 A0283/06 A0284/06 A0313/27
A0352/32 A0380/15 A0389/04 A0404/07
A0415/04 A0435/08 A0515/25 A0628/22
A0689/08 B0735/28 B0771/13 B0814/06
B0895/07 B0989/25 B1007/32 B1040/11
B1052/13 B1221/19 C0067/41 C0085/06
C0132/03 C0173/33 C0174/08 C0180/29
C0194/07 C0199/38 C0204/18 C0421/12
notices (4) B1129/14
B1135/34 B1138/18 B1143/26
noticing (4) A0090/23
A0400/21 B1120/08 C0415/36
notifying (1) B0756/26
notin (1) B0811/22
notion (15) A0096/14
A0226/36 A0231/10 A0267/08 A0386/19
A0432/21 A0486/04 A0583/11 B0850/31
B1034/19 B1186/29 B1219/12 B1295/28
C0071/37 C0112/13
notions (23) A0090/30
A0107/30 A0109/21 A0127/15 A0262/03
A0297/03 A0353/07 A0482/09 A0496/13
A0557/08 B0740/05 B0810/08 B0975/11
B0985/28 B1008/18 B1299/15 B1382/04
C0093/27 C0202/09 C0392/30 C0432/33
C0522/12 C0537/23
notoriety (8) A0262/32
B0726/29 B0749/14 B0864/14 B0915/14
B1360/30 B1380/02 C0403/36
notorious (9) A0033/10
A0061/01 A0122/23 A0135/12 B0726/03
B0757/15 B0864/08 B0915/13 B1384/06
notoriously (1) A0534/19
Notre (1) A0096/V
notre (2) A0611/04 C0430/29
notwithstanding (27) A0337/31
A0346/24 A0366/21 A0431/17 A0540/21

->A0601/04 A0624/22 A0627/25 A0684/22
A0691/33 B0747/30 B0758/14 B0763/16
B1052/32 B1079/05 B1093/01 B1154/02
B1346/10 C0056/03 C0139/08 C0432/31
C0538/10 C0540/16 C0553/07 C0556/31
C0561/09 C0576/10
noumena (2) B1295/17 B1311/10
noun (1) A0469/27
nouns (1) A0203/04
nourishes (1) C0179/11
nourishment (3) C0138/04
C0138/10 C0141/18
Nourjabad (1) A0313/V
Nourjahad (1) A0313/05
nous (Gr.) (5) A0089/30
A0108/15 A0108/21 A0108/V A0108/V
nouuellement (1) C0430/28
Nouvelette (1) B1137/36
Nouvelle/Heloise (1) A0568/26
Novalis (2) B0723/M B0946/08
novel (33) A0022/06
A0079/12 A0123/27 A0141/28 A0162/08
A0211/17 A0344/06 A0348/19 A0439/09
A0440/16 A0455/14 A0581/11 A0671/24
A0683/04 A0706/07 A0706/13 A0707/11
B0944/27 B1070/18 B1184/29 B1190/19
B1271/11 B1271/16 B1272/10 B1340/15
B1347/06 B1347/33 B1348/25 B1379/19
C0171/21 C0387/03 C0394/14 C0543/11
novel-hero (1) B1116/01
novelist (4) A0086/24
A0087/12 A0493/03 A0621/25
novelists (2) A0100/23 A0341/16
novels (4) A0079/05
A0630/V B1051/15 B1051/19
novelties (1) C0523/39
novelty (19) A0141/04
A0296/V A0408/04 A0459/32 A0507/28
A0608/09 A0711/16 B0808/10 B0866/08
B1047/28 B1078/30 B1276/17 B1335/20
C0093/28 C0203/22 C0522/06 C0523/18
C0550/27 C0574/08
November (6) A0227/27 B0723/13
B0942/16 B1100/01 C0156/29 C0159/13
novice (1) B0989/32
Now (1) B0772/20
now (1166)
now-a-days (2) A0089/29 B1291/08
nowhar (1) B0811/26
nowhere (3) A0312/14
B1335/02 B1374/27
Nu-Nu (6) C0204/06 C0204/22
C0205/03 C0205/06 C0205/20 C0206/02
Nubia (1) A0611/14
Nubian (4) A0578/34
A0638/14 B1291/08 B1310/06
nucleus (3) A0458/30
A0460/13 A0461/13
nudge (1) B1194/19
nues (1) A0035/10
nuff (2) B0820/13 B0821/05
nuisance (1) B1193/30
null (1) B0759/24
nullity (2) A0135/22 A0553/14
nullus (1) A0599/M

numb (1) B0963/03
Number (2) B0870/16 B0870/16
number (108)
numbered (9) A0264/35
B0903/17 B0903/18 B0980/21 B1055/19
B1059/15 C0531/11 C0551/36 C0561/41
numbering (1) C0551/21
numberless (1) B1214/35
numbers (13) B0764/23
B0946/33 B1096/29 B1384/08 C0056/10
C0151/09 C0152/09 C0172/29 C0417/38
C0428/21 C0530/22 C0561/38 C0567/07
numbness (3) A0437/17
C0119/13 C0204/33
numerous (46) A0026/03 A0070/18
A0081/40 A0122/08 A0211/08 A0243/07
A0268/05 A0409/17 A0500/03 A0508/06
A0556/08 A0591/31 A0663/18 B0727/11
B0736/29 B0752/11 B0754/01 B0762/34
B0887/V B0941/19 B0957/14 B0960/04
B0978/13 B0987/28 B1007/27 B1034/30
B1076/16 B1101/20 B1115/09 B1138/37
B1154/33 B1179/05 B1180/15 B1259/31
B1293/08 B1313/28 B1329/06 B1332/03
B1337/30 C0065/23 C0393/26 C0548/03
C0548/14 C0551/02 C0570/04 C0577/04
numerously (1) A0490/35
nunc (2) A0681/M A0681/M
nunquam (1) B0870/21
nuptials (1) A0214/15
nurse (7) A0214/17
A0482/11 A0483/V A0486/30 B1047/04
B1090/07 B1236/11
nursed (1) A0227/26
nurses (6) B1016/19 B1090/02
B1238/04 B1240/06 B1240/34 B1241/19
nurses' (1) B1241/34
nurtured (2) A0446/18 B1122/28
nutmegs (1) A0482/25
nutriment (3) B1162/35
C0396/10 C0535/37
nutritious (2) C0138/15 C0145/19
nutritive (1) C0535/41
nuts (6) A0356/21 A0625/V
C0181/36 C0181/39 C0188/22 C0192/24
nx (4) B1374/09
B1374/09 B1374/13 B1374/14
nxbxdy (1) B1374/12
nxne (1) B1374/17
nxr (3) B1374/18 B1374/18 B1374/18
nxw (3) B1374/07 B1374/09 B1374/16
C (18) A0035/28 A0035/28
A0053/27 A0061/M A0080/20 A0319/19
A0319/21 A0319/21 A0344/26 A0384/01
A0385/12 A0388/18 B1156/09 B1370/14
B1370/18 B1370/27 B1371/01 B1371/02
c (1) B0838/21
c (9) A0174/17
A0174/18 B0978/11 B1350/18 B1370/20
B1372/33 B1373/18 B1386/03 B1386/03
C (Gr.) (1) A0089/30
c (Gr.) (5) A0108/15
A0108/21 A0108/V A0108/V A0346/03
C-ing (1) B1370/18
c-o-o-o-gh (2) B1012/08 B1012/09

O-wy (2) B1371/02 B1371/02
o-wy (1) B1374/02
O' (1) A0621/22
o' (4) A0292/M
A0464/04 B0968/03 B1375/20
o'> (28) A0464/02
A0464/06 A0464/08 A0464/16 A0465/07
A0465/11 A0465/14 A0465/17 A0465/24
A0465/24 A0465/27 A0465/V A0466/09
A0466/10 A0466/15 A0466/15 A0466/31
A0466/33 A0467/11 A0467/30 A0468/09
A0468/11 A0468/13 A0468/26 A0469/03
A0469/07 A0469/14 A0469/19
o'clock (62)
o'er (3) A0162/23
A0162/27 A0163/11
o'ercast (1) A0228/07
O's (1) B1370/19
o's (1) B1372/30
O'Bumper, Bibulus (1) A0181/11
O'Connell, Daniel (1) B0870/31
O'Grandison, Sir Pathrick (11) A0464/03
A0464/13 A0465/14 A0465/23 A0466/13
A0467/03 A0468/03 A0468/13 A0469/23
A0470/15 A0470/16
O'Phlegethon, Andrew (1) A0356/25
O'Rafferty (1) A0374/V
O'Rourke, Thomas (1) C0432/47
O'Trump (3) A0384/30
A0384/31 A0384/33
O'Trump, Kathleen (1) A0384/13
oak (10) A0087/20 A0102/06
A0143/01 A0143/01 A0321/20 A0367/V
A0430/02 B1332/04 C0541/31 C0549/24
oak-plank (1) C0533/19
Oak/Hill (1) A0274/17
oaken (3) A0241/29
A0401/08 A0562/20
oaks (3) A0029/05
B0817/35 C0542/12
oakum (1) C0533/19
oar (5) A0151/28
A0155/24 A0604/19 C0088/23 C0168/05
oars (6) B0932/28 C0533/04
C0533/25 C0535/26 C0540/03 C0554/01
oarsman (1) B1281/05
Oasis (1) B1193/18
oasis (1) A0427/10
oat-meal (1) A0341/V
oath (15) A0035/16
A0101/20 A0253/16 A0346/14 A0447/14
A0469/25 A0628/19 A0653/V B0824/02
B1049/24 B1105/06 C0058/09 C0395/03
C0426/38 C0427/25
oaths (1) B0965/21
oatmeal (1) A0342/18
ob (15) B0811/V
B0812/07 B0812/28 B0812/29 B0812/29
B0812/30 B0814/18 B0820/18 B0821/02
B0821/07 B0821/22 B0826/26 B0826/27
B0826/28 B1103/03
ob'nt (1) B1055/21
obaysance> (1) A0466/32
obedient (13) A0264/20
A0267/21 A0269/27 A0274/01 A0274/23
->A0276/12 A0279/33 A0281/35 A0282/35
A0302/26 A0370/04 A0665/09 B1371/18
cbelisks (3) B1192/25
B1193/09 B1193/21
cbesity (1) A0298/V
cbey (3) A0652/28
B0915/30 C0108/08
cbeyed (8) A0318/05
A0398/28 B0819/08 B0899/22 B1015/25
B1238/31 B1347/21 C0557/31
cbject (143)
cbjected (2) B1002/09 C0105/22
cbjection (15) A0274/19
A0299/02 B0744/11 B1035/05 B1035/16
B1077/30 B1097/08 B1135/20 B1138/11
B1177/08 B1237/06 B1379/21 C0056/08
C0429/28 C0529/29
cbjectionable (5) A0299/32
A0711/05 B1121/03 B1276/07 B1278/17
cbjective (1) B1220/18
cbjectivity (1) A0341/24
cbjectless (5) A0410/33
A0437/19 A0546/17 B0753/02 B0947/V
cbjects (64)
cblate (1) C0417/28
cbligation (1) C0430/37
cbligation (5) B0875/10
B0875/11 B0892/V C0073/33 C0523/28
cblige (10) A0279/31 A0650/22
A0651/08 A0651/11 B0816/10 B0872/20
B0892/V B1045/16 C0523/15 C0555/13
cbliged (27) A0271/34
A0275/27 A0385/20 A0411/07 A0512/26
A0625/25 A0629/08 A0653/04 B0747/36
B0898/16 B0979/37 B1005/15 B1110/03
C0064/08 C0066/19 C0077/19 C0122/10
C0139/25 C0144/08 C0161/18 C0161/20
C0170/02 C0192/05 C0416/33 C0542/27
C0572/28 C0572/30
cbliging (4) A0268/03
C0180/04 C0564/09 C0565/13
cbligingly (1) A0352/14
cbliquely (1) C0402/06
cbliquity (1) A0379/17
cbliterated (2) B0764/14 C0172/12
cbliterates (1) B0880/08
cblivion (1) C0148/38
Cblong (1) B0922/T
cblong (15) A0501/03
B0826/01 B0831/17 B0924/31 B0924/35
B0927/24 B0929/14 B0929/33 B0930/03
B0931/31 B0932/23 B1179/21 C0178/22
C0399/18 C0573/36
cbras (1) A0621/04
cbsarve> (1) A0468/01
cbscenities (1) A0612/02
cbscure (7) A0054/34
A0064/01 A0531/28 B0771/16 B0862/15
B1385/24 C0392/07
cbscurity (1) A0366/21
observable (11) A0106/V
A0274/30 A0275/37 A0406/15 A0410/29
A0497/13 B1240/07 B1335/01 C0419/30
C0421/11 C0558/22
cbservant (1) B1219/18

observation (52)
observations (25) A0096/08
A0142/16 A0279/22 A0507/31 A0512/05
A0528/20 A0530/02 A0592/24 A0593/06
A0711/04 B0797/15 B0988/14 B1004/27
B1019/31 B1050/18 B1276/06 B1358/01
C0126/02 C0157/01 C0157/06 C0423/10
C0523/19 C0524/26 C0538/31 C0538/33
observe (48) A0024/08
A0064/15 A0107/10 A0123/13 A0286/07
A0293/22 A0324/10 A0346/08 A0387/05
A0512/19 A0527/V A0529/26 A0530/05
A0549/11 A0590/28 A0608/07 B0736/22
B0744/25 B0745/16 B0747/13 B0750/26
B0769/08 B0789/06 B0831/15 B0833/28
B0834/09 B0836/13 B0837/11 B0840/18
B0888/V B0932/31 B0977/36 B1012/08
B1051/12 B1055/06 B1116/10 B1135/10
B1259/02 B1339/09 B1339/12 B1380/23
C0146/26 C0207/23 C0425/05 C0533/22
C0546/30 C0568/24 C0569/26
observed (130)
observer (15) A0104/28
A0144/09 A0400/17 A0709/27 B0760/21
B0764/30 B0974/06 B1274/29 B1280/18
B1318/06 C0429/34 C0429/38 C0429/40
C0547/29 C0577/09
observers (2) A0458/02 C0545/02
observes (6) A0018/V A0705/32
B0977/11 B1269/36 C0160/09 C0162/07
observing (30) A0065/22 A0109/20
A0141/12 A0161/19 A0432/13 A0486/31
A0507/19 A0533/21 A0534/04 A0590/36
A0628/03 A0688/23 A0690/01 A0694/13
B0747/36 B0750/12 B0850/23 B0889/08
B1143/12 B1184/28 B1295/15 B1311/07
B1339/20 C0094/22 C0168/10 C0181/24
C0192/39 C0413/09 C0417/32 C0544/12
<u>obsol</u> (1) A0366/10
obsolete (3) A0143/18
A0144/22 B0840/30
obst-- (1) B1369/27
obstacle (8) B0902/22
B1074/18 B1322/20 C0074/37 C0075/10
C0076/08 C0402/23 C0537/01
obstacles (3) B0762/34
B1294/33 C0094/40
obstinacy (8) A0058/26
A0654/04 B0807/33 B0822/29 B0958/35
B1114/32 B1369/03 C0568/04
obstinate (8) A0059/06
A0097/08 A0211/11 A0413/29 A0649/01
A0654/V B0764/06 B1262/13
obstinately (5) A0212/07
B0892/20 B1053/26 C0201/11 C0205/09
obstreperous (4) A0177/V
A0249/07 B0823/12 B1018/06
obstreperously (1) C0168/37
obstructed (4) B1329/23
C0542/24 C0559/33 C0576/22
obstruction (2) A0685/20 B1329/11
obstructions (3) C0159/11
C0543/04 C0572/26
obtain (28) A0071/17
A0125/29 A0127/V A0128/29 A0404/25
->A0566/10 A0590/31 A0638/08 A0667/50
A0693/17 B0771/31 B0839/06 B0889/03
B0889/16 B0891/20 B0892/24 B0940/01
B0982/12 B1206/02 B1303/08 C0074/13
C0120/31 C0125/38 C0183/11 C0185/34
C0418/47 C0521/12 C0569/17
cbtained (68)
cbtaining (16) A0105/07
A0211/19 A0443/09 A0546/09 B1003/06
C0088/01 C0097/24 C0102/07 C0104/22
C0117/12 C0144/41 C0145/25 C0176/25
C0389/02 C0430/45 C0526/21
cbtains (1) B0878/16
cbtrude (1) C0413/02
cbtruded (2) B1219/13 B1224/V
cbtruding (1) C0564/39
cbtrusive (2) A0409/22 A0490/08
cbtrusively (2) A0371/21 B0990/04
obtuse (5) A0435/19
A0544/03 A0557/28 A0557/29 A0696/26
cbviated (1) A0300/14
cbvious (42) A0054/19 A0063/23
A0339/19 A0345/03 A0346/13 A0482/06
A0508/22 A0529/05 A0559/16 A0609/17
A0615/22 A0622/13 A0695/15 A0709/10
A0711/23 B0739/33 B0744/27 B0753/19
B0759/07 B0760/21 B0765/23 B0772/02
B0773/31 B0837/08 B0923/09 B0962/08
B0980/12 B0990/02 B1109/35 B1181/36
B1276/24 B1278/13 B1297/11 B1385/26
C0062/22 C0098/04 C0116/14 C0203/38
C0404/27 C0414/21 C0415/38 C0546/12
cbviously (15) A0054/27
A0063/27 A0203/10 A0491/06 A0500/05
A0696/20 B0739/23 B0745/11 B0745/21
B1093/09 B1219/03 B1240/25 B1281/24
B1294/31 B1383/34
cbviousness (1) A0552/16
occasion (49) A0105/14
A0110/09 A0125/35 A0126/14 A0225/15
A0249/24 A0296/16 A0343/18 A0349/12
A0379/12 A0435/28 A0436/09 A0528/21
A0548/19 A0584/13 A0629/18 A0673/18
A0709/18 B0733/24 B0747/26 B0750/26
B0809/V B0817/20 B0850/20 B0929/25
B1047/33 B1140/06 B1151/01 B1152/01
B1184/22 B1347/01 B1351/26 B1353/29
B1369/09 B1383/11 C0066/12 C0073/17
C0085/07 C0087/37 C0089/02 C0095/34
C0099/09 C0107/12 C0119/31 C0137/27
C0152/05 C0410/09 C0421/05 C0552/03
cccasional (23) A0136/08
A0244/V A0245/11 A0248/22 A0411/02
B0728/27 B0728/30 B1055/08 B1191/02
B1207/12 B1278/15 B1282/03 B1332/04
B1332/12 B1334/20 B1391/18 C0136/04
C0149/07 C0165/40 C0168/07 C0197/18
C0561/15 C0575/13
occasionally (53)
occasioned (64)
cccasions (19) A0081/19
A0098/14 A0123/19 A0127/17 A0156/10
A0161/24 A0429/17 A0441/15 B0911/20
B0960/13 B0986/01 B0988/09 B1234/13
B1350/12 B1379/18 B1381/01 C0123/23

->C0548/24 C0552/20
occidit (1) A0125/04
occiput (1) B1190/33
occultation (2) C0423/27 C0423/33
occultations (1) C0423/34
occupancy (1) A0537/10
occupant (5) A0204/13
A0386/31 B0734/01 B0959/03 C0389/11
occupants (1) B0732/37
occupation (12) A0088/15
A0100/31 A0484/03 A0488/10 A0490/05
A0535/13 B0749/22 B1096/22 B1141/03
C0116/20 C0146/11 C0391/02
occupations (8) A0151/11
A0405/09 A0410/31 A0482/30 A0483/07
A0485/29 A0528/06 C0439/V
occupied (57)
occupies (1) A0274/10
occupy (14) A0430/23 A0503/02
A0565/27 A0589/04 B0724/29 B0751/09
B0923/05 B1093/34 B1153/09 B1301/16
C0391/08 C0394/17 C0412/18 C0430/43
occupying (10) A0279/13 A0321/14
A0565/01 B0866/23 B0925/21 B1141/02
B1249/09 B1335/08 C0551/32 C0565/31
occur (16) A0053/10
A0497/18 A0704/16 B0724/15 B0743/27
B0898/21 B0955/28 B0961/10 B0961/12
B0988/09 B1269/16 B1373/29 C0075/09
C0084/22 C0099/01 C0149/04
occurred (82)
occurrence (24) A0021/19
A0028/20 A0053/16 A0062/24 A0072/22
A0074/19 A0081/19 A0370/23 A0414/34
A0544/16 B0726/31 B0746/31 B0956/01
B1047/28 B1249/07 B1373/27 C0149/03
C0149/17 C0397/22 C0403/12 C0407/11
C0419/26 C0422/14 C0539/14
occurrences (5) A0135/14
A0277/04 A0277/06 A0301/24 C0539/24
occurring (5) A0641/23
B0946/12 B1030/19 C0098/06 C0182/27
occurs (2) B0837/01 B0837/28
Ocean (3) C0053/T
C0055/29 C0057/20
ocean (50) A0137/20 A0138/28
A0139/11 A0145/09 A0146/08 A0146/12
A0314/16 A0578/33 A0579/14 A0580/07
A0587/24 A0588/22 A0589/11 A0592/22
A0594/10 A0601/31 A0638/13 B0966/25
B1069/07 B1078/21 B1079/07 B1080/09
B1106/21 B1123/27 B1155/29 B1159/20
B1293/12 B1310/05 B1391/17 C0065/12
C0065/21 C0071/27 C0124/08 C0153/22
C0163/29 C0205/29 C0205/38 C0397/16
C0399/17 C0399/23 C0407/33 C0412/04
C0416/18 C0417/01 C0417/16 C0422/25
C0525/19 C0526/12 C0526/12 C0542/10
ocean-crag (1) A0213/12
oceanic (4) C0126/15
C0153/14 C0155/21 C0191/11
oceans (1) C0429/12
och (7) A0464/11
A0465/13 A0467/11 A0468/17 A0468/30
A0469/15 A0470/10
cchre (1) A0498/10
Ccracoke/Inlet (1) B0931/15
cctagonal (1) A0502/24
cctaves (2) B0905/17 B0905/28
cctavo (4) A0283/36
A0283/37 A0301/08 A0409/05
Cctober (17) A0232/14
A0240/01 A0246/13 A0252/09 A0253/22
A0654/25 A0655/04 A0655/V B0808/01
B1136/07 B1136/30 B1137/26 B1138/24
B1304/14 C0058/22 C0150/04 C0560/18
ccular (4) A0379/15
B0823/02 B0906/30 B1351/02
cd/rot/me (3) B1046/06
B1046/07 B1046/08
Cdd (14) B1100/T B1103/25
B1103/35 B1104/15 B1104/20 B1106/04
B1106/16 B1107/02 B1107/34 B1108/34
B1109/29 B1109/34 B1110/08 B1110/23
cdd (60)
cdd-looking (4) A0370/22
A0386/32 B1291/06 C0389/04
cdder (1) B1109/19
oddest (1) B1102/03
cddities (4) A0262/05
A0295/V B0975/13 B1011/18
cddity (2) A0298/V B1008/11
cddly (5) B1303/18
B1303/23 C0157/23 C0387/27 C0390/24
cdds (6) A0436/30 B0773/22
B0946/30 B1046/03 C0105/12 C0187/08
cde (4) B1132/10
B1132/13 B1132/18 B1143/28
Cdenheimer (1) A0540/30
cdiosius (2) A0568/V B0974/M
cdious (9) A0500/07
B0760/08 B0854/33 B1138/13 B1154/29
B1194/10 B1292/06 B1300/18 B1371/31
cdor (20) A0081/08
A0217/V A0407/05 A0614/26 A0691/07
A0696/02 B0925/25 B0944/28 B0967/26
B1106/27 B1180/06 B1180/25 B1242/12
B1283/05 B1340/17 B1351/33 C0542/08
C0543/28 C0547/21 C0553/03
cdorless (1) C0394/02
cdorous (4) A0046/30
A0602/15 A0610/03 B1280/11
cdors (2) A0403/05 B0943/17
Cdyssey (1) A0710/30
Cedipus (2) A0639/03 B1044/01
Cegipans (1) A0409/08
ceufs (1) A0102/10
Ceuvres (1) A0100/30
cf (1) A0353/35
cf (20515)
cff (242)
cffal (1) B1130/10
cffence (8) A0127/15
A0249/09 A0272/01 A0299/13 A0440/25
A0707/32 B0813/15 B1272/33
cffend (2) B0893/22 B0955/02
cffended (8) A0165/23
A0497/15 B0747/29 B0748/12 B0767/33
B0893/20 B1009/01 C0067/20
cffending (3) B0852/V

->B1010/15 C0179/37
offends (1) A0499/01
offense (1) B0852/24
offensive (6) A0300/01 A0497/04
A0499/V A0624/31 B1242/12 B1371/16
offer (25) A0141/24
A0155/23 A0300/21 A0346/23 A0622/12
B0727/09 B0727/19 B0733/17 B0736/25
B0852/17 B0899/15 B1091/24 B1152/29
B1281/14 B1320/02 B1322/07 B1358/02
B1379/21 C0117/40 C0145/01 C0189/21
C0191/27 C0522/36 C0531/29 C0561/13
offered (50) A0025/24 A0108/09
A0141/03 A0249/14 A0302/10 A0303/11
A0444/29 A0491/03 A0593/02 A0613/08
A0624/05 A0626/31 A0627/23 A0642/09
A0707/08 B0737/20 B0768/16 B0841/08
B0851/10 B0854/17 B0866/17 B0899/09
B0907/03 B0980/27 B0982/07 B1021/05
B1054/16 B1054/23 B1107/13 B1164/02
B1188/14 B1272/07 B1294/09 B1338/24
B1348/29 C0065/38 C0101/02 C0104/17
C0105/22 C0109/04 C0128/24 C0176/08
C0200/07 C0207/22 C0439/V C0527/24
C0534/20 C0546/27 C0557/06 C0561/07
offering (10) A0043/11 A0165/13
A0299/02 A0302/17 A0311/08 B0727/25
B0871/33 B1260/33 B1357/04 C0179/40
offerings (1) A0044/23
offers (4) A0036/23
B0877/06 B1094/02 B1383/01
office (24) A0046/28
A0204/12 A0496/10 A0547/03 A0560/22
B0733/36 B0754/07 B0754/09 B0796/22
B0878/21 B0879/17 B0896/30 B1013/21
B1075/01 B1075/17 B1105/21 B1105/35
B1129/25 B1130/23 B1208/24 B1363/28
B1369/28 B1372/33 C0134/27
officer (14) B0753/16 B0754/18
B0769/05 B0770/03 B0770/11 B0770/21
B0931/22 B0946/31 B0949/21 B0949/22
B0958/19 B0958/32 C0526/27 C0539/32
officered (1) B0946/28
officers (12) B0754/08
B0796/19 B0796/22 B0796/33 B0797/11
B0858/13 B0949/19 B0981/04 B1362/12
B1362/23 B1362/35 B1363/23
offices (8) A0027/13
A0337/31 A0370/08 A0442/17 B0729/01
B0749/10 B1018/27 C0188/12
official (3) B0873/11
B0975/06 C0390/33
officiate (1) A0027/14
officious (1) A0435/23
officiousness (1) A0445/04
offing (1) A0579/17
offspring (3) B0760/20
B1131/07 B1131/11
often (89)
oftener (4) A0545/V
B0926/18 B1322/11 B1330/09
oggling> (2) A0464/22 A0469/03
ogs (1) B0879/28
oh (3) A0431/08 B1370/06 B1370/06
oh (107)
Chio (1) B0862/09
Cil (3) A0055/13 A0064/27 B1133/05
cil (10) A0136/02 A0491/15
A0503/04 B0956/35 B1145/21 B1371/26
C0064/19 C0155/29 C0155/40 C0156/17
cil-cask (1) C0144/20
cil-casks (7) C0069/03
C0074/09 C0091/31 C0094/11 C0099/27
C0099/30 C0116/14
cil-cloths (1) C0534/14
Cil-of-Bob (20) B1127/13
B1127/17 B1127/23 B1128/12 B1132/08
B1132/13 B1132/18 B1134/08 B1137/04
B1137/07 B1137/16 B1138/05 B1138/17
B1139/06 B1139/12 B1141/01 B1142/01
B1143/24 B1143/28 B1144/04
cil-tanks (1) C0099/40
ciled (1) B1071/16
cils (1) A0097/08
cily (3) A0369/08
A0694/06 B1345/06
Cinos (24) A0189/11
A0190/17 A0191/06 B1211/01 B1211/03
B1212/04 B1212/10 B1212/13 B1212/22
B1212/29 B1212/34 B1213/05 B1213/11
B1213/13 B1213/15 B1213/26 B1213/29
B1214/17 B1215/07 B1215/12 B1215/16
B1215/17 B1215/20 B1215/24
ciseau (1) A0034/01
Ckydandies (2) C0551/18 C0551/24
Cld (23) A0154/06
A0365/M A0481/M B0863/17 B1045/22
B1045/25 B1045/27 B1046/02 B1047/08
B1047/19 B1047/27 B1048/01 B1048/18
B1048/23 B1048/25 B1049/13 B1050/24
B1051/06 B1054/18 B1056/12 B1056/22
B1056/29 B1058/18
cld (285)
cld-fashioned (3) A0493/07
B1090/27 B1337/25
cld-womanish (1) A0654/07
Cld/Republic (1) A0153/07
Cldeb (3) B0949/02
B0949/22 B0950/27
olden (1) A0406/36
clder (4) A0431/13
B0841/03 C0057/17 C0545/08
cldest (6) A0261/20 A0366/24
A0585/04 A0585/32 B0865/35 C0176/20
cle (2) B0912/01 B0912/01
clfact (1) A0203/M
clive (2) A0033/13 A0622/28
clive-jars (1) C0141/29
clives (9) C0137/02
C0137/20 C0138/41 C0140/03 C0140/07
C0141/04 C0141/11 C0141/20 C0141/30
Cllapod (1) A0354/16
Clympia (1) A0080/03
Clympiad (1) A0128/29
clympiad (1) A0653/17
Clympics (1) A0127/07
Cmahas (1) C0548/12
omelette (1) A0102/11
cmelettes (2) A0096/09 A0098/32
cmen (6) B0737/06 B1078/23

->B1247/17 B1249/21 C0136/29 C0419/06
omens (1) B1247/06
Omicron (1) A0346/11
ominous (6) A0028/V A0090/08
A0153/24 A0349/28 A0349/32 B0843/27
ominously (1) A0102/05
omission (1) B1233/17
omit (11) A0629/30
B1140/11 B1358/18 B1380/29 B1386/07
C0101/27 C0522/12 C0539/29 C0546/29
C0560/17 C0565/39
omitted (5) A0441/15
A0488/V B1159/12 C0534/16 C0544/03
omitting (1) B0772/02
<u>Omne</u> (1) B1080/10
<u>omne</u> (2) A0534/27 A0654/08
omni-prevalent (2) A0460/35
A0610/19
Omnibus (4) B1089/01
B1089/03 B1091/20 B1091/23
omnibus (24) A0341/06
B1089/06 B1089/10 B1089/18 B1089/26
B1090/03 B1090/08 B1090/11 B1090/13
B1090/17 B1090/18 B1090/20 B1090/23
B1090/26 B1090/28 B1090/37 B1091/01
B1091/05 B1091/10 B1091/14 B1091/16
B1091/17 B1092/09 B1092/15
omnibus-driver (2) B0736/01
B0770/13
omnipotence (1) A0446/06
omnipraevalent (1) A0615/12
Omnipresence (2) A0068/06 B1106/13
omnipresence (1) A0446/05
omniprevalence (1) B1034/04
omniscience (1) A0383/13
On (1) A0301/03
on (1632)
on (Gr.) (2) A0225/M A0229/M
once (376)
<u>ond</u> (1) B0905/24
One (3) A0119/T B0870/16 C0387/T
one (1492)
one-and-twenty (2) C0437/V
C0437/V
one-eyed (1) A0356/27
one-fourth (2) A0251/16 B1136/15
one-half (7) A0485/14
A0488/24 A0499/17 B1137/33 C0400/30
C0400/30 C0579/10
one-idead (1) B1313/13
one-sided (1) B1313/13
one-third (3) B1136/36
C0400/28 C0577/21
one-thirtieth (1) C0400/27
one's (8) A0072/11
A0072/22 A0345/18 B1090/15 B1126/19
B1221/18 B1292/03 B1349/24
oneness (1) A0342/13
onerous (2) A0484/10 B1141/03
ones (31) A0091/08
A0091/36 A0110/14 A0111/12 A0156/17
A0218/14 A0500/03 A0510/34 A0529/11
A0550/26 A0583/25 A0584/32 A0592/16
A0654/V B0723/M B0749/26 B0898/05
B1038/03 B1038/04 B1038/05 B1038/06
->B1180/27 B1237/08 B1299/13 B1345/16
B1350/24 B1360/09 C0178/33 C0528/21
C0573/31 C0573/39
cngry (1) A0373/15
cnions (1) C0155/35
Cnly (1) B1127/13
cnly (640)
cnpleasant (1) B0812/16
cnset (2) C0186/28 C0563/12
cnward (15) A0162/23
A0195/06 A0244/13 A0244/13 A0244/15
A0244/15 A0316/10 A0514/35 A0685/10
A0686/05 A0697/02 B1214/29 B1214/30
B1282/22 C0574/27
onwards (2) A0145/24 A0195/V
cnyxes (1) B1280/26
cooogh (2) B1012/V B1012/V
cooooh (1) B0820/32
coze (1) B0742/31
cozing (3) B0807/02
C0406/03 C0415/34
cozy (1) A0195/08
cpal (1) B0828/01
cpals (1) B1280/26
cpen (175)
cpen-mouthed (2) C0388/02 C0577/33
cpened (58)
cpening (62)
openings (2) B1181/03 B1333/11
cpenly (6) A0435/25 A0436/02
B0933/26 B0977/29 B0992/29 B1375/16
cpenness (1) A0436/13
cpens (6) A0033/14 A0146/01
A0489/33 B0875/25 B0957/29 B0977/14
cpera (7) B0889/01
B0895/02 B0897/21 B0905/02 B0907/01
B0914/23 B1108/33
cpera-glass (5) A0487/17
B0891/25 B0891/28 B0891/29 B0892/01
cperate (5) A0403/14
B0744/20 B0769/19 B1223/26 B1223/V
cperated (8) A0327/09
A0378/09 A0446/08 B1132/29 B1249/05
B1295/29 B1311/26 C0406/31
cperates (1) B1119/18
cperating (4) A0433/07
B0762/31 B0960/07 B1093/11
cperation (20) A0142/08
A0437/08 A0565/05 A0601/28 A0616/03
A0625/18 B0870/09 B1005/12 B1005/18
B1007/12 B1018/20 B1019/25 B1070/07
B1071/23 B1078/19 B1181/10 B1293/34
C0406/35 C0410/39 C0544/37
cperations (28) A0046/23
A0059/17 A0067/08 A0067/17 A0105/16
A0206/02 A0296/V A0296/V A0459/22
A0478/16 A0486/03 A0528/14 A0601/17
A0691/33 B0870/03 B0878/35 B1142/33
B1182/11 B1213/15 B1236/15 B1362/11
C0108/25 C0126/31 C0203/01 C0428/36
C0534/06 C0545/03 C0546/09
cperator (1) B0941/34
cpined (1) A0087/03
cpinion (89)
cpinions (35) A0028/10

->A0135/11 A0160/04 A0203/05 A0262/03
A0266/01 A0271/35 A0297/02 A0298/V
A0299/08 A0299/14 A0299/14 A0299/34
A0299/34 A0302/17 A0366/05 A0408/24
A0544/10 A0547/15 A0625/V A0703/19
A0708/24 B0748/33 B0759/01 B0823/02
B0941/15 B0986/29 B1135/33 B1135/33
B1268/18 B1273/18 B1293/30 B1318/13
B1363/37 C0387/04
opium (18) A0035/14 A0078/30
A0136/04 A0211/V A0311/25 A0320/25
A0323/13 A0325/12 A0325/27 A0326/V
A0397/17 A0402/26 A0663/V A0667/13
A0667/23 A0667/35 A0667/64 C0078/09
opium-dream (1) A0311/V
Opium-eater (1) A0339/29
opium-engendered (1) A0326/07
Oporto (1) A0247/13
Oppodeldoc (23) B1129/04
B1129/13 B1129/16 B1129/19 B1129/21
B1129/28 B1129/31 B1130/02 B1130/04
B1130/06 B1130/11 B1130/17 B1130/22
B1130/24 B1130/24 B1130/29 B1130/30
B1130/35 B1131/03 B1131/08 B1131/14
B1131/21 B1131/34
opponent (4) A0529/09
B0984/14 B0984/30 B0985/05
opponent's (1) B0985/06
opponents (5) A0530/09
B0984/13 B0989/32 C0086/10 C0113/23
opportune (1) C0399/32
opportunely (3) B0757/24
C0092/21 C0165/22
opportunite (2) B0899/30 B0899/V
opportunities (9) A0073/24
A0501/04 A0583/24 A0707/09 B0760/12
B1233/06 B1272/08 C0070/06 C0393/28
opportunity (72)
oppose (3) A0409/27
A0650/16 A0654/01
opposed (3) A0527/V
B1237/06 B1294/34
opposite (54)
opposition (8) A0527/V
A0610/05 B1206/10 C0066/02 C0082/05
C0103/10 C0105/21 C0112/30
oppress (1) A0684/15
oppressed (23) A0054/28
A0063/29 A0079/29 A0157/24 A0214/27
A0217/V A0227/05 A0231/16 A0398/22
A0399/31 A0404/10 A0414/34 A0436/19
A0459/32 A0608/09 A0614/15 A0667/56
A0683/16 B0943/28 B0963/36 B0967/07
B0974/08 C0071/13
oppresses (1) A0080/14
oppression (10) A0023/V A0614/15
A0614/22 A0615/30 B0961/20 C0073/15
C0176/12 C0182/30 C0183/10 C0198/05
oppressive (9) A0028/V
A0403/06 A0409/33 A0411/05 B0944/18
B1283/05 C0094/16 C0420/40 C0542/08
oppressively (2) A0397/02 C0142/13
opprobrium (2) A0053/04 A0062/09
optic (1) B1038/05
optical (2) A0107/20 C0430/05

cptics (2) A0107/08 A0107/V
cpulence (2) A0705/28 B1270/26
cpulent (2) B0863/37 B1137/13
cr (1891)
cr-molu'd (1) A0500/27
cracles (1) B1115/24
Crang-Outangs (1) B1345/V
crange (7) A0175/20
A0181/09 A0349/14 A0672/01 A0676/14
B1331/07 C0542/10
crange-colored (3) A0336/08
A0349/32 A0368/06
crange-coloured (1) A0339/06
crange-jellies (1) A0345/14
crange-peel (1) B1244/07
cration (1) B1020/21
crations (3) A0175/32
A0181/31 B1207/30
Cratiunculae (1) A0366/15
Cratiunculis (1) A0515/34
crator (3) A0279/12
B1050/31 B1185/19
crators (1) A0654/16
cratory (1) B1013/07
crb (11) A0189/16
A0417/13 A0457/18 A0458/01 A0459/31
B1035/28 B1214/04 B1280/28 B1301/12
B1301/13 B1301/21
Crbis (1) A0601/33
crbit (9) B1301/01
B1302/06 B1321/06 B1321/17 C0400/05
C0401/31 C0402/08 C0419/09 C0420/15
crbits (3) A0457/25
B1322/01 B1322/02
crbs (11) A0313/10
A0313/23 A0314/11 A0615/08 B0940/20
B1181/31 B1259/05 B1301/15 B1301/25
C0402/17 C0426/06
crchestra (5) A0177/06
A0318/12 A0672/28 A0673/29 B1020/12
Crchideae (1) B1162/33
crchis (1) B1163/24
crder (76)
crdered (19) A0070/10
A0079/26 A0123/27 A0136/30 A0325/04
A0654/20 B0822/03 B0909/24 B1056/10
B1186/08 B1352/15 C0088/19 C0101/20
C0108/04 C0164/31 C0167/31 C0168/28
C0168/40 C0175/31
crderly (2) A0482/04 A0510/33
crders (10) A0024/27 A0320/26
A0338/22 B0827/03 B1258/23 B1258/24
C0061/38 C0108/08 C0110/34 C0527/30
crdinance (3) B1092/22
B1092/28 B1093/34
crdinarily (7) A0320/07
A0512/29 A0711/11 B1040/13 B1221/07
B1276/12 B1352/21
crdinary (120)
Crdonnance (1) A0301/01
Cregon (3) A0478/01
C0525/20 C0525/39
Crfeo (1) A0162/03
crgan (12) A0478/19
A0482/17 A0483/21 A0485/V A0527/V

->A0531/03 B0824/10 B0852/V B1219/24
B1219/24 B1220/03 B1220/05
organ-grinder (1) A0252/V
organ-grinders (1) A0510/25
organ-grinding (1) A0489/23
organic (6) B1038/28 B1039/08
B1039/14 B1039/17 B1039/24 B1040/06
organization (1) B1039/32
organized (2) A0203/14 B1037/27
organs (16) A0298/V
A0379/15 A0433/30 B1030/06 B1030/08
B1037/13 B1037/14 B1037/26 B1037/29
B1037/31 B1038/11 B1038/17 B1038/19
B1038/25 B1038/29 C0178/16
oriels (3) B0945/11
B0945/23 B1283/12
Oriental (2) B1151/01 B1340/02
origin (29) A0019/07
A0074/33 A0127/12 A0141/28 A0157/24
A0157/V A0209/09 A0323/25 A0365/18
A0365/19 A0403/34 A0413/04 A0426/13
A0562/23 A0610/14 A0612/20 A0688/08
A0695/18 B0772/18 B0871/24 B1033/32
B1190/23 B1281/16 B1322/15 C0124/35
C0387/23 C0401/41 C0404/03 C0539/08
original (81)
originality (3) A0158/12
B0870/02 B0871/06
originally (29) A0146/10
A0163/22 A0283/14 A0343/20 A0349/17
A0483/27 A0556/05 A0559/07 B0727/15
B0738/20 B0741/33 B0753/29 B0753/40
B0772/30 B0855/27 B0857/16 B0933/36
B0964/35 B1053/13 B1068/10 B1114/17
B1181/32 B1189/25 B1236/18 B1321/02
B1346/22 B1386/09 C0093/23 C0531/36
originate (1) A0441/13
originated (3) A0269/18
A0275/26 A0311/11
originator (2) A0071/24 B1311/01
originators (1) B0987/06
oriole (1) B1337/15
Orion (5) A0535/09
A0536/11 A0536/19 A0536/23 B1212/31
orlop (6) C0080/34 C0091/29
C0094/10 C0095/30 C0099/28 C0115/24
ornament (4) A0269/06
A0274/32 A0277/15 A0278/33
ornamental (1) A0486/12
ornamented (7) A0368/05
B0828/08 B0890/10 B1179/24 B1261/07
C0534/03 C0552/11
ornaments (3) A0671/31
A0672/08 B0828/05
Orndoff (1) B1390/18
orne (1) B1246/03
Orontes (1) A0121/06
orthodox (1) A0399/03
orthodoxy (1) B1044/06
orthographically (1) C0418/07
orthography (1) B1095/10
ortolan (1) A0033/02
ortolans (1) A0037/10
os (2) A0379/30 B1182/13
os (1) A0298/V
os (Gr.) (1) A0507/11
Osage (2) C0527/33 C0539/35
Osage/Femme/Rivers (1) C0538/08
Osborne (6) B1069/17 B1072/24
B1072/27 B1072/31 B1080/04 B1081/23
Osborne's (2) B1075/21 B1081/06
oscillation (1) B1334/07
oscillations (1) A0691/02
osier (1) C0202/22
osprey (1) C0151/32
Ossa (1) A0071/06
osseous (1) B1235/35
osservasse (1) A0662/V
ossi (1) A0352/12
ossification (1) B1235/30
ossified (1) B1235/26
ostensible (2) B0731/27 C0564/19
ostensibly (2) B0726/17 C0066/10
ostentatious (2) A0500/28 B1007/31
ostentatiously (2) A0269/01
C0181/21
Otello (1) B0905/14
other (571)
other's (3) A0613/02
A0640/19 C0153/11
others (88)
otherwise (71)
Otter (1) C0560/20
otter (1) C0536/22
Otterholm (2) A0579/27 A0584/02
Ottoes (1) C0540/30
ottoman (13) A0033/09
A0033/10 A0036/15 A0088/26 A0158/09
A0162/04 A0164/V A0166/13 A0166/20
A0325/17 A0327/V A0329/09 A0498/15
ottomans (4) A0087/32
A0321/29 A0322/11 A0324/21
ou (3) A0033/20 A0033/20 C0430/27
ought (16) A0092/19
A0262/23 A0302/23 A0338/07 A0346/09
A0366/07 A0563/V A0583/18 A0622/02
B0901/03 B1311/19 C0068/20 C0401/29
C0427/33 C0427/37 C0535/11
ould> (4) A0464/21
A0466/01 A0467/18 A0470/15
ounce (1) B1130/34
ounces (5) A0057/31
A0068/15 B1071/30 B1072/02 C0141/33
ounly> (3) A0466/04
A0467/31 A0467/V
our (1182)
ourang-outang (1) B1351/03
ourang-outangs (10) B1021/11
B1350/14 B1350/23 B1350/30 B1352/01
B1352/10 B1352/35 B1353/13 B1353/18
B1354/04
Ourang-Outang (14) A0559/20 A0559/27
A0560/12 A0560/28 A0561/20 A0561/21
A0562/03 A0562/25 A0564/22 A0565/12
A0565/28 A0567/02 A0567/24 A0568/03
Ourang-Outangs (1) B1350/07
ours (8) A0120/18
A0195/V B0769/32 B1299/12 C0433/05
C0532/29 C0534/35 C0536/21
ourself (1) A0250/20

ourselves (112)
out (662)
out-flowing (1) B1242/11
out-heroded (1) A0021/08
out-houses (2) B1337/07 B1338/17
out-of-the-way (4) A0365/04
A0482/03 B0985/33 B1048/26
out-Heroded (2) A0440/15 A0675/01
outbidding (1) A0033/10
outbreak (1) C0562/36
outburst (1) B0856/14
outcast (1) A0426/06
outcasts (1) A0426/06
outcry (1) B1138/27
outer (7) A0642/07
B0730/25 B0765/19 B0832/26 B0964/22
B1071/14 C0426/10
outfit (1) A0440/06
Outis (1) B1384/07
outlay (1) A0490/03
outlet (3) A0406/01
B1282/11 C0196/06
outline (19) A0023/10
A0214/24 A0246/V A0297/V A0313/12
A0328/17 A0434/19 A0613/17 A0704/34
B0829/12 B0829/16 B0829/20 B0855/30
B0889/28 B0956/18 B1248/09 B1269/33
B1279/36 C0522/30
outlines (9) A0089/04
A0103/20 A0196/23 A0204/27 A0312/13
A0689/06 A0695/26 C0194/01 C0420/19
outnumbered (1) C0086/11
outpouring (1) A0046/17
outrage (18) A0556/30 B0735/16
B0736/13 B0751/05 B0753/21 B0757/19
B0757/24 B0757/26 B0758/16 B0760/28
B0761/02 B0763/11 B0764/04 B0764/16
B0769/22 B0769/28 B1354/16 C0188/06
outrageous (4) A0072/29
A0373/V A0443/V C0557/03
outrageously (1) A0294/V
outrages (1) B0769/14
<u>outre</u> (11) A0090/30
A0109/21 A0430/27 A0430/V A0482/06
A0547/18 A0557/07 B0736/22 B0902/01
B1335/23 C0436/V
outre (1) A0494/01
outreaching (1) A0663/14
outridden (1) A0027/V
outrider (1) A0367/28
outriggers (1) C0186/35
outright (9) A0036/19
A0341/V A0342/16 A0413/31 A0470/12
B0875/25 B1057/16 B1154/11 C0187/32
outrun (1) A0683/21
outset (5) A0105/19
B0738/26 B0740/03 C0090/16 C0526/11
outside (16) A0057/17
A0067/34 A0437/11 B0732/07 B0734/17
B1014/14 B1020/05 B1182/13 B1349/34
B1351/22 C0077/14 C0141/05 C0152/26
C0175/13 C0409/20 C0411/09
outskirts (2) A0066/13 B0751/30
outspread (1) B1248/22
outstretched (13) A0165/24
->A0217/V A0461/12 A0579/02 A0614/26
A0685/20 A0691/20 A0697/09 B0865/34
B1020/25 B1110/17 C0195/14 C0208/12
cutstripped (1) A0029/08
cutward (20) A0025/19
A0086/26 A0099/24 A0161/09 A0235/10
A0241/08 A0303/26 A0310/14 A0530/26
A0692/26 B0824/21 B1102/28 B1106/06
B1212/30 B1321/24 B1321/26 C0059/32
C0124/39 C0397/04 C0398/22
cutwardly (5) A0104/10
A0315/08 B0878/05 B0956/28 C0398/26
cutwards (3) C0402/08
C0440/V C0552/10
cutwits (1) B0869/22
cutwitted (1) B0993/22
cv (4) B1103/25
B1103/35 B1109/34 B1109/34
Cval (1) A0662/T
cval (7) A0267/36
A0271/27 A0664/09 A0664/28 B0809/34
B1333/21 C0423/33
cven (4) A0340/06
A0340/27 A0340/28 B1167/09
cven-full (1) A0101/06
cver (487)
cver-acute (2) B0747/27 B0840/13
cver-conscientious (1) B0874/19
cver-curious (1) A0142/34
cver-effeminacy (2) A0270/37
A0281/03
cver-hanging (1) B1280/24
cver-largely (1) B0989/35
cver-profound (1) B1310/23
cver-rated (1) B1005/27
cver-shoes (1) A0513/21
cver-spreading (1) A0324/29
cver-topped (1) B0842/09
cver-value (1) B1249/34
cver-wise (1) C0427/11
cverarching (1) C0196/16
cverawed (2) A0405/21 B1222/23
cverboard (30) A0137/25 A0586/23
A0589/27 A0594/03 B0930/20 B0930/36
B0932/08 B1293/11 C0071/34 C0090/37
C0102/10 C0102/17 C0108/02 C0108/30
C0110/09 C0111/19 C0114/21 C0115/06
C0116/35 C0120/04 C0133/16 C0139/01
C0140/04 C0140/14 C0140/25 C0142/28
C0144/39 C0163/34 C0424/38 C0533/37
cverburthened (1) A0456/18
cvercame (2) B0865/15 C0528/38
cvercast (3) A0162/21
A0233/V A0585/28
cvercharged (2) A0484/25 B0794/09
cvercoat (12) A0349/03
A0349/05 A0351/03 A0351/04 A0351/05
A0356/22 A0511/27 B0808/11 B1185/34
C0067/23 C0416/33 C0579/07
cvercome (14) A0402/15 A0432/03
A0442/08 B0742/33 B0944/17 B1134/29
C0086/40 C0094/30 C0094/40 C0095/35
C0110/15 C0197/26 C0205/08 C0415/06
cvercoming (1) A0102/24
cverdo (1) B0840/14

overdone (3) A0401/21
A0508/11 C0396/30
overflowing (5) A0210/23
A0317/18 A0512/32 A0643/33 B0901/15
overflowings (1) A0151/12
overgrown (4) A0142/21
B0817/31 B1329/10 C0577/18
overhanging (3) B0947/15
C0538/25 C0544/21
overhasty (1) B0733/08
overhaul (1) C0542/27
overhauled (1) C0566/02
overhauling (2) C0549/30 C0570/35
overhead (27) A0088/04
A0103/17 A0195/21 A0248/17 A0326/10
A0587/09 A0665/11 A0687/12 A0689/24
B0866/12 B0959/15 B0968/20 B1073/30
B1108/27 B1261/06 B1279/25 B1292/21
B1292/23 B1329/11 B1331/10 C0182/23
C0184/25 C0410/23 C0416/19 C0420/16
C0425/15 C0539/08
overheard (6) A0081/18 A0126/02
B0768/07 B1059/05 C0095/34 C0556/26
overhung (4) B0947/03
B1281/35 C0181/28 C0549/24
overjoyed (1) C0096/03
overlapping (1) A0536/01
overlaying (1) A0501/29
overlook (1) C0553/37
overlooked (8) A0383/17
B0901/07 B0950/10 B1035/09 B1188/24
B1219/04 B1219/06 C0116/15
overlooking (1) A0043/05
overpower (1) A0165/V
overpowered (6) A0411/32 A0582/01
B0946/33 B1021/24 B1046/27 C0071/23
overpowering (3) A0122/12
A0159/20 C0073/12
overran (1) A0694/17
overrated (1) B0904/25
overreaching (3) A0209/02
A0209/04 B0982/03
overruled (3) A0198/23
B1077/31 B1351/01
overruling (1) C0161/20
overrun (1) C0098/25
overscored (3) A0163/23
A0264/37 B0923/13
overshadowed (8) A0215/05
A0236/04 A0295/07 A0297/V A0379/09
A0428/18 A0512/11 B1337/34
overshadowing (3) B0901/V
B0963/34 C0181/05
overshadows (1) A0033/16
overshot (2) A0177/26 A0183/21
oversight (8) A0528/28
A0529/05 B0765/15 B0765/15 B0771/13
B0990/02 C0079/02 C0200/27
oversights (1) A0528/30
overspread (9) A0159/V
A0235/25 A0327/22 A0400/07 A0404/14
A0408/15 A0689/05 B0963/27 B1282/01
overstowed (1) A0252/23
overstrained (1) A0413/17
overtake (3) B1003/04
->C0125/37 C0201/35
cvertaken (3) B0968/13
B1158/20 C0522/40
cvertakes (1) B1256/08
cverthrew (2) B0902/12 B1167/04
cverthrow (6) A0612/10 B0734/28
B0852/06 B0852/16 B1018/35 B1213/18
cverthrowing (1) B1178/28
cverthrown (2) A0090/02 B1110/19
cverthrows (1) A0611/18
cvertook (6) A0592/01 A0623/20
A0686/07 C0063/15 C0200/02 C0417/30
cvertouched (1) A0502/11
cverturn (1) A0203/04
cverturned (2) A0253/26 B1093/22
cverturning (3) A0102/13
A0103/01 C0145/12
cverwhelm (2) A0139/17 A0140/21
cverwhelmed (20) A0074/09
A0079/39 A0137/31 A0242/31 A0457/09
A0461/15 A0508/13 B0907/01 B0966/26
B1189/18 B1225/23 B1303/06 B1325/04
C0128/25 C0184/10 C0188/02 C0192/28
C0205/30 C0397/11 C0421/20
cverwhelming (10) A0022/16 A0053/37
A0063/08 A0245/V A0253/24 A0295/24
B0947/17 B1221/03 C0126/10 C0185/24
cverwhelms (1) B0961/24
<u>overzezet</u> (1) B1115/29
cw (1) B1103/07
ow'dst (1) A0384/07
cwe (1) A0268/23
cwed (4) A0435/18
B1052/30 B1297/32 C0395/40
cwes (1) A0600/14
cwing (33) A0046/22
A0276/24 A0302/09 A0367/06 A0381/07
A0584/11 A0591/03 B0727/12 B0923/32
B1073/15 B1076/01 B1163/36 B1184/28
B1186/02 B1354/18 C0064/26 C0115/05
C0117/06 C0119/25 C0121/25 C0121/33
C0141/23 C0154/15 C0155/21 C0161/33
C0164/40 C0177/22 C0187/12 C0417/27
C0426/11 C0558/29 C0560/04 C0570/19
Cwl (4) B1136/04
B1136/05 B1136/23 B1139/35
cwl (5) B1103/33
B1138/19 B1359/01 B1371/32 B1372/01
cwn (448)
cwned (4) A0583/20
B1158/25 C0057/26 C0202/27
cwner (14) A0023/25 A0027/13
A0103/25 A0247/12 A0479/10 A0560/28
A0568/06 B0770/29 B0874/04 B0876/30
B0977/18 B1049/23 B1137/08 C0148/05
cwner's (1) A0241/17
cwners (3) A0123/18
C0065/35 C0161/27
cwnership (1) C0166/02
cwning (1) C0156/18
ox-cart (1) A0294/V
cxen (1) A0294/V
Cxford (5) A0440/05
A0440/32 A0444/11 A0444/32 A0445/30
cxus (1) B0969/17

oxygen (5) A0460/24
A0460/25 A0460/26 A0460/31 C0403/16
Oyarvido, Manuel de (1) C0156/34
oyster (1) C0177/07
oysters (1) A0491/13
P (34) B1032/17 B1032/18
B1032/20 B1032/22 B1032/25 B1032/27
B1032/30 B1032/33 B1032/V B1033/02
B1033/08 B1033/12 B1033/15 B1033/17
B1033/31 B1034/07 B1035/05 B1035/31
B1036/06 B1036/11 B1036/14 B1036/18
B1036/26 B1036/29 B1037/01 B1037/04
B1037/11 B1037/21 B1037/28 B1038/20
B1039/03 B1039/10 B1039/18 B1039/27
p (1) B1381/27
p. (3) B1161/33 B1161/37 B1165/35
P./M. (11) A0204/33
A0585/07 B0879/12 B0931/07 B1069/16
B1081/14 B1081/31 C0413/08 C0418/37
C0419/17 C0565/14
P.R.E.T.T.Y. (1) A0338/12
P.S. (6) B1055/24 B1075/28
B1078/28 B1079/34 B1081/09 B1133/09
P-- (10) A0294/V A0301/22
A0301/25 A0302/06 B1235/03 B1380/17
B1380/32 B1381/19 B1382/34 B1384/03
P--/the/Versifier (1) B1379/03
P--/Theatre (1) B0888/29
P--'s (2) B1380/26 B1384/14
pa (2) C0180/32 C0180/32
pabulum (1) B1038/24
pace (1) B1263/26
pace (9) A0145/28
A0274/11 A0688/19 A0692/15 B1081/08
B1225/V B1226/02 C0144/04 C0563/22
paced (1) B0797/14
paces (21) A0138/32
A0310/08 A0514/02 A0629/26 A0685/07
A0686/13 A0686/15 A0686/16 A0686/27
A0688/18 B0896/22 B1052/09 B1260/30
B1330/16 B1332/02 B1335/09 B1337/06
C0086/31 C0182/13 C0200/03 C0201/05
Pacific (11) C0057/20
C0093/29 C0104/18 C0137/25 C0138/18
C0147/07 C0178/11 C0525/15 C0525/19
C0527/15 C0527/36
pacific (3) A0101/21
A0567/02 A0652/23
Pacific/Islands (1) B1277/21
Pacific/Ocean (4) C0101/38
C0525/06 C0527/24 C0574/32
pacifically (1) A0109/17
pacified (2) B1349/27 C0131/39
pacify (1) C0395/35
pacifying (1) C0558/12
pacing (1) A0412/03
pack (2) A0443/27 A0623/11
pack-thread (1) A0137/30
package (3) A0264/33
B0981/01 C0523/30
packages (5) A0443/12
B0745/30 B0746/18 B1155/28 C0534/26
packed (5) A0143/23
B0933/30 B1155/22 B1303/02 C0158/33
packet (4) A0381/28
->A0490/14 C0067/06 C0437/V
packet-ship (1) B0922/02
packets (1) B1081/05
packing (2) B0856/35 C0069/01
packs (1) A0443/22
pacquet (1) A0667/12
padded (1) B0965/32
paddings (1) B0967/25
paddle (2) B1281/05 C0201/31
paddle-blades (1) C0202/37
paddled (1) C0176/18
paddles (2) C0200/22 C0202/34
paddling (1) C0200/38
Paddy/O'Raferty (1) A0374/16
padlock (1) B1261/28
Padua (1) A0086/02
Paestum (2) A0228/25 A0233/06
Pagan (2) B0987/34 B0988/02
pagans (1) B0988/02
page (35) A0024/16
A0025/02 A0028/09 A0162/02 A0162/09
A0166/16 A0217/11 A0270/17 A0274/35
A0276/01 A0278/36 A0279/13 A0343/12
A0426/02 A0487/01 B1128/34 B1145/24
B1247/27 B1297/11 B1359/16 B1383/15
B1383/17 B1383/20 B1383/25 B1383/V
B1384/14 B1384/33 B1385/02 B1385/14
B1385/26 C0196/09 C0428/38 C0429/19
C0429/22 C0430/27
pageantries (1) A0644/06
pageants (1) B1347/05
pages (26) A0218/12 A0226/10
A0230/08 A0316/19 A0338/14 A0493/03
B0949/24 B1097/05 B1101/16 B1106/13
B1115/23 B1130/26 B1132/32 B1134/05
B1141/02 B1152/02 B1315/12 C0055/03
C0056/28 C0207/25 C0207/26 C0392/10
C0429/28 C0430/43 C0522/12 C0522/25
Pagoda (1) A0486/13
pagoda (1) B1303/20
paid (39) A0136/35
A0143/09 A0144/08 A0157/18 A0174/10
A0174/31 A0176/16 A0179/24 A0182/17
A0251/20 A0261/03 A0338/03 A0365/05
A0541/17 A0654/24 B0806/T B0875/28
B0876/09 B0877/09 B0877/20 B0877/23
B0878/33 B0879/02 B0914/20 B0958/34
B0981/33 B0990/29 B1005/29 B1130/31
B1135/15 B1208/13 B1208/29 C0088/40
C0097/17 C0158/24 C0174/14 C0201/02
C0395/39 C0561/14
pain (55)
pained (1) A0643/34
painful (12) A0078/04
A0210/26 A0499/15 A0608/21 A0691/20
B0949/30 B0956/10 B1037/07 B1165/28
C0088/20 C0406/02 C0418/44
painfully (5) A0405/13
A0641/V B0940/28 B1014/12 B1089/05
pains (17) A0081/31
A0092/07 A0123/13 A0266/08 A0430/31
A0534/20 A0670/04 B0744/34 B0941/13
B0988/31 B1128/30 B1131/32 B1132/07
B1384/08 C0098/36 C0407/24 C0411/26
paint (5) A0035/27

->A0461/04 B0925/23 B1168/05 B1372/22
paint-begrimed (1) A0510/10
painted (17) A0100/29
A0123/02 A0370/16 A0404/30 A0405/22
A0674/30 A0689/26 B0925/26 B1180/13
B1192/28 B1337/32 B1340/09 C0123/09
C0537/40 C0552/05 C0552/13 C0569/29
painter (15) A0273/21
A0282/25 A0282/27 A0665/01 A0665/08
A0665/11 A0665/18 A0665/23 A0665/26
A0665/34 A0666/V A0706/31 A0707/24
B1271/33 B1272/25
painters (2) A0157/21 A0160/V
painting (16) A0059/04
A0069/V A0070/04 A0160/14 A0164/09
A0164/10 A0164/25 A0435/19 A0497/11
A0663/22 A0663/29 A0664/11 B0923/15
B0949/06 B1257/10 C0065/18
paintings (16) A0035/25
A0035/28 A0035/28 A0160/02 A0209/17
A0405/14 A0405/17 A0502/03 A0502/10
A0662/12 A0662/13 A0663/02 A0664/27
B1179/08 B1179/25 B1180/13
pair (37) A0034/24
A0055/07 A0057/14 A0064/13 A0103/27
A0103/30 A0164/24 A0205/16 A0241/10
A0247/32 A0248/13 A0252/14 A0338/21
A0340/36 A0368/09 A0379/08 A0379/14
A0379/22 A0488/25 A0513/20 B0745/34
B0916/13 B0990/19 B1054/11 B1089/23
B1090/25 B1091/23 B1095/06 B1153/10
B1178/34 B1185/33 B1186/01 B1248/23
C0105/04 C0109/03 C0391/26 C0396/11
pairs (3) B1248/22
C0089/29 C0178/28
Paixhan (1) A0628/25
Palace (9) A0019/18
A0021/01 A0028/23 A0029/06 A0151/23
A0152/06 A0164/15 A0406/22 A0417/V
palace (31) A0021/21
A0023/16 A0024/17 A0025/04 A0025/18
A0029/18 A0122/21 A0123/07 A0123/30
A0124/07 A0152/15 A0154/21 A0155/12
A0155/20 A0210/08 A0250/09 A0406/27
A0406/28 A0407/17 A0429/22 A0486/05
A0486/11 A0486/21 B0947/03 B0947/04
B1156/09 B1192/20 B1192/25 B1192/33
B1193/13 C0069/27
palaces (10) A0087/36 A0122/06
A0151/05 A0515/02 A0671/17 A0683/02
B0864/34 B1160/10 B1160/11 C0174/34
Paladian (1) A0151/V
Palaeochori (1) A0159/02
Palais (1) C0430/31
Palais/Royal (3) A0533/32
B0725/26 B0753/07
palanquins (1) B0945/15
palatable (4) C0151/33
C0177/10 C0188/22 C0535/01
palate (2) A0250/26 A0388/30
palaver (2) A0251/29 A0466/06
Palazzo (1) A0156/30
palazzo (4) A0446/21
B1258/20 B1263/06 B1263/10
pale (49) A0028/03
->A0036/17 A0087/17 A0104/12 A0153/24
A0195/09 A0197/07 A0214/11 A0215/04
A0215/26 A0218/19 A0226/16 A0227/11
A0230/15 A0231/24 A0299/17 A0312/07
A0316/21 A0373/06 A0407/39 A0448/03
A0510/22 A0514/01 A0587/19 A0665/11
A0672/32 A0676/02 B0789/13 B0796/35
B0797/07 B0810/29 B0814/27 B0928/01
B1004/10 B1014/29 B1020/02 B1046/24
B1049/32 B1145/20 B1185/08 B1348/33
C0061/40 C0067/27 C0088/11 C0122/29
C0418/43 C0432/14 C0543/22 C0557/09
paleness (1) B0753/09
paler (4) A0459/21
C0059/02 C0061/06 C0124/12
Palfrey (1) A0272/32
Palfrey, J. G. (1) A0267/22
Paliggenesia (Gr.) (1) A0230/25
paliggenesia (Gr.) (1) A0226/26
palin (Gr.) (1) A0346/03
pall (3) A0022/17
A0246/02 A0319/13
pall-like (1) A0322/03
Palladian (1) A0151/05
palled (1) A0166/02
pallet (1) A0665/05
palliation (1) C0555/30
palliative (1) B1235/17
pallid (8) A0190/02
A0319/15 A0326/14 A0401/32 A0407/04
A0609/08 A0666/02 B0947/30
pallidly (1) C0205/41
pallor (10) A0154/26 A0159/V
A0190/05 A0324/29 A0402/07 A0410/33
A0442/04 A0509/19 B0826/20 B0956/19
palm (7) A0088/16
A0249/06 A0433/03 B0944/23 B0945/28
B1226/10 C0078/18
palmed (2) A0056/29 A0066/19
Palmer's/Land (2) C0159/34 C0160/01
palmetto (1) B0807/08
palms (2) A0625/16 C0124/38
palpabilities (1) B1038/33
palpability (2) B1034/20 B1223/02
palpable (16) A0070/15
A0070/29 A0080/13 A0081/16 A0104/34
A0217/V A0325/07 A0403/34 A0614/16
B0757/09 B0757/27 B0948/05 B0961/24
B1314/12 C0413/06 C0419/01
palpably (6) A0078/24 A0215/25
A0329/21 B0990/05 B1037/11 C0124/07
palpi (1) B1250/24
palpitate (1) A0195/06
palpitated (1) B0967/08
palpitates (1) B0961/30
palpitating (4) A0054/31
A0063/31 A0218/27 C0175/33
palsied (1) A0243/30
palsying (1) B1246/13
paltry (6) A0057/28 A0068/10
A0346/24 A0588/31 B0850/20 B0907/V
pamphlet (9) A0174/01
A0179/12 A0182/13 A0265/34 B1359/13
B1359/28 B1380/13 C0392/11 C0428/38
Pan (1) A0124/15

pan (6) A0101/10 B0834/31
B0834/32 B0834/33 B0835/01 C0170/12
Pandemonium (1) B1017/29
pane (2) A0158/01 A0321/16
panel (1) A0546/19
panels (1) A0689/25
panes (11) A0367/13
A0401/10 A0501/09 A0507/20 A0671/32
A0672/06 A0672/17 A0674/07 B1336/25
B1336/27 C0410/17
pangs (4) A0319/07
A0319/09 B1226/08 C0126/21
panic (1) C0187/26
panic-stricken (1) A0445/08
Pankey (1) C0058/29
pannels (2) A0245/V A0416/23
panorama (2) A0578/35 B1278/10
panoramic (2) B1278/03 B1280/25
pansies (1) B1212/31
pantaloons (14) A0034/16 A0034/23
A0488/26 A0508/33 B0869/22 B0878/02
B1185/33 B1194/29 C0083/15 C0105/06
C0119/20 C0121/06 C0398/04 C0552/16
pantaloons' (1) C0119/04
panted (3) A0254/05
A0458/22 A0696/05
Pantheism (3) A0079/07
A0226/25 A0230/24
pantheistical (1) A0625/04
panting (6) A0028/V B0826/13
B0944/05 C0081/30 C0526/15 C0563/24
pantomime (1) B1182/34
pantries (1) B1313/01
pants (1) A0485/08
Papa (1) A0656/16
papa (3) A0655/16
A0655/22 B0875/19
papal (1) A0021/27
Papaver/rhoeas (1) C0428/29
Paper (4) B0753/13
B0753/31 B0753/36 B0754/04
paper (140)
paper-hangings (1) A0498/V
papered (1) B1339/33
papers (34) A0093/14 A0093/16
A0102/03 A0102/26 A0112/25 A0263/13
A0263/16 A0263/17 A0280/08 A0284/21
A0337/34 A0338/11 A0538/06 A0547/03
A0566/16 B0726/08 B0728/08 B0738/02
B0876/22 B0876/31 B0980/32 B0990/31
B1138/36 B1302/26 B1304/06 B1360/06
B1363/03 C0085/07 C0207/06 C0427/24
C0428/10 C0448/V C0521/19 C0523/10
papier (3) A0034/02
B1114/02 B1179/24
papillon (1) A0071/01
papillotes (1) A0371/05
papyrus (1) B1292/32
papyrus (3) B1179/24
B1180/12 B1180/24
par (10) A0273/29 A0384/23
A0528/15 B0878/04 B0892/10 B0986/32
B1114/03 C0430/28 C0430/30 C0550/24
par (3) A0293/V B1014/22 B1190/04
Parable (1) A0188/T
parable (2) A0609/28 A0621/21
parachutes (1) A0381/26
paracutas (1) C0174/08
parade (2) A0496/15 A0545/04
paraded (1) A0428/27
Paradise (7) A0100/21
A0100/21 B1277/10 B1302/30 B1302/31
C0544/03 C0547/36
paradise (5) A0612/03
A0642/27 B0862/06 B1283/04 B1384/31
paradises (2) A0707/25 B1272/26
paradox (7) A0429/03
A0478/07 A0482/05 A0495/V B1183/28
C0438/V C0535/42
Paradox, Sir Positive (2) A0175/09
A0180/32
paradoxical (4) A0213/06
A0399/26 B1220/21 B1302/02
paradoxically (1) A0511/20
Paragrab (1) B1368/T
paragrab (5) B1373/10
B1373/15 B1374/01 B1374/03 B1375/15
paragraph (15) A0302/18
A0341/14 B0739/06 B0740/15 B0743/09
B0759/17 B1101/18 B1358/20 B1358/25
B1359/03 B1370/13 B1370/31 B1371/05
B1371/27 B1373/13
paragraphs (5) A0537/04
B0949/28 B1136/26 B1141/31 B1370/03
parallel (1) B0723/M
parallel (37) A0590/34
B0723/M B0749/26 B0772/25 B0773/02
B0773/14 B0773/16 B1080/32 B1156/24
B1160/29 B1248/17 B1339/32 B1384/11
C0053/T C0149/10 C0152/22 C0157/29
C0157/31 C0157/32 C0158/13 C0158/30
C0159/02 C0160/20 C0161/22 C0162/05
C0170/26 C0185/12 C0193/15 C0203/12
C0408/12 C0415/23 C0419/38 C0524/28
C0524/35 C0527/15 C0530/07 C0573/40
paralleled (2) A0281/24 B1122/14
paralleling (1) B0723/15
parallelipipedal (1) C0573/36
parallelism (3) B1080/37
B1279/18 C0408/18
parallelogram (3) A0501/06
B1008/29 C0152/17
parallels (2) C0161/02 C0528/15
paralysis (2) A0248/04 B0829/24
paralyze (3) A0547/29
B0765/14 C0109/35
paralyzed (4) A0137/28
A0329/25 B0960/27 C0060/07
paraphernalia (3) A0080/25
A0217/V A0248/29
paraphrased (1) A0125/07
Parasites (1) B1162/36
parasites (1) A0440/32
parasol (7) B0734/34
B0735/09 B0753/27 B0758/09 B0759/03
B0759/13 B0761/33
parcel (8) A0128/19
A0265/32 A0319/23 B0872/29 B0981/01
B1128/24 B1362/29 C0425/10
parcelled (1) B0863/36

parcels (1) C0430/48
parched (2) B0967/05 C0078/36
parchment (33) A0093/17
A0112/28 B0828/35 B0829/04 B0829/13
B0829/18 B0829/28 B0830/01 B0830/05
B0830/14 B0830/20 B0830/24 B0830/30
B0830/35 B0831/06 B0831/10 B0831/10
B0831/12 B0831/16 B0831/22 B0831/31
B0832/06 B0832/10 B0832/16 B0832/30
B0834/24 B0834/30 B0835/03 B0835/V
B0839/30 B1077/09 B1239/23 B1383/27
pardon (24) A0056/17
A0066/06 A0121/29 A0124/16 A0158/14
A0158/15 A0300/04 A0348/11 B0727/22
B0768/17 B0873/34 B1005/V B1127/21
B1127/23 B1189/29 B1189/31 B1211/01
B1212/01 C0104/22 C0426/21 C0426/26
C0426/37 C0427/06 C0521/15
pardonable (1) B0887/19
pardoned (6) A0250/18 A0271/33
A0278/23 A0428/13 B0763/05 B1152/11
pardonne (1) B0899/28
pardons (1) B1010/14
pardons (5) A0108/13
A0656/06 B1005/03 B1010/15 B1158/35
parent (5) A0429/19
A0625/29 A0626/V B1332/28 C0551/37
parent's (1) B1322/25
parentheses (1) B1222/01
parenthesis (1) B1101/34
parents (9) A0026/20
A0427/26 A0440/06 A0483/09 A0652/29
B0753/29 B0850/11 B1361/01 C0067/03
parfumerie (4) B0725/V
B0726/V B0753/06 B0753/16
Parian (1) A0510/09
parier (2) B0986/33 B0986/V
Paris (50) A0093/23 A0445/01
A0445/32 A0531/15 A0531/26 A0532/07
A0532/24 A0541/27 A0544/14 A0544/29
A0550/12 A0564/25 A0681/M B0727/17
B0740/14 B0749/09 B0750/03 B0750/04
B0753/19 B0757/14 B0758/22 B0759/29
B0760/08 B0760/25 B0763/25 B0773/02
B0887/24 B0892/12 B0897/28 B0898/28
B0914/12 B0941/11 B0957/15 B0974/01
B0978/17 B0987/12 B0992/33 B1002/04
B1004/13 B1005/05 B1008/17 B1075/13
B1077/03 B1077/28 B1261/07 B1380/06
B1380/14 C0423/23 C0526/15 C0526/22
Paris (1) C0430/30
parish (1) A0240/06
Parisian (18) A0019/02 A0297/03
A0545/01 A0546/18 A0554/11 A0562/23
B0723/14 B0725/02 B0727/03 B0728/13
B0735/05 B0898/28 B0901/13 B0915/11
B0974/15 B0978/10 B0983/21 B1007/33
Parisians (1) B0726/30
Park (2) A0464/15 A0512/30
park (4) A0021/03
C0561/32 C0561/34 C0562/13
Park/Theatre (1) B1244/01
Parker (24) C0112/33
C0114/10 C0118/10 C0118/24 C0118/40
C0119/11 C0119/16 C0119/24 C0123/02
->C0125/10 C0127/05 C0127/41 C0129/07
C0129/33 C0130/09 C0130/29 C0130/37
C0132/01 C0132/12 C0133/19 C0133/22
C0134/35 C0135/12 C0135/22
Parker, Richard (3) C0102/22
C0112/31 C0113/23
Parker's (1) C0115/04
parle (1) A0273/29
parlerebbe (1) A0662/V
parley (2) A0413/28 C0072/06
Parliament (1) C0525/34
parlor (10) A0354/06 B0909/25
B0916/21 B1004/02 B1008/06 B1014/09
B1339/18 B1339/24 B1339/25 B1339/28
parlors (1) B1313/01
parly-wouing> (1) A0468/27
parmi (1) A0035/10
Parmly's (1) A0388/14
Parnasse (1) A0033/18
paroquet (1) A0087/10
paroxysm (5) A0034/03
A0053/37 A0063/09 C0072/30 C0080/40
paroxysms (2) A0558/17 B0959/24
Parrish (1) A0464/04
parrot (4) B0750/30
B0750/31 B1349/18 B1349/34
parrotfish (1) C0174/07
Parry (1) C0535/33
pars (1) A0382/15
parsimonious (2) A0624/18 B1055/05
parsimony (1) B1093/02
parsley (1) C0138/11
part (240)
partaker (1) C0188/16
partakes (3) A0282/02
B1093/33 C0521/28
partaking (4) A0405/28
B1007/30 C0175/40 C0553/36
partant (1) A0037/V
parte (2) B0740/03 B0745/11
parted (8) A0137/29
A0215/11 A0484/25 A0489/22 A0627/34
B1390/11 C0176/25 C0552/25
parterre (1) A0429/16
Parthenon (2) A0108/14 B1275/33
parti-colored (3) A0321/28
A0326/10 A0603/11
parti-coloured (1) A0321/V
parti-striped (1) B1257/18
partial (22) A0276/17 A0293/09
A0328/07 A0438/30 A0458/16 B0966/21
B1010/31 B1242/09 B1381/08 C0065/28
C0097/19 C0097/37 C0098/03 C0098/16
C0098/38 C0098/40 C0118/11 C0119/15
C0119/18 C0148/38 C0185/16 C0552/21
partiality (5) A0064/15
A0204/01 B0850/23 B0855/07 B1139/19
partially (40) A0054/03
A0063/12 A0102/23 A0140/30 A0215/05
A0294/V A0298/V A0322/13 A0325/15
A0379/09 A0404/18 A0410/13 A0415/08
A0441/26 A0543/27 A0553/22 B0730/08
B0837/09 B0891/01 B0933/30 B0941/30
B0959/05 B1032/05 B1235/25 B1263/01
B1337/34 C0060/30 C0072/31 C0087/24

->C0109/17 C0113/39 C0114/39 C0125/21
C0144/14 C0155/18 C0173/13 C0192/34
C0397/14 C0442/V C0545/40
participants (1) B0844/18
participate (1) A0435/15
participated (3) C0152/21
C0537/08 C0565/07
participation (2) A0020/08 A0560/11
particle (14) A0303/19 A0535/04
A0580/28 B0827/27 B0980/19 B1107/27
B1213/35 B1347/15 C0122/34 C0134/22
C0160/21 C0164/14 C0164/23 C0203/12
particles (7) A0694/06
B1033/26 B1081/01 B1214/29 C0079/23
C0080/02 C0172/09
particolored (2) A0100/11 A0326/V
particoloured (1) A0157/V
particular (76)
particularized (1) C0428/28
particularizing (1) A0578/25
particularly (37) A0120/18
A0120/V A0123/04 A0163/26 A0204/10
A0212/32 A0261/25 A0261/28 A0262/04
A0262/21 A0269/23 A0301/07 A0382/14
A0414/07 A0535/28 A0628/15 A0628/16
A0630/14 A0631/01 B0735/20 B0735/28
B0751/07 B0926/33 B1010/22 B1010/30
B1016/06 B1141/32 B1234/07 B1236/08
B1300/02 B1310/09 C0055/28 C0093/31
C0110/11 C0429/43 C0530/21 C0541/15
particulars (36) A0024/21
A0078/14 A0078/15 A0209/14 A0299/33
A0352/32 A0398/06 A0538/27 A0544/14
A0559/30 B0832/14 B0933/17 B0979/14
B1068/07 B1069/21 B1073/02 B1081/19
B1191/06 B1191/10 B1234/02 B1240/15
B1300/35 B1329/15 B1340/V B1351/24
C0096/10 C0110/03 C0162/02 C0203/32
C0400/19 C0428/15 C0521/09 C0524/38
C0528/07 C0530/15 C0546/31
particuller> (1) A0464/24
parties (24) A0075/04
A0093/03 A0112/16 A0293/18 A0486/08
B0727/34 B0753/40 B0770/16 B0770/17
B1047/29 B1048/16 B1096/01 B1152/32
B1233/04 C0177/19 C0177/20 C0177/31
C0186/41 C0188/41 C0438/V C0528/19
C0547/07 C0560/23 C0563/05
parting (5) A0156/V
A0346/27 A0655/11 B1122/13 C0561/08
Partisan (1) A0282/26
partisan (2) B0993/02 C0102/12
partisans (1) C0093/22
partition (5) B1372/26
C0090/23 C0091/13 C0092/35 C0152/31
partitions (1) C0140/31
partly (22) A0152/V A0295/21
A0295/21 A0324/21 A0499/09 A0592/07
A0592/08 A0710/04 B0855/15 B0946/29
B0949/09 B1160/16 B1275/07 B1275/08
B1321/11 B1380/01 B1380/01 C0089/10
C0089/11 C0159/30 C0393/08 C0393/09
partner (9) A0311/04
A0384/19 A0384/V A0485/20 A0530/08
C0134/29 C0153/07 C0166/02 C0527/34
partook (10) A0213/01 A0213/26
A0322/16 A0436/08 B0891/06 B1004/33
B1089/25 C0100/36 C0418/42 C0578/20
parts (24) A0269/04
A0271/04 A0273/17 A0273/38 A0400/11
A0707/29 A0707/30 B0877/34 B0900/20
B0987/25 B1075/14 B1181/24 B1272/29
B1272/30 B1315/02 B1338/05 B1351/32
C0183/39 C0427/34 C0521/17 C0531/32
C0534/33 C0554/14 C0554/15
party (160)
party's (1) C0562/09
parvenu (3) A0440/36
A0441/23 A0496/22
Pas (1) A0062/32
pas (8) A0033/19
A0037/02 A0037/25 A0071/01 A0216/09
A0385/07 A0568/25 A0654/06
pas-de-zephyr (1) A0371/31
Pas/Seul (2) A0177/02 A0177/09
pasan (Gr.) (1) B1385/18
Pascal (1) A0611/03
Pasigono (1) B1160/15
Pasquinaded (1) A0534/19
pass (59)
passable (4) A0091/16
A0110/18 A0286/16 B0810/07
passados (1) A0292/M
passage (100)
Passages (1) A0178/V
passages (27) A0065/24
A0068/06 A0075/05 A0078/25 A0294/V
A0297/12 A0314/22 A0400/24 A0409/07
A0437/04 A0457/16 A0581/15 A0709/19
B0731/23 B0731/24 B0906/07 B1274/21
B1310/11 B1358/15 B1360/08 B1362/07
B1384/11 B1384/37 C0068/41 C0154/28
C0392/23 C0528/20
passant (1) C0448/V
passed (156)
passees (1) B0914/13
passenger (1) A0135/26
passengers (21) A0056/28
A0066/17 A0493/08 A0507/32 A0512/28
A0513/07 B0753/25 B0874/28 B0922/06
B0922/17 B0924/05 B0926/01 B0931/13
B0931/17 B0933/27 B0934/05 B1091/10
B1093/20 B1293/15 B1298/31 C0407/10
passerois (1) A0096/M
passers (1) B0874/27
passes (16) A0124/10
B0749/11 B0749/20 B0872/06 B1032/13
B1032/20 B1035/18 B1168/30 B1236/34
B1237/08 B1237/22 B1242/07 B1242/35
B1257/24 B1292/20 C0572/10
passing (55)
passion (47) A0020/V
A0053/23 A0055/36 A0065/18 A0156/06
A0156/23 A0156/26 A0156/26 A0225/08
A0229/08 A0262/06 A0262/29 A0279/20
A0299/27 A0313/22 A0315/09 A0315/10
A0317/16 A0323/17 A0379/24 A0638/02
A0644/18 B0764/21 B0789/10 B0890/25
B0894/18 B0898/11 B0899/05 B0901/19
B0902/15 B0913/13 B0913/V B0927/09

->B1013/07 B1050/06 B1105/05 B1122/10
B1122/25 B1122/25 B1123/05 B1163/05
B1223/14 B1223/V B1277/07 B1391/12
C0065/04 C0198/09
passionate (20) A0020/06
A0311/09 A0316/26 A0317/19 A0323/11
A0327/25 A0399/02 A0404/15 A0431/08
A0432/09 A0445/32 A0609/08 A0645/07
A0651/24 A0665/01 A0665/13 B0910/02
B1215/31 B1226/13 C0073/16
passionately (3) A0642/07
B0907/03 B1249/22
passions (2) A0053/14 A0062/21
passions (8) A0087/37
A0214/02 A0234/06 A0427/25 A0623/10
A0640/25 B1215/28 B1215/33
passive (4) A0613/27
B0764/01 C0129/12 C0429/24
passport (1) C0526/25
passports (2) B1075/14 B1075/18
passus (1) A0043/M
Past (1) B0773/26
past (43) A0078/21
A0144/19 A0162/23 A0209/08 A0228/08
A0228/24 A0252/28 A0298/08 A0355/26
A0436/22 A0438/13 A0507/25 A0535/23
A0577/05 A0608/25 B0813/20 B0843/04
B0903/24 B0941/01 B0944/01 B0948/17
B0949/33 B0977/26 B1075/22 B1105/20
B1105/33 B1138/29 B1138/31 B1168/39
B1181/13 B1195/09 B1311/16 B1321/V
C0081/16 C0132/06 C0167/35 C0404/35
C0412/07 C0526/39 C0537/38 C0549/40
C0556/19 C0561/10
paste (3) B0877/25
B1113/08 B1292/32
pasteboard (2) B0990/35 B1179/23
pastimes (1) A0431/05
pastor (1) A0428/29
pastoral (1) B1279/01
pastures (1) A0047/22
pat (2) A0053/25 A0062/29
Patagonia (1) C0158/11
patch (5) B1279/33
C0184/05 C0189/07 C0192/21 C0202/33
patches (3) A0087/08
A0510/15 C0150/26
pate (1) A0100/30
pate (1) B1107/18
pate-pans (1) A0102/03
patent (1) A0681/M
patent (2) A0498/V B0870/26
patent-blacking (1) A0483/V
patent-leather (1) B1185/35
paternal (5) A0179/11
A0210/22 A0311/03 B1132/16 B1140/19
pates (1) A0096/06
path (49) A0020/V
A0073/14 A0078/15 A0145/02 A0210/27
A0316/09 A0367/04 A0417/05 A0426/M
A0445/17 A0458/02 A0600/28 A0639/11
A0642/34 A0693/19 A0708/08 B0764/29
B0765/04 B0774/01 B0817/34 B0943/10
B0943/10 B0946/26 B0948/12 B1048/35
B1048/V B1160/29 B1296/21 B1302/05
->B1313/19 B1313/20 B1316/12 B1328/04
B1330/14 C0074/32 C0074/37 C0075/09
C0171/26 C0172/19 C0174/14 C0181/22
C0184/11 C0184/23 C0186/25 C0192/03
C0192/04 C0199/37 C0402/10 C0580/02
pathology (1) A0067/28
pathos (2) A0162/V B1133/05
Pathrick> (8) A0464/10
A0466/21 A0468/08 A0468/19 A0469/06
A0469/08 A0469/10 A0469/20
paths (12) A0244/22
A0640/33 A0643/10 B1297/25 B1299/12
B1316/09 B1329/07 B1337/03 C0152/32
C0152/34 C0542/18 C0543/31
pathway (5) A0198/04
A0323/18 A0591/10 C0094/28 C0206/05
patience (7) B0986/06
B1131/35 B1208/26 C0071/36 C0123/35
C0130/11 C0170/28
patient (25) B0856/15
B0941/14 B0941/31 B0950/05 B0959/21
B0959/32 B0960/21 B0962/10 B1006/08
B1010/02 B1011/19 B1021/21 B1032/17
B1233/19 B1235/34 B1236/06 B1237/06
B1238/03 B1238/17 B1239/05 B1241/22
B1242/28 B1242/32 C0129/23 C0535/40
patient's (4) B1235/22
B1236/27 B1237/16 B1242/14
patiently (3) B0794/26
B0808/12 B1352/02
patients (10) B1004/16 B1005/12
B1006/01 B1006/24 B1007/20 B1009/25
B1015/16 B1016/36 B1018/20 B1018/35
patria (1) A0681/M
patriarch (1) A0121/22
patrician (3) A0086/26
A0089/11 B1187/24
patrie (1) B1206/14
patrimony (3) A0159/15
A0399/15 A0531/23
patriots (1) A0127/20
patron (3) A0705/13
B1140/32 B1270/11
patronage (4) A0432/18
A0435/23 B1072/23 B1208/19
patronise (1) A0246/31
patronize (1) A0341/16
patronized (2) A0071/09 A0071/29
patronizing (1) B1133/17
patronym (1) B0887/19
patronymic (2) A0337/07 A0434/05
patted (1) C0079/17
Patten (1) C0155/24
Patten's (1) C0155/33
pattern (5) A0089/15
A0321/25 A0367/16 A0498/09 A0509/03
patterns (4) A0320/24
A0322/16 A0497/28 B1179/09
Patterson (1) C0153/31
patting (2) B0854/21 C0169/18
Paul (1) A0079/08
Paulding (1) A0281/20
Paulding, J. K. (1) A0266/33
Paulding's (2) A0267/06 A0267/08
pause (31) A0024/09

->A0028/V A0055/04 A0064/07 A0158/V
A0177/13 A0183/07 A0216/22 A0263/16
A0297/19 A0320/27 A0328/23 A0339/10
A0440/14 A0534/13 A0564/14 A0626/05
A0629/14 A0656/25 A0672/28 A0683/27
B0769/08 B0770/27 B0821/20 B0823/23
B0840/16 B1033/18 B1033/19 B1188/17
B1386/06 C0067/18
paused (26) A0074/08 A0140/16
A0166/06 A0339/18 A0350/07 A0352/09
A0397/21 A0414/02 A0414/26 A0514/19
A0534/11 A0629/33 A0683/22 A0692/04
B0903/20 B1004/06 B1214/16 B1250/09
B1259/25 B1260/06 B1262/20 C0079/15
C0189/38 C0388/09 C0388/10 C0421/28
pauses (6) A0162/01 A0411/31
B0764/32 B0955/31 B0983/10 B1032/V
pausing (4) A0154/08
A0161/25 B0817/17 B0871/28
pauvre (1) A0036/10
paved (4) A0366/32
A0535/33 A0538/20 B0980/29
Pavee (6) B0725/22 B0726/19
B0729/05 B0729/31 B0732/36 B0758/20
pavement (6) A0044/13 A0415/21
A0494/01 A0535/31 A0536/04 A0557/30
paving-stones (3) A0243/31
A0514/28 A0535/24
paw (3) A0470/10 A0650/05 B1338/24
Pawnees (1) C0540/31
paws (5) C0072/33
C0076/23 C0076/26 C0076/32 C0092/02
pay (46) A0340/19 A0485/13
A0486/11 A0539/02 A0563/08 A0631/22
A0655/11 B0808/26 B0821/10 B0841/08
B0872/28 B0874/34 B0875/05 B0876/05
B0876/07 B0876/13 B0924/10 B0982/35
B0992/26 B1091/13 B1092/18 B1094/03
B1094/05 B1127/32 B1129/07 B1129/22
B1130/07 B1130/08 B1130/10 B1130/30
B1131/04 B1131/16 B1132/30 B1134/17
B1135/12 B1207/22 B1207/25 B1208/02
B1208/04 B1208/04 B1257/27 B1373/11
C0069/38 C0081/26 C0179/34 C0554/20
payed (1) C0533/01
paying (8) A0490/22
A0560/30 B1160/05 B1206/09 C0099/06
C0393/10 C0439/V C0538/06
payment (5) B0735/30
B0767/17 B0767/20 B0878/31 C0395/35
Payne (1) B0729/34
pays (1) B0877/02
pe (13) B1102/19
B1102/37 B1103/01 B1103/25 B1103/28
B1104/03 B1109/07 B1109/07 B1109/11
B1109/18 B1109/18 B1109/19 B1109/31
pea (2) A0371/01 B1363/19
pea-green (1) A0100/05
pea-jacket (3) C0092/36
C0094/07 C0100/06
peace (9) A0043/V
A0209/06 A0216/13 A0384/18 A0641/07
A0645/06 A0696/31 B0976/31 C0522/09
Peace/River (1) C0527/11
peaceable (2) A0413/22 C0531/27
peaceful (2) A0603/17 B1370/08
peacefully (1) A0101/06
peach (1) C0081/10
peacock (1) B1300/21
peak (1) C0184/30
peaked (1) C0167/18
peaks (2) C0153/37 C0161/30
peal (1) A0674/10
peanuts (1) B1244/06
pear (3) C0165/26
C0559/19 C0576/05
pear-tree (1) B1337/10
Pearl (1) C0157/41
pearl (2) A0348/33 A0407/16
pearl-powder (1) B0914/10
pearly (2) A0328/02 A0639/24
pears (1) C0138/12
peasant (2) B0945/31 B0958/31
peasantry (1) A0399/19
Pease's (1) B1096/03
pebble (1) B1279/33
pebbles (4) A0639/24
A0639/31 B1280/14 B1333/25
Pectoral (1) A0047/20
pectoral (1) B0960/19
peculiar (110)
peculiar-looking (1) A0071/14
peculiarities (14) A0081/37 A0216/04
A0267/08 A0270/37 A0280/06 A0281/21
A0294/V A0298/07 A0328/17 A0403/26
A0664/16 A0706/07 B0940/25 B1271/11
peculiarity (24) A0098/12
A0123/11 A0161/12 A0246/15 A0246/15
A0275/37 A0284/06 A0313/06 A0379/21
A0433/27 A0549/17 A0549/20 A0654/13
B0745/26 B0745/26 B0746/11 B0850/13
B0960/35 B1240/18 B1248/27 B1337/27
B1391/02 C0137/30 C0429/35
peculiarly (19) A0053/11
A0065/16 A0093/37 A0113/21 A0247/31
A0439/V B0728/12 B0736/22 B0750/13
B0818/29 B0925/25 B0961/36 B1008/18
B1081/08 B1315/26 B1315/30 C0175/08
C0202/16 C0426/01
pecuniary (4) A0624/10
A0711/14 B1276/15 C0564/11
pedant (1) B1115/26
pedant's (1) B1115/25
pedants (1) A0609/33
peddling (1) A0099/05
pedestrian (1) B1328/01
pedestrians (2) B0864/12 B1090/16
pedis (1) B1182/13
pedlars (1) A0509/31
pedlers (1) B1312/27
Pedro (23) A0085/08
A0087/11 A0088/14 A0088/18 A0089/23
A0089/25 A0089/35 A0090/16 A0090/33
A0091/06 A0091/33 A0092/10 A0092/14
A0092/31 A0093/14 A0093/27 A0093/34
A0093/36 A0094/09 A0662/V A0663/03
A0667/16 A0667/40
Pedro's (2) A0089/13 A0090/24
Pedronist (1) A0086/10
peep (4) A0121/10

->A0122/25 A0371/20 B1191/34
peeper> (1) A0465/13
peepers (2) A0469/12 A0470/02
peepers> (3) A0464/13
A0465/10 A0468/29
peer (2) B1222/26 C0433/01
peered (4) A0045/14
A0312/28 A0640/09 B1331/12
peering (4) A0411/28
A0507/20 A0599/M B1003/26
peers (1) A0033/07
peevish (2) A0144/27 B0851/18
peevishly (2) B0810/26 B1184/16
peevishness (1) A0141/18
peg (17) B0822/05
B0822/08 B0822/09 B0822/10 B0822/12
B0824/31 B0824/34 B0843/15 C0196/34
C0196/36 C0197/01 C0197/04 C0197/06
C0197/07 C0197/13 C0197/14 C0198/10
pegs (2) C0175/02 C0197/29
pehabe (1) B1103/32
peine (1) A0430/07
pele-mele (1) B1021/09
Pelham (1) A0079/04
pelican (1) C0164/28
pelicans (1) C0173/40
pelief (3) B1109/26
B1109/26 B1109/29
Pelion (1) A0071/06
pell (1) B1103/15
pellucid (1) B0864/33
pelly (1) A0373/14
peltries (10) C0529/05 C0529/28
C0530/12 C0530/24 C0532/15 C0532/40
C0539/28 C0544/01 C0564/20 C0576/14
pemmican (4) C0396/10
C0534/29 C0535/02 C0535/31
pen (27) A0096/07
A0265/22 A0268/18 A0269/03 A0281/18
A0281/28 A0339/08 A0339/11 A0339/14
A0639/04 A0703/28 B0809/12 B0809/16
B0849/02 B0851/29 B0983/09 B1126/07
B1127/23 B1128/01 B1132/13 B1132/18
B1134/02 B1138/01 B1143/22 B1268/26
C0069/21 C0092/15
pen-holding (1) A0508/36
pen-knife (1) B0851/27
penalty (1) A0642/16
penblade (1) C0076/07
penchant (5) A0091/33
A0091/33 A0111/09 A0111/09 A0273/24
pencil (6) A0162/05 B0878/26
B0880/08 B0900/18 C0193/24 C0203/40
pencil-scratches (1) B1115/10
penciled (1) B1325/08
penciling (1) B1235/19
pencilled (1) B1114/12
pencilling (1) B1113/03
pencillings (1) B1114/25
Pendant (1) B1328/T
pendant (1) A0500/21
pendants (1) A0246/24
pendent (1) B1282/06
pendulous (2) A0602/31 A0615/06
Pendulum (6) A0481/V A0481/V
->A0484/V A0484/V A0488/V A0681/T
pendulum (10) A0020/15 A0672/22
A0689/29 A0690/12 A0691/15 A0691/30
A0692/23 A0693/15 A0694/18 A0694/31
Pendulum, Peter (2) A0481/V
A0483/V
pendulums (1) A0373/29
penetrate (8) A0145/21
A0611/29 A0638/12 B0734/31 B1282/14
C0082/21 C0121/24 C0181/06
penetrated (8) A0264/04
B0943/05 B1138/11 B1321/28 C0159/36
C0160/17 C0161/21 C0527/30
penetrating (9) A0107/09
A0461/17 A0583/04 C0158/21 C0159/05
C0160/30 C0162/14 C0564/23 C0565/01
penetration (2) A0064/31 A0434/31
Penguin (5) C0061/05
C0062/24 C0063/28 C0064/15 C0064/23
penguin (8) C0151/10
C0151/24 C0151/26 C0151/40 C0152/06
C0152/36 C0153/13 C0159/17
penguin's (2) C0152/35 C0152/37
penguins (5) C0151/09
C0151/22 C0152/02 C0152/37 C0153/23
peninsula (2) B1335/15 B1335/16
penknife (5) C0091/11
C0092/23 C0119/05 C0127/21 C0406/37
penmanship (5) A0268/37
A0271/04 A0272/11 A0272/37 A0273/12
pennant (1) A0240/23
penned (4) B0899/13
B0899/26 B1139/28 B1320/03
Pennicornis (1) B1163/33
pennies (2) A0485/16 B0878/30
Pennifeather (21) B1047/15
B1047/22 B1047/27 B1047/31 B1048/10
B1048/21 B1049/20 B1049/25 B1049/29
B1050/03 B1050/11 B1051/28 B1052/04
B1052/15 B1053/02 B1053/17 B1054/26
B1057/28 B1058/03 B1058/14 B1059/23
Pennifeather's (2) B1049/27
B1054/06
penning (3) A0533/26
B1195/11 B1322/14
Pennsylvania (1) B0888/V
penny (4) A0485/20
A0485/25 B1138/06 B1140/20
penny-a-liner (4) B1101/29
B1133/34 B1139/09 B1139/25
pense (1) A0036/06
pensiero (1) B0905/23
pension (3) B0729/13
B0729/14 B0756/01
pension (1) B0725/23
pensively (1) A0628/01
Penstruthal (2) B1072/31 B1075/21
pentagon (1) A0321/14
pentagonal (1) A0321/13
Pentateuch (1) A0043/16
penthouse (1) C0191/06
penuriousness (1) A0511/22
people (114)
people-less (1) A0513/32
people's (1) B1091/23

peopleless (1) A0189/24
pepper-castor (1) B1141/12
per (10) A0301/12 A0301/12
  A0301/12 A0302/19 A0302/19 A0302/19
  A0303/03 A0303/04 A0303/04 A0603/35
per (38) A0027/24 A0034/22
  A0044/04 A0485/08 A0485/08 A0485/26
  A0486/16 A0657/05 A0705/18 A0705/21
  A0705/22 A0705/23 B0872/02 B0924/11
  B1055/19 B1072/10 B1079/15 B1138/30
  B1164/39 B1166/31 B1270/17 B1270/19
  B1270/20 B1270/21 B1364/33 B1364/34
  C0138/36 C0141/33 C0161/05 C0163/09
  C0163/11 C0164/04 C0164/16 C0164/21
  C0164/21 C0167/37 C0400/16 C0400/21
perambulates (1) A0126/16
perambulations (1) A0431/04
perambulators (1) A0044/14
percave> (4) A0465/01
  A0467/16 A0467/31 A0470/02
percaved> (1) A0465/08
perceive (112)
perceived (75)
perceives (2) B0977/10 B1030/06
perceiving (28) A0056/25
  A0058/10 A0122/11 A0158/09 A0323/06
  A0345/01 A0356/16 A0412/24 A0412/27
  A0536/02 A0667/57 B0893/15 B0907/06
  B0967/24 B0990/10 B1006/08 B1031/19
  B1155/30 B1292/17 B1372/23 C0056/08
  C0131/24 C0157/28 C0174/19 C0194/12
  C0198/19 C0204/16 C0428/29
perceptible (36) A0136/26
  A0312/16 A0316/V A0326/27 A0328/08
  A0379/16 A0400/18 A0435/17 A0448/01
  A0458/14 A0459/18 A0591/21 A0691/14
  B0807/02 B0893/26 B0962/13 B1180/25
  B1224/30 B1235/15 B1237/02 B1280/09
  B1329/17 B1334/06 B1335/23 B1349/28
  C0061/18 C0078/03 C0079/39 C0098/28
  C0142/10 C0183/05 C0184/05 C0203/29
  C0416/32 C0419/41 C0428/31
perceptibly (3) A0460/08
  A0690/14 C0204/21
perception (20) A0047/28
  A0312/06 A0326/01 A0439/30 A0456/05
  A0530/22 A0663/24 B0926/31 B1030/06
  B1030/23 B1038/07 B1038/18 B1039/02
  B1039/31 B1137/23 B1167/14 B1302/06
  C0059/35 C0079/03 C0399/02
perceptions (4) A0234/09
  A0558/03 A0613/26 C0538/39
perceptive (2) A0479/35 B1312/25
percha (1) B1293/06
percha (1) B1298/26
perchance (1) A0320/17
perdidit (1) A0536/18
perds (1) A0037/07
perdu (1) A0037/08
perdus (1) C0524/10
Pere (1) A0037/06
peregrinations (2) A0241/22
  B1110/11
peremptorily (3) A0318/04
  A0442/12 A0623/13
peremptory (5) A0024/27
  A0385/19 A0386/25 B0904/30 B1184/16
perennial (1) B1277/06
perfect (86)
perfected (3) A0458/23
  B0862/18 B1037/09
perfection (17) A0100/21
  A0164/19 A0312/15 A0379/25 A0508/28
  A0529/22 B0871/27 B0983/30 B1036/05
  B1039/11 B1160/33 B1169/18 B1214/20
  B1215/02 B1215/05 B1273/31 B1338/30
perfectionists (2) A0703/07
  B1268/06
perfectly (55)
perfidy (1) C0180/06
perforate (1) C0573/29
perforating (1) B1163/18
perforations (2) A0321/26 B1235/28
perforce (3) A0672/30
  B0877/29 B1055/05
perform (7) A0496/09
  A0705/06 B1006/11 B1270/05 B1346/17
  C0111/22 C0406/35
performance (6) A0059/14 A0672/29
  B0905/31 B0910/19 B0913/18 B1244/03
performances (2) A0406/10 B0894/22
performed (17) A0067/21
  A0354/19 A0382/V A0688/20 B0879/04
  B0910/03 B0934/03 B1013/21 B1020/16
  B1020/29 B1069/15 B1142/33 B1166/22
  B1222/06 C0097/05 C0416/11 C0534/05
performer (2) A0056/04 A0065/28
performers (2) B0904/28 B1245/03
performing (4) A0387/15
  B0875/28 B0875/29 B1301/06
performs (1) C0559/10
perfume (14) A0055/14 A0064/28
  A0159/21 A0212/03 A0343/31 A0350/20
  A0615/29 A0642/30 A0643/26 A0683/04
  B0863/01 B1340/15 C0543/23 C0568/12
perfumed (2) A0503/04 A0533/01
perfumer (2) B0725/25 B0726/18
perfumery (2) B0725/30 B0726/12
perfumery-girl (4) B0730/02
  B0737/09 B0748/31 B0749/14
perfumes (2) A0157/25 B1333/06
perhaps (193)
pericranium (2) A0107/13 B1292/07
Perier (1) A0652/V
Perier, Casimir (1) A0652/10
perigee (2) C0400/09 C0420/14
perihelion (2) A0458/02 C0401/25
peril (10) A0023/17 A0144/V
  A0242/31 B0949/17 B1078/30 B1158/23
  C0063/07 C0199/36 C0398/23 C0424/22
perilous (11) A0098/18
  A0578/14 A0625/06 B0765/03 C0059/36
  C0062/28 C0065/10 C0139/08 C0420/39
  C0441/V C0528/20
perils (4) B0902/17
  C0120/17 C0145/07 C0405/36
period (214)
periodical (8) A0270/07
  A0429/07 A0431/03 B0958/15 B1130/V
  B1137/27 B1138/20 C0416/37

periodically (5) A0026/04
A0242/18 B1089/23 C0173/37 C0428/42
periodicals (5) B1130/09
B1130/14 B1131/31 B1145/03 B1206/11
periods (8) A0121/20
A0402/26 A0533/29 A0609/14 A0683/12
B0723/23 C0401/27 C0417/39
periphery (1) B0749/20
perish (21) A0020/V
A0138/07 A0403/10 A0403/10 A0685/15
A0687/27 B0969/18 B1152/26 B1213/31
B1371/01 C0074/41 C0083/09 C0090/05
C0117/35 C0119/03 C0127/34 C0132/25
C0146/27 C0183/06 C0185/32 C0186/04
perished (20) A0022/11
A0025/13 A0033/02 A0088/08 A0137/26
A0318/V A0430/07 A0456/28 A0684/24
A0691/27 B1123/21 B1215/18 C0086/23
C0117/05 C0118/03 C0126/06 C0190/11
C0191/30 C0207/06 C0522/23
perishing (4) A0609/32
C0072/41 C0072/41 C0119/40
periwig (1) C0431/05
periwigs (1) A0294/V
Perkins (1) C0147/28
permanent (6) B0770/33 B0929/05
B1006/03 B1142/07 B1235/28 C0571/28
permanently (2) C0409/27 C0524/32
permeate (1) B1128/17
permeates (4) B1033/24
B1033/28 B1038/06 B1038/16
permeation (1) B1033/27
Permission (1) A0301/03
permission (10) A0546/10 A0546/11
B1052/29 B1074/13 B1091/25 B1091/25
B1159/03 B1178/21 C0101/19 C0526/20
permit (28) A0490/03
A0506/02 A0506/03 A0624/24 A0642/17
A0662/02 A0667/10 B0739/05 B0743/16
B0818/27 B0956/34 B0960/01 B1003/14
B1018/04 B1051/12 B1052/30 B1207/06
B1280/15 C0112/13 C0134/06 C0145/33
C0146/17 C0180/15 C0181/14 C0202/10
C0395/06 C0433/10 C0550/15
permits (1) B0979/21
permitted (39) A0074/23
A0086/31 A0099/26 A0100/08 A0244/12
A0293/11 A0321/07 A0428/25 A0458/28
A0532/12 A0611/06 A0625/02 A0642/25
A0681/02 A0691/21 B0771/23 B0832/10
B0854/20 B0875/20 B0889/24 B0889/V
B0907/24 B1004/18 B1005/12 B1071/V
B1134/17 B1144/20 B1277/34 B1293/15
B1295/20 B1299/05 B1311/14 C0070/25
C0088/21 C0535/28 C0539/34 C0552/01
C0562/18 C0572/36
permitting (9) A0484/28
B0733/34 B0742/32 B0748/20 B0922/04
B1183/14 C0136/32 C0172/29 C0526/24
pernicious (4) A0212/08
A0217/V C0071/25 C0137/07
perpendicular (17) A0045/06
A0280/02 B0741/29 B1080/27 B1080/31
B1162/07 B1180/17 C0181/03 C0183/39
C0185/12 C0196/15 C0398/19 C0408/06
->C0408/11 C0422/33 C0573/33 C0578/26
perpendicularly (11) A0270/17
B1075/09 B1080/26 B1281/33 C0154/33
C0173/09 C0408/05 C0410/22 C0412/09
C0573/07 C0575/36
perpetrate (2) B1130/06 B1223/22
perpetrated (6) A0102/11 B0753/21
B0757/20 B0768/28 B1017/24 C0146/29
perpetrating (1) B0757/32
perpetration (3) A0244/07
A0548/12 B1139/08
perpetrator (4) A0544/V
A0548/11 A0556/31 A0564/10
perpetrators (3) B0758/21
B0761/02 B0763/15
perpetual (7) A0432/03
A0617/02 B0852/13 B0965/08 B1157/19
B1162/08 B1187/17
perpetually (8) A0478/06
B0984/03 B1010/05 B1169/15 B1213/07
B1225/06 B1380/27 C0150/32
perplex (1) A0545/29
perplexed (5) A0566/01
B0940/04 B0989/31 B1020/35 C0563/36
perplexing (6) A0102/09 A0231/12
A0234/22 A0355/34 A0544/13 B1050/14
perplexity (4) A0401/03
A0428/30 B0943/34 B0963/18
Perrine (1) C0561/03
Perriri (1) B1163/17
persecute (2) B1096/28 B1108/05
persecuted (2) B1012/22 B1096/32
persecution (4) A0351/03
B1096/27 B1096/29 B1096/29
persecutor (2) A0056/23 A0066/25
persecutors (1) A0689/21
Persepolis (2) A0145/05 A0161/18
perseverance (9) A0055/09
A0064/12 B0770/23 B0870/01 B0870/18
B0924/01 B1362/08 C0159/28 C0394/36
persevere (6) A0351/34 C0063/04
C0095/30 C0194/12 C0576/13 C0576/26
persevered (1) A0212/07
perseveres (1) B0870/18
persevering (5) A0545/11
B0832/32 B0983/22 B1178/18 C0166/21
perseveringly (5) A0327/01
A0439/31 A0513/01 B0898/18 B0902/15
Persia (2) A0035/12 A0068/13
Persian (2) A0057/29 A0343/30
Persians (1) A0165/V
persist (12) A0080/18
A0478/04 A0515/21 B0947/25 B1113/10
B1145/16 B1206/09 B1221/06 B1221/06
B1296/30 B1313/32 B1371/01
persisted (5) B0958/36
B1186/28 C0101/07 C0131/33 C0143/20
persists (1) B0748/01
person (194)
person's (1) C0090/22
personage (22) A0104/30 A0245/20
A0248/04 A0292/V A0370/32 A0378/16
A0652/20 B0873/V B0976/29 B0976/30
B0977/03 B0977/05 B0977/11 B0977/20
B0977/27 B0991/18 B0993/15 B1011/16

->B1012/33 B1102/23 C0532/27 C0569/24
personages (2) A0250/12 C0061/09
personal (76)
personally (10) A0278/25 A0286/03
A0294/05 A0409/29 A0621/05 B0956/27
B0978/18 B1143/07 B1361/19 C0558/13
personate (1) B0933/34
personified (1) B0889/22
persons (71)
perspicacity (1) A0160/08
perspicuity (1) C0203/39
perspicuous (1) C0208/07
perspiration (2) A0685/02 C0561/23
persuaded (6) A0226/07 A0230/05
B0734/10 B1018/34 B1031/24 C0408/25
persuasion (3) A0408/10
B0958/07 B1048/10
persuasions (2) C0169/41 C0205/04
persvaded (1) B1375/19
pert (1) A0652/10
perticcler (1) B1373/22
pertinaciously (9) A0212/26
A0324/12 A0445/21 A0515/11 A0613/21
B0759/16 B1011/19 C0179/35 C0559/01
pertinacity (9) A0059/07
A0408/05 A0624/26 A0692/05 B0746/32
B0824/11 B0855/08 B0923/05 B1206/05
pertinent (2) A0293/V A0343/02
pertinently (1) B0869/14
perturbation (1) C0421/33
perturbations (1) C0441/V
perturbed (4) A0195/20
A0323/23 A0324/V C0078/09
Peru (1) A0033/06
perusal (12) A0265/34
A0269/26 A0303/01 A0409/09 A0582/30
A0663/09 B0736/18 B0977/04 B0981/30
C0393/03 C0426/31 C0521/17
peruse (4) A0302/V
B1017/17 B1106/12 B1133/06
perused (7) A0218/16
A0302/02 A0663/V B1101/09 B1130/32
B1137/27 B1139/14
pervade (2) B1039/V C0060/38
pervaded (15) A0036/11
A0214/27 A0247/02 A0328/08 A0397/07
A0401/18 A0411/25 A0437/18 A0603/17
A0615/31 A0673/02 A0696/02 C0198/08
C0564/13 C0565/08
pervades (4) B1215/10
B1215/10 C0521/26 C0523/40
pervading (15) A0161/14
A0211/03 A0310/M A0312/04 A0314/27
A0318/V A0378/18 A0461/19 A0610/18
A0683/28 B1033/22 B1122/12 C0066/15
C0401/31 C0402/12
Perverse (2) B1219/T B1224/05
perverse (5) A0026/28
A0653/20 B0807/21 B1222/13 B1223/22
Perverseness (1) B0852/06
perverseness (6) B0852/08 B0852/15
B1220/22 B1221/15 B1223/25 C0082/31
perversion (4) A0405/13
A0498/27 A0610/27 B0745/24
perversity (6) A0054/19 A0063/22
->A0320/17 A0624/24 B1225/13 B1316/10
Pest (9) A0240/T
A0240/V A0250/04 A0250/11 A0251/12
A0252/12 A0252/21 A0252/33 A0253/15
pest (5) A0242/V
A0242/V A0242/V A0242/V A0670/06
pest-ban (1) A0243/19
pest-spirits (1) A0243/10
Pest-Iferous (1) A0250/14
Pest-Ilential (1) A0250/15
pestered (1) A0279/04
pestilence (10) A0189/09 A0190/14
A0243/16 A0244/20 A0445/08 A0670/01
A0671/12 B0854/34 B1278/23 B1294/08
pestilences (2) A0459/08 C0126/12
pestilent (1) A0400/01
pestilential (2) A0244/03 C0078/29
pestis (1) A0018/M
pesty (1) A0414/22
pet (5) A0340/02
B0850/35 B0853/36 B0866/21 B1095/02
pet> (1) A0470/16
Peter (2) A0347/08 A0481/V
peterel (4) C0151/30
C0151/31 C0151/32 C0159/18
peterels (2) C0151/27 C0164/03
Peters (107)
Peters, Dirk (14) C0087/01 C0087/35
C0089/01 C0089/27 C0090/29 C0090/36
C0092/39 C0093/22 C0099/38 C0100/17
C0101/36 C0102/19 C0164/32 C0181/26
Peters's (6) C0104/18 C0126/32
C0138/27 C0196/29 C0197/17 C0208/05
Petersham (1) A0485/04
Petershams (1) A0485/19
Peterson (2) C0067/16 C0179/30
Peterson, C. J. (1) B0735/37
petit (1) B1056/02
petit-maitre (1) A0036/15
Petite (13) C0529/05
C0529/31 C0530/01 C0530/25 C0530/35
C0530/37 C0532/39 C0533/13 C0533/38
C0533/41 C0534/30 C0535/24 C0536/26
petite (1) A0380/V
petite (3) A0268/17
A0281/02 A0284/12
Petite/Cote (1) C0561/04
Petite/Cote (1) C0535/22
petiteness (1) A0283/04
petition (1) A0490/34
Petrie (1) B1382/31
Petrie, William (1) B1382/29
petrifaction (1) B1160/18
petrified (6) B0896/29 B1160/14
B1160/16 B1160/20 B1160/24 C0570/26
pets (3) B0850/12
B0850/24 B0851/10
petted (1) B1346/35
petticoat (6) B0734/34 B0758/09
B0761/32 B0762/05 B0762/09 B0766/33
petticoats (4) A0374/04
B0734/24 B0750/18 B0766/04
Pettitt (1) A0388/06
petto (4) A0296/V
A0365/V B0870/09 B1017/29

petty (6) A0021/14 A0263/22
A0434/02 A0589/18 B0770/34 C0570/20
petulance (2) B1170/04 B1225/10
petulant (4) A0433/11
A0439/12 A0513/V A0535/30
petulantly (2) A0533/20 B0964/11
peu (3) A0019/04
B0914/13 B1105/09
peut (1) A0036/22
pew (3) A0382/20 A0383/04 A0428/31
Pfaal, Hans (1) C0441/V
Pfaall (3) C0388/40
C0428/06 C0428/10
Pfaall, Grettel (1) C0388/37
Pfaall, Hans (7) C0387/T
C0389/07 C0391/02 C0391/06 C0403/35
C0426/30 C0427/27
Phaall (4) B1386/08
C0447/V C0447/V C0447/V
Phalarian (1) A0066/V
Phalaris (2) A0056/21 A0066/10
phalaris (1) B1017/27
phantasies (3) A0311/26
B0965/06 C0118/14
phantasm (6) A0403/18 A0408/28
A0602/17 A0673/21 B0850/03 B0853/32
phantasma (1) A0216/18
phantasmagoric (6) A0322/26
A0323/26 A0400/29 A0405/28 A0411/V
A0430/31
phantasms (3) A0080/26
A0674/30 B0963/34
phantastic (1) A0323/V
phantasy (3) A0322/07
B0822/28 B0902/V
phantasy-pieces (1) A0473/18
phantom (7) A0054/18
A0063/V A0318/24 A0604/19 B1279/11
B1283/13 C0198/13
pharagges (Gr.) (1) A0195/M
Pharisee (10) A0043/02 A0043/12
A0044/10 A0045/14 A0046/05 A0046/26
A0047/06 A0047/23 A0048/V A0048/V
Pharonnida (1) A0426/M
Pharronida (1) A0426/V
phase (2) B1278/17 B1278/18
phaseless (1) B0940/16
phases (1) B1220/19
phenomena (2) B1295/18 B1311/11
phenomena (12) A0413/03
B0946/13 B1030/01 B1030/03 B1030/12
B1032/01 B1080/22 B1080/24 C0172/15
C0203/21 C0387/02 C0421/05
phenomenon (17) A0106/32
A0370/26 A0459/33 A0582/29 B1079/06
B1080/V B1182/01 B1249/11 C0388/09
C0388/24 C0402/03 C0405/27 C0412/11
C0417/12 C0421/34 C0422/10 C0423/36
pheugon (Gr.) (1) A0346/03
Phi (1) A0346/09
phial (1) B0736/13
Phil. (1) B1161/33
Philadelphia (18) A0265/05 A0270/25
A0273/33 A0273/35 A0277/21 A0278/22
A0337/12 A0337/25 A0347/20 A0354/05
->A0568/V B0735/37 B0863/33 B0864/06
B1089/19 B1097/07 C0155/25 C0522/40
Philadelphian (1) B0864/16
Philadelphians (1) B0864/10
Philip/Le/Bel (1) A0301/01
philippic (1) B1370/07
Philistine (2) A0044/20 A0045/19
Philistines (2) A0047/08 A0048/01
philological (1) C0208/23
philosopher (30) A0075/16 A0085/M
A0090/16 A0091/34 A0091/35 A0092/35
A0094/20 A0097/14 A0098/04 A0098/22
A0104/23 A0105/31 A0106/10 A0107/31
A0109/09 A0110/08 A0110/32 A0111/10
A0111/12 A0111/23 A0112/V A0114/01
A0114/06 A0114/V A0478/12 A0611/03
B1293/24 B1295/06 B1310/19 B1317/26
philosopher's (7) A0085/06
A0089/03 A0090/01 A0102/02 A0103/19
A0108/19 B1363/36
philosophers (18) A0054/36 A0064/03
A0123/05 A0128/19 A0175/10 A0175/10
A0180/33 A0180/33 A0527/V B1160/17
B1189/03 B1213/20 B1294/30 B1294/V
B1300/02 B1300/11 B1312/01 B1313/13
philosophic (3) A0099/07
A0458/18 A0609/28
philosophical (11) A0381/21
A0657/24 B0747/20 B0749/02 B0752/15
B0757/V B0773/35 B1143/31 B1246/17
C0387/02 C0429/29
Philosophical/Transactions (1) 423/26
Philosophie (3) A0109/31
A0109/32 C0430/37
philosophie (2) A0053/14 A0062/22
philosophizing (1) A0080/19
Philosophy (5) A0495/T
A0495/V A0495/V B1168/14 B1311/14
philosophy (39) A0054/36
A0061/02 A0064/04 A0064/V A0070/V
A0074/21 A0075/07 A0080/17 A0086/15
A0089/29 A0096/05 A0109/03 A0135/13
A0226/12 A0230/10 A0339/31 A0457/11
A0495/V A0495/V A0495/V A0498/25
A0533/22 A0703/23 B0743/01 B0752/04
B0852/07 B0900/14 B1031/24 B1182/25
B1215/13 B1234/26 B1249/30 B1268/22
B1294/07 B1310/27 B1312/34 C0145/09
C0392/27 C0432/08
Philpot, Philip (1) A0278/03
Phiz (1) A0071/32
Phlegethon (1) A0582/22
phlegmatic (1) A0027/25
Phoebus (2) A0045/28 A0046/07
phonetic (2) B1179/30 B1180/18
phonetical (1) B1317/07
phonetics (1) B1184/18
phosphorescence (2) B1078/22
B1163/23
phosphorescent (1) B1081/08
phosphoric (4) A0139/01
B0964/26 B0965/03 C0142/31
phosphorus (12) C0068/30
C0069/38 C0077/05 C0077/33 C0078/16
C0078/39 C0079/21 C0079/31 C0080/02

->C0080/06 C0081/24 C0094/03
phosphorus-box (2) C0074/01
C0074/15
phrase (21) A0344/16
A0345/17 A0345/29 A0354/01 A0547/05
A0553/10 A0587/30 A0624/21 A0641/24
A0707/03 B0762/13 B0842/15 B0880/04
B0905/26 B0923/33 B1051/13 B1051/23
B1090/22 B1225/07 B1275/19 C0089/34
phraseology (6) A0124/09 A0431/V
A0707/21 B0745/25 B0876/25 B1272/22
phrases (7) A0053/07
A0062/13 A0234/31 A0623/28 B0841/28
B1141/12 B1141/27
phrenes (Gr.) (1) A0097/33
phrenological (2) A0527/V B1221/09
phrenologists (2) A0531/02 B1219/02
phrenology (6) B0852/V B1191/13
B1219/16 B1219/21 B1220/20 B1221/08
phrensied (1) A0580/14
phrensy (1) C0123/18
phrenzy (3) A0567/05
B0858/30 B1005/V
phthisis (3) B1030/24
B1234/21 B1235/33
physic (1) A0631/17
physical (58)
physically (3) B0854/30
B0940/30 B1182/31
Physician (1) A0340/08
physician (15) A0026/24
A0059/16 A0066/24 A0090/16 A0092/04
A0111/16 A0218/09 A0401/02 A0482/34
A0539/23 A0543/18 B0816/23 B0941/02
B0941/32 B0982/29
physicians (14) A0324/07 A0325/04
A0404/17 A0483/22 B0956/14 B0961/03
B0962/05 B1234/20 B1234/36 B1235/36
B1236/18 B1238/02 B1239/14 B1241/20
physics (3) A0652/21
B0989/17 C0387/06
physiognomy (4) A0104/12
A0246/22 B1107/01 C0533/10
Physiological (1) B1163/42
physiologist (2) A0174/04 A0179/15
Physiology (1) B1165/35
physiology (1) B0810/09
physique (1) A0403/28
physique (1) A0265/18
piano (5) B0905/02
B0905/29 B0916/02 B1004/05 B1096/14
piano-forte (2) A0502/22 B1119/15
Piazza (1) A0151/20
piazza (2) B1294/19 B1337/17
piazzas (2) B1336/13 B1336/37
Piazzetta (1) A0151/24
Piazzo (1) A0155/V
Pibrac (1) A0096/M
pic-nics (1) B0865/20
pick (4) B1052/10
B1207/05 C0187/35 C0396/15
pick-pockets (1) A0509/07
picked (34) A0356/29 A0444/20
A0561/10 A0594/16 B0770/18 B0770/24
B0771/26 B0828/02 B0830/20 B0857/21
->B0869/13 B0869/14 B0869/19 B0903/26
B1052/14 B1081/04 B1154/14 C0064/14
C0074/04 C0099/21 C0100/23 C0120/18
C0147/26 C0148/26 C0165/33 C0167/12
C0178/14 C0190/30 C0195/18 C0205/16
C0208/17 C0420/32 C0532/08 C0570/26
picking (5) A0368/24
B0770/28 B1383/12 C0152/25 C0404/33
pickle (2) A0092/33 A0112/10
pickled (6) A0092/21 A0092/21
A0111/31 A0111/31 C0142/41 C0576/04
picks (1) B0873/21
pictorial (3) A0708/05
B0929/34 B1273/05
Pictorius (1) A0176/11
Pictorius, Hermanus (1) A0173/02
pictural (2) A0511/18 A0708/V
picture (23) A0370/17
A0398/07 A0405/30 A0497/08 A0497/09
A0502/08 A0662/V A0663/20 A0664/22
A0709/05 A0709/05 B0736/27 B0925/06
B0925/16 B0948/28 B0948/34 B1274/10
B1274/10 B1333/01 B1335/27 B1340/24
C0197/36 C0405/26
pictured (3) A0687/28
A0689/28 A0696/05
pictures (8) A0158/12
A0502/V A0568/20 A0663/09 B0925/06
B1303/26 B1330/31 C0093/34
picturesque (27) A0269/34
A0272/15 A0273/13 A0273/22 A0274/14
A0275/14 A0275/38 A0277/14 A0278/34
A0280/25 A0282/23 A0285/33 A0367/08
B0823/06 B0864/07 B0864/36 B0945/09
B1160/23 B1273/31 B1274/17 B1278/06
B1329/01 B1329/26 B1334/01 B1337/30
B1338/04 C0554/10
picturesque-hunters (1) B0864/16
picturesque-looking (1) A0298/V
picturesqueness (4) A0281/02
B1115/09 B1334/17 C0065/09
picul (2) C0179/04 C0179/14
piculs (2) C0177/40 C0179/05
pie (1) B1012/24
pie-crust (1) A0386/25
pie-men (1) A0510/24
piece (1) A0653/19
piece (58)
piecemeal (1) C0135/35
pieces (51)
piena (1) B0905/24
pierced (1) A0552/01
piercing (4) A0218/03
A0414/23 C0072/23 C0408/29
Pierre (12) A0107/25
B1011/06 C0529/19 C0529/23 C0530/30
C0531/14 C0531/30 C0532/30 C0532/31
C0533/14 C0537/27 C0549/09
Pierre's (2) C0531/29 C0531/32
pies (1) B1012/22
Pieta (1) A0160/V
piety (1) B0879/21
Pig (1) A0043/V
pig (12) A0285/06
A0368/17 A0368/23 A0372/26 A0467/28

->B0870/12 B0911/28 B1102/19 B1102/37
B1139/17 B1142/15 B1142/18
pig-sty (1) A0486/13
pigeon (1) C0408/22
pigeon-wing (2) A0627/17 A0629/30
pigeon-winged (1) A0371/31
pigeon-winger (1) A0627/18
pigeon-winging (1) A0630/20
pigeon-wings (1) B0913/26
pigeons (9) B1164/37
B1164/40 B1164/40 C0151/28 C0396/12
C0404/31 C0405/11 C0406/18 C0408/20
pigger (1) B1103/01
Pigs (2) A0271/34 B1136/18
pigs (4) A0347/30
A0370/12 A0373/30 B1096/10
Pike, Zebulon M. (1) C0527/28
Pilau (1) B1224/11
pile (9) A0141/17
A0142/10 A0280/08 A0535/23 A0535/27
B1167/34 B1181/16 B1262/04 C0165/34
piled (7) A0248/26
A0430/13 B1076/19 B1260/05 B1261/05
C0069/04 C0091/31
piles (5) A0156/V
A0253/27 A0253/V A0662/03 A0705/12
pilfering (1) C0179/41
Pilgrimage (1) B1101/04
pilier (1) C0430/31
pill (1) A0092/10
pill-box (1) A0111/23
pillaging (1) C0555/26
pillar (1) A0122/29
pillars (4) A0044/24
B1071/18 B1336/14 B1337/17
pillow (9) A0033/12
A0163/13 A0228/31 A0233/12 A0663/10
B0871/20 B1040/11 B1178/09 B1329/02
pillows (3) A0411/28
B1235/20 C0072/13
pills (2) A0341/03 B1195/02
pimpled (1) A0247/06
pin (1) A0443/15
pinch (6) A0072/06 A0356/04
A0356/07 B0811/27 B1012/17 B1155/05
pinchbeck (1) B0877/24
pinched (5) A0327/21
B0944/11 B0956/18 B1155/11 B1192/05
Pindar's (2) A0176/02 A0182/01
pine (5) A0162/14
A0582/05 B0924/31 C0090/24 C0533/02
pined (4) A0227/09
A0231/23 A0643/V A0665/16
pineknots (1) A0482/25
pining (1) C0426/16
piningly (1) A0609/35
pinion (2) A0406/31 B1071/22
pinioned (2) B1018/24 C0086/16
pinions (2) A0351/30 B0955/33
pink (6) A0368/10 A0464/02
A0464/05 B1153/32 B1185/33 C0151/16
pinnacle (6) A0046/21 A0140/16
A0349/26 A0582/22 B0817/25 B1126/17
pinnacles (4) A0195/M
A0271/25 B1076/18 B1283/13

pinned (1) C0113/08
pins (2) A0501/21 B1325/09
pint (2) C0071/20 C0141/36
Pinxit (2) A0069/V A0070/02
pinxit (1) A0059/02
pioneer (1) B1048/24
Piot (1) C0430/30
pious (2) A0642/14 C0062/07
piously (4) B0878/13
B0879/10 B0879/18 B0880/06
pipe (14) A0368/21 A0368/33
A0370/13 A0373/18 A0667/28 B0975/15
B0981/34 B1108/35 B1257/24 B1257/25
B1259/01 C0388/07 C0390/19 C0426/32
pipes (2) A0373/07 C0387/19
piquancy (1) A0673/21
piquant (6) A0343/01 A0343/16
A0343/17 A0343/20 A0344/04 A0344/06
pique (1) A0441/32
pique (3) A0026/15
A0432/14 C0093/16
piqued (1) B0728/11
pirate (4) A0628/31
B0831/08 B0834/11 B0836/11
pirates (3) B0833/07
B0833/08 C0102/41
piratical (6) B0843/25 C0088/37
C0093/21 C0102/04 C0103/10 C0109/37
piroque (16) C0530/31
C0532/41 C0533/37 C0534/15 C0538/04
C0538/06 C0548/30 C0548/32 C0549/30
C0554/02 C0566/02 C0568/19 C0568/31
C0569/22 C0572/39 C0576/35
Pirouette (5) A0385/06
A0385/07 A0385/17 A0385/20 A0385/24
pirouette (2) A0071/01 A0371/31
pirouette (1) A0354/22
pirouetted (1) A0062/31
pish (1) B1162/V
Pisistratus (2) A0093/05 A0112/17
pissel (1) B0813/11
pistil (1) B1163/28
pistol (11) A0387/V
A0563/17 B0992/11 B1046/V B1057/31
C0085/17 C0186/08 C0187/11 C0196/34
C0201/03 C0579/31
pistol-shot (1) B1046/22
pistols (12) A0548/18
A0548/20 A0562/06 B0895/11 C0105/05
C0109/31 C0180/25 C0184/14 C0199/16
C0199/22 C0577/31 C0579/20
Pit (1) A0681/T
pit (20) A0487/23
A0543/28 A0589/28 A0687/05 A0689/09
A0690/23 A0690/24 A0690/25 A0690/27
A0696/32 A0696/33 B0823/29 B0826/15
B0826/23 B0827/10 B0844/20 B1244/06
C0192/01 C0192/34 C0193/03
pitch (11) A0054/06
A0063/15 A0488/25 A0587/09 B0793/27
B1166/27 B1373/12 C0092/17 C0111/24
C0133/15 C0190/18
pitched (1) C0107/18
pitcher (13) A0686/09
A0688/02 A0689/19 B0945/32 C0093/02

->C0093/41 C0415/29 C0415/30 C0415/34
C0415/37 C0415/40 C0415/41 C0416/10
pitchers (2) A0245/15 A0253/28
pitches (1) A0489/33
pitchfork (1) A0107/19
pitching (5) B1093/34
C0074/08 C0110/22 C0149/30 C0399/22
pitchings (1) C0095/32
pitchy (2) A0138/31 A0152/01
piteously (5) A0127/26
A0351/14 A0506/05 C0085/41 C0406/19
pith (1) A0654/19
pithy (1) A0242/V
pitiable (14) A0317/03 A0373/V
A0378/13 A0398/V A0403/16 A0412/02
A0442/20 B1101/29 C0094/28 C0112/28
C0115/16 C0134/24 C0142/37 C0188/06
pitied (6) A0563/23 B0794/13
B0823/28 B0927/11 B1014/27 B1182/06
pitiful (5) B0964/17
B0965/01 B0965/05 B1370/20 B1370/V
pits (3) A0581/26
A0687/32 B0964/32
pittoresque (1) B1330/06
pity (17) A0160/23
A0227/12 A0231/25 A0385/34 A0401/25
A0416/06 A0427/06 A0442/17 A0456/18
A0627/11 B0750/30 B0993/11 B0993/23
B1012/08 B1183/06 B1207/09 B1317/25
pivot (1) B1077/16
pivots (1) B1071/20
pizziness (3) B1103/08
B1104/04 B1104/V
pizzness (1) B1104/02
placard (1) B0727/25
placarded (1) A0294/V
placards (1) B0990/01
place (211)
placed (91)
places (24) A0153/16
A0240/10 A0579/28 A0583/29 B0834/34
B0871/20 B0930/04 B0945/25 B0977/15
B1019/03 C0057/23 C0105/09 C0113/02
C0178/30 C0183/39 C0193/01 C0196/16
C0399/14 C0429/16 C0429/17 C0547/17
C0567/23 C0570/17 C0572/27
placid (6) A0020/V A0102/07
A0215/04 A0310/06 A0312/23 A0315/V
placidity (4) A0101/V
A0315/13 A0317/08 C0524/03
placidly (3) A0152/10
B1135/03 B1333/34
placing (16) A0053/02
A0062/07 A0090/04 A0411/15 A0555/03
B0758/27 B0824/10 B1136/23 B1237/27
B1250/30 C0068/31 C0109/19 C0141/05
C0191/07 C0202/38 C0415/23
plagiarism (2) B1384/07 B1384/09
plague (6) A0075/14 A0190/13
A0242/20 A0244/06 B0955/06 B1294/04
plague-goblins (1) A0243/11
plaid (1) B1185/33
plain (37) A0269/09
A0346/16 A0353/06 A0367/02 A0369/06
A0386/24 A0465/12 A0469/09 A0489/24
->A0499/06 A0503/08 A0552/31 A0621/04
A0709/25 B0811/22 B0817/04 B0820/10
B0877/36 B0945/01 B0975/31 B0979/22
B1192/18 B1274/27 B1298/13 B1316/06
B1316/22 B1336/14 B1340/09 B1340/15
B1390/18 C0541/33 C0557/13 C0566/19
C0573/01 C0573/03 C0574/22 C0575/11
plain-looking (1) B0924/23
plainly (21) A0106/26
A0295/15 A0371/16 A0460/07 A0582/07
A0694/26 B0826/02 B0838/27 B0849/06
B1011/33 B1014/20 B1031/18 B1031/31
C0061/36 C0103/18 C0111/14 C0124/22
C0142/32 C0399/20 C0401/13 C0524/06
plains (2) A0191/10 C0551/13
plaisir (1) B0913/08
plaits (2) B1339/32 C0552/01
plan (1) C0430/41
plan (33) A0303/24
A0367/22 A0437/15 A0443/09 A0687/33
A0690/31 B1017/04 B1046/28 B1048/19
B1051/18 B1091/11 B1115/34 B1129/07
B1143/17 B1143/21 B1295/14 B1311/07
C0066/08 C0066/25 C0067/08 C0076/13
C0092/11 C0104/04 C0104/08 C0108/12
C0110/30 C0151/41 C0168/26 C0173/01
C0180/08 C0392/01 C0415/38 C0439/V
plane (13) A0054/22
A0098/01 A0548/01 A0549/V A0559/12
B0736/36 B1070/03 B1070/10 C0398/20
C0418/29 C0419/13 C0419/40 C0420/09
planes (1) C0148/09
planet (11) A0189/14
B1321/15 B1321/V C0422/06 C0423/05
C0424/32 C0424/37 C0425/26 C0425/34
C0426/06 C0429/30
planetary (1) C0402/13
planets (11) A0457/25
A0600/28 B1038/23 B1038/24 B1168/06
B1322/05 B1322/26 C0157/33 C0400/03
C0401/26 C0402/14
plank (4) B1334/05
C0091/18 C0094/09 C0415/27
plank-work (1) A0243/24
plankings (1) A0413/32
planks (4) B0796/09
B0797/29 C0075/18 C0091/13
planned (3) A0436/29
B0909/01 B1340/12
plans (11) A0105/18
A0433/22 A0673/12 A0711/36 A0712/01
B1277/03 B1277/04 B1277/32 B1349/29
C0093/11 C0109/37
Plant (1) A0710/32
plant (6) B1093/30 B1163/16
B1163/19 B1293/01 C0150/25 C0150/26
Plantae (1) B1163/11
plantation (2) B0841/02 C0529/02
planted (2) A0429/16 C0155/35
Plantes (1) A0568/07
plants (2) B1163/11 B1334/24
plased> (1) A0464/08
plases> (1) A0464/02
plaster (6) A0486/16 B0853/26
B0857/06 B0857/17 B1180/12 B1185/27

plastered (5) A0297/V
B0857/05 B1262/35 B1263/24 B1351/05
plasterers (1) C0545/30
plastering (1) B0853/08
platanus (1) B1179/22
plate (3) B1008/31
B1011/01 B1011/06
plateau (3) B0864/35
B1281/28 B1282/04
plates (4) A0499/32
A0688/33 B0980/16 B1136/09
platform (7) B0817/30
C0184/05 C0184/23 C0189/07 C0191/06
C0192/15 C0578/24
platina (1) B1168/24
platinum (1) B1167/29
platitudes (1) C0130/20
Plato (18) A0091/16 A0091/16
A0091/17 A0091/17 A0101/09 A0108/10
A0108/12 A0108/13 A0110/19 A0110/19
A0110/19 A0110/20 A0225/M A0229/M
A0283/35 A0610/34 B0869/12 B0869/14
Platonist (4) A0086/08
A0097/04 A0176/05 A0180/27
Platte (7) C0527/33
C0528/18 C0539/19 C0539/38 C0540/01
C0540/32 C0541/29
platter (2) A0692/20 A0694/03
plausibility (5) B0736/32
B0738/17 C0055/34 C0428/05 C0433/06
plausible (2) A0582/30 B0844/13
plausibly (1) B1183/23
Plautus (2) A0091/19 A0110/21
play (33) A0037/18
A0071/08 A0126/10 A0228/26 A0233/07
A0279/25 A0319/17 A0434/33 A0441/04
A0441/21 A0442/13 A0444/07 A0485/31
A0489/01 A0528/07 A0528/27 A0530/12
A0625/06 A0639/03 B0796/21 B0899/02
B0946/23 B1044/01 B1044/12 B1046/18
B1140/24 B1141/15 B1314/31 B1347/04
C0106/34 C0133/32 C0184/18 C0533/35
play-ground (3) A0429/13
A0431/04 A0431/24
playbill (1) B0895/13
played (15) A0071/29
A0247/05 A0441/24 A0530/16 A0530/24
A0704/15 B0724/34 B0756/24 B0872/09
B0984/07 B0989/28 B1015/V B1101/22
B1269/15 C0406/30
player (6) A0528/31 A0529/19
A0530/06 B0773/22 B0984/08 B1119/16
players (1) A0529/06
playful (1) A0311/05
playfulness (1) B0825/19
playing (11) A0374/16
A0384/21 A0529/32 A0705/12 B0989/29
B1101/22 B1140/21 B1140/30 B1140/33
B1141/02 B1270/11
playmate (1) B0850/35
plays (2) B1096/35 B1128/25
plaything (1) B1168/02
plazer (1) A0344/24
plead (1) B1050/V
pleaded (2) A0386/28 B1050/29
pleading (1) B1002/09
pleadings (1) B0907/12
pleasant (27) A0205/06
A0349/21 A0490/32 A0512/15 A0650/18
B0904/14 B0927/26 B0943/09 B1153/21
B1154/18 B1154/19 B1154/19 C0120/11
C0120/22 C0126/30 C0136/04 C0138/38
C0158/02 C0158/20 C0163/03 C0164/22
C0166/09 C0166/35 C0553/07 C0563/33
C0570/02 C0576/10
pleasantly (4) B0797/20
B1246/07 B1329/18 C0560/27
pleasantry (2) B0927/30 B1353/02
please (31) A0123/12
A0182/11 A0251/14 A0251/21 A0264/06
A0264/32 A0273/05 A0284/01 A0285/03
A0345/06 A0345/16 A0384/21 A0386/03
A0443/10 A0624/13 A0624/16 A0651/06
A0657/30 B0876/09 B0988/09 B1010/08
B1016/26 B1221/25 B1322/30 B1385/37
C0391/05 C0404/17 C0409/11 C0425/19
C0426/09 C0432/12
pleased (21) A0074/01
A0100/01 A0100/22 A0271/11 A0339/21
A0381/13 A0473/15 A0604/15 A0629/01
B0728/17 B0907/10 B1032/27 B1257/20
B1360/34 B1370/31 C0101/19 C0396/20
C0407/11 C0408/34 C0560/25 C0566/10
pleases (1) B1155/07
pleasing (7) A0269/35
A0499/22 A0710/04 B1011/33 B1275/07
B1361/07 C0118/12
pleasurable (4) A0212/28
B0955/04 B0966/15 B1224/29
pleasurably (1) C0065/09
pleasure (70)
pleasures (5) A0251/10
A0430/31 A0608/12 A0622/27 B0855/06
plebeian (3) A0250/07
A0434/05 B0887/10
pledge (5) A0165/15
A0228/19 A0232/25 A0563/26 A0623/14
Pleiades (2) B1212/30 B1301/04
plein (1) A0650/07
plenitude (1) A0429/09
plentiful (7) C0090/07
C0100/35 C0101/22 C0174/11 C0177/08
C0566/26 C0572/08
plentifully (2) C0138/41 C0176/32
plentifulness (1) B1364/17
plenty (12) A0339/31
A0380/05 A0585/09 C0151/09 C0155/05
C0155/21 C0177/04 C0179/22 C0540/07
C0556/15 C0566/18 C0576/06
pleurez (2) A0378/M A0378/M
pliancy (1) C0087/21
Pliny (1) A0173/02
Pliny's (1) A0154/23
plot (6) A0203/M A0319/02
A0355/18 B0870/24 B0915/19 B1153/07
Plotinus (2) A0176/06 A0180/28
plotting (1) A0437/05
plover (1) C0559/41
plovers (1) C0566/23
plucking (1) B1104/06

plug (2) C0415/31 C0415/31
plugs (1) C0533/23
plum (8) A0651/12
A0651/13 A0651/17 A0653/11 A0653/26
A0657/29 C0542/17 C0543/30
plum-trees (1) C0541/34
plumage (9) A0152/V
A0641/01 A0643/11 C0125/02 C0151/11
C0151/14 C0151/24 C0164/04 C0191/12
plume (2) B0723/26 B1234/04
plume-like (1) B1279/24
plumed (1) A0407/04
plumes (1) A0034/01
plumes (3) A0081/04
A0249/12 B0963/29
plummed (1) C0114/08
plump> (2) A0467/01 A0467/20
plumped (1) A0249/18
plumped> (2) A0467/10 A0467/14
plunder (5) A0120/05
B0834/07 C0186/01 C0188/05 C0189/01
plunderer (2) A0243/14 A0244/06
plunge (20) A0029/16
A0143/31 A0244/21 A0355/32 A0587/35
A0588/17 A0591/35 A0687/10 A0687/30
A0690/27 A0692/V B1223/15 B1223/20
B1372/18 C0060/15 C0086/04 C0108/24
C0129/10 C0149/31 C0578/33
plunged (15) A0025/03
A0154/09 A0438/12 A0447/21 A0579/18
A0593/34 B0737/07 B0851/34 C0114/27
C0121/17 C0121/17 C0136/25 C0144/15
C0165/08 C0198/15
plunges (5) A0023/18
C0098/01 C0106/03 C0129/26 C0563/01
plunging (10) A0021/29 A0059/26
A0067/16 A0146/06 A0514/03 A0580/16
C0127/13 C0130/31 C0545/29 C0578/22
plural (1) B1359/21
plus (9) A0096/M
A0096/M A0135/M A0135/M A0379/27
A0652/12 B0987/01 B1105/09 B1121/03
plus (2) A0085/06 B0988/07
Plutarch (1) B1191/28
Pluto (8) A0045/24
B0850/35 B0851/12 B0851/17 B0851/18
B0854/10 B0854/10 B0855/01
ply (1) A0127/28
plying (1) A0240/04
pneumatics (2) A0071/28 C0392/18
pocket (35) A0067/34
A0068/04 A0093/12 A0106/03 A0106/17
A0110/16 A0262/19 A0356/03 A0369/01
A0371/21 A0563/17 A0563/V A0653/25
A0685/28 B0809/15 B0810/37 B0822/06
B0830/24 B0830/30 B0870/15 B0872/19
B0873/22 B0873/23 B0908/05 B0908/V
B0910/V B0992/16 B1052/12 B1057/V
B1109/33 B1207/05 B1362/30 C0083/34
C0119/04 C0426/35
pocket-book (12) A0112/23
B0872/18 B0873/24 B0874/02 B0874/16
B0876/21 B0876/26 B1053/22 B1057/33
B1058/01 B1235/19 C0390/01
pocket-comb (1) C0127/40
pocket-compass (1) B0842/06
pocket-handkerchief (10) A0057/16
A0057/21 A0299/18 A0629/11 B0734/26
B0734/35 B0758/09 B0761/33 B0762/24
B0766/08
pocket-handkerchiefs (5) B0750/21
B0750/23 B0750/28 B0766/06 C0196/20
pocket-knife (1) C0075/19
pocket-mirror (2) A0056/34 A0066/24
pocketbook (2) B0983/12 C0193/24
pocketing (1) B1363/29
pockets (13) A0241/26
A0371/06 A0443/13 A0443/21 A0494/09
B0830/34 B0871/11 B0877/03 B1184/02
C0085/27 C0093/41 C0397/28 C0427/30
poco (1) A0621/03
podagre (1) A0033/20
Poe (14) B1379/17 B1379/22
B1381/07 B1381/16 B1382/31 B1383/08
B1383/24 B1384/06 B1385/13 B1385/24
C0055/29 C0056/12 C0056/29 C0207/38
Poe, Edgar A. (6) A0527/V B0806/T
B0939/V B1002/V B1044/V B1291/11
Poe, Edgar Allan (1) B0886/V
Poe's (7) B0772/08
B1358/18 B1379/09 B1379/31 B1383/09
B1384/37 C0056/20
poem (20) A0055/24
A0269/19 A0269/25 A0280/32 A0280/34
B1127/12 B1130/34 B1132/17 B1133/02
B1133/19 B1134/08 B1134/15 B1134/18
B1135/35 B1137/07 B1138/05 B1139/04
B1139/08 B1385/01 B1385/07
Poems (7) A0280/15
A0621/02 A0621/09 B1383/30 B1384/14
B1384/33 B1385/14
poems (6) A0281/33 A0342/11
B1122/22 B1129/03 B1379/18 B1380/20
poesy (2) B1129/21 B1129/29
poet (38) A0091/17 A0110/19
A0162/02 A0218/14 A0354/29 A0356/V
A0652/15 A0706/03 A0706/14 A0706/28
A0707/06 A0707/19 A0711/14 B0863/23
B0869/24 B0979/09 B0986/18 B0986/21
B0986/24 B0986/25 B0986/V B0988/17
B0988/V B1122/06 B1123/08 B1123/14
B1127/19 B1127/23 B1127/34 B1138/01
B1271/07 B1271/17 B1271/30 B1272/06
B1272/18 B1276/14 B1304/30 B1384/27
poet-love (1) B1122/06
poet's (2) A0599/M A0621/13
poeta (1) A0652/15
poetaster (1) B1131/03
poete (1) A0652/10
poetic (15) A0127/06
A0128/27 A0397/09 A0609/22 A0609/26
A0611/34 A0706/05 A0706/12 A0707/01
A0707/03 B1271/09 B1271/15 B1272/02
B1272/19 B1277/30
poetical (9) A0385/21
A0621/08 A0706/32 B0843/26 B0843/29
B1128/09 B1137/04 B1271/34 B1317/36
poetizing (1) B1141/03
Poetry (1) A0628/26
poetry (5) A0070/32

->B1090/30 B1271/31 B1335/21 B1335/22
Poets (4) A0127/02
A0127/21 A0127/30 A0628/26
poets (4) A0609/31
A0609/34 B0986/18 B0986/20
poh/poh (1) B1371/32
poignancy (1) A0433/24
poignant (4) A0295/23
A0316/12 B0877/14 B1047/02
Poindexter (2) C0531/17 C0531/26
Point (2) C0529/02 C0530/27
point (1) A0037/25
point (265)
pointed (27) A0164/21
A0218/28 A0328/07 A0386/15 A0401/07
A0416/24 A0430/02 A0432/08 A0549/V
A0549/V A0593/16 A0703/33 B0767/13
B0864/10 B0877/02 B0895/20 B0927/02
B1092/12 B1250/26 B1268/32 B1381/19
C0068/21 C0069/28 C0130/34 C0131/14
C0536/04 C0555/16
pointedly (4) A0283/06
A0508/16 B1051/28 B1134/09
pointing (9) A0087/02
A0100/13 A0158/V B0842/06 B0933/04
B1163/27 C0118/38 C0168/31 C0176/10
points (92)
poised (1) C0390/01
poison (5) A0166/V
A0612/06 B0736/15 C0126/13 C0406/21
poisoned (7) A0166/19
A0166/19 B0947/21 B0949/21 B1224/12
C0103/31 C0107/25
poisonous (4) A0195/20
A0244/01 B0950/11 C0095/17
poke (1) B0911/28
poked (2) A0252/21 B1091/26
poking (1) A0374/02
Poland (1) C0526/29
Polar (4) C0185/33
C0202/01 C0204/32 C0416/24
polar (2) C0160/27 C0425/36
Polar/Gulf (1) A0146/13
Polar/Sea (2) C0521/06 C0527/05
polarized (1) A0138/25
Pole (6) A0146/13 C0207/18
C0416/26 C0417/25 C0417/34 C0418/30
pole (12) A0145/26
C0158/16 C0158/26 C0159/27 C0161/21
C0164/08 C0164/25 C0167/04 C0536/06
C0536/11 C0547/19 C0547/26
polecat (1) C0552/20
poled (1) C0536/01
polemics (1) A0101/05
poles (13) C0410/09
C0411/13 C0411/15 C0432/26 C0432/27
C0533/26 C0535/30 C0536/04 C0536/08
C0536/11 C0540/03 C0552/33 C0554/06
Police (1) A0546/08
Police (1) A0546/V
police (36) A0544/15
A0545/01 A0547/19 A0548/07 A0548/V
A0551/12 A0552/05 A0552/17 A0554/03
A0554/20 A0556/16 A0558/01 A0561/26
A0624/04 B0725/02 B0726/08 B0727/03
->B0727/17 B0734/28 B0753/30 B0754/16
B0756/V B0768/13 B0796/19 B0796/22
B0858/09 B0858/18 B0974/15 B0978/10
B0979/20 B0981/04 B0983/21 B0988/27
B1143/04 B1362/03 B1363/28
policial (4) B0725/11
B0986/08 B0988/20 B0988/32
policy (10) A0491/12 A0562/02
B0756/23 B0769/23 B1104/35 B1105/14
B1132/02 C0531/11 C0549/10 C0555/39
Polish (1) B1234/05
polish (3) A0053/35
B1009/32 B1160/43
polished (3) A0140/09
B1003/30 B1333/36
polishing (1) A0271/04
polite (5) A0265/32
A0270/03 A0274/18 B0871/34 B1137/07
politely (1) B1208/11
politeness (1) B1069/25
Politian's (1) A0162/03
politic (1) B1153/06
political (10) A0079/01 A0338/19
A0705/10 B0727/01 B0728/07 B0977/26
B0993/01 B0993/06 B1270/09 C0425/39
politician (1) B1127/32
politics (4) A0338/35
A0652/26 B1185/01 C0391/14
poll (2) B1372/02 B1372/07
polled (1) B1300/05
pollen (4) B1163/30
B1163/32 B1163/35 B1163/39
pollicis (1) B1182/13
polluted (2) B0760/08 C0171/29
pollution (2) A0120/07 B0760/09
Polly (1) C0146/31
Polybius (1) A0111/06
Polyglot (1) A0272/24
Polyglot, Delphinus (1) A0175/30
Polyglott (1) A0175/V
Polyglott, Delphinus (1) A0181/30
Polytechnic/Institution (1) B1070/20
pomatum (1) A0297/V
pomegranate (1) B1159/21
pomp (1) A0157/01
Pompeius (1) A0045/27
Pompey (35) A0043/08
A0044/06 A0347/19 A0348/28 A0348/28
A0349/06 A0349/16 A0349/19 A0350/03
A0350/27 A0350/29 A0350/32 A0350/34
A0351/04 A0351/13 A0351/35 A0352/01
A0352/03 A0352/04 A0352/10 A0353/02
A0353/15 A0353/30 A0353/V A0354/09
A0356/19 A0387/19 A0387/20 A0387/25
A0388/04 A0388/09 A0388/18 A0388/25
A0388/29 A0489/12
Pompey's (2) A0348/29 A0350/13
pomposity (2) A0301/04 A0380/15
pompous (5) A0124/09
A0345/30 A0651/24 B1297/23 B1316/07
pomps (1) A0644/06
pon (7) B0812/06
B0819/20 B0819/32 B0820/15 B0820/33
B0821/06 B0821/21
Ponca (2) C0549/35 C0550/09

Poncas (1) C0549/40
pond (6) B1079/28 B1333/31
B1334/15 C0540/20 C0546/21 C0547/28
ponder (6) A0055/15 A0064/30
A0146/05 A0189/04 A0213/23 A0692/07
ponderable (2) C0400/31 C0401/11
pondered (9) A0022/05
A0216/04 A0313/18 A0398/01 A0429/30
A0608/04 A0609/34 A0692/10 B1224/07
pondering (4) A0604/17
B0819/30 B1225/06 C0072/03
ponderous (9) A0088/01
A0353/28 A0353/35 A0416/25 A0429/04
A0429/04 A0614/22 B1282/34 C0546/18
ponders (1) A0683/04
ponds (1) B0950/08
Ponnonner (15) B1178/25
B1178/26 B1181/11 B1182/06 B1182/19
B1183/04 B1183/17 B1184/01 B1185/18
B1186/33 B1187/22 B1188/18 B1189/29
B1192/02 B1194/24
Ponnonner, Doctor (1) B1178/16
Ponnonner's (5) B1179/01
B1182/35 B1185/07 B1195/01 B1195/17
Ponte (1) A0151/14
pontifical (1) A0021/25
Ponto (2) B1329/04 B1338/24
poodle (6) A0174/13 A0179/28
A0348/21 A0349/16 A0350/34 B0871/14
pooh (1) B1162/23
pool (12) A0399/29
A0584/01 A0586/36 A0589/06 A0590/33
A0594/11 B1049/03 B1049/05 B1049/08
B1052/25 B1057/31 B1381/34
pools (1) C0572/29
poop (3) A0136/26
A0145/31 B1281/01
poor (74)
poor-devil (2) B1140/31 B1207/26
poorly (1) B0812/10
pop (1) B1011/27
Pope (1) B1385/19
popinjay (1) A0371/23
poplar (1) B1332/13
poplars (1) A0071/25
poppies (3) A0035/15
B1283/08 C0412/35
popping (2) B1011/30 B1020/28
populace (12) A0069/29
A0123/06 A0127/01 A0496/27 A0512/31
A0514/33 B0750/11 B0757/28 B0758/02
B0946/18 B1226/03 B1374/24
popular (18) A0056/04 A0065/28
A0243/11 A0459/07 B0727/13 B0734/08
B0757/03 B0757/22 B0850/31 B0987/02
B1091/22 B1122/18 B1242/04 B1247/06
B1247/10 B1346/32 B1374/29 C0056/24
population (7) A0507/25
A0601/11 B0750/04 B1374/05 C0153/14
C0156/16 C0176/13
populous (9) A0128/15
A0135/24 A0349/20 A0514/02 A0515/17
A0533/07 B0729/10 B1246/08 B1277/31
Porcupine (1) C0551/34
porcupine (2) C0552/12 C0552/15
Porcupiniana (1) B1141/V
pore (1) A0685/03
pored (5) A0144/23
A0234/18 A0316/20 A0325/14 A0408/29
pores (1) A0670/05
poring (4) A0160/12
A0226/10 A0230/07 A0507/18
pork (4) A0354/32
A0368/02 A0368/13 C0534/28
porker (1) A0047/31
porous (2) A0400/V B0959/14
porousness (1) A0142/30
Porphyrogene (1) A0407/12
Porphyry (2) A0176/05 A0180/27
porphyry (2) A0036/02 A0036/V
porpoise (1) A0650/03
Porque (1) A0344/24
Porrex (1) A0240/M
porridge (2) A0341/V A0342/19
Port (5) B1104/21
B1104/26 C0127/20 C0130/01 C0140/10
port (12) A0135/24
A0137/22 A0441/28 A0650/04 A0651/20
C0064/23 C0098/23 C0098/33 C0104/17
C0105/01 C0137/24 C0157/03
Port/Egmont (1) C0151/27
portage (2) C0526/40 C0547/24
portal (1) A0349/33
portals (2) B0956/28 B0965/28
portend (1) C0388/04
portended (1) A0028/V
portentous (4) A0027/05
A0088/17 A0241/31 B1247/16
portents (1) A0654/08
porter (7) A0539/23
B0856/37 B1155/24 B1155/32 B1157/34
B1157/37 B1158/13
porters (2) A0510/25 B1090/16
portico (2) B1192/12 B1192/23
porticoes (1) B1192/19
portion (176)
portionless (1) B1123/24
portions (26) A0103/28 A0298/V
A0320/10 A0545/23 A0582/16 B0742/34
B0863/03 B1017/02 B1031/14 B1036/22
B1036/24 B1139/15 B1160/40 B1181/23
B1352/29 C0078/01 C0087/20 C0087/39
C0097/01 C0130/41 C0160/02 C0181/04
C0207/12 C0418/43 C0438/V C0550/26
Portland (1) A0276/23
portly (2) B1003/29 B1090/01
portmanteau (1) B0873/19
Porto/Rico (1) C0088/40
Portrait (1) A0662/T
portrait (15) A0164/12
A0165/08 A0174/12 A0175/01 A0179/27
A0180/24 A0663/21 A0664/04 A0664/20
A0664/28 A0665/21 B0948/31 B0949/01
B1168/05 C0554/11
portraite (2) B0912/06 B0912/08
portraits (2) A0502/07 B1180/16
portraiture (6) A0240/07 A0435/05
A0708/04 B0853/28 B1273/04 C0533/06
portraitures (1) A0695/30
portray (4) A0311/19

->A0318/01 A0447/26 A0665/08
ports (2) A0140/09 C0098/40
Portuguese (1) C0154/25
position (113)
positions (5) A0604/13
A0687/28 B1075/05 C0126/09 C0533/20
positive (43) A0024/04
A0135/20 A0211/13 A0217/08 A0261/12
A0296/V A0380/10 A0386/15 A0386/24
A0405/04 A0427/23 A0436/09 A0482/04
A0482/18 A0507/15 A0540/10 A0550/04
A0652/01 A0656/14 A0712/06 B0763/17
B0764/13 B0962/02 B0966/20 B1039/12
B1039/21 B1127/09 B1139/16 B1191/20
B1207/07 B1240/02 B1277/12 B1292/11
B1294/13 B1314/34 C0387/07 C0399/29
C0401/22 C0404/05 C0404/27 C0439/V
C0446/V C0535/38
positively (47) A0111/06
A0173/21 A0173/V A0176/19 A0179/01
A0244/V A0264/15 A0279/21 A0365/17
A0389/05 A0499/V A0589/01 A0657/23
A0708/18 B0729/04 B0810/23 B0829/27
B0889/26 B0924/23 B0931/24 B0957/20
B1012/13 B1109/24 B1122/31 B1135/V
B1144/17 B1157/21 B1222/16 B1234/16
B1261/33 B1273/13 B1295/26 B1311/23
B1314/35 B1360/34 B1364/29 C0055/17
C0061/27 C0157/20 C0175/37 C0207/30
C0407/05 C0413/35 C0421/23 C0429/14
C0546/25 C0557/17
positiveness (2) B0746/10 B0773/15
possess (15) A0246/21
A0273/23 A0343/31 A0379/04 A0478/25
A0562/01 B0888/10 B0901/26 B1054/24
B1102/02 C0055/14 C0087/11 C0392/34
C0400/35 C0550/27
possessed (48) A0313/22
A0349/24 A0437/19 A0438/09 A0447/26
A0461/11 A0528/02 A0556/09 A0588/35
A0614/10 A0641/V A0644/12 A0651/30
A0711/14 B0813/33 B0825/15 B0827/23
B0851/24 B0855/03 B0903/10 B0928/17
B0943/23 B0966/28 B1012/34 B1057/32
B1102/29 B1123/06 B1155/21 B1169/20
B1182/05 B1191/35 B1258/18 B1276/12
B1346/02 B1346/35 B1362/01 C0058/18
C0133/25 C0135/11 C0393/01 C0421/19
C0429/33 C0524/01 C0532/33 C0537/03
C0564/33 C0569/33 C0578/06
possesses (1) A0568/V
possessing (6) A0282/26 B0770/18
B0957/28 B1034/19 B1045/17 C0577/36
possession (77)
Possession/Island (1) C0150/06
possessions (7) A0020/19
A0157/07 A0704/13 B0815/04 B1269/12
C0524/36 C0525/24
possessor (6) A0033/06 A0528/02
A0561/30 A0705/05 B0833/33 B1270/04
possessors (1) C0413/01
possibilities (1) B1101/32
possibility (32) A0096/15
A0136/27 A0366/26 A0437/30 A0558/04
A0693/14 B0901/27 B1051/07 B1101/13
->B1105/26 B1109/27 B1116/06 B1271/02
B1277/06 B1300/06 C0060/07 C0061/28
C0062/03 C0094/29 C0097/15 C0117/30
C0121/08 C0122/26 C0127/25 C0144/40
C0183/28 C0196/21 C0202/13 C0400/10
C0413/04 C0419/09 C0423/03
possible (204)
possibly (49) A0153/V
A0261/11 A0315/04 A0344/09 A0355/02
A0355/18 A0435/18 A0478/02 A0528/12
A0535/03 A0555/10 A0559/06 A0559/11
A0559/30 A0615/19 A0709/04 A0711/15
B0763/12 B0767/23 B0814/02 B0895/29
B0957/05 B1049/15 B1092/02 B1130/06
B1225/17 B1250/05 B1270/37 B1274/09
B1295/06 B1310/20 B1340/V C0064/02
C0076/32 C0107/16 C0111/39 C0116/21
C0129/05 C0129/37 C0133/31 C0134/15
C0186/09 C0388/04 C0400/20 C0413/24
C0416/25 C0533/35 C0537/26 C0562/05
possum (2) A0285/11 A0489/01
Post (1) B0754/35
<u>post</u> (4) A0704/28
B0959/35 B1053/34 B1269/27
post (7) B1105/V
C0064/07 C0188/13 C0525/17 C0525/21
C0527/38 C0545/27
Post/Office (3) A0264/28
A0277/27 B0872/35
postage (1) A0490/21
posted (3) C0544/04
C0549/29 C0568/37
<u>posteriori</u> (7) A0086/11
A0097/10 A0342/V A0552/13 B1220/20
B1295/14 B1311/06
posteriors (1) A0489/V
posterity (4) B1126/06
B1318/05 B1375/04 C0398/32
posting (2) C0539/15 C0558/34
postmarks (1) A0490/18
postpone (3) B1153/25
B1154/04 B1181/13
postponed (1) B1236/14
postponing (1) B1108/12
posts (1) C0062/01
postscript (1) A0544/21
posture (6) A0677/01 B0733/28
B0910/V C0117/13 C0422/01 C0545/19
postures (1) B0961/15
pot (3) A0085/09 A0368/01 C0163/07
pot-belly (1) C0569/15
pot-house (1) A0296/12
pot-houses (1) A0296/12
potatoes (5) C0083/34
C0091/06 C0093/02 C0094/01 C0155/35
potency (1) A0416/23
potent (4) A0126/06
A0439/V A0500/06 A0688/28
pots (3) B1004/03
B1334/23 B1337/30
pottle (2) B1109/10 B1109/19
<u>potu</u> (1) C0129/24
Poughkeepsie (1) B1291/05
poultry (1) C0156/23
pounce (1) B1292/22

pound (3) B0870/31
B1177/07 C0147/18
pounded (2) C0534/36 C0534/40
pounding (1) C0395/24
pounds (38) A0174/22 A0174/23
A0174/27 A0174/29 A0180/02 A0180/03
A0180/04 A0180/06 A0180/16 A0180/17
A0180/19 A0381/29 A0653/25 A0705/32
B0828/12 B1071/02 B1071/05 B1071/05
B1071/27 B1071/29 B1073/08 B1073/20
B1074/08 B1077/35 B1269/36 B1303/34
C0137/08 C0137/34 C0138/21 C0141/27
C0141/31 C0142/08 C0394/23 C0394/24
C0394/40 C0396/22 C0403/24 C0405/19
pour (3) A0545/06
A0602/07 C0430/41
pour (3) A0165/13
A0317/18 B1168/24
poured (15) A0035/12
A0054/23 A0108/08 A0157/28 A0316/V
A0405/04 A0602/24 A0644/20 B0899/04
B1057/27 B1104/21 B1106/22 B1348/29
C0111/01 C0124/05
pouring (11) A0102/01
A0107/23 A0124/05 A0249/18 A0250/32
A0253/07 B0834/30 C0141/30 C0142/40
C0200/14 C0562/13
pourtray (2) A0311/V A0318/V
Poussin (1) A0707/V
pouvoir (2) A0018/08 A0506/M
pover (2) A0344/31 A0356/13
poverty (7) A0103/28
A0514/24 A0531/19 A0624/07 B0856/18
B1055/06 B1208/08
powder (13) A0410/06
B1161/39 B1181/01 C0194/05 C0194/15
C0195/18 C0204/41 C0394/24 C0395/22
C0533/31 C0542/28 C0556/16 C0559/25
powdered (1) A0428/34
Power (1) B1211/T
power (126)
powerful (23) A0019/26
A0105/V A0164/V A0343/31 A0350/20
A0460/28 A0544/04 B0905/18 B0909/04
B0957/35 B0980/09 B1119/19 B1165/26
B1339/02 B1348/11 B1349/25 B1363/09
C0055/15 C0204/28 C0422/08 C0438/V
C0540/30 C0548/15
powerfully (2) A0528/27 C0411/16
powerfulness (1) A0413/27
powerless (2) A0080/22 A0612/35
powers (41) A0054/01
A0063/09 A0067/25 A0078/12 A0078/35
A0097/19 A0189/31 A0211/25 A0212/31
A0225/12 A0226/03 A0229/12 A0234/04
A0382/09 A0467/09 A0468/23 A0527/V
A0528/21 A0547/29 A0691/29 B0727/03
B0793/22 B0807/20 B0828/33 B0890/22
B1018/36 B1036/04 B1047/02 B1140/35
B1166/22 B1167/04 B1169/09 B1237/02
B1345/19 B1380/33 C0072/40 C0082/39
C0083/21 C0130/16 C0148/06 C0429/44
Powhatan (1) A0621/21
pp. (4) A0366/17
B1358/07 B1358/07 C0430/32

practicability (1) B1294/25
practicable (5) B1039/15
B1310/17 C0107/10 C0574/29 C0580/02
Practical (1) C0393/02
practical (17) A0295/10
A0296/V A0433/18 A0434/01 A0437/06
A0609/21 A0711/34 B0903/23 B0985/08
B1010/10 B1018/15 B1301/32 B1301/33
B1345/15 B1347/26 B1359/35 C0430/20
practically (1) B1090/31
practice (24) A0437/31
A0487/03 A0555/17 A0583/36 A0623/19
A0709/26 A0710/14 B0747/20 B0901/V
B0942/09 B0985/22 B1004/30 B1005/31
B1070/19 B1093/28 B1113/10 B1130/28
B1141/05 B1191/02 B1274/28 B1275/17
C0057/03 C0114/05 C0561/35
practices (1) B1206/09
practise (2) A0440/22 B1257/09
practised (6) A0055/32 A0065/14
A0303/30 A0434/04 C0112/38 C0156/41
practising (2) A0059/15 A0066/23
practitioner (1) A0056/33
practitioners (2) A0067/30 B0960/02
praenomen (1) A0434/06
praeter-nature (1) B0772/12
Praeter-Veteris (1) A0366/16
praeternatural (3) A0528/10
A0551/03 A0555/12
prairie (18) A0580/05 B1299/30
B1300/27 C0537/08 C0541/26 C0541/36
C0541/37 C0552/36 C0553/16 C0557/34
C0561/23 C0561/25 C0561/37 C0568/09
C0568/20 C0577/17 C0578/07 C0580/02
Prairie/du/Chien (1) C0528/13
prairies (6) B0862/10 C0540/11
C0542/04 C0542/37 C0548/03 C0559/18
praise (3) A0611/30
B1139/30 B1381/06
praised (2) B1081/17 B1385/13
praises (1) B1380/07
praiseworthy (2) A0295/25 B1380/20
prandian (1) B1105/V
prate (1) A0482/01
prating (2) B1298/08 B1316/15
pratique (1) A0296/V
Pratt (13) A0655/03
A0655/10 A0655/17 A0655/22 A0655/27
A0655/V A0656/01 A0656/06 A0656/12
A0656/21 A0656/25 A0657/17 A0657/22
prawns (1) C0177/07
pray (14) A0034/13 A0090/27
A0090/31 A0109/23 A0110/11 A0261/19
A0262/11 A0263/20 A0383/25 B1010/10
B1103/04 B1159/26 B1190/01 B1191/10
prayed (5) A0020/V
A0354/27 A0691/07 C0088/21 C0141/19
prayer (3) A0227/33
A0590/07 A0691/08
prayers (3) B1107/14
B1152/21 B1294/08
praying (2) C0131/18 C0132/12
pre-eminence (1) B1138/24
pre-eminent (5) A0372/15
A0703/26 B1129/29 B1268/25 C0530/39

pre-eminently (2) A0302/15 A0379/13
pre-existent (2) A0175/12 A0181/02
preached (3) A0624/03
B1295/13 B1311/05
preacher (1) C0531/36
preaching (1) A0479/08
precarious (3) C0089/03
C0114/29 C0197/29
precaution (19) A0247/30
A0409/28 A0586/04 B0732/18 B0744/24
B0763/09 B0771/11 B0879/23 B1075/13
B1352/12 C0094/05 C0108/20 C0116/03
C0143/41 C0153/09 C0168/40 C0171/10
C0180/14 C0191/05
precautions (12) A0671/04
B0796/05 B0815/27 B0965/25 B0967/20
C0097/38 C0098/22 C0098/41 C0109/18
C0149/24 C0544/03 C0546/29
preceded (3) B0728/33
B1219/05 C0564/37
precedes (2) B0838/13 B1075/10
preceding (8) A0157/15
A0164/15 A0609/15 B0962/26 B0992/10
B1068/08 B1177/01 C0196/09
precepts (1) B0747/12
precincts (6) A0135/17 A0159/18
A0217/V A0293/16 A0672/20 B0760/13
precious (6) A0097/06 A0301/06
A0316/10 B1155/23 B1259/13 B1303/04
precipice (24) A0045/14
A0046/06 A0578/11 B0865/33 B1108/20
B1222/26 B1223/15 B1281/33 B1332/02
B1334/11 B1334/34 B1338/15 C0164/09
C0181/28 C0184/40 C0191/32 C0196/14
C0196/30 C0198/11 C0199/16 C0578/25
C0578/33 C0578/33 C0579/11
precipice's (1) B1223/01
precipices (3) B0863/09
C0412/32 C0567/20
precipitancy (1) B1223/06
precipitate (8) A0024/18
A0327/11 A0692/30 B0879/20 B0993/07
C0110/29 C0187/34 C0424/20
precipitated (12) A0057/35
A0068/20 A0351/07 A0593/24 A0703/24
B0771/04 B0943/24 B1107/06 B1268/23
C0073/05 C0184/35 C0198/26
precipitates (1) A0582/35
precipitating (3) A0567/V
B0817/26 B1162/19
precipitation (4) A0058/06
A0068/28 A0626/06 B1322/19
precipitous (22) A0045/07 A0140/02
A0398/09 A0580/17 B0864/27 B0865/02
B1279/04 B1331/19 B1331/24 B1334/31
B1335/05 C0155/11 C0167/25 C0172/30
C0173/16 C0173/24 C0183/17 C0183/38
C0424/34 C0572/33 C0576/37 C0578/19
precise (36) A0069/02
A0073/V A0241/27 A0285/35 A0298/01
A0356/V A0484/18 A0622/07 B0728/18
B0758/16 B0767/18 B0770/04 B0822/05
B0830/35 B0833/31 B0873/04 B0877/34
B0910/07 B0925/02 B0929/17 B0993/13
B1034/07 B1102/34 B1192/15 B1214/03
->B1221/26 B1331/17 B1358/28 C0089/34
C0155/09 C0156/38 C0157/07 C0193/22
C0207/40 C0388/21 C0576/40
precisely (80)
precision (21) A0104/01
A0266/10 A0266/17 A0271/19 A0273/19
A0283/27 A0300/17 A0380/12 A0429/31
A0473/02 A0478/22 A0497/19 A0530/25
A0613/19 B0905/19 B1119/09 B1119/23
B1164/36 B1167/01 B1346/21 C0438/V
preclude (1) A0549/06
precluded (3) A0235/06
A0433/30 B1256/06
precocity (1) A0623/09
preconceived (6) A0667/60 B0740/04
B0822/32 B0842/01 B1220/10 C0387/04
preconcert (3) A0703/22
B0827/17 B1268/21
preconcertedly (1) A0654/24
pred (1) B1104/V
predecessor (1) B1314/28
predecessors (5) A0603/31
B0759/01 B0887/23 B1136/08 B1220/09
predestined (1) A0622/08
Predicament (1) A0347/25
predicament (6) A0127/24 B1108/25
B1108/26 B1353/03 B1372/27 B1382/13
predict (1) B1138/02
predicted (3) A0228/33
A0460/09 A0623/20
Prediction (2) B1320/04 B1320/T
prediction (1) A0019/22
predilections (1) B1020/23
predisposed (2) A0019/23 B1107/10
predisposes (1) B1345/08
predisposing (1) B0962/07
predominance (1) B0863/24
predominant (10) A0156/20 A0415/01
A0651/27 A0651/V A0692/16 B0826/18
B0836/19 B0837/09 B0963/35 C0118/15
predominate (1) B1300/09
predominated (1) A0226/03
predominates (2) A0145/22 B0837/03
predominating (1) A0073/14
preeches (1) B1109/33
Preface (2) B1113/T C0055/01
preface (5) A0265/11
A0473/T A0621/02 B1383/30 C0207/09
prefacing (1) A0528/19
Prefect (37) A0546/08
A0568/19 B0725/05 B0727/02 B0727/18
B0728/23 B0728/34 B0734/27 B0737/21
B0754/17 B0772/06 B0974/15 B0975/11
B0975/29 B0976/02 B0976/16 B0976/24
B0977/25 B0977/34 B0979/03 B0981/20
B0981/27 B0982/34 B0983/05 B0983/14
B0984/02 B0985/09 B0985/29 B0986/14
B0986/28 B0988/15 B0988/25 B0989/04
B0989/06 B0990/06 B0990/14 B0991/13
prefect (3) A0120/25
B0986/19 B0993/15
Prefect/of/Police (1) A0568/09
Prefect's (1) B0986/12
Prefecture (4) B0725/13
B0727/27 B0728/35 B0737/10

prefer (4) A0340/32
B0878/12 B1109/22 B1137/40
preferable (2) A0412/11 C0102/03
preference (4) A0657/25
B0766/13 C0058/04 C0065/34
preferred (11) A0026/14
A0086/13 A0366/09 A0381/21 A0511/17
A0583/29 B0771/14 B0879/10 B1299/04
B1345/14 C0152/14
preferring (2) A0160/23 C0199/16
Prefet (2) A0546/V A0568/V
prefixed (1) B1133/03
pregnancy (2) A0379/18 A0439/19
pregnant (1) B1226/14
Preignac (2) A0101/V A0181/14
prejudice (7) A0097/25
B0725/09 B0727/17 B0933/26 B1030/18
B1050/22 C0065/01
prejudiced (1) B1207/17
prejudices (3) A0459/08
C0105/24 C0438/V
preliminaries (1) A0074/13
preliminary (1) A0301/26
Premature (1) B0954/T
premature (5) B0956/03
B0961/10 B0962/20 B0963/24 C0076/01
prematurely (1) A0611/08
premeditated (2) B0769/V B1107/30
premier (1) C0430/31
premise (3) A0135/18
B1358/01 C0415/14
premised (1) B1223/V
premises (24) A0121/25
A0399/11 A0539/16 A0544/19 A0546/08
A0552/23 B0749/02 B0749/02 B0796/23
B0827/10 B0858/03 B0858/11 B0978/23
B0978/27 B0979/01 B0980/22 B0981/19
B0981/22 B0983/25 B0988/24 B0988/29
B1003/06 B1005/16 B1362/28
Premium (1) B0806/T
premium (1) A0491/03
Prentice's (1) B1141/08
preparation (7) A0057/12
B1075/29 B1075/33 B1299/13 C0114/22
C0149/36 C0170/38
preparations (12) A0080/33
A0217/01 A0286/08 A0327/11 B0832/17
B1274/06 C0108/07 C0131/34 C0177/32
C0390/08 C0394/37 C0550/15
preparatory (3) B0770/V
B1037/08 C0110/03
prepare (6) B0808/15 B1075/14
B1096/15 C0055/32 C0155/40 C0527/21
prepared (47) A0139/22
A0204/07 A0250/23 A0326/04 A0402/17
A0502/01 A0533/10 A0563/03 A0581/07
A0628/08 A0687/15 A0690/22 B0742/33
B0748/11 B0754/22 B0754/26 B0755/06
B0813/22 B0814/05 B0818/27 B0854/19
B0857/17 B0858/19 B0879/08 B0906/03
B0926/07 B0930/09 B0941/25 B0947/26
B0967/25 B0990/19 B0992/17 B1058/17
B1242/32 B1242/34 B1293/04 C0093/39
C0133/40 C0141/02 C0169/20 C0186/14
C0409/16 C0410/09 C0413/17 C0429/39
->C0535/34 C0543/38
preparees (1) A0037/10
prepares (1) B0891/13
preparing (13) A0053/03
A0062/08 B0750/12 B1181/12 B1302/29
C0139/17 C0178/02 C0179/20 C0189/24
C0207/20 C0549/32 C0568/39 C0579/27
preponderate (2) B0741/22 C0546/22
preponderated (1) C0546/28
prepositions (1) B1296/28
prepossessing (2) A0104/18 A0126/19
prepossession (1) A0473/08
prepossessions (1) B0993/01
preposterous (12) A0294/V
A0496/05 A0497/V A0499/28 A0499/V
B0739/15 B0923/03 B1131/13 B1138/25
B1169/01 B1297/25 C0078/11
preposterously (1) B1314/33
prerogative (1) B1215/04
pres (1) C0430/30
Presburg (5) A0225/15
A0229/14 B1360/21 B1360/33 B1361/01
prescience (1) A0611/12
prescribe (1) B0815/34
prescribed (2) A0296/V B0740/04
prescriptive (2) A0431/18 A0479/37
presence (63)
Present (1) B0724/31
present (191)
presentant (1) A0037/21
presentation (4) B0899/V
B0900/16 B0916/10 B1180/14
presented (59)
presenter (1) A0096/M
presentiment (2) A0136/33 B0833/23
presenting (12) A0226/28
A0231/02 A0613/16 B0762/27 B0865/27
B0965/06 B1079/06 B1259/24 C0172/01
C0203/25 C0554/09 C0559/15
presently (63)
presentment (1) B0874/23
presents (10) A0500/04 B1018/09
B1346/27 C0155/11 C0195/22 C0552/04
C0557/10 C0558/21 C0566/09 C0569/38
preservation (15) A0073/14
A0295/22 A0442/10 B0826/01 B0965/23
B1180/24 B1303/34 C0120/02 C0134/15
C0134/41 C0136/29 C0144/27 C0198/24
C0406/26 C0412/26
preserve (7) A0473/10
B1330/05 C0132/05 C0139/04 C0410/10
C0535/08 C0574/03
preserved (19) A0264/02
A0273/15 A0277/16 A0298/V A0711/29
B0742/24 B0831/20 B0889/V B0956/20
B1276/32 B1303/27 B1304/24 C0089/27
C0117/25 C0132/27 C0190/31 C0193/24
C0199/17 C0566/04
preserver (1) B0958/02
preserves (1) A0365/19
preserving (9) A0266/13
A0409/16 A0627/09 C0063/22 C0087/36
C0096/25 C0138/16 C0141/27 C0396/39
presided (3) A0311/13
A0311/14 B1104/30

President (3) B1195/15
C0390/33 C0390/37
president (12) A0175/27
A0181/22 A0204/11 A0205/10 A0245/20
A0246/17 A0247/24 A0249/10 A0249/22
A0249/33 A0250/34 A0252/03
presidents (1) B1089/20
press (20) A0140/12
A0154/18 A0203/04 A0276/10 A0412/23
A0508/03 A0512/25 B0735/05 B0758/15
B0811/08 B1059/11 B1138/06 B1358/21
B1369/28 B1371/24 B1373/17 B1374/03
B1380/12 C0162/36 C0207/02
pressed (20) A0035/23
A0248/07 A0324/16 A0329/14 A0353/13
A0515/04 A0552/26 A0553/04 A0609/08
A0694/20 A0694/31 A0697/02 B0947/16
B0992/03 C0068/23 C0068/26 C0075/26
C0075/27 C0100/10 C0166/21
presses (1) A0479/22
pressing (13) A0079/42
A0103/10 A0553/26 A0614/27 A0643/31
B0873/13 B0907/02 B1017/21 B1134/25
B1235/21 C0072/33 C0082/20 C0103/36
pressingly (1) A0667/51
pressure (29) A0078/01
A0078/34 A0137/12 A0155/11 A0353/13
A0354/35 A0404/20 A0543/29 A0613/23
A0694/23 A0696/34 B0814/03 B0856/09
B0902/12 B0965/27 B1040/14 B1352/20
B1359/19 B1359/25 C0090/20 C0118/31
C0175/13 C0178/40 C0182/17 C0404/04
C0404/14 C0407/15 C0411/31 C0413/16
Preston (3) A0441/08
A0444/20 A0444/30
presumable (2) B0986/04 B0986/V
presume (39) A0074/02
A0096/05 A0126/13 A0145/20 A0336/01
A0444/07 A0621/06 A0708/02 B0731/35
B0744/18 B0753/11 B0810/11 B0810/18
B0833/20 B0843/24 B0910/03 B0950/19
B0979/07 B0979/19 B0980/15 B0982/01
B1005/31 B1015/10 B1016/02 B1019/06
B1135/06 B1159/01 B1187/07 B1188/01
B1189/31 B1190/12 B1191/04 B1239/32
B1273/02 B1301/10 B1302/28 B1361/12
B1379/25 C0062/38
presumed (4) A0262/34
A0431/22 A0686/16 B0986/05
presumption (1) A0249/20
pretence (5) B0723/14
B0827/03 B0878/23 B1153/09 C0180/17
pretences (1) C0393/14
pretend (18) A0380/10 A0439/29
A0560/18 B0740/27 B0773/34 B0826/17
B1104/28 B1192/29 B1194/26 B1208/10
B1233/01 B1241/01 B1315/20 B1370/02
B1379/33 C0167/38 C0203/38 C0558/23
pretended (4) B0916/15
B0992/25 C0056/10 C0168/25
pretender (1) B1324/02
pretending (4) A0482/33
B0894/14 B0990/22 B1354/01
pretends (3) B0977/14
B1096/13 B1297/16
pretension (2) B1137/30 C0181/19
pretensions (3) A0431/32
B1104/33 B1359/10
preternatural (2) A0029/23 A0152/07
preterpluperfect (1) A0498/07
pretext (2) C0107/15 C0564/17
prettiest (1) A0485/18
pretty (33) A0034/12
A0072/28 A0074/04 A0091/08 A0107/10
A0110/14 A0174/18 A0176/17 A0182/18
A0280/32 A0280/35 A0285/07 A0300/V
A0343/02 A0346/01 A0348/10 A0384/16
A0482/17 A0489/24 A0628/17 B0833/11
B0833/12 B0930/24 B1016/25 B1056/30
B1079/23 B1091/02 B1338/06 C0163/25
C0536/32 C0543/05 C0553/07 C0574/09
prevail (3) A0459/09
C0148/22 C0169/41
prevailed (16) A0244/02
A0349/27 A0457/34 B0733/13 B0879/29
B0933/36 B0965/16 B1097/04 C0100/08
C0107/27 C0128/19 C0132/20 C0132/32
C0203/03 C0420/02 C0426/24
prevailing (9) A0212/30
A0273/12 A0402/05 A0671/28 B0837/05
B1153/23 C0156/28 C0160/11 C0203/09
prevails (3) B1221/V
B1222/21 B1281/22
prevalence (4) A0046/23
A0473/13 A0709/30 B1274/32
prevalent (8) A0473/02
A0497/16 A0502/02 B0963/14 C0087/30
C0153/10 C0428/20 C0552/40
prevarication (1) B0824/07
prevent (50) A0089/03 A0103/19
A0356/17 A0378/09 A0412/24 A0412/27
A0447/24 A0694/01 A0704/31 B0733/14
B0734/25 B0747/31 B0750/20 B0766/05
B0766/12 B0766/28 B0828/04 B0851/02
B0933/26 B0949/20 B1045/26 B1074/21
B1106/25 B1132/29 B1142/35 B1249/06
B1269/30 B1335/01 B1351/28 C0077/03
C0098/32 C0109/18 C0110/23 C0120/04
C0133/19 C0133/28 C0142/11 C0143/39
C0174/40 C0181/23 C0198/21 C0403/13
C0404/33 C0408/32 C0415/03 C0416/27
C0537/02 C0561/35 C0567/28 C0575/39
prevented (34) A0020/08 A0080/42
A0103/32 A0137/01 A0159/22 A0242/32
A0247/29 A0248/11 A0433/08 A0511/06
A0664/18 A0667/56 A0688/23 B0765/13
B0817/26 B0857/07 B0915/28 B0931/20
B0948/27 B1052/13 B1364/15 C0055/25
C0090/11 C0094/37 C0098/11 C0110/17
C0127/35 C0128/40 C0131/04 C0132/30
C0133/14 C0175/15 C0391/38 C0410/28
preventing (6) A0248/27 B0854/30
B0990/09 B1189/27 B1334/07 C0152/20
Prevention (1) B1131/33
prevention (2) A0295/22 B1300/06
previous (33) A0106/28
A0139/14 A0164/02 A0205/01 A0209/24
A0459/02 A0541/04 A0627/25 A0629/18
B0726/29 B0746/29 B0770/09 B0809/23
B0857/28 B1051/V B1053/06 B1072/12

->B1234/19 B1235/33 B1239/19 B1270/36
C0062/39 C0080/03 C0095/20 C0160/17
C0162/16 C0166/05 C0419/22 C0428/36
C0429/39 C0522/13 C0536/21 C0537/03
previously (25) A0406/15
A0408/11 A0409/17 A0446/29 A0459/25
A0461/05 A0541/14 A0565/06 A0693/23
B0894/28 B0962/21 B0991/26 B1019/32
B1051/02 B1141/17 B1178/34 B1239/29
B1315/13 C0077/08 C0080/06 C0164/05
C0448/V C0533/37 C0550/04 C0557/09
prey (15) A0315/09
A0329/09 A0427/24 A0442/01 A0509/27
A0693/31 B0965/08 B1165/09 B1292/22
C0134/24 C0142/33 C0151/38 C0547/08
C0547/25 C0547/32
prey'st (1) A0599/M
preys (1) A0604/08
Price (4) A0176/09
A0180/30 A0703/05 B1268/05
price (16) A0485/17
A0491/13 A0532/09 A0611/12 B0863/37
B0872/01 B0872/14 B1090/05 B1244/02
B1257/28 B1312/28 B1364/33 C0178/12
C0179/13 C0179/41 C0426/17
priced (1) A0513/23
priceless (2) B0907/10 B1317/32
prices (3) A0388/14
B1092/22 B1134/17
pricked (2) A0248/02 A0252/15
pricking (1) B0966/13
prickly (4) C0138/12
C0165/26 C0559/19 C0576/05
pride (7) A0097/19
A0297/01 A0369/20 A0433/05 B0887/19
B0957/17 B1332/23
prided (3) A0247/15
A0298/05 B1257/06
priest (2) A0044/15 B0916/16
priesthood (2) A0601/05 A0608/04
Priestley (3) A0180/30
A0703/05 B1268/05
Priestly (1) A0176/09
priests (1) A0021/25
prig (1) A0488/14
prim (1) B0910/24
prima (4) A0303/23
A0536/18 B0889/10 B1219/02
primaeval (1) A0610/03
primaries (1) B1322/19
primarily (2) A0212/17 B1314/26
primary (7) A0211/09
A0212/23 A0347/13 B0724/09 B0852/09
B1292/32 B1322/11
prime (4) A0486/09
A0486/16 A0510/07 B1348/15
primer (1) A0078/22
primeval (2) A0195/17 A0196/32
primitive (18) A0175/13 A0181/02
A0497/03 A0527/V A0531/03 A0709/04
B0852/08 B1039/25 B1184/24 B1219/04
B1220/21 B1221/05 B1273/29 B1273/32
B1274/04 B1334/04 C0173/18 C0550/29
primitively (1) A0286/05
primness (1) A0380/11
Primo's (1) C0527/01
primum (1) B1219/13
prin (Gr.) (1) A0507/11
Prince (15) A0034/20
A0127/02 A0127/21 A0127/30 A0182/15
A0183/02 A0670/10 A0671/13 A0675/18
A0675/27 A0676/17 A0676/26 A0705/31
B1269/35 C0525/30
prince (4) A0128/04
A0671/06 A0675/29 A0676/01
Prince/de/Foie-Gras (1) A0034/13
Prince/of/Wales (1) A0180/25
Prince/Edward's/Island (2) C0150/04
C0154/20
Prince's (2) A0705/35 B1270/34
prince's (3) A0670/15
A0675/02 A0676/09
princely (3) A0157/10
A0704/21 B1269/20
Princes (1) A0021/28
princes (1) A0029/V
Princess (1) C0156/35
Princesse (1) A0102/10
principal (37) A0021/03
A0023/16 A0123/06 A0124/03 A0126/17
A0263/36 A0400/05 A0428/29 A0430/04
A0507/21 A0514/05 A0589/02 B0850/15
B0878/30 B0904/16 B0909/23 B0962/27
B1127/03 B1129/06 B1192/15 B1247/25
B1249/33 B1282/32 B1302/30 B1310/26
B1332/32 B1336/21 B1339/14 B1361/14
C0055/25 C0093/17 C0144/22 C0150/20
C0162/14 C0179/23 C0546/34 C0548/02
principality (1) A0020/15
principally (20) A0087/28
A0136/31 A0499/09 B0949/09 B1015/10
B1048/10 B1079/17 B1234/06 B1321/12
B1351/18 B1358/26 C0097/24 C0105/29
C0137/27 C0168/18 C0178/34 C0203/39
C0530/11 C0536/17 C0538/36
principia (1) B1220/07
principium (2) A0226/36 A0231/10
principle (57)
principles (25) A0078/40
A0135/15 A0338/02 A0381/32 A0497/09
A0499/19 A0609/16 A0609/17 A0703/30
A0706/18 B0747/15 B0747/16 B0747/35
B0770/V B0835/33 B0985/22 B0985/27
B0986/14 B1089/03 B1153/24 B1164/25
B1268/28 B1271/21 C0186/11 C0433/09
print (14) A0264/35 A0283/24
A0547/16 A0621/09 B0731/V B0734/08
B0738/08 B0740/14 B1103/02 B1103/02
B1131/04 B1136/27 B1208/28 B1250/12
printed (13) A0265/10
B0739/07 B0739/16 B0875/01 B1091/26
B1115/22 B1133/02 B1314/04 B1320/04
B1380/13 B1390/17 C0427/26 C0534/24
printer (1) C0427/25
printer's (1) B1130/23
printers (1) B1373/34
printin> (1) A0465/30
Printing (1) B1167/37
printing (2) A0465/V C0415/12
printing-offices (2) B1184/19

->B1373/28
prints (4) A0107/04
B0752/29 B1137/29 B1139/10
prior (11) A0055/17
A0065/01 A0704/19 B0733/36 B0761/09
B0768/07 B0770/22 B1038/26 C0078/25
C0411/36 C0524/12
priori (11) A0086/10
A0097/10 A0103/V A0342/V B0871/22
B0955/36 B1219/17 B1295/08 B1310/27
B1313/19 B1313/35
priority (1) B1136/24
prism (1) B1248/19
prism-cut (1) A0499/25
prismatic (1) B1250/26
prison (22) A0081/27 A0153/06
A0154/06 A0416/14 A0589/18 A0602/21
A0686/01 A0686/11 A0686/33 A0688/09
A0688/31 A0689/23 A0695/07 A0695/20
A0696/03 A0697/04 C0078/04 C0080/26
C0083/30 C0182/37 C0192/26 C0195/26
prison-house (2) A0616/13 A0641/10
prison-like (1) A0428/22
Prison-House (1) B1206/T
prisoner (9) A0565/V
B1052/21 B1053/25 B1054/14 B1362/35
C0071/34 C0093/07 C0201/31 C0202/41
prisoners (6) A0123/29 A0124/26
B0955/08 C0086/27 C0088/05 C0561/31
prisons (2) B1163/06 B1337/16
privacy (4) A0033/08
A0155/05 A0235/11 B0760/05
private (35) A0059/23
A0062/33 A0067/14 A0085/03 A0120/12
A0142/01 A0203/05 A0250/19 A0432/08
B0726/12 B0727/25 B0733/17 B0863/07
B0871/18 B0878/13 B0889/11 B0904/27
B0960/03 B0960/08 B0982/28 B1002/03
B1003/10 B1058/34 B1072/33 B1089/23
B1090/23 B1134/09 B1179/05 B1189/23
B1242/03 C0055/08 C0093/16 C0425/29
C0529/06 C0576/39
privately (4) C0103/25
C0394/18 C0396/16 C0536/18
privation (2) C0145/05 C0148/34
privations (2) C0095/22 C0564/19
privilege (6) A0058/03 A0068/24
B0908/V B0910/11 B1005/13 B1093/06
privileges (5) A0251/09
A0382/10 B0865/20 B1153/01 C0153/15
privy (1) B0755/19
privy-councillors (1) B1354/14
Prize (1) B0806/T
prize (8) A0055/10
A0055/24 A0064/26 B0815/05 B0815/13
B0830/27 C0127/18 C0165/20
prized (1) B0807/11
prizing (1) C0213/V
pro (4) A0204/12
A0366/11 B1080/10 B1189/10
pro (2) B1144/22 C0065/01
pro-o-odigies (1) A0386/01
probabilities (5) A0528/33
A0556/24 B0724/02 B0773/13 B0836/04
probability (25) A0018/06
->A0055/19 A0065/03 A0080/42 A0145/27
A0548/17 B0740/28 B0740/29 B0745/15
B0746/13 B0746/18 B0771/02 B1051/25
B1051/26 C0055/22 C0059/37 C0093/36
C0122/15 C0189/15 C0202/14 C0389/07
C0403/17 C0418/04 C0420/31 C0546/27
probable (33) A0021/07
A0054/33 A0081/20 A0211/22 A0409/14
A0444/12 A0548/13 A0552/34 A0554/20
A0560/10 A0566/21 A0682/29 B0739/35
B0749/25 B0749/31 B0988/V B0990/07
B1123/03 B1154/11 B1187/02 B1364/05
C0058/38 C0065/27 C0075/39 C0079/25
C0095/14 C0132/26 C0153/38 C0208/01
C0394/13 C0402/33 C0404/01 C0578/35
probably (57)
Probant (1) A0495/04
probe (1) B1133/09
probed (5) B0979/26
B0980/16 B0980/V B0981/10 B1168/07
probes (1) B0989/03
probing (2) B0985/24 C0076/36
problem (8) A0478/32
A0479/04 B1069/06 B1081/15 B1164/25
B1164/31 B1375/11 C0166/23
problematical (1) B1079/21
problems (2) B1018/10 B1164/03
proboscis (14) A0073/10 A0108/06
A0173/08 A0174/16 A0177/29 A0177/29
A0178/13 A0180/24 A0183/25 A0183/26
B1248/10 B1248/17 B1248/35 B1250/22
procedure (1) B0766/24
proceed (71)
proceeded (136)
proceeding (40) A0065/15
A0126/23 A0252/03 A0409/19 A0499/14
A0657/08 B0758/04 B0772/28 B0816/14
B0840/32 B0909/22 B1044/14 B1076/27
B1162/02 B1310/01 B1332/06 B1362/27
B1381/15 C0061/25 C0064/19 C0075/24
C0077/21 C0105/13 C0121/36 C0148/20
C0150/41 C0181/01 C0194/13 C0194/22
C0393/24 C0430/17 C0430/18 C0526/28
C0535/26 C0545/06 C0549/08 C0554/03
C0560/20 C0574/25 C0577/28
proceedings (8) A0070/29
A0204/30 A0545/03 A0684/18 B0733/32
B0748/23 B0823/12 C0198/18
proceeds (11) A0413/23
B0732/19 B0865/03 B1071/21 B1102/10
B1160/25 B1183/26 B1281/18 B1311/23
C0430/13 C0531/31
process (24) A0226/01
A0229/18 A0339/03 A0388/10 A0685/24
B0773/11 B0826/03 B1073/12 B1127/08
B1127/11 B1167/12 B1182/07 B1187/08
B1187/13 B1187/18 B1189/25 B1233/23
B1241/27 B1350/38 C0152/31 C0196/22
C0535/39 C0535/41 C0538/19
processes (5) A0527/V
A0527/V B1292/33 B1312/16 B1317/23
procession (1) A0081/06
processions (1) C0118/13
proche (1) C0430/31
proclaimed (1) A0245/12

proclaiming (1) A0124/08
proclamation (1) B0727/22
Proclus (2) A0176/06 A0180/28
procrastinate (1) B1047/01
Procrustean (1) B0984/02
procure (15) A0269/25
A0325/05 A0388/10 A0531/24 A0537/12
A0561/26 A0650/V B0908/21 B1073/14
C0092/14 C0154/07 C0393/17 C0529/04
C0531/07 C0555/10
procured (18) A0138/10 B0728/35
B0841/31 B0959/01 B1059/08 B1073/09
B1106/31 B1241/19 B1351/06 C0151/06
C0155/06 C0179/24 C0533/40 C0534/01
C0534/04 C0535/15 C0542/37 C0558/04
procuring (5) A0490/11
B0850/24 B1022/05 C0078/08 C0156/22
prodigal (1) A0486/03
prodigies (6) A0189/08 A0380/33
A0382/31 A0384/02 A0384/25 A0385/13
prodigious (40) A0024/07
A0122/06 A0146/14 A0247/32 A0367/26
A0414/16 A0557/21 A0559/21 A0580/20
A0583/01 A0590/20 A0590/V B0828/08
B0930/19 B0930/31 B0948/30 B0980/27
B1009/01 B1013/30 B1020/07 B1069/02
B1156/35 B1159/19 B1165/02 B1165/14
B1167/03 B1194/08 B1301/02 B1346/15
B1352/07 B1360/30 B1381/32 C0087/31
C0138/26 C0397/16 C0398/14 C0412/13
C0428/34 C0429/22 C0577/36
prodigiously (4) C0118/31
C0205/23 C0389/20 C0403/26
produce (16) A0102/19
A0159/10 A0447/28 A0673/05 A0707/25
B0726/29 B0730/19 B0763/15 B0773/04
B0865/10 B0956/01 B1139/03 B1168/23
B1272/25 C0178/35 C0423/21
produced (38) A0112/24 A0204/08
A0206/03 A0213/17 A0241/01 A0245/V
A0435/10 A0459/19 A0543/28 A0544/03
A0623/05 A0663/17 A0672/14 A0672/18
B0742/29 B0822/06 B0894/06 B0905/07
B0929/28 B0949/23 B0978/31 B0978/34
B1039/10 B1096/19 B1161/25 B1250/22
B1321/31 B1322/23 B1350/22 C0083/33
C0091/41 C0111/28 C0127/34 C0150/16
C0172/02 C0187/16 C0187/29 C0421/41
produces (5) A0600/06
A0692/09 B0773/10 B0875/06 B0977/13
producing (8) A0500/06
A0613/13 A0629/11 B0726/31 B0981/27
B0983/01 B1039/07 B1260/28
production (1) B1133/V
productions (3) A0473/29
A0706/26 C0176/06
productive (2) C0071/10 C0122/21
productiveness (1) C0156/15
profanation (1) A0159/16
profane (2) A0250/34 A0250/35
profanely (1) A0250/05
profanity (1) A0438/29
professed (7) B0726/14
B0897/V B0909/11 B1236/09 B1278/25
B1312/02 C0157/39

professes (3) B1360/20
B1380/17 C0430/33
professing (2) B1345/17 C0429/04
profession (13) A0097/18
A0107/17 A0123/18 A0440/21 A0484/10
A0486/03 A0486/34 A0488/03 A0489/08
A0490/25 B1029/03 B1127/02 C0391/12
professional (2) A0509/33 B1345/27
Professor (16) A0281/17
A0283/21 A0284/05 A0284/06 A0284/10
A0284/27 A0295/12 B1002/T B1017/02
B1017/12 B1018/03 B1022/04 B1359/09
C0390/32 C0426/32 C0426/38
professor (1) C0427/03
proffered (2) B0909/12 B1107/35
Proffit, Peter (2) A0484/31
A0488/07
proficiency (4) A0105/11
A0529/19 A0529/21 C0393/04
proficient (1) A0315/18
profile (3) A0415/12
B0891/01 B0894/10
Profit (1) A0488/V
profit (11) A0044/21
A0121/24 A0438/19 A0487/30 A0489/20
B1113/11 B1142/09 B1143/08 C0093/28
C0176/07 C0530/23
profitable (4) A0243/02
A0484/08 B1245/03 C0170/21
profited (1) B1059/25
profits (3) C0086/35
C0531/31 C0564/06
profligacy (2) A0438/17 A0438/17
profound (69)
profoundest (5) A0300/27
A0411/09 B1164/25 C0169/32 C0397/38
profoundly (16) A0078/40
A0381/03 A0531/V A0565/19 A0612/29
A0626/23 A0706/29 B0878/25 B0924/15
B0975/35 B0986/V B1046/19 B1153/34
B1271/31 B1325/01 B1359/08
profundity (17) A0079/05
A0098/24 A0098/26 A0107/14 A0113/10
A0244/19 A0294/V A0303/26 A0304/V
A0338/05 A0346/08 A0545/29 A0577/M
A0628/21 B0964/03 B0985/02 C0438/V
profuse (6) A0401/14 A0502/V
A0670/04 B1242/11 B1279/05 B1332/36
profusely (6) A0245/16 A0508/13
A0602/28 B1281/35 C0387/14 C0542/07
profuseness (1) A0440/08
profusion (16) A0087/29
A0156/13 A0501/23 A0501/V A0503/01
A0672/08 A0702/02 A0704/07 B0872/05
B0945/12 B1008/01 B1008/32 B1269/07
B1334/32 C0542/14 C0576/08
progenitors (5) B0871/28
B1296/14 B1298/18 B1312/17 B1316/29
progeny (2) C0153/05 C0178/33
prognostic (1) B1274/01
progress (58)
progressed (3) B0742/10
B0743/16 B1193/30
progresses (1) A0530/12
progressing (1) C0088/02

progression (3) C0407/22
C0412/20 C0417/37
progressive (4) A0310/08
B1037/08 B1071/24 C0404/03
prohibited (3) A0243/16
B0891/24 B1293/14
project (18) A0484/06 A0486/08
B1018/07 B1049/12 B1070/24 B1072/26
B1079/19 C0066/14 C0103/35 C0136/17
C0151/19 C0177/29 C0177/36 C0393/11
C0404/19 C0415/18 C0523/16 C0523/16
projected (6) A0672/13 B0841/18
B0957/07 B1336/20 C0418/07 C0525/36
projecting (10) B1071/13 B1106/06
B1248/14 B1336/19 B1336/33 C0150/36
C0165/27 C0184/03 C0195/21 C0200/19
projection (3) A0046/17
B0857/08 C0577/40
projections (3) B0818/35
C0197/18 C0207/32
projector (1) B1069/20
projects (4) A0295/04
B0856/31 C0134/28 C0565/07
<u>prolegomena</u> (1) A0654/17
prolix (1) B1224/02
prolixity (1) A0413/11
prolongation (2) C0423/14 C0423/17
prolonged (1) C0204/08
promenade (5) A0484/17
A0484/32 A0485/10 B0901/06 C0152/29
promenade-ground (1) C0153/25
promenades (1) B1143/01
Prometheus (1) A0710/31
prominence (4) A0312/10
A0379/31 A0402/01 A0549/V
prominences (2) A0548/V B0736/35
prominency (1) A0097/32
prominent (7) A0120/09
A0227/11 A0231/24 A0401/11 B0955/12
C0076/02 C0178/15
promiscuous (2) A0507/19 C0099/26
promiscuously (3) A0253/29
B0827/22 B1261/09
promise (26) A0043/07 A0642/16
A0653/07 A0654/V B0729/19 B0816/20
B0816/24 B0820/07 B0872/27 B0875/05
B0879/26 B0904/05 B0910/05 B0910/07
B0910/19 B1059/07 B1082/05 B1130/10
B1238/04 C0093/07 C0101/13 C0133/38
C0176/25 C0179/36 C0393/10 C0558/17
promised (7) A0156/08
B0727/23 B0727/33 B1055/32 B1144/05
C0096/07 C0117/40
promises (8) A0643/24
B0807/29 B0874/34 B0965/20 B1079/33
C0086/06 C0392/03 C0395/35
promising (5) B1329/08
C0069/38 C0088/13 C0091/07 C0395/05
promontory (4) A0579/07
B0865/24 C0149/13 C0574/16
promote (1) A0346/31
prompt (5) A0107/01
B1129/07 B1129/22 B1208/32 C0557/29
prompted (6) A0235/05 A0235/18
A0411/30 A0586/12 A0686/21 A0692/31
promptings (2) B1220/24 B1220/27
promptitude (1) A0078/14
promptly (5) B0730/02
B0819/08 B0820/29 B1130/07 B1208/05
promptness (2) A0385/22 C0165/06
prompts (1) B1096/26
promulgate (1) B0987/02
promulgated (1) B0749/01
promulgation (2) B0987/04 B1311/17
prone (5) A0073/16
B0724/28 C0055/15 C0538/27 C0562/40
proneness (1) B0965/12
<u>prononces</u> (1) B1137/20
pronoun (1) B1096/37
pronounce (3) A0045/26
A0708/14 B1273/09
pronounced (14) A0035/04 A0056/35
A0066/25 A0293/17 A0385/22 A0557/27
B0926/20 B0959/07 B0961/03 B1030/13
B1040/07 B1143/25 B1296/06 C0082/36
pronouncing (1) B1110/09
pronouns (1) A0203/05
pronunciation (2) A0652/11 B0912/11
proof (16) A0098/26
A0432/02 A0582/19 A0665/22 B0731/33
B0734/23 B0745/29 B0746/20 B0746/24
B0746/25 B0758/31 B0768/23 B1338/22
B1369/01 B1379/22 C0105/26
proof-tones (1) A0609/25
proofs (2) A0533/16 B0751/V
proones (Gr.) (1) A0195/M
propagated (2) A0336/11 B1295/07
propagates (1) B1163/19
propagator (2) B1301/09 B1310/26
propel (2) B1070/08 B1077/07
propeller (6) B1070/16 B1077/12
B1078/19 B1079/24 B1079/32 B1080/15
propellers (1) B1293/11
propelling (3) B1070/09
B1070/13 B1070/20
propensities (11) A0026/30
A0034/V A0053/31 A0063/02 A0086/13
A0293/25 A0427/27 A0559/22 A0626/21
C0153/10 C0548/27
propensity (14) A0098/28 A0099/05
A0101/18 A0212/14 A0212/17 A0609/04
A0622/33 A0623/17 B0774/01 B1219/03
B1219/10 B1220/06 B1221/21 C0532/17
proper (108)
properly (66)
properties (5) A0101/05
A0211/21 C0392/34 C0400/39 C0426/02
property (20) A0023/24
A0218/09 A0431/19 A0444/05 A0539/15
A0541/13 A0561/32 A0563/04 B1049/20
B1054/12 B1054/25 B1108/18 B1144/34
B1360/16 B1361/34 C0057/08 C0393/13
C0529/07 C0535/42 C0575/42
prophecies (2) A0458/34 A0461/03
prophecy (7) A0019/08
A0019/24 A0370/20 A0478/25 A0623/07
B0755/16 B1391/05
Prophet (8) C0535/23
C0561/40 C0562/02 C0562/16 C0563/10
C0566/38 C0577/12 C0579/19

prophet (4) A0119/02
A0336/M B1152/15 C0531/37
prophetic (1) C0065/25
prophetical (1) B1317/36
propinquity (1) B1250/02
propitious (1) B1107/23
proportion (48) A0183/24
A0277/16 A0312/01 A0379/21 A0380/18
A0436/08 A0460/24 A0500/08 A0545/26
A0548/V A0615/12 A0667/72 A0709/26
A0710/15 B0752/V B0773/15 B0889/18
B0927/34 B0963/07 B1030/12 B1035/11
B1040/05 B1073/31 B1073/34 B1074/26
B1080/36 B1186/03 B1190/01 B1269/05
B1274/29 B1275/17 C0098/28 C0161/10
C0191/13 C0391/25 C0401/12 C0403/12
C0403/25 C0403/33 C0405/03 C0408/17
C0414/15 C0415/37 C0419/01 C0423/04
C0424/27 C0430/09 C0535/35
proportional (1) A0446/16
proportionally (1) C0389/17
proportionate (6) A0591/17 A0628/23
B0989/V B1074/14 C0147/14 C0533/31
proportioned (5) A0298/V
A0379/32 A0464/19 A0704/05 C0148/40
proportions (16) A0035/19
A0079/44 A0157/V A0246/V A0297/V
A0342/25 A0708/03 B1192/10 B1273/02
B1336/04 B1346/25 B1362/32 B1364/09
C0206/06 C0402/02 C0402/16
propos (1) A0344/29
proposal (5) A0279/27
A0441/13 B0902/07 C0133/34 C0526/20
proposals (4) B0725/30
B0754/25 B0754/29 B0899/24
propose (10) A0205/34 A0564/V
B0751/29 B0752/29 B0754/28 B0816/17
B0984/22 B1126/13 B1142/30 C0432/28
proposed (22) A0301/18 A0398/14
A0441/29 A0545/05 B0727/15 B0727/26
B0843/09 B1002/06 B1053/33 B1177/04
B1236/09 C0056/04 C0105/15 C0121/02
C0132/04 C0182/36 C0184/13 C0414/23
C0526/16 C0527/22 C0536/24 C0569/18
proposing (1) A0585/20
proposition (30) A0339/19 A0345/20
A0346/22 A0486/20 A0499/10 A0600/11
A0623/23 A0710/19 B0728/18 B0728/22
B1077/25 B1077/29 B1215/09 B1220/27
B1275/23 B1298/14 B1302/08 B1314/13
B1314/18 B1314/23 B1314/25 B1315/03
B1315/34 B1316/23 C0086/06 C0086/38
C0121/04 C0125/36 C0132/11 C0170/28
propositions (5) A0531/13
A0709/12 B0773/17 B1313/29 B1314/37
propounded (9) A0263/27
A0271/11 A0384/16 A0629/20 B1032/07
B1240/26 B1314/30 C0556/08 C0556/14
propounder (2) B1314/29 B1315/14
propounding (1) B0897/07
propped (3) B0857/15
B1235/19 C0410/08
proprieties (4) A0157/19
A0165/25 A0273/23 A0495/05
proprietor (13) A0021/05
->A0073/17 A0100/32 A0158/07 A0248/12
A0398/15 A0496/17 A0500/29 B0877/02
B1207/11 B1208/18 B1208/33 B1208/37
proprietor's (1) B1208/24
proprietors (1) B1207/25
propriety (18) A0053/13 A0062/21
A0078/41 A0099/04 A0127/15 A0266/19
A0302/07 A0568/13 A0609/12 A0675/08
B0916/04 B0955/02 B1013/30 B1131/12
B1241/24 B1279/32 B1335/20 C0059/11
propulsion (1) B1070/28
proscribing (1) B1311/15
proscription (2) B1297/24 B1316/07
prose (3) A0204/07
B1090/30 B1386/07
prosecute (4) A0382/12
B1132/06 C0177/28 C0522/38
prosecuted (3) B1131/32
C0447/V C0526/34
prosecuting (2) B1182/26 C0170/24
prosecution (4) A0437/14
A0486/02 B1221/02 C0564/13
prosoiso (Gr.) (1) A0455/M
prospect (25) A0242/30
A0352/08 A0352/33 A0653/17 B0865/25
B1032/27 B1080/30 B1080/36 B1278/03
B1278/13 B1291/20 B1294/17 C0090/12
C0117/19 C0128/24 C0131/19 C0132/06
C0143/26 C0185/28 C0186/10 C0404/36
C0408/09 C0408/18 C0575/09 C0575/13
prospective (1) B0752/12
prospectively (1) B1364/28
prospects (6) B0902/05 B1278/22
C0130/23 C0131/29 C0162/31 C0541/39
prosperity (5) A0251/06
A0703/01 A0703/02 B1268/01 B1268/02
Prospero (6) A0670/10 A0671/13
A0675/18 A0675/28 A0676/17 A0676/26
prostekonti (Gr.) (1) A0075/V
prostrate (14) A0023/03 A0235/27
A0566/27 A0612/30 A0676/25 A0686/06
A0686/32 B0963/04 B1160/32 B1223/19
B1226/17 C0074/23 C0095/24 C0125/31
prostrated (4) A0094/22
A0114/17 C0130/17 C0563/12
prostrating (2) A0125/28 A0404/23
protect (2) B1092/32 C0428/40
protected (6) A0103/31 A0410/09
A0442/17 B1104/09 C0082/19 C0536/08
protecting (1) A0469/07
protection (10) A0021/V A0086/16
A0243/05 A0432/18 A0626/26 B1207/36
C0150/40 C0540/31 C0558/07 C0558/16
protector (1) A0294/V
Protestantism (1) B0723/M
Protestantismus (1) B0723/M
Protestants (1) A0621/18
protestation (2) A0074/09 A0074/10
protestations (1) C0569/05
proticting> (1) A0469/V
prototypes (2) A0613/07 B1191/16
protoxide (1) B1359/17
protracted (9) A0296/16
A0414/30 A0438/24 A0441/18 B0942/21
B0965/18 B0991/29 B1349/08 C0083/38

protruded (8) A0140/08
A0294/10 A0543/26 B1156/22 C0184/04
C0396/17 C0406/05 C0437/V
protruding (7) A0241/03
B0927/34 C0087/24 C0394/28 C0420/36
C0551/40 C0569/14
protuberance (8) A0126/19
A0173/20 A0178/29 A0483/26 B1169/17
B1303/23 B1346/10 C0194/03
protuberances (1) C0422/32
proud (8) A0087/36
A0370/06 A0484/27 A0600/24 B0909/06
B1007/15 B1133/01 B1281/04
proudest (2) A0059/06 C0407/39
proudly (1) A0484/23
prove (38) A0021/13 A0263/36
A0267/33 A0270/07 A0280/16 A0441/33
A0551/26 A0561/28 A0642/11 A0642/16
A0667/47 B0727/20 B0744/28 B0925/05
B0956/05 B1029/05 B1119/M B1225/V
B1225/V B1236/14 B1358/13 B1369/09
C0056/22 C0080/05 C0087/31 C0158/15
C0178/02 C0180/07 C0207/06 C0401/19
C0403/08 C0408/32 C0424/03 C0430/08
C0534/21 C0534/32 C0555/41 C0558/40
proved (80)
proven (1) B0724/19
proverb (2) A0064/21 B1154/21
proverbial (2) B1018/07 B1138/20
proverbially (3) A0703/34
B1045/18 B1137/14
Proverbs (1) B0878/27
proverbs (1) B0880/10
proves (4) A0145/16
B0744/30 B1313/16 C0428/19
provide (2) C0105/19 C0391/29
provided (28) A0098/05
A0173/05 A0178/10 A0621/04 A0671/06
A0693/14 B0770/V B0965/32 B1135/21
B1142/13 B1156/21 B1339/04 B1379/28
B1379/29 C0069/35 C0070/33 C0098/08
C0104/06 C0126/34 C0155/04 C0395/39
C0403/06 C0403/07 C0526/20 C0530/21
C0534/11 C0534/13 C0554/08
Providence (5) A0090/15
B1049/11 B1055/33 B1361/12 C0062/08
providence (1) A0577/M
providential (1) C0428/40
providentially (3) B0753/17
C0139/14 C0397/07
providing (1) C0129/03
province (8) A0578/27
A0704/20 A0707/05 B0957/26 B1011/13
B1269/19 B1272/04 C0539/32
provinces (6) A0120/26 A0706/35
B1002/02 B1194/04 B1272/01 B1346/27
provincialists (1) B1008/17
proving (5) A0059/21
A0067/12 B0930/15 C0195/22 C0544/06
provision (17) B0931/25
B1073/25 B1310/23 C0093/01 C0096/36
C0121/10 C0126/27 C0137/17 C0140/11
C0144/01 C0144/39 C0146/40 C0176/33
C0177/05 C0191/19 C0202/01 C0546/35
provisional (1) B0728/23
provisioned (1) A0671/03
provisions (19) A0092/18
A0111/28 C0060/03 C0078/32 C0082/29
C0084/25 C0092/28 C0136/16 C0143/33
C0145/22 C0146/34 C0170/30 C0396/09
C0399/13 C0442/V C0534/26 C0539/12
C0540/03 C0547/10
proviso (1) B0888/08
provoke (1) C0555/38
provokingly (1) B1340/05
prow (4) B1281/12
C0165/35 C0165/38 C0168/24
prowess (1) C0555/27
prowling (2) B1373/02 C0570/33
proximate (1) B0949/35
proximity (8) A0437/21
A0458/03 A0693/12 B0832/11 B0896/09
B1282/05 C0207/18 C0564/35
prudence (3) A0073/13
B0870/30 B1005/08
prudent (4) B0810/35
B1073/29 C0104/01 C0554/20
prudential (1) B0916/05
prudently (1) C0199/22
pruderies (1) B0899/24
prudish (1) B1016/25
Prussian (1) A0350/19
pry (1) B1261/18
prying (2) B0929/14 C0075/20
Psalemoun (1) C0203/36
Psalm (1) A0188/M
psalm (1) A0047/24
psaltery (1) A0047/25
Psammitticus (2) A0059/11 A0062/01
pseudo-horror (1) A0473/26
pseudo/wife (1) B0934/02
pseudonym (2) B1133/10 B1137/09
pshaw (3) A0176/23
A0182/25 B1163/08
psychal (4) B0887/04
B0948/23 B0966/10 B1031/02
Psyche (7) A0336/04
A0337/06 A0341/V A0342/20 A0345/04
A0356/01 B0889/28
Psychological (1) A0195/V
Ptolemaiad (1) A0089/16
Ptolemais (2) A0189/19 A0191/09
Ptolemy (2) B1191/28 B1191/28
public (77)
public's (1) B0757/10
publican (1) B0876/14
publication (13) A0088/05
A0102/28 A0105/08 A0265/07 B0723/07
B0723/23 B1131/V B1135/19 B1141/35
B1208/30 C0056/15 C0403/35 C0428/36
publications (1) A0297/04
publicly (1) A0433/03
publique (1) B0986/34
publish (1) B1119/M
published (27) A0146/10
A0301/05 A0417/V A0473/03 B0723/13
B0729/02 B0751/01 B0763/23 B0772/30
B1068/10 B1133/01 B1143/30 B1270/36
B1357/03 B1359/26 B1364/05 B1380/03
B1380/18 B1385/08 B1386/08 C0055/30

->C0156/38 C0207/25 C0427/10 C0428/07
C0448/V C0524/39
publisher (2) B0862/23 B1209/09
publishers (6) B1207/09 B1207/11
B1207/19 B1207/22 B1207/22 B1208/02
publishing (5) B1130/28
B1131/18 B1369/22 B1379/15 C0056/07
puckered (3) A0245/27
A0368/11 B1102/33
pudding (1) C0100/35
pudding-stone (2) A0175/26 A0182/08
Puddington (1) B1166/31
puddle (1) A0488/22
pudicitiae (2) A0072/01 A0072/30
Pue's (2) A0630/V A0630/V
puerile (1) A0568/V
puff (17) A0248/22
A0368/22 A0368/23 A0585/34 B0976/03
B0982/21 B0982/21 B0982/21 B0982/21
B0982/22 B0982/22 B0982/22 B1101/22
B1101/25 B1165/10 B1239/28 C0101/35
puffed (10) A0252/14 A0254/05
A0373/21 B0742/09 B1108/35 B1156/35
B1375/21 C0189/40 C0388/09 C0388/10
puffing (1) B1380/02
puffs (1) B1207/12
puffy (4) A0070/22
A0247/11 A0368/30 C0389/22
puggish (1) B1157/20
pugnacious (1) A0089/19
pulcherrimus (1) A0072/30
Pulci (1) A0088/10
pull (14) A0047/07 A0047/08
A0056/33 A0066/23 A0174/01 A0176/24
A0179/11 A0337/02 A0372/04 A0487/19
B1054/04 C0121/38 C0201/06 C0553/28
pulled (22) A0047/11 A0173/V
A0178/26 A0344/02 A0351/21 A0353/22
A0465/19 A0537/31 A0624/04 B0795/27
B0932/29 B1182/29 B1363/15 C0068/32
C0118/36 C0173/11 C0200/41 C0409/21
C0415/32 C0535/27 C0557/35 C0566/31
pulling (6) A0340/15 A0343/10
A0413/33 B0892/03 B1183/17 C0185/18
pulls (3) A0173/08
A0178/13 B0871/13
pully-wou> (2) A0469/16 A0470/23
pully> (3) A0466/08
A0467/01 A0467/20
pulmonary (2) A0054/28 A0063/28
pulmonifera (2) C0178/10 C0178/21
pulpit (4) A0383/01
A0383/06 A0428/32 A0430/09
pulpits (1) B1313/02
pulpy (1) C0535/36
pulsation (6) A0328/09 A0328/14
A0615/06 B0796/03 B0956/20 B0962/12
pulse (5) B0815/30
B1235/14 B1237/10 B1238/09 B1239/06
pulseless (1) A0614/32
pulses (1) A0612/34
pumice-stone (1) C0572/12
pump (5) A0242/08
C0103/13 C0114/14 C0411/07 C0424/12
pump-handle (2) C0112/33 C0113/25
pump-handles (2) C0108/28 C0111/04
pumped (2) B0923/37 B1021/29
pumpkin (2) B1012/22 B1012/24
pumps (10) A0138/02 A0371/08
A0371/18 B0930/33 B0931/03 C0102/26
C0108/26 C0114/10 C0114/31 C0114/41
pun (2) B0836/07 B1116/10
punch (2) A0245/14 A0253/27
punch-bowl (1) B0828/08
puncheon (5) A0246/12
A0253/09 B1102/24 B1102/32 B1106/17
puncheon> (1) A0466/11
puncheons (1) B1260/05
punctilios (1) A0021/12
punctilious (2) A0654/09 B0904/06
punctual (1) C0416/36
punctuality (2) A0483/06 B1152/19
punctually (3) A0630/04
B0772/06 C0416/09
punctuate (1) B0840/08
punctuation (1) A0266/10
Pundit (16) B1293/22
B1293/26 B1293/28 B1294/01 B1294/24
B1296/34 B1297/01 B1299/07 B1299/18
B1299/24 B1300/36 B1302/25 B1303/02
B1303/37 B1304/22 B1314/05
Pundita (1) B1305/18
pungencies (1) A0536/20
pungency (1) B1381/12
pungent (4) B0738/11
B1137/16 B1139/24 B1242/12
pungently (2) A0689/22 B1130/13
punish (5) B0844/05
B1131/17 B1256/07 B1256/07 B1291/16
punished (1) B1129/31
punishing (1) B0915/18
punishment (2) A0567/12 B1131/19
punishments (3) A0690/26
B1004/15 B1006/22
punning (1) B0833/14
pupil (6) A0225/13 A0229/13
A0340/21 B0941/18 B1242/10 B1251/04
pupilless (1) A0215/09
pupils (4) A0313/21
B0940/17 B1115/25 B1239/22
puppets (1) A0318/17
puppy (5) A0357/02
A0367/24 A0368/29 B1370/29 C0073/30
pur (Gr.) (2) A0455/M A0612/37
puras (1) A0621/02
purchase (17) A0047/04
A0092/33 A0112/10 A0346/22 A0491/09
B0746/02 B0854/17 B0872/03 B0872/14
B0872/17 B1129/23 B1145/02 B1362/01
B1363/14 C0393/01 C0393/26 C0439/V
purchased (6) A0044/08 A0320/08
B1361/34 C0156/26 C0533/13 C0534/19
purchaser (2) A0067/08 B0872/30
purchases (5) A0093/03
A0112/15 B0875/01 B0880/07 B1360/15
purchasing (5) A0485/03
A0705/11 B1270/10 C0530/31 C0555/28
pure (34) A0078/31 A0108/01
A0110/24 A0156/12 A0217/V A0233/21
A0405/24 A0461/23 A0478/26 A0610/30

->A0610/33 A0621/05 A0710/03 A0711/05
A0711/21 B0987/19 B1071/02 B1091/18
B1095/08 B1122/02 B1137/15 B1219/05
B1220/06 B1248/19 B1275/06 B1276/07
B1276/22 B1361/23 B1363/31 B1364/07
C0096/37 C0394/02 C0543/28 C0572/23
purely (21) A0225/19
A0225/19 A0225/20 A0266/01 A0281/34
A0601/01 A0613/26 A0614/34 A0703/31
A0706/13 B0724/03 B0924/21 B1051/23
B1114/06 B1268/30 B1271/16 C0087/06
C0171/25 C0402/15 C0404/11 C0438/V
pures (1) B1122/01
purest (5) A0312/09
A0473/34 B0855/06 B1281/28 C0151/13
purgatory (1) A0621/07
purification (3) A0612/01
A0612/36 C0411/04
purifying (1) A0348/08
purity (9) A0086/18
A0096/17 A0154/27 A0323/10 A0343/27
A0458/24 B0742/17 B1073/19 B1122/11
purlieus (1) B1139/10
purlit> (1) A0469/V
purlite> (2) A0465/27 A0469/01
purliteness> (3) A0464/05
A0465/18 A0466/15
purloin (1) C0153/11
Purloined (1) B0974/T
purloined (4) B0976/12
B0976/13 B0982/01 B0986/11
purloiner (1) B1108/18
purple (24) A0087/01
A0100/12 A0106/24 A0190/09 A0235/20
A0241/15 A0329/V A0368/05 A0368/18
A0640/03 A0671/31 A0671/32 A0676/13
A0676/13 B1277/09 B1283/02 B1331/07
B1348/32 B1373/05 B1386/03 C0172/01
C0542/10 C0542/39 C0543/29
purplish (1) B1330/35
purport (1) A0383/19
purported (3) A0241/34
A0663/10 B1128/22
purports (1) B1358/21
purpose (143)
purposeless (1) B1036/34
purposely (7) A0303/31
A0554/01 B0762/15 B0915/19 B1188/24
B1188/27 C0069/10
purposes (37) A0098/21
A0250/10 A0340/25 A0410/05 A0432/08
A0439/33 A0489/28 A0495/V A0500/10
A0567/02 A0705/V B0756/09 B0771/31
B0831/13 B0954/02 B0977/26 B1073/10
B1074/36 B1079/18 B1102/26 B1219/19
B1235/25 B1272/18 B1350/31 B1364/24
C0080/36 C0105/32 C0134/22 C0387/08
C0394/35 C0395/01 C0402/22 C0409/15
C0410/40 C0413/23 C0442/V C0557/32
purraty-trap> (1) A0469/18
purraty> (1) A0465/25
purred (3) A0054/25
A0063/25 B0854/14
purse (8) A0500/20
A0651/25 A0652/03 B0871/08 B0876/21
->B0876/33 B1143/19 B1144/28
purse-strings (1) B0875/26
purses (2) A0293/25 A0293/V
purslain (1) C0138/12
pursuance (6) A0626/13 A0706/16
B0752/32 B1271/19 C0066/19 C0103/09
pursuant (1) A0347/14
pursue (8) A0560/15
B0771/25 B1281/10 C0080/11 C0081/40
C0523/01 C0529/24 C0575/29
pursued (18) A0242/16 A0444/34
A0514/20 A0671/26 B0738/07 B1048/20
B1158/18 B1183/23 B1183/25 B1189/26
B1226/04 B1333/19 C0063/15 C0152/10
C0201/27 C0202/03 C0439/V C0576/30
pursuer (2) A0565/17 A0676/23
pursuers (1) A0243/22
pursues (1) B0870/20
pursuing (9) A0548/03
B0840/13 B1313/19 B1328/03 C0093/23
C0166/18 C0203/20 C0527/10 C0547/37
pursuit (18) A0460/33 A0513/13
A0515/21 A0704/04 B0734/10 B0738/25
B0756/11 B1096/05 B1108/15 B1238/15
B1269/03 C0082/27 C0200/30 C0201/34
C0558/10 C0563/21 C0564/29 C0571/32
pursuits (4) A0268/28
A0482/32 A0495/V C0138/17
pursvaded (1) B1375/V
pursy (2) A0651/24 B1208/17
purticular> (1) A0467/05
purty> (2) A0464/23 A0465/07
purulent (1) B1235/27
Pusey (1) B1095/03
Puseyism (1) A0181/05
Puseyites (1) B1095/04
push (13) A0385/05
A0583/37 C0074/27 C0143/21 C0158/15
C0166/28 C0170/37 C0529/27 C0539/26
C0549/05 C0564/34 C0572/35 C0574/28
pushed (34) A0092/18 A0103/08
A0111/28 A0206/03 A0479/25 A0508/04
A0511/28 B1157/23 B1349/02 C0075/32
C0094/27 C0096/31 C0109/19 C0129/13
C0163/20 C0181/35 C0184/20 C0191/35
C0194/09 C0200/08 C0200/24 C0201/10
C0415/32 C0525/29 C0526/08 C0526/35
C0527/12 C0538/15 C0540/12 C0555/01
C0561/08 C0561/16 C0568/34 C0576/27
pushing (15) A0627/14
B0771/11 B0793/30 B1050/09 B1363/15
C0162/20 C0169/15 C0172/29 C0188/08
C0536/09 C0537/02 C0554/03 C0559/30
C0560/08 C0564/22
puss (3) A0479/18
C0409/03 C0413/31
put (200)
putares (1) A0603/35
Putnam (2) B1380/03 B1383/15
Putnam's (1) B1384/14
putrefaction (5) A0092/22
A0111/32 C0071/06 C0124/22 C0142/30
putrescent (1) B0742/34
putrid (4) A0244/V
B1057/07 C0141/21 C0142/15

putridity (1) B1243/06
puts (6) A0284/09 A0378/12
A0530/25 B0871/19 B0975/27 B1152/14
putting (43) A0034/09
A0124/25 A0373/03 A0373/07 A0444/07
A0486/04 A0510/08 A0511/27 A0513/28
A0547/29 A0639/12 A0642/31 B0767/16
B0830/01 B0866/13 B0912/V B0984/25
B1014/22 B1101/34 B1119/07 B1129/28
B1131/27 B1143/11 B1144/28 B1157/28
B1258/18 B1296/30 B1302/18 B1311/16
B1313/07 B1363/14 B1363/28 B1379/13
B1379/32 C0066/30 C0067/27 C0108/12
C0124/15 C0134/32 C0391/31 C0391/38
C0397/39 C0411/22
putty (2) B0819/33 B0826/26
puzzle (2) A0273/04 A0280/05
puzzled (15) A0388/26
A0547/21 A0553/08 A0628/15 A0628/16
B0809/24 B0810/22 B0822/35 B0926/29
B0975/25 B1056/11 B1103/05 B1297/29
B1298/02 B1317/01
puzzles (2) B0844/10 B0989/28
puzzling (1) A0527/M
px (1) B0988/07
pxh (2) B1374/11 B1374/11
pxll (2) B1374/15 B1374/20
pxxr (1) B1374/15
Pym (3) C0207/02 C0207/27 C0208/19
Pym, A. G. (1) C0056/32
Pym, A. Gordon (1) C0057/T
Pym, Arthur (1) C0058/09
Pym, Arthur Gordon (3) C0053/T
C0057/01 C0212/V
Pym's (1) C0207/15
Pyramid (1) A0045/12
pyramid (1) A0122/30
pyramids (2) A0108/17 B1160/13
Pyrrhonism (1) A0135/11
Pyrros (1) A0638/V
Pythagoreans (2) A0226/26 A0230/25
PRETTYBLUEBATCH (1) A0337/24
q (2) B0988/08 B0988/10
qu'il (2) A0033/19 A0033/20
qu'on (1) A0397/M
qu'un (2) A0019/02 A0135/M
quack (3) A0652/21
B1140/12 B1257/11
quackeries (1) B0959/22
quackery (1) B1359/31
quacking (1) B1134/24
quadrant (1) C0439/V
quadruped (1) A0099/25
quadrupeds (1) C0155/30
quadrupled (3) A0078/20
A0442/01 C0168/27
Quaere (1) A0365/V
quaffed (2) A0101/V A0249/19
quaint (6) A0143/18 A0211/32
A0301/10 A0399/17 A0429/21 A0664/29
quaintly (1) A0295/06
quaintness (1) A0314/24
qualification (1) C0418/16
qualifications (4) A0053/31
A0063/02 A0085/04 A0096/01
qualified (3) A0055/33
A0113/21 B0904/11
qualify (1) C0080/24
qualities (19) A0028/08
A0139/20 A0213/02 A0250/25 A0279/22
A0280/26 A0281/26 A0479/37 A0545/09
B0747/31 B0922/13 B0986/09 B1031/25
B1033/14 C0073/29 C0147/11 C0149/30
C0171/25 C0171/41
quality (18) A0100/09 A0245/16
A0265/25 A0278/37 A0405/04 A0432/04
A0485/01 A0530/04 A0556/09 B1033/11
B1034/06 B1039/31 B1056/09 B1073/18
C0101/05 C0179/13 C0179/14 C0542/39
Quand (1) A0096/M
quantities (4) A0539/10
C0205/22 C0395/39 C0442/V
quantity (62)
quantum (1) A0125/06
quantum (3) A0055/05
A0064/08 A0497/24
quarante (1) A0018/12
quarrel (7) A0019/24
A0351/24 A0433/02 B0753/17 B0754/21
B0987/11 B1316/04
quarrelled (2) A0484/25 A0489/21
quarrelling (1) C0104/03
quarrels (3) C0088/04
C0102/09 C0532/35
quarrelsome (1) C0558/06
quart (3) B1045/34
B1045/35 C0138/22
quarter (37) A0366/28
A0513/10 A0514/22 A0546/14 A0552/17
A0553/18 A0554/25 A0581/32 A0585/13
A0588/01 A0602/23 B0739/01 B0807/01
B0872/35 B0878/22 B0894/17 B0976/11
B0976/23 B1135/19 B1237/12 C0071/41
C0123/30 C0130/30 C0140/30 C0163/09
C0187/12 C0190/02 C0191/31 C0202/37
C0398/34 C0407/01 C0407/03 C0414/27
C0567/25 C0572/41 C0574/10 C0578/08
quarter-past (1) C0409/07
Quarterly (5) A0174/03
A0179/14 A0622/09 B1132/24 C0432/38
Quarterly/Review (1) A0628/10
quarters (13) A0369/25
B1059/01 C0095/19 C0101/41 C0103/13
C0110/41 C0163/30 C0164/21 C0167/06
C0200/15 C0404/23 C0560/22 C0578/39
Quartier (1) A0546/V
Quartier (1) B0726/24
Quartier/St./Roch (2) A0537/07
A0544/19
quarto (2) A0056/08 A0409/10
quartz (3) A0175/26
A0182/06 C0573/34
quasi (2) A0072/30 A0366/10
quasi (1) B0914/06
quatrain (1) A0681/M
quatre (1) A0018/12
quaver (1) A0411/03
quavering (1) B0819/35
Que (1) A0344/23
que (25) A0019/04

->A0033/20 A0034/01 A0034/02 A0036/05
A0037/02 A0037/10 A0037/24 A0096/M
A0096/M A0096/M A0216/08 A0216/10
A0344/15 A0344/21 A0352/12 A0431/08
A0602/07 A0611/04 A0621/01 A0621/03
B0986/34 B1114/02 B1122/01 C0430/41
Queen (2) A0250/11 A0337/05
queen (9) A0037/16
A0120/27 A0337/04 B1152/13 B1155/12
B1155/15 B1159/12 B1159/28 C0162/02
queen's (1) B1154/02
queenly (2) A0033/06 B0890/14
queer (8) A0126/20
A0337/22 A0625/02 A0655/12 B1016/23
B1016/24 B1295/01 C0387/26
queerest (3) B0810/09
B0812/04 B1299/31
quell (1) B1248/34
quelling (1) A0127/18
quelqu'un (1) A0602/07
quench (1) B1212/27
quenched (1) B1206/19
quere (1) A0113/31
queries (5) A0271/11
B0770/15 B1191/32 B1241/14 C0556/08
querulous (1) A0023/21
query (1) A0354/31
query (9) A0281/32
A0383/19 A0479/02 A0652/10 B0869/17
B0903/23 B1164/34 B1315/16 C0556/26
quest (2) B0807/24 B1163/34
question (180)
questionable (1) B1314/36
questioned (6) B1052/22 B1191/30
B1238/31 B1249/26 B1361/35 C0205/06
questioning (3) C0180/30
C0202/28 C0203/31
questionings (1) B0770/12
questions (18) A0384/16 A0445/11
A0478/35 A0527/M A0629/20 B0726/15
B0751/16 B0817/12 B1032/07 B1186/17
B1221/20 B1294/03 C0100/21 C0102/41
C0127/38 C0205/10 C0395/26 C0556/14
queue (2) A0103/30 C0389/20
queues (1) A0561/08
Qui (1) A0135/M
qui (9) A0033/19
A0036/16 A0125/04 A0498/02 A0568/24
A0568/25 A0600/01 B1122/01 C0430/36
quia (2) A0213/07 A0213/08
quick (28) A0055/27
A0065/07 A0081/16 A0099/04 A0139/29
A0166/14 A0540/06 A0541/07 A0541/V
A0543/05 A0550/15 A0579/19 A0587/37
A0604/14 A0687/12 B0795/09 B0795/V
B0797/09 B0812/27 B1057/25 B1242/24
B1242/24 B1242/25 B1242/25 C0074/31
C0108/25 C0164/37 C0199/18
quickened (1) B1226/02
quicker (3) A0081/06
B0795/16 B0795/16
quickly (40) A0020/12
A0021/11 A0103/16 A0105/16 A0344/26
A0413/32 A0508/04 A0535/23 A0562/11
A0562/V A0593/30 A0614/33 A0684/12

->A0696/27 B0764/14 B0793/20 B0797/11
B0822/15 B0859/02 B0866/11 B0911/01
B0963/02 B1032/26 B1052/11 B1106/31
C0078/19 C0085/15 C0089/24 C0096/05
C0100/41 C0106/41 C0125/15 C0126/37
C0135/18 C0136/26 C0179/27 C0186/40
C0421/25 C0544/36 C0546/01
quickness (1) B1167/14
quicksand (1) C0538/18
quicksands (1) C0536/02
Quicourre (1) C0548/01
quid (1) A0638/15
quidnuncs (1) B1068/12
quiescence (6) A0212/06 A0612/29
A0614/34 A0616/32 B0966/15 B1034/01
quiet (31) A0029/22
A0091/31 A0111/01 A0152/10 A0195/03
A0195/V A0196/02 A0311/19 A0347/27
A0433/23 A0473/22 A0533/08 A0537/19
A0565/10 A0565/19 B0862/15 B0878/11
B1008/36 B1047/16 B1056/35 B1090/30
B1090/31 B1090/32 C0074/19 C0081/33
C0093/38 C0096/19 C0119/11 C0168/39
C0175/21 C0545/34
quieted (2) A0674/16 B0891/06
quietly (24) A0025/17
A0080/34 A0123/14 A0317/10 A0317/V
A0437/15 A0532/27 A0563/15 A0563/16
A0627/14 A0684/16 B0844/06 B0866/19
B0894/09 B1047/04 B1075/19 B1107/03
B1108/31 B1183/13 B1191/33 B1349/14
B1369/22 C0058/05 C0390/23
quietude (2) B0893/23 B1280/19
quills (2) C0552/12 C0552/15
Quinault (1) A0135/M
quintessence (6) A0052/03 A0062/06
A0160/19 A0499/27 B1315/05 C0426/36
Quintillian (1) B1115/25
Quinty (3) A0091/19
A0091/19 A0110/23
Quirite (2) A0091/23 A0110/27
quit (4) A0642/06
B0899/11 B1014/02 C0188/17
quite (160)
quits (2) B1074/04 B1280/33
quitted (2) A0512/22 B0768/06
quitting (16) A0347/13
A0444/05 A0444/10 A0444/11 A0593/31
A0686/21 B0738/32 B0755/21 B0767/05
B0896/08 B1081/12 B1158/22 B1161/14
B1163/09 B1236/03 C0579/24
quiver (2) A0692/32 B1237/23
quivered (8) A0141/14
A0164/26 A0415/34 A0615/02 A0643/V
A0692/29 B0858/15 B1242/20
quivering (12) A0023/10
A0137/06 A0146/08 A0190/28 A0319/12
A0510/23 B0943/14 B0963/29 B0966/17
B1014/30 B1057/12 C0122/29
quivers (1) A0154/29
Quixotic (2) A0297/03 B1380/25
quiz (3) A0055/33
A0368/15 B0925/18
quizzed (3) A0279/20
A0284/32 A0487/17

Quizzem's (1) B1359/10
quizzes (1) A0303/29
quizzical (2) A0285/07 A0299/20
quo (2) B1051/21 B1364/06
quocunque (1) B1143/16
quoi (2) A0380/07 A0652/10
quondam (2) A0531/V A0534/17
quorum (1) A0382/15
quota (2) A0206/02 A0622/34
quotations (2) B0926/34 B1318/09
quote (7) A0342/11
A0709/19 B0734/09 B1115/37 B1154/27
B1370/12 B1381/03
quoted (12) A0176/05
A0176/08 A0180/27 A0180/29 A0356/12
A0536/16 B0759/17 B1151/04 B1274/21
B1275/19 B1293/28 B1360/08
quotes (2) B1051/16 B1382/34
quoting (4) A0652/11
B0986/33 B1293/37 B1304/30
r (1) B0838/09
R.S.A. (1) A0337/18
R-- (2) C0523/24 C0565/37
R--'s (2) C0523/25 C0538/26
Rabbins (1) B1095/02
rabbit (7) B1011/02
B1011/04 B1011/07 B1011/09 B1011/14
B1177/06 B1178/06
rabbit-berry (1) C0570/21
rabbits (3) B0850/25
B0851/14 C0156/23
rabble (10) A0123/03 A0125/30
A0125/34 A0126/01 A0262/04 A0490/08
A0498/18 B0946/30 B0947/16 B1224/03
Rabelais's (1) B1345/14
rabid (2) A0510/13 B0858/26
Raca (2) A0047/03 A0047/03
race (40) A0054/09
A0105/09 A0123/05 A0141/02 A0209/13
A0313/03 A0349/01 A0385/26 A0399/05
A0404/04 A0426/04 A0427/18 A0459/28
A0494/05 A0495/04 A0498/20 A0509/07
A0604/02 A0609/18 A0611/20 A0638/01
A0640/26 B0750/31 B0871/25 B1051/05
B1139/29 B1166/18 B1187/29 B1188/02
B1190/23 B1280/21 C0065/23 C0164/34
C0169/09 C0201/17 C0536/20 C0551/21
C0551/38 C0558/06 C0569/14
Race/street (1) A0388/V
races (3) A0495/07
B0943/26 C0172/37
rack (4) A0693/01
B0991/01 B0991/10 B0991/34
raconteur (1) A0600/07
racoon (1) C0536/23
racy (2) A0091/16 A0110/19
Radcliffe (1) A0662/06
rade> (1) A0465/30
radiance (7) A0311/24
A0417/08 A0503/11 A0590/23 B0964/26
B1138/02 C0402/04
radiant (10) A0228/09 A0299/20
A0312/24 A0316/17 A0406/28 A0603/06
A0608/29 A0644/07 A0664/07 B1385/30
radiantly (1) A0594/09
radiating (1) A0498/18
radiation (1) A0405/05
radical (8) A0104/22
A0580/19 A0641/V A0644/V B0851/07
B1219/04 B1221/04 C0555/30
radicalism (1) C0391/18
radically (7) A0460/18
A0499/12 A0704/17 B0991/13 B1190/07
B1269/16 B1318/12
radicalness (2) B0991/19 B1221/21
radii (3) B1071/12
B1071/13 C0400/03
radius (2) C0400/12 C0400/12
Rafaelle (2) A0035/26 A0035/26
Rafflesia (1) B1162/36
rafts (11) C0185/37
C0186/34 C0186/37 C0187/11 C0187/24
C0187/28 C0187/31 C0188/04 C0189/31
C0201/33 C0204/03
rag (3) A0143/22 A0686/02 A0686/15
ragamuffin (1) A0124/26
rage (28) A0023/26
A0139/03 A0159/14 A0262/19 A0373/20
A0447/07 A0499/29 A0675/22 A0676/17
B0856/25 B0896/29 B0911/20 B0913/23
B1101/27 B1165/10 B1348/32 B1353/32
B1372/23 B1373/05 C0067/31 C0075/33
C0079/01 C0149/15 C0188/01 C0190/20
C0201/14 C0201/20 C0562/30
raged (4) A0075/14
A0582/12 A0671/12 B1392/02
ragged (6) A0124/22 A0510/26
A0511/35 C0159/22 C0164/09 C0536/32
Ragged/Hills (1) B0943/26
Ragged/Mountains (3) B0939/T
B0942/15 B0950/01
raging (5) B1006/29
B1215/33 B1294/04 C0135/32 C0561/15
ragout (2) A0094/02 A0113/30
rags (3) A0373/17
A0510/10 C0109/04
rail (2) B1374/26 C0124/38
railroad (4) B0863/06
B1298/34 B1299/08 B1299/22
railroads (2) A0381/26 B1193/04
rails (2) B0765/29 B1299/13
Railway (1) B1166/30
railway (1) B1382/10
raiment (2) A0153/02 A0448/08
rain (32) A0087/33
A0196/04 A0196/04 A0196/06 A0197/24
A0355/04 A0413/30 A0512/09 A0512/14
A0513/08 A0513/35 B0729/16 B0735/07
B0759/02 B0769/V B1131/10 B1131/10
C0102/25 C0139/21 C0146/05 C0162/28
C0395/19 C0541/05 C0549/19 C0552/39
C0565/12 C0570/29 C0571/21 C0572/25
C0573/24 C0576/20 C0577/01
Rain/River (1) C0526/37
rainbow (6) A0209/02 A0209/04
A0227/28 A0232/14 A0591/08 A0594/07
rained (1) C0548/41
rains (4) A0044/23
C0573/12 C0573/17 C0578/27
rainwater (1) C0145/15

rainy (1) B1115/03
raise (13) A0047/24
A0252/01 A0538/22 A0552/01 A0552/04
A0552/21 A0578/30 B0818/23 B0827/01
B1361/31 C0060/29 C0130/10 C0549/03
raised (17) A0035/23
A0198/13 A0217/V A0553/26 A0586/16
A0693/24 B0924/14 B1076/11 B1106/31
B1193/15 B1194/15 B1259/25 C0059/24
C0061/01 C0068/28 C0410/07 C0553/30
raisin (1) B1106/03
raising (14) A0106/20 A0325/20
A0374/12 A0433/30 A0694/08 B1071/27
B1127/27 C0082/08 C0082/32 C0156/02
C0169/37 C0205/11 C0431/02 C0529/31
raisins (1) B1105/02
raisonnement (1) A0611/04
rake (3) A0180/25
A0226/12 A0230/10
rakish-looking (1) C0146/23
ralelly> (1) A0464/19
rallied (2) B0947/12 B1194/24
Ram (3) B1296/05 B1296/21 B1313/20
ram (3) A0047/16 A0388/17 B1312/07
Ram-ishly (1) B1317/30
ram's (1) B1296/21
ram's-horn (1) B1313/21
ramble (3) A0210/24
B0942/13 C0169/05
rambling (4) A0427/34
A0428/14 B1246/05 C0532/14
rammed (1) A0388/16
rampant (1) B1259/35
rampart (5) A0045/05
A0428/23 B1263/25 C0205/25 C0521/08
ramparts (8) A0043/04
A0044/22 A0045/30 A0145/14 A0294/V
A0407/04 A0478/22 A0579/03
rams (1) B1316/15
Ramus, Jonas (2) A0581/08 A0582/24
ran (48) A0058/29
A0080/40 A0214/26 A0301/19 A0355/04
A0406/22 A0484/28 A0513/31 A0534/30
A0584/31 A0610/02 A0654/27 A0663/25
B0789/14 B0813/12 B0814/22 B0899/27
B0928/05 B0944/04 B1076/10 B1108/17
B1132/12 B1158/12 B1158/13 B1160/08
B1178/16 B1225/21 B1372/14 C0067/28
C0081/24 C0104/25 C0115/30 C0115/35
C0134/28 C0169/15 C0173/26 C0183/35
C0184/31 C0200/08 C0200/19 C0200/20
C0411/37 C0417/41 C0537/38 C0539/15
C0542/25 C0548/39 C0571/01
rancid (2) A0092/01 A0111/13
Randolph, John (1) B1234/09
random (11) A0296/V
A0343/11 A0487/34 A0500/10 A0514/28
A0528/20 A0613/02 A0651/03 B1115/05
C0114/37 C0128/01
rang (6) A0059/19 A0067/10
A0546/26 A0672/32 A0675/28 B1186/07
range (28) A0245/10
A0613/10 A0639/10 B0752/15 B0911/16
B0983/31 B1015/24 B1160/28 B1184/01
B1261/01 B1359/08 C0087/40 C0113/41
->C0161/31 C0184/30 C0187/11 C0195/09
C0203/22 C0205/22 C0208/05 C0208/07
C0419/02 C0449/V C0527/02 C0530/03
C0572/19 C0575/14 C0575/16
ranged (4) A0070/19
A0081/40 C0205/26 C0415/20
ranges (1) C0159/25
ranging (1) C0185/04
rank (10) A0243/32 A0397/14
A0413/04 B1007/29 B1114/09 B1190/27
C0150/28 C0165/18 C0192/20 C0552/41
ranked (1) A0510/14
rankly-growing (1) A0514/29
ranks (1) A0128/16
ransack (1) B1362/28
ransacked (2) A0096/12 A0096/13
ransacking (1) B0978/18
rant (3) A0340/09
B1130/05 B1130/05
Rantipole (1) A0383/10
rap (3) A0346/13 B0812/30 B1103/32
rapacious (1) B1300/20
rapid (54)
rapidity (31) A0053/21
A0275/34 A0353/25 A0459/35 A0511/05
A0580/16 A0581/24 A0590/22 A0696/35
B0771/33 B1012/12 B1071/24 B1119/08
B1156/29 B1178/28 B1235/31 B1352/31
C0060/06 C0063/34 C0168/04 C0171/33
C0200/40 C0396/21 C0401/39 C0404/24
C0412/15 C0414/07 C0417/17 C0424/41
C0553/27 C0559/34
rapidly (69)
rapidly-growing (1) A0314/14
rapier (2) A0447/05 B1262/26
rapine (1) A0242/33
rapped (5) A0412/06
A0562/13 B0808/08 B0858/30 B1338/25
rapping (2) A0249/22 A0562/V
rapport (3) B0941/25
B0941/26 B1241/17
raps (2) A0489/27 B1104/11
rapt (2) A0712/07 B1277/12
rapture (3) A0644/V
C0146/15 C0524/04
rapturous (2) B0960/33 B1079/11
rara (1) B1345/09
rarae (1) A0500/V
rare (41) A0081/19
A0087/17 A0189/22 A0225/13 A0278/37
A0296/V A0310/05 A0345/17 A0379/21
A0409/10 A0429/17 A0444/04 A0444/06
A0444/16 A0444/16 A0460/01 A0532/01
A0584/10 A0691/12 A0705/V B0807/36
B0832/04 B0864/10 B0889/02 B0934/08
B1034/24 B1034/25 B1035/22 B1038/22
B1187/24 B1334/35 B1373/27 B1383/10
C0401/31 C0402/08 C0403/19 C0410/36
C0412/14 C0429/44 C0531/01 C0568/11
rarebit (1) B1178/V
rarefaction (4) C0400/33
C0401/17 C0403/09 C0403/12
rarefied (3) C0406/12
C0409/13 C0413/21
rarely (16) A0430/28

->A0497/21 A0554/12 A0665/27 B0723/M
B0746/35 B0807/22 B0831/12 B0837/04
B0841/25 B0864/17 B0941/22 B0961/11
B1006/25 B1179/16 B1350/32
rarer (1) B1038/14
rarest (4) A0458/31
A0664/30 A0665/02 B0762/15
rarified (1) B1035/04
rarity (3) B1033/25
B1034/29 C0424/09
rascal (8) A0058/15
A0069/04 A0092/06 A0111/18 A0240/M
A0371/29 A0388/29 A0650/15
rascality (2) A0262/15 B1300/09
rascally (4) A0262/09
A0374/07 A0486/18 B1300/11
rascals (4) C0556/11
C0556/18 C0556/37 C0557/03
rash (6) A0025/12 B0738/25
B0761/18 B0888/27 B0895/06 B0949/20
rashness (2) B0902/04 C0406/22
rason> (5) A0464/16
A0465/03 A0467/25 A0470/24 A0470/V
raspberry (1) A0470/22
rasps (1) C0148/10
rat (13) A0090/15
A0350/13 A0350/15 A0350/18 A0350/19
A0356/29 B1106/24 B1153/16 B1153/27
B1153/29 B1153/29 C0167/18 C0391/28
rat-traps (1) B0870/26
Rata (2) B1163/15 B1163/17
rate (32) A0138/11
A0337/24 A0370/30 A0466/06 A0491/11
A0585/14 A0657/05 B0909/17 B1077/20
B1078/03 B1080/06 B1159/19 B1164/39
B1166/05 B1167/16 B1292/18 B1298/29
C0058/36 C0060/09 C0164/15 C0164/20
C0167/04 C0400/16 C0400/20 C0402/28
C0402/39 C0405/21 C0406/11 C0407/22
C0412/12 C0534/21 C0540/16
rather (192)
ratio (11) A0073/18
A0500/09 A0548/07 A0652/05 B0746/11
B0746/14 B1035/17 B1116/11 B1169/19
C0401/14 C0424/33
ratiocination (4) B0738/12
B0745/14 B0773/04 B1031/33
rational (15) A0226/31
A0231/05 A0285/24 A0455/10 A0656/V
B0823/05 B0900/15 B1004/26 B1005/28
B1140/13 C0078/14 C0129/16 C0130/24
C0145/07 C0205/08
rationale (3) B0741/02
B0839/27 B1029/01
rationally (2) B1315/33 C0182/20
ratlin-stuff (1) A0142/10
Rats (1) B1244/T
rats (7) A0690/04
A0691/22 A0693/29 B1095/05 B1096/28
B1096/31 B1244/01
Rattle (2) B1052/03 B1054/20
rattle-snake (1) C0539/30
Rattleborough (11) B1044/01
B1044/03 B1044/13 B1045/10 B1045/22
B1047/07 B1048/09 B1052/19 B1054/27
->B1055/27 B1058/19
Rattleburghers (3) B1044/05
B1051/05 B1058/24
rattled (5) A0046/06
A0088/04 A0143/14 A0347/30 A0400/30
rattlesnakes (1) C0576/19
rattling (7) A0219/05
A0248/21 A0414/09 B0943/35 B0956/29
C0083/15 C0552/12
ravages (1) A0610/24
rave (1) C0438/V
raved (1) B0797/17
Raven (2) B1380/15 B1380/22
raven (2) A0297/V A0330/V
raven-black (2) A0312/11 A0594/21
raven-winged (1) A0210/28
raven's (1) A0215/V
ravenous (4) A0690/06
A0693/30 A0694/10 C0071/03
ravine (22) B0943/03 B0948/13
B1279/19 B1280/28 B1332/21 B1333/13
B1335/04 C0172/30 C0180/39 C0181/15
C0184/06 C0184/21 C0188/24 C0188/35
C0189/12 C0191/14 C0191/34 C0192/29
C0198/31 C0553/15 C0553/25 C0560/03
ravines (7) B0817/28
B0863/08 C0552/37 C0576/06 C0577/04
C0577/07 C0580/06
raving (4) A0135/20
A0558/14 A0589/33 C0124/27
ravings (1) B1131/16
ravishing (1) B0903/28
raw (4) B1096/20
C0085/40 C0115/01 C0565/17
ray (12) A0248/27
A0312/22 A0611/16 A0685/06 B0793/09
B0794/29 B0795/05 B0795/15 B1167/32
B1168/18 C0068/36 C0423/24
raylessness (1) B0967/03
rays (34) A0138/25 A0141/31
A0157/27 A0321/16 A0406/03 A0437/15
A0499/07 A0510/35 A0545/27 A0590/24
A0591/05 A0613/12 A0663/16 A0663/18
A0672/13 A0674/04 B0821/32 B0826/14
B0940/21 B1076/08 B1168/14 B1168/19
B1168/20 B1168/35 B1248/20 B1262/22
B1282/25 B1322/18 C0083/36 C0414/09
C0423/15 C0423/19 C0423/36 C0430/11
razor (8) A0537/28
A0544/08 A0557/24 A0565/04 A0565/15
A0566/26 A0690/18 A0690/19
razor-like (1) A0693/09
razors (2) C0128/07 C0148/10
re-appearance (1) B0726/11
re-appeared (4) A0512/33
B0744/03 B0753/08 C0544/31
re-appears (1) B0908/V
re-captured (1) A0560/14
re-capturing (1) A0566/V
re-commence (1) C0549/28
re-compose (1) B1242/27
re-cross (1) C0561/38
re-crossed (2) A0512/24 B0735/32
re-directed (1) B0992/06
re-echo (1) A0244/14

re-echoed (2) B1262/29 C0190/06
re-employing (1) A0549/V
re-enclose (1) A0276/25
re-enclosed (1) B1143/29
re-enforcement (1) C0186/28
re-entered (2) A0604/23 B1155/16
re-entering (1) B0873/07
re-erected (1) B1263/25
re-established (1) A0105/15
re-examination (2) B0731/07
B0982/04
re-examined (1) B0751/19
re-fastened (1) A0552/15
re-heated (1) B0835/03
re-instituted (1) B0841/03
re-interred (1) B0733/16
re-laid (1) B0857/16
re-melt (1) B1168/32
re-model (1) B1115/34
re-modelled (1) B1225/10
re-passage (1) B0808/06
re-procured (1) A0443/20
re-read (1) B1101/14
re-scription (1) B1189/25
re-sealed (1) B0992/06
re-search (1) B0981/22
re-searched (1) A0544/20
re-seated (1) A0090/05
re-sinking (1) B0966/16
re-solution (1) A0528/12
re-squeaked (1) A0387/15
re-stated (2) A0403/26 B0751/06
re-touching (2) A0102/27 C0523/15
re-writing (1) B1189/21
reach (62)
reached (92)
reaches (8) A0674/10
B0749/15 B0764/32 B0864/23 B0957/29
B1038/12 B1163/18 B1179/17
reaching (59)
read (67)
reader (34) A0064/07 A0075/07
A0078/42 A0090/07 A0120/13 A0211/24
A0348/11 A0348/16 A0366/15 A0484/28
A0487/33 A0531/12 B0731/23 B0773/20
B0855/09 B0855/26 B0895/14 B0955/15
B1114/12 B1115/32 B1152/10 B1209/04
B1240/02 B1241/01 B1277/14 B1333/01
C0062/04 C0095/25 C0161/23 C0203/34
C0207/34 C0208/03 C0431/10 C0524/24
reader's (3) B1091/25
B1091/26 B1310/03
readers (33) A0265/37
A0294/V A0297/20 A0365/05 A0621/10
B0724/11 B0772/02 B0956/09 B1030/16
B1073/01 B1074/02 B1082/05 B1119/01
B1131/20 B1133/04 B1137/04 B1139/07
B1248/01 B1318/05 B1339/04 B1384/26
C0056/29 C0097/03 C0137/28 C0152/04
C0158/24 C0178/03 C0521/02 C0521/21
C0521/28 C0522/07 C0528/07 C0535/32
readily (60)
readiness (4) B0875/10
C0171/08 C0177/23 C0179/33
reading (35) A0055/24
->A0096/14 A0143/03 A0261/14 A0265/08
A0300/31 A0303/04 A0328/13 A0338/05
A0339/16 A0342/08 A0343/09 A0344/19
A0532/05 A0533/03 A0548/15 A0559/26
A0629/23 B0754/10 B0838/08 B1101/03
B1101/12 B1106/11 B1137/21 B1153/06
B1224/10 B1224/13 B1247/02 B1374/06
B1378/02 C0078/21 C0080/13 C0129/22
C0392/15 C0417/10
readings (1) A0316/15
readjust (1) C0094/08
readjusted (2) C0090/22 C0099/35
readjusting (1) B1182/14
reads (2) A0108/21 B0838/15
readverting (1) B0748/04
ready (43) A0054/20
A0063/23 A0067/29 A0075/08 A0156/08
A0217/01 A0387/V A0388/09 A0562/06
B0812/08 B0900/02 B0923/35 B1049/24
B1075/22 B1126/10 B1129/24 B1141/14
B1185/18 B1208/31 B1292/05 B1314/22
B1345/20 B1359/35 C0058/25 C0065/37
C0111/05 C0121/15 C0145/26 C0165/02
C0177/41 C0186/14 C0187/27 C0393/01
C0393/16 C0395/03 C0395/39 C0407/30
C0530/26 C0530/33 C0531/03 C0533/32
C0534/41 C0549/33
real (64)
realities (6) A0055/03 A0064/06
A0210/16 A0599/M B0988/01 C0197/39
reality (18) A0217/V A0551/27
A0552/12 A0614/33 A0707/26 B0818/34
B0955/09 B1220/V B1272/26 B1352/10
C0109/12 C0111/31 C0111/40 C0135/31
C0148/37 C0199/29 C0392/34 C0543/12
realization (2) B0862/06 B1269/02
realize (4) A0683/V
A0691/V B1360/15 C0148/41
realized (2) B0726/02 B1363/35
realizes (1) B1122/07
really (111)
realm (4) A0195/14
A0407/14 B1295/21 B1390/14
realms (2) B0961/33 B0967/36
reanimation (1) C0073/13
reap (3) B1358/31
B1360/13 C0411/23
reaped (2) B1170/04 C0190/10
reappeared (1) B1134/34
reapplication (1) B0832/25
reapproached (1) B1262/28
rear (12) A0144/01
A0379/31 A0429/15 A0538/20 A0539/29
A0546/22 A0554/18 A0565/20 B0901/15
B1336/07 C0541/35 C0577/28
reared (5) A0406/28
A0579/05 B0902/13 B1219/V C0573/19
reascend (1) C0390/10
reascending (1) B1250/33
Reason (3) A0477/T
B0774/01 B0855/29
reason (175)
reasonable (23) A0026/31
A0160/V A0250/01 A0285/24 A0294/V
A0350/15 A0374/06 B0763/06 B0873/15

->B1014/27 B1110/05 B1142/02 B1206/14
B1315/10 C0058/21 C0078/11 C0204/28
C0207/33 C0388/07 C0392/31 C0402/27
C0402/36 C0523/31
reasonableness (1) B1322/07
reasoned (9) A0078/40
A0086/10 A0097/10 A0097/10 A0317/04
B0756/V B0831/29 B0984/21 B0986/27
reasoner (6) B0738/25 B0744/10
B0745/04 B0746/02 B0984/05 B1031/17
reasoner's (4) B0744/27
B0748/16 B0984/29 B0985/04
reasoners (3) A0551/25
B1296/32 B1313/35
reasoning (12) A0080/18
A0551/06 B0984/27 B0987/17 B1032/03
B1048/18 B1166/22 B1370/15 B1384/09
C0078/12 C0401/03 C0429/47
reasonings (1) C0392/22
reasons (32) A0018/V
A0069/27 A0093/11 A0112/22 A0150/V
A0204/22 A0225/21 A0299/03 A0380/05
A0427/22 A0527/V A0645/08 A0708/20
B0733/04 B0745/04 B0753/19 B0761/29
B0772/01 B1046/33 B1058/35 B1109/35
B1132/28 B1273/15 B1278/01 B1358/23
C0055/07 C0080/27 C0107/26 C0203/38
C0207/11 C0432/22 C0443/V
reassure (3) A0325/01
B0965/20 B1135/27
reassured (1) B1262/27
rebel (1) B1019/10
rebellion (3) A0431/30
B1021/18 C0175/38
rebellious (1) A0021/27
rebels (2) A0252/09 B1019/25
rebound (1) C0144/12
rebuilt (1) B1110/12
rebuke (1) C0067/26
rebukes (1) B1133/27
Rebus (1) A0366/16
rebut (1) B0740/20
rebuts (1) B0748/28
rebutted (1) B0728/21
recall (8) A0151/V
A0311/09 A0313/28 A0435/28 A0682/30
A0684/04 A0709/22 B1274/25
recalled (7) A0252/05
A0542/04 A0543/08 A0682/34 C0126/21
C0134/35 C0540/07
recalling (4) A0075/06
A0156/23 A0710/10 B1275/13
recalls (1) B0959/26
recapture (1) C0053/T
recapturing (1) A0566/02
recede (2) C0172/26 C0542/34
receding (1) C0178/30
receipt (9) A0059/16
A0067/06 A0074/15 B0872/03 B0878/18
B1055/13 B1055/25 B1056/11 C0092/10
receipted (1) B0879/23
receive (16) A0154/18
A0234/09 A0280/13 A0303/14 A0490/21
A0611/31 B0723/05 B0887/13 B0924/03
B1178/18 B1361/27 C0056/20 C0066/31
->C0124/26 C0177/39 C0206/05
received (96)
receives (3) A0397/10
C0106/26 C0573/09
receiving (9) A0044/04
A0088/06 A0354/06 A0556/20 B0733/12
B1055/31 B1160/43 B1351/16 C0177/21
recency (1) B0901/29
recent (4) A0297/03
B0980/10 B1235/30 C0528/24
recently (3) B0853/09
B0981/07 B1193/17
receptacle (1) A0071/14
receptacles (1) B0965/30
reception (4) B0738/18
B0956/26 B0965/31 C0555/23
recess (10) A0321/23 A0501/11
A0501/13 B0759/31 B0989/02 B1261/11
B1261/18 B1261/30 B1262/12 B1262/26
recesses (27) A0102/22
A0151/26 A0157/V A0197/13 A0197/15
A0235/22 A0243/28 A0323/16 A0401/13
A0405/01 A0429/12 A0436/30 A0501/08
A0529/25 A0590/26 A0639/11 A0641/15
A0642/06 A0696/12 B0807/15 B0943/05
B0947/15 B0964/27 B1260/06 B1331/32
C0080/26 C0186/23
recherche (6) A0300/25 A0343/23
A0345/18 A0529/07 B0986/04 B1115/07
Recherches (1) A0175/03
recherches (2) A0180/26 B0985/35
recipients (2) B1135/13 B1135/14
reciprocal (2) C0537/18 C0537/28
reciprocating (1) B1122/30
recital (1) B1058/05
recitations (1) A0431/03
recitative (1) B0905/12
recited (1) B1127/11
reciting (1) A0108/27
reckless (3) A0020/V
A0026/21 A0675/03
recklessly (1) A0438/12
reckoning (2) A0236/05 C0414/17
reclaimed (1) B0834/08
reclaiming (1) B0977/28
recline (1) C0173/07
reclined (3) A0033/09
A0101/10 B0817/28
reclining (2) A0248/12 A0664/20
reclosed (2) A0540/20 A0552/29
recluse (1) B0807/19
recognisable (4) A0399/04
A0509/14 B1160/40 C0108/38
recognise (8) A0078/42
A0283/26 A0428/17 A0445/34 A0473/25
A0550/10 B0958/09 B0958/10
recognised (16) A0089/15
A0155/20 A0314/V A0317/V A0412/05
A0498/26 A0588/05 A0613/24 B0898/13
B0958/01 B0959/08 B1049/19 B1052/15
B1081/22 B1272/13 C0067/14
recognises (2) A0530/16 B0977/10
recognising (4) A0162/12
B0961/05 B1263/03 C0119/36
recognition (5) B0730/23

->B0731/01 B0748/12 B0749/17 B0898/15
recognized (15) A0070/08
A0073/06 A0079/24 A0297/V A0314/13
A0317/25 A0707/02 A0707/14 B0724/10
B0730/02 B0734/16 B0735/36 B0747/16
B0749/12 B0755/08
recognizes (2) A0611/36 B0748/10
recognizing (1) B0732/22
recoil (3) A0028/01
B0961/31 C0169/09
recoiling (1) B1260/30
recollect (8) A0055/28
A0065/09 B0828/11 B0828/28 B0966/24
B1128/33 B1194/14 B1369/31
recollected (5) A0534/06
A0592/13 B0829/29 B1192/19 C0095/40
recollection (30) A0091/25 A0142/25
A0143/04 A0151/15 A0235/20 A0263/04
A0294/V A0311/02 A0348/16 A0354/07
A0638/21 A0644/04 A0685/11 B0906/27
B0906/29 B1139/08 C0064/11 C0067/30
C0070/38 C0077/06 C0081/02 C0089/10
C0109/12 C0118/21 C0131/23 C0134/04
C0199/30 C0392/16 C0397/39 C0406/29
recollections (11) A0020/V
A0209/21 A0210/30 A0218/01 A0323/10
A0348/01 A0348/13 A0427/33 A0428/11
B0759/08 B0765/04
recommandable (1) C0430/41
recommenced (2) A0249/35 B0823/25
recommencing (1) C0189/40
recommend (5) A0340/11
A0388/03 A0389/10 A0621/15 B1011/05
recommendation (3) B0876/21
B0926/13 B1045/19
recommendations (1) B0879/02
recommended (3) B0957/16
C0060/33 C0527/20
recommending (4) A0055/14
A0064/28 A0266/02 A0485/01
reconcile (5) A0086/09
A0145/22 A0158/10 B1091/08 C0522/11
reconciled (1) A0022/17
reconciles (1) B1035/20
reconciling (2) A0097/08 A0547/21
reconnoissance (1) C0188/14
reconnoitre (4) B1335/09
C0096/16 C0188/18 C0576/25
reconnoitred (1) B0752/27
reconsider (1) B0902/07
record (22) A0088/07 A0209/V
A0217/11 A0339/25 A0340/15 A0426/10
A0616/16 A0642/17 A0643/02 B0723/21
B0831/19 B0834/25 B0942/02 B0955/13
B0964/01 B1058/06 B1079/34 B1144/34
B1154/18 B1184/20 C0522/11 C0525/32
recorded (11) A0086/13
A0459/25 B0857/03 B0959/21 B1069/03
B1190/04 B1297/03 B1314/07 C0402/38
C0521/22 C0539/28
Recorder (1) B1303/14
recording (1) B1079/33
records (10) A0144/19 A0203/13
A0293/01 A0443/29 A0582/24 A0611/11
B0958/17 B1090/19 B1302/33 C0521/26
recorked (1) C0127/24
recount (2) B1104/28 C0083/38
recounted (2) A0081/38 B1057/30
recounting (1) C0532/19
recourse (3) A0705/17
B1132/16 B1270/15
recover (12) A0249/33
A0299/18 A0439/24 A0442/34 A0564/28
B1107/29 C0116/06 C0119/26 C0127/15
C0187/25 C0199/14 C0523/10
recovered (42) A0024/25 A0057/19
A0092/28 A0112/03 A0155/25 A0324/05
A0325/15 A0564/11 A0590/30 B0829/25
B0834/11 B0851/36 B0928/10 B0930/22
B0958/03 B0967/01 B1007/10 B1108/24
B1194/33 B1262/01 B1295/20 B1311/13
B1349/13 B1352/36 C0060/14 C0064/22
C0088/11 C0100/14 C0101/01 C0101/33
C0118/20 C0119/18 C0127/27 C0135/25
C0148/33 C0165/10 C0182/19 C0397/14
C0399/09 C0409/03 C0565/26 C0568/08
recovering (7) A0684/33
B0834/13 B0843/26 B0983/08 B1140/26
B1249/03 C0397/18
recovery (11) A0137/15
A0152/01 A0153/21 A0211/14 A0323/22
A0691/17 B0877/06 B0959/22 B0966/17
C0198/28 C0563/28
recreant (2) A0642/11 A0644/15
recrossed (2) A0325/14 B0767/21
recrossing (1) A0430/11
recruit (3) C0170/36
C0531/35 C0532/04
recruited (1) C0139/07
recruiting (1) C0540/11
recruits (6) A0058/08 A0058/12
A0068/29 A0068/34 C0530/14 C0532/07
rectangular (4) A0380/12
A0405/31 A0612/02 B0747/12
rectangularly (1) B0762/18
rectification (1) B1189/26
rectify (2) A0276/26 C0172/15
recue (1) B0986/34
recur (1) B1008/12
recurrence (1) A0324/06
recusant (1) A0690/25
Red (2) A0366/17 C0551/13
red (76)
red-bud (1) B1332/09
red-hot (3) B1167/09
B1168/04 B1168/32
red-litten (1) A0407/35
Red/Death (6) A0670/01 A0670/T
A0671/10 A0675/15 A0676/33 A0677/03
Red/River (2) A0270/02 C0551/01
reddened (2) A0675/22 A0675/V
reddish (1) B1180/25
redeem (1) B1152/25
redeemed (2) A0086/22 A0612/06
redivert (1) B0758/25
redness (2) A0670/03 B1180/31
redolent (3) A0217/V
B0773/33 B1246/12
redouble (1) B0764/29
redoubled (10) A0025/03 A0089/28

->A0092/26 A0112/01 A0328/10 A0440/12
A0508/10 C0115/19 C0169/31 C0200/39
redoubtable (1) A0254/04
redoubted (1) A0078/43
redresser (1) B1256/08
reduce (4) B0745/05
B0850/03 B1076/26 C0136/03
reduced (22) A0529/04 A0531/19
A0551/21 B0745/14 B0806/03 B0940/32
B0943/22 B0993/15 B1104/12 B1161/39
B1184/30 B1298/20 B1316/32 C0071/20
C0082/29 C0130/09 C0130/15 C0132/07
C0535/35 C0539/39 C0540/30 C0565/36
reducible (1) B1033/31
reductio (1) B1006/05
reduction (1) B0738/23
reduit (1) A0611/04
reduplication (1) A0408/17
reeds (2) A0087/18 B0807/03
reef (4) C0060/09
C0167/32 C0170/39 C0176/18
reefed (1) C0163/02
reefs (2) C0176/22 C0179/23
reeked (1) A0399/35
reeking (1) A0157/25
reel (1) A0327/V
reeled (10) A0035/08 A0217/V
A0244/11 A0317/10 A0417/14 A0437/25
B0947/22 B1352/24 C0083/12 C0440/V
reeling (8) A0137/23
A0243/30 A0416/30 A0510/15 A0514/33
A0667/52 A0667/54 C0397/01
reels (1) A0217/V
refastened (1) C0409/31
refer (11) A0267/20
A0302/17 A0339/22 A0366/15 B0766/01
B0837/27 B0842/16 B0915/22 B0956/06
B1152/09 C0541/16
referable (3) A0478/17
B1017/02 B1299/11
reference (50) A0065/15 A0135/15
A0203/13 A0268/16 A0278/05 A0283/13
A0303/06 A0369/32 A0457/18 A0536/19
A0582/16 A0612/36 A0667/68 A0683/13
A0711/07 B0724/01 B0740/01 B0740/15
B0745/19 B0746/05 B0747/32 B0840/34
B0841/24 B0876/34 B0894/20 B0988/18
B1009/25 B1048/08 B1131/13 B1134/V
B1135/33 B1137/17 B1153/31 B1178/05
B1186/22 B1190/26 B1215/09 B1276/08
B1312/30 B1325/10 B1357/04 B1358/06
B1359/16 B1371/05 C0064/34 C0152/13
C0208/25 C0424/35 C0524/16 C0524/39
referens (1) A0382/17
referred (12) A0313/15
B0773/13 B0862/20 B1140/30 B1192/11
B1215/08 B1295/14 B1301/01 B1311/07
B1360/09 B1381/23 B1383/06
referrible (2) B0871/24 B1017/V
referring (13) A0090/33
A0109/24 A0135/14 A0302/23 A0641/V
A0654/04 B0839/03 B0922/17 B1036/29
B1215/03 B1322/05 B1325/07 B1364/12
refers (1) B0753/14
refined (9) A0273/22
->A0545/28 A0709/15 B0895/V B0926/30
B1004/03 B1030/06 B1096/17 B1169/06
refinedly (3) A0300/27
A0301/13 A0302/09
refinements (1) B1345/10
refitted (1) C0566/03
reflect (13) A0080/41
A0346/32 A0588/30 A0686/09 B0755/24
B0763/28 B0961/10 B0963/31 B1333/28
B1384/23 C0079/24 C0134/20 C0189/15
reflected (24) A0035/02
A0070/V A0073/14 A0398/05 A0536/27
A0558/05 A0602/03 B0840/11 B0940/21
B0988/23 B0989/01 B0990/11 B1214/32
B1224/25 B1248/19 B1331/08 B1333/35
C0169/37 C0400/14 C0414/33 C0423/22
C0430/13 C0536/38 C0555/24
reflecting (4) B1101/33
B1282/25 C0391/30 C0430/22
reflection (49) A0057/22
A0068/05 A0138/24 A0204/23 A0300/08
A0300/17 A0302/07 A0315/01 A0385/03
A0443/18 A0500/04 A0502/18 A0534/04
A0560/16 A0566/06 A0589/16 A0592/04
A0629/33 A0692/05 A0711/22 B0766/32
B0773/30 B0830/02 B0831/14 B0841/16
B0853/19 B0896/13 B0910/01 B0916/25
B0975/08 B1077/29 B1170/03 B1223/17
B1276/23 B1277/23 B1300/08 B1364/14
C0075/40 C0081/03 C0082/30 C0085/09
C0107/17 C0153/27 C0153/28 C0396/36
C0403/34 C0406/27 C0408/04 C0421/28
reflections (15) A0054/12
A0063/19 A0107/12 A0158/02 A0213/26
A0534/16 A0624/20 A0630/24 B0832/01
B0896/05 B1093/37 C0128/22 C0197/31
C0537/16 C0578/15
reflective (4) A0478/05
A0479/36 A0528/21 A0531/V
reflector (1) A0500/06
reflux (2) A0582/09 A0582/34
refolded (1) B0992/03
Reformation (1) B0723/M
Reformation (1) B0723/M
Reforme (1) A0033/18
refract (1) C0423/20
refracted (2) A0212/25 C0423/36
refracting (1) C0423/24
refraction (1) C0423/18
refrain (11) A0427/11
A0710/28 B0817/05 B0909/02 B1013/07
B1275/31 B1358/15 C0067/24 C0122/13
C0131/20 C0166/27
refrained (2) B0795/13 B0795/22
refresh (1) C0432/29
refreshed (2) C0137/16 C0146/02
refreshing (1) A0428/04
refreshment (2) C0155/35 C0156/22
refreshments (1) B1004/33
refrigerator (1) C0068/20
refuge (3) B0946/33
B1301/19 C0579/25
refusal (6) A0251/27 A0441/31
B0822/22 C0107/27 C0179/37 C0554/21
refusals (1) B0960/02

refuse (8) A0217/V
A0431/24 A0696/13 B0931/36 B1006/09
B1094/03 B1192/34 C0547/04
refused (11) A0593/20
A0623/13 A0631/22 A0643/32 A0652/03
B0888/18 B0896/30 B0926/10 B1012/23
B1054/13 C0171/28
refuser (1) A0037/03
refuses (2) A0433/25 A0515/28
refusing (10) A0058/27 A0271/33
A0539/17 B0907/29 B0915/27 B1361/35
C0133/32 C0134/27 C0201/11 C0558/41
refutation (2) A0299/12 C0401/22
refuted (2) A0703/08 B1268/08
refutes (1) B1325/10
regain (9) A0691/28
B0834/17 B1077/16 C0097/23 C0100/27
C0114/34 C0117/24 C0182/09 C0199/33
regained (8) A0611/06
B0932/04 B0966/22 B1014/34 B1104/27
C0100/40 C0101/03 C0119/15
regaining (3) B0968/26
C0098/11 C0408/30
regal (4) A0159/11
A0250/19 A0320/19 B1127/15
regard (132)
regarded (70)
regarding (9) A0218/10
A0709/10 B0894/14 B0924/22 B0946/16
B0985/28 B1247/17 C0421/34 C0429/12
regardless (2) B0851/08 C0095/33
regards (33) A0097/30
A0250/17 A0268/27 A0271/03 A0496/17
A0498/06 A0545/16 A0650/22 B0724/08
B0759/24 B0769/11 B0770/08 B0835/33
B0870/15 B0992/16 B1035/17 B1036/02
B1070/18 B1167/36 B1221/11 B1257/05
B1300/34 B1315/04 B1331/37 B1371/10
C0055/35 C0145/23 C0171/39 C0433/08
C0530/22 C0532/32 C0538/41 C0575/21
regather (1) A0683/09
regathering (1) A0430/30
regenerate (1) C0414/39
regenerated (2) A0612/06 C0414/24
regenerating (2) C0412/24 C0413/08
regeneration (1) A0611/20
regia (1) B0832/20
regiment (3) A0058/08
A0372/08 B1092/16
region (56)
regions (43) A0045/24
A0145/22 A0210/08 A0242/21 A0298/V
A0312/10 A0402/03 A0426/05 A0514/21
A0601/18 A0611/16 A0639/17 A0641/06
A0643/22 B0897/02 B0924/21 B0964/15
B1316/11 C0055/05 C0093/26 C0158/25
C0159/30 C0160/27 C0198/35 C0202/08
C0207/18 C0207/19 C0393/27 C0401/31
C0402/12 C0403/27 C0412/29 C0417/29
C0418/09 C0418/17 C0422/28 C0426/10
C0426/11 C0528/28 C0528/31 C0538/32
C0561/37 C0572/21
registered (1) B0985/26
Registre (1) A0106/05
Regni (1) A0213/04

regret (16) A0265/06
A0268/27 A0281/11 A0323/08 A0351/17
B0853/34 B0877/15 B1110/03 B1158/23
B1222/04 C0094/36 C0120/16 C0143/11
C0146/06 C0413/27 C0561/02
regretful (1) B0949/09
regretted (4) B1144/05
B1192/14 B1234/23 C0207/17
regular (32) A0045/01
A0156/16 A0280/05 A0311/27 A0337/12
A0337/25 A0381/28 A0483/03 A0493/04
A0579/19 A0583/26 A0653/05 B0749/20
B1049/02 B1119/M B1154/11 C0056/15
C0097/03 C0167/39 C0173/08 C0177/14
C0401/29 C0412/25 C0415/09 C0416/12
C0445/V C0539/15 C0539/27 C0551/29
C0553/19 C0573/06 C0573/32
regularity (10) A0267/02 A0283/23
A0312/02 A0482/19 A0484/18 B1331/17
C0193/13 C0193/18 C0413/19 C0573/37
regularly (5) A0369/32
B1390/02 C0544/04 C0546/35 C0568/37
regularly-formed (1) C0194/15
regulate (3) A0225/06
A0229/06 A0497/10
regulated (6) A0283/07 A0582/09
B0737/05 B1092/22 B1119/21 B1245/03
regulating (1) C0400/39
regulations (2) A0205/33 B1003/10
Regulus (1) A0080/16
regulus (1) B0832/22
reheaded (1) B1143/26
reign (8) A0055/31
A0065/12 A0096/02 A0120/08 A0240/02
A0250/29 B1019/16 B1246/01
reigned (6) A0317/16 A0328/03
A0415/32 A0617/01 B0967/24 B1055/08
reigneth (1) A0645/06
reigning (5) A0086/31
A0100/08 A0215/08 B1018/36 C0569/35
reigns (2) A0144/15 B1079/04
Reihe (1) B0723/M
rein (1) B0929/32
Reine (1) A0102/11
reined (1) A0398/09
reinem (1) A0342/V
reinen (2) A0342/01 A0342/V
reins (1) A0299/V
reinstate (1) B0815/04
reinstation (1) B1051/34
reiterating (2) C0132/34 C0205/09
reject (9) A0054/19
A0063/22 A0530/07 A0551/25 A0710/10
B0849/03 B0855/29 B0957/18 B1275/13
rejected (6) A0435/34 B0747/13
B0773/24 B1224/08 B1277/35 B1296/25
rejecting (1) A0608/04
rejoice (7) A0455/10
B1178/18 B1278/11 B1293/17 C0101/07
C0115/08 C0128/39
rejoiced (6) A0566/01 B0823/15
B0922/08 B1077/07 C0189/18 C0554/28
rejoices (1) B1130/17
rejoicing (1) C0073/24
rejoicings (1) B1077/10

rejoinder (3) A0074/33
A0299/07 A0626/05
rejoined (1) B1159/26
rekindled (1) C0136/31
relapse (3) A0327/18
A0328/25 B0960/32
relapsed (4) A0684/32
B0724/27 C0063/37 C0081/33
relate (15) A0328/23
A0427/03 A0538/09 A0639/01 B0772/22
B0906/07 B1191/15 B1236/24 B1292/34
B1362/24 C0057/32 C0123/40 C0124/01
C0538/33 C0548/26
related (16) A0281/33
B0959/11 B1140/17 B1154/34 B1159/29
B1166/11 B1226/16 B1241/18 B1299/37
B1303/17 C0055/29 C0065/03 C0425/25
C0528/26 C0541/15 C0561/28
relates (5) A0075/16
B1159/09 C0430/43 C0526/14 C0527/24
relating (7) A0608/30
B0723/14 B1021/19 B1032/10 C0055/05
C0065/12 C0569/16
relation (30) A0263/30 A0276/09
A0346/16 A0348/17 A0431/15 A0538/29
A0550/V A0709/33 A0710/01 B0726/16
B0757/02 B0941/25 B0987/22 B0987/30
B1037/30 B1096/03 B1275/01 B1275/04
B1300/36 C0066/27 C0153/33 C0180/31
C0207/19 C0207/34 C0395/04 C0521/04
C0521/19 C0524/22 C0532/18 C0557/17
relations (10) A0282/15 A0507/33
A0709/26 A0710/14 B0940/01 B1180/19
B1274/28 B1275/17 C0057/16 C0066/10
relationship (2) A0434/20 A0434/25
relative (21) A0020/V
A0404/02 A0591/33 B0733/14 B0735/27
B0768/09 B0887/13 B0914/21 B0915/14
B0916/27 B1051/03 B1075/05 B1127/26
B1137/10 B1138/04 B1246/02 B1302/27
B1353/21 B1382/07 C0196/08 C0207/18
relatives (18) A0705/28 B0733/01
B0733/02 B0733/32 B0733/34 B0736/06
B0748/19 B0748/29 B0755/10 B0755/15
B0807/31 B0904/V B1122/23 B1234/27
B1270/26 C0522/15 C0523/25 C0537/14
relax (1) C0064/09
relaxed (3) A0328/01
A0329/13 B1055/04
relaxes (1) A0581/29
relaxing (2) A0154/02 C0197/41
release (5) A0073/09
B1363/34 C0095/15 C0118/41 C0562/25
released (5) A0568/08
B0760/11 B1059/24 C0141/19 C0199/21
releasing (2) A0047/V C0086/34
relented (1) B0902/22
relenting (1) A0696/06
relentless (1) A0023/13
relentlessly (1) A0692/17
relevancy (2) B0752/04 B0831/14
reliable (2) B1236/13 B1313/22
reliance (5) A0302/13
B0924/18 C0103/30 C0104/11 C0553/38
relics (1) B1304/05
relied (4) B1069/22
B1234/18 C0167/41 C0404/15
relief (1) B0853/14
relief (49) A0056/19
A0066/08 A0072/11 A0353/33 A0412/12
A0413/15 A0428/13 A0445/03 A0456/23
A0490/35 A0510/34 A0626/12 A0692/29
B0857/30 B0900/09 B0907/29 B0916/25
B0958/24 B1030/31 B1093/27 B1105/10
B1108/03 B1115/04 C0071/18 C0072/05
C0074/13 C0089/11 C0089/35 C0092/28
C0119/23 C0120/15 C0129/39 C0131/03
C0131/12 C0132/34 C0138/24 C0140/08
C0140/25 C0140/36 C0141/10 C0142/17
C0143/13 C0143/26 C0183/10 C0185/34
C0399/11 C0406/38 C0421/28 C0537/15
relieve (13) A0074/06
A0502/03 B0726/17 B0816/03 B0950/03
B1295/03 B1310/16 C0071/01 C0117/41
C0134/36 C0142/21 C0143/01 C0143/03
relieved (37) A0298/V
A0355/16 A0355/24 A0459/06 A0501/26
A0501/27 A0541/23 A0562/28 A0614/23
B0820/20 B0865/11 B0895/12 B0944/08
B1030/25 B1236/17 B1249/28 B1282/03
B1334/19 B1336/31 B1339/35 B1349/20
C0060/24 C0073/15 C0079/08 C0081/01
C0107/38 C0119/31 C0125/20 C0198/04
C0201/22 C0205/39 C0411/26 C0535/20
C0545/23 C0554/15 C0558/14 C0559/31
relieves (1) A0548/29
relieving (7) A0073/28
A0101/V A0711/19 B0769/26 B1242/06
B1276/20 C0077/03
relievo (1) A0273/28
religio (1) B0987/09
religio (1) A0018/V
religion (1) B0987/09
religious (2) B1152/19 B1153/24
relinquish (2) B1109/15 C0523/01
relish (2) A0135/12 B0822/17
relished (1) B1078/10
reloading (1) C0557/35
reluctance (5) A0441/30
B0772/07 B0874/20 B0887/18 C0134/01
reluctant (2) A0446/10 B1107/13
reluctantly (5) A0217/V
A0347/10 B0823/30 B1348/07 C0159/12
rely (1) B1005/17
relying (2) B1313/32 C0089/04
rem (1) B1143/14
remain (60)
remainder (11) A0355/28
B0827/10 B1049/26 C0091/17 C0103/24
C0126/19 C0128/11 C0129/36 C0187/33
C0409/30 C0550/12
remained (129)
remaining (31) A0058/03
A0068/24 A0350/33 A0553/27 A0558/V
A0616/02 B0741/18 B0834/06 B0916/04
B1145/04 B1186/11 B1263/20 C0073/41
C0075/02 C0079/31 C0080/02 C0086/27
C0112/26 C0112/36 C0129/12 C0135/14
C0141/04 C0141/29 C0169/04 C0184/37
C0185/05 C0207/03 C0393/14 C0394/29

->C0533/24 C0543/08
remains (21) A0357/11
A0708/21 B0839/29 B0861/07 B0976/14
B1032/05 B1163/19 B1163/20 B1182/22
B1261/05 B1273/16 B1315/36 B1360/08
B1360/10 C0082/10 C0116/19 C0117/21
C0120/32 C0153/06 C0548/04 C0548/06
remanded (3) A0067/30
A0684/26 B1054/35
remark (29) A0073/25
A0098/12 A0106/07 A0161/08 A0225/16
A0246/20 A0349/09 A0429/10 A0479/32
A0536/28 A0549/19 A0628/05 A0628/21
A0630/15 A0652/16 B0810/20 B0823/32
B0828/32 B0927/32 B0932/30 B1010/10
B1047/19 B1051/06 B1160/37 B1184/22
B1186/22 C0167/37 C0419/41 C0429/26
Remarkable (1) B1310/T
remarkable (99)
remarkably (32) A0055/12
A0064/V A0281/25 A0283/21 A0341/18
A0530/30 A0562/26 B0837/03 B0850/27
B0877/34 B0897/24 B1018/21 B1018/23
B1056/09 B1076/14 B1142/31 B1194/07
B1257/23 B1315/10 B1328/04 C0068/05
C0104/35 C0120/11 C0146/32 C0155/02
C0158/02 C0532/01 C0533/08 C0543/23
C0553/06 C0553/36 C0566/20
remarked (10) A0019/V A0161/05
A0549/12 A0585/08 B0748/06 B0751/10
B1047/18 B1350/09 C0123/18 C0429/43
remarking (2) A0533/09 A0534/14
remarks (12) A0265/01
A0280/15 A0533/29 A0628/09 B0863/30
B1004/23 B1089/15 B1190/15 B1209/08
B1357/04 B1369/36 C0207/22
remedied (2) B0765/16 B1074/26
remedies (5) A0611/18
A0667/02 B0941/13 B0941/16 B1074/19
remedy (10) A0402/32 A0708/28
B0771/13 B0888/17 B1074/25 B1155/04
B1273/22 C0103/02 C0207/08 C0430/11
remember (99)
remembered (47) A0020/01
A0064/09 A0073/23 A0191/15 A0325/02
A0406/17 A0413/24 A0479/12 A0534/32
B0734/13 B0831/19 B0850/34 B0853/19
B0925/04 B0943/25 B1008/16 B1051/01
B1114/05 B1152/12 B1225/15 B1240/27
C0061/23 C0063/19 C0070/39 C0074/17
C0078/28 C0081/27 C0084/03 C0088/09
C0095/34 C0107/22 C0113/24 C0136/09
C0136/20 C0138/32 C0145/04 C0149/02
C0192/33 C0207/41 C0398/23 C0405/25
C0421/08 C0423/02 C0522/36 C0546/13
C0547/34 C0570/01
remembering (2) B1128/31 C0131/04
remembers (1) A0336/13
remembrance (13) A0209/26
A0210/02 A0314/01 A0430/30 A0438/03
A0456/10 A0555/27 B0769/10 B0854/29
B0906/V B1049/22 B1055/09 C0193/27
remembrances (3) A0020/V
A0639/05 A0683/12
remets (1) B1114/03

remimbered> (1) A0466/13
remind (2) A0107/30 B0955/15
reminded (4) A0139/20
A0190/09 A0400/13 B1107/02
reminding (1) B1091/07
reminiscences (1) A0402/18
remissness (2) B0754/16 B0756/V
remnant (7) A0531/22
A0686/27 A0691/22 A0694/02 B0856/09
C0074/04 C0139/27
remnants (3) B0830/16
C0077/31 C0111/35
remodelled (3) A0398/12
B0965/26 B1080/16
remonstrance (3) A0560/07
A0625/10 A0627/26
remonstrated (3) A0624/01
B1054/16 C0128/12
remorse (4) B0851/32
B0852/22 B0853/34 C0108/03
remorseless (1) A0021/14
remote (37) A0315/02
A0320/14 A0322/19 A0404/06 A0409/23
A0410/04 A0414/04 A0428/31 A0429/32
A0430/02 A0432/25 A0436/23 A0441/10
A0579/17 A0583/05 A0662/08 A0674/11
A0704/20 A0709/06 B0807/16 B0829/34
B0871/26 B0957/26 B0986/16 B0989/01
B1126/19 B1128/19 B1214/24 B1214/28
B1261/04 B1269/19 B1299/11 B1299/18
C0112/10 C0180/41 C0186/07 C0577/05
remotely (5) A0310/12
A0312/30 A0511/15 B1190/22 C0166/31
remoteness (1) A0366/01
remoter (1) A0401/12
remotest (5) A0369/31
A0371/25 B1214/23 C0144/40 C0182/32
removal (10) A0075/15 A0205/31
A0243/06 A0317/21 A0440/01 A0613/24
B1352/22 C0404/03 C0411/31 C0413/25
remove (16) A0022/15
A0070/06 A0079/22 A0456/08 B0764/13
B0844/18 B0856/30 B0979/10 B1115/33
C0075/32 C0089/23 C0092/01 C0107/14
C0121/36 C0402/23 C0547/03
removed (39) A0059/23
A0067/14 A0121/23 A0298/V A0350/07
A0415/19 A0444/03 A0509/01 A0537/27
A0542/15 A0594/17 A0689/19 B0759/09
B0770/20 B0770/29 B0795/31 B0824/31
B0825/02 B0834/33 B0836/06 B0891/22
B0929/19 B0979/27 B0979/30 B0979/38
B0981/12 B1006/29 B1059/13 B1070/32
B1120/08 B1180/27 B1351/26 C0069/15
C0090/27 C0119/22 C0119/22 C0173/10
C0548/29 C0575/36
removes (1) B0771/30
removing (13) A0141/06
A0249/16 B0751/06 B0763/09 B0826/11
B0826/30 B0826/34 B1109/05 B1180/09
C0075/37 C0090/15 C0181/21 C0194/10
remplis (1) A0650/06
remunerated (1) B1127/15
remuneration (3) B1134/14
B1134/21 B1206/03

rencontre (2) A0535/07 C0405/16
rencontres (1) A0297/04
rend (1) C0097/32
render (41) A0189/27
A0265/36 A0268/05 A0401/10 A0562/01
A0604/06 B0747/27 B0753/38 B0858/21
B0887/01 B0965/22 B0978/30 B1054/08
B1157/08 B1241/01 B1261/34 B1300/08
B1346/33 B1354/07 B1364/18 B1373/33
B1381/11 C0069/36 C0073/25 C0080/25
C0082/06 C0113/09 C0114/32 C0116/35
C0120/37 C0139/36 C0177/24 C0189/04
C0196/19 C0406/25 C0425/09 C0428/31
C0530/16 C0538/17 C0565/10 C0579/14
rendered (70)
rendering (14) A0059/28 A0142/29
A0267/30 A0442/16 A0512/14 A0593/06
A0604/05 B0902/20 B1105/11 B1206/01
C0134/32 C0178/29 C0202/19 C0392/28
renders (3) A0564/05
B0723/09 B1360/22
rending (1) A0416/13
Renelle (3) B0957/18
B0957/V B0958/10
renew (5) B0755/02
B0914/29 C0126/27 C0139/17 C0140/28
renewal (3) B0754/24
B1105/17 C0140/10
renewed (5) B0894/26
B1188/17 C0122/18 C0137/17 C0159/13
renews (1) C0179/12
renounce (1) B1005/22
renovation (3) C0404/08
C0404/09 C0412/27
renown (10) A0121/28 A0271/26
A0298/01 A0382/31 A0384/01 A0384/25
A0665/18 B0986/18 B1126/18 B1135/32
renowned (3) A0286/05
A0295/05 C0551/17
rent (3) A0512/03
C0182/04 C0437/V
rented (1) B1369/28
renting (1) A0532/13
rents (5) B0762/19
B0878/21 C0202/32 C0205/35 C0205/35
repaid (1) C0073/32
repair (3) A0320/09
A0535/25 B0877/01
repaired (7) A0055/15
B0905/02 B0923/09 B1185/31 C0392/39
C0544/39 C0566/02
repairing (6) B1185/25 C0065/32
C0103/16 C0540/04 C0544/26 C0545/30
repairs (2) C0534/17 C0576/35
repast (3) B1008/15
B1009/08 C0135/29
repay (1) B1128/05
repayment (1) C0393/16
repealed (2) B1154/16 B1154/30
repeat (32) A0074/25
A0078/25 A0151/07 A0163/V A0212/03
A0228/19 A0232/25 A0277/25 A0314/13
A0318/04 A0329/11 A0348/12 A0513/04
A0667/48 A0685/14 A0691/33 A0708/31
A0711/07 B0752/20 B0760/22 B0761/24
->B0772/21 B0929/35 B1031/27 B1035/32
B1133/20 B1187/15 B1238/24 B1273/25
B1315/19 B1316/31 B1360/10
repeated (41) A0025/16
A0026/08 A0053/08 A0057/23 A0062/14
A0071/21 A0109/15 A0113/02 A0177/08
A0302/V A0328/25 A0372/28 A0399/01
A0409/V A0441/31 A0497/18 A0625/18
B0751/01 B0770/12 B0842/32 B0877/32
B0913/25 B1015/V B1188/09 B1190/15
B1239/19 B1260/17 C0063/05 C0076/23
C0081/34 C0083/20 C0123/26 C0172/33
C0203/31 C0204/10 C0410/39 C0422/38
C0556/39 C0566/36 C0567/21 C0569/30
repeatedly (19) A0161/19
A0447/21 A0512/24 A0541/10 B0926/10
B1163/39 B1165/34 B1233/13 B1313/33
C0086/38 C0094/17 C0095/11 C0121/32
C0127/38 C0146/28 C0388/35 C0397/24
C0400/16 C0579/35
repeater (2) A0368/14 A0368/25
repeaters (3) A0372/25
A0372/28 A0374/01
repeating (8) A0068/05
A0354/28 B1005/18 B1225/07 C0062/15
C0110/33 C0157/38 C0168/32
repel (2) C0165/05 C0555/34
repent (1) C0411/21
repented (3) A0098/18
B1158/22 C0184/17
reperuse (1) B0745/19
repetition (10) A0212/04 A0326/25
A0344/16 A0434/10 B0941/19 B1014/30
B1238/25 B1239/11 B1318/02 C0420/03
repetitions (3) B0837/17
B0837/19 B1293/30
repining (1) B0866/03
replace (2) B0930/02 C0128/12
replaced (12) A0164/V
A0410/25 A0552/28 A0552/30 A0553/23
A0664/25 B0796/10 B0979/32 B0992/16
C0092/37 C0388/07 C0576/39
replacing (2) B0992/27 B1260/32
replenished (1) B1104/20
replete (7) A0212/22
A0217/09 A0430/24 A0612/22 B0955/17
C0122/21 C0397/19
repletion (3) A0056/13
A0066/02 C0540/06
replied (128)
replies (6) A0262/34 A0264/02
B0872/24 B0873/30 B0984/15 C0556/34
reply (76)
replying (6) A0088/28 A0250/18
A0266/24 A0271/11 A0277/23 A0561/19
report (17) A0157/06
A0164/06 A0269/15 A0275/25 A0336/11
A0441/01 B0728/35 B0897/08 B0992/11
B1145/26 B1145/27 B1364/02 C0066/35
C0186/09 C0187/17 C0530/19 C0548/21
reported (3) A0058/25
A0098/14 B1136/17
reports (4) B0768/08
B0834/18 B1209/07 C0157/13
repose (17) A0294/14

->A0312/09 A0312/V A0502/09 B0827/16
B0891/07 B0893/24 B0909/22 B0948/07
B0964/33 B1006/18 B1126/04 B1259/27
B1277/29 C0126/25 C0138/41 C0414/38
reposed (7) A0247/12
A0602/28 B0796/32 B0967/18 B1110/18
B1237/28 C0184/20
reposing (1) B0854/03
reprehensible (3) A0626/21
C0114/05 C0388/24
represent (5) B0837/20
B0837/33 B1295/27 B1311/24 C0108/36
representation (5) B0855/31
B1248/28 C0056/03 C0195/13 C0208/02
representations (3) A0498/13
C0093/25 C0104/23
representative (2) A0055/34
B0985/15
representatives (1) B0733/33
represented (24) A0021/23
A0022/08 A0146/12 A0146/14 A0442/05
A0550/14 A0580/27 A0689/27 B0767/15
B0838/09 B0838/21 B0838/28 B0839/01
B0839/24 B0933/19 B1073/V B1123/06
B1179/30 B1180/13 B1351/04 B1362/11
C0061/28 C0089/06 C0170/31
representing (6) B0838/32 B1032/17
B1179/25 B1220/05 C0109/12 C0154/13
represents (6) B0837/22 B0837/23
B0837/23 B0839/12 B0903/30 B1279/16
repress (1) B1240/31
repression (2) B1296/10 B1312/14
reprinted (2) A0283/36 B1380/05
reproach (2) A0044/13 A0442/23
reproached (1) A0135/09
reprocured (1) C0523/29
reproof (2) B0916/09 B1014/07
reptiles (1) C0199/04
Repub. (1) A0611/27
republic (2) B1299/36 B1300/03
Republican (1) A0154/06
republican (3) A0500/19
B1094/05 B1300/10
Republicanism (1) B1300/25
republication (1) A0473/08
republish (1) B0958/17
republished (1) A0074/32
repugnance (4) A0435/26
A0652/16 B0888/06 B1249/05
repugnant (1) A0018/14
repulsive (4) A0327/21
A0689/02 B1122/31 B1349/25
reputable (4) A0057/12
B0763/25 B0878/22 B0898/18
reputation (11) A0120/12
A0297/27 A0380/23 A0568/23 B0728/12
B0986/22 B1137/22 B1139/21 B1140/21
B1380/34 C0531/19
reputed (2) A0539/04 A0539/20
request (16) A0271/33
A0277/05 A0278/26 A0285/24 A0301/23
A0301/25 A0302/23 A0398/26 A0409/29
A0489/33 A0490/01 A0652/01 B0872/04
B0908/08 B1129/06 B1236/05
requested (13) A0107/23
->A0301/07 A0353/02 B0755/23 B0959/35
B0983/18 B1057/02 B1130/07 B1208/12
B1208/34 B1237/32 B1239/06 C0127/40
requesting (10) A0056/16 A0066/06
A0091/31 A0111/01 A0275/04 B1250/11
B1258/30 B1371/22 C0133/35 C0136/11
requests (1) A0652/02
<u>requiescat</u> (1) B1263/26
require (16) A0282/03
A0343/18 B0732/08 B0740/09 B0743/04
B0743/11 B0746/35 B0837/09 B0840/16
B0878/35 B1091/11 B1168/36 C0394/34
C0409/10 C0414/39 C0432/01
required (34) A0066/01 A0478/32
A0478/36 A0513/19 A0555/16 A0626/16
A0690/07 B0762/23 B0762/35 B0844/21
B1049/25 B1054/17 B1108/15 B1164/15
B1166/23 B1169/34 B1315/21 B1322/02
B1322/03 B1337/11 B1345/24 B1358/13
B1369/06 C0075/31 C0111/06 C0147/21
C0156/22 C0177/34 C0391/27 C0419/32
C0420/39 C0424/07 C0430/07 C0538/01
requires (11) A0341/V
A0430/22 A0488/16 A0489/25 B0876/27
B0887/08 B0989/29 B1032/31 B1092/14
B1350/02 C0106/38
requiring (2) B0975/08 C0523/01
requisite (15) A0340/26
A0479/17 A0479/23 A0555/08 A0667/51
B1079/23 B1158/08 C0098/22 C0106/29
C0136/35 C0148/05 C0393/23 C0403/13
C0530/29 C0574/25
requisites (1) A0478/34
requisition (1) B1077/02
<u>res</u> (1) A0072/30
rescinding (1) B1053/13
rescue (6) A0025/12 A0483/11
B1194/25 C0184/14 C0198/23 C0399/05
rescued (2) C0062/05 C0073/30
research (3) A0250/23
A0478/36 A0556/25
researches (7) A0266/30
A0686/20 B0728/04 B1089/07 B1164/06
B1359/17 C0525/02
resemblance (38) A0057/37 A0068/21
A0124/14 A0213/12 A0233/18 A0234/19
A0271/01 A0274/08 A0275/12 A0285/19
A0297/21 A0434/15 A0494/07 A0553/25
A0665/21 B0725/17 B0735/27 B0810/24
B0830/18 B0841/20 B0914/25 B0950/09
B1302/21 B1329/16 B1350/15 C0137/41
C0138/06 C0150/29 C0151/19 C0165/28
C0165/37 C0171/38 C0193/09 C0195/15
C0207/29 C0208/04 C0399/19 C0543/35
resemble (12) A0675/10
B0829/20 B0857/09 B0929/29 B0950/14
B1030/02 B1030/02 B1031/29 B1102/30
B1134/23 B1282/18 B1304/03
resembled (18) A0087/10 A0246/12
B0789/12 B0825/13 B0828/29 B0940/V
B0947/19 B0957/22 B1012/04 B1076/19
B1293/06 B1346/19 C0167/19 C0171/18
C0173/29 C0419/21 C0542/12 C0543/11
resembles (14) A0277/34 A0281/01
A0282/22 A0284/27 A0368/32 A0479/20

->A0493/07 B0809/29 B0810/10 B1037/22
B1037/23 B1037/23 B1300/34 C0431/06
resembling (42) A0087/05 A0089/08
A0100/16 A0104/07 A0211/13 A0298/V
A0511/15 A0550/16 A0687/11 A0689/14
B0733/06 B0854/10 B1011/29 B1070/05
B1102/10 B1157/05 B1162/15 B1179/35
B1234/08 B1239/23 B1281/26 B1292/30
B1328/09 B1383/07 C0124/31 C0150/25
C0165/17 C0167/16 C0173/16 C0175/23
C0177/06 C0180/26 C0182/01 C0183/35
C0185/01 C0188/23 C0189/41 C0194/11
C0204/41 C0388/29 C0397/09 C0543/23
resented (4) A0374/01
A0436/02 A0444/13 B1313/10
resentment (2) A0074/27 A0300/12
reserve (4) A0380/17
A0398/30 A0622/17 B1122/34
reserved (3) A0350/31
A0687/22 B0889/04
reserving (2) B1141/11 C0405/19
reservoir (1) B1091/19
reside (1) C0572/04
resided (10) A0164/02 A0539/12
A0546/15 B0729/09 B1183/07 B1234/06
C0203/36 C0391/09 C0391/10 C0551/10
residence (30) A0085/02 A0120/24
A0121/23 A0155/25 A0268/25 A0293/28
A0296/08 A0429/31 A0436/06 A0541/21
A0560/24 A0564/25 A0625/30 B0726/19
B0729/05 B0749/33 B0806/05 B0808/04
B0899/02 B0901/V B1166/14 B1340/24
B1361/30 B1369/18 B1374/25 C0066/37
C0156/09 C0173/20 C0425/26 C0523/09
residences (1) A0495/02
resident (4) B0749/08
B0758/21 C0156/19 C0207/13
resides (2) A0273/37 A0542/25
residing (5) A0531/15
B0939/01 C0155/39 C0551/05 C0551/22
residue (2) B1351/11 C0535/36
resign (3) A0316/02
A0663/08 C0200/36
resignation (1) B1132/33
resigned (9) A0058/21
A0069/10 A0081/23 A0204/32 A0593/22
B0852/34 B1140/32 C0073/03 C0144/11
resignedly (1) B1015/27
resigning (4) A0057/23
A0068/07 B0865/15 B1108/30
resin (2) B1180/01 C0533/02
resined (1) B1096/16
resist (6) A0446/14 A0582/27
A0696/33 B0889/22 B1261/30 C0547/26
resistance (1) A0653/19
resistance (25) A0056/15
A0066/04 A0249/14 A0317/02 A0432/06
A0593/03 A0652/06 B0825/21 B0902/V
B0958/12 B1021/04 B1035/06 B1035/08
B1035/10 B1072/05 B1383/01 C0075/35
C0088/19 C0133/30 C0135/27 C0187/08
C0200/07 C0401/30 C0423/30 C0568/32
resisted (6) A0551/32 A0552/21
B0853/08 B0958/11 B1225/15 C0561/12
resisting (2) A0213/13 C0133/26
resistlessly (1) A0697/02
resolute (6) A0444/31 A0515/15
B1072/13 B1371/05 C0059/10 C0557/29
resolutely (8) A0327/01
A0369/05 A0458/04 B0888/18 B1054/15
B1077/32 C0187/05 C0545/27
Resolution (2) C0158/28 C0159/31
resolution (25) A0271/35
A0279/05 A0409/20 A0446/18 A0527/V
A0681/13 A0694/28 B1020/11 B1101/11
B1221/04 C0060/19 C0060/36 C0080/32
C0090/03 C0109/14 C0112/39 C0132/09
C0135/16 C0158/21 C0162/20 C0197/17
C0197/20 C0399/28 C0543/08 C0561/16
resolutions (2) A0369/13 A0627/25
resolve (8) A0386/16
A0411/07 A0435/16 B0835/28 B0923/05
C0063/14 C0074/14 C0085/10
resolved (70)
resolvent (1) A0533/24
resolving (5) A0501/20
A0527/V A0530/V A0687/27 B0931/18
resonant (1) B1294/22
resonne (1) A0397/M
resort (6) B0735/20 B0807/03
B1127/03 C0132/09 C0132/22 C0185/31
resorted (12) A0263/22
A0565/11 B0739/32 B0888/16 B0950/03
B0990/17 B1004/16 C0097/24 C0105/32
C0106/04 C0114/06 C0142/03
resorting (1) B0765/25
resounded (5) A0029/14
A0242/20 B0967/36 B1226/06 C0387/21
resource (10) A0386/20 B0900/27
B1074/12 B1154/04 B1347/20 C0106/41
C0143/13 C0196/26 C0399/33 C0425/01
resources (9) A0081/34
A0529/08 A0711/14 B0984/01 B1074/17
B1074/32 B1276/15 C0080/39 C0192/19
respect (93)
respectaable (3) B0912/19
B0912/28 B0913/11
respectability (1) A0509/04
respectable (21) A0286/22
A0483/16 A0483/24 A0485/28 A0489/08
B0872/16 B0878/04 B0878/13 B0878/31
B0879/24 B0896/01 B0914/13 B0956/12
B1044/10 B1045/13 B1045/21 B1056/18
B1136/23 B1300/17 C0057/01 C0391/11
respectably (1) A0490/35
respected (6) A0090/19 A0370/10
A0709/03 B1115/19 B1257/06 B1259/13
respectful (4) A0349/20
B0728/29 B0773/32 C0171/04
respectfully (20) A0265/13
A0267/21 A0268/32 A0269/27 A0272/03
A0274/01 A0275/07 A0276/12 A0277/28
A0278/08 A0281/12 A0282/17 A0282/34
A0283/16 A0284/01 A0284/35 A0285/27
B0874/26 B0875/17 B1130/22
respecting (40) A0263/02
A0265/07 A0294/04 A0294/V A0297/03
A0382/14 A0513/26 A0544/28 A0546/04
A0549/10 A0550/21 A0667/41 A0687/19
B0729/28 B0732/31 B0737/20 B0814/29

->B0815/19 B0914/27 B0949/11 B1069/26
B1073/02 B1152/04 B1189/35 B1303/30
C0073/23 C0101/38 C0102/08 C0156/31
C0156/40 C0161/22 C0202/09 C0532/26
C0537/23 C0538/29 C0538/36 C0546/32
C0548/26 C0556/26 C0565/40
respective (9) A0123/18
A0204/08 A0250/14 A0251/10 A0559/08
A0615/17 B1073/23 B1346/26 C0402/17
respectively (2) C0394/18 C0417/38
respects (23) A0101/12
A0240/21 A0277/34 A0299/11 A0346/26
A0368/07 A0496/V A0558/16 A0655/11
B0930/15 B0947/19 B1036/02 B1055/25
B1241/06 B1274/08 B1293/06 B1303/17
C0086/36 C0145/20 C0146/32 C0147/16
C0151/25 C0566/07
respiration (15) A0074/01
A0074/07 A0074/14 B1241/07 B1359/18
B1359/20 B1359/23 C0402/23 C0403/31
C0404/12 C0409/16 C0410/41 C0411/20
C0411/34 C0424/21
respiratory (2) A0056/21 A0066/10
respite (1) C0420/41
respited (1) C0086/28
resplendent (3) B0909/V
B1144/02 B1332/37
resplendently-blooming (1) B1340/16
responded (5) A0046/29
A0235/28 A0370/05 A0614/31 B1123/16
response (3) B0985/01
B1123/18 B1315/16
responsibilities (1) B0879/04
responsibility (1) A0508/20
responsible (4) A0056/30
A0066/19 B1259/15 C0558/13
resposes (1) B1281/05
ressemblance (1) A0019/04
Rest (1) B0856/04
rest (81)
restaurants (1) A0101/13
restaurateur (8) A0096/01
A0097/14 A0098/29 A0099/24 A0105/20
A0108/23 A0109/15 A0540/30
restaurateurs (1) A0100/06
reste (1) A0019/03
rested (19) A0088/16
A0157/20 A0190/29 A0190/32 A0191/02
A0241/16 A0244/28 A0294/11 A0410/20
A0641/08 A0686/33 B0827/07 B0853/07
B1009/V B1108/19 B1273/28 B1311/10
C0127/26 C0137/14
resting (6) A0241/29 B0819/01
C0125/17 C0136/34 C0545/20 C0568/22
resting-place (1) C0196/36
restive (1) A0436/01
restless (4) A0270/14
A0274/12 A0508/06 B1004/22
restlessness (2) A0081/06 A0135/27
restoration (2) A0328/11 B0877/08
restorations (1) A0160/18
restoratives (1) B0957/35
restore (6) A0216/13 A0323/18
A0327/10 A0374/19 A0589/08 B0747/37
restored (8) A0067/18
->B0960/28 B0960/30 B0963/01 B0968/08
B1056/35 C0168/39 C0175/21
restoring (2) B0959/28 C0177/02
restrain (6) A0033/13 B0851/13
B0903/09 B1139/14 C0130/30 C0137/11
restrained (11) A0021/27
A0204/27 A0412/09 B0825/28 B0858/20
B0907/15 B1020/20 C0086/40 C0089/09
C0131/38 C0555/26
restraining (2) A0023/18 C0558/10
restrains (2) B1034/17 B1221/28
restraint (4) A0123/17
B1122/34 B1337/20 C0093/30
restraints (2) A0440/13 B0760/15
restrict (1) C0141/33
restrictions (1) B1311/25
rests (1) B1392/08
result (90)
resulted (15) A0427/28
A0445/19 A0613/22 A0711/36 B0731/06
B0754/21 B0834/05 B0949/07 B1031/09
B1298/06 B1358/32 C0065/28 C0097/28
C0131/05 C0413/13
resulting (6) A0295/17 A0528/28
B1223/22 B1317/22 B1322/24 C0098/08
results (28) A0296/V
A0403/12 A0473/32 A0474/04 A0528/10
A0544/03 A0545/07 A0545/V A0710/27
B0747/33 B0832/22 B0976/17 B1032/06
B1168/20 B1168/23 B1213/09 B1214/08
B1214/09 B1234/14 B1275/30 B1295/10
B1310/32 B1357/11 B1364/11 B1364/32
C0071/11 C0157/06 C0523/14
resume (6) B0724/15 B0763/21
C0074/37 C0540/13 C0548/18 C0553/05
resumed (42) A0093/25 A0107/25
A0109/20 A0113/04 A0159/08 A0160/01
A0261/17 A0261/17 A0263/01 A0328/14
A0353/09 A0389/03 A0415/15 A0514/15
A0515/05 A0515/26 A0579/23 A0686/11
A0686/13 B0892/V B0893/31 B0905/30
B0907/07 B0989/28 B0992/09 B1012/02
B1014/08 B1021/32 B1102/18 B1123/11
B1142/19 B1159/16 B1186/22 B1190/08
B1249/25 B1250/13 B1262/18 B1349/05
C0077/20 C0104/36 C0129/05 C0560/28
resuming (6) A0165/17 B1188/11
B1189/11 C0068/34 C0076/29 C0086/39
resurrection (1) B0958/06
resurrexit (1) A0213/08
resuscitated (2) A0074/31 C0064/17
resuscitation (1) B0960/32
retail (3) A0488/18
B0870/04 B1293/25
retailed (2) B1155/19 B1312/28
retain (13) A0053/13
A0062/20 A0281/21 A0538/23 B0841/34
B0873/34 B1073/17 B1364/26 B1383/22
C0059/03 C0087/09 C0156/07 C0404/26
retained (23) A0156/25
A0281/22 A0415/02 A0559/06 A0613/22
B0762/05 B0809/17 B0828/20 B0851/12
B0914/08 B0934/02 B1095/07 B1235/15
B1250/25 B1345/19 B1345/23 C0056/09
C0064/04 C0072/38 C0189/29 C0207/04

->C0412/04 C0557/04
retaining (9) A0073/29
A0444/29 A0567/07 A0711/15 B0843/32
B1119/06 B1276/15 C0114/40 C0130/16
retains (1) B1160/33
retake (1) C0104/14
retaken (3) A0070/07
A0079/24 C0086/08
retaliation (2) B1048/03 B1379/17
retaliations (1) A0433/33
retard (2) B1295/29 B1311/26
retardation (2) B1035/20 B1035/25
retarded (1) B0742/15
retarding (2) B1035/28 C0401/32
retched (2) A0092/05 A0111/18
retchings (1) C0143/05
retention (1) A0554/02
retentive (1) A0529/30
retina (1) A0545/23
retina (5) A0613/12
B1038/04 B1167/32 C0078/02 C0438/V
retinue (1) A0028/06
retire (3) B1126/04
C0399/01 C0561/36
retired (13) A0157/15
A0532/16 A0539/20 A0556/07 A0670/13
B1106/11 B1160/28 B1372/13 C0134/10
C0389/05 C0393/28 C0416/11 C0575/34
retirement (3) A0532/21
B1246/03 B1279/02
retirements (2) A0709/34 B1275/02
retires (1) B0872/05
retiring (6) A0411/14 A0510/32
A0513/08 B1278/20 C0421/11 C0572/14
retorted (1) A0034/07
retouch (3) A0059/03
A0069/V A0070/03
retrace (4) A0535/06
C0076/11 C0183/24 C0191/33
retraced (4) A0513/03
A0515/12 B1242/29 C0096/01
retracing (6) A0535/12 A0546/25
B0948/12 C0095/07 C0154/18 C0548/28
retreat (9) A0141/07
A0303/13 A0385/25 C0110/29 C0161/21
C0169/39 C0187/34 C0200/17 C0549/01
retreated (4) B0947/12
B0947/13 C0206/02 C0555/09
retreating (6) A0241/02 A0298/V
A0404/10 A0676/21 C0126/20 C0181/37
retribution (1) B1256/08
retrieval (1) A0531/21
retro-gradation (1) A0609/21
retrogradation (3) B1214/11
B1215/01 B1215/02
retrograde (2) A0528/14 B1382/22
retrograding (1) B1214/05
return (91)
returned (67)
returneth (1) A0318/26
returning (24) A0151/23
A0212/27 A0429/28 A0507/08 A0510/03
A0564/30 A0581/33 B0756/01 B0756/05
B0756/26 B0835/10 B0851/20 B1036/33
B1044/15 B1279/27 C0080/30 C0100/36

->C0127/17 C0137/05 C0153/22 C0166/16
C0173/38 C0522/26 C0561/26
returns (4) B0765/04
B0877/21 B1222/24 B1325/05
Retzsch (1) A0511/17
reunions (1) B1055/07
reve (1) A0498/02
reveal (1) C0094/39
revealed (6) A0312/27 A0507/01
A0642/03 A0709/27 B1274/30 C0080/18
revealing (1) B0890/07
revel (5) A0190/01
A0673/10 A0674/13 A0676/35 B1224/26
Revelation (2) B1029/T B1219/08
reveled (1) B1224/V
revelled (7) A0213/29
A0323/10 A0674/20 B0865/18 B1337/14
C0412/29 C0523/38
reveller (1) A0397/16
revellers (3) A0675/13
A0676/27 A0676/35
revelry (1) A0151/V
revenge (8) A0351/09
A0445/31 B0927/14 B1051/33 B1256/02
B1354/26 C0391/36 C0550/03
revenged (1) B1110/22
revenue (1) B0754/05
reverberate (1) C0550/21
reverberated (1) A0413/35
reverberation (4) A0415/28
A0614/17 A0614/20 B0858/34
reverberations (1) A0687/08
reverence (7) A0125/22
A0144/10 A0180/09 A0370/12 A0467/03
B1385/06 C0169/32
reverenced (2) A0430/08 B1035/34
Reverend (1) A0430/05
reverend (3) A0382/18
A0428/32 A0627/31
reverent (1) A0664/24
reverently (1) A0614/01
reverie (4) A0498/V
A0629/24 B0724/28 B0811/05
reveries (6) A0135/21 A0162/01
A0345/29 A0405/27 A0665/14 B0963/23
reverse (9) A0100/29
A0294/07 A0366/06 A0370/17 B0829/14
B0854/25 B0909/08 B1207/21 C0131/29
reversed (3) A0594/V
B0992/03 B1161/15
reverses (1) B0807/28
revert (2) A0547/V A0555/33
revery (5) A0210/12
A0212/29 A0326/23 A0603/34 A0673/01
reviendrai (1) A0037/09
Review (1) C0432/38
review (4) A0265/07
B1141/01 B1379/15 B1381/26
Reviewed (1) B1378/T
reviewed (2) B1141/17 B1378/M
Reviewer (1) B1378/T
reviewer (1) B1379/16
reviewers (1) A0630/06
reviewing (3) B1379/03
B1379/06 B1379/31

reviews (2) B1141/22 B1206/05
revision (1) C0207/05
revival (2) A0683/33 B1242/08
revive (3) B1241/03
B1390/06 C0130/20
revived (9) A0514/31
B0956/31 B0958/01 B0959/08 B0960/30
B1108/32 C0116/18 C0129/15 C0560/29
revivication (1) A0328/V
revivification (2) A0328/24
C0112/02
revivified (1) B1189/10
reviving (5) B0928/08
C0061/04 C0063/38 C0083/21 C0121/05
revoir (1) A0034/29
revolt (1) A0440/13
revolted (2) A0485/V C0081/10
revolting (1) B0763/21
revolution (24) A0137/04
A0211/09 A0213/25 A0353/21 A0355/27
A0591/21 A0593/07 A0604/23 A0681/07
B1035/23 B1070/04 B1070/22 B1106/06
B1144/19 B1164/31 B1302/14 B1321/06
B1321/16 B1321/17 B1321/19 C0401/35
C0422/12 C0426/12 C0526/02
revolutionary (3) A0085/09
B1138/34 B1318/11
revolutions (6) A0589/06 B1035/07
B1321/19 B1322/03 B1322/04 C0391/21
revolve (3) B1071/20
B1071/23 C0432/25
revolved (6) A0591/04 B0891/19
B1321/06 B1321/32 C0078/07 C0392/21
revolves (4) A0622/31
A0656/29 B1301/26 B1322/11
revolving (8) A0601/21
B1164/30 B1301/05 B1301/25 B1301/36
B1321/08 C0079/34 C0136/07
revulsion (1) B0969/01
reward (30) A0055/09 A0064/12
A0563/09 A0563/12 A0563/V A0563/V
B0727/09 B0727/09 B0727/22 B0727/27
B0736/25 B0737/19 B0768/16 B0768/20
B0864/25 B0874/07 B0877/02 B0877/06
B0877/09 B0877/20 B0978/20 B0980/27
B0982/07 B0982/09 B0982/14 B0985/21
B0986/09 B1164/03 B1170/05 C0426/16
rewarding (1) B0874/04
Reynold's (1) A0276/17
Reynolds (2) C0160/09 C0162/07
Reynolds, J. N. (2) A0276/13
C0159/28
rhapsodical (1) B0943/19
rhapsodies (1) A0406/17
rhapsody (1) B1317/36
rhetoric (1) A0507/13
rhetorical (1) B0989/14
rheum (2) A0143/16 B1259/05
rheumatism (1) B0906/19
Rhine (3) A0310/11
A0320/05 B0862/12
rhinoceros (1) A0070/27
Rhode/Island (1) B1361/12
rhodomontades (1) C0123/04
rhomboids (1) B1092/17

Rhone (1) B0862/13
rhymed (1) A0406/13
rhymes (1) B1132/14
rhyming (2) B1128/02 B1244/07
rhythm (1) A0611/28
Rialto (2) A0087/03 A0157/02
riband (1) B0990/V
ribands (1) A0694/30
ribband (1) A0348/22
ribbon (5) A0371/09
A0561/06 A0561/10 A0561/12 B0990/36
ribbons (4) A0368/05
A0368/11 B0930/18 C0388/31
ribs (6) A0543/34 B0771/07
B0927/29 B1194/19 B1235/29 C0202/21
Ricara (1) C0560/23
Ricaree (2) C0556/39 C0556/39
Ricarees (6) C0556/11 C0556/18
C0556/37 C0557/03 C0557/13 C0560/32
Riccaree (1) A0498/09
rice (2) B0945/30 C0404/34
Rice, Joel (1) C0099/03
rich (53)
Rich-- (1) A0112/V
rich-ermined (1) A0021/24
Richbourg (2) A0101/V A0181/12
richer (5) A0696/04
A0706/26 B1162/05 B1271/28 B1279/04
riches (3) A0441/01
A0705/07 B1270/06
richest (9) A0087/19
A0322/13 A0502/24 A0707/04 B0863/09
B0864/37 B1272/03 C0083/16 C0083/31
richly (13) A0087/07
A0100/16 A0165/04 A0379/04 A0502/12
A0664/09 B0828/09 B0828/17 B0864/36
B0907/04 B1114/24 B1192/28 B1246/17
richly-embroidered (1) A0246/01
Richmond (4) B0968/10
C0055/04 C0055/31 C0099/04
richness (3) A0663/V
B1136/32 B1280/18
Ricketts (1) C0057/09
ricocheting (1) C0187/16
rid (23) A0073/22
A0210/04 A0355/20 A0487/14 A0586/19
A0588/27 A0589/17 B0771/15 B0789/16
B0797/04 B0853/32 B0855/32 B0930/30
B0965/19 B1142/14 B1143/09 B1164/18
B1224/31 C0105/11 C0113/04 C0114/22
C0395/12 C0425/02
ridden (1) A0587/31
riddle (8) A0262/01
A0435/16 A0548/15 A0553/30 A0560/09
A0639/03 B0828/25 B0841/23
riddles (2) B0835/26 B1189/15
riddy> (1) A0464/14
ride (14) A0026/13 A0026/14
A0028/15 B0965/09 B1003/03 B1003/13
B1007/10 B1090/14 B1090/17 B1091/17
B1091/17 B1379/23 C0106/27 C0106/36
rider (7) A0019/09
A0022/11 A0024/10 A0027/06 A0029/07
A0029/18 B1057/32
ridge (9) A0370/23

->A0582/34 A0589/13 B1054/11 B1337/21
C0116/24 C0184/38 C0541/35 C0541/37
ridge-beam (1) B1336/11
Ridge/Road (1) B0864/20
ridges (5) A0104/13
B0865/22 C0185/12 C0571/25 C0576/23
ridicule (3) B0886/01
C0167/08 C0537/21
ridiculed (1) B0763/24
ridiculer (1) A0297/15
ridiculous (14) A0107/04 A0123/01
A0157/08 A0247/26 A0283/38 A0300/22
A0355/08 A0399/30 A0428/15 A0482/27
A0630/13 B0926/34 B1167/06 C0427/11
ridiculously (3) A0483/V
B0889/19 B1008/09
riding (4) A0587/30
A0652/25 B1091/20 B1374/26
rien (1) A0135/M
rife (5) A0209/V
A0217/V A0457/33 B0760/V C0080/22
rifle (7) A0388/16
B1052/25 B1054/06 C0533/32 C0534/12
C0562/04 C0566/38
rifled (2) A0538/02 A0556/02
rifles (5) C0534/07
C0549/34 C0561/26 C0563/20 C0577/29
rift (6) A0587/10 A0590/24
B0842/09 B0842/10 B0842/30 B1280/32
rigged (8) A0249/27
B1071/07 C0057/27 C0115/29 C0115/29
C0163/07 C0389/16 C0393/25
rigging (9) A0140/10
A0140/26 A0142/18 B0930/27 C0110/17
C0114/26 C0147/34 C0169/06 C0189/27
right (193)
right-angle (1) C0408/07
right-angled (2) B1080/27 C0408/06
righted (4) A0137/13
C0104/28 C0114/39 C0146/39
righteous (3) A0252/10
A0371/22 B1170/05
righteously (1) B1379/02
rightful (2) B0877/02 B0977/18
rightly (8) A0295/07
A0348/08 B0763/10 B0869/27 B1070/29
B1369/21 C0394/40 C0413/05
rights (3) A0250/21
A0251/01 A0445/21
rigid (25) A0135/08
A0153/25 A0166/22 A0166/V A0217/V
A0235/06 A0296/06 A0326/15 A0327/09
A0365/12 A0415/11 A0428/34 A0484/11
A0567/09 B0730/07 B0879/21 B0947/31
B0961/22 B0964/35 B1003/11 B1005/15
B1238/12 B1238/30 B1242/21 C0064/29
rigidam (1) A0043/M
rigidity (5) A0328/16
A0415/32 B0956/21 B1040/12 B1181/24
rigidly (10) A0329/08 A0405/29
A0461/12 A0498/16 A0558/22 A0706/32
B0724/04 B1057/21 B1058/17 C0105/27
rigmarole (3) A0303/03
A0654/08 C0430/04
rigola (1) A0662/V
rigor (2) B0902/21 B1182/26
rigorous (12) A0234/14
A0327/23 A0460/16 A0485/30 A0531/24
B0747/18 B0855/30 B0858/11 B0962/17
B1016/32 B1058/34 B1335/22
rigorously (7) B0757/10
B0946/04 B0979/04 B1134/30 B1249/26
B1271/34 B1339/27
Riker (1) B1303/14
rilievo (1) A0097/32
rim (22) A0138/28 A0261/07
B0910/27 B1073/33 B1108/35 C0388/28
C0389/15 C0396/17 C0397/02 C0398/16
C0399/07 C0408/23 C0408/30 C0409/21
C0409/36 C0410/30 C0410/31 C0415/22
C0416/01 C0417/08 C0417/21 C0418/16
rims (1) C0415/29
rind (1) C0547/04
ring (20) A0165/11
A0189/14 A0215/V A0248/19 A0374/13
A0405/12 A0589/29 B0825/32 B0877/05
B0877/11 B0877/16 B0877/20 B0877/24
B0890/08 B0934/10 B1103/11 B1103/15
B1321/30 B1321/31 B1337/14
ring-bolt (3) A0586/11
A0589/24 A0593/21
ringbolt (2) C0060/31 C0063/20
ringing (14) A0154/16 A0218/03
A0415/24 A0562/09 B0797/01 B0797/02
B0905/15 B0929/30 B0966/12 B1119/08
B1160/31 B1178/12 B1225/02 C0198/01
ringlets (3) A0215/06
A0234/28 A0247/04
rings (5) B0826/07
B0828/06 B0944/03 B1008/01 B1322/18
rinsed (1) B0834/30
Rio (1) C0103/26
Rio/Janeiro (2) C0147/26 C0156/03
riot (1) B1091/16
rioters (1) A0124/07
riotous (2) A0631/19 B1049/33
riots (1) B0949/14
rip (1) C0396/35
ripe (8) A0242/14
A0441/06 A0708/10 B0818/31 C0118/13
C0542/14 C0542/38 C0576/07
ripened (3) A0436/05
A0663/V B0807/18
ripening (2) A0433/09 A0663/22
riper (1) A0430/25
ripped (4) A0413/33
A0469/24 B0732/25 C0188/07
ripping (1) A0414/07
ripple (1) B1282/32
ripples (3) A0236/09
B1281/13 C0167/29
rise (34) A0019/13 A0087/08
A0100/18 A0162/V A0273/19 A0295/31
A0582/06 A0587/34 A0657/08 A0689/03
B0742/21 B0742/32 B0771/34 B0773/07
B0894/04 B0903/02 B0933/01 B0948/04
B0956/03 B1044/12 B1044/19 B1213/17
B1242/03 B1281/V B1364/32 C0053/T
C0075/27 C0087/32 C0397/22 C0402/30
C0427/10 C0433/02 C0528/18 C0553/25

risen (6) A0151/01 A0157/27
A0157/V B0740/29 B0743/14 C0175/13
rises (7) A0582/36
B0732/10 B0740/11 B0743/07 B0818/30
B1244/04 C0154/32
rising (25) A0114/04
A0157/V A0411/22 A0413/30 A0582/34
A0657/07 A0657/09 A0657/13 B0743/13
B0809/19 B0905/29 B1075/23 B1138/01
B1282/19 B1385/05 B1385/10 C0159/09
C0163/37 C0164/01 C0405/40 C0414/13
C0417/12 C0539/01 C0547/20 C0573/07
risk (24) A0243/06
A0484/05 A0581/21 A0583/28 A0583/33
A0584/31 A0624/17 A0687/27 B0771/14
B0819/04 B0856/31 B0863/08 B1256/06
C0062/27 C0084/07 C0151/05 C0179/07
C0179/36 C0184/02 C0189/09 C0191/36
C0411/11 C0531/10 C0539/14
rites (1) C0108/05
ritual (1) A0409/13
Rituel (2) A0104/11 A0106/02
Ritzner (6) A0293/05 A0296/V
A0298/06 A0299/03 A0300/19 A0301/34
rival (17) A0019/15
A0020/06 A0022/09 A0433/29 A0434/16
A0435/29 A0437/05 A0445/35 A0446/01
A0665/05 B1133/32 B1133/V B1134/07
B1145/04 B1194/26 B1295/21 B1311/15
rivaling (1) A0312/V
rivalled (1) B0889/28
rivalling (1) A0312/09
rivalry (6) A0177/V A0204/10
A0432/10 A0432/32 A0496/22 B1132/10
rivals (1) B1136/11
river (181)
river's (4) A0195/08
B0739/31 B0764/32 B1260/09
riverence> (2) A0467/V A0470/17
rivers (12) A0602/11
A0610/01 B0863/25 B1161/01 C0527/33
C0528/11 C0551/14 C0551/16 C0551/22
C0551/34 C0574/28 C0575/17
rivet (2) B0810/28 B0890/21
riveted (19) A0027/01
A0029/01 A0153/06 A0166/23 A0211/29
A0214/29 A0327/01 A0429/05 A0536/01
A0664/20 A0689/25 B0826/06 B0887/05
B0889/11 B0892/23 B0903/09 B0932/28
B0991/32 B1181/29
rivets (1) B1339/03
rivetted (5) A0022/V
A0153/V A0325/V A0326/V A0327/V
rivulet (10) A0495/V A0602/13
B0864/08 B0864/18 B1302/33 B1333/12
B1334/08 B1334/13 C0180/34 C0561/29
rivulets (1) A0639/28
road (26) A0081/07 B0735/25
B0758/06 B0767/06 B1048/34 B1049/01
B1126/17 B1160/26 B1296/02 B1299/10
B1312/02 B1328/03 B1329/13 B1329/16
B1330/13 B1330/19 B1333/08 B1335/08
B1337/06 B1338/10 B1338/13 B1345/03
B1346/14 B1362/05 C0172/23 C0523/08
road-side (1) B0760/17

roads (16) A0365/03
B1295/04 B1295/22 B1297/24 B1297/30
B1298/03 B1298/04 B1298/08 B1310/17
B1311/18 B1316/08 B1316/16 B1316/18
B1317/03 B1317/09 B1329/29
roadside (1) B0735/18
roam (1) B1004/18
roamed (9) A0410/32
A0640/16 B0858/18 B0862/12 B0945/20
B1123/01 B1334/26 C0169/25 C0412/30
roaming (4) A0210/26
A0533/05 B0734/30 B1005/13
roams (1) B0963/09
Roanoke/Island (1) B0933/11
roar (10) A0088/04 A0125/16
A0249/07 A0428/08 A0580/34 A0581/24
A0583/17 B1158/09 C0061/20 C0072/29
roared (13) A0047/V
A0054/24 A0197/17 A0373/14 A0384/08
A0582/04 B0824/10 B0975/34 B1013/18
B1110/08 B1348/07 B1350/13 C0117/22
roaring (10) A0029/15 A0146/07
A0588/11 B1090/33 C0063/03 C0102/31
C0110/16 C0387/21 C0396/26 C0420/27
roarings (2) A0056/20 A0066/09
roars (1) B1092/36
roast (1) C0069/24
roasted (3) B1010/27
B1167/10 C0093/02
roasting (1) A0495/V
robbed (3) A0564/06
B0977/03 B0977/27
robber (3) A0555/01
B0976/33 B0977/24
robber's (3) B0976/18
B0976/33 B0977/23
robbers (2) B0793/29 C0549/42
robbery (3) A0244/07
A0564/05 C0569/01
robbing (1) B1207/31
robe (10) A0614/08 A0685/34
A0686/28 A0691/32 A0692/03 A0693/04
A0694/32 B0896/12 C0542/13 C0552/11
robe-de-chambre (3) A0034/16
A0034/25 A0545/06
robed (1) B0945/19
Robert (7) A0178/20
A0178/30 C0066/32 C0531/17 C0535/16
C0541/06 C0548/34
Robert's (1) A0656/03
robes (3) A0407/25
A0416/28 A0428/33
Robesp-- (1) A0112/26
robust (5) A0064/18
A0144/14 A0675/29 B0958/19 B1057/16
Rochefoucault (1) B0985/02
Rocher/de/Cancale (2) A0175/17
A0181/07
rock (49) A0044/30
A0146/14 A0195/17 A0196/10 A0196/11
A0196/12 A0196/17 A0196/20 A0196/30
A0197/04 A0197/12 A0197/17 A0197/20
A0197/28 A0197/31 A0198/07 A0198/10
A0198/14 A0198/16 A0578/11 A0580/36
B0841/07 B0841/17 B0841/32 B0843/02

->B1156/11 B1162/32 B1261/24 B1281/32
B1334/33 B1335/06 C0065/21 C0150/37
C0154/37 C0165/27 C0173/18 C0174/06
C0181/29 C0183/35 C0184/03 C0184/24
C0195/06 C0196/32 C0200/19 C0208/28
C0443/V C0538/37 C0570/24 C0572/37
rock-blaster (1) C0185/01
rocked (3) A0197/28
A0415/13 A0580/36
rocking (3) A0028/24
A0415/29 C0144/17
rocking-chair (1) B1340/08
rocks (18) A0579/13 A0579/22
A0581/22 A0581/29 A0582/08 A0582/34
A0583/30 A0600/23 B0841/12 B0942/34
B1162/17 B1332/20 B1333/14 C0171/21
C0199/10 C0200/08 C0538/16 C0543/34
rocky (9) B0865/26
B1160/21 B1281/18 B1331/24 B1335/08
C0155/16 C0165/24 C0180/37 C0571/20
Rocky/Mountains (17) C0521/T
C0522/38 C0524/11 C0524/35 C0527/09
C0527/23 C0527/32 C0528/27 C0528/35
C0529/T C0540/T C0550/T C0560/T
C0571/T C0572/03 C0574/29 C0576/13
rocs (1) B1164/20
rod (14) A0351/32 A0554/08
A0554/31 A0555/02 A0566/04 A0567/21
A0568/04 A0690/21 B1077/12 B1077/22
B1080/15 B1080/17 C0115/32 C0115/34
rode (11) A0298/06
A0400/21 B0896/26 B0930/14 B1003/19
B1003/25 B1314/08 B1378/M C0061/16
C0099/14 C0099/22
Rodman (15) C0522/13
C0522/21 C0524/12 C0524/37 C0528/33
C0528/38 C0533/05 C0535/31 C0539/34
C0544/03 C0544/11 C0544/39 C0548/18
C0560/17 C0574/39
Rodman, James (3) C0522/29
C0523/27 C0533/07
Rodman, James E. (1) C0521/27
Rodman, Julius (8) C0521/30
C0521/T C0522/24 C0529/T C0540/T
C0550/T C0560/T C0571/T
Rodman's (6) C0523/10 C0523/34
C0524/22 C0538/34 C0539/17 C0550/23
rods (2) B0761/16 C0192/22
Rogers (4) C0107/32
C0108/36 C0109/36 C0112/02
Rogers, Hartman (3) C0102/20
C0103/27 C0107/22
Rogers, Mary (1) B0723/16
Rogers, Mary Cecilia (3) B0723/10
B0724/11 B0772/23
Rogers's (1) C0111/17
Roget (12) B0723/18
B0723/T B0726/07 B0729/13 B0729/20
B0731/26 B0732/30 B0732/32 B0753/15
B0755/16 B0755/19 B0974/V
Roget, Estelle (1) B0725/18
Roget, Marie (22) B0725/14 B0729/05
B0731/21 B0731/31 B0731/35 B0732/05
B0732/25 B0734/36 B0736/02 B0737/18
B0737/29 B0738/16 B0743/35 B0745/09
->B0753/06 B0754/01 B0758/11 B0761/34
B0771/03 B0772/24 B0772/V B0974/12
Roget's (1) B0733/25
rogue (1) A0090/25
Roi (1) A0037/21
roisterers (1) A0514/16
role (1) A0534/18
role (2) A0675/20 A0675/V
roles (1) B1347/14
roll (18) A0195/22 A0236/V
A0345/31 A0613/10 B0980/03 B1143/03
B1237/19 C0062/13 C0071/27 C0074/31
C0112/26 C0113/18 C0113/39 C0116/05
C0139/26 C0141/02 C0143/40 C0541/18
rolled (42) A0078/36 A0139/V
A0158/02 A0197/27 A0210/12 A0219/05
A0234/17 A0236/01 A0242/12 A0244/15
A0248/14 A0252/17 A0253/23 A0355/19
A0355/30 A0406/03 A0489/13 A0508/04
A0512/34 A0538/V A0616/14 A0628/02
A0695/12 B0864/14 B0898/12 B0913/17
B0975/16 B1012/11 B1021/13 B1101/01
B1185/04 B1239/21 B1242/20 B1250/22
B1352/05 C0059/27 C0099/16 C0100/09
C0102/36 C0107/18 C0390/13 C0568/01
rolling (20) A0143/24
A0190/21 A0275/35 A0355/03 B0930/31
B1278/36 B1280/26 B1372/06 C0074/08
C0094/18 C0097/41 C0117/17 C0131/22
C0143/29 C0144/14 C0144/27 C0152/39
C0165/10 C0205/25 C0579/08
rollings (1) C0097/16
rolls (3) B1119/M
B1180/11 C0120/05
Roman (10) A0018/V A0044/06
A0044/V A0045/23 A0045/26 A0089/06
A0122/23 A0165/02 B1130/03 B1361/07
Roman/Empire (1) A0120/25
romance (11) A0151/18
A0311/12 A0533/26 B0747/25 B0866/21
B0905/14 B1123/09 B1123/13 B1338/34
B1339/04 B1339/05
romancer (1) A0414/33
romances (1) A0413/06
Romances B1381/26
Romans (4) A0046/21
A0091/22 A0110/25 B1089/06
romantic (12) A0311/08
B0748/15 B0893/03 B0899/07 B0899/18
B0908/17 B0910/13 B0957/27 B1076/15
B1122/26 C0521/25 C0565/08
romantic-looking (1) C0564/23
romanticist (1) B0955/01
Rombert (1) A0034/17
Rome (10) A0044/17 A0108/23
A0109/02 A0122/24 A0175/29 A0181/24
A0196/23 A0445/04 A0445/31 A0446/20
Ronald's, E. (1) C0057/12
roof (22) A0367/14 A0389/07
A0400/18 A0406/35 A0417/10 A0542/19
A0672/09 A0696/11 B0768/28 B0965/36
B1165/05 B1261/15 B1279/10 B1336/02
B1336/05 B1336/06 B1336/15 B1336/16
B1337/21 B1338/06 B1351/22 B1354/25
roofed (1) A0626/26

roofs (7) A0244/23
B0980/V B1160/11 B1336/10 B1336/12
B1336/13 B1336/20
rookeries (2) C0152/04 C0153/13
rookery (6) C0151/24 C0152/03
C0152/24 C0152/34 C0153/10 C0153/25
room (165)
rooms (19) A0174/32
A0176/25 A0180/23 A0182/28 A0446/23
A0539/15 A0542/10 A0543/09 A0546/33
A0551/16 A0671/16 A0673/29 A0675/29
A0676/10 B0726/03 B0904/18 B0928/22
B1258/28 B1362/14
roomy (4) B0922/19
C0068/08 C0070/25 C0539/07
rooster (1) B1159/02
root (13) A0612/36
A0614/32 B1093/04 B1163/18 B1163/19
B1182/14 B1248/12 C0138/07 C0173/04
C0174/38 C0207/43 C0207/43 C0208/06
rooted (3) A0217/V
A0438/19 C0112/28
roots (11) A0195/20
A0344/02 A0351/21 A0537/31 A0557/17
A0557/19 B0988/06 B1160/38 B1162/34
C0072/19 C0533/01
rope (59)
ropes (11) A0351/13
B0730/09 B1346/18 C0119/07 C0119/30
C0120/07 C0144/01 C0406/28 C0409/20
C0415/22 C0415/26
roguelaire (3) A0512/04
B1258/19 B1260/29
Rose (1) B1384/20
rose (22) A0137/11 A0140/14
A0515/16 A0533/19 A0585/23 A0587/33
B0734/02 B0748/18 B0854/28 B1076/04
B1156/15 B1353/20 C0060/15 C0068/26
C0072/18 C0073/13 C0082/24 C0086/38
C0405/20 C0444/V C0537/04 C0553/18
rose-bud (1) B1384/22
rose-bushes (3) C0566/18
C0577/19 C0577/34
rose-water (1) A0613/04
rose-wood (5) A0034/21
A0501/10 A0502/20 A0502/22 A0502/23
rosemary (1) A0603/25
roses (4) A0228/25
A0233/06 A0330/07 C0576/07
Ross (6) C0066/27 C0066/31
C0092/18 C0430/21 C0430/23 C0535/33
Ross, Alexander (2) A0173/02
A0176/11
Ross' (1) B1169/34
rot (1) B1373/04
rotate (2) B1322/10 B1382/22
rotated (3) B1321/04
B1321/05 B1321/32
rotating (2) B1382/08 B1382/17
rotation (10) B1321/04 B1321/06
B1321/16 B1321/21 B1321/22 B1322/24
B1322/25 B1382/23 B1382/26 C0426/12
rotted (3) A0400/14
B0957/08 B1243/04
rotten (5) B0735/10
->B0759/05 B0820/12 B0820/13 B0820/14
rottenness (1) A0142/32
Rotterdam (27) C0387/01
C0387/10 C0387/22 C0388/03 C0388/16
C0388/23 C0388/35 C0388/41 C0390/08
C0390/14 C0390/25 C0390/39 C0391/03
C0391/15 C0391/26 C0393/29 C0399/27
C0412/22 C0414/13 C0425/21 C0426/22
C0427/05 C0427/16 C0427/26 C0427/34
C0437/V C0443/V
Rotterdam/College (1) C0390/34
rotting (2) A0244/05 B1160/38
rotund (5) A0070/23
A0265/20 A0271/04 A0275/34 B1106/33
Rotunda (1) A0294/V
rotundity (3) A0099/30
C0097/35 C0389/18
Rouen (3) A0096/03
A0096/17 A0099/13
rouge (2) B0911/09 B0914/11
Rouge-et-Noir (2) A0204/33 A0205/25
rough (26) A0045/23 A0388/10
A0468/16 A0537/16 A0609/32 B0763/34
B0809/16 B0828/28 B0857/06 B0960/20
B1078/17 B1226/05 B1359/27 B1379/23
B1391/08 C0058/29 C0123/10 C0132/35
C0140/10 C0140/28 C0147/11 C0173/06
C0202/17 C0204/15 C0429/17 C0570/23
rough-looking (2) B0968/07 C0061/09
roughened (2) A0592/12 A0592/16
rougher (2) B1226/06 C0200/18
roughly (5) A0243/24
A0443/19 B1333/21 C0055/34 C0169/16
roughness (1) C0098/28
Roule (2) B0726/26 B0737/16
round (114)
roundabout (1) C0395/15
rounded (6) A0035/18 A0087/21
A0503/02 A0604/23 B1333/26 C0165/16
rounding (1) C0159/11
roundly (1) B1383/04
roundness (2) B0890/09 B1165/02
rounds (3) A0530/23
B1358/21 B1380/12
roused (1) C0133/15
rousing (1) A0368/01
Rousseau (3) A0053/14
A0062/V A0568/26
rout (3) A0319/03
A0385/05 B1260/V
route (32) A0490/20
A0490/26 A0514/20 A0577/04 A0626/25
A0655/18 B0735/30 B0749/25 B0763/19
B0767/20 B0864/16 B0865/13 B0872/29
B0909/22 B1002/02 B1052/06 B1260/34
B1299/07 B1317/17 C0148/20 C0176/31
C0177/35 C0199/10 C0420/01 C0525/25
C0526/25 C0527/10 C0527/36 C0536/22
C0558/26 C0565/02 C0569/39
routes (4) A0240/M
B0749/33 B1048/27 B1317/18
routine (6) A0434/11 A0485/34
A0489/12 A0532/18 B0985/30 C0414/34
roved (1) C0551/35
roving (2) C0532/17 C0547/13

row (5) A0140/08
A0366/33 A0657/30 B1259/23 C0556/24
row-de-dowed (1) B1017/25
Rowdy-dow (1) B1129/V
Rowdy-Dow (13) B1129/25
B1129/32 B1130/28 B1131/22 B1131/26
B1134/19 B1136/11 B1136/32 B1137/28
B1138/25 B1144/25 B1145/03 B1145/07
rowed (1) C0533/03
Rowena (10) A0323/21 A0325/13
A0325/20 A0325/24 A0326/20 A0327/11
A0329/16 A0329/V A0330/02 A0330/03
rowers (1) C0200/23
rowing (5) B0753/23
C0536/03 C0538/05 C0556/10 C0569/39
rows (2) B1156/24 C0091/34
Royal (2) A0179/29 A0337/18
royal (14) A0122/21 A0174/14
A0174/V A0175/02 A0179/35 A0250/08
A0250/13 B0976/12 B0977/03 B0991/18
B1153/10 B1345/22 C0151/10 C0151/21
Royal/Geographical/Soc. (1) C0162/03
Royal/Hydographical/Soc. (1) C0156/38
Royal/Philippine/Co. (1) C0156/35
rub (2) A0489/15 B1131/28
Rubadub (4) C0390/32
C0390/37 C0426/32 C0426/38
rubbed (10) A0035/01 A0694/07
B0732/27 B0854/15 B0944/11 B1372/23
C0061/21 C0078/18 C0080/06 C0081/24
rubber (3) B0880/07
B1293/07 B1293/08
rubbing (8) B0808/22
B1178/15 C0079/15 C0081/23 C0109/05
C0141/10 C0191/09 C0569/28
rubbing-post (1) B1107/05
rubbish (11) A0090/02
A0243/V A0244/26 B0857/21 B1128/19
C0077/32 C0152/25 C0181/22 C0183/08
C0183/28 C0389/04
Rubens (2) A0175/24 A0181/21
rubicund (2) A0510/18 B1057/20
rubies (2) B0827/35 B1280/25
Rubini (1) B0925/10
rubs (1) C0547/22
ruby (3) A0035/11
A0325/23 A0407/16
ruby-colored (1) A0325/V
ruby-drops (1) A0326/02
ruby-red (3) A0640/03
A0640/33 A0643/07
rudder (22) A0137/16 B0754/08
B0770/21 B0770/24 B0770/25 B0771/29
B0815/09 B1071/25 B1071/30 B1071/V
B1073/34 B1075/25 B1077/01 B1077/04
B1079/18 B1315/24 C0106/31 C0106/33
C0115/24 C0115/28 C0115/33 C0162/33
rudderless (2) A0638/12 B0771/30
ruddier (1) A0674/07
ruddy (2) A0022/23 C0405/31
rude (6) A0249/10 A0251/03
A0479/16 B0822/13 B0841/20 C0195/13
rudely (6) A0046/19 A0689/01
B0835/04 B1011/28 B1281/20 C0552/13
rudeness (5) A0379/29
->A0443/01 A0676/31 B0894/12 B1107/31
rudiment (1) B1296/37
rudimental (16) B1037/05
B1037/13 B1037/14 B1037/15 B1037/17
B1037/24 B1037/32 B1038/08 B1038/10
B1038/18 B1038/20 B1038/20 B1038/25
B1038/26 B1038/28 B1039/03
rudiments (3) B1158/29
B1160/38 B1250/24
Rue (11) A0561/01
B0723/T B0724/12 B0725/22 B0726/19
B0726/24 B0729/05 B0729/09 B0729/31
B0732/36 B0758/20
rue (1) A0603/25
Rue/des/Dromes (8) B0729/10
B0729/24 B0731/28 B0734/16 B0755/22
B0755/32 B0756/13 B0756/27
Rue/C-- (2) A0535/01 A0535/21
Rue/Deloraine (1) A0541/11
Rue/Dubourg (1) A0563/02
Rue/Dunot (1) B0974/04
Rue/Montmartre (1) A0531/28
Rue/Morgue (16) A0527/T
A0527/V A0537/09 A0538/28 A0542/26
A0546/12 A0563/14 A0563/28 A0565/20
A0566/14 B0725/01 B0725/16 B0736/20
B0737/33 B0974/11 B1380/04
Rue/Richelieu (1) A0546/13
Rue/St./Denis (1) A0534/17
Rue/St./Roch (1) A0546/13
Rue/Trianon (1) A0544/V
ruffian (4) B0760/04
B1103/18 B1109/10 C0101/15
ruffianly (1) C0085/33
ruffians (11) A0510/05
B0749/05 B0750/24 B0757/20 B0757/32
B0763/24 B0763/33 B0768/18 B0769/23
C0088/16 C0091/12
ruffle (2) A0246/28 B0810/21
ruffles (1) C0431/05
ruffling (1) A0446/26
rug (2) A0054/25 A0063/25
rugged (7) A0047/17
A0711/20 B1276/21 B1281/33 C0172/19
C0192/03 C0424/05
ruin (11) A0140/21
A0145/06 A0249/28 A0442/16 A0457/19
A0461/15 A0611/11 A0623/08 A0623/19
C0398/37 C0443/V
ruined (1) B1092/24
ruinous (4) A0121/22
A0489/03 B1222/07 C0414/27
ruins (8) A0159/03
A0210/29 B0853/04 B1192/17 C0184/33
C0190/07 C0198/36 C0565/33
rule (22) A0250/03 A0458/29
A0482/23 A0529/32 A0592/25 A0710/26
A0710/27 B0740/25 B0740/25 B0740/26
B0740/31 B0741/01 B0741/02 B0741/35
B0743/29 B1115/32 B1135/17 B1183/27
B1208/29 B1275/28 B1275/30 B1315/25
rule-of-three (1) A0483/02
ruler (2) A0407/14 A0642/13
rules (5) A0269/08
A0302/14 A0529/28 B0979/24 B1116/03

ruleth (1) A0645/06
ruling (3) B1380/24
C0087/21 C0087/23
rum (7) B0760/20
B0854/04 B1102/24 B1106/17 C0086/29
C0101/16 C0111/01
rum-puncheon (1) A0337/16
rumbling (4) A0696/27
B1102/07 B1102/35 C0396/26
Rumgudgeon (12) A0649/03
A0651/23 A0652/23 A0653/12 A0654/24
A0654/V A0655/05 A0655/10 A0655/V
A0656/26 A0657/02 A0657/23
ruminate (1) B1047/05
ruminating (1) A0212/13
rummaged (1) B1363/02
rummages (1) B1163/35
rummaging (4) A0055/11
A0064/26 C0079/13 C0085/29
rummer (1) A0340/02
rumor (4) A0434/20
A0674/25 A0690/26 B0728/03
rumors (8) A0685/11
B0731/19 B0834/02 B0834/03 B0834/04
B0834/08 B1361/22 C0427/09
rump (1) C0534/40
rumpled (2) B0766/20 B0766/20
run (60)
runaway (1) B1101/11
rung (1) B0980/05
rungs (1) B0980/07
running (43) A0127/21
A0242/15 A0267/30 A0274/29 A0274/34
A0285/01 A0285/34 A0314/15 A0374/04
A0399/09 A0483/V A0484/05 A0487/08
B0864/20 B0873/20 B0879/31 B0932/16
B1091/24 B1105/32 B1235/27 B1336/32
B1339/34 C0060/10 C0061/12 C0084/06
C0088/27 C0102/35 C0108/40 C0124/17
C0158/32 C0161/31 C0162/05 C0163/30
C0173/34 C0185/12 C0409/28 C0420/13
C0425/38 C0527/02 C0530/07 C0537/07
C0574/32 C0578/08
runs (13) A0128/05
A0366/09 A0535/08 A0554/08 A0581/23
A0622/14 A0628/31 B0837/02 B1122/10
B1209/05 B1250/20 C0152/22 C0430/27
rupture (1) C0185/16
rural (1) B0760/14
ruse (1) C0056/14
ruses (1) B0988/26
rush (19) A0195/22
A0319/14 A0349/24 A0407/40 A0515/08
A0694/16 B0963/33 B0966/25 B1057/15
B1069/01 B1134/32 B1352/14 B1372/28
B1374/25 C0073/12 C0086/07 C0105/20
C0186/18 C0579/05
rushed (37) A0138/28
A0217/V A0245/05 A0254/02 A0326/15
A0415/30 A0513/11 A0537/15 A0567/V
A0590/06 A0605/04 A0651/20 A0676/18
A0691/23 A0696/10 A0696/16 A0697/09
B0809/21 B0944/01 B0947/11 B0983/16
B0992/14 B1021/10 B1182/22 B1352/04
C0124/15 C0174/17 C0190/19 C0190/40
->C0199/13 C0201/21 C0206/04 C0422/39
C0539/10 C0568/30 C0572/10 C0579/20
rushes (1) B0738/26
rushing (32) A0101/25
A0137/07 A0146/12 A0195/13 A0253/21
A0324/24 A0324/28 A0327/30 A0329/25
A0330/14 A0416/25 A0417/14 A0442/29
A0456/04 A0507/25 A0565/23 A0676/03
A0682/16 A0683/33 A0691/02 B0862/13
B0932/13 B1223/07 B1350/24 C0060/19
C0063/24 C0134/31 C0197/38 C0205/37
C0396/33 C0536/35 C0562/35
rushlight (1) B0898/02
Russell/Square (1) A0464/04
russet (1) B1053/22
russet-leather (1) B1053/V
Russia (4) A0543/07
A0550/03 C0160/05 C0524/36
Russian (4) A0543/06
A0550/03 C0526/17 C0526/21
Russians (1) A0496/04
rust (1) A0553/21
rustled (1) A0411/23
rustling (5) A0081/04
A0195/21 A0197/01 B0964/32 C0188/26
rusty (3) A0500/22
A0649/01 C0398/05
ruts (1) A0535/31
rxlling (1) B1374/19
RICHEL (1) A0093/15
S (1) A0337/20
S. (19) A0138/16
C0150/05 C0150/07 C0150/38 C0154/23
C0155/09 C0155/15 C0157/08 C0157/09
C0157/10 C0157/26 C0158/14 C0160/31
C0161/03 C0161/29 C0162/23 C0163/04
C0166/03 C0399/22
S./E. (2) A0138/15 C0540/14
S./W. (1) C0527/02
S.C. (3) B0922/01
B1068/03 B1069/13
S.D.U.K. (2) A0337/18 A0337/21
S-- (3) B0896/27 B0900/20 B0991/16
s'echapper (1) A0036/22
s'il (3) A0033/19
A0037/25 B0993/27
sa (2) A0654/06 C0430/41
sabage (1) B0826/27
Sabbath (3) B0750/14
B0760/11 B0771/34
sable (15) A0081/11
A0088/16 A0090/09 A0091/10 A0190/22
A0190/24 A0246/04 A0249/11 A0532/28
A0674/08 A0674/09 A0676/24 A0682/01
A0684/02 B0963/34
sable-bound (1) A0090/04
sable-feathered (1) A0152/04
Sabretash (1) B1179/12
Sabretash, Arthur (1) B1178/34
sac (1) A0096/M
sack (2) B1165/11 B1185/34
sackbut (1) A0047/26
sacking (4) A0543/19
A0553/02 A0557/V B1053/28
sacks (1) B0827/09

sacre (6) A0101/V A0540/11
A0541/10 A0541/31 A0541/V A0541/V
sacred (9) A0085/03
A0250/10 A0429/17 B0945/21 B0961/35
B0965/21 B1318/01 B1318/08 C0132/15
sacrifice (12) A0227/32
A0346/24 A0589/01 A0684/27 B0728/14
B0902/25 B0902/26 B0908/13 B0910/09
B1089/23 B1152/28 C0529/02
sacrificed (6) A0033/09 A0357/10
A0600/08 C0092/12 C0100/08 C0107/12
sacrifices (1) A0043/09
sacrificing (2) C0175/19 C0558/11
sacrilege (1) A0675/V
sacrumstance (1) B0821/05
sad (37) A0089/29
A0127/24 A0180/25 A0210/02 A0234/30
A0413/10 A0602/11 A0603/19 A0609/06
A0609/06 A0613/32 A0614/12 A0616/12
A0622/12 A0622/23 A0631/08 A0641/19
A0653/08 A0664/V A0667/43 A0683/03
B0729/03 B0757/02 B0772/28 B0814/34
B0879/31 B0933/16 B0964/28 B0964/31
B0969/12 B1046/06 B1133/07 B1263/03
B1385/36 C0076/12 C0131/29 C0547/32
saddened (2) B0726/11 C0537/14
saddle (2) A0027/01 A0028/13
saddle-bags (2) B1044/17 B1046/21
sadly (7) A0321/10
A0643/12 B0822/34 B0932/28 B1009/01
C0115/18 C0130/09
sadness (1) B0892/29
safe (19) A0538/03
B0820/26 B1018/04 B1105/23 B1157/14
B1225/07 B1225/10 B1225/11 B1298/26
B1390/06 B1391/30 B1391/31 C0068/20
C0096/32 C0109/16 C0135/22 C0202/19
C0399/12 C0530/16
safeguard (1) B1221/10
safely (16) A0053/29
A0062/33 A0564/25 A0610/31 A0667/10
B0739/18 B0924/33 B0930/14 B1010/24
B1082/05 B1386/06 C0099/35 C0179/28
C0393/02 C0536/20 C0575/42
safer (3) A0074/24
B1115/34 B1220/12
safety (25) A0127/10
A0265/32 A0585/36 B0827/05 B0931/15
B1076/22 B1078/32 B1106/33 B1352/19
C0067/35 C0070/32 C0082/01 C0121/31
C0129/04 C0133/30 C0144/31 C0170/39
C0186/10 C0198/30 C0397/37 C0409/03
C0424/02 C0425/22 C0555/29 C0568/05
saffron (2) A0195/05 A0245/23
saffron-like (1) C0126/05
sagacious (7) A0350/03
A0670/10 B0747/10 B0850/16 B0850/28
B0977/32 B0990/17
sagaciously (3) A0704/23
B1052/02 B1269/23
sagacity (17) A0027/V
A0055/16 A0098/09 A0301/08 A0434/02
B0793/22 B1035/10 B1049/14 B1052/27
B1136/04 B1294/32 C0079/08 C0086/14
C0532/33 C0546/13 C0546/24 C0547/08
sage (1) A0096/M
sage (2) B1115/01 B1181/18
sages (1) B1189/26
said (750)
sail (55)
sail-boat (2) B0770/25 C0057/26
sailed (16) A0135/23
A0657/18 A0657/19 C0057/14 C0099/04
C0099/08 C0146/33 C0148/06 C0148/12
C0156/36 C0157/12 C0157/18 C0158/28
C0160/29 C0161/27 C0164/17
sailer (1) C0147/10
sailing (2) B0923/30 C0071/40
sailor (13) A0560/29
A0561/04 A0561/13 A0562/16 A0562/28
A0564/11 A0566/01 A0566/08 A0566/24
B0769/02 B0835/21 B1154/33 B1155/17
sailor's (5) A0563/19
A0564/V A0567/21 B0730/34 B0768/32
sailors (4) A0560/24
A0561/08 A0561/09 C0064/32
sailors' (1) A0564/30
sails (15) A0136/30
A0142/10 A0585/33 B0754/06 B1164/29
C0101/34 C0105/37 C0106/16 C0123/16
C0123/32 C0131/14 C0170/11 C0188/07
C0189/27 C0566/28
Saint (10) B0751/V B0751/V
B0752/V B0755/V B0755/V B0755/V
B0756/V B0756/V B0756/V B0756/V
saint (2) A0075/12 A0642/15
Saint/Andree (3) B0725/22
B0726/19 B0726/24
Saint/Benoist (1) C0430/30
Saint/Vitusse (1) B0911/27
saints (1) A0044/12
sais (1) A0380/07
saith (2) A0085/10 A0311/V
sake (31) A0248/10
A0532/26 A0534/21 A0549/03 A0600/12
A0629/09 B0852/18 B0870/14 B0873/28
B0903/29 B0903/29 B0907/19 B0907/26
B0908/01 B0908/07 B0908/13 B0910/09
B1078/32 B1114/11 B1115/17 B1139/11
B1191/33 B1221/03 B1242/24 B1278/12
B1345/13 C0059/18 C0083/23 C0093/15
C0411/08 C0546/34
Sal (1) C0148/14
salad-bowl (1) A0345/14
Salamanca (1) C0432/29
salamander (1) B1370/02
salamanders (1) B1167/08
salary (2) B0879/02 B1142/09
sale (2) A0485/19 B1129/24
Sale's (1) B1165/33
Salem/Mass. (1) B1163/13
salis (1) B1364/03
Salle (1) A0216/08
salle (2) B1007/27 C0430/31
sallied (1) A0533/04
sallies (1) B0811/05
sally (4) B0947/11
B0947/28 B0949/20 B1244/06
Salmanezer (2) A0059/07 A0061/03
Salmon (1) C0527/14

salmon (1) C0174/05
->C0167/28 C0171/01
saloon (5) A0209/15
B1351/15 B1351/30 B1352/13 B1354/26
saloons (1) B1298/37
Salsafette (2) B1014/18 B1014/22
Salsafette, Eugenie (1) B1014/11
salt (15) A0488/14
B0866/15 B0866/17 B0933/02 B0933/03
B0933/31 C0067/33 C0078/32 C0091/06
C0137/10 C0148/15 C0535/01 C0535/37
C0570/19 C0577/24
salt-cellar (1) B1104/06
salted (1) B1181/09
salts (4) A0174/14
A0179/29 C0553/02 C0572/13
salubrity (1) C0156/15
salusque (1) A0681/M
saluted (2) B1078/13 B1133/16
salva (1) A0638/M
salvation (7) A0057/31
A0068/15 A0137/10 A0483/27 B0932/02
B1020/31 C0187/37
Salvator (1) B0865/27
Salvatorish (1) B1332/08
Salvinam (1) A0072/32
Samaria (2) A0059/08 A0061/04
same (273)
sameness (3) A0226/30
A0231/04 B1347/34
San/Carlo (1) A0079/08
San/Carlos (1) B0905/18
San/Marco (1) A0151/25
San/Miguel (1) C0157/40
Sanconiathon (2) A0090/25 A0090/26
Sancta (1) A0227/31
sanctified (1) A0479/14
sanctify (1) B0955/03
sanctimoniousness (1) B0888/21
sanction (1) B0959/35
sanctity (5) A0099/18
A0104/17 A0105/24 B1298/01 B1317/34
sanctuary (2) A0046/18 A0124/11
sanctum (4) A0099/12
A0100/26 A0100/27 A0430/04
sanctum (1) A0261/04
sand (16) B0806/08
B0830/15 B1081/26 B1160/27 B1161/29
B1165/11 B1192/18 C0155/04 C0389/35
C0437/V C0540/22 C0559/36 C0573/34
C0576/22 C0577/22 C0578/03
sand-bar (3) C0533/38
C0559/23 C0559/31
sand-bars (2) C0543/03 C0559/17
sand-island (1) C0542/33
sand-plains (1) C0072/25
sandalled (1) A0035/22
sandals (1) A0089/14
Sandflesen (2) A0579/27 A0584/02
sandhills (1) B1160/28
sands (4) A0045/15
A0163/01 B1155/28 C0559/34
sandstone (2) C0573/09 C0573/22
Sandwich (1) C0162/10
Sandwich/Land (1) C0160/14
sandy (3) B1361/06

sane (5) A0693/26
B1004/22 B1016/09 B1018/11 B1363/36
sang (6) A0190/07 A0190/19
A0510/26 A0527/M B0904/29 B1123/01
sangsue (1) B0950/11
sangsues (1) B0950/07
sanguine (2) B0842/14 B0888/26
sanguinis (2) A0125/06 A0681/M
sanity (7) A0643/02
B0844/05 B1004/29 B1018/09 B1247/32
C0078/26 C0087/32
sank (24) A0235/V
A0316/23 A0325/16 A0594/02 A0604/10
A0609/07 A0641/08 A0682/14 B0865/17
B0913/24 B0932/31 B0932/35 B0962/33
B0963/32 B1013/12 B1134/28 B1135/03
B1161/35 B1161/36 B1354/10 C0074/06
C0074/22 C0076/15 C0567/39
sans (1) A0096/M
Sanscrit (1) A0344/10
Santa/Croix (1) C0146/34
Sante (6) A0558/15 B1002/03
B1003/19 B1006/34 B1007/08 B1009/22
Saonie/Sioux (1) C0561/31
Saonies (3) C0551/18
C0551/26 C0562/32
sap (1) B1160/40
sapientiae (2) A0568/V B0974/M
sapphires (2) B0827/36 B1280/25
Saracen (2) A0022/09 A0023/14
Saracenic (1) A0321/25
saracenic (1) B1282/V
Saratoga (2) B0941/04 B0949/04
sarcasm (3) A0299/05
A0568/12 B1380/33
sarcastic (3) A0435/09
A0437/32 A0444/01
sarcophagi (1) A0326/08
sarcophagus (2) A0322/04 B0956/26
Sardanapalus (2) A0059/09 A0061/04
Sarmatic (1) A0125/35
sartain (3) B0812/21
B0820/01 B0824/09
sarvant> (1) A0465/29
sarvice> (1) A0465/16
sash (8) A0068/19
A0367/13 A0552/05 A0552/21 A0552/27
A0552/33 A0553/23 A0553/26
sashes (3) A0414/09
A0552/15 A0552/18
Saskatchawine (5) C0526/04
C0526/40 C0550/32 C0551/35 C0572/05
sassafras (2) B0761/18 B1332/09
sasso (1) B0905/14
sat (85)
Satanic (3) A0034/30
A0035/24 A0090/12
sate (5) A0414/16
A0608/13 A0665/V B0905/01 B0909/V
satellite (10) A0417/13 C0422/06
C0424/05 C0424/28 C0425/28 C0426/06
C0428/22 C0429/23 C0432/02 C0432/47
satellite's (1) C0426/12
satellites (5) A0457/23

->A0458/32 B1322/12 B1322/16 C0423/27
satiata (1) A0681/M
satiated (1) B1391/14
satiating (1) B1277/07
satin (8) A0336/07
A0339/05 A0349/12 A0371/09 A0464/02
B1093/31 B1279/10 C0389/25
satin-like (2) A0087/04 A0100/15
satin-wood (1) B1281/05
satire (2) B1130/12 B1381/05
Satires (2) A0172/M A0178/M
satirical (1) C0433/04
satirically (1) B1133/32
satirist (2) A0088/11 A0536/15
satisfaction (29) A0098/04
A0104/35 A0354/20 A0356/07 A0379/02
A0469/19 A0484/27 A0487/21 B0748/32
B0814/19 B0816/22 B1105/25 B1133/01
B1155/15 B1206/13 B1219/19 B1224/25
B1262/16 B1271/10 B1378/02 C0069/26
C0088/21 C0175/31 C0188/15 C0397/35
C0409/05 C0419/05 C0569/26 C0575/23
satisfactorily (4) A0560/30
B0731/17 B0733/21 B0879/09
satisfactory (20) A0104/20
A0107/02 A0272/02 A0303/12 A0366/07
B0729/27 B0940/01 B0983/26 B1021/16
B1089/08 B1101/14 B1116/03 B1135/23
B1135/35 B1140/07 B1141/34 C0080/29
C0177/31 C0207/10 C0420/05
satisfied (53)
satisfy (15) A0302/23
B0751/18 B0874/08 B0966/30 B1031/02
B1126/10 B1137/10 B1257/33 B1359/15
C0135/20 C0146/09 C0176/23 C0191/20
C0393/09 C0569/06
satisfying (5) A0121/26
A0383/11 C0158/09 C0195/25 C0397/25
sattinet (1) A0485/02
saturated (3) B1350/37
C0146/10 C0578/27
Saturday (8) A0337/35
A0428/24 B1044/13 B1069/15 B1072/33
B1075/20 B1075/33 B1236/02
Saturday/Evening/Post (1) B0735/37
Saturn (3) B1322/13
C0423/32 C0429/29
Saturnian (1) A0316/18
saturnine (2) A0104/12 C0533/11
Saturnus (1) A0189/15
Satyr (1) B1136/11
satyr (1) A0124/14
Satyr-like (1) A0153/18
satyrs (1) A0409/07
sauce (3) A0175/19
A0181/08 B1007/24
saucer (1) A0369/09
sauer-kraut (3) A0368/02
A0368/13 A0370/06
Sauerkraut (1) C0391/09
sauntered (4) A0160/02
B0927/16 B1329/04 C0392/21
sauntering (2) B0807/24 B1225/08
sausage (2) B1305/03 B1305/05
sausages (4) B1119/M
->C0069/23 C0071/21 C0081/11
Sauterne (12) A0086/14
A0090/04 A0091/26 A0092/11 A0092/37
A0099/01 A0101/V A0110/27 A0112/V
A0181/14 B1017/22 B1017/30
savage (25) A0320/11
A0347/05 A0383/31 A0385/33 A0628/17
A0649/02 A0711/21 B1130/16 B1158/06
B1276/22 B1350/24 B1375/21 C0169/38
C0172/37 C0173/05 C0185/18 C0187/15
C0427/05 C0524/02 C0548/26 C0551/20
C0553/10 C0557/39 C0558/23 C0579/03
savages (67)
savans (3) B1191/20
B1295/21 B1296/01
savans (6) B1294/32 B1296/06
B1311/15 B1312/07 B1312/26 B1316/15
savant (1) A0096/M
savants (1) A0096/12
save (45) A0028/27
A0029/12 A0121/V A0189/20 A0189/34
A0190/12 A0235/10 A0310/M A0311/22
A0314/29 A0315/10 A0319/24 A0320/01
A0323/25 A0329/13 A0429/07 A0439/05
A0487/02 A0498/V A0586/32 A0602/18
A0611/20 A0625/07 A0639/19 A0640/11
A0641/04 A0643/17 A0665/31 A0673/32
A0682/04 A0685/14 A0689/27 A0693/19
B0931/26 B0961/26 B0966/04 B1169/10
B1321/25 C0083/10 C0102/18 C0114/38
C0119/02 C0132/27 C0200/35 C0565/07
saved (15) A0483/24
B0813/25 B0962/20 B1129/08 B1209/02
C0060/22 C0062/03 C0089/02 C0099/22
C0116/03 C0117/31 C0119/40 C0133/16
C0142/20 C0165/06
saving (6) A0466/08 B0931/07
C0061/28 C0073/33 C0096/24 C0202/39
savoir (1) A0033/19
savor (2) A0380/14 B0888/22
saw (263)
saw-dust (1) B0980/V
sawed (1) A0585/35
saws (3) B0871/29
B1096/26 C0148/09
sawyer (1) C0542/25
sawyers (1) C0534/10
sax (1) A0372/31
saxifrage (1) C0150/25
Saxony (2) A0498/07 A0501/24
say (609)
sayest (1) A0034/24
Saying (2) A0365/M A0481/M
saying (57)
sayings (2) A0026/16 A0198/24
says (102)
scabius (1) B1163/24
scaffold (1) A0068/22
scale (6) A0367/10 A0509/30
B0870/04 B1248/24 C0110/03 C0525/35
scales (7) B0809/09
B0815/16 B0905/20 B1156/16 B1248/24
B1250/21 C0127/41
scalp (1) A0557/20
scalpel (1) B1185/26

scalping (3) A0388/09
B1140/30 C0552/18
scaly (1) A0414/15
scamp (1) A0388/18
scamper (1) C0188/15
scampered (1) C0563/05
scampering (1) A0374/02
scampers (1) A0124/22
scan (1) B1130/24
scandalous (1) B1370/21
scanned (1) A0400/05
scant (2) A0581/01 B0807/04
scantily (1) C0078/30
scantlings (1) B0796/10
scanty (2) A0034/25 C0136/01
scapegrace (2) A0374/07 A0651/18
Scarabaei (3) B1187/30
B1188/03 B1188/23
scarabaei (1) B0808/23
Scarabaeus (9) B1187/21
B1187/22 B1187/23 B1187/25 B1187/26
B1187/31 B1188/05 B1188/13 B1188/21
scarabaeus (18) B0808/19 B0809/27
B0810/09 B0810/09 B0810/12 B0814/30
B0814/32 B0815/08 B0815/12 B0817/02
B0821/33 B0822/29 B0828/28 B0829/19
B0829/29 B0830/06 B0831/26 B0831/30
scarabaeus (1) B1180/22
scarce (6) A0159/V A0457/15
A0514/27 A0581/25 B1119/01 C0192/24
scarcely (154)
scare (1) A0690/08
scared (1) A0243/14
scarf (7) B0734/34
B0735/27 B0735/36 B0758/09 B0761/33
B0762/05 B0762/09
scarlet (11) A0641/01
A0643/11 A0670/05 A0672/06 A0675/17
B1281/01 C0151/16 C0167/16 C0167/21
C0190/29 C0543/29
scarred (1) A0580/13
scars (1) B0732/27
scattered (16) A0087/29
A0143/17 A0219/07 A0240/11 A0245/16
A0401/16 A0514/14 A0672/09 B0761/33
B1122/22 C0124/21 C0144/21 C0182/05
C0404/34 C0563/15 C0570/27
scattering (2) C0153/16 C0563/03
scene (73)
scenery (20) A0318/19
A0353/12 A0600/17 A0707/24 A0709/04
A0709/24 B0861/01 B0862/04 B0863/02
B0863/17 B0863/21 B0864/04 B0942/30
B1272/25 B1274/09 B1274/26 C0537/10
C0537/24 C0543/11 C0574/05
scenes (13) A0384/10
A0601/32 A0711/21 B0760/01 B0862/19
B0865/16 B1179/25 B1276/22 B1385/32
C0537/16 C0537/16 C0543/37 C0564/39
scenic (1) A0319/06
scent (4) A0553/10
A0690/07 B0734/10 B0843/21
scented (2) A0034/22 C0539/12
scentless (2) A0343/32 A0350/21
scents (1) C0547/22

sceptical (3) A0295/27
B1031/04 B1031/10
sceptre (2) A0021/27 B1126/05
Scheherazade (19) B1151/T
B1152/05 B1152/24 B1153/01 B1153/19
B1153/28 B1154/12 B1154/15 B1154/22
B1155/09 B1155/19 B1159/09 B1159/16
B1159/25 B1159/34 B1160/05 B1169/03
B1169/14 B1169/30
Schelling (5) A0078/43
A0079/13 A0226/27 A0231/01 A0342/V
scheme (7) A0437/08
B0747/37 B1018/22 B1070/01 B1070/30
B1350/28 C0066/19
schemes (6) A0441/06 A0445/18
A0545/10 B0891/19 B1224/08 B1300/04
Schiedam (1) B1110/22
Schiller (2) A0345/09 A0357/04
Schiller's (1) A0150/V
Schiraz (1) A0641/22
schist (2) A0175/26 A0182/06
Schlemil, Peter (1) A0054/14
Schnellpost (1) B1360/21
scholar (9) A0162/02
A0271/21 A0431/15 A0473/25 B1095/09
B1139/13 B1139/38 B1140/17 B1385/17
scholars (1) A0429/33
scholarship (1) B1380/23
scholiasts (1) A0621/20
school (18) A0079/03 A0428/12
A0428/29 A0429/18 A0430/24 A0431/V
A0432/21 A0434/12 A0435/14 A0437/01
A0710/35 B0984/11 B1003/30 B1034/26
B1096/24 B1275/35 C0057/09 C0057/12
school-boy (2) A0445/34 B1250/18
school-life (1) A0427/33
school-master (1) A0592/32
school-phraseology (1) A0431/22
school-room (1) A0429/34
schoolboy (6) A0445/V B0984/04
B0984/15 B0984/27 B0985/01 C0429/30
schoolboys (1) C0064/29
schoolfellows (1) A0434/27
schoolmates (2) A0431/12 A0436/04
schools (8) A0313/27
A0341/23 A0342/V A0610/28 A0611/07
B0752/19 B1036/02 B1036/03
schooner (37) A0240/03
C0053/T C0099/03 C0099/13 C0110/01
C0110/02 C0137/24 C0146/24 C0147/08
C0148/12 C0148/26 C0149/11 C0149/29
C0154/11 C0154/17 C0156/18 C0158/06
C0158/07 C0160/29 C0163/23 C0163/36
C0165/12 C0166/03 C0167/06 C0168/32
C0169/18 C0171/09 C0176/25 C0176/31
C0177/14 C0177/19 C0177/34 C0180/15
C0186/24 C0187/19 C0189/32 C0190/30
schooner-rigged (1) A0583/20
schooner's (1) C0170/11
schooners (1) C0103/14
schorl (2) A0175/26 A0182/07
Schouw (1) B1163/11
Schrevilius (1) B1092/04
Schroeter (1) C0423/10
Schuylkill (2) B0863/32 B0864/04

Science (3) A0599/M
C0429/26 C0429/31
science (45) A0105/11
A0135/16 A0144/22 A0173/04 A0173/13
A0176/13 A0178/09 A0178/21 A0211/21
A0295/01 A0295/02 A0313/26 A0315/27
A0399/04 A0440/22 A0527/V A0609/21
A0652/19 B0724/04 B0743/12 B0747/34
B0752/07 B0871/26 B0877/28 B0987/16
B0987/24 B1069/07 B1070/02 B1164/01
B1185/11 B1189/04 B1191/06 B1191/11
B1270/12 B1294/34 B1294/35 B1311/26
B1312/27 B1313/01 B1359/07 C0088/02
C0166/32 C0426/20 C0426/40 C0528/30
Sciences (1) B0869/T
sciences (3) B0869/05
B1303/16 B1313/11
scientific (12) A0478/23
B0815/14 B0875/31 B1072/24 B1093/21
B1357/06 B1359/30 B1361/15 B1381/20
B1381/28 C0428/05 C0433/09
scimetar-like (1) A0353/20
scimitar (2) A0691/10 A0695/03
scion (1) A0293/03
scissors (2) A0074/31 C0148/10
scoffed (2) A0710/35 B1276/01
sconces (2) B1258/27 B1351/31
scope (3) B1030/07
B1140/35 B1379/04
score (9) A0474/01
A0483/09 A0628/21 B1156/22 B1185/13
B1248/14 B1379/20 C0056/24 C0104/20
scored (1) A0241/33
scores (1) C0395/36
scoria (1) C0198/40
scorn (8) A0269/05
A0283/28 A0426/03 A0442/23 A0609/32
B0871/07 B1298/17 B1316/28
scorned (2) A0609/34 B0899/24
scorning (1) B1337/20
scorns (1) B0870/13
scorpions (1) C0199/04
Scotch (2) A0496/01 B1312/20
Scotland (1) B1160/36
Scott, Walter (1) A0205/27
Scotts, Leonard (1) B1206/10
scoundrel (12) A0094/21
A0356/23 A0374/09 A0384/11 A0447/07
A0447/08 A0650/25 A0657/V B0820/20
B0824/05 B0876/11 B0900/19
scoundrelly (2) A0355/16 A0371/23
scoundrels (3) A0073/23
A0631/22 B0916/19
scourge (1) B1219/24
scourged (1) B1379/04
scourges (1) A0081/33
scouring (1) B1244/06
scouts (1) C0535/14
scowl (2) A0303/01 A0444/31
scowling (1) A0509/34
scramble (8) B1391/05
C0091/31 C0169/06 C0191/36 C0567/30
C0572/31 C0577/30 C0579/34
scrambled (7) B0808/03
C0144/34 C0180/38 C0182/13 C0183/07
->C0553/31 C0578/21
scrambling (7) A0243/20
B0983/16 B1020/14 B1353/08 C0181/40
C0187/40 C0579/09
scrap (7) A0344/12
B0809/15 B0828/35 B0829/01 B0830/13
B0831/10 B1363/29
scrape (3) A0340/26
A0583/32 B0907/25
scraping (4) A0374/14
A0541/32 B1180/33 C0076/08
scraps (1) A0343/13
scratch (5) A0265/22
A0387/25 A0388/11 A0388/12 B1160/42
Scratchaway, Augustus (1) A0204/32
scratched (2) A0268/18 C0173/16
scratches (3) A0272/34
A0538/15 A0543/24
scratching (7) A0341/27
A0342/V A0374/02 B0809/20 B1021/09
B1107/04 C0092/01
scratchy (1) A0272/13
scrawl (2) A0275/05 A0490/15
scrawled (1) C0092/30
scream (11) A0139/30
A0384/02 A0697/05 B0797/26 B0859/02
C0060/37 C0061/19 C0124/32 C0206/01
C0571/01 C0579/01
screamed (15) A0253/02
A0353/30 A0373/16 A0384/27 A0586/25
A0587/18 B0820/30 B0914/02 B0968/08
B1353/04 C0059/19 C0083/22 C0123/23
C0198/13 C0579/19
screaming (8) A0128/18
A0347/29 A0414/30 B1017/34 B1353/13
C0064/07 C0067/24 C0187/36
screams (18) A0540/04 A0566/21
A0566/28 A0566/V B0734/26 B0735/34
B0735/35 B0750/20 B0766/05 B0766/12
B0768/02 B0768/04 B0768/07 B0992/13
B1014/24 B1262/23 C0188/31 C0191/01
screeching (1) A0374/03
screen (1) B1282/08
screw (16) A0388/18
B1070/28 B1071/10 B1071/15 B1071/18
B1071/22 B1071/23 B1071/V B1073/35
B1075/25 B1077/01 B1077/06 B1077/16
B1079/18 C0097/20 C0410/31
screw-driver (1) A0080/35
screwed (8) A0080/39
A0387/21 A0388/04 A0410/25 B1141/19
C0097/21 C0097/31 C0410/31
screwing (2) C0097/23 C0097/28
screws (4) A0080/38
A0081/09 A0081/29 A0479/27
scribble (1) B1129/25
scribbler (1) B1131/18
scribbling (1) B1115/18
scribblings (1) B1115/17
scribe (1) A0089/07
scripta (3) A0301/10
A0302/20 A0303/17
scriptural (1) A0491/11
scroll (4) A0164/V
A0271/28 B1304/02 B1322/30

scruple (12) A0073/24
A0107/24 A0382/17 A0654/12 B0851/14
B1078/12 B1167/09 B1354/15 C0093/10
C0153/11 C0164/36 C0578/40
scrupled (1) B1078/35
scruples (4) A0490/27
B0874/08 B1185/20 B1234/27
scrupulous (12) A0283/26
A0484/12 B0752/32 B0767/15 B0897/05
B1168/07 B1169/31 B1330/04 C0171/24
C0428/18 C0552/02 C0577/15
scrupulously (7) A0286/17
A0434/22 A0445/24 A0499/23 A0509/16
A0510/20 B0877/36
scrutinize (3) B0810/30
B0829/13 B1354/01
scrutinized (11) A0055/07
A0064/25 A0312/24 A0445/13 A0546/31
A0709/08 B0832/26 B0894/17 B0894/V
B0980/21 B1274/13
scrutinizing (6) A0142/20 A0163/24
A0400/17 A0511/10 B0985/25 B0991/36
scrutiny (31) A0089/03
A0102/24 A0103/19 A0234/13 A0314/03
A0314/19 A0445/13 A0515/15 A0546/02
A0552/17 A0675/11 A0709/14 B0753/02
B0818/08 B0827/20 B0833/02 B0915/01
B0915/01 B0962/17 B0981/06 B0990/32
B1010/26 B1274/18 B1312/05 B1337/11
C0064/29 C0076/38 C0090/16 C0167/24
C0208/24 C0426/14
scud (5) A0127/29
A0242/09 C0106/01 C0106/09 C0107/01
scudded (2) A0137/31 A0587/05
scudding (1) C0106/08
scuffle (4) A0173/25
A0179/05 B1056/29 C0113/40
scuffling (1) A0541/32
scull (1) A0057/08
sculleries (1) B1313/01
scullion (2) B1139/10 B1139/26
scullions (3) A0263/03
A0263/05 A0263/27
sculls (1) A0253/V
sculptor (1) A0380/02
sculptural (3) A0708/06
B0914/09 B1273/05
sculpture (6) A0160/14 A0322/06
A0706/32 A0708/04 B1271/33 B1273/03
sculptured (2) A0322/02 A0367/25
sculptures (1) A0157/21
scum (1) A0085/10
scuppers (2) C0108/10 C0111/20
scurrilous (1) A0272/22
scurvy (4) C0166/14
C0176/37 C0177/02 C0192/21
Scythas (1) A0081/17
Scythe (1) A0347/V
Scythe (1) A0353/35
scythe (6) A0689/27 B0814/06
B0816/28 B0817/32 B0822/01 B0822/12
scythes (2) B0814/16 B1162/15
Scythian (1) A0123/29
se (7) A0161/04
A0301/12 A0302/20 A0303/04 A0611/04

->A0662/V B1379/07
se'n (1) A0344/31
Sea (2) B1385/01 C0147/16
sea (194)
sea-beast (1) B1158/02
sea-biscuit (3) C0069/22
C0078/34 C0088/22
sea-boat (2) A0252/23 C0147/11
sea-brilliancy (1) A0139/02
sea-burial (1) C0108/06
sea-chest (1) B0810/32
sea-coal (1) A0054/24
sea-coast (1) B0831/05
sea-gull (1) A0144/01
sea-kelp (1) C0138/12
sea-parlance (1) C0105/31
sea-shell (1) B1156/31
sea-shore (2) A0045/15 B1155/25
sea-sickness (2) C0074/11 C0102/38
sea-stores (4) C0057/02
C0089/19 C0091/21 C0126/13
sea-turtle (1) A0241/13
sea-weeds (1) B1391/20
sea/boat (1) B0930/15
seaboard (1) B0862/02
seaboat (1) C0149/30
Seabright (2) A0704/32 B1269/31
seacoast (2) B0807/10 C0199/07
Seadrift, Solomon (1) A0205/19
seafaring (1) C0087/30
seagull (1) C0125/01
seagulls (1) C0151/28
seahens (1) C0151/27
seal (22) A0265/25 A0266/19
A0267/36 A0269/08 A0269/37 A0271/27
A0273/25 A0276/02 A0280/29 A0282/10
A0670/03 B0833/17 B0991/06 B0991/14
B0992/18 B1055/19 C0151/07 C0153/32
C0154/01 C0154/06 C0154/11 C0155/20
sealed (8) A0274/14
A0280/09 A0283/30 A0490/18 A0558/03
B0932/19 C0153/36 C0390/04
sealing (2) C0137/24 C0147/06
sealing-wax (1) C0390/04
sealskins (4) C0155/27
C0155/40 C0156/17 C0156/27
seam (4) B1054/09
B1054/10 C0183/15 C0183/32
seaman (11) A0143/07
A0144/26 A0241/08 A0253/14 A0585/04
B0768/33 B0769/05 C0065/16 C0097/07
C0098/36 C0176/20
seaman's (3) C0067/12
C0105/06 C0180/25
seamed (1) A0580/13
seamen (25) A0240/02
A0240/13 A0242/06 A0243/23 A0244/29
A0248/29 A0249/33 A0580/06 A0585/32
B0841/26 B1069/20 B1072/36 B1076/24
B1077/14 B1077/30 B1081/22 B1392/02
C0063/04 C0086/20 C0093/35 C0111/13
C0123/30 C0138/17 C0146/36 C0147/22
seams (7) C0076/04
C0102/26 C0103/04 C0106/06 C0533/01
C0552/17 C0572/24

sean (2) A0621/02 A0621/03
seaports (1) A0251/19
search (80)
searched (10) A0542/15 A0542/17
B0830/34 B0979/04 B0979/15 B1022/03
B1058/35 B1181/03 B1362/13 B1362/28
searches (1) B0988/32
searching (11) A0028/04
B0903/25 B0970/05 B0983/24 B0985/13
B1054/03 B1133/27 C0063/12 C0085/27
C0108/27 C0167/33
seared (1) A0697/02
Seas (1) C0178/07
seas (18) A0139/24 A0142/32
A0586/05 A0587/06 B0930/19 B0930/V
C0060/24 C0106/06 C0106/34 C0108/23
C0115/09 C0117/02 C0117/09 C0117/12
C0117/22 C0149/28 C0202/36 C0420/19
seashore (2) C0191/22 C0200/09
season (24) A0087/16
A0227/25 B0742/16 B0865/30 B1019/19
B1106/25 B1257/16 B1351/17 C0152/08
C0153/32 C0155/19 C0158/15 C0159/10
C0159/38 C0160/10 C0161/17 C0161/35
C0191/10 C0202/11 C0387/11 C0431/14
C0540/10 C0552/39 C0562/12
seasonable (2) C0138/24 C0530/33
seasoned (1) A0689/22
seasons (2) B0942/17 C0178/27
seaswallows (1) C0151/28
seat (42) A0056/09 A0065/31
A0088/20 A0092/27 A0094/08 A0102/26
A0104/21 A0112/02 A0114/04 A0158/08
A0216/24 A0249/12 A0302/02 A0385/17
A0413/02 A0491/19 A0563/21 B0734/33
B0758/07 B0761/14 B0796/31 B0809/17
B0810/32 B0839/31 B0841/34 B0842/29
B0843/30 B0905/30 B0916/19 B1009/15
B1056/31 B1072/31 B1075/21 B1093/30
B1134/28 B1249/09 B1329/35 B1340/10
B1348/34 B1383/22 C0062/14 C0562/19
seated (22) A0021/25 A0173/V
A0178/17 A0240/05 A0245/17 A0247/11
A0261/05 A0303/06 A0368/30 A0382/21
A0384/15 B0809/11 B0944/18 B1009/05
B1133/19 B1294/18 C0100/02 C0109/26
C0168/31 C0175/06 C0204/22 C0431/05
seating (1) B0829/12
seats (10) A0191/11 A0252/32
A0502/21 B0840/03 B0889/04 B1014/21
B1014/29 B1054/33 B1250/11 C0550/29
seawater (3) C0129/10
C0143/04 C0169/19
seaweed (4) C0131/35
C0145/36 C0145/40 C0153/01
seaworthy (1) C0065/33
seben (1) A0372/31
seceders (2) C0551/30 C0551/37
secluded (5) A0564/27
B0726/25 B0735/20 B0926/08 B0943/01
seclusion (9) A0234/14
A0235/06 A0532/20 A0600/15 A0670/14
A0671/11 B0759/29 B1277/25 B1278/19
seclusions (1) A0098/32
second (137)
second-handed (1) A0512/04
secondary (8) A0457/25
A0458/04 A0473/28 A0711/30 B0724/10
B1213/23 B1276/33 B1314/34
seconded (1) B1077/26
secondly (12) A0496/19
A0555/10 A0682/28 B0763/18 B0985/10
B1220/01 B1233/20 B1236/20 B1383/05
C0427/18 C0556/09 C0556/23
seconds (22) A0106/04 A0253/10
A0355/31 A0447/19 A0590/10 A0615/15
A0630/17 A0686/32 A0687/08 B0825/22
B0960/23 B1106/14 B1261/29 C0078/23
C0098/13 C0144/11 C0396/07 C0405/22
C0411/06 C0412/10 C0418/32 C0544/31
secrecy (4) B0976/05
B1298/04 C0393/13 C0395/04
secret (56)
secretary (1) A0337/12
secrete (1) B0985/34
secreted (4) B0808/09
B0844/15 C0394/32 C0523/26
secreting (2) A0140/31 C0067/11
secretly (7) A0431/32
B1004/16 B1119/22 B1325/08 C0132/07
C0133/21 C0537/01
Secrets (1) B1206/T
secrets (7) A0151/06
A0506/03 A0616/13 B0925/15 B1038/31
B1317/32 C0166/32
sect (3) A0044/11
B1095/03 B1095/04
section (2) B1293/33 B1369/16
sections (2) A0176/02 A0182/01
sects (1) A0128/17
seculare (2) A0091/20 A0110/24
secundum (1) A0409/11
secure (25) A0486/09
A0589/31 B0796/28 B0858/11 B0947/01
B1057/35 B1113/08 B1158/25 B1261/29
B1299/17 B1392/01 C0098/36 C0098/37
C0099/07 C0104/29 C0105/21 C0116/34
C0116/37 C0143/34 C0189/04 C0189/18
C0199/13 C0200/17 C0533/23 C0564/20
secured (34) A0081/13 A0410/26
A0590/05 A0593/24 B0730/27 B0730/31
B0738/18 B0765/22 B0766/16 B0771/18
B0808/19 B0826/05 B0858/08 B0866/19
B1059/12 B1077/22 B1082/02 B1336/27
B1350/35 C0082/11 C0085/34 C0098/30
C0108/29 C0111/05 C0113/30 C0119/32
C0139/03 C0165/11 C0175/02 C0396/11
C0399/13 C0529/28 C0552/33 C0558/33
securely (13) A0542/19
A0551/16 A0551/32 A0555/03 A0565/03
A0589/26 A0593/13 A0689/14 B0830/01
B1008/25 C0122/06 C0139/27 C0415/20
secures (2) A0711/18 B1276/19
securing (11) A0139/10
B0771/19 B0771/20 B0992/24 C0070/31
C0098/20 C0126/24 C0143/28 C0144/40
C0390/30 C0573/39
securities (1) B0966/04
security (20) A0021/13
A0137/27 A0243/08 A0435/18 A0671/09

->B0962/27 B1224/26 B1225/06 C0093/30
C0099/22 C0136/11 C0139/34 C0172/26
C0175/16 C0188/13 C0189/10 C0202/32
C0203/05 C0398/13 C0563/20
sedan (1) A0493/08
sedate (1) A0672/33
sedge (1) A0398/12
sedges (1) A0397/14
Sedgwick (1) A0268/37
Sedgwick, C. M. (1) A0268/33
Sedgwick's (1) A0269/06
sediment (1) B1374/30
sedition (1) A0621/14
seduce (1) A0529/11
seduced (5) A0441/31
B0859/14 B0871/01 B1108/09 B1155/02
seductions (1) A0438/25
see (293)
see-saw (1) A0694/03
seed (1) C0150/29
seed-vessels (1) B1293/01
seed> (1) A0469/02
seeds (1) B1247/01
seeing (38) A0066/15 A0069/02
A0261/21 A0269/20 A0342/06 A0513/12
B0729/33 B0811/07 B0890/24 B0894/24
B0905/06 B0915/26 B1101/27 B1133/02
B1139/30 B1143/01 B1158/32 B1159/07
B1168/11 B1183/13 C0061/07 C0061/15
C0061/36 C0144/40 C0145/39 C0161/24
C0169/29 C0169/37 C0175/35 C0187/14
C0188/04 C0188/41 C0189/09 C0198/22
C0392/08 C0417/25 C0429/33 C0429/40
seek (24) A0209/26
A0385/24 A0427/09 A0440/20 A0444/08
A0545/18 A0551/01 A0551/11 A0599/M
B0746/22 B0746/23 B0760/05 B0863/05
B0946/33 B0949/06 B1017/16 B1034/19
B1140/06 B1277/31 B1278/20 C0074/36
C0438/V C0522/08 C0537/15
seekers (2) B0986/07 B1048/15
seeking (9) A0152/12
A0347/16 A0428/13 A0446/26 A0532/07
A0533/06 B0774/02 B0853/01 C0191/14
seeks (5) A0709/22
B0760/13 B0989/32 B1096/27 B1274/25
seem (50) A0099/V A0143/27
A0251/29 A0266/08 A0270/14 A0277/15
A0282/14 A0371/24 A0431/18 A0432/31
A0509/26 A0553/15 A0558/01 A0587/28
A0588/19 A0639/02 A0655/06 A0673/29
B0850/01 B0862/01 B0890/30 B0904/01
B0962/09 B0983/23 B0993/18 B1038/33
B1047/02 B1080/08 B1080/12 B1274/16
B1281/13 B1281/14 B1294/31 B1298/11
B1339/06 B1360/19 B1370/23 B1380/31
C0097/08 C0116/13 C0163/21 C0204/28
C0387/25 C0406/05 C0410/02 C0415/10
C0419/11 C0432/16 C0433/07 C0532/16
seemed (302)
seemeth (1) A0045/20
seeming (17) A0435/30
A0537/30 A0547/19 A0547/21 A0683/09
A0683/14 B0940/21 B0959/35 B1057/21
B1213/06 B1219/V B1283/13 C0152/19
->C0408/02 C0408/20 C0523/20 C0574/02
seemingly (22) A0215/09 A0299/29
A0458/12 A0685/21 A0686/23 A0686/34
B0723/03 B0736/09 B0752/06 B0773/17
B0820/03 B0959/03 B0966/14 B0990/27
B1014/31 B1020/13 B1081/04 B1237/27
B1248/19 B1311/28 B1334/01 C0399/18
seems (67)
seen (286)
Seer (1) B1291/05
sees (4) A0153/15
A0529/10 B0871/16 B0990/24
segar-girl (1) B0725/V
segment (3) C0404/39
C0404/40 C0405/01
segonde (1) B0912/07
Seine (8) B0726/23
B0729/31 B0731/22 B0733/06 B0736/03
B0741/04 B0753/24 B0754/06
seize (10) A0318/25 A0382/17
A0675/25 A0676/08 B0757/28 B0932/07
B1260/07 C0117/40 C0186/19 C0188/31
seized (42) A0055/36 A0091/10
A0110/16 A0216/27 A0330/11 A0349/25
A0372/03 A0443/19 A0447/02 A0566/24
A0567/16 A0603/33 A0676/20 A0692/22
B0749/04 B0753/27 B0755/02 B0795/24
B0824/02 B0851/22 B0947/23 B0956/13
B0968/05 B0983/09 B0992/29 B1013/16
B1104/06 B1226/06 B1354/11 B1362/24
C0088/16 C0089/25 C0108/18 C0109/13
C0112/34 C0113/19 C0133/12 C0201/05
C0389/33 C0406/14 C0421/19 C0579/01
seizing (20) A0053/02
A0062/07 A0182/33 A0253/06 A0254/01
A0351/10 A0381/02 A0439/12 A0511/28
A0676/28 B0818/35 B0830/10 B0830/V
B1093/13 B1353/09 C0061/40 C0093/19
C0105/18 C0165/04 C0199/24
seizure (2) A0670/08 B0963/08
seldom (34) A0019/16 A0020/19
A0025/V A0244/27 A0277/36 A0435/V
A0438/07 A0539/28 A0556/07 A0584/07
A0624/10 A0704/17 B0724/01 B0749/11
B0807/35 B0878/24 B0903/22 B0904/13
B1004/16 B1005/09 B1045/25 B1046/07
B1050/18 B1269/16 B1291/08 B1314/16
B1329/20 B1334/14 B1358/27 B1380/30
C0106/04 C0162/27 C0559/39 C0564/20
Select (1) B1092/23
select (4) A0366/06
B0964/01 B1314/32 B1314/35
selected (9) A0093/16
A0112/27 A0488/19 B0955/16 B1128/34
C0070/33 C0152/11 C0179/22 C0575/35
selecting (1) C0546/35
selection (2) A0710/13 B1275/16
selects (1) B0989/34
self (10) A0121/21 A0464/V
A0467/V A0532/04 A0605/09 B0815/10
B0948/16 B1212/28 B1271/06 C0169/38
self-agency (1) A0445/21
self-amendment (1) B1379/05
self-balanced (1) A0402/24
self-cognizance (2) B1032/09

->B1032/11
self-complacency (2) A0303/03
B1300/02
self-conceit (1) A0432/17
self-congratulation (1) A0205/07
self-consequence (1) A0026/23
self-consistent (1) B0946/04
self-defence (3) B1221/10
C0428/06 C0448/V
self-demonstration (1) B0746/33
self-destruction (2) A0549/07
B0736/17
self-esteem (1) A0601/24
self-evidency (1) A0097/01
self-evident (7) A0582/25
B0975/33 B0989/09 B0990/05 B1295/09
B1310/28 B1310/29
self-existing (1) A0615/18
self-gratulation (1) B1346/01
self-identity (1) A0079/14
self-imposed (1) A0365/11
self-interest (1) B0870/13
self-love (1) A0478/04
self-movement (1) B1034/02
self-moving (1) A0071/09
self-murder (3) A0054/21
A0063/24 B0737/15
self-possession (7) A0140/19
A0155/25 A0295/19 A0327/10 A0589/09
C0132/02 C0399/03
self-sacrificing (1) B0850/19
self-same (1) A0318/27
self-satisfaction (2) A0241/17
A0371/14
self-satisfied (1) B0873/07
self-suggestion (1) B1225/16
self-willed (2) A0020/V A0427/24
sell (4) A0564/29
C0110/14 C0529/05 C0530/12
sellers (1) A0513/17
selling (2) A0539/10 C0393/08
Selten (1) B0723/M
semblance (9) A0514/27
A0538/24 A0553/28 B0818/33 B0927/22
B0969/12 C0198/39 C0389/23 C0550/19
'sembled (2) A0702/M B1267/M
semi-axis (1) C0400/07
semi-circular (1) A0439/06
semi-metal (1) C0393/32
semi-osseous (1) B1235/23
semi-spiral (1) B1071/11
semi-syncope (1) B0962/33
semi-Druidical (1) A0321/22
semi-Gothic (2) A0321/22 B1283/10
semi-Saracenic (1) B1283/10
semicircle (1) C0423/18
semicircular (1) A0651/24
semicolon (2) B0837/22 B0837/29
Senate (1) A0491/04
send (19) A0264/26
A0268/06 A0270/06 A0279/03 A0631/06
B0872/23 B0878/17 B0923/35 B1010/21
B1046/09 B1053/19 B1130/10 B1131/21
B1131/23 B1132/28 B1234/35 C0171/13
C0527/22 C0530/26
sending (11) A0281/09
A0580/33 B0872/20 B1046/33 B1140/14
B1291/02 C0092/05 C0154/16 C0522/37
C0575/06 C0576/24
sends (1) B0966/19
Seneca (3) A0080/16
A0568/V B0974/M
Seneca (1) A0109/31
senior (1) A0432/22
sens (1) B1105/09
sensation (30) A0057/20 A0097/07
A0141/22 A0142/23 A0144/11 A0182/35
A0245/V A0340/24 A0397/15 A0399/31
A0404/09 A0431/06 A0436/19 A0510/29
A0674/32 A0683/28 A0692/09 B0738/06
B0944/27 B0959/31 B0963/02 B0966/14
B1295/15 B1299/01 B1311/07 B1359/24
B1380/10 C0060/18 C0204/33 C0411/28
sensation-paper (1) A0346/12
sensations (33) A0069/14
A0078/07 A0078/14 A0078/42 A0079/10
A0079/37 A0080/18 A0081/01 A0145/20
A0244/08 A0339/26 A0340/15 A0340/16
A0340/17 A0340/19 A0341/03 A0347/07
A0354/04 A0354/12 A0355/22 A0402/34
A0415/01 A0443/17 A0590/17 A0614/29
A0682/16 B0944/14 B1223/06 C0063/31
C0075/38 C0129/01 C0397/18 C0404/14
sense (125)
senseless (4) B0962/11
C0060/27 C0135/24 C0563/12
senses (53)
sensibilities (1) B0902/V
sensibility (6) A0282/04 A0398/32
A0613/20 B0905/11 B0922/13 C0523/32
sensible (1) A0019/03
sensible (11) A0080/26
A0264/09 A0457/24 B1013/25 B1037/30
B1184/31 C0117/27 C0146/02 C0406/38
C0418/40 C0532/02
sensibly (7) B0873/08
B0931/05 C0129/19 C0131/32 C0418/19
C0560/07 C0561/24
Sensitive (1) A0710/32
sensitive (9) A0216/06
A0415/03 B0726/30 B0942/04 B1007/21
B1054/30 B1135/26 C0167/08 C0537/29
sensual (5) A0510/18
A0613/25 A0613/26 A0613/26 A0614/34
sent (46) A0034/23 A0057/11
A0067/10 A0173/09 A0174/32 A0180/23
A0271/35 A0276/25 A0329/V A0460/21
A0483/18 A0541/17 A0542/17 A0591/19
A0631/21 B0732/30 B0760/32 B0770/06
B0770/08 B0808/29 B0815/22 B0815/23
B0872/04 B0872/07 B0872/29 B0899/03
B0899/26 B1019/15 B1031/01 B1119/M
B1129/16 B1129/18 B1135/05 B1193/24
B1321/09 B1322/17 B1346/27 B1347/20
C0056/20 C0057/09 C0067/02 C0086/29
C0150/17 C0156/05 C0539/31 C0549/41
sentence (30) A0108/21 A0143/03
A0161/25 A0213/06 A0218/13 A0252/04
A0252/10 A0252/10 A0252/10 A0272/35
A0279/15 A0299/16 A0346/14 A0414/01

->A0623/23 A0623/29 A0681/03 A0681/03
A0684/02 A0684/19 B0739/14 B0739/20
B0837/04 B0840/06 B1020/02 B1054/35
B1141/13 B1359/22 B1383/23 B1383/33
sentences (9) A0218/22
A0281/05 A0303/V A0341/12 A0356/11
B0959/09 B1215/32 B1226/14 C0080/11
sentience (6) A0408/06 A0408/12
A0408/18 A0612/28 A0616/01 A0617/04
sentient (2) A0216/06 A0600/26
sentiment (1) A0611/04
sentiment (60)
sentiments (1) A0216/09
sentiments (21) A0054/06
A0063/14 A0069/11 A0079/41 A0203/09
A0301/28 A0302/17 A0302/25 A0399/27
A0400/27 A0436/08 A0459/30 B0723/05
B0852/10 B0891/05 B0893/26 B0984/37
B1122/07 C0066/13 C0095/26 C0537/18
sentries (3) C0544/04
C0558/34 C0568/37
sentry (3) B1329/02
C0549/29 C0549/36
senty (1) A0354/31
sep (1) B0809/03
Sep. (4) B1136/02
B1136/21 B1137/13 B1138/09
separate (13) A0246/18
A0496/28 A0531/03 A0608/21 A0641/V
A0693/08 B0929/04 B1129/05 B1141/18
B1167/15 B1181/15 B1321/07 C0430/46
separated (12) A0544/06
A0603/29 A0695/21 B0807/01 B0898/06
B0928/22 B0929/04 B1332/28 C0133/18
C0162/35 C0190/25 C0409/25
separately (1) A0417/V
separates (1) C0155/18
separation (4) A0293/12
A0355/29 C0172/14 C0181/23
sepoys (1) B0949/19
Sept (1) B1139/13
September (14) A0324/16 C0149/10
C0150/23 C0547/38 C0548/19 C0548/20
C0548/41 C0548/41 C0549/15 C0550/06
C0553/06 C0559/08 C0559/38 C0560/07
sepulchral (5) A0023/07
A0056/01 A0065/21 B0963/35 B0969/14
sepulchre (3) A0074/30
A0079/27 A0081/36
sepulchres (1) B1179/04
sepulchrum (2) A0209/M A0218/15
sepulture (3) A0081/12
B0733/17 B0968/33
sepultus (1) A0213/08
Sequel (1) B0723/T
sequel (4) A0203/11
A0263/33 B1155/07 C0443/V
sequence (5) B0724/08
B0747/19 B0829/23 B0853/01 B1107/20
sequitur (1) B0744/18
sequuntur (1) A0495/04
ser'ts (2) B1055/21 B1055/V
sera (1) A0356/13
seraglio (1) B1164/22
serai (2) A0037/07 A0037/V
seraph (2) A0406/31 A0644/22
Seraphic (2) A0055/12 A0064/V
seraphic (2) B0893/02 B0898/14
Seraphim (1) A0641/12
seraphim (1) A0641/V
seraphs (1) A0319/09
serenading (1) B1097/01
serene (5) A0250/11
A0250/16 A0312/23 A0348/07 B1178/08
serenity (2) A0102/10 A0252/V
serge (6) A0685/30 A0686/12
A0688/20 A0691/32 A0692/V A0694/32
series (41) A0303/29
A0402/15 A0543/25 A0559/02 A0631/12
A0706/24 B0723/M B0724/09 B0773/36
B0806/03 B0824/14 B0833/27 B0849/07
B0927/23 B0940/31 B0943/02 B0946/05
B0965/25 B0992/13 B1014/24 B1019/31
B1032/07 B1071/12 B1164/07 B1179/27
B1186/17 B1233/15 B1271/26 B1296/09
B1312/14 B1321/27 B1333/19 C0055/02
C0096/08 C0176/05 C0193/25 C0201/21
C0405/14 C0409/28 C0409/33 C0425/19
seringa (1) B1334/21
serious (51)
seriously (19) A0018/12
A0216/09 A0248/05 A0434/22 A0442/07
A0625/20 A0650/16 B0819/29 B0942/20
B1053/02 B1194/26 B1247/07 B1348/19
B1351/28 C0059/04 C0125/36 C0532/36
C0561/11 C0563/08
seriousness (1) B0815/02
sermon (2) A0382/19 B1313/04
sermonic (2) A0297/22 A0354/16
serpent (5) A0321/27
B0914/01 B0947/20 B1259/35 C0138/01
serpent-like (1) A0640/20
serpentine (1) B1330/14
serpents (4) A0640/14
C0072/14 C0174/13 C0534/03
servant (36) A0059/19
A0216/26 A0263/19 A0264/21 A0265/13
A0266/32 A0267/21 A0268/09 A0269/27
A0274/01 A0275/28 A0276/12 A0279/33
A0281/35 A0282/35 A0296/V A0301/29
A0302/26 A0400/22 A0438/31 A0539/07
B0852/32 B0872/07 B0877/12 B0877/18
B0901/11 B0923/07 B0923/10 B0923/12
B0924/29 B0933/19 B1059/18 B1371/18
B1382/28 C0426/29 C0430/44
servants (3) A0327/14
B0978/13 B1009/04
serve (18) A0205/11 A0212/34
A0625/07 A0627/07 A0627/15 A0709/12
B0762/26 B0944/25 B1050/20 B1074/36
B1123/07 B1126/15 B1275/18 C0129/30
C0188/40 C0430/47 C0549/03 C0552/16
served (34) A0240/23 A0345/14
A0399/25 A0401/10 A0405/33 A0458/33
A0484/15 A0610/04 A0625/08 A0631/12
A0644/04 A0644/15 B0826/09 B0894/30
B0898/10 B0900/28 B0931/09 B0943/08
B1102/14 B1123/20 B1129/09 B1156/34
B1165/27 B1168/01 B1241/26 C0081/08
C0120/11 C0129/16 C0191/07 C0207/41

->C0392/30 C0399/02 C0415/05 C0421/33
serves (1) C0150/36
servi (1) A0034/02
service (21) A0058/37
A0155/23 A0263/21 A0264/12 A0275/06
A0282/33 A0349/04 A0428/28 A0546/07
B0754/05 B1089/19 B1089/24 B1206/04
B1360/12 C0063/09 C0077/33 C0097/08
C0127/05 C0147/13 C0534/22 C0566/07
serviceable (3) B0908/18
B0910/14 B1091/07
services (15) A0300/21
A0705/33 B0725/12 B0753/23 B0878/35
B0879/22 B1270/33 B1346/33 C0085/07
C0177/26 C0179/31 C0393/12 C0395/40
C0432/01 C0522/36
servile (1) A0021/12
serving (3) C0152/29
C0174/39 C0571/06
servitude (1) B1157/15
Servius (1) A0599/M
ses (5) A0034/01
A0036/21 A0119/M A0216/09 A0216/10
sesamoideum (1) B1182/13
session (1) A0490/36
session-room (1) A0369/18
sessions (1) B1054/28
set (149)
sets (6) A0152/02 B0871/11
B0955/32 B1090/35 B1136/08 C0538/16
settee (3) A0054/11
A0088/36 B1340/09
settees (1) A0087/31
setting (34) A0019/23 A0102/20
A0217/07 A0241/20 A0293/23 A0312/12
A0417/08 A0482/30 A0484/01 A0508/25
A0594/09 A0625/22 A0654/12 B0727/22
B0746/28 B0817/22 B0821/32 B0828/02
B0942/21 B1038/15 B1090/25 B1280/V
B1331/28 B1372/16 C0159/14 C0160/07
C0163/09 C0164/15 C0164/20 C0167/03
C0170/27 C0175/36 C0414/09 C0526/22
settings (2) B0828/01 B0877/08
settle (11) A0478/01
B0895/18 B1045/11 B1105/17 B1206/13
B1369/14 B1385/04 C0098/33 C0157/22
C0172/05 C0545/39
settled (29) A0018/04
A0024/26 A0029/24 A0156/20 A0203/03
A0227/10 A0231/23 A0270/14 A0404/17
A0509/02 A0512/09 A0638/03 A0696/03
B0728/23 B0748/32 B0816/21 B0910/27
B0924/30 B0925/12 B0976/03 B1020/21
B1051/05 B1220/02 B1256/05 C0115/23
C0205/31 C0522/18 C0524/32 C0565/32
settlement (7) B1364/31
C0153/19 C0156/03 C0156/21 C0525/22
C0533/40 C0571/28
settlements (4) C0564/14
C0564/35 C0568/11 C0574/19
settling (4) A0641/07
B0878/14 B1206/12 C0098/27
seul (3) A0096/M
A0506/M A0599/03
seule (1) A0019/02
seulement (1) C0430/38
seuls (1) A0018/08
seven (87)
seven-eighths (1) A0389/08
seventeen (5) A0122/01
B1071/04 B1154/V C0407/20 C0537/37
seventeenth (4) C0069/39
C0135/36 C0192/31 C0421/15
seventh (15) A0177/22
A0183/17 A0411/15 A0672/02 B0819/23
B0839/33 B0840/23 B0842/15 B1079/13
B1107/12 B1262/19 C0084/23 C0179/16
C0418/01 C0423/32
seventy (18) A0120/04 A0175/06
A0175/06 A0181/27 A0348/30 A0511/12
A0583/21 B0729/20 B0819/05 B0941/03
B0968/17 B1007/35 B1248/11 C0138/20
C0181/03 C0181/33 C0186/34 C0578/26
seventy-five (9) A0487/30
B1068/06 B1069/11 B1081/32 B1138/30
C0057/26 C0179/14 C0394/40 C0396/21
seventy-fours (1) B1248/08
seventy-nine (1) A0460/25
seventy-second (1) C0160/20
seventy-seven (1) B1154/25
sever (1) A0355/27
several (199)
severas (1) A0621/03
severe (25) A0101/16
A0135/17 A0403/34 A0538/15 B0807/36
B0812/12 B0958/21 B1089/05 B1092/31
B1129/27 B1131/19 B1157/09 B1184/07
B1258/12 B1369/34 B1380/32 C0114/15
C0118/07 C0137/15 C0141/34 C0191/20
C0394/36 C0405/09 C0557/31 C0578/01
severed (6) A0094/22 A0114/16
A0557/23 A0567/04 A0694/27 C0546/01
severely (3) A0142/22
B0879/28 C0557/40
severest (4) C0064/24
C0202/07 C0523/41 C0527/07
severities (1) A0296/04
severity (6) B0955/03 B1016/33
B1054/16 B1129/31 C0438/V C0447/V
Sevres (2) A0503/01 A0503/V
sew (1) C0108/05
sewed (2) B1185/26 C0532/41
sewer (1) B1021/30
sex (3) A0284/26 B0888/V B1015/14
Sexagesima (1) A0582/11
sexes (2) B1090/13 B1097/02
sexton (1) A0070/12
Seymour (1) C0102/19
sha'nt (1) A0284/34
shabby (1) B1019/20
shackles (1) A0323/14
shade (24) A0081/10
A0215/20 A0325/11 A0357/02 A0437/11
A0485/06 A0499/06 A0499/07 A0499/12
A0499/26 A0503/09 A0603/17 A0603/26
A0604/08 A0604/22 A0604/27 A0605/07
A0613/17 A0629/26 A0663/20 B0904/21
B1340/16 C0172/01 C0172/02
shaded (3) A0322/13
A0412/16 B0904/15

Shades (1) A0071/25
shades (6) A0033/V A0397/05
A0515/23 A0560/16 B0755/13 B1078/16
Shadow (8) A0188/T
A0188/M A0191/08 A0317/03 A0318/V
A0608/28 A0616/26 B0964/V
shadow (83)
shadow-like (1) A0326/07
shadowed (2) A0100/31 A0405/29
shadowing (1) B0901/08
Shadows (1) A0071/25
shadows (32) A0079/10
A0080/27 A0102/23 A0122/15 A0142/25
A0145/04 A0153/11 A0156/12 A0188/02
A0210/27 A0214/04 A0216/20 A0227/23
A0232/10 A0234/21 A0236/07 A0302/12
A0417/07 A0499/03 A0533/06 A0603/30
A0614/14 A0682/32 A0683/14 B0902/10
B1040/16 B1122/33 B1246/19 C0065/08
C0111/34 C0444/V C0444/V
shadowy (11) A0021/23
A0397/23 A0403/25 A0477/03 A0479/34
A0639/21 B0955/26 B1122/26 B1317/23
C0412/31 C0575/20
shady (1) C0207/44
shaft (2) B1071/21 B1391/26
shafts (2) A0075/08 A0086/16
shaggy (2) B1248/13 C0168/16
shaggy-haired (1) A0356/28
shags (1) C0151/28
shake (9) A0436/20
A0439/17 A0586/18 B0856/08 B0981/03
B1110/03 B1141/20 B1225/20 C0413/03
shaken (7) A0213/11
A0317/08 A0329/16 A0664/14 B0968/06
B1020/07 C0083/14
Shakespeare (3) A0121/29
A0383/28 B1126/02
shaking (12) A0078/V
A0384/08 A0400/04 A0411/26 A0649/03
A0687/26 B0913/V B0964/11 B1110/06
C0067/31 C0082/24 C0397/24
shall (247)
shallow (12) B0771/05
B0959/02 B0984/04 C0152/38 C0173/15
C0178/17 C0178/26 C0178/30 C0178/32
C0536/15 C0554/02 C0559/16
shallowness (2) B0742/17 C0575/30
shalt (6) A0228/18 A0228/26
A0228/27 A0232/23 A0233/07 A0233/08
sham (2) A0490/14 A0490/18
Sham-Post (1) A0490/12
shame (9) A0047/16
A0444/33 A0588/34 A0676/17 B0826/28
B0854/29 B0923/02 B1166/21 C0094/36
shamed (1) B0818/22
shameful (4) A0021/10
A0355/11 A0443/V C0097/05
shamefully (3) B0959/02
B1008/02 B1293/13
shameless (1) B1121/02
shank (2) A0553/18 A0553/19
shape (54)
shaped (5) A0100/05
B1072/01 B1156/33 C0387/27 C0393/31
shapeless (2) A0246/V C0198/40
shapes (3) A0603/20
B1169/10 C0540/22
share (7) A0067/22
A0071/23 A0251/30 B0863/26 C0073/24
C0531/30 C0564/07
shared (2) C0137/03 C0531/32
sharing (2) C0086/35 C0128/41
shark (1) C0141/14
sharks (9) C0140/20
C0140/39 C0142/19 C0142/32 C0143/08
C0143/25 C0143/36 C0144/22 C0145/40
sharp (35) A0081/08
A0352/32 A0354/03 A0410/10 A0501/16
A0544/08 A0588/10 A0670/04 A0671/23
A0676/24 A0691/07 A0694/06 A0694/33
B0830/09 B0855/13 B1011/31 B1110/09
B1193/20 B1280/01 B1280/23 B1281/02
B1339/32 B1345/20 C0074/29 C0082/20
C0113/33 C0147/09 C0178/18 C0194/11
C0423/14 C0536/35 C0558/20 C0559/39
C0563/09 C0563/35
sharp-pointed (1) C0572/32
sharpen (1) A0055/23
sharpened (1) B0789/03
sharpers (1) A0509/24
sharply (5) A0029/14
A0602/20 C0387/24 C0418/31 C0577/05
sharply-defined (1) B0864/32
sharpness (1) B1279/35
shattered (10) A0137/33 A0138/06
A0153/15 A0543/33 A0544/07 A0592/11
B1110/21 C0113/26 C0115/15 C0117/01
shattering (1) A0300/17
shave (2) A0044/15 B1195/16
shaved (3) A0247/27
B1181/08 C0551/41
shaving (1) A0565/05
shawm (1) A0047/24
she (2) A0357/06 A0357/06
she (571)
sheath (2) B1180/12 C0562/06
sheathed (1) A0410/08
shed (3) B1294/06
C0558/39 C0559/02
sheep (7) A0498/V
A0629/24 B1115/03 B1278/35 B1334/25
B1335/03 C0156/23
sheep-bells (1) C0388/29
sheer (12) A0336/11
A0447/19 A0578/11 A0589/34 B0957/06
B1057/16 B1114/32 B1207/09 B1334/11
C0065/13 C0073/01 C0113/20
sheet (19) A0135/M
A0249/18 A0252/14 A0274/38 A0281/29
A0321/15 A0340/18 A0346/23 A0485/22
A0681/11 B0993/24 B1141/15 B1354/03
C0135/40 C0139/20 C0139/21 C0141/39
C0407/33 C0418/18
sheets (1) C0145/28
shefa (1) A0626/12
shekels (3) A0044/04
A0045/22 A0047/05
shelf (6) A0621/09 B0956/33
B1340/19 C0415/24 C0415/27 C0415/28

shell (7) A0128/V
A0544/32 B1037/17 B1037/19 B1374/01
C0061/24 C0178/15
shelled (4) A0091/36
A0092/02 A0111/13 A0111/14
Shelley (1) A0710/33
shellfish (1) C0177/06
shells (5) B0807/25
B1160/27 C0145/38 C0153/01 C0177/08
shelter (8) A0197/02
B0726/19 B0769/V B0968/15 C0150/40
C0173/14 C0555/07 C0561/36
sheltered (2) A0323/16 B0899/25
shelves (4) A0503/05
A0582/35 B0762/09 C0068/18
shepherd (2) B1295/13 B1311/05
Sherry (3) A0181/16
B1258/03 B1258/17
Shetland (1) C0159/34
Shetland/Islands (1) C0162/11
Shetlands (1) C0160/24
shew (1) B1267/M
shicken (2) B1103/29 B1103/33
shield (10) A0075/08 A0267/37
A0414/18 A0414/20 A0415/18 A0415/21
A0415/26 A0416/12 B0858/33 C0425/14
shields (1) C0554/09
shift (5) A0295/29
A0318/19 A0584/22 C0098/30 C0099/19
shifted (3) A0555/30
A0696/28 C0114/36
shifting (7) A0138/03
C0097/15 C0097/26 C0097/30 C0097/38
C0098/15 C0559/34
shifting-boards (5) A0141/06
C0098/18 C0098/30 C0098/36 C0212/V
shifts (1) B1361/31
shilling (4) A0490/04
A0653/08 B1053/14 C0066/04
shilling's (1) B0880/07
shillings (1) B0875/23
shine (2) A0228/09 B0947/16
shingles (1) B1337/26
shining (14) A0313/23 A0414/18
A0578/11 A0580/30 A0639/26 B1107/17
B1165/03 B1212/20 B1348/09 C0062/12
C0062/24 C0072/15 C0193/20 C0443/V
shins (4) B1010/V
B1010/V B1010/V B1015/20
ship (81)
ship-builders (1) C0114/06
ship-furniture (3) C0069/07
C0074/35 C0089/19
ship's (3) B0830/17
C0061/35 C0131/36
shipmate (2) A0241/18 A0249/28
shipped (9) A0137/21
A0251/19 B0930/19 C0085/40 C0099/15
C0102/31 C0104/28 C0113/39 C0533/27
shipping (5) A0560/23
B0930/16 C0060/24 C0106/02 C0106/28
ships (4) A0581/35
B0945/27 C0118/17 C0147/17
shipwreck (2) C0053/T C0065/19
Shiraz (1) A0641/V
shirt (15) A0103/34
A0485/03 A0627/33 B1053/29 B1058/04
B1058/27 B1184/04 C0108/30 C0108/36
C0124/41 C0197/22 C0413/31 C0552/05
C0552/28 C0552/30
shirt-collar (3) A0056/24
A0066/14 A0089/12
shirts (8) B0750/26
B1350/37 C0119/20 C0128/07 C0145/28
C0146/10 C0146/16 C0202/40
shivered (2) B1046/25 B1160/02
shivering (2) B1185/30 B1238/25
shoal (1) C0146/37
shoals (7) C0155/01
C0188/05 C0189/33 C0548/37 C0571/20
C0572/31 C0576/11
shock (18) A0058/33 A0079/16
A0137/15 A0140/23 A0144/V A0439/24
A0615/31 A0664/V B0948/02 B0948/14
B0956/27 B0966/18 B1182/10 C0106/27
C0115/38 C0129/21 C0189/36 C0396/31
shocked (1) B0815/02
shocking (5) A0025/17
A0053/10 A0179/34 B1007/21 C0109/07
shocks (1) B1119/21
shod (1) B1379/23
shoe (3) B0745/29
B0811/27 C0579/15
shoe-buckles (2) A0369/10 A0370/13
shoe-marks (1) B1049/02
shoes (12) A0103/26
A0368/10 A0368/19 A0508/35 B0745/29
B0746/16 B0746/17 B0747/04 B0878/02
B1008/07 B1048/33 C0534/23
shone (10) A0196/16 A0196/V
A0316/19 A0417/09 A0585/03 B0793/01
B1050/01 B1328/08 B1348/10 C0536/30
shook (24) A0102/02
A0104/20 A0155/21 A0181/15 A0247/25
A0437/22 A0586/28 A0587/18 A0593/20
A0629/03 B0811/09 B0913/18 B0944/03
B0963/28 B0963/29 B0968/27 B1003/27
B1046/25 B1182/35 B1185/23 C0059/03
C0059/17 C0074/07 C0128/36
shoot (4) B0839/33
B0840/23 B0842/16 C0200/06
shooting (4) A0183/V
B1280/27 C0150/29 C0201/02
shooting-stars (1) B1322/21
shop (13) A0174/11
A0179/25 A0245/09 A0248/25 A0250/06
A0489/13 A0513/22 A0513/23 B0726/06
B0872/17 B0873/07 B1127/22 B1293/25
shop-doors (1) B0989/25
shop-keeper (4) A0513/28
B0872/09 B0872/19 B0872/24
shop-shutters (1) B1008/27
shopkeeper (2) B0726/02 B0872/05
shops (2) A0243/07 B0725/26
shore (100)
shore-party (1) C0180/23
shores (15) A0196/02
A0286/05 A0594/11 A0654/22 B0864/31
B1164/12 B1179/17 B1278/34 B1279/18
C0155/02 C0155/19 C0157/21 C0525/15

->C0525/31 C0572/29
short (138)
shorter (7) A0103/25
B0832/23 B0836/16 B0962/10 B1163/29
B1380/20 C0401/28
shortest (3) C0134/40
C0135/07 C0148/23
shortly (29) A0059/15
A0156/29 A0356/08 A0487/06 A0584/12
A0686/11 B0746/29 B0761/09 B0900/11
B0915/24 B1075/30 B1135/31 B1213/18
C0063/02 C0103/32 C0104/32 C0117/27
C0118/11 C0119/14 C0122/20 C0159/19
C0189/25 C0207/19 C0428/30 C0522/23
C0525/12 C0558/24 C0566/30 C0574/09
shot (45) A0025/10
A0029/23 A0177/14 A0183/09 A0384/32
A0384/32 A0417/05 A0470/09 A0588/10
A0590/23 A0628/24 A0694/34 B0794/30
B0839/35 B0840/24 B0842/21 B0843/15
B0843/16 B0843/17 B0933/01 B1046/V
B1057/31 B1332/30 C0099/20 C0112/32
C0112/35 C0164/27 C0165/02 C0187/30
C0200/01 C0396/20 C0405/23 C0413/34
C0531/20 C0535/19 C0550/17 C0555/08
C0558/33 C0566/32 C0566/38 C0568/12
C0570/15 C0570/32 C0577/38 C0579/28
shot-towers (1) A0071/24
shots (4) C0164/37
C0187/15 C0531/28 C0579/35
should (543)
should'st (1) A0151/V
shoulder (19) A0080/40
A0089/24 A0107/26 A0279/28 A0311/23
A0415/33 A0446/33 B0892/03 B1013/11
B1107/04 B1226/07 B1298/19 C0076/40
C0082/16 C0083/27 C0118/32 C0137/40
C0142/05 C0536/08
shoulder-blades (1) B0730/12
shoulders (37) A0035/02
A0037/09 A0080/37 A0080/44 A0087/07
A0100/17 A0143/13 A0155/07 A0196/22
A0217/V A0240/18 A0247/12 A0297/V
A0352/05 A0352/11 A0379/22 A0379/24
A0388/06 A0388/06 A0413/30 A0469/16
A0568/21 A0625/17 A0664/05 B0771/06
B0809/21 B0832/08 B1057/26 B1157/14
B1190/31 B1316/30 C0121/08 C0182/14
C0531/22 C0552/02 C0552/09 C0552/29
shouldn't (5) A0286/21
A0387/14 A0387/19 B0898/01 B1373/15
shouldst (2) A0151/02 A0151/07
shout (11) B1181/35
B1249/15 B1298/17 B1316/28 B1353/02
C0136/18 C0146/15 C0165/21 C0172/33
C0387/20 C0544/08
shouted (11) A0044/10
A0045/23 A0180/01 A0252/12 A0252/33
A0387/06 B0914/V B1165/08 B1348/31
C0123/23 C0557/21
shouting (9) A0123/02
A0417/15 A0461/19 A0627/08 C0124/23
C0131/22 C0190/21 C0541/22 C0560/11
shoutings (1) B0992/13
shouts (12) A0123/31
->A0124/08 A0243/27 B1020/03 C0061/15
C0124/05 C0143/18 C0168/07 C0174/17
C0199/31 C0199/34 C0569/30
shoved (1) A0469/16
shovel (1) B0818/21
show (45) A0088/13
A0205/06 A0324/25 A0342/12 A0344/18
A0346/07 A0374/15 A0399/30 A0434/15
A0436/10 A0441/30 A0485/07 A0485/21
A0496/12 A0500/11 A0555/09 A0562/07
A0702/M A0710/05 B0738/21 B0743/10
B0743/13 B0744/16 B0744/28 B0747/34
B0752/05 B0754/15 B0763/17 B0766/25
B0878/24 B1003/34 B1039/20 B1096/09
B1122/V B1221/09 B1275/08 B1311/27
B1314/01 B1359/26 B1371/10 B1380/23
B1380/30 C0117/15 C0428/14 C0571/07
showd> (1) A0465/05
showed (12) A0346/25
A0380/29 A0593/01 B0796/28 B0830/22
B0967/10 B1007/18 B1130/36 C0069/14
C0069/29 C0404/35 C0441/V
shower (9) A0152/27
C0135/38 C0139/18 C0141/34 C0142/03
C0145/27 C0190/07 C0205/31 C0542/32
shower-bath (1) C0129/23
showers (1) C0387/13
showing (14) A0056/03 A0065/25
A0272/14 A0303/23 B0948/27 B1046/14
B1093/37 B1186/25 B1297/18 B1297/22
B1314/20 B1315/20 B1383/13 C0570/24
showman (1) B1096/12
shown (23) A0157/02
A0386/28 A0546/26 A0621/23 B0732/07
B0740/08 B0743/21 B0752/04 B0752/10
B0809/22 B0909/25 B0948/26 B1039/23
B1071/V B1092/05 B1096/31 B1315/37
B1369/08 B1374/33 C0177/03 C0196/08
C0561/01 C0574/18
shows (5) A0582/08
A0621/15 B0743/03 B0746/32 B1120/06
showy (1) B1334/20
shrank (10) A0215/09 A0567/21
A0610/23 A0640/32 A0643/06 A0676/10
A0694/11 A0696/07 A0697/01 B0946/25
shredded (1) B1141/17
shredding (1) B1141/16
shreds (4) A0510/15
B0930/23 B1141/10 B1141/19
shrew (3) A0052/01
A0062/03 B1195/12
shrewdness (1) C0055/33
shriek (20) A0029/12
A0151/27 A0153/23 A0218/03 A0219/02
A0414/23 A0414/32 A0515/05 A0580/34
A0588/13 A0692/14 A0696/16 B0796/20
B0796/25 B0859/03 B0944/01 B0967/05
B0967/36 B1225/22 C0208/19
shrieked (11) A0105/30
A0197/26 A0235/V A0253/05 A0319/19
A0330/18 A0416/19 A0461/13 B0795/26
B0797/28 B1017/25
shrieking (12) A0029/15
A0139/31 A0145/17 A0146/V A0482/14
A0579/06 B0945/22 B1057/17 B1156/36

->C0116/22 C0131/37 C0203/04
shrieks (10) A0105/32 A0128/07
A0245/02 A0249/32 A0537/08 A0540/03
A0541/02 A0566/13 A0614/06 B1354/05
shrill (24) A0088/35
A0103/15 A0218/02 A0244/30 A0540/11
A0540/22 A0540/28 A0541/05 A0541/09
A0541/09 A0541/33 A0542/30 A0543/05
A0549/14 A0549/20 A0550/14 A0550/21
A0555/20 A0588/12 B1262/23 B1353/04
B1353/16 C0072/23 C0408/29
shrill-sounding (1) C0198/13
shriller (1) A0540/08
shrilly (1) A0029/15
shrimps (1) C0177/07
shrine (4) A0075/17
A0162/16 A0311/09 A0314/09
shrines (2) A0159/05 B0945/10
shrink (5) A0692/32
A0708/02 B1163/41 B1222/27 B1273/01
shrinking (5) A0330/12
A0510/04 A0695/02 B1014/29 B1239/35
shrivelled (3) A0143/14
A0327/21 C0107/37
shroud (13) A0022/V
A0029/22 A0034/25 A0080/37 A0081/09
A0228/28 A0233/09 A0243/14 A0246/28
A0252/16 A0254/02 B0956/30 B0957/06
shrouded (6) A0326/05 A0426/V
A0672/02 A0675/09 B0964/28 C0206/06
shrouds (1) A0405/V
shrub (4) A0602/15
B0807/12 B1334/20 C0150/28
shrubberies (7) A0210/33
A0428/05 B0761/17 B0765/07 B1279/25
B1283/07 B1329/10
shrubbery (6) A0196/32 B0864/28
B0866/12 B1332/12 C0192/09 C0542/17
shrubs (6) A0429/16 A0578/16
B1280/17 C0155/13 C0181/34 C0188/28
shrugged (4) A0035/01
A0037/09 A0625/17 B1190/31
shrunk (6) A0028/03 A0567/V
A0692/25 B0946/V B1243/03 C0142/35
shrunken (2) A0215/11 C0107/37
shud> (2) A0464/05 A0468/31
shudder (24) A0020/V
A0028/14 A0080/40 A0154/29 A0218/10
A0327/24 A0328/20 A0398/11 A0403/13
A0415/33 A0437/32 A0461/14 A0513/29
A0547/11 A0675/21 B0851/29 B0855/31
B0964/17 C0064/36 C0074/39 C0125/15
C0132/02 C0135/14 C0397/09
shuddered (15) A0023/11
A0054/21 A0063/24 A0198/16 A0214/11
A0216/05 A0226/16 A0230/15 A0234/24
A0405/16 A0405/17 A0558/V A0681/17
A0687/04 B0963/31
shuddering (11) A0191/12
A0683/31 A0696/15 A0696/18 B0966/26
B1223/15 B1240/32 C0087/27 C0203/03
C0208/18 C0399/08
shudderingly (1) A0412/34
shuffled (3) A0037/14
A0053/26 A0441/24
shuffling (2) A0056/02 A0065/26
shunned (3) A0225/08
A0229/09 A0323/05
shut (23) A0053/29
A0181/16 A0189/23 A0356/21 A0625/18
A0663/24 A0664/26 A0670/07 A0702/M
B0927/03 B0928/28 B1008/25 B1019/04
B1021/25 B1105/02 B1185/04 B1267/M
B1279/24 B1282/21 B1338/23 C0070/07
C0085/02 C0111/03
shutter (8) A0513/28
A0554/27 A0554/32 A0555/04 A0565/25
A0565/27 A0566/22 B1336/27
shutters (11) A0532/31
A0539/28 A0546/17 A0554/10 A0554/17
A0558/02 A0663/04 B0793/28 B1008/25
B1020/07 B1336/25
shutting (6) A0215/16 A0217/V
A0639/10 A0641/10 A0663/25 C0109/20
Shuttleworthy (21) B1044/10
B1044/12 B1044/24 B1045/20 B1045/24
B1046/06 B1046/14 B1046/18 B1046/32
B1048/12 B1048/29 B1050/05 B1050/33
B1053/12 B1055/25 B1055/31 B1056/04
B1057/07 B1057/35 B1058/35 B1059/17
Shuttleworthy, Barnabas (1) B1055/16
Shuttleworthy's (8) B1045/33
B1046/29 B1047/13 B1049/23 B1049/28
B1052/23 B1053/07 B1056/03
shy (2) C0151/33 C0154/06
Shylock (1) B1208/07
si (7) A0036/17
A0037/07 A0037/09 A0209/M A0218/15
B0993/26 C0180/32
Siam (1) A0087/18
Sibyls (1) A0144/V
sich (2) A0506/01 A0515/32
sich (2) B0812/09 B0812/24
sich> (4) A0466/32
A0467/V A0468/26 A0470/16
Sicily (1) B1101/05
sick (18) A0157/V A0587/35
A0681/01 A0681/01 A0691/18 B0811/23
B0811/24 B0811/30 B0812/33 B0963/03
B1091/09 B1091/10 B1195/13 B1222/27
B1263/22 B1390/04 C0073/01 C0083/13
sick-list (1) C0177/04
sickened (5) A0217/V
A0227/13 A0232/01 A0612/12 B0933/22
sickening (5) A0080/41
A0397/18 A0590/08 B0927/20 C0397/01
sickly (3) A0138/19
A0195/05 A0415/34
sickness (9) A0026/33
A0456/02 A0684/02 B0760/07 B0947/23
B1222/28 C0101/33 C0197/36 C0563/36
Siculus, Diodorus (1) B1191/34
side (172)
side-dishes (1) B1011/03
side-long (1) A0545/22
side-piece (1) B1011/07
side-pocket (1) C0389/38
sideboard (1) B1020/11
sidelong (4) A0582/20
A0695/01 C0567/13 C0579/11

sidereal (2) B1035/23 C0426/12
sides (59)
siding (1) C0104/02
sidled (1) A0510/01
sie (6) A0150/V A0150/V
A0345/08 A0345/08 B0723/M B0723/M
siecle (1) A0431/08
siege (3) A0059/13
A0652/05 B1107/22
sienta (1) A0344/23
siestas (1) B1105/22
Sieur (1) A0302/18
Sieur (1) C0430/39
sieve (1) B1141/10
sift (1) B0770/02
sifted (2) B1141/10 B1316/32
sigh (28) A0020/V
A0073/24 A0092/28 A0104/16 A0112/03
A0162/09 A0195/09 A0195/13 A0264/11
A0327/30 A0447/16 A0514/03 A0600/24
A0629/10 B0826/25 B0875/19 B0902/07
B1005/24 B1237/14 B1278/07 B1349/05
B1373/13 B1384/19 B1384/19 B1384/24
B1384/24 C0413/19 C0564/21
sighed (10) A0045/14 A0046/26
A0174/17 A0179/32 A0196/06 A0198/07
A0351/15 A0642/19 B1249/28 B1347/31
sighing (3) A0642/28
B0929/29 C0198/15
sighs (6) A0197/08 A0198/02
A0294/V A0319/28 A0643/28 A0645/04
sight (107)
sights (2) B0886/02 B0964/21
sign (16) A0057/03
A0066/29 A0079/28 A0100/28 A0102/03
A0240/07 A0251/21 A0337/17 B1033/04
B1235/31 B1240/04 B1260/27 C0076/27
C0150/27 C0157/28 C0409/06
signal (16) A0047/06
A0047/07 A0414/14 A0460/15 A0562/07
A0694/15 B0823/32 B1059/19 B1068/02
B1078/12 C0111/10 C0111/25 C0121/20
C0121/30 C0146/16 C0185/21
signalizing (1) B1126/05
signals (3) A0382/25
C0063/05 C0568/41
signature (10) A0144/25 A0282/02
A0282/07 A0623/14 B0833/14 B0833/15
B0833/21 B0836/06 B1138/01 B1139/04
signatures (2) A0264/01 A0264/36
signed (8) A0113/01
A0490/35 A0491/08 B0874/34 B0983/03
B0983/10 B1129/03 B1132/20
significant (2) B1133/03 B1190/32
significantly (2) A0624/14 C0388/10
signification (2) A0611/33 B1096/02
signified (2) C0086/15 C0176/12
signifies (2) A0043/V A0621/05
signifieth (2) A0048/V A0048/V
signify (1) B1155/13
signing (2) A0490/16 B1130/02
Signor (13) A0088/18
A0089/35 A0091/06 A0091/33 A0092/14
A0093/27 A0093/34 A0093/36 A0175/21
A0181/18 C0431/05 C0432/10 C0432/43
Signor's (1) C0431/09
Signora (7) A0336/01
A0336/V A0337/09 A0337/11 A0349/10
A0356/01 A0357/11
signs (21) A0059/19
A0067/10 A0189/08 A0261/02 A0303/26
A0593/16 B0823/22 B0930/26 B0989/25
B0989/35 B1131/03 B1237/18 B1358/17
C0114/20 C0119/27 C0119/36 C0145/30
C0168/24 C0175/07 C0189/37 C0543/09
Sigourney (2) A0267/01 B1385/07
Sigourney, L. H. (1) A0266/04
Sigourney's (2) A0266/15 A0267/05
Silence (3) A0195/T
A0198/11 A0198/16
silence (52)
silenced (1) B0823/17
silent (32) A0028/29
A0028/V A0139/08 A0151/06 A0151/22
A0195/M A0197/V A0210/28 A0294/V
A0297/08 A0299/28 A0400/01 A0408/22
A0444/01 A0542/07 A0625/14 A0644/10
A0673/32 B0724/23 B0763/34 B0947/30
B0963/05 B1052/31 B1191/32 B1194/18
C0072/23 C0083/19 C0083/23 C0118/02
C0124/25 C0134/18 C0412/36
silentio (1) A0662/V
silently (14) A0085/11 A0089/21
A0417/17 A0437/33 A0600/23 B0728/32
B0770/28 B0770/29 B0854/33 B1241/02
B1280/26 C0108/16 C0134/11 C0205/25
silex (1) B1162/32
silf> (4) A0464/17
A0465/06 A0466/22 A0467/10
silicified (1) B1160/42
Silk (1) B1183/06
silk (31) A0036/V
A0447/06 A0501/13 A0502/20 A0503/06
A0628/04 B0734/34 B0735/08 B0758/09
B0759/03 B0761/33 B0863/13 B0911/02
B0968/30 B1049/18 B1071/16 B1071/30
B1073/03 B1074/07 B1074/11 B1074/23
B1076/02 B1258/19 B1292/27 B1292/28
B1292/33 B1293/03 C0172/02 C0389/29
C0395/01 C0534/22
silk-buckingham (1) B1293/03
silk-velvet (1) A0246/02
silk-worms (1) B1207/37
silken (3) A0234/28
A0247/20 A0402/09
silks (1) B0945/12
silky (2) C0167/17 C0168/16
sill (1) C0186/38
Silliman's/Journal (1) B1357/02
silly (14) A0019/22 A0026/15
A0120/10 A0263/02 A0279/32 A0556/04
B0833/25 B0852/12 B0915/27 B1013/23
B1114/14 B1115/01 B1131/03 B1257/27
silver (36) A0044/04
A0045/22 A0087/23 A0155/01 A0158/03
A0163/15 A0165/05 A0279/17 A0368/20
A0414/17 A0415/21 A0415/23 A0415/27
A0501/11 A0501/14 A0502/01 A0537/32
A0640/10 A0641/01 A0643/14 B0820/27
B0825/27 B0827/27 B0872/34 B0945/17

->B0955/33 B1009/02 B1283/09 B1332/12 B1339/33 B1363/04 B1364/27 B1364/34 C0388/34 C0389/26 C0575/20
silver-like (1) A0138/27
silver-smith (1) A0540/17
silvery (2) A0152/24 A0164/V
Simeon (5) A0043/02 A0043/10 A0045/08 A0048/V A0048/V
Simia (1) A0124/21
similar (120)
similarity (10) A0414/05 A0434/23 A0434/26 A0478/15 B0829/11 B0829/16 B0949/05 C0428/01 C0448/V C0448/V
similarly (7) A0410/09 A0552/04 B0979/29 B1139/08 B1144/03 C0131/06 C0145/03
simile (2) A0209/06 B0989/14
similes (3) A0343/17 A0343/20 A0344/04
similitude (5) A0234/21 A0270/34 A0410/15 B1137/05 C0388/26
Simmond's (1) B1162/28
Simms (3) A0282/22 A0282/26 C0102/16
Simms, W. T. Gilmore (1) A0282/18
Simoom (3) A0136/V A0138/V A0195/V
simoom (2) A0211/V B0932/V
Simoon (3) A0136/34 A0138/13 A0195/V
simoon (2) A0145/10 A0211/01
simpering (1) C0130/18
simple (77)
simple-minded (1) C0564/08
simplest (3) B0839/28 B0855/05 B1074/19
simpleton (4) B0984/14 B0984/17 B0984/20 B0984/24
simplicity (10) A0274/37 A0349/02 A0405/20 A0459/01 A0582/23 B0876/20 B0975/27 B0989/05 B1072/14 B1383/10
simply (27) A0091/30 A0106/29 A0110/32 A0315/21 A0340/31 A0501/26 A0528/19 A0688/30 B0745/23 B0929/36 B1089/16 B1092/34 B1179/30 B1193/15 B1213/13 B1219/09 B1240/03 B1298/20 B1312/29 B1339/07 B1354/17 B1357/06 B1371/22 B1375/09 B1384/10 C0401/04 C0547/16
Simpson (16) B0887/10 B0887/18 B0887/V B0888/06 B0897/29 B0898/04 B0899/28 B0900/02 B0909/16 B0910/23 B0911/14 B0911/18 B0911/22 B0911/V B0913/13 B0914/06
Simpson, Adolphus (1) B0887/14
simultaneous (1) B1015/06
simultaneously (7) A0057/25 A0370/05 B1021/06 B1190/29 B1221/12 B1221/13 A0387/19
sin (4) A0319/01 B0852/25 B0852/25 B1224/28
Sinbad (9) B1154/33 B1155/16 B1155/18 B1159/04 B1159/13 B1159/17 B1159/28 B1159/34 B1160/06
Sinbad (1) B1158/33
since (165)
sincere (3) B1050/04 B1257/12 C0096/32
sincerely (4) A0071/12 A0106/10 A0654/01 B0823/28
sincerest (1) B1052/31
sincerity (4) A0295/27 A0401/24 B0915/V C0089/07
sinciput (3) A0482/17 A0483/20 B1190/34
sind (1) B0723/M
sind> (1) A0465/27
sine (1) A0599/M
sine (2) C0404/40 C0404/41
sinecure (1) A0370/08
sinecures (2) A0369/28 A0370/10
sinews (1) C0062/35
sing (6) A0125/12 A0125/13 A0407/21 B0905/06 B0915/29 B1021/01
Sing, Cheyte (2) B0949/16 B0949/18
Singapore (1) C0179/18
singed (1) B1107/09
singer (1) B0905/11
singing (11) A0124/29 A0127/04 A0343/22 B0904/05 B0904/26 B0906/04 B0993/09 B1004/05 B1096/14 C0530/38 C0560/11
Single (1) A0301/01
single (108)
single-minded (1) B1051/05
singles (1) B1337/32
singly (3) A0294/13 B1282/04 C0547/07
singular (138)
singular-looking (5) A0141/17 A0388/33 C0167/14 C0193/01 C0195/09
singularity (7) A0142/11 A0144/14 B0829/21 B0949/36 C0076/19 C0429/39 C0574/08
singularly (29) A0026/16 A0054/05 A0063/13 A0088/25 A0155/14 A0215/04 A0248/03 A0297/V A0315/22 A0378/17 A0397/03 A0434/18 A0511/24 A0536/08 A0544/25 A0557/01 A0604/18 A0608/10 A0639/V B0796/34 B0887/28 B0940/08 B0942/05 B1106/05 B1137/16 C0398/35 C0436/V C0524/37 C0531/26
singularly-marked (1) A0603/04
sinister (5) A0019/V A0262/33 A0371/17 A0409/25 A0631/20
Sinivate (3) A0386/07 A0386/12 A0386/17
Sinivate, Theodore (1) A0385/28
sink (13) A0052/03 A0062/05 A0588/19 B0732/18 B0741/11 B0741/35 B0743/15 B0743/23 B0743/29 B0744/24 B0760/09 C0116/15 C0534/08
sinking (14) A0138/25 A0140/22 A0214/28 A0373y20 A0397y18 A0602y18 A0692/30 B1236/21 C0064/39 C0075/40 C0141/17 C0411/02 C0559/28 C0559/31
sinks (3) B0732/11 B0740/12 B0743/08
sinned (3) A0034/08 A0474/03 A0474/03

sinner (2) A0075/12 A0252/26
sinner's (1) A0227/32
sins (2) B1291/14 B1292/04
sinuous (2) A0247/06 B0943/11
Siope (1) A0195/V
Sioux (32) C0548/18
C0548/23 C0549/03 C0549/07 C0549/14
C0549/42 C0550/07 C0550/23 C0551/13
C0551/16 C0551/17 C0551/29 C0551/37
C0551/38 C0552/04 C0552/21 C0553/14
C0553/14 C0554/05 C0555/14 C0555/25
C0556/10 C0556/25 C0556/28 C0557/10
C0557/14 C0558/01 C0558/05 C0558/21
C0560/08 C0560/26 C0565/36
Sioux (1) C0550/27
Sioux/Tetons (1) C0556/24
sipped (2) B1102/14 B1105/11
sipping (1) A0099/02
Sir (33) A0158/19
A0158/20 A0173/03 A0176/12 A0183/06
A0183/07 A0205/27 A0413/09 A0414/07
A0415/16 A0468/08 A0469/06 A0469/08
A0469/10 A0469/20 A0527/M B1069/16
B1069/33 B1070/15 B1070/18 B1070/30
B1070/34 B1072/23 B1072/30 B1080/04
B1114/19 B1114/19 B1358/16 B1359/12
B1359/29 C0428/28 C0525/07 C0526/33
sir (153)
sire (2) A0023/24 A0399/15
Sirius (1) B1168/V
sis (1) B0814/12
Sissytoonies (1) C0551/10
sister (12) A0404/01
A0410/15 A0639/06 B0877/18 B0877/22
B0924/11 B1153/09 B1153/17 B1154/26
B1154/28 B1155/09 C0529/20
sister-in-law (2) B0877/19 B0877/22
sisters (9) B0922/18
B0923/19 B0924/07 B0926/03 B0926/07
B0933/04 B0933/18 C0522/18 C0529/01
sit (24) A0072/10
A0105/14 A0250/18 A0262/22 A0318/11
A0339/06 A0369/22 A0385/14 A0409/08
A0415/07 A0493/08 A0508/33 A0562/24
A0578/20 A0578/29 A0621/24 A0656/14
A0681/02 B0824/28 B0911/V B0931/32
B0931/33 B0932/06 B1167/24
site (4) A0366/27
A0681/M B1303/09 C0198/35
sitot (1) A0397/M
sits (3) A0250/11
A0369/03 A0467/08
sittin> (1) A0466/V
sitting (38) A0071/19 A0174/12
A0174/22 A0179/27 A0180/02 A0217/04
A0217/04 A0248/12 A0296/16 A0329/08
A0353/16 A0357/03 A0407/11 A0441/18
A0466/29 A0487/16 A0565/04 A0566/19
A0650/04 A0664/19 B0728/28 B0794/03
B0797/18 B0905/V B0958/32 B0975/02
B1045/31 B1057/06 B1100/03 B1167/09
B1247/21 B1249/08 B1347/22 C0060/30
C0069/20 C0136/06 C0175/10 C0532/18
sitting-places (1) A0502/19
sittings (1) A0443/23
Situ (1) A0601/33
situated (23) A0044/29
A0053/11 A0248/03 A0369/07 A0374/17
A0501/V B0928/32 B1248/10 B1277/33
B1301/18 B1352/27 C0099/34 C0131/06
C0145/03 C0152/12 C0174/35 C0180/36
C0400/07 C0410/25 C0418/10 C0537/35
C0555/34 C0574/16
situation (81)
situations (3) C0438/V
C0543/10 C0559/34
six (1) A0036/21
six (122)
sixes (3) B0773/21
B0773/23 B0773/27
sixpence (2) A0489/18 A0489/33
sixpences (1) B1090/04
sixpennies (1) B0878/30
sixteen (10) A0120/17 A0483/30
A0578/12 B0887/26 B1093/17 B1335/35
C0057/12 C0068/25 C0537/37 C0576/31
sixteen-hundredth (1) C0405/05
sixteenth (9) B1143/17
B1251/03 B1251/04 B1335/16 C0129/38
C0149/10 C0164/18 C0192/25 C0421/11
sixth (20) A0068/29
A0138/29 A0175/05 A0177/21 A0181/27
A0183/16 A0276/11 A0314/18 A0614/36
A0615/21 A0671/11 A0672/01 B0864/21
B0941/29 B1262/19 C0129/41 C0159/39
C0179/16 C0423/32 C0531/34
sixthly (1) A0248/03
sixty (29) A0045/02
A0366/33 A0367/02 A0673/06 B0819/05
B0874/30 B0968/17 B1077/21 B1130/19
B1161/06 B1192/25 B1192/30 B1248/10
B1351/34 C0156/01 C0161/02 C0161/11
C0181/33 C0186/34 C0193/13 C0200/23
C0400/16 C0400/21 C0415/35 C0416/09
C0432/06 C0525/37 C0545/09 C0578/26
sixty-eighth (1) A0578/27
sixty-fifth (1) C0161/09
sixty-five (5) A0511/12
C0138/20 C0161/11 C0405/19 C0418/32
sixty-four (2) C0159/34 C0160/35
sixty-fourth (1) C0159/02
sixty-seven (1) C0162/06
sixty-six (1) C0162/06
sixty-two (2) B1137/36 C0161/02
size (65)
sized (1) A0485/22
sizes (5) B1073/23
B1119/05 C0178/22 C0540/22 C0573/35
Skarholm (1) A0579/28
skate (1) C0174/06
skeered (1) B0812/05
skeleton (7) A0244/27
A0248/17 A0253/18 A0689/04 B0956/29
B1119/M C0072/22
skeletons (4) B0825/23
B0844/11 B0961/14 B1260/V
skeptic (1) B1104/32
skeptical (2) A0027/24 B1044/07
skepticism (1) A0438/10
sketch (12) A0059/03

->A0069/V A0070/03 A0174/31 A0180/22
A0501/01 A0558/27 B0828/28 B0829/06
B0829/14 B0829/28 B0830/32
sketched (2) B1185/01 C0554/13
sketching (2) B0831/26 B1246/05
sketchy (2) C0428/02 C0448/V
skewers (1) C0175/01
skies (7) A0123/32
A0124/27 A0189/15 A0599/M A0702/M
B1267/M C0423/31
skiff (4) B0817/14
B0864/23 B0865/14 B0866/09
skilful (3) B0914/12
B1119/21 B1257/13
skilfully (2) A0105/18 B0770/15
skill (12) A0341/V
A0404/16 A0441/03 A0444/09 A0530/01
A0707/29 B0956/14 B1108/01 B1272/30
C0059/06 C0168/16 C0544/41
skilled (1) A0096/05
skillful (2) A0478/23 C0188/13
skim (1) A0588/20
skimmed (1) A0037/06
skin (31) A0103/23
A0312/09 A0355/22 A0402/08 A0460/17
B1157/07 B1180/25 B1235/13 B1239/22
C0081/12 C0087/16 C0123/35 C0142/11
C0173/04 C0174/31 C0174/34 C0180/28
C0186/26 C0188/16 C0190/31 C0206/07
C0395/29 C0405/15 C0549/19 C0552/10
C0552/16 C0552/19 C0552/20 C0564/22
C0569/29 C0575/39
skins (11) A0143/14
C0154/07 C0168/15 C0174/20 C0175/01
C0203/37 C0536/16 C0552/05 C0570/06
C0575/32 C0575/42
skipped (1) A0567/13
skipping (1) A0627/07
skirmish (1) C0560/24
skirt (3) A0351/05
B0735/13 B0763/03
skirts (3) A0366/32
C0068/40 C0571/15
skulking (2) A0356/29 C0186/22
skull (42) A0067/01 A0248/08
A0248/16 A0249/19 A0250/32 A0253/07
A0651/25 B0809/28 B0810/07 B0810/08
B0821/01 B0821/03 B0821/06 B0821/10
B0821/18 B0821/21 B0821/22 B0821/22
B0824/21 B0829/18 B0829/19 B0829/31
B0831/06 B0831/08 B0831/21 B0831/23
B0831/30 B0831/33 B0832/16 B0832/32
B0834/31 B0842/13 B0842/16 B0842/19
B0843/13 B0843/24 B0843/31 B0844/03
B0958/22 B1191/08 B1383/27 C0579/22
skull's (1) B0843/25
sky (21) A0145/15
A0228/04 A0349/24 A0578/17 A0585/28
A0587/10 A0587/33 A0594/08 A0602/26
B0819/14 B0819/16 B1080/11 B1280/26
B1391/17 C0166/11 C0184/05 C0189/07
C0399/23 C0416/19 C0536/37 C0575/20
sky-blue (9) A0087/05
A0100/15 A0175/07 A0181/28 A0336/07
A0349/13 B1165/15 B1185/33 C0389/25
sky-light (3) B1351/20
B1353/19 B1354/24
Skylark (1) B1291/12
slab (3) B1303/36
B1304/01 B1304/09
slabs (2) A0235/27 B1337/02
slack (7) A0583/37
A0584/25 A0585/11 A0586/35 A0586/38
A0587/25 A0594/12
slack-lime (1) B1073/27
slack-water (1) A0584/04
slackened (1) C0563/21
slain (3) A0125/10
A0125/35 A0346/06
slake (1) B0760/01
slaked (1) C0188/20
slammed (1) A0253/16
slamming (1) B0876/17
Slang-Syllabus (1) B1141/07
Slang-Whang (4) A0338/24
A0338/25 A0338/26 A0338/27
slant (1) A0603/07
slanted (1) A0640/08
slap (1) C0101/12
slapped (2) A0114/02 B1046/01
slapping (2) C0168/36 C0546/07
slashed (1) A0086/30
slashes (1) A0086/31
slate (3) B0734/03
B0748/18 B0812/04
slaty (1) C0184/03
slave (4) A0320/25
A0403/10 A0427/08 C0414/33
Slave/river (1) C0527/03
Slave/Lake (1) C0527/04
slavery (1) B1316/14
slayeth (1) A0414/20
sledgehammer (1) B1020/06
sleep (62)
sleep-producing (1) B0941/27
sleep-waker (9) B1030/20
B1032/09 B1035/33 B1040/07 B1040/15
B1238/32 B1239/07 B1239/21 B1241/33
sleep-waker's (1) B1241/18
sleep-waking (2) B1032/02 B1237/21
Sleeper (1) B1380/21
sleeper (6) A0166/21 A0195/V
A0437/16 A0614/11 A0616/22 B0946/08
sleepers (1) B0964/29
sleeping (9) A0137/02
A0410/03 A0429/32 A0503/04 A0602/12
B1090/02 B1240/29 C0126/25 C0535/09
sleeping-place (1) C0091/19
sleeping-room (1) B1363/02
sleepless (1) C0143/24
sleepy (3) B1155/01
C0070/35 C0414/20
sleet (1) B1093/07
sleeve (6) A0106/16 A0443/11
A0443/20 B0732/25 B0732/29 C0413/31
sleeves (5) A0086/30
A0100/07 B0890/03 B0913/18 B1108/14
slender (22) A0087/22 A0094/21
A0101/V A0114/16 A0156/07 A0190/02
A0243/05 A0297/V A0311/18 A0503/10

->A0603/09 A0640/07 A0641/V A0644/V
A0682/04 B1283/06 B1336/17 B1338/28
C0137/38 C0173/31 C0397/04 C0412/35
slept (26) A0137/26 A0436/27
A0688/21 B0728/31 B0793/18 B0794/10
B0851/30 B0857/34 B0857/34 B0928/18
B0934/02 B0968/16 B0968/22 B1081/11
B1105/34 B1153/15 B1240/28 C0071/01
C0071/08 C0073/39 C0078/31 C0084/40
C0100/38 C0101/32 C0192/16 C0416/36
slice (1) B1011/21
slices (1) C0534/34
slid (6) A0292/M A0695/02
B0928/27 B1331/03 B1363/16 C0578/29
slide (5) A0195/V
A0587/35 A0591/15 A0671/18 C0578/32
Slidell (1) A0283/08
Slidell, Alexander (1) A0282/36
Slidell's (1) A0283/01
sliding (7) A0546/19
B0826/12 B0908/V B0928/23 B0928/26
B0928/29 C0579/17
slight (77)
slightest (44) A0079/17
A0249/14 A0295/26 A0326/27 A0366/25
A0378/11 A0500/01 A0538/26 A0561/27
A0585/15 A0615/11 A0624/01 A0693/12
A0710/07 B0815/31 B0857/20 B0893/21
B0965/27 B1079/29 B1097/08 B1152/34
B1275/10 B1302/07 B1310/30 B1354/07
B1358/12 B1359/15 B1360/10 B1362/12
B1363/31 B1391/21 C0064/31 C0074/07
C0130/05 C0134/03 C0179/38 C0180/14
C0388/06 C0398/35 C0409/06 C0413/19
C0415/17 C0569/22 C0579/15
slightly (37) A0261/15
A0264/18 A0300/05 A0313/06 A0313/12
A0328/V A0443/24 A0443/25 A0501/27
A0503/02 A0508/35 A0510/17 A0535/26
A0629/34 B0823/26 B0826/10 B0875/33
B0891/12 B0894/12 B0906/18 B0958/22
B1003/25 B1016/05 B1133/16 B1190/33
B1237/30 B1282/22 B1332/29 B1333/13
B1340/10 C0063/22 C0078/02 C0113/28
C0189/37 C0399/18 C0406/18 C0566/32
slim-legged (1) C0175/34
slime (3) A0686/24
B0807/03 C0142/39
slimy (1) A0685/22
sling (4) A0379/V
A0464/T A0465/02 A0470/25
slings (1) C0168/20
slip (39) A0046/15
A0093/16 A0098/01 A0112/27 A0151/28
A0341/26 A0342/V A0344/29 A0388/06
A0587/29 B0730/25 B0730/29 B0730/32
B0730/32 B0730/34 B0762/25 B0765/20
B0766/18 B0766/33 B0812/07 B0813/23
B0831/18 B0832/33 B0834/33 B0835/10
B0843/07 B1077/08 B1113/07 B1362/06
C0067/09 C0076/38 C0077/39 C0078/15
C0079/06 C0079/19 C0092/32 C0105/10
C0143/16 C0392/05
slip-knot (1) C0138/28
slipknot (1) C0090/28
slipped (13) A0058/11
A0219/04 A0468/11 A0535/25 A0580/28
B0793/32 B0852/20 B1108/13 C0069/15
C0090/17 C0142/30 C0163/36 C0188/11
slippers (3) A0086/34
A0100/11 A0155/06
slippery (8) A0578/10
A0686/05 C0183/37 C0567/19 C0571/22
C0572/27 C0577/01 C0578/27
slipping (8) A0085/11
A0152/08 A0559/05 A0692/V B0766/29
C0120/04 C0121/09 C0138/27
slips (6) A0037/19 A0383/16
C0545/17 C0546/40 C0546/41 C0547/02
sloop (4) B0968/13
B0968/17 B0968/28 C0099/21
sloop-fashion (1) C0057/27
slope (7) A0270/17
A0282/23 A0591/16 A0594/04 A0603/01
B1280/23 B1330/25
sloped (8) A0590/35
B1280/08 B1331/24 B1332/01 B1333/27
B1381/34 C0543/13 C0567/15
slopes (6) A0278/34 B0862/35
B1281/24 B1331/18 B1331/34 B1385/35
sloping (5) B1338/14
C0181/31 C0196/32 C0555/07 C0573/12
slouched (2) B1102/32 B1105/05
slouching (1) A0297/V
slow (26) A0316/08 A0323/22
A0388/19 A0411/11 A0428/31 A0431/12
A0591/21 A0653/15 A0675/19 A0689/34
A0695/02 B0854/27 B0855/28 B0958/02
B0963/07 B1222/28 B1298/33 B1299/04
B1371/33 C0073/20 C0074/24 C0137/36
C0143/40 C0396/16 C0401/28 C0534/34
slow-match (1) C0394/26
slow-paced (1) B1136/10
slower (2) A0081/06 B1292/14
slowly (48) A0025/14
A0029/V A0037/V A0047/30 A0140/15
A0152/04 A0215/12 A0217/V A0330/16
A0404/06 A0416/24 A0437/15 A0512/23
A0592/19 A0592/31 A0594/08 A0604/17
A0604/22 A0612/31 B0793/03 B0793/03
B0818/07 B0823/30 B0851/36 B0894/12
B0895/05 B0897/21 B0927/33 B0966/09
B1057/10 B1212/17 B1239/21 B1279/01
B1281/11 B1282/34 B1382/22 B1385/10
C0077/21 C0111/21 C0123/17 C0124/03
C0125/26 C0184/20 C0188/28 C0387/25
C0444/V C0559/02 C0562/21
sluggish (2) A0400/02 A0458/19
sluggishly (1) B1238/27
slumber (31) A0028/18
A0195/21 A0195/M A0312/20 A0324/18
A0501/02 A0566/13 A0643/30 A0643/30
A0664/15 A0682/21 A0682/24 A0689/12
B0827/16 B0865/17 B0963/16 B0963/33
B0968/08 B0968/27 B0969/18 B1178/10
C0070/36 C0084/30 C0085/10 C0128/20
C0415/09 C0416/05 C0416/12 C0419/18
C0421/14 C0422/09
slumbered (6) A0612/29 A0688/01
A0702/M B0724/31 B0964/30 B1267/M

slumberer (2) A0616/24 B1237/27
slumbering (5) A0311/26
A0610/25 A0612/16 A0663/15 B1107/03
slumbers (9) A0087/37
A0139/28 A0322/25 A0600/24 A0605/04
A0616/12 B0858/16 B0964/28 B1105/23
slung (1) B1057/34
slur (1) B1035/24
sluts (1) B1096/38
Sluys (1) A0240/04
slxw (1) B1374/12
Slyass (5) B1136/17
B1136/19 B1136/25 B1137/02 B1139/01
smack (9) A0583/21
A0583/35 A0584/27 A0585/08 A0585/30
A0590/02 A0590/32 A0593/32 B1381/33
smacked (1) A0110/15
small (231)
small-clothes (1) A0628/04
small-pox (2) C0522/23 C0565/35
smaller (27) A0152/03
A0537/32 A0579/11 A0582/32 A0591/26
B0828/11 B0989/19 B1073/31 B1073/35
B1130/32 B1130/33 B1336/03 B1340/21
C0090/20 C0136/20 C0141/25 C0151/24
C0153/21 C0154/10 C0156/21 C0162/37
C0172/22 C0394/17 C0394/22 C0396/17
C0560/04 C0574/17
smallest (12) A0387/02
A0662/07 B0738/24 B0741/25 B1131/27
B1207/26 B1321/03 B1363/29 C0088/07
C0155/14 C0203/36 C0532/41
smart (4) A0489/27
B1004/32 C0135/38 C0139/18
smarter (1) A0346/10
smell (9) A0081/08
A0092/22 A0111/32 A0217/V A0345/27
A0613/02 A0687/03 B0968/29 C0124/09
smelled (2) A0350/15 A0350/18
smells (1) A0244/01
smelt (4) A0092/07
A0111/19 A0350/13 A0694/15
Smif (1) A0387/V
smile (32) A0025/10
A0098/07 A0098/15 A0215/11 A0215/22
A0217/V A0234/23 A0247/05 A0303/02
A0407/41 A0410/24 A0415/34 A0438/08
A0444/09 A0467/27 A0508/11 A0536/24
A0600/23 A0664/V B0744/18 B0773/32
B0815/04 B0871/03 B0895/19 B0927/20
B0940/14 B1030/33 B1040/10 B1135/03
B1257/03 B1257/04 C0125/24
smiled (15) A0249/10
A0299/13 A0356/07 A0624/02 A0629/34
A0665/17 A0673/03 A0690/33 B0795/28
B0796/24 B0797/20 B0901/22 B0927/28
B1135/14 B1191/23
smiles (16) A0037/19
A0164/17 A0303/05 A0312/24 A0435/09
A0509/29 A0629/08 A0641/V A0644/V
A0650/09 A0665/03 B0797/25 B0898/14
B0903/28 C0123/40 C0130/19
smiling (10) A0227/08 A0231/20
A0261/15 A0469/14 A0582/23 A0612/03
A0691/11 B0947/25 C0123/36 C0559/04
smirked (1) B1348/33
smirking (1) A0468/26
Smith (20) A0380/19
A0382/08 A0382/27 A0382/27 A0382/31
A0383/18 A0383/19 A0383/20 A0383/30
A0383/32 A0384/19 A0385/07 A0385/08
A0385/14 A0385/31 A0385/32 A0386/06
A0386/10 B1370/11 B1370/35
smith (1) B1305/12
Smith, Horace (1) A0205/29
Smith, John (4) B1369/21
B1370/01 B1370/30 B1370/34
Smith, John A. B. C. (8) A0378/03
A0380/02 A0381/11 A0382/24 A0382/28
A0385/02 A0388/24 A0389/17
Smith, Thomas (1) A0172/03
Smith's (2) A0379/01 A0386/09
Smitherton (11) A0655/07
A0655/09 A0655/17 A0655/23 A0655/28
A0656/08 A0656/13 A0656/19 A0656/25
A0657/04 A0657/17
smitten (3) A0065/18
A0262/28 B0963/03
smock (1) C0108/38
smoke (18) A0029/24 A0044/24
A0071/11 A0368/34 A0373/22 A0374/10
B0943/06 B0974/08 B0977/32 B1157/25
B1157/26 B1167/09 C0086/06 C0187/18
C0189/24 C0189/40 C0388/14 C0440/V
smoke-blackened (1) A0240/08
smoked (2) A0373/19 A0667/28
smoking (5) A0023/26
A0372/02 A0610/22 A0667/15 A0667/20
smoky (2) A0507/20 B1328/09
smooth (24) A0405/32
A0580/20 A0580/30 A0590/21 A0603/10
A0685/21 B0818/29 B0902/19 B1081/26
B1165/03 B1180/26 B1363/18 C0062/23
C0120/23 C0126/29 C0129/40 C0140/34
C0141/06 C0152/28 C0152/33 C0159/24
C0166/35 C0203/10 C0204/15
smoother (1) A0640/11
smoothing (1) C0169/18
smoothly (2) A0086/27 A0100/04
smoothness (1) A0312/15
smote (1) A0108/17
smother (1) A0154/19
smothered (3) A0409/33
C0072/12 C0182/12
smothering (1) B0897/06
Smug (2) B1127/03 B1137/13
smuggle (1) B0925/16
smuggling (1) B0904/07
snags (1) C0534/09
snail (2) B1311/31 B1312/15
snail-paced (1) B0896/17
snake (2) B0950/14 B1016/21
snake-like (1) C0575/18
snakes (1) A0625/V
Snap (7) A0205/10
A0205/31 A0206/03 A0487/05 A0487/09
A0487/26 A0487/32
snapped (1) C0198/25
Snapping-Turtle (2) B1143/18
B1143/28

snappish (1) A0341/13
snares (1) A0441/06
snarl (1) C0081/25
snarling (1) C0081/37
snatch (1) C0126/24
snatched (1) A0234/13
snatches (2) A0638/10 B1225/03
snatching (1) C0146/04
sneak (1) A0622/18
sneaking (1) B1093/04
sneer (5) A0299/06
A0435/15 B0828/33 B1184/08 B1370/25
sneered (2) A0624/03 B1130/33
sneering (1) B1383/14
sneers (2) B0871/12 B1381/01
sneezed (2) A0254/05 B1182/34
sneezing (4) A0091/11
A0108/05 A0110/16 B1310/23
Snob (13) B1132/20
B1133/10 B1136/19 B1137/02 B1137/04
B1137/09 B1137/10 B1137/39 B1138/01
B1138/02 B1139/01 B1139/04 B1139/13
Snobbs (4) A0336/09
A0336/10 A0337/03 A0337/08
Snobbs, Suky (3) A0336/03
A0337/09 A0349/11
snore (5) A0056/19
A0066/09 B1155/14 B1178/12 C0085/04
snores (1) B1154/31
snoring (3) B1155/11
C0084/29 C0094/21
snort (1) B1165/10
snout (3) C0165/16
C0165/17 C0173/30
snow (12) A0055/01
A0064/09 A0101/V B1093/07 C0150/32
C0155/01 C0161/30 C0162/28 C0163/21
C0206/08 C0571/25 C0576/29
snow-ball (1) B1334/21
snow-capped (2) C0521/07 C0575/14
snow-white (1) A0406/V
snowed (1) A0101/24
snowy (1) B1339/30
snowy-white (1) A0152/28
snub (1) A0294/09
Snubbing (1) B1141/07
snubby (1) B1157/20
snuff (6) A0090/20 A0371/13
A0489/11 A0539/10 B1012/17 B1312/20
snuff-box (7) A0108/09
A0108/11 A0356/03 A0371/11 B0992/08
B0992/09 B1102/30
snuff-color (1) A0370/33
snuffed (1) C0091/41
snuffy (1) A0429/01
snug (4) A0249/28
B0930/11 C0104/33 C0149/29
snugger (1) A0486/35
snugly (2) C0104/39 C0407/07
so (5) A0150/V
A0345/07 A0357/05 B0723/M B0723/M
so (1) B0873/12
so (1702)
So-and-so (2) A0174/13 A0174/18
So-and-So (1) A0179/28
so-called (1) B1294/34
soaked (1) C0547/21
soap-boiler (1) A0482/33
soapstone (9) C0180/36
C0183/36 C0184/30 C0185/08 C0193/11
C0196/14 C0196/24 C0196/31 C0197/29
soar (3) A0163/03
B1297/27 B1316/11
soared (4) A0599/M
B0924/20 B1076/23 B1108/29
soaring (3) B1145/01
C0390/22 C0573/04
soars (1) B1298/31
sob (4) A0319/09
A0326/22 A0328/21 B0929/35
sobbed (1) A0348/15
sobbing (3) B0859/01
B0929/26 B0929/29
sober (16) A0240/23
A0240/V A0299/26 A0371/V A0439/15
A0485/34 A0663/28 B0748/01 B0767/34
B0844/06 B0914/07 B0969/11 B1109/24
B1301/33 C0058/15 C0148/37
sober-sided (1) B0878/03
sobs (2) A0613/30 C0130/38
sociable (1) A0466/16
sociably (1) C0100/19
social (8) A0025/26
A0381/31 A0703/16 A0704/16 B0926/03
B1268/15 B1269/15 B1293/21
Society (3) A0337/18
A0337/18 B1093/19
society (40) A0026/14
A0093/08 A0105/01 A0112/20 A0204/04
A0204/16 A0204/27 A0205/08 A0205/34
A0225/02 A0225/09 A0227/04 A0229/02
A0229/09 A0296/04 A0337/17 A0337/22
A0338/09 A0338/33 A0339/02 A0346/24
A0398/24 A0508/18 A0532/08 A0623/33
A0626/20 B0760/15 B0896/01 B0902/06
B0927/06 B0960/31 B1233/08 B1390/09
B1390/10 B1390/11 C0055/04 C0162/13
C0174/27 C0537/17 C0563/37
socket (7) A0479/26
A0479/28 A0665/32 B0851/29 B0851/36
C0074/01 C0095/06
sockets (10) A0078/07 A0355/01
A0613/10 A0685/06 B0928/01 B0947/32
B0983/08 B1156/22 C0397/11 C0406/06
socle (1) A0159/03
Socrates (1) A0160/24
sod (3) B1337/04 C0575/36 C0576/39
sodales (2) A0209/M A0218/14
sodden (1) A0509/18
sods (1) B0942/34
sofa (9) A0401/19
A0500/30 B0871/31 B0871/35 B0872/06
B0872/08 B1021/14 B1249/10 B1340/08
sofas (2) A0502/20 A0502/25
soft (30) A0033/14 A0088/18
A0154/24 A0155/V A0247/05 A0271/26
A0312/20 A0613/32 A0640/01 A0643/28
A0645/04 A0681/18 B0742/31 B0878/05
B0929/15 B1165/03 B1333/09 C0090/24
C0145/38 C0178/19 C0181/28 C0183/35

->C0184/01 C0191/09 C0415/31 C0543/14
C0572/28 C0573/08 C0573/18 C0579/34
soften (3) B0902/21
B0958/04 B1050/13
softened (6) A0047/09 A0178/24
B1104/16 B1109/25 B1331/25 B1332/01
softening (2) A0427/05 C0086/33
softer (4) A0643/16
B1281/23 B1332/09 C0573/25
softest (2) C0196/14 C0542/13
softly (1) B0965/32
softness (4) A0312/25
A0402/02 B1280/19 C0536/30
sofy> (5) A0466/29
A0466/30 A0467/07 A0468/11 A0469/28
soho (2) A0125/13 A0125/16
soi (Gr.) (1) A0455/M
soient (2) A0037/10 C0430/36
soil (23) A0600/20
B0817/26 B0862/34 B0959/14 B1161/35
B1162/16 B1162/25 B1190/27 B1332/28
B1334/23 B1334/35 C0156/16 C0166/20
C0185/01 C0185/11 C0185/16 C0530/10
C0540/26 C0553/01 C0566/20 C0573/12
C0577/20 C0578/21
soiled (2) B0991/03 B0991/20
soils (1) B1090/04
soiree (3) A0384/13
B0908/22 B0915/27
sojourn (4) A0369/11
A0398/15 B1054/20 C0576/36
sojourned (1) A0046/09
solace (2) A0317/05 A0402/29
solar (6) B0904/16 B1322/18
B1340/15 C0423/15 C0423/24 C0442/V
sold (9) A0484/34
A0631/23 B0745/30 B0746/18 B0865/21
B0872/08 B1128/21 C0529/02 C0533/41
soldier (3) A0045/23
A0381/20 B0795/12
soldiers (1) B0812/01
sole (67)
Soledad (1) C0157/03
solely (13) A0206/01
A0210/19 A0229/M A0432/11 A0642/02
A0710/27 B0737/20 B0962/20 B1219/07
B1223/22 B1321/20 B1369/23 C0522/08
solemn (27) A0081/04
A0141/19 A0150/V A0153/12 A0162/28
A0165/13 A0195/V A0241/06 A0320/23
A0323/17 A0405/06 A0428/31 A0429/10
A0429/10 A0439/20 A0515/26 A0603/19
A0614/13 A0616/12 A0616/V A0675/19
A0676/11 B0911/V B0964/28 B0965/20
B1278/29 C0524/06
solemnity (11) A0161/20
A0196/07 A0244/14 A0294/14 A0339/10
A0642/14 A0643/19 B0817/29 B0948/20
C0175/05 C0552/03
solemnly (8) A0319/27
A0483/14 A0487/33 A0604/V A0609/37
A0674/10 B1053/14 C0104/21
soles (2) A0534/26 C0174/07
solicit (2) B0849/02 C0426/20
solicited (3) A0156/27
->B1072/23 C0393/12
soliciting (1) B1011/21
solicitous (1) B1113/01
solicitously (1) A0441/12
solicitude (1) C0116/32
solid (34) A0044/30 A0087/23
A0102/06 A0107/33 A0322/03 A0352/31
A0428/21 A0430/05 A0438/14 A0667/39
A0667/64 A0685/20 A0686/24 A0690/20
B0809/02 B0828/05 B0833/26 B0878/24
B0967/16 B1156/11 B1156/27 B1157/12
B1160/02 B1193/09 B1261/16 B1262/28
B1322/29 B1391/29 B1392/06 C0076/09
C0115/37 C0178/20 C0182/03 C0387/26
solid-looking (1) A0508/34
solidiforms (2) A0175/V A0182/06
solidity (7) A0271/20
A0478/37 B1034/20 B1138/V B1165/14
B1168/08 B1191/08
solidly (1) B0858/29
soliloquized (1) A0070/22
soliloquy (4) A0071/20
A0387/24 A0548/21 B0826/25
solitary (17) A0029/12
A0216/17 A0348/20 A0602/01 B0755/14
B0766/21 B0859/13 B0945/31 B0964/01
B0983/V B0991/02 B1108/08 B1163/06
B1304/29 C0072/03 C0532/22 C0560/12
solitude (2) A0602/06 A0602/07
solitude (19) A0195/10
A0196/29 A0197/03 A0197/11 A0197/19
A0197/30 A0242/28 A0319/06 A0412/11
A0508/08 A0567/23 A0600/07 A0600/18
B0760/01 B0942/32 B1277/27 B1279/02
B1391/12 C0073/24
solitudes (2) A0610/02 C0412/34
solo (1) A0161/04
Solomon (2) B0878/28 B0880/10
soluble (1) B0839/26
solus (1) B0813/24
solution (28) A0384/17
A0386/22 A0387/13 A0429/03 A0547/18
A0548/06 A0548/V A0560/08 A0568/17
B0736/24 B0828/24 B0835/12 B0835/14
B0836/01 B0836/05 B0836/18 B0839/25
B0840/13 B0923/09 B0926/23 B0926/23
B1164/03 B1164/35 B1183/28 B1293/05
B1317/04 C0080/29 C0415/02
solutions (3) A0528/08
B1164/05 B1164/08
solve (4) A0434/03
A0478/32 A0708/34 B1273/28
solved (6) B0835/23 B0835/24
B0842/15 B1069/06 B1164/04 B1206/17
solving (5) A0479/04
A0707/22 B0831/28 B1272/23 C0166/23
sombre (4) A0400/28
A0603/17 B1279/05 C0538/36
Some (2) A0178/V B1177/T
some (1160)
somebody (19) A0072/23
A0175/05 A0176/26 A0176/27 A0176/28
A0181/26 A0182/29 A0182/30 A0182/31
A0489/33 A0586/22 A0651/24 A0652/19
B0821/01 B0913/15 B1012/16 B1012/V

->B1324/01 C0389/12
somehow (4) A0341/12
A0490/05 A0584/31 B1050/25
something (159)
sometimes (53)
somewhat (136)
somewhere (16) A0055/02
A0172/03 A0178/03 A0273/37 A0284/20
A0350/18 A0584/02 A0621/26 B0812/21
B0834/02 B0843/22 B0877/05 B1095/05
B1206/19 C0083/04 C0525/20
somnolency (1) B0941/28
Son (1) A0048/V
son (4) A0096/M
A0096/M A0397/M B0905/24
son (26) A0026/19 A0048/V
A0120/01 A0160/V A0160/V A0173/10
A0177/25 A0178/17 A0183/20 A0190/20
A0312/28 A0399/15 A0468/20 A0469/26
A0584/28 A0624/08 B0735/34 B0768/01
B1142/11 C0057/13 C0057/16 C0087/01
C0522/24 C0529/12 C0566/08 C0568/40
song (14) A0126/23 A0190/24
A0246/07 A0489/26 A0527/M A0651/23
B1004/06 B1128/21 B1143/17 B1225/03
B1384/15 C0387/M C0544/07 C0550/21
songs (7) A0190/08
A0190/20 A0190/21 A0641/22 B0916/06
B1123/01 C0530/39
sonn (1) B0913/07
Sonnambula (1) B0905/21
Sonnet (1) B1385/27
sonorous (2) A0190/20 B1129/04
sonorously (1) A0615/11
sons (5) A0228/12
A0232/17 A0577/04 B0734/30 C0066/33
sont (1) B1121/03
Sontag (1) A0294/V
sonum (1) A0536/18
soon (213)
sooner (39) A0019/V
A0080/42 A0268/24 A0295/11 A0384/15
A0403/17 A0415/25 A0430/06 A0468/01
B0756/20 B0823/01 B0854/07 B0858/34
B0907/25 B0923/08 B0925/03 B0959/18
B0988/27 B0991/11 B1040/10 B1048/06
B1049/17 B1056/27 B1108/10 B1110/06
B1164/18 B1225/12 B1352/03 B1379/26
C0058/18 C0082/14 C0085/16 C0091/40
C0110/09 C0113/13 C0119/22 C0190/39
C0555/31 C0564/32
sooppose (1) B0913/V
soot (1) A0538/08
sooth (3) A0413/29
A0415/22 A0665/21
soothed (2) A0317/04 B1018/05
soothing (11) B0900/12
B1004/14 B1005/19 B1005/25 B1005/31
B1008/13 B1016/32 B1017/36 B1018/19
B1021/31 B1281/15
sooty (1) C0569/10
sophist (1) A0151/09
sophistry (1) B1221/19
sophists (2) A0710/34 B1275/35
Sophocles (1) A0608/M
soporific (1) C0084/35
soprano (1) B0905/18
sorcery (1) A0431/05
sore (1) A0414/14
sorely (2) B0833/17 C0184/17
sorrow (32) A0026/19
A0053/37 A0063/09 A0153/15 A0154/03
A0196/28 A0209/06 A0209/07 A0216/24
A0228/22 A0228/22 A0233/03 A0233/04
A0320/03 A0366/04 A0401/17 A0407/25
A0457/03 A0603/20 A0604/21 A0605/05
A0608/25 A0614/31 B1004/09 B1047/02
B1096/12 B1145/25 C0065/20 C0095/27
C0148/39 C0148/39 C0567/36
sorrowful (3) A0398/08
A0641/21 C0183/30
sorrowfully (1) B1057/08
Sorrows (1) A0342/V
sorrows (4) A0320/18
A0613/34 B1360/23 B1372/07
sorry (22) A0074/22 A0088/06
A0093/36 A0203/01 A0266/26 A0285/23
A0355/28 A0381/06 A0563/06 A0627/23
B0811/20 B0816/15 B0816/15 B0910/V
B1005/29 B1019/05 B1044/08 B1050/10
B1089/22 B1153/23 B1154/31 B1271/04
sort (29) A0252/28
A0483/23 B0730/27 B0765/22 B0819/11
B0878/05 B0904/13 B0940/26 B0984/02
B1009/14 B1016/26 B1017/28 B1052/11
B1055/33 B1128/28 B1129/23 B1130/08
B1180/11 B1194/03 B1294/29 B1299/18
B1299/29 B1346/08 B1363/01 C0391/19
C0427/12 C0530/03 C0562/06 C0573/10
sorts (3) B1050/19
B1092/17 B1132/19
Sospiri (1) A0151/14
sospite (1) A0681/M
sotticism (1) B1315/28
sottise (1) B0986/34
sottish (1) A0247/31
sotto (1) A0382/26
soufflee (1) A0113/26
sought (22) A0294/02 A0316/07
A0404/11 A0413/22 A0458/22 A0532/08
A0536/V A0560/23 A0591/32 A0664/26
A0667/17 A0685/27 A0694/12 A0694/22
B0726/19 B0808/08 B0914/26 B1059/04
B1115/04 B1183/26 C0143/06 C0540/31
Soul (1) A0533/22
soul (170)
soul-passion (1) B1123/12
soul-stirring (1) A0079/12
soul's (2) B1031/05 B1212/28
soulless (2) A0438/21 A0617/05
souls (19) A0033/02
A0091/08 A0110/14 A0111/33 A0189/17
A0196/V A0311/26 A0321/06 A0489/05
A0494/09 A0533/02 A0611/V A0640/25
A0641/V A0642/27 B1222/11 C0116/08
C0124/05 C0146/35
Sound (1) C0526/18
sound (120)
sounded (11) A0086/20
A0151/21 A0337/15 A0372/20 A0533/19

->A0627/27 A0628/18 A0674/18 B0796/16
B1138/14 C0164/19
soundest (5) B1004/27
B1295/27 B1296/32 B1296/33 C0416/05
sounding (5) A0674/14
B0979/34 B0985/24 C0163/07 C0164/14
sounding-gear (1) C0167/02
soundless (2) A0397/01 C0205/37
soundly (10) A0372/06 B0728/32
B0857/33 B0934/08 B0968/22 B1032/19
C0100/39 C0192/16 C0416/37 C0575/43
sounds (30) A0161/28 A0190/24
A0210/01 A0235/29 A0245/03 A0248/V
A0314/21 A0323/24 A0324/13 A0324/13
A0324/22 A0403/07 A0411/30 A0415/04
A0514/31 A0537/18 A0550/16 A0600/03
A0608/11 A0613/19 A0613/32 A0614/12
A0643/25 B0764/29 B0929/13 B1092/07
B1096/19 B1168/02 B1240/14 C0447/V
soup (2) B0875/02 C0535/35
souper (1) B1056/02
sour (1) A0429/01
source (34) A0067/23 A0406/02
A0431/30 A0461/06 A0528/03 B0855/05
B0926/25 B0943/34 B0986/16 B0987/33
B1137/14 B1143/11 B1160/21 B1215/14
B1215/14 B1233/08 B1249/33 B1322/21
B1346/01 C0061/01 C0064/12 C0081/19
C0087/03 C0438/V C0525/39 C0527/22
C0527/29 C0527/33 C0528/03 C0528/22
C0530/23 C0544/17 C0551/10 C0562/08
sources (12) A0106/32
A0141/28 A0473/32 A0500/09 A0507/15
A0529/23 A0545/20 B0753/38 B0761/01
B0850/15 C0525/23 C0551/13
sourit (1) A0036/17
sous-cuisinier (1) A0099/13
South (11) A0071/27
A0380/31 B1016/25 B1075/24 B1076/21
B1076/27 B1246/12 C0057/20 C0147/16
C0208/21 C0541/07
south (72)
south-east (1) C0417/05
south-eastern (1) B1338/02
south-west (1) A0585/03
south-western (1) C0540/18
South-West (1) B1392/03
South/Carolina (2) B0806/06
B1081/15
South/East (1) B1076/19
South/Orkney (1) C0162/11
South/Orkneys (1) C0160/14
South/Pacific (1) C0093/24
South/Sea (1) C0151/37
South/Seas (7) B1277/22
C0053/T C0055/02 C0147/07 C0148/06
C0161/27 C0178/05
South/Shetland/Islands (1) C0160/15
Southampton/Row (1) A0464/03
southeast (8) C0146/38
C0148/32 C0150/11 C0158/32 C0161/38
C0162/26 C0163/24 C0203/06
southeastern (2) C0170/41 C0176/14
southerly (4) B0923/36
C0155/05 C0155/14 C0203/07
Southern (8) B0822/27
B1299/21 B1386/10 C0055/30 C0056/07
C0428/07 C0448/V C0540/15
southern (41) A0145/26
A0321/14 B0862/05 B1002/02 B1008/17
B1281/33 B1331/18 B1331/33 B1332/11
B1332/17 B1333/20 B1334/07 B1334/10
B1335/33 C0053/T C0148/02 C0150/15
C0155/15 C0157/09 C0157/28 C0158/26
C0159/07 C0159/21 C0159/27 C0162/15
C0165/33 C0166/12 C0171/20 C0173/38
C0180/27 C0186/36 C0188/39 C0191/26
C0196/13 C0203/23 C0205/27 C0416/23
C0419/38 C0551/12 C0551/14 C0554/04
Southern/Indian/Ocean (1) C0150/08
Southern/Ocean (2) C0202/25
C0207/21
southward (46) A0121/08 A0139/14
A0145/18 A0583/27 B0942/14 B1160/25
C0149/23 C0156/30 C0158/12 C0158/21
C0159/01 C0159/14 C0159/19 C0159/23
C0159/35 C0160/02 C0160/12 C0160/36
C0161/19 C0162/20 C0163/06 C0163/12
C0163/16 C0164/17 C0164/27 C0166/04
C0166/34 C0167/05 C0170/24 C0170/27
C0170/37 C0173/24 C0177/29 C0185/37
C0198/32 C0201/32 C0202/13 C0203/08
C0203/18 C0204/19 C0204/27 C0205/22
C0407/32 C0419/16 C0542/03 C0554/27
southwardly (9) B1331/16
B1331/22 B1332/06 C0160/26 C0161/37
C0162/21 C0164/15 C0164/20 C0553/17
southwest (12) B0930/09
C0058/10 C0058/33 C0088/37 C0103/08
C0148/16 C0149/21 C0149/34 C0149/38
C0202/30 C0204/05 C0528/16
sovereign (8) A0021/26
A0250/28 A0297/17 A0407/V A0600/29
A0640/15 B1298/32 C0155/41
sovereignty (1) A0120/04
sow (1) B1372/01
space (42) A0021/08 A0027/06
A0106/28 A0219/02 A0267/32 A0274/10
A0296/V A0478/34 A0478/37 A0579/14
A0601/05 A0601/14 A0616/20 A0654/V
B0822/02 B0837/33 B0893/18 B0894/01
B0979/23 B1035/07 B1038/34 B1038/35
B1040/02 B1078/25 B1114/25 B1215/10
B1243/02 B1315/01 B1321/10 B1333/37
C0068/17 C0068/24 C0069/19 C0099/29
C0099/30 C0099/33 C0113/14 C0163/01
C0179/21 C0387/26 C0410/41 C0546/19
space-penetrating (2) C0428/24
C0430/10
spaces (5) A0639/30
B0838/18 B1034/28 B1322/19 C0099/31
spacious (2) B1160/10 B1261/05
spade (4) B0814/10
B0814/12 B0822/14 B0825/25
spades (7) B0814/06
B0814/16 B0816/28 B0824/04 B0825/06
B0959/01 B1049/15
Spain (3) A0496/03
A0542/26 C0407/37
spake> (2) A0465/12 A0465/13

spalpeen> (5) A0465/01
A0467/09 A0469/19 A0470/20 A0482/14
spalpeeny> (3) A0466/01
A0469/26 A0470/10
Spaniard (4) A0549/21
A0549/27 A0549/32 A0550/06
Spaniards (1) C0533/37
Spanish (19) A0087/03
A0143/01 A0143/01 A0246/03 A0344/11
A0344/26 A0447/04 A0540/14 A0540/V
A0549/28 B0825/26 B0827/28 B0836/09
B0836/11 B1052/14 C0087/16 C0137/29
C0156/37 C0539/31
spanked (1) A0585/14
spanker (1) B0930/12
spanned (2) B1334/05 B1338/07
spar (1) C0149/40
spare (12) A0347/10
A0498/22 B1071/05 B1105/20 B1348/35
C0074/05 C0086/01 C0201/07 C0393/03
C0534/07 C0535/08 C0559/30
spared (8) A0433/28
A0621/25 A0691/22 B0869/12 B0979/06
B1131/31 C0529/22 C0563/28
spareness (1) B1234/08
spark (1) C0569/34
sparkle (2) A0702/M B1267/M
sparkled (3) A0090/01
B0890/08 B1260/03
sparkling (2) A0407/19 B0862/36
sparks (2) A0702/M B1267/M
Sparks, Jared (1) A0279/34
Sparks' (1) A0280/01
spars (1) A0142/21
sparsely (1) B1329/01
Sparta (3) A0159/01
A0159/02 A0159/05
spasm (4) A0248/02
A0588/07 B0898/24 C0406/14
spasmodic (7) A0054/08
A0063/16 A0319/20 B0967/21 B1138/26
C0081/18 C0407/29
spasmodically (1) A0692/28
spasms (5) A0069/29
B1030/30 C0103/28 C0107/23 C0424/19
spattered (1) C0125/03
speak (120)
speaker (18) A0025/06 A0144/28
A0299/13 A0416/24 A0534/05 A0540/26
A0543/04 A0548/08 A0676/05 B0949/23
B1010/08 B1011/28 B1012/05 B1013/10
B1050/27 B1221/24 B1222/05 C0059/16
speaketh (1) A0046/11
speaking (56)
speaks (16) A0357/04
A0502/09 A0556/17 A0609/25 B0751/V
B0766/15 B1106/08 B1360/32 B1361/10
C0137/35 C0159/31 C0207/27 C0428/28
C0429/40 C0522/04 C0538/34
spear (2) C0199/19 C0387/M
spears (6) B0945/17 B0947/17
C0168/19 C0169/11 C0554/10 C0557/24
special (10) A0369/12 A0709/31
A0710/19 B0924/10 B1092/22 B1214/01
B1214/01 B1274/33 B1275/22 C0062/07
specie (1) B0875/26
species (108)
specific (5) B0741/04
B0741/08 B0741/13 B0742/05 B0742/12
<u>specificae</u> (1) A0638/M
specifically (3) B0743/22
C0387/08 C0403/15
specification (1) A0299/34
specified (5) A0303/07
A0498/27 B0759/27 C0084/40 C0160/11
specify (3) A0093/19
A0112/30 B0772/01
specifying (1) B1075/15
specimen (11) A0086/33
A0273/20 A0344/12 A0387/V B0839/28
B1140/35 B1145/30 B1179/06 C0176/10
C0432/08 C0432/32
specimens (8) A0321/22
A0383/12 A0705/12 B0807/25 B0810/08
B0827/29 B0864/03 B0890/19
specious (2) A0400/13 B1153/09
speciousness (1) A0104/27
speck (5) A0215/20
B1155/36 B1391/21 C0077/34 C0443/V
speckled (1) A0640/10
specks (1) C0416/18
spect (1) B1373/02
spectacle (16) A0106/19
A0121/17 A0123/10 A0123/27 A0140/01
A0317/03 A0447/27 A0537/22 A0581/17
B0964/23 B1160/22 B1195/07 B1331/05
B1382/27 C0124/19 C0563/01
Spectacles (1) B0886/T
spectacles (21) A0029/04
A0103/31 A0106/16 A0124/17 A0205/16
A0261/08 B0728/30 B0888/V B0907/30
B0908/05 B0908/V B0910/21 B0910/27
B0911/12 B0916/31 B0990/20 B0990/26
B1292/05 C0067/27 C0107/34 C0426/34
spectator (4) A0037/12
C0111/31 C0151/20 C0423/37
spectators (5) A0154/14
A0441/22 B0859/12 B1096/11 C0186/32
spectral (7) A0080/32
A0153/24 A0445/04 A0603/20 A0675/18
A0695/30 B0966/27
spectre (2) A0426/M A0608/13
spectres (1) A0682/07
spectrum (2) A0215/19 B1167/33
speculate (3) B1316/27
B1316/31 B1364/28
speculated (2) C0057/04 C0564/12
speculating (2) A0399/12 A0591/32
speculation (20) A0021/06
A0214/10 A0296/V A0339/31 A0439/29
A0457/19 A0482/27 A0490/31 A0509/31
A0583/33 B0724/06 B0870/05 B1364/10
B1364/18 C0134/29 C0167/06 C0169/27
C0170/22 C0208/13 C0401/09
speculations (16) A0070/20
A0080/28 A0081/42 A0151/09 A0151/09
A0608/14 A0705/02 A0706/09 B1190/23
B1270/02 B1271/13 B1310/30 B1360/03
C0413/05 C0423/03 C0427/09
Speculative (1) C0392/11

speculative (8) A0212/33
A0225/16 A0225/20 A0234/07 A0456/20
A0457/11 B1249/30 C0438/V
speculatively (1) B1357/11
speculum (1) C0430/21
speech (28) A0067/25
A0105/21 A0161/22 A0234/30 A0249/23
A0251/27 A0252/30 A0315/04 A0353/04
A0356/08 A0624/12 A0710/15 B0728/16
B0822/33 B0913/12 B1135/29 B1139/19
B1183/20 B1184/21 B1275/18 B1354/20
C0061/35 C0082/39 C0083/21 C0175/22
C0426/02 C0426/02 C0556/05
Speeches (1) B1141/06
speeches (6) A0175/32 A0181/32
A0345/26 A0628/23 C0391/18 C0395/37
speechless (5) A0158/V
A0594/17 B0911/16 B0983/06 B1134/31
speed (21) A0128/02
A0580/09 A0591/03 A0592/28 A0630/27
B0837/13 B0873/20 B1108/17 B1158/12
B1166/28 B1166/30 B1178/29 C0200/20
C0200/40 C0400/17 C0412/19 C0421/32
C0553/30 C0557/35 C0563/19 C0568/20
speediest (1) C0438/V
speedily (13) A0388/27
A0612/14 B0753/11 B0872/04 B0988/11
B1021/06 B1049/16 B1222/06 C0062/16
C0108/13 C0108/16 C0120/18 C0133/33
speeding (1) A0580/32
speedy (7) A0386/17
A0691/08 B0927/11 B1129/06 B1129/22
B1241/29 C0095/15
spell (7) A0022/20
A0227/05 A0231/16 A0338/07 A0416/23
A0664/22 B1339/03
spellbound (1) B1244/05
spelled (1) B1095/08
spelling (1) B0950/19
spells (1) A0337/20
spelt (2) B0950/24 B1095/10
spend (6) A0655/27 B0729/09
B0756/12 B1177/03 B1246/02 C0066/32
spending (3) A0090/19
B0813/24 C0066/28
spendthrifts (1) A0440/15
spent (25) A0120/28
A0135/23 A0347/15 A0405/07 A0438/01
A0513/06 A0587/04 B0726/15 B0826/33
B0827/19 B0850/12 B0865/14 B0904/24
B1209/02 C0102/06 C0120/37 C0126/19
C0146/03 C0149/01 C0391/30 C0402/24
C0419/25 C0528/27 C0550/13 C0575/31
spermaceti (1) C0149/09
sperrits> (1) A0464/12
sphere (10) A0080/31 A0479/06
A0479/07 A0592/28 A0592/34 A0600/27
B0840/32 C0404/39 C0404/40 C0404/41
spheres (2) A0318/13 B1120/07
spherical (3) A0273/15
A0592/27 C0404/38
spheroid (1) C0417/28
Sphinx (2) B1246/T B1250/27
<u>Sphinx</u> (1) B1250/18
Sphynx (1) A0639/V

sphynxes (2) A0165/24 B1192/24
spice (1) B1096/30
spices (1) C0535/36
spicing (2) A0339/32 A0343/15
spicy (1) A0694/07
spider (4) A0090/15
B0794/30 B0940/V B1251/02
spiders (1) A0478/14
spikes (5) A0429/06
C0143/30 C0143/33 C0144/01 C0144/36
spin (2) B1013/18 B1207/34
spinal (1) C0165/08
spines (1) B1156/18
spinning (2) B1020/24 C0198/12
spins (1) A0656/29
spiral (3) A0136/22
A0350/06 B0980/03
Spirit (2) A0033/03 A0601/23
spirit (126)
spirit-land (1) A0594/20
spirit-lifting (2) A0311/25
A0644/19
spirit-soothing (1) A0428/03
spirit-stirring (2) A0431/08
A0644/V
spirited (4) A0662/12
B1009/18 B1090/25 B1340/03
spirits (44) A0023/15
A0092/23 A0092/34 A0111/V A0112/11
A0296/V A0402/21 A0407/09 A0431/28
A0455/V A0460/32 A0514/33 A0551/04
A0611/22 A0626/30 A0665/16 B0926/02
B0931/10 B0942/23 B0981/31 B1014/34
B1076/04 B1108/31 B1194/33 B1246/16
B1390/06 C0107/24 C0114/16 C0119/01
C0127/23 C0139/07 C0142/25 C0398/39
C0412/22 C0416/38 C0537/04 C0537/15
C0547/36 C0549/02 C0549/20 C0553/07
C0560/30 C0561/20 C0576/09
spiritual (14) A0189/27 A0210/01
A0313/17 A0413/12 A0600/13 A0643/31
A0682/28 A0703/09 A0711/17 B1122/10
B1212/18 B1276/18 B1339/08 C0112/03
spirituality (8) A0312/26
A0338/06 A0500/24 A0704/05 A0712/02
B0724/05 B1269/05 B1277/04
spit (2) A0101/11 C0130/41
spite (31) A0078/07
A0247/07 A0295/21 A0371/16 A0431/31
A0432/31 A0435/01 A0584/14 A0673/10
A0694/01 B0761/27 B1034/13 B1034/25
B1166/03 B1316/15 C0056/16 C0058/41
C0072/09 C0089/12 C0114/30 C0131/32
C0140/04 C0144/39 C0146/07 C0149/36
C0395/21 C0414/14 C0423/06 C0423/07
C0557/18 C0559/24
spitefully (1) A0071/13
spitting (2) C0128/34 C0569/28
splash (1) C0125/09
splashed (1) C0144/24
splendid (1) A0511/02
splendor (9) A0021/01
A0157/04 A0159/21 A0406/04 A0640/10
B0904/18 B1128/12 B1136/31 B1332/36
splendours (1) A0640/V

splinter (3) A0564/28
C0118/39 C0135/20
splintered (2) A0487/23 A0543/33
splinters (7) A0592/13
C0134/08 C0134/26 C0134/37 C0134/40
C0135/06 C0135/15
split (5) A0468/24
B0930/18 C0178/37 C0185/11 C0188/07
splitting (3) A0581/21
C0101/36 C0169/13
splotch (1) B0854/12
splotches (2) C0107/39 C0107/40
splotching (1) C0109/05
spoil (1) B1007/22
spoiled (5) A0497/20
B1010/09 C0074/05 C0082/32 C0137/10
spoilers (1) C0547/32
spoils (2) A0497/V C0188/16
spoilt (2) A0599/M B1010/V
spoke (124)
spoken (64)
spokeshaves (1) C0148/10
sponges (1) C0534/15
sponsors (1) B1346/05
spontaneity (1) B1247/11
spontaneous (3) B0757/05
B1190/26 B1190/28
spoons (1) A0537/32
sport (6) A0099/02 B1096/26
B1097/02 B1346/32 B1350/08 C0547/34
sported (2) A0312/21 B1122/35
sporting (1) A0553/09
sports (1) A0431/23
spose (1) B0820/17
spot (86)
spots (20) A0204/26
A0543/25 A0559/02 A0583/29 A0639/32
B0808/33 B0809/33 B0815/14 B0828/31
B1120/03 B1239/24 B1277/35 B1300/34
C0157/14 C0157/16 C0184/37 C0184/39
C0425/17 C0429/11 C0577/23
spotted (5) A0322/14
A0502/02 B0834/34 B1334/25 B1339/29
spotting (1) B1278/35
spotty (1) A0502/10
spouse (1) B1107/V
spout (1) B1009/V
sprang (31) A0045/06
A0151/27 A0217/V A0243/33 A0416/18
A0565/12 A0610/20 A0640/07 A0640/32
A0643/08 B0767/03 B0793/32 B0932/09
B1020/13 B1057/06 B1057/25 B1123/26
B1162/26 B1248/15 B1333/14 B1337/19
C0058/22 C0072/27 C0082/15 C0085/15
C0091/40 C0112/23 C0125/15 C0131/15
C0200/01 C0578/17
sprawling (4) A0265/19
A0285/34 A0498/18 B0925/24
spray (4) A0580/28
A0585/29 A0589/15 A0591/10
spread (25) A0136/14
A0142/15 A0159/V A0189/09 A0249/04
A0352/14 A0406/31 A0537/19 A0559/12
A0625/16 A0640/12 A0665/28 A0674/26
B0818/02 B0853/09 B1332/06 C0072/17
->C0139/21 C0189/28 C0412/36 C0417/14
C0432/12 C0443/V C0546/03 C0566/16
spreading (5) A0249/06
A0559/03 A0580/22 B1161/30 C0575/11
sprightly (1) B0726/03
spring (41) A0325/22
A0356/23 A0479/29 A0531/15 A0541/14
A0552/22 A0552/26 A0552/30 A0553/04
A0553/26 A0554/02 A0554/03 A0630/18
A0638/05 B0855/10 B0932/08 B0944/12
B1071/22 B1071/23 B1071/26 B1077/06
B1077/12 B1130/20 B1337/06 C0128/26
C0130/22 C0180/34 C0188/19 C0188/21
C0522/24 C0527/09 C0534/38 C0536/30
C0543/33 C0547/05 C0547/13 C0561/38
C0563/22 C0563/25 C0568/10 C0573/14
spring-guns (1) A0381/27
spring-house (1) B1338/06
springing (11) A0382/03
A0555/03 B0905/28 B1167/15 B1213/08
B1332/20 B1334/35 C0131/41 C0139/02
C0145/35 C0165/22
springs (11) A0210/14
A0433/V A0479/19 A0552/33 B0965/34
B1212/26 B1221/08 B1277/06 C0171/02
C0187/09 C0547/23
springy (2) A0510/21 A0603/08
sprite (1) A0599/M
spruce (1) C0533/01
sprung (9) A0416/V
A0615/03 B0752/21 C0103/07 C0114/03
C0122/36 C0146/38 C0199/11 C0199/20
spun (1) A0590/22
spunging (1) B0982/26
spurious (1) B0985/02
spurned (1) A0440/12
Spurzheim (1) B1191/17
Spurzheimites (1) B1220/08
spy (1) C0553/19
spy-glass (5) A0465/11
A0465/13 C0439/V C0443/V C0568/24
spyglass (1) B1300/31
squabbles (1) B1189/15
squall (7) A0252/01
C0104/27 C0104/29 C0139/24 C0149/26
C0149/39 C0162/28
squalling (1) A0374/03
squalls (4) C0102/24
C0163/22 C0163/39 C0570/29
squandering (1) A0151/02
square (29) A0045/01
A0151/21 A0273/28 A0351/27 A0367/22
A0430/03 A0512/32 A0513/02 A0688/31
A0696/25 B0901/07 B0980/22 B0985/26
B1164/40 B1185/27 B1336/18 B1340/14
C0068/17 C0068/25 C0136/23 C0152/02
C0152/17 C0152/36 C0192/22 C0387/09
C0391/08 C0430/22 C0533/28 C0573/36
square-looking (1) B1157/10
square-rigged (1) C0106/15
squared (1) B0988/07
squares (4) B1092/17
B1120/04 C0152/32 C0403/25
squashish (2) B1158/33 B1159/03
squat (3) A0241/10

->B0819/10 B1092/09
squaw (3) C0087/02
C0552/24 C0561/07
squaze> (7) A0468/15
A0468/22 A0468/23 A0469/05 A0469/08
A0469/09 A0470/22
squazes> (1) A0468/18
squazing> (3) A0468/01
A0468/05 A0469/23
squeak (1) B1158/33
squeak (1) A0387/03
squeaked (1) A0388/29
squeaking (1) A0374/03
squeeze (1) B0968/21
squeezed (5) B1192/32
C0077/24 C0194/13 C0534/41 C0544/32
squeezing (3) C0090/18
C0091/34 C0181/30
Squibalittle (1) B1139/02
squibbing (1) B1047/25
squint (2) A0353/31 A0387/V
squirrel (1) B1346/20
squirrels (1) C0545/20
St./Andree (4) B0729/06
B0729/31 B0732/36 B0758/20
St./Andrew's/Stair (1) A0242/16
St./Andrews (1) A0240/06
St./Austin's (1) A0213/05
St./Bartholomew (1) B0955/07
St./Bruno (1) A0662/V
St./Charles (1) C0530/40
St./Eustache (15) B0729/13
B0731/13 B0732/37 B0733/11 B0736/12
B0751/19 B0751/24 B0752/34 B0755/07
B0755/22 B0755/31 B0756/04 B0756/13
B0756/17 B0756/23
St./Eustache, Jacques (1) B0729/08
St./Florentin (2) A0175/20
A0181/09
St./George (2) A0101/V A0181/13
St./Germain (1) A0561/02
St./Helena (2) C0430/45 C0431/12
St./Louis (1) C0528/13
St./Mark's (1) A0086/20
St./Mark's/Place (1) A0268/02
St./Menehoult (5) A0175/19
A0181/08 B1007/23 B1010/21 B1010/31
St./P-- (2) A0294/V C0526/25
St./Patrick (1) A0625/07
St./Peray (3) A0099/02
A0101/V A0181/15
St./Peter's/river (1) C0528/23
St./Peters' (2) C0551/06 C0551/07
St./Petersburgh (1) C0526/22
St./Pierre (1) A0079/04
St./Pierre, Bernardin de (1) B1114/02
St./Urfino (1) A0087/12
St./Vincent (1) B1161/30
stab (3) A0447/10
C0133/13 C0188/33
stabbed (2) C0113/01 C0135/27
stability (1) B1164/27
stable (3) A0027/11
A0563/02 B1053/32
stables (7) A0021/15
->A0022/05 A0022/24 A0023/26 A0024/11
A0024/13 A0025/04
stadium (1) A0128/V
Stael (5) A0180/V
A0712/V A0712/V B1277/V B1277/V
staff (1) B1248/18
stage (25) A0055/36
A0056/10 A0065/19 A0065/32 A0246/11
A0383/17 A0383/26 A0682/30 A0682/34
B0832/01 B0889/07 B0889/16 B0892/02
B0892/22 B0894/09 B0894/14 B0894/22
B1045/07 B1090/27 B1090/27 B1119/20
B1350/38 C0093/09 C0402/29 C0423/03
stage-box (1) B0892/04
stage-coach (1) B0863/06
stage-mad (1) A0534/18
stage-player (1) A0252/27
stage-struck (1) A0072/21
stages (1) A0682/27
staggered (14) A0023/12 A0166/23
A0245/06 A0297/14 A0387/11 A0439/02
A0447/13 A0686/05 B0818/05 B0859/07
B1058/07 B1108/10 C0406/20 C0579/11
staggering (5) A0137/12
A0140/20 B0896/22 B0912/03 C0397/02
stagnant (3) A0139/27
B1049/03 C0572/29
stagnation (2) A0210/14 B0742/18
staid (3) B0877/35
C0540/27 C0570/02
stain (3) A0164/18
A0600/21 B0796/13
stained (6) A0036/V A0165/06
A0671/27 B1049/21 B1058/04 B1280/34
stains (1) A0670/05
stair (2) A0176/26 A0416/17
stair-case (1) A0054/30
staircase (14) A0063/30 A0157/03
A0166/14 A0182/29 A0350/22 A0350/26
A0350/35 A0356/23 A0409/26 A0412/05
A0562/10 A0567/25 B1182/23 B1258/29
staircases (5) A0029/17
A0152/06 A0350/01 A0401/02 C0573/23
stairs (24) A0173/25
A0179/07 A0470/09 A0470/21 A0470/V
A0537/16 A0540/06 A0541/28 A0542/27
A0543/02 A0543/14 A0546/27 A0547/23
A0548/28 A0551/10 A0558/18 A0562/05
A0565/13 B0856/19 B0859/08 B1336/31
B1337/24 B1372/15 B1391/24
stairway (1) A0080/44
stake (1) B0728/13
stakes (9) A0441/30
C0184/39 C0185/02 C0185/05 C0185/07
C0185/16 C0185/19 C0190/24 C0190/39
Stale (1) A0337/21
stale (4) A0337/20
A0343/27 B0871/08 C0142/02
stalk (1) C0405/30
stalked (8) A0151/19
A0244/13 A0515/06 A0610/12 A0673/27
A0675/20 B0794/22 C0524/03
stalking (3) A0018/01
A0068/17 A0242/25
stall (5) A0027/15

->C0392/08 C0392/39 C0395/05 C0399/32
Stamboul (3) A0175/04
A0181/25 B0896/18
stamen (1) A0568/20
stamens (2) B1163/29 B1163/29
stammered (1) C0059/20
stamp (8) A0028/02
A0144/18 A0276/03 A0338/18 A0340/24
A0509/34 B0833/17 B0833/20
stamped (5) A0276/02
A0430/33 A0490/18 B0866/19 C0576/38
stamping (2) B1021/09 C0131/17
stanchions (3) A0102/05
C0098/19 C0098/30
stand (41) A0046/01
A0088/01 A0088/21 A0090/05 A0090/08
A0120/02 A0145/09 A0165/02 A0191/12
A0338/22 A0352/02 A0353/02 A0384/09
A0416/26 A0447/10 A0489/21 A0586/16
A0623/06 A0673/33 B0812/13 B0839/11
B0875/29 B1020/35 B1081/12 B1106/12
B1106/25 B1169/23 B1222/26 B1348/18
C0059/10 C0059/18 C0059/25 C0108/22
C0115/20 C0136/33 C0140/15 C0163/14
C0175/37 C0184/12 C0555/38 C0578/05
stand-still (1) C0105/34
Standard (1) B0754/35
standard (2) A0089/05 A0667/61
standing (37) A0053/01
A0058/14 A0062/07 A0069/03 A0174/15
A0216/25 A0249/03 A0367/27 A0441/22
A0442/33 A0485/07 A0503/04 A0509/01
A0583/34 B0865/33 B0902/06 B0924/34
B0931/35 B1157/27 B1183/13 B1185/03
B1192/17 B1330/24 B1336/04 C0061/05
C0067/15 C0070/02 C0071/02 C0075/04
C0085/36 C0159/36 C0163/17 C0185/02
C0195/13 C0199/29 C0522/15 C0577/09
stands (17) A0337/20
A0337/21 A0339/07 A0368/13 A0416/21
A0564/03 A0656/27 A0673/31 A0703/23
B0739/21 B0807/06 B0864/30 B1163/31
B1207/36 B1268/22 B1298/22 B1316/33
Stanfield (2) A0502/05 A0707/V
stanzas (6) B1127/17 B1127/23
B1128/11 B1132/08 B1133/04 B1139/28
staples (1) B1261/26
Stapleton (2) B0960/29 B0960/36
Stapleton, Edward (1) B0959/32
star (22) A0162/V A0314/18
A0314/19 A0545/21 A0545/24 A0599/M
B0898/02 B1035/14 B1035/18 B1035/18
B1168/35 B1168/V B1215/25 B1215/29
B1301/02 B1301/02 C0187/30 C0395/19
C0430/17 C0430/19 C0438/V C0439/V
star-beloved (1) A0151/04
star-shadows (1) B1039/01
star-shaped (2) A0640/29 A0643/05
starboard (14) A0585/13 A0588/21
A0590/06 B0928/26 C0062/21 C0068/11
C0071/41 C0099/18 C0115/14 C0117/09
C0123/12 C0123/33 C0165/21 C0187/10
starched (2) A0089/12 A0246/27
stare (8) A0215/10
A0370/25 A0513/24 B1180/29 B1181/32
->B1348/13 C0131/30 C0550/22
stared (8) A0089/25
A0094/09 A0114/04 A0241/19 A0412/14
A0548/08 B0927/31 C0554/23
stares (2) A0241/20 B0983/10
stares> (1) A0470/03
staring (2) A0103/02 A0387/12
starry (3) A0162/20
B1212/31 B1213/26
stars (29) A0036/01
A0078/39 A0189/10 A0189/24 A0236/05
A0313/24 A0314/17 A0412/28 A0601/07
A0702/M B1038/33 B1039/04 B1040/03
B1080/11 B1122/29 B1168/36 B1212/16
B1213/27 B1267/M C0088/26 C0416/20
C0423/32 C0423/32 C0423/36 C0430/06
C0430/19 C0432/12 C0432/18 C0443/V
start (9) A0126/20
A0191/11 A0629/32 B0816/18 B0893/06
B1093/18 B1184/11 C0545/32 C0549/33
started (44) A0087/34
A0092/27 A0112/02 A0154/26 A0249/31
A0300/18 A0383/04 A0389/06 A0408/19
A0414/01 A0415/V A0513/33 A0563/20
A0585/10 A0627/28 A0630/26 A0644/V
A0684/33 B0816/26 B0856/05 B1070/03
B1089/18 B1168/39 B1295/09 B1299/30
B1310/27 C0058/08 C0058/32 C0062/30
C0067/26 C0077/22 C0421/21 C0526/34
C0530/35 C0533/08 C0540/14 C0542/30
C0545/37 C0550/18 C0558/26 C0559/08
C0561/18 C0577/12 C0577/28
starting (21) A0057/33
A0078/06 A0088/20 A0103/01 A0235/25
A0355/01 A0584/26 A0630/17 B0737/24
B0827/08 B0947/32 B0983/08 B1015/03
B1044/18 B1076/13 B1188/07 C0062/13
C0186/40 C0397/10 C0527/10 C0536/29
starting-point (1) A0535/16
startle (6) A0354/35 A0616/27
A0664/03 A0704/16 B1269/15 C0415/05
startled (27) A0021/30
A0137/03 A0151/27 A0210/10 A0210/30
A0326/23 A0353/13 A0402/09 A0410/V
A0436/16 A0500/17 A0511/24 A0534/23
A0566/13 A0616/24 A0694/10 B0723/02
B0724/20 B0793/26 B0829/26 B0865/30
B0866/01 B1033/16 B1240/02 C0124/33
C0188/29 C0189/38
startles (1) B1278/15
startling (22) A0106/06 A0166/21
A0213/29 A0266/18 A0312/22 A0325/06
A0444/15 A0533/16 A0557/01 A0593/05
A0664/23 A0686/31 A0695/29 B0763/07
B0853/30 B1029/02 B1160/17 B1300/03
C0122/24 C0404/01 C0419/29 C0422/10
startlingly (2) A0211/14 A0327/25
starvation (4) A0685/15
B1208/16 B1208/37 C0144/38
starve (3) A0092/33
A0112/10 B1207/04
starved (1) B1208/15
starving (3) A0584/11
B1208/19 C0147/35
State (2) C0531/20 C0532/12

state (113) ->A0126/12 A0144/12 A0233/18 A0233/23 A0241/09 A0245/21 A0294/V A0311/17 A0329/24 A0438/20 A0511/34 A0559/21 A0641/V B0958/19 B1300/19 C0087/07 C0112/12 C0168/13 C0533/09
state-room (13) B0922/05 B0923/04 B0924/27 B0925/20 B0927/03 B0928/20 B0928/29 B0929/01 B0929/06 B0929/09 B0930/05 B0933/36 B0934/02
state-rooms (5) B0922/16 B0922/19 B0922/22 B0926/09 B0928/32
stated (24) A0409/16 A0542/22 A0544/18 A0546/30 A0547/13 A0549/29 A0551/20 A0564/18 B0733/15 B0739/21 B1053/16 B1152/V B1240/16 B1383/04 C0078/25 C0099/29 C0117/08 C0125/40 C0179/10 C0401/13 C0423/26 C0430/06 C0441/V C0522/26
stateliest (1) A0153/07
stately (13) A0122/06 A0196/22 A0349/04 A0354/05 A0406/27 A0644/06 A0676/05 A0709/34 B0815/11 B0945/15 B1275/02 B1333/02 C0151/17
statement (11) A0269/18 A0270/28 A0705/35 B1270/34 B1357/03 B1358/24 C0055/12 C0055/28 C0056/18 C0207/09 C0430/35
statements (7) B1325/09 C0088/03 C0157/17 C0207/19 C0207/35 C0538/29 C0565/40
Staten/Land (1) C0157/12
stateroom (12) C0068/11 C0068/35 C0069/33 C0072/08 C0075/29 C0076/06 C0084/27 C0085/16 C0089/17 C0107/16 C0110/26 C0113/26
staterooms (4) C0068/04 C0068/06 C0084/06 C0085/29
states (3) B0862/17 B1194/09 C0160/19
States'/College (2) C0390/38 C0425/29
statesman (2) A0271/20 C0522/37
stating (3) A0561/V B0736/16 B0756/27
station (29) A0102/08 A0120/25 A0249/16 A0322/23 A0593/12 A0593/21 A0629/02 A0639/26 B0976/29 B1136/24 B1312/35 C0083/05 C0101/31 C0105/27 C0108/32 C0110/32 C0116/37 C0134/11 C0158/18 C0176/17 C0190/25 C0197/02 C0197/14 C0198/18 C0203/27 C0394/20 C0395/15 C0408/30 C0579/10
stationary (7) A0191/01 B1075/09 B1076/34 C0105/37 C0118/16 C0389/37 C0410/14
stationed (5) B0753/19 B1354/25 C0058/34 C0108/14 C0186/26
stations (4) A0322/01 B0874/26 C0153/17 C0189/29
statistical (1) C0521/26
statt (1) B0723/M
statu (1) B1364/06
statuary (1) A0160/24
statue (6) A0035/21 A0154/26 A0160/24 A0165/02 A0510/08 B1057/21
statue-like (2) A0022/10 A0153/01
statues (5) A0035/19 A0158/12 B1179/09 B1192/24 C0573/21
stature (20) A0064/19 ...
statures (1) A0021/28
statute (1) B1093/14
staunch (1) A0508/31
stave (1) B0905/27
staves (1) A0591/27
stay (21) A0112/23 A0128/21 A0150/M A0166/10 A0244/09 A0347/03 A0412/15 A0532/11 A0584/09 B0808/29 B0816/16 B0872/21 B0873/28 B0932/07 B1045/29 B1096/22 C0084/21 C0124/25 C0127/04 C0170/36 C0526/24
stay-sail (1) B0930/23
stayed (4) B0856/22 B0991/05 C0057/11 C0176/22
staying (2) A0622/11 C0128/03
stays (3) A0140/27 C0062/09 C0114/24
stead (4) A0414/15 A0617/01 A0703/24 B1268/23
Steadfast (1) B1314/14
steadfast (1) B0747/17
steadfastly (1) A0515/25
steadied (5) A0251/14 B1007/25 C0111/07 C0115/12 C0415/25
steadier (1) C0544/10
steadiest (1) A0021/30
steadily (48) A0190/19 A0191/05 A0199/02 A0213/13 A0227/10 A0231/23 A0310/08 A0314/12 A0404/20 A0513/01 A0556/33 A0557/V A0590/03 A0615/16 A0692/12 A0707/32 B0728/28 B0750/02 B0793/30 B0793/30 B0795/14 B0797/12 B0797/14 B0797/16 B0823/10 B0854/06 B0866/15 B0870/20 B0895/18 B0930/11 B0930/25 B0932/V B0944/16 B1075/23 B1076/04 B1080/18 B1272/33 B1281/18 C0078/19 C0124/03 C0125/27 C0126/36 C0197/31 C0388/08 C0391/11 C0419/16 C0444/V C0559/06
steadiness (1) C0415/16
steady (16) A0212/01 A0499/24 A0508/32 A0584/06 A0585/02 A0695/01 B0976/03 B1076/12 B1157/14 B1234/26 C0060/13 C0071/41 C0075/30 C0120/22 C0122/01 C0166/09
steaks (1) A0622/27
steal (3) A0612/31 B0925/15 B0929/01
stealing (3) A0663/V A0664/02 C0188/27
stealthily (7) A0310/08 A0639/19 A0682/11 B0794/28 B0794/29 B0866/14 C0544/22
stealthy (6) A0080/32 A0400/23 A0692/15 B1225/V C0549/29 C0568/36
steam (4) A0498/24 A0588/14 B1194/16 B1194/21
steam-boats (1) A0381/27
steam-engine (1) C0415/12
steam-vessels (1) A0588/14

steamboat (4) B0863/06
B0873/18 B0874/21 B1089/11
steaming (1) B0862/26
steed (8) A0023/01
A0023/22 A0025/02 A0027/06 A0027/16
A0027/V A0029/06 A0029/17
steel (22) A0081/09 A0104/09
A0268/18 A0352/31 A0690/17 A0691/03
A0691/07 A0692/07 A0693/03 A0693/12
B0944/03 B1071/12 B1071/21 B1077/12
B1080/17 B1136/09 B1161/21 B1161/38
B1180/33 B1193/19 B1193/20 C0431/04
steel-bound (1) B1053/22
Steen, Jan (2) A0175/24 A0181/21
steep (15) A0044/29
A0355/03 A0594/05 B0856/19 B0865/26
B1336/10 C0541/35 C0543/34 C0553/36
C0555/02 C0567/11 C0567/18 C0570/35
C0574/16 C0577/03
steeped (1) A0428/12
steeple (17) A0071/03
A0294/V A0349/23 A0352/22 A0355/04
A0355/30 A0366/13 A0369/07 A0369/18
A0369/19 A0369/25 A0370/27 A0372/10
A0372/17 A0374/08 A0374/21 A0428/09
steer (3) C0058/38
C0158/12 C0202/12
steerage (5) C0077/15
C0082/37 C0089/30 C0095/17 C0212/V
steered (4) B1077/32
C0123/18 C0148/16 C0160/36
Steering (1) B1068/05
steering (3) C0131/26
C0148/32 C0154/21
steersman (1) C0536/11
stem (6) A0137/08 A0399/05
B0818/32 B1332/30 C0115/13 C0202/23
stemming (1) A0124/05
stems (6) A0640/07 A0643/06
B1105/03 B1106/03 B1333/02 C0542/13
stench (4) A0122/14
C0084/35 C0094/14 C0124/09
stentorian (1) A0244/19
step (64)
Stephanie (1) B0914/V
stepped (30) A0033/M A0070/16
A0104/16 A0108/17 A0154/07 A0179/25
A0325/05 A0351/04 A0445/05 A0448/02
A0535/25 A0547/02 A0552/19 A0562/13
A0686/28 A0695/06 B0753/25 B0814/21
B0896/20 B0944/10 B0960/22 B0992/15
B1183/34 B1250/09 B1261/21 B1261/30
B1339/13 C0114/05 C0532/03 C0533/27
stepping (6) A0100/33 A0383/12
A0685/22 B0909/02 B1045/28 C0545/12
steps (54)
sterb'ich (2) A0345/07 A0345/07
sterbich (2) A0150/V A0150/V
stereotomic (1) A0536/V
stereotomy (4) A0535/09
A0536/03 A0536/05 A0536/V
steril (3) C0155/12
C0155/17 C0166/20
sterling (1) A0381/29
stern (32) A0137/08
->A0137/33 A0142/23 A0315/09 A0316/27
A0318/V A0401/17 A0446/18 A0486/29
A0589/25 A0681/14 B0866/06 B0878/04
B0891/23 B0931/18 B0932/04 B1040/12
B1052/29 B1338/20 C0106/02 C0115/13
C0124/18 C0125/26 C0126/02 C0131/25
C0134/04 C0134/18 C0188/09 C0200/37
C0202/23 C0413/01 C0536/06
stern-post (4) A0137/16
C0115/31 C0115/33 C0115/35
stern-sheets (1) B0931/29
Sterne (1) B1378/M
sterner (3) A0328/25
B0817/29 B0967/23
sternest (1) A0397/10
sternly (3) A0412/19
A0628/14 B0931/32
sternutamentis (1) A0091/13
stertorous (3) B1237/11
B1237/15 C0128/20
stertorousness (1) B1237/15
stew (3) A0093/37
A0102/13 A0113/24
steward's (1) C0122/08
stick (9) A0369/17
B0812/08 B0813/22 B1102/11 B1338/25
B1373/18 C0175/18 C0396/09 C0547/15
sticking (1) B0830/15
sticks (3) C0547/05
C0561/33 C0575/41
stiff (20) A0079/42
A0240/V A0249/20 A0252/17 A0253/31
A0300/24 B0910/24 B0923/36 B0928/25
B0992/02 B1059/08 B1079/23 B1163/27
B1250/25 C0102/13 C0139/31 C0536/04
C0544/32 C0559/18 C0572/28
stiff-frozen (1) A0673/33
stiff-looking (1) A0248/03
stiffened (2) A0675/11 B1237/26
stiffer (1) B1157/17
stiffly (4) A0297/V
A0381/03 B0926/04 B1195/08
stiffness (2) A0327/23 A0380/11
stifle (1) A0684/15
stifled (5) A0414/06
A0694/22 B0724/01 B0794/08 C0147/35
stifling (6) A0153/09 A0299/27
B0955/07 B0961/21 C0072/30 C0182/30
stigma (3) B1163/28
B1163/30 B1163/39
stigmatise (1) A0338/07
stile (6) A0627/16 A0629/29
A0629/33 A0630/05 A0630/21 A0630/26
Stiletto (3) A0177/03
A0177/09 A0183/01
stiletto (1) A0086/32
still (461)
still-increasing (1) A0610/11
stillness (5) A0428/08
A0443/14 A0682/17 A0683/19 B0929/24
stimulate (2) A0689/21 B1165/28
stimulates (1) B0795/12
stimulus (2) C0128/17 C0392/31
sting (3) A0298/V
A0435/11 B0916/09

stingings (1) B1158/08
stint (1) B1017/23
stipping> (1) A0464/14
stipulated (2) B0862/25 C0177/39
stipulating (1) C0056/09
stir (11) A0353/33
A0675/V B0827/03 B0962/35 B0967/14
B1046/30 B1047/09 B1258/24 B1363/09
C0056/05 C0100/40
stirred (15) A0053/34
A0063/06 A0153/02 A0217/V A0329/05
A0329/11 A0329/23 A0329/26 A0348/13
A0639/25 A0653/21 C0072/37 C0111/23
C0118/37 C0206/02
stirring (4) A0401/01
C0387/11 C0395/25 C0574/23
stitch (1) C0391/27
stock (6) A0069/22 A0349/02
C0082/29 C0144/39 C0177/09 C0576/01
stock-jobbers (1) A0508/18
stocked (2) B1019/21 C0560/15
stockinet (1) B1350/37
stockinett (1) C0108/39
stocking (1) A0387/17
stockings (7) A0057/15
A0067/33 A0368/09 A0368/19 A0371/08
A0464/18 B0863/14
stocks (2) A0582/05 C0057/04
stoical (1) C0145/09
stole (4) A0437/03
A0682/09 C0184/25 C0205/29
stolen (1) B1318/07
stolid (3) A0458/10
B1298/23 B1316/34
stomach (22) A0059/22 A0067/13
A0091/18 A0097/20 A0099/30 A0110/20
A0367/29 A0370/14 A0543/28 A0628/01
B0741/32 B0742/27 B1106/33 B1166/14
B1346/11 C0081/10 C0107/35 C0108/41
C0117/35 C0133/13 C0175/38 C0535/40
stomachs (2) B1119/M C0128/17
Stone (1) B0740/33
stone (43) A0122/29
A0196/13 A0196/15 A0329/26 A0557/29
A0684/30 A0685/21 A0689/09 A0695/06
A0708/11 B0734/33 B0758/08 B0761/32
B0796/01 B0796/01 B0796/03 B0890/15
B1040/13 B1089/20 B1127/35 B1160/02
B1160/16 B1160/30 B1262/06 B1262/35
B1263/24 B1281/35 B1304/10 B1304/29
B1321/09 B1334/38 B1335/33 B1338/01
B1363/36 C0112/25 C0152/25 C0152/25
C0173/16 C0173/20 C0184/01 C0184/34
C0421/04 C0573/38
Stone, W. L. (1) A0285/28
Stone's (2) A0285/32 A0285/35
stone's (2) C0554/04 C0568/19
stones (33) A0081/38
A0244/23 A0400/12 A0408/11 A0408/14
A0535/09 A0535/32 A0582/12 B0734/32
B0758/07 B0761/14 B0762/06 B0828/01
B1089/23 B1166/03 B1166/12 B1322/V
B1329/23 B1330/01 B1337/05 C0152/14
C0165/34 C0168/21 C0181/22 C0186/37
C0189/29 C0191/07 C0420/33 C0422/39
->C0534/36 C0559/15 C0573/34 C0576/23
stony (3) A0415/32
B0956/21 B1181/23
stood (131)
stool (1) C0113/16
stoop (3) A0240/18
A0297/V B1052/09
stooped (3) A0299/18
B0940/09 C0390/06
stoopide (3) B0913/V
B0913/V B0913/V
stooping (6) A0249/05 A0444/03
A0536/25 B0854/21 B0944/13 C0396/15
stoops (1) B0873/21
stop (26) A0341/13 A0354/02
A0388/V A0464/08 A0489/31 A0489/32
A0552/16 A0675/V A0696/30 B0818/14
B0866/10 B0909/20 B1035/14 B1035/22
B1155/06 B1169/23 B1311/33 B1328/07
B1372/06 C0168/06 C0548/11 C0554/18
C0554/21 C0555/12 C0555/14 C0579/10
stoppage (1) C0148/25
stopped (17) A0243/V
A0354/02 A0566/09 A0696/29 B1335/09
C0067/29 C0159/20 C0191/32 C0526/01
C0540/17 C0541/36 C0561/24 C0566/29
C0566/35 C0567/12 C0568/21 C0579/17
stopper (1) C0396/08
stopping (8) A0056/36
A0486/05 A0515/24 A0565/16 C0170/29
C0526/29 C0559/39 C0563/19
stops (2) B0864/19 B1090/33
store (2) B0746/01 C0546/35
store-room (1) B1336/36
stored (2) A0245/12 C0547/02
storeroom (11) C0121/13
C0121/18 C0122/27 C0126/33 C0127/30
C0136/15 C0136/37 C0138/19 C0139/18
C0140/11 C0140/29
stores (4) A0135/05
A0243/05 C0139/01 C0530/32
stories (14) A0098/17 A0429/25
A0473/04 A0473/25 B0834/01 B0834/09
B0943/25 B1009/24 B1303/03 B1362/09
B1380/08 C0057/23 C0065/12 C0549/06
storing (1) C0093/41
storm (17) A0029/V
A0079/11 A0088/14 A0319/14 A0411/31
A0412/17 A0414/11 A0417/04 A0581/14
A0581/34 A0585/27 B0767/30 B0930/23
B0968/13 B1090/34 C0060/02 C0134/19
storm-staysails (1) C0106/16
storm-tormented (1) B1123/27
storms (3) A0228/04
C0149/15 C0202/17
stormy (2) A0087/33 C0432/21
Story (1) B0806/T
story (48) A0018/02
A0088/02 A0198/29 A0386/04 A0407/31
A0413/21 A0414/12 A0479/09 A0537/09
A0537/21 A0539/08 A0539/30 A0542/13
A0542/18 A0543/09 A0554/11 A0565/23
A0578/23 A0583/17 A0593/30 A0594/23
A0599/M A0652/22 A0652/22 A0654/19
A0654/V B0789/07 B0887/08 B0901/22

->B0957/12 B0958/36 B0982/22 B1153/16
B1154/17 B1155/08 B1159/27 B1345/02
B1350/32 B1361/24 B1386/08 C0064/32
C0080/18 C0428/15 C0428/28 C0448/V
C0541/12 C0541/12 C0569/17
Story, Joseph (1) A0275/29
Story's (2) A0275/33 A0275/37
stout (21) A0080/35
A0152/11 A0205/27 A0271/26 A0552/02
A0553/06 A0562/16 A0584/29 B0789/M
B0827/09 B0859/10 B1015/11 B1141/32
B1361/06 C0098/18 C0115/30 C0123/34
C0124/35 C0124/39 C0143/30 C0534/12
stoutest (2) A0459/28 C0531/19
stove (2) C0068/05 C0140/31
stow (1) A0251/15
stowage (19) A0136/04
C0069/11 C0091/36 C0094/13 C0095/31
C0096/01 C0097/02 C0097/03 C0097/09
C0097/14 C0097/19 C0098/03 C0098/08
C0099/07 C0099/25 C0099/26 C0099/31
C0114/04 C0114/37
stowage-room (1) A0252/01
stowed (6) A0249/28 C0089/21
C0098/17 C0190/34 C0407/07 C0533/32
stragglers (2) B0823/14 C0152/20
straggling (1) A0248/V
straight (35) A0056/05
A0244/11 A0271/23 A0276/36 A0277/36
A0283/24 A0285/02 A0297/V A0298/V
A0497/16 A0622/04 A0629/04 A0671/18
B0825/01 B0842/20 B1018/12 B1045/04
B1092/15 B1282/19 B1296/21 B1301/30
B1302/04 B1302/07 B1313/21 B1315/01
B1330/08 C0067/07 C0085/35 C0167/17
C0174/25 C0181/31 C0183/13 C0193/05
C0432/02 C0432/23
straight-forward (1) A0489/24
straight-jacket (1) A0065/29
straightaway (1) B1051/09
straightening (1) B1182/18
straightest (1) B1316/17
straightway (2) A0627/23 C0432/45
strain (6) A0164/V A0614/24
B0940/27 B1050/16 B1159/07 C0083/16
strained (3) A0326/25
A0535/26 B0930/28
straining (6) A0271/02 A0282/09
A0685/06 A0696/11 C0103/03 C0106/07
strains (3) A0022/03
A0615/27 A0615/28
Strait (1) C0158/10
strait-forward (1) C0532/20
strait> (1) A0465/06
Straits (1) B1392/05
straits (2) C0525/21 C0525/40
strange (89)
strangely (12) A0228/35
A0233/17 A0233/23 A0435/09 A0457/32
A0550/07 A0608/07 B0834/24 B1079/30
B1152/04 C0070/37 C0413/13
strangeness (5) A0312/01
A0312/04 A0313/12 A0711/26 B1276/30
stranger (45) A0081/32
A0081/34 A0089/23 A0090/23 A0091/07
->A0091/09 A0091/15 A0091/32 A0092/05
A0092/12 A0092/27 A0093/25 A0094/07
A0094/19 A0140/26 A0142/28 A0154/20
A0154/V A0155/13 A0155/20 A0156/02
A0156/03 A0156/04 A0340/34 A0434/09
A0439/16 A0442/31 A0512/06 A0512/33
A0513/14 A0514/01 A0514/19 A0515/21
A0675/07 B0950/26 B0957/11 B1093/30
B1151/M B1184/29 B1361/26 C0123/24
C0124/31 C0125/39 C0147/03 C0532/08
stranger's (3) A0089/04
A0089/32 A0103/20
strangers (4) A0250/21
B0897/12 B0967/29 C0168/06
strangest (2) A0314/06 C0190/20
strangle (1) A0589/15
strangled (2) A0557/03 C0113/20
strap (1) A0689/14
strapped (2) A0485/08 B1044/18
straps (3) B0878/02
B1185/33 B1194/28
strata (1) C0402/35
strata (3) C0413/25
C0424/24 C0573/11
stratification (4) C0171/22
C0181/28 C0185/07 C0185/14
stratum (1) C0406/12
straw (2) C0069/04 C0134/39
straw-colored (1) B1185/35
straws (2) C0134/08 C0545/17
stray (5) A0368/24
B0945/31 B1101/08 B1279/33 B1335/03
strayed (3) A0602/02
A0602/04 C0570/33
streak (5) B1156/13
B1156/24 C0109/06 C0416/22 C0543/22
streaked (1) C0543/29
streaks (4) A0580/21
A0580/22 B0827/14 C0203/24
stream (58)
stream's (1) B1281/33
streamed (6) A0139/33 A0143/16
A0330/14 A0590/25 A0672/16 B1161/05
streamer (1) B1078/05
streaming (4) A0023/09
A0029/22 B0852/21 B1215/30
streamlets (1) B1283/09
streams (11) A0158/V
A0163/09 A0639/31 A0643/26 B0862/35
B0863/29 C0163/30 C0171/22 C0171/30
C0548/11 C0574/26
street (49) A0072/24
A0078/23 A0085/01 A0124/03 A0124/04
A0174/32 A0242/12 A0248/27 A0254/03
A0352/25 A0355/32 A0487/05 A0488/06
A0489/30 A0507/20 A0509/34 A0511/28
A0512/20 A0512/26 A0512/V A0513/30
A0513/34 A0515/18 A0515/23 A0533/31
A0534/30 A0535/09 A0535/22 A0541/25
A0542/V A0546/21 A0551/23 A0565/14
A0652/19 B0796/17 B0875/13 B0877/05
B0897/07 B0897/21 B0915/10 B0915/20
B0989/25 B0990/01 B0992/19 B1093/18
B1103/12 B1182/21 C0067/08 C0067/31
street-crossing (1) A0488/19

street-door (1) B1178/13
street-robber (1) C0073/35
streets (25) A0122/14
A0189/24 A0242/29 A0244/01 A0347/28
A0349/21 A0490/08 A0533/04 A0565/19
B0734/14 B0750/07 B0750/10 B0750/15
B0851/03 B0945/06 B0945/08 B0945/23
B0947/15 B0963/09 B1092/33 B1160/13
B1225/08 B1370/09 C0392/07 C0392/21
strength (70)
strengthen (6) A0059/25 A0608/19
A0610/05 A0631/12 B0989/15 C0116/18
strengthened (9) A0623/21
A0663/V B0746/10 B0814/26 B1054/29
C0137/16 C0172/21 C0176/31 C0423/10
strengthening (1) B0832/31
strengthens (1) C0179/11
strenuous (3) A0244/17
A0337/31 A0650/05
strenuously (5) A0054/26
A0063/25 A0127/01 B1223/V C0175/24
stretch (5) A0044/03
A0195/10 A0282/03 B0989/34 C0546/18
stretched (8) A0103/06
A0136/32 A0351/01 B1057/12 B1096/16
C0124/40 C0196/30 C0536/36
stretches (2) A0121/07 C0521/06
stretching (9) A0165/V
A0686/08 B0913/01 B1382/19 C0070/02
C0122/37 C0148/17 C0417/22 C0575/14
strewed (4) A0592/09
B1160/34 C0175/03 C0559/14
strewn (3) A0144/21
C0190/13 C0198/38
stricken (6) A0163/03 A0615/35
A0672/25 B0758/22 B0771/25 B0819/29
strict (13) A0081/05
A0242/03 A0347/12 A0408/28 A0461/11
A0485/30 A0496/20 A0616/26 B0827/03
B0989/13 B1362/03 C0167/38 C0203/38
strictest (3) A0217/V
A0486/32 B0747/01
strictly (20) A0086/08
A0097/05 A0301/13 A0410/22 A0482/02
A0527/V A0531/09 A0599/05 B0757/05
B0962/35 B1089/02 B1089/14 B1268/28
B1328/08 C0098/09 C0139/16 C0428/01
C0428/24 C0448/V C0563/38
strictness (1) A0432/23
stride (1) A0427/01
strides (1) B0797/15
strike (7) A0372/14
A0372/18 B0854/31 B0864/22 B1354/15
C0165/37 C0197/40
strikes (9) A0033/12
A0142/29 A0144/V A0673/30 B0732/41
B1092/13 B1221/29 B1222/22 C0570/08
striking (24) A0209/14
A0285/18 A0300/16 A0349/02 A0351/07
A0373/28 A0388/25 A0410/14 B0929/21
B0957/04 B1279/16 B1350/15 B1352/04
C0063/36 C0070/40 C0086/22 C0114/33
C0137/41 C0140/24 C0151/20 C0187/16
C0422/24 C0526/19 C0552/04
strikingly (6) A0274/37 A0282/28
->A0283/05 A0367/08 B0891/17 C0416/17
string (13) B0818/20
B0818/25 B0821/25 B0821/26 B0821/31
B0822/04 B0947/05 B0949/17 B1096/17
C0076/37 C0076/39 C0197/13 C0552/29
stringed (3) A0314/21
A0403/07 A0406/07
strings (6) A0630/01 B0730/32
B0730/33 B1096/18 C0175/28 C0431/07
strip (9) A0034/11
A0034/12 A0034/12 A0136/16 A0675/V
B0766/15 B1183/14 C0121/05 C0417/18
stripe-interspersed (1) A0498/18
striped (1) B1165/03
stripes (2) C0108/40 C0151/15
stripped (3) A0242/33
C0108/30 C0547/03
stripping (1) B1180/24
strips (3) B0735/14
B0762/12 B0762/14
strived (1) A0218/01
striving (2) A0299/28 C0197/25
strode (8) A0253/17
A0400/30 A0439/11 A0510/23 A0514/35
B0824/02 B1258/34 C0061/39
stroke (6) A0274/34 A0568/23
A0693/09 A0694/31 B1153/29 B1237/01
stroked (1) B1184/03
strokes (7) A0269/03
A0372/20 A0674/18 A0694/19 B0825/25
C0201/08 C0411/06
stroll (3) A0489/29
B0756/22 C0539/05
strolled (4) A0347/27
A0626/24 B0897/07 C0542/03
strolling (1) A0533/31
Strom (6) A0585/11 A0586/04
A0586/31 A0586/33 A0587/26 A0594/14
strong (109)
stronger (10) A0088/14 A0381/05
A0434/14 B0748/05 B0761/29 B0900/13
B1077/31 C0093/22 C0127/03 C0543/24
strongest (6) A0354/35 A0611/29
B1052/01 B1160/42 C0531/19 C0537/28
strongly (26) A0044/28 A0427/22
A0458/32 A0503/V A0533/01 B0745/31
B0755/24 B0941/24 B0991/27 B1080/18
B1101/25 B1122/11 B1221/16 B1239/25
C0055/31 C0065/16 C0075/32 C0081/38
C0169/17 C0170/27 C0420/12 C0443/V
C0533/09 C0537/08 C0553/01 C0561/13
strongly-knit (1) C0531/22
strove (1) A0684/08
struck (54)
structure (15) A0142/16
A0152/09 A0430/05 A0436/30 A0631/12
A0670/15 A0690/20 B0857/16 B1164/27
B1336/03 B1337/18 B1391/31 B1392/08
C0173/30 C0202/18
structures (4) A0156/30
A0486/15 C0198/39 C0573/27
struggle (30) A0027/19 A0029/11
A0329/01 A0329/02 A0329/08 A0403/18
A0411/27 A0416/28 A0432/03 A0510/36
A0593/22 A0644/17 A0693/12 A0694/25

->B0734/38 B0758/13 B0762/07 B0763/28
B0763/31 B0763/31 B0764/06 B0963/30
B1049/06 B1222/21 C0082/27 C0086/11
C0144/10 C0165/10 C0197/37 C0567/21
struggled (29) A0215/28
A0313/19 A0316/24 A0327/16 A0328/02
A0401/12 A0411/06 A0411/18 A0578/17
A0684/14 A0691/09 A0691/27 A0692/18
A0692/25 A0697/04 B0855/29 B0941/17
B0947/23 B0967/34 B1242/29 B1262/35
C0074/24 C0088/20 C0182/09 C0197/32
C0406/19 C0408/28 C0567/30 C0567/39
struggles (23) A0140/22
A0152/22 A0253/12 A0316/25 A0318/V
A0402/15 A0416/14 A0529/21 A0566/28
A0582/02 A0683/09 B0741/26 B0743/23
B0743/26 B0829/23 B0956/32 B0959/05
C0064/10 C0096/08 C0138/26 C0183/14
C0188/31 C0399/06
struggling (22) A0029/V A0165/V
A0344/30 A0541/32 A0563/19 B0762/07
B0958/33 B0964/30 B0966/16 B0967/09
B0983/16 B1079/09 B1208/07 B1221/26
B1353/18 C0063/16 C0083/02 C0144/06
C0149/31 C0182/16 C0190/13 C0567/17
strugglingly (1) C0188/28
strung (1) A0588/28
strut (1) C0153/24
stubborn (2) A0061/02 A0652/26
stubbornly (1) A0058/27
stubbornness (1) A0652/06
Stubbs (1) B0900/23
stubby (2) A0357/05 A0357/05
stuck (9) A0246/03
A0248/20 A0340/30 A0592/13 B0735/07
B0759/02 B1141/21 C0427/22 C0547/19
stud (2) A0023/28 A0025/13
studded (2) A0429/05 C0542/16
studded-sail (1) A0143/20
studding-sail (3) A0142/13
A0142/13 A0143/23
Student (2) A0176/09 A0180/30
student (10) A0295/05 A0438/02
A0709/28 B0922/11 B0960/18 B1145/20
B1236/16 B1240/34 B1274/30 C0415/03
students (3) A0296/11
A0436/28 A0438/22
studied (8) A0036/21
A0054/17 A0071/28 A0086/02 A0251/V
A0299/07 A0304/02 B1031/11
studies (14) A0070/31 A0078/26
A0099/10 A0210/24 A0226/09 A0230/07
A0268/28 A0310/13 A0311/05 A0316/07
A0405/09 A0431/23 C0066/11 C0393/04
studio (2) A0400/25 B0925/33
studious (1) A0665/01
study (25) A0086/22
A0135/05 A0173/09 A0173/11 A0177/25
A0178/16 A0178/19 A0183/20 A0226/01
A0229/18 A0295/01 A0311/22 A0339/02
A0339/23 A0342/14 A0495/V A0528/13
A0611/35 B0987/16 B1018/10 B1031/10
B1115/04 B1132/07 B1181/21 B1339/16
stuff (6) A0251/20 B0812/30
B1090/30 B1129/23 B1131/23 B1165/12
stuffed (1) A0345/13
stuffing (2) C0109/01 C0190/31
stuffs (1) A0251/17
Stuffundpuff (1) A0366/19
Stultz (2) A0034/V A0034/V
stumble (2) B1352/06 C0392/07
stumbled (5) A0244/29
A0351/05 A0686/05 B0823/09 B0825/31
stumbling-block (1) A0044/14
stumbling-blocks (1) A0556/22
stump (3) A0139/10
A0281/28 B1185/03
stumped (1) A0628/V
stumpy (2) A0241/10 A0371/18
stumpy-looking (1) A0371/08
stunned (5) A0137/15
B1110/16 C0074/30 C0113/29 C0116/04
stunning (1) A0057/19
stunted (2) C0155/13 C0181/34
stupefying (1) A0058/23
stupendous (11) A0028/22
A0139/24 A0140/V A0143/32 A0145/14
A0430/18 A0456/25 B0913/V B0948/23
B1082/08 B1372/09
stupid (11) A0069/10
A0203/03 A0245/V B0923/33 B0984/34
B1018/30 B1101/07 B1144/01 C0126/19
C0199/30 C0398/33
stupid-looking (1) B1019/12
stupide (3) B0913/05
B0913/07 B0913/07
stupidity (7) A0622/10
B0821/12 B0843/12 B1006/08 B1300/12
C0432/41 C0554/14
stupidly (2) A0378/V B1261/24
stupified (10) A0023/08 A0029/V
A0153/21 A0372/V B0826/22 B0829/21
B0854/02 B0944/22 C0125/06 C0420/23
stupor (15) A0404/10
A0455/12 A0456/02 A0586/20 A0664/02
B0829/25 B0958/26 C0072/10 C0081/01
C0081/21 C0081/33 C0096/22 C0190/17
C0204/24 C0421/41
sturdily (1) A0413/33
sturdy (4) A0509/33
A0652/04 B1010/23 C0388/02
Sturgeon/Lake (1) C0526/40
stxp (1) B1374/19
style (52)
styled (3) B1127/08
B1130/14 C0427/28
styles (6) A0341/19 A0709/21
A0709/33 B1129/17 B1274/24 B1275/02
stylish (1) A0494/03
stylus (1) A0104/07
stylus (2) A0089/08 A0189/05
Styx (2) A0092/08 A0111/20
Suarven (1) A0579/26
suavity (2) B0796/19 B1191/09
sub (1) A0638/M
sub-collectors (1) A0043/11
sub-commentaries (1) A0366/20
sub-divided (1) C0551/01
subdivided (1) A0081/36
subdivisions (2) A0429/23 A0436/26

subdue (3) A0165/14
A0663/27 B1096/27
subdued (9) A0158/05
A0503/V A0664/24 B0891/V B0929/10
B1004/08 B1069/07 B1278/29 C0082/36
subduing (1) B1236/35
subjacent (1) B1076/15
subject (110)
subject's (1) B1182/28
subjected (16) A0460/19
A0499/16 B0730/21 B0762/06 B0826/02
B0832/20 B0832/30 B0963/25 B0988/23
B1074/04 B1133/27 B1187/13 B1187/18
C0145/06 C0428/42 C0540/26
subjectivity (1) A0341/24
subjects (10) A0087/13 A0156/04
A0342/V B0830/28 B0969/04 B1179/26
B1180/13 C0193/26 C0392/27 C0428/20
subjoined (5) B1068/08
B1116/04 B1133/04 B1235/02 B1370/12
sublimate (1) B1122/16
sublimated (1) A0263/28
sublimating (1) B1078/30
sublimation (1) A0166/02
sublime (13) A0099/31
A0352/08 A0397/20 A0705/34 A0711/03
B0862/34 B1076/16 B1132/10 B1156/09
B1270/34 B1273/31 B1297/30 B1317/09
sublimest (1) A0495/V
sublimity (3) A0140/17
B1133/05 C0405/26
sublunary (1) A0427/16
submission (4) A0021/12
A0431/25 A0446/10 B1104/12
submissive (2) A0104/15 C0200/07
submit (7) A0446/19
A0609/18 B0731/23 B0874/29 B0941/19
B1382/03 C0133/34
submitted (9) A0383/07
A0708/26 B0731/09 B0731/16 B0835/03
B1169/31 B1273/21 C0086/11 C0394/07
submitting (1) C0086/16
subscribe (2) B1136/20 B1207/08
subscribers (1) B1378/03
subscription (1) B1136/36
subscription-list (3) B1136/15
B1137/33 B1138/30
subsequent (23) A0315/01
A0326/02 A0326/04 B0723/23 B0733/21
B0828/19 B0831/25 B0956/25 B0989/19
B1049/28 B1184/22 B1314/25 B1359/21
C0053/T C0137/26 C0145/07 C0155/32
C0161/24 C0184/16 C0193/25 C0208/22
C0546/31 C0554/13
subsequently (7) A0314/08
A0568/06 B0731/16 B0877/32 B1274/06
B1292/36 B1359/01
subserved (1) B1068/11
subservience (1) B1136/28
subserviency (1) B1207/12
subservient (1) A0499/13
subside (1) A0588/09
subsided (11) A0155/19
A0580/24 B0828/23 B1079/14 B1140/12
B1262/18 B1278/36 B1374/30 C0205/03
->C0420/29 C0556/07
subsidence (1) B1080/22
subsiding (2) B1391/07 C0120/01
subsist (1) C0196/11
subsisted (1) B1047/29
subsistence (1) A0138/10
subsisting (1) B1162/35
substance (39) A0347/24
A0403/27 A0410/07 A0564/18 A0602/33
A0604/07 B0853/25 B0929/16 B0948/15
B0967/12 B0967/16 B1030/19 B1038/12
B1039/30 B1040/02 B1057/30 B1162/26
B1163/20 B1165/03 B1165/35 B1168/08
B1222/20 B1293/05 B1320/03 B1321/10
B1362/31 B1362/33 C0063/37 C0125/08
C0127/16 C0167/16 C0178/05 C0178/20
C0193/19 C0387/26 C0393/32 C0394/09
C0437/V C0570/18
substances (7) A0219/07
B1246/18 B1321/29 B1364/09 C0199/38
C0420/32 C0553/01
substantial (7) A0457/27
A0509/03 B1039/08 B1053/16 B1123/21
B1279/13 B1340/07
substantiality (2) B1039/14
B1040/03
substantive (3) B1038/35
B1039/28 B1220/19
substitute (6) A0491/05 B0838/18
B1322/30 B1373/30 C0092/22 C0426/02
substituted (2) B1180/28 B1224/16
substituting (1) B0838/15
substitution (1) B1373/33
substructure (1) B0752/17
subtend (1) C0421/16
subtended (3) C0418/31
C0420/06 C0421/08
subtends (1) B1300/31
subterfuge (1) B1379/29
Subterranean (1) A0409/01
subterranean (2) A0074/33 A0685/15
subterrene (3) A0195/13
A0685/V B0967/36
subtle (3) A0211/04
C0180/10 C0546/15
subtlety (1) B1073/16
suburb (1) B1192/20
suburban (1) A0515/01
suburbs (3) A0068/23
B0759/30 C0427/29
subversive (1) C0390/27
subvert (1) A0203/04
succeed (12) A0102/24
B0816/08 B1078/31 C0066/25 C0080/34
C0088/33 C0127/07 C0159/05 C0187/04
C0199/34 C0530/26 C0555/28
succeeded (91)
succeeding (8) A0026/21
A0138/12 B0837/31 B0853/04 B1225/22
B1238/18 C0186/21 C0212/V
success (40) A0055/19
A0065/03 A0268/08 A0268/31 A0337/33
A0346/31 A0413/20 A0435/13 A0529/20
A0555/08 A0683/11 B0737/06 B0771/32
B0817/08 B0877/32 B0941/14 B0966/22

->B0984/06 B0984/32 B0988/26 B1072/18
B1078/23 B1078/31 B1129/08 B1132/26
B1242/31 B1268/24 B1348/14 B1372/19
C0104/16 C0120/41 C0121/29 C0128/08
C0137/18 C0154/05 C0187/37 C0394/37
C0419/06 C0532/36 C0539/26
successes (1) A0703/25
successful (11) A0102/15
A0433/21 A0683/33 B0725/V B0746/07
B1079/19 B1213/19 B1242/30 C0402/26
C0521/04 C0526/15
successfully (7) A0315/26
A0440/35 A0496/22 B0958/23 B1225/15
C0057/04 C0523/04
succession (30) A0021/05 A0092/12
A0165/16 A0204/19 A0245/02 A0249/31
A0321/27 A0322/24 A0501/28 A0537/08
A0593/33 A0615/20 A0649/V A0651/V
B0773/21 B0837/02 B0850/06 B0865/04
B1262/23 C0072/18 C0115/30 C0118/19
C0140/18 C0164/37 C0184/21 C0199/18
C0528/11 C0562/28 C0573/33 C0577/03
successive (3) A0121/20
B0746/24 C0401/24
successively (4) A0484/19
B0962/25 B1351/08 C0402/34
successor (1) A0321/01
succinctly (2) B0849/06 B1233/12
Succoth-Benith (1) A0046/12
succour (1) C0094/23
succumb (1) A0610/21
succumbed (7) A0318/V
A0404/22 A0446/03 A0531/19 A0612/21
B0856/10 B0941/31
such (521)
sucked (1) B1162/20
suction (3) A0583/01
A0593/03 B1383/02
sudden (51)
suddenly (121)
suddenness (5) B0963/07
B1013/12 B1107/32 B1239/26 C0190/15
Sue's (1) B1270/37
Sues (1) C0550/28
Suez (1) B1160/26
suffer (22) A0074/07 A0456/11
A0489/V A0507/01 B0741/13 B0741/14
B0816/02 B0852/01 B1032/15 B1039/22
B1207/28 B1291/14 C0105/24 C0110/15
C0132/08 C0135/23 C0403/13 C0405/11
C0407/17 C0413/04 C0413/11 C0522/09
sufferance (1) A0403/27
suffered (52)
sufferer (7) A0053/10
A0406/06 B0941/18 B0962/19 B1237/09
B1243/02 C0142/04
sufferers (5) B0856/16
B1209/07 C0088/29 C0147/29 C0389/07
suffering (28) A0310/03
A0324/03 A0687/23 A0691/28 A0704/22
B0744/12 B0900/08 B0931/15 B0955/17
B0956/15 B0963/21 B1030/28 B1223/10
B1269/21 C0065/17 C0071/20 C0071/33
C0076/30 C0080/22 C0111/38 C0128/33
C0129/24 C0146/09 C0148/34 C0406/24
->C0408/20 C0421/03 C0567/23
sufferings (11) B1360/23
C0053/T C0074/11 C0117/39 C0120/14
C0141/19 C0142/21 C0143/04 C0143/23
C0145/33 C0169/17
suffers (2) B0829/24 B0990/04
suffice (8) A0018/02
A0440/15 A0497/11 B0772/11 B0966/V
C0135/31 C0186/08 C0566/26
sufficed (15) A0215/22
A0459/29 A0547/29 A0705/17 B0728/31
B0730/19 B0958/04 B0966/04 B0980/14
B1078/06 B1181/30 B1270/16 B1300/08
C0180/07 C0408/04
sufficiency (2) A0612/31 B1073/14
sufficient (109)
sufficiently (102)
sufficing (1) B1382/27
suffocated (1) C0182/06
suffocating (4) A0446/23
A0696/02 B1106/27 C0124/10
suffocation (12) A0056/22
A0058/35 A0066/11 A0071/05 A0080/14
A0176/25 A0182/28 A0189/28 A0217/V
A0563/19 B1226/08 C0076/01
suffrage (2) B1193/34 B1300/04
suffuse (1) A0295/25
suffused (1) B0730/03
sugar (2) A0340/03 C0577/23
sugar-cane (1) C0156/02
sugar-loaf (1) A0368/04
sugarhousemolasses (1) B1092/12
suggest (26) A0204/23 A0302/08
A0328/13 A0446/09 A0555/31 A0627/04
A0650/11 A0708/29 A0710/29 B0739/34
B0773/02 B0916/04 B0961/15 B0984/24
B0992/32 B1005/29 B1052/34 B1079/08
B1134/13 B1142/34 B1275/31 B1311/29
B1315/20 B1348/24 C0093/25 C0427/03
suggested (54)
suggesting (2) B0986/11 B1347/05
suggestion (32) A0055/37
A0056/35 A0065/20 A0066/21 A0264/37
A0325/26 A0366/26 B0728/27 B0731/23
B0736/08 B0740/02 B0748/16 B0750/05
B0752/32 B0755/24 B0757/09 B0773/23
B0844/15 B0892/20 B0943/18 B1185/08
B1247/12 B1301/19 B1349/20 B1351/01
B1351/26 B1352/16 B1359/29 C0059/13
C0133/01 C0198/20 C0546/22
suggestions (10) A0212/20 A0408/01
A0435/29 B0731/19 B0822/31 B0862/32
B1185/19 C0055/25 C0166/26 C0430/01
suggestive (2) B0838/35 B0991/22
suggests (1) B0738/11
sui (1) A0493/06
suicidal (1) B1108/13
suicide (7) A0054/18
A0063/21 A0549/02 B0737/13 B0751/24
C0392/01 C0399/28
suis (2) A0033/19 A0096/M
suit (12) A0103/22
A0484/19 A0487/29 A0530/16 A0627/32
A0705/34 B0740/04 B1257/09 B1270/34
B1277/24 B1370/35 C0152/17

suitable (8) A0057/13
A0707/05 B0933/31 B1277/33 C0093/19
C0152/11 C0177/26 C0178/03
suite (5) A0671/17
A0671/27 A0672/10 A0672/11 B0904/18
suited (8) A0090/21
A0532/13 A0653/20 A0710/20 B0878/10
B0916/14 B1275/23 B1345/15
suites (2) A0671/17 B1258/28
suitor (3) B0729/13
B0748/24 B0755/31
suitors (2) B0755/09 B0957/14
suits (3) A0142/22
B0864/24 C0546/39
Suky (1) A0336/03
<u>Sul</u> (1) B0905/14
sulky (3) A0535/26
B0811/04 B1348/28
sullen (11) A0078/10
A0138/24 A0139/32 A0153/01 A0244/24
A0400/20 A0402/20 A0428/07 A0687/10
C0125/09 C0205/28
sullenly (4) A0029/21
A0081/16 A0417/17 A0603/29
sullied (3) A0053/35
A0063/07 A0426/02
Sullivan's/Island (4) B0806/06
B0807/35 B0840/29 B1068/03
Sully (2) A0502/07 A0664/06
sulphur (2) B1158/02 C0553/02
sulphureous (1) A0405/11
sulphuric (1) B1168/25
sulphurous (5) A0074/26
A0405/V A0688/08 A0695/18 B1168/29
sultry (4) A0092/19
A0111/29 A0240/V B0865/14
sum (32) A0093/19
A0120/11 A0276/25 A0346/24 A0350/26
A0443/08 A0490/02 A0529/31 A0541/16
A0541/17 A0556/13 A0568/07 A0654/18
A0705/04 A0705/32 A0705/33 B0727/15
B0727/19 B0727/28 B0768/26 B0872/01
B0874/04 B0875/27 B0879/08 B0903/06
B0987/28 B1053/10 B1137/34 B1269/35
B1270/04 B1270/33 C0057/06
sum'mat (1) C0067/21
summary (4) B0877/30
B1048/04 B1152/11 B1357/02
summat> (1) A0465/01
summed (4) A0611/26
A0703/28 B1092/35 B1268/27
Summer (1) B1384/20
summer (13) A0087/16
A0293/07 A0531/15 A0604/26 B0807/07
B0904/13 B1044/09 B1246/04 B1328/01
B1328/10 C0536/28 C0547/09 C0552/38
summer's (2) A0211/31 A0482/18
summers (1) A0653/15
summing (1) B1031/16
summit (39) A0045/08
A0071/02 A0122/30 A0140/04 A0146/04
A0196/19 A0294/V A0322/09 A0350/24
A0366/12 A0366/29 A0370/22 A0577/01
A0580/03 A0581/14 B0817/23 B0841/17
B0947/01 B1127/01 B1161/07 B1247/30
->B1278/21 B1280/09 B1294/16 B1294/20
B1330/29 B1391/26 C0153/02 C0163/28
C0184/29 C0189/20 C0192/18 C0193/08
C0196/01 C0203/25 C0204/11 C0204/40
C0205/32 C0577/16
summits (2) A0195/19 A0640/13
summon (8) B0966/29
C0075/02 C0075/40 C0109/13 C0119/01
C0134/25 C0135/16 C0197/20
summoned (5) A0670/11
B0877/19 B1030/26 C0060/18 C0135/08
summoning (2) A0327/15 A0676/26
summons (3) A0398/28
A0431/02 B1347/21
sumptuous (2) A0122/08 B1056/21
sumptuously (1) A0662/08
sums (8) A0441/05
A0442/06 A0541/15 B1136/16 B1136/37
B1138/31 B1361/31 C0393/14
Sun (6) A0080/03 A0122/22
A0409/04 B1321/02 B1321/16 B1321/23
sun (79)
sun-dial (1) A0367/04
sun-rise (1) A0155/V
sun-set (1) C0542/20
Sun's (1) B1322/27
sun's (6) B1076/07 B1321/20
B1321/27 C0401/34 C0402/07 C0423/19
sunbeams (3) A0195/V
A0195/V A0604/20
sunburnt (1) A0562/18
Sunda/islands (1) A0135/25
Sunday (42) A0382/19 A0428/26
A0582/11 A0651/13 A0654/25 A0656/02
A0656/04 A0656/07 A0656/09 A0656/11
A0656/12 A0656/14 A0656/19 A0656/21
A0656/22 A0657/21 A0657/22 A0657/22
B0729/06 B0731/15 B0731/26 B0735/20
B0735/22 B0736/03 B0739/01 B0739/04
B0739/25 B0745/10 B0750/10 B0750/11
B0751/22 B0754/02 B0755/11 B0758/33
B0759/28 B0760/23 B0769/28 B0958/29
B1044/21 B1046/17 B1079/13 B1236/01
Sundays (5) A0649/T
A0651/15 A0651/17 A0656/23 A0657/30
sunder (1) A0692/02
sundown (5) B0931/05
B1079/17 C0100/24 C0137/18 C0163/19
sundry (3) A0262/31
A0262/32 B1130/04
sung (5) A0091/20
A0110/24 A0125/34 A0127/01 B0890/16
sunk (17) A0198/06
A0316/V A0328/19 A0351/15 A0594/V
A0674/22 B0744/02 B0744/02 B0858/34
B1338/35 C0120/16 C0142/10 C0198/15
C0396/29 C0444/V C0540/19 C0575/36
sunken (3) A0327/06
A0328/16 B0956/18
sunlight (5) A0210/05
A0603/07 A0639/11 B1283/12 B1331/07
sunrise (15) A0043/07
A0045/30 A0155/17 A0156/29 A0165/12
A0675/26 B0808/30 B0808/31 B0816/19
B1239/04 B1292/23 C0102/34 C0103/07

->C0139/17 C0550/18
suns (5) B1038/23
B1038/24 B1212/33 B1301/23 B1322/27
sunset (9) A0136/14
A0602/25 B0808/03 B1328/12 C0086/30
C0149/32 C0423/12 C0545/27 C0559/21
sunshine (5) B0944/19
B1074/10 B1145/27 B1332/22 C0425/35
Sunship (2) A0122/27 A0122/27
sunt (1) A0638/14
sup (3) A0033/08 C0127/22 C0137/07
super-eminent (1) C0389/30
superabundance (2) A0705/29
B1270/27
superabundant (1) B1373/31
superadded (1) A0245/26
Superadditis (1) A0515/34
superb (8) A0035/04
A0174/04 A0176/15 A0179/15 A0182/16
A0298/V A0379/26 B0828/14
superbly (1) B1008/31
supercilious (2) A0264/18 A0508/25
supererogation (3) A0552/07
B1030/15 B1219/10
supererogatory (1) A0444/08
superficial (4) A0107/16
A0545/18 C0404/05 C0438/V
superficiality (1) A0263/24
superficially (1) A0651/28
superficies (1) C0412/02
superfluities (3) A0074/07
A0240/20 A0531/25
superfluity (2) A0072/09 A0286/22
superfluous (17) A0034/02
A0107/V A0108/06 A0262/15 A0269/05
A0271/23 A0278/33 A0283/28 A0705/28
B0731/02 B0765/31 B0916/12 B1075/18
B1126/19 B1270/26 B1310/24 C0202/34
superhuman (9) A0029/11
A0128/26 A0164/14 A0416/22 A0558/07
B0932/11 B0932/V B1020/17 B1133/30
superinduced (3) A0211/08
B0757/13 B0963/15
superinduces (1) B0959/25
superintend (1) C0177/36
superintended (1) B1330/04
superintendence (5) A0711/27
B1072/29 B1276/30 B1277/03 B1351/24
superintendent (4) B1003/08
B1004/01 B1009/22 B1021/20
superior (19) A0078/38
A0126/16 A0204/14 A0265/25 A0298/V
A0301/17 A0529/03 A0711/28 B0904/28
B1090/26 B1191/08 B1250/25 B1276/31
B1278/30 B1293/04 B1296/11 B1302/22
C0201/02 C0402/31
superiority (8) A0029/V
A0432/02 A0432/04 A0478/08 A0592/28
A0707/12 B1192/35 B1272/11
superlatively (1) C0388/33
supernal (2) A0342/13 B1123/26
supernatural (4) A0025/V
A0140/13 A0152/V B0723/03
supernaturally (1) A0212/30
supernumerary (1) B0923/03
superscription (1) B0991/17
superseded (3) B1019/28
C0403/28 C0422/06
superstition (11) A0018/09
A0135/18 A0242/24 A0322/25 A0399/24
A0459/11 A0654/07 A0689/02 B0810/11
B0850/30 B1247/02
superstition's (1) A0139/V
superstitions (3) A0532/15
B0822/27 C0111/12
superstitious (5) A0139/07
A0326/24 A0403/22 C0105/24 C0107/21
supervene (1) B1239/16
supervened (6) A0327/23 A0616/33
A0682/15 B0896/07 B0960/12 B1030/23
supervision (3) A0436/02
A0445/14 B0807/34
supinely (3) A0446/03
C0182/24 C0568/01
supineness (1) C0145/10
supped (1) C0138/41
supper (6) B0808/16 B0827/08
B1056/21 B1177/05 B1177/06 C0558/35
suppers (1) B1129/18
supplicating (1) C0132/14
supplied (16) A0094/10
A0114/05 A0157/10 A0616/02 B0975/15
B1056/21 B1107/16 B1157/06 B1248/13
C0078/30 C0081/07 C0136/01 C0176/33
C0411/07 C0548/30 C0566/16
supplies (2) C0530/27 C0557/15
supply (28) A0108/25
A0689/17 B0743/25 B0854/01 B1009/30
B1186/08 C0069/37 C0072/08 C0073/42
C0077/30 C0078/33 C0084/28 C0090/07
C0095/13 C0096/35 C0100/35 C0101/22
C0136/16 C0138/08 C0145/21 C0170/30
C0188/36 C0200/22 C0203/15 C0415/19
C0417/10 C0556/16 C0566/03
supplying (4) A0204/17
B0771/11 B0903/21 B1038/24
support (12) A0460/28
A0664/V B0741/24 B0759/23 B0817/27
B1070/17 B1071/02 B1336/13 C0174/37
C0197/30 C0423/30 C0424/29
supported (9) A0088/02
A0181/28 A0241/10 B1071/18 B1165/15
B1382/21 C0410/05 C0552/29 C0552/33
supporters (1) B0861/04
supporting (5) A0350/04
A0460/30 B1073/06 B1073/20 C0120/07
supports (2) B1261/14 C0552/08
supposable (4) B0754/20
B1051/32 B1208/35 B1322/23
suppose (90)
supposed (111)
supposes (5) A0549/26
A0568/18 B0744/03 B0744/13 B0758/29
supposing (29) A0023/27
A0282/08 A0479/36 A0527/V A0531/03
A0549/12 A0552/33 A0592/16 A0686/19
A0688/22 B0729/17 B0758/21 B0771/10
B0815/01 B0915/16 B0987/18 B1049/15
B1057/33 B1093/31 B1164/39 C0090/37
C0123/27 C0171/28 C0401/40 C0413/21

->C0416/23 C0417/34 C0420/29 C0424/28
supposition (23) A0142/18
A0145/27 A0281/26 A0369/30 A0548/14
A0684/21 A0705/24 B0733/02 B0737/15
B0748/30 B0754/03 B0762/32 B0773/05
B0812/23 B0837/11 B0948/24 B0986/17
B1206/18 B1270/23 B1321/03 C0094/24
C0413/04 C0523/29
suppositions (1) B0794/20
supposititious (1) A0403/25
suppress (1) A0209/V
suppressed (1) B0929/26
Suppression (1) B1093/19
supremacy (3) A0021/27
A0316/01 A0478/06
supreme (27) A0126/V
A0204/20 A0380/08 A0431/27 A0495/02
A0496/V A0511/24 A0610/08 A0705/08
A0706/05 A0708/01 B0858/04 B0895/25
B0898/20 B0963/27 B1055/08 B1079/04
B1137/28 B1257/15 B1270/08 B1271/08
B1273/01 B1295/12 B1311/04 B1317/34
B1371/11 C0156/13
supremely (2) A0326/20 B0892/V
supremeness (2) B0961/19 C0182/28
sur (7) A0096/07
A0096/08 A0096/08 A0109/31 B1114/02
C0430/37 C0430/41
surcingle (5) A0689/15
A0693/07 A0693/18 A0694/15 A0694/30
surcoat (1) A0247/V
sure (183)
surely (31) A0034/07
A0109/07 A0123/24 A0128/15 A0143/29
A0151/07 A0214/01 A0227/28 A0232/15
A0261/24 A0310/11 A0311/14 A0401/25
A0414/11 A0612/11 A0641/V B0767/28
B0816/16 B0849/04 B0865/29 B0906/24
B0912/29 B1010/11 B1017/10 B1338/30
C0071/31 C0077/11 C0113/05 C0125/22
C0153/28 C0388/16
surer (2) B0906/15 B1054/08
surest (4) A0298/V
B0737/06 B0769/26 B1345/03
surety (1) B1054/17
surf (6) A0139/05 A0579/05
A0588/15 A0589/11 A0614/17 C0167/29
surface (131)
surfaces (8) A0140/09
A0412/29 A0601/10 A0601/12 A0662/14
B1070/21 B1168/39 B1303/36
surge (4) A0579/10
A0588/20 A0589/23 C0064/06
surgeon (8) A0067/05
A0067/18 A0067/33 A0068/28 A0544/09
B0763/22 C0062/37 C0535/38
surgeon's (1) A0067/32
surgery (1) A0219/06
surges (1) B1079/08
surmise (3) B0750/V
C0124/13 C0407/12
surmises (2) C0080/28 C0094/27
surmising (2) A0350/03 A0350/05
surmount (1) A0073/15
surmounted (8) A0086/27
->A0100/04 A0350/22 A0350/32 A0429/05
B1257/19 C0400/30 C0401/11
surname (3) A0267/19
A0431/16 B0887/12
surnamed (4) B1127/26
B1295/12 B1310/19 B1311/05
surpass (4) B0902/28
B0903/12 B1137/30 B1332/33
surpassed (7) A0021/09
A0139/17 A0664/V B0817/35 B1157/02
B1262/30 C0176/34
surpasses (4) A0507/12
B0903/V B1136/07 B1136/31
surpassing (14) A0160/12 A0244/17
A0327/V A0379/12 A0407/22 A0459/24
A0461/22 A0705/07 A0711/13 B0923/23
B1166/05 B1270/06 B1276/13 B1278/04
surpassingly (4) A0401/32
A0665/24 B0897/18 B0909/05
surplus (3) B1073/22
B1120/02 C0530/32
surprise (47) A0022/V
A0107/V A0163/18 A0245/V A0303/20
A0352/28 A0500/18 A0530/14 A0627/28
A0656/V A0674/28 A0690/28 B0755/30
B0771/33 B0829/15 B0854/07 B0893/27
B0906/01 B0911/04 B0911/04 B0986/29
B1008/06 B1009/23 B1016/03 B1031/04
B1181/04 B1234/29 B1234/30 B1260/17
B1329/29 C0059/21 C0066/13 C0067/20
C0100/25 C0107/08 C0109/23 C0168/35
C0171/11 C0175/29 C0180/29 C0182/19
C0388/38 C0390/02 C0407/08 C0421/41
C0426/33 C0429/38
surprised (33) A0158/V
A0439/02 A0513/01 A0583/08 A0624/27
A0656/08 A0705/30 B0810/21 B0834/23
B0872/01 B0875/09 B0906/02 B0907/08
B0943/32 B1007/01 B1055/13 B1076/24
B1090/14 B1183/03 B1270/30 C0073/37
C0077/15 C0159/31 C0159/39 C0174/19
C0204/16 C0411/25 C0412/16 C0417/21
C0554/28 C0561/30 C0568/18 C0569/09
surprises (2) B1310/09 B1390/12
surprising (11) A0389/02
A0545/08 B0724/20 B0725/06 B1078/14
B1080/01 B1159/12 B1168/09 C0130/16
C0166/07 C0574/06
surprized (1) A0159/V
surr (1) B1092/36
surrender (4) B1304/15
B1304/33 B1304/36 B1305/04
surrendered (3) B1304/36
B1305/01 B1305/05
surround (3) B0752/25
B0760/02 C0409/12
surrounded (17) A0217/V
A0271/28 A0273/28 A0293/25 A0322/23
A0350/28 A0366/29 B0947/11 B0962/36
B0988/18 B1168/27 C0116/22 C0117/16
C0142/32 C0152/36 C0187/02 C0545/08
surrounding (17) A0244/25
A0405/23 A0616/20 A0709/24 B0947/02
B1073/16 B1163/29 B1274/26 B1282/27
B1293/01 B1294/17 B1301/14 C0074/34

->C0184/26 C0403/20 C0566/12 C0575/09
surrounds (1) A0588/15
surtout (4) A0247/17
A0368/20 C0389/25 C0389/38
survey (21) A0104/20
A0124/12 A0314/13 A0349/26 A0351/25
A0352/21 A0511/19 A0555/33 B0752/29
B0894/26 B1102/18 B1294/16 B1335/32
B1338/09 C0112/07 C0153/26 C0192/38
C0397/20 C0416/28 C0564/41 C0574/26
surveyed (9) A0216/03
A0261/06 A0581/13 A0689/23 B0980/V
B0990/27 B1247/35 C0411/40 C0564/31
surveying (5) A0180/11
B0911/25 B0914/24 B1188/28 C0078/02
survive (2) A0081/21 A0631/16
survived (4) A0159/07
A0577/06 B1131/27 C0094/16
survivers (3) C0053/T
C0086/31 C0146/42
surviving (2) A0053/10 B0914/V
survivors (1) A0137/24
sus (1) A0621/03
susceptibility (8) A0708/33
B0978/31 B0978/34 B1030/10 B1030/22
B1181/25 B1233/19 B1273/26
susceptible (13) A0135/15
A0527/02 A0545/23 A0600/04 A0707/30
A0708/32 B0877/28 B1080/25 B1272/31
B1273/26 C0397/37 C0422/02 C0438/V
suspect (11) A0272/10
A0432/06 B0793/17 B0876/34 B0956/16
B0978/07 B0991/28 B1224/24 B1313/24
B1361/15 C0065/13
suspected (25) A0056/06
A0065/29 A0295/09 A0440/30 A0561/25
B0727/34 B0753/40 B0758/27 B0797/22
B0864/12 B0888/15 B0906/V B0946/12
B0956/15 B1048/27 B1050/25 B1050/32
B1051/32 B1235/34 B1300/37 B1360/02
B1361/18 B1363/23 C0059/29 C0397/26
suspecting (3) B0946/11
C0107/29 C0112/10
suspects (1) B0946/07
suspend (2) A0344/02 A0351/22
suspended (19) A0069/21
A0078/01 A0079/21 A0101/V A0248/17
A0459/22 B0956/02 B0965/36 B1051/36
B1071/08 B1073/30 B1110/10 B1333/34
B1353/19 C0198/27 C0388/31 C0398/27
C0409/29 C0411/09
suspenders (1) B0823/19
suspending (1) B1292/24
suspendu (1) A0397/M
suspense (3) A0685/04
C0077/12 C0135/17
suspension (1) A0489/02
suspensions (1) B0955/30
suspicion (54)
suspicions (10) A0067/12 A0105/04
A0234/10 B0814/26 B0844/05 B0858/24
B0961/16 B1049/30 B1058/13 C0105/09
suspicious (12) A0024/08
A0261/07 B0748/14 B0762/13 B0767/14
B0823/07 B0857/12 B1047/12 B1050/09
->B1053/01 C0180/05 C0437/V
suspiciously (2) A0410/24 C0390/01
suspict> (1) A0467/18
sustain (14) A0503/06 A0675/19
A0709/13 B0955/03 B1136/13 B1136/34
B1137/31 B1138/28 B1161/21 B1246/16
C0149/04 C0187/07 C0409/26 C0412/14
sustained (23) A0059/13
A0079/18 A0104/05 A0279/23 A0546/02
B0749/26 B0958/12 B1132/24 B1185/25
B1314/19 C0126/01 C0132/25 C0187/27
C0207/31 C0400/35 C0404/10 C0405/17
C0413/32 C0540/04 C0544/38 C0545/40
C0550/03 C0579/24
sustaining (6) A0126/11 A0447/05
A0479/30 B1070/14 B1279/13 B1283/11
sustenance (5) A0044/08
A0458/21 B1162/27 C0132/37 C0419/33
suture (1) B1054/09
sutures (1) A0688/33
swagger (3) A0286/19
A0286/22 A0510/17
swaggerers (1) A0354/21
swaggers (1) B0871/10
swallow (11) A0251/23
B1045/34 B1195/16 B1347/30 B1349/26
C0128/32 C0130/40 C0141/21 C0142/16
C0178/14 C0178/18
swallow-tailed (2) A0371/06
A0371/22
swallowed (25) A0092/11
A0092/31 A0112/06 A0126/22 A0143/29
A0165/15 A0178/13 A0325/24 A0340/29
A0388/15 A0442/09 A0604/28 A0651/20
A0663/V A0667/35 A0667/70 A0667/71
A0682/16 B0767/16 B0852/34 B0942/07
B1282/16 C0061/21 C0078/35 C0137/12
swallowing (1) C0142/12
swallows (2) A0033/13 B1039/01
swam (13) A0643/14
B1158/21 B1159/19 B1159/28 B1161/04
C0073/01 C0140/23 C0144/25 C0164/39
C0188/10 C0541/06 C0567/19 C0567/26
Swammerdamm (1) B0807/26
swamp (9) B0932/07
C0544/19 C0544/20 C0544/28 C0545/01
C0545/14 C0545/30 C0546/04 C0547/33
swamp-fight (1) A0380/30
swamping (2) B0931/20 C0062/27
swampy (1) C0577/20
swan (1) B1281/04
swan-like (1) A0022/01
swans (1) C0431/07
swar (1) B1373/22
sward (1) B1281/25
swarm (3) A0128/V
B1158/18 B1293/12
swarmed (3) A0694/21
B0945/08 B1157/37
swarming (8) A0123/09
A0693/29 B0945/23 B0946/30 B1161/01
C0142/15 C0185/35 C0186/22
swarthiness (2) A0509/19 B0769/10
swarthy (2) B0768/31 B0769/09
swate> (9) A0464/17

->A0465/05 A0465/21 A0466/22 A0466/30
A0467/27 A0467/31 A0467/V A0468/12
swatest> (1) A0467/08
sway (2) A0415/14 A0580/12
swayed (2) A0411/22 C0125/18
swaying (3) A0580/32
A0590/03 B1077/13
swear (5) A0466/12
A0653/V B1019/19 B1143/05 C0541/17
swearing (4) A0092/30
A0112/05 A0623/17 B1046/07
Swede (3) A0137/21
A0138/30 A0139/08
Swedenborg (1) A0409/01
sweep (12) A0567/03
A0587/35 A0590/08 A0689/34 A0690/11
A0691/10 A0692/01 A0692/26 A0695/V
B1212/17 B1282/13 C0556/03
sweeping (5) A0265/22
B1223/06 B1335/14 B1336/10 C0115/40
sweeping-brushes (1) A0543/11
sweepings (1) A0603/13
sweeps (7) A0510/25
A0542/17 A0543/10 A0584/30 A0590/04
B1282/30 B1333/19
sweet (47) A0055/12
A0064/V A0152/21 A0228/10 A0310/14
A0311/22 A0312/18 A0343/31 A0348/28
A0350/20 A0354/07 A0357/10 A0384/06
A0407/03 A0407/20 A0503/02 A0600/02
A0604/03 A0608/07 A0610/25 A0613/05
A0613/15 A0613/23 A0614/01 A0614/27
A0616/05 A0640/22 A0643/15 A0644/04
A0645/05 A0682/10 B0737/V B0807/11
B0901/09 B0901/18 B0902/10 B0902/13
B0924/12 B1283/05 B1328/06 B1337/12
B1337/17 B1351/33 C0138/10 C0138/22
C0543/25 C0543/33
sweet-scented (3) A0603/08
B1162/09 B1181/02
sweeter (2) A0641/04 B0863/03
sweetest (5) A0034/15
A0348/21 A0639/11 B0903/11 B0903/V
sweetly (5) A0653/11
B0967/19 C0083/16 C0100/39 C0192/16
sweetness (1) B1092/13
sweets (1) C0543/39
swell (9) A0138/07
A0139/17 A0509/07 A0579/19 B1391/07
C0102/35 C0129/27 C0129/40 C0139/32
swelled (6) A0078/05 A0079/43
A0143/V A0316/23 A0641/03 A0694/24
swelling (8) A0036/V
A0104/33 A0139/24 A0154/27 B0859/02
B1346/11 C0098/26 C0397/23
swells (2) A0587/31 A0674/02
sweltering (2) A0139/06 A0580/32
swelters (1) A0590/04
swept (14) A0137/08 A0137/25
A0211/03 A0233/22 A0246/24 A0589/27
A0591/18 A0691/06 B0932/14 C0114/01
C0115/13 C0116/24 C0140/32 C0144/39
swerving (1) B0747/16
swift (1) B1166/04
swift-flying (1) C0208/19
swiftly (3) A0515/14
B0946/26 C0186/41
swiftness (4) A0513/31
B1156/03 C0532/04 C0567/02
swilling (1) A0249/27
swim (4) A0582/03
B0741/16 C0547/25 C0567/39
swimmer (2) A0080/06 A0152/12
swimmers (1) C0567/02
swimming (13) A0593/02
B0741/27 B1156/01 B1165/19 B1383/01
C0125/37 C0130/31 C0140/39 C0143/18
C0187/36 C0555/11 C0567/12 C0568/33
swimmingly (2) A0488/19 C0412/18
swindling (1) A0485/25
swing (1) A0372/04
swinging (11) A0089/01
A0092/26 A0112/01 A0122/16 A0482/13
A0643/25 B0843/34 C0100/12 C0112/20
C0115/33 C0184/02
swings (2) A0591/19 B1281/11
Swiss (4) B1119/01
B1119/03 B1119/T B1119/M
swivel (1) C0171/14
swivels (2) C0180/19 C0180/22
swollen (11) A0298/V
B0730/14 B0948/08 B1239/32 C0078/36
C0107/35 C0109/01 C0118/31 C0541/10
C0565/19 C0569/14
swoon (13) A0682/22
A0682/27 A0684/02 A0691/16 B0960/29
B0962/34 B1183/21 B1226/17 C0074/25
C0135/25 C0197/37 C0397/12 C0578/41
swooned (10) A0069/V A0070/01
A0566/28 A0682/19 A0683/01 B0957/05
B1240/34 B1352/11 C0119/28 C0198/17
swooning (4) B0859/07
B0961/04 B1157/34 C0111/17
swoop (1) B1212/30
sword (2) A0447/21 B1096/33
sword-handles (1) B0828/10
swore (10) A0047/03 A0373/18
A0489/16 A0624/04 B0797/17 B1105/06
C0058/08 C0061/27 C0388/35 C0426/38
sworn (4) A0339/28
A0372/08 B1346/31 B1349/21
swung (25) A0021/22
A0035/11 A0047/11 A0087/23 A0100/28
A0101/V A0102/04 A0103/17 A0140/10
A0241/12 A0253/18 A0554/28 A0555/04
A0555/05 A0565/26 A0672/22 A0690/21
A0694/33 B0797/17 B0844/07 B0956/28
B1354/21 C0125/21 C0127/24 C0572/36
sx (8) B1374/07
B1374/07 B1374/09 B1374/11 B1374/12
B1374/17 B1374/19 B1374/20
sxrrxws (1) B1374/20
sxw (1) B1374/14
sybils (2) A0144/20 A0198/25
sycamore (5) A0604/13
B1179/22 C0545/04 C0545/13 C0545/26
sycophancy (1) B1136/28
syfe (2) B0814/10 B0814/12
syllabification (5) A0555/22
A0558/11 A0558/20 B0960/25 B1240/25

syllable (23) A0062/30
A0072/25 A0191/15 A0191/15 A0214/25
A0301/14 A0342/13 A0447/08 A0533/33
B0983/18 B1014/08 B1050/26 B1101/13
B1349/02 C0072/37 C0078/22 C0083/03
C0083/10 C0083/11 C0111/26 C0112/24
C0123/02 C0425/09
syllables (12) A0144/27
A0217/V A0235/23 A0385/32 A0415/25
A0416/19 A0439/22 A0681/16 B0824/05
B1102/12 B1225/09 C0080/25
syllabub (1) A0338/01
syllogism (1) A0099/02
sylph (1) A0210/32
sylph-like (1) A0164/V
Sylphs (1) B1283/14
symbols (1) B1188/14
symmetrical (1) C0573/35
symmetry (3) A0156/07
B0890/02 B1279/31
sympathies (2) A0410/18 B1030/09
sympathising (1) B0900/08
sympathize (2) A0071/12 B1317/36
sympathized (1) B1131/35
sympathy (19) A0070/09
A0079/25 A0355/13 A0365/08 A0427/06
A0670/07 A0712/04 B0866/03 B0887/03
B0890/21 B0993/11 B1054/22 B1094/05
B1208/09 B1234/32 B1277/08 B1277/30
C0065/18 C0169/17
symphonies (1) A0036/V
symphony (1) B1119/10
Symposium (2) A0225/M A0229/M
symposium (1) B1177/01
symptom (1) A0508/05
symptoms (15) A0211/V
A0297/22 A0667/29 B0959/33 B0982/30
B1030/30 B1235/35 C0141/08 C0166/14
C0168/35 C0175/38 C0177/03 C0404/01
C0406/08 C0406/39
synonym (1) B1314/14
synonyme (1) B1115/29
synonymes (1) A0079/03
synonymous (2) A0703/03 B1268/03
synopses (1) B1250/10
syphon (2) B0812/02 B0812/04
Syrens (1) A0527/M
Syria (5) A0120/17
A0122/22 A0125/19 A0126/05 A0640/14
Syrian (2) A0120/02 A0120/24
Syrians (3) A0122/28
A0124/17 A0127/19
Syrianus (2) A0176/07 A0180/28
syrups (1) A0384/05
System (2) B1002/T B1163/42
system (47) A0018/13
A0321/11 A0482/19 A0484/11 A0485/25
A0486/32 A0487/14 A0488/18 A0512/14
A0610/14 B0747/34 B1004/14 B1005/12
B1005/15 B1005/18 B1005/20 B1005/25
B1005/35 B1006/33 B1007/11 B1008/13
B1016/31 B1016/32 B1017/01 B1017/35
B1018/19 B1018/32 B1019/29 B1021/28
B1021/31 B1141/04 B1295/13 B1295/19
B1296/08 B1300/37 B1301/26 B1301/29
->B1301/35 B1302/06 B1311/06 B1311/12
B1312/12 C0172/24 C0179/12 C0179/12
C0402/13 C0404/06
systematic (3) B0840/32
B1051/18 C0176/30
systematical (1) A0482/08
systematized (1) B1298/20
systems (1) B1219/21
T (1) A0264/07
t (1) B0838/02
t (4) A0266/09
A0653/21 B0916/14 B1139/13
t. (4) B1136/02
B1136/21 B1137/13 B1138/09
T-- (1) A0294/V
T--, Tabitha (2) A0382/21 A0382/25
t/ee (1) B0838/06
T's (1) A0267/34
t's (2) A0265/21 A0267/06
taba (1) A0120/08
tabac (1) A0096/M
Tabbies (1) A0491/09
tabby (4) A0054/25
A0063/25 A0105/29 A0368/14
tabernacle (1) A0047/05
table (91)
table-land (1) B1278/02
tableau (1) A0298/V
tableland (2) C0154/33 C0154/35
tables (7) A0087/30
A0367/23 A0368/29 A0622/19 B0827/26
B0979/27 B1011/13
tablets (2) A0340/15 C0397/28
tabular (1) B0839/11
tac (1) A0096/M
tacit (1) B0907/27
tacitly (1) B0740/13
Tacitus (2) A0386/25 A0654/V
Tacitus-ism (1) B1114/28
tack (1) C0123/22
tacks (1) C0068/29
tact (3) A0339/V
B0728/17 B0898/04
tactics (1) C0553/10
Tadmor (1) A0145/05
taffety (1) C0389/27
taffrail (1) A0136/11
Taglioni (1) A0079/09
tail (24) A0091/29
A0099/15 A0104/34 A0107/14 A0110/31
A0126/17 A0127/26 A0127/V A0127/V
A0285/06 A0348/25 A0368/14 A0368/26
B0870/11 B1096/22 B1096/22 B1156/33
B1338/23 C0140/24 C0167/17 C0173/31
C0544/34 C0566/25 C0566/26
tailor (3) A0484/15
A0541/26 B1305/12
Tailor's (1) A0484/08
tailor's-shears (1) A0338/21
tailors (1) A0484/30
tails (8) A0286/19
A0372/25 A0374/01 A0491/05 A0491/13
C0151/18 C0431/08 C0546/07
taint (4) B0811/32
B0813/02 B0821/01 B1312/23

tainted (2) A0162/07 A0230/14
take (194)
taken (181)
takes (12) A0368/22
A0507/02 A0591/35 B0852/07 B0874/19
B0977/17 B1090/04 C0151/38 C0539/22
C0548/02 C0548/13 C0578/15
taking (109)
tal (1) A0621/01
Talbot (23) B0889/01
B0891/28 B0892/03 B0892/26 B0896/08
B0896/13 B0896/20 B0896/24 B0896/26
B0898/17 B0898/23 B0898/29 B0900/06
B0900/V B0908/20 B0908/27 B0909/02
B0909/10 B0909/19 B0915/06 B0915/11
B0915/19 B0916/19
Talbot's (4) B0892/19
B0896/21 B0915/24 B0916/16
Talbots (1) B0897/02
talc (1) A0182/07
Tale (6) A0018/V A0043/T
A0043/V A0378/T B0939/T B1151/T
tale (28) A0061/T
A0096/V A0099/12 A0135/19 A0150/V
A0172/T A0204/07 A0204/14 A0204/34
A0209/V A0210/34 A0240/T A0242/18
A0292/V A0413/19 A0417/V A0426/V
A0621/T A0622/07 A0622/07 A0622/15
B0723/09 B1138/34 B1208/06 B1223/03
C0414/04 C0433/02 C0550/09
talens (1) A0600/01
talent (7) A0053/28
A0273/24 A0293/02 A0297/28 A0528/07
A0600/04 B1380/24
talented (2) A0380/01 B1127/14
talents (11) A0058/37
A0092/15 A0111/25 A0225/11 A0229/11
A0265/11 A0435/31 A0600/06 B0904/28
B0957/15 B1347/03
Tales (4) A0599/02
B1380/03 B1383/15 B1386/08
tales (10) A0198/20 A0234/12
A0243/12 A0286/21 A0473/02 A0473/14
A0687/19 B0969/06 B1152/12 C0542/05
talk (30) A0341/22 A0342/V
A0484/01 A0568/14 A0626/23 B0747/11
B0813/05 B0892/11 B0933/05 B0975/29
B0993/08 B1102/36 B1103/08 B1103/23
B1114/11 B1114/16 B1114/17 B1154/14
B1154/23 B1188/10 B1249/29 B1292/01
B1313/18 B1314/37 B1359/04 B1375/07
C0058/13 C0066/23 C0100/19 C0111/12
talk's (1) B1114/11
talked (21) A0056/04
A0071/28 A0175/11 A0175/14 A0175/25
A0176/11 A0181/04 A0467/23 A0508/07
B0797/03 B0797/07 B0797/11 B0923/21
B0963/22 B1009/19 B1104/35 C0064/35
C0093/03 C0099/39 C0127/37 C0564/06
talker (1) A0381/14
talking (17) A0345/23
A0347/29 A0384/29 A0484/V A0535/20
B0811/29 B1013/12 B1103/05 B1103/08
B1143/15 B1192/19 B1293/10 B1293/20
C0057/19 C0067/20 C0093/10 C0529/18
tall (54)
taller (3) A0214/V
A0240/17 A0330/10
tallest (1) A0297/V
tallies (1) C0548/07
tallow (1) C0094/02
tally (2) A0558/18 B0748/15
talons (3) A0567/07
B1165/04 C0125/02
tam> (1) A0470/23
tam'd (1) B1109/11
tame (6) A0024/10 B1129/19
C0173/34 C0174/01 C0560/01 C0566/23
tamed (1) B1334/27
tamely (3) A0057/01
A0066/27 A0253/14
tan (2) A0344/22 A0354/30
tan-bark (1) A0489/30
tan> (1) A0469/V
tangent (4) A0105/29
A0387/06 A0482/26 A0652/21
tangible (1) A0019/04
tangible (4) A0054/35
A0064/03 A0676/32 B1039/34
tangled (1) A0400/08
tank (1) B0945/31
tantalistical (1) A0654/V
tantalization (1) A0651/30
tantalize (1) B1221/24
tantalizing (2) A0080/05 C0077/12
tantum (1) A0125/05
tap (2) A0218/19 B1103/19
tap-houses (1) A0241/23
tap-room (1) A0240/05
tape (1) C0390/04
tape-measure (2) B0822/07 B0824/33
taper (8) A0035/22
A0276/18 B1224/22 C0068/30 C0068/36
C0069/29 C0070/27 C0073/42
taper-wax (1) C0077/28
tapering (7) A0272/13
A0273/14 A0275/14 A0285/02 A0690/19
C0415/31 C0423/14
tapers (5) A0532/31
C0069/37 C0074/15 C0074/16 C0077/06
tapestried (2) A0023/22 A0157/V
tapestries (6) A0209/16 A0324/14
A0324/25 A0400/28 A0671/31 A0672/02
tapestry (10) A0021/22 A0022/08
A0022/21 A0023/11 A0024/19 A0160/05
A0211/32 A0322/10 A0498/15 A0662/10
tapestry-hangings (1) A0087/18
tapis (2) A0298/10 B1133/26
tapping (3) A0089/23
A0107/26 A0182/18
taps (2) B0929/21 B1057/04
tar (6) A0241/02 B0925/23
B1021/27 B1350/37 B1351/05 B1354/18
tar-brush (1) A0142/12
Tarantula (1) B0806/M
tardily (2) A0613/21 B0963/10
tardy (2) B0729/25 B0767/13
target (1) B1101/23
tariff (1) B1154/16
tarn (8) A0398/10

->A0399/22 A0400/01 A0400/20 A0403/29
A0408/18 A0413/04 A0417/16
tarns (2) A0602/12 B0865/05
Tarpaulin (9) A0242/12
A0244/16 A0245/V A0246/19 A0247/26
A0250/31 A0251/26 A0252/18 A0253/06
Tarpaulin, Hugh (5) A0241/28
A0243/20 A0249/04 A0253/22 A0254/04
Tarr (5) B1002/T
B1017/03 B1017/12 B1018/03 B1022/04
tarred (1) B1021/24
tarried (2) A0216/15 A0415/22
Tartak (1) A0046/11
task (28) A0102/27
A0328/06 A0328/11 A0479/24 A0549/04
A0625/09 A0665/19 B0823/20 B0836/14
B0856/29 B1140/33 B1179/33 B1222/06
B1236/12 B1262/32 B1298/15 B1316/25
C0075/05 C0075/15 C0090/13 C0111/09
C0111/22 C0136/36 C0186/21 C0207/10
C0430/08 C0522/33 C0532/23
tasked (2) A0528/22 B0727/03
tasking (2) A0529/17 A0536/V
tasks (1) B1163/07
tassel (1) C0388/27
tassels (3) A0086/28
A0100/05 A0503/06
taste (44) A0090/22
A0091/26 A0110/27 A0265/36 A0296/V
A0299/05 A0320/20 A0339/27 A0473/08
A0473/16 A0496/13 A0496/17 A0496/21
A0497/24 A0498/08 A0498/27 A0499/13
A0499/27 A0499/V A0500/21 A0500/V
A0610/28 A0610/29 A0610/32 A0611/36
A0613/02 A0670/16 A0673/19 B0890/12
B0904/11 B0904/17 B0924/25 B1004/03
B1004/10 B1007/34 B1008/35 B1258/04
B1278/11 B1330/11 B1345/15 C0150/30
C0171/28 C0177/06 C0553/04
tasted (6) A0091/07 A0110/13
A0111/02 A0111/18 B1349/31 C0129/41
tasteful (1) B1280/21
tastefully (1) A0500/17
tasteless (1) C0394/02
tastes (4) A0273/22
A0673/11 A0709/32 B1275/01
tasting (2) C0171/24 C0188/22
tasty (1) A0486/11
tat (1) B1109/31
tattered (3) A0401/15
A0411/21 A0662/09
Tattle (2) A0384/22 A0384/24
tattoo (2) A0372/09 B0795/15
tattooing (1) B1163/21
Tau (2) A0045/19 A0346/11
taught (15) A0311/28
A0473/27 A0609/18 A0611/11 A0703/11
B1004/28 B1134/14 B1215/13 B1300/23
C0079/12 C0079/23 C0139/32 C0430/48
C0532/22 C0541/21
taunt (1) C0557/22
Tauta (1) B1291/T
tauta (Gr.) (1) A0608/M
Tavern (1) C0537/39
tavern (3) A0066/30
->B0841/06 B0875/32
tavern-keeper (1) B0876/03
tawdry (1) C0123/09
tawny (3) A0559/29
A0559/V A0560/27
tawny-colored (1) A0560/V
tax (4) A0300/07
A0473/14 B1152/25 B1154/29
taxed (1) A0528/V
taxing (1) A0473/22
Taylor, Jeremy (1) B1114/19
<u>te</u> (2) A0344/23 A0354/31
te (31) B1103/24
B1103/25 B1103/25 B1103/28 B1103/28
B1103/33 B1103/33 B1103/33 B1103/33
B1103/34 B1103/34 B1103/34 B1103/34
B1103/34 B1103/35 B1103/35 B1103/35
B1104/16 B1104/17 B1104/18 B1109/10
B1109/18 B1109/26 B1109/27 B1109/27
B1109/29 B1109/29 B1109/31 B1109/31
B1109/34 B1109/34
te (Gr.) (2) A0195/M A0195/M
tea (6) A0337/12 A0337/25
B0928/18 B0930/01 B1045/30 C0561/22
tea-pot (4) B1009/27
B1009/30 B1009/31 B1369/17
Tea-Pot (11) B1369/31
B1370/12 B1371/04 B1371/06 B1371/07
B1371/09 B1371/10 B1371/13 B1371/18
B1371/24 B1374/06
Tea-Pot's (1) B1370/03
teaching (1) B1158/29
teachings (1) B1219/V
teak (1) A0136/01
teal (1) C0151/27
tear (12) A0092/11
A0111/23 A0126/31 B0762/22 B0762/25
B0762/27 B0766/33 B0797/29 B0991/04
C0106/10 C0106/37 C0134/25
tearfully (1) A0510/04
tearing (7) A0072/04
A0123/30 A0253/17 A0557/17 B0913/19
C0131/18 C0205/37
tears (35) A0154/22
A0154/24 A0162/09 A0216/26 A0294/V
A0318/10 A0346/30 A0351/17 A0404/15
A0484/23 A0587/24 A0613/35 A0623/02
A0626/22 A0631/20 A0641/19 A0641/V
A0644/21 A0644/V B0762/18 B0817/05
B0852/21 B1052/28 B1104/14 B1133/06
B1134/01 B1135/24 B1348/04 C0061/08
C0065/20 C0073/16 C0122/13 C0123/06
C0128/13 C0130/38
technical (1) B1358/15
technicality (2) A0711/20 B1276/21
technically (6) A0157/18 A0211/26
A0443/24 A0664/05 A0707/33 B0724/02
tedious (2) B1291/16 C0071/17
tedium (2) A0081/40 A0430/21
tee-totum (7) B1013/15
B1013/15 B1013/17 B1013/24 B1015/V
B1020/23 B1020/26
teemed (1) A0514/30
teeming (1) A0430/22
teeth (70)

Teian (2) A0228/26 A0233/07
Teios (1) A0190/20
Tekeli-li (3) C0204/25
C0204/25 C0208/16
Tekeli-li (6) C0190/22 C0190/22
C0191/01 C0191/02 C0203/04 C0206/01
Telegraph (1) B1119/18
telegraph (4) B1089/11
B1293/33 B1293/34 B1294/01
telegraphed (1) A0382/25
telescope (15) B0841/25
B0841/26 B0841/32 B0842/12 B1081/06
B1167/29 B1169/33 B1391/17 C0396/05
C0399/20 C0405/06 C0415/12 C0423/34
C0430/21 C0430/22
telescopes (3) A0601/03
B1073/24 C0426/14
telescopic (2) A0314/19 B1301/07
tell (118)
Tell-Tale (1) B0789/T
telles (1) A0096/V
tellin (1) B0809/01
telling (9) A0337/23
A0562/30 A0613/35 A0624/01 B0820/21
B0890/11 B1390/03 C0057/22 C0170/25
Tellmenow (1) B1151/02
tells (5) A0593/27
A0609/28 B0950/28 B1300/36 B1302/24
tem (1) A0204/12
tem. (1) B1189/10
Tem-Pest (1) A0250/15
temerity (2) B1134/03 B1245/02
temoins (1) A0600/02
temper (13) A0102/07
A0107/32 A0299/33 A0323/04 A0446/12
A0446/26 A0532/14 B0810/21 B0810/36
B0851/19 B0856/12 B0969/02 B1104/27
temperament (20) A0161/11
A0278/38 A0324/11 A0398/33 A0402/19
A0427/19 A0440/11 B0742/18 B0851/05
B0888/26 B0893/03 B0922/12 B0934/07
B0942/04 B1234/11 B1246/15 B1380/26
C0065/14 C0521/29 C0538/34
temperance (3) A0621/16
A0623/14 B1089/02
temperate (1) C0171/19
temperature (11) B1168/25
C0160/41 C0161/03 C0161/07 C0163/10
C0164/16 C0164/22 C0166/08 C0167/01
C0203/13 C0203/28
tempered (1) A0499/07
tempers (2) A0097/29 A0433/07
Tempest (2) A0029/08 A0710/31
tempest (20) A0026/33
A0029/20 A0044/24 A0079/11 A0102/04
A0137/13 A0138/14 A0139/03 A0143/17
A0146/08 A0197/22 A0197/24 A0411/22
A0413/31 A0587/04 B0932/18 B1078/36
C0063/04 C0112/15 C0185/24
tempestuous (3) A0028/17
A0412/19 A0437/V
tempestuously (2) A0078/06 C0116/28
Temple (2) A0045/13 A0122/22
temple (16) A0046/07
A0047/02 A0075/17 A0120/06 A0120/20
->A0122/26 A0123/30 A0124/10 A0402/03
B0945/31 B0947/22 B0948/07 B0950/09
B1166/05 B1185/26 B1302/19
Temple, William (1) B1114/19
temples (23) A0078/06
A0122/08 A0126/31 A0159/05 A0161/18
A0195/V A0215/06 A0235/21 A0298/V
A0298/V A0312/10 A0328/11 A0329/V
A0515/01 B0760/07 B0950/04 B0966/19
B1160/13 B1193/09 B1294/09 C0073/12
C0396/33 C0573/21
Templeton (9) B0941/02
B0941/07 B0941/10 B0941/23 B0946/15
B0947/31 B0948/20 B0948/34 B0950/03
tempora (2) B1293/37 B1370/06
tempora (1) B1370/14
temporal (5) A0021/26
A0601/25 A0615/23 B1181/23 B1219/15
temporarily (2) A0662/06 B1107/16
temporary (12) A0399/08
A0409/30 A0428/14 A0626/11 B0829/24
B0955/30 B1037/08 C0098/19 C0523/09
C0555/28 C0571/27 C0575/34
temporize (1) B1047/01
temps (2) A0431/08 B1104/V
tempt (1) B0814/32
temptation (2) A0427/12 B0769/V
temptations (1) A0644/13
tempted (5) A0381/20
A0427/13 A0578/13 B0870/05 C0074/03
tempting (1) C0166/23
ten (118)
ten-knot (1) C0139/38
tenable (1) A0600/09
tenacity (2) B0742/33 C0577/37
tenant (11) A0190/10
A0217/01 A0218/20 A0328/18 A0410/14
A0539/17 B0963/32 B1339/22 C0173/11
C0173/19 C0178/40
tenantable (1) B1003/21
tenanted (8) A0327/13
A0403/23 A0406/26 A0662/V B0807/07
B0943/27 B1038/28 B1038/30
tenanting (1) B1224/01
tenants (1) C0174/34
tended (5) A0589/08
B0761/01 B1051/10 B1128/14 B1331/16
tendency (13) A0019/20
A0312/16 A0550/29 B0963/12 B1050/26
B1073/15 B1076/25 B1191/03 B1207/21
B1221/03 B1312/24 C0167/04 C0207/24
tender (1) A0352/12
tender (5) A0344/15
A0352/11 C0165/17 C0176/35 C0546/40
tendered (1) B1185/22
tenderly (1) A0404/01
tenderness (4) A0613/04
B0850/09 B0893/02 B1122/11
tending (5) A0327/03
A0434/15 B1052/07 B1074/05 C0160/25
tendre (3) A0344/15
A0344/16 A0344/21
tendrils (1) B1337/22
tends (3) A0283/08
B0769/04 C0159/35

Tenebrarum (3) A0578/35
B1291/07 B1310/05
tenebrarum (1) A0638/14
tenement (3) A0227/18
A0232/05 A0554/21
tenements (1) A0514/26
Tenera (1) A0072/30
Teneriffe (1) C0154/35
tenfold (2) A0512/13 B0893/04
tenor (5) A0304/01
A0473/02 A0533/19 B0985/33 B1054/19
tenor/G (1) B0905/26
tense (1) A0498/08
tent (3) C0175/13
C0175/32 C0176/13
tenth (16) A0043/02
A0584/35 A0654/25 A0655/05 A0655/V
B0727/14 B1181/19 B1262/33 C0148/12
C0414/01 C0420/04 C0533/31 C0539/20
C0539/38 C0560/18 C0560/27
tenths (1) B1181/20
tents (1) C0552/31
tenty (1) A0356/14
tenuity (6) A0064/20 A0402/02
A0457/26 A0460/06 A0461/05 B0940/V
tenure (5) A0500/25
A0578/09 A0641/V C0095/23 C0134/17
tepid (1) C0178/29
Teraphim (1) A0046/10
terapin (1) C0137/30
Terence (1) A0091/23
Terentius (2) A0110/22 A0111/03
term (55)
termed (46) A0211/22 A0230/22
A0231/03 A0295/06 A0300/27 A0348/08
A0435/06 A0445/32 A0479/16 A0483/15
A0497/05 A0508/16 A0508/26 A0509/30
A0529/14 A0549/14 A0550/14 A0581/05
A0612/26 A0615/33 A0631/04 A0664/05
A0682/34 A0706/09 A0706/21 A0707/33
B0724/02 B0886/04 B0902/07 B0942/18
B0948/21 B0984/28 B1004/14 B1122/26
B1143/31 B1241/27 B1247/24 B1271/13
B1271/23 B1272/33 B1293/02 B1295/08
B1310/26 C0174/25 C0420/32 C0525/20
terminate (2) B0949/34 C0565/21
terminated (7) A0279/15
A0553/16 B0890/06 C0159/25 C0195/06
C0404/02 C0578/33
terminates (2) C0150/37 C0418/30
terminating (5) A0122/29
A0211/12 A0273/13 B1163/26 C0575/15
termination (15) A0102/15
A0212/28 A0414/01 A0627/12 A0670/08
B0838/12 B0864/22 B1128/08 B1234/34
B1261/18 B1280/24 B1280/30 C0195/10
C0395/37 C0572/19
terminations (1) B0837/27
terming (1) B1145/16
terms (31) A0074/11
A0098/06 A0155/26 A0157/07 A0157/07
A0252/04 A0279/27 A0320/V A0403/02
A0403/25 A0433/06 A0496/V A0539/01
B0772/07 B0878/13 B0905/31 B0993/15
B1005/35 B1045/23 B1105/17 B1109/01
->B1138/12 B1139/24 B1184/17 B1220/26
B1314/34 B1316/28 B1339/06 C0166/36
C0177/37 C0555/25
terns (1) C0151/28
terra (2) B1292/01 C0389/35
terra-firma (1) B1108/19
terrace (9) A0710/05
B1275/09 B1335/18 C0577/10 C0577/13
C0578/22 C0579/16 C0579/25 C0580/06
terraces (3) A0709/35
B1275/03 C0577/03
terre (1) B1335/18
terrestrial (4) A0412/30
C0429/08 C0432/46 C0544/03
Terrible (1) B0852/28
terrible (83)
terribly (8) A0143/16
A0401/26 A0582/05 B0961/18 B1020/34
C0061/16 C0125/22 C0197/28
terrific (27) A0101/23
A0137/18 A0138/14 A0140/01 A0143/22
A0243/18 A0244/14 A0246/24 A0318/V
A0328/25 A0353/35 A0537/08 A0580/29
A0590/29 B0955/22 B0965/07 B1057/15
B1108/25 B1248/31 C0072/11 C0109/12
C0111/16 C0134/07 C0182/30 C0397/03
C0419/19 C0578/32
terrifically (2) A0692/01 B1106/15
terrified (11) A0411/11
A0565/07 A0694/10 B0824/10 B0849/08
B0992/V B1164/19 B1350/17 C0420/04
C0424/06 C0562/40
terrify (1) A0165/26
terris (1) B1345/09
territories (1) A0286/06
territory (9) B1162/09
B1164/38 C0521/10 C0524/30 C0528/31
C0536/38 C0536/39 C0550/32 C0553/10
terror (92)
terror-inspiring (1) A0430/03
terror-stricken (3) A0036/07
A0243/09 C0420/24
terrors (21) A0080/07
A0080/27 A0228/16 A0228/17 A0232/V
A0232/V A0235/14 A0317/01 A0417/01
A0457/21 A0591/29 A0642/02 A0687/27
A0696/25 B0794/12 B0944/09 B0965/23
B0969/15 C0081/20 C0107/21 C0204/33
tertiary (2) A0175/V A0182/05
Tertullian (1) A0511/03
Tertullian's (1) A0213/06
test (11) A0311/06
A0496/30 A0497/01 B0743/02 B0850/20
B1072/20 B1076/35 B1234/02 B1314/30
B1315/13 C0407/12
testator (1) B0887/15
tested (1) B0946/12
testified (3) A0543/08
B0735/18 B0736/02
testify (3) B0875/20
B1049/24 C0162/12
testimonials (1) B0879/09
testimony (18) A0265/09 A0351/17
A0538/33 A0540/19 A0540/31 A0543/06
A0544/10 A0549/09 A0549/11 A0550/08

->A0550/21 A0558/29 B0730/19 B0734/18
B0956/04 B1054/14 C0424/34 C0544/40
testing (1) B0960/18
tests (2) B0946/05 B0962/18
tete (1) B1145/23
tete (1) B1145/V
tete-a-tete (3) A0381/13
A0381/V A0382/26
Teton (5) C0551/23
C0551/26 C0557/37 C0559/38 C0560/12
Teton/Sioux (1) C0552/32
Tetons (9) C0551/11
C0551/17 C0553/12 C0556/17 C0557/11
C0557/17 C0558/06 C0558/08 C0560/25
Teufel (2) A0177/05 A0177/08
teufel (1) A0183/03
teufel (2) A0373/06 A0373/09
teuffel (2) B1109/07 B1110/08
Texas (1) B1160/14
text (5) B0833/19
B1115/20 B1115/36 B1189/18 B1313/04
textilem (1) B0889/30
Textor, Ravisius (2) A0158/21
A0158/V
texture (10) A0081/09 A0267/11
A0402/10 A0403/05 A0498/06 A0512/02
B1281/26 B1339/28 C0174/29 C0543/22
th (2) B0838/01 B0838/04
Thames (2) A0240/04 A0242/22
Thammuz (1) A0043/03
than (1075)
thank (13) A0261/15
A0261/16 A0265/32 A0276/08 A0282/14
A0388/01 B0955/21 B1005/08 B1010/07
B1010/30 B1011/10 B1013/34 C0569/40
thanked (4) A0056/24
A0066/14 B1003/16 B1159/17
thankful (1) A0483/23
thankfully (1) B1207/27
thankless (1) B1206/07
thanks (8) A0047/24
A0087/12 A0268/08 A0271/12 A0485/V
C0096/32 C0127/20 C0138/24
thanksgiving (1) C0124/05
that (5301)
that'll (4) A0464/17
A0465/16 A0465/23 A0469/06
that's (30) A0109/11 A0109/15
A0109/15 A0336/05 A0344/04 A0344/26
A0344/33 A0345/09 A0346/06 A0464/01
A0464/10 A0464/22 A0464/23 A0465/09
A0467/22 A0468/20 A0470/07 A0470/11
A0470/24 A0534/01 A0630/11 A0650/28
A0650/28 B0820/06 B0896/26 B0914/02
B0914/02 B0914/03 B1373/05 C0447/V
thatched (1) B0945/30
The (16) A0018/V
A0146/10 A0162/03 A0213/05 A0284/18
B0724/12 B1122/12 B1212/10 B1380/04
B1380/06 B1380/09 B1385/01 B1385/08
C0412/04 C0551/23 C0553/14
the (34485)
Theatre (3) A0301/02
A0534/02 A0537/02
theatre (9) A0318/11
->A0383/11 A0487/15 B0761/V B0877/31
B0891/23 B0894/03 B0898/19 B0915/17
theatres (1) A0514/05
Theatrical (1) B1244/T
theatrical (2) A0053/28 B1331/05
Theban (2) B1179/04 B1191/20
Thebes (2) B1179/03 B1192/19
thee (30) A0034/21 A0034/23
A0127/27 A0150/03 A0150/M A0151/10
A0163/11 A0164/V A0166/11 A0228/06
A0228/10 A0228/28 A0233/09 A0251/05
A0319/23 A0345/10 A0345/10 A0348/29
A0357/09 A0357/09 A0384/06 A0455/M
A0599/M A0599/M A0645/08 B0964/13
B0964/21 B0964/22 B1046/05 B1385/31
theft (2) B0977/01 B1384/13
their (988)
theirs (6) A0368/34 A0509/03
A0604/03 B1363/16 C0137/12 C0549/13
Thelluson (2) A0704/35 B1269/34
them (817)
theme (20) A0069/17
A0214/09 A0315/20 A0366/14 A0381/16
A0532/05 A0641/21 A0709/20 B0726/08
B0727/01 B0731/07 B0751/08 B0863/23
B0863/35 B0924/20 B1014/09 B1132/10
B1274/23 C0433/04 C0576/14
themes (4) A0338/16
A0509/31 B0954/01 C0429/47
themselves (155)
then (774)
thence (34) A0122/24 A0142/02
A0236/01 A0349/26 A0400/23 A0429/18
A0565/13 A0605/11 A0641/06 A0676/15
B0737/23 B0754/08 B0822/09 B0842/22
B0983/13 B0986/20 B1294/16 B1295/10
B1330/33 B1338/15 B1353/11 B1361/16
C0056/21 C0084/27 C0089/22 C0410/37
C0431/12 C0526/37 C0527/24 C0528/12
C0528/13 C0528/13 C0528/16 C0547/01
thenceforward (9) A0021/13
A0026/V A0138/30 A0427/29 A0530/25
A0641/20 B0852/34 B1213/35 B1312/09
Theo (Gr.) (1) A0075/V
Theocritus (1) A0111/05
theological (2) A0226/23 A0230/22
theologists (1) A0458/33
Theology (1) A0295/12
Theology, Theologos (2) A0175/14
A0181/04
Theophrastus (2) A0176/01 A0181/33
theoretical (1) B1313/09
theories (10) A0067/27 A0079/04
A0173/07 A0178/12 A0234/12 A0536/06
B1298/20 B1300/13 B1316/31 C0423/06
theorist (5) B1296/06
B1297/37 B1312/08 B1313/09 B1317/33
theorize (4) B1298/17
B1298/20 B1316/27 B1316/31
theory (16) A0099/03
A0458/22 A0556/23 A0556/24 B0744/11
B0747/31 B0748/01 B0960/18 B1120/08
B1160/18 B1220/28 B1303/10 B1313/09
C0403/38 C0407/18 C0413/20
there (1361)

there'll (1) B1373/10
there's (3) A0343/34
A0468/03 B1046/11
thereabout (3) A0593/31
C0174/38 C0196/33
thereabouts (7) A0173/17
A0178/26 A0513/18 B1045/10 C0551/10
C0573/13 C0577/03
thereafter (4) A0027/20
A0098/07 A0325/19 B0925/18
thereby (7) A0085/M
A0189/34 A0226/34 A0231/08 A0262/33
A0292/V B1131/28
therefore (172)
therefrom (7) A0199/01
A0212/21 A0538/10 A0567/V C0150/12
C0390/03 C0397/28
therein (20) A0037/02
A0047/10 A0071/05 A0089/15 A0198/21
A0218/13 A0234/29 A0262/15 A0310/M
A0314/26 A0318/V A0328/V A0388/33
A0552/02 A0603/27 A0640/21 A0641/18
B1068/11 C0391/10 C0524/40
thereof (3) A0044/04
A0414/15 A0581/30
thereto (1) A0069/10
thereunto (2) A0216/22 C0398/36
thereupon (4) B0854/08
B0966/18 C0390/27 C0396/33
therewith (2) A0413/33 A0529/09
thermometer (6) A0485/05 C0159/03
C0162/28 C0164/23 C0396/06 C0396/24
These (1) A0213/26
these (859)
thesis (1) A0473/30
they (981)
they'll (1) A0347/06
thick (56)
thick-headed (1) B0871/28
thick-soled (1) B0878/01
thicker (2) A0241/16 C0173/14
thickest (1) C0190/25
thicket (32) B0734/32
B0734/39 B0735/36 B0736/06 B0758/05
B0758/06 B0758/15 B0758/26 B0758/30
B0759/24 B0759/26 B0760/24 B0760/27
B0761/08 B0761/12 B0761/15 B0761/25
B0763/08 B0763/11 B0764/02 B0764/10
B0765/04 B0765/28 B0766/12 B0766/22
B0767/05 B0767/05 B0767/06 B0767/08
B0768/29 B0769/V B0866/13
thickets (1) A0047/16
thickly (15) A0144/20
B0817/30 B1179/24 B1180/12 B1248/24
C0145/18 C0163/19 C0425/06 C0549/24
C0558/31 C0559/14 C0560/15 C0572/15
C0574/11 C0577/18
thickly-wooded (2) C0184/06
C0549/18
thickness (7) A0269/03
A0270/18 B0981/04 B1160/34 B1167/30
C0405/01 C0573/05
thief (4) A0556/10
A0676/34 B0976/35 B0978/21
thievery (1) C0170/06

thieves (1) B0869/22
thievish (1) C0153/10
thigh-bone (1) A0246/06
thighs (4) A0057/05
A0368/19 C0168/36 C0552/08
thimble-rig (1) A0509/15
thin (22) A0088/26 A0196/08
A0215/10 A0240/21 A0247/06 A0298/V
A0367/23 A0401/32 A0511/34 A0681/12
A0681/12 B0793/09 B0829/04 B0940/09
B0980/03 C0087/20 C0410/38 C0415/27
C0416/22 C0533/11 C0534/34 C0573/11
thin> (27) A0465/10
A0465/11 A0465/19 A0465/20 A0466/03
A0466/04 A0466/05 A0466/20 A0466/31
A0467/08 A0467/09 A0467/16 A0467/V
A0468/03 A0468/09 A0468/30 A0468/V
A0469/14 A0469/15 A0469/18 A0469/21
A0469/27 A0469/V A0469/V A0469/V
A0470/11 A0470/11
thine (11) A0073/33
A0074/07 A0150/02 A0150/02 A0151/03
A0151/12 A0227/31 A0228/06 A0228/10
A0448/16 B1385/31
thing (240)
Things (1) A0269/19
things (171)
Thingum (6) B1126/T B1127/25
B1137/11 B1138/04 B1142/10 B1142/19
thingum (3) B1127/26
B1127/27 B1127/28
think (198)
thinker (3) A0179/18
A0213/16 B1312/08
thinkers (5) A0556/23
B0723/01 B1298/16 B1310/24 B1316/25
thinking (61)
thinks (15) A0281/18
A0286/20 A0467/22 A0468/19 A0488/14
A0540/22 A0543/05 A0549/31 B0744/15
B0772/13 B1380/33 C0428/06 C0448/V
C0546/14 C0546/16
thinned (1) C0565/35
thinner (3) C0411/02
C0575/19 C0575/19
thinnest (1) C0574/04
thins (1) B1096/29
Third (1) B1321/21
third (83)
thirdly (5) B1233/21
B1383/07 C0427/22 C0556/11 C0556/25
thirds (1) B0826/35
thirst (34) A0081/32 A0226/11
A0321/07 A0688/02 A0689/20 A0689/20
B0760/01 B1145/26 B1212/26 B1277/07
C0071/21 C0073/40 C0076/01 C0076/30
C0081/09 C0083/29 C0083/33 C0090/05
C0120/14 C0126/22 C0135/32 C0137/13
C0140/37 C0141/09 C0142/14 C0142/17
C0143/01 C0143/23 C0143/35 C0145/31
C0145/39 C0146/02 C0146/09 C0188/20
thirteen (18) A0373/05 A0373/28
A0705/19 B0838/35 B0839/32 B0840/22
B0841/29 B0842/02 B1070/35 B1194/03
B1194/09 B1270/18 C0102/19 C0141/34

->C0161/01 C0429/02 C0429/23 C0429/27
thirteenth (4) B0728/10
C0101/08 C0150/04 C0421/08
thirtieth (1) C0101/08
thirty (42) A0044/04 A0120/14
A0121/14 A0501/03 A0539/34 A0557/18
A0671/24 A0689/24 A0692/01 B0727/27
B0828/06 B1007/28 B1079/15 B1080/07
B1160/08 B1248/18 B1332/23 B1334/09
B1334/13 B1353/17 C0064/33 C0124/20
C0146/33 C0148/18 C0179/05 C0179/15
C0187/31 C0194/14 C0201/04 C0396/24
C0430/43 C0432/05 C0441/V C0441/V
C0526/09 C0528/15 C0533/14 C0538/22
C0540/32 C0559/11 C0567/06 C0578/19
thirty-first (1) B0879/16
thirty-five (3) C0147/22
C0162/29 C0559/12
thirty-four (1) C0164/17
thirty-nine (2) A0121/V C0421/16
thirty-seven (2) B1136/18 B1192/22
thirty-six (6) A0121/V A0581/19
A0705/21 B1141/02 B1270/20 C0159/04
thirty-three (2) A0121/V C0163/10
thirty-two (3) A0219/06
C0180/24 C0184/31
This (2) B0831/14 C0071/06
this (2843)
This-and-that (2) A0174/14 A0174/19
This-and-That (1) A0179/28
thistles (1) B1010/04
thither (12) A0195/18
A0318/16 A0440/05 A0603/22 A0612/13
B0880/01 B0905/V B0916/03 B1181/21
B1329/06 B1337/05 C0563/16
Thomas (4) A0173/12
A0173/21 A0388/01 C0433/01
Thomas, Don (1) A0621/06
Thompson (3) A0382/01
A0382/05 A0382/07
Thompson, David (1) C0527/34
thongs (2) C0562/17 C0563/18
thorn (6) A0044/13 B0735/14
B0762/17 B0762/17 B0762/20 B0762/29
thorns (4) B0762/29
B0762/30 B0762/35 B0763/04
Thornton (21) C0532/25
C0537/08 C0537/18 C0539/04 C0541/12
C0541/15 C0541/22 C0542/02 C0544/16
C0544/39 C0548/34 C0549/09 C0554/13
C0561/10 C0563/35 C0565/07 C0565/14
C0565/20 C0565/26 C0568/07 C0575/08
Thornton, Andrew (2) C0532/10
C0535/23
Thornton's (3) C0535/07
C0535/24 C0561/19
Thorntons (1) C0532/11
thorough (20) A0107/27
A0112/07 A0496/24 A0538/18 B0750/27
B0941/17 B0963/16 B0978/04 B0981/22
B0984/32 B0988/27 B1048/16 B1069/10
B1144/20 B1250/04 B1315/32 B1338/09
C0069/12 C0156/30 C0170/20
thorough-bred (1) A0243/23
thoroughfare (5) A0512/17
->A0513/33 A0535/01 B0729/11 B1316/18
thoroughfares (4) A0507/21
A0546/12 B0862/27 B1226/03
thoroughly (61)
thoroughness (1) B1277/24
those (343)
Thou (1) B1044/T
thou (77)
though (32) A0037/12
A0188/M A0203/M A0250/02 A0387/14
A0387/19 A0388/15 A0466/12 A0470/18
A0483/05 A0510/01 A0532/15 A0612/14
B0731/31 B0789/M B0888/05 B0905/18
B0908/02 B0984/24 B1090/06 B1092/37
B1093/32 B1139/02 B1168/25 B1225/V
B1298/36 B1320/03 B1353/23 B1382/27
B1392/05 C0193/24 C0404/18
thought (351)
thought's (1) A0406/29
thoughtful (4) A0674/20
A0683/08 B0929/12 B0979/11
thoughtfully (6) A0160/15 B0823/25
B0913/25 C0070/33 C0079/34 C0444/V
thoughtless (2) A0142/14 A0438/11
thoughtlessly (1) C0408/02
thoughtlessness (1) B1005/11
Thoughts (2) B0969/05 B1385/07
thoughts (53)
thousand (172)
thousand-and-second (1) B1154/26
Thousand-and-Second (1) B1151/T
thousands (11) A0639/13
B0734/12 B0745/28 B0746/25 B0749/06
B0942/01 B1162/04 C0138/16 C0188/10
C0387/20 C0564/17
Thrace (2) A0175/28 A0181/23
thrashed (1) B0875/29
thrashing (2) A0384/11 B0875/15
thread (9) A0072/14
A0448/08 B0794/29 B1011/17 B1160/36
B1251/01 C0094/35 C0148/11 C0534/22
threaded (2) B1279/37 C0193/05
threading (1) C0199/10
threads (3) B0735/09
B0759/04 C0575/19
threat (9) B0765/01
B1051/08 B1051/30 B1051/35 B1058/16
B1103/17 B1105/06 B1256/04 B1371/20
threaten (1) C0202/37
threatened (6) A0139/16 A0457/30
A0624/03 A0653/05 B0949/34 B1051/29
threatening (4) A0461/12
A0512/V C0182/08 C0391/35
threats (7) A0034/09
A0144/03 B0807/29 B0930/10 B1051/01
B1051/08 C0086/06
Three (3) A0057/04
A0057/09 A0058/06
three (375)
three-cornered (1) A0368/17
three-gallon (1) C0129/29
three-hundred-and-twentieth (1) 12/01
three-inch (1) B0932/25
three-quarter (2) C0399/16 C0422/32
threshold (8) A0023/12

->A0100/33 A0321/07 A0416/30 A0439/07
A0615/22 B1338/27 C0085/17
threw (85)
thrice (2) A0182/33 A0428/24
thricks> (1) A0468/09
thrifle> (1) A0470/18
thrill (8) A0162/08
A0428/06 A0460/21 A0616/32 A0638/09
A0682/06 B0955/04 C0058/19
thrilled (7) A0443/04
A0613/36 A0615/02 A0695/31 B0851/26
B0890/02 C0122/34
thrilling (12) A0144/16
A0226/15 A0234/12 A0310/06 A0315/22
A0380/27 A0398/11 A0692/09 B0723/02
B0810/10 B0960/35 B1279/31
thrillingly (5) A0218/25
A0313/26 A0405/16 B1075/30 B1240/25
thrills (1) A0154/25
thrive (4) B1096/27
B1206/15 B1206/16 C0138/13
throat (39) A0053/02
A0054/09 A0062/07 A0063/17 A0089/11
A0104/02 A0245/01 A0251/V A0328/08
A0506/06 A0538/15 A0538/21 A0543/23
A0544/07 A0557/22 A0558/30 A0559/13
A0559/14 A0567/07 A0694/22 B0730/06
B0851/28 B1059/09 B1101/26 B1262/24
C0072/29 C0078/36 C0082/15 C0085/21
C0089/25 C0108/18 C0113/11 C0113/19
C0113/33 C0133/12 C0138/29 C0389/29
C0398/38 C0411/29
throats (5) A0124/01
A0339/33 A0370/04 B0859/05 C0060/37
throbbed (2) A0078/06 A0615/03
throbbing (1) A0155/10
throne (11) A0068/13
A0120/03 A0227/34 A0324/V A0406/21
A0407/11 A0459/12 B0761/22 B1212/31
B1214/33 C0569/35
thrones (2) B1385/05 B1385/10
throng (5) A0318/09
A0407/40 A0507/23 A0515/07 A0676/27
thronged (7) A0512/21
A0515/17 B0750/10 B0750/15 B0958/30
B1081/28 B1107/25
thronging (7) A0235/16
A0436/18 A0439/23 A0514/06 A0640/26
A0685/11 A0694/23
throth> (1) A0467/23
throttled (3) A0538/17
A0543/30 B1169/28
throttling (1) A0123/21
through (1) B0838/20
through (535)
throughout (63)
throw (43) A0057/07
A0066/33 A0073/27 A0105/14 A0121/01
A0155/07 A0156/24 A0234/09 A0327/03
A0345/24 A0405/25 A0538/32 A0593/15
A0663/06 A0663/16 B0732/03 B0733/22
B0738/29 B0739/02 B0739/11 B0773/26
B0810/27 B0828/36 B0855/12 B0874/18
B1163/30 B1223/V B1305/16 B1312/24
B1321/24 C0078/05 C0101/26 C0105/16
->C0131/36 C0133/11 C0142/27 C0192/08
C0207/24 C0405/18 C0426/19 C0430/15
C0554/04 C0568/19
throwing (44) A0054/11
A0063/18 A0068/19 A0101/V A0105/26
A0158/08 A0164/11 A0216/24 A0356/22
A0567/14 A0608/12 B0739/32 B0773/27
B0856/20 B0894/29 B0907/16 B0930/36
B1069/28 B1101/15 B1141/10 B1156/03
B1180/33 B1261/28 B1262/05 B1321/29
B1332/21 B1337/22 C0073/14 C0105/36
C0113/07 C0113/18 C0122/16 C0133/16
C0138/28 C0140/22 C0170/01 C0192/15
C0197/01 C0197/23 C0389/35 C0398/15
C0412/07 C0424/38 C0568/33
thrown (117)
throws (5) A0503/10
A0529/08 B0773/25 B0773/29 B0874/20
thrue> (4) A0465/21
A0466/20 A0469/08 A0469/09
thrummed (1) C0103/04
thrumming (1) A0153/19
thrust (30) A0080/45 A0143/08
A0352/23 A0447/13 A0535/23 A0538/14
A0543/22 A0547/25 A0551/31 A0557/03
A0557/11 A0567/17 A0684/34 B0793/01
B0793/02 B0830/24 B0877/21 B0927/22
B0967/31 B0977/06 B0991/08 B1059/08
B1178/15 B1184/02 B1262/24 B1263/20
B1353/22 C0075/18 C0143/17 C0545/21
thrusting (5) A0549/04
A0557/06 B1015/26 C0092/20 C0199/19
thrusts (2) A0479/21 B0871/11
thruth> (5) A0465/09
A0465/V A0469/V A0470/19 A0470/24
Thumb (1) A0621/22
thumb (11) A0071/18
A0136/27 A0509/22 A0625/21 B0793/32
B1011/29 B1012/19 B1184/05 B1184/10
B1184/12 B1184/13
thumb-latch (2) A0479/16 A0479/22
thumbed (1) A0078/22
thump (4) A0056/31
A0066/20 A0383/01 A0622/33
thumped (3) A0486/29
B1056/32 C0115/26
thumping (3) B1178/13
B1372/24 C0058/29
thunder (13) A0048/V
A0048/V A0197/27 A0197/V A0198/02
A0198/04 A0380/33 A0468/18 A0583/13
B1090/34 B1157/26 C0072/29 C0141/35
thunder-blasted (1) A0163/02
thunder-cloud (2) C0189/41 C0563/14
thunderbolt (3) A0588/11
B0893/19 C0446/V
thundering (1) A0146/08
thunders (4) A0145/18
A0697/09 C0420/27 C0422/38
thunderstricken (2) B0826/22
B0983/05
thunderstruck (4) A0173/22
A0179/01 C0421/17 C0436/V
Thursday (1) B0958/29
Thursday, (1) B0754/09

thus (513)
thwart (1) A0432/12
thwarted (5) A0102/14
A0105/19 A0250/08 A0386/19 A0445/31
thy (37) A0034/25
A0056/20 A0127/26 A0127/28 A0127/V
A0128/10 A0150/03 A0151/10 A0151/10
A0159/19 A0163/07 A0163/V A0227/34
A0228/06 A0228/15 A0228/21 A0228/22
A0228/24 A0228/28 A0232/V A0233/02
A0233/03 A0233/05 A0233/09 A0251/01
A0251/03 A0251/05 A0349/31 A0426/09
A0599/M A0645/07 A0645/09 B1385/29
B1385/35 B1385/37 B1386/01 B1386/02
Thyeste (1) B0993/27
tibia (1) A0543/33
tic (1) A0096/M
tickets (1) B1090/04
ticking (2) A0354/11 A0367/26
tickings (1) A0615/11
tickling (1) A0367/V
tide (12) A0124/05
A0145/17 A0154/28 A0385/03 A0563/V
A0592/18 B0741/09 B0741/10 B0873/27
B1081/25 B1160/27 C0060/01
tide's (1) C0178/30
tides (4) A0235/V
A0316/23 A0507/25 A0601/33
tidings (2) B0729/24 B0731/29
tie (3) A0561/09 B0916/15 C0537/28
Tieck (2) A0293/03 A0409/04
tied (36) A0057/16
A0057/21 A0067/33 A0068/04 A0104/01
A0247/27 A0248/18 A0252/08 A0253/03
A0348/22 A0368/14 A0368/26 A0374/01
A0693/08 B0730/16 B0734/20 B0734/25
B0750/19 B0766/04 B0768/32 B0823/18
B1351/07 B1351/07 B1379/09 C0063/19
C0085/22 C0092/32 C0196/20 C0196/29
C0197/01 C0390/04 C0398/12 C0404/32
C0406/41 C0415/22 C0562/02
tier (5) A0487/16
B1262/09 B1262/14 B1262/19 B1262/33
tiers (3) B1248/26
C0091/31 C0164/01
Tiger (21) C0073/10
C0073/22 C0073/26 C0074/03 C0074/19
C0076/15 C0077/36 C0079/09 C0080/32
C0081/13 C0081/30 C0090/29 C0091/33
C0091/40 C0096/17 C0096/31 C0100/13
C0101/01 C0101/31 C0113/06 C0118/25
tiger (5) A0123/16
A0692/15 B1338/20 C0135/11 C0438/V
tight (12) A0103/23
A0252/22 A0387/V A0465/11 A0508/24
A0625/19 B0812/06 B1157/07 C0085/20
C0119/30 C0196/31 C0389/25
tight-fitting (3) A0371/06
B1257/18 B1350/36
tightened (5) A0590/09
A0629/34 B0746/27 B0746/29 B1071/17
tightening (2) B0747/02 B1170/02
tightly (13) A0247/27
B0730/16 B1134/25 B1291/06 C0063/35
C0089/29 C0097/21 C0097/31 C0124/39
->C0165/15 C0398/13 C0410/14 C0415/22
tightness (4) C0117/34
C0118/34 C0415/33 C0562/23
tile (1) B0980/V
tiled (1) B1362/27
tiles (3) A0366/33
A0367/14 A0367/22
till (31) A0079/01
A0080/25 A0165/03 A0228/34 A0469/12
A0469/16 A0470/20 A0483/30 A0487/17
A0489/32 A0629/28 A0650/26 A0651/18
A0651/18 A0683/16 B0743/32 B0809/10
B0822/08 B0933/01 B1119/M B1163/31
B1163/35 B1163/39 B1178/08 B1213/34
B1321/30 C0091/37 C0391/33 C0399/06
C0526/29 C0545/39
tiller (3) C0059/04
C0059/21 C0060/12
tillers (2) A0703/34 B1268/33
tilling> (1) A0466/07
tills (1) A0601/26
tilt (2) C0067/28 C0389/14
tilting (1) B1380/27
Timarchus (1) A0124/04
timber (10) A0591/25 B0741/25
C0063/18 C0115/30 C0541/29 C0542/36
C0559/18 C0566/16 C0571/14 C0574/11
timber-bolts (1) C0062/30
timbered (2) C0541/27 C0574/17
timbers (5) A0141/07
A0142/27 B0830/18 C0063/25 C0098/20
Timbuctoo (1) A0381/30
Time (2) A0347/V B0789/M
Time (1) A0353/35
time (610)
time-eaten (1) A0532/14
time-honored (4) A0209/12
A0320/12 A0399/06 C0412/32
time-piece (5) A0367/18
A0367/26 A0367/28 A0373/25 B1105/26
time-pieces (2) A0367/25 A0615/15
time-servers (1) A0498/20
time-worn (1) A0430/13
time's (1) A0642/34
timely (4) A0687/16
C0113/04 C0127/20 C0144/33
Times (4) A0338/22
A0338/25 A0338/26 A0338/26
times (108)
timid (6) A0123/15 A0165/25
A0583/32 C0059/41 C0166/25 C0562/33
Timon (1) B1277/27
timorously (1) B1090/11
tin (7) B0793/32
B0809/01 B0834/31 B1101/23 B1141/12
C0109/29 C0393/30
tincture (4) A0158/V
A0226/05 A0230/03 C0392/13
tinctured (3) A0099/09
A0135/13 B0850/29
tinder-works (1) C0148/08
ting (3) B0812/25
B0821/27 B1103/09
tinge (4) A0327/05
A0442/03 A0601/31 C0553/03

tinged (6) A0226/16 A0241/04
A0246/33 A0442/23 A0706/08 B1271/12
tingling (2) A0683/28 B0966/13
Tinian (1) C0057/23
tink (3) B0813/01
B0912/23 B1103/09
tinkling (2) A0128/18 C0388/30
tinned-ware (1) C0439/V
tinsel (1) A0276/35
tint (22) A0267/11 A0268/19
A0269/08 A0276/01 A0313/12 A0502/01
A0502/V A0603/21 A0665/31 A0665/33
A0696/04 B0832/22 B0835/05 B1281/27
B1337/33 C0151/12 C0204/36 C0407/34
C0416/40 C0418/42 C0419/15 C0538/42
tinted (4) A0321/16
A0672/13 A0674/03 B1331/07
Tintontintino (2) A0175/21 A0181/18
tints (5) A0100/14
A0501/22 A0640/31 A0643/07 A0665/28
tiny (4) A0155/06
A0155/V A0367/13 C0389/15
tip (3) B0927/01 B1182/28 B1185/27
tip> (3) A0465/13
A0466/31 A0468/13
tipped (1) C0425/15
tipping (1) A0468/29
tippling (1) C0427/29
tips (1) B1157/09
tiptoe (5) A0053/02
A0062/07 A0218/20 C0417/03 C0443/V
Tipula (1) B1163/33
tirade (1) A0536/14
tirade (1) B1129/16
tire (1) C0430/41
tired (3) B1119/M
C0058/15 C0058/24
tiresome (1) A0300/28
tis (5) B0814/18
B0819/32 B0820/17 B0821/14 B0912/16
tissue (6) A0150/V A0501/11
A0501/14 B0730/05 B0742/34 B0743/09
tissues (1) B0742/09
titanic (1) B1301/34
tithe (1) C0080/19
Titian (2) A0175/23 A0181/20
titillating (1) B1312/20
title (38) A0023/29 A0026/02
A0088/08 A0093/21 A0106/05 A0112/32
A0120/V A0122/23 A0156/03 A0250/04
A0284/17 A0292/V A0301/10 A0337/15
A0365/14 A0385/21 A0385/23 A0399/17
A0431/21 A0609/33 A0622/15 B0942/15
B0962/06 B1115/37 B1137/05 B1138/05
B1139/06 B1185/29 B1207/10 B1207/33
B1314/14 B1317/33 B1369/12 C0150/21
C0174/33 C0430/27 C0432/42 C0448/V
titled (1) A0163/12
titles (8) A0235/15
A0235/17 A0250/14 A0301/01 B0810/13
B1180/19 B1180/19 C0429/10
tittle-tattle (1) A0298/V
tiz (1) B1103/02
to (11276)
to (Gr.) (1) A0075/V

to-day (43) A0044/21
A0209/08 A0426/10 A0435/32 A0584/17
A0655/04 A0655/08 A0656/20 B0813/08
B0849/05 B0948/22 B1030/16 B1079/25
B1168/38 B1186/34 B1222/11 B1226/18
B1257/23 B1293/32 B1302/26 B1391/15
C0057/31 C0103/27 C0145/35 C0167/22
C0203/31 C0204/20 C0204/38 C0205/14
C0419/14 C0420/12 C0420/34 C0422/41
C0541/01 C0542/23 C0565/12 C0566/22
C0567/04 C0568/07 C0569/41 C0570/17
C0570/22 C0570/34
to-day's (3) A0651/13
A0656/03 A0656/11
to-morrow (16) A0456/22
A0584/17 A0655/28 A0656/01 A0656/21
A0657/22 B0809/10 B0849/05 B0892/17
B0923/30 B1222/12 B1222/14 B1226/19
B1235/05 B1371/08 B1391/10
to-morrow's (2) A0656/07 A0656/12
to-night (12) A0416/11
A0443/07 B0808/22 B0808/29 B0813/28
B0904/04 B0908/13 B1030/32 B1031/01
B1119/12 B1178/23 B1373/10
Toad (5) B1136/27
B1137/15 B1137/21 B1138/19 B1139/35
toad (1) A0625/08
toast (1) A0438/29
toasted (2) A0091/21 A0110/24
toasting (2) A0101/08 A0107/19
tobacco (18) A0482/32 A0539/10
A0667/13 A0667/23 B0875/33 B0875/35
B0876/07 B0876/10 B0876/12 B0876/12
C0097/20 C0097/25 C0097/34 C0534/24
C0556/09 C0556/16 C0557/13 C0558/17
tobacco-pouches (1) C0552/22
tobacconist (1) A0539/09
Toby (12) A0629/23
A0630/18 C0532/08 C0532/26 C0535/22
C0548/33 C0569/10 C0569/12 C0569/24
C0569/33 C0569/35 C0569/40
Toby's (1) A0622/34
today (1) A0657/21
todder (1) B0812/06
toddy (1) A0253/10
toe (4) A0487/10
B0825/32 B1180/30 B1182/12
toes (8) A0087/02
A0100/13 A0172/M A0178/M A0385/10
A0626/13 B0819/01 B1091/15
toga (3) A0089/06
A0089/11 A0196/23
together (122)
toil (4) A0410/26
A0686/12 B0827/06 B0843/08
toiled (2) A0616/28 B1145/18
toilet (1) B0915/05
toiling (3) B0859/10
C0070/29 C0192/03
toils (1) A0442/01
toilsome (2) B0764/28 B0765/03
Token (1) B1385/08
token (13) A0231/22
A0400/16 A0469/21 A0515/08 A0557/20
A0683/09 B1109/34 B1281/22 B1338/21

->C0165/38 C0558/15 C0563/28 C0568/38
tokens (5) A0283/03
B1140/05 B1158/28 B1234/31 C0424/13
told (98)
Toledo (3) A0684/30
A0685/12 A0697/11
tolerable (10) A0271/06 A0284/12
A0369/15 B0797/24 B1079/32 B1248/09
C0057/06 C0066/16 C0139/34 C0405/10
tolerably (15) A0283/02
A0346/03 B0810/03 B0869/10 B1071/17
B1102/28 B1339/12 B1339/31 B1361/29
C0163/03 C0167/01 C0196/34 C0565/37
C0570/07 C0574/16
tolerated (1) C0182/34
toll (3) A0683/22
B0874/28 B0874/31
tolling (2) A0078/09 A0340/14
Tom (3) A0347/08 B0876/V B1183/14
Tom-Fool (1) A0627/06
Tom/street (1) B0876/28
Tom/O'Bedlam's (1) C0387/M
tomahawk (2) B1140/29 B1140/30
Tomas (1) A0621/V
tomb (21) A0080/27
A0081/13 A0081/20 A0198/28 A0198/30
A0198/32 A0218/20 A0236/11 A0326/05
A0328/18 A0416/07 A0682/33 A0685/02
B0858/35 B0859/15 B0956/35 B0962/30
B0965/28 B0965/36 B1179/01 C0198/32
tombeau (1) A0378/M
tombs (5) A0322/05
A0604/03 B0963/23 B1160/24 B1188/25
tomes (1) A0088/01
Tommy (1) B1140/28
tomorrow (2) A0455/12 A0675/V
Tompkins, Bobby (2) A0490/17
A0490/29
Toms (1) A0491/09
ton (4) A0247/02
A0508/28 A0650/06 A0650/07
ton (1) B0877/04
tone (65)
tones (22) A0046/05 A0055/29
A0056/01 A0065/10 A0065/21 A0191/13
A0191/13 A0218/25 A0226/17 A0227/06
A0230/16 A0234/30 A0342/04 A0342/25
A0435/02 A0550/09 A0615/17 A0640/04
B0905/16 B1106/17 B1212/35 C0067/21
tong (1) B0899/28
Tongue (1) B1141/09
tongue (32) A0072/23
A0074/04 A0144/27 A0175/18 A0181/08
A0247/08 A0262/27 A0389/08 A0414/16
A0543/27 A0550/06 A0625/25 B0836/04
B0863/35 B0892/18 B0896/30 B0901/19
B0911/23 B0927/01 B0967/05 B1011/31
B1015/26 B1183/10 B1221/27 B1226/05
B1239/32 B1240/07 B1241/12 B1242/20
B1243/01 C0406/20 C0541/19
tongues (8) A0157/27
A0175/06 A0315/17 A0663/05 B0836/09
B1015/23 B1051/16 C0387/17
tonight (1) B0910/09
tonnage (1) C0057/28
tonnerres (1) A0183/02
tonnish (1) B0908/V
tons (11) A0135/28
A0140/03 A0583/21 B0968/17 B1166/31
B1293/13 C0146/33 C0147/09 C0147/15
C0184/34 C0430/24
too (391)
Too-wit (23) C0169/12
C0169/35 C0170/05 C0170/17 C0170/38
C0171/04 C0171/27 C0172/04 C0172/20
C0172/27 C0174/16 C0174/31 C0174/35
C0175/06 C0175/16 C0175/17 C0176/25
C0177/25 C0179/35 C0180/31 C0181/17
C0186/27 C0188/12
Too-wit (1) C0168/41
Too-wit's (1) C0188/17
took (272)
Tooke, Horne (1) B1115/01
tool (1) B1260/32
tools (1) B0823/33
tooth-pick (1) C0397/29
toothpick (1) C0092/15
top (63)
top-gallant (1) A0143/24
top-heavy (1) A0251/30
topaz (1) A0537/32
topic (38) A0069/15 A0297/07
A0311/16 A0346/19 A0356/03 A0379/01
A0379/01 A0441/14 A0550/V A0705/05
A0706/01 A0709/09 B0725/10 B0772/11
B0817/11 B0863/35 B0875/06 B0902/27
B0950/16 B0961/34 B0961/35 B0991/30
B1009/23 B1031/05 B1133/07 B1138/07
B1152/09 B1190/11 B1247/06 B1270/04
B1295/01 B1297/02 B1298/07 B1311/17
B1314/06 C0058/06 C0423/25 C0523/21
topical (1) B0950/03
topics (12) A0296/V
A0321/10 A0381/21 A0460/20 A0533/05
A0655/01 B0727/01 B0747/32 B0974/10
B1004/24 B1359/31 B1361/14
topmost (3) C0197/07
C0546/04 C0577/13
topography (1) C0429/04
topped (1) A0428/21
tops (6) A0641/09 A0643/21
B0979/27 B0979/32 C0150/32 C0185/19
topsail (2) C0146/24 C0147/08
topsiturviness (1) B1144/20
topsy-turvy (2) A0128/14 B1115/29
torch (6) A0406/02 B1261/17
B1263/20 B1353/12 B1353/22 B1354/22
torches (2) A0409/32 B1161/29
tore (11) A0351/11
A0413/34 A0685/33 B0735/11 B0759/06
B0766/33 B0825/21 C0102/32 C0115/25
C0115/34 C0182/17
torment (2) A0690/28 C0196/12
tormented (4) A0197/25
B1221/23 C0183/11 C0411/27
tormenting (2) A0225/04 A0229/05
tormentor (5) A0056/35
A0066/13 A0445/23 A0446/15 B0858/01
tormentors (1) A0696/06
torments (3) B0856/09

->C0076/30 C0083/29
torn (40) A0557/16
A0567/01 A0582/07 A0599/M A0686/27
B0730/24 B0730/25 B0730/26 B0730/29
B0730/30 B0734/19 B0734/25 B0735/11
B0735/14 B0750/19 B0762/10 B0762/12
B0762/14 B0762/16 B0762/21 B0762/35
B0763/01 B0763/03 B0765/20 B0766/04
B0766/32 B0991/03 B0991/20 B1049/20
B1226/05 B1369/35 C0079/06 C0079/20
C0106/33 C0115/14 C0119/29 C0124/41
C0142/33 C0188/03 C0579/15
tornado (2) A0074/08 A0145/10
torne (1) A0344/25
torny (1) A0354/33
torpid (3) B0962/15
B0966/11 B1047/03
torpor (2) A0609/07 A0612/25
torrent (2) A0099/03 C0181/01
torrents (7) A0235/21
A0329/V A0684/31 B0966/19 B1161/05
C0541/05 C0552/38
Torres, Thomas De Las (1) A0621/01
torrid (1) C0171/19
tortoise (15) B0966/10
B1311/V C0137/22 C0137/27 C0137/32
C0139/04 C0140/05 C0141/04 C0141/22
C0141/25 C0141/31 C0142/41 C0165/37
C0170/16 C0174/11
tortoise-meat (1) C0143/28
tortoises (4) C0176/27
C0176/33 C0191/22 C0203/14
Tortoni's (1) A0345/15
tortorum (1) A0681/M
torture (7) A0397/20
A0681/14 A0687/25 A0690/23 B0963/26
B1158/07 B1292/11
tortured (7) A0227/19
A0232/06 A0403/06 A0411/21 A0612/16
B0849/08 B1079/07
torturer (1) A0693/13
tortures (2) B0968/32 C0413/26
toss (1) A0264/17
tossed (3) A0351/12
C0086/03 C0108/19
total (31) A0120/11
A0138/05 A0210/15 A0213/23 A0299/24
A0337/12 A0337/26 A0427/29 A0442/16
A0442/32 A0460/34 A0529/31 A0615/32
A0688/28 B0726/14 B0752/01 B0753/41
B0955/28 B0963/05 B0964/06 B0966/08
B1104/33 B1144/18 B1168/19 B1242/28
B1331/10 B1336/01 C0190/17 C0194/21
C0411/03 C0445/V
totality (1) A0400/13
totally (28) A0054/02
A0055/30 A0063/11 A0088/14 A0089/09
A0090/25 A0121/19 A0498/28 B0763/24
B0808/20 B0890/17 B0906/07 B0926/21
B0940/23 B1092/20 B1190/07 B1303/06
B1360/24 C0062/36 C0082/39 C0096/29
C0126/10 C0130/07 C0207/42 C0396/18
C0445/V C0521/11 C0564/16
tote (1) B0818/16
totter (2) A0198/03 C0198/23
tottered (10) A0023/08 A0035/15
A0101/24 A0140/17 A0141/13 A0217/V
A0437/18 A0510/01 A0697/06 C0421/20
tottering (10) A0029/17 A0324/V
A0329/19 A0406/21 A0448/04 A0514/26
A0532/16 A0591/09 B1126/16 C0198/11
Tottle (1) B1310/19
touch (21) A0213/15
A0227/05 A0231/17 A0330/13 A0381/16
A0405/15 A0405/16 A0412/07 A0613/20
A0673/16 A0683/28 B0896/12 B1076/34
B1167/13 B1168/27 B1169/27 B1240/22
C0075/26 C0141/32 C0203/03 C0204/37
Touch-and-go (2) B1371/04 B1372/10
touch-and-go (1) A0483/22
Touch-me-not (3) A0174/15
A0174/20 A0175/02
Touch-me-Not (1) A0179/29
touche (1) A0397/M
touched (21) A0164/22
A0181/11 A0553/17 A0675/04 A0682/06
A0687/01 B0824/26 B0854/08 B0906/16
B0927/29 B0931/20 B0932/03 B1016/05
B1137/13 B1190/32 B1191/33 C0100/09
C0108/03 C0155/34 C0574/12 C0576/18
touches (4) A0088/06
A0142/14 A0493/09 B1006/05
touching (22) A0180/09 A0263/29
A0271/34 A0281/32 A0348/15 A0366/03
A0382/13 A0385/21 A0386/20 A0434/20
A0498/08 B0748/28 B0759/15 B0844/05
B0854/14 B0902/V B0985/22 B1016/05
B1135/10 B1292/01 C0113/27 C0206/03
tough (3) A0622/27
C0191/11 C0202/22
toughest (1) A0059/05
Toughkeepsie (1) B1291/V
tould> (3) A0465/29
A0466/08 A0468/31
Tour (2) A0705/31 B1269/35
tour (10) A0686/11 A0688/24
B0908/27 B1002/01 B1328/01 C0521/09
C0522/30 C0523/14 C0527/27 C0539/23
tourist (2) B0863/12 C0522/33
tourists (2) B0861/08 B0862/22
tourniquet (2) C0410/15 C0424/16
tournure (2) B0889/27 B0914/11
tous (3) A0216/08
A0216/10 A0600/01
tousand (1) A0183/03
tousand (2) A0177/05 A0177/08
tout (8) A0037/08
A0087/08 A0100/18 A0273/29 A0281/05
A0386/V A0611/04 C0430/37
tout-ensemble (3) A0266/10
A0280/07 A0283/22
tout/ensemble (3) A0035/20
A0269/35 B1335/19
toute (2) B0986/34 B0986/34
toutes (1) A0036/06
tow (1) C0538/01
tow-line (2) C0535/28 C0560/05
toward (25) A0435/23
A0545/22 A0548/09 A0563/16 A0564/26
A0566/19 A0581/20 A0591/33 A0671/11

->B0894/10 B0942/16 B1003/V B1004/V
B1102/33 B1105/26 B1140/18 B1185/05
B1272/22 B1278/24 B1279/23 B1281/12
B1321/22 C0392/17 C0398/25 C0401/39
towards (107)
towed (3) B0729/32
B0754/07 C0088/24
tower (3) A0045/08
A0157/01 C0570/25
towered (4) A0247/33
A0349/23 A0589/12 B0865/22
towering (5) A0145/14
A0146/14 C0116/24 C0159/26 C0572/41
towers (5) A0045/01
A0087/36 A0122/20 A0209/12 B1160/13
towing (3) C0165/12
C0188/09 C0571/22
towing-line (1) C0534/14
town (33) A0121/01
A0123/09 A0128/14 A0428/03 A0488/21
A0490/28 A0510/06 A0515/18 B0750/13
B0760/13 B0760/13 B0814/13 B0851/21
B0877/34 B0878/22 B0879/29 B0892/11
B0896/28 B0897/10 B0908/21 B0909/17
B0916/19 B0945/05 B0989/30 B1046/09
B1053/09 B1128/20 B1138/07 B1303/06
B1369/14 B1375/09 B1385/04 C0064/32
town-lamps (1) A0565/V
Town-Council (4) A0366/13
A0369/07 A0369/08 A0372/01
toy (3) A0368/14 B0907/04 B0908/01
toys (3) B0984/09
C0399/20 C0534/25
trace (33) A0312/06
A0315/02 A0438/16 A0544/31 A0561/27
A0601/19 A0681/12 B0731/29 B0732/13
B0744/08 B0744/17 B0770/18 B0770/23
B0817/16 B0831/23 B0871/26 B0887/20
B1031/31 B1048/29 B1048/30 B1048/31
B1181/11 B1214/28 B1214/28 B1281/34
B1330/15 B1331/31 C0069/34 C0145/39
C0152/16 C0397/16 C0407/38 C0527/22
traceable (3) A0322/19
A0497/02 B1214/09
traced (16) A0380/09
A0403/33 A0553/12 A0558/28 A0559/28
A0560/12 B0771/35 B0830/19 B0835/04
B0899/02 B1248/29 B1280/22 B1362/08
C0158/05 C0420/20 C0544/17
traces (30) A0236/12 A0326/13
A0366/12 A0538/07 B0744/20 B0757/09
B0763/28 B0763/29 B0763/32 B0764/07
B0765/30 B0765/35 B0769/13 B0962/13
B0980/10 B1004/08 B1247/11 B1299/10
B1299/11 B1329/09 C0068/35 C0158/19
C0172/12 C0184/36 C0189/13 C0199/02
C0425/16 C0563/26 C0571/30 C0575/39
tracing (6) A0296/V B0737/23
B0772/29 B1214/22 C0076/37 C0527/29
track (12) A0693/15
A0705/24 B0862/21 B1048/34 B1049/05
B1270/22 B1299/12 B1299/16 B1299/17
B1359/34 C0148/23 C0528/09
tracked (2) A0553/V B1048/32
tracks (2) B1329/17 C0578/02
Tracle (8) A0464/23
A0465/08 A0465/22 A0466/10 A0466/23
A0466/30 A0466/31 A0467/02
tracle (1) A0466/11
tract (8) A0397/04
B0817/15 C0162/04 C0524/32 C0524/34
C0540/21 C0551/15 C0551/25
trade (20) A0098/05
A0098/06 A0482/32 A0484/20 A0485/31
A0486/07 A0486/23 A0488/24 A0489/11
A0510/13 A0540/17 B1127/33 C0147/12
C0147/21 C0147/24 C0525/23 C0526/03
C0534/20 C0536/18 C0549/41
traded (1) C0156/17
trader (2) C0057/02 C0125/41
traders (2) C0537/39 C0575/33
tradesmen (1) A0508/17
trading (6) A0240/03 C0147/07
C0527/18 C0527/38 C0530/12 C0531/10
trading-posts (1) C0087/05
traditions (3) B1189/24
B1189/35 B1190/11
traduced (1) B1115/28
<u>traduit</u> (1) B1115/28
traffic (3) A0046/02
C0148/02 C0170/14
tragacanth (1) B1113/08
tragedian (1) A0383/14
tragedies (6) A0055/27 A0056/02
A0175/31 A0176/03 A0181/31 A0182/02
Tragedy (1) A0240/M
tragedy (19) A0065/08
A0065/21 A0162/03 A0162/04 A0164/10
A0319/17 A0344/17 A0438/05 A0534/15
A0534/19 A0538/28 B0723/08 B0724/25
B0751/30 B0767/12 B1021/17 B1133/35
C0133/32 C0135/26
trail (2) B0753/30 B1074/20
trailing (3) A0351/05
B1077/33 B1337/23
train (18) A0211/08 A0293/06
A0408/02 A0458/14 A0592/04 A0683/21
B0723/M B0724/17 B0758/01 B0910/01
B0943/19 B0988/30 B0988/33 B1031/33
B1048/18 B1166/31 B1299/04 C0128/39
trained (3) A0027/V
A0123/17 B0979/20
training (2) B1244/03 C0430/46
trains (1) C0394/25
trait (8) A0054/19
A0063/22 A0073/14 A0099/07 A0432/19
B0855/05 B1281/21 C0538/31
traitor (1) B1384/27
traitorous (1) A0642/16
traits (5) A0402/18
A0445/14 A0446/07 A0509/20 B1279/19
trallala (1) B1092/30
trammels (1) A0320/25
trampled (5) B0734/37
B0758/12 B0762/03 B0762/08 B0913/22
trampling (2) B0913/V C0175/15
trance (10) A0211/12 A0211/12
B0962/16 B0963/12 B0964/02 B0964/08
B0965/15 B0967/28 B1238/01 B1242/07
trances (1) A0163/04

tranquil (7) A0437/12
A0503/10 B1239/16 B1278/34 C0085/11
C0138/40 C0398/35
tranquillity (5) A0058/22
A0081/23 A0252/30 A0581/31 B1155/20
tranquillize (1) C0076/12
tranquilly (7) A0642/23
B0724/31 B0857/33 B0964/20 B0964/33
B1279/20 B1349/31
trans (1) A0265/26
transact (2) B0814/02 C0153/35
transacting (1) B0892/22
transaction (6) A0058/13 A0069/02
A0074/17 A0093/02 A0112/14 B0872/08
transactions (2) A0560/11 B0977/12
transcendental (1) A0342/05
Transcendentalism (1) B1311/01
transcendentalism (3) A0080/28
A0316/16 A0621/22
Transcendentalist (1) B1316/03
Transcendentalists (1) B1310/07
transcendentalists (2) A0631/22
B1291/09
transcendentally (1) A0629/30
transcendentals (3) A0626/34
A0629/22 B1129/11
transcribe (1) B1310/11
transcribed (1) B1075/26
transcribing (1) B1318/03
transfer (2) B1072/04 C0425/36
transferred (2) B1115/28 B1312/35
transferring (2) A0642/06 B1115/19
transforming (1) B1385/37
transfusion (1) C0430/02
transient (1) A0404/18
transition (5) A0104/23
A0298/V A0496/11 B0905/27 C0148/38
transition-thought (1) B1115/15
transitions (1) A0266/18
translate (2) B0958/17 B1159/03
translated (6) A0088/10 B1091/01
B1115/28 B1296/36 C0430/33 C0432/48
translates (1) B1385/19
translating (4) B0838/32
B0839/06 B0929/12 B1179/29
translation (8) A0043/M
A0346/04 A0652/15 B0732/23 B0839/29
B1128/22 B1291/04 B1304/22
translations (2) A0599/02 B0731/24
translator (2) B1360/20 B1360/22
transmission (1) A0399/15
transmits (1) B1167/35
transmitted (2) B1055/15 B1131/05
transmitting (1) A0142/04
transmuted (1) A0036/12
transparency (2) B1162/05 B1279/06
transparent (6) A0136/20 A0316/21
A0613/08 B1280/12 B1316/05 C0204/13
transpired (1) A0538/31
transport (5) A0550/31
A0644/V B0891/06 B0895/22 B0903/09
transports (2) B0900/12 C0083/31
trap (31) A0182/07
A0253/15 A0353/24 A0566/03 C0068/28
C0070/07 C0070/15 C0071/14 C0072/06
->C0074/13 C0074/19 C0075/27 C0077/08
C0080/31 C0084/08 C0084/20 C0084/26
C0084/31 C0085/02 C0085/02 C0085/15
C0089/23 C0107/15 C0531/10 C0543/08
C0547/16 C0547/23 C0547/24 C0547/31
C0548/11 C0558/02
trap-door (2) A0245/09 A0542/18
trapdoor (1) C0069/33
trapper (4) C0547/09
C0547/17 C0547/27 C0550/04
trappers (1) C0575/33
trapping (8) C0522/04
C0529/03 C0529/09 C0529/27 C0536/18
C0539/25 C0544/11 C0546/33
trash (4) A0096/11
B1130/07 B1130/07 B1373/19
travel (8) A0135/23
A0654/23 B0863/24 B1122/13 C0065/39
C0066/18 C0402/28 C0578/14
traveler (1) B1188/09
travelers (2) B1184/30 B1192/05
traveling (6) B1292/19 B1298/33
B1298/35 B1299/04 B1302/03 B1302/04
travelled (7) A0205/14
A0493/03 B1009/14 B1160/26 B1183/07
B1277/33 C0564/17
traveller (10) A0056/30 A0594/20
B0863/04 B0873/19 B0941/10 B1160/24
B1278/07 C0523/38 C0526/22 C0538/27
traveller's (1) B1338/11
travellers (10) A0407/34 B0862/07
B0876/19 C0198/34 C0539/34 C0545/12
C0547/34 C0548/08 C0550/06 C0564/04
travelling (5) B1002/06
B1021/22 B1382/10 C0400/15 C0400/20
travels (7) B1163/17
B1164/40 B1168/34 C0057/24 C0068/19
C0524/41 C0528/21
traverse (1) C0574/36
traversed (9) A0078/24
A0315/26 A0514/22 B1078/17 B1164/36
C0171/20 C0400/13 C0524/37 C0528/30
traversing (5) A0690/04
B0749/27 B1163/39 B1294/26 C0200/10
tray (1) B1004/32
treacheries (1) A0021/10
treacherous (5) A0043/15
A0686/24 C0185/15 C0530/20 C0536/20
treachery (1) C0190/11
tread (5) A0514/35
A0626/13 B0943/24 B1091/14 C0528/34
treading (1) B0866/14
treads (1) B0871/12
treason (8) A0252/33
A0253/01 A0253/02 A0253/03 A0253/04
A0253/05 A0253/05 B1374/24
treasure (27) A0152/13
A0532/09 A0599/M B0765/01 B0823/22
B0825/13 B0826/13 B0826/30 B0827/18
B0828/21 B0833/33 B0834/06 B0834/15
B0834/19 B0842/18 B0843/16 B0843/22
B0844/16 B0873/25 B0876/27 B0877/03
B0929/34 B1056/34 B1179/11 B1346/03
C0138/23 C0524/08
treasures (2) A0250/26 B0796/28

treat (4) B1006/15
C0129/19 C0177/01 C0392/03
treated (17) A0173/V
A0302/21 A0346/26 A0709/20 B0753/28
B1019/05 B1055/04 B1106/19 B1165/25
B1274/23 C0062/37 C0089/01 C0101/37
C0148/30 C0180/06 C0558/37 C0564/15
treating (3) A0431/32
A0473/23 C0562/07
Treatise (1) A0271/34
treatise (17) A0069/19
A0071/25 A0074/32 A0172/06 A0172/07
A0178/07 A0213/03 A0301/03 A0303/06
A0303/16 A0303/32 A0528/19 A0601/33
B1297/05 C0392/11 C0392/18 C0399/31
treatises (3) A0109/10
A0176/01 A0181/33
treatment (9) B1007/02
B1016/35 B1016/35 B1019/24 B1019/24
B1019/27 B1019/28 B1021/33 B1052/32
treats (1) C0167/40
Trebizond (2) A0086/12 A0097/12
treble (2) A0533/19 B0905/27
trebled (3) B0982/14
B1345/28 C0141/12
trebly (1) C0080/23
tree (89)
tree-stems (1) A0398/13
tree-top (1) C0547/31
tree-tops (1) B0827/14
trees (82)
trefoil (1) B0943/15
trellice-work (2) A0157/V A0321/19
trelliced (2) A0087/26 A0401/V
trellis (1) A0554/15
trellis-work (2) A0555/02 B0826/06
trellised (2) A0214/04 A0401/10
trellissed (1) A0401/V
Tremaine (6) A0321/03 A0323/02
A0329/V A0330/04 A0330/06 A0330/09
tremble (3) A0578/04
A0592/04 B1222/18
trembled (25) A0140/17
A0143/13 A0145/08 A0157/23 A0197/03
A0197/10 A0197/19 A0197/30 A0198/26
A0213/15 A0227/29 A0232/V A0234/09
A0329/23 A0415/09 A0461/13 A0580/36
A0642/20 A0687/23 B0947/30 B1246/11
B1262/25 C0071/24 C0162/34 C0421/01
trembles (3) A0154/22
A0154/V B0764/24
trembling (15) A0021/11
A0088/01 A0155/11 A0191/12 A0246/31
A0416/30 A0563/21 A0684/33 A0695/16
B0826/12 B0983/15 C0077/04 C0083/01
C0083/23 C0396/29
tremendous (22) A0138/07 A0380/30
A0382/14 A0482/V B0932/15 B1090/34
B1136/14 B1136/35 B1137/31 B1138/28
C0098/01 C0110/16 C0110/25 C0113/14
C0114/25 C0115/34 C0115/39 C0149/27
C0184/22 C0188/31 C0201/14 C0546/03
tremendously (3) B0930/08
C0113/36 C0139/32
tremolite (1) A0182/09
tremor (7) A0219/04
A0228/31 A0233/12 A0328/01 A0411/25
B0943/24 B1238/23
tremour (1) C0109/13
tremulous (12) A0104/33
A0143/15 A0145/28 A0218/21 A0378/V
A0402/21 A0411/02 A0439/16 A0640/13
A0640/23 A0666/02 B0906/02
tremulously (1) A0614/28
tremulousness (2) A0615/27 A0673/09
trench (1) A0044/30
trencher (1) B1010/24
trepanning (1) B0958/23
trepidancy (1) A0402/15
trepidation (13) A0106/01
A0161/21 A0401/04 A0530/21 B0893/06
B1102/15 B1158/01 B1183/32 C0059/09
C0110/15 C0197/25 C0198/28 C0389/34
trespassed (1) A0408/08
tressel (2) A0248/13 A0249/16
tressels (2) A0253/26 A0410/12
tresses (8) A0312/12
A0537/29 A0557/15 A0557/16 A0558/V
A0644/V B0957/28 B1107/15
Trevanion, Rowena (2) A0321/03
A0330/04
trial (16) A0053/37
A0063/09 A0559/11 A0629/08 A0684/01
A0684/26 B0984/16 B0984/17 B1005/28
B1018/34 B1054/05 B1054/14 B1054/28
B1181/26 C0104/20 C0398/15
triangle (5) B1080/27
B1080/30 C0154/27 C0408/06 C0408/10
triangular (2) B1340/19 C0196/04
Trianon (5) A0542/V
A0563/V A0563/V A0565/V A0566/V
tribe (22) A0313/04 A0508/22
B0808/23 B0897/01 B0940/19 B1029/04
B1188/21 B1303/13 B1304/05 C0087/02
C0177/27 C0540/30 C0546/36 C0547/06
C0548/15 C0548/24 C0549/35 C0549/38
C0550/08 C0550/25 C0551/11 C0552/34
tribes (9) C0151/08
C0153/21 C0527/18 C0530/19 C0548/25
C0551/18 C0551/30 C0565/31 C0571/29
tribulation (1) B0873/32
Tribunal (1) A0546/V
Tribunal (1) A0537/V
tribunal (1) B0958/12
Tribunaux (2) A0537/04 A0546/31
tribunes (1) A0108/29
trice (2) A0387/21 B1056/27
trick (6) A0530/15 B0872/12
B1379/29 C0134/38 C0406/30 C0541/21
trickle (3) B1260/10
C0146/11 C0573/24
trickled (1) A0404/15
trickling (1) C0573/17
tricks (5) A0295/14
A0530/20 B0876/18 B1191/19 C0079/12
tried (16) A0092/06
A0312/05 A0353/28 A0447/23 A0487/20
A0489/23 B0795/14 B0930/30 B1015/V
C0064/18 C0073/22 C0121/01 C0143/01
C0192/04 C0412/07 C0579/35

trifle (15) A0090/29
A0243/24 A0252/22 A0348/13 A0371/20
A0624/14 B0741/22 B0870/31 B0931/37
B1128/31 B1141/11 B1153/22 C0395/40
C0428/02 C0448/V
trifled (1) C0556/23
trifles (8) A0086/23
A0270/06 A0688/15 B0797/13 B0923/01
B1073/30 B1384/02 B1384/03
trifling (10) A0057/11 A0138/15
A0354/13 A0367/16 A0399/08 A0487/11
B0773/06 B0908/03 B1361/31 C0424/07
trim (1) B0930/14
trimmed (1) A0587/27
trimmings (2) A0336/08 A0349/13
Trinculo (1) B1031/19
trink (2) B1104/17 B1104/18
trinket (2) B0903/30 B1093/01
trinkets (3) B0828/20
C0148/11 C0177/12
trio (5) A0047/31
B0897/14 B0897/25 B0898/06 B0898/V
trip (3) B1091/07
C0427/30 C0530/30
triple (5) A0080/25
A0217/V A0370/15 A0426/V C0124/19
triple-stemmed (1) B1332/26
triple-tinted (1) B1212/33
triplicate (2) B1212/32 B1346/02
tripod (1) A0672/12
tripods (2) A0674/04 A0677/03
Trippetta (6) B1346/33 B1347/04
B1347/20 B1348/33 B1353/28 B1354/25
Trippetta's (2) B1347/09 B1351/23
trips (2) A0381/29 C0529/19
Trist (2) A0413/08 A0413/22
Tristan (2) C0155/38 C0156/20
Tristan/d'Acunha (4) C0154/22
C0154/29 C0155/25 C0158/12
triumph (24) A0019/10
A0019/25 A0057/35 A0124/24 A0126/23
A0312/18 A0316/05 A0427/29 A0511/23
A0530/14 B0737/09 B0793/23 B0796/31
B0858/21 B0859/04 B0941/31 B1057/20
B1068/02 B1078/33 B1195/05 B1318/06
B1372/18 C0136/27 C0165/12
triumphant (7) A0023/13
A0028/15 A0098/07 A0706/26 B0815/03
B0967/24 B1271/28
triumphantly (3) B0759/22
B0857/22 B1358/10
triumphed (1) B1154/16
triumphs (3) A0644/01
A0693/01 B1144/28
trivial (22) A0019/13 A0145/10
A0161/14 A0213/11 A0324/11 A0346/V
A0403/13 A0426/15 A0428/15 A0528/06
A0649/05 A0685/32 B0756/06 B0843/20
B0910/19 B0991/35 B1107/24 B1114/14
B1133/24 B1143/19 C0094/34 C0167/10
trod (4) A0141/30
A0487/09 B0865/21 B0942/34
trodden (5) A0639/11
B0752/23 B0942/34 B1162/18 C0188/02
trois (1) B1339/35
troisieme (3) A0561/02
B0974/04 B0974/V
trombones (2) B1009/06 B1017/26
troof (2) B0811/18 B1103/02
troop (2) A0124/27 A0407/20
troops (5) A0690/06
A0694/17 A0705/28 B1270/26 C0118/14
trophies (3) A0400/30
A0662/11 C0552/18
trophy (1) C0165/13
Tropic/of/Cancer (1) C0148/13
tropical (2) A0639/07 C0425/18
tropics (4) A0139/02
C0072/26 C0402/04 C0419/04
troth> (2) A0467/V A0469/28
Trotter (3) B0872/32
B0873/01 B0873/05
troubadour (1) B1096/36
trouble (75)
troubled (9) A0070/17
A0090/07 A0216/23 A0389/16 B0754/17
B0906/19 B0989/08 B1345/11 C0418/48
troubles (5) C0074/08
C0076/17 C0081/13 C0438/V C0575/03
troublesome (7) A0073/18
B0874/32 B1010/02 B1095/05 B1169/26
C0407/29 C0549/08
troubling (2) A0531/25 C0061/25
trough (1) B0930/18
trout (2) B0870/26 B1333/30
trove (1) B0873/25
trowel (4) B1260/28
B1262/07 B1262/18 C0544/34
trowsers' (1) B0871/11
Troy (2) A0059/10 A0061/06
truant (1) A0228/05
trubble (2) B0815/09 B0824/V
truce (1) B1384/02
trucks (1) A0143/23
true (164)
truer (1) B1123/12
truest (5) B0863/09
B0887/02 B0922/14 B1040/03 B1272/03
truffe (2) B1100/02 B1100/V
truism (3) B1297/09
B1297/19 B1314/12
truly (33) A0098/29
A0113/06 A0226/30 A0231/04 A0273/07
A0276/28 A0280/18 A0295/08 A0298/V
A0311/30 A0348/09 A0378/02 A0382/03
A0386/08 A0442/04 A0473/06 A0531/10
A0611/03 B0811/20 B0853/15 B0901/13
B0957/17 B1012/17 B1038/35 B1039/28
B1102/25 B1178/29 B1277/05 B1291/10
B1294/06 B1339/06 C0073/27 C0204/12
trump (5) A0037/15
A0530/10 A0530/10 B0943/33 B1127/28
trumpery (4) A0046/03
A0089/30 B0990/35 B1292/26
trumpet (4) A0487/02
B1157/27 B1158/25 C0396/07
trumpet-tongued (1) B1222/08
Trumpeter (1) B1119/15
trumpets (2) A0125/20 A0697/08
truncheon (1) A0249/22

trunk (26) A0057/07 A0057/10
A0067/04 A0297/V A0603/29 B0818/06
B0818/13 B0818/29 B0818/V B0819/17
B0822/07 B0824/34 B0842/21 B1163/18
B1248/12 B1248/21 B1337/10 B1363/05
B1363/07 B1363/11 B1363/16 C0128/04
C0128/31 C0174/40 C0545/10 C0551/39
trunks (8) A0066/34
A0397/14 A0591/26 B1332/03 B1332/28
C0072/17 C0444/V C0543/18
trust (17) A0141/02
A0243/08 A0345/03 A0384/12 B0737/22
B0816/08 B0874/02 B0924/17 B0931/18
B0965/10 B1155/03 B1379/20 C0055/33
C0129/25 C0179/28 C0199/16 C0408/25
trusted (3) B0771/05
B0988/05 C0107/02
trusting (5) A0551/14
B0816/29 B1007/06 C0088/02 C0181/16
trustingly (1) B1221/19
trusty (1) C0416/09
truth (179)
truthfulness (2) B1122/16 B1350/35
truths (16) A0609/23
B0987/19 B0987/20 B0987/29 B0987/29
B0987/30 B1295/10 B1297/31 B1298/05
B1310/28 B1310/29 B1310/31 B1312/10
B1313/30 B1317/06 B1317/10
try (15) A0286/21
A0484/03 A0559/15 A0624/06 B0746/01
B0816/15 B0816/16 B0820/11 B0824/29
B1011/02 B1011/21 B1093/20 C0076/12
C0529/04 C0550/12
trying (9) A0285/11
A0586/20 A0625/V B0794/16 B0794/20
B1163/38 C0080/34 C0132/28 C0200/17
trysail (2) A0579/17 C0102/15
Tsalal (6) C0205/13 C0205/15
C0207/25 C0208/17 C0208/21 C0208/22
Tsalal (2) C0204/07 C0204/08
Tsalalian (1) C0208/18
Tsalemon (2) C0203/36 C0204/08
tu (2) A0034/01 A0034/02
tua (1) A0018/M
tub (5) A0245/14
A0253/26 B0796/14 B1091/34 B1091/35
tube (12) B1071/10
B1071/18 B1101/23 B1101/24 B1106/20
B1163/34 B1163/41 B1362/19 B1362/21
C0410/34 C0410/35 C0423/36
tubercles (1) B1235/27
tuberoses (1) B1283/09
tubes (2) B1071/19 C0393/30
tubular (2) B1163/25 B1163/27
Tuckerman's (1) B1101/05
Tuclid (1) B1310/33
tue (1) A0036/21
Tuesday (9) A0204/30
B0732/13 B0744/08 B0745/13 B0753/20
B0754/04 B0770/30 B1069/16 B1081/14
tuft (4) A0558/22
A0559/29 C0552/01 C0552/02
tufted (1) A0320/24
tufts (1) C0552/18
Tula (1) C0161/28
tulip (5) A0708/03
B1273/02 B1332/34 B1333/16 B1334/05
tulip-tree (4) B0817/34
B0818/28 B0824/19 B1337/33
Tulipiferum (3) B0818/28
B0864/31 B1332/26
tulips (4) A0603/15
B1283/08 B1332/37 C0543/30
tumble (4) A0340/29
B1305/09 C0085/38 C0443/V
tumbled (14) A0047/31 A0355/03
B1110/12 B1335/06 C0061/02 C0116/05
C0117/02 C0165/09 C0184/34 C0190/08
C0390/12 C0425/06 C0571/03 C0579/16
tumbler (2) A0651/V C0111/01
tumblers (1) C0109/29
tumbles (1) C0098/10
tumbling (4) A0070/22
B1334/11 C0412/33 C0417/02
tumuli (2) C0198/38 C0199/10
tumult (17) A0021/19
A0022/22 A0054/28 A0063/29 A0080/07
A0123/24 A0155/10 A0155/19 A0197/21
A0330/01 B0896/07 B0946/27 B0948/06
B0959/17 B0965/04 B1352/18 C0190/07
tumultuous (14) A0120/08 A0125/27
A0195/07 A0210/30 A0234/01 A0315/09
A0417/15 A0507/27 A0683/26 B1382/24
C0134/19 C0188/06 C0396/26 C0421/22
tumultuously (2) A0461/10 A0695/01
tun> (1) A0464/06
tune (4) A0374/15
A0611/34 B1020/16 C0388/30
tunica (1) B1181/33
tunnel (2) A0405/31 B1382/20
Tupper, Martin Farquhar (1) B1380/06
turba (1) A0681/M
turbaned (1) B0945/19
turbans (3) B0947/05
B0949/18 B1157/11
turbulent (6) A0326/17 A0611/15
A0644/01 B1215/28 B1215/34 C0553/40
turf (4) A0602/14
A0603/01 B1334/19 B1337/02
turfed (1) B0759/13
turgid (2) A0138/26 A0594/V
Turgot (4) A0176/08
A0180/29 A0703/05 B1268/05
Turk (3) A0175/04
A0181/25 A0313/10
Turkey (1) A0498/08
turkey-cock (1) B1303/28
turkeys (1) C0540/06
turkies (1) C0542/41
Turkish (3) A0336/M
B1295/06 B1310/19
turmoil (2) A0515/23 A0612/20
turn (73)
Turnapenny (1) B1051/20
turned (139)
turning (52)
turnip (2) A0336/13 A0337/01
Turnip, Tabitha (3) A0336/11
A0336/12 A0337/08
turns (13) A0412/04

->A0656/28 B0765/06 B0831/27 B0932/24
B1279/06 B1282/23 B1321/22 C0078/10
C0129/33 C0131/18 C0136/31 C0172/23
turnstile (4) A0627/13
A0629/27 A0630/29 A0631/09
Turpin, Dick (1) B0870/30
turpitude (2) A0426/13 B1143/V
turret (7) A0321/12
A0321/20 A0323/25 A0327/12 A0662/09
A0665/15 A0665/25
turret-chamber (1) A0665/10
turrets (3) A0045/09
A0403/29 A0412/24
Turtle (2) B1143/31 B1144/15
turtle (3) A0491/13
C0145/13 C0199/08
turtles (2) C0200/22 C0202/01
tusks (1) B1248/15
twang (1) A0111/05
'twas (3) B0812/16
B0812/17 B0824/27
twattle (4) B1129/22
B1130/27 B1143/26 B1166/07
tweaking (1) B1142/27
tweedle (1) A0177/06
tweedle-dee (2) A0177/06 A0177/06
tweedle-dum (1) A0177/06
twelfth (5) A0674/V
B0941/30 C0146/34 C0154/18 C0158/16
twelve (44) A0101/16
A0121/08 A0240/01 A0242/14 A0370/04
A0372/35 A0483/29 A0508/28 A0514/16
A0622/19 A0674/17 A0686/27 A0693/03
B0731/34 B0793/17 B1092/24 B1161/06
B1162/07 B1248/25 B1299/12 B1373/25
C0121/13 C0131/09 C0137/33 C0142/22
C0147/18 C0147/18 C0171/07 C0171/13
C0174/30 C0174/37 C0175/09 C0179/16
C0393/18 C0418/36 C0420/20 C0424/15
C0530/06 C0533/03 C0541/25 C0567/04
C0569/41 C0573/06 C0573/32
twelves (1) C0147/19
twentieth (10) A0584/20 A0704/14
B1269/V C0070/18 C0084/02 C0135/37
C0146/41 C0157/25 C0196/10 C0419/38
twenty (85)
twenty-eight (3) B1338/27
C0148/18 C0560/14
twenty-eighth (1) C0161/28
twenty-fifth (5) A0293/16
B0729/28 C0148/13 C0149/10 C0156/09
twenty-first (6) A0704/31 B1269/31
C0136/03 C0156/41 C0158/20 C0161/40
twenty-five (25) A0355/25
A0484/32 A0487/29 A0494/03 A0501/03
A0688/11 A0705/20 B1007/28 B1092/15
B1093/34 B1105/20 B1192/22 B1270/19
B1364/33 C0124/20 C0203/28 C0394/19
C0420/07 C0421/09 C0533/07 C0538/10
C0541/32 C0568/07 C0570/11 C0571/10
twenty-four (22) A0264/35 A0367/04
A0656/27 A0656/29 A0657/01 A0657/12
A0657/13 A0657/19 A0657/20 B0744/03
B0759/21 B0904/V B1154/04 B1234/35
B1335/35 C0071/17 C0072/04 C0081/04
->C0112/07 C0176/26 C0196/02 C0414/18
twenty-ninth (1) C0148/14
twenty-one (11) A0294/06
A0460/25 A0653/16 B0827/36 B0839/31
B0840/21 B0841/29 B0842/02 B0842/07
B1071/02 C0156/14
twenty-second (4) B0725/24
B0729/07 B0745/10 C0136/06
twenty-second, (1) B0731/26
twenty-seven (6) B0909/09 B0912/04
B1015/16 B1105/31 C0086/19 C0142/08
twenty-seventh (4) C0157/01
C0157/11 C0162/29 C0547/36
twenty-sixth (1) C0162/23
twenty-third (3) B0770/19
C0136/40 C0138/40
twenty-three (2) B0903/16 B0955/07
twenty-two (3) B0887/09
B0903/15 C0086/23
twice (30) A0096/10 A0101/24
A0228/25 A0228/25 A0233/06 A0233/07
A0242/12 A0265/07 A0270/15 A0280/14
A0428/26 A0539/23 A0584/08 A0694/33
B0773/21 B0979/03 B1049/09 B1104/32
B1109/21 B1143/03 B1293/29 B1330/09
C0070/01 C0096/24 C0123/20 C0200/29
C0392/16 C0529/16 C0530/26 C0532/35
twig (3) A0346/11
B1329/23 C0547/23
twilight (10) A0066/03 A0214/22
A0227/35 A0611/23 A0614/18 A0642/03
B0901/05 B0902/11 C0102/27 C0423/21
twin (1) A0313/24
twine (3) C0393/19
C0393/24 C0534/23
twinge (1) B0906/20
twinkled (1) A0241/13
twinkling (4) A0068/34
A0465/24 A0702/M B1267/M
twins (2) A0410/18 A0432/26
twirl (4) A0248/21
A0271/05 A0285/06 A0498/24
twirled (2) A0385/07 B0906/31
twirling (1) B0817/03
twist (5) A0069/25
A0077/02 A0182/26 A0242/04 C0534/24
twisted (2) A0056/26 A0066/16
twistical (1) A0625/04
twisting (4) A0174/27
A0180/10 A0629/12 C0410/13
twists (1) B0875/32
twittering (1) C0573/28
Two (1) B0870/16
two (587)
two-fold (3) A0074/01
A0100/31 A0696/23
two-reef (1) C0139/31
two-thirds (3) A0667/29
A0705/27 B1007/32
twofold (3) A0243/25
A0434/10 B0974/02
twoness (1) A0342/14
tx (3) B1374/09 B1374/10 B1374/12
txld (2) B1374/07 B1374/19
txxeeth (1) B0837/34

tying (5) A0512/15
A0561/07 A0629/11 C0120/33 C0197/13

type (7) A0099/32
A0209/05 A0515/28 A0675/14 B1184/19
B1369/28 C0207/04

types (1) A0301/05

typhus (1) B0959/33

typical (1) A0690/25

typified (1) A0545/20

typographical (2) B0950/22 B0950/28

typography (3) A0211/30
B1136/08 B1304/07

tyranny (2) A0445/07 A0687/20

tyrant (4) B1194/13
B1348/06 B1348/27 B1348/36

tyrant's (1) B1349/14

tyrants (1) B1313/03

Tyrian (1) A0150/V

Tyrius (1) A0176/06

Tyrius, Maximus (1) A0180/28

u (1) B0838/21

ubi (1) A0681/M

Ude (1) A0653/20

ugh (37) A0092/06
A0092/06 A0092/07 A0092/07 A0111/17
A0111/17 A0111/19 A0111/19 A0111/19
A0252/18 A0252/18 A0252/18 A0252/19
A0252/19 A0252/19 A0252/19 A0252/19
A0252/19 A0252/19 A0252/20 A0252/20
A0252/20 B1259/08 B1259/08 B1259/08
B1259/08 B1259/08 B1259/08 B1259/08
B1259/08 B1259/08 B1259/08 B1259/08
B1259/08 B1259/09 B1259/09 B1259/09

ugliness (1) C0425/40

ugly (8) B0924/23
B1157/06 C0064/21 C0088/27 C0425/08
C0551/38 C0569/13 C0569/32

Ugolino (2) B1128/24 B1129/17

ult (7) A0265/31
A0266/24 A0267/17 A0268/24 A0272/23
A0273/03 A0273/34

ulterior (2) B1221/04 C0565/05

Ultima/Thule (1) A0690/26

ultimate (36) A0553/12
A0555/17 A0564/29 B0955/19 B0959/22
B1033/27 B1036/17 B1037/09 B1037/09
B1037/16 B1037/16 B1037/20 B1037/24
B1037/27 B1037/33 B1037/36 B1038/11
B1038/18 B1038/26 B1038/31 B1039/26
B1072/18 B1128/10 B1312/31 B1364/10
C0060/27 C0089/35 C0093/12 C0120/01
C0136/29 C0198/07 C0397/37 C0414/31
C0419/06 C0424/02 C0575/21

ultimately (9) A0067/12
B1090/15 B1362/33 C0063/21 C0112/40
C0185/33 C0207/07 C0417/25 C0430/08

ultimatum (1) A0346/14

ultimo (1) A0286/04

ultra (3) A0300/24
A0379/27 A0652/12

ultra (3) A0075/V
A0085/06 A0297/02

ultra-marine (1) B1279/10

ultras (1) A0159/12

uman (1) B0905/23

umbrageous (1) B0761/21

umbrella (2) B1091/13 C0067/28

umbrellas (1) A0512/12

un (15) A0019/02
A0019/03 A0019/03 A0019/03 A0036/V
A0037/03 A0037/V A0096/M A0161/04
A0397/M A0621/01 A0652/10 B0914/13
B0993/26 B1105/09

un (2) B1372/33 B1372/34

un-written (1) B1190/05

Una (19) A0608/01
A0608/02 A0608/06 A0608/07 A0608/13
A0608/23 A0608/25 A0608/29 A0608/T
A0609/01 A0609/03 A0609/09 A0610/25
A0612/09 A0612/13 A0614/01 A0614/25
A0616/05 A0616/30

unabated (2) A0139/04 B0927/18

unable (26) A0033/12 A0058/24
A0128/11 A0266/28 A0270/36 A0500/15
A0623/10 A0708/34 B0723/05 B0726/06
B0733/11 B0829/24 B0835/12 B0931/02
B0958/09 B1273/28 B1374/29 C0121/24
C0123/02 C0127/09 C0159/32 C0161/32
C0398/30 C0420/05 C0563/25 C0580/04

unaccommodating (1) A0248/05

unaccompanied (1) A0138/V

unaccountable (29) A0028/13
A0098/19 A0102/16 A0138/27 A0142/25
A0161/24 A0293/27 A0411/32 A0432/05
A0529/15 A0629/12 B0751/26 B0890/19
B0927/08 B0948/26 B0956/13 B0988/04
B1035/20 B1050/31 B1182/24 B1233/17
B1294/31 B1303/04 B1318/09 C0077/02
C0122/30 C0389/01 C0391/04 C0422/24

unaccountably (6) A0378/06 B0810/15
B0825/08 B1222/28 B1272/05 B1303/24

unaccustomed (1) B1239/33

unacquainted (2) A0261/18 A0285/25

unadapted (1) B1273/36

unadulterated (2) A0078/31 A0629/05

unaffected (1) C0573/12

unaided (1) A0609/26

unaltered (3) B1051/35
B1073/18 B1237/12

unanimity (1) B0758/15

unanimous (2) A0021/16 A0549/19

unanimously (2) A0021/V A0560/04

unanswerability (1) B1035/17

unanswerable (2) A0628/09 A0629/20

unanticipated (4) A0457/10
A0457/13 A0663/17 B1358/05

unappeasable (1) A0330/02

unapproachable (1) C0065/21

unarmed (3) A0562/21
C0181/17 C0186/30

unassassinated (1) B0737/25

unassisted (1) A0216/07

unassuming (1) A0433/23

unattainable (4) A0711/09
A0711/10 B1276/11 C0401/02

unattempted (1) A0435/03

unattended (4) B0872/11
B1018/04 B1360/04 C0189/37

unauthorized (1) B1095/13

unavailing (1) A0545/09

unavoidable (2) A0127/27 C0055/14
unavoidably (1) B1154/07
unaware (5) B0725/28
B0759/18 B0941/35 B0993/04 C0413/24
unawares (2) C0107/16 C0553/22
unawed (1) A0410/21
unbarred (1) A0081/21
unbecoming (3) A0126/13
B0907/22 B0976/36
unbecomingly (1) B1317/28
unbent (1) A0299/22
unbidden (2) A0250/02 A0682/35
unblemished (1) B1279/35
unblushingly (1) B1207/05
unbonneted (1) A0029/07
unborn (1) A0436/19
unbound (3) A0681/02
A0684/06 C0562/04
unbounded (4) A0282/05
B0896/05 B1239/04 C0404/37
unbridled (1) A0440/33
unbroken (6) A0321/15 A0442/V
B0932/30 B1054/31 C0418/17 C0418/18
unbrokenly (1) A0614/24
unburied (1) B0956/21
unburthen (5) B0849/05
B1114/13 C0537/19 C0537/20 C0563/40
unbuttoning (1) A0262/18
uncalculating (2) A0440/05 B0896/04
uncarpeted (1) B1008/23
unceasing (6) A0405/05 A0704/04
A0712/01 B0940/16 B1269/03 B1277/03
unceasingly (2) A0411/04 A0692/24
unceremoniously (1) B0983/17
uncertain (8) A0066/02
A0081/31 A0214/22 A0244/V A0589/19
B1073/13 B1206/06 C0112/19
uncertainty (6) A0349/31 A0604/31
B0901/V B1328/11 C0125/39 C0185/23
uncharitable (1) A0158/15
unchecked (1) B0760/18
unchoked (1) A0138/02
uncircumcised (2) A0043/06 A0045/15
uncivilized (1) B1303/15
uncle (29) A0649/03
A0650/08 A0650/15 A0650/21 A0650/23
A0650/29 A0650/V A0651/01 A0651/06
A0651/10 A0653/12 A0654/24 A0654/V
A0655/12 A0655/19 A0655/24 A0655/V
A0656/05 A0656/11 A0656/20 A0657/03
A0657/16 A0657/27 B1047/25 B1051/02
B1051/29 B1051/35 B1053/21 B1059/25
uncle's (3) B1047/23
B1047/31 B1047/32
unclosed (3) A0684/12
A0688/07 B1238/26
unclosing (2) A0438/30 B0957/31
unclouded (1) C0429/03
uncomfortable (7) A0261/16
A0630/13 B1008/15 B1157/06 C0140/16
C0175/08 C0395/20
uncomfortably (2) A0626/28 B0895/11
uncommon (3) A0096/01
A0413/03 A0430/27
uncommonly (1) C0560/01
uncomplaining (1) B0856/15
uncomplainingly (2) A0665/17
B1079/07
uncomprehended (1) B0961/05
uncompromising (1) B0896/03
unconceivable (1) C0122/25
unconceived (1) C0122/25
unconditionally (1) B0988/07
uncongenial (1) B0850/23
unconnected (3) A0266/14
A0695/17 C0127/37
unconquerable (1) B1221/01
unconscionably (1) A0342/V
unconscious (7) A0024/06
A0143/10 A0416/01 A0616/07 A0694/04
C0060/18 C0186/02
unconsciously (4) A0091/09
A0110/15 B1096/35 B1101/34
unconsciousness (2) A0683/14
B0966/08
uncontrollable (5) A0029/10
A0349/25 B0795/21 B1222/03 C0198/10
unconvulsive (1) B0960/21
uncounted (1) B1224/05
uncourteously (1) B0926/04
uncourtly (1) A0434/05
uncouth (2) A0413/11 B0943/26
uncouthness (1) C0055/35
uncovered (6) A0196/26 A0371/04
B0825/22 B1249/23 B1262/05 C0153/08
unction (1) A0161/22
unction (1) C0521/15
uncto (1) B0870/21
uncurtained (1) A0036/08
und (7) A0150/V
A0150/V A0183/07 A0345/07 A0366/10
B0723/M B0723/M
und (14) A0177/V A0373/03
A0373/V B1103/33 B1103/33 B1103/34
B1104/03 B1104/18 B1109/07 B1109/11
B1109/26 B1109/29 B1109/31 B1109/31
undammed (1) A0610/02
undaunted (1) A0599/M
undauntedly (1) A0244/12
undecayed (1) B0960/10
undeceive (1) A0612/24
undecided (1) B1242/26
undefinable (1) A0428/06
undefined (1) A0190/25
undeniability (1) B1315/05
undeniable (5) A0096/06
A0293/20 B1164/35 B1313/30 B1314/17
under (252)
under-jaw (1) A0241/03
under-let (1) A0539/14
under-rate (1) B1249/34
under-tone (4) A0227/29
A0232/V B1153/17 B1225/07
under-tow (1) A0144/06
Underduk (1) C0390/15
Underduk, Superbus Von (3) C0388/05
C0390/05 C0426/33
undergo (4) A0456/10
B1330/16 C0395/28 C0408/20
undergoing (6) A0136/19 A0535/24

->A0592/22 B0931/14 C0097/34 C0204/13
undergone (11) A0080/14
A0080/15 A0203/10 A0612/01 A0613/20
B1279/31 C0055/33 C0085/12 C0115/02
C0127/36 C0414/29
underground (1) B1021/25
undergrowth (2) B0807/10 B1329/10
underlined (1) A0162/05
underneath (1) A0248/V
underrated (1) A0280/27
underscored (1) A0218/13
understand (89)
understanding (39) A0018/14
A0096/15 A0284/29 A0389/14 A0458/10
A0459/V A0482/01 A0529/26 A0549/30
A0550/19 A0555/11 A0560/19 A0613/28
A0615/01 A0695/25 A0706/35 A0710/25
B0737/V B0768/15 B0825/06 B0946/23
B0948/18 B0990/06 B1006/19 B1035/03
B1046/15 B1101/12 B1102/01 B1138/21
B1140/08 B1155/13 B1214/20 B1214/27
B1219/18 B1241/18 B1249/34 B1272/01
B1275/28 B1358/34
understands (1) B0870/24
understood (60)
undertake (4) C0056/15
C0196/26 C0427/07 C0522/33
undertaken (2) B1222/11 C0425/23
undertaker (8) A0057/11
A0080/34 A0080/39 A0245/09 A0248/26
A0249/29 A0250/06 A0542/25
undertaking (10) A0346/32 A0347/22
B1082/09 B1358/14 C0075/04 C0090/10
C0121/09 C0523/03 C0526/01 C0526/30
undertakings (1) A0529/20
undertone (1) A0088/35
undertook (2) B1107/22 C0525/13
undervalue (1) A0555/15
undervalued (1) B0828/21
underwent (5) A0446/16
A0456/09 B0940/18 C0406/24 C0572/13
underwood (5) A0195/16
C0548/40 C0577/28 C0578/09 C0578/11
undeviating (4) A0399/15
A0497/09 C0415/15 C0438/V
undeviatingly (1) A0319/22
undid (3) B0793/07
B0793/08 C0409/29
undignified (2) A0626/06 B0910/25
undiminished (1) B1237/16
undiscovered (2) B0760/23 B0761/25
undisputed (1) B1044/04
undistinguishable (1) A0190/22
undisturbed (7) A0408/16
A0415/30 B0796/28 B0956/25 B0980/31
B1238/06 B1239/15
undivided (4) A0213/09
A0250/03 B0889/07 C0413/07
undivulged (1) A0507/04
undo (1) C0197/12
undone (1) B1225/V
undoubted (1) A0380/16
undoubtedly (34) A0069/15 A0072/15
A0088/08 A0090/33 A0108/07 A0109/25
A0123/27 A0127/26 A0157/V A0159/04
->A0160/13 A0298/03 A0336/06 A0402/33
A0508/17 A0586/12 A0695/10 B0891/15
B1019/36 B1045/21 B1130/09 B1130/10
B1305/02 B1329/28 B1391/29 C0080/27
C0092/10 C0186/30 C0388/15 C0416/18
C0417/27 C0418/05 C0425/22 C0447/V
undreamed (1) B0865/20
undubitably (1) B0968/32
undue (10) A0055/04 A0064/08
A0212/11 A0266/11 A0273/19 A0282/09
A0497/19 A0545/29 B0863/26 B1074/29
undulated (1) B1328/04
undulation (2) B0862/34 B1038/08
undulations (1) B1214/28
une (3) A0602/06
A0602/08 B0986/34
unearthed (4) B0825/35
B0834/19 B0960/06 B1303/32
unearthly (6) A0027/05 A0226/17
A0230/15 A0250/28 B1240/17 C0446/V
unearths (1) B0957/29
uneasily (4) A0102/20
A0411/23 A0643/09 B0960/23
uneasiness (26) A0064/16 A0081/32
A0137/01 A0514/15 A0614/11 A0667/45
B0813/32 B0825/17 B0940/29 B0943/23
B0966/11 B1032/15 C0070/04 C0084/10
C0129/01 C0397/31 C0403/32 C0406/04
C0407/17 C0409/06 C0411/30 C0412/21
C0413/12 C0413/20 C0419/07 C0575/05
uneasy (20) A0145/01
A0274/11 A0322/28 A0323/23 A0433/13
A0585/18 A0600/24 A0625/01 A0626/33
A0674/16 B0949/10 B0964/35 B1237/20
C0070/12 C0071/22 C0075/31 C0395/30
C0405/38 C0408/23 C0410/07
unedged (1) B0763/04
uneducated (1) B0926/21
unemployed (1) A0529/01
unencumbered (1) B1316/33
unendurable (3) A0411/33
A0459/30 B0961/20
unequal (11) A0279/14
A0410/33 A0499/14 A0541/07 A0549/04
A0550/15 A0555/20 A0614/21 B0832/29
B0962/15 C0187/06
unequalled (1) A0379/09
unequivocal (7) A0053/03
A0510/07 A0551/24 B0895/20 B0962/25
B1237/18 C0419/37
unequivocally (6) A0104/18 A0113/03
A0215/23 A0303/12 B1047/24 B1080/13
unerring (1) A0078/14
uneven (3) B0818/31
B0940/12 C0180/37
unevenly (1) A0543/05
unevenness (1) C0079/36
uneventful (1) C0547/37
unexampled (1) B1337/19
unexpected (12) A0073/03
A0159/21 A0654/15 B1075/17 B1280/01
C0082/37 C0124/06 C0165/01 C0187/17
C0387/03 C0407/11 C0562/33
unexpectedly (8) A0105/06
B0858/10 B0942/22 C0184/10 C0432/01

->C0554/15 C0559/31 C0562/15
unexplored (8) A0610/03
B0759/31 B0858/14 B1331/32 C0418/10
C0521/12 C0521/13 C0524/33
unexposed (1) B0977/08
unfair (1) A0073/24
unfamiliar (1) A0400/33
unfastened (6) A0154/12 C0091/10
C0196/37 C0398/03 C0409/36 C0415/21
unfathomable (7) A0138/28
A0232/02 A0313/V B0852/16 B1222/16
C0126/18 C0405/31
unfavorable (1) B1052/21
unfeeling (1) A0020/V
unfeigned (2) B1016/03 C0561/02
unfeignedly (1) B0906/01
unfilled (1) B0827/12
unfinished (1) A0160/07
unfit (2) A0142/29 C0410/42
unfitted (2) A0534/14 B1312/35
unflinching (1) A0230/06
unflinchingly (1) B1374/03
unflogged (1) A0622/30
unfold (3) B0894/24
B0964/22 B1208/06
unfolded (3) B0747/31
B1140/09 B1214/21
unforeseen (2) B0752/08 B1077/11
unforgotten (1) A0321/02
unformed (2) A0268/15 A0693/22
unfortuate (1) B0962/27
unfortunate (22) A0026/10 A0070/24
A0077/02 A0204/18 A0253/06 A0631/14
B0725/17 B0731/22 B0734/24 B0750/18
B0754/01 B0766/03 B0769/06 B0825/14
B0932/18 B1010/12 B1138/05 B1242/02
C0088/29 C0166/29 C0408/32 C0556/36
unfortunately (12) A0066/34
A0102/11 A0121/V A0264/02 A0264/24
A0344/28 A0351/02 A0565/13 B1106/13
B1350/02 B1385/07 C0390/12
unfrequently (10) A0211/12 A0314/22
A0406/13 A0529/10 A0545/04 A0545/07
B0759/31 B1114/10 B1181/06 C0106/18
unfruitful (2) A0296/15 B0752/24
unfulfilled (1) B1215/33
unfurnished (1) A0242/32
ungenteel (1) B1127/32
ungentlemanly (6) A0094/14 A0114/13
A0114/V A0386/17 A0623/19 B1169/04
ungovernable (10) A0028/25 A0053/12
A0062/20 A0140/13 A0154/28 A0427/25
A0563/V A0567/V A0580/11 B0856/13
ungoverned (1) A0142/08
ungracious (1) A0435/25
ungrammatical (1) B1131/04
ungrateful (3) A0546/07
B0808/11 B1128/04
ungratefully (1) C0128/10
ungreeted (1) B1107/31
unguarded (1) C0200/21
unguided (2) A0639/08 B0834/16
unhallowed (3) A0251/04
A0323/02 B1215/34
unhandsome (2) A0114/09 B1123/23
unhandsomely (1) B1183/13
unhappily (5) A0611/10
A0627/02 B1031/15 B1271/05 C0430/09
unhappiness (4) A0018/07
A0703/26 B0903/03 B1268/25
unhappy (15) A0024/30
A0055/20 A0065/04 A0070/24 A0074/07
A0213/17 A0626/30 B0772/23 B1005/10
B1053/28 B1054/34 B1133/28 B1169/08
B1371/05 B1374/31
unheard (1) A0062/26
unheard-of (4) A0021/11
A0053/18 B0757/33 C0425/20
unheeded (3) A0402/10
A0616/V B0872/13
unhemmed (1) B0762/32
unhesitatingly (6) A0053/16
A0062/V A0243/25 A0325/24 B1223/V
B1358/12
unhewn (1) A0610/02
unholy (1) A0163/13
unhurried (1) A0402/23
uniform (15) A0266/13
A0267/35 A0269/04 A0278/34 A0415/14
A0499/07 A0591/18 A0685/27 B0946/29
B1071/17 B1168/21 C0171/41 C0173/01
C0193/19 C0203/25
uniformity (10) A0267/02 A0273/15
A0497/18 A0500/07 A0694/04 B1279/32
B1280/19 B1282/02 B1330/10 C0151/41
uniformly (6) A0433/21 A0437/07
C0161/07 C0166/06 C0179/39 C0573/25
unimaginable (1) A0379/05
unimaginative (1) A0413/11
unimagined (1) B0752/18
unimpaired (1) B1074/33
unimpeded (1) A0676/08
unimportant (1) C0079/04
unimpressive (2) B1214/32 B1225/03
unincorporate (1) B1036/20
unincumbered (1) C0577/30
unindividualized (1) B1036/32
uninformed (2) A0443/06 C0433/07
uninjured (2) C0136/23 C0399/12
unintelligible (11) A0025/V
A0102/25 A0213/V A0217/12 A0339/32
A0583/13 A0707/34 B0892/27 B0960/24
B1272/34 C0392/22
unintentionally (1) A0104/03
uninterrupted (5) A0703/20
B0724/33 B0906/06 B1268/19 B1330/08
uninterruptedly (6) A0497/16
A0676/11 B0752/09 B1123/11 C0084/40
C0545/35
Union (1) B0877/33
union (3) A0650/16
A0653/24 B0901/V
unique (7) A0293/20
A0301/06 A0528/32 A0693/08 B1034/26
B1039/06 B1299/03
uniquely (1) A0248/06
uniquity (1) A0293/21
unison (2) A0320/13 B1038/15
unit (2) B0955/20 B1178/01
unite (5) B0927/09

->B1277/18 C0110/01 C0182/31 C0521/21
United (1) B0862/16
united (18) A0074/30 A0278/18
A0365/16 A0543/16 A0557/12 B0826/09
B0922/14 B0987/27 B1073/21 B1089/12
B1145/04 B1166/23 B1276/29 B1299/21
B1363/08 C0121/39 C0403/18 C0412/16
United/States (11) A0261/22
A0261/24 A0497/05 A0500/V B0862/03
B0864/10 B0914/20 B1164/40 C0055/01
C0526/19 C0528/29
uniting (2) C0431/01 C0538/05
unity (5) A0175/11
A0181/01 A0473/10 B1034/03 B1212/21
universal (22) A0337/13 A0337/26
A0370/24 A0460/21 A0610/16 A0710/34
B0834/17 B0894/V B0933/26 B0984/07
B1036/08 B1036/08 B1036/12 B1137/08
B1139/04 B1145/10 B1190/11 B1275/35
B1300/03 B1324/02 C0182/04 C0523/17
universality (1) B0987/21
universally (8) A0583/09
B0738/14 B0864/27 B1029/02 B1044/25
B1122/18 B1346/34 C0111/13
Universe (4) A0127/02
A0127/23 A0128/01 B1317/32
universe (23) A0079/32
A0145/15 A0211/28 A0298/V A0304/06
A0314/07 A0314/V A0405/05 A0431/07
A0601/26 A0642/14 A0682/18 B0913/16
B0943/18 B0963/05 B1109/02 B1134/01
B1190/20 B1212/19 B1213/07 B1214/26
B1299/33 B1317/19
University (2) A0181/22 B0922/11
university (9) A0292/V
A0293/24 A0293/28 A0295/08 A0296/10
A0297/27 A0299/10 A0440/18 A0440/36
Unjigah (1) C0527/11
unjust (2) B0763/24 B1380/29
unjustly (1) A0528/14
unkind (1) B1090/08
unkindest (1) B1129/28
unknown (57)
unlearned (3) A0226/24
A0230/23 A0338/06
unless (33) A0025/27
A0092/21 A0111/31 A0226/06 A0230/04
A0706/24 B0724/01 B0759/30 B0770/32
B0809/28 B0841/34 B0865/11 B0871/02
B0929/25 B0963/14 B1003/07 B1033/14
B1188/33 B1238/10 B1271/26 B1300/26
B1310/07 B1331/19 B1332/25 B1347/17
B1383/21 C0106/04 C0129/02 C0130/02
C0142/01 C0404/08 C0557/11 C0577/38
unlettered (1) B1313/16
unlike (9) A0274/28
A0434/V A0614/17 A0651/23 B1156/10
B1248/16 C0171/20 C0172/37 C0174/03
unlikely (1) B1169/31
unlimited (6) A0250/29 A0675/01
B1037/33 B1038/17 B1134/05 C0175/31
unload (1) B0968/28
unlocked (1) B0808/09
unlocking (1) B0983/13
unlooked (1) B0752/18
unlooked-for (1) C0069/35
unloosened (1) A0330/V
unloveliness (1) A0209/05
unlucky (1) A0070/08
unmanacled (2) A0058/03 A0068/25
unmanageable (3) A0584/27
B0958/20 B1076/02
unmanned (1) A0588/27
unmannerly (1) B1383/11
unmask (1) A0675/25
unmeaning (7) A0026/16
A0080/22 A0155/14 A0499/25 A0568/V
A0692/27 B1130/05
unmentionable (2) A0065/27 B1137/07
unmentioned (1) A0404/28
unmerited (1) A0317/24
unmingled (1) A0404/08
unmistakeable (3) B0895/03
B0946/03 B1247/12
unmitigated (3) A0294/14
C0425/35 C0440/V
unmolested (3) C0102/06
C0395/16 C0558/16
unmouldered (1) B0956/30
unmuzzled (1) B0823/34
unnameable (1) B1222/29
unnatural (18) A0023/V A0025/27
A0026/32 A0081/02 A0098/20 A0143/01
A0214/V A0246/10 A0402/34 A0409/28
A0412/31 A0414/32 A0460/30 A0591/28
A0683/19 B0814/28 B0903/02 C0145/03
unnaturally (1) A0022/08
unnecessarily (4) A0563/25
B0902/20 B1259/20 B1380/32
unnecessary (24) A0055/30
A0065/11 A0093/18 A0112/29 A0204/22
A0226/20 A0230/19 A0274/32 A0302/V
A0433/14 A0554/04 A0704/V B0723/08
B0736/25 B0839/24 B0916/05 B1145/28
C0056/30 C0106/30 C0132/25 C0411/15
C0526/24 C0539/22 C0546/29
unnerved (6) A0235/12 A0397/21
A0403/16 A0415/29 A0558/24 B1242/26
unnoticed (7) A0141/33
A0154/21 A0310/09 A0444/30 A0663/21
B0990/04 B1334/12
unnumbered (1) B1130/21
unobserved (5) B0905/05
B0908/25 C0084/22 C0089/17 C0544/24
unobstructed (4) A0551/28
A0552/20 A0578/11 A0590/31
unobtrusive (1) A0399/02
unoccupied (1) C0153/03
unoffending (1) B0852/19
unopened (3) A0409/32
B0899/26 B1181/06
unorganized (3) B1037/28
B1037/33 B1038/11
unostentatious (2) A0528/22
B0877/36
unpacked (2) B1369/28 C0407/29
unpaid-for (1) A0241/31
Unparalleled (1) C0387/T
unparalleled (10) A0021/06 A0157/03
A0212/09 A0213/32 A0426/05 B1131/15

->B1371/27 C0404/21 C0421/24 C0425/20
unpardonable (4) A0249/30
A0295/13 A0426/11 B0899/10
unparticled (15) B1033/25
B1033/27 B1033/34 B1034/03 B1034/05
B1034/08 B1034/26 B1036/06 B1036/17
B1036/24 B1037/35 B1038/06 B1038/16
B1040/01 B1040/05
unperceived (4) A0140/29
B0794/23 B1382/25 C0396/18
unphilosophical (3) A0054/37
A0064/04 B0740/19
unpicturesqueness (1) B1274/17
unpleasant (9) A0497/18
A0500/05 A0500/V A0564/26 B0812/15
B1078/25 B1233/08 C0204/37 C0565/17
unpleasantly (2) B1328/09 C0565/19
unpleasing (1) B0940/14
unpleasingly (1) B1004/10
unpossibility (2) A0251/11 A0251/15
unpractised (1) C0547/29
unprepossessing (1) A0562/18
unpretending (2) B1335/25 B1379/18
unprincipled (3) A0372/12
B0993/12 B1207/33
unprofitable (2) A0490/12 B1029/04
unproportionably (1) A0322/08
unpublished (1) C0524/17
unqualified (4) A0105/02
A0431/27 A0439/18 C0569/31
unquenchable (1) B1212/27
unquestionability (1) B1314/36
unquestionable (8) B0748/24
B0772/14 B0877/24 B1045/01 B1298/24
B1315/04 B1316/35 B1329/08
unquestionably (11) A0379/19
A0560/01 A0612/18 B0766/29 B0771/12
B0863/21 B0904/24 B0978/26 B1078/28
B1082/08 B1358/05
unquiet (10) A0102/21 A0144/23
A0145/28 A0161/23 A0190/05 A0196/32
A0324/18 A0326/08 A0499/21 B0827/16
unransacked (1) B1179/16
unrasonable> (1) A0469/20
unravel (2) A0099/02 C0388/06
unreal (4) A0022/03
A0212/25 A0695/34 A0696/01
unrealities (1) B1246/18
unreason (1) B1314/01
unreasonable (7) A0027/23
A0353/03 A0485/17 A0486/22 B1077/25
B1220/28 B1379/26
unreasoning (2) B0748/13 B0765/13
unredeemed (1) A0397/19
unredressed (2) B1256/07 B1256/08
unrelieved (4) A0139/01
A0140/07 A0397/08 A0500/05
unremitting (2) A0059/33 C0394/36
unremittingly (1) B0894/11
unreserved (2) B0906/07 C0094/38
unreservedly (3) A0405/01
B0901/16 C0093/10
unresistingly (2) A0447/12 C0075/41
unrest (1) B0964/31
unrestricted (1) B1122/33
unriddled (2) A0553/30 B0839/30
unriddles (1) B1298/03
unrigged (1) C0424/18
unrivalled (1) A0380/25
unroll (1) B1178/23
unrolled (2) B0822/08 B0822/09
unrolling (1) B1185/12
unrounded (1) B1337/26
unruffled (3) A0398/10
C0405/06 C0407/33
unsatisfactory (5) A0398/02
A0477/03 A0582/31 B1291/17 C0078/22
unscathed (1) A0349/35
unscrew (1) C0424/16
unscrewed (1) A0410/13
unscrupulous (1) A0446/28
unsearchableness (1) A0577/M
unseasonable (1) A0251/03
unseasonably (1) A0214/17
unseemly (1) A0057/27
unseen (11) A0157/V
A0640/34 B0863/09 B0872/13 B0890/27
B0955/32 B0961/24 B0964/24 B1281/16
B1317/31 B1352/32
unselfish (1) B0850/18
unsettled (3) A0282/06
B0807/32 B0814/04
unshackled (1) C0412/30
unsheathing (1) B1262/25
unshipped (1) C0533/27
unsightly (2) A0603/23 B1351/21
unskillful (1) A0667/07
unslacked (1) C0396/09
unsocial (1) A0320/15
unsolved (1) B0723/12
unspeakable (6) A0328/22 A0426/11
A0692/29 B0863/10 B1162/05 C0080/18
unstable (2) B0902/09 C0412/31
unsteadily (1) B1261/22
unsteadiness (1) C0099/16
unsteady (8) A0138/22
A0141/11 A0210/03 A0499/01 A0510/17
B1258/33 C0129/28 C0577/20
unstring (1) A0578/04
unstrung (3) A0687/23
B0965/08 C0578/41
unsuccessful (7) A0437/07
B1069/20 B1242/08 C0121/19 C0121/40
C0141/16 C0197/10
unsuitable (1) B1044/08
unsuited (2) A0673/22 A0673/24
unsundered (1) C0545/40
unsupported (2) C0055/18 C0136/33
unsurpassed (2) B1333/35 C0524/09
unsuspectedness (1) A0296/V
unswathe (1) B1178/21
<u>unt</u> (2) A0357/05 B1158/34
untameable (1) C0577/36
untenable (2) B1296/29 B1313/31
untenanted (2) A0242/32 A0676/31
untended (1) B1317/30
untie (3) C0119/02
C0197/07 C0398/09
untied (4) C0088/18
C0088/40 C0090/21 C0408/21

until (304)
untimely (3) A0026/20
A0445/04 A0603/20
untiring (1) A0061/01
unto (24) A0195/09
A0195/13 A0196/07 A0196/14 A0197/14
A0197/17 A0310/M A0314/29 A0319/24
A0320/01 A0426/12 A0447/09 A0515/24
A0580/23 A0604/05 A0604/07 A0608/16
A0639/03 A0643/28 A0643/V A0645/09
A0681/01 A0695/11 B1109/34
untold (1) B1170/03
untorturing (1) A0616/V
untouched (4) B0751/16
B0851/34 B1317/31 C0545/38
untoward (3) A0531/18
A0665/06 B1055/09
untractable (2) A0024/08 A0027/V
untravelled (2) B1184/25 C0521/11
untried (1) C0207/08
untrodden (2) A0296/V A0316/09
untrue (1) B0987/24
untutored (1) A0157/22
unus (1) A0125/01
unused (1) B0741/27
unusual (59)
unusually (26) A0026/17 A0241/11
A0245/25 A0267/31 A0297/08 A0314/17
A0410/10 A0491/01 A0613/01 A0630/22
A0662/11 B0761/13 B0873/12 B1053/10
B1072/16 B1076/12 B1100/02 B1238/01
C0115/29 C0147/09 C0158/20 C0387/10
C0521/22 C0540/17 C0562/11 C0562/32
unusualness (3) B0737/05
B0746/11 B0746/33
unutterable (13) A0048/02
A0217/V A0326/17 A0327/06 A0329/23
A0676/30 B0771/26 B0854/32 B0856/06
B1240/32 B1302/01 B1372/15 C0083/31
unvarying (3) A0703/29
B0749/18 B0834/09
unveiling (1) A0319/16
unvollkommen (2) B0723/M B0723/M
unwarranted (1) B1242/04
unwashed (1) B0760/06
unwavering (1) C0111/40
unwearied (1) A0211/29
unwelcome (4) A0025/09
A0071/15 A0432/16 B0808/V
unwell (1) B0815/27
unwetted (1) A0349/35
unwholesome (1) C0192/20
unwieldy (4) A0241/10
A0551/30 B1345/34 C0075/11
unwilling (4) A0074/11
A0141/02 B0817/10 C0065/39
unwillingly (1) C0186/31
unwisely (1) A0609/35
unwitting (1) B1050/26
unwittingly (7) A0022/07
A0142/12 A0294/V A0444/24 A0534/03
B0745/04 C0130/27
unwomanly (1) B1277/08
unwonted (2) A0043/13 A0329/12
unworldliness (1) B1338/34
unworthily (1) A0317/24
unworthy (7) A0086/23
A0099/19 A0299/11 A0446/27 C0422/35
C0563/41 C0564/16
unwound (1) A0693/10
unwounded (1) C0557/37
unwrought (2) A0703/14 B1268/13
unyielding (1) C0075/34
up (892)
up-side-down (1) B1141/28
upbraid (3) A0227/07
A0231/19 A0416/16
upheld (2) B1165/32 C0061/36
upholstery (2) A0158/13 A0498/15
uplift (2) B0928/05 B0966/34
uplifted (13) A0217/V
A0399/28 A0411/27 A0413/31 A0414/21
A0439/17 A0615/30 B0741/23 B0959/05
B0966/34 B1102/15 C0067/28 C0076/23
uplifting (7) A0214/19
A0623/07 B0856/20 B1017/10 B1135/01
B1247/27 B1261/17
upon (2261)
upper (63)
upper-lip (1) A0241/16
uppermost (6) A0085/11 B0957/02
B0977/08 B0991/V C0197/01 C0577/10
upraise (1) A0552/27
upraised (1) B1074/30
upreared (1) A0140/04
uprearing (1) A0190/01
upright (11) A0058/15
A0069/03 A0153/22 A0252/11 A0387/V
A0640/08 B0741/16 B0910/24 B0911/V
B1163/31 C0063/20
uprightness (1) B1136/27
uprise (1) A0594/08
uprising (1) A0319/16
uproar (10) A0022/05 A0123/31
A0128/12 A0174/02 A0179/13 A0373/12
A0580/12 B1020/17 B1374/22 C0387/05
uproarious (1) C0550/20
uproariously (1) A0105/27
uprooted (1) B1303/06
uprooting (1) A0557/21
uprose (2) A0594/V A0643/20
Upsaroka (1) C0087/19
Upsarokas (1) C0087/02
upset (2) A0099/03 B1090/18
upsetting (1) A0088/20
upside (4) A0108/21
A0342/10 B1279/12 C0388/26
upside-down (1) A0265/23
upsprang (1) B1332/03
upspringing (6) A0608/18 A0615/21
B0759/14 B0759/21 B1190/29 B1283/10
upstart (1) A0044/17
upthrew (1) A0616/28
upturned (4) A0047/30
B0825/25 B1353/32 C0387/18
upward (25) A0350/23
A0496/27 A0536/11 A0578/16 A0602/23
A0689/23 A0689/31 A0690/11 A0690/17
A0692/26 B0730/25 B0765/21 B0944/22
B1105/18 B1214/29 B1214/30 B1280/22

->B1281/24 B1352/33 C0063/36 C0125/13
C0144/13 C0183/16 C0402/36 C0403/21
upwardly (1) B1239/22
upwards (24) A0035/08
A0047/11 A0122/V A0139/34 A0166/08
A0196/19 A0353/27 B0741/28 B0826/15
B1072/03 B1156/18 B1163/26 B1260/16
C0396/21 C0398/14 C0399/06 C0402/06
C0412/19 C0415/15 C0420/34 C0422/39
C0425/12 C0442/V C0552/27
Uranus (1) B1322/13
urbanity (2) B1209/10 C0148/01
urchin (1) A0124/22
urchins (1) A0368/26
urge (4) A0696/33
B0765/02 B0902/24 B0985/34
urged (35) A0226/27
A0231/01 A0235/19 A0432/09 A0459/04
A0473/32 A0513/01 A0566/06 A0604/19
B0741/01 B0745/22 B0761/30 B0764/02
B0825/30 B0852/18 B0893/11 B0901/22
B0926/10 B0949/09 B0966/33 B0985/20
B1236/10 B1315/25 C0065/38 C0100/30
C0128/01 C0134/35 C0403/38 C0423/09
C0521/16 C0522/08 C0529/24 C0536/10
C0558/39 C0561/11
urgency (1) B0960/28
urgent (7) A0156/28
A0386/28 B0760/32 B0769/02 B0900/11
B1236/19 C0559/07
urges (2) B0749/06 B1223/17
urging (6) B0745/07 B1315/28
C0055/06 C0076/17 C0132/16 C0557/02
Urion (1) A0536/20
urry (1) B1109/18
us (789)
usage (3) A0135/01
A0300/05 A0555/17
usages (1) B1005/25
usbande (2) B0912/08 B0912/09
use (92)
use-up (1) B1140/34
Used (1) A0378/T
used (49) A0090/26
A0248/17 A0266/09 A0268/20 A0273/27
A0277/15 A0283/03 A0328/12 A0356/V
A0389/18 A0399/19 A0410/04 A0443/22
A0493/05 A0508/36 A0561/07 A0584/03
A0612/36 A0623/10 A0667/25 A0667/37
B0746/26 B0766/30 B0841/21 B0841/27
B0924/09 B1013/08 B1015/01 B1090/14
B1137/17 B1183/13 B1383/28 C0057/20
C0063/11 C0069/01 C0084/38 C0100/24
C0139/20 C0144/32 C0156/40 C0174/21
C0180/27 C0202/22 C0388/22 C0534/31
C0535/28 C0566/28 C0567/27 C0577/25
Useful (1) A0337/18
useful (6) A0270/07 A0382/02
A0382/03 B1091/14 B1091/16 C0070/16
usefully (1) A0528/22
useless (23) A0058/19
A0139/09 A0495/V B0888/08 B0895/22
B0930/34 B1082/11 B1158/24 B1235/24
C0061/24 C0075/37 C0078/35 C0094/20
C0114/40 C0116/22 C0117/37 C0126/16
->C0127/08 C0134/32 C0142/38 C0199/16
C0201/20 C0425/41
uses (5) A0600/13
B1130/18 B1158/06 B1300/23 B1383/20
Usher (17) A0397/06
A0397/22 A0397/T A0399/05 A0399/18
A0401/19 A0404/29 A0405/07 A0406/21
A0409/08 A0409/29 A0410/16 A0412/06
A0413/01 A0415/30 A0416/27 A0417/17
usher (1) A0430/10
Usher, Roderick (4) A0398/15
A0401/27 A0404/V A0405/22
Usher's (2) A0408/03 A0413/09
ushered (2) A0401/05 B1004/01
Ushers (1) A0404/05
ushers (1) A0428/25
using (14) A0273/14 A0555/14
A0584/30 B1090/15 B1222/13 B1383/14
C0145/22 C0163/07 C0173/38 C0199/22
C0536/11 C0544/34 C0557/23 C0577/15
using-up (2) B1129/13 B1140/31
usual (117)
usually (62)
usurpation (1) A0120/04
usurped (2) A0616/19 B1018/27
usurping (1) B1194/13
usury (1) B0869/02
Ut (1) B0870/21
Utawas (1) C0528/10
Utawas/river (1) C0526/35
Utica (1) B1360/35
utilitarian (1) B0866/06
utilitarians (1) A0609/32
utility (1) A0609/21
utmost (18) A0374/08 A0551/32
B0727/04 B0826/09 B0982/18 C0074/21
C0074/33 C0075/34 C0114/30 C0122/11
C0130/30 C0137/05 C0190/09 C0200/33
C0424/12 C0438/V C0538/02 C0556/40
utter (35) A0104/17
A0139/21 A0141/33 A0144/16 A0251/11
A0251/15 A0274/36 A0320/14 A0329/07
A0397/15 A0404/08 A0405/20 A0414/V
A0442/14 A0446/09 A0532/V A0623/23
A0691/13 B0760/16 B0961/07 B0967/03
B1105/31 B1247/09 B1295/34 B1302/12
B1311/34 C0076/21 C0083/11 C0088/01
C0096/08 C0108/18 C0112/29 C0182/06
C0186/20 C0398/37
utterance (16) A0054/01
A0063/10 A0315/14 A0318/02 A0402/24
A0411/04 A0416/22 A0439/20 A0555/22
A0624/31 B0905/13 B1221/27 B1241/02
B1256/04 C0072/37 C0083/02
uttered (33) A0053/04
A0108/18 A0155/15 A0214/25 A0249/31
A0315/15 A0317/10 A0317/V A0447/08
A0541/07 A0564/12 A0630/15 A0675/28
B0825/31 B0858/27 B0902/10 B0960/24
B0983/18 B1020/32 B1050/26 B1051/02
B1057/10 B1105/06 B1225/V B1240/33
B1353/16 C0091/41 C0128/37 C0136/17
C0388/37 C0425/09 C0429/38 C0557/20
uttering (7) A0217/V
B1349/02 C0111/26 C0112/24 C0123/04

->C0130/19 C0408/28
utterly (100)
uttermost (5) A0317/06
A0426/04 B0878/08 B0966/04 B1145/11
utterness (1) A0413/V
utters (1) B1250/28
V (38) A0268/01 A0407/24
B1032/16 B1032/19 B1032/21 B1032/23
B1032/26 B1032/28 B1032/31 B1032/V
B1033/01 B1033/03 B1033/06 B1033/07
B1033/09 B1033/13 B1033/16 B1033/18
B1033/33 B1034/09 B1035/16 B1035/34
B1036/08 B1036/12 B1036/16 B1036/20
B1036/27 B1036/31 B1037/03 B1037/05
B1037/12 B1037/23 B1037/29 B1038/22
B1039/05 B1039/11 B1039/19 B1039/29
V-- (1) A0093/08
Va. (1) C0055/04
vaat (1) A0365/V
vacancy (4) A0411/08
A0685/08 B0838/03 B1057/22
vacant (6) A0397/13 A0398/13
A0513/24 A0533/18 A0548/25 B0983/10
vacantly (1) B1348/22
vacated (2) B0913/24 C0545/12
vacillating (3) A0214/24
A0556/31 B0962/15
vacillation (6) A0514/15 A0608/08
C0415/18 C0416/32 C0419/41 C0420/01
vacuo (1) C0425/37
vacuum (4) C0207/10
C0404/10 C0410/37 C0411/03
vagabond (5) B1103/11
B1138/06 B1138/12 B1138/14 B1370/17
vagabond's (1) B1349/22
vagabonds (2) A0389/05 A0389/06
vagaries (3) A0212/08
A0411/08 B0825/15
vague (50) A0054/13 A0054/29
A0063/20 A0063/29 A0080/21 A0098/20
A0141/04 A0156/22 A0190/30 A0210/03
A0217/10 A0225/06 A0225/19 A0229/06
A0324/19 A0327/28 A0400/26 A0413/13
A0496/V A0536/09 A0555/24 A0609/27
A0612/18 A0612/27 A0614/11 A0643/V
A0664/08 A0664/29 A0683/18 A0685/11
A0686/21 B0723/02 B0748/09 B0766/17
B0834/02 B0943/08 B0943/27 B0943/29
B0955/26 B1031/07 B1280/23 C0064/12
C0080/25 C0109/11 C0182/02 C0392/29
C0412/38 C0429/10 C0530/19 C0565/05
vaguely (2) A0684/04 B1033/V
vagueness (2) A0405/16 A0710/15
vaguenesses (1) B1275/18
vaguest (1) B0900/07
Vah (1) A0047/V
vain (68)
vainly (2) A0608/17 C0125/38
Valdemar (24) B1233/02
B1233/T B1234/06 B1234/25 B1235/02
B1235/07 B1235/36 B1236/07 B1236/19
B1236/28 B1238/06 B1238/14 B1238/22
B1238/33 B1239/08 B1239/15 B1239/35
B1240/04 B1240/25 B1241/13 B1241/28
B1242/06 B1242/17 B1380/09
Valdemar, M Ernest (1) B1234/03
Valdemar's (4) B1235/21
B1237/32 B1241/05 B1241/32
vale (14) A0150/M A0166/11
A0639/09 A0643/12 B0863/02 B1331/12
B1331/18 B1331/25 B1331/34 B1332/17
B1333/11 B1333/22 B1334/26 B1335/04
Valence (4) B0736/02
B0736/04 B0769/11 B0770/13
Valens (1) A0120/28
valet (1) A0159/17
valet (12) A0386/29
A0400/23 A0401/04 A0662/01 A0663/15
A0667/05 B0824/15 B0826/30 B0843/08
B0900/25 B0901/14 B0931/23
valets-de-chambre (1) A0123/19
valiant (1) A0253/16
valiantly (2) A0345/02 A0356/V
valid (1) A0098/26
validity (4) A0530/04
B0751/21 B0752/25 B0752/34
Valley (1) A0608/28
valley (53)
valleys (7) A0195/M
A0406/25 A0545/18 A0600/22 B0817/27
B1328/06 C0572/18
vallisneria (1) B1163/24
valor (9) A0124/28
A0128/24 A0356/17 A0380/33 A0382/31
A0384/02 A0384/26 A0385/13 A0386/01
valorously (1) A0415/20
valourously (1) A0059/12
valuable (15) A0087/18
A0088/07 A0268/06 A0382/10 A0562/26
B0752/11 B0913/20 B0976/24 B1053/23
B1137/03 B1138/34 B1310/25 C0068/05
C0155/31 C0163/35
valuables (1) B0828/11
value (31) A0263/20
A0561/21 A0561/32 B0747/33 B0826/13
B0827/25 B0827/32 B0828/08 B0842/24
B0872/17 B0873/25 B0877/05 B0890/09
B0907/06 B0908/03 B0985/08 B0987/08
B0987/13 B0987/27 B0987/27 B1114/08
B1214/07 B1312/29 B1345/28 B1360/16
B1364/17 B1364/26 B1364/27 B1381/12
C0073/30 C0180/01
valueless (2) A0073/17 B0828/16
values (2) A0528/25 B0987/28
valve (8) B1074/14
C0406/28 C0411/01 C0411/05 C0411/10
C0412/08 C0413/10 C0413/31
Valz (1) C0401/40
van (1) C0570/37
Van/Diemen's/Land (2) C0156/10
C0161/36
vanes (9) B1070/05
B1070/05 B1070/11 B1070/22 B1070/22
B1070/31 B1080/17 B1081/V B1164/30
Vanilla (1) C0543/24
vanilla (1) B1092/31
vanilla-perfumed (1) A0640/01
vanish (2) A0546/01 B1034/31
vanished (9) A0212/23
A0410/31 A0682/13 B0842/30 B0969/09

->B1374/27 C0198/29 C0413/34 C0575/20
vanishes (1) B1282/11
vanishing (2) B1032/04 B1330/31
vanities (1) A0644/01
vanity (1) A0440/06
Vankirk (4) B1030/22
  B1032/14 B1032/30 B1032/V
vapid (1) B0940/23
vapor (17) A0136/16
  A0153/02 A0400/02 A0412/30 A0578/31
  A0687/02 A0696/02 B1168/30 B1222/31
  B1321/10 B1321/10 B1321/13 B1321/29
  B1322/16 B1331/09 B1362/23 C0418/50
vapors (1) B1076/18
vapory (3) A0064/02
  A0244/03 A0457/26
vapour (9) C0166/12
  C0192/40 C0203/23 C0203/27 C0204/19
  C0204/35 C0204/40 C0205/02 C0205/22
vapour-like (1) A0036/V
vapours (1) C0444/V
vapoury (2) A0054/35 C0208/20
variability (1) B1314/13
variable (7) A0210/03
  A0302/12 A0528/25 B0736/32 C0157/24
  C0425/17 C0425/38
variance (10) A0019/06 A0019/23
  A0415/13 A0482/27 A0527/V B0773/11
  C0387/04 C0429/05 C0429/06 C0429/46
variation (20) A0399/09
  A0528/33 A0530/12 A0613/32 A0641/23
  B0773/06 B0841/27 B0940/15 B0984/23
  B0984/25 B0985/19 C0161/05 C0161/09
  C0163/11 C0164/04 C0164/21 C0166/06
  C0167/10 C0172/02 C0401/36
variations (6) A0081/10 A0138/15
  A0324/27 B0877/27 B0962/09 C0203/26
varied (15) A0156/12
  A0296/V A0402/20 A0431/07 A0445/26
  A0671/27 B0836/02 B0865/04 B1164/32
  B1331/14 B1340/20 C0087/22 C0402/15
  C0536/13 C0572/09
varies (4) A0270/16
  A0275/36 B1281/28 B1303/01
Varietes (2) A0534/02 A0537/02
varieties (10) A0489/11 A0497/10
  A0507/34 A0709/32 B1274/34 B1311/30
  B1332/11 B1333/31 B1334/22 C0174/08
variety (41) A0024/25
  A0111/03 A0128/17 A0163/V A0273/16
  A0296/V A0341/04 A0367/16 A0509/14
  A0514/04 A0531/18 A0583/30 A0592/08
  A0663/V B0827/27 B0850/11 B0871/33
  B0923/02 B0945/12 B1009/08 B1019/13
  B1038/28 B1179/26 B1215/05 B1292/33
  B1330/10 C0089/19 C0153/14 C0155/20
  C0156/23 C0159/08 C0173/34 C0427/10
  C0538/28 C0552/13 C0553/02 C0554/17
  C0559/40 C0568/12 C0572/06 C0573/17
various (62)
variously (3) A0173/16
  A0178/25 A0542/22
varlet (1) A0250/34
varnish (4) C0393/19
  C0394/41 C0395/21 C0403/03

varnished (4) B1073/03
  B1292/26 B1293/05 C0403/02
vary (5) A0490/26
  B0985/23 B1038/29 B1167/02 B1193/24
varying (7) A0191/14
  A0326/09 B1164/30 B1168/21 B1180/04
  B1363/18 C0418/32
vas (3) B0913/03 B0913/04 B1375/19
vase (5) A0164/21
  A0165/V B1340/16 B1340/19 B1340/20
vases (4) A0165/06
  A0165/19 A0503/01 B1179/09
vassal (1) A0025/16
vassals (2) A0021/11 A0025/01
vast (135)
vaster (2) B0827/23 B0989/21
vastly (4) A0322/26
  B0837/26 B1078/03 C0202/25
vastness (7) A0557/V
  A0577/M A0711/26 B1039/01 B1039/28
  B1078/33 B1276/28
vat (15) B0900/V
  B0911/27 B0911/27 B0911/28 B0912/12
  B0912/12 B0912/16 B0912/22 B0913/04
  B1102/06 B1103/02 B1103/08 B1103/08
  B1103/28 B1104/02
Vathek (1) B1335/18
Vathek, Rabbi (1) A0089/17
Vaudeville (1) A0096/M
vaudeville (1) B0898/06
vault (17) A0070/11
  A0075/02 A0081/19 A0235/28 A0400/14
  A0405/31 A0409/31 A0416/15 A0686/18
  A0686/18 A0688/20 B0956/24 B0957/23
  B0965/26 B0967/28 B1261/06 C0387/15
vault-door (1) B0965/33
vaulted (6) A0028/13 A0087/20
  A0321/21 A0401/13 A0503/09 C0405/30
vaulting (1) A0321/24
vaults (6) A0409/18 B1258/08
  B1258/13 B1258/29 B1259/30 B1260/09
vaunted (1) A0478/06
veal (5) A0175/19
  A0181/08 B1007/23 B1010/21 B1010/31
veered (1) B1079/16
vegetable (5) A0408/06
  A0460/11 B0742/27 C0138/13 C0429/46
vegetables (5) B1162/25
  B1162/26 C0155/36 C0156/24 C0535/02
vegetation (14) A0459/17 A0460/08
  B0807/03 B0862/36 B1282/20 B1331/37
  B1332/14 C0150/27 C0165/25 C0199/02
  C0566/13 C0574/02 C0576/32 C0577/11
vehemence (2) A0317/27 C0408/28
vehement (2) A0356/24 B1182/29
vehemently (4) A0664/13
  B0770/09 B0797/12 B1057/27
vehicle (9) A0057/05
  A0058/11 A0066/32 A0068/31 A0081/11
  A0460/27 A0494/01 B0908/23 B1329/13
vehicles (2) A0493/01 B1093/12
veil (6) A0397/18 B0795/03
  B0924/15 B1275/18 C0206/01 C0428/38
veiled (3) A0035/21
  B0924/14 B0945/15

veils (1) A0318/10
vein (4) A0473/19
B1119/M B1122/10 C0406/36
veins (14) A0078/05 A0218/18
A0227/10 A0231/24 A0316/22 A0327/06
B1167/08 C0060/41 C0172/07 C0172/07
C0172/10 C0172/10 C0172/13 C0397/23
vell (5) B0899/29
B0911/25 B0911/26 B1373/21 B1373/23
veller (1) B1104/18
vellum (4) B0832/19
B0832/27 B0833/15 B0834/27
vellum-paper (1) A0301/06
velocities (2) A0591/33 C0412/16
velocity (36) A0088/17
A0137/32 A0139/26 A0145/18 A0412/25
A0580/09 A0585/23 A0588/18 A0690/13
A0692/13 B1072/10 B1075/08 B1075/11
B1078/04 B1281/13 B1282/22 B1292/16
B1321/19 B1321/20 B1382/25 C0205/34
C0397/01 C0400/18 C0401/33 C0402/30
C0402/36 C0403/26 C0408/35 C0412/10
C0421/25 C0421/32 C0423/01 C0538/01
C0562/38 C0566/34 C0578/29
Veloute (1) A0175/19
veloute (2) A0181/08 B1007/24
velvet (14) A0087/19 A0100/11
A0447/04 A0509/15 A0663/07 A0672/02
A0673/31 A0676/22 B1049/18 B1281/26
B1329/19 B1334/25 C0107/41 C0542/13
velvety (2) B1333/09 B1337/04
Ven (1) A0344/22
ven (2) B0912/07 B0913/06
vended (1) A0510/26
venders (1) B1092/29
venerable (6) A0344/06 A0348/18
A0349/23 A0428/03 A0430/20 A0627/30
veneration (2) B1033/05 B1127/05
Venetian (1) A0155/07
vengeance (11) A0372/11
A0696/23 B0765/02 B1048/04 B1054/36
B1058/16 B1106/18 B1354/20 C0208/27
C0392/04 C0555/31
vengeful (1) B1158/09
Venice (10) A0085/01 A0086/16
A0086/30 A0089/18 A0151/04 A0151/13
A0152/17 A0153/08 A0165/21 A0321/15
venir (1) A0344/23
Venitian (1) A0155/V
venny (1) A0354/31
venom (1) A0434/06
venomous (3) B0950/06
C0126/15 C0174/15
vent (5) A0697/05
B0727/18 B0913/06 B1048/07 C0537/07
vented (1) C0201/20
ventilators (1) A0071/09
ventricle (1) C0404/08
ventriloquial (1) B1059/21
ventum (1) B0889/30
ventur (2) B0819/32 B0820/14
venture (21) A0151/V
A0271/25 A0327/16 A0435/06 A0444/17
A0624/06 A0667/07 A0674/06 B0820/25
B0942/02 B0976/22 B1090/11 B1320/02
->C0061/12 C0071/13 C0086/05 C0092/29
C0121/28 C0189/13 C0202/06 C0393/35
ventured (30) A0027/13 A0142/01
A0142/09 A0157/07 A0241/26 A0366/30
A0403/24 A0566/03 A0609/12 A0662/01
B0739/26 B0927/19 B0927/22 B0967/13
B1014/35 B1044/07 B1091/22 B1103/26
B1134/13 B1178/02 B1188/30 B1256/02
B1313/06 C0145/40 C0181/13 C0182/21
C0188/38 C0424/16 C0427/03 C0566/38
ventures (3) B1094/04
B1325/03 C0153/07
venturing (2) B0747/30 B1104/32
Venus (10) A0160/14 A0160/15
A0160/15 A0160/16 A0546/01 A0641/V
B1014/23 B1039/34 B1039/34 C0402/09
Venus/Aphrodite (1) B1123/26
Venuses (1) A0160/V
Ver (1) A0581/20
ver (11) B0912/01
B0912/06 B0912/16 B0912/17 B0912/19
B0912/27 B0913/04 B0913/04 B0913/06
B0913/07 B0913/10
veracity (4) A0143/06
A0625/31 C0055/22 C0569/19
veranda (1) A0501/09
verandahs (1) B0945/10
verb (2) B0869/07 B1383/15
verbal (6) A0295/10 A0406/13
B1069/26 B1345/16 C0207/43 C0208/05
verbatim (3) A0264/35
B1069/23 B1370/03
verbatim (5) A0302/V
B1131/18 B1154/27 B1236/25 B1304/22
verborum (1) A0345/26
verbose (1) B0876/26
verbosity (1) A0629/18
verdant (4) A0320/16
A0602/19 B0877/33 B1385/35
verdict (2) B1054/33 B1224/19
verdure (3) A0612/02
C0150/24 C0575/12
verdured (1) A0602/28
verge (10) A0140/02 A0154/08
A0314/01 A0514/21 A0555/26 A0638/10
B0746/18 B0865/33 B0948/23 B1332/03
verging (1) A0018/10
veriest (6) A0438/15 A0445/28
A0500/13 A0687/31 B1313/16 C0414/33
verified (3) A0138/09
B1293/27 C0207/20
verify (2) B0837/11 C0088/02
verily (9) A0043/12
A0045/14 A0046/15 A0047/08 A0159/V
B0813/25 B1360/01 C0064/30 C0395/31
verisimilitude (1) C0433/09
verisimillima (1) A0091/14
veritable (2) A0053/15 A0062/22
veritable (2) A0433/05 B1333/32
veritably (1) A0429/22
verite (1) B1122/01
vermicular (2) B0950/07 B0950/13
vermin (5) A0319/09
A0694/05 B1158/04 B1158/06 C0142/15
Vernunft (2) A0342/01 A0342/V

verre (2) A0650/06 A0650/07
Versailles (2) A0709/34 B1275/03
verse (4) A0536/V
B1132/12 B1135/16 B1386/08
versed (4) A0627/01
B0983/23 C0404/40 C0404/41
verses (14) A0057/23 A0284/17
A0284/20 A0303/24 A0318/04 A0354/29
A0406/22 B1093/07 B1128/31 B1129/02
B1130/19 B1130/34 B1379/03 B1379/06
versez (1) C0430/36
version (1) C0430/41
version (2) B1152/12 B1360/23
versions (1) B1234/05
vertical (2) B1075/07 C0140/17
vertically (2) B1294/18 B1382/22
Vertu (1) A0160/V
vertu (1) C0430/41
vertus (1) A0119/M
Verulam (3) A0311/30
A0311/V A0313/02
Verus (1) A0120/27
Ververt (1) A0408/29
very (1311)
vessel (116)
vessel's (5) C0067/40
C0117/10 C0133/15 C0142/30 C0187/10
vessels (29) A0591/25
B1078/07 B1078/12 B1080/08 B1081/03
B1160/40 C0065/35 C0067/01 C0088/34
C0097/12 C0098/14 C0098/39 C0099/40
C0105/27 C0106/13 C0106/16 C0107/01
C0148/19 C0149/23 C0157/39 C0158/34
C0159/04 C0159/15 C0160/17 C0176/23
C0398/38 C0525/41 C0526/17 C0536/14
vest (2) B1185/34 C0389/26
vested (1) A0108/29
vestibule (5) A0124/11
A0349/34 A0439/03 B1339/12 B1339/16
vestige (3) A0156/25
A0215/01 B1049/05
Vestris, Ronzi (1) A0079/09
vesture (1) A0675/15
vestures (1) A0675/V
veto (1) A0021/26
veulent (1) A0600/01
vex (4) A0434/02
B0795/30 B0852/16 B1224/15
vexation (5) A0434/14
B0872/18 B0897/06 B1056/20 B1104/14
vexatious (1) C0077/11
vexed (5) A0535/26
B0793/12 B0822/34 B0828/29 B0875/09
via (1) B1068/01
viand (1) A0694/07
vibrated (4) A0616/32
A0692/17 B1167/33 C0420/25
vibrates (3) A0020/15
A0150/V B1038/15
vibration (11) A0104/34
A0136/28 A0157/23 A0691/17 A0691/30
A0692/25 B0742/30 B1038/02 B1213/33
B1213/34 C0075/17
vibrations (4) A0691/V
A0693/03 B1038/03 B1262/15
vibratory (2) B1240/06 B1241/12
vice (7) A0438/19
A0440/11 A0440/34 A0510/14 A0623/09
A0624/07 B1275/27
vice-like (1) C0399/07
Vice-President (2) C0390/33
C0390/38
vices (3) A0440/17
A0622/24 B0906/12
vicinage (2) B0760/V B0866/05
vicinity (71)
vicissitudes (2) A0102/16 B0843/33
victim (34) A0152/10 A0211/06
A0417/01 A0427/15 A0441/17 A0443/29
A0557/30 A0559/06 A0670/06 B0726/28
B0734/05 B0754/01 B0757/03 B0764/01
B0766/34 B0771/07 B0794/23 B0796/32
B0853/25 B0927/25 B0959/22 B1053/30
B1057/31 B1182/23 C0059/32 C0061/19
C0086/22 C0108/07 C0111/33 C0135/33
C0182/30 C0199/13 C0547/31 C0567/03
victim's (1) B1224/13
victims (8) A0298/02
A0546/32 A0566/18 A0684/28 A0687/20
B0857/03 B1157/18 B1224/05
Victoria (2) B1068/05 B1069/03
victorious (1) A0254/01
victory (5) A0127/06
A0128/28 A0433/03 A0529/06 C0188/14
vid (2) B0900/01 B0913/08
vida (2) A0344/25 A0650/06
vide (1) A0650/07
Vidocq (1) A0545/10
vie (1) A0378/M
vie (2) A0440/08 A0500/26
vieille (1) B1007/31
viele (1) B1360/21
Vienna (4) A0445/05
B0904/27 B0993/19 B1380/14
vient (1) A0018/08
view (162)
viewed (8) A0071/03
A0511/17 A0709/05 B1076/25 B1274/10
B1378/M C0109/09 C0430/16
viewing (1) B0750/01
views (21) A0025/22
A0105/13 A0458/23 A0621/22 A0705/34
B0728/24 B0815/24 B0871/35 B0916/05
B0928/13 B1072/23 B1135/28 B1167/29
B1270/34 B1293/21 B1320/01 C0102/01
C0103/19 C0170/33 C0527/19 C0565/06
vigilance (6) A0061/03 A0438/18
A0551/14 B0966/03 C0089/13 C0439/V
vigilant (1) B1334/28
Vigiliae (1) A0409/11
vignette (1) A0664/06
vignetting (1) A0664/16
vigor (16) A0127/28
A0211/18 A0283/08 A0297/05 A0310/M
A0314/27 A0318/V A0459/12 A0557/12
A0557/14 A0638/01 A0692/02 B0727/11
B0928/04 B1014/32 B1123/20
vigorous (15) A0022/01
A0054/32 A0063/33 A0164/26 A0195/V
A0442/28 A0552/04 A0609/15 B0942/05

->B0969/03 B1016/V B1141/32 B1301/37
C0064/19 C0533/08
vigorously (11) A0329/05
A0329/11 B0944/04 B1225/21 B1237/25
B1249/V B1262/07 C0082/20 C0091/13
C0144/24 C0561/08
vigour (6) A0296/V C0101/04
C0122/18 C0130/23 C0194/09 C0197/25
vile (5) A0441/14
B0852/11 B0853/35 B1300/23 B1371/01
vilest (1) A0440/21
vill (2) B0899/28 B0900/01
villa (1) B0866/23
village (40) A0057/02
A0058/01 A0120/20 A0366/27 A0369/20
A0370/15 A0371/18 A0427/34 A0428/28
B0909/20 B0957/24 B0957/27 B0957/34
B1303/07 B1328/12 B1338/10 C0171/06
C0172/18 C0172/34 C0173/17 C0173/23
C0173/38 C0174/16 C0174/35 C0175/35
C0176/14 C0176/31 C0177/16 C0179/35
C0180/13 C0180/36 C0189/01 C0192/07
C0200/14 C0528/14 C0540/30 C0547/01
C0548/12 C0548/13 C0561/06
village/of/B-- (1) B1328/06
villagers (2) C0174/23 C0174/30
villages (4) C0172/35
C0560/23 C0565/31 C0565/33
villain (20) A0092/08
A0114/16 A0346/15 A0347/08 A0374/11
A0445/03 A0447/09 A0487/28 A0623/02
A0653/02 B0824/06 B1108/28 B1128/04
B1133/34 B1138/13 B1183/17 C0073/31
C0108/16 C0111/20 C0427/27
villainous (3) A0251/V
B0911/30 B1300/07
villains (9) A0486/22
B0732/16 B0744/22 B0753/30 B0797/28
C0085/33 C0086/25 C0090/38 C0557/05
villainy (1) B0755/01
villanous (2) A0251/24 B1103/16
Villanova (1) A0294/V
villany (2) B0755/V C0086/15
Villaret (1) A0173/03
villas (1) B0863/37
Vin (1) A0108/V
Vin (2) A0105/V A0439/V
vin (1) A0096/M
Vin/de/Barac (1) A0165/V
Vin/de/Bourgogne (1) A0098/32
vindicate (1) A0203/11
vindicating (1) C0569/19
vindictive (2) B1207/17 C0201/17
vine (6) A0228/27 A0233/08
A0236/04 A0314/14 A0321/19 C0185/05
vine-leaves (1) B0828/09
vinegar (3) C0141/11
C0141/30 C0142/41
vines (3) C0542/14
C0543/19 C0543/35
vini (1) A0125/05
vintages (1) B1257/13
violate (3) A0251/02
B0852/14 B1039/12
violated (3) A0123/20
->A0218/26 B0767/25
violating (1) A0482/02
violation (4) A0703/12
B0769/V B1039/15 B1268/10
violations (1) A0615/13
violator (1) B0764/05
violence (53)
violent (58)
violently (41) A0092/05
A0111/18 A0315/08 A0416/V A0439/19
A0442/08 A0447/02 A0459/28 A0498/27
A0563/21 A0584/15 A0594/14 A0686/29
A0692/18 B0810/29 B0814/31 B0854/31
B0911/13 B0967/14 B1057/05 B1223/12
B1226/V B1242/20 B1262/24 B1349/02
B1353/17 C0059/17 C0062/25 C0063/36
C0074/29 C0082/17 C0094/19 C0107/18
C0112/20 C0121/20 C0134/27 C0139/26
C0140/24 C0144/15 C0197/40 C0204/23
Violet (1) B1294/24
violet (8) A0157/27
A0640/03 A0672/01 A0676/15 B1055/18
B1167/32 B1168/19 B1168/21
violet-coloured (1) A0086/28
violets (4) A0643/09
B1212/32 B1283/08 B1340/22
Virgilius (1) A0111/05
virgin (2) B0942/33 B1363/31
Virginia (7) B0939/01
B0968/10 C0055/27 C0099/04 C0522/27
C0524/18 C0532/12
Virginian (3) B1329/12
C0531/35 C0532/11
Virtu (3) A0160/05
A0174/30 A0705/12
Virtu (1) A0160/V
virtu (2) A0180/21 B1270/11
virtual (2) B1295/33 B1311/33
virtually (3) B0819/03
B0907/28 B0929/03
virtue (6) A0266/02 A0426/15
B0822/35 B1275/27 B1275/29 B1369/05
virtues (3) A0097/30
A0710/28 B0949/32
virtuoso (1) B1257/08
virtuous (3) A0055/23
A0065/06 B0730/20
virulence (1) B1354/08
virulent (1) C0126/07
vis (1) B0989/16
vis (2) A0493/09 A0493/09
vis-a-vis (2) A0105/17 A0384/16
visage (17) A0057/31
A0068/10 A0126/03 A0245/V A0247/32
A0298/V A0298/V A0429/01 A0498/V
A0507/35 A0510/16 A0511/07 A0665/V
A0675/10 B0826/21 B0911/10 B1003/26
viscera (2) A0059/23 A0067/14
visible (63)
visibly (6) A0215/25 A0321/05
A0610/18 A0642/26 A0665/16 B1299/32
vision (59)
visionaries (1) A0209/14
Visionary (1) A0150/V
visionary (4) A0151/10

->B0823/02 B1249/27 C0565/07
visions (19) A0151/03
A0166/05 A0210/17 A0210/17 A0326/07
A0327/26 A0328/19 A0427/17 A0436/17
A0638/08 A0683/03 B0865/18 B0889/23
B1106/15 B1385/34 C0065/19 C0065/22
C0066/18 C0125/28
visit (34) A0090/18 A0176/16
A0182/17 A0261/03 A0338/33 A0365/05
A0386/30 A0402/28 A0654/24 B0753/10
B0755/22 B0756/12 B0756/27 B0808/26
B0811/12 B0813/08 B0863/13 B0914/20
B0923/26 B0981/33 B0991/29 B0992/28
B1005/29 B1152/21 B1292/07 C0069/38
C0155/33 C0170/08 C0171/06 C0174/05
C0179/34 C0180/38 C0194/09 C0395/04
visitant (1) C0111/34
visitarem (2) A0209/M A0218/15
visitation (4) A0090/15
A0459/25 B1224/19 C0111/36
visitations (1) A0081/33
visited (30) A0164/03 A0645/02
B0723/21 B0759/31 B0808/04 B0853/04
B0865/06 B0865/13 B0923/25 B0933/21
B1002/05 B1045/25 B1291/08 B1294/10
C0055/05 C0057/11 C0057/24 C0072/02
C0093/26 C0101/39 C0154/25 C0155/23
C0155/38 C0171/17 C0524/30 C0527/26
C0560/23 C0566/06 C0566/40 C0568/35
visiter (20) A0108/09
A0109/20 A0111/01 A0111/24 A0112/07
A0114/14 A0161/28 A0263/05 A0263/33
A0322/23 A0562/08 A0562/V B0728/06
B0733/36 B0975/15 B0975/34 B0991/25
B1278/32 B1280/27 B1331/22
visiter's (5) A0104/31
A0105/10 A0105/21 A0106/07 A0107/27
visiters (5) B0796/26
B0872/12 B0958/30 B1278/28 C0169/22
visiting (10) A0218/V A0461/16
B0863/13 B0991/02 B1155/21 C0084/07
C0084/22 C0085/09 C0180/13 C0558/01
visitor (8) A0089/20
A0090/05 A0090/21 A0092/31 A0322/V
A0383/10 A0458/31 B0877/14
visitor's (2) A0091/28 A0104/20
visitors (4) A0532/21
B1005/11 B1019/08 B1019/11
visits (1) B0809/23
vist (1) B1103/33
vista (10) A0036/07 A0316/08
A0602/27 A0671/18 B1247/22 B1280/31
B1281/18 B1282/10 B1282/19 C0198/37
vistas (1) B1212/16
visual (3) A0613/11
B0967/02 C0438/V
vita (1) A0681/M
vital (4) B1187/15
B1298/12 B1312/23 B1317/15
vitality (11) A0157/V
A0321/27 A0322/V A0401/16 A0601/16
B0955/29 B0957/32 B1188/21 B1235/25
B1240/04 C0072/22
vitally (2) A0458/09 B1316/20
vituperate (1) A0622/22
vituperative (2) A0057/24 A0068/08
vivacious (2) A0401/20 A0402/20
vivacity (7) A0081/03
A0284/08 A0413/18 A0437/26 A0460/05
A0510/28 A0695/32
vivat (1) A0125/04
vivente (2) A0092/34 A0112/11
Vivian (3) A0079/06
A0079/06 A0079/06
Vivian/Grey (2) A0079/05 A0079/05
vivid (34) A0215/06 A0216/19
A0248/24 A0274/13 A0293/04 A0293/04
A0316/05 A0325/26 A0399/31 A0405/18
A0430/33 A0438/09 A0439/26 A0439/27
A0498/11 A0503/02 A0507/13 A0532/07
A0613/13 A0640/10 A0663/20 B1278/35
B1281/01 B1329/21 B1331/08 B1332/33
B1337/33 B1338/32 B1354/03 C0065/08
C0190/01 C0197/33 C0405/22 C0542/08
vividly (9) A0210/30
A0316/16 A0417/09 A0437/16 A0641/V
A0671/30 B0955/14 B1223/11 B1234/29
vividness (1) B0948/17
vivo (1) A0662/V
vivre (1) A0135/M
vivus (1) A0018/M
vixen (2) A0052/01 A0062/03
viz (6) B0744/11 B0761/01
B1077/26 B1299/31 B1358/04 B1383/01
viz. (1) C0207/31
vizier (5) B1152/22
B1152/29 B1152/32 B1152/33 B1152/33
vizier's (1) B1152/04
vocal (4) A0244/18
B0905/20 B0905/29 B1337/16
vocalists (1) B0904/28
voce (1) A0382/26
vociferate (1) A0075/13
vociferated (7) A0088/25
A0092/35 A0103/04 A0112/V B0824/13
B0931/35 B1312/04
vociferation (1) B1056/35
vociferations (2) C0175/16 C0201/21
vociferous (1) A0294/V
voice (170)
voiceless (1) A0600/21
voices (33) A0047/24
A0074/31 A0143/15 A0216/23 A0373/02
A0387/02 A0407/22 A0537/16 A0540/07
A0541/28 A0542/21 A0542/28 A0543/02
A0547/22 A0548/27 A0548/28 A0549/08
A0549/10 A0550/21 A0558/17 A0559/31
A0681/05 A0697/07 A0697/V B0944/31
B1014/18 B1102/07 B1191/12 B1294/23
C0086/33 C0123/24 C0190/22 C0550/21
void (4) A0080/21
A0616/31 A0643/32 B0963/04
voila (1) A0037/08
Voissart (11) B0887/28
B0888/04 B0912/17 B0912/18 B0912/20
B0912/22 B0912/24 B0912/30 B0913/02
B0913/25 B0913/27
Voissart, Victor (1) B0887/27
volant (1) C0430/29
volatile (2) B1168/25 C0537/29

volatilized (1) C0402/16
volcanic (6) B1161/29 B1321/28
  B1322/17 C0420/30 C0422/30 C0422/34
volcano (2) B1161/30 B1321/09
volcanoes (4) B1215/28
  B1215/33 B1321/V B1322/V
volition (12) A0315/05
  A0478/19 A0612/35 A0613/09 B0941/34
  B0948/10 B0948/15 B1034/03 B1037/34
  B1038/32 B1039/07 B1241/14
volley (1) A0245/07
Voltaic (2) B1167/34 B1181/16
Voltaire (1) B1345/14
voluble (1) B0871/34
volume (38) A0088/16 A0090/04
  A0090/21 A0091/10 A0100/29 A0104/08
  A0110/16 A0164/V A0301/06 A0303/17
  A0303/23 A0314/23 A0348/18 A0409/05
  A0413/08 A0473/09 A0497/23 A0532/01
  A0615/28 A0663/10 A0664/27 B0981/02
  B1247/26 B1250/12 B1262/30 B1282/31
  B1314/09 B1384/14 B1386/10 C0392/10
  C0401/41 C0421/16 C0423/26 C0432/09
  C0432/38 C0536/35 C0575/07 C0575/25
volumes (20) A0101/07
  A0198/20 A0198/21 A0209/22 A0225/14
  A0226/21 A0230/20 A0278/24 A0283/36
  A0283/37 A0300/30 A0343/11 A0501/12
  B0981/09 B1115/05 B1115/20 B1128/21
  B1246/22 C0189/25 C0393/01
voluminous (4) A0088/05
  A0102/27 A0641/05 A0643/20
voluminousness (1) A0509/11
volunteered (4) A0540/30
  C0127/06 C0136/41 C0179/31
voluptuary (1) C0179/12
voluptuous (9) A0022/01
  A0036/11 A0312/20 A0663/V A0671/15
  B0863/02 C0093/32 C0536/30 C0542/04
voluptuousness (3) B1122/08
  B1280/20 B1340/02
volutes (1) A0322/12
volution (2) B0730/10 B0766/31
Von (2) A0292/V A0299/09
von (13) A0372/22
  A0372/23 A0372/24 A0372/24 B0912/18
  B0912/25 B0912/26 B0912/V B0913/04
  B0913/04 B0913/06 B0913/07 B0913/10
Von/C-- (1) A0294/V
Von/Hardenburg (1) B0723/26
Von/Jung (2) A0302/27 A0303/09
Von/Kempelen (15) B1357/07
  B1357/T B1358/11 B1360/09 B1360/13
  B1360/17 B1360/26 B1361/04 B1361/20
  B1361/29 B1361/33 B1362/24 B1364/04
  B1364/22 B1364/26
Von/Kempelen's (3) B1357/05
  B1363/33 B1364/15
Von/Underduk (3) C0390/28
  C0390/37 C0426/39
Von/Weber (1) A0405/14
Vonder (1) A0366/09
vonder (1) A0365/V
Vondervotteimittiss (17) A0365/02
  A0365/17 A0366/03 A0366/22 A0367/17
  ->A0369/11 A0369/15 A0369/21 A0369/28
  A0370/09 A0370/16 A0370/32 A0371/15
  A0372/10 A0372/23 A0373/12 A0374/20
Vondervotteimittiss (1) A0366/09
vool (3) B1102/06
  B1103/01 B1109/31
Vopiscus, Flavius (1) A0125/34
vor (8) B1102/37
  B1103/02 B1103/07 B1103/08 B1103/09
  B1103/24 B1103/29 B1104/03
voracious (1) C0143/17
voracity (2) A0694/05 A0694/13
vord (1) B1103/03
vortex (8) A0438/11
  A0581/07 A0582/16 A0582/37 A0593/02
  A0703/26 B1268/25 B1383/01
vortices (4) A0580/15
  A0580/24 A0581/26 A0582/32
vot (3) A0373/14 A0373/16 A0373/18
voted (1) B1299/34
votes (1) B1300/05
Votteimittiss (1) A0366/10
vouchsafe (1) B1381/19
vouchsafed (1) B0817/12
voudrait (1) A0033/19
Vougeot (1) B1017/30
Vougeot (2) B1007/24 B1016/28
vould (1) B1375/V
vour (1) A0372/31
vous (2) A0037/20 A0602/07
vow (8) A0642/09
  A0642/14 A0642/21 B1152/14 B1152/18
  B1152/34 B1153/25 B1154/08
vowed (4) A0625/07
  B1256/02 C0066/04 C0391/36
vowel (2) B1370/32 B1371/15
vows (5) A0644/09
  A0645/09 A0654/11 A0673/04 B1107/13
Voyage (1) A0409/01
Voyage (1) C0430/27
voyage (75)
voyager (6) B1079/01 B1279/28
  B1280/33 B1281/16 B1282/23 C0432/35
voyager's (1) B0865/03
voyagers (13) B1075/13
  B1081/21 C0535/33 C0539/37 C0540/01
  C0540/12 C0544/02 C0545/25 C0547/30
  C0551/20 C0560/23 C0561/01 C0564/03
voyages (8) B1074/18
  B1164/21 C0068/19 C0099/05 C0148/08
  C0432/36 C0534/31 C0550/10
voyageur (1) C0529/18
voyageur (1) C0553/20
voyageurs (1) C0549/07
vrai (2) A0034/08 A0036/05
Vredenburg's (1) C0067/38
Vredenburgh (2) C0057/15 C0065/30
Vredenburgh, Peter (1) C0163/34
Vrinch (1) B1296/12
vrow (2) A0372/24 C0388/37
vrows (2) A0373/16 C0436/V
vs (1) A0477/T
vulgar (11) A0161/07
  A0336/04 A0337/16 A0432/18 A0459/08
  A0527/V A0623/32 B0810/08 B0926/21

->B1092/01 B1250/27
vulgarly (3) B1004/14
B1096/20 B1293/01
vull (1) B1109/34
vulnerable (1) A0433/26
vulture (6) A0078/32 A0599/M
B0789/13 B0793/09 B0794/30 B0940/V
vultures (1) A0315/09
Vurrgh (5) A0579/24
A0579/27 A0580/10 A0581/20 A0583/23
vy (4) B0911/28
B0912/V B1103/09 B1104/02
VI (2) A0268/22 A0407/33
VII (1) A0269/13
VIII (1) A0270/01
W. (25) C0136/05
C0147/27 C0148/27 C0154/23 C0155/10
C0155/15 C0157/08 C0157/09 C0157/10
C0157/27 C0158/14 C0159/16 C0160/07
C0161/39 C0162/05 C0162/24 C0163/04
C0163/38 C0164/19 C0166/03 C0167/22
C0399/22 C0399/22 C0412/04 C0526/07
W./V./B. (1) A0024/01
W-- (6) A0057/37 A0058/09
A0058/16 A0068/21 A0068/32 A0069/04
wadded (1) C0533/19
wadding (1) B0979/36
waddle (1) A0070/25
waddled (2) C0388/09 C0388/10
wade (1) C0572/30
waded (1) A0197/13
wading (1) C0536/14
wafer (1) A0268/19
wafered (21) A0270/22
A0271/06 A0272/17 A0272/38 A0274/14
A0274/38 A0275/18 A0276/20 A0276/37
A0277/17 A0277/37 A0278/19 A0279/17
A0281/06 A0281/29 A0282/29 A0283/09
A0284/13 A0284/29 A0285/08 A0285/37
wafted (1) C0124/08
wag (1) C0541/19
wager (5) A0624/25
A0626/09 B0761/19 B0761/19 B0761/22
wagers (1) A0623/24
wagged (1) B1338/23
waggeries (2) A0175/24 A0181/21
wagging (2) A0091/29 A0110/31
wagon (2) B1055/24 B1329/12
wagoner's (1) A0565/V
wags (2) B1293/36 C0427/16
wailing (1) B0859/03
wailings (1) A0036/13
wainscoting (1) A0447/20
waist (17) A0254/02
A0447/05 A0629/11 B0730/26 B0730/27
B0765/21 B0765/22 B0910/V B1180/23
B1261/28 B1351/06 C0060/31 C0063/19
C0118/33 C0196/29 C0552/06 C0552/30
waist-coat (2) B0908/V B0910/V
waistband (4) C0083/14
C0105/06 C0119/20 C0398/04
waistcoat (10) A0509/15 B0809/15
B0830/24 B0878/01 B0908/05 B1049/18
B1049/20 B1051/10 B1052/26 B1058/01
waistcoat-pocket (1) B0851/27
waistcoats (2) A0368/18 A0508/34
wait (22) A0088/31 A0103/10
A0486/10 A0586/35 A0629/28 A0650/26
B0810/01 B0873/27 B0873/30 B0984/37
B1046/30 B1208/34 B1236/18 B1318/05
C0072/04 C0091/37 C0105/34 C0133/38
C0550/01 C0551/20 C0556/19 C0561/12
waited (14) A0105/17 A0138/29
A0413/28 A0483/30 A0693/31 B0754/12
B0794/26 B0808/V B0923/27 B1208/35
B1318/06 B1352/01 C0168/03 C0176/15
waiters (1) B1010/23
waiting (12) A0035/01
A0043/V A0046/02 A0164/V A0400/22
A0468/13 B0908/26 B1372/12 C0067/07
C0079/16 C0186/27 C0187/35
wake (3) A0123/14
B1155/05 B1238/29
waked (1) B1090/34
wakeful (1) B0929/08
wakefulness (1) B0963/30
waken (2) B1242/25 C0416/04
wakes (1) B1090/32
wakes> (1) A0464/08
waking (7) A0327/26
A0437/26 A0638/V A0664/03 B0944/10
B0946/09 B0965/07
Wales (3) B1072/32
B1075/22 C0063/11
Wales' (1) C0525/30
walk (25) A0070/25
A0071/30 A0080/08 A0188/M A0228/27
A0348/20 A0490/25 A0513/04 A0515/26
A0554/06 A0686/14 B0814/23 B0855/11
B0863/08 B0875/18 B0965/09 B1090/14
B1105/21 B1161/28 B1346/07 C0151/17
C0152/28 C0536/09 C0559/20 C0571/23
walked (18) A0071/30 A0174/10
A0174/16 A0196/13 A0510/20 A0512/18
A0512/23 A0514/02 A0515/22 A0546/21
A0563/16 A0641/16 B0818/07 B0858/17
B0872/27 B0943/20 B1225/21 C0181/23
walker (1) B0741/17
walking (7) A0072/20
A0261/04 A0488/13 B1185/34 B1372/12
C0429/37 C0533/26
Walking-Advertisement (1) A0484/08
walking/gentlemen (1) B1045/07
Walking/Advertiser (1) A0484/31
walks (5) A0428/25
B0749/09 B0749/16 B0749/18 B0749/23
wall (85)
walled (5) B0761/13
B0857/03 B0857/V B0859/15 C0561/33
Wallenstein (1) B1234/05
<u>Wallenstein</u> (1) A0150/V
wallet (3) A0112/24
B0810/37 C0085/28
walls (73)
Walnut (1) B1092/32
walnut (2) B1282/06 C0541/31
walnuts (2) B1332/04 B1332/05
Walsh, Robert (1) A0265/14
waltz (1) A0405/14
waltzers (3) A0672/30

->A0674/16 A0675/20
Wampoo (1) C0174/33
Wampoos (1) C0173/02
wan (8) A0198/13
A0227/06 A0231/17 A0234/29 A0311/12
A0319/15 A0401/28 A0412/08
wand (1) B0944/34
wander (2) C0387/M C0392/06
wandered (6) A0078/15 A0157/19
A0328/04 A0639/24 B1338/10 C0198/07
wanderer (6) A0033/04 A0513/09
A0515/25 B0760/08 B0807/34 B0823/16
wanderers (2) A0407/07 A0457/26
wandering (6) A0320/08 A0347/15
A0567/08 A0599/M B1247/26 C0551/33
wanderings (2) A0078/16 A0601/32
waned (9) A0197/04
A0197/11 A0197/20 A0197/31 A0326/18
A0411/17 A0411/17 A0614/10 B0796/06
waning (1) A0674/06
wanness (2) A0327/20 A0404/14
want (41) A0091/21
A0110/25 A0246/15 A0261/09 A0274/12
A0284/33 A0387/V A0388/02 A0401/34
A0402/01 A0487/11 A0497/07 A0497/13
A0508/26 A0625/01 A0650/29 B0766/09
B0806/03 B0818/23 B0819/24 B0871/31
B0872/34 B1034/22 B1072/08 B1076/24
B1143/10 B1206/01 B1219/07 B1220/22
B1347/32 B1348/28 C0067/22 C0081/39
C0084/19 C0097/14 C0141/17 C0183/06
C0404/13 C0420/33 C0425/41 C0537/12
wanted (20) A0097/16
A0370/21 A0370/28 A0371/28 A0372/13
B0878/34 B1105/29 B1105/31 B1157/36
B1236/26 C0070/09 C0110/21 C0156/25
C0391/23 C0411/18 C0419/31 C0428/17
C0432/17 C0530/16 C0568/13
wantin> (1) A0464/05
wanting (17) A0044/02
A0044/23 A0086/17 A0096/16 A0098/24
A0316/17 A0438/25 A0464/V B0760/26
B0765/10 B1331/06 C0075/23 C0092/22
C0148/23 C0174/24 C0391/16 C0401/19
wanton (3) A0020/V
A0673/25 C0568/14
wants (2) A0478/33 A0609/36
Wappatomies (1) C0551/06
Wappytooties (1) C0551/08
war (12) A0125/35
A0142/17 A0381/17 A0600/21 B0870/28
B1278/19 B1294/04 B1294/07 B1318/12
C0548/25 C0551/37 C0557/14
war-coursers (1) A0021/29
war-party (1) C0561/30
war-whoop (1) A0244/15
wardrobe (2) B1019/20 B1185/31
warehouse (1) B1127/03
warehouses (2) B0871/32 B0872/11
wares (2) A0248/25 B0945/12
warlike (2) C0548/23 C0550/13
warm (29) A0214/17
A0227/27 A0232/13 A0496/01 A0499/03
A0502/08 A0538/12 B0759/11 B0810/16
B0834/30 B0922/10 B0942/16 B0958/27
->B1050/02 B1091/18 B1247/21 B1260/04
B1328/09 B1351/27 C0120/11 C0126/30
C0136/04 C0139/36 C0167/01 C0203/13
C0387/10 C0542/22 C0555/23 C0568/06
warm-hearted (1) B1050/18
warmest (2) A0297/13 B0922/14
warming (1) B1073/27
warmly (3) B0965/32
B1054/16 C0166/21
warmth (10) A0328/08 A0401/20
A0709/10 B0956/20 B0962/13 B1054/22
B1123/12 B1257/17 B1280/19 C0127/23
warn (1) C0535/14
warned (3) A0533/03
A0667/31 B0978/06
warning (5) A0058/28
A0610/18 C0061/15 C0080/21 C0186/05
warped (1) C0163/18
warrant (7) A0180/07
A0209/20 A0282/08 A0612/11 B0809/08
B0957/10 C0162/08
warranted (3) A0136/33
B0746/05 B1360/28
Warreconne (1) C0551/28
warring (1) A0145/09
warrior (2) A0125/10 C0552/13
warriors (7) C0180/28
C0186/26 C0188/16 C0203/37 C0551/04
C0551/27 C0558/10
wars (1) A0459/08
wary (4) A0102/21
B0796/14 C0172/28 C0545/11
was (5326)
wash (1) B0796/13
washed (13) A0438/13
A0490/29 A0538/35 B1181/09 C0108/09
C0117/07 C0118/28 C0139/35 C0140/04
C0140/13 C0142/40 C0178/41 C0559/15
washing (6) A0092/08 A0111/20
C0110/17 C0117/38 C0169/19 C0536/34
Washington (7) A0275/22
A0277/02 A0279/02 B1192/09 B1304/17
B1304/20 B1305/06
Washington, George (1) B1304/12
washingtubs (1) B1092/01
Washish (2) B1158/33 B1159/03
wasn't (16) A0336/10
A0383/31 A0384/20 A0385/09 A0385/33
A0466/14 A0468/14 A0468/17 A0468/28
A0468/30 A0470/10 A0470/11 A0470/12
A0470/14 A0470/17 A0656/09
Wasp (2) C0158/07 C0160/29
Wasp/Bay (2) C0151/01 C0151/05
Wassatoons (1) C0565/38
wast (1) A0034/22
waste (4) A0097/06
A0591/22 A0604/04 B1029/05
waste-pipes (1) A0588/13
wasted (2) A0246/32 B1073/13
wasteful (1) B1008/34
wasting (5) A0151/11
A0404/17 A0495/V A0604/07 C0134/34
watape (1) C0534/17
Watarhoo (1) C0551/26
watch (54)

watch-box (1) A0546/19
watch-house (1) B1143/05
watch's (1) B0793/20
watched (17) A0136/14
A0234/15 A0509/08 A0513/22 A0515/11
A0565/06 A0616/15 A0641/06 A0689/34
A0695/10 B1004/17 B1302/17 C0096/02
C0169/30 C0189/21 C0547/30 C0553/11
watchers (1) B1362/05
watches (9) A0352/26
A0370/02 A0372/25 A0372/V A0373/04
A0509/02 A0615/10 A0642/26 B0828/14
watchful (1) A0600/24
watching (12) A0212/01
A0234/02 A0324/19 B0894/33 B0901/05
B0901/V C0061/30 C0084/11 C0095/31
C0549/39 C0568/25 C0579/14
watchman (1) B1093/06
water (327)
water-casks (1) B1073/25
water-clock (1) C0416/36
water-colour (1) B0948/25
water-dog (5) A0054/25
A0063/26 A0091/30 A0099/16 A0102/20
water-fall (1) A0602/25
water-gate (2) A0153/18 A0155/24
water-jug (1) C0141/04
water-kegs (1) C0424/39
water-lilies (8) A0195/09
A0196/13 A0196/20 A0197/07 A0197/08
A0197/26 A0198/02 A0198/07
water-logged (1) A0137/10
water-melon (1) B1292/31
water-tight (1) C0147/19
water's (2) B1280/08 C0152/22
watercask (1) A0589/25
waterfall (1) B1186/01
waterfalls (1) C0412/32
waters (45) A0087/27
A0088/04 A0097/09 A0106/25 A0144/01
A0151/06 A0152/10 A0157/01 A0195/05
A0197/07 A0198/06 A0213/14 A0227/27
A0232/13 A0343/27 A0400/20 A0408/17
A0408/21 A0417/16 A0456/04 A0578/34
A0580/13 A0600/23 A0612/03 A0640/20
B0771/05 B1079/06 B1122/28 B1160/20
B1333/24 B1382/18 C0072/23 C0178/17
C0417/16 C0443/V C0444/V C0527/24
C0527/25 C0527/31 C0528/17 C0536/37
C0536/39 C0547/33 C0553/18 C0574/30
watery (1) A0139/27
Waukerassah (3) C0566/06
C0566/39 C0568/40
wave (12) A0079/13
A0079/13 A0140/04 A0587/34 A0640/24
A0694/03 A0694/35 B1225/22 C0117/17
C0118/05 C0139/12 C0149/32
waved (1) A0252/14
waver (2) A0512/12 C0578/37
wavering (3) A0277/13
C0093/27 C0112/19
wavers (1) A0456/23
waves (11) A0195/15
A0582/33 A0587/28 A0588/09 A0594/13
B0864/33 B1156/03 C0106/27 C0115/39
->C0444/V C0567/39
waving (8) A0078/36
A0675/30 A0682/01 B1078/14 C0072/22
C0118/13 C0542/11 C0575/11
wavy (2) A0644/V C0076/09
Wawandysenche (1) C0548/10
wax (11) A0265/25
A0266/20 A0267/36 A0269/09 A0269/37
A0271/27 A0273/26 A0276/02 A0283/30
B1009/02 C0077/31
wax-light (1) B1224/17
waxen (2) A0316/22 B1351/27
way (410)
waylaid (1) B0979/03
waylayings (2) B0979/08 B0988/22
ways (9) A0092/32
A0112/09 A0514/04 A0577/M A0577/M
A0639/29 A0650/11 B0869/06 C0123/03
wayward (1) C0107/27
waywardness (1) A0514/12
<u>we</u> (1) C0180/32
we (1) B0928/23
we (2696)
we'll (3) A0343/33
A0466/21 A0655/29
weak (22) A0190/22 A0430/30
A0441/02 A0499/08 A0651/23 A0654/03
A0665/20 A0691/18 B0763/33 B0888/14
B0989/01 B0990/25 B1090/12 B1213/20
B1257/05 B1360/15 C0074/39 C0094/20
C0120/05 C0146/17 C0184/12 C0430/18
weak-minded (3) A0427/25
A0440/24 A0483/09
weaken (1) A0578/03
weakened (6) A0663/V B1069/33
B1273/35 C0125/33 C0132/10 C0144/31
weakening (1) C0401/33
weaker (3) A0020/01
B0946/30 C0391/24
weakest (1) A0387/V
weakness (27) A0227/08
A0231/19 A0310/M A0314/29 A0319/24
A0320/02 A0428/14 A0433/29 A0446/09
A0654/06 A0686/04 B0853/01 B0888/15
B0899/06 B0906/21 B0907/20 B0907/21
B0907/V B0915/04 B0915/27 B1003/23
B1211/01 C0094/37 C0122/16 C0128/35
C0145/02 C0399/03
weaknesses (1) A0098/22
Weal-Vor/House (1) B1075/20
Wealth (1) B1303/21
wealth (23) A0135/03
A0157/09 A0296/19 A0320/06 A0496/09
A0496/18 A0704/22 A0705/02 A0705/15
A0711/34 B0827/23 B0852/34 B0890/12
B0926/22 B0957/13 B1093/02 B1179/10
B1269/22 B1270/01 B1270/13 B1270/28
B1277/01 C0525/34
wealthier (1) B0874/30
wealthiest (2) A0440/09 B1044/10
wealthy (14) A0019/21 A0157/06
A0442/06 B0806/03 B0892/11 B0895/30
B0899/20 B0914/17 B0941/06 B1045/21
B1047/23 B1127/26 B1138/03 B1304/35
weapon (5) A0544/03

->A0544/05 A0565/07 C0199/26 C0579/22
weapons (8) B0946/31
B1352/12 C0105/20 C0174/21 C0186/39
C0556/01 C0557/28 C0578/06
wear (14) A0250/13 A0403/05
A0587/13 B0746/16 B0869/21 B0907/30
B0907/31 B0908/07 B0908/13 B0908/16
B0910/09 B0910/13 B1049/25 B1226/18
wearer (3) A0248/08
B0890/13 C0553/25
wearer's (1) C0552/14
wearers (1) B1008/04
wearied (7) A0515/24
A0612/19 A0689/35 A0691/08 B1345/13
B1347/33 C0399/31
wearily (1) B0963/10
weariness (2) A0196/28 B0892/29
wearing (8) A0379/V
A0447/04 A0485/05 A0623/16 B0888/17
B1008/07 B1224/01 C0095/03
wearisomeness (1) A0683/22
wears (11) A0126/V
A0280/03 A0368/04 A0369/04 A0464/T
A0465/02 A0470/24 B0840/04 B0877/36
B0897/24 B1250/29
weary (7) A0320/08
B0825/06 B0896/16 B1318/02 B1384/34
C0086/26 C0412/36
weasel (1) B0869/22
weather (82)
weather-beaten (1) A0143/04
weather-forechains (1) C0122/05
weather-lanyards (1) C0114/25
weathercock (1) A0294/V
weathered (1) C0139/33
weathering (2) C0164/13 C0203/07
weathers (1) B1093/05
weaving (1) B0724/31
web (3) A0682/25 A0682/26 B0940/V
web-feet (1) B1156/30
web-like (1) A0402/02
web-work (2) A0400/08 B1259/02
wed (2) B0901/29 B0957/18
wedded (4) A0644/V
A0645/01 A0665/01 B0887/V
Weddel, James (1) C0157/11
Weddell (2) C0160/26 C0162/09
Weddell, James (1) C0160/16
wedding (4) A0052/02
A0062/04 A0650/24 B1153/08
wedge (1) B1248/21
wedged (4) A0543/15
C0069/05 C0074/34 C0159/22
wedges (1) C0098/35
Wednesday (6) B0729/28 B0731/32
B0731/33 B0732/31 B0744/14 B1030/26
weed (1) A0667/16
weehawken (1) B0726/33
week (42) A0203/07 A0428/24
A0438/21 A0583/32 A0584/11 A0649/T
A0651/15 A0651/17 A0656/24 A0667/53
B0726/10 B0726/15 B0727/08 B0727/16
B0728/01 B0750/09 B0753/03 B0753/07
B0753/12 B0753/15 B0759/14 B0759/27
B0760/10 B0789/21 B0896/28 B0924/04
->B0933/11 B0949/28 B0979/17 B1006/09
B1046/31 B1048/29 B1137/34 B1143/34
B1241/30 B1347/14 B1361/11 C0065/06
C0156/27 C0170/36 C0188/37 C0543/40
weekdays (1) B0760/01
weekly (2) B0731/06 B0735/03
weeks (41) A0213/09
A0227/19 A0232/05 A0303/32 A0398/15
A0439/28 A0483/22 A0616/14 A0654/26
A0665/10 A0665/30 B0726/32 B0735/06
B0751/04 B0756/28 B0759/24 B0808/04
B0843/04 B0854/31 B0897/10 B0925/07
B0962/16 B0963/04 B1005/21 B1073/19
B1079/29 B1131/13 B1143/10 B1166/14
B1181/09 B1224/07 C0066/28 C0107/36
C0149/06 C0154/02 C0155/29 C0158/01
C0428/08 C0448/V C0522/23 C0567/10
weep (1) B1215/24
weeping (7) A0153/V
A0696/17 C0085/40 C0123/06 C0130/38
C0131/16 C0144/41
weeps (1) A0163/15
weigh (3) C0070/10
C0137/33 C0142/09
weighed (5) A0584/04
A0585/10 B1071/29 B1168/07 C0142/08
weighing (6) A0047/04 B1089/20
B1166/31 B1303/33 C0137/35 C0138/20
weight (71)
weightier (1) A0578/08
weights (3) B1073/21
B1073/24 C0403/18
weighty (4) A0402/23
A0690/20 B1166/05 B1329/14
Weilburg (1) B1070/26
weird (6) A0608/31 B0943/V
B0945/29 B0955/15 B1039/V B1279/31
welcome (7) A0098/16
A0158/11 B0796/24 B0808/14 B0901/V
B0974/16 B0982/25
welcomed (2) A0205/06 A0412/12
Weld, H. Hastings (1) B0731/38
welded (1) A0671/01
welfare (4) A0250/28
A0282/14 B1140/19 B1222/22
well (559)
well-arranged (2) B0863/15 B1331/05
well-being (1) B1221/11
well-built (1) C0531/25
well-concerted (1) A0114/15
well-conditioned (1) C0387/10
well-considered (1) B1318/13
well-contrived (1) B1353/02
well-digested (1) B0986/31
well-directed (1) B1032/07
well-dressed (1) B0872/16
well-feigned (1) A0441/30
well-flavoured (1) C0176/35
well-frequented (1) A0055/32
well-furnished (1) A0497/06
well-grounded (1) A0316/13
well-informed (1) A0491/01
well-knit (1) A0144/13
well-known (10) A0105/10 A0385/31
A0413/21 A0498/13 A0602/06 B0831/08

->B1053/V B1069/18 B1234/03 B1244/01
well-meant (1) B0813/21
well-merited (2) A0055/22 A0065/06
well-modelled (1) C0106/35
well-oiled (1) A0508/24
well-regulated (3) A0486/32
A0622/26 C0153/28
well-settled (1) B1318/13
well-sized (3) A0266/12
A0269/01 A0278/14
well-sustained (1) A0296/V
well-timed (1) C0546/23
well-to-do (1) B0878/03
well-tuned (1) A0407/10
welled (2) B0794/10 B1279/34
Wellingtons (1) A0489/15
wells (3) A0687/27
B1193/15 C0196/06
Welsh (2) B1177/06 B1178/06
weltering (1) A0158/04
went (202)
wept (7) A0172/06
A0178/07 A0348/14 A0642/20 B1020/34
B1142/02 C0094/31
were (2010)
Wertemuller (1) A0294/V
Werther (1) A0342/V
wery (2) B1373/15 B1373/20
West (3) B1077/32
B1369/12 C0093/20
west (43) A0159/02
A0368/07 A0594/10 A0602/18 A0655/25
A0657/01 A0657/18 A0657/20 B1079/17
B1081/08 B1330/36 B1331/27 B1331/35
B1335/13 B1336/03 B1336/21 B1336/23
B1336/28 B1337/19 B1339/24 B1339/25
B1339/26 C0088/31 C0102/14 C0148/14
C0157/24 C0157/30 C0159/33 C0160/15
C0160/34 C0193/05 C0203/24 C0203/25
C0432/26 C0524/29 C0524/36 C0526/04
C0526/05 C0565/34 C0567/16 C0568/09
C0575/15 C0575/17
West/India (1) C0103/09
westerly (3) C0148/23
C0162/27 C0570/09
Western (1) B1166/30
western (24) A0603/04
A0604/18 A0672/15 A0672/22 B0807/05
B0807/09 B0862/05 B1333/18 B1334/30
B1336/09 B1336/17 B1336/37 B1392/05
C0154/08 C0157/34 C0158/11 C0164/12
C0180/27 C0184/38 C0193/03 C0418/38
C0526/31 C0529/11 C0532/14
Westminster (1) A0179/15
westward (26) A0136/15 B0824/33
B0863/33 B0942/13 B1192/19 B1281/31
C0104/32 C0140/35 C0149/14 C0151/05
C0153/33 C0154/19 C0156/28 C0156/30
C0157/29 C0159/35 C0160/03 C0160/12
C0163/26 C0164/10 C0165/29 C0407/32
C0417/19 C0527/12 C0528/32 C0536/37
westwardly (5) A0195/22
A0674/05 B0864/20 C0155/08 C0527/31
wet (7) A0135/M
B1091/13 C0148/18 C0183/37 C0395/29

->C0405/34 C0552/10
wetting (1) C0405/15
whale (2) C0093/24 C0149/08
whale-fishery (1) C0138/17
whale-ship (1) C0161/27
whaleboat (1) C0091/01
whaleboats (1) C0088/07
whalebone (2) B1059/08 B1059/10
whales (5) A0581/37
A0582/25 C0155/21 C0160/08 C0167/11
whaling (6) C0057/18 C0063/09
C0065/32 C0078/29 C0084/38 C0099/40
whaling-ship (2) C0061/04 C0061/11
whaling-ships (1) C0149/07
whaling-vessel (1) C0068/03
whar (1) B0811/26
wharf (11) B0771/17
B0771/19 B0771/23 B0814/06 B0873/19
B0873/20 B0923/32 B0924/31 C0058/28
C0058/37 C0067/11
what (996)
whatever (89)
whatsoever (14) A0106/27 A0279/06
A0366/02 A0431/26 B1167/26 B1383/03
C0158/02 C0199/02 C0401/20 C0405/12
C0422/26 C0437/V C0441/V C0445/V
Wheal-Vor (1) B1081/12
wheel (3) A0057/05
A0066/32 B1059/18
wheel-route (1) B1329/22
wheel-tracks (1) B1329/16
wheeled (2) A0090/05 A0566/17
wheels (6) A0351/30 A0351/33
B0955/33 B1089/03 B1092/02 B1329/09
wheezed (2) A0054/26 A0063/26
wheezing (2) A0247/11 C0081/30
whelmed (2) A0603/16 A0605/08
when (1001)
whence (20) A0403/23
A0411/32 A0417/06 A0439/33 A0445/11
A0513/33 A0529/23 A0553/24 A0639/21
A0682/35 A0685/26 B0940/02 B1353/29
B1382/12 C0190/23 C0192/02 C0207/44
C0208/06 C0552/01 C0575/09
whenever (23) A0486/03
A0532/04 A0653/11 B0789/14 B0855/09
B0928/25 B1096/26 B1144/15 B1161/27
B1241/12 B1257/14 B1280/15 B1292/17
B1292/20 B1346/36 B1347/02 C0060/15
C0094/22 C0162/26 C0422/04 C0432/23
C0541/14 C0541/22
where (330)
where's (1) A0387/V
whereabout (1) A0035/V
whereabouts (8) A0035/03
B0731/15 B0751/21 B0770/04 B0823/09
B1052/22 C0184/19 C0580/05
whereas (3) B1096/18
C0136/22 C0429/13
whereby (1) A0122/30
wherein (8) A0153/05
A0293/21 A0296/V A0366/18 A0408/02
C0097/01 C0423/36 C0438/V
whereof (2) A0414/25 C0387/M
whereupon (3) A0191/01

->B0876/24 B1015/24
wherever (11) A0367/20
A0694/08 B0727/24 B0851/01 B0959/31
B1009/03 B1304/34 C0088/14 C0138/14
C0153/16 C0571/16
wherewith (3) A0067/20
A0623/29 B1303/10
whether (77)
whetting (1) B1349/18
which (3552)
whiff (1) B0979/11
whiffs (2) B0982/16 C0390/19
Whig (1) A0074/32
whig (1) B1185/V
while (446)
whilst (1) B1225/08
whim (8) A0296/03
A0440/33 A0445/25 A0651/27 A0651/V
A0704/22 B1113/09 B1269/21
whims (4) A0262/05
A0532/28 A0547/04 B1009/25
whimsical (6) A0120/11 A0122/V
A0296/V A0298/10 A0432/11 C0433/10
whimsicalities (1) A0295/14
whimsically (1) C0387/27
whine (5) C0073/07
C0073/10 C0076/21 C0091/41 C0169/16
whining (1) A0102/30
whip (4) A0565/11
A0567/11 A0622/31 B0916/17
whip-cord (1) B0817/03
whipcord (3) C0069/30
C0070/15 C0074/36
whipped (3) A0264/22
A0338/01 B1129/18
whipper-snapper (1) A0062/05
whippersnapper (1) A0052/02
whirl (19) A0329/09
A0341/17 A0580/27 A0582/21 A0583/15
A0586/31 A0586/34 A0587/26 A0588/03
A0588/16 A0588/21 A0588/35 A0590/04
A0591/20 A0591/24 A0592/18 A0594/06
B1078/36 C0144/13
whirled (4) A0582/09
A0592/22 B1166/31 C0396/40
whirligig (1) A0371/24
whirling (7) A0035/07
A0146/02 A0166/V A0354/22 A0580/15
B1381/29 C0063/33
whirlingly (1) A0674/13
whirlpool (8) A0137/19
A0146/07 A0253/11 A0581/04 A0582/37
A0588/01 A0593/10 A0594/04
whirlpools (3) A0580/20
A0584/14 C0144/19
whirls (1) A0692/26
whirlwind (5) A0029/18
A0412/20 A0417/12 A0447/V B0977/31
whisk (1) A0099/15
whisker (1) A0562/19
whiskers (8) A0371/03
A0379/06 A0379/08 B1097/03 B1184/04
B1186/01 B1234/09 B1361/06
whiskey (8) B1096/32
C0533/41 C0535/03 C0549/37 C0556/09

->C0556/15 C0557/12 C0558/35
whisper (13) A0089/33
A0324/22 A0433/31 A0435/04 A0443/04
A0446/33 A0448/11 A0487/18 A0685/14
B1013/20 B1015/30 B1238/28 C0142/26
whispered (16) A0024/18
A0088/18 A0102/30 A0218/26 A0235/23
A0300/20 A0380/19 A0439/13 A0439/22
B0964/04 B0966/31 B1013/11 B1013/14
B1191/26 B1212/25 C0559/01
whispering (2) A0218/05 A0673/04
whisperingly (1) A0674/26
whisperings (1) C0555/19
whispers (6) A0081/04 A0381/07
A0383/06 A0435/34 A0614/01 A0693/01
whiss (1) B1158/34
whist (7) A0384/21
A0529/13 A0529/19 A0529/28 A0655/29
A0656/01 B1293/08
whistle (2) A0387/03 B1353/16
whistled (3) A0387/08
B1225/V C0058/39
whistling (2) A0102/19 A0347/30
whit (2) A0246/09 C0427/36
White (1) C0551/23
white (115)
white-apparelled (1) B0956/28
white-dressed (2) C0552/09 C0552/33
white-plumed (1) B1119/03
White-Paint (1) C0548/10
White-Stone (1) C0548/09
White/river (1) C0551/33
White, Thomas W. (1) C0055/31
B0843/32
whiteness (5) C0208/07
B1234/09 C0107/38 C0206/08
whiter (1) A0681/11
whites (6) A0248/14 A0467/30
C0548/24 C0549/41 C0549/42 C0557/41
whitest (1) B1161/11
whither (6) A0126/22 A0166/05
A0320/28 A0416/15 B0992/24 B1258/07
whither> (3) A0465/27
A0466/22 A0466/22
whiting (1) B1009/32
Whitmore, Richard (1) C0525/33
Whittington (1) B1097/06
whizz (1) B1145/29
Who (1) A0374/11
who (803)
Who's (1) B0793/33
whoever (16) B1129/16
B1129/19 B1129/21 B1130/02 B1130/04
B1130/22 B1130/29 B1130/31 B1131/08
B1131/14 B1131/21 B1131/34 B1131/36
B1191/28 B1318/12 C0134/40
Whole (1) B1141/07
whole (420)
whole-number (1) B1168/17
wholesome (2) A0491/02 C0555/24
wholly (4) A0551/29
B0756/18 B1329/26 C0422/20
whom (166)
whomsoever (2) A0532/V A0534/29
whooping (1) B1021/04
whose (210)

why (186)
wick (1) B0975/09
wicked (7) A0058/26
A0086/17 A0498/20 A0626/22 B0984/34
B1158/10 C0201/16
wickedly (1) A0105/27
wickedness (3) A0427/01
A0622/34 A0703/V
wicker (4) A0253/29
B1071/08 B1073/32 B1337/14
wicker-work (6) A0046/16 C0393/20
C0397/06 C0398/16 C0408/23 C0415/22
wickliffe's (1) B1101/V
wid (9) B0811/33
B0811/34 B0812/04 B0812/29 B0812/29
B0818/23 B0820/18 B0821/15 B0821/24
wid> (31) A0464/09
A0464/10 A0464/17 A0465/07 A0465/09
A0465/20 A0465/29 A0466/03 A0466/16
A0466/17 A0466/24 A0466/25 A0467/07
A0467/15 A0467/17 A0467/25 A0468/02
A0468/08 A0468/10 A0468/16 A0468/22
A0468/24 A0468/27 A0469/04 A0469/11
A0469/16 A0469/22 A0469/22 A0469/24
A0470/02 A0470/12
<u>widdy</u> (1) A0354/33
widdy> (9) A0464/23
A0465/06 A0465/28 A0466/10 A0466/10
A0467/07 A0469/22 A0469/22 A0470/14
widdy's> (2) A0466/18 A0466/25
wide (72)
wide-spreading (1) C0072/19
widely (7) A0098/15
A0153/06 A0398/19 B0956/11 B1239/31
B1336/33 B1378/01
widened (3) A0417/12
B1302/34 C0575/37
widening (2) C0204/20 C0558/29
wider (6) A0265/10 A0479/07
B1157/16 B1337/28 C0575/25 C0576/25
widest (9) A0611/11
A0611/35 A0706/03 B1072/02 B1187/14
B1271/07 B1331/17 B1331/31 B1333/23
widout (1) B0824/24
widow (9) A0026/10
A0384/13 B0725/18 B0892/12 B0914/18
B0915/09 B0915/21 B1107/11 B1107/19
width (16) A0551/18
A0695/20 A0696/36 B0968/19 B1162/06
B1261/12 B1280/04 B1281/28 B1299/16
B1334/14 C0163/18 C0181/06 C0537/38
C0552/07 C0572/08 C0578/04
wield (1) A0156/10
wielded (2) A0544/04 B0977/26
wields (1) A0368/13
wife (76)
wife's (5) A0054/29
A0055/16 A0064/31 A0227/04 A0231/16
wig (8) A0295/12
A0388/09 A0428/34 B0913/20 B1012/02
B1185/07 B1234/11 C0087/15
Wiggins (1) B1293/20
wigless (1) B1107/18
wild (137)
wild-looking (1) A0122/V
wilder (1) A0166/05
wilderness (29) A0020/14
A0020/14 A0045/16 A0045/19 A0121/04
A0121/05 A0128/15 A0137/06 A0158/V
A0195/V A0197/14 A0212/20 A0427/10
A0431/06 A0437/04 A0579/10 A0588/V
B0807/02 B0945/10 C0149/37 C0387/M
C0397/16 C0444/V C0522/08 C0524/04
C0532/19 C0543/39 C0564/18 C0564/32
wildernesses (3) A0640/06
A0711/20 B1276/22
wildest (13) A0027/08
A0137/19 A0320/10 A0321/22 A0427/16
A0427/24 A0515/14 A0537/25 A0558/17
B0862/06 B0889/23 B0946/20 B0946/27
wildly (13) A0311/08
A0311/25 A0317/26 A0412/20 A0439/01
A0512/34 A0683/02 A0684/34 B0899/13
B0940/12 B0945/09 C0124/04 C0190/19
wildness (1) C0198/33
Wiley (3) B1380/03
B1383/15 B1384/14
wilful (1) B1384/12
Wilhelm (1) A0020/03
Wilkie's (1) B1101/04
Wilkins', Peter (1) C0429/20
Will (14) B0807/31 B0809/01
B0811/28 B0811/33 B0812/21 B0812/26
B0814/12 B0814/16 B0818/15 B0819/06
B0820/10 B0820/28 B0821/27 B0824/09
will (814)
will-I (1) B1220/01
will/'o/the/wisp (1) B0902/08
Will/o'/the/Wisp (1) A0482/08
will> (1) A0464/19
willain> (2) A0466/V A0467/15
William (2) A0431/20 A0434/07
William/IV (1) C0162/01
Williams (1) A0388/20
Williams, J. B. (1) B1163/13
willian> (2) A0466/03 A0469/15
willing (32) A0073/22
A0099/23 A0534/24 A0563/08 A0626/03
B0728/15 B0747/23 B0982/35 B1008/14
B1009/21 B1032/31 B1077/29 B1092/17
B1093/05 B1101/06 B1126/09 B1178/04
B1186/23 B1236/10 B1236/28 B1380/08
C0133/34 C0177/30 C0190/38 C0195/15
C0203/01 C0390/21 C0415/01 C0428/13
C0532/30 C0564/29 C0569/03
willingly (7) A0250/01
A0430/07 B0822/18 B0902/V B1010/V
C0426/15 C0555/14
willingness (2) B1349/26 C0104/07
Willis (3) A0280/19
A0280/23 B1380/16
Willis's/Rooms (1) B1070/32
willow (6) A0163/15 B1332/12
C0566/17 C0566/17 C0577/19 C0578/10
willows (5) C0536/34
C0544/20 C0544/22 C0545/01 C0577/19
Wilson (18) A0431/20 A0432/24
A0432/32 A0433/14 A0434/07 A0434/26
A0436/34 A0439/32 A0444/03 A0444/04
A0444/06 A0445/02 A0445/28 A0446/06

->A0448/06 A0448/11 C0102/22 C0112/35
Wilson, William (6) A0426/01
A0426/T A0437/22 A0439/13 A0440/31
A0445/34
Wilson's (3) A0431/30
A0432/19 A0433/33
Wimble, Will (2) A0249/29 A0250/06
win (3) A0414/20 A0441/05 A0629/07
wind (132)
wind-harp (1) A0643/16
wind-sails (1) A0071/09
Windenough (7) A0064/14
A0064/16 A0073/06 A0073/21 A0073/30
A0074/09 A0075/03
Windenough's (1) A0073/10
Windham (1) A0071/31
winding (11) A0157/02
A0249/17 A0252/14 A0639/19 B0724/25
B0945/08 B1142/26 B1258/29 B1282/17
C0068/41 C0543/31
winding-sheet (1) A0247/03
windings (13) A0081/07
A0429/23 A0671/26 B0865/01 B0942/29
B1279/26 C0069/31 C0070/28 C0074/26
C0077/25 C0193/04 C0208/26 C0410/31
windlass (13) B1078/01
C0115/14 C0116/02 C0116/19 C0117/02
C0117/21 C0118/40 C0119/12 C0119/30
C0119/32 C0120/08 C0139/04 C0139/28
windmill (3) B1070/06
B1164/29 B1380/28
windmills (1) C0118/17
window (60)
window-panes (1) A0036/13
window-sash (1) B1251/02
windowless (1) A0244/05
windows (47) A0019/18
A0022/24 A0036/V A0058/06 A0068/27
A0072/20 A0151/05 A0152/06 A0157/28
A0248/27 A0351/25 A0367/12 A0397/13
A0398/13 A0401/07 A0407/08 A0407/35
A0430/02 A0501/07 A0533/15 A0539/28
A0542/08 A0551/21 A0551/28 A0552/08
A0552/14 A0558/04 A0626/27 A0671/27
A0671/30 A0672/05 A0674/03 B0901/07
B0992/12 B1008/24 B1008/28 B1008/30
B1020/03 B1021/06 B1021/08 B1057/15
B1299/05 B1336/23 B1339/30 B1340/22
C0410/29 C0420/35
winds (25) A0029/16
A0044/V A0054/22 A0213/14 A0227/24
A0232/11 A0236/08 A0426/05 A0578/19
A0580/33 A0594/08 A0642/29 A0643/27
B0724/31 B0871/15 C0071/36 C0088/15
C0140/19 C0148/23 C0150/41 C0156/28
C0160/11 C0162/25 C0205/37 C0570/10
windward (15) B0930/29
B0931/08 C0062/13 C0106/26 C0114/33
C0118/05 C0119/33 C0120/03 C0123/14
C0136/10 C0141/05 C0143/31 C0143/41
C0144/13 C0187/12
windy> (2) A0465/07 A0465/09
wine (80)
wine-bibbing (1) A0247/31
wine-bottle (1) C0141/29
wine-box (1) B1059/V
wine-cellars (1) A0245/10
wine-pipe (1) B1102/24
wine-table (1) A0446/22
wines (7) A0243/05
A0245/15 A0250/26 B1017/28 B1257/12
C0058/12 C0091/21
wing (22) A0599/M B0809/03
B1008/28 B1103/28 B1103/28 B1103/33
B1103/33 B1103/34 B1103/34 B1103/35
B1248/22 B1336/09 B1336/15 B1336/17
B1336/28 B1336/30 B1336/37 B1337/19
B1338/05 B1339/23 B1339/26 C0151/38
winged (4) A0033/04
A0407/05 A0407/V B1180/22
wings (30) A0164/25 A0189/09
A0316/13 A0318/20 A0330/16 A0599/M
A0603/15 B0963/34 B1013/30 B1103/27
B1153/32 B1156/31 B1164/35 B1215/25
B1248/22 B1248/26 B1250/21 B1250/25
B1282/34 B1311/32 B1337/25 C0151/18
C0151/35 C0178/17 C0191/13 C0408/24
C0409/01 C0429/19 C0429/20 C0543/01
wink (6) A0098/08 A0355/14
A0467/16 A0468/08 A0468/29 B1373/08
winked (7) A0465/20
A0487/21 A0625/17 B0927/29 B1012/12
B1182/33 B1193/16
winking (2) A0355/09 A0469/22
Winowacants (2) C0551/02 C0551/05
wins (4) B0984/10
B0984/16 B0984/20 B0984/27
wint> (3) A0466/25
A0468/09 A0470/08
winter (23) A0101/17
A0214/16 A0243/03 A0249/28 A0531/V
A0604/26 B0888/29 B0963/10 C0161/35
C0170/32 C0185/33 C0204/32 C0447/V
C0522/22 C0526/23 C0546/35 C0547/02
C0547/10 C0560/09 C0560/22 C0560/26
C0561/01 C0566/04
winters (1) B0807/35
wiped (5) A0106/16
A0487/V B0823/25 B0911/01 C0426/34
wire (9) A0682/06
B0960/20 B1071/12 B1071/14 B1119/20
B1167/13 B1167/29 B1181/26 B1182/30
wires (3) B1163/37
B1293/33 B1293/35
Wirklichkeit (1) B0723/M
Wirt, William (1) A0275/08
Wirt's (2) A0275/12 A0275/16
Wisconsin/river (1) C0528/12
wisdom (17) A0075/10
A0075/14 A0128/24 A0234/05 A0316/10
A0323/10 A0407/23 A0435/32 A0446/05
A0568/19 A0638/11 B1018/08 B1047/08
B1092/28 B1127/07 B1212/02 B1345/25
wise (25) A0098/21
A0205/08 A0235/15 A0386/14 A0458/24
A0458/28 A0458/28 A0460/10 A0473/22
A0491/02 A0599/M A0609/11 A0609/11
B0793/06 B0796/05 B0984/34 B1164/02
B1169/03 B1194/06 B1345/25 B1368/01
B1369/01 B1369/08 B1369/10 C0062/07

wiseacre (2) B1296/15 B1312/17
wisely (2) B0789/19 B1127/33
wiser (6) A0622/16 B1104/34
B1177/04 B1220/12 C0168/26 C0427/37
wisest (2) A0370/18 C0558/40
wish (67)
wished (19) A0324/25
A0352/06 A0586/30 A0625/25 A0653/23
A0663/07 B0797/01 B0808/20 B0856/24
B1014/14 B1015/V B1018/33 B1139/23
B1189/34 C0127/41 C0404/26 C0535/08
C0556/08 C0558/04
wishes (20) A0021/26
A0092/15 A0111/25 A0268/31 A0339/01
A0383/16 A0653/27 B0744/28 B0749/04
B0923/14 B1096/06 B1114/13 B1242/18
B1360/02 B1360/04 B1384/28 C0176/36
C0414/03 C0529/26 C0563/41
wishing (12) A0080/22
A0268/07 A0356/10 B0762/01 B0808/23
B0810/21 B0979/30 B1093/19 B1105/08
C0080/27 C0141/19 C0399/31
wisiting> (1) A0464/01
Wissahiccon (7) B0861/T
B0863/31 B0863/33 B0864/13 B0864/22
B0865/05 B0865/18
wissahiccon (1) B0864/02
wit (18) A0087/09 A0344/19
A0407/23 A0434/01 A0437/06 A0650/28
A0652/12 A0675/08 B0747/25 B0923/23
B1012/30 B1045/35 B1055/07 B1127/07
B1345/11 C0102/19 C0430/16 C0527/38
wit's (1) A0433/28
witch (3) A0052/02
A0062/04 A0599/M
witches (2) A0479/12 B0850/31
With (1) B0795/25
with (4276)
withal (2) A0413/27 A0414/23
withdraw (4) A0022/20
A0552/07 B0893/08 B1181/07
withdrawal (1) A0510/32
withdrawing (3) B0893/30
B1261/30 C0172/11
withdrawn (1) B0832/13
withdrew (6) A0094/19 A0114/14
A0437/15 A0552/20 B0856/25 B1011/29
withered (4) A0643/08
A0665/15 B1279/33 C0173/06
withering (2) B1133/27 B1371/11
withersoever (1) A0512/07
withheld (2) B0855/15 B0960/32
withhold (2) B1014/21 B1054/31
withholding (1) B1154/31
within (341)
without (491)
withstand (3) A0696/34
B1322/25 C0188/01
witness (18) A0294/V A0539/18
A0540/06 A0540/15 A0540/22 A0540/30
A0544/06 A0549/30 A0550/14 A0550/16
A0642/14 B1053/14 B1053/15 B1108/08
B1382/10 C0541/16 C0545/26 C0567/32
witness' (1) B0745/25
witnessed (7) A0298/V
->A0299/V A0479/31 B0942/01 B1007/12
B1008/34 C0095/21
witnesses (8) A0542/04
A0542/22 A0543/08 A0544/21 A0549/12
A0549/18 A0560/06 B1236/13
witnessing (1) C0535/39
wits (3) A0509/26
B1101/32 B1347/35
witticism (1) B0927/32
witticisms (1) B1345/21
wittily (3) A0093/11
A0112/22 A0433/22
witty (3) A0204/03
A0435/13 B1325/02
wives (3) B1101/10
B1169/02 B1169/05
wizard (2) B0955/33 B1279/32
wo (8) A0153/16
A0318/21 A0326/17 A0614/07 B0856/03
B0955/19 B0964/23 B1248/37
woe (2) A0228/01 A0326/V
woes (2) A0675/V B1130/21
woful (1) A0046/17
wofully (1) A0240/V
Wolf (1) B0832/07
wolf (3) C0536/23
C0560/03 C0570/32
Wollaston (1) B1167/29
wolly-wou> (1) A0469/15
wolverine (1) C0536/23
wolves (3) C0567/03
C0567/08 C0575/12
woman (41) A0151/18
A0154/25 A0162/08 A0227/09 A0231/22
A0234/04 A0315/17 A0315/25 A0368/02
A0383/02 A0540/13 A0544/04 A0557/03
A0622/29 A0644/07 A0704/03 B0734/12
B0744/02 B0749/07 B0889/20 B0891/18
B0892/05 B0893/22 B0894/16 B0897/28
B0902/24 B0903/22 B0915/18 B0924/19
B0924/23 B0933/20 B1004/06 B1005/02
B1121/01 B1169/22 B1269/02 B1277/08
B1338/27 B1339/04 B1339/07 C0395/08
woman's (4) A0540/10
A0540/24 A0542/02 B0958/03
womanhood (3) A0510/07
A0663/22 B1339/07
womanliness (1) B1339/05
womanly (1) A0317/23
womb (1) C0429/24
women (30) A0128/V A0315/07
A0347/29 A0510/06 A0527/M A0548/28
A0704/13 B0741/07 B0745/33 B0841/04
B0888/28 B0992/21 B1015/17 B1016/11
B1016/11 B1016/17 B1016/19 B1045/15
B1047/V B1092/29 B1269/12 B1303/22
B1303/26 B1350/12 B1350/26 B1352/11
C0093/33 C0156/14 C0174/24 C0180/03
won (3) A0443/07 A0626/09 B0984/11
won't (6) A0630/11 B0820/18
B1142/22 B1142/23 B1169/23 C0067/32
wonder (56)
wonder-stricken (2) A0154/13
A0372/02
wonder-working (1) A0213/24

wondered (9) A0153/13 A0234/10 A0400/33 A0590/11 A0644/V B0927/21 B1346/29 C0111/29 C0397/22
wonderful (38) A0072/29 A0098/10 A0141/27 A0144/16 A0174/03 A0179/14 A0198/28 A0210/13 A0210/14 A0295/18 A0296/V A0379/21 A0381/25 A0381/26 A0381/34 A0385/11 A0478/15 A0478/31 A0588/32 B0757/21 B0772/26 B0826/02 B1157/21 B1162/36 B1163/03 B1165/21 B1166/24 B1278/02 B1316/19 B1346/17 C0425/30 C0425/34 C0441/V C0536/12 C0543/35 C0569/17 C0576/08 C0577/37
wonderfully (16) A0047/23 A0382/29 A0383/32 A0386/01 B0931/09 B1030/09 B1073/33 B1180/28 B1240/24 B1293/27 C0138/13 C0139/07 C0179/11 C0421/16 C0524/20 C0554/22
wondering (3) B0866/04 C0077/27 C0390/25
wonderingly (1) B0944/21
wonderment (2) A0172/M A0178/M
wonders (17) A0343/33 A0455/13 A0457/32 A0499/03 A0593/10 A0709/31 A0710/19 B0897/27 B1006/11 B1274/33 B1275/22 B1298/25 C0057/31 C0060/11 C0064/30 C0412/31 C0564/32
wondrous (1) B1382/27
wont (15) A0098/15 A0098/31 A0143/05 A0235/20 A0402/06 A0428/30 A0459/09 A0533/15 A0608/11 A0615/14 A0624/31 B0927/16 B1257/03 B1352/32 B1371/32
wonted (1) A0438/29
woo> (2) A0467/01 A0467/01
wood (52)
wood-cut (1) A0273/18
wood-cutters (2) C0545/37 C0547/30
wood-cutting (1) C0546/09
wood-work (1) A0400/13
Wood/river (1) C0538/43
wooded (5) B0817/24 B1281/20 C0167/26 C0549/24 C0558/31
wooden (7) A0514/25 A0695/06 B0929/22 B0967/16 B1119/M C0175/01 C0534/34
woodland (1) B1048/35
Woods (2) C0526/37 C0528/23
woods (13) B0734/31 B0735/25 B0759/31 B0760/18 B1057/36 B1246/05 B1371/29 B1371/31 B1371/31 C0532/08 C0550/21 C0552/40 C0563/06
woodwork (2) A0081/28 A0367/14
woody (2) C0541/35 C0541/37
wool (6) A0351/10 A0351/16 A0351/16 A0489/16 C0165/14 C0569/29
woollen (7) A0368/19 B0825/25 B0929/15 C0082/20 C0109/03 C0119/20 C0202/34
woolly (1) C0168/15
woolly-wou> (1) A0469/V
woolly> (1) A0466/08
Woolwich (1) B1069/21
word (178)
worded (2) A0273/05 B1047/11
wording (1) A0302/11
wordly (1) B0899/14
Words (2) B1177/T B1211/T
words (264)
wore (43) A0023/04 A0189/11 A0205/15 A0246/25 A0247/02 A0328/26 A0401/03 A0439/09 A0508/29 A0509/02 A0509/14 A0509/33 A0513/20 A0513/34 A0514/23 A0533/15 A0578/34 A0582/31 A0602/17 A0603/21 A0628/03 A0682/03 B0728/28 B0728/29 B0811/04 B0825/29 B0826/20 B0940/29 B1008/02 B1049/29 B1080/05 B1157/05 B1235/12 B1257/18 B1345/19 C0087/15 C0105/06 C0108/38 C0131/07 C0204/31 C0559/02 C0560/26 C0562/21
worf (1) B0811/32
work (94)
worked (10) A0343/23 A0399/31 A0554/15 A0610/27 A0631/20 B0796/06 B0825/34 C0118/32 C0393/24 C0395/31
working (12) A0056/02 A0065/26 B0760/10 B0913/13 B1081/V C0107/20 C0114/02 C0114/07 C0114/41 C0136/38 C0395/23 C0545/23
workings (1) A0324/20
workmanship (4) A0086/33 A0189/22 C0202/27 C0534/02
workmen (1) B1303/32
Works (1) B1141/07
works (25) A0135/06 A0271/35 A0283/06 A0301/01 A0399/01 A0408/29 A0489/27 A0502/11 A0577/M B0828/16 B0862/18 B1017/15 B1022/04 B1031/11 B1141/09 B1144/34 B1220/16 B1220/17 B1279/32 B1298/12 B1316/20 B1329/30 C0169/23 C0524/13 C0536/41
World (1) B0861/03
world (183)
world's (2) A0431/01 A0609/12
worldly (9) A0409/18 A0435/31 A0458/08 A0532/11 A0703/02 B0852/33 B1224/28 B1268/02 B1276/21
Worlds (1) B0863/17
worlds (5) A0151/07 A0214/25 A0217/V B1213/26 C0083/02
Worm (2) A0319/18 B0961/24
worm (12) A0107/07 A0228/17 A0232/V A0235/02 A0616/12 A0616/34 A0616/V B0964/28 B1037/06 B1037/12 B1163/15 B1292/30
worm-eaten (2) A0142/31 A0514/25
worm-holes (1) B1160/39
worm's (1) B1037/11
wormed (1) A0298/V
Wormley (3) C0548/34 C0549/08 C0579/15
Wormley, Alexander (2) C0531/35 C0535/23
worms (5) B0963/23 B1165/27 B1165/34 C0142/39 C0178/17
wormwood (1) B1131/30
worn (30) A0086/27 A0086/29 A0089/15 A0100/03 A0100/06 A0329/04 A0444/16 A0444/27 B0731/11 B0735/26

->B0735/27 B0746/21 B0827/06 B0827/30
B0890/05 B0908/05 B0916/12 B1049/22
B1141/26 B1262/11 C0411/31 C0416/41
C0552/05 C0552/10 C0552/15 C0552/19
C0562/06 C0572/36 C0577/05 C0579/08
worried (1) C0391/34
worry (1) A0284/19
worse (28) A0139/09
A0326/03 A0373/29 A0623/01 A0623/01
A0631/18 A0652/07 A0695/11 B0851/07
B0866/04 B0911/V B0942/23 B1017/27
B1017/28 B1132/05 B1139/27 B1153/13
B1249/21 B1278/16 B1390/04 C0121/29
C0141/17 C0190/14 C0388/30 C0531/01
C0561/20 C0565/09 C0565/15
worship (5) A0122/24
A0311/28 A0644/17 B1188/15 B1303/20
worshipped (3) A0035/13
A0122/29 C0524/02
worshippers (2) A0043/14 A0498/21
worst (16) A0410/05
A0488/10 A0490/25 A0514/23 A0515/30
A0548/12 A0585/11 A0684/13 B0844/17
B1050/14 B1139/28 B1278/18 C0079/08
C0095/36 C0406/39 C0549/32
worsted (1) B1101/23
worth (32) A0028/11
A0069/28 A0091/22 A0110/26 A0160/V
A0285/11 A0339/16 A0340/18 A0379/14
A0703/33 B0732/34 B0828/14 B0828/17
B0863/13 B0880/07 B1054/24 B1079/33
B1092/23 B1189/20 B1244/02 B1268/31
B1364/24 B1364/24 C0057/26 C0091/12
C0179/04 C0179/13 C0196/01 C0196/05
C0442/V C0531/04 C0574/38
worthless (3) B0991/05
B1297/22 B1316/06
worthlessness (1) B0991/23
worthy (32) A0044/26
A0098/23 A0241/23 A0243/20 A0245/V
A0250/35 A0252/11 A0295/28 A0297/V
A0382/20 A0495/V A0557/27 A0703/20
B0748/35 B0823/05 B0862/03 B0862/11
B0926/27 B0987/04 B1050/05 B1050/32
B1052/02 B1053/07 B1054/21 B1206/07
B1250/08 B1268/19 C0165/32 C0173/23
C0401/23 C0402/04 C0419/41
wou> (4) A0466/08
A0466/08 A0467/20 A0467/20
would (981)
Would-be (1) B1324/T
would-be (1) B1324/02
wouldn't (12) A0072/24
A0345/12 A0384/09 A0464/12 A0465/27
A0487/19 A0488/28 A0651/03 B0812/28
B0982/11 B1046/32 B1046/32
wouldst (1) A0599/M
woully> (1) A0467/20
wouly-wou> (1) A0470/23
wound (21) A0564/28
B0730/26 B0765/21 B0851/23 B0945/01
B1053/33 B1071/29 B1077/35 B1153/33
B1185/26 B1328/05 C0064/20 C0071/15
C0076/33 C0085/23 C0088/11 C0111/24
C0113/33 C0180/40 C0535/40 C0575/18

wounded (17) A0626/07
A0662/02 B1044/18 B1107/12 C0119/29
C0127/08 C0136/32 C0141/07 C0143/20
C0187/33 C0557/27 C0557/33 C0557/40
C0558/11 C0558/19 C0563/09 C0566/32
wounds (5) A0058/24
A0549/06 C0092/25 C0141/10 C0141/18
wrap (2) A0559/14 C0416/33
wrapped (16) A0139/08
A0141/32 A0196/22 A0246/02 A0437/03
A0439/28 A0489/31 A0611/22 A0630/28
B0830/20 B0830/25 B0890/31 B1106/29
C0063/34 C0130/33 C0397/38
wrapper (4) A0087/05
A0443/13 A0443/22 A0685/30
wrapping (1) A0048/V
wrapt (1) A0139/V
wrath (14) A0383/05 A0417/04
A0447/01 A0567/03 B0765/08 B0795/V
B0856/21 B0897/01 B0898/24 B1107/18
B1128/32 B1130/20 B1158/08 C0392/03
wreath (4) A0127/06
A0128/28 A0128/28 B1282/26
wreathed (2) A0162/17 A0217/V
wreathing (3) A0029/V
A0603/19 B1339/02
wreaths (2) B1330/25 C0192/40
wreck (15) A0213/23
A0591/36 A0604/02 A0614/35 B0830/17
B0931/16 B0932/10 B0932/20 B1110/19
C0115/06 C0139/13 C0146/42 C0189/23
C0198/38 C0572/32
wreckers (1) B0933/12
wrenched (1) B1020/07
wrenching (2) C0122/06 C0126/31
wrestled (2) A0317/02 A0696/14
wretch (19) A0052/01
A0055/22 A0062/03 A0065/06 A0071/16
A0092/10 A0111/22 A0242/31 A0250/35
A0336/12 A0416/06 B0771/25 B0911/29
B0914/V B0966/05 B1054/34 B1058/06
B1059/22 B1138/13
wretched (10) A0092/08 A0111/19
A0515/03 A0653/22 B0855/36 B0957/21
B1101/30 B1131/03 B1177/02 B1360/02
wretchedly (3) B1183/15
B1310/21 B1313/14
wretchedness (7) A0209/01
A0703/12 B0855/36 B0857/25 B0955/18
B0966/32 B1268/11
wretches (9) A0382/30
A0383/31 A0384/21 B1157/08 C0180/11
C0181/20 C0188/10 C0190/14 C0201/16
wriggle (2) A0623/05 B1346/08
wriggled (1) B0819/02
wriggles (1) B1251/01
wriggling (2) A0373/28 A0627/07
wrigglings (1) B1165/28
wring (1) B1153/13
wringing (4) A0506/04
B1257/20 C0120/09 C0146/10
wrinkled (3) A0144/18
A0510/10 C0389/22
wrinkles (3) A0252/13
B0911/10 C0410/24

wrist (9) B0730/08
B0730/10 B0890/09 B0964/11 B0964/25
B0965/02 C0118/31 C0142/05 C0398/13
wristband (1) A0509/11
wrists (7) A0078/05
A0103/26 A0247/29 B0967/15 B0967/22
C0168/17 C0411/28
write (51)
writer (37) A0174/05
A0175/11 A0179/17 A0204/11 A0282/03
A0283/29 A0339/07 A0339/28 A0341/19
A0398/21 A0479/10 A0581/12 A0709/19
B0723/20 B0738/21 B0743/20 B0840/11
B1119/11 B1119/13 B1250/06 B1274/22
B1310/13 B1318/12 B1359/14 C0055/24
C0207/23 C0207/33 C0391/05 C0392/23
C0428/11 C0428/11 C0429/07 C0430/33
C0448/V C0448/V C0522/01 C0524/13
writer's (1) B1359/27
writers (5) A0071/31
A0150/V A0531/06 B1206/04 C0433/06
writes (14) A0093/10 A0112/22
A0271/24 A0276/33 A0280/23 A0281/04
A0284/26 A0285/01 A0285/18 A0286/16
A0709/21 B1138/01 B1380/25 C0423/31
writhe (5) A0161/17
A0674/02 A0681/16 B1156/32 B1337/22
writhed (9) A0157/V
A0321/26 A0616/V A0643/09 A0673/28
A0694/21 B0967/20 B1239/29 C0399/07
writhes (4) A0319/05
A0319/07 A0319/07 B1079/07
writhing (9) A0166/04
A0195/20 A0215/26 A0326/10 A0588/22
A0602/12 A0697/03 B0947/19 B0950/13
writhings (2) A0317/07 B1165/28
writin> (1) A0465/28
writing (44) A0088/33
A0103/13 A0266/16 A0267/03 A0267/28
A0268/15 A0269/07 A0270/13 A0272/09
A0272/12 A0273/20 A0274/08 A0274/28
A0275/12 A0275/15 A0277/14 A0278/34
A0279/12 A0279/31 A0281/01 A0281/27
A0283/04 A0283/21 A0284/08 A0296/V
A0338/04 A0338/10 A0338/14 A0338/31
A0465/V A0473/07 A0528/19 A0533/03
B0831/13 B0835/32 B1059/16 B1091/19
B1164/06 B1166/29 C0056/27 C0078/20
C0080/04 C0080/04 C0430/03
writing-desk (1) B0811/01
writing-table (1) B0990/29
writings (10) A0059/08 A0061/04
A0225/16 A0225/20 A0229/15 A0269/24
A0271/03 A0280/27 A0457/17 B1017/16
Written (1) B0806/T
written (63)
Wrong (1) B0806/M
wrong (36) A0058/30
A0075/04 A0090/25 A0090/25 A0093/26
A0369/14 A0459/26 A0500/15 A0553/17
A0561/12 B0751/23 B0757/33 B0757/35
B0763/12 B0769/V B0796/12 B0852/17
B0946/14 B0984/10 B1013/05 B1039/12
B1101/24 B1140/16 B1183/33 B1190/07
B1195/15 B1220/08 B1221/01 B1221/03
->B1256/07 B1256/10 C0059/04 C0186/08
C0424/28 C0574/39 C0575/02
wrong's (2) B0852/18 B1221/03
wronged (1) B0789/11
wrote (26) A0069/V A0109/09
A0174/01 A0179/12 A0263/27 A0302/03
A0339/14 A0340/01 A0343/19 A0621/12
B0869/02 B0900/10 B0900/16 B0901/18
B0911/19 B1145/14 B1145/18 B1145/25
B1145/25 B1145/26 B1145/27 B1145/28
B1145/28 B1383/33 B1383/35 B1384/02
wrought (23) A0029/02
A0213/30 A0322/15 A0613/28 A0665/19
A0666/01 A0708/25 B0737/V B0826/05
B0866/04 B0905/V B0923/06 B0969/01
B1133/17 B1193/21 B1214/01 B1224/06
B1235/11 B1251/02 B1273/20 B1280/18
B1364/19 C0178/20
wrought-iron (1) C0115/32
wrung (1) C0120/12
wud> (9) A0465/17
A0465/18 A0466/07 A0466/18 A0466/32
A0467/11 A0467/15 A0468/V A0469/12
wully> (1) A0467/01
wxnt (1) B1374/11
wxxds (3) B1374/08
B1374/10 B1374/10
Wyatt (28) B0923/25
B0923/29 B0924/14 B0924/22 B0924/28
B0925/14 B0926/03 B0926/12 B0926/18
B0926/22 B0926/24 B0926/35 B0927/30
B0928/33 B0928/34 B0929/01 B0929/09
B0929/31 B0930/02 B0930/05 B0931/21
B0931/28 B0931/32 B0931/35 B0932/06
B0932/09 B0933/17 B0933/33
Wyatt, Cornelius (2) B0922/09
B0925/27
Wyatt, W. (1) C0524/18
Wyatt's (6) B0923/19 B0924/06
B0925/20 B0926/05 B0928/16 B0928/21
<u>Wyatt's</u> (1) B1165/35
X (2) A0271/08 B1375/13
x (7) B0988/07
B1373/30 B1373/31 B1373/35 B1374/01
B1374/03 B1375/11
X-ample (1) B1375/04
X-asperation (1) B1375/03
X-cellent (1) B1374/32
X-centric (1) B1375/01
X-ed (1) B1375/15
x-ed (1) B1374/04
X-ing (1) B1368/T
X-press (1) B1375/02
X-traordinary (1) B1375/09
X-treme (1) B1375/22
x-tremity (1) B1375/V
X-uberance (1) B1374/34
X/(cross) (1) B1375/21
xdixus (1) B1374/10
Xerxes (2) A0534/18 A0534/27
<u>Xerxes</u> (1) A0119/M
xf (5) B1374/08
B1374/10 B1374/16 B1374/17 B1374/20
xh (3) B1374/09 B1374/11 B1374/13
xld (5) B1374/10

->B1374/10 B1374/15 B1374/17 B1374/20
xnce (2) B1374/09 B1374/12
xnly (1) B1374/14
xr (1) B1374/15
xut (3) B1374/08 B1374/09 B1374/16
xwl (2) B1374/11 B1374/14
xwns (1) B1374/13
xx (1) A0277/22
xxult (2) A0275/03 A0277/24
XI (1) A0271/31
XII (1) A0272/19
XIII (1) A0273/01
XIV (1) A0273/32
XIX (1) A0276/22
XV (1) A0274/16
XVI (1) A0275/01
XVII (1) A0275/21
XVIII (1) A0276/06
XX (1) A0277/01
XXI (1) A0277/20
XXII (1) A0278/01
XXIII (1) A0278/21
XXIV (1) A0279/01
XXIX (1) A0281/31
XXV (1) A0279/30
XXVI (1) A0280/12
XXVII (1) A0280/31
XXVIII (1) A0281/08
XXX (1) A0282/12
XXX/ale (1) B1375/20
XXXI (1) A0282/31
XXXII (1) A0283/12
XXXIII (1) A0283/33
XXXIV (1) A0284/15
XXXV (1) A0284/31
XXXVI (1) A0285/10
XXXVII (1) A0285/22
XXXVIII (1) A0286/01
y (2) A0621/03 B0986/33
yachts (1) A0581/35
Yampoos (1) C0173/02
Yankee/Doodle (1) B1020/15
Yankee's (1) B1375/02
Yankees (2) A0496/05 B1191/07
Yanktons (1) C0551/11
yard (15) A0347/04
  A0538/20 A0546/33 A0557/30 A0593/08
  A0676/09 A0686/16 A0690/12 B0841/17
  B0856/35 B1164/40 C0175/36 C0175/36
  C0185/03 C0202/39
yard-arms (1) A0143/24
yards (49) A0367/02
  A0578/13 A0591/V A0671/24 A0686/17
  A0688/11 B0822/02 B0825/02 B0865/26
  B0943/10 B1161/35 B1248/23 B1280/04
  B1281/29 B1331/13 B1331/17 B1331/30
  B1331/36 B1332/23 B1333/23 B1334/09
  B1336/05 C0144/16 C0169/04 C0181/01
  C0184/32 C0188/18 C0191/28 C0193/04
  C0193/07 C0193/21 C0194/23 C0195/05
  C0196/07 C0199/09 C0200/12 C0200/26
  C0393/18 C0396/25 C0408/26 C0541/25
  C0542/24 C0559/12 C0559/13 C0570/13
  C0570/37 C0571/19 C0572/09 C0577/03
yards' (1) B1335/05

yaw (2) C0124/16 C0124/33
yawed (1) C0123/19
yawl (1) A0142/11
yawling (1) B0968/V
yawned (3) A0035/01
  A0101/14 A0689/09
yawning (5) A0080/27
  A0697/01 B0990/21 C0205/35 C0405/29
yawns (3) A0153/10
  A0703/26 B1268/25
ycleped (1) A0087/06
ye (33) A0188/01
  A0249/26 A0249/27 A0251/08 A0351/15
  A0357/01 A0381/01 A0381/02 A0464/05
  A0464/12 A0465/08 A0465/14 A0465/15
  A0465/17 A0466/12 A0466/20 A0466/25
  A0466/31 A0466/33 A0467/13 A0468/04
  A0468/13 A0469/02 A0469/11 A0469/26
  A0470/08 A0470/18 A0639/02 B1046/10
  B1046/10 B1046/11 B1046/13 B1145/19
ye're (1) A0466/21
ye've (1) A0470/06
yea (1) A0188/M
yea-nay (1) B1139/16
year (75)
year's (2) A0654/22 C0138/09
yearning (1) C0198/09
years (202)
yell (10) A0244/30 A0591/12
  B0795/25 B0913/21 B0967/36 C0060/37
  C0124/30 C0201/14 C0553/31 C0554/17
yelled (1) A0353/31
yelling (2) B1021/04 C0187/36
yellings (2) A0243/27 C0189/39
Yellow (1) B1294/24
yellow (25) A0087/08
  A0087/17 A0100/15 A0106/23 A0138/19
  A0197/06 A0215/06 A0245/23 A0283/29
  A0368/05 A0368/11 A0406/34 A0498/10
  A0559/V A0640/02 B0945/19 C0126/07
  C0389/27 C0418/43 C0419/15 C0543/01
  C0543/22 C0543/29 C0559/36 C0576/07
Yellow/Stone (2) C0574/20 C0574/41
yellowish (2) B1242/11 C0572/12
Yellowstone (2) C0528/18 C0571/09
yells (8) A0244/14
  B1014/24 B1014/26 B1015/05 B1019/32
  B1262/29 C0184/22 C0200/39
yelpings (1) B0823/11
yer> (2) A0465/21 A0470/07
yes (109)
yesterday (19) A0265/08
  A0370/21 A0384/07 A0473/21 A0540/16
  A0656/09 A0656/10 A0656/14 A0656/19
  A0657/21 B0753/14 B0753/22 B0900/20
  B1079/22 B1091/22 B1160/28 B1370/12
  C0129/40 C0539/12
yesterday's (1) A0536/14
yet (474)
yeux (1) A0378/M
yield (17) A0059/06
  A0061/01 A0310/M A0314/28 A0319/23
  A0320/01 A0448/13 A0583/30 A0604/03
  A0604/04 B0907/11 C0059/34 C0076/11
  C0086/13 C0090/20 C0561/13 C0568/01

yielded (8) A0642/31
A0644/16 B0907/18 B0910/02 B1107/13
B1234/30 C0569/22 C0579/34
yielding (4) A0154/02
A0433/02 B1035/13 B1370/33
yields (3) A0479/23
A0708/17 B1273/12
yon (3) A0153/09 A0165/13 A0252/09
yonder (8) A0046/17
A0122/19 A0122/28 A0124/22 A0217/V
A0300/09 A0300/11 A0579/25
York (5) B1081/04
B1192/08 B1328/02 C0428/09 C0522/18
York-Town (1) B1138/34
Yorktown (2) B1304/17 B1304/34
you (1531)
you'd (1) A0468/10
you'll (1) A0629/V
you're (6) A0651/07 B1127/28
B1371/29 B1371/30 B1371/34 B1372/01
you've (1) B1371/32
young (124)
younger (10) A0241/08 B0891/18
B0897/22 B0915/07 B0915/22 B0915/29
B0925/10 B0941/10 B1014/08 C0529/20
youngest (2) A0577/04 A0585/35
your (464)
yours (31) A0089/23
A0090/30 A0107/25 A0107/28 A0109/22
A0266/03 A0268/32 A0270/08 A0271/13
A0272/03 A0273/07 A0276/28 A0277/28
A0278/08 A0278/27 A0279/03 A0279/07
A0280/18 A0280/36 A0284/01 A0284/35
A0650/17 B0813/30 B0816/21 B0844/08
B0870/15 B0900/23 B1142/20 B1178/24
B1291/10 B1305/17
yourself (48) A0072/12
A0072/13 A0090/27 A0173/25 A0179/05
A0251/29 A0272/25 A0299/10 A0299/32
A0300/03 A0340/26 A0347/01 A0534/14
A0536/05 A0536/26 A0536/V A0563/25
A0578/30 A0589/10 A0612/12 A0650/23
A0651/02 A0656/V B0768/11 B0820/16
B0826/28 B0844/12 B0870/17 B0892/09
B0903/17 B0907/27 B0913/05 B0949/05
B0949/11 B0979/06 B0982/17 B1005/30
B1007/05 B1010/07 B1010/09 B1013/34
B1014/01 B1032/30 B1091/03 B1093/34
B1093/35 B1103/32 B1109/10
yourselves (2) A0250/22 B0816/16
yourzelf (1) B1103/10
youself (1) B0913/V
youth (17) A0023/20
A0025/17 A0085/12 A0150/03 A0210/11
A0410/22 A0430/25 A0439/07 A0440/33
A0510/11 A0639/04 B0726/28 B0893/01
B0914/08 B0916/07 B0940/05 B1133/18
youthful (3) B0888/17
B1122/28 B1123/13
yowling (1) B0968/04
yr./mo./ob./sts (1) B1055/V
yur> (5) A0465/03
A0465/16 A0465/19 A0465/24 A0470/08
Yurope (1) B1294/05
yxu (11) B1374/07
->B1374/07 B1374/11 B1374/12 B1374/13
B1374/13 B1374/13 B1374/16 B1374/19
B1374/19 B1374/19
yxu're (4) B1374/08
B1374/09 B1374/13 B1374/14
yxu've (1) B1374/11
yxur (5) B1374/10
B1374/10 B1374/17 B1374/20 B1374/20
yzur (1) B1374/08
Zacchary (1) B1305/12
Zadig (1) B1345/14
zaffre (1) B0832/20
Zahara (1) C0072/25
Zaiat, Ebn (2) A0209/M A0218/14
Zaire (7) A0195/03
A0196/02 A0197/06 A0344/15 A0344/V
A0344/V A0344/V
Zaire (3) A0344/15
A0344/16 A0344/21
Zante (2) B1385/27 B1386/03
zay (1) B1103/01
zeal (8) A0495/V
B0738/04 B0823/04 B1050/20 B1052/08
B1128/08 B1182/26 C0545/41
zealous (2) A0044/13 B0753/35
zee (5) B1102/19
B1103/01 B1103/10 B1103/24 B1103/25
zenith (2) C0410/26 C0420/08
Zenobia (8) A0337/03
A0337/04 A0337/05 A0337/08 A0340/11
A0340/19 A0346/30 A0356/01
Zenobia, Psyche (8) A0336/02
A0336/V A0337/09 A0337/11 A0339/09
A0339/22 A0349/10 A0357/12
zenzes (1) B1109/20
Zephyr (1) A0062/32
zephyr (2) A0385/07 A0385/V
Zephyrs (1) A0640/13
Zeros (1) B1300/16
zest (1) A0352/13
zide (1) B1102/20
zig-zag (1) B1339/34
zigzag (2) A0400/19 A0417/11
Zimmerman (1) A0602/06
Zion (1) A0044/29
zit (5) B1102/19
B1102/37 B1103/01 B1103/24 B1103/32
zober (1) B1109/19
Zodiac (1) C0432/27
zodiacal (2) C0402/03 C0423/09
Zohar (1) B1151/03
Zoilus (2) A0190/10 A0191/03
zone (1) C0425/38
zones (2) C0171/19 C0425/18
zoophytes (1) C0178/34
Zopyrus (1) A0068/14
zorry (1) B1104/17
zubmizzion (1) B1109/34
Zufalle (1) B0723/M
zusammen (1) B0723/M
0.0000157 (2) B1168/16 B1168/20
0.05484 (1) C0400/06
1 (7) A0487/05
B0876/28 C0142/13 C0194/01 C0203/21
C0207/39 C0566/12

1-- (1) B1390/01
1/2 (5) A0485/08
A0485/08 B1055/29 B1168/19 C0430/24
1/3 (1) C0179/05
1/4 (2) B1168/18 B1168/18
1, (2) B1291/13 C0162/30
1" (1) C0423/28
10 (5) A0484/32
B1079/14 C0103/26 C0163/33 C0570/22
10, (1) C0560/29
10,600 (1) C0400/28
10' (3) C0159/32 C0163/04 C0163/14
10th (1) C0419/18
100,000 (1) B1136/15
1000 (4) B1168/37
B1168/38 B1168/39 C0400/26
101 (1) B1381/27
102 (1) C0526/05
103 (1) C0526/07
106 (1) C0159/33
1080 (1) C0400/13
11 (6) A0283/37 A0484/33
B1069/15 B1075/22 C0561/18 C0570/29
11th (1) C0419/29
110 (1) B0879/14
117,000,000 (1) B1301/06
118 (1) C0160/31
12 (10) A0283/36 A0484/34
A0485/08 B1081/07 C0154/23 C0155/10
C0155/15 C0164/07 C0563/32 C0570/34
12' (1) C0155/15
12th (1) C0419/35
1200 (2) B1073/21 B1073/22
13 (6) A0485/01 B1359/16
C0147/27 C0428/38 C0563/32 C0571/09
13th (2) C0420/03 C0574/18
1300 (1) B1073/22
132,000 (1) C0411/39
133 (1) C0179/05
1356 (1) C0423/23
14 (7) B1383/15
C0161/05 C0163/11 C0164/12 C0540/14
C0563/32 C0574/23
14' (2) C0159/02 C0161/03
14th (2) B1381/23 C0420/11
142 (1) C0159/16
143 (1) B1165/35
15 (4) A0485/05
A0487/26 C0541/01 C0563/32
15-1 (5) B1136/02
B1136/21 B1137/13 B1138/09 B1139/13
15,000 (1) B1076/14
15' (9) C0157/10
C0157/26 C0159/06 C0160/07 C0160/22
C0160/37 C0161/38 C0163/13 C0163/38
15" (3) C0157/08 C0157/09 C0157/10
15th (1) C0420/19
150 (1) B1358/07
16 (4) A0485/07
A0487/28 C0541/24 C0565/12
16th (1) C0420/34
160 (1) B1391/24
161 (1) C0400/18
1643 (1) C0154/26
1645 (1) A0582/11
1666 (1) A0301/05
167,000 (1) B1168/34
168th (1) C0524/29
1698 (1) C0525/01
17 (4) A0485/10
C0164/26 C0542/01 C0565/16
17' (1) C0155/09
17th (1) C0421/07
1749 (1) C0525/10
1758 (1) C0525/09
176 (1) C0430/32
1762 (1) C0156/33
1763 (1) C0525/11
1766 (1) B1161/25
1767 (1) C0154/26
1769 (2) C0157/40 C0525/30
1770 (1) C0525/30
1771 (1) C0525/30
1772 (3) C0150/13
C0158/28 C0525/30
1773 (1) C0159/04
1774 (2) C0157/40 C0525/33
1775 (1) C0526/03
1776 (1) C0526/06
1777 (1) C0150/19
1778 (1) C0526/08
1779 (1) C0157/41
1780 (2) B0948/35 B0949/16
1781 (1) B1304/18
1781-8, (1) A0283/36
1783 (1) B1161/24
1784 (1) C0522/17
1789 (1) C0526/34
1790 (6) B1161/34 C0155/24
C0155/26 C0156/34 C0157/41 C0522/22
1791 (4) C0155/26
C0522/24 C0530/34 C0539/38
1792 (2) C0528/39 C0560/29
1793 (4) C0527/10
C0527/26 C0527/37 C0528/37
1794 (3) B1161/28
C0156/36 C0522/26
1796 (1) B1390/01
18 (7) A0485/12
B0728/10 B1383/18 C0166/34 C0542/23
C0565/16 C0576/10
18-- (14) A0135/24 A0293/08
A0301/32 A0302/29 A0446/20 A0531/16
A0584/35 B0729/07 B0731/26 B0808/01
B0974/02 B1002/01 B1044/09 B1055/23
18,000 (1) C0400/29
18th (4) A0301/32
A0302/29 C0422/41 C0527/21
180 (1) B1391/26
1803 (2) C0160/04 C0527/17
1804 (1) C0527/17
1805 (2) C0527/17 C0527/31
1806 (2) C0527/17 C0527/31
1807 (1) C0527/31
1809 (1) C0156/39
1810 (2) B0957/09 C0527/34
1811 (4) C0146/34
C0155/38 C0430/23 C0528/05
1812 (1) B1161/29
1813 (1) A0432/28

1817 (1) C0156/04
1820 (1) C0157/11
1822 (2) C0158/05 C0160/16
1823 (2) C0160/28 C0528/22
1824 (1) C0156/10
1825 (1) C0099/05
1827 (3) B0939/01
C0053/T C0066/29
1828 (1) C0162/30
1829 (1) B1385/08
1831 (3) A0146/10
B0959/30 C0161/26
1832 (3) A0089/12
C0161/37 C0528/26
1836 (1) A0279/18
1837 (2) B1070/27 C0056/11
1838 (1) C0056/32
1839 (1) B1234/07
1841 (1) A0568/V
1842 (1) B0723/13
1845 (1) B0942/01
1846 (1) B1381/23
1847 (1) B1304/14
19 (5) A0485/13
C0167/22 C0396/24 C0542/30 C0576/21
19th (2) B1304/14 C0424/10
190 (1) B1391/10
193 (1) C0207/26
194 (1) C0207/26
195 (1) C0207/26
2 (20) A0485/04
A0487/09 A0593/35 A0611/27 B0876/29
B1069/16 B1081/09 B1081/31 B1168/18
B1168/19 B1293/32 B1391/11 C0142/36
C0163/03 C0194/19 C0194/20 C0203/31
C0207/39 C0548/20 C0566/28
2,230,272,000 (1) B1164/40
2' (1) C0157/09
2" (1) C0423/28
2d. (1) B1382/06
20 (8) A0485/03
B1168/37 B1168/38 B1168/39 B1385/26
B1391/27 C0543/03 C0576/30
20,000,000 (1) B1169/35
20' (5) C0088/31
C0158/14 C0163/04 C0166/03 C0167/22
200 (1) B1391/10
200,000 (1) B1136/36
2045 (1) B1195/16
2050 (1) B1303/06
21 (2) C0205/28 C0429/19
21' (1) C0164/19
21st, (1) B1055/23
215 (1) B1161/33
22 (2) B1385/02 C0205/39
22" (1) C0157/10
221 (1) B1161/37
23 (2) B0753/13 C0429/22
23' (2) C0159/18 C0162/23
231,920 (1) C0400/14
237,000 (2) C0400/04 C0400/11
24 (3) B0753/20 B1384/14 C0139/07
24' (1) C0155/10
24" (1) C0157/08
240 (1) B1164/39
240,000 (2) C0428/21 C0428/26
25 (8) A0484/33
A0484/35 A0485/06 A0485/12 B0753/31
B1383/25 C0139/38 C0565/25
25,000 (5) B1079/25
B1080/10 B1080/26 B1080/29 C0401/05
25' (1) C0162/24
2500 (2) B1073/08 B1073/20
26 (3) B0754/09 C0140/27 C0158/31
26,400 (1) C0404/36
26' (1) C0155/15
27 (2) A0366/17 C0140/34
27' (2) C0160/31 C0161/05
28 (3) B0753/36 C0141/01 C0147/27
28' (1) C0163/11
2848 (1) B1291/13
29 (1) C0141/07
29' (2) C0161/39 C0162/05
3 (13) A0487/15
B0876/29 B1168/18 B1294/15 B1391/19
C0101/29 C0143/26 C0195/02 C0195/03
C0204/12 C0207/39 C0430/24 C0548/41
3. (1) A0611/32
3,000,000 (1) B1169/33
3rd (1) C0416/16
30 (1) C0141/14
30' (4) C0088/30
C0161/29 C0162/05 C0163/38
300 (1) C0403/23
300,000 (1) B1137/33
31 (3) B0754/04 C0141/23 C0148/27
31' (2) C0159/15 C0161/29
32 (1) C0423/22
322 (1) C0441/V
33 (1) B0836/21
34 (1) B1383/20
35 (1) C0088/30
37 (5) A0485/08
C0150/05 C0154/23 C0155/09 C0155/15
37.4 (1) C0394/01
37' (1) C0157/08
38 (1) C0159/02
39 (1) A0464/03
4 (10) B0837/23 B1298/25
B1392/10 C0143/38 C0195/22 C0195/24
C0204/20 C0207/45 C0548/41 C0568/06
4th (2) C0102/05 C0416/38
40 (2) C0163/38 C0527/32
40,000 (1) B1073/04
40' (2) C0150/38 C0159/14
40" (1) C0157/09
40th (1) C0527/15
4000 (3) A0541/16
A0541/21 C0400/12
4071 (1) C0430/22
41 (2) C0158/14 C0162/24
42 (5) C0150/07
C0163/04 C0163/14 C0164/19 C0166/03
42,000 (1) C0428/25
43 (1) C0167/22
43' (1) C0157/08
46 (1) C0150/05
46' (1) C0150/05
46th (1) C0528/15
47 (6) C0157/08 C0157/09

TOTAL WORDS = 468687

->C0157/10 C0157/27 C0161/29 C0162/05
47th (1) C0528/15
48 (3) C0150/07 C0150/38 C0570/09
5 (13) B1299/24
C0145/35 C0163/12 C0195/03 C0196/09
C0204/26 C0207/39 C0419/10 C0430/24
C0430/24 C0549/15 C0567/05 C0568/29
5' (1) C0167/22
5th (2) C0102/13 C0417/12
50 (3) A0485/11 B1392/07 C0430/25
50' (1) C0166/03
5010 (1) A0366/17
5080 (1) C0400/13
51 (1) B1166/32
52 (1) C0157/08
52' (1) C0160/31
53 (6) B1166/32 B1358/07
C0157/09 C0157/10 C0157/26 C0526/05
53' (1) C0150/05
5376 (1) C0423/24
54' (2) C0159/16 C0159/33
55 (1) C0526/07
55' (1) C0157/09
56 (1) C0527/13
56th (1) C0524/29
57' (2) C0157/10 C0158/31
58' (2) C0157/27 C0160/06
59 (2) C0159/14 C0160/06
59.9643 (1) C0400/03
59' (1) C0150/07
6 (7) A0485/13
B1055/29 B1300/30 C0146/05 C0204/35
C0430/23 C0553/06
6' (1) C0150/39
6th (5) B1069/15
B1075/20 B1075/33 C0102/24 C0417/21
60 (1) C0158/14
60th (1) C0524/34
61 (2) B1168/34 C0088/31
63 (2) B1385/14 C0162/23
64 (1) C0160/31
66 (1) C0161/29
67 (3) C0159/06 C0159/15 C0161/38
69 (6) B1384/33 C0150/39
C0160/37 C0161/39 C0162/05 C0163/04
7 (6) B1075/22 B1302/16
C0146/13 C0163/25 C0205/06 C0559/08
7th (2) C0102/35 C0417/33
70 (3) C0159/18 C0160/07 C0161/03
70th (1) C0524/28
706 (1) A0485/06
71 (2) B1166/30 C0159/32
7254 (1) C0418/02
73 (1) C0163/13
74 (1) C0160/22
75 (1) A0485/02
78 (1) C0163/38
8 (10) B0836/21 B0837/10
B0837/11 B0837/16 B0837/19 B0837/23
B1302/25 C0205/14 C0559/38 C0570/10
8' (2) C0154/23 C0154/23
8'48" (1) C0419/10
8th (3) B1080/14 C0103/07 C0418/40
81 (1) C0164/19
82 (2) B1358/07 C0166/03
83 (1) C0167/22
9 (3) C0205/21 C0560/07 C0570/17
9th (5) B1069/16
B1081/14 C0103/16 C0419/14 C0524/28
90 (1) B1166/31
900,000,000 (1) B1167/33
96 (1) A0485/14

TOTAL INDEXED WORDS = 25906

POE'S COMPOUND WORDS

The following list which gives all the words containing hyphens is derived from the sorted words in the main section of this Index. They are here printed in reverse or "flapped back" order, with the very last element in the word given first. The last hyphen has been cancelled and a comma has been inserted by a special computer program, *after* the last element, here placed alphabetically. Thus:

blood-tinted	becomes	tinted, blood
Bowling-Green	becomes	Green, Bowling
Opium-eater	becomes	eater, Opium
sea-biscuit	becomes	biscuit, sea

The last element is usually a word, hereby revealed to the student of Poe in its alphabetical place, but not separately given in the Frequency List. In part the reason is that several of Poe's words with hyphens do not yield full words for the final element, as we see in ma-a-an (an, ma-a), moon-hoax-y (y, moon-hoax), cock-a-doodle-doo (doo, cock-a-doodle), x-ed (ed, x), O-wy (wy, O). Clearly Poe uses the hyphen for humorous and rhetorical divisions. He also uses it to link the prefix elements as in re-appeared (appeared, re) and semi-axis (axis, semi) and sometimes to link a suffix, as in Hog-ishly (ishly, Hog) or Carlyle-ism (ism, Carlyle). He also joins an adverb to its governing adjective, as in neatly-folded (folded, neatly) and distantly-observed (observed, distantly). All of these hyphenated words can be checked in the main text of the Index for their location(s) and frequency via the first element, which follows the comma.

abiding, long
able, come-at
abouts, gad
absorbing, all
acquired, lately
Act, Cat
acute, not-over
acute, over
adapted, ill
admeasurement, ill
admeasurement, non
ado, despera-a
Advertisement, Walking
advised, ill
aged, middle
agency, self
agitated, highly
agonies, death
ahead, go
air, mid
aisy, Look
amendment, self
ample, X
an, ma-a
Andrewism, Merry
angel, arch
angels, earth
angle, right
angled, right
animal, land
animal, man
animals, man
ant, lion
aplasm, cat
apparelled, white
appearance, non
appearance, re
appeared, re
appears, re
arms, man-at
arms, yard
arranged, well
asperation, X
aw, he
axis, semi
back, canvass
back, draw
backed, high
backed, hollow
backs, canvas
bag, balloon
bags, carpet
bags, saddle
bail, leg
balance, counter
balanced, self
ball, billiard
ball, snow
balloon, Nassau
balls, eye
balls, musket
ban, pest
Bank, New
bar, crow
bar, sand
barber, merchant
barbers, merchant
bark, birch
bark, tan
bars, sand
bass, double
bat, man
bath, shower
bats, man
be, would
be, Would
beam, ridge
bear, bug
beast, sea
beaten, weather
beating, brow
bed, death
bedewed, blood
begrimed, paint
being, well
bell, church
bells, hand
bells, sheep
belly, pot
beloved, star
Benith, Succoth
berry, rabbit
bethumbed, much
Bezek, Adoni
bibbing, wine
bill, board
biography, auto
biscuit, sea
black, boot
black, jet
black, lamp
black, raven
blackened, smoke
blacking, patent
blacks, boot
blades, paddle
blades, shoulder
Blas, Gil
blasted, thunder
blaster, rock
blende, horn
Bleu, Bas
Bleus, Bas
block, stumbling
blocks, stumbling
blooming, resplendently
blossoming, ever
blossoms, flower
blue, sky
board, chess
board, head
boards, shifting
boat, ferry
boat, jolly
boat, keel
boat, long
boat, sail
boat, sea
boats, life
boats, steam
Bob, Oil-of
bodied, able
body, busy
bodyism, busy
boiler, soap
bolt, ring
bolts, timber
Bon, Bon
Bon's, Bon
bone, chicken
bone, thigh
boned, large
bones, cheek
Bonist, Bon
book, check
book, day
book, memorandum
book, note
book, pocket
Book, Day
Book, Jest
boom, jib
bottle, wine
bottomed, flat
bottomed, leather
bound, elegantly
bound, iron
bound, sable
bound, steel
bowl, punch
bowl, salad
box, phosphorus
box, pill
box, snuff
box, stage
box, watch
box, wine
boxes, air
boy, school
break, day
bred, ill
bred, thorough
breeches, knee
breed, half
breeding, ill
bridle, chain
brilliancy, sea
brows, eye
Brules, Bois
brush, tar
brushes, sweeping
bubble, air
buckingham, silk
buckles, shoe
bud, red
bud, rose
bug, goole
Bug, Cold
builders, ship
built, cottage
built, well
burial, sea
burned, hard
burthened, deeply
bushes, briar
bushes, currant
bushes, filbert
bushes, rose
buttoned, closely
by, by-and
by, by-the
by, good
bye, by-the
bye, good
cabin, after
cabin, cuddy
cable, chain
calculation, mis
called, mis
called, so
Cameleopard, Homo
cane, sugar
canopy, fog
cap, fool's
cap, funnel
cap, night
capped, snow
captured, re
capturing, re
care, devil-me
cart, ox
case, book
case, dressing
case, stair
cask, oil
casks, oil
casks, water
castor, pepper
ceasing, never
cellar, salt
cellars, wine
cellent, X
centric, X
chain, chandelier
chains, fore
chains, main
chair, arm
chair, rocking
chairs, arm
chamber, ante
chamber, bed
chamber, dais
chamber, turret
channel, mid
chat, chit
cherished, long
chest, iron
chest, sea
chests, arm
chief, commander-in
chilling, blood
chloride, Bi
circular, semi
citizens, fellow
clack, click
clasped, iron
clock, water
closet, book
clothes, bed
clothes, night
clothes, small
cloths, floor
cloths, oil
cloud, thunder
Clout, Dish
coach, stage
coal, sea
coast, sea
coat, waist
cock, chicken
cock, turkey
cognizance, self
collar, shirt
collectors, sub
collegians, fellow
color, snuff
colored, blood
colored, copper
colored, fiery
colored, gaudy
colored, many
colored, orange
colored, parti
colored, ruby
colored, straw
colored, tawny
colour, water
coloured, light
coloured, orange
coloured, parti
coloured, violet
comb, curry
comb, pocket
commence, re
commentaries, sub
commoner, fellow
communication, inter
compass, pocket
complacency, self
compose, re

conceit, self
conceived, ill
concentrated, highly
concerted, well
condemned, death
conditioned, well
congratulation, self
conscientious, over
consequence, self
considered, well
consistent, self
constructed, ill
continued, long
contrived, ill
contrived, well
cord, whip
corn, hot
cornered, three
Council, Town
councillors, privy
course, matter-of
coursers, war
cover, book
covered, moss
crag, ocean
cream, ice
creature, fellow
credence, half
cross, re
crossed, re
crossing, street
crowing, cock
crust, pie
cry, death
cuffed, hand
cuffing, hand
curious, over
curling, naturally
curtain, drop
cushioned, luxuriously
cut, prism
cut, wood
cutters, wood
cutting, wood
d'esprit, jeu
dabble, mud
Dabbling, Mud
dancers, ballet
daughter, grande
dauns>, Maiter-di
day, birth
day, every
day, hey
day, mid
day, moon
day, noon
day, to
day's, to
days, dog
days, now-a
dealers, double
deck, half
decks, between
dee, tweedle
deer, mule
defence, self
defined, sharply
demons, fever
demonstration, self
desired, long
desk, writing
destruction, self
detailed, faintly
devil, dare
devil, poor
devouring, all
dial, sun
Did, Katy
Diddle, Hey-Diddle
Didn't, Katy
digested, well
directed, ill
directed, re
directed, well
discernible, barely
dishes, side
disposed, ill
distant, far
distinction, contra
divided, sub
do, well-to
dog, bull
dog, lap
dog, water
dogs, fire
doo, cock-a-doodle
doo, cock-a-doodle-de
doo, cock-a-doodle-de-doo
doo, eighty
doodle, cock-a
doodleing, cock-a
doooooh, cock-a-doodle-de
door, next
door, street
door, trap
door, vault
doors, folding
doors, shop
doux, billet
Dow, Rowdy
dow, Rowdy
dowed, row-de
down, eider
down, knock
down, up-side
down, upside
dozen, half-a
draping, linen
drawn, long
dream, after
dream, day
dream, opium
dreamer, day
dreams, day
dressed, well
dressed, white
driver, omnibus
driver, screw
drop, dew
drops, ruby
Druidical, semi
Drum, Hum
drum, Hum
dum, tweedle
dust, gimlet
dust, saw
dying, never
ease, heart's
East/Review, Down
east, down
east, south
East, Down
east, North
Easter, Down
eastern, north
eastern, south
Eastern, North
eaten, time
eaten, worm
eater, fire
eater, Opium
echo, re
echoed, re
ed, x
ed, X
educated, generally
effeminacy, over
egory, cat
eight, fifty
eight, forty
eight, twenty
eighth, sixty
eighth, twenty
eighths, seven
elastic, gum
embroidered, richly
eminence, pre
eminent, pre
eminent, super
eminently, pre
employing, re
empty, half
enamelled, flower
enclose, re
enclosed, re
encumbered, law
end, butt
ends, beam
enduring, long
enemy, arch
enemy, Arch
enforcement, re
engendered, half
engendered, opium
engendered, Bacon
engine, steam
engrossing, all
enkindled, fear
entered, re
entering, re
entity, non
epistolary, non
erect, cat
erected, re
ermined, rich
established, re
esteem, self
evidency, self
evident, self
examination, re
examined, re
exhibiters, monkey
exist, co
existent, pre
existing, self
exquisite, hyper
eyed, blue
eyed, one
faced, fiery
fact, matter-of
fall, foot
fall, night
fall, water
famed, far
Farm, Chalk
fashion, sloop
fashioned, old
fastened, copper
fastened, re
fated, ill
favored, ill
feathered, sable
feet, web
feigned, well
fervid, all
fiend, arch
Fiend, Arch
fifth, eighty
fifth, sixty
fifth, twenty
fight, swamp
finders, money
finding, fault
finger, fore
first, thirty
first, twenty
fish, flying
fish, gold
fishery, whale
fitted, ill
fitting, close
fitting, tight
five, fifty
five, forty
five, seventy
five, sixty
five, thirty
five, twenty
fizzitistical, hyper
flavoured, well
fledged, new
flowered, gold
flowing, gently
flowing, out
fly, dragon
Fly, Gad
flying, swift
fold, two
folded, neatly
Fool, Tom
footed, four
footed, leaden
footfall, gentle
for, unlooked
for, unpaid
forechains, weather
forgotten, long
forgotten, never-to-be
formed, half
formed, regularly
forte, piano
fortune, ill
forward, straight
forward, strait
founded, ill
four, eighty
four, fifty
four, forty
four, ninety
four, sixty
four, thirty
four, twenty
fours, seventy
fourth, eighty
fourth, ninety
fourth, one
fourth, sixty
fox, kitt
Fred, Man
frequented, well
Friday, Man
fringed, lily
Frog, Hop
Frog's, Hop
frozen, stiff
Fudge/University, Fum
Fudge, Fum
ful, goblet
full, basin
full, oven

furnished, ill
furnished, well
furniture, death
furniture, ship
Gabalus, Elah
gallant, top
gallon, three
garden, flower
garden, landscape
Garden, Landscape
gardener, landscape
Gardener, Landscape
gardening, landscape
gardens, landscape
garter, clasp
gas, coal
gate, garden
gate, water
gear, sounding
gh, o-o-o-o
girl, cigar
girl, perfumery
girl, segar
glass, cut
glass, eye
glass, ground
glass, looking
glass, opera
glass, spy
glasses, burning
glasses, looking
go, touch-and
go, Touch-and
goblins, plague
god, demi
gone, by
goods, dry
Gothic, semi
gown, morning
gradation, retro
granulated, delicately
Gras, Prince/de/Foie
gratulation, self
green, pea
Green, Bowling
grinder, organ
grinders, organ
grinding, organ
grooved, iron
ground, above
ground, back
ground, burial
ground, fore
ground, play
ground, promenade
grounded, well
grouping, color
growing, rankly
growing, rapidly
Growing, Cat
grown, full
grown, grass
gull, sea
gun, ninety
guns, fire
guns, spring
gurdy, hurdy
Gush, Mige
haired, fair
haired, shaggy
half, one
hand, minute
handed, left
handed, second
handedly, left
handkerchief, neck
handkerchief, pocket
handkerchiefs, pocket
handle, pump
handles, pump
handles, sword
hanging, over
hangings, paper
hangings, tapestry
hardiness, fool
harp, jews
harp, wind
hatch, companion
hatchway, main
hauled, close
hazard, hap
Head/Lake, Dog
head, death's
head, fountain
head, heels-over
head, mast
head, Bullet
head's, Bullet
headed, addle
headed, bullet
headed, button
headed, double
headed, dunder
headed, light
headed, thick
headed, Death's
headedness, hot
heads, cat
heads, death's
health, ill
hearted, best
hearted, frank
hearted, good
hearted, hard
hearted, kind
hearted, light
hearted, warm
heartedness, light
heated, re
heavers, coal
heavy, top
heeled, high
hen, marsh
Henna, Ge
hens, marsh
hero, novel
Heroded, out
heroded, out
Hill, Bunker
himself, every-man-for
hire, cab
hoax, moon
Hoax, Balloon
Hoax, Moon
hold, foot
holding, pen
hole, bung
hole, gimlet
hole, key
hole, loop
holes, arm
holes, worm
holidays, half
honored, time
hopper, grass
horn, big
horn, ram's
horn, French
horror, pseudo
horse, mill
hot, red
hour, death
house, ale
house, charnel
house, compting
house, counting
house, dwelling
house, fowl
house, glass
house, light
house, manor
house, pot
house, prison
house, spring
house, watch
House, Coffee
House, Light
House, Prison
houses, mad
houses, out
houses, pot
houses, tap
hued, leaden
humor, ill
humored, good
humoredly, good
humour, good
humouredly, good
hundred, eighty-two
hundredth, sixteen
hunter, fox
hunters, picturesque
I, nill
I, will
ian, Hog
idead, one
identity, self
Iferous, Pest
Ilential, Pest
imparted, never-to-be
important, all
imposed, self
imprisoned, long
inch, three
increasing, still
Indian, half
informed, well
ing, O
ing, X
insane, half
inspiring, awe
inspiring, horror
inspiring, terror
instituted, re
interest, self
interlocking, closely
interred, long
interred, re
interspersed, stripe
interspersed, Asphodel
introduction, cab
iron, wrought
ish, Neufchatel
ishly, Hog
ishly, Ram
island, sand
ism, Carlyle
ism, Montesquieu
ism, Tacitus
ites, Hog
izing, lion
jacket, pea
jacket, straight
jackets, leather
jars, olive
jaw, under
jellies, orange
jobbers, stock
jockey, horse
jug, water
keep, donjon
keeper, game
keeper, shop
keeper, tavern
kegs, water
kelp, sea
kimbo, a
klock, Klock
knife, carving
knife, pen
knife, pocket
knit, strongly
knit, well
knives, case
knot, bow
knot, eleven
knot, slip
knot, ten
known, well
kraut, sauer
ladder, companion
laid, deeply
laid, re
lamps, gas
lamps, town
land, spirit
land, table
lantern, battle
lanterns, battle
lanyards, weather
largely, over
latch, thumb
law, brother-in
law, sister-in
leaf, dog
leather, patent
leather, russet
leaved, broad
leaves, vine
lee, hard-a
leg, chair
legged, slim
legs, bow
Legs, Daddy-Long
length, full
less, people
let, under
Levi, Ben
Levi, Buzi-Ben
Li, Ju-Kiao
li, Tekeli
lids, eye
life, school
lifting, spirit
light, fire
light, sky
light, wax
lighted, gas
like, beast
like, business
like, cat
like, chasm
like, child
like, corpse
like, demon
like, diamond
like, dream
like, eye
like, fairy
like, fang

like, frog
like, gauze
like, gentleman
like, glass
like, glow-worm
like, hair
like, lath
like, laughter
like, life
like, liver
like, mirror
like, pall
like, plume
like, prison
like, razor
like, saffron
like, satin
like, scimetar
like, serpent
like, shadow
like, silver
like, snake
like, statue
like, swan
like, sylph
like, vapour
like, vice
like, web
like, Madonna
like, Satyr
likeliness, life
likeness, life
lilies, water
lime, slack
line, bee
line, boundary
line, tow
line, towing
liner, penny-a
lip, upper
list, sick
list, subscription
litten, gas
litten, red
litter>, love
load, canoe
loaf, sugar
logged, water
Lol, Fol
long, side
looking, black
looking, bleak
looking, cabalistic
looking, cadaverous
looking, cosy
looking, crooked
looking, effeminate
looking, fairy
looking, fantastical
looking, ferocious
looking, fine
looking, foreign
looking, frightful
looking, gallant
looking, ghastly
looking, gloomy
looking, good
looking, hearty
looking, humar
looking, ill
looking, indifferent
looking, ivory
looking, light
looking, lily
looking, liquid
looking, magical
looking, massive
looking, misty
looking, muscular
looking, odd
looking, peculiar
looking, picturesque
looking, plain
looking, rakish
looking, romantic
looking, rough
looking, singular
looking, solid
looking, square
looking, stiff
looking, stumpy
looking, stupid
looking, wild
looking, Eastern
lost, long
love, ladye
love, poet
love, self
lovers, money
luck, ill
luminosity, non
luminous, non
lunatic, lunar
lurch, lee
Lussac, Gay
lustre, lack
mad, stage
made, ill
Magnetic, Electrc
maid, lady's
maker, attaghan
maker, bellows
man, belfry
man, frog
manager, line
mannered, ill
manufacture, dollar
marcy, Lor-gol-a
Mare, Night
Margaux, Chateau
marine, ultra
marked, singularly
marks, shoe
mast, mizen
mast, mizzen
master, school
match, slow
mates, co
mathematicians, men
meal, oat
meant, well
measure, tape
meat, dog
meat, tortoise
meeting, camp
melon, water
melt, re
memorable, ever
men, fellow
men, pie
mender, bellows
mentioned, above
mentioned, first
merited, well
metal, bell
metal, semi
mill, music
mind, master
minded, beautiful
minded, bloody
minded, carnal
minded, fickle
minded, high
minded, simple
minded, single
minded, weak
mindedness, fickle
mindedness, high
minds, master
mirror, pocket
model, re
modelled, re
modelled, well
moles, ground
morrow, to
morrow's, to
mottled, gray
mouthed, open
moved, mechanically
movement, self
moving, self
murder, self
n, Ma-a-a-a
nail, door
nails, finger
naked, half
name, flash
named, above
nature, praeter
natured, good
natured, ill
nay, yea
needle, knitting
negligent, half
neighs, Cock
nettings, boarding
new, nearly
nics, pic
night, to
nine, forty
nine, ninety
nine, seventy
nine, thirty
ninth, ninety
ninth, twenty
nip, cat
nobody, good-for-nothing-to
Noir, Rouge-et
nopolis, Alexander-etc.
north, half
nose, hawk
nosed, bottle
nosed, carbuncle
Not, Touch-me
not, Touch-me
note, chanticleer
note, foot
notes, bank
notes, foot
nothing, good-for
Nu, Nu
number, whole
nurtured, gin
nut, hickory
nuts, cocoa
nxbxdy, gxxd-fxr-nxthing-to-
O, capital
o, little
o, no-o
observed, distantly
odigies, pro-o
of, unheard
off, cast
office, barge
offices, printing
oil, fish
oiled, well
omened, ill
on, mo-o
on, mo-o-o
one, dot-and-carry
one, fifty
one, forty
one, ninety
one, twenty
os, Kickapo-o-o
osseous, semi
out, look
outang, ourang
Outang, Ourang
outangs, ourang
Outangs, Orang
Outangs, Ourang
paced, slow
paced, snail
padded, double
Paint, White
painter, landscape
panes, window
pannelled, curiously
paper, sensation
paper, vellum
parlance, sea
part, bi
part, hinder
Part, Bi
parted, half
party, shore
party, war
passage, re
passages, love
passion, soul
past, half
past, quarter
path, by
path, foot
paths, by
pearl, mother-of
pedler, fig
peel, orange
peltries, cat
penetrating, space
Peor, Baal
perfectibility, human
perfumed, vanilla
Perith, Baal
pervading, all
Pest, Ana
Pest, Tem
Phittim, Abel
phraseology, school
pick, tooth
piece, a
piece, head
piece, mantel
piece, side
piece, time
pieces, mantel
pieces, phantasy
pieces, time
pigeons, carrier
pinny>, forty
pipe, wine
pipes, bag
pipes, waste
pitched, low
pits, arm
place, common
place, dwelling
place, fire

place, hiding
place, lurking
place, resting
place, sleeping
places, bathing
places, common
places, fire
places, sitting
placid, ever
plains, sand
planetary, inter
plank, oak
plant, coffee
plate, copper
plate, dial
plates, forechain
player, automaton-chess
player, chess
player, stage
player, Chess
pleasurable, half
plicable, in-X
plumed, brilliantly
plumed, white
plumes, hearse
plused, non
pocket, breast
pocket, coat
pocket, side
pocket, waistcoat
pockets, pick
poems, love
point, starting
pointed, sharp
polished, highly
poplars, lombardy
position, juxta
possession, self
post, bed
post, rubbing
post, stern
Post, Sham
posts, bed
posts, trading
pot, flower
pot, tea
Pot, Tea
Pot's, Tea
pouches, tobacco
pound, five
powder, pearl
pox, small
practice, mal
precise, half
preserver, life
President, Ex
President, Vice
press, X
prevalent, ever
prevalent, omni
procured, re
producing, death
producing, sleep
profound, over
proof, bullet
Puddle, Mud
puncheon, rum
purged, death
quarter, three
questioning, cross
quill, goose
quizzical, half
race, foot
race, mill
rack, card
rate, under
rated, over
read, re
received, generally
red, blood
red, dusky
red, ruby
reef, two
reefed, close
reefed, double
refined, death
regulated, ill
regulated, well
reliefs, bas
remembered, dim
remembered, ever
rending, heart
ribbon, bonnet
ridden, demagogue
rig, thimble
rigged, barque
rigged, schooner
rigged, square
right, down
Right, Copy
ring, ear
ringers, Bell
rings, ear
rise, sun
riveted, iron
road, carriage
road, main
roarings, bull
robber, mail
robber, street
robed, black
rod, lightning
rods, lightning
room, ball
room, bed
room, dining
room, dissecting
room, drawing
room, school
room, session
room, sleeping
room, state
room, store
room, stowage
room, tap
rooms, drawing
rooms, state
rope, bell
rope, drag
rope, guide
ropes, drag
route, wheel
sac, cul-de
sacrificing, self
sail, stay
sail, studded
sail, studding
sails, after
sails, wind
same, self
Saracenic, semi
sash, window
satisfaction, self
satisfied, self
saturated, brandy
saving, labor
saw, see
Saxon, Anglo
scarred, art
scattering, brain
scented, highly
scented, sweet
Scented, Highly
scratches, pencil
scription, re
sealed, re
search, re
searched, re
searching, far
seat, devil's
seated, deep
seated, re
second, eighty
second, seventy
second, thousand-and
second, twenty
Second, Thousand-and
second,, twenty
seeing, far
seeker, gold
seekers, money
sense, common
sentiment, half
servant, negro
servers, time
set, deep
set, sun
settled, well
seven, eighty
seven, forty
seven, ninety
seven, seventy
seven, sixty
seven, thirty
seven, twenty
seventh, twenty
sevenths, five
Shade, Horse
shadowed, deeply
shadows, star
shaped, coffin
shaped, lenticular
shaped, star
shears, tailor's
sheet, winding
sheets, stern
shell, sea
shells, egg
ship, packet
ship, whale
ship, whaling
ship>, leddy
ships, amid
ships, whaling
Shittim, Abel
shoes, over
shore, sea
shot, cannister
shot, pistol
shotted, double
shut, half
shutters, shop
sick, heart
sickness, sea
side, bed
side, hill
side, road
sided, one
sided, sober
sides, hill
sighted, clear
similes, fac
sinking, fast
sinking, re
sites, building
six, eighty
six, fifty
six, sixty
six, thirty
sixth, forty
sixth, twenty
sized, well
skelteriness, helter
skin, elk
skin, ham
skinning, eel
skins, bear
slate, mica
slide, land
slopes, mountain
Slow, Jo-Go
slumber, half
slumberous, half
smith, silver
snake, rattle
snapper, whipper
snatchers, body
So, So-and
so, So-and
sojourners, fellow
soled, thick
solution, re
soothing, spirit
sore, eye
Soul, Bless-my
soul, Bless-my
sounding, hollow
sounding, shrill
Spattering, Cur
spike, marlin
spike, marling
spiral, semi
spirited, high
spirited, noble
spirits, pest
splitting, hair
spot, blood
spread, freshly
spreading, over
spreading, wide
squeaked, re
stained, blood
stalking, deer
stall, book
stars, shooting
stated, re
staysails, storm
steeple, Christchurch
stemmed, triple
stems, tree
still, stand
stirring, heart
stirring, soul
stirring, spirit
stock, joint
stone, key
stone, mile
stone, pudding
stone, pumice
Stone, White
stones, corner
stones, paving
stores, sea
Story, Moon
street, bye
stretched, far
stricken, awe
stricken, horror
stricken, panic
stricken, terror

stricken, wonder
strings, leading
strings, purse
striped, black
striped, parti
stroke, master
strom, Moskoe
struck, stage
struggles, death
stuff, humming
stuff, ratlin
stuffin/University, Gutt
sty, pig
style, new
subdued, half
sufferers, fellow
sufficient, all
suggestion, self
summer, mid
sustained, long
sustained, well
svigging, a
Syllabus, Slang
syncope, hemi
syncope, semi
table, card
table, dining
table, dinner
table, wine
table, writing
tail, coat
tailed, black
tailed, cur
tailed, swallow
tails, coat
Tale, Tell
talked, much
tanks, oil
tattle, tittle
Telegraph, Electro
tempered, finest
tempered, good
tenths, nine
teuffel, head
That, This-and
that, This-and
third, forty
third, one
third, twenty
thirds, two
thirstiness, blood
thirsty, blood
thirtieth, one
thought, transition
thousandth, eighteen
thread, pack
threaded, gold
three, eighty
three, fifty
three, rule-of
three, thirty
three, twenty
throat, cut
throthing>, bog
throtting>, bog
tide, low
tight, air
tight, water
time, day
time, life
timed, happily
timed, ill
timed, well
tinted, blood
tinted, crimson
tinted, myriad
tinted, triple
tintinnabulic, Electro
to, flapping
tone, under
toned, deep
toned, high
toned, loud
tones, bell
tones, proof
tongue, mother
tongued, trumpet
tools, edge
top, hill
top, humming
top, mountain
top, tree
topped, over
tops, hill
tops, mountain
tops, tree
tormented, storm
totum, tee
touch, new
touching, re
tow, under
towers, shot
Town, York
track, carriage
tracks, wheel
trader, fur
traordinary, X
trap, mouse
trap>, purraty
traps, beaver
traps, man
traps, rat
traveller, fellow
treated, ill
tree, pear
tree, tulip
trees, plum
treme, X
tremity, x
tressels, coffin
trigger, gun
Tritonic, inter
trot, jog
tuned, well
turtle, sea
Turtle, Snapping
turvy, topsy
twentieth, three-hundred-and
twenty, five-and
twenty, one-and
two, eighty
two, fifty
two, sixty
two, thirty
two, twenty
uberance, X
un, Club/Vingt
uncle, grand
up, dammed
up, use
up, using
used, ill
value, over
veiled, close
velvet, silk
ventilated, ill
vermin, men
vessel, whaling
vessels, blood
vessels, seed
vessels, steam
victorious, ever
vine, grape
vines, grape
visaged, dusky
Vor/House, Weal
Vor, Wheal
waker, sleep
waker's, sleep
waking, sleep
walnut, black
war, man-of
war, men-of
ware, crockery
ware, tinned
ware, Britannia
warm, luke
warmer, coffee
watches, death
water, back
water, bilge
water, fresh
water, high
water, low
water, rose
water, slack
waving, naturally
wax, sealing
wax, taper
way, arch
way, companion
way, forecastle
way, gate
way, half
way, out-of-the
wayfarers, fellow
weed, milk
weeds, sea
weight, make
West/Company's, North
west, north
west, south
West, South
western, north
western, south
Western, North
westwardly, north
Whang, Slang
wheat, buck
wheel, mill
wheels, chariot
while, ere
white, grayish
white, snow
white, snowy
whoop, war
will, good
willed, self
winded, double
wing, pigeon
winged, misty
winged, pigeon
winged, raven
winger, pigeon
winging, pigeon
wings, pigeon
wires, cage
wise, over
wit, Too
wit's, Too
witnesses, eye
womanish, old
wondrous, half
wood, cotton
wood, rose
wood, satin
wooded, thickly
wool, cotton
woolsey, linsey
word, catch
work, brick
work, frame
work, iron
work, lead
work, mason
work, net
work, plank
work, trellice
work, trellis
work, web
work, wicker
work, wood
working, wonder
works, tinder
worm, coral
worm, earth
worms, silk
worn, time
worshippers, cat
wou>, pully
wou>, wolly
wou>, woolly
wou>, wouly
wouing>, parly
wow, bow-wow
wrapper, dressing
wreathed, ivy
writer, letter
writing, hand
writing, re
written, un
wxw, bxw-wxw
wy, o
wy, O
y, moon-hoax
yard, lumber
Yard, Court
yards, church
year, leap
York/Sun, New
York, New
zag, zig
Zebub, Baal
1, 15

FREQUENCY LIST IN DESCENDING ORDER

(34485)
the
(20515)
of
(13921)
and
(11276)
to
(10861)
a
(9631)
in
(7883)
I
(5326)
was
(5301)
that
(5166)
it
(4276)
with
(3934)
as
(3702)
my
(3614)
at
(3552)
which
(3414)
is
(3306)
had
(3160)
for
(3084)
he
(3039)
his
(2853)
by
(2843)
this
(2838)
not
(2696)
we
(2616)
but
(2578)
be
(2410)
from
(2342)
have
(2261)
upon
(2010)
were
(1958)
all
(1891)
or
(1876)
no
(1851)
me
(1811)
an
(1702)
so
(1632)
on
(1588)
been
(1531)
you
(1492)
one
(1361)
there
(1311)
very
(1222)
more
(1205)
its
(1182)
our
(1166)
now
(1162)
are
(1160)
some
(1145)
could
(1143)
him

(1079)
her
(1075)
than
(1018)
into
(1001)
when
(996)
what
(988)
their
(981)
they
would
(939)
about
(897)
any
(892)
up
(859)
these
(817)
them
(814)
will
(803)
if
who
(789)
us
(783)
most
(774)
then
(750)
said
(669)
much
(666)
great
made
(662)
out
(640)
only
(632)
has
little
(618)
however
(614)
found
(610)
time
(609)
say
(598)
before
(587)
two
(582)
being
here
(571)
other
she
(559)
well
(551)
even
Mr
(543)
first
should
(535)
through
(521)
after
such
(513)
thus
(502)
might
(495)
man
(491)
without
(488)
long
myself
(487)
over
(474)
yet
(470)
having
(465)
every

(464)
your
(461)
still
(457)
did
(448)
own
(446)
while
(441)
down
(438)
do
(423)
never
(420)
whole
(413)
length
(410)
way
(406)
many
(400)
may
(391)
too
(389)
although
(377)
must
(376)
once
(375)
good
indeed
three
(365)
day
like
(363)
nothing
(360)
far
(357)
can
(356)
himself
(351)
thought
(347)
again
(344)
how
(343)
those
(341)
within
(335)
eyes
(331)
am
(330)
where
(327)
water
(326)
just
(325)
large
(324)
came
(317)
head
(315)
feet
(304)
until
(303)
let
(302)
seemed
(295)
few
(294)
make
means
(293)
see
(291)
manner
(289)
night
(286)
among
seen
(285)
old
(283)

during
(282)
left
(281)
hand
(278)
course
(277)
less
(273)
same
(272)
took
(270)
mind
(265)
matter
nearly
point
(264)
words
(263)
saw
(260)
body
(255)
ever
itself
(254)
fact
(252)
full
under
(247)
shall
(242)
off
(240)
part
thing
(236)
back
know
(235)
doubt
immediately
(231)
least
small
(230)
also
(229)
each
nature
(228)
men
(225)
lay
(224)
moment
(222)
became
(221)
called
(219)
felt
idea
(217)
light
(216)
half
(214)
period
(213)
air
soon
(212)
between
(211)
place
(210)
whose
(209)
altogether
(207)
character
(205)
appearance
(204)
possible
(202)
life
went
years
(200)
appeared
fell
nor
put
(199)

several
(198)
hundred
last
think
(196)
days
(195)
death
friend
gave
(194)
name
person
sea
take
(193)
perhaps
right
(192)
rather
(191)
present
(188)
account
four
(186)
above
why
(185)
end
face
(184)
attention
(183)
around
both
general
sure
world
(182)
earth
(181)
another
certain
heard
heart
river
taken
(180)
question
(179)
truth
(178)
either
word
(176)
portion
(175)
open
reason
(173)
difficulty
latter
(172)
case
side
therefore
thousand
(171)
things
(170)
done
soul
voice
(169)
away
(168)
come
letter
(167)
beyond
go
(166)
near
whom
(165)
discovered
room
since
(164)
true
(162)
hour
view
(161)
always
(160)
eye
kind

party
quite
(159)
five
morning
something
(157)
merely
(156)
door
passed
(155)
cannot
themselves
(154)
brought
known
scarcely
(153)
sir
(152)
find
mere
(151)
against
get
hold
(150)
knew
(149)
minutes
set
(147)
black
(145)
distance
human
(144)
form
(143)
object
purpose
(142)
high
miles
(141)
continued
given
(140)
believe
better
entirely
paper
(139)
alone
turned
(138)
short
singular
(137)
attempt
deep
looked
second
wild
(136)
impossible
proceeded
somewhat
(135)
already
house
making
vast
(134)
degrees
effect
(133)
gentleman
(132)
degree
home
regard
wind
(131)
best
stood
surface
(130)
circumstances
longer
observed
(129)
remained
(128)
Augustus
replied
(127)
give
(126)

farther
mouth
necessary
power
spirit
(125)
sense
(124)
spoke
young
(122)
condition
six
together
(121)
beneath
grew
look
low
suddenly
(120)
bed
hands
ordinary
similar
sound
speak
(119)
direction
hours
(118)
close
fine
tell
ten
(117)
dark
God
thrown
usual
(116)
boat
corpse
especially
vessel
(115)
getting
natural
white
(114)
instant
people
round
(113)
de
position
state
(112)
ourselves
perceive
(111)
extent
hope
really
supposed
(110)
almost
peculiar
subject
(109)
city
strong
sufficient
taking
yes
(108)
force
horror
lady
next
nose
number
proper
single
species
times
(107)
arose
late
oh
Peters
sight
towards
(106)
dead
mean
(105)
chamber
entire
interest
(104)
beauty
below
(103)
neither
(102)
balloon
call
finally
love
says
sufficiently
(101)
apparently
lost
(100)
design
passage
shore
utterly
(99)
bottom
foot
fully
going
Madame
remarkable
remember
(98)
common
cut
enough
told
(97)
able
along
apparent
beautiful
dear
entered
figure
king
(96)
evident
huge
looking
received
(95)
board
Captain
exceedingly
(94)
arm
deck
extreme
feel
work
(93)
anything
business
considered
country
none
respect
(92)
because
easily
except
floor
heavy
new
points
reached
terror
use
(91)
aware
countenance
main
placed
return
succeeded
table
(90)
box
expression
fancy
fifty
greater
leaving
result
suppose
(89)
atmosphere
clear
evidence
fall
held
minute
often
opinion
strange
tree
understand
whatever
(88)
animal
bring
others
(87)
seven
(86)
events
fire
island
mentioned
perfect
spot
(85)
absolutely
line
sat
threw
twenty
wall
(84)
feeling
individual
(83)
afterwards
breath
frequently
land
moon
shadow
terrible
third
(82)
began
brig
escape
ground
height
lying
occurred
trees
weather
(81)
met
original
rest
ship
situation
(80)
extraordinary
family
precisely
proved
search
wine
(79)
accident
brief
formed
hair
narrow
sun
(78)
ago
arms
company
evidently
intense
kept
led
(77)
coming
eight
example
gone
hung
possession
public
simple
slight
thou
whether
(76)
age
become
carefully
meaning
meantime
order
particular
personal
red
reply
wife
(75)

astonishment
perceived
trouble
voyage
year
(74)
arrived
blood
got
greatly
knowledge
poor
(73)
keep
scene
turn
walls
(72)
cause
determined
evening
greatest
immediate
opportunity
south
wide
(71)
amid
discovery
ha
lips
memory
otherwise
persons
proceed
vicinity
weight
(70)
art
does
ears
friends
instance
material
pleasure
regarded
rendered
resolved
strength
teeth
(69)
aid
article
care
certainly
distinct
excellent
existence
help
imagine
nevertheless
profound
rapidly
(68)
Dupin
forced
leave
obtained
vain
(67)
across
besides
cabin
consideration
conversation
different
former
giving
imagination
read
returned
savages
seems
sole
wish
(66)
apartment
expected
influence
properly
(65)
actually
appear
book
dog
excited
size
tone
(64)
behind
car
distinctly
fellow
following
generally
MS.
objects
occasioned
real
spoken
step
(63)
action
change
died
forth
horrible
living
presence
presently
throughout
top
upper
visible
written
(62)
<u>de</u>
despair
doing
excessively
hear
important
measure
o'clock
opening
quantity
reach
sleep
usually
various
(61)
absolute
ah
chief
danger
filled
genius
gold
lie
mass
thinking
thoroughly
(60)
asked
bosom
exception
islands
loud
lower
matters
months
motion
murder
odd
readily
remain
run
sentiment
understood
window
(59)
bore
early
green
immense
letters
pass
presented
reaching
rope
sides
unusual
vision
(58)
afterward
bear
enabled
experienced
opened
physical
piece
progress
stream
violent
(57)
answer
broken
completely
corner
don't
ear
else
feeble
ice
latitude
note
occupied
principle
probably
saying
unknown
(56)
<u>a</u>
appears
circumstance
feelings
finding
gigantic
necessity
north
region
secret
speaking
thick
wonder
(55)
desire
difficult
effort
employed
fallen
followed
importance
middle
pain
passing
perfectly
sail
term
(54)
carried
darkness
descent
drew
fate
forward
frame
glass
intellect
mad
Monsieur
opposite
rapid
shape
steps
struck
suggested
suspicion
tall
watch
(53)
cat
conclusion
crowd
described
Esq.
everything
excitement
extremity
failed
falling
fifteen
hills
inches
neck
occasionally
rich
satisfied
senses
sometimes
thoughts
valley
violence
(52)
acquaintance
alive
buried
color
covered
experience
gale
gentle
gradually
happened
limbs
loss
observation
silence
style
suffered

turning
wood
(51)
afforded
building
characters
closed
equal
fail
father
gentlemen
joy
Jupiter
lines
pieces
serious
sudden
write
(50)
accomplished
centre
companions
concluded
fair
fear
hole
imagined
intention
moments
mystery
narrative
ocean
offered
Paris
prevent
reference
seem
vague
(49)
absence
afford
alas
big
blue
brain
chance
comprehend
current
editor
forthwith
hideous
hitherto
intended
intervals
iron
mate
notice
occasion
pale
path
possibly
reflection
relief
rock
street
used
yards
(48)
act
admit
admitted
articles
attained
bodies
caught
committed
departed
error
etc.
evil
extended
fashion
fastened
glance
honor
ideas
innumerable
Marie
money
nine
observe
possessed
proportion
ran
slowly
steadily
story
yourself
(47)
April
author
cold
curiosity
die
features
movement
need
passion
positively
prepared
remembered
surprise
sweet
system
windows
(46)
arrested
Baron
ceased
chair
commenced
companion
consequence
epoch
exertion
food
horse
mental
noise
numerous
pay
sent
southward
termed
(45)
closely
heaven
increased
language
magnificent
month
Mrs
noon
save
science
shot
show
stranger
waters
(44)
books
conceive
conduct
deposited
direct
edge
entertained
escaped
fool
forever
fro
hard
larger
Legrand
live
mention
mile
slightest
spirits
started
taste
throwing
twelve
writing
(43)
confusion
depth
exact
fairly
flowers
fortune
fourth
fury
happy
impression
information
keeping
lies
lofty
makes
mistaken
naturally
past
positive
putting
ready
regions
running
stone
throw
to-day
west
wore
(42)
beheld
behold
bottle
chain
conceived
deal
dream
forgotten
French
frequent
gazed
girl
gloom
grass
horizon
laid
method
mine
moral
obvious
recovered
resembling
resumed
rolled
seat
seized
skull
space
Sunday
thirty
week
(41)
accordingly
approached
astonished
crew
daily
departure
descended
details
directly
drawing
dreams
facts
fearful
free
ghastly
grave
moreover
powers
rare
render
repeated
series
southern
spring
stand
variety
violently
want
weeks
woman
(40)
affair
agony
anxiety
banks
complete
elevation
examination
forget
hardly
ill
interior
interrupted
mode
mother
partially
proceeding
prodigious
quickly
race
respecting
society
success
torn
village
(39)
consequently
contrived
convinced
English
excessive
fat
folly
habit

Indians
lived
midnight
paid
permitted
philosophy
presume
removed
slip
sooner
substance
summit
throat
understanding
(38)
assured
birds
broad
burst
child
coast
contemplation
difference
exactly
fancied
forms
holding
instantly
investigation
la
per
poet
pounds
produced
prove
resemblance
seeing
sitting
title
topic
V
volume
wonderful
(37)
aroused
beast
Bon-Bon
brilliant
broke
cases
connected
daughter
dress
easy
endeavored
examined
existed
faint
heads
labor
leading
loose
mankind
pair
parallel
particularly
plain
Prefect
principal
purposes
quarter
relieved
remote
rushed
sad
schooner
shoulders
slightly
standing
thy
ugh
writer
(36)
animals
assistance
clearly
clock
contents
delight
diameter
duty
earnest
east
expedition
grace
hero
herself
lamp
legs
particulars
perceptible
police
precise
servant
silver
tied
ultimate
velocity
wrong
(35)
amount
analysis
ancient
approaching
arrangement
attempts
beginning
bodily
bringing
capital
coffin
delicate
Doctor
dollars
Dr
drawn
engaged
game
growing
induced
longitude
opinions
page
pocket
Pompey
private
reading
sharp
straight
tears
urged
utter
(34)
adapted
afternoon
arranged
boats
captain
courage
dat
description
devil
dropped
dying
effected
energy
enter
fingers
follow
forehead
highly
hill
hurried
interval
it's
London
Missouri
mountains
P
papers
picked
prevented
pure
pushed
rays
reader
required
rise
secured
seldom
served
setting
solid
source
thence
thirst
undoubtedly
victim
visit
vivid
(33)
absorbed
actual
angles
anxious
applied
approach
arrangements
aspect
bearing
believed
bit
bold
bright
caused
charge
chiefly
conception
confess
directions
distant
effects
event
exist
experiment
flew
gang
gas
gray
health
host
increase
maintained
majesty
master
necessarily
noticed
novel
owing
parchment
plan
play
pretty
previous
probable
readers
regards
sensations
Sir
stones
surprised
town
trace
truly
unless
uttered
voices
ye
(32)
abandoned
accompanied
affairs
affected
allow
attended
bad
circle
contrary
crossed
exhausted
fancies
fit
hesitation
history
knees
lately
limits
Lollipop
meet
melancholy
northern
possibility
rain
rate
reasons
regular
remarkably
repeat
route
rushing
shadows
silent
Sioux
smile
sorrow
stern
suggestion
sum
thicket
though
tongue
willing
worth
worthy
(31)
adventure
agitation
agreed
artist
awe

bound
breeze
bug
burning
calm
canoe
concealed
crowded
detail
discover
dozen
due
Ellison
equally
floated
front
heavens
heavily
inch
intensity
Ligeia
modern
motionless
nervous
ones
palace
pause
please
quiet
rapidity
remaining
sake
scrutiny
silk
skin
slumber
spite
sprang
surely
te
terms
till
total
trap
value
wid>
yours
(30)
anticipated
ascertain
assumed
attempting
circular
completed
creation
creature
diddler
dim
distinguished
exertions
figures
forest
forming
furniture
glorious
group
happiness
hue
identity
incident
invention
liberty
Morella
observing
overboard
philosopher
proposition
recollection
relation
residence
reward
sensation
sentence
soft
sounds
stepped
struggle
succession
talk
that's
thee
thrust
traces
twice
ventured
visited
wings
women
worn
(29)
American
arising
carry
confined
consequences
convey
dense
directed
distinguish
eastward
eh
entrance
especial
fast
fellows
field
forecastle
instances
journal
knowing
L'Espanaye
Lalande
level
literary
M
machine
negro
northward
origin
originally
pressure
remark
satisfaction
settled
shortly
singularly
sixty
sort
square
stars
station
struggled
supposing
unaccountable
uncle
vessels
warm
wilderness
(28)
ability
according
admiration
alarmed
alteration
angle
ask
ballast
becomes
borne
breadth
calling
chasm
continually
Count
drop
drowned
enveloped
expectation
exquisite
faith
fantastic
firm
flat
floating
forty
further
General
gently
gives
grounds
highest
Hop-Frog
knife
laws
learned
limb
loveliness
lustre
marked
monster
move
music
neighborhood
c'>
obtain
operations
perceiving
permit
provided
quick
rage
range
results
sigh
solution
speech
suffering
supply
tale
task
totally
worse
Wyatt
(27)
absurd
abyss
acquainted
acute
amazement
apart
artificial
ascertained
attached
attempted
belonging
bitter
bow
breathing
busied
caution
channel
consider
cook
crimson
date
deadly
deceased
deeply
demeanor
describe
disease
drink
encountered
endeavor
express
extending
future
golden
grow
heat
I'll
July
June
law
leaves
madness
Miss
noble
notwithstanding
obliged
overhead
passages
pen
picturesque
pleasant
pointed
published
recesses
Rotterdam
simply
smaller
solemn
startled
supreme
terrific
thin>
treasure
weakness
(26)
added
addressed
beings
cliff
cloud
consciousness
creatures
demanded
destruction
dignity
dragged
ease
eighteen
ensued
extensive
external
fragments
Frenchman
glimpse
hiccup
higher

intolerable
lives
marble
meeting
moved
pages
paused
portions
promise
road
rough
slept
slow
son
stop
strongly
suggest
trunk
unable
uneasiness
unusually
westward
wrote
(25)
advantage
attending
avoid
base
beloved
blow
born
brains
can't
canoes
consisted
Crab
cried
cross
disorder
driven
dull
eastern
efforts
ejaculated
entering
erect
exercise
expressed
gloomy
Greek
haste
headlong
houses
Indian
ingenuity
magazine
mistake
momentary
observations
offer
patient
previously
principles
probability
prospect
que
resistance
resolution
rigid
rising
safety
savage
seamen
secure
severe
spent
spread
stage
streets
study
suspected
swallowed
swung
toward
trembled
twenty-five
upward
W.
walk
winds
wise
works
yellow
(24)
advanced
agitated
asleep
attributed
beetle
breast
breathed
bulk
cast
class
composed
composition
constantly
copy
crime
cutting
D--
definite
desired
desperate
dinner
double
dreary
earth's
enthusiasm
ere
evinced
expect
explanation
faculties
final
globe
Goodfellow
Goosetherumfoodle
gorge
grasp
habits
impressed
impressions
inconceivable
infinite
laughed
loved
Mademoiselle
Majesty
moderate
nearer
occurrence
office
Oinos
omnibus
pardon
Parker
parties
parts
peculiarity
places
practice
precipice
premises
process
purple
quietly
reflected
represented
returning
revolution
risk
sank
season
seek
shade
shook
shrill
shudder
sit
smooth
stairs
stated
striking
tail
triumph
unnecessary
unto
upwards
Valdemar
western
(23)
angels
aperture
becoming
belief
bell
bewildered
bones
bottles
bowed
branch
carpet
cats
celebrated
chin
coat
conceal
confidence
conviction
decided
diddle
disappeared
ebony
elapsed
execution
explain
favorite
fires
fish
fresh
gorgeous
hereafter
hint
humanity
hurry
ignorant
increasing
ingenious
injury
inspired
instruments
journey
L'Etoile
laugh
lest
letting
listen
mark
mirror
mortal
multitude
natives
notions
occasional
Old
Oppodeldoc
oppressed
Pedro
picture
powerful
reasonable
respects
retained
rid
shown
shut
situated
soil
struggles
subsequent
supposition
sustained
syllable
Talbot
temples
Too-wit
universe
useless
wealth
whenever
winter
wrought
(22)
add
adventures
advice
Agathos
ascend
aside
attack
August
bank
Beauvais
bent
berth
blind
breaking
calculated
cargo
ceiling
comparatively
creek
curtains
customary
dare
deed
delicious
depended
disturbed
endeavoured
enormous
fifth
firmly
freely
holy
horrors
inconvenience
insult
involved

issued
jist>
larboard
largest
leaped
massa
member
merit
Miller
names
partial
partly
personage
precipitous
prison
proposed
pulled
ravine
record
reduced
rim
Roget, Marie
roof
rose
rudder
rule
seal
seated
seconds
seemingly
slender
sorry
sought
star
startling
steel
stomach
struggling
suffer
thin
tint
tones
touching
tremendous
tribe
trivial
twenty-four
unfortunate
universal
wait
weak
wing
(21)
accustomed
affection
aloud
appalling
application
arrive
awake
bears
Blackwood
British
capacity
changed
comparison
confounded
considerable
considerations
contact
continuous
couple
deceived
descending
determine
diminished
discussion
disposition
divine
employ
en
exciting
explained
female
fever
German
glare
government
gravity
guilty
Guy
hearing
hereupon
illustrious
impulse
inclined
individuals
inhabitants
intelligence
Italian
Journal
justly
knows
lead
Maillard
margin
metaphysician
Metzengerstein
morrow
nearest
nobody
paces
passengers
Pennifeather
perish
phrase
plainly
pleased
precision
purely
relative
remains
respectable
sentiments
service
Shuttleworthy
signs
sky
spectacles
speed
starting
stay
stout
survey
talked
terrors
Thornton
Tiger
tomb
touch
touched
venture
views
wafered
wound
(20)
advance
alluded
Angel
ascending
ascent
assume
barely
boys
certainty
circumference
cliffs
cloth
clothes
conditions
constructed
contempt
continent
convenient
cry
dared
deny
derived
determination
difficulties
disappearance
dread
dreamed
dropping
eleven
emotion
empty
et
ether
examine
exceeding
finger
finished
flesh
foam
follows
handkerchief
hopes
humble
husband
identical
infinitely
inquiries
inspection
interested
interesting
January
jaws
knocked
likely
madman
man's
materially
meditation
musical
nail
odor
Oil-of-Bob
operation
outward
overwhelmed
passionate
perception
perished
pit
plunge
poem
press
pressed
principally
property
respectfully
ring
rolling
satisfactory
scenery
security
seizing
shriek
sixth
Smith
speculation
spots
stature
stiff
strictly
temperament
tempest
theme
therein
thorough
trade
uneasy
variation
villain
visiter
volumes
wanted
whence
wishes
2
(19)
abandon
address
admirable
adopted
altitude
amused
amusement
answered
anticipate
arise
ascended
assure
bandage
bill
bird
brass
capable
children
circuit
coincidence
comprehension
confused
constant
construction
custom
Dammit
dangerous
designed
diminutive
dis
discourse
doors
drunk
dwarf
edges
Egyptian
elevated
endeavors
endured
favor
fearfully
fiction
flame
formerly
furious
garden
handed
happen

Heaven
hesitate
hidden
holes
hulk
hurled
hurriedly
informed
inquiry
inside
intimate
introduction
judge
ledge
leg
lose
louder
lovely
mathematical
May
medical
mercy
mighty
mingled
mountain
mysterious
novelty
occasions
ordered
outline
peculiarly
precaution
preserved
provisions
qualities
repeatedly
rested
riveted
rooms
rush
S.
safe
Scheherazade
send
seriously
sheet
shoulder
solitude
somebody
souls
Spanish
stowage
superior
suspended
sympathy
tragedy
Una
visions
whirl
wished
wretch
yesterday
(18)
acquired
alarm
allowed
ambition
Amontillado
apparatus
argument
arisen
arrival
atrocity
attend
bade
bay
beat
beating
beg
benefit
borough
built
century
Charley
collected
colors
concealment
connection
conscience
considerably
containing
convince
covering
decidedly
decision
delay
Deluc
demand
discovering
disposed
distinctness
division
draw
dreadful
dry
duration
endure
England
exclaimed
existing
extend
false
familiar
fatal
fault
flames
France
freedom
G--
glasses
grief
guess
hanging
hearts
heir
images
in
indebted
indignation
jug
justice
lid
listened
lungs
March
medium
metal
minutely
named
nerves
O
opium
outrage
Parisian
Philadelphia
philosophers
Plato
popular
prairie
pretend
primitive
procured
project
propriety
pursued
pursuit
quality
questions
reality
relatives
resembled
rocks
roll
scarabaeus
school
screams
seas
serve
seventy
shock
sick
smoke
speaker
testimony
thirteen
tobacco
train
united
unnatural
utmost
walked
Wilson
wit
witness
(17)
accomplish
accuracy
ages
apprehension
attracted
bark
beaver
blackness
branches
brink
brother
Canadians
careful
casual
cautiously
chest
cloak
comes
comfortable
consequent
conveyed
credit
dawn
decease
deprived
destiny
detailed
dimensions
disturbance
earlier
Egypt
elbow
elements
endeavoring
entitled
est
Europe
examining
excess
flashed
fools
furiously
goes
graceful
grotesque
grown
horses
hot
humor
indefinite
inevitable
inevitably
infinity
insisted
introduced
invariably
irregular
key
learn
Legs
lip
locality
majestic
marvellous
meant
minds
miraculous
monarch
October
pains
painted
peg
perfection
performed
perpendicular
phenomenon
pity
practical
profundity
provision
puff
purchase
raised
report
repose
rival
sagacity
seeming
solitary
stands
steeple
stopped
storm
sunk
superfluous
surrounded
surrounding
talking
treated
treatise
trust
tumult
Usher
vapor
vault
visage
Vondervotteimittiss
waist
wanting
watched
wisdom
wonders
wounded
yield
youth

(16)
abruptly
absent
abundant
accidentally
accompany
acknowledge
albatross
America
analogous
angel
antique
ashamed
assert
awaited
awful
axioms
begin
behavior
Berenice
Bob
bows
boy
bridge
bundle
calamity
centuries
cheek
chimney
clouds
complexion
concerning
contained
continual
court
dangers
death's-head
deliverance
demon
den
desolate
display
distressing
doubted
drank
dreaded
Duc
dwelling
eagerly
edition
Eleonora
ends
entombed
equivocal
expressions
faded
fathoms
fissure
foliage
fortunate
frightful
gained
gasped
gleaming
granite
ho
hollow
honest
ignorance
imminent
impeded
incidents
indication
inquired
instead
interruption
kinds
knot
ladies
lapse
le
legitimate
lifted
Lord
luminous
maiden
masses
melody
mille
missing
model
modes
Moissart
mon
mud
MSS.
nights
obtaining
occur
organs
ought
outside
painting
paintings
palpable
passes
pirogue
placing
prevailed
price
produce
Professor
profoundly
profusion
proof
proportions
Pundit
quitting
rarely
receive
recognised
regret
related
remove
request
require
roads
rudimental
safely
sailed
sand
scattered
screw
sign
signal
Simpson
smiles
sober
somewhere
speaks
spectacle
speculations
steady
subjected
supplied
temple
tenth
The
theory
to-morrow
traced
trial
tried
truths
utterance
vigor
wasn't
whispered
whoever
width
wonderfully
worst
wrapped
(15)
accordance
actions
anchor
apartments
appellation
armed
atmospheric
au
avoided
bag
battery
blew
brilliancy
brute
calls
Canadian
cannon
carcass
cards
carriage
carrying
Charmion
clambered
closet
compared
concluding
confirmed
connexion
consistency
consists
consumed
criticism
daybreak
deliberately
des
discharge
dogs
downward
Dutch
dwell
eating
encampment
energetic
enthusiastic
established
eternal
expedient
farthest
feature
fierce
fiery
fled
flower
fly
forcibly
forcing
friendship
furnished
gate
gay
gaze
God's
harsh
hoop
hourly
hu
hurricane
image
imitation
impossibility
impress
indescribable
innocent
inserted
instinct
invisible
joined
joke
lantern
lasted
Latin
lights
loaded
locked
luckily
mesmeric
Mississippi
mist
motive
mutineers
nails
naked
notes
notion
oath
ob
objection
oblong
observer
obviously
onward
painter
paragraph
pervaded
pervading
physician
played
plunged
poetic
Ponnonner
portrait
possess
poured
preservation
prey
Prince
procure
pushing
puzzled
rational
recognized
reflections
relate
requisite
respiration
resulted
Rodman
sable
sails
salt
satisfy
saved
screamed
services
seventh
shirt

shores
shuddered
smiled
steep
stirred
structure
stupor
sufficed
sunrise
symptoms
taught
telescope
termination
thickly
thinks
tolerably
tortoise
trembling
trifle
try
un
unhappy
uniform
unparticled
valuable
varied
vat
vigorous
windward
wont
wreck
yard
(14)
accidents
accurately
afraid
agency
aghast
agonies
allude
allusion
altered
analogy
angry
apprehended
august
axe
axiom
Barnard
beasts
behaved
betook
bless
bloody
blowing
cab
candle
cap
causes
chains
citizens
civilized
closer
closing
cognizant
comfort
conscious
convulsive
cool
created
decomposition
delighted
depends
depths
designs
destroyed
Diana
dint
disgust
draperies
drawer
drinking
echo
education
egress
elk
enclosure
enduring
epistle
estimate
exalted
eye-glass
faces
faculty
fashioned
fitted
fitting
flight
flood
folds
fond
forbear
forbidden
foreign
Fortunato
gathering
glances
Gliddon
goods
Greely
gulf
habitual
happens
hat
Hermann
Hum-Drum
il
impatience
incomprehensible
incredible
indicated
indications
instrument
investigations
lake
legible
leisure
Lewis
liquid
magnificence
married
members
miserable
Monos
Nantucket
neat
needless
neighboring
non
occupy
Odd
officer
Ourang-Outang
overcome
owner
pantaloons
particle
peculiarities
perfume
Peters, Dirk
physicians
pipe
pitiable
Poe
pray
print
proboscis
pronounced
propensity
prostrate
pull
raising
rendering
resembles
ride
ridiculous
ringing
rod
royal
September
shining
showing
silently
silly
sinking
song
spiritual
staggered
staircase
starboard
stories
studies
surpassing
sustain
swept
tumbled
tumultuous
und
using
vale
vegetation
veins
velvet
verses
waited
wealthy
wear
whatsoever
Will
wrath
writes
18--
(13)
abstract
accurate
addition
additional
ahem
aided
anger
architecture
arousing
assembled
assembly
assuredly
Atlantic
attendance
authority
axis
Berlifitzing
boldly
buffalo
buildings
bullet
bursting
bushes
calmly
camp
career
cautious
cents
chambers
collecting
command
commence
commencement
communication
comprehended
consented
constitution
contain
Cote
Death
decayed
declared
delirium
density
descend
detect
dirty
doctrines
dwelt
eager
earliest
earthly
East
effectually
elsewhere
establish
everlasting
exaggerated
experiments
expiration
expired
extravagant
failure
finds
Gazette
glory
glow
hem
hull
hunters
imaginative
indistinct
inferior
inform
intelligible
intoxication
issue
Jupiter's
later
laughter
leaping
lightning
limit
lunatic
managed
manners
Massa
measured
Mill
million
millions
Minister
misery
momently
moods
mother's
movements

Mummy
neglected
newspapers
nonsense
noted
numbers
obedient
ottoman
outstretched
pe
Petite
pitcher
plane
pockets
poles
powder
Pratt
preparing
pressing
printed
profession
proprietor
publication
push
quarters
raise
rat
referring
reflect
relieve
remembrance
removing
requested
retain
retired
richly
roared
root
Rowdy-Dow
runs
sailor
scenes
securely
separate
shop
shroud
Signor
sink
slipped
Snob
solely
speedily
state-room
stately
strict
string
sublime
summer
susceptible
swam
swimming
swoon
temper
tendency
thank
thunder
tightly
token
trepidation
turns
unutterable
uplifted
von
voyagers
washed
whisper
wildest
wildly
windings
windlass
woods
3
5
(12)
academy
activity
admired
affectation
affording
aged
agreeable
Antarctic
apparition
apprehensions
arch
ardent
area
assassins
assertion
association
audience
awakened
awaking
band
bare
basis
basket
begged
bet
blade
blessed
bliss
blush
Bon-Bon, Pierre
break
breathe
brothers
Buckingham
burden
burned
claim
clay
coach
communicated
communications
companion-way
conclusive
confession
contemptible
content
cord
corners
cost
crossing
deeper
define
defined
deliberate
deliberation
delicacy
disappointed
discoveries
disgusting
displayed
document
domain
downwards
draught
dusk
eighty
Eiros
elicited
exceeded
Excellencies
exists
facility
fears
feathers
fiend
fog
founded
fullest
gathered
glad
glossy
gradual
granted
guard
hath
he's
heel
hence
herd
hesitated
hotel
household
hunting
immortal
inability
indispensable
insect
intend
intuition
John
Jones
killed
labour
Lady
lamentable
landscape
lastly
library
limited
loathsome
lover
mansion
match
mathematician
mattress
medicine
meditations
merits
Messenger
miracle
mixture
momentarily
murderers
murmur
mysteries
nation
Nosology
occupation
officers
organ
overcoat
painful
paths
persist
perusal
phenomena
phosphorus
Pierre
pig
pistols
plenty
pocket-book
pole
pool
populace
port
precautions
precipitated
preparations
preposterous
presenting
president
quivering
quoted
ray
rear
reasoning
recover
referred
remarks
replaced
resemble
resorted
rigorous
rivers
Roget
romantic
Rumgudgeon
sacrifice
Sauterne
scientific
scoundrel
scruple
scrupulous
secondly
separated
shaking
shallow
sheer
shoes
shouts
showed
shrieking
sister
sketch
skill
smallest
snow
sources
southwest
spare
stateroom
strangely
succeed
suffocation
suit
support
suspicious
sweep
syllables
takes
tear
temporary
thither
thrilling
tide
tight
to-night
Toby
topics
track
tremulous
tube
unexpected
unfortunately
valet

volition
waiting
war
watching
wave
wishing
working
worm
wouldn't
(11)
accepted
adjusted
advantages
Ainsworth
alike
apply
arouse
associates
astronomical
beach
beauties
behaviour
birth
bitterly
bounded
brow
Bullet-head
bustle
busy
canvass
casting
cataract
cheeks
Clarke
classical
cleared
clever
climate
clothed
colour
comet
contention
continue
contour
control
converse
cotton-wood
countenances
counter
cries
critical
crooked
currents
damp
dashed
daylight
deficiency
deficient
development
devoted
devoured
disappointment
disaster
discernible
dismay
disposal
dispute
dissolution
distress
dragging
driving
dug
dust
duties
earnestly
elopement
embarrassment
embrace
employment
essence
essentially
ethereal
eventful
every-day
exposed
fabric
faintly
fanciful
fashionable
fastening
feared
fiendish
fill
finest
flitted
flying
folded
foresail
forty-five
francs
frequented
Froissart
fruitless
ghost
glowing
Grampus
guns
happily
heels
heightened
hereditary
hiding-place
hit
hum
illness
impetuous
improbable
incision
indicate
indicative
ineffectual
inner
inspire
instructions
insufferable
interference
intermingled
isn't
je
jest
Kate
kick
King
labors
laughing
leddyship>
lids
livid
loosely
loudly
luck
lumber
maintain
masquerade
mast
meself>
mesilf>
monsieur
motions
moving
murdered
mutiny
nerve
newspaper
nice
nostrils
O'Grandison, Sir Pathrick
observable
omit
orb
orbs
outre
Pacific
panes
perilous
perpendicularly
philosophical
pistol
pitch
planet
planets
plans
playing
pouring
preferred
prior
priori
proceeds
profit
propensities
rafts
random
ratio
Rattleborough
recollections
recorded
recovery
refer
refrain
refused
remainder
reputation
requires
restrained
rode
romance
roots
ropes
rubbish
Rue
ruffians
ruin
scarlet
scream
scrutinized
seaman
searching
securing
sending
sensible
settle
shadowy
shout
shouted
shrieked
shuddering
shutters
singing
skins
Smitherton
solemnity
soothing
sounded
South
specimen
springing
springs
statement
stir
storeroom
streams
stupendous
stupid
subsided
successful
sufferings
sullen
superstition
surprising
suspect
swallow
swinging
swollen
talents
Tea-Pot
temperature
tenant
terrified
test
thine
thousands
throne
thumb
tons
tore
twenty-one
undergóne
unequal
unintelligible
unquestionably
unseen
upright
vengeance
ver
vibration
vigorously
vitality
Voissart
vulgar
waves
wax
wears
wharf
wherever
winding
yxu
(10)
abroad
abrupt
absurdity
abundance
accosted
accounts
acumen
adjoining
advertisement
agent
ahead
alley
annoyed
appearances
appearing
appreciate
appreciation
aright
ascertaining
assuming
astronomers
attendants
avenue

barometer
barrel
Bedloe
behalf
believing
belonged
berry
bid
bitterness
boisterous
boundary
bounds
bout
bread
breakfast
Brigadier
Cape
catching
cell
cent
chances
chaos
chateau
check
classes
claws
coincidences
columns
comment
comments
commotion
compass
conformation
consisting
constituted
contributions
conversed
cotton
couldn't
counted
create
Croissart
cunning
d--d
damned
decay
declined
deduced
defect
defence
defiance
Deity
delivered
deposes
deposit
depressed
desperately
detecting
Devil
diagonally
disagreeable
distances
dollar
drama
drapery
drawers
dressed
drove
Duchess
dungeon
E.
eagerness
eat
eaten
echoes
elaborate
electric
enable
endeavour
endless
enjoying
enshrouded
entertain
erected
erudition
essential
Eugenie
everybody
exceed
expense
explore
extremely
falls
feather
ferocity
fervor
fired
flowing
forebore
formation

fortnight
frail
frank
frivolous
funeral
fur
Gad-Fly
gain
giddy
glanced
god
grain
grand
grasped
gross
gruff
guilt
guttural
hairs
hall
hast
hearty
hell
hinted
holds
hut
idiosyncrasy
impatient
impetuosity
impetuously
improvement
impulses
incapable
included
indulged
insinuate
intoxicated
jewels
Jung, Ritzner Von
Jup
keel
kill
kindness
lashed
lean
lef
liable
lighted
linen
load
Locke
Lofoden
logic
logical
longing
looks
lot
madmen
magic
magnetic
mainly
maintaining
malady
Man
masonry
measures
meat
Messieurs
metaphysics
midst
misfortune
modified
Moneypenny
monthly
Morella's
mortality
Moskoe-strom
mountainous
muffled
murderer
neglect
neighbor
nephew
net-work
northeast
oak
oblige
occupying
offering
oil
oppression
orders
ourang-outangs
overwhelming
P--
palaces
pallor
par
parlor
partook

patients
peltries
pendulum
per
peril
permission
personally
pestilence
Pharisee
plunging
pocket-handkerchief
policy
political
predominant
presents
projecting
propose
protection
puffed
pumps
rabble
radiant
rank
recess
records
redoubled
reeled
refusing
regularity
relations
remarked
remedy
removal
renown
repetition
requesting
resided
resource
rigidly
rivulet
roar
roaring
robe
Roman
Rome
rotation
Rowena
rubbed
Saint
satellite
searched
seats
seize
self
shattered
shield
shone
shrank
shrieks
sighed
signature
similarity
simplicity
sixteen
smiling
sockets
soundly
special
sphere
stronger
student
stupified
subjects
suggestions
suspicions
swooned
swore
tales
tapestry
texture
theories
timber
tolerable
tottered
tottering
tour
trance
traveller
travellers
trifling
twentieth
twilight
undertaking
undue
unfrequently
ungovernable
uniformity
unparalleled
unquiet
uproar

variance
varieties
Venice
Venus
verge
visiting
vista
waistcoat
warmth
well-known
worked
wretched
writings
yell
younger
12
4
8
(9)
accursed
actuated
advisable
aft
after>
agreement
aint
alarming
Allen
altar
amazed
ample
anomalous
antelope
antiquity
apology
appended
applicable
apt
Arabesque
arabesque
archway
aristocracy
arrange
arrest
arrives
arriving
arts
ascension
asking
assertions
assigned
attainable
attraction
audacity
authors
average
awaiting
ball
bar
bargain
belt
berths
beside
bidding
Bob, Thingum
brambles
Brevet
bride
brook
bulwarks
bumper
burthen
busily
butchery
caresses
carved
cask
catacombs
cavern
ce
chairs
charity
Charleston
chirography
church
cipher
clean
clew
colossal
combination
conceptions
concerned
concerns
condenser
conducted
confessed
confine
consent
consigned
converted
convulsively
copper
cords
correct
cousin
cover
creating
crisis
crown
crystal
curse
deeds
deer
definition
demeanour
demonstrate
demonstration
desert
deserted
deserved
designated
detestable
devices
Diary
didn't
dignified
dilemma
discharging
disturb
dreamy
droll
dwellings
eccentric
ecstasy
effectual
eighth
eloquence
embalmed
embarrassed
eminent
empire
encompassed
encouraged
enemy
Englishman
enigma
enjoyed
enjoyment
enterprise
escaping
eternity
everywhere
exaggeration
excuse
exercised
exterior
extinguished
extra
fails
filthy
flash
flipper
float
Fly
friend's
friendly
fulfilled
fulfilment
funnel
gallons
garment
garments
gazing
gesticulations
gilt
glee
Gothic
grant
guesses
guidance
guide-rope
habited
hail
ham
handkerchiefs
hang
harmless
hastened
headway
hi
hovered
humph
ideal
illuminated
imbedded
imbued
immortality
imperceptible
impetus
import
imprisoned
indentures
inimitable
injured
inn
insert
insist
instantaneously
intentions
interests
interpreter
issuing
judgment
keepers
lashings
lateral
leaning
leather
les
liberal
liquor
literally
longed
machinery
manage
manifest
marks
mask
memories
mentioning
merriment
minister
ministers
minutest
miracles
misty
moaning
momentous
Monday
Moskoe
Mounseer>
muscle
muscles
muslin
narration
native
Nature
navigation
ne
negative
neighbors
noises
noticeable
notorious
numbered
o
odious
olives
opportunities
oppressive
orbit
outlines
outright
overspread
pace
Palace
pamphlet
parents
partner
peace
penetrating
permitting
perseverance
pertinaciously
pertinacity
Pest
pigeons
pile
pillow
plumage
plus
poetical
pointing
pondered
ponderous
populous
preserving
prevailing
prisoner
propounded
protracted
purity
pursuing
queen
query
qui
reasoned
receipt
receiving
refined

regain
regarding
reject
resigned
resources
respective
retaining
retreat
reverse
revived
richest
ridge
rigging
roamed
rocky
sacred
Scarabaeus
scholar
score
seclusion
seeking
selected
semblance
sensitive
sentences
seventy-five
shake
shame
sharks
shipped
shouting
shower
sickness
Sinbad
sisters
sixteenth
sky-blue
sleep-waker
sleeping
slumbers
smack
smell
soapstone
sofa
sold
southwardly
splendor
sprung
stakes
start
stick
strengthened
stretching
strikes
strip
stuck
subdued
submitted
sunset
superhuman
supported
surveyed
swamp
swate>
swell
Tarpaulin
telling
Templeton
terrace
territory
Tetons
theatre
thenceforward
thread
threat
traversed
treatment
tribes
troubled
trying
Tuesday
ultimately
university
unlike
unpleasant
valor
vanes
vanished
vapour
vehicle
verily
villains
vividly
voluptuous
waned
watches
ways
wid
widdy>
widest
widow
wire
wondered
worldly
wretches
wrist
writhed
writhing
wud>
15'
(8)
abnormal
abominable
abstraction
access
accidental
accomplishment
accounting
accused
acquaintances
active
adaptation
adduced
adrift
afar
agility
aim
alleys
allowing
alter
alternately
althegither>
ami
amounted
amphitheatre
announcement
annual
anon
antagonist
antelopes
apathy
appalled
apple
ardor
arguments
arm-chair
arranging
assurance
astounding
attacked
attacks
attaining
attainment
attendant
attentively
awaken
awoke
axes
bags
balloons
Barronitt>
Bas-Bleu
beads
beam-ends
beavers
bells
beset
betrayed
bigger
blank
bluffs
boasted
bought
bowels
boxes
breathless
bricks
brilliantly
brown
build
butter
buttons
bye
capitals
catch
causing
central
ceremony
Chantilly
Chinese
choice
choose
cities
clung
coats
cognizance
collar
complain
compositions
composure
concealing
concussion
confirmation
conscientiously
conspicuous
consuming
contrive
coolly
copied
corn
costume
courtesy
courtiers
covert
crawling
creditors
crescent
cursed
curtain
d--n
damage
dancing
De
dearest
deception
decisive
decks
declining
declivity
deductions
deemed
deepest
defects
denied
depend
depending
desolation
devotion
diddling
differ
diminution
dismal
disordered
distinction
distinctive
disturbances
divested
divide
divided
divisions
doctor
dogged
dominion
dominions
doomed
doubled
doubly
doubtful
downright
drag
drunken
Eds.
elder
emaciated
emergency
emitted
emphasis
employing
endurance
enjoy
ensue
epigram
errors
establishment
eternally
evincing
expanse
explicit
extends
extremities
F--
fable
fairest
falsity
fastenings
feat
February
ferocious
fight
finer
finish
flies
flow
flowed
fluid
folding
footsteps
forcible
fork
foul

fowl
framework
frock
fumes
G--n
gaining
gait
galvanic
glaring
gleamed
gradation
grandeur
grape
grossly
guests
guided
gutter
gx
habitually
halls
handsome
harmony
headed
hearth
heartily
helm
hissing
Hog
hook
horrid
House
hues
I'm
identification
idle
immensely
imperfect
impunity
inclination
inconvenient
incumbent
indicating
indistinctly
induce
inexpressible
infancy
infirmity
initials
ink
inquire
insisting
instantaneous
instinctively
instituted
insufficient
intelligent
intending
intensely
internal
interspersed
irresistible
Jane
Jules
kicked
Kidd
knives
ladder
lady's
leaf
leaned
leap
listening
losing
lowered
ludicrous
luxuriant
luxury
madam
magazines
magnitude
mais
manoeuvre
marl
marriage
massive
massy
materials
mathematicians
mein
memorandum
merest
meridian
merry
Messrs
mild
mob
modification
moon's
morbid
mouths
muscular
musingly
musket
New
news
niche
nobility
notoriety
obeyed
obstacle
obstinacy
obstinate
occupations
offence
offended
offices
one's
operated
opposition
ours
overlooked
overshadowed
oversight
pallid
parcel
parted
pas
passions
Pathrick>
paying
penetrate
penetrated
penguin
periodical
periods
perpetually
pictures
plum
Pluto
preceding
precipitate
prevalent
prize
problem
proceedings
producing
promises
Prophet
protruded
protuberance
proud
province
proximity
purse
pursue
queer
quivered
radical
ramparts
rascal
razor
reaches
recall
recognise
recollect
reeling
refuse
regained
reign
repeating
resolutely
resolve
restaurateur
restored
revenge
revolving
riddle
rigged
rightly
ripe
Rodman, Julius
rubbing
ruins
rumors
sash
satin
Saturday
schools
scorn
scramble
screaming
screwed
sealed
secondary
Seine
Shadow
shelter
shirts
shutter
Shuttleworthy's
signed
slippery
slipping
sloped
Smith, John A. B. C.
social
solemnly
southeast
Southern
sovereign
spared
specimens
speculative
spirituality
stalked
stamp
stare
stared
steed
stopping
stretched
strode
studied
succeeding
suffice
suitable
suited
summon
sums
superb
superiority
surfaces
surgeon
surmounted
susceptibility
swarming
swelling
sx
tails
taper
tarn
tenanted
terribly
thanks
threshold
thrill
titles
toes
tongues
tout
Tracle
tract
trait
translation
trapping
travel
treason
tresses
trifles
trunks
ugly
uncertain
undertaker
unexpectedly
unexplored
universally
unquestionable
unsteady
valve
victims
viewed
violet
visitor
vor
vortex
vow
voyages
wan
water-lilies
waving
weapons
wearing
whereabouts
wherein
whim
whirlpool
whiskers
whiskey
wig
witnesses
wo
yells
yielded
yonder
zeal
Zenobia
Zenobia, Psyche
20
25
(7)

abated
Abel-Phittim
abeyance
abilities
accompanying
accomplishing
accord
accounted
acknowledged
acted
acting
adieu
advised
affinity
affixed
afloat
ague
Americans
analytical
animated
ankles
anomaly
Antioch
ape
apex
appetite
appointed
appreciable
approaches
arises
ascendancy
ashes
Assiniboins
asunder
ate
atrocious
attitude
attribute
autographs
autumn
avail
ave
awkward
axiomatic
backwards
bands
barriers
bathed
bathing
beds
bedstead
bees
belfry
bestowed
bethought
bizarre
blackguards
blaze
blazing
blown
blushed
boots
Boston
breeches
buffaloes
burghers
butt
cabinet
cambric
candles
cant
Capt
card
careless
cart
cellar
censers
chafed
chagrin
changing
Charlottesville
chasms
Chateau-Margaux
childhood
chosen
circles
circulate
circumstantial
civility
club
collateral
commit
common-place
communion
compare
conceivable
conclusions
condensation
conference
confinement

conflicting
consolation
constitute
constitutional
constrained
consult
contemplated
contest
contrast
conversant
convulsions
Cook
cork
cornices
corresponding
couch
crack
cravat
creeping
crept
cruel
curling
Daddy-Long-Legs
darker
dashing
daughters
decent
deepened
delirious
Demon
demons
depart
depicted
detained
device
dilate
dining-room
discoursed
disgusted
distorted
distressed
divil>
dose
drifted
dxn't
echoed
effecting
eldest
emendation
emerged
encamped
encircled
encumbered
ended
enemies
engendered
ennui
enormously
entangled
Epicurus
estate
esteem
exchange
excitable
excite
exclusively
exerted
expansion
exploring
explosion
exquisitely
extension
eyelids
fainted
faintest
faithful
famine
fasten
fatigue
feebly
fiercely
filling
fire-place
firmament
fist
fits
fixed
flatter
foreman
foreseen
fortunately
forty-one
fourteenth
fragment
Frederick
freshened
fright
frightened
frog
fruiterer

Fum-Fudge
furnish
furs
futile
garters
gasping
gates
generosity
genuine
glowed
goblet
gods
Grace
grateful
gratification
grating
gratitude
gravitation
Greely, John
grim
grinning
groping
growl
guide
gum
gunwale
habiliments
hailed
hatch
hatchway
hatred
Hawk, Thomas
headache
heavenly
hemisphere
herein
hers
hideously
hind
hinges
hither
hostility
howling
humming
hunger
hurrying
hush
hypothesis
icy
ideality
illimitable
imaginable
immersion
impalpable
imply
inadequate
incoherent
inconsiderable
indecent
indulge
indulging
inflicted
ingress
inscription
insensibility
interment
intricate
Irish
Isitsoornot
ivory
Jan.
jester
jetty
Joyeuse
judged
judges
jumped
junction
keen
keeps
keg
Kepler
kingdom
kittens
knee
laden
lain
landing
leaden
leads
leagues
leak
leeward
lesson
lilies
lion
list
literature
lodged
lonely

lunatics
lurch
Ma'mselle
madly
magical
Maiter-di-dauns>
many-colored
masse
masts
mate's
Medoc
melted
memorable
memoranda
merchant
merged
messenger
metallic
metaphysical
methodical
microscope
minor
minuteness
missed
misunderstood
mixed
modest
modifications
modify
moisture
moonlight
morals
mos
mus
muskets
muttered
mystification
N.
navigator
navigators
needed
Neptune
nests
No.
nobleman
nodded
nurse
obscure
och
oil-casks
one-half
opera
orange
ordinarily
ornamented
outer
oval
palm
Paradise
paradox
parasol
particles
patience
perform
perpetual
perused
Pfaall, Hans
phantom
philosopher's
phrases
piled
platform
Platte
pleasing
plentiful
Poe's
Poems
poisoned
pon
population
porter
possessions
post
posteriori
poverty
prejudice
preparation
preserve
pride
primary
professed
prominent
promised
prophecy
protruding
Psyche
purposely
quarrel
quote
rabbit
radiance
radically
rats
rattling
ravines
recalled
recovering
rejoice
relating
relieving
remnant
repaired
replete
reposed
researches
revelled
reverence
rider
rifle
rigorously
rises
Robert
roofs
rugged
rum
sadly
sagacious
salvation
sanity
scales
scarf
scheme
scrambled
scrambling
scrap
scratching
scrupulously
se
seams
secretly
secrets
self-evident
self-possession
sensibly
settlement
shaken
share
sheep
shell
shifting
shoals
shorter
shrubberies
si
Signora
similarly
simultaneously
singularity
skeleton
skies
slack
sliding
slope
Snap
snuff-box
socket
solidity
songs
spades
spasmodic
spectral
speedy
spell
splinters
squall
squaze>
stables
statements
stationary
stealthily
stockings
strike
strokes
stupidity
submit
subsequently
substances
substantial
successfully
succumbed
sufferer
suicide
sur
surpassed
sweeps
tables
talent
tapering
tearing
tee-totum
terminated
thereabouts
thereby
therefrom
thickness
threats
thrilled
thronged
thronging
tin
torrents
torture
tortured
tranquil
tranquilly
travelled
travels
tremor
triumphant
troublesome
turret
type
ult
uncomfortable
unconscious
und
undisturbed
unequivocal
unfathomable
unique
unmeaning
unnoticed
unreasonable
unsuccessful
unwittingly
unworthy
uplifting
urgent
uttering
valleys
variable
varying
vastness
vice
Virginia
vivacity
vociferated
waking
walking
warrant
warriors
Washington
wearied
weary
weeping
welcome
wept
wet
whirling
whist
wicked
widely
willingly
Windenough
wines
winked
Wissahiccon
witnessed
wooden
woollen
wretchedness
wrists
x
Zaire
1
14
18
6
(6)
a
abounded
abounding
abstruse
achieved
acid
addressing
adequate
adjusting
admission
admitting
adopt
adorned
advances
advent
adventurer
adventurers
aeronaut
affect
affidavits
agents

agree
akin
Alexander
alleviation
ammunition
amounting
angular
animal's
animation
annoyance
anxiously
Apollo
apothecary
applause
applying
appointment
Aries
Arnheim
assassin
assassination
assent
asserted
asserts
assign
assist
assumptions
astounded
atrocities
attachment
attain
audible
Augustus's
aunt
availed
avenues
avidity
await
awhile
baffled
balustrade
barrels
based
beard
beaten
bee
begun
beholding
bestow
betray
betrothed
bewildering
bias
bitten
blankets
blast
bleeding
blindly
blood-red
boards
bolt
bon
bonnet
bono
bordering
brandy
brave
breeding
brick
brightest
brim
brings
brows
bruises
buckle
Bugaboo
burn
busying
by-and-by
cabbage
cabbages
cakes
cane
caoutchouc
captive
cares
carpets
casement
castle
caverns
cavity
cease
censer
Chambertin
champagne
channels
chaotic
characteristic
characterized
charcoal
chase
chased
chicken
chicken-bone
chilly
choked
chose
Christian
circulation
clamber
cleverly
clue
Columbia
combinations
communicate
comparative
competition
complex
compliment
comply
comprehensive
concern
conclude
condensed
confident
confidently
confound
confusedly
congratulated
conical
continuing
continuously
contributed
convexity
conveying
convincing
convulsion
copies
cordiality
corpses
corruption
cough
craggy
crags
creator
criterion
critics
crotchet
crowding
crowned
cuddy
cui
cultivated
culture
curve
customs
cutter
cylinder
damme
dampness
dance
danced
dans
dat's
dates
dawned
day-break
dealt
deaths
decline
decorations
deity
delightful
delivery
demonstrated
depression
der
derivation
derive
desirous
despatched
despite
destined
dew
dexterity
didst
Dieu
din
directing
discerned
discordant
discrepancy
displaying
disquietude
dizzy
domestic
doom
dreading
dried
driver
drowning
drowsy
e
ecarte
economy
Edinburgh
Egyptians
ejaculation
ellipse
enamored
enchanted
enclosed
endowed
endowments
enraptured
ensuing
estimated
Ethelred
ethical
evils
evince
ex
exaltation
excellence
excluded
excursion
excursions
executed
exhaustion
exhibited
expresses
expressing
extremes
fainting
fairy
fait
fancying
fangs
fantastically
fastidious
favorable
favourable
Fay
fields
fifteenth
filagreed
firing
First
fishing
fitful
fixedly
flashing
floors
flourish
flushed
follies
footman
forbade
fore
forefathers
foreigner
forenoon
forgetting
fortitude
foundation
fourteen
frames
frankly
frantic
freak
Frinchman>
fronting
frustrated
fuel
gable
gallows
gardening
garret
geological
gets
giant
girl's
giv'd>
glancing
glared
glories
gloves
goat
Goodfellow's
goole-bug
graces
grasshopper
gratified
gratify
grey
grieved
grin
groan
groups
groves
gum-elastic

ha>
habiliment
harassing
Hardy
haunted
hazards
he-aw
heated
heavier
helpless
hemmed
heterogeneous
hid
hieroglyphical
hieroglyphics
highway
hog
Holland
hopeless
horns
horribly
houl>
hundreds
hypothenuse
hysterics
identified
idiot
illegible
imitate
impediment
impertinent
impressive
include
including
inducing
inference
infernal
inflation
inherited
inhumation
insinuations
instructed
insulated
interposed
interview
intonation
introduce
intruder
intrusion
intuitive
invented
invited
Islands
iz
jeu
jib
journals
Jxhn
Kant
Kickapoo
kicking
killing
Kissam
knocking
L--l
lack
lakes
landed
lane
Laplace
largely
latch
learning
lee
leisurely
lend
lethargy
levity
likewise
limitless
links
Literary
loftiest
loops
loosened
lord
Luchesi
Luchresi
lunar
lustrum
Magazine
maintains
male
manifold
Mann
manoeuvres
map
Marie's
marrow
marry
massacre
mechanical
Mem
mentally
meteoric
metropolis
miscellaneous
miserably
monstrous
moody
mortification
moss
motley
mould
mournful
multiform
multiplied
murmuring
myriads
mystical
nameless
namesake
narrowly
nations
neighbourhood
nest
newly
nigger
nineteenth
ninety
nitre
nook
nooks
noses
November
Nu-Nu
nurses
nuts
oars
observes
odds
offensive
oldest
omen
ominous
openly
opens
organic
orlop
Osborne
overheard
overpowered
overthrow
overtook
P.S.
palpably
paltry
pan
panting
pardoned
pauses
Pavee
pavement
pencil
Pendulum
performance
permanent
perpetrated
perplexing
persevere
persuaded
perverseness
perversity
Peters's
petrified
petticoat
petty
phantasm
phantasmagoric
phraseology
phrenology
pickled
pinch
pink
pinnacle
piquant
piratical
pitied
placid
plague
plant
plaster
player
plot
Poe, Edgar A.
poems
Pole
pond
ponder
poodle
portraiture
possessing
possessor
posture
practised
prairies
precincts
precious
preconceived
predicament
prepare
preventing
prisoners
privilege
prodigies
profuse
profusely
projected
prompted
propeller
proportionate
prospects
Prospero
protected
provinces
publishers
pulling
pulsation
pupil
purchased
pursuance
puts
quaint
questioned
quiescence
quintessence
ragged
rainbow
rang
rash
realities
reasoner
recherche
recruits
refusal
regulated
reigned
rejected
rejoiced
repairing
replies
replying
representing
represents
rescue
resist
resisted
resolute
resort
respected
resting
restore
restrain
resulting
resume
resuming
retiring
retracing
retreating
revealed
reveries
revolutions
revolved
ribs
Ricarees
rift
risen
Ritzner
rivalry
Rodman's
rookery
Ross
rounded
routine
rude
rudely
sacre
sacrificed
sang
Sante
savans
saving
scale
scarce
schemes
schoolboy
scrutinizing
sculpture
scythe
sensibility

sentience
serge
sets
severed
severity
shades
shalt
shelf
shrouded
shrubbery
shrubs
shrunk
shutting
sic
sighs
sing
sleeper
sleeve
slid
slips
slopes
slumbered
snuff
softened
solar
solved
spears
speeches
spend
sport
stained
stanzas
startle
statue
stealthy
stem
stems
stepping
stifling
stile
stock
stooping
stowed
strain
straining
streamed
strengthen
stricken
strikingly
strings
stroke
Strom
strongest
stuff
styles
substitute
Sun
sun's
supervened
supper
surf
sustaining
swelled
Tale
tame
tapestries
tar
tasted
tea
technically
Tekeli-li
tenuity
theirs
thermometer
Thingum
thirty-six
thorn
thoughtfully
threatened
timid
tinged
tissue
tops
torch
tracing
trading
tragedies
transaction
translated
transparent
traveling
Tremaine
trick
Trippetta
Tsalal
turbulent
twenty-first
twenty-seven
unaccountably
unbroken
unceasing
uncertainty
uncovered
undergoing
unearthly
unequivocally
unfastened
ungentlemanly
unhesitatingly
uniformly
uninterruptedly
unlimited
unnerved
unspeakable
uppermost
upspringing
urging
useful
vacant
vacillation
variations
vaulted
vaults
veil
venerable
verbal
veriest
vigilance
vigour
vine
virtue
visibly
viz
volcanic
voyager
vulture
W--
wandered
wanderer
wandering
washing
weakened
Wednesday
weighing
weird
whaling
wheels
whimsical
whispers
whites
whither
wicker-work
wider
willow
Wilson, William
wink
wiser
withdrew
won't
wool
Wyatt's
you're
11
13
1790
47
53
69
7
(5)
a-kimbo
ab
abbey
abounds
absorbing
abuse
abysses
accept
acquiescence
ad
adds
admirably
adored
adventitious
aff>
affords
affright
agreeing
Aidenn
airs
alabaster
ale
Allamistakeo
allotted
allowance
alludes
aloft
alternative
Amrican
analyst
analytic
ancestors
anchcrage
anecdotes
anguish
animcsity
ankle
antennae
Antiochus
anywhere
appeal
appertaining
appertains
applies
appreciated
apprchend
approcriate
Arabic
arbitrary
Arch
architect
Arctic
Aristotle
arrant
articulate
ass
assault
assemblage
assented
astonish
astonishing
astronomy
Athenaeum
athwart
atoms
attach
attentive
attract
attracting
Aug.
autograph
aversion
averted
avowed
awakening
azure
backed
backs
balls
banker
barbarous
Baron's
barren
bars
beautifully
begins
behave
behould>
belfry-man
Bell-ringers
bellows
belly
Ben-Levi
bend
bien
bin
Bishcp
bite
bitterest
blame
blended
blinded
blocked
blocks
bloom
blows
Bob, Thomas
boiling
bolder
bolted
bolts
bone
borders
bosoms
boudoir
boundaries
boyhood
brazen
breezes
brisk
broach
bruised
brushes
bulkhead
bulls
bureau
burgomaster
Buzi-Ben-Levi
by-the-by
cabman

calamities
calculation
calculations
cameleopard
canal
candelabrum
candor
capabilities
capacities
caprices
capture
carelessly
carries
casks
catalepsy
catastrophe
category
cave
cavities
cells
cessation
chandelier
changes
chap
Charles
chart
chess
chime
chimera
clasped
clerk
climb
clocks
clubs
coal
coat-pocket
coincident
coins
collect
college
colored
coloring
comet's
comets
commences
commencing
commentary
commission
commonest
commonly
compact
compliments
compound
condescended
Condorcet
confining
conjecture
consummation
contemptuously
context
continues
contrivance
convenience
conversing
convulsed
cordage
cordially
corroboration
corroborative
cottage
counsel
counterfeit
counting
countries
cow
crash
crate
crawled
crevice
cripple
crow
crucible
cruelly
cryptograph
cue
cup
cured
curious
curiously
cursory
cylindrical
d'esprit
dam
dangling
daring
data
decanter
decaying
December
decide
declare
decorum
Dee, Dubble L.
default
definitiveness
demanding
demonstrations
denominate
densely
denying
depict
der
des
describing
destinies
destitute
destroyer
detailing
detected
determining
devil's
devils
devise
devoid
diamond
differing
differs
diffusion
digging
diminishing
dirt
disappear
disappears
discharged
disconcerted
disguise
dish
dismissed
displaced
distended
district
districts
distrust
disturbing
divest
dizzily
domination
donkey
dost
doubts
dragon
drained
dreadfully
dresses
drifting
drops
drum
duck
ducks
Dumas
duplicate
Earl
Eastern
ebb
editorial
effective
effusion
eggs
egregious
eighteenth
elastic
elbows
embraced
eminence
enchanting
encountering
engagement
engraving
ensconced
entertaining
entertainment
entombment
entrails
entranced
entrusted
Epidaphne
epithets
equator
Ermengarde
escapes
estin (Gr.)
eventually
evidences
exchanged
exit
expectations
expenses
expensive
expose
extinct
extracts
extravagance
extravagances
eyeing
fables
fac-simile
families
far-distant
fates
feels
felon
fervid
Fether
fiddle
fiercest
finder
flaring
flitting
flock
floe
flourished
followers
foolscap
footing
footstep
forefinger
forests
foretopsail
forgive
fort
forwards
fraction
fractured
fragrance
frantically
frequency
fretted
frozen
fruit
functions
Gallipago
gather
gaudy
gem
gendarme
generous
George
gintleman>
glassy
gleams
Glendinning
glimmer
glimpses
glitter
gloriously
goats
goodly
goodness
gossamer
Gott
gracious
gradations
grandfather
grandmother
Greece
Greelys
groaned
growled
Gruff
guessed
hammer
hand-writing
handle
hangs
harbour
hats
hazard
heading
Helseggen
henceforward
Henson
hide
hints
hippodrome
histories
hoax
Homer
honorable
honour
hoped
horizontal
horseback
hould>
Hudson
hurt
hydrogen
hymn
idees
idiotic
idolatrous

ignoramus
imaginations
imbibed
immersed
impediments
impenetrable
implements
implicit
implied
inaccessible
incalculable
incipient
incoherence
income
inconceivably
inconsistency
inconsistent
indecision
indecorous
independent
individually
industry
ineffable
infected
inferences
inferred
influences
inhabited
inheritance
inmost
innermost
inordinate
inorganic
inquisitive
insanity
insensible
insinuated
insoluble
instigation
instinctive
intellectual
interred
intimacy
invested
involve
issues
item
jacket
Jefferson
jokes
juncture
Kickapoos
king's
kiosk
kissed
knxw
laboring
Lafitte
Lalande, Stephanie
lamps
landlady
landscape-gardening
lashing
latitudes
laudable
Law
laying
leather-bottomed
lift>
lighter
lightning-rod
lingering
link
liqueur
lit
Liverpool
location
locks
log
longitudinal
look-out
lots
lucid
luminiferous
lunacy
lurid
lurking
Madeline
mainmast
majority
management
Mandans
mangled
maniac
manifested
mantle
march
Marchesa
Mason
masqueraders
masthead
matches
matured
maturity
mavourneen
meadows
meaningless
meerschaum
metaphysicians
methods
midway
mildew
mineral
Minnetarees
mirth
Misquash
miss
Misthress>
modelled
modestly
Mole
moment's
monkey
morality
morass
morsel
motives
moves
muddy
multitudinous
mummies
munificent
Murders
murmurs
musician
muttering
mutton
neatly
necks
needle
nervousness
Newfoundland
Newton
nil
nitrogen
noblest
nonchalance
noose
nous (Gr.)
o (Gr.)
oar
objectionable
objectless
obligation
obstinately
obtuse
occupant
occurrences
occurring
oddly
omitted
opera-glass
operate
opponents
orchestra
Orion
ounces
outset
outwardly
overflowing
owl
Oxford
oxygen
packages
packed
painfully
paint
paradise
paragrab
paragraphs
pardons
parent
paroxysm
partiality
parting
partition
patch
paternal
pathway
pattern
paws
payment
penchant
Penguin
penguins
penknife
penmanship
peremptory
periodically
periodicals
perplexed
persevering
perseveringly
persisted
perverse
pest
pet
Philosophy
piano
picking
piles
pinched
pine
Pirouette
pitching
piteously
pitiful
plastered
plausibility
pleasures
pledge
plunder
plunges
pocket-handkerchiefs
poetry
poison
polite
pompous
Ponnonner's
pored
Port
positions
potatoes
practicable
prayed
pre-eminent
predecessors
preface
premature
Presburg
pretence
privileges
probabilities
probed
processes
procuring
produces
profoundest
progenitors
promenade
promising
prompt
promptly
prone
properties
proportioned
proposal
propositions
prosperity
Providence
proving
publishing
pulse
pump
puncheon
punish
puppy
purchases
purchasing
purest
putrefaction
Quarterly
queries
raging
rampart
rapped
rason>
rattled
reared
recognition
recollected
recommend
reconcile
regularly
reigning
relates
release
released
reliance
reluctance
reluctantly
remedies
remotely
remotest
renew
renewed
rents
represent
representation
residing

resolving
resounded
responded
retina
revel
revery
reviving
ribbon
richer
ridges
rife
rifles
rigidity
rings
rivetted
robust
rose-wood
rotten
rotund
roughly
row
rowing
rudeness
rules
rustling
sailor's
saloon
sanctity
sane
Saskatchawine
sate
satellites
satisfying
Schelling
scratch
scud
secluded
seduced
seeks
sensual
sepulchral
sequence
serene
serpent
ses
seventeen
shaped
sharply
shells
shift
shifting-boards
shipping
shocking
shouldn't
shows
shrink
shrinking
sickened
sickening
Simeon
similitude
singular-looking
sinister
sixty-five
sizes
sleeves
slide
sloping
slumbering
Slyass
smoking
sneer
snore
so
sofy>
solving
sons
soundest
sounding
spaces
spalpeen>
spasms
specific
specified
speck
spectators
speechless
spikes
split
spoiled
spotted
spreading
spy-glass
squeezed
Stael
staggering
staircases
stall
stamped
state-rooms
stationed
statues
steadied
steerage
stifled
stillness
strangeness
stray
streak
strenuously
stretch
stumbled
stunned
subjoined
suddenness
sufferers
suite
sulphurous
summoned
Sundays
sundown
sung
sunlight
suns
sunshine
superintendence
superstitious
supporting
supposes
surcingle
surveying
sustenance
swear
sweeping
sweetest
sweetly
sycamore
syllabification
Syria
tapers
Tarpaulin, Hugh
Tarr
tells
temporal
tempted
tended
tender
tending
tenor
tenure
terminating
Teton
text
theorist
thinkers
thirdly
thoroughfare
thrillingly
throats
throng
throws
thrusting
thruth>
thwarted
tier
tiger
tightened
timbers
time-piece
tints
tiptoe
tis
Toad
tokens
tombs
tormentor
towering
towers
traits
trampled
tranquillity
transition
transport
travelling
traversing
treacherous
tread
triangle
Trianon
tricks
trio
triple
trodden
troops
troubles
truest
trump
trusting
tub
tulip
twelfth
twenty-fifth
twist
tying
unaware
unburthen
uncontrollable
undeniable
underwent
underwood
unhappily
uninterrupted
unite
unity
unobserved
unsatisfactory
uses
uttermost
vagabond
vary
vase
veal
vegetable
vegetables
vell
vent
verbatim
vermin
vessel's
vestibule
vexation
vexed
victory
vile
visiter's
visiters
vizier
vows
Vurrgh
wager
walks
walled
warning
wasting
water-dog
weapon
weighed
westwardly
whales
whine
whirlwind
whiteness
wife's
willows
wiped
wooded
worlds
worms
worship
wounds
writers
writhe
xf
xld
yawning
York
yur>
yxur
zee
zit
10
15-1
19
20'
25,000
37
42
6th
9th
(4)
abating
abdomen
Abernethy
abject
abound
absurdities
Academy
accelerated
accents
accommodated
accommodation
accruing
accusation
accuse
acres
acts
adapting
adding
adept
adjustment

admire
admissible
adoration
adore
advantageous
advise
aerial
affections
afflicted
affront
affronted
aggravated
aiding
Alexander-etc-nopolis
algebraic
alluding
alongside
altercation
altering
alternate
ambiguous
ambitious
amounts
amply
amuse
amusing
analyzing
ancestor
ancients
anecdote
angelic
announced
anomalies
answering
antiquarian
anybody
apparel
appliances
applicability
apprehensive
Archimedes
Ariel
Aristotelian
array
arrow
arrows
artistical
Ashimah
ashore
asks
asphodel
assassinated
assumption
assures
astern
Atrevida
attired
attributing
audacious
Auroras
author's
authorities
avarice
avoiding
awfully
ay
azimuth
baboon
backward
Baconian
balance
banter
Bartholinus
baseless
basin
battlements
bawled
bedclothes
bedecked
Bedlo
bell-rope
bending
benefits
benignity
bequeathed
bequest
besprinkled
bewilderment
bind
black-looking
blackguard
blazed
blissful
block
blossoms
bluff
bluish
blunder
bookseller's
boon
border
bored
bowl
bowsprit
Bransby's
briefly
brig's
broadest
broadside
Browne, Thomas
brush
bull
Bullet-head, Touch-and-go
buoyed
burial
burnished
burnt
bushel
buzz
cache
Cafe
calculate
Calculus
calf
California
Caligula
calmness
caloric
caprice
Captains
captured
carcasses
cared
carvings
cathedral
Catullus
causeway
ceasing
celebrity
cellars
centres
centrifugal
chafing
chained
chalk
chanced
changeable
chapter
chapters
characteristics
charged
charitable
charm
charms
chateau
chatted
cheerful
cheerless
chemical
chess-player
chickens
childish
chilled
chilliness
chimneys
chivalrous
Christendom
chuckled
Cimabue
citizen
civil
clambering
clearer
clenched
clerks
clotted
clumsily
cluster
clutched
Co.
coating
coffins
coin
Coleridge
collation
collection
collision
colloquy
combat
combativeness
combined
combining
comfortably
commanded
commander
commanding
commerce
commingled
commiseration
community
companion-hatch
companion-ladder
companion's
Company
compassion
compelled
compliance
compose
composing
compression
concavity
concocted
condemned
condensing
cone
confines
confirm
confronted
connecting
conquered
considerate
consist
consoling
constituent
consummate
consummated
contemplative
contented
contracted
contradiction
contrivances
conversations
convex
conveys
cook's
coral
Cornwallis
corpulent
correspond
costly
council
count
counterpart
countless
coupled
courses
covers
crackling
crag
crates
Crebillon's
creep
critic
crude
cruise
crypt
cudgel
cultivating
cum'd
cum'd>
cure
customer
cuts
Cuvier
cypress
d--l
dabbled
Daddy
dagger
Dammit, Toby
dandy
dares
darkest
dash
dazzling
deaf
deceive
declares
decoration
decrease
deduce
deepening
defective
deformed
deformity
delicately
delightfully
deliver
deluge
deluged
demands
demolished
Demosthenes
denouement
denser
departs
deplorable
deprive
derision
descried

descriptions
desires
despairing
desperado
despised
despotism
destination
destroy
detain
detection
deter
dev--
deviations
devout
Diable
diabolical
diagnosis
Dial
diamonds
diddler's
diddles
differed
dig
dimness
diplomacy
disbelief
disburses
discarded
disclose
disclosing
discomfort
discouraged
discretion
discussed
discussing
disengaged
disfigured
dislike
dismiss
dispelled
dispense
dispose
dissimilar
dissipated
distortion
distracted
diverted
divinity
dizziness
dog's
domesticated
Don
doth
dotted
Double
double-reefed
doubtless
downfall
dram
dreaming
drenched
dromedary
dronk
drums
drying
dudgeon
duello
Duke
duly
dungeons
durch
dusky
earthquake
easterly
ebber
ecstasies
ecstatic
eddies
Edina
edited
editors
educated
efficient
egg
ejaculations
elapsing
elasticity
electricity
elegance
elephant
elephants
elevate
elicit
Ellison's
elm
eloquent
em
embalmment
embellishments
embodiment
embody
emerald
emotions
emphatically
emptied
enchantment
encounter
endeavouring
energies
enkindled
enlightened
enraged
enters
entity
entreaties
enunciation
Epiphanes
epistles
epithet
equivalent
era
err
erred
essay
establishing
estates
esteemed
estimating
estimation
ethics
etiquette
evermore
Examiner
excel
excellence
excepting
exceptions
exclamation
exhibition
expanded
expediency
expenditure
experimental
expire
explanations
explored
exposition
extort
extorted
extract
extracted
eye-sore
fabulous
faithfully
fame
farewell
fatality
father's
fathom
Fatquack
faut
feast
feasting
feeblest
feed
felled
felling
females
feminine
fence
fervent
fibre
fiends
figuratively
filberts
filmy
filth
fine-looking
firmness
fishermen
fit
fitfully
five-and-twenty
flag
flakes
flaming
flapping
flattened
flavor
flee
flights
flippant
Florence
flown
foaming
folio
footstool
forces
fore-finger
foremast
foremost
forgot
formal
formally
formidable
forthcoming
fortunes
forty-eight
fought
foundations
fowls
Frank
freaks
freed
frenzy
Frogs
frolic
fulfil
full-length
fuller
fulness
fun
functionary
furnishing
gales
gall
gallant
Garcia, Pedro
gash
gate-way
gaunt
genii
gentleman's
gentleness
gibbering
gilded
gill
gimlet-hole
Gizbarim
Glass
glazed
gleam
glides
glittering
Glory
gondola
Goodfellow, Old Charley
gore
gout
governor
grammar
granting
gravel
graves
Greely, Poindexter
groped
grows
guest
guineas
handcuffs
handful
handiwork
handled
handsomely
hangman
Hans
harangue
harassed
harm
hastening
hastily
hasty
hazy
he'll
hearkened
heathen
hectic
helped
Henderson
heretofore
hermit
Herschel
highness
historian
History
hitch
hitting
hoaxes
Hogs
hoisted
homewards
hon>
horn
hover
howl
Humanity
hunter
hushed
hybrid
identify

idiots
illiberality
illigant>
illumined
imagining
imitated
immeasurably
immensity
immoderate
impaired
impelled
impels
impertinence
implicated
implicitly
imposed
impotent
improve
incessantly
inclinations
incongruities
incontrovertible
increases
indefinable
indefinitely
independently
indeterminate
India
inexplicable
inexpressibly
infant
infants
infatuation
infested
inflated
inflict
influenced
initial
injuries
inny>
inordinately
inquiring
inquisitiveness
inquisitorial
insertion
insight
insists
inspiration
institutions
instrumental
insulted
integrity
intellects
intent
intercept
intercourse
interfere
interruptions
interspaces
intervention
intimately
intrinsically
introducing
intrude
invalid
inventive
inventor
invitations
involves
involving
inwardly
Ionic
iron-bound
irrelevant
irritated
Irving
Island
islanders
isle
islet
items
iver>
jagged
Java
jaw
jealous
jerk
jerked
Jerusalem
jet
Jew
join
joint
joking
jump
jumping
Junot, Pierre
keenly
kegs
Kentucky
key-hole
keys
kindred
kipt>
Kirschenwasser
knell
knit
L'Etoile's
labored
laboured
lace
laconic
Lake
landlord
lands
landscape-garden
landscapes
lanterns
latterly
lavished
leader
league
lecture
lengthen
lens
Leslie
lesser
lessons
letter-writer
liberality
lifeless
lift
lifting
lighten
likes
lions
listener
litten
lively
lo
local
loins
loses
loudest
Louisiana
loves
lowest
lozenge
lurches
luxuriance
luxurious
lynx
Machiavelli
Madeira
Maelstrom
magi
magistrate
mainsail
Maison
major
Maltese
man-animal
manifestations
mantel-piece
manufactured
manuscript
marginal
Mary
masked
Mason, Monck
master's
mathematics
mature
mazes
me
meal
Mediterranean
medley
mentions
Mercury
merge
message
Michau
mid
midsummer
milder
mildewed
military
mines
miniature
miraculously
mirrors
mischief
miseries
misled
mistress
mistrust
moccasins
mockery
models
moderns
Montreal
mood
moons
morphine
mostly
motto
moulded
Mousseux
moveable
multiple
Mumblethumb
mummy
murderous
murders
murmured
mute
Mynheer
nailed
nare
narratives
naval
neatness
nebulae
nether
New-York
nicety
nigh
nightly
nine-tenths
niver>
no
noffin
noisome
nom
Nopolis
North
nothingness
notices
noticing
novelist
novels
Nubian
nx
o'
obliging
obstreperous
obstructed
oceanic
octavo
ocular
odd-looking
oddities
ode
odorous
offers
oftener
older
Omnibus
operating
opponent
ornament
ottomans
ould>
out-of-the-way
outrageous
ov
oven
overgrown
overhung
owed
Owl
owned
packet
palatable
palazzo
paler
palpitating
pangs
Paper
paradoxical
paralyzed
parfumerie
park
parrot
partaking
passable
passive
patient's
patronage
patterns
pausing
paved
pebbles
pecuniary
peep
peered
peering
pemmican
penned

penny
penny-a-liner
percave>
perceptions
performing
perfumery-girl
perils
perishing
permeates
pernicious
perpetrator
perplexity
persecution
perturbed
peruse
pervades
perversion
peterel
petticoats
petto
petulant
Phaall
phosphoric
physiognomy
pick
picturesqueness
piercing
pigs
pillars
pined
pinnacles
piously
pirate
placidity
plank
planks
plates
Platonist
pleasantly
pleasurable
Poets
poets
poignant
pointedly
poisonous
Polar
policial
politics
pollen
pondering
poring
pork
portentous
portray
post
posterity
potent
pp.
precipitation
Prefecture
prefer
preference
presentation
presumed
pretended
pretending
prevalence
Price
prickly
prima
prime
prince
prints
privacy
privately
pro
prodigiously
proficiency
profitable
progressive
projects
prominence
promontory
prophet
proposals
proprieties
prosecute
prosecution
prostrated
proves
prow
prudent
psychal
puffy
pulpit
pungent
pupils
purloined
pursuits
putrid

qualifications
quantities
quit
quoting
rack
raged
railroad
rains
rambling
ranged
rarefaction
rarest
rascally
rascals
ratiocination
ravenous
raving
raw
re-appeared
readiness
realize
realm
reasoner's
recalling
recent
reception
recognisable
recognising
recommending
reconnoitre
rectangular
reduce
reef
reflecting
reflective
regal
regretted
relapsed
relied
reminded
remorse
reports
repugnance
repulsive
reputable
resented
reserve
resident
resigning
respectful
responsible
restless
restraint
retrace
retraced
retreated
returns
reverberation
reverie
review
revolves
ribbons
Richmond
riding
righted
ripped
river's
roaming
Rogers
Romans
roomy
roses
routes
Rubadub
ruffian
ruinous
rumbling
rummaging
rumor
Russia
Russian
sacking
sailors
sally
salts
sanctum
sands
satisfactorily
sauntered
sausages
scent
scraping
screws
scroll
scruples
scuffle
scurvy
sea-stores
sealskins
seam

seaweed
secrecy
secreted
sees
select
sell
senseless
Sep.
separation
sequel
serpents
settlements
settling
seventeenth
severest
shameful
shelled
shelves
shilling
shins
ships
shoot
shooting
shop-keeper
shots
shreds
shrine
shrub
shrugged
sich>
sidelong
silf>
simpleton
sin
sincerely
sincerity
site
skeletons
skiff
Slang-Whang
slave
sling
sloop
smart
smelt
Smith, John
sneezing
Snobbs
snug
soared
sob
softer
softness
sojourn
soliloquy
solve
sombre
somehow
son
sorrows
southerly
spade
Spaniard
spasm
spectator
spider
spirited
sprawling
spray
squalls
squares
stale
starvation
staterooms
stations
stayed
stead
steam
steamboat
steered
stench
stereotomy
stern-post
stiffly
stirring
stole
stores
strangers
stratification
streaks
streaming
strewed
strolled
structures
sturdy
submission
successively
suffccating
sullenly
sultry

summary
summed
superficial
superintendent
supernatural
supplying
supposable
surest
surge
surnamed
surpass
surpasses
surpassingly
surrender
surtout
survived
swearing
swiftness
swim
Swiss
swooning
sworn
t
t.
tabby
taint
Talbot's
Tales
tangent
tangible
tastes
tax
tea-pot
telegraph
tenderness
terrestrial
thanked
that'll
themes
theorize
thereafter
thereupon
thief
thighs
thirteenth
Thomas
thorns
thoroughfares
thoughtful
threatening
thrive
thrue>
thump
thunders
thunderstruck
tides
tightness
time-honored
timely
Times
tincture
tinge
tinted
tiny
toe
toil
ton
tormented
tortoises
touches
towered
Town-Council
translating
trapper
trash
treat
trod
tropics
trowel
trumpery
trumpet
tuft
tulip-tree
tulips
tumble
tumbling
tune
turf
Turgot
turnstile
twattle
twenty-second
twenty-seventh
twinkling
twirl
twisting
tyrant
unanticipated
unattainable
unattended

unbounded
unconsciously
under-tone
undergo
undertake
undeviating
undivided
unearthed
uneasily
unhappiness
unheard-of
Universe
unnecessarily
unobstructed
unpardonable
unperceived
unqualified
unreal
unrelieved
untied
untouched
unwelcome
unwieldy
unwilling
upside
upturned
urge
Usher, Roderick
vacancy
vacuum
Valdemar's
Valence
validity
Vankirk
varies
varnish
varnished
vases
vastly
vehemently
vein
vellum
veracity
verdant
verse
versed
vex
vibrated
vibrations
Vienna
villages
violation
violets
visionary
visitation
visitors
vital
vocal
void
volcanoes
voluminous
volunteered
vortices
vowed
vy
waistband
wary
waste
wedded
wedding
wedged
weighty
welfare
whims
whip
whirled
wholly
wicker
winged
wins
withdraw
withered
woman's
workmanship
wou>
wrapper
wreath
wringing
writhes
yielding
yxu're
1000
15
16
17
1791
1793
18th
1811
30'

(3)
A--
aback
abandoning
abandonment
abhor
abide
abstracted
abstractions
abundantly
accelerating
acceleration
accentuation
acceptable
accessible
accomplice
accomplishments
accumulations
accusing
acquaint
acquainting
acquirements
acquisition
acuteness
Adam
addicted
adequately
adhered
adjacent
adjective
adjust
admeasurement
administration
admirari
admonition
ado
adopting
advert
adverted
Aeris
aerostation
Aeschylus
affectedly
affectionateness
affirmative
afflatus
aforesaid
Africa
African
aggregate
aimed
aims
Ainsworth, Harrison
airy
alert
algebra
alighting
alit
aliterque
allay
allayed
Almacks
almighty
alphabet
altitudes
amiable
amity
Amricans
amusements
Ana-Pest
analogies
analyze
Anamoo-moo
Anfangsgrunde
annexed
annihilated
annihilation
anointed
answers
ante-chamber
anticipation
anticipations
antipodes
antiquities
apes
apout
appellations
appendages
applicationem
apprentices
approbation
apprcved
apron
Arabian
argued
argues
Aristophanes
army
arrogance
Art

artistic
ascendency
ascensions
aspects
asphaltum
asserting
assisted
associate
assumes
astral
astronomer
Astronomers
Astronomy
Athenian
Athens
atomic
attentions
attorney
au-chat
augmented
augos (Gr.)
auriculas
authenticity
Automaton
autumnal
availability
available
averse
B--
B--'s
babies
baboons
baby
baggage
bald
balderdash
ballad
Balloon
Baltimore
bandages
banish
banners
baptismal
bard
barrier
Barriere
bas
Batavia
beaming
bearer
bearings
bed-chamber
bed-room
bedizzened
bee-line
beer
befallen
beholder
belied
believes
belle
belles
bellowed
belong
Bentham
bereavement
berries
beseech
besieged
betting
Bible
bidden
bigoted
binding
birch
bird's
biscuit
bittern
Black
blackened
blacker
blandest
blemish
Bless-my-soul
Block
blood-chilling
bloodthirsty
blotted
Bluddennuff
blunders
blurred
boar
boarding
boatmen
bobbing
Bobby
bog
Boggs
boiled
boldness
Bon-Bon
bond
bonds
bookseller
boot
booty
boring
botheration
bouche
bounden
Bourdon
bower
Bowie
bowing
boyish
braggadocio
bravado
bravo
breach
breathes
breed
Bremen
brethren
bridal
brighter
Bringhurst, Everard
briskly
Broadway
brutal
buck
buckles
buckskin
Bugaboos
bulkheads
bulky
bump
Buonaparte
bury
bush
butterfly
by-path
C--
cable
cadaverously
cadences
calculating
caliph
caliphs
calmest
candid
canisters
canopy
capacious
caps
capsized
captain's
carboy
card-rack
carelessness
cargoes
Carlyle
Carnac
carnival
carnivorous
casements
castellated
Castle
castles
Cat
Catalani
cataracts
cauliflowers
causality
causeless
ceases
celery
cellular
cemetery
chain-cable
Channing's
charnel
Chateau
Chayenne
che
cheap
cheer
cheers
chef
Chevalier
chiefs
chimerical
chiming
China
chisel
choking
chopping
chose
chrysalis
cigar
circumscribed
City
civilization
claimed
clapped
clasp
classic
Claude
clearing
clearness
Cleomenes
clergyman
click-clack
clinging
closest
clothing
cloudy
clump
clutches
coarse
coasts
cocked
coeur
coffee
coffin-shaped
coincide
coldness
collated
colorless
combine
comforts
commendable
commensurate
commented
committing
commodities
comparing
compartments
compels
compensation
complained
complaint
complying
comprehensible
compressed
comprising
concave
concentration
concert
concerted
confiding
conflagration
conflict
confronting
congratulate
Congress
conjectures
conjoined
Connaught
connections
consecrated
consigning
consolatory
console
conspicuously
constables
constitutes
construct
constructing
constructionem
contend
contenting
continents
continuance
contradicted
contradictions
contradistinction
contributors
controversy
controvert
conventional
coolness
copious
cordial
cordials
cornice
corporations
correcting
correction
correspondence
correspondent
correspondents
corroborated
costumes
Cotopaxi
councils
counteracted
countrymen
craving
creates
creative

creeks
Crichton
crimson-tinted
crow-bar
Crows
crows
crucibles
cruelty
crying
cryptographist
cubic
cud>
Cul-de-Sac
cum
cum
cursing
curt
curved
cut-throat
cxxl
cycle
Cyrus
d'ye
dainty
Damascus
dames
Dammit's
damnable
damning
dan
dangerously
dangled
dar
darkened
darkly
darlint>
daughter's
David
Day-Book
day's
days'
dazzled
dealer
debaucheries
decreasing
decree
deductive
deem
deepen
defeat
defend
defended
deference
definitely
definitively
delicacies
deliciously
Delight
delineated
delineation
deliverer
demonstrable
demure
denizens
descends
deserves
desirable
desperation
despise
destroying
desultory
detaching
detachment
deterred
deuced
developed
devious
devoting
devour
devouring
dexterous
dial-plate
diary
Dick
dickey
dies
dieth
differences
diffused
diligence
diligent
Diogenes
dirteen
disappearing
disastrous
discard
disciples
disclosed
discolored
discomfited
disconcert
discrimination
disdain
diseased
disinheritance
dislocated
dismissing
dispirited
displeased
disproved
disputed
disregarded
dissatisfaction
dissection
dissipate
dissolute
distasteful
distempered
distending
distinguishing
Divine
Doctor's
Doctors
dogma
doings
dolt
domains
dotage
dots
drain
draughts
drawing-room
dreamer
dressing
drive
drives
drowsiness
drug
drunkard
du
Ducal
Duelli
duk
duns
dupe
Dupin, C. Auguste
dx
e
e.g.
earnestness
eastwardly
eats
eaves
ebery
eccentricities
eccentricity
eddy
Editor
effrontery
eh
eighty-three
ejected
elementary
elenchi
eleventh
Elizabethan
elliptical
emaciation
embalming
embellishment
emerge
emitting
enables
enacted
encamp
encampments
encircle
enclose
encrusted
endeared
engage
engaging
enlighten
ennuye
enormities
enormity
ensemble
entreated
entreating
envelops
envy
enwrapped
Epiphanes, Antiochus
equalled
equatorial
equerries
equipment
equipments
erecting
erection
Eros
erudite
essays
et
Eton
Eusebius
evapcrated
Evening
everlastingly
exacted
exactions
exaggerate
examples
exasperated
excelled
excesses
excites
exclusion
exclusive
excoriations
execrable
exemption
exercises
exhausting
exhibiting
exigency
expatiate
expecting
expedients
expeditions
explaining
Exposition
expostulation
exposure
extinguish
extravagantly
extricate
extricating
exultation
eye-like
fac-similes
facilities
failing
failings
fain
fair-haired
fairy-like
falsely
familiarity
famous
fans
fantastical
fastnesses
fatigued
favourite
fearing
feasible
feasted
feathered
fed
feebleness
fellow-men
ferry
fertile
fetid
fetters
fewer
fibe
fictitious
fidelity
fierceness
fiery-colored
fifty-three
fifty-two
fighting
film
finesse
finishing
fins
fire-guns
fireplace
Fitche
fitness
flags
flambeau
flambeaux
flannel
flapped
flattered
flattering
flaw
flayed
fleshly
flexible
flickering
flints
flocks
floes
flogging
Flos

floundering
flour
flourishes
flourishing
flows
fluctuating
fluently
foamed
focal
focus
foe
fois
foothold
forbidding
forbore
formality
formations
formless
Forsyth
fragile
frame-work
framed
frankness
freestone
freight
freshly
fricasseed
friction
friendliness
fringed
frivolity
Froissart, Napoleon B.
fruits
funds
Furies
furnace
furrenner>
furtherance
furthermore
fuss
futility
galaxy
gallon
galloped
gangs
ganzas
gaping
gaseous
gasp
gasps
gateway
gelatinous
generalization
gentler
genus
geographer
geometry
Georgia
Germany
germination
gesture
ghosts
gib
giddiness
gifts
girdle
girls
git>
gived>
gladly
glean
gloomily
glove
goading
goblets
Gonzales
Goodfellow, Charles
goole
goose
goot
gorgeously
Gorgias
gossip
Gotham
gotten
gouge
gracefully
grade
Grand
grand
grapnel
graven
Great
greatness
Grecian
greedy
Greeks
Grey
grieve
grisette
grope
grosser
ground-glass
grovelling
growth
grumbling
guessing
guitar
gull
gun
gust
Guy's
habitation
habitations
hairy
half-formed
half-sentiment
hammers
handwriting
hanged
hangings
hangman's
happening
happier
hardships
hardware
hark
harkened
hasn't
hasten
hate
hated
haughty
hauled
hauling
haunts
hauteur
havoc
hazardous
hazel
heaped
hearken
hearse
heartfelt
heaving
hebby
Hebrew
Hell
hellish
helping
hen
herds
hereby
heretical
Herod
hesitating
Hey-Diddle-Diddle
hickory
Highness
hilarity
hinder
Hippocrates
His
historical
hobby
Hog-ian
hogshead
hogsheads
holder
honey
hoo
hoofs
hooks
hopelessness
hoping
horizontally
horse's
hose
hospital
Hotel
hotly
hour's
hovering
howlings
humbled
humbug
Hungarian
husband's
husky
hyena
hypochondriac
hypocrisy
hysterical
I've
identically
idols
ignited
ignoratio
illusion
imaginary
imbecile
immeasurable
impatiently
imperatively
imperceptibly
imperfectly
imperial
implored
impossibilities
impregnation
impresses
improper
impropriety
improved
inaccurate
inadmissible
inappropriate
inasmuch
incapacity
incarnate
incensed
incredulity
incubation
incubus
indentation
Independence
index
indicates
indifferent
indignant
indiscretion
indisputably
inditer
individuality
indolent
indubitably
inducement
inductions
inductive
indulgence
inexperience
infamous
infamy
inferiority
Inferno
infest
infirm
ingeniously
Inglitch
iniquity
injudicious
injunction
injure
Injuriae
inland
innate
innocence
inquisition
inscriptions
insensibly
inseparable
insignia
insignificant
insolent
inspecting
inspires
institution
instruct
insuperable
insurance
insure
intends
intently
intentness
interfered
intermediate
interments
internally
interpretation
interrupt
interrupting
intervened
intimation
intirely>
intolerably
intricacies
intricacy
intrigues
intrinsic
intruded
inventions
invigorated
invoked
inward
irascibility
irrecoverably
irredeemable
irregularity
irregularly
irrepressible

irrevocable
irrevocably
Ise
isolated
Italic
II
jabbering
jail
jarred
jars
Je
Jews
jingled
jist
joining
jollyboat
journeyed
jugs
Jung
junk
justifiable
justified
Kabbala
kai (Gr.)
Kanadaw
keener
keenest
Kennedy
kid
kindled
kindly
kings
kiss
kitchen
Knickerbocker
knowest
knoweth
knowingly
L'Enclos, Ninon De
labelled
laborers
labours
labyrinth
Lackobreath
Lama-Lama
lambs
lame
lamented
lasting
Late
lattice
lawyer
leaps
legislature
Leibnitz
lengths
lent
lethargic
lets
Letter
lettered
lettres
levelled
Lex
licking
Lieber
lieth
lieu
Lieutenant
Life
life-like
Ligeia's
lightly
lined
lion-ant
liqueurs
liquors
listlessly
lit>
literal
little-o
livery
Lloyd
loam
localities
lodging
loftier
Logs
logs
long-continued
longitudinally
looking-glass
looking-glasses
lookout
loosening
loveliest
lovers
lucrative
lump
lustily
lustreless
Mackenzie
maddening
Maelzel's
magically
magicians
magnanimous
magnetism
mail
Major
males
malice
man-animals
Man-Fred
managing
manhood
mania
manifestation
manipulations
manly
manoeuvring
manufacture
manuscripts
marbles
Mare
market
Marsyas
marvel
maskers
mason
masters
maternal
mates
meandering
meanwhile
Mecca
mechanism
medals
Median
mediate
Melodies
melodious
mended
Mennais
Mentoni
Mentoni, Marchesa di
merchants
merrily
mesmerism
mesmerized
metamorphosis
methinks
mid-air
mieux
Mignaud
milky
Miller, Joseph
Miller, Joseph A.
Miller, Joseph B.
Miller, Joseph C.
Miller, Joseph D.
Miller, Joseph W.
minarets
mingling
ministerial
minute-hand
Mirror
mis
misadventure
misanthropy
miscalculation
misconceived
miscreants
mistakes
mistaking
misunderstanding
Mob
moiety
moist
molest
mollusca
molten
monomania
monotonous
monotonously
monotony
monsters
monuments
moodily
moodiness
moralists
More, Thomas
Morgue
mornin>
Morning
mortified
mosaiques
Moslemin
moss-covered
mouff
mought
mounds
moustaches
mummer
muse
mused
musically
musicians
musing
mutilated
mystic
mysticism
n'est
Nantz
nap
narrated
narrower
Naso
Nassau
nate>
national
nativity
Natural
navy
nay
Neal
Neal, John
necessaries
necromancy
needles
neighbouring
Nep
Nero
network
Niagara
nicely
niches
Nicolino
night's
nightmare
Nile
nincompoop
ninety-nine
ninety-one
Ninon
ninth
nobody's
nondescript
nonentity
noonday
northwardly
Norwegians
note-book
nourishment
nowhere
nucleus
numbness
nutriment
nxr
nxw
o'er
O'Trump
oaken
oaks
obelisks
obey
obsolete
obstacles
obstructions
Ocean
offending
official
offspring
oh
Oil
oily
old-fashioned
Oldeb
One
one-third
oozing
opportunely
oppose
opposed
orange-colored
orations
orator
orbits
ordinance
Oregon
oriels
originality
originated
ornaments
other's
ou
ounly>
outlet
outwards
overcast

overdone
overhanging
overpowering
overreaching
overruled
overscored
overshadowing
overtake
overtaken
overturning
owners
p.
pacific
package
pairs
pall
panted
Pantheism
papa
papier
papyrus
par
parallelism
parallelogram
paralyze
paraphernalia
Parker, Richard
partakes
parti-colored
participated
parvenu
passionately
paste
patches
patiently
patrician
patrimony
patron
paving-stones
paw
pea-jacket
pear
peepers>
pelief
penning
pension
perceptibly
peremptorily
perfected
perforce
perpetration
perpetrators
persuasion
petite
pets
peu
pew
Pfaall
phantasies
phantasms
phantasy
philosophic
Philosophie
phrenzy
phthisis
physically
physics
pictorial
pictured
pillows
pique
pirates
pits
pizziness
placidly
planned
plate
plateau
play-ground
plebeian
plumes
polish
polished
poop
poppies
posted
postpone
pot
pots
pound
pour
pour
praeternatural
praise
prayer
prayers
preached
precarious
preceded
precipices
precipitating
precluded
preconcert
predicted
prefect
prejudices
premise
preparatory
presided
President
Preston
pretends
pretensions
prevail
prevails
prices
prided
Priestley
prince's
princely
productions
professes
profile
profits
progressed
progression
prohibited
projection
projections
promiscuously
pronounce
propelling
propped
prose
prosecuted
proverbially
providentially
prudence
pshaw
puckered
pulls
pully>
punctually
punishments
purification
purliteness>
purported
purred
puss
Pym
Pym, Arthur Gordon
quack
quadrupled
qualified
quantum
quarrels
quart
quartz
queerest
questioning
quicker
Quinty
quiz
quizzed
rabbits
races
radii
rag
rags
rake
Ram
ram
ramble
rant
rap
rapport
rapture
rarefied
rarity
rationale
Rattleburghers
reader's
reap
Reason
reasoners
reassure
rebellion
receives
recently
reckless
reclined
recoil
recommendation
recommended
recourse
recruit
red-hot
redolent
referable
refinedly
refuge
regaining
regiment
regulate
rejoinder
relapse
relaxed
remanded
remembrances
remnants
remodelled
remonstrance
remonstrated
remuneration
renders
Renelle
renewal
renovation
renowned
rent
repair
repast
repeaters
repented
repetitions
repletion
reported
reprehensible
representations
republican
research
reserved
resign
respectaable
resplendent
response
retail
retaken
retire
retirement
retouch
retrogradation
revellers
reverend
reversed
reviewing
revive
revolutionary
revolve
Rhine
riches
richness
ridicule
ridiculously
righteous
rights
rigmarole
ring-bolt
ringlets
ripened
ripples
roasted
robbed
robber
robber's
robbery
robe-de-chambre
robes
rocked
rocking
Rodman, James
Rogers, Hartman
Rogers, Mary Cecilia
rolls
rooted
roquelaire
rose-bushes
rotated
rotted
rotundity
Rouen
rounds
Rousseau
rout
rubber
ruby
ruby-red
rudiments
ruling
rusty
S.C.
S--
s'il
Sabbath
safer
sagaciously
sameness
sand-bar
sandy
Saonies

sarcasm
sarcastic
sartain
sashes
Satanic
saturated
Saturn
sauce
sauer-kraut
savans
saws
scalping
Scarabaei
sceptical
Science
sciences
scope
scoundrels
scrape
scratches
scripta
scrutinize
scullions
sculptural
sea-biscuit
seaman's
seawater
sect
segment
self-defence
self-murder
Seneca
sentries
sentry
sepulchre
sepulture
servants
serviceable
serving
settee
seul
severely
sex
shaded
Shakespeare
shamefully
shapes
shaved
shed
shekels
Sherry
shifted
ship-furniture
ship's
shirt-collar
shoe
shortest
shrew
shrivelled
shuffled
shunned
sickly
siege
sighing
signals
Silence
silken
similes
Simms
Simoom
Simoon
simplest
sincere
sinciput
singly
Sinivate
sinks
sinned
sits
situations
sixes
skilful
skirt
skirts
sky-light
slab
slain
slate
sleepy
slime
slippers
smitten
smothered
Snobbs, Suky
snoring
snout
soar
soaring
sobbing
Society
sod
soften
soiree
soldier
solicited
solutions
sooth
sorrowful
sorts
Spain
spalpeeny>
sparkled
Sparta
specifically
specify
speculate
spending
spherical
spiral
splinter
splitting
spontaneous
squat
squaw
squazing>
squeezing
stab
stable
stagnant
staid
stain
stalking
Stamboul
stanchions
starry
starve
starving
states
stating
stays
steal
stealing
steer
steering
steril
sterner
sternly
stertorous
stew
sticks
stigma
Stiletto
sting
stolid
stony
stoop
stooped
stoopide
storms
strained
strains
stranger's
straps
strata
strayed
strenuous
strewn
strictest
stringed
stripped
strips
stroll
studding-sail
students
stump
stupide
styled
subdue
sublimity
subscription-list
substantive
subtended
subterrene
subtle
suburbs
successive
suction
suitor
suits
sulky
sullied
summons
sunbeams
sundry
sunken
sup
supererogation
superfluities
superinduced
superseded
superstitions
supervision
supinely
supremacy
surmise
surname
surplus
surrendered
surround
survivers
suspecting
suspense
swagger
swarm
swarmed
swaying
Swede
sweet-scented
swiftly
symmetry
Syrians
systematic
tact
tailor
taller
talons
tamely
tapping
tassels
tattered
tavern
tawny
Tekeli-li
telescopes
temperance
tempestuous
tendre
tends
Tenebrarum
tenement
tent
terraces
terror-stricken
testified
testify
tete-a-tete
Theatre
there's
thereabout
thereof
thingum
thinker
thinner
thirty-five
thirty-two
Thompson
Thornton's
threads
Three
throttled
thumped
thumping
thunderbolt
tie
tiers
tight-fitting
tiles
tiller
tinctured
ting
tink
tip
tip>
tired
to-day's
toga
toiling
Toledo
toll
Tom
topmost
torments
torpid
tossed
Touch-me-not
tough
tould>
tous
tout-ensemble
towed
tower
towing
toy
toys
traceable
traditions
traffic
trailing
trained
transcendentalism

transcendentals
treating
treatises
trebled
tremble
trembles
tremendously
trickle
trinkets
trip
triumphantly
triumphs
troisieme
trophies
Trotter
truism
trusted
Tulipiferum
turbans
Turk
Turkish
Turnip, Tabitha
turrets
turtle
twas
twenty-eight
twenty-third
twenty-two
twig
twine
two-fold
two-thirds
twofold
tx
typography
ultra
ultra
unaltered
unarmed
unbecoming
unbound
uncle's
unclosed
uncommon
unconnected
Underduk, Superbus Von
undid
une
unendurable
uneven
unfold
unfolded
ungrateful
unhallowed
unheeded
union
unlearned
unmanageable
unmistakeable
unmitigated
unmolested
unopened
unorganized
unphilosophical
unprincipled
unreservedly
unruffled
unsettled
unstrung
untie
untimely
untoward
unusualness
unvarying
upbraid
usage
vacillating
vagaries
vapory
variously
vas
veiled
venomous
ventures
verbatim
verdure
verified
Verulam
vestige
vibrates
vices
villainous
vinegar
vines
violate
violated
Virginian
Virtu
virtually
virtues

virtuous
visual
Vivian
voluptuousness
vool
vot
vulgarly
wake
Wales
wallet
waltzers
wanton
warmly
warned
warranted
Waukerassah
wavering
we'll
weak-minded
weaker
wearer
web
weigh
weights
well-regulated
well-sized
wells
West
westerly
wheel
whereas
whereupon
wherewith
whipcord
whipped
whirlpools
whistled
whither>
wickedness
widened
wildernesses
Wiley
Willis
Wilson's
win
windmill
wint>
wires
witch
withdrawing
withstand
wits
wittily
witty
wives
wolf
wolves
womanhood
won
wondering
Wormley
worshipped
worthless
wreathing
wretchedly
wrinkled
wrinkles
wxxds
xh
xut
yawned
yawns
yields
yon
youthful
Zaire
10'
15"
1772
1794
1827
1831
1832
24
26
28
31
4000
48
50
67
70
8th
9
(2)
Aaraaf
abatement
abbreviation
abhorrence
abnormally

abode
abortion
abortions
abortive
above-mentioned
abreast
abruptness
absolved
abstractedly
abstractly
Absurdities
absurdly
abused
acceptation
accepting
accession
accessory
accommodate
accompanies
accoutrements
accredited
accumulate
accumulating
accumulative
accusations
ached
achievement
Achilles
Achilles'
acknowledging
acknowledgment
acme
acquintance>
acquirement
acrid
acumine
acutely
adamant
Addison
addresses
adherence
adhesion
admirers
admiring
admits
admittance
advancement
advancing
Adventure
adventurous
advertisements
advertiser
advertisers
Aeolus
aeriforms
aeronauts
affability
affecting
affirm
agencies
agile
agonizing
agraffas
agreeably
ah
Ahnahaways
ai
aiei (Gr.)
ails
aiming
air
ajar
alarmingly
Albano
Albany
albatrosses
Alcmaeon
ale-house
ales
algebraists
alien
alienation
alight
alighted
aliquantulum
all-absorbing
Allah
allaying
alleged
alleviating
allies
alloy
Almack's
Almighty
alphabetical
alterations
alternation
alto
amassed
Amatory

amazing
ambiguity
Ambitious
amendment
amenity
amiability
amicae
an>
analogical
analyzed
anatomical
Anaxagoras
ancestral
anchors
ancles
Andromache
anemone
anew
anges
angrily
Animae
animalculae
Animals
Annals
annals
Annian
Annie
announcing
annoying
another's
antagonistical
antediluvian
anticipating
antimony
Antinous
antiquarians
antiquated
anxieties
apathetic
Aphrodite, Marchesa
Apollonius
apologies
apologize
apotheosis
Appalachia
appealing
appeals
appease
appeased
appendix
apprehending
appurtenance
appurtenances
aquiline
Arabella
Arago
arch-enemy
Archangels
arched
arches
Archimedean
Archipelago
architects
architectural
archives
Archytas
areas
Argand
Argostino
argue
argumentation
Arianus
Ariel's
Ariosto
Aristotelians
arm-chairs
arm-pits
armorial
armory
aromatic
Arpino
arresting
arrests
arrowy
Artemis
artery
artifices
artillery
artists
artizans
as
asafoetida
ashy
aspirations
asquint
assailed
asses
asseverations
Assiniboin
assistant
astonishingly
astute
atom
attaching
attains
attractive
attributable
auburn
aulos (Gr.)
Aurora
auspices
austere
authenticated
authorship
auto (Gr.)
autocrats
autres
avaricious
avast
avenging
averred
avert
avoidance
awe-inspiring
awe-stricken
awkwardly
azote
Azoth
Azrael
Baal
Baal-Zebub
Babylon
bac
badly
Bag
Bagdad
bail
bales
ball-room
balm
ban
bandaged
Bank
baptism
Barac
barb
barbarian
barbaric
bargaining
bargains
barge
barge-office
bargeman
bargemen
barnacles
Barnard's
baron
barred
barricade
Barronit>
Barry, Littleton
basement
bases
basest
baskets
battle
battle-lanterns
bazaar
beak
beams
bear's
beau
beaucoup
beckoned
becomingly
bed-side
bedding
beetling
befell
beggary
begging
begirt
belay
Belial
belligerents
Bellini
belongs
benches
Bendis
bends
Benevenuta
benign
Benjamin
benumbed
bepuffed
Berlin
besieging
besmeared
besought
bestowing
bestudded
bewilder
bewitched
Bi-chloride
bi-part
Bianca
bibliographical
bienseance
bigots
bijou
bilge-water
billow
billows
binary
Bird, Robert M.
birth-day
bishop's
bizarre
Blab
blacking
blandly
blanket
blanks
bleak
bled
Bleitziz
blend
Bless-my-Soul
blindness
blinking
Blitzen
Blitzen
blood-thirsty
bloodless
blooming
Bludenuff
blue-eyed
blushing
Boanerges
boarding-nettings
boating
bobby
Bois
boisterously
boldest
Bologna
bona
bonne
Bonner, Jim
Bonneville
booked
bordered
Borneo
Bossarion
botanical
Bottle
bottoms
boudoir
bouleversement
Boullard
Boulogne
boundless
bow-legs
bow-wow-wow
Bowling-Green
bowstring
brace
Brandreth's
brands
Bransby
Brantome's
breakers
breaks
breathings
bred
breeched
brick-work
brightened
brightly
Briscoe
bristly
broader
brocade
broils
Brooks
broth
Brougham
Brougham's
Brownson
bruise
brushed
brushing
Brussels
brute's
Brutus
Bubastis
buck-wheat
bucket
Buckingham, Silk
Buffon

bug-bear
bugbears
Bullet-head's
bullets
bulwark
bumpkin
bunch
bundles
buoys
bureau
bursts
Business
bust
Butler
buts
butt-end
button
buttresses
by-gone
bye-street
Byron
bystanders
c'est
cabalistical
cabinets
cabins
cabmen
caboose
cadaverous
Caesar
cages
Cain
cake
camel
Cameleopards
campaign
Campanella
candelabra
candidly
canister
canst
canvas
canvass-back
capered
capricious
Capricornuto
capsizing
captives
captivity
Caravaggio
carboys
carcases
careered
careering
carousals
carousing
Carpaccio
carpeted
cartel
carving
carving-knife
Caryatides
cascade
Case
cash
Casneau
casually
cat's
cataleptic
cataleptical
catalogue
catapult
catechism
caterpillar
caterpillars
catholic
Catholique
cavalier
caved
caves
Cayley, George
Cayley's, George
cedar
ceilings
celebration
Cerberus
cerements
ces
cessations
chagrined
Chained
chair-leg
chambermaids
champion
Champollion
chapeau-de-bras
chapel
characterize
characterizes
charges
Charley's
charnal
charnel-house
charts
chasm-like
chassez
chastity
chattered
chatty
Chaworth
Chaworth, Mary
cheek-bones
cheered
cheerfully
cheerily
cheering
chemically
chemin
chemist
chequered
cher
cherub
Chess-player
Chestnut
chew
chez
Chichester
Chickasaw
Chief
chien
child-like
childishly
chill
chilling
chimed
chimpanzees
chins
chiselled
cholera
chooses
chorus
christened
Christmas
chronic
chronometer
chuckle
chuckling
ciphers
circuitous
circulated
circumambient
circumgyratory
circumnavigating
cited
civilities
civilize
clad
claims
clamminess
clammy
clamor
clandestinely
clangor
clapper
clapping
clashing
clasps
classify
classifying
clattering
clause
cleanest
cleanly
cleft
cleverest
Climax
climax
climbing
clime
cloaks
Clos
close-reefed
closeness
closets
clouded
Club
clumps
clumsy
clustered
coachman
coalescence
coasting
cobbler's
cock
cock-a-doodle
cock-a-doodle-de-dco
cock-a-doodle-doo
cocks
cod
coexist
cognomen
cohesion
collapsed
colleges
collccation
colony
Columbiad
column
columnar
com'd
com'd>
combed
combing
combustion
cometh
comic
commands
comme
commendation
commenting
communicates
communicating
communicative
companionship
compares
comparisons
compartment
competent
complimented
component
comprehending
con
conceit
conceiving
concentrative
concise
Concord
concubines
concurrence
condense
condor
conduit
confectioner
conferred
confessions
confide
confided
confidential
confounding
confounds
confutation
conglomeration
congregated
conic
conjointly
conjunction
conjured
conjuror
conjurors
connect
connivance
conquer
Conqueror
conqueror
conquers
consecutive
consenting
considering
considers
consistent
conspiracy
consternation
constriction
constructiveness
construed
consubstantialism
consulting
consumption
contains
contemporaries
contemporary
contemptuous
contended
contending
contentedly
continuation
contortions
contract
contradictories
contre-temps
convalescent
conveniences
conveniently
convert
conveyance
convict
convictions
convolutions
cooking
cooks

copiously
copper-fastened
coppered
coppice
coquettish
corked
corolla
corporal
corporate
corporation
corpore
corporeal
corps
corrected
corrective
correctly
corridors
corroborates
corrumpitur
corrupted
corvette
cotch
cotemporaries
cottage-built
couldst
Council
councillors
counterbalance
counts
county
courageous
Courier
courts
cove
cows
Crabbe
cracked
cracks
cradle
craft
crafty
crammed
cramped
Cratinus
cravings
crawl
creaked
creations
credulity
creed
crevices
Cribalittle
crimes
criticise
cronies
crosses
crotchets
Crow
crowbar
Cruelty
crumbled
crumbling
crumple
crushed
crushing
cubits
cuff
culpable
culprit
cultivation
cunningly
curas
Curiosities
curls
currency
curses
Curtis, Adelaide
curvature
curves
cusps
customers
cut-glass
cutlasses
cutlery
Cxncxrd
cycles
d'etre
d'oeuvres
d'or
d'un
daggers
dallying
damaged
damages
dangle
dank
darling
dart
daubed
Davy, Humphrey
deaden
dearly
death-bed
death-condemned
death-furniture
Death's
deceit
decently
deciding
declaration
declaring
declivities
decollavimus
decora
decreased
decreases
decrees
decrepitude
decrying
decypher
deep-set
defeated
defenceless
defer
deferred
deficiencies
defining
definitive
defy
defying
degage
Dei
deities
dejected
dejection
del
delectable
deleterious
deliberations
Delos
Deluc's
Democracy
democracy
Democratic
Democritus
demoniac
demonstrably
demonstrates
demur
demurely
denial
denizen
denn
denominated
denuded
departing
dependence
deplorably
depopulated
deportment
deposed
depositing
depressions
deputed
derivable
derives
deriving
descant
Descent
descents
descriptive
deserting
deserts
deserve
designates
desist
despaired
despatch
desperadoes
despises
dessert
deters
detested
detriment
deux
developing
deviate
devised
devising
devoutly
Dew
dews
dey
di
diable
dialect
diamond-like
Dian
dice
dicebant
dictates
die
diet
diffuse
diggers
digne
dignitaries
dilation
diligently
diluted
dimension
diminish
dimples
dingy
dining
Diodorus
Dionysius
dios
diplomatist
dipped
dips
dire
directness
directors
direful
disadvantage
disadvantages
disagreed
disagreement
disarmed
disasters
disbelieving
disburse
disclosure
discoloration
discomfiture
discomposed
discord
discordantly
discourage
discoursing
discriminating
discursive
discuss
discussions
diseases
disentangled
disgrace
disguised
disinter
disinterring
disjointed
disk
dismally
disobey
displaces
displays
displeasing
displeasure
disproportion
disputing
disquisitions
disregard
disrepute
dissatisfied
dissemble
dissipation
dissuade
distaste
distension
distention
distinguishes
dit
dived
diver
diverging
divers
diverse
diversion
diversity
diverting
divinely
diving
divinities
Dobson, Tom
doch
doctor's
doctrine
documents
doesn't
doffed
dogmas
dogmaticians
Domain
dominator
domino
donned
doo
doorway
dormant

dormant
dormitories
doting
dough
doze
drab
drawings
dream-like
dreaminess
dreariness
dressing-case
drift
drivel
drollery
droop
drooping
dropsy
dross
drown
drugged
Drummummupp
du
Dub--
duel
duellist
Duels
duke
dulled
dully
dumpy
dunder-headed
Dupin's
durability
durable
Dutchman
dvelf
dwarf's
dwarfish
dwelled
dwells
dyed
eagle
earn
earthen
earthy
easier
eater
echoing
eclat
eclipse
Eden
Edgarton
editing
Editors
educed
eels
eend
efface
efficiency
efficiently
effulgence
eides (Gr.)
Eight
eighty-fourth
eighty-six
eighty-two
elaborately
elbowed
Eleatic
electrical
Electro-Telegraph
Eleithias
element
eliciting
elite
elks
ellipsoid
Ellison, Seabright
elongation
eloped
elp
elucidation
elude
eluded
eluding
Elysium
emanation
embarrass
embittered
emblem
embodied
embodies
embolden
embouchure
embroidered
emerging
emit
Emperor
emperor
emperor's
employer
employs
Empress
empressement
enamelled
encamping
encased
enchained
encircles
Encke's
encompass
encored
encourage
encroachments
encumber
endeavours
Enderby
endow
endowing
endued
enfeeble
enfeebled
enforced
engagements
engine
engirdled
engrossed
enigmas
enlisted
enriching
ensues
ensured
entablature
entailed
entangle
enterprize
enthroned
entrapped
entry
envelop
envelope
enveloping
enviable
environed
environs
epilepsy
equality
equip
equipped
equipping
er
era
errand
erroneous
erroneously
errs
eruption
eruptions
eschew
eschewed
escondida
escorted
escritoire
escutcheon
escutcheons
estrange
etaient
Ethiopian
Etienne
etre
Etruscan
Ettrick
Euclid
euphonious
European
evanescent
Eve
ever-memorable
evidencing
evolution
evolutions
examinations
excavated
excavation
excellences
Excellencies'
Excellency
excellently
Exchange
exchanging
excitability
exclamations
excrescence
excruciating
excuses
execute
executing
executors
exemplifying
exert
exhorted
exigencies
exorbitant
expanding
expatiating
expeditious
explains
explicitly
explcit
exploits
expose
expound
expressive
externally
Extravaganza
extremeness
extricated
exultingly
eye-brows
eyeballs
eyebrow
eyed
eyelid
eying
faced
facie
facing
facsimiles
factions
facto
faggots
fainter
fait>
fallacy
falsities
faltered
fama
Fame
familiarly
fanatico
fandango
fang-like
fanned
fantasy
farce
fare
farrago
fascinated
fascination
faster
fatally
Fate
fathers
fathcmed
fathomless
fatigues
faugh
faultless
favors
favour
fay
Fays
fearlessly
Feb.
feint
felicity
Felix, Minutius
fellow-sufferers
fellow's
fences
fermentation
ferocious-looking
ferrades
fete
fettered
feudal
fibres
fiddles
fide
fiery-faced
fifty-four
fifty-one
figgurs
filbert
filbert-bushes
files
filliping
finely
fire-eater
fire-light
firma
fishy
fists
five-pound
fix
fizz
fizzing
Flaccus
flagon
flagons

flagrant
flagstones
flamingo
flashes
flask
flat-bottomed
flatu
flaunted
flavour
flaws
flax
fleet
Fletcher, Giles
flickered
Flimen
flimsy
Flint's
flirting
floods
flooring
flounces
floundered
fluidiforms
fluido
flung
flurry
fluttered
flux
foes
foible
foils
Folio
fondness
foolish
foolishly
foot-note
forbid
forbids
fore
forebodings
forechains
forego
forerunner
foresee
foreshadowing
foresight
forethought
foretold
forgetfulness
forlorn
formulae
forte
fortified
fortuitous
Fortune
forty-four
forty-seven
Found
foundered
Fountain
fountain
fountains
fours
fox
fox-hunter
fracture
fragility
fraternity
fraud
freebooters
frenzied
frequenting
freshness
fricaseed
Fricassee
frightfully
frigid
frind>
fringe
Frog
frost
froth
frothing
frown
frowned
frows
fru
fugitive
fuit
fulfilling
fulfillment
fullness
fund
funereal
fungi
fungus
Fur
furies
furnaces
Furniture
furrener>
furthering
fusion
fustian
fut
fut>
Future
G
gables
gaily
gallery
galley
Gallipagos
gallop
galloping
Galvanic
gambler
gangway
Garcia
gardens
Gargantua
garter
gasteropeda
gathers
gazes
Ge-Henna
geese
gems
genera
generalities
generality
generate
generated
generation
generic
generously
gentaal>
gentlemanly
gentry
genus
germ
Germanic
Germanism
germen
gift
gifted
gimlets
gin
girdled
girlhood
git
gits>
Glanvill
Glanvill, Joseph
glaringly
gleaned
glide
glided
glimmering
glistened
glistening
globes
globular
glutinous
gnarled
gnashed
gnawed
gnawing
goaded
goal
Godhead
Gods
Godwin, William
goggling>
Good
good-for-nothing
good-hearted
good-humour
Gordon
gorges
Gottingen
gouty
governed
gown
grammarians
grand-uncle
granulated
grapple
grasping
grasshoppers
gratifying
Grave
gravely
gravitating
grease
Grecque
Greely, Meredith
Green
greenest
greet
greeted
grievous
grind
grins
grizzly
groans
grocery
grooms
grossest
grotesquerie
grottoes
ground-moles
grouse
grunted
guarda
guarded
guardian
guerre
guesser
guest's
guides
guiding
Guido's
gulled
gully
gums
gunning
gypsum
gyrations
Hades
hag
haggard
Halcyon
half-credence
Hall's
Halleck's
hallooed
halt
ham-skin
handling
handsomest
handspike
haply
harder
hardy
hare
harken
harp
harshness
Hartley
Hastings
hatchways
Haubrion
haunches
Haunted
haven't
hawk
hazarded
head-board
heap
heaps
hearers
hearse-plumes
heartless
heartlessness
heartrending
heaved
Heaven's
Hebrews
Hedelin
heed
heeded
heeding
heeled
heighten
helas
helplessness
Helusion
Henson's
Hephestion, Ptolemy
herbage
Herculean
here's
heresy
Hermann, Johan
Hermann's
hero's
hesitates
hesitatingly
Hesper
Hewitt's
hewn
Hicks, Absalom
hid>
hideousness
hiding
Hierocles
highlands
hillo
hillocks

Hills
Him
himsilf>
Hindoo
hippopotami
hips
hist
hoarsely
hoary
hobbies
hobbling
hogs
Holland, Robert
hollo
hollow-sounding
Holy
homage
homes
homme
homo
homoeopathists
Homouioisios
Homousios
honesty
honeysuckle
honors
hooked
Horace
hordes
hornblende
horrendum
Horreur
Horror
horror-stricken
Hortulus
hospitable
hospitality
hospitals
hostel
hostilities
Houri
hours'
hubbub
huddled
Hugh
human-perfectibility
humanities
Humdrum
humility
humming-stuff
humour
hump
Hungary
hunt
Hunt, John
hunted
hurl
Hurlygurly, Tim
hurrah
hxme
hxw
hyacinth
hyacinthine
hydrophobia
hypocritical
I'd
I's
i's
icebergs
iciness
id
ideal
idealized
idee
identifying
idiocy
idleness
idly
ignoble
iligant>
ill-breeding
ill-favored
ill-health
ill-luck
ill-timed
ill-treated
illustration
illustrations
illy
imagines
imbecility
imbue
immaculate
immaterial
immateriality
immature
immolation
immutable
Imp
impalpability
impart
imparted
imparts
impassioned
impended
impending
imperious
imperishable
impertinences
implacable
implanted
implicate
implies
implore
imploring
importunate
importunities
imposing
impositions
imprecations
impressing
impressively
improperly
improvements
improvisations
improvisatrice
imprudence
imprudently
impudence
impudent
impulsive
inaccuracy
inanimate
inapplicable
inappreciable
inarticulate
inaudible
inaudibly
incarceration
incarnation
incidental
includes
incognizant
incoherently
incommoding
incomparably
incongruous
inconsequential
incurring
ind>
indefinitive
indemnify
indentations
independence
indescribably
indigenous
indignantly
indignity
indiscriminate
indisputable
indistinguishable
indite
indited
inditing
individualities
individuationis
indivisible
induces
induction
indulges
inestimable
inexorable
inextricable
infallible
infallibly
infantry
infesting
infinitude
infirmities
inflamed
inflections
inglorious
ingulfed
inhabit
inhabitant
inhalation
inhaling
inherent
inkling
inmates
innuendo
inquietude
Inquirer
Inquisition
inquisitively
inscribed
insects
insignificance
insignium
inspect
inspiring
inst.
instalments
instanced
instanter
instantiae
institute
instrumentality
insufferably
insulation
insulting
insults
insupportable
insurmountable
intangible
intellectually
intelligences
intelligibility
intemperance
intensest
intensities
intercepted
interim
interjectional
interloper
interminable
intermingling
interpreters
interrogatories
intersected
intersection
intersperses
intervening
interweaving
intimated
intractable
intrigue
invaluable
invariable
inversion
inverted
invest
investigate
investiture
investment
inviolate
involuntarily
inwards
iota
iris
irksome
irons
irrational
irreconcilable
irreducible
irregularities
irreparably
irresistibly
irresolute
irritability
irritable
irritation
Isaeus
Italians
italics
ivy
III
IV
J--
j'irois
Jacques
jaggeree
Japan
jar
jealousy
jellies
jerkin
jesters
jesting
jests
jewel
jewelled
jewelry
jiffy
jingling
Johannisberger
joints
joker
jokers
joli
jolly
jolly-boat
jostled
jostling
journalist
Journey
journeys
jòyful
judgments
judicial

judicious
juicy
Junius
junto
Justice
justification
jutting
juxtaposition
K
kabos
Kamschatka
Kanzas
Kate's
kath'auto (Gr.)
Keats
keenness
Kennedy, John P.
kennel
Keplers
kerseymere
kettle
kindle
knee-breeches
knight
knock
knocker
knuckles
Koran
kraut
Kreutzenstern
Kritik
l'histoire
L'homme
la
labels
laborious
labyrinths
lac
lacerated
lachrymatory
lack-lustre
laffin>
Lalande, Eugenie
land-slide
landlocked
landmarks
Landor
Landor's
Landscape
Landscape-Garden
lanes
lap
lapsed
lash
lasst
laste>
latent
lather
Latour
latter's
laudanum
lauding
laughingly
Launcelot
launch
laurels
layer
lazily
lazy
Le
leapt
learnedly
ledger
Ledyard
lee-lurch
leech
leeches
leetle
left-handed
legacy
legal
legally
leggings
legion
legions
legislative
Legrand, William
lending
lenses
Leonville
lesen
Leslie's
levatas
levique
lib.
liberties
license
licked
life-likeliness
life-likeness

light-house
lightened
lightest
lighting
lightness
likeness
liking
lily
limpid
line-manager
lineaments
linger
lingered
linked
lintels
lionizing
Lionship
Liriodendron
lisped
listens
litterateur
littleness
livelihood
loaf
loathed
lock
Locke's
locking
locusts
lodges
lodgings
logically
loiter
loitered
lone
lonesome
longboat
longest
loop
loosen
Lord's
lorgnette
loser
loser's
Loss
lounging
low-pitched
lowering
lowness
Lucan
luce
lull
lulled
lulling
luminary
lurked
lustra
lustrous
Luther, Martin
luxuriantly
luxuries
Lyceum
Lysias
ma
mace
Mackenzie, Alexander
Maelstroom
Magellan
magnifying
mahogany
mail-robber
Maisons
maker
maladies
Malcontent
malevolence
maliceful
malicious
malignant
mallet
maltreating
Mam'selle
mamma
Man-Friday
Mandeville
mania
maniere
mansions
mantel
mantel-pieces
manual
maple
maps
Marchioness
Margaux
marginalia
Maria
Marinade
Markbrunnen
markedly

marriages
marsh
marshy
Marston's
marvels
masculine
Mason's
master-stroke
mastered
mastery
mastiff
materialism
mattered
maximum
mazy
meals
meas
medallions
meddled
medicinal
meditate
meek
meekly
meetings
Mela, Pomponius
melee
Mem.
meme
memoirs
memorandum-book
memorials
menages
mender
mendicant
mending
menial
mercantile
merchandise
merciful
Meredith
meridians
meritorious
mes
Mesmer
mesmerizing
metal
Metamora
metaphysicianism
Metaphysische
Metempsychosis
meth'auton (Gr.)
methought
mica-slate
mice
microscopes
mid-summer
midday
Mige-Gush
migrated
mihi
mill
mill-horse
mill-wheel
Mille
milled
Miller, Joseph E.
Miller, Joseph F.
Miller, Joseph G.
Miller, Joseph H.
Miller, Joseph I.
Miller, Joseph K.
Miller, Joseph L.
Miller, Joseph M.
Miller, Joseph N.
Miller, Joseph O.
Miller, Joseph P.
Miller, Joseph Q.
Miller, Joseph R.
Miller, Joseph S.
Miller, Joseph T.
Miller, Joseph V.
Miller, Joseph X.
Miller, Joseph Y.
Miller, Joseph Z.
millionaires
Milton
mimes
mimic
mind's
minding
mingle
minute's
mirror-like
misanthrope
misanthropic
misapprehended
miser
misfortunes
misrepresentations
Misses

mistook
mists
mixing
mobile
moderately
modesty
molestation
momentum
monarch's
monks
mono (Gr.)
monosyllable
monstrosities
monstrum
Montesquieu
Montresors
Monument
monument
Moon-Hoax
Moon-Story
Moore's
moralist
morbidly
morbus
morceau
Morgan
morning's
Morrell
mors
mortally
mortar
mortem
Moscow
Most
motionlessness
mouldering
mourn
mourned
mournfully
mourning
mouse
mousike (Gr.)
Mudler
mulct
multicolor
multiplication
multiply
Mummy's
Muriton
Murray
muses
Muset
mushrooms
musique
Muskau, Puckler
mustachios
mustard
muster
musty
mutteringly
myriad
myrmidons
myrtle
mysteriously
Mystery
mystified
n'a
n'etait
Naiad
nakedness
narcotic
narrating
Narrative
narrowed
National
nationality
natur>
Naturwissenschaft
naught
nausea
nautical
Neal's
nebber
neber
nebulous
needn't
negro's
negroes
nemo
nervously
net
nettled
nibblers
nicht
nihil
nihility
nihilo
nill
nimio
Nimrod

ninety-ninth
Nineveh
ninny
nixt>
nod
nodding
noiselessly
non-appearance
nonce
noodle
Nordland
Norfolk
normal
north-west
northwest
northwesterly
Norway
notre
noumena
Novalis
novelists
now-a-days
nuff
nullity
Number
nunc
nurtured
nutritious
o-o-o-o-gh
O-wy
objected
obliterated
observers
obstruction
obtruded
obtrusive
obtrusively
occultation
occurs
octaves
oddity
odiosius
odors
Oedipus
offend
oggling>
Okydandies
ole
olive
omelettes
omne
omni-prevalent
omnibus-driver
Omnipresence
on (Gr.)
one-and-twenty
one-fourth
onerous
onset
onwards
oooogh
open-mouthed
openings
opportunite
oppressively
opprobrium
optical
optics
opulence
opulent
orderly
organized
Oriental
originator
os
Osage
Osborne's
ostensible
ostensibly
ostentatious
ostentatiously
Otterholm
out-houses
out-Heroded
outskirts
over-acute
over-effeminacy
overawed
overcame
overcharged
overhauling
overshot
overthrew
overthrown
overturned
overwhelm
P--'s
pa
pacified
pack

packing
paddle
paddles
Paestum
Pagan
painters
palate
palaver
palmed
palms
palpability
pane
pannels
panorama
panoramic
parable
parade
paradises
Paradox, Sir Positive
paralleled
parallels
paralysis
parched
parier
Park
parley
paroxysms
parsimonious
parte
Parthenon
participation
particolored
partisan
passions
passports
pasteboard
pat
patent
pathos
patronized
patronymic
patting
Paulding's
pea
peaceable
peaceful
peaks
pearl
pearly
peasant
pedestrians
Pedro's
peepers
peer
peevish
peevishly
pegs
pendulous
Pendulum, Peter
penetration
penguin's
peninsula
pennies
Pennifeather's
Penstruthal
perceives
perceptive
peregrinations
perfectionists
perforations
performances
performer
performers
perfumed
perfumer
perfumery
perfumes
pericranium
perigee
perihelion
permanently
perpetrate
persecute
persecuted
persecutor
Persepolis
Persia
Persian
personages
perspiration
persuasions
pertinent
pervade
Perverse
pestilences
pestilential
Peter
peterels
Peterson
petulance

petulantly
Phalaris
phase
phenomena
Philistine
Philistines
philosophie
Phoebus
phonetic
phosphorescence
phosphorus-box
phrenological
phrenologists
physiologist
piano-forte
piazza
piazzas
pickle
pictural
picul
piculs
Pierre's
pigeon-wing
Pigs
pills
Pindar's
pinion
pinioned
pinions
pins
pint
Pinxit
pious
pipes
pirouette
Pisistratus
pitchers
pitchy
plagiarism
plains
plaits
plantation
planted
plants
platter
plausible
Plautus
plays
pleaded
pleasantry
Pleiades
plentifully
pleurez
Plotinus
plug
plume
plump>
plumped>
plunderer
plus
pneumatics
pocket-mirror
pocketbook
poesy
poet's
Poindexter
Point
poked
polar
poll
polluted
pollution
Pompey's
pomposity
Ponca
ponderable
Ponto
poor-devil
popping
porcupine
porous
Porphyry
porphyry
porridge
portage
portals
porters
portico
portly
portraite
portraits
ports
positiveness
possum
posting
pottle
pounded
pourtray
pouvoir
pover

powerfully
powerless
practise
practising
practitioners
praised
praiseworthy
prating
praying
pre-eminently
pre-existent
precedes
Prediction
predisposed
predominates
Preface
preferable
preferring
Prefet
pregnancy
Preignac
premeditated
preponderate
prepossessing
prescribed
prescriptive
presentiment
presumable
pretension
preternatural
pretext
prevention
priceless
pricked
priest
priesthood
primarily
primeval
Prince's
principium
printing
printing-offices
prison-house
prisons
privation
privations
pro
probing
problems
Proclus
productive
profane
professing
professional
proffered
Proffit, Peter
profligacy
progeny
prolongation
prominences
promiscuous
promptings
promptness
promulgation
pronunciation
proofs
propagated
propagator
propel
prophecies
propounder
proscription
prosecuting
prostrating
protect
protestation
prototypes
proudest
proverb
proverbial
provide
prowling
prying
Psammitticus
pseudonym
Ptolemais
Ptolemy
publisher
pudding-stone
pudicitiae
Pue's
pully-wou>
pulmonary
pulmonifera
pump-handle
pump-handles
pumped
pumpkin
pun
punch

punctilious
punctuality
pungently
punishment
pur (Gr.)
purchaser
purlite>
purses
pursuer
pursy
purty>
Putnam
putty
puzzle
puzzles
pxh
pxll
pyramids
Pythagoreans
q
qu'il
qu'un
quaffed
quarrelled
quarto
quasi
Queen
queenly
quest
queue
quia
quieted
quietude
quills
Quirite
quits
quitted
quiver
Quixotic
quizzical
quo
quoi
quondam
quota
quotations
quotes
R--
R--'s
rabid
Raca
racy
radicalness
radius
Rafaelle
ragout
rail
railroads
rails
raiment
rallied
Ramus, Jonas
rancid
ransacked
rapier
rapping
raps
rapt
rapturous
rascality
rashness
Rata
rationally
Rattle
Raven
raven
raven-black
razors
re-crossed
re-echoed
re-entered
re-examination
re-stated
re-touching
readjusted
reads
realization
realized
realms
reaped
rebels
recede
recherches
recipients
reciprocal
reckoning
reclining
reclosed
recognises
recognizes
recommenced

reconciling
recount
recounted
recreant
recrossed
rectify
Red
reddened
redeemed
redness
reeds
reefs
referrible
reflux
refracted
refrained
refreshed
refreshment
refuses
refutation
refuted
regardless
regenerated
regenerating
regulations
reigns
reinen
reiterating
relationship
relaxing
releasing
relevancy
reliable
religious
relinquish
relish
reluctant
relying
remarking
remedied
remembering
remind
remissness
rencontre
repairs
repealed
repeater
repel
replace
replacing
representative
repression
reprinted
reproach
reproof
republic
reputed
requiring
rescued
resentment
reserving
resides
residue
resin
resisting
Resolution
resolutions
respectively
respiratory
restlessness
restoration
restoring
restraining
restrains
restraints
resuscitated
retailed
retaliation
retard
retardation
retarding
retched
retirements
retrograde
Revelation
reverenced
revert
reviewed
reviews
revival
revivification
revolted
Reynolds
Reynolds, J. N.
rheum
rhyming
Rialto
Ricaree
rice
Richbourg

riddles
rifled
right-angled
rightful
rigor
ringbolt
riotous
ripening
Rituel
riverence>
rivet
roarings
robbers
rods
role
rookeries
Ross, Alexander
rotate
rotating
rotting
rouge
Rouge-et-Noir
rough-looking
roughened
rougher
Roule
roundness
roving
rows
Royal
rub
Rubens
rubicund
rubies
rudderless
ruddy
ruffle
rug
ruler
rumpled
S.D.U.K.
sa
sack
sacrificing
saddened
saddle
saddle-bags
saffron
sage
sail-boat
sailing
saint
saith
salary
sale
salle
Salmanezer
Salsafette
saluted
Samaria
Sanconiathon
sanctuary
sand-bars
Sandflesen
sandstone
sanguine
sanguinis
sapientiae
sapphires
Saracen
Saratoga
sarcophagus
Sardanapalus
sassafras
satin-like
satire
Satires
satirist
saturnine
sauntering
sausage
savor
Saxony
Saying
sayings
scant
scanty
scapegrace
scattering
scented
scentless
sceptre
Schiller
schist
school-boy
schoolmates
schorl
Schuylkill
scimitar
scissors

scoffed
sconces
scorned
Scotch
scoundrelly
scowl
scratched
scrawl
screwing
scudded
scullion
sculptured
scuppers
scythes
Sea
sea-boat
sea-shore
sea-sickness
Seabright
seacoast
sealing
sean
seashore
seasonable
seasons
seceders
secreting
section
sections
seculare
secures
seekers
seizure
selection
self-cognizance
self-complacency
self-destruction
self-satisfaction
self-willed
selling
sembled
semi-Gothic
semicolon
sentient
sepulchrum
ser'ts
serai
seraph
Seraphic
seraphic
serenity
sermon
sermonic
settings
Sevres
sewed
sexes
shadowed
shaft
shafts
shaggy
shallowness
sham
shank
shapeless
shared
sharing
shave
she
sheath
sheltered
shepherd
shicken
shine
shipmate
shipwreck
shivered
shivering
shoe-buckles
shopkeeper
shops
shouldst
shrines
shrunken
shud>
shuffling
shy
sich
sich
sidereal
sifted
sights
signatures
significant
significantly
signification
signified
signifies
signifieth
signing

Sigourney
Sigourney's
silky
silvery
simile
simoom
simoon
sine
sinecures
Sing, Cheyte
sinner
sins
sinuous
sipped
sire
sister-in-law
sixpence
sixty-four
sixty-two
skeptical
sketched
sketching
sketchy
skilfully
skillful
skulking
slabs
slapped
slapping
sleep-waking
slouched
slower
sluggish
slumberer
small-pox
smelled
Smith's
smoked
smoky
smoothly
Smug
snail
snake
Snapping-Turtle
snatches
sneered
sneers
sneezed
snow-capped
snugly
So-and-so
sobs
sodales
sofas
softening
softest
soho
soient
soiled
solace
soles
solicit
solidiforms
solitude
solitudes
Solomon
Some
sonorous
soothed
sophists
sorely
soul's
soulless
soundless
soup
southeastern
space-penetrating
spacious
spake>
spanned
sparkle
sparkling
sparks
spear
specious
spectre
spectrum
speculated
speculating
spelt
spheres
Sphinx
sphynxes
spicing
spin
spinning
Spirit
spirit-lifting
spirit-stirring
spit

spitting
splintered
splotches
spoils
spoilt
sported
springy
squashish
squint
stabbed
stagnation
stair
stamens
stamping
standard
Stanfield
Stapleton
star-shaped
starched
stares
staring
startlingly
State
statesman
statue-like
staying
Steen, Jan
sterb'ich
sterbich
stiffened
stiffness
stimulate
stimulus
stipulated
stocked
stocks
stomachs
Stone's
stone's
stops
store
stored
stormy
Story's
stoutest
stove
stragglers
straightway
straits
strangest
strangled
strapped
straw
straws
stretches
stripes
striving
stubborn
stubby
stud
studded
Student
studio
stuffing
Stultz
stumble
stumpy
stunted
stupidly
stylus
Styx
suavity
subdivisions
submissive
subscribe
subsiding
substantiality
substituted
subterranean
succinctly
suffers
sufficiency
suffrage
sugar
suggesting
suggestive
suis
suites
suitors
Sully
sulphur
summer's
summits
summoning
sumptuous
Sunship
superabundance
supercilious
superfluity
supernal

supplies
supports
supremely
supremeness
surer
surmises
surmising
surprises
survive
surviving
suspend
suspiciously
swallow-tailed
swallows
swamping
swarthiness
swarthy
sway
swayed
sweeter
swells
sweltering
swimmer
swimmingly
swings
swivels
sword
sybils
syfe
sympathies
sympathize
Symposium
synonymous
syphon
Syrian
Syrianus
System
T--, Tabitha
t's
tableland
tablets
Tacitus
tainted
talented
tally
tan
tantalizing
tap
tape-measure
tapestried
tapis
taps
tardily
tardy
tarns
tarried
tasked
tasking
tasting
Tattle
tattoo
Tau
te
te (Gr.)
technicality
tedious
tedium
Teian
telescopic
temerity
tempers
Tempest
tempestuously
Temple
tempora
temporarily
temps
temptation
tenacity
tenfold
Terentius
terminate
terminates
terra
terrifically
tertiary
tests
Teufel
teufel
teuffel
Textor, Ravisius
th
Thames
theatrical
Theban
Thebes
theft
Thelluson
theological
Theology, Theologos

Theophrastus
thereunto
therewith
thicker
thickly-wooded
thirty-nine
thirty-seven
thirty-three
This
This-and-that
thongs
Thornton, Andrew
thoughtless
Thoughts
Thrace
thrashing
threaded
three-quarter
thrice
throbbed
thrones
thrusts
thumb-latch
thunder-cloud
thunderstricken
ticking
tidings
Tieck
tightening
tillers
tilt
timbered
Time
time-pieces
tingling
tinkling
Tintontintino
Titian
to-morrow's
toasted
toasting
toiled
toilsome
tolling
tomahawk
tomorrow
Tompkins, Bobby
topsail
topsy-turvy
torches
torment
tormenting
tornado
torpor
torrent
tortures
totter
Touch-and-go
Tour
tourist
tourists
tourniquet
tournure
tousand
toute
tow-line
tracked
tracks
trader
traders
trail
training
trampling
transact
transactions
transcendentalists
transfer
transferred
transferring
translate
translations
translator
transmitted
transparency
transports
trap-door
travelers
treasures
Trebizond
treble
trellice-work
trelliced
trellis-work
trellised
tremulousness
tressel
tressels
Trevanion, Rowena
triangular
Tribunaux
trice
trimmings
trink
trinket
triplicate
tripods
Trippetta's
trips
Trist
Tristan
trombones
troof
troop
tropical
troth>
troubling
trout
Troy
trubble
truffe
trumpets
truthfulness
trysail
Tsalal
Tsalemon
tu
tubes
tubular
tumbler
tumuli
tumultuously
tunnel
turgid
turmoil
turnip
turpitude
Turtle
turtles
tweedle-dee
twenty-three
twins
twirled
twisted
txld
typographical
tyranny
Ugolino
ulterior
umbrella
un
unabated
unacquainted
unadulterated
unanimous
unanimously
unanswerable
unavoidable
unawares
unbidden
uncalculating
unceasingly
uncircumcised
unclosing
uncomfortably
uncomplainingly
unconsciousness
uncouth
undergrowth
undertaken
undertook
undignified
undiscovered
undulation
unfeigned
unfit
unfitted
unforeseen
unformed
unfruitful
unguided
unhandsome
unimpressive
uninformed
uninjured
unison
unit
uniting
University
unjust
unmanacled
unmentionable
unostentatious
unpacked
unpleasantly
unpossibility
unpretending
unprofitable
unravel
unreasoning
unredressed
unremitting
unreserved
unresistingly
unriddled
unrolled
unsightly
unstable
unsuited
unsupported
unsurpassed
unt
untenable
untenanted
untractable
untravelled
untrodden
unvollkommen
unwonted
unwrought
upheld
upholstery
uplift
uprose
upset
urbanity
urges
usbande
Usher's
ushered
using-up
usurped
vacated
vagabonds
vaguely
vagueness
vainly
valiantly
valueless
values
vanish
vanishing
vapoury
Varietes
vassals
vaster
vehemence
vehement
vehicles
velocities
veloute
velvety
ven
veneration
ventur
venturing
verb
verdict
verify
veritable
veritable
vermicular
Vernunft
verre
Versailles
version
vertical
vertically
vest
vibratory
Vice-President
vicinage
vicissitudes
Victoria
vid
vida
vie
vill
villagers
villanous
villany
Vin
vindictive
virgin
virtu
virtual
vis
vis-a-vis
viscera
visitarem
visitor's
vitally
vituperative
vivacious
vivente
vixen
vociferations
volatile
volcano
Voltaic
volution

Von
voracity
Vougeot
vous
vowel
vrai
Vredenburgh
vrow
vrows
VI
waddled
waggeries
wagging
wagon
wags
waist-coat
waistcoats
waken
walnut
walnuts
wander
wanderers
wanderings
wanness
wants
wardrobe
warehouses
wares
warlike
warmest
warrior
Washish
Wasp
wasted
water-gate
water's
waver
wavy
waxen
waylayings
wealthiest
weariness
weathering
web-work
wed
Weddell
weekly
welcomed
well-arranged
well-merited
welled
Welsh
wery
whale
whalebone
whaling-ship
wheeled
wheezed
wheezing
whelmed
whereof
whiffs
whispering
whistle
whistling
whit
white-dressed
wholesome
whomsoever
widdy's>
widening
wielded
willain>
William
willian>
willingness
Wimble, Will
windy>
winking
Winowacants
Wirt's
wiseacre
wisely
wisest
witches
withal
withering
withheld
withhold
wizard
woe
woes
wonder-stricken
wonderment
woo>
wood-cutters
Woods
woodwork
woody
worded

Words
world's
Worm
worm-eaten
Wormley, Alexander
worshippers
wrap
wreathed
wreaths
wrenching
wrestled
wriggle
wriggling
writhings
wrong's
Wyatt, Cornelius
X
Xerxes
xnce
xwl
xxult
y
Yankees
yaw
year's
yelling
yellings
yellowish
Yellowstone
yer>
Yorktown
youngest
yourselves
Zaiat, Ebn
Zante
zealous
zenith
zephyr
zigzag
zodiacal
Zoilus
zones
0.0000157
1,
1200
13th
14'
14th
1769
1774
1780
1792
1803
1805
1806
1810
1822
1823
1837
19th
21
22
23
23'
237,000
240,000
2500
27
27'
29'
31'
4th
40
40'
41
5th
54'
57'
58'
59
61
63
7th
71
8'
82
(1)
A.D.
a-piece
a-svigging
a's
abandonnement
abased
abasement
abashed
Abbe
abbeys
abdication
abductor
Abel-Shittim

aberration
abet
abetting
abiding
Abingdon
able-bodied
aboard
abolish
abolished
abomination
abominations
aboriginal
aborigines
above-ground
above-named
aboveboard
abridgment
absconded
absences
absented
absorptive
abstains
absterrebitur
abstruseness
abstrusities
absurdum
abuses
abusing
abutting
abxut
abysmal
academies
acanthus
accede
accelerate
accent
acceptance
accepts
acclamation
accommodating
accommodations
accomplices
accomplishes
accorded
accorto
accost
accoutred
accumulation
accurse
acetous
achievements
achieves
aching
achlus (Gr.)
acknowledgement
acquires
acquisitions
acquit
acquitted
acre
acrimonious
Act
actively
actors
ad
adage
Adam
Adam's
Adams, J. Q.
adapts
addenda
adders
addle-headed
addling
adduce
Adelaide
ademptum
admeasured
administer
administered
admirer
admires
admixture
admonisher
Adommin
Adonai
Adoni-Bezek
adorn
Adramalech
Adriatic
adroitness
Aduanturier
adult
adventuring
advertise
Advertisement
advertising
advisedly
advisers
advising

advocated
advocates
adzes
Aedepol
aerienne
aerolites
aeronautic
aethera
Aetna
affaire
affectations
affectionate
affectionately
affects
affianced
afficiantur
affidavit
afflict
afflicting
affluence
affray
affrighted
afoot
afore
Afrasiab
Africans
after-cabin
after-dream
after-sails
afterlife
aftersail
afterwords
ag
aggregated
agin
agin>
agir
agitating
agitations
agog
Agony
agraffas
agreements
agrees
agressi
aground
aha
Ahmateaza
aides-de-camp
aids
aight
aigrette
ailment
aimable
aime
aimless
Ainsworth's
air-boxes
air-bubble
air-tight
airing
aisles
aisy>
akimbo
Al
al
alacrity
Aladdin's
alarmedly
alarummed
albeit
Albert
albuginea
Alceus
alchemy
Alcman
Alcohol
alcun
Alcyone
Aleph
Alex--
Alexan
Alexandria,
Alfred
Algae
aliment
alimentiveness
Aliquibus
Alive
All
all-devouring
all-engrossing
all-fervid
all-important
all-pervading
all-sufficient
Allamistakeo
Allamistakeo's
Allbreath
allegorical
allegorically
allegory
Allen, Colonel Ethan
Allen, William
Allen, Wilson
alleviate
alliance
allied
allowances
allured
allusions
alluvia
alluvial
alow
Alpheus
Alraschid, Haroun
alterest
alternations
alternatively
aluit
alum
Amateaza
amativeness
amazingly
Ambaaren
amber
ambitus
ambuscade
Amen
amenable
amending
amends
amerement
Americanism
Amerique
amicable
amicably
amid-ships
amidships
amiss
ammonia
Ammonites
amongst
amour
amplification
Amplitudine
Amsterdam
an
Anacharsis
Anacreon
Anakim
analogically
analogist
analyse
Anamalech
Anamoo-moos
anarchy
anatomists
anchored
and
andava
Anderson
Andromache
Andronicus
anemonae
anemonoe
aner (Gr.)
aneurism
Angelo
angler
Anglo-Saxon
anglois
anima
animadversion
animadversions
animalculae
animate
animaux
annales
annihilate
anniversary
annotations
announce
annoy
annoyances
annoys
annually
Anonymous
Ansichten
ant
antagonists
Antares
Antediluvians
antennae
Anthon
Anthon, Charles
anticipative
Antigone
antipathies
antipathy
antiquum
Antoeus
Antony, Mark
antro
anxther
anyone
Aoede
aorta
apeak
Apennines
aper
aphelion
Aphrodite
Apicius
apocryphal
apologetic
apologie
apologizing
apostrophising
apothegm
appals
Apparatus
appending
Appennine
appertain
appetency
appetites
apples
applications
appoint
appointments
apposite
appreciating
apprize
approbatory
appropriated
appropriately
appropriating
approval
apropositions
apsides
Apuleius
aqua
aqueduct
Arab
Arcadians
arch-angel
Arch-enemy
arch-fiend
arch-way
Arch-Fiend
Archangel
archbishop
Archilochus
architecture
ardency
ardently
ardour
arduous
Aregan
aren't
arena
Argelais
argent
argumentative
argumentum
aria
Arickara
aridity
Aripao
Aristaeus
aristocratic
Aristoeus
Aristolochia
arithmetic
arithmetical
Arkansas
arm-chests
arm-holes
armchair
armful
arming
Arnoldi
arointed
Arouet
Arouet, Francois Marie
arranges
arrivals
arrogated
arronde
arrondees
arrowhead
arrowheads
art
art-scarred
arter
artesian
arth>
Arthur
Article

articles'
articulation
articulo
artificers
artificialities
artificiality
artificially
artisan
artist's
artista
artizan
artless
Arts
asbestic
ascendere
ascribed
ash
Ashtophet
Asiatic
Asiatic
Asiatics
askance
askant
aslant
Asphodel-interspersed
asphodels
asphyctic
aspires
aspiring
assailants
assassinations
assaulting
assemble
asseveration
assiduity
assiduously
assignable
Assignation
assimilate
assistants
assisting
assists
associated
Association
assoilzie
assorted
assorting
assuaging
assunder
assurement
assuring
assurity
Assyria
Ast
Astarte
asteroids
asthma
Astor's
Astor's, John Jacob
Astoreth
Astoria
astound
astoundingly
astride
astrologer
astrologers
astrology
astronomically
astuteness
asylum
Atalanta
Atalantic
Athenians
atomies
Atree
attacking
attaghan-maker
attainments
Atticus, Herodes
attorneys
attractions
attributes
Atys
auction
audacities
audibly
Audiguier
auditory
aught
augment
augmentation
augmenting
aujourd'huy
aunt's
auram
Aurelian
auricle
auricula
auriculas
Aussi
aussi
austerity
Austrian
authentic
authorized
auto-biography
Autobiographists
autocrat
autographical
Autography
automaton
automaton-chess-player
autor
autos (Gr.)
autos-da-fe
autremet
auyos (Gr.)
av
availing
avails
avait
avalanche
avatar
ave>
avec
aven>
avenged
avenger
averaged
Averni
aves
avis
avoids
avoirdupois
avowedly
awakes
awed
awfulest
awry
aye
Ayesher
Aznac
Azrael's
B
b
B.A.T.C.H.
B.L.U.E.
Baal-Peor
Baal-Perith
Baalzebub
Babbage's
Babel
Bacchanalian
Back
back-ground
back-water
backing
backwoods
Bacon
Bacon-engendered
Baconianism
Bad
badger
Badger, Samuel
badges
baffles
baffling
bag-pipes
bagatelle
bah
Baiae
bailed
bailing
baissee
bait
bait>
baize
baked
balanced
balancez
balancing
Balbec
balconies
ballast's
ballet-dancers
balloon-bag
Balloon-Hoax
balloon's
Balzac
Balzac
bamboozled
banditti
bandy
bank-notes
banked
banking
bankrupt
banned
Banquo
Baptista
Baptiste
Barac
Barbadoes
barbarians
barbarity
barber
barbers
Barclay
bards
barefooted
barely-discernible
Bargain
Barlow's
Barnabas
Barnard, Augustus
Barnes
barometers
baron's
barque-rigged
barques
Barrett
barricaded
barring
Barronissy>
barroques
barrow
Barry, Lyttleton
Bartas
barterings
bas-reliefs
Bas-Bleus
baseness
Bashan
bashfulness
basin-full
basinful
basso
batch
bate>
bath
bathe
bathing-places
Batrachomyomachia
battalions
batten
batter
Battery
battle-lantern
battledoor
battlement
bauble
bawling
bayonet
bazaars
beaker
beam
bean
beant
bear-skins
beards
bearskins
beast-like
beastly
Beasts
Beati
beautiful-minded
beautifullest>
Beauvais'
beaver-traps
becalmed
Beckford
beckoning
bed-clothes
bed-post
bed-posts
bedevilled
bedewed
bedight
Bedlam
bedlam
Bedlamite
bedlamite
Bedlo, Augustus
Bedloe, Augustus
bedposts
bedroom
bedside
bee'nt
beef
beefsteak
beetle's
befall
befitting
befriended
befriends
befxre
Begebenheit
Begebenheiten
begetting
beggar

beggarly
beggars
begin'd>
beginned>
begirdled
begrimed
begs
beguile
behaves
behaving
behemoth
behild>
beholds
behooved
bei
bejewelled
Bekker
bel-esprit-ism
belabor
belave>
belaved>
beldame
Belfry
Belgium
Bell
bell-metal
bell-tones
Belles
bellies
bellowing
bellowings
bellows-maker
bellows-mender
Belphegor
belted
Belus
Benares
bended
beneficial
benevolence
benevolent
Bengal
Bengalee
benighted
benignly
Bennett's
Bentham, Jeremy
Benthams
Bentinck's
Bentley
Benton
bequeath
Beranger
bereft
Beresina
Bergerac
Berlifitzing, Wilhelm Von
Berlifitzings
Bermuda
Berwick
beseamed
beseechingly
besets
besotted
bespeak
bespotted
bess
Bessarion
Bessop
best-hearted
bestir
bestows
bestrode
betaken
Bete
bete
bethinking
betrayal
betrayer's
betrays
bets
Betsey
betwane>
between-decks
betwixt
beverage
bevy
beware
bewinged
bewitching
bewitchingly
Bi-Part
Bias, Fanny
bible
biblical
bibliotheque
Bichloride
bickering
bids
big-horn
biggest
bight
bigness
bignonia
billet
billet-doux
billets
billets
billets-doux
billiard-ball
Billingsgate
bills
Billy
binder
bindings
biography
Biot
biped
bipeds
Bipont
birch-bark
Bird, Robert
Bird, William
Birds, Robert
birds'
birthday
bisected
bishop
bismuth
bison
bits
bitther>
bituminous
bivalve
bivouac
bizarrerie
bizarreries
black-robed
black-striped
black-tailed
black-walnut
blackamoor
blackberries
blacken
blackest
blackfish
blackish
blacksmith
Blackwood, Blackwood
Blackwood's
bladders
blades
blarney
Blas, Gil
blasphemer
blasphemies
blaspheming
blasphemous
blasphemy
blazoned
bleak-looking
bleating
bleed
blemishes
blende
blessing
blessings
blieve
blindfold
blink
bliss>
bloated
Block, E. T. V.
blockading
blockhead
blood-bedewed
blood-colored
blood-spot
blood-stained
blood-thirstiness
blood-tinted
blood-vessels
bloodshed
bloody-minded
bloomed
Bloomsbury
blossoming
blossomy
blot
blotting
blowpipe
Bludenuff, Baron
bludgeon
Blue
blueish
blunderbuss
blunderbusses
Blunderbuzzard
blundering
blunt
blushes
bluster
blustering
board-bill
boarded
boast
boasting
boatman
Bob's
Bobby's
bobolink
bobtail
boded
bodiless
boding
body-snatchers
body's
bog-throthing>
bog-throtting>
boggy
Bogs
bogs
bogthrotter>
boilings
Bois-Brules
Bolingbroke
bolsters
bomb
bombarded
bombast
Bombay
bombshell
Bon-Bon's
Bon-Bonist
bona
Bond, Peter
Bones
Bonfanti's
bonfire
bonheur
Bonhomme
bonhommie
bonnet-ribbon
bonum
bonus
Book
book-case
book-closet
book-cover
book-stall
booksellers
bookshelves
bookworm
boomed
booming
booms
boosed
Booshoh
boot-black
boot-blacks
boquets
Bordeaux
boredom
Bornese
borrow
borrowed
borrows
bosky
Bossuet
Bossuet, Julien
Bostonians
botanically
botanist
Botany
bote
bothered
Bothnia
bottle-nosed
Bougive
bould>
bounced
Bound
boundary-line
bounding
bouquets
Bourdeaux
Bovis
bow-knot
Bowen, Walter G.
bowstringing
bowstrung
Box
boxed
Boy
Boz
bracelet
bracelets
brackets
bragging
brain-scattering

bran
brand
branded
branding
brandish
brandished
brandishing
brandy-saturated
brant
bras
brat
brats
brawling
brawny
braying
brazier
Brazil
breaches
breakbones
breakfasted
breast-pocket
breasts
Breath
breathlessly
breeches'
breve
brevity
brewing
Brewster
briar-bushes
bribing
briefer
brighten
brilliantly-plumed
brimful
brimfull
brimming
brinks
Brisky>
bristles
Britain
Britannia-ware
Britannica
broached
broaching
Broad
broad-leaved
broadcloth
Brobdingnag
brochures
Broglio, Duke Di
brooded
Brooks, James
broom
broomstick
brother-in-law
brother's
brotherhood
brow-beating
Bruges
bruin
bruited
Brunswick
brushwood
brusquerie
brutality
brutally
Brutii
Bryant
bubbled
bubbles
Buchan
Buckholm
Buckhurst's
buds
Buffalo
buffoon
buffooneries
buffoonery
buffoons
Bug
bugaboo
building-sites
builds
bull-dog
bull-roarings
bulldog
bullet-headed
bullet-proof
bullock
bullocks
bully
Bulwer
bumpers
bunches
bung-hole
Bunker-Hill
Buonaparte, Napoleon
buoy
buoyancy
buoyant
buoyantly
buppy
burdens
Buren, Vanny
burgher
burglars
burgomaster's
burgomasters
Burial
burial-ground
buries
burning-glasses
burnings
burns
burr
burthened
burthening
burthens
Burton
Bury
burying
bushy
busies
business-like
buskin
Bussy
bustled
busy-body
busy-bodyism
butcheries
butefulle
buttercup
butterflies
button-headed
buy
buyers
buying
buzzard
buzzing
bxg
bxw-wxw-wxw
bxwl
by-paths
by-the-bye
bypaths
Byron's
C
c eiling
c
c.o.r.d.a.
C'est
c'etait
c's
Cab
cab-hire
cab-introduction
caba
cabalistic-looking
cabbaged
cables
caches
cachinnated
cachinnatio
cachinnatory
cadaverous-looking
cadaverousness
cadence
Cadet
Cafe
Cafes
cage
cage-wires
caged
Cairo
cajole
cajoled
calamitous
calamo
Calbrinachus
calc
calcedony
Calculating
Calcutta
calcutta
calico
calicoes
calmer
calms
calumet
calumny
Calvin, John
Cambyses
Cameleopard
camelopard
cameos
camp-meeting
Campaign
Campanile
camphor
Can
Canada
Canadas
canaille
canaries
cancel
candlestand
candy
canine
caning
canis
cannibal
cannibals
Canning, Launcelot
cannister
cannister-shot
canoe-load
canoe's
canonicals
canos
Canova
Cant
canteen
canteens
Canton
canvas-backs
capability
caparisoned
capers
capital-O
capitally
Capitol
Capitols
capon
Capricornutti
caprioles
capsising
capsize
captains
captious
captivated
captivating
capturing
Capuletti
caput
car
carabine
Caraccas
caracols
Carathis
carbuncle-nosed
carcase
card-table
carded
Careme
caressed
caressing
Carey
Carey, Matthew
caricature
Carlyle-ism
carnal-minded
Carne
Carnival
carols
carousal
carouse
carped
carpenter
carpenters
carpet-bags
carpets
carriage-road
carriage-track
carriages
carrier-pigeons
carriers
carronades
carrot
carrots
cars
Carson, John
carted
cartes
Carthaginian
cartilaginous
carts
carve
Carver
Carver, Jonathan
Carver's
carvers
case-knives
Caserta
Cask
cassimere
Cassini
cassock
cast-off
castas

caste
castor
cat-aplasm
cat-au-rabbit
cat-egory
cat-erect
cat-heads
cat-like
cat-nip
cat-peltries
cat-worshippers
Cat-Act
Cat-Growing
catalpa
catalpas
catamites
catch-word
caterwauled
caterwauling
cathead
Cato
Catone
Cats
Catskills
cattymount
Caus, Solomon de
causeways
caustic
cautioned
cavalierly
cavalry
cavernous
cavilled
caving
ceaseless
Cecil
ceder
celeste
Cemeteries
cemeteries
centigrade
centime
centripetal
cents
centurion
cerebral
cerement
ceremonial
ceremonies
certum
Cervantes, Miguel de
Cervantes, Miguel De
cet
cette
Chabert
Chacun
chaff
chain-bridle
chaining
chaise
chaise-longue
Chaldaea
Chaldaean
chalice
Chalk-Farm
chalky
challenge
challenged
Chamberlaine's
Chamberlayne's
chambermaid
Chamfort
chandelier-chain
chandeliers
Channing
Channing, W. E.
chanticleer-note
chanting
Chapman
Chapman's
Chapter
characteristically
characterization
charadrai (Gr.)
chargeable
chargee
charger
chariot-wheels
charioted
Charite
charities
charlatanerie
charming
Charon
Charonian
Chartreuse
chas'd
chasing
chastened
chastise
chastisements
Chateau
Chateaubriand
chatter
chattering
Chaucer
Chaussee
cheat
cheats
check-book
checked
checking
cheerfulness
cheese
chef-d'oeuvres
chefs
chemise
chemist's
chemistry
Chenes
Cheops
cherished
cherishing
cherry
chesnut
chess-board
chestnut
chestnuts
cheval
Chevalier's
chewing
Chian
chibouc
chicanery
chicken-cock
chided
chieftain's
Chienne
child's
Childe
childlike
Chili
chillily
chills
chimaeras
Chimerique
chimes
chip
Chiponchipino
Chiromancy
chirp
chiseled
chiselling
chisels
chit-chat
chivalry
cho-o-ose
chocolate
Choctaw
Choctaws
chokeberries
Cholera
cholic
chopped
chops
chords
Chorum
chorused
choses
Christ
Christchurch-steeple
Christi
chronicle
chronicled
Chronicles
chronicles
Chronology, Chronologos
chronometers
chucking
chum
chums
church-bell
church-yards
churches
Cicero
Cicero
cigar-girl
cigars
circled
circonscriva
circumjacent
circumlocution
circumscribing
circumscription
circumstanced
circumvallatory
circumvents
circumvolutions
citadel
citation
citing
citizenship
cito
claimant
claiming
clairvoyance
clamored
clamorer
clamorous
clamorously
clang
clanging
clangorous
clanking
clans
clap
claret
Clarke, Lewis G.
Clarke's, Lewis
clasp-garter
clasping
classically
classics
classification
clatter
clayey
cleanness
clear-sighted
clearest
clefts
clematis
Clematitis
clerically
clerk's
cleverness
Climah
climates
climber
clinched
cling
clip
cliverly>
clockwork
clod
cloister
close-fitting
close-hauled
close-veiled
closely-buttoned
closely-interlocking
closes
clothe
cloths
club's
clutch
clutching
co-exist
co-mates
coadjutor
coadjutors
coal-gas
coal-heavers
coalesce
coals
coarser
coastmen
coat-tail
coat-tails
coated
coatings
cobalt
Cobbett
Cobbett's
cobbler
cobler
Cocaigne
cock-a-doodle-de-doo-doo
cock-a-doodle-de-doooooh
cock-a-doodleing
cock-crowing
Cock-neighs
cock's
cocking
cocoa
cocoa-nuts
code
codfish
codicil
coffee-plant
coffee-warmer
Coffee-House
coffer
coffin-tressels
Cognoscenti
Cognoscenti, Miranda
coherence
cohort
coinage
coincided
coir

Col.
Col--e
colder
coldly
Coleridegy
collars
collate
collaterally
collectedly
collectedness
collectively
collector
College
collocations
colloquialism
Colloquy
Cologne
Colonial
colonnades
color-grouping
colouring
colourless
Colquhoun
Combat
combat
combating
combats
combattendo
Combe
combings
combustibility
combustible
come-at-able
comedies
comers
cometary
comforted
comforter
comfortless
comicality
commandant
commander-in-chief
commemorated
commemorates
commencements
commentaries
commentators
commincement>
commingle
commingling
Commire, P.
commits
committal
committee
commodious
Commodus
Common
common-places
common-sense
commonalty
commoner
compactly
compacts
companies
companionless
company's
comparable
compassionating
compassless
compatible
compeers
compel
compendious
compendium
compensated
compete
competing
competitors
compilation
compilations
compiled
compiler
complacent
complacently
complaining
complains
complaisance
complate>
complately>
Complete
completeness
completes
completing
completion
complexity
complicate
complicated
complied
composedly
composite
comprehind>
compressing
compromised
comptant
compting-house
comptoir
compulsory
computation
computations
computed
comrades
Comus
con
concated>
concealments
conceals
conceded
conceited
conceits
concentrate
concentrated
concentrations
concentric
concerto
concessions
concetto
concierge
conciliate
conciliation
concision
conclave
concludes
conclusively
concocting
concoctor
concordance
concrete
concretely
concur
concurred
concussions
Condamnes
condemn
condemnation
condemning
condescends
condescension
condiment
conditionally
conditioned
conducting
conductor
cones
confederacy
confederation
confer
confessing
Confessions
confessor
confessors
confidentially
configuration
conformity
confront
confronts
Confucius
confute
confuted
congeal
congealed
congealing
congenial
congeniality
conger
congratulating
congregation
conjoining
conjurer
connexions
connings
connoisseur
connoisseurship
conoissance
conquerors
consated>
Conscience
conscientiousness
consekvence
consequence
conservatione
conservatories
considdeble
Considered
consignee
Consistory
consolations
consoled
consoles
consolidation
consort
conspire
conspired
Constantinople
constituting
constitutionally
constraint
constructive
constructs
consul
consultation
Consultations
consults
consumptive
contagion
contaminated
contemns
contemplate
contemplating
contemplations
contento
Contes
contested
contiguous
continental
contingencies
continuity
contra-distinction
contraction
contradictory
contraries
contrasted
contrasting
contre
contree
contretemps
contribute
contribution
contusion
conundrums
conveniency
convention
conventionalities
convenu
converge
Conversation
conversational
converses
conversible
convertible
converting
convicted
convinces
convolute
cooing
cooked
cooled
cooler
cools
coop
cooped
Cooper, J. Fenimore
Cooper's
Copernicus
copper-colored
copper-plate
copperas
Copy-Right
copying
copyist
coquet
coquetries
coquetry
coquetted
coral-worm
coralliferi
corded
Cordova
Corinnos
coric
corned
Corneille
cornelian
corner-stones
corns
coroner's
corps
corpse-like
correctness
corresponded
corridor
corroborate
corrosion
corrosive
Corsican
corslet
corty
cosmogony
costliness
costs
costumbres

costumed
cosy-looking
cot>
cotch'd>
cotelette
cotemporary
Cottage
cottage
Cottle
cotton-wool
cottons
cottonwood
Councils
counsels
count's
countenanced
counter-balance
counteract
counterbalanced
counterbalances
counterfeiting
counterfeits
counters
counties
counting-house
coup
coup-de-grace
coupa
couples
couplet
couplets
cour
courageously
Courier
Court-Yard
courteous
courtezan
courtier
Cousin
cousins
covenant
coverings
coveted
cowardice
cowardly
cowards
Cowper
coxcombry
crabs
cracking
cramp
cranium
crank
crannies
crashing
crature>
cravats
craved
crayons
crazy
creak
creaking
cream
creamy
creases
Creation
Creator
creature's
credence
credential
credentials
credibile
credible
credited
creek's
creese
Creoles
Crepuscularia
cresset
crest
Crichton's
cricket
Crime
criminal
criminate
criminating
crimped
crimpled
crimsoned
crisp
critic's
criticisms
critique
critiques
croak
croaked
crockery-ware
croit
Crommelin
crone
crony
crooked-looking
crops
cross-questioning
crouch
crouched
crouching
Crowd
crowds
crowing
Crozet
crucifixes
cruised
cruises
cruising
crumbs
crumpled
crumpling
crushes
crustily
crusty
crxw
crxwing
Cry
cryptogamous
cryptographs
crystallic
cub
cubical
cucumber
cuddy-cabin
cuffed
cuffs
cul-de-sac
cul-de-sac
Cunningham
cupboard
cupola
cur-tailed
Cur-Spattering
curbstone
curdled
Curio, Caelius Secundus
curiosities
curiously-pannelled
curl
curlin>
curly
curmudgeon
curous
currant-bushes
currants
currente
curry-comb
curtail
curtained
curtchy>
curveted
curvets
curvetted
cushion
cushioned
cushions
custody
customarily
cuteness
cxck
cxme
cxw
cyanite
Cybele
cycloid
Cygni
cynic
cynosure
cypher
cyphers
cypresses
cythern
D
d
d
D.C.
D.U.K.
D--'s
d--dest
d'autre
d'ecarte
d'expliquer
d'objection
d'oeil
d'oeuvre
d'oreon (Gr.)
d'oro
d'une
d'Alger
D'Ambois
d'Amerique
D'Anan, Thomas
D'Antin
d'Atree
D'Avisson
D'Avisson
D'Indagine, Jean
D'Israeli, I.
dabble
dabbler
Daddyship
Dagon
Daguerreotype
daintiest
daintiness
dais-chamber
daisies
daisy
dalliance
dallied
damaging
damascus
dammed-up
damming
damn
damnation
dampened
damps
damsel
damsels
dancer
dances
dandies
dandled
danseuse
Dante
Dante's
Daphne
Daphnis
dapperness
dar
dar's
Darcotas
Darcotas
dare-devil
dare's
Darien
darkling
darned
darry
darted
darting
darty
das
Dashers
dashes
dass
dastardly
dated
dating
daunt
daunted
dauntless
Davidson
Davy, Sir Humphrey
dawdling
dawns
day-book
day-dream
day-dreamer
day-dreams
day-time
daydreams
dazzle
Dead
deadened
deafen
deafening
dealers
dealings
deals
death-agonies
death-cry
death-hour
death-producing
death-purged
death-refined
death-struggles
death-watches
Death's-headed
death's-heads
deathful
deathlike
debasement
debated
debating
debauch
debbil
debbil's
debbils
debilitated
debility
debouche

debouches
debris
debt
debtor
debts
debut
decade
decadence
decamped
decamps
decays
deceased's
deceitful
decency
Decided
decides
deciphering
decisions
decisively
decked
declines
decomposed
decorative
decorist
decorists
decorously
decouuert
decrepid
decyphered
decyphering
deducible
deducing
deduct
Dee's, Dubble L.
deed's
deep-seated
deep-toned
deeply-burthened
deeply-laid
deeply-shadowed
deer-stalking
defaced
deferring
defied
defies
defines
definiteness
deflect
deformities
defraud
Defuncti
degenerating
degradation
degraded
deigning
dejeuner
Delaware
delayed
delegates
deliberated
deliberateness
deliberating
delicately-granulated
deliciousness
delighting
delights
delikittest>
delineate
deliverers
delivers
dell
delly
delude
deluging
delusion
delusive
dem
demagogue-ridden
demande
demarcates
demented
demerit
demeure
demi-god
demijohns
demnition
demolition
demon-like
demoniacal
demoniacally
demonstrating
demureness
denies
denominating
denomination
denoted
denoting
denounce
denouncement
denouncing

dens
denseness
densest
densities
dental
dents
denunciations
department
dependance
dependencies
dependent
depicting
deplored
depopulating
deposite
deposition
deposits
depot
depot
depraved
deprecates
depredations
depresses
depressing
deprivation
depriving
deputes
deranged
derangement
derided
deriding
derisive
Derivationibus
derogate
Derome
descanted
descendant
descendants
descensus
dese
desecrate
desecrating
desecration
desertion
deshabille
desideratum
designate
designation
designations
designedly
desk
deskism
desks
Desolation
Desoulieres
Desoulieres
Desoulieres, Jules
despairingly
despatches
despera-a-ado
despicable
despising
despoiled
despondency
despondingly
desposition
despotic
dessein
Desultory
detach
detached
detachments
detaining
detects
detention
deteriora
deteriorate
determinate
determines
detestably
detestation
detract
detracts
detrimental
devastated
develop
develope
developments
devil-me-care
Devil's
devil's-seat
devilish
devolving
devote
devotedly
devotees
devotional
devours
devoutest
dew-drop

Dew, T. R.
dexterously
DeGrat's
diablerie
diablerie
diagonal
dial
dialects
dialogue
diameters
diametrically
Dianam
diaphragm
diaries
diatribe
Diavolo
Diavolo
diavolo
Dickens
dickeys
dicta
dictate
dictated
dictation
dictatorial
diction
dictionary
Dictu, Horrible
dictum
did'st
didactic
Didcot
diddle
diddled
Diddler, Jeremy
dieu
Differential
differently
diffident
diffuseness
Diffusion
diffusive
digest
digested
digestion
digestive
digits
dignitary
dignitary's
dignities
digress
digression
dilapidated
dilapidation
dilatation
dilemma'd
dilikittest>
dillikittest>
dim-remembered
diminutively
dimmer
dimpled
dine
dined
dining-table
dinner-table
dinners
Dios
dip
dipping
Directorium
direst
dirges
disabled
disabuse
disabused
disagreeably
disapprobation
disarrangement
disastrously
disbelieve
disc
discern
discernment
discharges
disciple
discipline
disclaim
disclosures
disconsolate
disconsolately
discontinuance
discountenanced
discourages
discoverable
Discovery
discreditable
discredited
discredits
discretionary

discussion
disdained
disdaining
disembogued
disemboweled
disembowelling
disenchained
disenchanted
disenfranchised
disengage
disengagement
disentangle
disentangles
disfigure
disfigures
disfiguring
disgraceful
disgracefully
disguising
Dish-Clout
dishearten
disheartened
dished
dishevelled
dishonored
dishonour
disinclined
disingenuous
disinterested
disinterment
disinterred
diskiver>
diskivered>
dislikes
dislodged
dislodging
dismasted
dismayed
dismembered
dismounted
disorders
disorganization
disorganized
disparity
dispassionate
dispelief
dispensation
dispensations
dispensed
dispeptic
disperate>
disperse
dispersed
dispersing
dispirate>
displace
displacing
displeases
disported
disposes
disposing
dispossessed
disputes
disquieting
disregardful
disregarding
disreputable
disrespect
disruption
disruptured
dissect
dissecting-room
dissension
dissent
dissertation
dissertations
disservice
disshevelled
dissimulation
dissimuler
dissipating
dissolved
dissolves
dissonant
dissuaded
Distance
distantly
distantly-observed
distemper
distend
distillation
distilled
distinctions
distingue
distinguishable
distorting
distresses
distressingly
distribute
distributed
distributio
disturber
disuse
ditch
Dithyrambics
dithyrambics
ditty
divarsion>
divarted>
dive
diverged
divergent
diversified
divert
divesting
divests
divides
dividing
divilish>
divinest
divining
divorce
Divorum
divulge
divulged
dizzying
docility
dod
dodged
Dodona
Dodona's
doer
doers
Dog
dog-days
dog-leaf
dog-meat
doggedly
doggrel
dogless
dogmatic
dogmatically
dogmatizing
dolce
doll
dollar-manufacture
dollar's
Dollars
Dolores
dolphins
dome
domes
Domestic
domestication
domestics
domiciliary
dominant
Dominican
Dominie
donations
donc
donce
Donder
Donder
Dondergat
donjon
donjon-keep
donkeys
donna
Donner
Donner
dont
doomsday
door-nail
dot-and-carry-one
double-bass
double-dealers
double-headed
double-padded
double-shotted
double-winded
doublet
doublets
doubters
doubting
doughty
doux
Dover
down-east
down-right
Down-East
Down-Easter
downcast
Downing, Jack
downwardly
downy
dozing
Draco
Draconian
drag-rope
drag-ropes
draggled
dragon-fly
dragon's
drags
draining
dramas
drams
Draper
draperied
draping
draw-back
drawing-rooms
drawling
drawlingly
draws
dreads
Dream
dreamers
Dreamland
dree
drenching
dresser
dressing-wrapper
driftwood
drill
drily
drinks
dripped
drippings
drissed>
drizzling
drole
drolleries
drollest
Dromeo
Dromes
droopingly
drop-curtain
dropsical
drown'd
drownthed>
drowsily
Drs.
drummers
drunkards
drunkenness
drxwn
dry-goods
dryness
Du
dub
dubiously
Dublin
Dubourg, Pauline
Duc
Duc's
ducal
Duchess'
Duchess's
Duck
Ducrow
Dudevant
duelling
duello
duke's
duller
Dumas, Paul
dumb
Dumbarton
dun
Dundergutz
Dunderheadism
duodecimal
duodecimo
duguel
dure
duskily
dusky-red
dusky-visaged
dusted
Duval, Henri
dwarfs
dweller
dwellers
dwelleth
dwelling-house
dwelling-place
dwindled
dxes
dxg
dxll
dye
dynamically
Dynamics
dynamics
dyspeptic
DOMITIAN
e-clench-eye
Eac

eagle's
ear-ring
ear-rings
earl
earldoms
earned
earns
earth-angels
earth-worm
earthenware
earthliness
earthquakes
easiest
easing
Eastern-looking
eau
eave
ebbing
eberry
ebon
ebullition
Eccaleobion
eccentrically
Ecclesiae
ecclesiastic
ecclesiastical
ecclesiastics
Eccossois
eclipsed
eclipses
ecliptic
economic
economize
ecrivaient
ecstacies
eddying
Edens
eder
edge-tools
edgeways
edible
edifices
edified
Edinburg
edit.
editions
editor's
editorials
Edmund's
Edouard
educe
Edward
eel-skinning
effaced
effeminacy
effeminate-looking
Effendi
effervescent
efficacious
efficacy
effudit
Egaeus
Egeria
egg-shells
egg'd
eglantine
egli
egotism
egotist
egressions
Egyptian's
eider-down
eighteen-thousandth
eighty-doo
eighty-fifth
eighty-four
eighty-second
eighty-seven
eighty-two-hundred
eine
ejaculating
ejecting
ekidnato (Gr.)
el
elaboration
Elah-Gabalus
elapse
elapses
elated
elbowing
Eld
elderly
elders
eleben
Elector
elector
electrified
electrify
Electro-tintinnabulic
Electro-Magnetic
electrometer
Electrotype
elegant
elegantly
elegantly-bound
elephantfish
elevates
elevating
eleven-knot
elfin
Elizabeth
elk-skin
elle
Elline
elongated
else's
eludes
Elwood
Elzevir
emanate
emanated
emanating
emancipated
embalm
embankment
embark
embarrassing
embellish
ember
embers
emblematic
emblematical
emboldened
embossed
embraces
embracing
embroidery
embryo
emendations
emeralds
Emeritus
Emerson
emeutes
emigrate
emigrated
eminences
emissaries
emits
Emmet
Emmons
Emmons, William
emperors
emphasized
emphasizing
emphatic
empires
empirical
employers
employments
empties
emptying
enact
enactments
enamel
enchanter
enchantingly
encircling
Encke, Professor
enclosing
encoffined
encompassing
encore
encounters
encouragement
encouraging
encrimsoned
encroached
Encyclopaedia
endanger
endangered
ending
endings
enditing
endlessly
endorsed
endorsement
endowment
enduing
endurable
endures
endureth
enemy-werrybor'em
enflamed
enforce
enforcing
Engedi
engender
engendering
engenders
Engine
engineer
engineers
enginery
engirdle
engraved
engraven
engravings
engrosses
engulfed
enigmatically
enim
enjoyments
enkindle
enkindling
enlarged
enlisting
enmity
ennuied
enrapt
Ens
ensanguined
ensconce
ensheathed
enshrine
enshrined
enslaved
enslaving
entanglement
entangling
entende
entendre
entereth
enterprises
entertainments
entertains
enthral
enthralling
enthusiast
enthusiastically
enthusiasts
enticed
enticing
entitle
entitling
entomological
Entozoa
entrances
entrancing
entrapment
entre
entreats
entrust
enuff
enumerated
enunciated
envelopes
envied
enwrapt
enwreathed
enwritten
eo
eos (Gr.)
ep'aian (Gr.)
epeen (Gr.)
ephemera
ephemeron
Ephesus
Epic
epics
Epictetus
epicures
Epidaphnians
Epidendron
Epidendrum
epidermis
Epigoniad
epigrammatic
epilepsis
epileptic
Epimanes
Epimanes, Antiochus
Epimenides
epistolary
epitaphs
Epizoae
epochs
Epsilon
equalization
equalling
equals
equanimity
equations
equerry
equilibrium
equilibrium
Equinoctial
equitably
equity
equivocation
eradicated

<u>eram</u>
erase
<u>erat</u>
ere-while
Erebus
erections
ermined
<u>ero</u>
<u>Errant</u>
erring
<u>erry</u>
<u>erscheint</u>
erysipelas
<u>Es</u>
eschewing
escort
escorting
escrutoire
<u>Espagnol</u>
espouse
<u>esprit</u>
Esqr
Esquimau
Esquimaux
Esquire
<u>essais</u>
essentiality
<u>esset</u>
<u>est-il</u>
establishes
<u>estomac</u>
estranged
estray
<u>Et</u>
<u>etait</u>
etait
<u>ete</u>
Eternity
ethereality
etherial
Ethix, Aestheticus
Etienne, Alexandre
Etoile
<u>eu</u>
eudosin (Gr.)
Euenis
<u>Eulalie</u>
eulogies
Eupatrids
euphonous
<u>euphorbium</u>
eureka
Euripides
Europeans
ev'ning
evacuation
evade
evaporates
evaporating
evaporation
eve
evening's
evenly
evenness
eventuality
ever-blossoming
ever-placid
ever-prevalent
ever-remembered
ever-victorious
Everard
everchanging
Everett, Edward
evergreens
every-man-for-himself
everybody's
Evil
evinces
evolving
Ex-President
exacerbate
Exact
exactitude
exaggerations
exalt
exalting
examines
excadingly>
exceeds
excellencies
excellency
excelling
excepted
excipting>
excitation
exclaims
exclude
excluding
exclusiveness
excoriated
excretory
excused
execrations
executioner
executive
exemplary
exemplification
exemplifications
exequy
<u>exergues</u>
exerting
Exeter
exhalation
exhalations
exhaling
exhaust
exhibitions
exhort
exhumed
exile
existences
existent
exonerate
exonerated
expand
expectoration
expedite
expel
expelled
expence
expending
experiences
Experimentalist
experimentally
experimenting
expert
expiated
expiring
explanatory
expletive
expletives
exploded
exploration
<u>exploraturi</u>
explorer
exposes
exposing
expostulated
expostulating
expounded
Express
expressly
extacy
extant
extensively
exterminated
externals
extinction
extinguishment
extolled
extortion
extortions
Extract
extraction
extraneous
extravaganza
extrinsic
exuberance
exuberant
exult
exults
Eye
eye-balls
eye-lids
eye-witnesses
eyebrows
eyelashes
eyrie
Ezekiel
ELIZABETH
Fable
<u>fables</u>
fabricated
fabrication
fabrications
fabrics
facetious
<u>facili</u>
<u>facilis</u>
facilitate
facsimile
factory
Facts
fag
faileth
failures
faintly-detailed
faints
<u>faire</u>
Fairies
fairies
Fairmount
fairy-looking
<u>faisant</u>
Fall
<u>fallen</u>
falsehood
Falstaffian
familiarised
fan
fancifully
<u>fanfaronnade</u>
fanning
fantasias
fantastical-looking
<u>far</u>
far-famed
far-searching
far-seeing
far-stretched
fared
Farmers'
farmhouse
farming
Farnesian
<u>farrago</u>
farthing
farthingale
fascinating
Fashion
fashionably
fashioning
fashions
fast-sinking
fastens
fastest
fastidiously
fastness
fatalities
fated
Father
fathered
fatherly
fatness
fatted
fattened
fatter
fatty
<u>fatui</u>
<u>Faubourg</u>
faucial
fault-finding
faults
faulty
favored
favoring
Favyn
fawn
Fay, Theo.
fear-enkindled
feasibility
feasts
Featherstone
Featherstonhaugh
feathery
feats
feebler
feeding
feerd
feered
feigned
felicitous
feline
fellow-citizens
fellow-collegians
fellow-commoner
fellow-creature
fellow-sojourners
fellow-traveller
fellow-wayfarers
<u>felo</u>
felon's
felons
Feltspar, F. F.
Feltzpar
<u>feminis</u>
<u>femoris</u>
fender
fens
<u>fer</u>
fer
ferment
ferments
ferret
Ferrex
Ferroe
ferry-boat
fertility
ferule
fervour

feshionable>
festered
festivals
festooning
fetter
fetterless
fever-demons
feverish
feverishly
fewest
fiat
Fibalittle
fibula
Fichte
fickle-minded
fickle-mindedness
fiddlestick
fiddling
fide
fidgetty
fie
Fiend
fier
fiercer
fierte
fievre
fifes
fiftieth
fifty-eight
fifty-five
fifty-six
fig-pedler
figgur>
figs
figurative
figurehead
filamentous
file
filed
filius
fillagree
filleted
fillip
fills
Fils
filtered
finale
finale
finances
financial
financier
fineness
finery
finest-tempered
finger-nails
finicky
finite
finnicky
Fior
fioriture
fir
fire-dogs
fire-places
firearms
Firefly
firmamental
firmer
firmest
firms
firs
first-mentioned
firstling
fish-oil
fished
fisher
fishes
fiss
fissures
fitly
fitter
five-sevenths
fixtures
fizzes
flaccid
Flaccus, Quintus
flacon
flambeaux
flannels
flapping-to
flash-name
flashiness
flashy
flasks
flatboats
flatness
Flotplatz
flatteringly
flattish
flaunting
flaxen
fledged
Fleece
fleeces
fleeing
flees
fleeting
fleets
fleshy
flexibility
flicker
flickeringly
flickerings
Flight
fling
flinging
flint
Flint, Timothy
flinty
flirt
flirtations
flit
floats
flocked
flog
flogged
floggings
flooded
floor-cloths
florem
Florentine
florid
flos
flounders
flow'rs
flower-blossoms
flower-enamelled
flower-garden
flower-pot
flowering
flowery
Floyd's
Flud, Robert
flue
fluency
fluent
flummery
flurried
flush
fluttering
fluvial
flying-fish
foamless
fob
fog-canopy
fogs
foible
foibles
foiled
Fol-Lol
fold
folder
folding-doors
Folgen
folios
folks
follower
fondez-vous
font
Fontaine
Fonthill
fool-hardiness
fool's
fool's-cap
foot-fall
foot-hold
foot-notes
foot-path
foot-race
footfall
footpads
foppery
foraging
forbearance
fore-chains
fore-ground
foreboded
foreboding
forecastle-way
forechain-plates
foredoomed
foregoing
foreground
foreheads
Foreign
foreign-looking
foreruns
foresaw
foreshadowed
foreshortened
foresters
foretopmast
foretopsails
forevermore
forfeit
forfeiting
forgave
forged
forgery
forgetful
forgets
forgettest
forgiveness
forked
forks
formae
formalities
formula
formulae
forsaken
forsooth
Fort
forten>
fortification
fortin>
fortunittest>
fortunnittest>
forty-nine
forty-pinny>
forty-sixth
forty-third
forwarding
fosse
Fosters
fouled
foulness
founder
foundering
fount
fountain-head
Four
four-footed
fourpence
fourthly
fourths
fowl-house
foxes
fracto
fractures
fragmentary
fragrant
frailness
framings
France
Francis
Francois
frank-hearted
frankest
Frankfort
frankincense
Fraser
frauds
fraudulent
fraught
fray
fraying
Frazer's
Frederick's
freeman
freer
freezing
freighted
French-horn
Frenchman's
Frenchwoman
frequents
fresco
frescos
fresh-water
fresher
freshets
freshly-spread
fret
fricandeau
fricandeaux
fricasee
fricassee
fricassee
Friday
friendless
frieze
frighten
frightening
frightful-looking
frigidity
Frinch>
frisked
frisking
Frobisher, Joseph
frocks
frog-like

frog-man
frogged
Frogpondium
frogs
frolicksome
frolics
frontal
frontem
frontis
fronts
frosts
frosty
frowningly
frowns
froze
frugal
fruitful
frustrate
frxq
frxwn
Fry
frying
Fuci
fudder
fuddled
fudge
fugitive's
fugitives
full-grown
fuller's
fulsomely
fulvous
fumbled
functionaries
fundamental
funeris
funeste
fungi
fungus
funnel-cap
funniest
funnin
funny
fur-trader
furled
furlong
Furneaux
furores
Furrier
furrowed
furrows
furtively
Fuseli
fusty
futmen>
futurity
fxr
fxwl
fxxl
fy
g
G--, Lieutenant
G--'s
G'zette
gad-abouts
gagged
gagne
gaieties
Gaillard, Petit
gains
gainsay
gainsayed
gaiters
gala
gale's
Gall
gallant-looking
galled
Gallery
galling
Gallows
Galvanism
galvanized
gamble
gambler's
gamblers
gambols
game-keeper
game's
gammoned
gander's
gannets
garb
garbled
Garcio, Alfonzo
Garden
garden-gate
Gardening
garish
garnered
Garnier
garrets
garter's
gas-lamps
gas-lighted
gas-litten
gases
gashes
gaspingly
gaudiness
gaudy-colored
gauntlet
gauntleted
gauze-like
Gay-Lussac
gayest
gaze
gazelle
gazette
Gazette's
Gazetteer
gear
gelasma (Gr.)
gelebt
geliebet
gemmary
gendarmes
gender
gendering
General's
generalizing
generally-educated
generally-received
generals
generical
generis
Geneva
Genii
genio
Genius
geniuses
Genoa
Genoese
gentaalest>
genteel
Gentiles
gentilhomme
gentility
gentle-footfall
gentleman-like
gentlest
gentlewoman
gently-flowing
Genuine
geographer's
geography
geologist
geometrical
geometrician
Georges
geranium
geraniums
Germans
germinated
gesticulate
gesticulated
gesticulating
gesticulation
gewohnlich
ghastliest
ghastlily
ghastliness
ghastly-looking
Gheber
ghee
ghostly
giants
gibbous
Gibraltar
giddiest
giebt
Gil-Blas
gilden
gilding
giltwork
gimlet-dust
Gin
gin-nurtured
gingerly
gingham
gintaal>
girded
girdles
Gironne, Eymeric de
girt
girth
girting
gitting
gitting>
giunge
givers
gizzard
gizzards
gladdens
glades
gladiatorial
glass-house
glass-like
glauber
Glaumba
gleichfalls
glens
Gliddon's
gliding
gloaming
gloominess
gloomy-looking
glorifying
gloss
Glover's
glow-worm-like
glowworm
Gluck
glueing
glut
gluttony
gnashing
gnawings
Gnomes
go-ahead
gobble
goblet-ful
gobletful
goblin
goblins
Goddess
goddesses
Goddin
godlike
Goethe
Gog
goggle
Golconda
Gold
gold-fish
gold-flowered
gold-seeker
gold-threaded
Gold-Bug
Golden
golly
Gondola, Convulvulus
gondolier
gongs
Gonzales, Dominique
good-by
good-bye
good-for-nothing-to-nobody
good-humored
good-humoredly
good-humouredly
good-looking
good-natured
good-tempered
good-will
Goodfellow, Charley
goodwill
goose-quill
Goose's
gooseberries
Gore
gores
gorging
gose
gospel
gossiping
gouges
Gould
gould>
Gould , H. F.
grabs
grace's
gracefulness
graciously
gradu
graduated
Graham
grains
Grand, Bouffon Le
grandames
grande
grande-daughter
grandest
grandiloquence
grandiloquent
Grandjean
Grandjean's
grandly
grandmother's
granc

Grant
Grant's
grape-vine
grape-vines
grapes
graphic
grass-grown
grass-hopper
grate
grated
gratis
gravelly
gravest
graveyard
gravities
gray-mottled
grayer
grayish
grayish-white
grayness
grazed
greasy
greedily
Greely, Robert
Green, Charles
Green's
greenish
Greenwich
greeting
Grenouille
Gresset
gridiron
griefs
grimace
grimaces
Grimm
Grimm's
grinders
grinding
grip
gripings
grisette
Griswold's
gritting
grog
groggy
Grogswigg
groin
grooming
Grotesque
grotesquely
grotesqueness
grotesquerie
grotesques
groundlessness
groundwork
grove
grovelled
growling
gruffest
grumble
grumble
Grunninger
grunt
grunt
Gruntundguzzell
grxwl
gry
Gualtier
guarantee
guarda
guardianship
guarding
guards
guffaw
guile
guiltlessness
Guinea
gulfs
gullet
gulley
Gulley's
gullibility
Gulliver
gummy
gun-trigger
gurnards
gush
gushed
gusty
Gutsmuth
gutta
gutta
gutters
guzzle
gwine
gxt
gxxd
gxxd-fxr-nxthing-tx-
gxxse
nxbxdy

gymnastic
gymnastics
gypsy
gyrating
gyratory
h
ha
hab
habe
habet
habituated
habitudes
hack
hackmen
hackneyed
hacknied
hadn't
hadst
haematite
hailing
hair-like
hair-splitting
hake
Hale
Hale, Sarah J.
half-a-dozen
half-breed
half-deck
half-empty
half-engendered
half-holidays
half-insane
half-naked
half-negligent
half-north
half-parted
half-past
half-pleasurable
half-precise
half-quizzical
half-shut
half-slumber
half-slumberous
half-subdued
half-way
half-wondrous
half-Indian
halibut
Hall, Lieut. F.
Halleck
Halleck, Fitz Greene
halloo
hallooing
hallucination
halted
halter
halts
Hamadryad
hammering
hammock
hampers
hams
hand-bells
hand-cuffed
hand-cuffing
handcuff
handing
handmaiden
handsommest
handspikes
hangeth
hangmen
hap-hazard
haporth>
happily-timed
harangues
haranguing
harbours
hard-a-lee
hard-burned
hard-hearted
hardening
hardest
hardihood
hardness
Hardy's
harem
Harlaem
Harlem
harmonies
harmoniously
harmonized
Harold
Harpies
harpooner
harpooners
Harris, Alfred
harrowing
Harry
harsher

Hartford
harvest
hashish
hasp
hastens
Hastings, Warren
hatchet
hatchets
hating
haughtiest
haul
haunt
haunting
haut
have
hawk-nose
Hawk, Tommy
hawk's
hawthorn
hay
Haydn
haze
head-piece
head-teuffel
headboard
headland
headless
headsail
heady
healthily
healthy
hearer
hearin>
hearkening
Hearne, Samuel
hears
Heart
heart-rending
heart-sick
heart-stirring
heart's
heart's-ease
hearths
heartiest
Hearts
hearty-looking
heaviest
heaviness
Hebrides
Hebron
Hecla
heedlessness
heeling
heels-over-head
heerd
Hegel
heigho
heiress
heirs
Heliogabalus
Hellofagabaluses
helmsman
helplessly
helter-skelteriness
hemi-syncope
hemispheres
hemispherical
hemlock
henceforth
hencoop
Hennepin
Henry
hens
Heraclides
Heraclitus
Herald
herald
heralded
heraldic
herbaged
herbs
Hercules
hereditarily
hereinafter
herewith
hermaphrodite
hermetically
hermit's
Hernani
Hero
heroes
heroine
heroines
Herr
Herschel's, John
hervor
Hessian
heterodox
Hetty
Hevelius

hey
hey-day
hey-diddle
Heywood
hic
hickories
hickory-nut
Hicks
Hieronymus
Hieronymus
High
high-backed
high-heeled
high-minded
high-mindedness
high-spirited
high-toned
high-water
highly-agitated
highly-concentrated
highly-polished
highly-scented
Highly-Scented
highways
hill-side
hill-sides
hill-top
hill-tops
hillock
hillsides
hilly
hinc
hinder-part
hindrances
Hinnom
Hinnon
hinting
hip
hipped
Hippocratian
Hippodrome
hire
hiss
hissed
hisses
hissingly
Histoire
historian's
historians
Histories
hitched
hoarded
hoarhound
hoarse
Hoax
hobbled
Hock
Hoeyholm
Hog-ishly
Hog-ites
hog's
Hogarth
Hoggishly
Hoggs
Holberg
holders
holiday
Hollander
Hollanders
Hollands
hollow-backed
holydays
homely
Homeric
homily
homines
hominis
hommes
hommy
Homo-Cameleopard
Homocameleopard
Homoomeria
homoomeria
honesti
Honor
honorable
honorably
Honourable
honourable
honourably
hood
hoof
hookah
hookahcase
Hop
Hop-Frog's
Hopkinson, Joseph
hopperer>
horn-blende
Hornet
horresco
horridly
horrific
horror-inspiring
horrorless
Horse
horse-jockey
Horse-Shade
horseman
horses'
Horsley
horticulturists
host's
hostages
hostelrie
hostess
hostile
hosts
hot-corn
hot-headedness
hot>
hotels
Hotte
Hottentot
Hottentots
houly>
hound
housed
housekeeper
houseless
hove
hovel
hovels
howiver>
howled
howls
Hoyle
huddling
Hudibras
Hudson's
hugely
huggab
Hugo, Jacobus
Huguenot
Hull
Hum-drum
human-looking
humane
humanely
humbly
Humboldt
Hume, David
humid
humming-top
humored
humorous
Humphrey's
Hundred
hundredth
hundredths
Hungarians
hungry
hunks
Hunt
Hunt, Wilson Price
hunter's
huomo
hurdy-gurdy
hurling
hurting
hurts
husbands
hushing
huskiness
huts
huzzy
hx
hxg
hxllx
hxmx
hxwl
hyacinths
Hyde
hydrangea
Hymns
hymns
hyper-exquisite
hyper-fizzitistical
hyperbole
Hyperion
hyperobtrusive
hyperquizzitistical
hypochondria
hypothetical
hysteria
i.e.
i'
I'en
Iago
Iamblichus
Iamblicus
ibid.
Ibis
ice-cream
Iceland
ices
ich
ichor
iddication>
idealische
idealischer
identifies
idiom
idiosyncracy
idiosyncratic
idolaters
idolator
idolatry
idolised
Iflesen
ignes
igniting
ignoramus
ignoramuses
ignotum
igualmente
ihre
Il
ill-adapted
ill-admeasurement
ill-advised
ill-bred
ill-conceived
ill-constructed
ill-contrived
ill-directed
ill-disposed
ill-fated
ill-fitted
ill-fortune
ill-founded
ill-furnished
ill-humor
ill-looking
ill-made
ill-mannered
ill-natured
ill-omened
ill-regulated
ill-used
ill-ventilated
illae
illegibility
Illinois
illnesses
illuminating
illumination
illumine
illusions
illustrate
illustrated
Illustrious
Ils
ilse>
imaged
imaginings
imbecilities
imbibe
imbibes
imbitter
imbodied
imitating
Imitation
imitations
imitative
immemorial
immerse
immethodical
imminency
immoderately
immoral
immortalize
immortalized
immovably
immoveable
immoveably
imp
impartiality
impassable
impede
impeding
impelling
impends
imperfection
imperiously
imperiousness
imperor>
impia
impiety
impinging

impious
impiously
impliedly
imploringly
implying
impolicy
impolitic
importa
importuning
impose
imposition
impossibile
impost
impostor
imposts
imposture
impracticable
impregnated
impregnating
impressiveness
imprimis
imprinted
imprisonment
improbabilities
improbability
impromptus
improves
improvisatori
improvised
improviso
imprudent
imps
impulsion
impune
impurity
imputed
in-X-plicable
inaccessibility
Inaccessible
inadapted
inadvertence
inadvertent
inadvertently
inanition
inapplicability
inapprehension
inartistical
inattention
incantations
incapacitated
incarnated
incarnations
incautiously
incendiary
incense
inception
incessant
Incidentibus
incidentibus
incitamentum
incited
inciting
inclines
inclusive
incommunicativeness
incomparable
incongruity
inconnue
inconsequence
inconsiderately
incontestably
incontrollable
incontrovertibly
inconveniences
inconveniently
incredibly
incredulous
incredulously
incrustations
incrusted
inculpate
incumbrance
incurred
indecisive
indefatigability
indefatigable
indelible
indelicate
indemnification
indemnity
indented
indenture
indeterminately
Indiana
indifference
indifferent-looking
indigestible
indigo
indirect
indirectly
indiscernible
indiscretions
indisposed
indisposition
indissolubly
indistinctness
individualized
indubitable
induct
indulgences
industriously
Industry
indwelling
inebriates
ineffective
inefficient
inelastic
ineptum
inequalities
inertia
inertiae
inessential
inexhaustible
inexpressibles
inexpressive
inextinguishable
inextricably
infantine
infarm>
infatuate
infect
infection
infer
infernally
inferorum
inferring
infidelity
infinitesimally
infinitum
inflammatory
inflicting
infliction
inflictions
influencing
influential
informality
informe
informing
informs
infuriated
infusion
infusions
ingens
ingenuous
ingrain
ingrates
ingratitude
ingredients
ingressions
ingulfs
inhale
inherit
inhuman
inhumed
iniquities
injuria
inky
inlaid
inlet
inmate
innocently
innocui
inopportuneness
inorganization
inornate
inquest
inquirendo
inquirer
inquiringly
Inquisitorial
Inquisitorum
insane
inscrutability
inscrutable
Insecta
inserting
inserts
insignium
insinuating
insipid
insipidity
insolence
insolubility
insommary
insomnia
inspected
Inspector
instability
installed
instanter
instigated
instil
Instinct
Institute
instituting
instruction
insultingly
insurrection
Intemperance
intemperate
intemporal
intentional
intentionally
inter
inter-communication
inter-planetary
inter-Tritonic
interchange
interchanging
interestingly
interfering
interiorly
interlarding
interleaf
interlinked
intermedium
interminableness
intermixed
International
interpose
interpret
interpretations
interpreted
interregnum
interrupts
intersperse
interspersing
interstices
interstriped
intertangled
intertwining
intervene
interviews
intervolved
interwoven
interwreathed
intestinal
intestines
intheristhin>
intheristhing>
inthroduction>
intimates
intolerability
intolerant
intonsos
intreated
intrench
intriguant
intriguing
Introductory
intruders
intruding
intuitively
inuendoes
inutility
invalid's
invalids
invent
invents
inventus
investigated
inveterate
invidious
invigorate
inviolable
invitation
invitingly
invoice
invoke
Involuntary
involute
involutions
io
Ionia
irae
Irdonozur
Ireland
iron-chest
iron-clasped
iron-grooved
iron-riveted
iron-work
ironed
ironmongery
irradiating
irreclaimable
irreconcileable
irrecoverable
irresolution
irreverence

irritate
irritating
Irving, Washington
Irving's
Isis
Isle
islets
Isola
Ispan, Pan
Israelitish
iss
Isthmus
istorein (Gr.)
it'll
Italia
italian
italicised
Italicus, Silius
Itchiatuckanee
ither>
itmost>
ivory-looking
ivy-wreathed
ixpicted>
izzards
IX
j'advoue
j'ai
j'ay
jabberings
jackanapes
jackass
Jacobin
jaconet
jade
jaded
jam
jammed
jangling
Jardin
jargon
jarring
jasmine
jauntily
jaunty
Jefferson's
Jeffrey
Jehoshaphat
Jehovah
Jennings'
jeopardize
jeopardized
Jeremiad
Jeremy
Jeremys
jerking
jerks
Jermyn
Jeruschalaim
Jest-Book
jested
jet-black
jeu-d'esprit
jeune
jeweller
Jewish
jews-harp
jib-boom
jig
jis
Jo-Go-Slow
Job
job
Jochaides, Simeon
jocular
Jod
Joe
jog-trot
jogged
Johnson
joint-stock
jointings
jollity
Jones, Davy
Jones, Robert
Joseph
jostle
jostlers
jottings
joue
jouissent
Jourdain's
journal's
journalists
journeyings
Jove
Jovis
joyfully
joyous
joys
Ju-Kiao-Li
Judge
judging
jugglers
Juif
Julie
Julien's
Julius
jumble
jumps
junior
juniors
Juniper
Junot
Junot's
Junto
jurisprudence
Jurmains
jury
justify
jut
jutted
juxta-position
k
kaleidoscope
kam
kanadaw
Kanawdian
Kanawdians
Katholim
Katy-Did
Katy-Didn't
keel-boat
keer
Keith, Rev. P.
Kemble, Fanny
Kempelen
ken
Kennebeck
Kennedy's
Kepler's
Kerguelen
Kerguelen's
Kergulen
key-stone
keyhole
Khoda
Kickapo-o-o-os
kicks
Kidd's
Kieldholm
Kilkenny
kind-hearted
kinder
kindest
King, Henry
King's
Kingdom
kingly
kip>
Kircher
Kissam's
kisses
kissing
kitt-fox
kitten
Klimm, Nicholas
Klock-klock
Klock-klock
Klock-Klock
knack
knapsack
knelt
Knickerbockers
knights
knitting-needle
knob
knock-down
knocks
knoll
knots
Knowledge
Knowles, Ned
koruphai (Gr.)
kraken
krokopepeplos (Gr.)
Kroutaplenttey
Kupris
L
L--l, Theodore
L'an
l'autre
l'ennemi
l'etudier
l'oiseau
l'original
l'ottimo
l'oublie
l'Ame
l'Andromache
L'Espanaye, Camille
L'Espanaye's
l'Esprit
l'Etoile
L'Omelette
L'Omelette
La
labor-saving
laborer
lacerating
lacessit
lachrymose
Lacko'breath
Lacroix
ladle
lady's-maid
ladye-love
Laertes, Diogenes
Laertius
Lafourcade, Victorine
laider>
lair
lakelet
Lakes
Lama-Lamas
Lamartine
Lamartine's
lamb
lambent
Lambert, Jonathan
lament
lamentation
lamenting
lamentingly
lamma
lamp-black
lampoon
lances
lancet
Land
land-animal
landlady's
Landon
landscape-gardener
landscape-gardens
landscape-painter
Landscape-Gardener
landsman
landward
languages
languidly
langve
lank
lanyards
lap-dog
Laplaces
lapsing
large-boned
largeness
lark
las
Lasalle
lashes
lasm (Gr.)
lasping
Last
latches
lately-acquired
lateness
laterally
latest
lath-like
lathered
latticed
laudatory
lauded
lauft
laughable
laughably
Laughter
laughter-like
laundress
Lauzanne, Jacques
lave>
laved
Laverna
lavish
law-encumbered
lawn
lawn's
Laws
lawyers
laxity
layers
lbs
Le
lead-work
leaden-footed
leaden-hued
leading-strings

leafless
leafy
leaky
leans
leant
leap-year
leather-jackets
leavestaking
lecturer
lecturing
Leda
leddy-ship>
leddyship's>
ledges
Ledyard's
Lee, Nat
leer
lees
left-handedly
leg-bail
legacies
lege
legend
legging
legislatively
legitimately
Legrand's
Leipsic
lemon
Lempriere
lenticular-shaped
Leonardo's
Leonidas
leopard
leper
lepidolite
Lepidoptera
lessen
lessened
lessening
letter's
lettest
Lettres
Levante
levee
levelling
levem
lever
leverage
levities
Lewis's
liability
liars
libel
liber
liberally
liberate
libitum
libraries
Library
library's
libre
Libya
lice
lichen
Lieber, Francis
lied
lieden
Lieut
life-boats
life-likeliness
life-preserver
life-time
life's
lifelessly
lifetime
lifts
Ligeia, Lady
Light
light-coloured
light-headed
light-hearted
light-heartedness
light-looking
Light-House
lightening
lightning-rods
ligulate
liked
liken
likened
likens
lilach
Lilienthal
lily-fringed
lily-looking
line
limestone
limiting
limped
limpidity
limping
linden
lineally
lineament
linen-draping
lingeringly
lingers
lingo
lining
linings
linsey-woolsey
Lion
lion-izing
lion's
liqueur
liquid-looking
liquidum
liriodendron
Lisbon
Lisiausky
lisping
listless
listlessness
litera
Literati
literati
literatim
Literature
lithe
lithographs
litter
litters
Little
liveliest
liveliness
Lively
liver-like
livers
liveth
Livius, Titus
Livre
loading
loan
loathing
loathsomeness
lobe
locale
Locke, Richard Adams
lockers
locomotion
locomotive
locus
locust
locution
lodge
loft
loftily
loge
Logic
logician
logicians
loll
lolls
lombardy
lombardy-poplars
Londonderry
long-abiding
long-boat
long-cherished
long-desired
long-drawn
long-enduring
long-forgotten
long-imprisoned
long-interred
long-lost
long-sustained
Long, Stephen H.
longas
Longfellow
longings
Longinus
longitudes
longue
Lonon>
Look-aisy
loom
loop-hole
looped
loophole
loosed
Lor-gol-a-marcy
Lord
lore
Lost
loth
Lothario
Lotophagi
lottery
loud-toned
loudness
louis
love-litter>
love-passages
love-poems
loving
low-tide
low-water
lowed
lowing
loyalty
lozenges
lubber
lubbers
Lucian
Lucilius
lucky
Lucretius
luggage
lui
lui-meme
luke-warm
lulls
Lully, Raymond
lumber-yard
Lumberskull
lumen
luminousness
lunae
lunar-lunatic
Lunarian
lunarians
lunatico
lung
lurking-place
lustrums
lute's
luth
Lutheranism
Lutherthum
Luxor
luxuriously-cushioned
luxuricusness
Lyne
lyne
lxg
Lxrd
lxxk
Lybian
lyceum
Lyell
lynching
lynn
Lyons
Lyra
lyre
lyrics
M.
M.S.
M--
M--'s
m'avoir
Ma-a-a-a-n
ma-a-an
macaroni
Macassar
maces
mache
Machi--
Machiavelian
Machine
mackerel
Mackinaw
maculae
Mad
mad-houses
Mad'selle
madame
maddened
maddest
Madonna-like
Madrid
Maelzel
Magazine
Magian
magical-looking
magna
magnanimity
magnetoesthetics
magnificently
magnifico
magnifiers
magnolias
Magpies
Maguntinae
Mahomet
maid
Maillard's
mails

maimed
main
main-chains
main-hatchway
main-road
mainchains
Maine
mainland
majestically
Majesty's
make-weight
makesetai (Gr.)
mal
mal-apropos
mal-practice
Malabar
Malay
Malays
malevolent
malheur
Malibran
maliciously
malignancy
malignity
Malninas
maltreated
Mam'selle
mammalia
Mammon
man-at-arms
man-bat
man-bats
man-of-war
man-traps
manacle
manacles
manageable
manages
Manchester
mandate
mandibles
mandragora
manganese
manger
maniacal
manifesting
Manilla
manned
mannerisms
manor
manor-house
mansarde
mansardes
mantelet
mantelet
mantled
manufacturer
manufacturing
manumitted
Manuscrit
mar
marcescit
marches
marching
mare
mares
Mareschino
Margaux
Marginalia
marginalic
margins
Marian
marine
mariners
marking
marlin-spike
marling-spike
marmo
Marmontel
Marquis
marquis
marrying
marsh-hen
marsh-hens
Marshall
mart
marten
Martial
martins
martyrdom
marvellously
Marx, Issachar
mashed
masks
mason-work
Mason's, Monck
masons
Masque
masquerader
masquerades
Mass
massive-looking
mast-head
master-mind
master-minds
masterly
masterpiece
masticating
mastication
Mastodon
mat
materiality
matronly
Mattee
matter-of-course
matter-of-fact
matting
mattock
mattresses
maturing
Maury, Lieutenant
Mavis, Martin Van Buren
mavoureen
maxime
Maximus
maybe
Mayor
Maza--
mazurka
Mazurkiad
McHenry's
meadow
meagre
meandered
meanness
measurable
measurement
meats
mechanically
mechanically-moved
mechanician
Mechanics
Mechanics'
medallion
medecin
media
Medicean
Medici
medicines
medii
meditated
meditates
meditating
meditatively
meee
meets
Melancthon, Philip
melanges
Melanie
melee
Melete
meliora
Mellen
Mellen, G.
Mellonta
mellonta (Gr.)
Melnotte
melodies
melodrama
melodrame
Melrose
melt
melting
melts
Melty
membrane
membranous
memoire
Memoirs
memorandum
memorial
men (Gr.)
men-mathematicians
men-of-war
men-vermin
menace
menaced
menagais
menageais
Menander
mendicants
menials
Menschen
Mentoni's
mer
Mercator
merchandize
merchant-barber
merchant-barbers
Mercier
mercies
Merciful
merciless
Mercurie
mercury
Merry-Andrewism
Mesmeric
mesmerical
mesmerist
metals
metaphor
Metaphysics
metempsychosist
meteor
methodically
methodise
mets
Metzengerstein, Frederick Von
meuble
mewed
Mexican
Miantinimoh
miasma
Michael
Michau, Andre
Michau's
Michilimackinac
microscopical
mid-channel
mid-day
middle-aged
midehed
mienne
mightiest
Mignaud, Jules
migrate
Milan
mile-stone
militates
militating
Milk
milk-weed
mill-race
Mill's
Miller, Joseph A. etc.
Miller, Joseph E. F.
Miller, Joseph G. H.
Miller, Joseph J. K.
Miller, Joseph L. M.
Miller, Joseph N. O.
Miller, Joseph P. Q.
Miller, Joseph R. S.
Miller, Joseph T. V.
Miller, Joseph W. X.
Miller, Joseph Y. Z.
Miller's
millstone
mimicking
mineralizing
minerals
minion
minions
minister's
Ministerial
ministry
mink
Minnackenozzies
Minnakenozzies
Minnetaree
minnows
minutes'
mio
Miranda
mirthful
mis-calculation
mis-called
misadmeasurement
misapprehensions
miscalculations
mischievous
misconception
misconduct
misdemeanor
misdemeanors
misguided
mishap
misinformed
misjudged
mislaid
misrepresented
misrule
misshapen
Missinipi
missionaries
missure>
Mister
mister
mistranslated
mistress'
misty-looking

misty-winged
mit
mitigating
mittens
mizen-mast
mizzen-mast
Mneme
mo-o-o-on
mo-o-on
moanings
moans
moat
mobilia
moccasin
mock
mocking
modelling
moderated
moderation
modeste
modificiren
modifies
modistes
modo
modulated
modulation
moeurs
Mogul
moistened
moitie
mole
moles
molesting
mollified
molluscae
Molucca
moment
moments'
monarchical
monarchs
monarchy
monastic
Monday's
Monde
money-finders
money-lovers
money-seekers
mongers
monitions
monk
monkey-exhibiters
monkish
Monody
monologue
monomaniac
monopoly
monotone
Monsieur
monsters'
monstrosity
monstrously
Montani
Montani, Alberto
montantes
Montesquieu-ism
Montfleury
Monticello
Montresor
Moon
moon-day
moon-hoax
moon-hoax-y
moonless
moonshine
Moore's, Tom
Moral
morale
Moralische
morally
morasses
Moraux
moraux
morbidity
Moreau, Pierre
Moresque
moriens
morir
morn
morning-gown
mornings
Morocco
morocco
morose
Morrell, Benjamin
morry
mort
mortalium
mortals
mortify
mortis

morto
mortuis
Mortuorum
Mortuus
mortuus
morty
morus
Mosaic
mosaics
Moses
Moses
moshe
mosques
moth
Mother
mother-of-pearl
mother-tongue
mothers
motioned
motioning
motivirt
moulds
mound
Mountain
mountain-slopes
mountain-top
mountain-tops
Mountains
mountebanks
mounted
mounting
mouse-trap
mouser
Mousseux
mouthful
mouton
Moving

much-bethumbed
much-talked
mud-dabble
Mud-Dabbling
Mud-Puddle
mud>
muerte
mulberries
Mulciberian
mule-deer
mullets
multicaulis
multicoloured
multifarious
multiplicity
multiplies
multiplying
mum
mumble
mumbled
munching
Munday, George
Munroe
Murchison
Murder
murdering
murky
murmurings
muscular-looking
Muse
Musee
Muset, Isidore
Museum
museums
Music
music-mill
Musing
musings
Musique
Muskau's
musket-balls
muslins
musn't
musquash
musquitoes
Musselmen
Mussulman
Mussulmen
mustache
mustachio
mustachio
mustn't
mutability
mutantur
mutely
mutilation
mutineer
mutter
mutual
mutually
muy
muzzle

mxther
My
myriad-tinted
Myrmeleon
myrmeleon
myrtles
mystific
Mystification
mystifique
mystify
Mythology
MACHIA
MAZA
MDCXLVIII
n.e.i.
N.B.
n'aurait
n'eut
n'ose
Naevius
naiteral
naive
naivete
nape
Naples
Napoleon
Napoleons
Napoli
nare
narrations
narrator's
narrowness
nascent
nascitur
Nassau-balloon
nasty
Natura, De Rerum
Naturae
naturae
naturalibus
naturalists
naturally-curling
naturally-waving
naturalness
Nature
Naturelle
nauseated
nauseous
navigable
Naxos
ne
Neal's, John
Neapolitans
nearing
nearly-new
neatly-folded
nebula
nebular
nebulosity
necessities
neck-handkerchief
necked
neckerchief
necromancers
necromantic
needing
needs
nefarious
neglects
negligence
negligently
negotiation
negro-servant
neider
neighbour
neighed
Nellies
nelly
Neopolitan
nephew's
Neptune's
Neptunian
Nereus
Nergal
nerving
nestled
nestling
nethermost
nettings
Neuclid
Neufchatel-ish
neuralgia
neuralgic
neutral
neutralize
never-ceasing
never-dying
never-to-be-forgotten
never-to-be-imparted
new-fledged

new-style
new-touch
New-Bank
next-door
ni
nib
nibble
nibbled
nibbling
nibblings
Nibhaz
Nicander
Nicanor, Seleucus
nicer
nicest
niceties
Nichol
Nick
Niebuhr
niece
niente
nier
Niger
niggardly
niggerless
Night
night-cap
night-clothes
night-fall
Night-Mare
nightcap
nightfall
Nightingale
Nil
nill-I
nimbleness
nimbly
Nimmy
ninety-four
ninety-fourth
ninety-gun
ninety-seven
Niobe
nisi
No
No
no-o-o
Noah
Noah, M.
noble-spirited
noblemen
nobles
Noblet
nocturnal
Nodaway
nods
noin
noisy
nom-de-guerre
nom-de-plume
nombre
nommy
non-admeasurement
non-entity
non-epistolary
non-luminosity
non-luminous
non-plused
nonchalance
nonchalant
nonentities
nonplussed
noon-day
nooses
Nootka
noovers
Norland
Norman
North-east
north-eastern
north-western
north-westwardly
North-Eastern
North-Western
northerly
Northern
Northman
northwestern
northwesternly
Norwegian
nosology
nostril
not-over-acute
notable
notebook
Notes
notifying
notin
notoriously
Notre
noun
nouns
nourishes
Nourjabad
Nourjahad
nouvellement
Nouvelette
novel-hero
novelties
novice
Now
nowhar
Nubia
nudge
nues
nuisance
null
nullus
numb
numbering
numberless
numerously
nunquam
nuptials
nursed
nurses'
nutmegs
nutritive
nxbxdy
nxne
o
O (Gr.)
O-ing
o-wy
O'
o'ercast
O's
o's
O'Bumper, Bibulus
O'Connell, Daniel
O'Phlegethon, Andrew
O'Rafferty
O'Rourke, Thomas
O'Trump, Kathleen
oak-plank
oakum
oarsman
Oasis
oasis
oat-meal
oaths
oatmeal
ob'nt
obaysance>
obesity
objective
objectivity
oblate
obligation
obligingly
obliquely
obliquity
obliterates
oblivion
Oblong
obras
obsarve>
obscenities
obscurity
observant
obsol
obst--
obstreperously
obtains
obtrude
obtruding
obviated
obviousness
occidit
occiput
occultations
occupancy
occupants
occupies
ocean-crag
oceans
ochre
octagonal
odder
oddest
Odenheimer
odorless
Odyssey
Oegipans
oeufs
Oeuvres
of
offal
offends
offense
offerings
officered
officiate
officious
officiousness
offing
ogs
Ohio
oil-cask
oil-cloths
oil-tanks
oiled
oils
oiseau
old-womanish
olden
olfact
olive-jars
Ollapod
Olympia
Olympiad
olympiad
Olympics
Omahas
omelette
omens
Omicron
ominously
omission
omitting
Omne
omnipotence
omnipraevalent
omnipresence
omniprevalence
omniscience
On
ond
one-eyed
one-idead
one-sided
one-thirtieth
oneness
ongry
onions
Only
onpleasant
onyxes
oooooh
ooze
oozy
opal
opals
openness
operates
operator
opined
opium-dream
Opium-eater
opium-engendered
Oporto
opponent's
opportune
oppress
oppresses
optic
or-mclu'd
oracles
Orang-Outangs
orange-coloured
orange-jellies
orange-peel
oration
Oratiunculae
Oratiunculis
orators
oratory
Orbis
Orchideae
orchis
Ordonnance
Orfeo
organ-grinder
organ-grinders
organ-grinding
organization
originate
originators
oriole
ornamental
Orndoff
orne
Orontes
orthodox
orthodoxy
orthographically
orthography
ortolan
ortolans
os

os (Gr.)
oscillation
oscillations
osier
osprey
Ossa
osseous
osservasse
ossi
ossification
ossified
Otello
Otter
otter
Ottoes
ounce
ourang-outang
Ourang-Outangs
ourself
out-flowing
out-heroded
outbidding
outbreak
outburst
outcast
outcasts
outcry
outfit
Outis
outlay
outnumbered
outpouring
outrageously
outrages
outre
outreaching
outridden
outrider
outriggers
outrun
outspread
outstripped
outwits
outwitted
Oval
oven-full
over-conscientious
over-curious
over-hanging
over-largely
over-profound
over-rated
over-shoes
over-spreading
over-topped
over-value
over-wise
overarching
overburthened
overcoming
overdo
overflowings
overhasty
overhaul
overhauled
overjoyed
overlapping
overlaying
overlook
overlooking
overpower
overran
overrated
overruling
overrun
overshadows
oversights
overstowed
overstrained
overtakes
overthrowing
overthrows
overtouched
overturn
overwhelms
overzezet
ow
ow'dst
owe
owes
owner's
ownership
owning
ox-cart
oxen
oxus
Oyarvido, Manuel de
oyster
oysters
p
P.R.E.T.T.Y.
pabulum
pace
paced
pacifically
pacify
pacifying
pacing
pack-thread
packet-ship
packets
packs
pacquet
padded
paddings
paddle-blades
paddled
paddling
padlock
Padua
pagans
pageantries
pageants
Pagoda
pagoda
pained
paint-begrimed
Paixhan
Paladian
Palaeochori
Palais
palanquins
Palazzo
paleness
Palfrey
Palfrey, J. G.
Paliggenesia (Gr.)
paliggenesia (Gr.)
palin (Gr.)
pall-like
Palladian
palled
pallet
palliation
palliative
pallidly
palmetto
palpabilities
palpi
palpitate
palpitated
palpitates
palsied
palsying
Pan
Pandemonium
panel
panels
panic
panic-stricken
Pankey
pansies
pantaloons'
pantheistical
pantomime
pantries
pants
Papa
papal
paper-hangings
papered
papillon
papillotes
papyrus
Parable
parachutes
paracutas
paraded
paradoxically
Paragrab
parallel
paralleling
parallelipipedal
paraphrased
Parasites
parasites
parcelled
parcels
pardonable
pardonne
pardons
parent's
parentheses
parenthesis
Parian
Paris
parish
Parisians
Parker's
parle
parlerebbe
Parliament
parlors
parly-wouing>
parmi
Parmly's
Parnasse
paroquet
Parrish
parrotfish
Parry
pars
parsimony
parsley
partaker
partant
parterre
parti-coloured
parti-striped
participants
participate
particoloured
particularized
particularizing
particuller>
Partisan
partisans
partitions
party's
Pas
pas-de-zephyr
pasan (Gr.)
Pascal
Pasigono
Pasquinaded
passados
Passages
passant
passees
passenger
passerois
passers
passport
passus
Past
pastimes
pastor
pastoral
pastures
Patagonia
pate
pate
pate-pans
patent
patent-blacking
patent-leather
pates
pathology
patria
patriarch
patrie
patriots
patronise
patronize
patronizing
patronym
patted
Patten
Patten's
Patterson
Paul
Paulding
Paulding, J. K.
pauvre
Pawnees
payed
Payne
pays
pea-green
peacefully
peach
peacock
peak
peaked
peal
peanuts
pear-tree
Pearl
pearl-powder
pears
peasantry
Pease's
pebble
Pectoral
pectoral
peculiar-looking
pedant
pedant's
pedants
peddling

pedestrian
pedis
pedlars
pedlers
Pedronist
peeper>
peers
peevishness
pehabe
peine
pele-mele
Pelham
pelican
pelicans
Pelion
pell
pellucid
pelly
pen-holding
pen-knife
penalty
penblade
pencil-scratches
penciled
penciling
pencilled
pencilling
pencillings
Pendant
pendant
pendants
pendent
pendulums
pennant
Pennicornis
Pennsylvania
pense
pensiero
pension
pensively
pentagon
pentagonal
Pentateuch
penthouse
penuriousness
people-less
people's
peopleless
pepper-castor
perambulates
perambulations
perambulators
percaved>
percha
percha
perchance
perdidit
perds
perdu
perdus
Pere
perennial
perfidy
perforate
perforating
performs
Perier
Perier, Casimir
periphery
periwig
periwigs
Perkins
permeate
permeation
Permission
permits
perpetrating
perplex
Perrine
Perriri
persecutors
persevered
perseveres
Persians
persists
person's
personate
personified
perspicacity
perspicuity
perspicuous
persvaded
pert
perticcler
pertinently
perturbation
perturbations
Peru
Perverseness
pest-ban
pest-spirits
Pest-Iferous
Pest-Ilential
pestered
pestilent
pestis
pesty
pet>
Petersham
Petershams
Peterson, C. J.
petit
petit-maitre
petite
petiteness
petition
Petrie
Petrie, William
petrifaction
petted
Pettitt
peut
Pfaal, Hans
Pfaall, Grettel
Phalarian
phalaris
phantasma
phantastic
phantasy-pieces
pharagges (Gr.)
Pharonnida
Pharronida
phaseless
phases
pheugon (Gr.)
Phi
phial
Phil.
Philadelphian
Philadelphians
philippic
philological
philosophizing
Philpot, Philip
Phiz
Phlegethon
phlegmatic
phonetical
phonetics
phosphorescent
phrenes (Gr.)
phrensied
phrensy
physic
Physician
Physiological
Physiology
physiology
physique
physique
Piazza
Piazzetta
Piazzo
Pibrac
pic-nics
pick-pockets
picks
Pictorius
Pictorius, Hermanus
picturesque-hunters
picturesque-looking
pie
pie-crust
pie-men
piece
piecemeal
piena
pierced
pies
Pieta
piety
Pig
pig-sty
pigeon
pigeon-winged
pigeon-winger
pigeon-winging
pigeon-wings
pigger
Pike, Zebulon M.
Pilau
pilfering
Pilgrimage
pilier
pill
pill-box
pillaging
pillar
pimpled
pin
pinchbeck
pineknots
pining
piningly
pinned
pinxit
pioneer
Piot
piquancy
pique
piqued
pirouette
pirouetted
pish
pissel
pistil
pistol-shot
Pit
pitched
pitches
pitchfork
pitchings
pith
pithy
pittoresque
pivot
pivots
pizzness
placard
placarded
placards
plague-goblins
plaid
plain-looking
plaisir
plan
planes
planetary
plank-work
plankings
Plant
Plantae
Plantes
plased>
plases>
plasterers
plastering
platanus
platina
platinum
platitudes
plausibly
playbill
players
playful
playfulness
playmate
plaything
plazer
plead
pleading
pleadings
pleases
pleasurably
plein
plenitude
plentifulness
pliancy
Pliny
Pliny's
plotting
plover
plovers
plucking
plugs
plum-trees
plume-like
plumed
plumes
plummed
plumped
plural
Plutarch
ply
plying
pocket-comb
pocket-compass
pocket-knife
pocketing
poco
podagre
Poe, Edgar Allan
poet-love
poeta
poetaster
poete
poetizing
Poetry
poignancy
point

poised
poke
poking
Poland
polarized
polecat
poled
polemics
Police
Police
Polish
polishing
politely
politeness
Politian's
politic
politician
polled
pollicis
Polly
Polybius
Polyglot
Polyglot, Delphinus
Polyglott
Polyglott, Delphinus
pomatum
pomegranate
pomp
Pompeius
pomps
Poncas
ponders
ponds
Ponnonner, Doctor
Ponte
pontifical
pooh
pools
poorly
pop
Pope
popinjay
poplar
poplars
Porcupine
Porcupiniana
pore
pores
porker
porousness
Porphyrogene
porpoise
Porque
Porrex
portal
portend
portended
portents
porticoes
portionless
Portland
portmanteau
Portrait
portraitures
Portuguese
possesses
possessors
possibilities
Post
postage
posteriors
postmarks
postponed
postponing
posts
postscript
postures
pot-belly
pot-house
pot-houses
potency
potu
Poughkeepsie
poultry
pounce
pounding
Poussin
powdered
Power
powerfulness
Powhatan
practicability
Practical
practically
practices
practitioner
praenomen
praeter-nature
Praeter-Veteris
praises
prandian
prate
pratique
prawns
pre-eminence
preacher
preaching
precepts
precipice's
precipitancy
precipitates
preclude
precocity
preconcertedly
pred
predecessor
predestined
Predicament
predict
prediction
predilections
predisposes
predisposing
predominance
predominate
predominated
predominating
preeches
prefacing
Prefect's
prefixed
pregnant
prejudiced
preliminaries
preliminary
Premature
prematurely
premier
premised
Premium
premium
Prentice's
preparees
prepares
preponderated
prepositions
prepossession
prepossessions
preposterously
prerogative
pres
prescience
prescribe
Present
presentant
presenter
presentment
preserver
preserves
presidents
presses
pressingly
presumption
pretences
pretender
preterpluperfect
prettiest
prevarication
Prevention
prey'st
preys
priced
pricking
Priestly
priests
prig
prim
primaeval
primaries
primer
primitively
primness
Primo's
primum
prin (Gr.)
Princes
princes
Princess
Princesse
principality
principia
printer
printer's
printers
printin>
Printing
priority
prism
prism-cut
prismatic
prison-like
Prison-House
privy
privy-councillors
Prize
prized
prizing
pro-o-odigies
Probant
probe
probes
problematical
procedure
procession
processions
proche
proclaimed
proclaiming
proclamation
procrastinate
Procrustean
prodigal
production
productiveness
profanation
profanely
profanity
professor
proficient
Profit
profited
profuseness
prognostic
progresses
progressing
projector
prolegomena
prolix
prolixity
prolonged
promenade-ground
promenades
Prometheus
prominency
promote
promptitude
prompts
promulgate
promulgated
proneness
prononces
pronoun
pronouncing
pronouns
proof-tones
proones (Gr.)
propagates
propellers
prophetic
prophetical
propinquity
propitious
proportional
proportionally
propos
proposing
propounding
proprietor's
proprietors
propulsion
proscribing
prosciso (Gr.)
prospective
prospectively
prostekonti (Gr.)
protecting
protector
Protestantism
Protestantismus
Protestants
protestations
proticting>
protoxide
protuberances
proudly
proven
Proverbs
proverbs
providence
providential
providing
provincialists
provisional
provisioned
proviso
provoke
provokingly
prowess
proximate
prudential

prudently
pruderies
prudish
Prussian
pry
Psalemoun
Psalm
psalm
psaltery
pseudo-horror
Psychological
Ptolemaiad
public's
publican
publications
publicly
publique
publish
pudding
Puddington
puddle
puerile
puffing
puffs
puggish
pugnacious
pulcherrimus
Pulci
pulpits
pulpy
pulseless
pulses
pumice-stone
punch-bowl
puncheon>
puncheons
punctilios
punctual
punctuate
punctuation
Pundita
pungencies
pungency
punished
punishing
punning
pupilless
puppets
puras
pures
purgatory
purifying
purlieus
purlit>
purloin
Purloined
purloiner
purplish
purport
purports
purposeless
purraty-trap>
purraty>
purse-strings
purslain
pursuant
pursuers
pursues
pursvaded
purticular>
purulent
Pusey
Puseyism
Puseyites
putares
Putnam's
putrescent
putridity
puzzling
px
pxxr
Pym, A. G.
Pym, A. Gordon
Pym, Arthur
Pym's
Pyramid
pyramid
Pyrrhonism
Pyrros
PRETTYBLUEBATCH
qu'on
quackeries
quackery
quacking
quadrant
quadruped
quadrupeds
Quaere
quaintly
quaintness
qualification
qualify
Quand
quantum
quarante
quarrelling
quarrelsome
quarter-past
Quartier
Quartier
quasi
quatrain
quatre
quaver
quavering
Que
queen's
quell
quelling
quelqu'un
quench
quenched
quere
querulous
query
questionable
questionings
queues
Qui
quickened
quickness
quicksand
quicksands
Quicourre
quid
quidnuncs
Quinault
Quintillian
quivers
Quizzem's
quizzes
quocunque
quorum
r
R.S.A.
Rabbins
rabbit-berry
Rabelais's
raconteur
racoon
Radcliffe
rade>
radiantly
radiating
radiation
radicalism
Rafflesia
ragamuffin
Railway
railway
rained
rainwater
rainy
raisin
raisins
raisonnement
rakish-looking
ralelly>
Ram-ishly
ram's
ram's-horn
rammed
rampant
rams
Randolph, John
ranges
ranging
ranked
rankly-growing
ranks
ransack
ransacking
Rantipole
rapacious
rapidly-growing
rapine
rara
rarae
rarebit
rarer
rarified
raspberry
rasps
rat-traps
ratlin-stuff
Rats
rattle-snake
rattlesnakes
ravages
rave
raved
raven-winged
raven's
ravings
ravishing
raylessness
razor-like
re-appearance
re-appears
re-captured
re-capturing
re-commence
re-compose
re-cross
re-directed
re-echo
re-employing
re-enclose
re-enclosed
re-enforcement
re-entering
re-erected
re-established
re-examined
re-fastened
re-heated
re-instituted
re-interred
re-laid
re-melt
re-model
re-modelled
re-passage
re-procured
re-read
re-scription
re-sealed
re-search
re-searched
re-seated
re-sinking
re-solution
re-squeaked
re-writing
readings
readjust
readjusting
readverting
realizes
reanimation
reappeared
reapplication
reapproached
reascend
reascending
reasonableness
reasonings
reassured
rebel
rebellious
rebound
rebuilt
rebuke
rebukes
Rebus
rebut
rebuts
rebutted
recalls
recapture
recapturing
receding
receipted
recency
receptacle
receptacles
Recherches
reciprocating
recital
recitations
recitative
recited
reciting
recklessly
reclaimed
reclaiming
recline
recluse
recognizing
recoiling
recommandable
recommencing
recommendations
reconciled
reconciles
reconnoissance
reconnoitred
reconsider
Recorder
recording

recorked
recounting
recrossing
recruited
recruiting
rectangularly
rectification
recue
recur
recurrence
recusant
red-bud
red-litten
reddish
redeem
redivert
redouble
redoubtable
redoubted
redresser
reducible
reductio
reduction
reduit
reduplication
reefed
reeked
reeking
reel
reels
refastened
referens
refers
refinements
refitted
reflector
refolded
Reformation
Reformation
Reforme
refract
refracting
refraction
refresh
refreshing
refreshments
refrigerator
refusals
refuser
refutes
regather
regathering
regenerate
regeneration
regia
registered
Registre
Regni
regretful
regularly-formed
regulating
Regulus
regulus
reheaded
reigneth
Reihe
rein
Reine
reined
reinem
reins
reinstate
reinstation
rejecting
rejoices
rejoicing
rejoicings
rejoined
rekindled
relax
relaxes
relented
relenting
relentless
relentlessly
relics
relief
relieves
relievo
religio
religio
religion
relished
reloading
rely
rem
Remarkable
remembers
remets
remimbered>
reminding
reminiscences
remorseless
remoteness
remoter
removes
remplis
remunerated
rencontres
rend
rending
renews
renounce
rented
renting
repaid
repay
repayment
repent
reperuse
repining
replenished
reposing
representatives
repress
reproached
reprocured
reptiles
Repub.
Republican
Republicanism
republication
republish
republished
repugnant
requests
requiescat
requisites
requisition
res
rescinding
reservoir
reside
residences
resignation
resignedly
resined
resistance
resistlessly
resolvent
resonant
resonne
resorting
respectability
respectably
respite
respited
resplendently-blooming
responsibilities
responsibility
resposes
ressemblance
Rest
restaurants
restaurateurs
reste
resting-place
restive
restorations
restoratives
restrict
restrictions
rests
resurrection
resurrexit
resuscitation
retains
retake
retaliations
retarded
retchings
retention
retentive
retina
retinue
retires
retorted
retribution
retrieval
retro-gradation
retrograding
returneth
Retzsch
reunions
reve
reveal
revealing
reveled
reveller
revelry
revenged
revenue
reverberate
reverberated
reverberations
Reverend
reverent
reverently
reverses
reviendrai
Review
Reviewed
Reviewer
reviewer
reviewers
revision
revivication
revivified
revoir
revolt
revolting
revulsion
rewarding
Reynold's
rhapsodical
rhapsodies
rhapsody
rhetoric
rhetorical
rheumatism
rhinoceros
rhodomontades
rhomboids
Rhone
rhymed
rhymes
rhythm
riband
ribands
ribband
Ricara
Riccaree
Rice, Joel
Rich--
rich-ermined
richly-embroidered
Ricketts
ricocheting
ridden
riddy>
ridge-beam
ridiculed
ridiculer
rien
right-angle
righteously
rigidam
rigola
Riker
rilievo
rims
rind
rinsed
Rio
riot
rioters
riots
rip
riper
ripping
ripple
rites
ritual
rivaling
rivalled
rivalling
rivals
rivets
rivulets
road-side
roadside
roam
roams
roars
roast
roasting
robbing
robed
Robert's
Robesp--
Rochefoucault
rock-blaster
rocking-chair
rocs
Rodman, James E.
Rogers, Mary
Rogers's
Roget, Estelle
Roget's
rogue

Roi
roisterers
role
roles
rollings
romancer
romances
Romances
romantic-looking
romanticist
Rombert
Ronald's, E.
roofed
rooster
Rose
rose-bud
rose-water
rosemary
Ross'
rot
rottenness
Rotunda
roughness
roundabout
rounding
roundly
roused
rousing
roved
row-de-dowed
Rowdy-dow
rowed
rowers
rubbing-post
Rubini
rubs
ruby-colored
ruby-drops
ruddier
rudiment
rue
ruffianly
ruffles
ruffling
ruined
rule-of-three
ruleth
rum-puncheon
ruminate
ruminating
rummaged
rummages
rummer
rump
runaway
rung
rungs
rupture
rural
ruse
ruses
rushes
rushlight
russet
russet-leather
Russians
rust
rustled
ruts
rxlling
RICHEL
S
s'echapper
sabage
sable-bound
sable-feathered
Sabretash
Sabretash, Arthur
sac
sackbut
sacks
sacrifices
sacrilege
sacrumstance
sadness
safeguard
saffron-like
sage
sages
sailer
sailors'
saints
sais
Sal
salad-bowl
Salamanca
salamander
salamanders
Sale's
salis
Salle
sallied
sallies
Salmon
salmon
saloons
Salsafette, Eugenie
salt-cellar
salted
salubrity
salusque
salva
Salvator
Salvatorish
Salvinam
Sancta
sanctified
sanctify
sanctimoniousness
sanction
sanctum
sand-island
sand-plains
sandalled
sandals
sandhills
Sandwich
sangsue
sangsues
sans
Sanscrit
sap
Saracenic
saracenic
sarcophagi
Sarmatic
sarvant>
sarvice>
sasso
satellite's
satiata
satiated
satiating
satin-wood
satirical
satirically
sattinet
Saturnian
Saturnus
Satyr
satyr
Satyr-like
satyrs
saucer
Sauerkraut
savant
savants
savoir
saw-dust
sawed
sawyer
sawyers
sax
saxifrage
sayest
scabius
scaffold
scalp
scalpel
scaly
scamp
scamper
scampered
scampering
scampers
scan
scandalous
scanned
scantily
scantlings
scarabaei
scarabaeus
scare
scared
scarred
scars
scenic
scents
Schiedam
Schiller's
Schiraz
Schlemil, Peter
Schnellpost
scholars
scholarship
scholiasts
school-life
school-master
school-phraseology
school-room
schoolboys
schoolfellows
schooner-rigged
schooner's
schooners
Schouw
Schrevilius
Schroeter
Sciences
scimetar-like
scion
scored
scores
scoria
scorning
scorns
scorpions
Scotland
Scott, Walter
Scotts, Leonard
scourge
scourged
scourges
scouring
scouts
scowling
scraps
Scratchaway, Augustus
scratchy
scrawled
screeching
screen
screw-driver
scribble
scribbler
scribbling
scribblings
scribe
scriptural
scrupled
scudding
scuffling
scull
sculleries
sculls
sculptor
sculptures
scum
scurrilous
Scythas
Scythe
Scythe
Scythian
se'n
sea-beast
sea-brilliancy
sea-burial
sea-chest
sea-coal
sea-coast
sea-gull
sea-kelp
sea-parlance
sea-shell
sea-turtle
sea-weeds
seaboard
seaboat
Seadrift, Solomon
seafaring
seagull
seagulls
seahens
sealing-wax
seamed
seaports
searches
seared
Seas
seasoned
seaswallows
seating
seaworthy
seben
seclusions
second-handed
seconded
secretary
secrete
Secrets
sects
secundum
securities
sedan
sedate
sedge
sedges
Sedgwick
Sedgwick, C. M.
Sedgwick's

sediment
sedition
seduce
seductions
see-saw
seed
seed-vessels
seed>
seeds
seemeth
Seer
segar-girl
segonde
Select
selecting
selects
self-agency
self-amendment
self-balanced
self-conceit
self-congratulation
self-consequence
self-consistent
self-demonstration
self-esteem
self-evidency
self-existing
self-gratulation
self-identity
self-imposed
self-interest
self-love
self-movement
self-moving
self-sacrificing
self-same
self-satisfied
self-suggestion
sellers
Selten
semi-axis
semi-circular
semi-metal
semi-osseous
semi-spiral
semi-syncope
semi-Druidical
semi-Saracenic
semicircle
semicircular
Senate
sends
Seneca
senior
sens
sensation-paper
sensibilities
sensible
Sensitive
sentiment
sentiments
senty
sep
separately
separates
sepoys
Sept
sepulchres
sepultus
Sequel
sequitur
sequuntur
sera
seraglio
Seraphim
seraphim
seraphs
serenading
seringa
seriousness
serpent-like
serpentine
serves
servi
servile
servitude
Servius
sesamoideum
session
session-room
sessions
settees
seule
seulement
seuls
seven-eighths
seventy-fours
seventy-nine
seventy-second
seventy-seven

sever
severas
severities
sew
sewer
Sexagesima
sexton
Seymour
sha'nt
shabby
shackles
Shades
shadow-like
shadowing
Shadows
shady
shaggy-haired
shags
Sham-Post
shamed
shameless
shark
sharp-pointed
sharpen
sharpened
sharpers
sharply-defined
sharpness
shattering
shaving
shawm
sheathed
sheep-bells
sheets
shefa
Shelley
shellfish
Shetland
Shetlands
shew
shields
shifts
shilling's
shillings
shingles
ship-builders
Shiraz
shoal
shocked
shocks
shod
shoe-marks
shooting-stars
shop-doors
shop-shutters
shore-party
shot-towers
should'st
shoulder-blades
shoutings
shoved
shovel
showd>
shower-bath
showers
showman
showy
shredded
shredding
shrewdness
shrill-sounding
shriller
shrilly
shrimps
shrouds
shudderingly
Shuttleworthy, Barnabas
Shylock
Siam
Sibyls
Sicily
sick-list
Siculus, Diodorus
side-dishes
side-long
side-piece
side-pocket
sideboard
siding
sidled
siecle
sienta
siestas
Sieur
Sieur
sieve
sift
signalizing
signify
Signòr's

Sigourney, L. H.
silenced
silentio
silex
silicified
Silk
silk-buckingham
silk-velvet
silk-worms
silks
sill
silver-like
silver-smith
Simia
Simmond's
Simms, W. T. Gilmore
simpering
simple-minded
Simpson, Adolphus
simultaneous
Sinbad
sincerest
sind
sind>
sine
sinecure
sinews
Singapore
singed
singer
Single
single-minded
singles
singularly-marked
Sinivate, Theodore
sinner's
Siope
Sioux
sipping
Sirius
sis
Sissytoonies
sitot
sittin>
sitting-places
sittings
Situ
six
sixpences
sixpennies
sixteen-hundredth
sixthly
sixty-eighth
sixty-fifth
sixty-fourth
sixty-seven
sixty-six
sized
Skarholm
skate
skeered
skeptic
skepticism
skewers
skilled
skim
skimmed
skipped
skipping
skirmish
skull's
Skylark
slack-lime
slack-water
slackened
slake
slaked
slammed
slamming
Slang-Syllabus
slant
slanted
slap
slashed
slashes
slaty
slavery
slayeth
sledgehammer
sleep-producing
sleep-waker's
Sleeper
sleepers
sleeping-place
sleeping-room
sleepless
sleet
slice
slices
Slidell

Slidell, Alexander
Slidell's
slim-legged
slimy
slings
slip-knot
slipknot
sloop-fashion
slouching
slow-match
slow-paced
sluggishly
slung
slur
sluts
Sluys
slxw
smacked
small-clothes
smarter
smells
Smif
smirked
smirking
smith
Smith, Horace
Smith, Thomas
smock
smoke-blackened
smoother
smoothing
smoothness
smote
smother
smothering
smuggle
smuggling
snags
snail-paced
snake-like
snakes
snapped
snappish
snares
snarl
snarling
snatch
snatched
snatching
sneak
sneaking
sneering
snores
snort
snow-ball
snow-white
snowed
snowy
snowy-white
snub
Snubbing
snubby
snuff-color
snuffed
snuffy
snugger
so
So-and-So
so-called
soaked
soap-boiler
soars
sobbed
sober-sided
sociable
sociably
socle
Socrates
sodden
sods
softly
soi (Gr.)
soils
sojourned
soldiers
Soledad
soliciting
solicitous
solicitously
solicitude
solid-looking
solidly
soliloquized
solo
soluble
solus
somnolency
Son
sonn
Sonnambula
Sonnet
sonorously
sont
Sontag
sonum
sooppose
soot
sooty
sophist
sophistry
Sophocles
soporific
soprano
sorcery
sore
sorrowfully
Sorrows
Sospiri
sospite
sotticism
sottise
sottish
sotto
soufflee
Soul
soul-passion
soul-stirring
Sound
sounding-gear
souper
sour
sourit
sous-cuisinier
south-east
south-eastern
south-west
south-western
South-West
sovereignty
sow
Spaniards
spanked
spanker
spar
spareness
spark
Sparks, Jared
Sparks'
spars
sparsely
spasmodically
spattered
speaketh
specie
specificae
specification
specifying
speciousness
speckled
specks
spect
Spectacles
spectres
Speculative
speculatively
speculum
Speeches
speediest
speeding
spellbound
spelled
spelling
spells
spendthrifts
spermaceti
sperrits>
spheroid
Sphinx
Sphynx
spice
spices
spicy
spiders
spinal
spines
spins
spirit-land
spirit-soothing
spitefully
splash
splashed
splendid
splendours
splotch
splotching
spoil
spoilers
spokeshaves
sponges
sponsors
spontaneity
spoons
sporting
sports
spose
spotting
spotty
spouse
spout
sprightly
spring-guns
spring-house
sprite
spruce
spun
spunging
spurious
spurned
Spurzheim
Spurzheimites
spy
spyglass
squabbles
squalling
squandering
square-looking
square-rigged
squared
squazes>
squeak
squeak
squeaked
squeaking
squeeze
Squibalittle
squibbing
squirrel
squirrels
stability
stadium
staff
stage-box
stage-coach
stage-mad
stage-player
stage-struck
stages
stains
stair-case
stairway
stake
Stale
stalk
stamen
stammered
stand-still
Standard
staples
Stapleton, Edward
star-beloved
star-shadows
stares>
starting-point
startles
starved
stateliest
statistical
statt
statu
statuary
statures
statute
staunch
stave
staves
stay-sail
Steadfast
steadfast
steadfastly
steadier
steadiest
steadiness
steaks
steam-boats
steam-engine
steam-vessels
steaming
steel-bound
steeped
Steering
steersman
stemming
stentorian
Stephanie
stereotomic
sterling
stern-sheets
Sterne
sternest
sternu+amentis

stertorousness
steward's
sticking
stiff-frozen
stiff-lookino
stiffer
stifle
stigmatise
stiletto
still-increasing
stimulates
stingings
stint
stipping>
stipulating
stitch
stock-jobbers
stockinet
stockinett
stocking
stoical
stolen
Stone
Stone, W. L.
stool
stoops
stoppage
stopper
store-room
storing
storm-staysails
storm-tormented
Story
Story, Joseph
stow
stowage-room
straggling
straight-forward
straight-jacket
straightaway
straightening
straightest
Strait
strait-forward
strait>
Straits
strangle
strap
strata
stratum
straw-colored
streaked
stream's
streamer
streamlets
street-crossing
street-door
street-robber
strengthening
strengthens
strictness
stride
strides
stripe-interspersed
striped
stripping
strived
stroked
strolling
strongly-knit
strove
strugglingly
strung
strut
stubbornly
stubbornness
Stubbs
studded-sail
studious
stuffed
stuffs
Stuffundpuff
stumbling-block
stumbling-blocks
stumped
stumpy-looking
stunning
stupefying
stupid looking
sturdily
stxp
stylish
stylus
Suarven
sub
sub-collectors
sub-commentaries
sub-divided
subdivided
subduing
subjacent
subject's
subjectivity
sublimate
sublimated
sublimating
sublimation
sublimest
sublunary
submitting
subscribers
subscription
subserved
subservience
subserviency
subservient
subside
subsidence
subsist
subsisted
subsistence
subsisting
substituting
substitution
substructure
subtend
subtends
subterfuge
Subterranean
subtlety
suburb
suburban
subversive
subvert
successes
successor
Succoth-Benith
succour
succumb
sucked
Sue's
Sues
Suez
sufferance
sufficing
suffocated
suffuse
suffused
sugar-cane
sugar-loaf
sugarhousemolasses
suggests
sui
suicidal
Suky
Sul
sulphureous
sulphuric
sum'mat
summat>
Summer
summers
summing
sumptuously
sun-dial
sun-rise
sun-set
Sun's
sunburnt
sunder
sunt
super-eminent
superabundant
superadded
Superadditis
superbly
supererogatory
superficiality
superficially
superficies
superinduces
superintend
superintended
superlatively
supernaturally
supernumerary
superscription
superstition's
supervene
supineness
supped
suppers
supplicating
supporters
suppositions
supposititious
suppress
suppressed
Suppression
surcoat
surety
surgeon's
surgery
surges
surmount
surprized
surr
surrounds
survivors
sus
suspects
suspenders
suspending
suspendu
suspension
suspensions
suspict>
suture
sutures
swaggerers
swaggers
swallowing
Swammerdamm
swamp-fight
swampy
swan
swan-like
swans
swar
sward
swatest>
Swedenborg
sweeping-brushes
sweepings
sweetness
sweets
swelters
swerving
swift
swift-flying
swilling
swimmers
swindling
swing
swivel
swoop
sword-handles
sxrrxws
sxw
sycophancy
syllabub
syllogism
sylph
sylph-like
Sylphs
symbols
symmetrical
sympathising
sympathized
symphonies
symphony
symposium
symptom
synonym
synonyme
synonymes
synopses
Syrens
syrups
systematical
systematized
systems
T
t
T--
T's
taba
tabac
Tabbies
tabernacle
table-land
tableau
tabular
tac
tacit
tacitly
Tacitus-ism
tack
tacks
tactics
Tadmor
taffety
taffrail
Taglioni
Tailor's
tailor's-shears
tailors
tal
Talbots
talc

talens
talk's
talker
tallest
tallies
tallow
tam>
tam'd
tamed
tan-bark
tan>
tangible
tangled
tank
tantalistical
tantalization
tantalize
tantum
tap-houses
tap-room
tape
taper-wax
tapestry-hangings
tar-brush
Tarantula
target
tariff
tarred
Tartak
tasks
tassel
tasteful
tastefully
tasteless
tasty
tat
tattooing
taunt
Tauta
tauta (Gr.)
Tavern
tavern-keeper
tawdry
tawny-colored
taxed
taxing
Taylor, Jeremy
Tea-Pot's
teaching
teachings
teak
teal
tearfully
technical
teemed
teeming
Teios
Telegraph
telegraphed
Tell-Tale
telles
tellin
Tellmenow
tem
tem.
Tem-Pest
temoins
temperate
tempered
Temple, William
tempora
temporize
tempt
temptations
tempting
ten-knot
tenable
tenantable
tenanting
tenants
tender
tendered
tenderly
tendrils
tenebrarum
tenements
Tenera
Teneriffe
tense
tenths
tents
tenty
tepid
Teraphim
terapin
Terence
terminations
terming
terns
terra-firma
terre
Terrible
terrify
terris
territories
terror-inspiring
Tertullian
Tertullian's
testator
tested
testimonials
testing
tete
tete
teufel
Texas
textilem
Thammuz
thankful
thankfully
thankless
thanksgiving
thatched
theatres
Theatrical
Theo (Gr.)
Theocritus
theologists
Theology
theoretical
there'll
thereto
These
thesis
they'll
thick-headed
thick-soled
thickest
thickets
thievery
thieves
thievish
thigh-bone
thimble-rig
Things
thinned
thinnest
thins
Third
thirds
thirtieth
thirty-first
thirty-four
This-and-That
thistles
Thomas, Don
Thompson, David
Thorntons
thorough-bred
thoroughness
Thou
thought's
thoughtlessly
thoughtlessness
thousand-and-second
Thousand-and-Second
thrashed
threading
threaten
three-cornered
three-gallon
three-hundred-and-twenti
three-inch
thricks>
thrifle>
thrills
throbbing
throth>
throttling
through
thrummed
thrumming
Thumb
thumbed
thunder-blasted
thundering
Thursday
Thursday,
thwart
Thyeste
tibia
tic
tickets
tickings
tickling
tide's
tile
tiled
tilling>
tills
tilting
Timarchus
timber-bolts
Timbuctoo
Time
time-eaten
time-servers
time-worn
time's
Timon
timorously
tinder-works
Tinian
tinned-ware
tinsel
tipped
tipping
tippling
tips
Tipula
tirade
tirade
tire
tiresome
tissues
titanic
tithe
titillating
titled
tittle-tattle
tiz
to (Gr.)
toad
toast
tobacco-pouches
tobacconist
Toby's
today
todder
toddy
toilet
toils
Token
tolerated
Tom-Fool
Tomas
tombeau
tomes
Tommy
Toms
ton
tong
Tongue
tonight
tonnage
tonnerres
tonnish
Too-wit
Too-wit's
Tooke, Horne
tool
tools
tooth-pick
toothpick
top-gallant
top-heavy
topaz
topical
topography
topped
topsiturviness
tormentors
torne
torny
Torres, Thomas De Las
torrid
tortoise-meat
Tortoni's
tortorum
torturer
toss
totality
tote
Tottle
touch-and-go
Touch-me-Not
touche
toughest
Toughkeepsie
tousand
toutes
tow
towing-line
town-lamps
tracle
traded
tradesmen
trading-posts
traduced
traduit

tragacanth
tragedian
Tragedy
trains
traitor
traitorous
trallala
trammels
trances
tranquillize
trans
transacting
transcendental
Transcendentalism
Transcendentalist
Transcendentalists
transcendentally
transcribe
transcribed
transcribing
transforming
transfusion
transient
transition-thought
transitions
translates
transmission
transmits
transmitting
transmuted
transpired
trapdoor
trappers
traveler
traveller's
traverse
tray
treacheries
treachery
treading
treads
Treatise
treats
trebly
tree-stems
tree-top
tree-tops
trefoil
trellis
trellissed
tremolite
tremour
tremulously
trench
trencher
trepanning
trepidancy
trespassed
tribulation
Tribunal
Tribunal
tribunal
tribunes
trickled
trickling
trifled
trim
trimmed
Trinculo
triple-stemmed
triple-tinted
tripod
triumphed
trois
trophy
troubadour
trough
trove
trowsers'
truant
truce
trucks
truer
trumpet-tongued
Trumpeter
truncheon
trustingly
trusty
Tsalalian
tua
tubercles
tuberoses
Tuckerman's
Tuclid
tue
tufted
tufts
Tula
tumblers
tumbles
tun>
tunica
Tupper, Martin Farquhar
turba
turbaned
turfed
Turkey
turkey-cock
turkeys
turkies
Turnapenny
Turpin, Dick
turret-chamber
tusks
twang
tweaking
tweedle
tweedle-dum
twelves
twenty-eighth
twenty-ninth
twenty-second,
twenty-sixth
twin
twinge
twinkled
twirling
twistical
twists
twittering
Two
two-reef
twoness
txxeeth
types
typhus
typical
typified
tyrant's
tyrants
Tyrian
Tyrius
Tyrius, Maximus
u
ubi
Ude
ugliness
ultimatum
ultimo
ultra-marine
ultras
uman
umbrageous
umbrellas
un-written
unaccommodating
unaccompanied
unaccustomed
unadapted
unaffected
unaided
unanimity
unanswerability
unappeasable
unapproachable
unassassinated
unassisted
unassuming
unattempted
unauthorized
unavailing
unavoidably
unawed
unbarred
unbecomingly
unbent
unblemished
unblushingly
unbonneted
unborn
unbridled
unbrokenly
unburied
unbuttoning
uncarpeted
unceremoniously
uncharitable
unchecked
unchoked
uncivilized
unclouded
uncommonly
uncomplaining
uncomprehended
uncompromising
unconceivable
unconceived
unconditionally
uncongenial
unconquerable
unconscionably
unconvulsive
uncounted
uncourteously
uncourtly
uncouthness
unction
unction
uncto
uncurtained
undammed
undaunted
undauntedly
undecayed
undeceive
undecided
undefinable
undefined
undeniability
under-jaw
under-let
under-rate
under-tow
Underduk
underground
underlined
underneath
underrated
underscored
understands
undertakings
undertone
undervalue
undervalued
undeviatingly
undiminished
undisputed
undistinguishable
undivulged
undo
undone
undoubted
undreamed
undubitably
undulated
undulations
unearths
unedged
uneducated
unemployed
unencumbered
unequalled
unerring
unevenly
unevenness
uneventful
unexampled
unexposed
unfair
unfamiliar
unfavorable
unfeeling
unfeignedly
unfilled
unfinished
unflinching
unflinchingly
unflogged
unforgotten
unfortuate
unfulfilled
unfurnished
ungenteel
ungoverned
ungracious
ungrammatical
ungratefully
ungreeted
unguarded
unhandsomely
unheard
unhemmed
unhewn
unholy
unhurried
unimaginable
unimaginative
unimagined
unimpaired
unimpeded
unimportant
unincorporate
unincumbered
unindividualized
unintentionally
Union
uniquely
uniquity
United
universality

Unjigah
unjustly
unkind
unkindest
unlettered
unlikely
unload
unlocked
unlocking
unlooked
unlooked-for
unloosened
unloveliness
unlucky
unmanned
unmannerly
unmask
unmentioned
unmerited
unmingled
unmouldered
unmuzzled
unnameable
unnaturally
unnumbered
unobtrusive
unoccupied
unoffending
unpaid-for
Unparalleled
unpicturesqueness
unpleasing
unpleasingly
unpractised
unprepossessing
unproportionably
unpublished
unquenchable
unquestionability
unransacked
unrasonable>
unrealities
unreason
unredeemed
unremittingly
unrest
unrestricted
unriddles
unrigged
unrivalled
unroll
unrolling
unrounded
unscathed
unscrew
unscrewed
unscrupulous
unsearchableness
unseasonable
unseasonably
unseemly
unselfish
unshackled
unsheathing
unshipped
unskillful
unslacked
unsocial
unsolved
unsteadily
unsteadiness
unstring
unsuitable
unsundered
unsuspectedness
unswathe
untameable
untended
untiring
untold
untorturing
untried
untrue
untutored
unus
unused
unveiling
unwarranted
unwashed
unwavering
unwearied
unwell
unwetted
unwholesome
unwillingly
unwisely
unwitting
unwomanly
unworldliness
unworthily

unwound
unwounded
unyielding
up-side-down
upper-lip
upraise
upraised
upreared
uprearing
uprightness
uprise
uprising
uproarious
uproariously
uprooted
uprooting
Upsaroka
Upsarokas
upsetting
upside-down
upsprang
upstart
upthrew
upwardly
Uranus
urchin
urchins
urgency
Urion
urry
usages
use-up
Used
Useful
usefully
usher
Ushers
ushers
usurpation
usurping
usury
Ut
Utawas
Utica
utilitarian
utilitarians
utility
utterness
utters
V--
Va.
vaat
vacantly
vacuo
vagabond's
vaguenesses
vaguest
Vah
Valdemar, M Ernest
Valens
valet
valets-de-chambre
valiant
valid
Valley
vallisneria
valorously
valourously
valuables
Valz
van
Vanilla
vanilla
vanilla-perfumed
vanishes
vanities
vanity
vapid
vapors
vapour-like
vapours
variability
varlet
vassal
Vathek
Vathek, Rabbi
Vaudeville
vaudeville
vault-door
vaulting
vaunted
veered
veils
veller
vellum-paper
Veloute
Ven
vended
venders
Venetian

vengeful
venir
Venitian
venny
venom
vented
ventilators
ventricle
ventriloquial
ventum
Venuses
Ver
veranda
verandahs
verborum
verbose
verbosity
verdured
verging
verisimilitude
verisimillima
veritably
verite
versez
version
versions
Vertu
vertu
vertus
Verus
Ververt
vested
Vestris, Ronzi
vesture
vestures
veto
veulent
vexatious
via
viand
vice-like
victim's
victorious
vide
Vidocq
vie
vieille
viele
vient
viewing
vigilant
Vigiliae
vignette
vignetting
vilest
villa
villainy
Villanova
Villaret
villas
Vin
vin
vindicate
vindicating
vine-leaves
vini
vintages
violating
violations
violator
Violet
violet-coloured
Virgilius
Virtu
virtuoso
virulence
virulent
vis
visionaries
Visionary
visitant
visitations
visits
vist
vistas
vita
vituperate
vivat
vividness
vivo
vivre
vivus
viz.
vizier's
vocalists
voce
vociferate
vòciferation
vociferous
voiceless

voila
Voissart, Victor
volant
volatilized
volley
Voltaire
voluble
voluminousness
voluptuary
volutes
Vonder
vonder
Vondervotteimittiss
Vopiscus, Flavius
voracious
vord
voted
votes
Votteimittiss
vouchsafe
vouchsafed
voudrait
Vougeot
vould
vour
Voyage
Voyage
voyager's
voyageur
voyageur
voyageurs
Vredenburg's
Vredenburgh, Peter
Vrinch
vs
vull
vulnerable
vultures
VII
VIII
wadded
wadding
waddle
wade
waded
wading
wafer
wafted
wag
wagers
wagged
wagoner's
wailing
wailings
wainscoting
waistcoat-pocket
waiters
waked
wakeful
wakefulness
wakes
wakes>
Wales'
walker
Walking-Advertisement
Wallenstein
Wallenstein
Walnut
Walsh, Robert
waltz
Wampoo
Wampoos
wand
waning
wantin>
Wappatomies
Wappytooties
war-coursers
war-party
war-whoop
warehouse
warm-hearted
warming
warn
warped
Warreconne
warring
wars
wash
Washington, George
washingtubs
Wassatoons
wast
waste-pipes
wasteful
watape
Watarhoo
watch-box
watch-house
watch's
watchers
watchful
watchman
water-casks
water-clock
water-colour
water-fall
water-jug
water-kegs
water-logged
water-melon
water-tight
watercask
waterfall
waterfalls
watery
waved
wavers
Wawandysenche
wax-light
waylaid
wayward
waywardness
we
we
weaken
weakening
weakest
weaknesses
Wealth
wealthier
wearer's
wearers
wearily
wearisomeness
weasel
weather-beaten
weather-forechains
weather-lanyards
weathercock
weathered
weathers
weaving
web-feet
web-like
Weddel, James
Weddell, James
wedge
wedges
weed
weehawken
weekdays
weep
weeps
weightier
Weilburg
Weld, H. Hastings
welded
well-being
well-built
well-concerted
well-conditioned
well-considered
well-contrived
well-digested
well-directed
well-dressed
well-feigned
well-flavoured
well-frequented
well-furnished
well-grounded
well-informed
well-knit
well-meant
well-modelled
well-oiled
well-settled
well-sustained
well-timed
well-to-do
well-tuned
Wellingtons
weltering
Wertemuller
Werther
Western
Westminster
wetting
whale-fishery
whale-ship
whaleboat
whaleboats
whaling-ships
whaling-vessel
whar
Wheal-Vor
wheel-route
wheel-tracks
where's
whereabout
whereby
whetting
whiff
Whig
whig
whilst
whimsicalities
whimsically
whining
whip-cord
whipper-snapper
whippersnapper
whirligig
whirlingly
whirls
whisk
whisker
whisperingly
whisperings
whiss
White
white-apparelled
white-plumed
White-Paint
White-Stone
White, Thomas W.
whiter
whitest
whiting
Whitmore, Richard
Whittington
whizz
Who
Who's
Whole
whole-number
whooping
wick
wickedly
wickliffe's
widdy
wide-spreading
widout
wield
wields
Wiggins
wigless
wild-looking
wilder
wildness
wilful
Wilhelm
Wilkie's
Wilkins', Peter
will-I
will>
Williams
Williams, J. B.
wind-harp
wind-sails
Windenough's
Windham
winding-sheet
windmills
window-panes
window-sash
windowless
wine-bibbing
wine-bottle
wine-box
wine-cellars
wine-pipe
wine-table
winters
Wirklichkeit
Wirt, William
wisiting>
wissahiccon
wit's
With
withdrawal
withdrawn
withersoever
withholding
witness'
witnessing
witticism
witticisms
woful
wofully
Wolf
Wollaston
wolly-wou>
wolverine
womanliness
womanly
womb
wonder-working
wonderingly

wondrous
wonted
wood-cut
wood-cutting
wood-work
woodland
woolly
woolly-wou>
woolly>
Woolwich
wording
wordly
worf
workings
workmen
Works
World
Worlds
worm-holes
worm's
wormed
wormwood
worried
worry
worsted
worthlessness
Would-be
would-be
wouldst
woully>
wouly-wou>
wrapping
wrapt
wreckers
wrenched
wriggled
wriggles
wrigglings
wring
wristband
writer's
writin>
writing-desk
writing-table
Written
Wrong
wronged
wrought-iron
wrung
wully>
wxnt
Wyatt, W.
Wyatt's
X-ample
X-asperation
X-cellent
X-centric
X-ed
x-ed
X-ing
X-press
X-traordinary
X-treme
x-tremity
X-uberance
xdixus
Xerxes
xnly
xr
xwns
xx
XI
XII
XIII
XIV
XIX
XV
XVI
XVII
XVIII
XX
XXI
XXII
XXIII
XXIV
XXIX
XXV
XXVI
XXVII
XXVIII
XXX
XXXI
XXXII
XXXIII
XXXIV
XXXV
XXXVI
XXXVII
XXXVIII
yachts

Yampoos
Yankee's
Yanktons
yard-arms
yards'
yawed
yawl
yawling
ycleped
ye're
ye've
yea
yea-nay
yearning
yelled
Yellow
yelpings
yesterday's
yeux
York-Town
you'd
you'll
you've
yourzelf
youself
yowling
Yurope
yxu've
yzur
Zacchary
Zadig
zaffre
Zahara
zay
zenzes
Zephyr
Zephyrs
Zeros
zest
zide
zig-zag
Zimmerman
Zion
zober
Zodiac
Zohar
zone
zoophytes
Zopyrus
zorry
zubmizzion
Zufalle
zusammen
0.05484
1--
1"
10,
10,600
10th
100,000
101
102
103
106
1080
11th
110
117,000,000
118
12'
12th
1300
132,000
133
1356
142
143
15,000
15th
150
16th
160
161
1643
1645
1666
167,000
168th
1698
17'
17th
1749
1758
176
1762
1763
1766
1767
1770
1771

1773
1775
1776
1777
1778
1779
1781
1781-8,
1783
1784
1789
1796
18,000
180
1804
1807
1809
1812
1813
1817
1820
1824
1825
1828
1829
1836
1838
1839
1841
1842
1845
1846
1847
190
193
194
195
2,230,272,000
2'
2"
2d.
20,000,000
200
200,000
2045
2050
21'
21st,
215
22"
221
231,920
24'
24"
240
25'
26,400
26'
28'
2848
29
3.
3,000,000
3rd
30
300
300,000
32
322
33
34
35
37.4
37'
38
39
40,000
40"
40th
4071
42,000
43
43'
46
46'
46th
47th
5'
50'
5010
5080
51
52
52'
53'
5376
55
55'
56
56th